# *Principles of* INTERNATIONAL ACCOUNTING

**SAMUEL FOX**
Research Professor of Accounting
Roosevelt University

**NORLIN G. RUESCHHOFF**
Professor of Accountancy
University of Notre Dame

# *Principles of* INTERNATIONAL ACCOUNTING

SAMUEL FOX
NORLIN G. RUESCHHOFF

**AUSTIN PRESS**
Educational Division of Lone Star Publishers, Inc.
P.O. Box 9774, Austin, Texas 78766

Library of Congress Card Number: 85-080012
ISBN: 0-914872-22-2

PRINTED IN THE UNITED STATES OF AMERICA

To

Genevieve, Jeffrey, Jennifer
and
Ottilie and Sandra

# Table of Contents

# Foreword

Suitable materials for class use in international accounting courses and seminars have had a gratifying increase in quality and quantity in the past decade. The publication of this text adds a new volume to the growing body of excellent textbooks and reference items. Each year brings more curriculum addition to the offerings available for student instruction in English-speaking institutions of higher learning throughout the world. It has been heartwarming to observe this favorable trend, which accompanies the vast increase in international trade and investment, travel and the sharing of ideas and concepts relating to the world dimensions of business.

The number of people working in, or interested in, international accounting matters has multiplied rapidly and the publication of this text will undoubtedly add to this favorable trend. The inauguration of the International Section of the American Accounting Association, some years ago, with its membership now encompassing persons from many countries, along with the founding of the International Association for Accounting Education and Research, will give additional emphasis to instructional demand for, and supply of, courses and seminars with broader than domestic emphases. In the United States the adoption by the American Assembly of Collegiate Schools of Business of a standard of curriculum requiring that all accredited business school students become familiar with the "world-wide dimension" of the subject matter studied, has added to the need for thoughtfully and carefully prepared textbooks such as the one herein presented.

This new text has an imaginative approach, including subdivisions based on Macro vs. Micro aspects. These terms, so well known in economics terminology, have an immediate appeal since so much of the popular literature in general makes reference to Macro and Micro.

Since the text is divided into parts, students and faculty instructors have the option of emphasizing selected chapters if time is not sufficient to cover thoroughly all of the materials. This is especially important because institutions have such a variety of instructional patterns with varying lengths of terms. Also, the level of student study, whether undergraduate or graduate, can be accommodated with the flexible features of this text.

Some special and perhaps even unique coverage features of this text may be emphasized in this Foreword. The first of these is that world organizations and their background relating to international accounting development over the past fifty years or so have been covered thoroughly. Students should therefore be more aware of these organizations and their accomplishments after studying this section of the book, over and above the lectures of the instructor. The impact of these organizations, and their world congresses held from time to time, dating back to the early years of the 20th century, is not so well known to the rank and file of students. At the same time, these organizations have contributed mightily to the tremendous progress now obvious in the harmonization of accounting.

The growth of world or international accounting has developed in response to the practical and social needs. This text emphasizes that aspect of growth and includes coverage of the contributions made by international firms to the progress of world standards.

It is now almost taken for granted that the development of accounting world-wide accompanies the improvement in the social and economic living standards of the peoples of the world. This has come to be called "economic development accounting," and dedicated individuals such as Dr. Adolf Enthoven have devoted almost a lifetime to this salient aspect of human development. The authors of this text therefore should be commended on stressing this topic and coverage in several of the chapters.

Since this text has been tried and tested several times in classroom relationships, it can be adopted and used with confidence by students and instructors in many countries.

International accounting has indeed come of age and it has promise of even more significant growth in professional and social consciousness in the last two decades of the 20th century. The availability of this text will assist in this objective and attainment.

I consider it a distinct honor to be invited to present this Foreword to what I hope will be a wide audience.

**PAUL GARNER**

Dean and Professor of Accountancy, Emeritus
    Graduate School of Business
    The University of Alabama
Charter Member of the International Section of the
    American Accounting Association
First President of the International Association for
    Accounting Education and Research

# Preface

Perhaps no area in the field of Accountancy is or has been as dynamic or multi-faceted as that known as International Accounting. Any textbook written in this area in the 1960s or 1970s could very easily be rendered obsolete in two to three years. Such is not the case in other areas in Accountancy; transitions have taken place but on a more gradual basis. Broad principles of accounting have been more stable with little metamorphosis.

The reason for this is not only the relative recency and celerity with which international operations of very large corporations have developed but also the advent of supersonic transport causing the shrinkage of the earth, making distant markets relatively close and easy to supply. Aided and abetted by advanced modern technological development, it is not difficult to recognize the profusion of conglomerates and key operational structures that have sprung up in our economic society, commonly referred to as Multinational Corporations (MNCs), which have contributed to the growth of International Accounting.

While the simple aspects of international accounting have been treated in texts for several decades, the subject matter centered principally in a discussion of foreign exchange, supplemented by a cursory treatment of currency translation for consolidated statements of companies with foreign subsidiaries. The subject matter accordingly was quite narrow in scope. It is only since the close of World War II, during the two decades from the mid-1940s to the mid-1960s, that International Accounting developed into sufficient proportions to assume a place in accounting as an independent discipline.

The rebuilding under the Marshall Plan of the European destruction wrought by the war, together with the explosion of business in the Orient, made it inevitable that the medium for reconstruction and expansion would have to be the affluent and prodigious corporate business enterprises centered principally in the United States.

The culmination of this trend indicated that by 1971 MNCs had reached such status as to encourage a study of them by the United Nations. This study (in the Dec. 1973, FINANCIAL EXECU-TIVE, page 32) revealed that of the 25 largest corporations, 15 were U.S. firms and that there were a total of 200 multinationals in the U.S. The U.S. Senate Committee on Finance found in 1973 that the sales volume of General Motors in 1969 was greater than all countries in the world except the top 22.

A subsequent study reported in the Nov. 1, 1975 issue of FORBES magazine evinces the international aspects that have developed by a substantial reversal of the original trend under which U.S. corporations dominated the international scene. This study indicates the invasion of the U.S. by foreign enterprises numbering some 85 large corporations from a widespread area, including the United Kingdom, Netherlands, South Africa, Germany, Canada, France, Switzerland, Belgium, Japan, Sweden, Saudi Arabia and Italy. As recently as 1984, the oil-rich Arab countries have been investing substantially in U.S. enterprises--banks, real estate, etc. Ironically the FORBES article is entitled "The U.S.' Unnaturalized Citizens." Obviously this flow reversal manifests a further complication of international accounting in that it now will attain a far greater degree of heterogeniety.

Prior to the decade of the 1970s, the presentation of International Accounting was primarily local in character--the subject matter would be approached from a United States viewpoint in U.S. colleges, from the British viewpoint in Great Britain, etc. Beginning with the mid-1970s the shift in investment from U.S. MNCs investing in foreign countries to foreign investors coming to the U.S. as foreign MNCs causes a shift from the local viewpoint to a heterogeneous approach, or from a UNI-LATERAL presentation to a MULTILATERAL one based on different interpretations in different countries resulting in a more complex treatment.

This shift in direction has had a definite impact on the study of International Accounting because the principal difficulty that has plagued this area has been the constant lack of uniformity of accounting principles in the divers countries. This factor has been further aggravated by a disparity of professional, academic, and legal fiats relating to the subject.

By the decade of the 1980s the subject of International Accounting has caught on in a tidal wave. Universities are offering the course in greater numbers. It seems likely that by the end of this decade it should be adopted by several hundred colleges.

At this point there are several options influencing the direction the course should take. Presently it is offered in colleges at the advanced undergraduate level, the master's level, and the doctoral level. It is not feasible to present the material in three different forms to each level separately. Therefore, in order to accommodate all of them in one volume, this book is designed as an intermediate level text intended for use at both the graduate and undergraduate levels as well as for accounting majors, international business majors, and/or general business students desiring an international orientation. It can be used within an MBA program, as well as in graduate programs in accounting and international business. At the undergraduate level, the primary prerequisite for a course using this text is a basic or elementary background in financial and managerial accounting.

The material is arranged in a flow pattern so that each chapter leads into the following one naturally, thereby ultimately presenting an unified whole. As you will note in the Table of Contents, there are four Parts which are divided into Chapters and Sections. At the end of each chapter are a number of theory questions, exercises, practice problems and/or cases. These are intended for the customary homework assignments. Many of the problems are adapted from AICPA and CMA exams. Material from Uniform CPA Examination Questions, copyright 1918 through 1985 by the American Institute of Certified Public Accountants, Inc., is reprinted with permission. Permission has been received from the Institute of Management Accounting of the National Association of Accountants to use Questions from past CMA Examinations, copyright 1981.

The extensive coverage of all aspects of international accounting, together with the problem material, will permit adoption of the text as a self-contained package with a minimum amount of outside readings. Where research is needed, particularly on the graduate level, there is a bibliography of references at the end of each chapter.

The extensive breadth of coverage in the book enables an unlimited flexibility that may be used to tailor the course to the preferences of the instructor. While the basic subject matter through the first 12 chapters, including international accounting theory, is the core of the course, from there on the instructor may select other chapters as time permits. This is particularly the case with such recent additions as the Social, Political, Inflation, and Taxation areas. In short, the text may be tailored to fit the time allotted to the course.

If outside readings and research are necessary and it is deemed desirable to cover all of the material in this book, two quarters or semesters are recommended. However, by selecting the preferential material in international accounting, a full coverage of the most important aspects can be effected in one semester.

Three novel features are incorporated into the material for the convenience of both the instructor and the student. The first relates to footnotes, which are stated within the text material and also listed in a Summary of Footnote References at the end of each chapter. The second is the sectionalization of the material identifying each section by a number that may be used as a handy reference rather than a page reference. The third identifies the content of each Section # with a subheading indicating exactly what subject matter is being treated so that the student will know what it is about.

The authors wish to acknowledge the inspiration furnished to them by three giants in the area of International Accounting, whose association with the area seems to be "ever since the memory of man runneth not to the contrary." First is the great southern gentleman, venerable Paul Garner, Dean Emeritus of the College of Business Administration of the University of Alabama; and second, Vernon Zimmerman, Dean of the College of Business Administration of the University of Illinois, Urbana Campus. The third is Joseph P. Cummings, the first U.S. representative and second chairman of the International Accounting Standards Committee.

The authors wish to express their appreciation to the American Institute of Certified Public Accountants, Inc., for granting us permission to reprint questions from CPA Examinations. Our gratitude is also extended to the Institute of Management Accounting of the National Association of Accountants for permission to reprint questions from past CMA Examinations.

An invaluable aid in gathering material, particularly CPA and CMA problems, organizing paper work, and coordinating multifarious text copy, has been Professor Mark Holtzblatt of the accounting faculty of Roosevelt University.

Deep appreciation is directed to Mrs. Mary R. Wingo of Austin, Texas, whose assistance in editing and correcting was extremely helpful. Thanks are due to the typists, Linda Nuccio and Mrs. Mary Holtzblatt, who deserves special gratitude for producing a presentable manuscript from a hopelessly scribbled original. Finally, the authors are indebted to the encouragement, suggestions, and help of the publisher, Mr. A.J. Lerager.

# PART I

# INTRODUCTORY ASPECTS OF INTERNATIONAL ACCOUNTING

Part I commences with a definition of "International Accounting" and a presentation of its nature and characteristics in the first chapter. In this discussion the relationship of Accounting to Business and Economics is pointed out, followed by a terse outline of the origins and historical development of international accounting. The metamorphoses in accounting principles and practices will manifest the inherent nature and characteristics of international accounting as having resulted from changes and advancements of business and accounting on an international basis. Chapter 1 concludes with a classification of international accounting into two major categories -- Micro and Macro International Accounting -- which sets the pattern for the subject matter of the book.

Part I concludes in Chapter 2 with a discussion of the Sources of International Accounting. Pointed out is not only the magnitude in numbers of sources but also their very great heterogeneity. The basic background of the Sources of International Accounting will point out the reasons for the great disparity that presently exists in the area of international accounting. While Chapter 2 may appear to be inordinately lengthy, it is believed that without a comprehension of the sources of international accounting, the student will be unable to comprehend the reasons for the various impasses and other conflicts that must necessarily result in a heterogeneous international political environment. Thus, by learning the diverse sources from which international accounting principles emanate, the student will have the necessary background to more readily see how the derivative international accounting principles have been created and have a better understanding of them.

# Nature, Characteristics and Classification of International Accounting

**#1-1....Basis of Accounting**

International Accounting on a broad unspecialized basis is the most recent addition to the spectrum of courses offered in the accounting area. At the outset, therefore, international accounting should be defined, which entails two aspects -- first, what is accounting, and second, what are its international implications.

It is common knowledge that Accountancy is not an end in itself. It generates no products or productive services that have any income-producing attributes. It is strictly a SERVICE INSTRUMENTALITY in the nature of a tool, and is subservient to the substance for which it acts as a tool. This substance basically is the economic order or business world. This material is therefore aimed at the class which directs the economic order activities, principally MANAGEMENT.

If accounting is to be an effective tool, it must be fashioned to fit the mold it is intended to serve. This means that if business is a heterogeneous collection of activities, as it so happens to be, then accounting must be a flexible device aimed at serving such heterogeneous activities, if it intends to succeed.

**NATURE OF ACCOUNTING**

**#1-2....What is Accounting?**

To carry out its objectives, the discipline of accounting must formulate a set of principles which are to be utilized in implementing the accounting processes. The question that immediately arises is: "Is Accounting an ART or is it a SCIENCE?"

Accounting authors have taken the position that since Accounting is based on Business, which in turn is the source of the discipline of MANAGEMENT, Accountancy must accordingly follow the character of Management; that Management has been developed from a pragmatic approach which perforce makes Management an ART; that since Accounting springs from Management, it must follow the same pattern; hence Accounting is an ART.

#1-3....Accounting As an Art

This view has been broadly accepted for many decades. Thus, as far back as 1953 the Commission on Terminology of the AICPA in ACCOUNTING TERMINOLOGY BULLETIN NO. 1, REVIEW AND RESUME, p. 9, defined Accounting as: "the ART of recording, classifying, and summarizing in a significant manner and in terms of money, transactions and events which are, in part at least, of a financial character, and interpreting the results thereof." Until 1970 this definition was commonly adopted by most of the introductory and intermediate accounting textbooks and it was generally accepted amongst accountants that accounting was an ART.

The revised definition of Accounting in 1970 was stated in STATEMENTS OF THE ACCOUNTING PRINCIPLES BOARD, APB #4, para. 40, as follows:

Accounting is a service activity. Its function is to provide quantitative information, primarily financial in nature, about economic entities that is intended to be useful in making economic decisions, in making reasoned choices among alternative courses of action.

This revised definition appears to adhere to the notion that Accounting is an Art as stated in its predecessor definition.

#1-4....Accounting As a Science

From time to time, various writers have had the opinion that Accounting is not an Art but a SCIENCE. To be a Science, a discipline does not necessarily have to be a NATURAL science. A Natural Science is one created by the laws of nature, not by man, whose rules are immutable. There are many sciences, in fact, which are not natural sciences, and there is a constellation of such sciences known as SOCIAL SCIENCES, including Political Science, Social Science, Law, Anthropology, etc. Accounting appears to be just as much a social science as is Law, Political Science, Sociology, or any other social science. A close examination will reveal that Accounting follows a somewhat similar pattern to Law which establishes its rules pursuant to actual economic and sociological developments. Because economic conditions are not static, the law must be flexible. When situations become obsolete or are dissipated, the laws relating to them must likewise be discharged. Conversely, as

new situations arise, new laws must be created. Therefore the
basic economo-legal philosophy with which the modern business
executive has become involved is the close observance of economic metamorphoses and the need to protect themselves by the
institution of law, through the enactment of the legal changes
required to meet such economic changes.

A close analysis of the pattern of accounting will disclose
that accounting treads a similar path. In the preceding paragraph, substituting the word "accounting" for where the word
"law" appears will show a striking similarity between the two
disciplines. This is manifested first by the issuance of APB
pronouncements, supplanted by the FASB announcements, whose
very essence is the congealing of experience in a particular
area into its ultimate form, viz., an FASB pronouncement. Although the FASBs do not carry legal fiat force, they nevertheless become a sort of so-called COMMON LAW of accounting. When
they are conjoined into a body, they have come to be known as
GAAP -- GENERALLY ACCEPTED ACCOUNTING PRINCIPLES, a term so
pervasive as to be universally employed in auditing certifica-
tions. Thus the rules of accounting produce statements for business operational decisions just as the rules of law are guidelines for the decisions rendered in litigation.

The basic problem is that in defining "Accounting," a distinction should be made between Accounting as an ART and Accounting as a SCIENCE. In formulating the rules by which the
game of Accounting is to be played, Accounting is a SCIENCE;
but in the actual performances of carrying out the rules, Accounting, in its practice, is an ART. Since we are concerned
with the creation and establishment of the rules, we are looking at Accounting as a Science.

That accounting has adopted a scientific approach may be
evidenced by the fact that during the 18th and 19th centuries,
when greater emphasis was placed on scientific method with respect to business relationships, accounting, too, followed the
path of business. The emphasis shifted from pragmatism to the
solution of problems theoretically before testing them in practice. The shift in essence was one in the direction away from a
trial and error procedure of testing whether the application of
a rule would or would not work to one which relied on a logical
and rigorous thinking.

It is surprising that accounting has not been recognized as
a science in the light of a letter written as far back as May
1, 1900, by Charles Waldo Haskins to the Massachusetts Society
of Public Accountants and published in May-June 1979 in the
MASSACHUSETTS CPA REVIEW, reprinted in Oct. 1979 in the JOURNAL
OF ACCOUNTANCY, page 76:

        Accountancy--the higher accountancy, if we must thus
    distinguish it--is a SCIENCE, and erudition; and not, as
    some seemed to suppose, a mere collection of approximate and

hardly certain rules indicated by observation and intuition,
and to be applied with tact and wariness. It thinks out, and
thus finds out, with logical and mathematical accuracy, the
condition  of affairs of any business enterprise; and therefore  is nonetheless a SCIENCE whether  it  works  with the
knotted  strings of the old Peruvians,  or the jacknife  and
tally stick  of the  European  baker, or the checkered cloth
and counters of the  Norman-English Exchequer, or the logis-
mography of the Italian Government, or the human brain alone
without even a slate or a pencil.

Accountancy--shall I still say the higher accountancy?--
gives account, not only  of  its employer's  affairs, but of
its  own accounts; so that  a manager or proprietor, whether
nation, municipality,  company, body of voters, or individual,  may know how matters stand; may render in turn the same
intelligent account to any third interested or disinterested
party; and  may  keep  a complete surveillance over  all the
accountable agents of the enterprise. Out of this SCIENCE OF
ACCOUNTANCY  has arisen, in the development of modern  business, our young and sturdy profession.
The Science of Accounting then can be defined as "setting forth
the  rules  for establishing and operating  accounting  systems
(sets of  books), directed toward summarizing all of the transactions an economic entity engages in during a specified period
of  time  into financial statements to enable management to use
such statements as a tool for making managerial decisions."

## #1-5....Accounting and Economics

Accounting has basically been associated with  the  area of
business, which has over the  past two centuries  been regarded
as  an  offshoot of the  discipline of economics.  It is common
knowledge that conventional Western economic thought sprang out
of the  thinking of the great  economists of the 19th century--
Adam Smith, Mill,  Locke,  Hume, Marshall, Ricardo, inter alia.
All of the economic thinking of these men was  in the direction
of private enterprise based on microeconomic principles. It was
inevitable that  accounting would follow in the wake of the development of economics.
Many accountants are  of  the  opinion that there  is little
relationship between  accounting  and economics, but it  is not
too difficult to see  that the same  ideas that pervade  economics run through  the training of accounting thought.  In fact,
in Germany for many  years there were no accounting courses offered as such.  Students desiring to study accounting in German
universities took such courses through the Economics curriculum
as a tool of  Business Economics.  Thus on the  basis that  accounting parallels  the area  of economics,  which is generally
conceded to be a social science, accounting too must be regarded as a social science.

## #1-6....Accounting and Social Responsibility

In the 1970s accounting has expanded into the social science
area, as will be seen later, opening up another new and complete vista of the emergence of accounting as a science. And
singularly enough international accounting for multinational
and transnational corporations has had a good deal of responsibility for this type of thinking. This viewpoint was expressed
in great depth at the 4th International Conference on Accounting Education in West Berlin, October 5-7, 1977. Some several
hundred of the world's leading accounting professors partici-
pated in that conference, which gave consideration to five subjects: (1) Development and State of Conventional Accounting
Education Systems; (2) New Demands on Educational Systems in
Accountancy; (3) Inflation Accounting; (4) Forecast Audit; and
(5) Social Accounting.

The general conclusion was reached that the area of account-
ing would henceforth have to be expanded to include Inflation
and Social Accounting. The leading discussants of these various
subjects were Prof. Louis Perridon of the Univ. of Augsburg;
Prof. Adolf Enthoven; Dr. Michael Chetkovich; Maurice Lorton,
Chairman of the Commission de Formation Professionelle de
l'Institut Francais des Experts Comptables; Prof. GGM Bak;
Prof. Andre Zund; Prof. Raymond J. Chambers of the Univ. of
Sydney, Australia; Prof. Peter Standish; Prof. O. Wanik; Prof.
J. R. Small and Mr. A. T. McLean of Heriot-Watt Univ. of Edin-
burgh; Prof. E. de Lembre; Dr. Ernest J. Pavlock; Prof. R. Lee
Brummet of the Univ. of North Carolina; Prof. G. Sieben; and R.
G. Palim.

The 4th Conference seemed to point to the thesis that accounting must now be regarded as a science. Thus on page 7 of
Subject 1, Prof. Louis Perridon states:

> I should like, with all necessary caution, to make the fol-
> lowing contention: The importance of accountancy as a SCIEN-
> TIFIC discipline, and as an instrument of management, and of
> economic and social policy, will increase more than ever as
> the economic sciences expand into the field of behavioral
> sciences, and will entail a fundamental change in the ap-
> proaches in research and the solution of economic issues.
> Such a development would be conducive to interdisciplinary
> research solution of practical issues.

In fact, Prof. Lee Brummet has indicated that the scope of accounting has so broadened in the direction of socio-economic
accounting in the late 1970s as to render the AICPA definition
of accounting obsolete. At the 4th Conference in the proceedings in Subject 5, pp. 4-6, Prof. Brummet declares:

> The entry of the accounting profession into social per-
> formance measurement and communication or social accounting
> may seem natural or unnatural, depending on our definition

of the field of accounting. The AICPA definition of some 40
years ago has constrained us to money or financial matters
and to tranactions and events.

Alternatively, I believe we should define our subject of
accounting broadly, and only in terms of its role in society. *** I suggest the following definition: "Accounting is a
systematic symbolic process which enables individuals, organizations and societies to articulate objectives, to provide projections and feedback information to assist in monitoring efforts to accomplish such objectives and to provide
high credibility performance and condition accountability
information to legitimate constituencies."
Prof. Brummet goes on to observe that "this proposed definition
is general enough to include national or world-wide economic or
social accounts and economic or social indicators--areas of
concern in all our countries and which have not enjoyed adequate participation of accountants."
On page 57 of Subject 1, Dr. Michael Chetkovich says: "Accounting, as an applied SCIENCE, must function within real
world constraints."
The latest expression on the subject is a book entitled TO-
WARD A SCIENCE OF ACCOUNTING, by Robert R. Sterling, Scholars
Book Co., Houston, TX, reviewed in the April 1982 JOURNAL OF
ACCOUNTANCY on pages 99-102.

## CHARACTERISTICS OF INTERNATIONAL ACCOUNTING

### #1-7....Basis for Development of International Accounting

Having discussed the nature and characteristics of accounting, the next consideration is the definition of "international
accounting." As pointed out above, accounting serves as a tool
for business and by itself would be a meaningless exercise. In
the early stages of Business Economics, starting with the 15th
century, when businesses were conducted on a simple and small-
scale basis, accounting concepts were sparse. When double-entry
accounting first originated, it was related to keeping records
of such simple forms of enterprise as sole proprietorships and
partnerships as well as for individual personal records. As
industry developed and became more complex, it expanded all
along on a microeconomic plane and accounting moved right along
with it, resulting in the proprietary and transaction theories
of accounting.

Thus in economies based on free enterprise, a microeconomic
aspect would dictate that there be private ownership of property with the perpetuation of ownership through the generation of
profits. The profit motive in turn could only be expanded
through an enlargement of the capital structure resulting in a
greater volume of operations thereby generating more and great-

er profits.  The inevitable medium through which this was to be
accomplished was the corporate form of structure.

In recent years the growing involvement of corporate multinational structures, stretching out beyond the confines of
their home countries into foreign lands, has inevitably created
an obligation to society at large, as pointed out by Prof.
Brummet.  The result has been an enlargement in scope of the
horizons of corporations beyond the sole profit-making purpose.
The enlargement has embraced the establishment of standards for
economic well-being, the development of scientific and technical innovations for progress, and for social responsibility to
the employees as well as the people of the lands in which they
operate.  Thus it is quite common to find corporations participating in the areas of national security, public health, education, monetary systems, and political matters.  These latter
concepts have created an aspect to international accounting
that would fall within the purview of macroeconomics.

#1-8....Evolution of International Accounting

From the foregoing, we find that international accounting
is a branch of the total field of the discipline of accounting,
much the same way as international law is in the curriculum of
law, and international economics is in the field of economics.
Before attempting to define international accounting, it is
necessary to trace its evolution to make for a clearer comprehension as to what it is about. Actually accounting is international in character because no one country developed from beginning to end all of the area as a package by itself.  The development of accounting bounced around from one country to another, a process that continues to this day and will continue
every day in the future.  Many authorities are of the opinion,
in fact, that there should be uniformity in accounting principles in the form of a set of international accounting standards
that must be adhered to by all countries.

HISTORICAL ASPECTS OF ACCOUNTING

#1-9....Accounting in the Bible

The history of accounting in general indicates that the development of all accounting has had its roots in countries all
over the world.  The history of international accounting therefore parallels the history of accounting in general.  It seems
anomalous then that it has been only recently that international accounting has been regarded as a separate offering in U.S.
universities.

It appears that as long as there have been people on the
earth, there has been a need for accounting. This is manifested

by an article entitled "Accounting in the Bible," by Prof. Robert Hagerman in the Fall 1980 issue of THE ACCOUNTING HISTORI-
ANS JOURNAL, pp. 71-76. It indicates that the Bible discusses
the objectives of accounting, internal control procedures, and
managerial accounting topics. The article also links the Bible
to current accounting thought. The full context of this article
is beyond the scope of this book. Only those expressions from
the Bible that are applicable will be presented. Prof. Hagerman
initiates his article by pointing out:

> The beginnings of modern accounting are commonly traced to
> Pacioli in the 15th century. Actually many of the fundamen-
> tal ideas that underlie modern accounting may be traced much
> further back. The Bible, which is generally viewed as cover-
> ing events between 1800 B.C. and 95 A.D., contains several
> references, both direct and indirect, to accounting and bas-
> ic accounting concepts.

FINANCIAL ACCOUNTING--The Bible points out that accounting is necessary to reduce fraud in 2 Kings 12:16 in a negative way regarding the building of the Temple: "No accounts
were kept with the men to whom the money was paid over to be
spent on workmen since they were honest in their dealings."

In the New Testament in Luke 16:2 appears a parable
about a steward wasting money: "What is this I heard about
you? Draw me up an account of your stewardship." This indicates that accounting was used as a control device to monitor performance and suggests that the owner should have in-
sisted on periodic accounting reports.

Accounting also serves the purpose of resolving disputes
between parties, ensuring that debtors and creditors agree
on the amounts due, and that partners and other classes of
owners know their share of the earnings. The Bible makes
this point in Eccles. 4:1-2, where it states: "These are
things you should not be ashamed of -- keeping strict accounts with a traveling companion." The idea is that accounts will reduce conflicts between the travelers.

There is one place where the Bible requires a particular
accounting system. Eccles. 14:7 states: "Whatever stores you
issue do it by number and weight, spending and taking put
everything in writing."

INTERNAL CONTROL--The Bible provides an extensive discussion of internal control: The rationale is that if employees have an opportunity to steal they may succumb to the
temptation. On this point the Bible says in Micah 7:5-6,
"Put no trust in a neighbor, have no confidence in a
friend." The dual custody of assets as an internal control
measure is graphically described in 2 Chronicles 24:11-12
as follows: "When the chest was taken to the royal office of
control, run by the Levites, they would check the amount of
money in it, then the King's secretary would come with a

representative of the chief  priest; they would take up  the
chest and carry it away."

The Bible also  discusses  the fact  that custodians  of
funds should be men of integrity.  In 2 Corinthians 8:16-17,
St.  Paul says he is sending Titus and two brothers to collect a  fund  the Corinthians have gathered,  and in  2 Cor.
8:20 says he is sending the  three so that "we hope that  in
this way there will be no accusations  made about our administering such a large fund; for  we are trying  to  do right
not only in the sight of God but also in the sight of men."

The lack of  honest employees and dual  custody  is described in John 12:7-8 discussing Judas as the treasurer: "he
was in charge of the common fund and used to help himself to
the contributions."

The basic internal control procedure of physically safe-
guarding  assets by providing limited access to them is suc-
cinctly stated in Eccles. 42:6-7 as:  "Where there are  many
hands, lock things up."

The value of  surprise audits as an internal control device is discussed in the Gospels of Luke and Matthew.  Matt.
24:46 summarizes the behavioral implications of these audits
or inspections as  follows: "Happy  is that  servant if  his
master's arrival finds him at his employment."

MANAGERIAL ACCOUNTING--The budgeting process is provided
for in Luke 14:28-29:  "Which of you here intending to build
a tower would not  first sit  down  and work out the cost to
see if you had enough to complete it?"

Regarding  participatory  budgeting,  Proverbs  15:22
states:  "Without deliberation plans  come to nothing, where
counselors are many, plans succeed."

Finally, the Bible  provides a very accurate description
of whether to  retain or drop  a  product.  Eccles. 7:22-23
states:  "Have you cattle? Look after them; if they are making you a profit, keep them."
In concluding, Prof. Hagerman makes the interesting observation
that  the Bible "shows that economic logic  was used in product
decisions,"  and that "it  is interesting  to see  how ideas we
consider to be modern were used by an ancient civilization."

## #1-10....Beginnings of the Science of Accounting

As Prof.  Hagerman indicated, "The beginnings  of modern accounting are commonly traced to Pacioli  in  the 15th century."
Frater Lucas Bartolomes Pacioli,  commonly referred to  as  Fra
Pacioli, has been regarded as the  father  of double-entry  accounting.  He was  highly respected as a writer, a teacher, and
an expert in such fields as commerce, mathematics,  and theology, and was truly a Renaissance man.

While most of  his writings deal with the topics of geometry and arithmetic, Pacioli is best known for his treatise on double-entry bookkeeping contained in his SUMMA DE ARITHMETICA, GEOMETRIA, PROPORTIONI ET PROPORTIONALITA, published in 1494. Pacioli's treatise met the need for a standardized system of describing business transactions. The following excerpts from John B. Geijsbeek's translation of the treatise reveal the practicality of Pacioli's suggestions for succeeding in business:

> to arrange all the transactions in such a systematic way
> that one may understand each one of them at a glance, i.e.,
> by the debit (debito--owed to) and credit (credito--owed
> by) method. This is very essential to merchants, because,
> without making the entries systematically it would be impos-
> sible to conduct their business, for they would have no rest
> and their minds would always be troubled. Pacioli's princi-
> ples remain the foundation of our present methods of book-
> keeping.

#### #1-11....Accounting in the Middle Ages

The beginnings of the science of accounting had their origin in the 14th and 15th centuries in the Italian city states. They then moved into Germany where they were espoused by the Hanse-atic League during the Fugger era. Contemporaneously the French adopted the Italo-German principles for governmental manage-ment, and the Dutch carved out the methodology for showing fis-cal period income. Inevitably the Italian, German, French, Dutch conglomeration entered the shores of Britain, whose pre-eminent economic status in the world during the 17th and 18th centuries made it a natural to develop accounting to a very high state.

The British brought with them their highly developed princi-ples to all of their colonies, including the United States, Canada, Australia, New Zealand, South Africa, as well as all others in the British Commonwealth. Just as the British sent its accounting methods to its colonies, so, too, did the Ger-mans, the French, and the Dutch. German accounting spread to Russia where the rulers of the two countries were related, as well as to Sweden and even far off Japan. French accounting spread to all French African countries and Polynesia. Dutch accounting was transported to Indonesia and African colonies.

#### #1-12....Accounting and the Industrial Revolution

The colonial spreading takes us to the 19th and 20th centur-ies, during which the United States began to develop into the most powerful economic country in the world. Accounting had to keep pace with the U.S. industrial boom, and this resulted in an expansion in depth as well as in variety of accounting prin-

ciples.  This required appropriate  training  resulting in  the
creation of  colleges  of finance and  commerce, as  they  were
known at the beginning of the 20th century.  Course offerings in
accounting  were  expanded, and eventually separate departments
of accountancy were established in all major universities.  The
latest  development  in  the  1980s  has  resulted in  separate
schools of  accountancy, which  no doubt eventually will become
professional colleges.

#1-13....Development of International Accounting

    After  World War II when  the largest  corporations could no
longer expand in accordance with the strict purposes and objectives stated in their corporate charters, and the United States
became so powerful  industrially,  such corporations mushroomed
into other areas of business.  They took the form of conglomerates spanning the entire globe. The result of this international explosion  of business was international ownership of corporate securities. This required responsible international financial statements that would be predicated  on some semblance  of
international accounting methodology.
    THE WALL STREET JOURNAL,  May 25,  1976., p. 8,  states  that
"the Securities and  Exchange Commission has approved  a previously proposed set of  standards  designed  to  encourage major
foreign companies to list securities on the New York Stock  Exchange."
    By 1984, the New York Stock Exchange had  172 foreign secur-
ities listed, consisting of 58 foreign  stocks  and 114 foreign
government  and  private bonds.  In 1984, total transactions in
foreign equities by overseas investors on U.S. markets equalled
$30.2 billion.  Foreign  purchases of U.S. stocks totaled $60.5
billion.  These foreign investors, both individual and institutional, bought  and  sold a record volume  of securities on all
U.S. securities  markets in 1984.  The  foreign transactions in
domestic markets,  including U.S.  and foreign  bonds, totaled
$789 billion, 46% above the 1983 level (NEW YORK STOCK EXCHANGE
FACT BOOK, 1985, pages 37-39, 64).
    Further, more U.S.  investors than ever are investing in the
world securities markets.  Between 1981 and 1984, international
investments by U.S.  pension funds  tripled from  $5 billion to
$15.7 billion. At least 39 U.S.-based mutual funds now special-
ize in  foreign investments, compared to nine in 1980.  (Marcia
Berss, "Just How Alluring Are Foreign Stocks Now?" FORBES, July
29, 1985, page 154).
    It would thus appear  that the prodigious trading in securi-
ties would result in the creation of a set of accounting standards for each of the countries  involved  that would be uniform
in character.  Such, however, is not the  case. Different coun-

tries have developed different sets of accounting principles,
although there is agreement on basic accounting standards. However, there are differences in different countries that militate against a uniform set of rules for all countries.

#1-14....International Accounting Clusters

As a result of the propagation of accounting principles
from dominant countries to their colonies, it appears that the
adoption of accounting principles seems to have followed a pattern of clustering into groups which follow a leader country.
In a similar vein, to determine the member countries of various
clusters, a study was made by H. M. Abu-Jbarah entitled A SUB-
ENTITY BASIS FOR FINANCIAL REPORTING BY MULTI-NATIONAL FIRMS: A
CLUSTER ANALYSIS APPROACH, as an unpublished doctoral dissertation, Univ. of Wisconsin, 1972. The study results in eight
clusters of countries. Eight economic factors were used as the
basis for determining the clusters: (1) per capita national
income; (2) private consumption expenditure as a percent of
GNP; (3) gross capital formation as a percent of GNP; (4) balance of trade as a percent of GNP; (5) share of agriculture of
all gross domestic products; (6) rate of growth of real domestic products; (7) change in foreign exchange rate; and (8)
change in consumer price index.

#1-15....Cluster Groupings

The foregoing study shows the following clusters:

GROUP #1--Burma, Republic of China, Costa Rica, Cyprus, Egypt,
    Greece, Guyana, Ireland, Jamaica, Mauritius, Nicaragua,
    Panama, Peru, Portugal, South Africa, Spain, Syria, Thai-
    land, Trinidad-Tobago, Tunisia
GROUP #2--Bolivia, Cameroon, Ceylon, Colombia, Dominican Repub-
    lic, Ecuador, El Salvador, Guatemala, Honduras, Iran, Ivo-
    ry Coast, Kenya, Malaysia, Mexico, Morocco, Paraguay,
    Philippines, Sierra Leone, Turkey
GROUP #3--Australia, Austria, Belgium, Canada, Denmark, Eng-
    land, Finland, France, Germany, Iceland, Italy, Japan,
    Luxembourg, Netherlands, New Zealand, Norway, Sweden,
    Switzerland  & U.S.
GROUP #4--Ethiopia, Ghana, India, Nigeria, Pakistan, Sudan,
    Tanzania
GROUP #5--Jordan, Korea, Malawi, Singapore, Vietnam
GROUP #6--Argentina, Brazil, Chile, Uruguay
GROUP #7--Iraq, Venezuela, Zambia
GROUP #8--Israel, Puerto Rico, Malta
    Obviously the member countries in each group do not neces-
sarily have the same accounting principles as every other coun-

try in the group. The countries are matched according to the eight criteria, but may have different accounting standards. What the study apparently attempts to show is that if accounting standards were to be adopted, the clusters should have similar standards due to similarity in structure.

Under the circumstances, it would appear that the propagation of accounting principles of a single country to a cluster of other countries would have a tendency to create uniform accounting principles in all of the clustered countries. However, such is not the case. On the contrary, intense chauvinism has resulted in national standards being profoundly rooted into a set of principles which have veered away from general uniformity. The result has been a great resentment on the part of individual countries which have been asked to espouse the principles of the more powerful countries.

## INTERNATIONAL ACCOUNTING

### #1-16....Definition of International Accounting

With the background material presented above, we are now prepared to define "International Accounting." International accounting must be designed to serve business that is carried out on the international level. To effectively accomplish its mission, then, international accounting must devise a set of principles aimed at presenting the financial results of business enterprises operating on the international level. International accounting basically differs from the conventional accounting to which the student has been oriented that has been directed to a single total accounting system for a specific country, in that it is a bifurcated problem. On the international level, there must first be a set of principles for a specific country, which must then be related to another country where operations take place, and where another set of principles are established.

### #1-17....Range and Extent of International Accounting

Thus international accounting is a conglomeration of the principles of accounting developed by all countries. Because each country may have its own set of principles that may differ in varying degrees, from slightly to greatly, it could very easily be a frightening subject if it should attempt to embrace all of the principles enunciated in all of the countries of the world.

Evidence of this may be supplied by a compendium compiled by the AICPA entitled PROFESSIONAL ACCOUNTING PRACTICES IN 30 COUNTRIES, which demonstrates basic accounting statements and principles in 30 countries. Obviously if international accounting is intended to cover all the countries in the world, the subject matter could run into over 150 countries. This points up the range that a course in international accounting could pursue.

If the course in international accounting is to cover accounting in more than one country, as the word "international" implies, the question is: "How many countries should be covered?" The following factors must be taken into consideration to answer the questions: How much time is to be devoted to the course?; Is the primary and basic interest in the course to be totally academic centering on a comparative philosophical treatment?; How much pragmatism is to be attached to the course?; and A combination of any or all of the three foregoing factors.

## APPROACHES TO INTERNATIONAL ACCOUNTING

### #1-18...Approaches to the Study of International Accounting

In an article in the INTERNATIONAL JOURNAL OF ACCOUNTANCY, 1971, by Weirich, Avery, and Anderson, three approaches to the study of international accounting are presented: (1) a universal approach; (2) an approach covering all the methods and standards of all the countries; and (3) practices of foreign subsidiaries and parent companies--called respectively, World Accounting, International Accounting, and Foreign Subsidiary Accounting. These approaches are described in the following terms:

WORLD ACCOUNTING--In the framework of this concept, international accounting is considered to be a UNIVERSAL system that could be adopted in all countries. A world-wide set of generally accepted accounting principles (GAAP), such as the set maintained in the United States, would be established. Practices and principles would be developed which were applicable to all countries. This concept would be the ultimate goal of an international accounting system.

INTERNATIONAL ACCOUNTING--A second major concept of the term "international accounting" involves a descriptive and informative approach. Under this concept, international accounting includes all varieties of principles, methods and standards of accounting of ALL countries. This concept includes a set of GAAP established for each country, thereby requiring the accountant to be multiple principle conscious when studying international accounting. No universal or perfect set of principles would be expected to be established. A collection of all principles, methods, and standards of all countries would be considered as the international accounting system. These variations result because of differing geographic, social, economic, political, and legal influences.

FOREIGN SUBSIDIARY ACCOUNTING--The third major concept
that may be applied to international accounting refers to
the accounting practices of a parent company and a foreign
subsidiary. A reference to a particular country or domicile
is needed under this concept for effective international
financial reporting. The accountant is concerned mainly with
the translation and adjustment of the subsidiary's financial
statements. Different accounting problems arise and different accounting principles are to be followed depending upon
which country is used as a reference for translation and
adjustment purposes.
An examination must be made of these three approaches to determine which would be the most effective to follow.

#1-19....The World Accounting Approach

This approach requires a set of universal or global principles which would be the same for all countries in the world.
Since such a set of principles does not exist at the present,
in order to implement this system it would be necessary to develop a set of global or universal principles. Ideally this
should be done, and if and when it is, it will then serve capa-
bly as the best approach for the study of international accounting.

#1-20....The International Accounting Approach

This approach is a multiple principle approach--in essence a
conglomeration of the GAAP in a multiplicity of countries. The
problem with this approach is to determine how many countries
are to be selected, and even more importantly, which ones they
should be. Manifestly, it would be infeasible and impractical
to take them all. So in order to follow this approach there
would have to be an arbitrary selection of the number and the
countries.
This could only be done from a partial viewpoint, meaning
that the probable base country to be selected would be that in
which the course in international accounting is offered, and
the other countries chosen would have to be either on a comparative basis with the base country, or to represent various sam-
plings or segments of countries, such as those highly developed, those medium-developed, and some developing countries. Such
an approach obviously would be a Comparative International Accounting study.

#1-21....The Foreign Subsidiary Accounting Approach

This approach is a far narrower one than the other two. It
confines the discussion to the narrow topic of Parent-Foreign

Subsidiary relationship.  While  it could  be developed into  a
course of its own, it would overlook the broader GAAP viewpoint
as well  as  the Comparative  study of the  relationship of accounting between different countries.  Accordingly, the Foreign
Subsidiary Approach, which is an absolute requirement in international accounting, would  have  to be  covered  as  a partial
treatment of the international accounting course.

### #1-22...Comparative International Foreign Subsidiary Approach

With a nationalistic attitude, pointed out above in the discussion of Cluster Groupings,  the study of  international  accounting  in universities should be  geared to  the  principles
established in  the country in which the university is located.
When a  foreign subsidiary approach is added, it  would form  a
Combined International with Foreign Subsidiary Approach.  Under
such an  approach  it would be necessary to expand the international  approach to include,  in addition  to the local country
principles, a comparative  study with whatever  additional foreign countries are regarded as desirable to be matched with the
local country.  This would result in  a number of presentations
related to the number of countries desired to be covered.

Since the  material in this book  is U.S. oriented, the  approach to be used will be to select the U.S. GAAP as the  basis
for development  of the discussion, and  build  the Comparative
Approach,  using about  a dozen other representative countries,
principally  those in the  European  Economic  Community (EEC),
upon the base.  Such would be a Comparative International Foreign Subsidiary approach.

### THE INTERNATIONAL ACCOUNTING STRUCTURE*

### #1-23....International Accounting Expertise Need

International accounting basically embraces  the application
of accounting principles for such business activity  of  an enterprise which crosses national boundaries or is conducted in a
location other than its domicile country. Excluded would be the
local aspects that would not  relate to the international business activity.  This however  may  not necessarily  be ignored,
inasmuch as they may have some utility in the study of comparative accounting principles.  It definitely is an element of international accounting because of its relation to transnational
reporting for investors.

The trends  resulting from the mutual interchange of invest-

------

*See Summary of Footnote References -- #1-23 thru #1-25

ments have created not only added responsibilities, but also prospective directions for the international accountant. Thus, international accounting becomes an invaluable tool to the professional accountant in his international financial responsibilities. Certainly international accounting encompasses all areas of accounting--financial, theory, managerial, auditing, and taxes.

### #1-24....Duties of the International Accountant

The duties of the international accountant within the international enterprise are both financial and managerial. On the financial side, the accountant is responsible for the accountability or stewardship of the firm's assets. The stewardship task requires a knowledge of the principles and practices of accounting for international activities.

On the managerial side, the accountant is responsible for supplying accounting information to assist in management decision-making, involving multinational control, referred to as International Financial Management. These duties are divided between the controller and the treasurer. They are not only carried out at the top level but also throughout the lower levels of the multinational organization. The experiences of a broad cross section of international companies with respect to the delegation of these tasks among the various levels can be viewed in Figure 1-1, prepared as Management Monograph No. 35, entitled ORGANIZING FOR INTERNATIONAL FINANCE, Business International Corp., N.Y., 1966, pp. 21-23.

### #1-25....Dimensions of International Accounting

International financial reporting may be made to internal or external sources. The investors in an international firm may be stockholders, creditors, other indirect claimants; other interested parties include government agencies, employees, labor unions, customers and suppliers. The creditors and stockholders may be private individuals, institutional investors, and governmental partners. Financial reporting to a world-wide audience of such breadth requires a more profound understanding than the mere knowledge of the accounting principles and practices within the domicile country.

As international business expands, international financial reporting becomes more important as an external tool of communication amongst traders, entrepreneurs, financiers, and investors. The professional responsibilities of both the public and the management accountant are no longer limited to fiscal matters, but extend to social, environmental and political responsibility.

FIGURE 1-1

MULTINATIONAL ENTERPRISE ACCOUNTING TASKS

## CONTROLLERSHIP

CORPORATE LEVEL ASSIGNMENTS
1. Consolidations policy & procedures (e.g., translation methods, which affiliates to include in consolidation)
2. Formulation and installation of standard chart of accounts
3. Accounting procedures & techniques (e.g., depreciation methods for types of assets, inventory valuation)
4. Internal auditing techniques and procedures
5. Format and timing of operating and capital budgets
6. Format and timing of reporting and control systems
7. Selection & use of EDP equipment for the accounting function(e.g., use of standard hardware & programming)
8. Selection of local certified public accountants for foreign subsidiaries

DIVISIONAL ASSIGNMENTS
1. Guidelines for formulation of subsidiary budgets
2. Review and consolidation of subsidiary budgets
3. Analysis of subsidiary performance, & action recommendations
4. Advisory services & training for subsidiary controllers
5. Establishment of divisional controllership policies
6. Supervision of pricing practices

SUBSIDIARY ASSIGNMENTS
1. Preparation of financial reports and consolidations
2. Analysis of financial performance
3. Preparation of budgets & financial forecasts
4. Maintenance of books, ledgers, journals, and other accounting records including EDP equipment
5. Auditing of subsidiary operations
6. Preparation of tax returns

## TREASURERSHIP

CORPORATE LEVEL ASSIGNMENTS
1. Provision of capital for projects & unusual cash needs (e.g., bank loans for medium & long-term financing,bond issues & stock issues)
2. Coordination of short-term financing to ensure optimum use of working capital on a global basis (e.g., maximum use of overdraft where necessary, & standards for dividend payment)
3. Policies & procedures for protection of exposed assets in inflationary countries with currency deterioration
4. Relations with domestic and foreign bankers
5. Stockholder relationships throughout the world
6. Policy & procedures for credit & collections (to ensure that multidivision customers do not exceed normal credit lines, and to standardize risk limits)
7. Policy & procedures on investments to be made with excess cash (e.g., what types of securities are acceptable, what balance should be in portfolio)
8. Insurance coverage, a function often assumed by corporate staff to take advantage of overall or blanket policies that can reduce insurance costs

DIVISIONAL ASSIGNMENTS
1. Review of cash & working capital positions & recommendations
2. Review of exposed asset protection
3. Coordination of borrowing practices
4. Advisory & training services for subsidiary treasurers

SUBSIDIARY ASSIGNMENTS
1. Analysis of working capital needs & cash requirement forecasts
2. Day-to-day banking operations for short-term funds
3. Operations to protect exposed assets
4. Administration of credit and collection operations
5. Investment of excess cash in approved investments
6. Provision of local insurance policies and contracts

Source: Reprinted from ORGANIZING FOR INTERNATIONAL FINANCE, Management Monograph No. 35, 1966, pp. 21-23, with the permission of the publisher, Business International Corporation, New York.

## CLASSIFICATION OF INTERNATIONAL ACCOUNTING

### #1-26...General Classification of International Acctg.

To set the pattern for the material to follow, we must establish a classification of the subject of international accounting. Basically, like the discipline of economics, international accounting can be divided into two principal areas: Micro International Accounting and Macro International Accounting. However, in this day of governmental influence, the significant aspects of each are often closely related and intertwined, because the dimensions are not readily distinguishable nor segregatable. Areas such as taxation and parastatal enterprise accounting certainly include elements of Macro as well as Micro Accounting. Social, Political, and Inflation Accounting also fall in this category of a mixed, hybrid, or quasi Macro-Micro accounting classification.

The primary distinction between Micro and Macro international accounting is that Micro is basically concerned with the private enterprise profit motive aspects of the business whereas Macro is regarded as being primarily oriented toward the governmental welfare-of-the-public concepts unrelated to the profit motive of free enterprise. Because it is difficult, if not impossible, to draw a clear line between Micro and Macro accounting indicating the sphere in which each lies, there are certain aspects of international accounting which are partly Micro and partly Macro, or MIXED MICRO-MACRO. There are two aspects to such mixed situations: QUASI MACRO and HYBRID MICRO-MACRO. The Quasi Macro occurs where the private profit-seeking enterprise is automatically linked to the welfare-of-the-community in which it operates and is there confronted with the welfare and public-good consideration that is slanted in the direction of Macro, hence may be termed QUASI MACRO INTERNATIONAL ACCOUNTING.

The HYBRID MICRO-MACRO aspect occurs where enterprise activities are part Micro and part Macro in character which is exemplified by TAXATION ACCOUNTING. The Micro aspects of taxation have a significant effect on the financial operating income, yet the government has an interest in the income in the same operations, making it Macro. Because the enterprise is the target of the accounting, it necessarily becomes Micro; and the governmental taxation aspect, automatically subjecting the private enterprise to government control, makes it at the same time Macro.

### #1-27....Micro International Accounting

The bulk of the material will naturally be applicable to enterprises involved in international business activities--Mi-

cro International Accounting.  This will be covered in three
parts: International Financial Accounting Theory; International
Financial Accounting Practice; and International Managerial
Accounting Control.

#### #1-28....Macro International Accounting

   Macro international accounting represents that area which is
unrelated to the financial gain objective of the enterprise.
Within recent years, the Macro aspects have been enlarged from
PURE Macro to include Quasi Macro International Accounting.
This relates to the accounting which is dictated by the govern-
ment involved, which injects into private enterprise operations
the government welfare aspects previously pointed out as Social
Responsibility Accounting by Prof. Lee Brummet.

#### #1-29....Pure Macro International Accounting

   Pure Macro Accounting is that dictated by the government to
be followed by enterprises within the society.  It falls into
two broad categories--Controlled Economy Enterprises and Free
Enterprise Societies.  In the Controlled Economy Enterprises,
the businesses are either owned or totally controlled by the
state, and private enterprise and profit motives are nonexistent. In the Free Enterprise Societies the enterprise is' responsible for ancillary aspects that derive from business operations, subjecting the accounting to principles which place the
welfare of the state above that of the individual enterprise.

#### #1-30....Quasi Macro International Accounting

   The following are the ancillary classes of activities resulting from the free enterprise society concept of Macro international accounting: International Socio-Economic Accounting; International Political Accounting; and International Inflation Accounting.

#### #1-31....Hybrid Mixed Macro Accounting

   International taxation represents an area which affects the
financial results of the enterprise, but in which government
policies are also involved.  Therefore International Taxation
Accounting falls within the area of Hybrid Micro-Macro international accounting.  There are two categories of international
taxation: taxation by the country of domicile, and taxation by
countries foreign to that of domicile.  Knowledge of both sets
of taxation laws--domicile and foreign--is desirable.

## #1-32...Chart of Classification of International Accounting

A chart of classification following the pattern above is outlined in Figure 1-2.

FIGURE 1-2
INTERNATIONAL ACCOUNTING CLASSIFICATION CHART

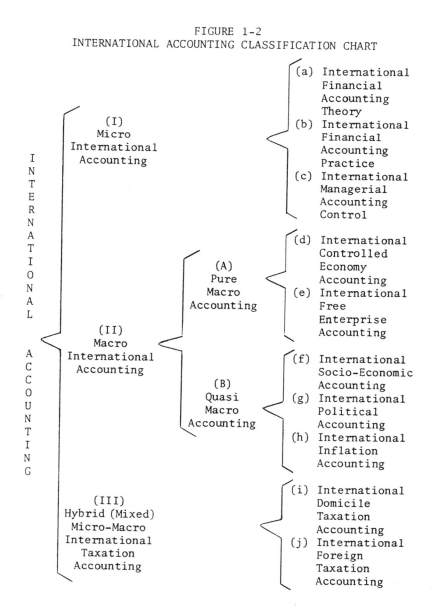

#1-33....The International Accounting Horizon

What is on the horizon for the international practice of
accounting and auditing is described by William S. Kanaga, the
1980-81 chairman of the AICPA Board of Directors, in the article "International Accounting: The Challenge and the Changes,"
on pp. 55-60, Nov. 1980, JOURNAL OF ACCOUNTANCY. The concluding
remarks indicate the future of international accounting:
    In Nov. 1905, an editorial in the first issue of the JOURNAL
    OF ACCOUNTANCY declared that future issues would "contain
    news of accountants in all countries where the profession is
    practiced." Today, keeping abreast of such news is a formid-
    able task, and there is every reason to believe that the
    pace of international commerce will continue to accelerate.
    "The old civic, state and national groupings have become
    unworkable." Realizing this, the world's governments in time
    will dismantle many of the artificial barriers to the inter-
    national practice of accounting and auditing. And those pro-
    fessionals who react well to change and to its new opportun-
    ities are in for an exciting future.
That international accounting has come of age may be evidenced
by the fact that it is on the threshold of becoming a topic to
be regularly included in the Uniform CPA Examination of the
AICPA. In June 1981,the WISCONSIN CPA JOURNAL, p. 23, the article "Representation of International Accounting Topics on the
CPA Examination," by Professors Pearson, Ryans, and Hicks,
points out:
    As more organizations begin to conduct business on a
    multinational level, it would appear there would be an in-
    creased demand for accountants who have expertise in the
    areas of international accounting and reporting. Not all
    accountants have such expertise, however; some probably have
    a reasonable familiarity and some might have no familiarity
    at all.
    METHODOLOGY--CPA examinations administered during the
    past 5 years were analyzed to determine current representa-
    tion of international topics. *** Short, highly-structured
    mail questionnaires were then sent to a random sample of 100
    CPAs, 100 management accountants, and 100 accounting acade-
    micians to seek their views regarding a proposed increase in
    international emphasis on the CPA exam.
    TIME DEVOTED TO INTERNATIONAL ACCOUNTING TOPICS, CPA
    EXAMS FROM MAY 1975 TO NOVEMBER 1979--It is quite evident
    that very little CPA exam time is allocated to topics with
    an international focus. The analysis of the past 5 years'
    exams shows that NO international questions have been asked,
    and very few international questions have been incorporated
    into the three other parts. The average allotted time of 16
    minutes for the entire exam represents less than 2% of the
    total exam time of 1170 minutes.

INCREASING INTERNATIONAL ACCOUNTING COVERAGE--Respondents to the questionnaires who supported an increase (31%), as against those against (42%), believed the Practice and Theory sections lend themselves best to internationalization. Very few perceive a need for a new separate international part.

CONCLUSION--The number of international business transactions and the resulting accounting problems are increasing dramatically. Because of this changing business environment, almost one-third of all the survey respondents believe that international accounting should be given GREATER emphasis on future CPA examinations.

## SUMMARY OF FOOTNOTE REFERENCES
(References are to Paragraph #'s)

#1-3    ACCOUNTING TERMINOLOGY BULLETIN # 1, REVIEW AND RESUME, p. 9
#1-3    STATEMENTS OF ACCOUNTING PRINCIPLES BOARD, APB #4, para. 40
#1-4    MASSACHUSETTS CPA REVIEW (May-June 1979); (AICPA) JOURNAL OF ACCOUNTANCY (Oct. 1979): 76
#1-6    4th International Conference on Accounting Education, Subject 1, p. 7, Louis Perridon; Subject 5, pp. 4-6, Lee Brummet; Subject 1, p. 57, Michael Chetkovich
#1-9    Robert Hagerman, "Accounting in the Bible," THE ACCOUNTING HISTORIANS JOURNAL (Fall 1980): 71-76. Reprinted with permission.
#1-10   Frater Lucas Bartolomes Pacioli, SUMMA DE ARITHMETICA, GEOMETRIA, PROPORTIONI ET PROPORTIONALITA, 1494, translated by John B. Geijsbeek
#1-13   THE WALL STREET JOURNAL (May 25, 1976): 8
#1-13   NEW YORK STOCK EXCHANGE FACT BOOK, 1985, pp. 37-39, 64
#1-13   Marcia Berss, "Just How Alluring Are Foreign Stocks Now?" FORBES (July 29, 1985): 154
#1-14   H.M. Abu-Jbarah, A SUBENTITY BASIS FOR FINANCIAL REPORTING BY MULTINATIONAL FIRMS: A CLUSTER ANALYSIS APPROACH, 1972, doctoral dissertation, University of Wisconsin
#1-18   Weirich, Avery and Anderson, "Approaches to Study of International Accounting," INTERNATIONAL JOURNAL OF ACCOUNTANCY (1971)
#1-23 thru #1-25:   "The International Accounting Structure," adapted from Norlin G. Rueschhoff, INTERNATIONAL ACCOUNTING AND FINANCIAL REPORTING, 1976, Praeger Publishers, Inc., by permission.
#1-24   Reprinted from ORGANIZING FOR INTERNATIONAL FINANCE, Management Monograph No. 35, 1966, pp. 21-23, with the permission of the publisher, Business International Corp., New York
#1-33   William S. Kanaga, "International Accounting: The Challenge and the Changes," JOURNAL OF ACCOUNTANCY (Nov. 1980): 55-60. Copyright © 1980 by the American Institute of Certified Public Accountants, Inc. Opinions expressed in the JOURNAL OF ACCOUNTANCY are those of editors and contributors. Publica-

tion in the JOURNAL OF ACCOUNTANCY does not constitute en-
dorsement by the AICPA or its committees.
#1-33   Pearson, Ryans and Hicks,   "Representation of International
Accounting Topics on the  CPA  Examination," WISCONSIN  CPA
JOURNAL (June 1981): 23

## BIBLIOGRAPHY

AICPA (American Institute of Certified Public Accountants). PROFES-
SIONAL ACCOUNTING IN 30 COUNTRIES.   AICPA, 1975
Brennan, W. John.  THE INTERNATIONALIZATION OF THE ACCOUNTING  PRO-
FESSION.  Toronto: Canadian  Institute of Chartered Account-
ants, 1979
Burton, John C. THE INTERNATIONAL WORLD OF ACCOUNTING. Arthur Young
Professors' Round Table, Council of Arthur Young Professors,
1981
Choi, Frederick.  "Multinational Challenges for Managerial Account-
ants," JOURNAL OF CONTEMPORARY BUSINESS (Autumn 1975): 51-67
Cummings, Joseph and Chetkovich, Michael.  "World Accounting Enters
a New Era," JOURNAL OF ACCOUNTANCY (April 1978): 52-61
Mueller, Gerhard G.  "Academic Research  in International Account-
ing," INTERNATIONAL JOURNAL OF ACCOUNTING (Fall 1970): 67-81
Qureshi, Mahmood.  "Pragmatic and Academic Bases of  International
Accounting," MANAGEMENT INTERNATIONAL  REVIEW, Vol. 19, No.
2 (1979): 61-67
Schoenfeld, Hanns-Martin. "International Accounting  Development,
Issues and Future Directions," JOURNAL  OF  INTERNATIONAL
BUSINESS STUDIES (Fall 1981): 83-100
Seidler, Lee.  "International Accounting--The Ultimate Theory
Course," ACCOUNTING REVIEW (Oct. 1967): 775-781
Sterling, Robert R.  TOWARD A SCIENCE OF ACCOUNTING. Houston, TX:
Scholars Book Co.  Reviewed in JOURNAL OF ACCOUNTANCY (April
1982): 99-102

## THEORY QUESTIONS
(Question Numbers are Keyed to Text Paragraph #'s)

#1-1   Discuss the nature of ACCOUNTING and the basic  purposes
that it serves.
#1-2   What  position have accounting practitioners  taken with
respect to its relationship to management and the nature
of the discipline of accounting?
#1-3   What definition  of ACCOUNTING  has  been promulgated by
the AICPA and been revised by the APB, and what has been
the general conclusion drawn from these two definitions?
Comment on the validity of such conclusion.
#1-4   Do you agree with Charles Waldo Haskins' appraisal as to
the nature of accounting, and if so, how  would you  define accounting as a social science?
#1-5   Many accountants are of the opinion that there is little
relationship between  accounting  and economics.  How do

you feel about such contentions?

#1-6    What new direction indicating the relationship between
        accounting and both economic and social aspects has ac-
        counting been taking in the decade of the 1980s? Ex-
        plain.

#1-9    What three areas of accounting are pointed out and il-
*p 10-11*  lustrate in the Bible? Give examples of each. *FINANCIAL*
        *INTERNAL CONTROL*
        *MANAGERIAL*

#1-10   Who was Fra Pacioli (Paciolo), what were his accomplish-
        ments, what system of accounting did he promulgate that
        is used to the present day?

#1-16   Define International Accounting. How does it differ
        from conventional accounting generally presented in the
        undergraduate accounting program?

#1-18   Define the different approaches to the study of Interna-
        tional Accounting, and indicate which is most appropri-
        ate to use and why.

#1-32   Construct a chart classifying the subject of Interna-
        tional Accounting.

#1-33   Discuss the future of International Accounting.


## CASES

### CASE 1-1

In any type of organizational situation, whether the company
follows an international, regional, or world-wide product division pattern, the success of the financial organization will
largely depend on the relationships among the financial staff
groups at the corporate, divisional, regional and subsidiary
levels.

The first requisite for optimum relationships is to determine the responsibilities in the financial area that should be
assigned at each level. The checklist shown in Chapter 1 as
Figure 1-1 gives an indication of how the financial functions
can be assigned for international operations. These determinations cannot fit the requirements of every firm, but they represent the experiences of a broad cross-section of international firms now implementing or planning specific areas of action
for each level of operations.

**Required**:
Prepare an organizational chart presenting the structure of the
international accounting function, including job titles.

*US Sources*
*FASB*
*SEC*
*IRS*
*FASB*
*Gov't Cost Acctg Stds*
*Industry Custom or Practice*

# Sources of International Accounting

#2-1....Classification of Sources of International Accounting

Because of the heterogeneous nature and characteristics of International Accounting as pointed out in Chapter 1, the question that immediately arises is: "Where do the various rules to be applied in international accounting come from?"

Basically there are six principal sources from which international accounting rules emanate: (I). Laws, enacted in the form of Codes, in the various countries which stipulate the required accounting principles and procedures; (II). General Accounting Principles promulgated in various countries resulting from acceptance of recognized practice application and not from legislative fiat; (III) Pronouncements of Recognized National and International Professional Accounting Organizations; (IV). Pronouncements of Recognized National and International Accounting Professors and Academic Bodies; (V). Limited Scope Organizations, in the form of Non-Accounting International Professional and/or Academic Bodies and Organizations; and (VI). Recognized Principles set forth by mutually agreed International Special Purpose Bodies expressly established for the purpose of creating pronouncements resulting in international accounting standards.

This very great diversity of sources of international accounting has resulted in an overwhelming number of bodies that have had a hand in the creation of international accounting principles. Frequent reference to this great proliferation of bodies is a sine qua non to the proper understanding of international accounting. It is of the utmost importance that the reader have a knowledge of the specified sources inasmuch as reference to them will be frequently made in the remainder of this material. The reader will therefore have to bear with the extensive listing in order to have the proper comprehension of the effect of the body source and the country on the nature and character of the principle evolved as well as its impact on the establishment of international accounting principles.

## (I).  STATUTORY OR CODE ACCOUNTING PRINCIPLES

### #2-2....International Accounting Principles by Legislative Fiat

In many countries the legislatures create laws relating to accounting principles that must be observed by accountants in such countries. Basically, these countries are centered in Europe--principally Germany, England, France, Sweden, Holland, Switzerland, Belgium and Italy. While there may be a difference in the degree or extent to which these principles are promulgated, nevertheless one can perceive a relationship between the difference in law with respect to what are known as "Civil Law" countries and those known as "Common Law" countries.

In the Civil Law countries, the underlying basis for law is in CODE or STATUTORY law, per se, which goes to great lengths and detail outlining not only what the law is but also how it is to be effectuated. In the Common Law version there is a minimum of statutory or Code control, with emphasis on a more flexible attitude and judgment by facts surrounding particular case situations. The Civil is more or less rigidified and the principal problem with it is to interpret the meaning of the language surrounding the particular law. Under the Common Law version, there is more flexibility and less need to be involved with interpretations of stiff legal language, but rather a greater reliance on equity and propriety.

### #2-3....Code Civil Law Countries

Prior to the 1940s, the typical Civil Code countries which had their basic origins in the French Napoleonic Code were France and Germany. They exerted influence on the other Code countries, viz., Switzerland, Sweden, Belgium, and far off Japan. The medium through which the accounting control was maintained, as indicated above, was detailed laws, such as National Charts of Accounting and Uniform Financial Statement Laws.

The extent to which Codes control the practice of accounting will of course depend upon the nature of the government. Where all business was under the virtual control of the government, accounting practice would be totally dictated by laws of the country. The same situation exists today in Communist Russia where all business is virtually under the control of the government.

However, in the more democratic governments, where a considerable part of business operations falls under the aegis of free enterprise, we find only a portion of accounting practice controlled by law and codes. Such part would, of course, be slanted toward the public interest, in the direction of having statements presented, and books and records kept, in a manner that would not be repugnant to the interests of the public and/

or the country.    Thus, Code countries accounting may fall into
two groups--total code control or partial code control.

#### #2-4....Total Code Control Countries

Under a total code  control concept, micro-accounting merges
with macro-accounting.   The concepts of total control countries
allow for a centrally controlled economy.   The micro-accounting
is not profit-oriented but based on control centers. Insofar as
Russia, or any of its  Eastern  European  satellites,  is  concerned, a brief illustrative  example  presented in the chapter
on Macro  Accounting should suffice  for the purposes  of  this
material.

#### #2-5....Partial Code Control Countries

It would be infeasible to treat  all of the practices of accounting in  all countries which have  accounting code control.
Under the circumstances, the student can get a fairly good picture from a treatment of the more prestigious countries. Illustrations will be given of England, Germany and France.

#### #2-6....England Code Accounting

Basically  a  good deal of  the accounting rules of  England
are of  the Common Law type--those developed  and  accepted by
the accounting profession through the  various professional institutes of chartered accountants.   The Code portion of English
accounting falls under what is  known as  the BRITISH COMPANIES
LAWS.    There has  been a  succession of British Companies Acts
which have diverse accounting requirements, and the development
of  the  accounting  practice in  England  has closely followed
these Company Acts.
Because  England is representative of the  Common Law aspect
of development of accounting principles,  the Accountancy  Laws
result  from  the establishment of principles  carried  out  in
practice,  which formed the basis for the enactment of the law.
The procedure that was followed was to form a committee to make
a study of a particular situation and offer recommendations for
formulating  it  into a law.   The committee  constituency  was
drafted from members of parliament, civil  servants, other professionals including attorneys, and business executives.
The Gladstone Committee was  the first one of this sort appointed,  as indicated by  Leonard W.  Hein in the article "The
Auditor and the British  Companies Acts," in the ACCOUNTING RE-
VIEW, July 1963, p. 508. The first Companies Act was promulgated in 1844 by the Gladstone Committee.  It was entitled "AN ACT
FOR  THE REGISTRATION, INCORPORATION AND  REGULATION OF  JOINT
STOCK COMPANIES," and was the foundation  for modern  business
incorporation methods.

Other similar Companies Acts were passed in 1855, 1856, 1862, 1867 and 1879. The Davey Committee Act was passed in 1895, followed by the Acts of 1900, 1907, and the Consolidation Act of 1908. Next came the Wrenbury Committee in 1918, and the Greene Committee in 1926, resulting in the Companies Act of 1928. Then followed the Cohen Committee, resulting in the Acts of 1947 and 1948, and more recently the Jenkins Committee of 1962 and the Act of 1966.

It may be observed that the great frequency of these Acts would be indicia of constant updating and upgrading of the subject matter involved. They were concerned with the following matters: financial statements, balance sheets and income statements; consolidated financial statements; regulation of public auditors; and corporate security issuances and dissolutions.

An illustration of the scholarly work may be evidenced in the Company Act of 1966 resulting from the Jenkins Committee report:

The proper function of the financial statements is admirably explained in the following passage from the RECOMMENDATIONS OF ACCOUNTING PRINCIPLES issued to its members by the Institute of Chartered Accountants in England and Wales: "The primary purpose of the annual accounts of a business is to present information to the proprietors, showing how their funds have been utilized and their profits derived from such use."

"It has long been accepted in accounting practice that a balance sheet prepared for this purpose is an historical record and not a statement of current worth. Stated briefly, its function is to show in monetary terms the capital, reserves, and liabilities of a business at the date at which it is prepared and the manner in which the total moneys representing them have been distributed over the several types of assets."

"Similarly a profit and loss account is an historical record. It shows as the profit or loss the difference between the revenue for the period covered by the account and the expenditure chargeable in that period, including charges for the amortization of capital expenditure. Revenue and expenditure are brought into the account at their recorded monetary amounts. This basis of accounting is frequently described as the historical cost basis."

#2-7....Impact of British Company Acts on Other Countries

The British investments in the U.S. in the 19th century resulted in British auditors coming to the U.S. to examine financial statements there. It was only natural to expect that these British auditors would leave an imprint on the U.S. accountants that would definitely bear the stamp of the principles promul-

gated by the Companies Acts. Thus the British Companies Acts
had a decided impact on U.S. accounting principles.

With respect to Companies Acts passed in other European and
South American countries, they were few and far between, resulting not only in outdated laws existing on the books, but
also in the creation of a lack of pragmatic application. This
was in contrast to the English Code resulting from the utilization of pragmatic experience as the basis for creating legislation applicable to the situations they were designed to cover--
the keystone for the passage of the British Companies Acts.

## #2-8....German Code Accounting

Just as England is typical of the Common Law approach, Germany has been typical of the Civil Code approach, discussed by
Hans W. Singer in his book STANDARDIZED ACCOUNTANCY IN GERMANY,
Cambridge Univ. Press, 1944. Between 1937 and 1945, there was
complete centralized control of all economic activity resulting
in a pure Macro Accounting situation, viz., all accounting was
totally geared to government policies, since virtually all business was either owned or controlled by the central government.
All accounting was subject to the government decree of 1937
which declared:

> The new aims of the German economy call for increased output
> and efficiency from business undertakings. The fulfillment
> of this great task required a thorough knowledge and a CLOSE
> CONTROL of all business transactions. Thus, a well develop-
> ed accounting system is a primary factor in the reorganiza-
> tion of industry. The PUBLIC INTEREST and in particular the
> aims of the Four-Year Plan demand that the accounting system
> of all firms should be arranged on uniform principles. Sys-
> tematic mutual exchange of experience, especially in the
> form of comparative analysis of companies, will help towards
> this end.

There will be no further discussion of total Macro Accounting,
except for Russia, which will be treated later.

At this point we are concerned with accounting methodology
under the democratic West German economy from 1946 as an example of Micro Accounting under a Code System. The development of
accounting principles in the German Federal Republic was predicated on the base of accounting that had been established in
the late 1920s and early 1930s before the Great Depression.

## #2-9....The Schmalenbach Model Chart of Accounts

The dominant accounting philosophy created during the 1920s
and early 1930s was academic in character. It was based on the

work of Prof. Eugen  Schmalenbach of the Univ. of  Cologne, resulting in his book  THE MODEL  CHART OF ˙ACCOUNTS published in
1929.   It culminated from the confusion existing in German accounting, resulting  from different companies  using  different
methods of accounting and his attempt to unify accounting principles. The issue was resolved by the creation by Prof. Schmalenbach of a national  uniform chart of accounts.  Modern German
accounting follows  the  Schmalenbach pattern, as do many other
European countries.

     The Schmalenbach  pattern was based  on  the principle  of a
NATIONAL CHART OF ACCOUNTS established on an industry-wide basis.  Prof. Kenneth Most in the  article "Official Charts of Accounts in Germany and France" in THE ACCOUNTANT, Jan. 26, 1957,
pp. 81-91, points out that current German  accounting is predicated substantially on CHARTS OF ACCOUNTS developed in over 100
industries. These Uniform Charts of Accounts are accompanied by
explanations of procedures and methodology for  their implementation. However, in May 1965 the German Bundestag (Parliament),
after 6 years of background work, passed a German Companies Act
which became effective on Jan. 1, 1966.   This Act provided for
many reforms involving the  tightening  up  of  loose reporting
methods by German companies as well as greater consideration of
the interests of stockholders.

     In this respect, then, Germany has followed the English pat-
tern but with more emphasis on a Code approach.  Since the Uniform Charts of Accounts may also fall within  the second  group
of  sources of international  accounting mentioned above--viz.,
Accounting Principles  Resulting From  Acceptance of Recognized
Practice  Application  But Not  From Legislative  Fiat--further
detailed discussion  will  be deferred to the treatment of this
Second Source of International Accounting.


#2-10....French Code Accounting

     In July 1962,  the CANADIAN CHARTERED ACCOUNTANT, pp. 56-57,
Pierre Garnier points out, in  the article "Uniform  Accounting
Systems in France," that the first  French  accounting regulations were  enacted in 1930 for a  few  specific types of businesses  and professions.  In 1938 a code was  passed regulating
insurance  businesses,  and in 1942 model  financial statements
were required for the banking businesses. In 1946 a ministerial
commission was appointed  to examine the  adoption  of  uniform
accounting methods, which  in 1947 proposed  a  PLAN COMPTABLE
GENERAL officially approved by a decree of September 14, 1947.

     Subsequently in the same year  (1947)  a CONSEIL NATIONAL DE
LA COMPTABILITE  (NATIONAL  COUNCIL  OF  ACCOUNTING) was formed
under whose jurisdiction all  accounting matters were  brought.
In 1950 and  again  in  1957, the National Council updated  the

PLAN COMPTABLE GENERAL and its function  was made to review the
Plan periodically and see that it meets current requirements.

#2-11....The Plan Comptable General

   The PLAN is outlined in the handbook  published by  the Conseil National de la Comptabilite entitled PLAN COMPTABLE GENER-
AL.  It was published  in 1960 in Paris,  and  some of its more
important features are stated on pages 95-98:
    First, it established a uniform chart of accounts;
    Second, it specifies the rules for recording transactions;
    Third, it promulgates reporting procedures and valuation
        accounting;
    Fourth, it sets forth standard forms for financial state-
        ments, and account classifications for preparation of
        statements.
It can readily be  seen that such an  integrated  and complete
set of standards comprises, as it were, a statement of codified
accounting principles.
   Under such codified  plan, the  result has  been that  since
1947 all businesses publicly owned, and where 20 percent of the
outstanding capital stock is  owned by the government or a public agency, are required to  follow the uniform accounting designated  in the Plan.   In addition any companies that have received 10 million or more francs of subsidies from the  government,  as well as busineses which have revalued their fixed assets  under a price-level adjustment permitted by the Plan, are
subject to the provisions of the Plan.

#2-12....Voluntary Espousal of Plan Comptable General

   Although only the types of  business operations specifically
stated in the Plan were  subject to it,  the Plan had worked so
well for those companies  which were required to use it, that a
great many other French companies voluntarily espoused it. In a
technical paper delivered before the 8th International Congress
of Accountants in  New York in  1962,  Joseph Loore points out
that  "in 1962 between  80  and 90 percent  of large  companies
adopted the Plan; between 60 and 80 percent of medium companies
also did; and 40  to 60 percent of smaller businesses  utilized
it."   The result of this overwhelming response was the passing
of a  decree on Dec. 28, 1959, which made the Plan required for
all French enterprises after a waiting period of 5 years.  Subsequently in Dec. 1961, the Plan was  adopted  in Belgium which
closely follows French policies.

#2-13....Code Accounting in the U. S.

   It should be noted that there is a glaring  contrast between
the British, German and  French provisions on the  one hand and

the virtually complete absence of similar Code provisions in the U.S. Whatever Code provisions or statutes that exist in the U.S. are to regulate certain industries (principally banking and insurance), to protect the public, as well as to avoid fraud in the issuance of corporate securities as exemplified by the Securities and Exchange Act. These legal codes are aimed at regulation of procedures of businesses and are not directly targeted for accounting as such. Any accounting provisions contained in these laws are incidental to effectuation of the purposes of the Act.

### (II). UNIFORM INDUSTRIAL ACCOUNTING PRINCIPLES

#### #2-14...Voluntary Industry Association Accounting Principles Adopted Either As Law or Required For Industry Recognition

A second source of international accounting has resulted from certain specific industries in many countries having vol- untarily legislated codes of accounting standards that the in- dustries themselves have sought to apply to firm members of the industry. On some occasions such industry regulations became so forceful as to be enacted in the form of legal legislation, such as the German Model Chart of Accounts.

#### #2-15....Swedish Metalworking Industry

Perhaps the most well-known case of development of industri- al accounting principles is demonstrated by what is known as the "Swedist M-Chart." One of the proteges of Prof. Schmalen- bach, who developed the GERMAN MODEL CHART OF ACCOUNTS, was Swedish Prof. Albert ter Vehn, who naturally adapted the German Chart to Swedish industry. However, instead of on a national basis, Vehn did so on a sectional basis by relating it to in- dustries. While there was no development of a national chart such as in Germany, the first Swedish industry that was con- fronted with intricate accounting principles due to complex production processes was the Metalworking industry. As a result the Swedish Association of Metalworking Industries selected a committee in 1940 to establish a uniform set of accounts for the industry. This was accomplished in 1945 and was labeled the M-CHART. It was successfully adopted overwhelmingly in the Swedish metalworking industry.

As a consequence of the success of the M-CHART, there fol- lowed in its wake adoption of similar uniform sets of accounts which were referred to as an "E-CHART" by electricity generat- ing plants, an "S-CHART" by the shoe industry, and a "T-CHART" by the textile industry. The result was that a very large seg- ment of all Swedish industrial enterprises is governed by the

accounting procedures based on  Uniform Charts of Accounts.  In
addition the  Chart Arrangement has been adopted on a less formal  basis  in other  industries,  such as SAS, the Scandinavian
Airlines System.  The Swedish accounting firm of Stockholm Horwath & Horwath has developed a uniform system of hotels adapted
from  the  American  uniform  system designed to  meet  Swedish
standards and  requirements.  This new national.system  of  accounts for hotels was introduced by the Swedish Hotel and Rest-
aurant Association during 1983.

#2-16....Legal Industrial Accounting Procedures

    In the United States, many  accounting rules are established
in the  course  of  regulation  of public  service  industries,
viz., those affected with  a public interest, as previously indicated.  In such cases regulatory bodies or commissions set up
by law  are  appointed to enforce  the application of these accounting principles to the practices of  these industries.  The
railroads, utilities, banks, insurance companies,  oil and  gas
are examples.  As early as 1917 the U.S. Federal Reserve Board
issued a recommendation of this kind entitled "Approved Methods
for the Preparation of Balance Sheet  Statements" in its WORLD
WAR I BULLETIN.  Many industries have made suggested accounting
procedures desirable, though not mandatory.  They have resulted
in the establishment of principles practiced by the bulk of the
members  of  the particular industry, notable of which were the
American Hotel Association, the American  Pétroleum  Institute,
and the Meat Packing Industry.
    In England too, as early as  1919, the printing industry set
forth its guidelines for accounting for members of the industry
by the British  Federation of Master Printers.  Many other fed-
erations, industries, and business associations in England have
followed the pattern.
    As  was  seen in the cases of Germany and France, accounting
principles have been  established on  a wider basis, being more
nationwide in character, and more or less disregarding specific
areas of business.  Nevertheless, rules were created which were
expected to be followed to receive recognition.

### (III).   PROFESSIONAL ACCOUNTING ORGANIZATIONS:
### (A).   INTERNATIONAL BODIES

#2-17....International Professional Accounting Bodies

    What appears to  be  what might become  the most influential
and  potent  source of international accounting  principles are
the professional accounting groups spread around  the world who
have periodic meetings and  conventions  in different areas of
the world on  a more or  less regular basis.  These  groups, of

which there are many  and are in a constant process  of change,
may be divided,  on a geographical criterion, into two groups--
International and  Regional.  The  principal objective of these
groups  is to improve the standards that presently exist in the
various countries, and not only to unify these standards toward
obtaining  some  uniformity in their adoption, but also in some
way to have them accepted on a global basis.

   Although the international conferences and conventions  have
been held on a  regular periodic basis and considerable discussion in the direction of the objectives stated above has  taken
place, no definite pattern  of  global acceptance  has  jelled.
This  was  because of the lack of continuity, in the sense that
each meeting has constituted a separate and distinct confabula-
tion, thereby lacking the persistence and cohesion  required to
come to conclusions as to a definite subject matter.

   Nevertheless  there  have been  advantages that have accrued
from these meetings:  (1) they recognize that there is a definite need  for  the establishment of  general accounting principles; (2) there is  a  considerable amount of discussion  about
them; (3) many different  concepts are advanced; and (4) definite thinking along these lines is  manifested from the many and
varied papers  that have been presented and discussed.  Many of
these papers receive  publication in both professional and academic journals,  which  in turn become the  subject  matter for
discussions  between professionals  and  professionals, professionals and academicians, and academicians and students.

#2-18...Classification of International Professional Bodies

   These international professional accounting bodies fall into
two groups--World-wide and Regional.  The most prominent world-
wide bodies have been the INTERNATIONAL CONGRESS OF ACCOUNTANTS
and the INTERNATIONAL FEDERATION OF ACCOUNTANTS. Of the regional groups,  the following organizations have  met on a periodic
basis in the regions they represent: the INTERAMERICAN ACCOUNT-
ING ASSOCIATION;  the UNION  EUROPEENNE DES EXPERTES COMPTABLES
ECONOMIQUES  ET  FINANCIERS  (UEC); the CONFEDERATION (formerly
Conference) OF  ASIAN AND PACIFIC ACCOUNTANTS (CAPA);  the AC-
COUNTANTS  INTERNATIONAL  STUDY GROUP (AISG);  and the INTERNA-
TIONAL COMMITTEE FOR ACCOUNTING COOPERATION (ICAC).

PROFESSIONAL WORLD-WIDE ACCOUNTING BODIES

#2-19....The International Congress of Accountants

   What was, but no longer is, the largest and most prestigious
group of international accountants has  been the  International
Congress of Accountants, which was replaced in 1977 by the  International Federation of Accountants (IFAC). The numbers, ven-

ues, and dates of the Congresses were as follows:

| | | | |
|---|---|---|---|
| 1st | St. Louis, 1904 | 7th | Amsterdam, 1957 |
| 2nd | Amsterdam, 1926 | 8th | New York, 1962 |
| 3rd | New York, 1929 | 9th | Paris, 1967 |
| 4th | London, 1933 | 10th | Sydney, 1972 |
| 5th | Berlin, 1938 | 11th | Munich, 1977 |
| 6th | London, 1952 | 12th | Mexico City, 1982 |

Until 1977 the meetings were scheduled for every five years and the degree of growth may be evidenced by the fact that there were 3,000 in 1957, 4,000 in 1962, and over 6,000 from over 60 different countries in 1977.

## #2-20...The International Coordination Committee For the Accountancy Profession (ICCAP)

Since the Congresses were individual, disconnected meetings, there was no continuity, resulting in a failure to pursue certain principles to a conclusion. For this reason, at the 1972 meeting it was decided to organize a committee known as the ICCAP, with representatives from Australia, Canada, West Germany, France, India, Japan, Mexico, Netherlands, Philippines, United Kingdom and Ireland, and the United States.

The purposes of the ICCAP were to arrange subsequent meetings, set up liaison between various bodies, relations with regional bodies, recommend any alterations in committee setup or deliberations, and to attempt to establish a permanent international office. Between 1972 and 1976, the ICCAP held five meetings and at the final one in Hawaii recommended that it be discontinued together with the International Congress of Accountants, and that it be replaced by the IFAC.

## #2-21...International Federation of Accountants (IFAC)

The IFAC was organized into two segments: (1) an ASSEMBLY, to take the place of the International Congress; and (2) an EXECUTIVE COMMITTEE, to take the place of the ICCAP. At the 1977 meeting which created the IFAC, the location of the secretariat was designated as New York.

The Constitution of the IFAC declares the following objectives: set a goal of international, technical, ethical and educational guidelines for the accounting profession; promote regional organizations; arrange Congress meetings for the purpose of interchanges of accounting principles between accountants from all over the world; disseminate principles of development; and attempt to reach conclusions that may be adopted for practice.

In 1976, prior to the meeting in which the IFAC was created, various sources, such as THE WALL STREET JOURNAL and the CANADIAN CHARTERED ACCOUNTANT, were of the opinion that the IFAC

would result in international accounting harmony.   However, in
the CONGRESS  DAILY NEWS,  published daily during the meetings,
issue of Oct. 12, 1977, the keynote speaker, German Minister of
Economics, Otto Lambsdorff, stated:

> International  harmonization of  criteria  is  a painstaking
> endeavor  and has  all too often  been  accompanied by dis-
> appointments.  Thus, West Germany is disciplined to go along
> with those  E.C.  countries  still  experiencing high infla-
> tionary rates which want  to abandon  the principles of his-
> torical cost accounting.   To  do so  would be tantamount to
> capitulating to inflation and raise the danger of its insti-
> tutionalization.   The importance of accountants  has  never
> been greater as a means to gain public confidence in balance
> sheet reporting.

These remarks are, of course, ominous with  respect  to  future
prospects for international accounting harmonization.  The second meeting of  the  IFAC was held  in  Mexico City in  October
1982.   The CPA LETTER, July 1982,  Vol. 62, No. 13, p. 2, indicates that "IFAC's membership consists of 80 accounting  bodies
from 59 countries which  represent more than  750,000 qualified
accountants engaged in public  and private practice, government
and education."

The 13th International Congress, which would be the 2nd IFAC
Congress, is  scheduled to take place  in  Tokyo  in October of
1987  under the auspices of the Japanese Institute of CPAs with
the proposed motto  "The  Public Accountant  and  Technological
Evolution."


## (III).   PROFESSIONAL ACCOUNTING ORGANIZATIONS:
### (B).   REGIONAL BODIES

### #2-22....The Interamerican Accounting Association (IAA)

As  the  name implies,  this group is regional in  character
having a Western Hemisphere  coverage of North and South America.  Since the bulk of the countries south of the United States
use Spanish as their national language, the meetings of the IAA
have been conducted in Spanish.  Such is the case with the IAA,
which before  1975 was known  as  the Inter-American Accounting
Conference.

As with other groups, many papers are presented and published, mostly in Spanish. Also because most of these countries are
in the developmental stage, as will be discussed in the chapter
on  Social Accounting, this aspect is emphasized in the papers.
The Interamerican  Accounting  Association has  had meetings at
the following locations:

| 1st  San Juan, P.R., 1949        | 9th  Bogota, Col., 1970              |
|-----------------------------------|--------------------------------------|
| 2nd  Mexico City, Mex., 1951      | 10th Punta del Este, Urug., 1972     |
| 3rd  Sao Paulo, Brazil, 1954      | 11th San Juan, P.R., 1974            |
| 4th  Santiago, Chile, 1957        | 12th Vancouver, Canada, 1977         |
| 5th  Havana, Cancelled            | 13th Panama City, Panama, 1979       |
| 6th  New York, 1962               | 14th Santiago, Chile, 1981           |
| 7th  Mar del Plata, Arg., 1965    | 15th Rio de Janeiro, Arg., 1983      |
| 8th  Caracas, Ven., 1967          | 16th Miami, Florida, 1985            |

The IAA functions through a group of technical and coordinating committees with headquarters location rotating among various countries, although it does maintain a secretariat in New York. The group has made some definite contributions toward advancing accounting standards in university education programs and professional accounting standards.

A report of the 7th Conference has been presented in the JOURNAL OF ACCOUNTANCY, Feb. 1966, p. 12, entitled "Inter-American Conference Adopts Auditing Resolution," which resulted in a resolution adopting "generally accepted auditing standards" resulting from a book published by the Instituto Mexicano de Contadores Publicos entitled AUDITING STANDARDS AND PROCEDURES. The IAA publishes a newsletter issued quarterly called BOLETIN INTERAMERICANO DE CONTABILIDAD. The IAA is also referred to as the "Asociacion Interamericana de Contabilidad" (AIC).

### #2-23...The Union Europeenne Des Expertes Comptables Economiques et Financiers (UEC)

The UEC was begun in Paris in November 1951 by 12 professional certified accounting associations as charter members from the following countries: Austria, Belgium, France, West Germany, Italy, Luxembourg, Netherlands, Portugal, Spain, and Switzerland. In 1963 professional societies from England, Yugoslavia, and the Scandinavian countries joined this group. The UEC Congresses have been held at the following locations:

| 1st  Florence and Rome, 1953 | 5th  Vienna, 1964        |
|-------------------------------|--------------------------|
| 2nd  Brussels, 1955           | 6th  Copenhagen, 1969    |
| 3rd  Nice, 1958               | 7th  Madrid, 1973        |
| 4th  Zurich, 1961             | 8th  Dublin, 1978        |
|                               | 9th  Strasbourg, 1983    |

Originally the secretariat was located at Paris but a permanent one was set up in Munich. Although the Congresses are relatively few and far between, the UEC maintains a continuous flow of activity through 12 permanent committees whose members are appointed on a rotating basis. The reports of the committees presented to the UEC executive committee result in resolutions regarding recommendations in the following areas each represented by a committee: accounting practices; accounting law; auditing practices; professional rules; publications; tax systems; and terminology. In the middle 1960s it published the UEC JOURNAL on a quarterly basis in German, French and English.

    Just as the IAA is geared to the Americas, the UEC is natur-
ally related to operations in the European theater. This has
been emphasized by the article "UEC" in THE ACCOUNTANT, Aug.
31, 1963, pp. 246-248, in which on its 10th anniversary it was
stated that: "This Working Group has for 3 years supplied the
Common Market authorities with countless information required
by them, and submitted important suggestions to them concerning
the methods for applying the Treaty of Rome to the profession."
As a result, the UEC is recognized by the European Economic
Community, and was recognized by the IFAC at its initiation
meeting in Munich in 1977.

    The UEC has been a prolific source of accounting material
in the form of brochures, paperbacks, UEC JOURNAL, and several
publications which have been very successfully circulated.
Among them are the ACCOUNTING DICTIONARY in the language of
eight countries, including Denmark, Netherlands, England,
France, Germany, Italy, Portugal and Spain, in its 1974 second
edition; and the 1974 third edition of the AUDITING HANDBOOK.

    Finally, the UEC has been an effective source of interna-
tional accounting through its study conferences and seminars.
Thus the 3rd UEC Study Conference in Yugoslavia in 1975 covered
broad aspects of international accounting cooperation and exchanges. The Euro-Seminars, as they are called, are held on an
annual basis involving pairs of countries, e.g., England and
Germany, England and Scandinavia, Germany and France, Germany
and Holland, etc. The first British-German seminar was held in
1972 in Wiesbaden and has been held annually since.

    The effectiveness of the UEC can best be summed up by the
following quotation from the article "UEC - Union Europeenne
Des Expertes Comptables, Economiques et Financiers" in THE AC-
COUNTANT, Aug. 31, 1963, p. 246:

    The profession of auditors and business counselors has been
    the liberal profession to be organized on an European plan
    with the creation between its members of an European spirit
    as a fundamental aim. As proved by the results already
    achieved by its Council, by its committees, by its Congress-
    es, the UEC has well shown its efficiency while working
    steadfastly with a feeling of European brotherhood.
Two significant thoughts may be drawn from this quotation: (1)
the recognition of accounting as a profession; and (2) the regional character of international accounting in the sense of
promoting European brotherhood.

#2-24....European Congress of Accountants (ECA)

    The foregoing European brotherhood had a profound effect on
Sir Thomas Robson, an eminent British accountant, who, in 1963,
had the feeling that the 9th International Congress of Accountants to be held in 1967 might follow the 8th held in New York

in a country outside Europe.  He accordingly called for an ECA, which was held in Edinburgh in 1963. Pursuant to this Congress, Sir Thomas wrote "Cooperation  in Europe," published in THE AC-COUNTANT, March 28, 1964, pp. 381-383, in which he stated:

> There might not  for some 10 or 15 years be a common meeting point  at  which  substantial  numbers  of  accountants could come together from all Western European countries, including Britain. The upshot  was that  the Scottish Institute gener-ously  undertook the task  of organizing the  Edinburgh Con-gress of last year (1963) and carried it through to the suc-cessful conclusion of which we all know.

As a result of the Edinburgh  ECA, many European countries were represented who formed close enough  ties which resulted in the admission into the UEC of the Chartered Accountants of  England and  Ireland, Holland, and  the Scandinavian countries.   These countries, through an amendment of the UEC CHARTER, were admit-ted to membership in the UEC in April 1963.  The net effect was a merger of the ECA into the UEC.

#### #2-25...Confederation of Asian and Pacific Accountants (CAPA)

This group, originally named the FAR EAST CONFERENCE OF  AC-COUNTANTS, held its first Asian and  Pacific Accounting Conven-tion in 1957 in Manila.  The title was later changed to CONFER-ENCE OF ASIAN AND PACIFIC ACCOUNTANTS, and finally to CONFEDER-ATION OF ASIAN AND PACIFIC ACCOUNTANTS (CAPA).  Its conventions have been held in the following locations:

| | | | | |
|---|---|---|---|---|
| 1st | Manila, 1957 | | 6th | Singapore and |
| 2nd | Canberra and | | | Kuala Lumpur, |
| | Melbourne, 1960 | | | 1970 |
| 3rd | Kyoto and Tokyo, 1962 | | 7th | Bangkok, 1973 |
| 4th | New Delhi, 1965 | | 8th | Hong Kong, 1976 |
| 5th | Wellington and | | 9th | Manila, 1979 |
| | Christchurch, 1968 | | 10th | New Delhi, 1983 |

The principal objective  of the CAPA is to create a uniform re-gional accounting  profession and is  therefore  professionally oriented. A by-product would be the creation of regional inter-national accounting  principles as  guidelines for  the practi-tioners of the region.  The  meetings of CAPA have followed the pattern of  the International Congresses of Accountants, and it is common to find a duplication of attendance by members of the profession and academic circles at both. The natural difference is that the CAPA papers center around the problems in the Asian and Pacific theater rather  than a broader international  scope as represented by the International Congresses.

The  organizational structure of the  CAPA has  an executive committee with membership representing the Pacific countries of Australia, Hong  Kong,  Japan, New Zealand, Philippines, Singa-pore, and the United States.   In 1976 a  permanent secretariat was established in New Zealand, which in 1978 was moved to Hong Kong, and is now in Manila, Philippines.

#2-26....The Accountants International Study Group (AISG)

The AISG is made up of practitioners from the U.S., England and Canada. Its purpose is "to institute comparative studies as to accounting thought and practice in the participating countries; to make reports from time to time which, subject to approval of the sponsoring institutes (AICPA, CHARTERED AC-COUNTANTS OF ENGLAND AND CANADA), would be issued to members of those institutes." It thus appears that the studies are made by professional English-speaking practitioners for the benefit of the members of the professional institutes, and that such stud-ies are directed only to English-speaking countries' accounting principles. Nevertheless they may have utility not only for application to international accounting clients but also for academicians.

#2-27....Accounting Studies

When a study is completed, it is given a number and publish-ed as a Study. These studies have been used as references not only for international accounting courses but also for courses in the regular areas of the accounting curriculum in U.S. uni-versities and texts written therefor. During the ten years of its existence, twenty studies have been published, as follows:

ACCOUNTANTS INTERNATIONAL STUDY GROUP STUDIES

| No. | Date | Title |
|-----|------|-------|
| 1 | 1968 | Accounting and Auditing Approaches to Inventories in Three Nations |
| 2 | 1969 | The Independent Auditor's Reporting Standards in Three Nations |
| 3 | 1969 | Using the Work and Reports of Another Auditor |
| 4 | 1971 | Accounting for Corporate Income Taxes |
| 5 | 1972 | Reporting by Diversified Countries |
| 6 | 1972 | Consolidated Financial Statements |
| 7 | 1973 | The Funds Statement |
| 8 | 1974 | Materiality in Accounting |
| 9 | 1974 | Extraordinary Items, Prior Period Adjustments, & Changes in Accounting Principles |
| 10 | 1974 | Published Profit Forecasts |
| 11 | 1975 | International Financial Reporting |
| 12 | 1975 | Comparative Glossary of Accounting Terms in Canada, U. K. and U. S. |
| 13 | 1975 | Accounting for Goodwill |
| 14 | 1975 | Interim Financial Reporting |
| 15 | 1975 | Going Concern Problems |

| 16 | 1976 | Independence of Auditors |
|----|------|--------------------------|
| 17 | 1976 | Audit Committees |
| 18 | 1977 | Accounting for Pension Costs |
| 19 | 1978 | Revenue Recognition |
| 20 | 1978 | Related Party Transactions |

#2-28...International Committee for Acctg. Cooperation (ICAC)

The ICAC, formed in 1966, has as its basic objective the improvement of accounting education and practice in underdeveloped countries, particularly in South America. It was the product of an accounting statement issued by the AICPA in January 1966 suggesting that Third World countries be given some attention in the development of accounting education and practice. This, of course, required considerable financial assistance, so that the statement had to be directed to international lending and finance organizations. They were requested to designate representatives to serve on a special committee organized to set up and implement the accounting assistance program. This resulted in the organization of the ICAC. Representatives to the committee come from the AICPA, Canadian Institute of Chartered Accountants, the Mexican Institute of CPAs, the U.S. Agency for International Development, the Inter-American Development Bank, and the International Finance Corporation.

The basic objectives of the ICAC have been stated in the following terms:

The importance of accounting is illustrated by the fact that aggregate national figures must be supported by accurate economic data recorded at the source by industry and commerce. The absence of such economic data often discourages the granting of credit and reduces the flow of essential loan and equity capital from domestic and foreign sources. The success of many economic development programs is also dependent on the existence of accurate and reliable accounting data and the competency and skills of accounting professionals.

This statement definitely indicates the strong relationship between accounting and economics as discussed in Chapter 1.

In 1967 Colombia was designated as a target for a major study project for accounting development, which resulted in an exhaustive and comprehensive report. In addition, a number of other projects involving educational interchanges, proposed seminars through South and Central America, and publications were all started. The results were disappointing inasmuch as nothing tangible was accomplished. A similar proposal was advanced for Third World African countries which will be discussed in the chapter related to Social and Developmental Accounting.

## #2-29...Opinions of Individual Professional Accounting Firms

Accounting professionals in many countries have issued pronouncements which have definitely had an impact on international accounting. Thus, the AICPA has, as one of its principal operating arms, the INTERNATIONAL PRACTICE DIVISION. To implement this, all of the larger international accounting firms issue regularly pamphlets, booklets, and newsletters regarding international accounting matters in an abundant fashion, keeping abreast of all developments as they arise. This has been a most fruitful source of international accounting material. The first such professional group to initiate international accounting concepts was the Canadian Institute of Chartered Accountants in its official monthly journal. Other similar organizations are the Dutch Institute (NIVRA) and the Chartered Accountants Institutes of England, Scotland, Wales, and Ireland.

## (IV).  ACADEMIC ACCOUNTING BODIES

## #2-30....Classification of Academic Accounting Bodies

Extremely active in the international accounting scene have been the professors of accounting in universities around the world. Next to the accounting practitioners--and participating with them equally both in international conferences and publications--the university professors of accounting have been a potent force in the development of international accounting principles. Like the professional accountants, the objectives of the professors have been to improve present standards in the various countries, to attempt to attain uniform standards, and to seek global adoption of generally accepted accounting principles.

The academicians may be classified from two points of view: (1) Nature of the body, and (2) Geographical scope. From the viewpoint of Nature, there are two groups: (a) Accounting Organizations and (b) Non-Accounting Organizations. From the viewpoint of Scope, the academic bodies, like the international professional groups, may be (c) International or (d) Regional.

The Accounting Organizations comprise the following two groups: the INTERNATIONAL CONFERENCES ON ACCOUNTING EDUCATION, which is the most influential; and the International Section of the American Accounting Association. The Non-Accounting Organizations are the ACADEMY OF INTERNATIONAL BUSINESS, and two professional organizations which are not solely accounting practitioner professional groups nor academicians. They are the NATIONAL ASSOCIATION OF ACCOUNTANTS (NAA) and the FINANCIAL EXECUTIVES INSTITUTE (FEI), which are nonetheless affiliated with accounting concepts that have contributed to international accounting literature.

From the viewpoint of Scope, the group which is internation-
al, as indicated above, is the INTERNATIONAL CONFERENCES ON
ACCOUNTING EDUCATION. The Regional or Local academic bodies may
be classified as (i) those affiliated with a Professional Aca-
demic Organization, and (ii) those affiliated with a University
Centre. The organization affiliated with a professional academ-
ic organization is the INTERNATIONAL ACCOUNTING EDUCATION AND
RESEARCH COMMITTEES OF THE AMERICAN ACCOUNTING ASSOCIATION.
Those affiliated with a University Centre are (a) CENTER FOR
INTERNATIONAL EDUCATION AND RESEARCH IN ACCOUNTING of the Univ.
of Illionois at Urbana; (b) INTERNATIONAL ACCOUNTING STUDIES
INSTITUTE (INTASI) of the Univ. of Wash. at Seattle; (c) INTER-
NATIONAL CENTRE FOR RESEARCH IN ACCOUNTING of the Univ. of Lan-
caster in England; and (d) CENTER FOR INTERNATIONAL ACCOUNTING
DEVELOPMENT of The Univ. of Texas at Dallas.

### #2-31...International Conferences on Accounting Education

The reason for the existence of the International Conferences on Accounting Education is that the International Congresses of Accountants catered principally to professional
practicing and industrial accountants, and the academic professors were a residual factor. Thus in 1962 the Univ. of Illinois
at Urbana, under the leadership of Dr. Vernon Zimmerman, established a CENTER FOR INTERNATIONAL ACCOUNTING AND RESEARCH just
prior to the 8th Interntl. Congress of Accountants in New York.
Since most of the academicians meeting at the Univ. of Illinois
were planning to attend the 8th Congress, it was decided to
arrange a separate meeting basically for academicians to be
held immediately prior to the N.Y. Congress meeting. This was
the inception of the INTERNATIONAL CONFERENCE ON ACCOUNTING
EDUCATION (ICAE) in Urbana in 1962. Since 1962 the ICAE has
been held immediately prior to the International Congresses
although in different venues. Thus the 2nd ICAE Conference was
held in 1967 in Guild Hall in London and sponsored by the City
of London Poly-Technic Institute just prior to the Paris Congress. The 3rd ICAE Conf. was held in the greater Sydney area
co-sponsored by the Universities of Sydney, New South Wales,
and Macquarie, but was scheduled after the 1972 Congress. The
4th ICAE Conf. was held in W.Berlin in 1977 the week before the
11th Cong. in Munich, where the IFAC was given birth.
These conferences draw around 300 academicians from all over
the world; the Berlin meeting was conducted in simultaneous
translations of English, German and French. The obvious emphasis in these meetings, as the term EDUCATION in the title of
the organization indicates, is on the academic aspects of international accounting (detailed in Chapter 1 in the description of the West Berlin Conference).
The 5th ICAE was held in Monterey, Mexico, in October 1982

immediately after the IFAC Conference in Mexico City. There
were 145 registrants from all continents, dominated by 70 from
Mexico and 22 from the U.S.A. The past attendance records disclose that in 1962 in Champaign there were 101; in 1967 in London, 121; in 1972 in Sydney, 211; and in 1977 in Berlin, 243.
This was the first conference in a developing country.

Just as the Regional Professional Associations, e.g., IAA,
CAPA, UEC, etc., are related to the International IFAC, so too
the academicians have Regional Academic Associations attached
to the Regional Professional Associations. Thus, immediately
following the Rio de Janeiro XV Inter-American Accounting Association Conference in Sept. 1973, the XI Inter-American Congress of Accounting Education was held at and sponsored by the
Univ. of Sao Paulo in Brazil.

## #2-32....American Accounting Association (AAA)

Between 1962 and 1976, the AAA had Committees on International Accounting Education and Research, and at the Atlanta
meeting in 1976 a formal INTERNATIONAL ACCOUNTING SECTION, with
a great degree of autonomy, was organized. Many of the members
of this group also attend the international professional and
academic meetings around the world and are prolific contributors to international accounting literature.

The Section publishes a newsletter called THE FORUM on a
periodic basis. Eventually there is a possibility that the Section may become sufficiently large enough to warrant its organization into a completely separate group called, perhaps, something like the INTERNATIONAL ACCOUNTING ASSOCIATION. One of the
authors recommended such a group be formed over a decade ago.

## #2-33....European Accounting Association (EAA)

The EAA was founded in 1977 under the auspices of the European Foundation for Management Development (EFMD) and in close
cooperation with the European Institute for Advanced Studies in
Management (EIASM). The aim is to create a European-wide community of accounting scholars and researchers. Although European
by name, the EAA has members from Australia, Canada, Colombia,
Hong Kong, India, Japan, Kenya, Libya, New Zealand, Nigeria,
Singapore, U.S.A., and Zambia. As of 1984 there are more than
490 members from 39 countries. The Association organizes a major accounting CONGRESS every year, providing a forum for academicians and accountants from industry and profession. This
event has taken place in major cities all over Europe:

| | | | |
|---|---|---|---|
| 1st | Paris, 1978 | 5th | Aarhus, Denmark, 1982 |
| 2nd | Cologne, 1979 | 6th | Glasgow, 1983 |
| 3rd | Amsterdam, 1980 | 7th | Saint Gallen, Switzerland, 1984 |
| 4th | Barcelona, 1981 | 8th | Brussels, 1985 |

## #2-34....Miscellaneous Regional Academic Associations

Regional academic accounting  bodies have sprung up in various parts of the world which function similarly  to the AAA and
European group.  Most notable of these are Canadian Association
of  Academic Accountants  (CAAA), Japan  Accounting Association
(JAA), the United Kingdom  Association of University Accounting
Instructors (UKAUAI), and the Australia-New Zealand Association
of University Accounting Instructors (ANZAUAI).

## #2-35....Academy of International Business  (AIB)

The AIB  is  a group of  university professors that embraces
all functional areas of international business,  viz., finance,
marketing,  management, etc.  It has had a very good sprinkling
of international  accounting  in its annual sessions which have
been held  around  the  world, in such cities as Paris in 1976;
Alexandria, Egypt in 1977; Seoul,  Korea in 1978; and in Mexico
City in 1983.
   It publishes its own journal, JIBS, the  JOURNAL OF INTERNA-
TIONAL BUSINESS STUDIES, and articles  appear  in  the  various
issues on the subject of International Accounting.  Many of the
academic  and professional members are  also frequenters of the
AIB meetings, and many excellent papers in the area of interna-
tional accounting have been presented at these meetings.

## #2-36...Non-Professional Accounting-Related Organizations

Other organizations, which are not solely accounting practitioner groups but  nonetheless  affiliated with accounting concepts, that have contributed to international accounting literature,  are the  NAA  and the FEI.  Thus, the NAA was the first
organization to  propose a change in  the technique of currency
translation, from the Current-Noncurrent  to the  Monetary-Nonmonetary  method subsequently adopted in FASB #8,  as discussed
later.
   The FINANCIAL EXECUTIVES INSTITUTE (FEI)  is  basically concerned  with the financial aspects of business management.  Because many accounting concepts are inextricably interwoven with
the financial aspects,  this organization  is  necessarily concerned with such accounting aspects.  The FEI has created a FI-
NANCIAL EXECUTIVES  RESEARCH  FOUNDATION (FERF) as its research
arm. The basic objective of the Foundation is to sponsor fundamental research and publish authoritative material in the field
of business  management with particular emphasis on the principles and  practices of financial  management  and  its evolving
role in the management of business.
   Some  of its  more prominent  publications  are "Joint  Ventures," "Effects of  Tax Policy on Capital Formation," and "The

Concept of Materiality in Financial Reporting." Its most important publication from the viewpoint of this text is entitled
ACCOUNTING FOR THE MULTINATIONAL CORPORATION published in 1977
by FERF. Three partners experienced in international accounting
from Price Waterhouse & Co. co-authored "THE STUDY", namely,
George C. Watt, Richard M. Hammer, and Marianne Burge. As
stated in its preface:

> The purpose of the study is to present current accounting
> consolidation practices and recent related changes in tax
> regulations. It is intended for two groups of readers—for
> chief financial officers, and for members of their staffs
> who implement policy decisions. The material designed for
> the chief financial officers poses policy questions and pro-
> vides alternative courses of action. The more technical
> material will be of interest to the second group.

This thoroughly comprehensive practical study of multinational
operations will be an extremely useful reference volume for
students of international accounting.

### #2-37...University Centre Affiliated Organizations

A few universities early recognized the impact that Multinational Enterprises would have on accounting, and for many years
have operated special centers of international accounting. The
two most prominent have been the Univ. of Illinois at Urbana
and the Univ. of Washington at Seattle.

### #2-38...Center for International Education and Research
###        (CIER)

The CIER was created by Dean Vernon Zimmerman of the College
of Business of the Univ. of Illinois at Urbana over a decade
and a half ago. Prof. Zimmerman has been the Director of the
Center since its inception. The Center conducts an annual seminar at Urbana, issues research monographs, and publishes semi-
annually the INTERNATIONAL JOURNAL OF ACCOUNTING.

### #2-39...International Accounting Studies Institute (INTASI)

INTASI, Univ. of Wash. at Seattle, has been under the very
capable leadership of Prof. Gerhard Mueller. The scholarly
Prof. Mueller has been the Director of INTASI and was the auth-
or of the first book written in the area of INTERNATIONAL AC-
COUNTING, which was updated in 1978 by a new volume co-authored
with Prof. Frederick Choi of New York University. Like the Center at Illinois, INTASI publishes research monographs and bib-
liographies, and also sponsors many international accounting
research activities.

### #2-40...International Centre for Research in Accounting

In England, the University of Lancaster has created the International Centre for Research in Accounting under the directorship of Professor Edward Stamp. Its activities follow the pattern of those of INTASI.

### #2-41...Center for International Accounting Development (CIAD)

A recent addition to the university group is the CIAD established in 1976 by Professor A.J.H. Enthoven, its director, at the University of Texas at Dallas. Professor Enthoven opened the center with a very impressive study pamphlet which was presented at the 60th meeting of the AAA in Atlanta on August 23, 1976, at its plenary session. The study was entitled SOCIAL AND POLITICAL IMPACT OF MULTINATIONALS ON THIRD WORLD COUNTRIES AND ITS ACCOUNTING IMPLICATIONS.

### #2-42...Centre for International Business Studies (CIBS)

In Canada, a recent and very prolific source of international business material has been the CIBS, created at the University of Western Ontario in its School of Business Administration, at London, Ontario. This Centre is famous for its excellent case studies in the various international functional areas.

### #2-43...Center for Transnational Accounting and Financial Research

The Center was established on September 1, 1980 at the University of Connecticut School of Business Administration. A major feature was its computerized data bank containing financial information on the international activities of 5,000 U.S. and non-U.S.-based multinational firms.

The Center's collection of financial and accounting data will be useful to scholars dealing with international trade and finance. It is also intended to assist financial managers, investors in non-U.S. stocks, and auditors responsible for auditing international companies.

The Center has conducted research in the areas of foreign operations disclosures by multinational corporations, cost of capital of multinational corporations, international portfolio management strategies, and the structure of the accounting profession world-wide. It also published monographs and working papers and sponsor an annual conference to disseminate findings of the research projects.

### (V).  LIMITED SCOPE BODIES--NON-ACCOUNTING INTERNATIONAL PROFESSIONAL AND/OR ACADEMIC BODIES AND ORGANIZATIONS AND GOVERNMENTAL AGENCIES

#### #2-44....Classifications of Limited Scope Organizations

There is a group of governmental bodies which have arms involved in connection with business dealings on an international basis that require accounting regulations. These governmental bodies, whose purposes are broad in scope, are therefore involved in setting accounting standards for transactions in which they are involved. They may be international, regional, or local in character.

The international group involves principally the United Nations (U.N.), the Organization for Economic Cooperation and Development (OECD), the European Economic Community (EEC), and The Center for International Business (CIB). The regional and local group comprises the OFFICE OF INTERNATIONAL OPERATIONS of the Securities and Exchange Commission (SEC), the INTERNATIONAL SECTION of the Internal Revenue Service (IRS), and the MULTINATIONAL DIVISION of the General Accounting Office (GAO).

#### #2-45...United Nations Expert Group on International Accounting and Reporting Standards

That international accounting standards are regarded as of great importance on the international scene may be evidenced by the commissioning of a study by the U.N. to determine "the impact of multinational corporations on the development process and on international relations." One of the results of the study was the proposal that a group of experts on international accounting should be selected to develop the international standards. Such a group was selected from almost the total spectrum of all aspects of life, viz., accountants, business management, academicians, economists, labor, lawyers, government, social scientists and public interest. The first operation was a review of current reporting practices by multinational corporations, and the reporting requirements of different countries.

The first meeting to set up the committee was held in Geneva in Sept. 1976. The next meeting, at which the Report was issued, was in N.Y. in 1977. In issuing the report the use of non-financial data was also injected apparently to emphasize the Macro Accounting aspects. The report indicates the issuance of two provisional lists of disclosure items that must be at a minimum for general purpose reporting by multinational corporations. First, as to enterprise as a whole: (a) consolidation of all group companies expected, with any exceptions to be justified; (b) disaggregation of certain consolidated information by geographic areas; (c) disaggregation of certain consolidated information by lines of business; (d) complete disclosure of the identity of individual member companies comprising the group. Second, as to Individual Member Companies: (a) separate list of minimum items to be disclosed in the general purpose reports of individual member company; (b) disclosure of sales by lines of business, amount of export sales, an extent of transactions with other companies in the group; (c) designated primary financial statement. The report was recommended favorably by the Secretary-General of the U.N.

#### #2-46...Organization for Economic Cooperation and Development (OECD)

The U.N. recommended lists for presentation of minimum items for disclosure in general purpose reports includes the views of not only the developed countries but also of the developing countries. On the other hand the guidelines for disclosure of information of the OECD, issued in 1976, represents the views only of the developed countries. In addition, as indicated previously, the U.N. is, unlike the OECD, coequally interested in disclosure of non-financial information.

The OECD is an organization of 24 of the most industrialized countries in the world. It provides a basis for harmonizing national policies in many areas, especially associated with the less developed countries. In Feb. 1975 it approved the formation of a Committee for International Investment and Multinational Enterprises, which was to be responsible for studying the relationship between multinational activities and governmental investment policies. Pursuant thereto it adopted a Declaration on International Investment and Multinational Enterprises on June 21, 1976, which was an important step for improving the climate for foreign private investment in OECD, as well as developing countries.

The guidelines set the accounting dimensions in requiring annual publication of financial statements for each enterprise in its entirety, entailing also supplementary disclosures on a consolidated basis, as well as the requirement set forth in FASB #14--Financial Reporting for Segments of a Business Enterprise. The OECD is also making investigations into tax issues, intercompany transfer pricing, tax incentives, and tax havens.

Two advisory bodies, viz., the BUSINESS AND INDUSTRY ADVISORY COMMITTEE (BIAC) and the TRADE UNION ADVISORY COMMITTEE (TUAC) assist the OECD in its work programs. The U.S. delegate sitting in on the BIAC is known as the USA-BIAC, which is sponsored by three prominent U.S. organizations--the U.S. Chamber of Commerce, the U.S. National Association of Manufacturers, and the U.S. Council of the International Chamber of Commerce. The principal purpose served by the USA-BIAC is to monitor responses to OECD guidelines and obtain views on how OECD governments are responding to the provisions of the Declaration in support of international investment.

The OECD has its secretariat and venue in a palace in Paris. Although the OECD Code is voluntary, it is supported by very weighty individuals and prominent professional accountants, which would appear to indicate that in order to operate in member countries the multinational corporations will have to abide by the accounting principles promulgated by it.

### #2-47....The European Economic Community (EEC).

*doesn't include, Finland, Norway, Sweden, Yugoslavia*

There has been a constant flux in the desire for membership in the EEC which presently consists of 12 countries--Belgium, Denmark, England, France, Greece, Italy, Ireland, Luxembourg, Netherlands, Portugal, Spain, and West Germany. Many countries, contiguous to those which are members, have been, and are, pressing for membership and most likely will be admitted. The original purpose of the organization was as a customs union to abolish restrictions on trade of industrial and agricultural products among the member countries, and creation of a common external tariff.

The EEC was established on March 25, 1957, as a product of the TREATY OF ROME with the following objective: "the approximation of their respective national laws to the extent required for the Common Market to function in an orderly manner." Upon creation of the EEC Commissions, the first order of business was to attempt to unify all of the Companies Laws, Corporation Laws, and Codes of Commerce of all member countries into one universal EEC COMPANY LAW. The Commission submitted the draft of the COMPANY LAW to all member states for ratification subsequent to approval from the EEC Council of Ministers.

Since the directives issued by the EEC involve corporations operating within the jurisdictions of its members, accounting regulations have the force of law and must be abided by by these corporations. To aid in enforcement, the EEC Commission drafted a statute in 1970 creating a new type of company, to be known as a SOCIETE EUROPEENE (SE), which was presented for approval to the European Council of Ministers.

The basic objective of the proposal was to make any companies that operate within the framework of the EEC subject to control extending beyond the borders of any one country in which the company was domiciled. To thoroughly regulate such companies, a Statute consisting of 284 Articles under 14 Titles was drafted. Included in the Statute were requirements for accounting and financial reporting, and proposals for standardization of financial statements and disclosures; harmonization of corporate tax systems; treatment of dividend and interest income; and cross-frontier mergers. Two other areas given attention were tax circumvention through artificial intercompany transfer prices and through tax haven companies.

## #2-48....The Center For International Business (CIB)

The Center is an independent, non-profit organization founded in 1976. It is a forum for sharing insights in international
business operations, amongst a select group of senior executives from private corporations operating on a world-wide
basis. Its philosophy is stated to be: "Over the course of
history, human progress and development have been achieved in
large measure by the INTERCHANGE OF IDEAS AND CONCEPTS as well
as by the exchange of economic resources and wealth."
    The purpose of the CIB is "to identify, analyze, and evalu-
ate the world-wide forces and trends affecting the corporation,
and to assist the global corporate decision maker at the most
senior level to interpret and integrate these factors into the
strategic management process. To accomplish these goals, the
Center provides for business executives a select series of professional and business development opportunities and publications which are made available to its members and, selectively,
to businesses, governments and academe world-wide."
    Membership in the CIB is extended to multinational corpora-
tions, international companies, firms, and individuals who are
heavily engaged in many fields of global trade and investment.
As of 1982 it totaled 280 corporate and individual members from
throughout the U.S., and in Europe, Japan, Mexico, Saudi
Arabia, Kuwait, Canada and Australia.
    The CIB conducts an ANNUAL INTERNATIONAL TRADE CONFERENCE
every April which is designed as a signal symposium for senior
executives from globally oriented companies. It is strucured to
identify, analyze and evaluate the critical policy issues and
trends that will shape the turbulent global environment in
which strategic corporate decisions must be made. Over 4,500
delegates have attended the annual conferences.
    The CIB publishes THE INTERNATIONAL ESSAYS FOR BUSINESS DE-
CISION MAKERS, used at both the graduate and undergraduate level in several universities, and by numerous corporations in
management development programs. It also publishes a series
known as THE OCCASIONAL PAPERS.

## #2-49....Regional Non-Accounting Governmental Agencies

Many governmental agencies, in the course of effectuating
their activities, are necessarily involved with accounting procedures and principles. In such cases, the accounting regulations must be adhered to in business practice. Most common and
typical of these agencies are the OFFICE OF INTERNATIONAL OPER-
ATIONS of the Securities and Exchange Commission (SEC), the
INTERNATIONAL SECTION of the Internal Revenue Service (IRS),
and the MULTINATIONAL DIVISION of the General Accounting
Office (GAO).

## (VI). INTERNATIONAL SPECIAL PURPOSE BODY ACCOUNTING PRONOUNCEMENTS

### #2-50....Special Purpose Boards and Committees

The final source of international accounting principles are the special boards and committees which have been created expressly to promulgate accounting principles through formal announcements. In the U.S. these announcements have come principally from the AICPA and FASB. They have been interwoven into the textbook principles advanced by academia, forming a set of ideas which has come to fall under the heading of GENERALLY ACCEPTED ACCOUNTING PRINCIPLES, referred to as GAAP.

### #2-51....Financial Accounting Standards Board (FASB)

The first pronouncements came in the 1930s and became formalized through the publication by AICPA of a series of ACCOUNTING RESEARCH BULLETINS (ARB) from 1939 to 1959, when the ACCOUNTING PRINCIPLES BOARD (APB) was formed. The Board gave more formality to the pronouncements and issued two series of publications, one known as APB OPINIONS and the other as APB STATEMENTS. Between 1959 and 1973 the APB issued 31 Opinions. Some dispute arose amongst accountants as to the strict validity of some of the opinions, and in 1964 the AICPA stated that deviations could be justified through explanatory footnotes to financial statements. The STATEMENTS were more in the nature of suggestions or recommendations and did not carry the weight of the OPINIONS.

The most influential Statement was #4—BASIC CONCEPTS AND ACCOUNTING PRINCIPLES UNDERLYING FINANCIAL STATEMENTS OF BUSINESS ENTERPRISES. In addition to the OPINIONS and STATEMENTS, the Director of Accounting Research of the AICPA published 15 ACCOUNTING RESEARCH STUDIES (ARS) designed to provide the APB with background material to support and aid in the establishment of accounting principles.

In 1972, after it was confirmed that accounting pronouncements should be based on opinions of other experts in the business world instead of purely on those of accountants, a FINANCIAL ACCOUNTING FOUNDATION was created to establish a new FINANCIAL ACCOUNTING STANDARDS BOARD. The Foundation consisted of nine trustees, four of whom were to be professional accountants and the other five to come from the ranks of business executives, financial analysts, and accounting educators.

The FASB was created in 1972 consisting of seven full-time paid members as contrasted to the 21 members of the APB who served without compensation. The principal purpose of the FASB is to issue STATEMENTS, which are regarded as the proper theory for the GAAP. Before a formal statement is drafted, a Discus-

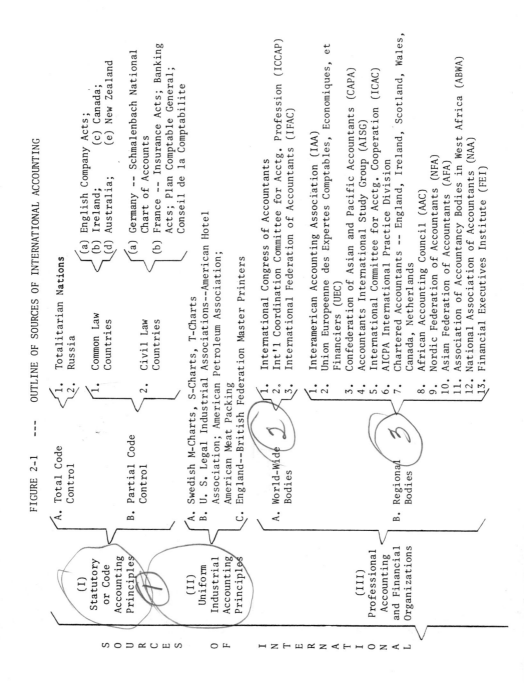

FIGURE 2-1 --- OUTLINE OF SOURCES OF INTERNATIONAL ACCOUNTING

SOURCES / INTERNATIONAL

**(I) Statutory or Code Accounting Principles**

A. Total Code Control
  1. Totalitarian Nations
  2. Russia

B. Partial Code Control
  1. Common Law Countries
    (a) English Company Acts;
    (b) Ireland;   (c) Canada;
    (d) Australia;   (e) New Zealand
  2. Civil Law Countries
    (a) Germany -- Schmalenbach National Chart of Accounts
    (b) France -- Insurance Acts; Banking Acts; Plan Comptable General; Conseil de la Comptabilite

**(II) Uniform Industrial Accounting Principles**

A. Swedish M-Charts, S-Charts, T-Charts
B. U. S. Legal Industrial Associations--American Hotel Association; American Petroleum Association; American Meat Packing
C. England--British Federation Master Printers

**(III) Professional Accounting and Financial Organizations**

A. World-Wide Bodies
  1. International Congress of Accountants
  2. Int'l Coordination Committee for Acctg. Profession (ICCAP)
  3. International Federation of Accountants (IFAC)

B. Regional Bodies
  1. Interamerican Accounting Association (IAA)
  2. Union Europeenne des Expertes Comptables, Economiques, et Financiers (UEC)
  3. Confederation of Asian and Pacific Accountants (CAPA)
  4. Accountants International Study Group (AISG)
  5. International Committee for Acctg. Cooperation (ICAC)
  6. AICPA International Practice Division
  7. Chartered Accountants -- England, Ireland, Scotland, Wales, Canada, Netherlands
  8. African Accounting Council (AAC)
  9. Nordic Federation of Accountants (NFA)
  10. Asian Federation of Accountants (AFA)
  11. Association of Accountancy Bodies in West Africa (ABWA)
  12. National Association of Accountants (NAA)
  13. Financial Executives Institute (FEI)

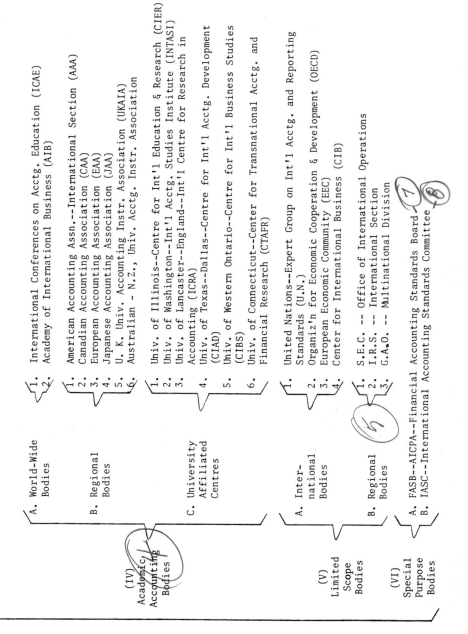

ACCOUNTING

(IV) Academic Accounting Bodies

A. World-Wide Bodies
1. International Conferences on Acctg. Education (ICAE)
2. Academy of International Business (AIB)

B. Regional Bodies
1. American Accounting Assn.--International Section (AAA)
2. Canadian Accounting Association (CAA)
3. European Accounting Association (EAA)
4. Japanese Accounting Association (JAA)
5. U.K. Univ. Accounting Instr. Association (UKAIA)
6. Australian - N.Z., Univ. Acctg. Instr. Association

C. University Affiliated Centres
1. Univ. of Illinois--Centre for Int'l Education & Research (CIER)
2. Univ. of Washington--Int'l Acctg. Studies Institute (INTASI)
3. Univ. of Lancaster--England--Int'l Centre for Research in Accounting (ICRA)
4. Univ. of Texas--Dallas--Centre for Int'l Acctg. Development (CIAD)
5. Univ. of Western Ontario--Centre for Int'l Business Studies (CIBS)
6. Univ. of Connecticut--Center for Transnational Acctg. and Financial Research (CTAFR)

(V) Limited Scope Bodies

A. International Bodies
1. United Nations--Expert Group on Int'l Acctg. and Reporting Standards (U.N.)
2. Organiz'n for Economic Cooperation & Development (OECD)
3. European Economic Community (EEC)
4. Center for International Business (CIB)

B. Regional Bodies
1. S.E.C. -- Office of International Operations
2. I.R.S. -- International Section
3. G.A.O. -- Multinational Division

(VI) Special Purpose Bodies

A. FASB--AICPA--Financial Accounting Standards Board
B. IASC--International Accounting Standards Committee

sion Memorandum is issued and an Exposure Draft is circulated.
After public hearings are held on the Exposure Draft, a new
Financial Accounting Standard is issued.

## #2-52...International Accounting Standards Committee (IASC)

The reason for the above detailed explanation of the creation and operation of the FASB is that it has followed the same
pattern on the local United States level as what was subsequently created in its wake--the IASC. The IASC purports to
perform the same functions on an international level as the
FASB does on the local U.S. level. Thus the FASB and the IASC
are both special purpose bodies created for the express aim of
establishing generally accepted accounting principles. The pronouncements emanating from either of these bodies are not legal
statutory fiats that are enforceable by law. They supposedly
carry the weight of the profession behind them, thereby rendering them in the nature of common law principles that are enforced through moral and ethical suasion rather than by legal
force. Because the pronouncements of the IASC will have prime
force in the establishment of GAAP on an international scale,
it must necessarily be given detailed attention. This will be
done in the discussion in the chapter on International Accounting Standards.

## #2-53....Outline of Sources of International Accounting

At this point there has been a thorough discussion of the
sources of international accounting. It may be seen that these
sources are greatly varied as to geographical origins, economic
philosophy, political structure, and social development.

Throughout the remainder of the material in this book, some
reference will be made to one or more of these sources, which
hopefully will enable the reader to have a better comprehension
of the overall panorama of the area of International Accounting, outlined in Figure 2-1.

### SUMMARY OF FOOTNOTE REFERENCES
(References are to Paragraph #'s)

#2-6    Jenkins Committee Report, RECOMMENDATIONS OF ACCOUNTING
        PRINCIPLES issued by Institute of Chartered Accountants in
        England and Wales, Companies Act of 1966
#2-8    Hans W. Singer, STANDARDIZED ACCOUNTANCY IN GERMANY (Cam-
        bridge Univ. Press, 1944)
#2-9    Kenneth Most, "Official Charts of Accounts in Germany and
        France," THE ACCOUNTANT (Jan. 26, 1957): 81-91
#2-10   Pierre Garnier, "Uniform Accounting Systems in France,"
        CANADIAN CHARTERED ACCOUNTANT (July 1962): 56-57
#2-11   PLAN COMPTABLE GENERAL (Paris: Conseil National De La

Comptabilite, 1960), pp. 95-98
#2-12  Joseph Loore, 8th International Congress of Accountants, New
York, 1962
#2-21  Otto Lambsdorff, CONGRESS DAILY NEWS (Oct. 12, 1977)
#2-21  CPA LETTER, Vol. 62, No. 13 (July 1982): 2
#2-23  "UEC--Union Europeenne Des Expertes Comptables, Economiques
et Financiers," THE ACCOUNTANT (Aug. 31, 1963): 246-248
#2-24  Sir Thomas Robson, "Cooperation in Europe," THE ACCOUNTANT
(Mar. 28, 1964): 381-383
#2-36  George C. Watt, Richard M. Hammer, and Marianne Burge, AC-
COUNTING FOR THE MULTINATIONAL CORPORATION, Copyright 1977
by Financial Executives Research Foundation, Morristown,
N.J. Reprinted with permission.

## BIBLIOGRAPHY

AICPA (American Institute of Certified Public Accountants). PROFES-
SIONAL ACCOUNTING IN 30 COUNTRIES. N.Y.: AICPA, 1975
Al Hashim, Dhia and Robertson, James. ACCOUNTING FOR MULTINATIONAL
ENTERPRISES. Indianapolis: Bobbs-Merrill, 1978
Arpan, Jeffrey and Radebaugh, Lee. INTERNATIONAL ACCOUNTING AND
MULTINATIONAL ENTERPRISES. Boston: Warren, Gorham & Lamont,
1981
Arpan, Jeffrey and Al Hashim, D.D. INTERNATIONAL DIMENSIONS OF AC-
COUNTING. Boston: Kent Publishing Co., 1984.
Berg, Mueller, and Walker. READINGS IN INTERNATIONAL ACCOUNTING.
Boston: Houghton, Mifflin Co., 1969.
Business International Corporation. INTERNATIONAL ACCOUNTING,
AUDITING AND TAX ISSUES. New York: 1979
Carty, James. "Accounting Standards and the United Nations," WORLD
ACCOUNTING REPORT (September 1982): 9-15
Choi, Frederick. "ASEAN Federation of Accountants: A New Interna-
tional Accounting Force," INTERNATIONAL JOURNAL OF ACCOUNT-
ING (Fall 1979): 53-75
Choi, Frederick. MULTINATIONAL ACCOUNTING: A RESEARCH FRAMEWORK FOR
THE EIGHTIES. Ann Arbor, Mich: UMI Research Press, 1981
Choi, Frederick and Mueller, Gerhard. AN INTRODUCTION TO MULTINA-
TIONAL ACCOUNTING. Englewood Cliffs, N.J.: Prentice-Hall,
Inc., 1978
Choi, Frederick and Mueller, Gerhard. ESSENTIALS OF MULTINATIONAL
ACCOUNTING: AN ANTHOLOGY. Ann Arbor, Mich: University Micro-
films International, 1979
Choi, Frederick and Mueller, Gerhard. INTERNATIONAL ACCOUNTING.
Englewood Cliffs, N.J.: Prentice-Hall, Inc., 1984
Cummings, Joseph and Rogers, William. "Developments in Internation-
al Accounting," CPA JOURNAL, 48 (May 1978): 15-19
Denman, John H. "The OECD and International Accounting Standards,"
CA MAGAZINE (February 1980): 56-59
Eiteman, David and Stonehill, Arthur. MULTINATIONAL BUSINESS
FINANCE, 3rd ed. Reading, Mass: Addison-Wesley Publishing
Co., 1982

Enthoven, Adolph.  SOCIAL AND POLITICAL IMPACT OF MULTINATIONALS ON
      THIRD WORLD COUNTRIES AND ITS ACCOUNTING IMPLICATIONS, 1976
Gray, S.J.    INTERNATIONAL   ACCOUNTING AND TRANSNATIONAL DECISIONS.
      Stoneham, Mass: Butterworth Publishers, 1983
Hein,  Leonard W.   "The  Auditor and the  British  Company Acts,"
      ACCOUNTING REVIEW (July 1963): 508
Holzer, H.P.  INTERNATIONAL ACCOUNTING. N.Y.: Harper & Row, 1984
IAA  7th Conference, Mar del Plata, Argentina, "Inter-American Con-
      ference Adopts Auditing  Resolution," JOURNAL OF ACCOUNTANCY
      (February 1966): 12
International Accounting Section, American  Accounting Association,
      NOTABLE CONTRIBUTIONS  TO THE  PERIODICAL INTERNATIONAL  AC-
      COUNTING LITERATURE, 1975-1978.  Sarasota: AAA, 1979
Miller,  Elwood.  ACCOUNTING PROBLEMS OF MULTINATIONAL ENTERPRISES.
      Lexington: D.C. Heath & Co., 1979
Mueller,  Gerhard.  INTERNATIONAL ACCOUNTING. N.Y.: Macmillan  Co.,
      1967
Nobes, C.W. and Parker, R.H.  COMPARATIVE INTERNATIONAL ACCOUNTING.
      Homewood, Ill: Richard D. Irwin, Inc., 1981
O.E.C.D.   ACCOUNTING PRACTICES  IN  OECD MEMBER  COUNTRIES. Paris:
      O.E.C.D., 1980
Rueschhoff, Norlin.  INTERNATIONAL ACCOUNTING AND FINANCIAL REPORT-
      ING.  N.Y.: Praeger Publishers, 1976
Schmalenbach, Eugen. THE MODEL CHART OF ACCOUNTS. 1929
Sycip,  Washington. "The Role of  CAPA in Achieving Harmonization,"
      SGV JOURNAL, Manila, No. 1 (1982): 2-7
Union   Europeenne   Des   Expertes   Comptables,   Economiques   et
      Financiers.  U.E.C. ANNUAL REPORT. Munich, Germany: 1982
United Nations Center on Transnational Corporations. TOWARDS INTER-
      NATIONAL STANDARDIZATION OF CORPORATE ACCOUNTING AND REPORT-
      ING.  N.Y.: United Nations, 1982
United Nations Economic & Social Council  (U.N.-ECOSOC), Commission
      on Transnational Corporations.  INTERNATIONAL STANDARDS  OF
      ACCOUNTING AND REPORTING.  N.Y.: May 27, 1981
U.S. Federal Reserve Board.   "Approved Methods for the Preparation
      of Balance Sheet Statements," WORLD WAR I BULLETIN (1917)
Watt, George C.; Hammer, Richard M.; and Burge, Marianne.  ACCOUNT-
      ING FOR THE MULTINATIONAL CORPORATION.  Morristown,  N.J.:
      Financial Executives Research Foundation (FERF), 1977
Yoshida, Hiroshi and Sumita, Kazutoyo. AN INTRODUCTION TO INTERNA-
      TIONAL ACCOUNTING.  Tokyo: Zeimukein Kyokai, 1982

## THEORY QUESTIONS
(Question Numbers are Keyed to Text Paragraph #'s)

#2-1   Basically how  many  principal sources  do international
       accounting rules emanate from and what are they?
#2-2   Into  how many countries  may  legislative code countries
       be classified, what are  they, and discuss their differ-
       ences.

#2-3    What does the extent to which Codes control the practice
        of accounting depend upon?  Illustrate the difference.
#2-6    Describe the operation of Code Accounting in England.
#2-7    Discuss the impact of the British  Company Acts on other
        countries.
#2-9    Who  was  Professor  Eugen Schmalenbach  and  what effect
        did he have on Germany International Accounting?
#2-11   Discuss the French Plan Comptable  General and the  Con-
        seil National De La Comptabilite and its  impact on Code
        Accounting in France.
#2-13   Make a  comparative analysis  of Code Accounting  in the
        U.S. with the British, German and French.
#2-15   Trace  the  evolution of the Swedish M-Chart and distin-
        guish it  from  the Schmalenbach  National Chart  of Ac-
        counts.
#2-17   What  appears  to  be the most  influential  and  potent
        source of international accounting  principles, into how
        many groups may they be divided, and what are they?
#2-19   What was the International Congress  of Accountants, its
        modus operandi, and results?
#2-20   Discuss the nature  and operation  of the  International
        Coordination Committee for  the  Accountancy  Profession
        and its ultimate resolution?
#2-21   Trace  the evolution of  the International Federation of
        Accountants and its present  position in the  accounting
        firmament.
#2-22   Outline the nature  and  operation  of the Interamerican
        Accounting Association.
#2-23   Discuss the nature of the Union Europeenne Des  Expertes
        Comptables, Economiques Et Financiers (UEC). Make a com-
        parative  analysis  of it with the Interamerican Account-
        ing Association.
#2-25   What is the nature  and makeup  of the  Confederation of
        Asian  and Pacific Accountants, how does it operate, and
        compare it with the IAA and UEC.
#2-26   Make a comparative analysis of the Accountants  Interna-
        tional Study Group with the IAA, UEC, and CAPA.
#2-30   Make a chart classifying Academic Accounting Bodies.
#2-31   Discuss the characteristics of the International Confer-
        ences on Accounting Education and how it operates.
#2-32   Discuss the relationship  of the American Accounting As-
        sociation with international accounting.
#2-35   How is  the Academy of International Business related to
        international accounting?
#2-37   Name  six University Centre affiliated organizations re-
        lated to development of international accounting outlin-
        ing how each contributes.
#2-44   Into  how many classes  may  international  governmental
        agencies fall and  what  are they?  What  agencies  are

represented in each of the groups?

#2-45  Discuss the nature, characteristics, and modus operandi
       of the United Nations Expert Group on International Ac-
       counting and Reporting Standards.

#2-46  Discuss the nature, characteristics, and modus operandi
       of the Organization for Economic Cooperation and Devel-
       opment (OECD).

#2-47  Discuss the nature, characteristics and modus operandi
       of the European Economic Community (EEC).

#2-48  How does the Center for International Business (CIB)
       relate to international accounting? Discuss its makeup
       and operation.

#2-51  What is the Financial Accounting Standards Board, how
       does it operate and what impact does it have on Interna-
       tional Accounting Standards?

#2-52  What is the International Accounting Standards Commit-
       tee, how does it operate, and what impact does it have
       on International Accounting Standards?

# PART II

# MICRO INTERNATIONAL ACCOUNTING

Part II is directed at international dealings involving financial and operating aspects of private enterprises with the profit-making objective. Obviously it is the most dominant aspect of business relations in our economic society and will represent the most important part of the material. Part II is covered in three sections: Micro International Financial Accounting Theory; Micro International Financial Accounting Practice; and Micro International Managerial Control Accounting.

MICRO INTERNATIONAL FINANCIAL ACCOUNTING THEORY initiates the discussion by establishing the underlying theory that is the basis for the recording of international business transactions in the books of account. This is the springboard from which all accounting originates. The first prerequisite is to establish the formal Standards of Accounting, and then add to them the Generally Accepted Accounting Principles (GAAP) that supplement the standards. Such standards are treated in Chapter 3, which describes how they are established, the attempt to harmonize them amongst the various nations, and the standards promulgated by special purpose bodies such as the International Accounting Standards Committee (IASC) and the European Common Market (EEC). Chapter 4 discusses the supplemental GAAP established in major countries, with a comparative analysis with U.S. GAAP. These will be directed at the underlying asset valuation concepts and items, as well as operating income statement principles.

Having established the basic accounting standards and GAAP in Chapters 3 and 4, Chapter 5 translates the theory into the financial statements required--Financial Statement Presentation Principles. Section One concludes in Chapter 6 with a discussion of International Accounting Reporting Standards, treating the auditing standards in various countries, their professional organizations, and those in the EEC countries.

MICRO INTERNATIONAL FINANCIAL ACCOUNTING PRACTICE is presented in the Section Two of Part II. It is one of the most important in the book, dealing with the accounting transactions in international operations and how they are handled on the books of account. It is covered in six chapters. Chapter 7 treats the basic ingredient in International Business Transactions, viz., Foreign Exchange. Chapter 8 explains the basis for implementation of international business transactions, viz., Foreign Exchange Rates and Markets. It discusses the nature of foreign exchange; the necessity for foreign exchange markets in the trading of foreign exchange; conversions and translation of foreign exchange; instruments of foreign exchange; classifications of foreign exchange rates; foreign currency quotations and their classification; causes of market rate fluctuations; effects of fluctuations on currencies; classification of currencies; and accounting for foreign exchange.

Chapter 9 presents the accounting for international foreign trade and investment transactions. This covers letters of credit, export-import transactions, and foreign investments. Chapter 10 treats that part of international accounting referred to as Multinational Accounting, primarily dealing with the definition of the multinational corporation and transnational business transactions. Chapter 11 discusses the problems arising from currency differences, the reporting currency, and methods of translation. Chapter 12 establishes translation principles and presents a complete parent and foreign branch accounting cycle illustrative case.

MICRO INTERNATIONAL MANAGERIAL CONTROL ACCOUNTING--the Third Section of Part II--contains three chapters. Chapter 13 is entitled "International Investment Accounting," Chapter 14 is "International Working Capital Management Accounting," and Chapter 15 is "International Intercorporate Transactions Accounting." These chapters treat the working capital stewardship; exchange exposure analysis; exchange risk control; hedging through Forward Exchange Contracts; analysis and evaluation of risk; transfer policy; transfer settlement; the netting process; and the need for centralized control.

# PART II

# SECTION ONE

# MICRO INTERNATIONAL FINANCIAL ACCOUNTING THEORY

# International Accounting Standards

#3-1....Establishment of International Accounting Standards

At this point we are concerned with the establishment of international accounting standards to serve as the basis for effectuation of the accounting processes and residually for determining GAAP on the international level. Thus a distinction should be made between International Accounting STANDARDS and International GENERALLY ACCEPTED ACCOUNTING PRINCIPLES.

#3-2....International Accounting Standards and GAAP

Technically, International Standards may be said not to have existed before the creation of the IASC, whose basic function it is to propogate the standards. Therefore, prior to IASC, it may be contended that whatever international rules existed were the result of an International GAAP. As a new IASC standard was promulgated, it eliminated the GAAP rule that it replaced. Obviously the apparent aim of the IASC eventually is to create a complete set of standards that will cover every aspect of international accounting theory, and that will be binding on operations in all countries, at which time we will have Global Accounting. Until that time is reached, which is a considerable length in the future, international accounting theory will be a mixture of IASC Standards and International GAAP. The international GAAP is and will be a mixture of principles of the various countries, which may result in contradictions and a comparative point of view. Since the Standards will replace the GAAP, we will first observe the nature of the Standards problem, and then proceed in the next chapter to an examination of the GAAP presently existing on the international level.

ESTABLISHMENT OF INTERNATIONAL ACCOUNTING STANDARDS

#3-3....Nature of International Accounting Standards

These immediate questions arise with respect to STANDARDS: What should they be? What should be their scope? Who should set

them? What criteria should be used for their establishment? The
ideal situation of course is to have a set of standards that is
universal or global in character, which at this point is
virtually impossible of attainment.  Basically the world is
divided into two camps--the free-enterprise democracies and the
totalitarian communist countries.  On the basis of this
division alone, it would be a sheer impossibility to extract
any universal or global accounting standards.

Since this material is oriented toward the free-enterprise
society, the next most feasible situation would be to have a
set of universal accounting standards for the free-enterprise
countries only.  This too, because of variations between countries, is not possible of attainment at this point in time.  To
be able to set such standards, the following problems would
arise:  Who would have the authority to establish them--legal
fiat or private expert? Would it be feasible to create one set
of standards for all of the heterogeneous types of business
operations? What bases would be used for establishing the
standards--practice, ethics, theory, equity, social desirability, or mores and customs. of the diverse countries? What criteria would be used for their establishment?

## #3-4....Criteria for Standards Establishment

To compound the problem, a multiplicity of criteria may
enter into the judgment of the establishment of accounting
standards.  Among the commonly known are the following:

(a) the legal system of the various countries, e.g., code or
common law
(b) the political basis for the governments, e.g., degree of
freedom of operation
(c) nature of economy, e.g., whether industrial, commercial,
agricultural, trade, tourist, etc.
(d) social aspects, e.g., duties of multinationals socially
as in the U.S.; or a more conservative laissez-faire
philosophy concerning control over the accounting methodology, as in the Middle or Near East; or the South
American philosophy where accounting is developing as a
profession
(e) degree of control by government fiat, e.g., Companies
Laws, German Charts of Accounts, regulation by such
agencies as SEC
(f) extent of business ownership--large corporate enterprise
vs. small individual ownership, e.g., large spread of
ownership vs. close ownership
(g) size of business, e.g., General Motors vs. single owner
proprietor
(h) complexity of operations, e.g., requiring inventive

skills vs. trading, requiring no technical training
- (i) stability of currency, e.g., current inflation accounting problem
- (j) professional status, a corollary of development of the
economy
- (k) educational basis for accounting

The foregoing possible criteria would seem to indicate that
attaining a set of accounting standards applicable uniformly to
a segment of the world is almost impossible of attainment under
current conditions.

## THE BASIC DILEMMA OF ESTABLISHMENT OF INTERNATIONAL
## STANDARDS -- UNIFORMITY VS. HARMONIZATION

### #3-5....Comparative Accounting Standards

Because different nations have different accounting principles, there is no uniformity between them. Nevertheless there
has been a constant flow of suggestion that there be a uniform
set of standards, the proponents stressing that uniformity be
synonymous with universal or global. Since we have in effect
what are comparative accounting standards between nations, the
question arises as to what situations to uniformity exist.

### #3-6....Comparative Standard Possibilities

There are three such possible situations: Uniformity, Flexibility or diversity, and Harmonization.

As indicated above, when the term UNIFORMITY is used it is
ordinarily meant to be universal or global, i.e., international
standardization of accounting rules.

FLEXIBILITY or diversity is the opposite of uniformity,
which is rigid in character. Flexibility or diversity supposedly permits better adaptability of accounting methods in each
firm, each industry, and/or each type of transaction. Furthermore, as long as a single method is not indicated, experimentation is allowed. New and better theories may result, which may
even allow the adaptation of the accounting recording policies
in a managerial control system.

HARMONIZATION lies somewhere between uniformity and flexibility, perhaps tilted more in the direction of uniformity.
This could result in what might be called a "conditional uniformity." Accounting principles between nations until the past
decade have been geared more in the direction of flexibility or
diversity. However, there has been some movement toward uniformity. Because of national pride, it has been considered more
tactful not to swing the pendulum to the other extreme, from
flexibility to uniformity. Hence a sort of compromise was settled on in the form of harmonization. Thus harmonization in

effect  says we want uniformity to the  extent that it does not
upset  local  national  principles deeply entrenched over  many
years.  In other words, if uniformity of standards  between nations results in  more  or  less innocuous metamorphoses, there
would be no objection.

## THE INTERNATIONALIZATION PROCESS

### #3-7....Historical Aspects of Internationalization

That internationalization  of  accounting  principles may be
salutary has been recognized by many prominent accounting authorities. Thus, F.M. Richard, President of the 9th International
Congress of Accountants, Paris, 1967, in the article "New Horizons of Accounting," p. 11, states:
> Almost all of the international  and national authors are in
> favor of the  harmonization of accounting and auditing prin-
> ciples,  and some even considered that this harmonization is
> essential  and really  urgent.  The rare exceptions to  this
> opinion come from those authors who have taken harmonization
> to  mean standardization,  uniformity, or unification, which
> is obviously out of the question.

During the discussions in  Paris,  influential professional accountants were enthused about the internationalization efforts.
This led to  the formation  of  an international  working party
from 14  countries resulting in the  issuance of a proclamation
of harmonization in Dec. 1971.  In Nov. 1972 the  ICCAP was established.  At its first  session  in Dusseldorf in April 1973,
the  11  members of  the  ICCAP  (Australia,  Canada,  Germany,
France, India,  Japan,  Mexico,  Netherlands, Philippines, U.K.
and the U.S.) formed the IASC.  In June 1973, nine  representatives of member accounting institutes formalized the  constitution of the IASC.

## UNIFORMITY OF STANDARDS

### #3-8....History of Uniformity

One of the  most ardent advocates of uniformity was a prominent independent accounting practitioner  named Jacob  Kraayenhof.  He was a Past  President of the  Netherlands Institute of
Accountants, as well as the President of the 7th Interntl. Congress of Accountants, Amsterdam, 1957. In the article "International Challenges for  Accounting" published in the  JOURNAL OF
ACCOUNTANCY,  Jan. 1960, pp. 34-38,  Kraayenhof  reiterated the
principles enunciated by him in his keynote address to the 1959
annual meeting of the AICPA in San Francisco. He contended that
there was an  urgency for  close international cooperation, and
for work on international accounting standards and theory based

on global assumptions.  He  further suggested the establishment
of standing  committees to research and study accounting standards in various countries which would exchange their results to
promote any  areas  of disagreement,  and that the AICPA be the
body to implement the arrangement.

   This desire for uniformity was the offspring of the development  of the scientific approach  to accounting that evolved in
the 18th and 19th centuries as pointed out in Chapter 1.   Under
this interpretation, the attempt  to  attain uniformity was the
exercise of  scientific methodology for accounting, in that all
principles were standardized.

### #3-9....Cameralistic Nature of Uniformity

   In the more bureaucratic  countries  (such  as Germany)  the
scientific approach was later stretched to the theory that uniformity could  be an excellent administrative device for carrying  out government  administrative duties.  In such sense,  by
attaining uniformity  this would establish one set of rules for
handling  not only all types of enterprise but also  every type
of transaction.  The term used  in these European countries for
uniformity was CAMERALISTIC.  The  establishment of one set  of
standards is thus cameralistic in nature because of its univer-
sality of application.  Under such a philosophy, uniformity becomes an ideal tool for dictatorial governments.

### #3-10....Advantages of Uniformity

   As indicated, uniformity of accounting standards is a desid-
eratum  announced at many of the  international accounting congresses.   However, the term that was emphasized was HARMONIZA-
TION and the word UNIFORMITY circumvented. The uniformity aimed
at, of course, was the same rules being applicable for the same
situations  in  different  nations--a world-wide  compatibility
between  countries of  similarity of rules for  the same situation.  Although current  trends  point toward a world-wide uniformity of accounting principles, particularly for corporations
with wide stockholder distribution, many international accountants are careful to use  the term harmonization.  In some cases
it almost appears as though the terms uniformity and harmonization are used interchangeably.

   Uniformity results  in many advantages.  It  expedites the
training of accounting  apprentices,  increases the reliability
of national statistics, and aids in  federal  and local tax administration.  As previously  indicated, it also tends toward a
rational development of accounting theory.   The  trends toward
uniformity are stimulated by a desire for comparability in  the
world-wide investment community.  An  understanding of the differences among  nations is  necessary  if an  advanced state of
uniformity is to develop.

#3-11....Objections to Uniformity

Accounting writers have raised objections to the term UNI-
FORMITY in its strict sense on an international basis. They are
(1) overemphasis of the clerical aspects of bookkeeping; (2)
stifling the development of accounting principles; (3) tendency
toward rigidity when established, thereby militating against
the making of changes where warranted; (4) rigidity in accounting contravenes the tendency that business is conducted on a
flexible basis; (5) dampening of managerial accounting methods;
(6) failure to recognize that economic and political differences between countries require different principles.
    One of the leading opponents of uniformity has been Prof.
Irving Fantl, who, in an article in the May 1971 issue of MAN-
AGEMENT ACCOUNTING, at page 13, states:
    Although the growth of multinational business interests
    make the prospect of compatible world-wide accounting most
    appealing, unfortunately the solution is too simple and the
    problem too complex. However desirable such a monolithic
    concept appears, practical impediments to such uniformity
    must be clearly recognized so that accountants and users of
    financial information will not rely on the prospect of uni-
    formity as a cure-all for the problems accruing from inter-
    national accounting diversity. Basically there are three
    impediments: (1) background and traditions, (2) economic
    environments, and (3) state sovereignty.
Prof. Fantl is of the opinion that any one of such three impediments, and most certainly all of them, would militate against
any nation wanting to be bound by universal accounting standards.

HARMONIZATION OF STANDARDS*

#3-12....Establishment of International Objectives

    At the 9th International Congress of Accountants, T.K.
Cowan, in a book entitled NEW HORIZONS OF ACCOUNTING, Paris,
1967, discussing "Harmonization of Accounting," at page 156,
recommended the formulation and acceptance of a statement of
broad accounting objectives as follows:
    (1) that it be recognized that the primary addressees of the
        external accounting reports of the businesses are the
        stockholders;
    (2) that the balance sheet be a statement of the resources
        entrusted to management;

------
*See Summary of Footnote References -- #3-12 thru #3-18

(3) that an income statement should show primarily the income which arose during the period covered, from the viewpoint of the resources of the undertaking with a subsequent adjustment for special practice such as effective price changes; and,

(4) that the basic objective in preparation be truth, and in presentation, fairness.

It is interesting to note that in the issuance of International Accounting Standard #1, and its accompanying Preface, certain of these broad objectives have been adopted, particularly the one that the stockholders of public companies are identified as the primary report users. Although specific definitions of a balance sheet and an income statement are not given, those two statements, as well as other statements and notes, are included in the overall definition of financial statements. The internationalization process began with the issuance of IASC #1; and if the international standards derived therefrom can be properly streamlined to the user needs under a holistic approach, true internationalization will prevail.

There are three approaches that may be employed to establish a holistic objective to accounting principles: Legalistic, Situationistic, and Principled. All three are in existence today in some form.

## #3-13....Legalistic Approach

This approach is exemplified by the company statements found in the British Commonwealth and German countries as indicated in Chapter 2. This approach can easily be identified by viewing the auditors' reports given in those countries which merely state that the financial reports are prepared IN ACCORDANCE WITH THE LAW.

## #3-14....Situationistic Approach

This approach is common throughout the world. It involves a loose type of structure that develops principles according to the situation involved. Thus, under specific situations that occur over a period of time, certain principles related to those situations become prevalent and ultimately result in standard principles that become generally accepted. This follows the common law approach described in Chapter 2 and is prevalent in the U.S.

## #3-15....Principled Approach

This approach would require that established principles be in consonance with a common and total objective. Thus the accountant should take a holistic view, viz., the application of

theory should be based on total awareness of user needs.  Eventually this approach should receive attention.  One method of
achieving the goals of a principles total approach is to establish a holistic simulation model.  Since principles affect economic decisions, such a model would help accountants to antici-
pate the effects of new accounting principles on  the firm and
the total economy before they are promulgated.

## #3-16....Definition of Harmonization

In the book ACCOUNTING FOR MULTINATIONAL ENTERPRISES, Bobbs-
Merrill, 1978, Seymour M. Bohrer, managing partner of Peat,
Marwick, Mitchell & Co., states on page 198:
        Harmonization, as defined in WEBSTER'S DICTIONARY, is
    "an interweaving of different accounts into a single narra-
    tive."   As defined by Prof. Schoenfeld, harmonization is "a
    reconstruction of different points of view." Both defini-
    tions are quite similar.  Harmonization differs from stand-
    ardization since the latter implies adherence to a rigid
    code and is not in concert with the concept of a profession.
    No profession could ultimately endure in an environment of
    rigid rules nor would it serve the public interest. Account-
    ing itself is evolutionary and not conducive to rigidity or
    uniformity.
        As a practical matter, uniformity does not exist nation-
    ally let alone internationally. Consequently, the concept of
    harmonization is a more realistic approach and has a greater
    likelihood of prevailing over standardization.  However,  as
    pointed out by Prof. Schoenfeld, meaningful harmonization
    will generally by necessity be limited to the Western indus-
    trialized nations.

## #3-17....Uniformity vs. Harmonization

Because it has frequently been said that uniformity and harmonization are terms that are used interchangeably, a distinction should be made between them. Perhaps the basic distinction
is the rigidity with which accounting principles are expected
to be adhered to on the international level.  To compound the
attempt at preciseness, it should be noted that the term UNI-
FORMITY, standing by itself, appears to have a double meaning;
hence, we must establish which of the two meanings is to be
used in making a comparison with harmonization.
Thus in Chapter 2 it was pointed out that Uniform Charts of
Accounts for various industries and businesses in general were
established in Sweden, Germany and France.  The Sweden M-Chart
and German Schmalenbach Chart are charts of accounts, and the
French Plan Comptable General embraces not only a chart of accounts but prescribes the procedures required to carry out the

accounting processes. All of these charts are national in character, within a single country, and therefore represent uniformity WITHIN the nation itself, applicable to all of the business enterprises within the nation. On the other hand, the
UNIFORMITY now being discussed is that between nations rather
than within a single nation.

## #3-18....Efforts Toward Harmonization

In Chapter 10 of the book ACCOUNTING FOR THE MULTINATIONAL
CORPORATION, FERF, 1977, entitled "Efforts to Develop World-
Wide Accounting Standards," co-author George Watt on pages
166-169 points out:
    Accounting standards in some countries have developed
through the influence of concepts and practices imported
from other countries with close trade relationships. The
multinational corporations have played an important role in
an evolutionary process that has resulted in establishing a
base, however uneven, from which world-wide accounting
standards may some day be developed. The thought of harmonizing accounting standards on an international level is not
a new idea in professional accounting circles. The impact
of, and concern with, international accounting standards is
also demonstrated by the commissioning of a study by the
United Nations to determine the impact of multinational corporations on the development process and on international
relations. ***
    The following organizations of professional accountants
are working toward HARMONIZATION in specific regions: the
Accountants International Study Group (AISG); the Groupe
d'Etudes des Experts-Comptables de la CEE of the EEC; the
Union Europeenne des Expertes Comptables, Economiques, et
Financiers (UEC).
On page 170, Mr. Watt sresses the RECOGNITION OF A NEED FOR
HARMONIZATION BY OTHER THAN PROFESSIONAL ACCOUNTING ORGANIZA-
TIONS, referring to the INTERNATIONAL ASSOCIATION OF FINANCIAL
EXECUTIVES INSTITUTES (IAFEI) organized in 1969 and extended to
17 developed countries. The IAFEI holds annual international
congresses at which representatives from all Institutes ex-
change information. Another international organization is the
NATIONAL ASSOCIATION OF ACCOUNTANTS, comprising 1,600 members
in 16 NAA international chapters. A third organization is the
INSTITUTE OF INTERNAL AUDITORS, which has 32 chapters in ten
areas.
    Perhaps the most prestigious and influential organization
involved in the process of HARMONIZATION, as indicated by Mr.
Watt on page 171, is the EEC:
    Harmonization of financial presentation in a major segment
    of the industrialized world promises to become an establish-

ed fact within the foreseeable future as a part of the overall coordination efforts taking place in the European Economic Community (EEC).  Article 51 of the proposed 4th  Directive (as amended Feb.21,1974) requires that  the nine Member
States amend their laws, regulations and administrative provisions to comply  with the provisions of the  Directive and
place such amendments in effect  within 30  months after the
Directive is enacted by the appropriate EEC authorities.

Because  of  the great importance  attached to  the EEC by  Mr.
Watt, the provisions relating to the accounting standards to be
set by the  EEC will be presented in more  detail shortly.  The
frequent use of the term HARMONIZATION by Mr. Watt,  and  the
conspicuous absence of  the term UNIFORMITY  in  his chapter on
World-Wide Accounting Principles,  would seem to indicate  that
the future trend will be more common use of the term HARMONIZA-
TION and  away from UNIFORMITY.  At this point in time, the two
media which appear to have the greatest impact on attainment of
harmonization are the IASC and the EEC.

## THE INTERNATIONAL ACCOUNTING STANDARDS COMMITTEE (IASC)

### #3-19....Historical Aspects of IASC

Perhaps the single most important element in the development
of harmonized accounting standards has been the IASC.  By  June
1973, the IASC  constitution was formalized  and signed by nine
representatives of  member accounting  institutes, representing
Australia, Canada, France, Germany, Japan, Mexico, Netherlands,
United Kingdom and Ireland, and the United States.
At its first meeting in June  1973, the IASC selected topics
for its first three international standards:  disclosure of accounting  policies;  valuation of inventories;  and consolidated
financial statements.  The committee agreed that the first subject  should be disclosure  of accounting policies for the purpose of having the advantage  of  clarifying the  policies currently  pursued in  different countries throughout  the  world.
With the  help of  the IASC secretariat located  in London, the
steering  committees which  had  been established  prepared the
exposure drafts  on the  first three standards for deliberation
by all IASC committee  members at the  regular meetings.   They
were then finalized into Standards.
In  January 1983, the IASC in  celebrating its 10th anniversary published a  statement entitled  COMMITTEE OBJECTIVES  AND
PROCEDURES, which includes  its history, and the mutual commitments of the IASC and the  IFAC.  It also includes a PREFACE TO
STATEMENTS OF INTERNATIONAL ACCOUNTING STANDARDS.

## #3-20....IASC Member Countries

Since their organization, the nine founding member countries
of the IASC have admitted a substantial number of additional
members, which by the end of 1984 included the following
countries:

Argentina, Austria, Bahamas, Bangladesh, Barbados, Belgium,
Brazil, Chile, Colombia, Cyprus, Denmark, Dominican Repub-
lic, Ecuador, Egypt, Fiji, Finland, Ghana, Greece, Hong
Kong, Iceland, India, Indonesia, Israel, Italy, Jamaica,
Kenya, Korea, Lebanon, Luxembourg, Malawi, Malaysia, Malta,
New Zealand, Nigeria, Norway, Pakistan, Paraguay, Peru,
Philippines, Portugal, Republic of China, Republic of Pan-
ama, Singapore, South Africa, Spain, Sri Lanka, Sweden,
Thailand, Trinidad and Tobago, Turkey, Uruguay, Venezuela,
Yugoslavia, Zambia, and Zimbabwe.

Each of these countries, like the nine founding members, has
its top ranked professional society or institute of professional accountants representing it.

## #3-21....IASC Objectives

The objectives of the IASC as stated in its constitution
are to:

(1)   establish and maintain an International Accounting Stand-
      ards Committee with a membership and powers set forth
      whose functions will be to formulate and publish, in the
      public interest, standards to be observed in the presenta-
      tion of audited financial statements and to promote their
      world-wide acceptance and observance
(2)   support the standards promulgated by the Committee
(3)   use their best endeavors (a) to ensure that published fi-
      nancial statements comply with these standards or that
      there is disclosure of the extent to which they do not,
      and to persuade governments, the authorities controlling
      securities markets, and the industrial and business commu-
      nity that published financial statements should comply
      with these standards; (b) to ensure (i) that the auditors
      satisfy themselves that the financial statements comply
      with these standards, or, if the financial statements do
      not comply with these standards, that the fact of noncom-
      pliance is disclosed in the financial statements, (ii)
      that in the event of non-disclosure, reference to noncom-
      pliance is made in the audit report; (c) to ensure that,
      as soon as practicable, appropriate action is taken in

respect of auditors whose audit reports do not meet the
requirements of (b) above
(4)   seek to secure similar general acceptance and observance
      of these standards internationally.
The definitions of the technical terms used in the Constitu-
tion--e.g., financial statements, audited accounts, basic
standards scope, working procedures, voting, authority, etc.--
are presented in an IASC brochure entitled PREFACE TO INTERNA-
TIONAL ACCOUNTING STANDARDS published in 1975 and revised in
January 1983.

#### #3-22....Definition of Accounting Standard

In an "Address at the Accountants-Dag Amsterdam," July,
1976, the meaning of the term ACCOUNTING STANDARDS is described
by the first chairman of IASC, Sir Henry Benson, in the IASC
NEWS, 4, No. 5, August 2, 1976, p. 3:
     An ACCOUNTING STANDARD is a clear definite directive as
to how financial statements should be presented; what
should be contained in them; and how the multifarious items
which go to make up financial statements should be dealt
with.
     Standards are based on a consensus of informed opinion
as to what is most appropriate, having regard to the normal
conduct of business by management, the needs of users of
financial statements, comprising creditors, employees, investors, and governments; and the rights and obligations of
shareholders. It does not mean that they are merely the lowest common denominator of what happens in practice. Standards are not absolute and immutable; they change, sometimes
quite quickly, because circumstances and opinion change.

#### #3-23....IASC Pitfalls

As for the pitfalls expected to be encountered by the IASC,
Sir Henry Benson, its founding chairman from 1973 to 1976,
issued the following remarks:
     The step from national standards to international stand-
ards looks to be a short one, but it has grievous pitfalls.
Nationals of every country prefer their own ways just as
they prefer their own food, wine and customs. There is an
even more formidable obstacle--national government. No government will willingly give up its sovereignty and yield the
right to decide what will happen in its own country. The
written standards prepared in the last three years and those
now under exposure are far from perfect.
     They are sometimes too permissive and allow for alterna-
tives; sometimes they are not sufficiently penetrating. But
the mere fact of preparing them has the merit of pointing

out to us in different countries how illogical some of our own existing standards are. Another advantage is that the profession in many countries does not have the money or resources in manpower to write standards, who can now adopt these international standards as their own standards which would have otherwise taken them years to achieve.

## #3-24....IASC Limitations

In the book ACCOUNTING FOR MULTINATIONAL ENTERPRISES, Bobbs-Merrill, 1978, Prof. Schoenfeld of the University of Illinois at Urbana, on page 185, observes:
> The standards issued by the IASC raise a number of questions. The first concerns quality; since standards are based on consensus, it is apparent that sometimes too much rigidity is avoided. However, it can be assumed that future amendments will eventually clarify and tighten these rules.
> The second question concerns the relationship between international standards and national laws or standards set by national professional bodies. This problem is of particular importance because international standards, in some instances, may be contrary to national law or standards. For example, the use of the equity method in consolidated statements (IASC #3) is clearly illegal in Germany.
> Since general accounting policies to be followed are stated in the international accounting standards, only deviations have to be reported. International standards thus will at least provide users of financial statements with basic points of reference on which they can base their evaluations; every major deviation will be noted. Of course, the reliability of such judgment will directly depend on the quality of available standards and compliance by the local professional accountants.

## #3-25....IASC Standards' Conflicts With Local Laws

The second question raised by Prof. Schoenfeld, whereby there arises a conflict between an IASC Standard and Local Law, requires a response. Sir Henry Benson's attempt to answer this question was presented in his address to the Accountants-Dag in Amsterdam in IASC NEWS 4, No.5, Aug. 2, 1976, p. 3, as follows:
> A question which can be asked at this point is how can international standards be applied when the local laws, either Company or Taxation Regulations, require accounts to be produced in a way which differs from the international standards. This is a practical difficulty but not one which is by any means insuperable.
> In such cases the local laws must of course prevail, but what can and should be done is for the financial state-

ments to disclose the extent to which the adoption of the local laws or regulations has required divergence from international standards. This will have the salutary effect of drawing to the attention of the users of the financial statements those areas where an international standard has not been observed; it will put the users on notice to make appropriate allowances and adjustments before arriving at their business judgments or making comparisons. In course of time, as international standards grow in stature, the number of such divergences can be expected to be reduced.

## #3-26....IASC Results

In ACCOUNTING FOR MULTINATIONAL ENTERPRISES, Professor Schoenfeld makes the following comments on page 186, appraising the efforts of the IASC to date:

In evaluating the work of the IASC, it must be noted that these are the first international standards which have been developed. At the very least, the issuing of these new standards has brought out differences of approach in various countries. For the first time, a common basis for comparison of national practice with WORLD-WIDE STANDARD PRACTICE has been created. This in itself represents a major improvement over the past situation. However, it would be overly optimistic to expect that IASC standards will immediately result in more uniform financial statements.

Undoubtedly, if international standards are followed, then deficiencies in information contained in published financial statements will come to light. Whether this is sufficient to allow users of financial statements to make valid comparisons without difficulties remains to be seen, because while deviations from standards must be mentioned, inclusions of adjusted data are not demanded. Nevertheless, all major divergences will be noted and users will not entirely depend on their sometimes limited knowledge of accounting practice in other countries.

On its record the IASC is generally regarded as having been successful in its efforts to date. Both professional and non-accounting professionals have given it their hearty endorsement, which has come from many different sources (the more prominent of which are the World Federation of Stock Exchanges, the London Stock Exchange, and the AICPA). In the August 1975 CPA LETTER issued by the AICPA, the following remarks indicate its observations:

At its July 1975 meeting, the AICPA's Board of Directors reaffirmed its support for the work of the IASC and adopted a revised statement on the Institute's position on implementation of international standards, which includes the following points:

(1) to achieve acceptance in the U.S., international accounting standards will have to be specifically adopted by the Financial Accounting Standards Board;
(2) if there is no significant difference between an international standard and U.S. practice on a subject, compliance with U.S. GAAP will constitute compliance with the international standard; if there is a significant difference between the two, the Institute will urge the FASB to give early consideration to HARMONIZING the differences;
(3) published pronouncements of the IASC will be included in the appropriate volume of AICPA PROFESSIONAL STANDARDS with an indication as to whether there are any significant differences between the international standards and U.S. GAAP;
(4) the AICPA will continue to encourage government authorities, stock exchanges and the business community to put forth their views on IASC draft proposals.

Two matters are significant in these remarks: (1) where there are differences between a U.S. standard and an IASC, the term used to reconcile them is HARMONIZATION, indicating that the AICPA favors harmonization rather than uniformity; and (2) that international standards will have to be adopted by the FASB, indicating the IASC remains subservient to the FASB in the U.S. community.

For an update on IASC developments to 1982, J.A. Burgraaff, IASC Board Chairman, presents a detailed description in the Sept. 1982 issue of the JOURNAL OF ACCOUNTANCY, pp. 104-110.

## #3-27....IASC Modus Operandi

The operating methods of the IASC follow the same pattern as those of the FASB. The principal difference between the two is that FASB members are paid on a full-time basis, a luxury the IASC, at this point in time, cannot afford. Because of its full-time participation, the FASB can indulge in a greater in-depth procedure in establishing its standards than the IASC, by issuing DISCUSSION MEMORANDA and carrying on other research.

The procedure for establishing Standards by both the FASB and the IASC is that a list of problems is issued to them by the profession at large. Then special committees are appointed, which review these topics and choose one on the basis of urgency. The topic selected for study is formally announced and the appropriate study is conducted. DISCUSSION MEMORANDA are then issued which are released to appropriate interested parties in the form of EXPOSURE DRAFTS, which generally run for a six-month period. During such period various comments and suggestions are made regarding their validity, amendment, alteration, correction, etc. This feedback, together with an interim study

of the proposed standard, results in the issuance of the final
IASC STANDARD.

#3-28....IASC Standards Issued

As of 1984, the IASC has issued 24 standards:
1.  Preface to Statements on International Accounting Stand-
    ards and Disclosure of Accounting Policies (1974)
2.  Valuation and Presentation of Inventories in the Context
    of the Historical Cost System (1975)
3.  Consolidated Financial Statements and the Equity Method of
    Accounting for Investments (1976)
4.  Depreciation Accounting (1976)
5.  Information to be Disclosed in Financial Statements (1976)
6.  Accounting Responses to Changing Prices (1977)
7.  Statement of Changes in Financial Position (1977)
8.  Unusual and Prior Items and Changes in Accounting Policies
    (1978)
9.  Accounting for Research & Development Activities (1978)
10. Contingencies and Events Occurring After the Balance Sheet
    Date (1978)
11. Accounting for Construction Contracts (1979)
12. Accounting for Taxes on Income (1979)
13. Presentation of Current Assets & Current Liabilities(1979)
14. Accounting for Foreign Transactions and Translation of
    Foreign Financial Statements (1977)
15. Reporting Financial Information by Segment (1980)
16. Accounting for Property, Plant and Equipment in the Con-
    text of the Historical Cost System (1980)
17. Accounting for Leases (1980)
18. Revenue Recognition (1981)
19. Accounting for Retirement Benefits in Employers' Financial
    Statements (1981)
20. Accounting for Government Grants and Disclosure of Govern-
    ment Assistance (1981)
21. Accounting for Effects of Exchanges in Foreign Exchange
    Rates (1981)
22. Accounting for Business Combinations (1981)
23. Capitalization of Borrowing Costs (1982)
24. Disclosure of Related Party Transactions (1983)

    Summaries of these IASC Standards will be presented in Chap-
ter 4 in connection with the GAAP with which they are associated. In addition to the IASC Standards, the FASB has issued
Statements directly related to international accounting. FASB
#52 (which supplanted FASB #8) relating to Accounting for the
Translation of Foreign Currency Transactions and Foreign Currency Financial Statements is the most important one presently
in force. It will be discussed in later chapters dealing with

the translation of foreign currency financial statements and recording of forward exchange contracts.

#3-29....IASC Consultative User Group

In order to involve the various users of accounts in the standard setting process, the IASC in Jan. 1981 invited a wide variety of international bodies to join a new consultative group. These bodies were to be asked to participate in the discussions that lead to the issue of IASC Standards. The following bodies have been asked to join the group: U.N.; OECD; principal national stock exchanges; International Chamber of Commerce (ICC); International Federation of Trade Unions; World Federation of Labor; World Bank; and the International Associations of Financial Executives Institutes and Financial Analysts. The reason for formation of the group is that the IASC is identified exclusively with the accounting profession, which creates a narrow perspective, and which in many countries has no responsibility for setting standards. An example is the AICPA, which is a member of the IASC board but is governed by the FASB, which in turn is not a member of the IASC for setting standards. This group was formalized at the 12th International Congress of the IFAC held in Mexico City in 1982.

## THE EUROPEAN ECONOMIC COMMUNITY (EEC)

#3-30....Historical Aspects of EEC

At the time EEC was created (TREATY OF ROME, March 25, 1957) all of the member countries had either COMPANY LAWS, CORPORATION LAWS or COMMERCIAL CODES in existence which differed from each other in many respects. This made it necessary from the outset for the EEC Commission, which was established, to create some harmonization between the diversity of Codes. The procedure followed was similar to that for IASC, viz., an exposure draft, or DRAFT DIRECTIVE, as it was called, was issued.

Hearings and investigations were held and conducted, causing revised drafts to be issued, which ultimately constituted the FINAL DRAFT. The Final Draft then required approval by the EEC Council of Ministers for presentation to the member states for ratification.

At this point, distinction must be made in two directions: (1) the Draft Directives were general in nature in that they covered every channel of company activity; and, (2) Draft Directives were of five different classes.

#3-31....Classes of EEC Draft Directives

The five classes are decisions, directives, opinions, recommendations, and regulations. DECISIONS are directives which are

binding on the parties named regardless of whether they are
private individuals, business enterprises, or governments. DI-
RECTIVES are orders issued to member states requiring them to
perform specific objectives, leaving the modus operandi of effectuation of the objectives to the discretion of the member
state involved. OPINIONS are mere statements of advice and not
binding on any member. RECOMMENDATIONS are stronger than opinions in that they make positive suggestions but are also not
binding. REGULATIONS are, as the term indicates, rules that are
aimed generally and equally at all member countries and are
binding with equal force and effect on all of them.

#### #3-32....Accounting-Oriented Draft Directives

Since Draft Directives were aimed at every functional activity of member country business organizations, it is necessary
to be concerned here only with those draft directives related
to accounting standards, of which there are four: Fourth Directive, Draft Fifth Directive, Seventh Directive and Eighth Directive. However, in a broad way the directives issued have
also been related to the harmonization of company laws, which
indirectly affect the accounting aspects.

Thus, as Professor Schoenfeld indicates in the book ACCOUNT-
ING FOR MULTINATIONAL ENTERPRISES, at page 187:

Several Directives have presently been issued by the
EEC. The First Directive (March 1968) requires that limited
companies and partnerships limited by shares must publish
annual balance sheets and profit and loss accounts.

The Second Directive specified rules governing maintenance and alteration of equity capital as well as minimum
paid-up share capital, and restricts both the payment of
dividends and the right of the company to purchase its own
shares.

The Third Directive applies to mergers; it requires management to publish specific data concerning the contemplated
merger, and to issue an independent accountant's report at-
testing to the fairness of the share exchanges.

The Fourth Directive specified details to be disclosed
in the annual financial statements--consisting of balance
sheet, profit and loss account, and explanatory notes--by
all companies whose liability is limited through share capital, excluding banks and insurance companies.

The Fifth Directive deals with the auditor's responsibilities, his liabilities for inaccuracies in reports and
prospectuses,and his right to practice in all EEC countries.

Additional directives are in the planning state, which
will address such issues as consolidated accounts, transnational mergers, insurance companies, credit institutions,
and minimal educational requirements for statutory auditors.

## #3-33....Nature and Types of Directives

To date there have been eight directives PUBLISHED. However,
a distinction must be made--concerning directives that have
been PUBLISHED--between those that have been PROPOSED and those
which have been ADOPTED. All eight have been published, but not
all of them have been ADOPTED. The current status of the eight
published directives is:
(1) The First Directive deals with the basic matters of company laws, and was adopted in March 1968.
(2) The Second Directive was published originally in March
1970 and amended in October 1973. It deals with the subject of Capital Stock. It was adopted in December 1976.
(3) The Third Directive was issued in June 1970 and amended in
Jan. 1973. It deals with mergers of companies subject to
the same member state laws. It was adopted in Oct. 1978.
(4) The Fourth Directive was published in Nov. 1971 and amended in Feb. 1974. It treats the subjects of form and content of financial statements, which obviously is of basic
concern to accounting. It was adopted in July 1978.
(5) The Fifth Directive also is related to accounting. It was
published in Oct. 1972 and amended in Aug. 1983. It treats
the subject of the corporate structure. It has been proposed but not yet adopted.
(6) The Sixth Directive was published in Oct. 1972 and amended
in Dec. 1975. It is concerned with prospectuses for issuances of securities on stock exchanges. It was adopted in
December 1982.
(7) The Seventh Directive is also related to accounting. It
was published in April 1976 and adopted in June 1983. It
is regarded as an extension of the Fourth Directive in
that it deals with Consolidated Accounts.
(8) The Eighth Directive was published in 1978 and adopted in
April 1984. It deals with auditors' qualifications.

## #3-34....Draft Fourth Directive

The 4th Directive had its original publication in Nov. 1971
and a revised draft was issued in Feb. 1974 entitled AMENDED
PROPOSAL FOR A FOURTH DIRECTIVE ON THE ANNUAL ACCOUNTS OF LIM-
ITED LIABILITY COMPANIES. It was presented by the Commission to
the Council on Feb. 26, 1974, published as Supplement 6/1974,
Bulletin of the European Communities, Commission of the EC,
Brussels, Belgium.
The Fourth Directive Revision consists of 12 Sections broken
down into 52 Articles. Strangely, the first provision is entitled Article 1 rather than Section 1; it makes reference to
the types of legal organizations that the various corporate
structure enterprises take in EC countries, which will be

treated in detail later.  The Sections  and Articles under each
Section are as follows:

| SEC.# | TITLE OF SECTION | ARTICLE NOS. IN SEC. |
|---|---|---|
| 1 | General Requirements | Art. 2 |
| 2 | Layout of The Annual Accounts | Art. 3 - 6 |
| 3 | Balance Sheet Layout | Art. 7 -11 |
| 4 | Specl. Prov. Relating to Balance Sheet Items | Art. 12-18 |
| 5 | Layout of the Profit & Loss Account | Art. 19-24 |
| 6 | Specl. Prov. of Profit & Loss Items | Art. 25-27 |
| 7 | Valuation Rules | Art. 28-39 |
| 8 | Contents of the Notes on the Accounts | Art. 40-42 |
| 9 | Contents of The Annual Report | Art. 43 |
| 10 | Publication | Art. 44-47 |
| 11 | Specl. Prvsns. Related to Limited Liability Companies | Art. 48-50 |
| 12 | Final Provisions | Art. 51-52 |

Article 51 (in the Final Provisions) requires that the 9 member
states amend their laws and regulations to comply with the provisions of the 4th Directive and  place  such amendments in effect  within  30 months after the Directive  is enacted  by the
appropriate EEC authorities.

#3-35...Interntl. Forms of EEC Country Corporate Organizations

    Article 1 of the 4th  Directive makes a listing of the legal
form titles of  the  limited  companies in  the  ten countries,
which  should  be of interest  to International Accounting students.  Certainly they should be familiar with this terminology
if  they intend to  enter the area of international accounting.
Article 1 declares:
    The  coordination measures prescribed by Articles 2 to 47 of
    this Directive apply  to the laws, regulations and  adminis-
    trative provisions of the Member States relating to the fol-
    lowing types of company:
    GERMANY--Die  Aktiengesellschaft,  die Kommanditgesellschaft
        auf Aktien (AG);
    BELGIUM--la  societe anonyme, de  naamloze vennootschap, la
        societe en commandite par actions, de commanditaire ven-
        nootschap op sandelen (SA);
    DENMARK--Aktieselskab, Kommandit-Aktieselskab (AS);
    FRANCE--la  Societe anonyme, la  societe  en  commandite par
        actions (SA);
    IRELAND  AND U.K.--Companies incorporated with  limited lia-
        bility (LTD.)
    ITALY--la societa per azioni, la societa in accomandita  per
        azioni (SPA);
    LUXEMBOURG--la  societe  anonyme, la  societe  en commandite
        par actions (SA);

NETHERLANDS--de naamloze vennootschap, de commanditaire vennootschap op aandelen (NV).

## #3-36....Draft Fifth Directive

The 5th Directive turned out  to be controversial in character and  for this reason was withdrawn temporarily  on Jan.  1,
1973, which  was the date that the U.K. and Ireland and Denmark
were admitted to membership in the EEC. This directive was concerned with the management and structure of larger corporations
and outside audits for them.   The controversy arose due to the
fact that the British structural pattern based on a single-tier
corporate board  system differed from the German and  Dutch arrangement of a two-tier system. In order to avert any difficulties, the 5th Draft Directive was withdrawn, with future action
supposed to be taken thereon.

## #3-37....Seventh and Eighth Directives

The 7th Directive issued in May  1976 by the EEC  Commission
deals with the  subject of  consolidated financial  statements.
After 7 stormy years, it was finally adopted on June 13, 1983.
The 8th  Directive aims to  harmonize  education and professional training requirements for auditors.

## SOCIETA EUROPA (SE)

## #3-38....Statute for European Companies

To supplement the foregoing directives in  order to maintain
better control over the various corporations doing  business in
the  EEC, the proposed STATUTE FOR  THE EUROPEAN COMPANY,  consisting of  284 articles  under 14  titles was issued June 1970
and amended  in May 1975.   The proposed Statute provides for a
SOCIETE EUROPEENE (SE) to be called by the Latin, SOCIETA EURO-
PA, a  company amenable to a legal arrangement common to all of
the EEC states.
Provision  is made for a  SUPERVISORY BOARD consisting of  a
representation  from three equal groups:  shareholders, employees, and  general interests other than the shareholders and employees.  Another section deals with the preparation of  annual
statements and  their audit comparable to the provisions in the
Fourth Directive.
It  should be  noted that the STATUTE is a PROPOSAL  that is
being considered for adoption. Accounting-wise, the two principal  sections are Section  6 ("Preparation of Group  Accounts")
and Section 7 ("Audit").
Section 6 consists of seven articles as follows:
Art. 196--Group Accounts and Part Group Accounts

Art. 197--Non-Consolidation of Accounts of Under-
      taking Within Group
Art. 198--Drawing Up of Group Accounts
Art. 199--Presentation of Group Accounts
Art. 200--Valuation
Art. 201--Information Contained in Note on Con-
      solidated Accounts
Art. 202--Incorporating of Art. 195 by Reference
Section 7 consists of 11 articles as follows:
Art. 203--Audit by Auditors
Art. 203(a)--Independence of Auditor
Art. 203(b)--Independence of Auditor
Art. 204--Appointment and Removal of Auditor
Art. 204(a)--Remuneration
Art. 205--Object of Audit
Art. 206--Auditor's Right of Examination
Art. 207--Auditor's Certificate
Art. 208--Auditor's Report
Art. 209--Auditor's Liability
Art. 210--Audit of Consolidations

## #3-39....Objectives of European Companies Statute

The Statute was designed ostensibly to make for a smooth
conduct of business between companies engaging in business in
the EEC countries by:
(1) eliminating the present legal framework in European
    dealings which would cause hindrance to the community
    development because it militates against the political
    and economic framework;
(2) creating uniformity within the operation framework of
    the EEC; and
(3) creating amenability to control of companies operating
    within the EEC domain that would be outside the juris-
    diction on an individual country basis.

## #3-40....European Companies Requirements

To attain the foregoing objectives, SE's would be limited
liability companies showing the term SE after their names (similar to Ltd. or Inc.) and would be required to be registered in
the European Commercial Register as well as the EEC Court of
Justice. They could only be created in one of three ways: a
merger of existing EEC companies; formation of a holding company
for existing EEC companies; or formation as a joint subsidiary.
They would also be subject to the following requirements of
legal capital: (a) for a merger or holding company, the sum of
500,000 European currency units of account; (b) for a joint
subsidiary, the sum of 250,000 European currency units of ac-

count; or (c) for a subsidiary of an SE, the sum of 100,000 European currency units of account. Such legal capital amounts must be fully paid up in cash or in kind. An SE is forbidden to reacquire its own shares or engage in reciprocal shareholdings with other SE's. An SE may issue non-voting shares up to 50% of the legal capital. Finally, shares that are issued may be bearer shares or registered shares. In the case of bearer shares, if more than 10% is owned by one party, there must be public notice given.

## #3-41...Impact of EEC and European Companies Law on International Accounting

It may be seen from the outline of the contents of the 4th Directive, together with the European Companies Statute, that considerable attention has been given to accounting in the EEC countries. Many accounting authorities are of the opinion that the EEC accounting regulations will have a salutary affect on harmonization of at least a regional European set of international accounting standards.

As to the relationship between U.S. companies desiring to work in an arrangement with the EEC, James J. Quinn, National Director of Accounting, Auditing and SEC Practice (Coopers and Lybrand) points out in ACCOUNTING FOR MULTINATIONAL ENTERPRISES, Bobbs-Merrill, 1978, at pages 102-103, that:

It is clearly premature to evaluate the impact of the EEC proposals on U.S. issuers wishing to raise capital within the EEC. Registration and listing could be more complicated than heretofore in terms of the individual nations; on the other hand, multinational offerings could be less complicated.

In sum, a U.S. company encounters considerably greater difficulties in raising money within the U.S. than does a U.S. company going overseas. In the major capital markets of the world, any well-run U.S. company meeting the stringent SEC requirements should have no problem in the regulatory area when raising capital, providing, of course, that market conditions are right.

In his discussion of efforts to develop world-wide accounting standards, Mr. Watt, in ACCOUNTING FOR THE MULTINATIONAL CORPORATION, published by Financial Executives Research Foundation, 1977, at page 171, declares:

The proposed Fourth Directive recognizes the principle that a company's financial statements present a "true and fair view and results." This is a step forward since in some of the countries in the group this concept is presently recognized neither in law nor in practice, because the concept of "compliance with legal requirements" is the overriding influence.

## SUMMARY OF FOOTNOTE REFERENCES
(References are to Paragraph #'s)

#3-7    F.M. Richard, "New Horizons of Accounting," 9th International Congress of Accountants, Paris, 1967, p. 11

#3-8    Jacob Kraayenhof, "International Challenges for Accounting," JOURNAL OF ACCOUNTANCY (January 1960): 34-38

#3-11   Irving Fantl, MANAGEMENT ACCOUNTING (May 1971): 13

#3-12 thru #3-18:   "Harmonization of Standards," adapted from Norlin G. Rueschhoff, INTERNATIONAL ACCOUNTING AND FINANCIAL REPORTING, 1976, Praeger Publishers, Inc., by permission.

#3-12   T.K. Cowan, "New Horizons...", op. cit., p. 156

#3-16   Seymour M. Bohrer, ACCOUNTING FOR MULTINATIONAL ENTERPRISES (Indianapolis: Bobbs-Merrill, 1978), p. 198

#3-18   George C. Watt, "Efforts to Develop World-Wide Accounting Standards," ACCOUNTING FOR THE MULTINATIONAL CORPORATION, pp. 166-171. Copyright 1977 by Financial Executives Research Foundation (FERF), Morristown, N.J. Reprinted with permission.

#3-22   Sir Henry Benson, "Address at the Accountants-Dag, Amsterdam," IASC NEWS, 4, No. 5 (Aug. 2, 1976): 3

#3-23   Sir Henry Benson, IASC Chairman, 1973-1976

#3-24   Hanns-Martin Schoenfeld, ACCOUNTING FOR MULTINATIONAL ENTERPRISES, op. cit., p. 185

#3-25   Sir Henry Benson, IASC NEWS, op. cit.

#3-26   Schoenfeld, op. cit., p. 186

#3-26   AICPA, CPA LETTER (August 1975)

#3-32   Schoenfeld, op. cit., p. 187

#3-34   EEC 4th Directive, AMENDED PROPOSAL FOR A FOURTH DIRECTIVE, Supplement 6/1974, Bulletin of the European Communities, EC Commission, Brussels, Belgium

#3-41   James J. Quinn, ACCOUNTING FOR MULTINATIONAL ENTERPRISES, op. cit., pp. 102-103

#3-41   Watt, op. cit., p. 171. Reprinted by permission from FERF.

## BIBLIOGRAPHY

Bartlett, Ralph T. "Current Developments of the IASC," THE CPA JOURNAL, 51 (May 1981): 20-27

Benson, Sir Henry. "The Story of International Accounting Standards," ACCOUNTANCY (July 1976): 34-39

Burgraaff, J.A. "IASC Developments," JOURNAL OF ACCOUNTANCY (Sept. 1982): 104-110

Choi, Frederick. "A Cluster Approach to Accounting Harmonization," MANAGEMENT ACCOUNTING, 63 (August 1981): 26-31

Choi, Frederick and Bavishi, V.B. "Financial Accounting Standards: A Multinational Synthesis and Policy Framework," INTERNATIONAL JOURNAL OF ACCOUNTING EDUCATION & RESEARCH (Fall 1982): 159-184

Choi, Frederick and Bavishi, V.B. "International Accounting Standards," JOURNAL OF ACCOUNTANCY (March 1983): 62

Cowperthwaite, Gordon H. "Prospectus for International Harmonization," CA MAGAZINE, 108 (June 1976): 22-31

DeBruyne, D. "Global Standards: A Tower of Babel?", FINANCIAL EXECUTIVE, 48 (February 1980): 30-37

Evans, T.G. and Taylor, M.E. "Bottom Line Compliance With the IASC: A Comparative Analysis," INTERNATIONAL JOURNAL OF ACCOUNTING EDUCATION & RESEARCH (Fall 1982): 115-128

Fantl, Irving L. "The Case Against International Uniformity," MANAGEMENT ACCOUNTING (May 1971): 13-15

Fitzgerald, R.D. "International Accounting and Reporting," PRICE WATERHOUSE REVIEW, 2 (1983): 16

Fox, Samuel and Holtzblatt, Mark. "The Basic International Accounting Dilemma: Uniformity vs. Harmonization," BUSINESS & SOCIETY, Vol. 22-1 (Spring 1983): 43-49

Mahon, J.J. "Whither International Accounting Standards," THE CPA JOURNAL (December 1983): 30-37

McClean, Alasdair. "Societas Europa," ACCOUNTANTS MAGAZINE (December 1971): 631-640

McComb, D. "International Accounting Standards and the EEC Harmonization," INTERNATIONAL JOURNAL OF ACCOUNTING EDUCATION & RESEARCH (Spring 1982): 35-48

McMonnies, P.N. "EEC, UEC, ASC, IASC, IASG, AISG, ICCAP, IFAC, Old Uncle Tom Cobbleigh and All," ACCOUNTING AND BUSINESS RESEARCH, 7 (Summer 1977): 162-167

Steinhauer, William. "Confusing Encounter," PRICE WATERHOUSE REVIEW (1976)

Thomas, B.S. "International Harmonization," BUSINESS LAWYER (August 1983): 1397

Turner, John N. "The Need for International Harmony in Accounting Standards," CA MAGAZINE (January 1983): 40-44

Turner, John N. "International Harmonization," JOURNAL OF ACCOUNTANCY (January 1983): 58

Vincent, Geoff. "Towards International Standards for Accountants," THE AUSTRALIAN ACCOUNTANT, 51 (March 1981): 98-99

## THEORY QUESTIONS
(Question Numbers are Keyed to Text Paragraph #'s)

#3-3    What problems are encountered in the process of establishing standards?

#3-4    What are the common criteria for establishment of standards?

#3-6    What three possibilities exist for setting standards? Define each and make a critical comparative analysis of them.

#3-8    Trace the history of uniformity of standards.

#3-9    What is meant by the Cameralistic Nature of Uniformity?

#3-10   What are the advantages of Uniformity?

#3-11   What are the objections to Uniformity?

#3-17  Define Harmonization.  Are the terms Uniformity and Har-
       monization interchangeable?  Explain.

#3-18  Trace the efforts that have  been made toward Harmoniza-
       tion.

#3-21  What are the objectives of the IASC?

#3-22  Define the term Accounting Standard.

#3-23  What difficulties are  anticipated  to be encountered by
       the IASC?

#3-24  What are the limitations of the IASC?

#3-25  What  situation prevails where  there  is a conflict be-
       tween IASC Standards and local laws?

#3-26  Make an appraisal of the IASC results to date.

#3-27  What  procedures are followed  by  the  IASC in creating
       standards?

#3-29  What is  the  IASC Consultative Users Group and how does
       it function?

#3-30  Trace the history of the European Economic Community.

#3-31  How many classes of EEC Draft Directives are  there  and
       what are they?  Define each class.

#3-32  How many of the EEC Draft Directives are directly relat-
       ed to accounting and which are they?

#3-33  Briefly describe the eight published EEC Directives.

#3-34  Discuss the content, makeup and significance of the  4th
       Draft Directive.

#3-35  What are the major  forms  of Corporate Organizations in
       the EEC member countries?

#3-37  What is the nature of the 7th EEC Draft Directive?

#3-38  What is the  Societa Europa  and  what function  does it
       serve?  What is its relationship to accounting?

#3-39  What  are  the requirements  of  the  European Companies
       Statute?

#3-40  What is  the impact  of the  EEC and  European Companies
       Statute on international accounting?

# International Comparative Generally Accepted Accounting Principles

## #4-1....Standards vs. GAAP

Up to this point  we have discussed the matter  of Standards as separate from GAAP. Technically the basic difference between the two would be the matter of formality.   STANDARDS are written  principles issued by a formal body established to  produce them. GAAP are principles not declared in writing by any formal body but  result from  usage and custom practiced over a period of  years.  Neither standards nor  GAAP have  any fiat or legal force behind them.  Pronouncements by the IASC may, and in many cases have to, be avoided where  they are in conflict with  the laws of the nation in which they are being applied. This is why Mr. Watt is so optimistic in his appraisal of the effect of the EEC Directives on standards to be observed by  the member countries being enacted into "laws, regulations  and administrative provisions."

## #4-2....International Accounting Necessarily Comparative

Because there are  differences in accounting principles  between nations, we do not have  uniformity, hence it becomes necessary to state the principles on a comparative basis. In such case they may be referred to as international COMPARATIVE accounting principles.  As  indicated in Chapter 1, we must begin by selecting one country as the base  domicile to which foreign principles are to be related, which  has been designated as the United States.   Hence the term "comparative" as used here will be  a comparison between the principles established in the U.S. with other countries selected on a basis of comparability.

## #4-3....GAAP

In the U.S.,  accounting theory and principles are generally referred to under the title GAAP--generally  accepted account-

ing principles. The GAAP pattern of accounting follows that of
the common law approach with respect to law as discussed in
Chap. 2. These principles have arisen and been followed through
custom and usage as practiced over many years in the U.S.

GAAP is not the result of any statutes and the law has no
control over them. Nevertheless as pointed out in Chapter 1,
there has been a liberal international flavoring sprinkled into
the U.S. GAAP concoction. As a result we find many U.S. accounting theories of GAAP equally accentuated in many of the
other developed countries. Hence in the remainder of this chapter we will treat accounting theory on a comparative basis with
such other selected countries. Particular emphasis will be giv-
en to the EEC, because the advanced states of present-day commercial and industrial systems resulted from developments in
the countries comprising the EEC. Several of the more prominent
countries representing the continents of Asia, Africa, and
South America will be interwoven in the comparative discussion.
The standards issued to date by the IASC will also be included.

## #4-4....Nature of International Principles

International principles from the viewpoint of acceptability
fall into two categories--some are accepted internationally,
others vary among nations. The former are uniform in character;
the latter are comparative. With reference to international
accounting principles, the IASC has promulgated international
accounting standards that are basically of two types: accounting principles and policies, and financial statement presentation principles. The former will be discussed in this chapter
and the latter in Chapter 5.


## FUNDAMENTAL ACCOUNTING ASSUMPTIONS*

### #4-5....Basic Assumptions

IASC #1 declares three basic assumptions--Going Concern,
Consistency, and Accrual--defined as follows:
(a)  GOING CONCERN--The enterprise is normally viewed as a go-
     ing concern, that is, as continuing in operation for the
     foreseeable future. It is assumed that the enterprise has
     neither the intention nor the necessity of liquidation or
     of curtailing materially the scale of its operations.
(b)  CONSISTENCY--It is assumed that the accounting policies
     are consistent from one period to another.

------
*See Summary of Footnote References -- #4-5 thru #4-47

(c)  ACCRUAL--Revenue and costs are accrued, that is, recogniz-
     ed as they are  earned or incurred (and not  as  money  is
     received or paid) and recorded in the financial statements
     of the periods  to which they relate.  (The considerations
     affecting the  process  of matching  costs  with  revenues
     under the  accrual assumption are not  dealt with in  this
     statement.) (IASC #1, DISCLOSURE OF ACCOUNTING PRINCIPLES,
     London, 1974.)
These three assumptions  have  world-wide acceptance.  However,
in several countries, including Switzerland and Italy, the consistency assumption is not required. Further, the disclosure of
the effect of a change in accounting principles is not required
to be disclosed in many countries.

Nevertheless, as international accounting  standards receive
recognition, these variations may be expected to diminish.  The
first international accounting  standard  does  point out  that
disclosure of the  assumptions is not required because of their
fundamental nature.

## #4-6....Basic Concepts

IASC  #1 also  states that  three  considerations govern the
selection and application by management of the  appropriate accounting policies in the  preparation of financial statements--
Prudence, Substance Over Form, and Materiality--as follows:
(a)  PRUDENCE -- Uncertainties inevitably surround many  trans-
     actions.  This should be recognized by exercising prudence
     in preparing financial statements. Prudence does not, how-
     ever,  justify the  creation  of  secret  or forbidden re-
     serves.
(b)  SUBSTANCE  OVER  FORM  --  Transactions and  other  events
     should be  accounted for and presented  in accordance with
     their substance and financial  reality and not merely with
     their legal form.
(c)  MATERIALITY  --  Financial statements should  disclose all
     items which are material  enough to affect evaluations  or
     decisions.

## #4-7....The Prudence Concept

The Prudence concept is related to the  principle of conservatism in the  U.S.  It comes into play in situations where uncertainties require some choice in applying a principle demanding the use of proper judgment.   In all parts of the world the
intuitive  but conservative  use of proper judgment  is  widely
accepted as necessary.

The term PRUDENCE has its origins  in Great Britain, and the
principle  of conservatism is exactly the  same as the Prudence
concept.  The term PRUDENCE appears  to be more acceptable than

CONSERVATISM, as may be evidenced by the mere statement that
accountants are prudent, rather than to state that accountants
are conservative. For this reason, Prudence should eventually
be the term to be used in such connection. The Prudence concept, as well as the concepts of Substance Over Form, and
Materiality, do have rather general acceptance around the
world.

### #4-8....The Materiality Concept

The Materiality concept assumes the proper disclosure of all
relevant financial statement items. In some countries the lack
of disclosure of departures from the consistency concept
assumes a similar lack of adoption of the Materiality concept
with its basic inherent disclosure requirement. A major exception is the lack of disclosure for hypothecated or pledged assets. The Materiality concept is widely accepted around the
world.

Although these assumptions and governing considerations
have world-wide acceptance, the more detailed accounting principles are not as widely uniform on a worldwide basis. The comparative study of these differences, to follow, will show some
of the diversity.

### UNDERLYING ASSET VALUATION CONCEPTS

### #4-9....The Historical Cost Concept

The Historical Cost concept for recording initial transactions and exchanges has had traditional acceptance. In double-
entry accounting, each transaction between the two parties is
recorded at its exchange value, which is historical cost.

### #4-10....Definition of Historical Cost for Inventories

In IASC #2, historical cost for inventories is defined as
follows:
   (a) HISTORICAL COST OF INVENTORIES is the aggregate of costs
       of purchase, costs of conversion, and other costs incur-
       red in bringing the inventories to their present loca-
       tion and condition.
   (b) COSTS OF PURCHASE comprise the purchase price including
       import duties and other purchase taxes, transport and
       handling costs, and any other directly attributable
       costs of acquisition less trade discounts, rebates, and
       subsidies.
   (c) COST OF CONVERSION are those costs, in addition to costs
       of purchase,that relate to bringing the inventories to
       their present location and condition.

This definition can assumedly be applied to other assets recorded at cost. In IASC #4, the historical cost becomes the depreciable amount for determining the allocation of depreciable assets over their useful life.

## #4-11....Ascertainment of Historical Cost

The above definition is readily determinable for purchased items and generally is applicable on a world-wide basis. Variations occur however in the ascertainment of historical costs of manufactured and constructed assets.

## #4-12....Ascertainment of Manufactured Inventory Cost

IASC #2 gives a definite specification concerning manufactured inventories. It states:

(a) The historical cost of manufactured inventories should include a systematic allocation of those production overhead costs that relate to putting the inventories in their present location and condition. Allocation of fixed production overhead to the costs of conversion should be based on the capacity of the facilities. If fixed production overhead has been entirely or substantially excluded from the valuation of inventories on the grounds that it does not directly relate to putting the inventories in their present location and condition, that fact should be disclosed.

(b) Overheads other than production overhead should be included as part of inventory cost only to the extent that they clearly relate to putting the inventories in their present location and condition.

(c) Exceptional amounts of wasted material, labor, and other expenses should not be included as part of inventory cost.

Manufactured inventory costs include all direct materials and direct labor, plus all variable and fixed factory overhead based on a normal capacity. The various cost concept relationships can readily be seen in Figure 4-1.

Of interest is the fact that in certain countries inventories may be shown at prime costs or only all of the variable costs. However, departures from cost, such as appraised values or market values, also are quite often used. Unfortunately departures from cost are not always disclosed in the financial statements. The lack of disclosure is most often coupled with the fact that the departures are in accordance with tax provisions requiring that tax accounting and accounting for financial reporting purposes be synchronized. This is a reporting requirement in West Germany and Colombia.

==

FIGURE 4-1

DIAGRAM OF VARIOUS COST CONCEPT RELATIONSHIPS

Direct Materials.........................$100
Direct Labor*............................$150
   PRIME COST...........................$250
Variable Factory Overhead*..............$ 75
   DIRECT COST (Variable Cost).........$325
Fixed Factory Overhead* (based on
       normal capacity).............$125
REPORTED INVENTORY COST** (in
      accordance with IASC #2)......$450


*Conversion Costs represent total costs of direct labor
and variable and fixed factory overhead.
**In the United States, this Inventory Cost is often
called "absorption cost."

============================================================

## #4-13....Constructed Asset Cost Determination

IASC #11 (1978) on accounting for construction contracts
specifies that historical cost includes:
  (a) Costs that relate directly to a specific contract. Exam-
      ples of such costs include site labor cost, including
      supervision; materials used for project construction;
      depreciation of plant and equipment used on a contract;
      and costs of moving plant and equipment to and from a
      site.
  (b) Costs that can be attributed to the contract activity in
      general and can be allocated to specific contracts.
      Examples of such costs include insurance, design and
      technical assistance, and construction overhead.
In contrast, costs that relate to the activities of the enterprise generally--such as general, administrative, and selling
costs; finance costs; research and development costs; and depreciation of idle plant and equipment--are usually excluded
from the historical cost of a constructed asset. These latter
general costs are not accumulated because they do not relate to
reaching the present stage of completion of the specific constructed asset.

## #4-14....Cost Formulas Used for Assigning Costs

Several different formulas are in use around the world for
the purpose of assigning costs. They include first-in, first-

out (FIFO); weighted average; last-in, first-out (LIFO); base
stock; specific identification; next-in, first-out (NIFO); and
latest purchase price. However, NIFO and latest purchase price
use costs that have not at all been incurred and are therefore
not based on historical cost.

#4-15....Specific Identification Method

The Specific Identification formula attributes specific
costs to identified items of inventory. The method can be appropriately used for purchased or manufactured assets that are
segregated.

#4-16....Interchangeable Inventory Items

For interchangeable items, the selection of the items for
determining historical cost can be so arranged as to obtain
predetermined effects on profits. Thus IASC #2 declares that:
   (a) the historical cost of inventories should be accounted
      for by using the FIFO formula or a weighted average
      cost formula, except as follows:
      (1) Inventories of items that are not ordinarily inter-
      changeable or goods manufactured and segregated for spe-
      cific projects should be accounted for by using specific
      identification of their individual costs;
      (2) The LIFO or base stock formulas may be used provided
      that there is disclosure of the difference between the
      amount of the inventories as shown in the balance sheet
      and either (a) the lower of the historical cost and net
      realizable value or (b) the lower of current cost at the
      balance sheet date and net realizable value.
   (b) Techniques such as the standard cost method of valuing
      products or the retail method of valuing merchandise may
      be used for convenience if they approximate conveniently
      the results of valuing at the lower of historical cost
      or net realizable value.

#4-17....Inventory Methods Used

The weighted average and FIFO cost formulas for inventories
are the most generally acceptable in all parts of the world.
The LIFO and base-stock methods are allowed and used in a few
countries. The retail method is widely acceptable for determining costs of resale merchandise.

#4-18....Departures From Cost

Showing inventories at net realizable value when that value
is below historical cost is an internationally declared princi-

ple.  However, other departures from cost can be found  in some
countries.  In Switzerland and Sweden, for example, inventories
may be written down below net realizable value in  order to establish inventory reserves permitted by tax laws.  On the other
hand, inventories may be reported in the Netherlands above cost
at replacement cost. In the U.S. they may be reported below net
realizable value  if that amount  is  greater than  replacement
cost, except where replacement cost is the best available means
for measuring net realizable value.

### #4-19....Valuation of Receivables

In the  valuation of receivables, the world-wide practice is
to report  the  receivables  at net realizable  value, which is
determined by  deducting an estimated allowance for uncollectible accounts from the  transaction amounts.   The amount of the
allowance is based on past experience and future projections of
expected uncollectibles.

Where  tax laws do not permit  such allowances, such  as  in
Italy, Spain, and  the Philippines, the uncollectible  accounts
are not  deducted until definitely  deemed  uncollectible.  The
enterprises in these  countries are forced to  use  the  direct
write-off method, whereas the allowance method is permitted and
generally acceptable in most parts of the world.

When the U.S. Securities Act  was passed in  1933,  the  accounting  profession  decreed the requirement  that receivables
from officers and directors  be shown separately on the balance
sheet.  A considerable number of countries  do  not follow this
requirement though many countries do require such separate disclosure.  Singularly standards that compel the separate reporting  of receivables from affiliated companies have been adopted
in more countries.

### #4-20....Valuation of Construction Contracts

In the case of construction contracts, there is a dual problem of valuation.  Equally as important as the valuation of the
contract at stages of completion that extend generally over two
or more accounting periods is the consideration of the recognition of revenue on such contracts.  According to the definition
of  ACCRUAL as pointed  out in IASC #1, revenues  and costs are
recognized as they  are earned or incurred and recorded  in the
financial statements of  the periods to which they relate.  The
problem of applying the accrual concept therefore arises in the
case of construction contracts extending for  more than one accounting period.

A completed contract recording policy would dictate that the
revenue  is to be recognized only when the contract is complete
or substantially so with only minor possible  expected warranty

work left to be done. Under this generally accepted accounting method, costs and progress payments received are accumulated during the course of the contract, but revenue is recognized only when the contract activity is substantially complete.

On the other hand, revenue could be considered earned as the construction is in the process of being completed. Recognizing revenue as the contract activity progresses is accomplished by the percentage-of-completion method of revenue recognition. Under this principle, costs incurred at each stage of completion are matched with the revenue, reporting the revenue attributable to the work completed. IASC #11 permits the use of this method only if the outcome of the contract can be reliably established. The degree of reliability is provided only if certain conditions are satisfied.

In the case of fixed price contracts, where the contractor agrees to a fixed contract price or rate, the conditions are (a) total contract revenues to be received can be reliably estimated; (b) both the costs to complete the contract and the stage of contract performance at the reporting date can be reliably estimated; and (c) the costs attributable to the contract can be clearly identified so that actual experience can be compared with prior estimates.

For Cost-Plus contracts, where the contractor is reimbursed for allowable or otherwise defined costs, plus a percentage of those costs or a fixed fee, the conditions are (a) the costs attributable to the contract can be clearly identified; and (b) costs other than those that will be specifically reimbursable under the contract can be reliably estimated.

In all types of construction contracts, and regardless of the method of revenue recognition, a foreseeable contract loss must be accrued both for the stage of completion and for future work on the contract.

## #4-21....Investments

On a world-wide basis, marketable securities held on either a short-term or long-term basis have been valued under the rule of cost or market, whichever is lower. Any impairment in value of the long-term investment would require a write-down to reflect the net realizable value, i.e., what it will bring on the current market. Its application has been extended to investments reported on the EQUITY BASIS under which the carrying value of an investment includes the original cost plus the investor's share of undistributed earnings since acquisition.

It may thus be seen that the Equity Method is another special revenue recognition principle in that it requires ascertainment of profits on investments in associated companies. This method originated in the U.S. and was subsequently adopted in Canada and Mexico, and has spread to other parts of the

world. This principle is now receiving international acceptance
with the promulgation of IASC #3 (1976), CONSOLIDATED FINANCIAL
STATEMENTS AND THE EQUITY METHOD OF ACCOUNTING FOR INVESTMENTS.

#4-22....Equity Method of Accounting for Investments

Under the Equity method, the investment account of the investor is adjusted in the consolidated financial statements for
the change in the investor's share of net assets of the company
in whose voting power the investor holds an interest. The investment account is adjusted for the increase or decrease to
recognize the investor's share of the profits or losses of the
investee after the date of acquisition. Dividends received from
the investee are then recorded by reducing the carrying amount
of the investment.

#4-23...Equity Method:  Consolidation Concept or
           Accrual Concept?

The equity method had been spreading as a consolidation concept requiring its use for investments in affiliates effectively controlled through partial ownership, e.g., of between 20 to
50% of the voting shareholder interest. It would apply to unconsolidated subsidiaries and joint ventures, although in many
countries such investments are reported at cost. Where the reported amount varies materially from the market value, in most
countries such investments are reported at cost.

As an accrual concept, the method would require recording
by the parent company so that if the parent company statements
are prepared without consolidation, the retained earnings and
reported earnings would be the same as if the financial statements were consolidated.

Thus, IASC #3 should give impetus to some uniformity in the
use of the equity method as well as in the consistency in the
practice of the preparation of consolidated financial statements.

#4-24...Applicability of Equity Method to
           Associated Companies

IASC #3 defines an ASSOCIATED COMPANY as "an investee company that is not controlled by the investor but in respect of
which (a) the investor's interest in the voting power of the
investee is substantial; (b) the investor has the power to
exercise significant influence over the financial and operating
policies of the investee; and (c) the investor intends to retain its interest as a long-term investment."

Under this definition, significant influence and control
means:

(a)   control is ownership, directly or indirectly through sub-
      sidiaries, of more than one-half of the voting power of
      the subsidiary.
(b)   significant influence is participation in the financial
      and operating policy decisions of the investee but not
      control of those policies.   An investor may exercise sig-
      nificant influence in several ways, usually by representa-
      tion on the board of directors but also by participation
      in policy-making processes, material intercompany transac-
      tions, interchange of managerial personnel, or dependency
      on technical information. If the investor holds less than
      20% of the voting power of the investee, it should be pre-
      sumed that the investor does not have power to exercise
      significant influence, unless such power can be clearly
      demonstrated.

Basically, this can be simply interpreted to indicate that an
associated company over which another company has a significant
influence must be reported by using the equity method of accounting.

## #4-25...Applicability of Equity Method to
##          Unconsolidated Subsidiaries

   Generally, controlled subsidiaries are consolidated, but
IASC #3 does state that "a subsidiary may be excluded from consolidation if its activities are so dissimilar from those of
the other companies in the group that better information for
the parent company shareholders and other users of the statements would be provided by presenting separate financial statements in respect of such subsidiary with the consolidated
financial statements."
   The investor's share of the profits or losses of such unconsolidated subsidiaries must be accrued under the equity method
of accounting. The types of companies that may be excluded depend on national tradition. Typically U.S. parent companies do
not consolidate finance subsidiaries. In Canada, regulated
utilities are not to be consolidated if owned by non-utility
companies.

## #4-26....Property, Plant, and Equipment

   The generally accepted amount for reporting property, plant
and equipment is at cost less accumulated depreciation. In a
few countries, certain assets such as land may be recorded at
fair economic value. In Brazil the asset carrying value must
annually be adjusted according to a federally determined price-
level coefficient. Conversely, a depreciable asset may be
written down if the book value exceeds the fair economic value.

Notwithstanding, the cost-less-accumulated depreciation principle is so totally adopted in many countries that even fully
depreciated assets are kept intact in the accounts.

## #4-27....Definition of Depreciable Assets

IASC #4, DEPRECIATION ACCOUNTING (1976), defines depreciable
assets as those which (a) are expected to be used during more
than one accounting period; (b) have a limited useful life; and
(c) are held by an enterprise for use in the production or supply of goods and services, for rental to others, or for administrative purposes.

This definition does not apply to forests and similar regenerative natural resources; expenditures on the exploration for
and extraction of minerals, oil, natural gas and similar non-
regenerative resources; and goodwill. It does, however, apply
to buildings, plant and equipment, and various intangibles.
When land has a limited useful life, the accrual of depreciation would be applicable to such land too.

The generally accepted rule for reporting fixed or depreciable assets assumes a full disclosure of the amount of accumulated depreciation. Also it is customary, as a world-wide practice, to segregate assets among main categories (such as land)
as a separate balance sheet item. Usually we find disclosure of
capital expenditures currently made, as well as those firmly
contracted, in a footnote or on a funds statement.

## #4-28....Intangible Assets

Intangibles are generally recorded when acquired and amortized over their useful life. However, this general world-wide
practice is not found in recording and amortizing Goodwill.
Expense recognition for goodwill varies from immediate write-
off to no write-off at all. In some cases of immediate write-
off, the total amount is charged directly to retained earnings
instead of to expense. When goodwill is amortized, the term of
amortization is often arbitrary and frequently in accordance
with specific corporation laws.

The determination of the amount of goodwill also varies. In
the United States and Mexico, the difference between cost and
book value of acquired net assets is first assigned to
identifiable assets and liabilities. Any remaining difference
is termed "negative goodwill." Negative goodwill is recorded
only if all non-current assets are written off and all current
assets are first written down to net realizable value. In
contrast, a few countries do not permit the recording of
negative goodwill or the amortization to income but require
such amount to be credited directly to the shareholders'
equity.

## UNDERLYING EQUITY CONCEPTS

### #4-29....Liabilities

It is widespread practice to present the amounts of both definitely determinable and estimated liabilities on the balance sheet. In most countries the amounts of payables to affiliates and officers and directors, and the existence of contingent liabilities, are also disclosed. In some countries, such as Spain and Italy, there is relatively little disclosure, if any. Insofar as self-insurance is concerned, the amount beyond the normal risk is disclosed in only a few countries.

### #4-30....Bond Premium and Discount Amortization

Generally the payment terms, including interest rates, are disclosed for long-term liabilities. However, there is an important variation as to the handling of bond discount and issue costs. Three different methods are utilized around the world for amortizing bond discount or premium and bond issue costs: the DIRECT WRITE-OFF method; the STRAIGHT-LINE method; and the BONDS-OUTSTANDING method. Under the Direct Write-Off method, the amounts are written off at the time of issuance. Under the Straight-Line method, the amounts are amortized over the life of the debt in equal amounts each year, even if the amount of bonds outstanding declines. Under the Bonds-Outstanding method, the amounts are amortized over the life of the bonds in relation to the amount of bonds outstanding.

The significance of the variation reflects primarily in the reporting of interest expense. On the balance sheet the difference between the various methods would probably not significantly distort the amount of liabilities reported.

### #4-31....Invested Capital

In countries where stock options, stock warrants, and preferred stocks are issued, disclosure is usually made as to the respective preferences and the potential effect on the number of outstanding shares. The re-acquisition of issued shares as treasury stock is prohibited in the open market in many countries. When corporations do disclose the amounts of legally acquired treasury stocks, various treatments that have been made are: treasury stock shown as an asset, or as a deduction from stockholders' equity at cost, or as retired.

### #4-32....Stock Dividends

Another accounting practice that varies among countries is the treatment of stock dividends. Only a few countries use the

U.S. method of charging the retained earnings for the amount at market value. A more prevalent practice is to charge retained earnings for the amount of the par or legal value of the shares.

#4-33....Equity Reserves

Among the many types of equity reserves utilized around the world are Expense Liability, Revaluation, Legal, Appropriated Retained Earnings, and General. Since the various reserves serve different purposes, an understanding of each is necessary for an investor analysis of owners' equity.

#4-34....Expense Liability Reserves

In several countries, notably Switzerland and Sweden, the economy is quite centrally controlled. This macroeconomic control is manifested in a desired goal of stability. In order to achieve stability in an economy that has some cyclical phenomena, enterprise income stability is achieved by established reserves that are increased proportionately more in good profit years. In such an environment, income smoothing is considered more important than strict adherence to the accrual concept. Variations in accounting principles and reporting evolve when the policy for establishing secret reserves is adjusted frequently. The consistency concept is then also abandoned.

Besides reserves for possible future expenses, another manifestation in such macroeconomic influence is found in INVENTORY RESERVES. They are established to reduce inventories below cost and net realizable value. Similarly, depreciation can be accelerated beyond the expected normal rate to create excessive DEPRECIATION RESERVES.

#4-35....Revaluation Reserves

Although Revaluation Reserves have been used in a number of countries, they are most prevalent in the Netherlands where replacement value accounting has been used with some success. Replacement Value accounting can be applied to inventories and to long-term assets. The balance sheet effect is to adjust upward for increases in the replacement value of the asset, recording a corresponding amount in a revaluation reserve account--an equity capital account. As the asset is used, the increased depreciation or the increased cost of sales on replacement cost is charged against income.

The revaluation reserves are established to write up depreciable assets to replacement cost. Because the incremental depreciation expense is not deductible for income tax purposes, the depreciation charges on the incremental write-up are not

recorded through the income but are charged directly to the
revaluation reserves. An alternate procedure is to charge the
incremental depreciation as an allocated expense with a parallel entry transferring an equivalent amount from the revaluation reserve to retained earnings. An illustration of the procedure is shown in Figure 4-2.

```
============================================================
                         FIGURE 4-2
             ILLUSTRATIVE REPLACEMENT VALUE ACCOUNTING

Price Increment Equipment                10,000
    Revaluation Capital                               10,000
(To write up asset to replacement value)

Deprec. on Price Increment Equip.        1,000
    Accum. Deprec. on Price Increment                  1,000
(To record depreciation on Price Increment)

Revaluation Capital                      1,000
    Retained Earnings                                  1,000
(To record reduction in revaluation
       capital due to depreciation)

      ALTERNATIVE PROCEDURE AFFECTING BALANCE SHEET ONLY*

Price Increment Equipment                10,000
    Revaluation Capital                               10,000
(To record write-up Replacement Value)

Revaluation Capital                      1,000
    Accum. Deprec. on Price Increment                  1,000
(To record depreciation)

    *Under this method, the income statement remains
       at historical cost.
============================================================
```

## #4-36....Impact of Inflation on Revaluation Reserves

Although the impact of inflation has been sporadic around
the world in the decade of the 1970s, it appears that most of
the countries in the world are experiencing high rates of inflation in the 1980s. Because of inflation, accounting has tak-
en on new dimensions as will be seen in more depth in the chapter on Inflation Accounting. In some countries the effects of
inflation are being integrated into the accounts. Generally,
two methods have been advocated--general price-level and specific price-level changes. In Brazil, for example, accounts

have been adjusted by a coefficient on a regular basis as determined by a governmental body.

To take steps to harmonize the price adjustment procedures, in March 1977, IASC #6, ACCOUNTING RESPONSES TO CHANGING PRICES, was issued requiring disclosure of the practices used. IASC #6 declares:

In complying with International Accounting Standard #1, Disclosure of Accounting Policies, enterprises should present in their financial statements information that describes the procedures adopted to reflect the impact on the financial statements of specific price changes, changes in the general level of prices, or of both. If no such procedures have been adopted, that fact should be disclosed.

This is one of many accounting policies that should be disclosed. IASC #6 was superseded by IASC #15 in November, 1981.

## #4-37....Legal Reserves

Many countries require LEGAL, or Statutory, reserves. The legal provisions for the reserves vary among countries. Generally an annual percentage of income (e.g., 10%) must be credited to the LEGAL reserve, with a maximum provision (e.g., 20%) of total paid-in or legal capital required. Because dividends cannot normally be charged against legal reserves, the amount acts as an additional protection to creditors.

## #4-38....Appropriated Retained Earnings Reserves

These are voluntary reserves which can later be transferred back to the unappropriated retained earnings account. The amounts so established merely act as a temporary restriction of retained earnings. Normally such reserves are not used to absorb charges to income.

## #4-39....General Reserves

The General Reserve is quite widespread in usage. It is in some respects similar to the appropriated retained earnings reserve. However, in some countries, notably Switzerland, the reserve can be utilized to smooth income among periods. The movement in reserve accounts generally is fully disclosed in the financial statements.

## #4-40....Retained Earnings and Dividends

In many countries, any restriction of retained earnings is disclosed. An excellent example of such a restriction is an amount of cumulative preferred dividends in arrears. In a number of countries, furthermore, provisions must be established

for dividends proposed for ratification at the subsequent annual meeting.

Where the pooling-of-interest method is used in accounting
for mergers as in the U.S. and Mexico, the retained earnings
of the merged company are accumulated retroactively. Since the
pooling method is not a generally accepted international principle, an awareness of its effects may be important for an investor's analysis.

## OPERATING INCOME STATEMENT PRINCIPLES

### #4-41....Revenues

With respect to sales, the generally accepted accrual concept assumes a proper cutoff, which in most cases is assumed to
take place at the time of delivery--the purported exchange date
of the transaction. Where the collection on credit transactions
is not reasonably assured, exceptions to this rule are made in
most countries, as is the case with real estate sales where
unrealized gains are generally deferred until collections are
assured.

As seen earlier, accruing profits on the basis of percentage
of completion for long-term contracts is generally accepted. In
the U.S., when ordinary risks and rewards of a lessor are
transferred to the lessee, the transaction is recorded as an
installment sale rather than as an operating lease. This financing method of accounting for lease revenue follows the accounting principle under which the substance of the transaction
takes precedence over the legal form.

### #4-42....Expense Recognition

The two revenue recognition principles discussed above, in
connection with construction contracts and consolidations, represent special situations which now occur rather frequently in
many countries. The international standards for these principles will have a favorable effect on comparability of international financial statements. Conversely, expense recognition
principles which have international acceptance further enhance
the comparability.

Under the accrual concept, expenses are recognized as they
are incurred. For costs which obtain benefits through more than
one accounting period, accrual accounting dictates that the
allocation of these costs be reported over the periods benefited. Two definite expense recognition principles have been given
attention by the IASC, viz., depreciation, and research and
development costs. After discussing these two standards, some
significant international variations will be pointed out.

## #4-43....Depreciation

The concept of depreciation is generally a rational and systematic allocation of the cost of buildings, equipment, and
other depreciable assets. Under IASC #4, the depreciable amount
of a depreciable asset must be allocated on a systematic basis
to each accounting period of the asset's useful life. The useful life is estimated upon giving consideration to expected
physical wear and tear, obsolescence, and legal or other limits
on the use of the assets. The useful life is either (a) the
period over which a depreciable asset is expected to be used by
the enterprise; or (b) the number of production or similar
units expected to be obtained from the asset by the enterprise.
The most commonly used method throughout the world is the
straight-line. Although no depreciation allocation method is
specified in IASC #4, other methods in use include: accelerated, such as the percentage-of-declining balance and sum-of-the-
years' digits, which have found some acceptance; the unit-of-
production; sinking-fund; and composite-rate methods, which are
used infrequently. The methods assumed to be applied are those
considered to best allocate the original cost in a systematic
and rational manner.
There are some exceptions to the general concept of depreciation, notable of which are those in Switzerland and South
America. The Swiss concept is an ultraconservative one by which
an excess depreciation charge is made in the early years of an
asset's life. On the other hand, in a number of South American
countries, the depreciation expense is exaggerated by the upward adjustment of the asset cost with a centrally determined
index. In such cases, the policies, charges, rates, and accumulated amounts with respect to depreciation, and the original
costs, in addition to the written-up value increments, should
all be disclosed in the financial statements as well as footnotes. Where the depreciation charge for most firms is significant in amount, the disclosure requirement should be mandatory.

## #4-44....Research and Development Costs

The expensing of research and development (R&D) costs varies
among nations. In the U.S., the present practice is to expense
all such costs immediately. This is a policy commenced only recently with the promulgation of FASB #2 (1974). Prior to that,
the costs of successful research were permitted to be deferred
and allocated in the periods benefited or matched against the
revenues derived. The past and the present U.S. practice, and
variations therefrom, are utilized in other countries.
The IASC seeks to harmonize these practices by the issuance
of IASC #9 ACCOUNTING FOR RESEARCH AND DEVELOPMENT COSTS (July
1978). Definitions for the terms are (a) Research is original

and planned investigation undertaken with the hope of gaining new scientific or technical knowledge and understanding; (b) Development is the translation of research findings or other knowledge into a plan or design for the production of new or substantially improved materials, devices, products, processes, systems or services prior to the commencement of commercial production.

Research and development costs include: (a) the salaries, wages and other related costs of personnel engaged in R&D activities; (b) the costs of materials and services consumed in R&D activities; (c) the depreciation of equipment and facilities to the extent that they are used for R&D activities; (d) overhead costs related to R&D activities; (e) other costs related to R&D activities, such as amortization of patents and licenses.

Such R&D costs are to be charged to expense in the period in which incurred, except for certain development costs of a project if all of the following criteria are satisfied:

(a)    the product or process is clearly defined and the costs attributable to the product or process can be separately identified;

(b)    the technical feasibility of the product or process has been demonstrated;

(c)    the management of the enterprise has indicated its intention to produce and market, or use, the product or process;

(d)    there is a clear indication of a future market for the product or process or, if it is to be used internally rather than sold, its usefulness to the enterprise can be demonstrated; and

(e)    adequate resources exist, or are reasonably expected to be available, to complete the project and market the product or process.

The amount of the deferral of development costs is to be limited to the amount which can be reasonably expected to be recovered from future related revenues.

IASC #9, though rather basic, is quite specific, so that if adopted on a world-wide basis will result in the establishment of considerable harmony for this particular accounting situation.

## #4-45....Income Taxes

There are basically two methods for handling income tax expense—the accrual, or liability, method; and the deferred method. In the U.S., income tax expense is recorded on an accrual basis and shown on the income statement, a practice prevalent in most countries. The principal exception in the handling of income tax charges is in tax allocation accounting.

In those countries that require accounting records to be

maintained in accordance with tax regulations, tax allocation
is inappropriate. However, when tax regulations do not require
the synchronization of tax records with the accounting records,
tax allocation may become necessary. Thus in the U.S. and Canada, tax allocation is required to account for timing differences between time of accrual and payment. The liability method,
allowed in the U.K., dictates an adjustment of the amount of
deferred tax to reflect current tax rates.

The deferred technique, in contrast to the liability method,
utilizes comprehensive tax allocation whereby deferred taxes
are not adjusted for future tax rate changes. In other countries no deferred taxes whatever are established but are merely
mentioned in footnotes. Whereas the division of such deferred
taxes between the current and the long-term portion is required, such as in the U.S., it is not always disclosed in other
countries.

In March 1979, IASC #12, ACCOUNTING FOR TAXES ON INCOME,
was issued to take effect as of Jan. 1, 1981. It appears that
U.S. GAAP in the area of income tax accounting are compatible
with IASC #12, but paradoxically the reverse is not the case.
The reason is that IASC #12 permits both the liability and deferred methods of inter-period tax allocation. Both the liability and deferred methods are predicated on the concept that
comprehensive inter-period tax allocation is to be made. However, IASC #12 permits partial allocation to be made if there is
assurance beyond a reasonable doubt that timing differences not
accounted for will result in no payment or reduction of taxes
in the foreseeable future. The Standard requires disclosure of
the current and cumulative amount of timing differences not
accounted for where partial allocation is used.

#4-46....Other Expenses

Although the accrual concept has world-wide adoption, as a
general proposition any differences in recording expenses is
relatively insignificant, but notwithstanding do exist. Some of
the more noteworthy include:

SWITZERLAND -- The accrual concept is not followed dogmati-
    cally hence costs of sales may not be matched with
    sales.
GERMANY -- All unrealized exchange gains and losses and ex-
    change adjustments on unsettled balances are charged to
    income in the period of the exchange rate change. The
    nature of the exchange gains and losses and exchange
    adjustments is discussed in a later chapter.
ITALY -- Bonuses to corporate directors are recorded as di-
    rect charges to retained earnings, and estimated pension
    costs must be accrued over the term of employment rather
    than the pay-as-you-go practice followed in many coun-
    tries.

JAPAN AND CANADA  -- The pension cost plan used in Italy  is
also used in these countries.

U. S. -- The practice of accruing losses on purchase commitments is not universally followed.

## #4-47....Earnings Per Share

Finally, an important statistic used by sophisticated security analysts is the earnings-per-share computation. Its presentation on  the income  statement  has gathered momentum and  is
currently found  on financial statements prepared  in the U.S.,
Canada, U.K.,  Netherlands, Philippines, and a few other  countries.  Most of these statements show a  fully diluted earnings
per share when complex capital structures exist.

However, the simple, most important  earnings-per-share figure is computed differently among the leading countries. A primary  earnings-per-share computation is based on an average  of
common shares  outstanding plus  common  share  equivalents  as
practiced in the U.S.,  Mexico and the  Philippines.  In Canada
and the U.K.,  a fundamental earnings-per-share  computation is
based only on common shares outstanding.

## EEC GENERALLY ACCEPTED ACCOUNTING PRINCIPLES

## #4-48...Comparative EEC General Accounting Principles Analysis

How the  EEC GAAP  compare with those outlined above may  be
observed from  the requirements in the 4th Directive.  To begin
with,  it recognizes the  principle that a company's  financial
statements  should present a  "true and fair view of its assets
and liabilities, financial  position and results."  In  a good
number of  EEC countries the principle influence is the concept
of "compliance with legal requirements,"  so  that the true and
fair  concept  is not  recognized either in law  or in practice.
For this  reason, the requirement in  the 4th Directive is  regarded as a step forward.

## #4-49....EEC Concept of Consistency

With respect to consistency, the language reads  "methods of
valuation may not  be changed  and departure is permitted  only
in  exceptional cases."  Thus consistency is recognized  and is
accompanied by the requirement  that  any  change  in principle
must be disclosed.

## #4-50....EEC Accrual Principle

Accrual accounting is specifically  recognized through Article  28, Paragraph 1(f), which  provides  for  the  fundamental

principle of balance sheet continuity in the following
language: "The opening balance sheet for each year shall correspond to the closing balance sheet for the preceding year."

#### #4-51...Basic Accounting Principles in Section 7

The basic accounting principles are provided  for in Section
7 of the EEC 4th Directive, Articles 28 - 39:

ARTICLE 28:   (1) The Member States shall ensure that the valua-
      tion of the items shown in the annual  accounts is made in
      accordance with the following general principles:  (a) the
      company  shall  be presumed to continue its business as  a
      going  concern; (b) the  methods of  valuation may  not be
      changed from one  year  to another;  (c) valuation must be
      made on a conservative basis,  and in particular (aa) only
      the profits earned at the date of the balance sheet may be
      included  in it, but account shall be taken of all contin-
      gencies  foreseeable at  that date; (bb) account  shall be
      taken of any deficiencies that do not  become apparent un-
      til  after the date of the balance sheet but do become ap-
      parent before it is drawn  up if they arise in  the course
      of the year to which the annual  accounts relate; (cc) ac-
      count shall be taken of any depreciation, whether the year
      closes with a  loss or with a profit; (d) account shall be
      taken of earnings  and charges arising during the  year to
      which  the accounts relate,  irrespective of  the date  or
      receipt of  payment of such earnings or  charges;  (e) the
      components  of  the  asset and liability  items  shall  be
      valued separately; (f) the opening balance sheet  for each
      year shall correspond to the closing balance sheet for the
      preceding year.
          (2) Departures from  these general principles shall be
      permitted  in  exceptional cases.  Where they are departed
      from, an indication thereof shall be given in the notes on
      the accounts together  with an  explanation of the reasons
      and an assessment  of  the effect on  the assets, liabili-
      ties, financial position and result.
ARTICLE  29:   provides for  valuation to be based on  purchase
      price or production cost.
ARTICLE 30:   authorizes  the valuation of tangible fixed assets
      with a limited useful life, and stocks, by the replacement
      value method, and that  the  difference between the valua-
      tion by the replacement value and  purchase price shall be
      shown under liabilities  as  a Revaluation Reserve, subdi-
      vided into Reserve for  Tangible Fixed Assets, Reserve for
      Participating Interests, or Reserve for Stocks.
ARTICLE 31:   makes further provision for revaluation reserves.
ARTICLE 32:   relates  to  the inclusion of  formation expenses

under national law and provides that they be written off over a maximum period of five years.

ARTICLE 33: stipulates that items of fixed assets shall be valued at purchase price or production cost which should be reduced by value adjustments when they have a limited useful life. The value adjustments should be calculated according to a method that satisfies the requirements of good management.

ARTICLE 34: relates to Cost of Research and Development.

ARTICLE 35: states that tangible fixed assets, raw and auxiliary materials constantly being replaced and of a value of secondary importance, may be shown under assets at a fixed quantity and value.

ARTICLE 36: relates to items of current assets which shall be valued at purchase price or production cost.

ARTICLE 37: provides for calculation of cost of stocks of goods either on the basis of weighted average prices or by FIFO or LIFO, or some similar method.

ARTICLE 38: states that where the amount of any debt repayable is greater than the amount received, the difference may be shown as an asset. Such amount shall be written off not later than the time when repayment of the debt is made.

ARTICLE 39: declares that provisions for contingencies and charges shall not exceed in amount the sums which a reasonable businessman would consider necessary. If substantial in amount they should be shown in the balance sheet under the item OTHER PROVISIONS.

It is not too difficult to see that the accounting principles outlined in Sec. 7 of the 4th Directive of the EEC closely follow the GAAP of the U.S. as well as whatever international accounting standards have been promulgated by the IASC. This should have a very salutary effect on harmonization and prove to be a boon in international financial reporting.

## #4-52....EEC Seventh Directive Lack of Harmonization

The EEC 7th Directive (an outgrowth of the 4th Directive), adopted in June 1983, offers some guidelines for more standardization of reporting. However, experience seems to indicate that the prospects for harmonization in this area appear discouraging. Whereas standard procedure in the U.S. and England follow the requirement of filing consolidated financial reports, such has not been the practice in Germany and France where there is separate reporting for parents and for subsidiaries, which is contrary to the 7th Directive. Under it, companies in EEC countries and non-EEC corporations with subsidiaries in a member country are required to file consolidated financial reports in that country.

The 4th Directive (adopted in 1978) required stricter financial reporting standards and was   not   implemented until   1982.
The 7th Directive requires each of the ten countries in the EEC
to pass legislation to  implement the Directive  within 5 years
and  annual reports do not have to conform until 1990.  Despite
the appearance that the 7th Directive intends to seek more harmonization in financial reporting, the  hiatus in time that extends to 1990 would appear to militate against harmonization.

### SUMMARY OF FOOTNOTE REFERENCES
(References are to Paragraph #'s)

#4-5 thru  #4-47:    "Accounting Assumptions,  Asset  Valuation Con-
     cepts,  Equity Concepts, Income Statement Concepts," adapted
     from  Norlin G. Rueschhoff, INTERNATIONAL ACCOUNTING AND FI-
     NANCIAL REPORTING, 1976,  Praeger Publishers, Inc., by  per-
     mission.
#4-5    IASC #1, DISCLOSURE OF ACCOUNTING PRINCIPLES, London, 1974
#4-10   IASC #2
#4-12   IASC #2
#4-13   IASC #11, 1978
#4-16   IASC #2
#4-24   IASC #3
#4-25   IASC #3
#4-27   IASC #4, DEPRECIATION ACCOUNTING, 1976
#4-36   IASC #6, ACCOUNTING RESPONSES TO CHANGING PRICES, 1977
#4-43   IASC #4, op. cit.
#4-44   IASC #9, ACCOUNTING FOR RESEARCH AND DEVELOPMENT COSTS, 1978
#4-50   EEC Fourth Directive, Article 28, para. 1(f)
#4-51   EEC Fourth Directive, Sec. 7, Articles 28-39

### BIBLIOGRAPHY

Bartholomew, E.G.   "Harmonization of  Financial Reporting in  the
     EEC," ACCOUNTANCY, 90 (October 1979): 48-53
Cairns, David;  Lafferty,  Michael;  and Mantle,  Peter. "Survey of
     Accounts and  Accounting, 1983-1984," MANAGEMENT ACCOUNTING
     (August 1984): 46-56
Elsea, Carole Ann. "Progress Toward International GAAP," THE WOMAN
     CPA (July 1979): 22-23
Gaertner, James  F.  and Rueschhoff, Norlin. "Cultural Barriers to
     International Accounting Standards," CA MAGAZINE,  113 (May
     1980): 36-39
Gray, S.J. "Multinational Enterprises and the Development of Inter-
     national Accounting Standards," CHARTERED ACCOUNTANT IN AUS-
     TRALIA, 52 (August 1981): 24-25
Meek, Gary.   "Competition Spurs World-Wide Harmonization," MANAGE-
     MENT ACCOUNTING (August 1984): 47-49
Perridon,  Louis.   "Accounting  Principles, An Academic  Opinion,"
     JOURNAL UEC (October 1974): 213-224

Smith, Willis A. "International Accounting Standards--An Update," THE CPA JOURNAL, 50 (June 1980): 22-27
Stillwell, M.I. "Generally Accepted Accounting Principles: Why the Americans Report As They Do," THE ACCOUNTANT, 175 (Nov. 25, 1976): 607-608

## THEORY QUESTIONS
(Question Numbers are Keyed to Text Paragraph #'s)

#4-1    Distinguish between Accounting Standards and Generally Accepted Accounting Principles.

#4-2    What effect do different standards of different countries have on international accounting? Explain.

#4-5    What are the three basic accounting assumptions expressed in IASC #1? Define them.

#4-6    What three considerations stated in IASC #1 govern the selection and application by management of appropriate accounting policies in the preparation of financial statements? Define them.

#4-7    Define the Prudence Concept.

#4-8    Define the Materiality Concept.

#4-9    Define the Historical Cost Concept.

#4-10   How does IASC #2 define historical cost for inventories?

#4-12   How does IASC #2 provide for ascertainment of Manufactured Inventory cost?

#4-13   What provision does IASC #11 make for accounting for construction contracts?

#4-16   What provision does IASC #2 make for interchangeable inventory items?

#4-21   What provision is made under IASC #3 for valuation of Investments under the equity method of accounting?

#4-27   How does IASC #4 make provision for Depreciation Accounting?

#4-28   What GAAP rules are followed for handling of Intangible Assets?

#4-29   What is the general practice with respect to handling of Liabilities?

#4-30   What three methods are used for amortizing bond premiums and discounts? Briefly describe each.

#4-31   How is Invested Capital generally handled?

#4-32   Discuss the treatment of Stock Dividends.

#4-33   Enumerate 5 different Equity Reserves used around the world and briefly outline the handling of each.

#4-40   Discuss the treatment of Retained Earnings & Dividends.

#4-41   How are Revenues generally handled?

#4-42   In general how is the matter of Expense Recognition treated?

#4-43   What provision is made for handling Depreciation under IASC #4?

#4-44  What is the accounting treatment for Research and Devel-
       opment Costs under IASC #9?
#4-45  Discuss the treatment of Taxes on Income under IASC #12.
#4-47  What is the status of Earnings Per Share reporting?
#4-49  How are the Concept of Consistency and the Accrual Prin-
       ciple treated under the EEC?
#4-51  Briefly outline how Basic Accounting Principles are
       handled under Sec. 7 of the EEC 4th Directive.


**EXERCISES**

**EX-4-1**
On an international level as substantiated by the promulgation
of International Accounting Standard No. 1, three fundamental
accounting assumptions that have world-wide acceptance are:
   a. Going-concern, consistency and accrual
   b. Accrual, matching, and historical cost
   c. Revenue realization, historical cost, & materiality
   d. Consistency, materiality, and prudence

**EX-4-2**
Three governing considerations as expressed in International
Accounting Standard No. 1 are:
   a. Materiality, consistency, and prudence
   b. Prudence, substance over form, and materiality
   c. Conservatism, consistency, and materiality
   d. Consistency, substance over form, and prudence

**EX-4-3**
The following is the normative accounting basis for presenting
inventories in accordance with international standards:
   a. At cost
   b. At lower of cost or net realizable value
   c. At lower of cost or replacement cost (i.e., market)
   d. At net realizable value

**EX-4-4**
The following inventory accounting method is not internationally acceptable as a method for determining the inventory.
   a. First-in, first-out method
   b. Average cost method
   c. Last-in, first-out method
   d. Retail method

**EX-4-5**
The term "inventory" includes tangible property
   a. Held for sale in the ordinary course of business or in the
      process of production for such sale.

b. In the process of production for sale or to be consumed in the production of goods or services for sale
c. Held for sale in the ordinary course of business or to be consumed in the production of goods or services for sale
d. All of the above

## EX-4-6
Costs of conversion are
a. The costs of raw materials and direct labor
b. The purchase costs including import duties and other purchase taxes, transport and handling costs, and any other directly attributable costs of acquisition less trade discounts, rebates, & subsidies
c. The costs, in addition to the costs of purchase, that relate to bringing the inventories to their present location and condition
d. The costs of completion and other costs necessarily to be incurred in order to make the sale

## EX-4-7 (CPA EXAM, 5/80, THEORY #26)
The principle of objectivity includes the concept of
a. Summarization
b. Classification
c. Conservatism
d. Verifiability

## EX-4-8 (CPA EXAM, 5/80, THEORY, #29)
What is the underlying concept that supports the immediate recognition of a loss?
a. Conservatism
b. Consistency
c. Judgment
d. Matching

## EX-4-9 (CPA EXAM, 11/79, THEORY, #19)
Which of the following is an example of the concept of conservatism?
a. Stating inventories at the lower of cost or market
b. Stating inventories using the FIFO method in periods of rising prices
c. Using the percentage of completion method in the first year of a long-term construction contract
d. Using the interest method instead of the straight line method to record interest in the first year of a long-term receivable

## EX-4-10 (CPA EXAM, 11/79, THEORY, #27)
Continuation of an accounting entity in the absence of evidence to the contrary is an example of the basic concept of
a. Accounting entity
b. Consistency
c. Going-concern
d. Substance over form

## PROBLEMS

**P-4-1**

Certain fundamental accounting assumptions and governing considerations that are outlined in International Accounting Standard No. 1 are listed and numbered below. A series of statements related to the numbered items appears below that. In the blanks to the left of each statement, write the number of the listed assumption or considerations that most closely associates with the statement.

1. Going-concern
2. Consistency
3. Accrual
4. Prudence – Conservatism
5. Substance over form
6. Materiality
7. Periodicity

_2_ a. Enhances comparability of statements of successive accounting periods.

_6_ b. Causes an asset with a three-year life and a cost of $5 to be expensed when incurred.

_4_ c. Is exemplified by the rule of "lower of cost or net realizable value."

_7_ d. Requires the measurement of the average earnings progress and financial position of business entities at regular intervals.

_1_ e. Assumes continuity of sufficient length to carry out planned operations and commitments.

_2_ f. Assumes the same accounting policies are followed from one year to another.

_3_ g. Assumes that revenues and costs are recognized as they are earned or incurred (and not as money is received or paid) and recorded in the financial statements of the periods in which they relate.

_4_ h. Does not justify the creation of secret or hidden reserves for uncertainties which inevitably surround many transactions.

_5_ i. Accounts for and presents transactions and other events in accordance with their financial reality and not merely with their legality.

_1_ j. Assumes that the enterprise has neither the intention nor the necessity of liquidation or of curtailing materially the scale of its operation.

**P-4-2**

The Holland Company, incorporated in the Netherlands, used the following standard costs in manufacturing its product, Dutcho:

|                                             |         |
|---------------------------------------------|---------|
| Raw Materials: (2 parts @ f 10.00)          | f 20.00 |
| Conversion Costs: (4 hours @ f 5.00)        | 20.00   |
| Total: one unit Dutcho                      | f 40.00 |

The company uses the replacement value theory with a standard cost system. All cost variances are recorded in a separate nominal account; all increments for price-level adjustments are recorded in separate balance sheet accounts. On Jan. 1 the index numbers for raw materials & finished goods were at 100. The index numbers were recalculated to be 110 on raw materials and 105 on its finished goods on June 30. There were no beginning inventories on January 1. The following transactions occurred:

Jan. 15 Purchased 2000 parts at total cost of f 20,500
Jan. 20 Transferred 1,200 parts to work-in-process
June 20 Incurred total (5 months) conversion costs of
        2,000 standard hours, f 10,000
June 25 Transferred 500 units to finished goods
June 30 Revalued the inventories for index number changes
July 5  Transferred 200 parts to work-in-process
July 30 Incurred 800 standard hours of conversion costs,
        f 4,000
July 31 Transferred 200 units to finished goods.

**Required:**
Prepare general journal entries to record the above transactions.

**P-4-3**

The following are Class Company's unit costs of making and selling a given item at normal capacity:

|                              |        |
|------------------------------|--------|
| Manufacturing:               |        |
|     Direct Materials          | $2.00  |
|     Direct Labor              | 1.20   |
|     Variable Overhead         | .80    |
|     Fixed Overhead            | 1.00   |
| Selling and Administrative:  |        |
|     Variable                  | 2.25   |
|     Fixed                     | .90    |

**Required:** (Assume there are 10,000 units on hand)

a. What would be the inventory amount to be shown on the balance sheet in accord with United States generally accepted accounting principles?

b. What would be the amount of the inventory shown on balance sheets of companies in several European countries where the inventory is presented at prime costs?

c. If the inventory were presented at direct cost, what would be the amount?

## P-4-4

After 15 years the accounts of Philip Jones Company included the following as of January 1:

| Account | Balance |
|---|---|
| Building (salvage value $25,000) | $700,000 |
| Accumulated depreciation, Building | 225,000 |

A competent appraisal firm engaged to examine the building delivered a report reflecting the following appraisal figures as of January 1:

| | |
|---|---|
| Reproduction cost new | $1,200,000 |
| Estimated salvage value | 50,000 |
| Accumulated depreciation (30%) | 345,000 |

**Required**: (Show all computations)

1. Assume the company's management decided to reflect the change in life estimate by revising the depreciation rate:
    a. Prepare the depreciation entry on December 31
2. Assume the company's management decided to reflect the appraisal with respect to the changes in life estimate and salvage value, but not as to reproduction cost:
    a. Prepare the depreciation entry on December 31
3. Assume the circumstances in 2 above, except that the appraisal is to be reflected fully in separate asset and contra-asset accounts for the appraisal increments:
    a. Prepare the adjusting entry necessary to record the appraisal increment.
    b. Prepare the depreciation entry on December 31 on the historical cost basis.
    c. Prepare the December 31 entry writing-off the amount of the depreciation on the appraisal increment.
4. Assuming entry 3a has been made:
    a. Prepare the depreciation entry on December 31 on the reproduction cost basis.
    b. Prepare the December 31 entry transferring the appropriate amount to retained earnings.
5. Assuming entry 3a and 4a:
    a. Prepare a December 31 entry transferring the portion of the appraisal increment realized into a special income account.
6. Comment on the relative merits of the 5 approaches.

## P-4-5

A Canadian corporation with common shares listed on the Montreal, Toronto, Alberta, and Vancouver Stock Exchanges in Canada, on the New York Stock Exchange in the United States, and on the Antwerp and Brussels Stock Exchanges in Belgium, has $47,156 income in 1985 and $35,074 income in 1984. The weighted average number of shares used in calculating earnings per common share is as follows:

|  | Canadian | | United States | |
|  | 85 | 84 | 85 | 84 |
|---|---|---|---|---|
| Basic and Primary: | | | | |
| Weighted average | | | | |
| common shares | 11,364 | 11,031 | 11,364 | 11,031 |
| Shares pertaining to | | | | |
| stock options | | | 73 | 38 |
|  | 11,364 | 11,031 | 11,437 | 11,069 |
| Fully Diluted: | | | | |
| Weighted average | | | | |
| common shares | 11,364 | 11,031 | 11,364 | 11,031 |
| Shares pertaining to | | | | |
| −conversion of debt | 266 | 507 | 266 | 507 |
| −conversion of | | | | |
| preferred shares | 1,119 | 1,157 | 1,119 | 1,157 |
| −options & warrants | 450 | 469 | 73 | 38 |
|  | 13,199 | 13,164 | 12,822 | 12,733 |

Basic and primary earnings per common share are calculated after reducing net income by $1,314 in 1985 and $1,319 in 1984 being the dividends on Series A and B preferred shares.

Net income used in determining fully diluted earnings per common share are increased by $120 in 1985 and $229 in 1984 being the after-tax effect of interest on debt assumed to be converted. Net income is further increased for purposes of calculating Canadian fully-diluted earnings per common share by $430 in 1985 and $402 in 1984 to give effect to an imputed return of six percent on funds which would have been available on the exercise of options and warrants.

## Required:
Determine the following earnings per share computations for years 1985 and 1984:
a. The primary earnings per share, by the U.S. method.
b. The basic earnings per share by the Canadian method.
c. The fully-diluted earnings per share by U.S. method.
d. The fully-diluted earnings per share, by the Canadian method.

# International Financial Statement Presentation Principles

FORM AND CONTENT OF FINANCIAL STATEMENTS*

#5-1....General Financial Statement Presentation Principles

The financial statements are the culmination of all of the accounting processes. They are the basic objectives of the accounting procedures. While there is uniformity in the basics as to the form and content of the financial statements, we find there is variation in their presentation amongst different countries. The differences in the choices of principles as well as in the method of applying them may be caused by such factors as the choice of the currency, the translation of foreign currency values into terms of domestic currency, and in financial statement consolidation.

Furthermore, there may be inconsistencies in the choice of accounting policies within an overall perspective, as pointed out by Joseph P. Cummings in his article "Beware of the Pitfalls in Foreign Financial Statements," PMM & Co., WORLD, 6, No. 1, Winter 1972, pp. 45-47; and also by I.N.S. Sharp in "International Variations in Presentation and Certification of Accounts," in THE ACCOUNTANT, 165, No. 5040, July 1971, pages 124-126.

THE BALANCE SHEET

#5-2....Statement of Financial Condition

The most basic financial statement is the Balance Sheet, or Statement of Financial Condition. It has been used since the

------

*See Summary of Footnote References -- #5-1 thru #5-11

medieval origins of double-entry record keeping. Its use, however, has developed into varied formats. Examples of the typical formats used in four different countries are presented in
Figure 5-1, as illustrated in the 1975 AICPA book, PROFESSIONAL
ACCOUNTING IN 30 COUNTRIES, pages 51, 125-126, 169, 629, and
746-749. The Canadian format is the one used in the United
States, as well as many other countries, including Brazil, Denmark, Japan, and Mexico.

An upside-down arrangement of balance sheet categories, such
as that shown in the typical German balance sheet is used in
France and the Netherlands. The upside-down arrangement is also
used in Australia, although the two sides of the statements are
reversed. The most unique arrangement is that of the United
Kingdom.

## #5-3....Variations in Balance Sheet Format

The variations in format show only the surface differences.
Within the segregations other variations exist. For example the
Brazilian current asset category excludes liquid assets which
are presented separately. In Germany the long-term liabilities
must be due beyond four years, so that obligations due within
four years are shown with Other Liabilities which include those
most currently due.

Also in Germany, as well as in France, the current year's
profit is shown separately at the bottom of the balance sheet.
Should the results of the current year's operations show a
loss, the amount is listed at the bottom of the asset side of
the balance sheet. Thus a study showing how the balance sheet
presentation policies evolved may be quite interesting, and may
even be necessary if a consistent, theoretically sound, universally applied presentation principle were to be established.

## #5-4....Current Assets and Current Liabilities

In July 1979, IASC #13, CURRENT ASSETS AND CURRENT LIABILI-
TIES, was issued to be effective Jan. 1,1981. Current assets
were defined as "resources that are reasonably expected to be
realized or consumed within one year from the date of the balance sheet." Current liabilities are defined as "obligations of
the enterprise that are payable on the demand of the creditor
or that are reasonably expected to be liquidated within one
year from the date of the balance sheet." Obviously both of
these definitions coincide with those currently used in the
U.S. IASC #13 conforms to U.S. practice in the presentation of
the current asset and current liability sections of the balance
sheet. Both show the current assets and current liabilities
presented as groups and subtotalled; and where no current/non-
current distinction is made, there should be no subtotals that
might imply a distinction.

# FIGURE 5-1
## COMPARATIVE BALANCE SHEET FORMATS

### United Kingdom

Net Assets Employed:
  Fixed Assets
  Subsidiaries
  Associated Companies
  Current Assets
  Less: Current Liabilities
  Less: Deferred Liabilities
Assets Represented by:
  Share Capital
  Reserves

### Australia

Share Capital & Reserves &
    Liabilities:
  Share Capital & Reserves
  Long-Term Debt and Defer-
    red Income Taxes
  Current Liabilities
Assets:
  Fixed Assets
  Investments
  Current Assets

### Canada

Assets:
  Current Assets
  Investments
  Fixed Assets
  Other Assets

Liabilities and Stock-
    holders' Equity:
  Current Liabilities
  Long-Term Debt
  Deferred Income Taxes
  Shareholders' Equity

### West Germany

Assets:
  Outstanding Payments on
    Subscribed Share
    Capital
  Fixed Assets & Investments
  Revolving Assets
  Deferred Charges and
    Prepaid Expenses
  Accumulated Net Loss (of
    period)
Liabilities & Shareholders'
    Equity:
  Share Capital
  Open Reserves
  Adjustments to Assets
  Reserves for Estimated
    Liabilities and Ac-
    crued Expenses
  Liabilities
  Liabilities, contractually
    payable beyond 4 yrs
  Deferred Income
  Accumulated Net Profit (of
    period)

Source: PROFESSIONAL ACCOUNTING IN 30 COUNTRIES, pp. 51, 125-126, 169, 629, 746-749. Copyright © 1975 by the American Institute of Certified Public Accountants, Inc. Reprinted with permission.

IASC #13 also suggests that current assets be listed in order of liquidity and current liabilities in order of liquidation as is the U.S. practice. However, one difference is that the Standard does permit the exclusion from current liabilities of the current portion of long-term liabilities intended to be refinanced in specified circumstances.

## #5-5....Occurrences After Balance Sheet Date

In October 1978, IASC #10, CONTINGENCIES AND EVENTS OCCURRING AFTER THE BALANCE SHEET DATE, was issued to be effective December 31, 1979. IACS #10, in brief, fully conforms to U.S. GAAP primarily found in FASB #5.

## THE INCOME STATEMENT

## #5-6....The Income Statement

A second basic financial statement is the Income Statement. Its presentations can be very simple and limited as in the U.K., or very elaborate as in Germany. Examples of statements showing the extremes in presentation are given in Figure 5-2, as illustrated in the AICPA book PROFESSIONAL ACCOUNTING IN 30 COUNTRIES, pages 52, 350, 351, 630, and 750-753.

Generally the basic sales-oriented format used in the U.S., Canada and Japan has been widely adopted. Variations do exist as to the content of the cost of goods sold and the expense breakdowns. Quite often the depreciation charges are excluded from the cost-of-goods-sold section and presented as separate one-line items. In most countries the income tax expense is disclosed separately.

=================================================================
FIGURE 5-2
COMPARATIVE INCOME STATEMENT FORMATS

### United Kingdom

Group Turnover
Profit Before Taxation and Extraordinary Items
   Less: Taxation Based on Profit for the Year
Profit After Taxation and Before Extraordinary Items
   Less: Extraordinary Items
Profits Attributable to Shareholders of Parent Company

### Japan

Sales
   Less: Cost of Goods Sold
Gross Profit on Sales
   Less: Selling and Administrative Expenses

Operating Income
     Add:  Nonoperating Revenue
Gross Profit for the Period
     Less:  Nonoperating Expenses
Net Income for the Period

## Australia

SALES AND REVENUE
     Less:  Cost of Sales
Operating Profit
     Add:  Income From Investments
     Less:  Interest to Other Persons
Pretax Profit
     Less:  Provision for Income Tax
NET PROFIT BEFORE EXTRAORDINARY ITEMS
     Less:  Extraordinary Items
NET PROFIT AFTER EXTRAORDINARY ITEMS
Unappropriated Profits, Previous Year
Prior Year Adjustments
Transfer From General Reserve
Available for Appropriation
Dividends
Transfer to General Reserve
Transfer to Capital Profits Reserve
Unappropriated Profits, End of Year

## West Germany

Net Sales
Increase or Decrease of Finished and Unfinished Products
Other Manufacturing Costs for Fixed Assets
TOTAL OUTPUT
Raw Materials & Supplies, Purchased Goods Consumed in Sale
GROSS PROFIT
Income From Profit Transfer Agreements
Income From Trade Investments
Income From Other Long-Term Investments
Other Interest and Similar Income
Income From Retirement and Appraisal of Fixed Assets
Income From the Cancellation of Lump Allowances
Income From the Cancellation of Overstated Reserves
Other Income, Including Extraordinary in the Sum of DM (    )
Income From Loss Transfer Agreements
TOTAL INCOME
Wages and Salaries
Social Taxes
Expenses for Pension Plans and Relief
Depreciation and Amortization of Fixed Assets and Investments
Depreciation and Amortization of Finance Investments
Losses by Deduction or on Retirement of Current Assets

Losses on Retirement of Fixed Assets and Investments
Interest and Similar Expenses
Taxes, on Income and Net Assets, and Other
Losses Arising From Loss Transfer Agreements
Other Expenses
Profits Transferable to Parent Company Under Profit Transfer
        Agreement
PROFIT OR LOSS FOR THE PERIOD
Profit or Loss Brought Forward From Preceding Year
Release of Reserves
Amounts Appropriated to Reserves Out of Profit of Period
ACCUMULATED NET PROFIT OR LOSS

Source: PROFESSIONAL ACCOUNTING IN 30 COUNTRIES, pages 52, 350, 351, 630, 750-753. Copyright © 1975 by the American Institute of Certified Public Accountants, Inc. Reprinted with permission.

================================================================

In Germany, the income statement is based on a unique production-oriented concept principle. However, in France a simplified income statement is accompanied by a general operating statement that is also production oriented. Such statements do not readily identify the cost of goods sold and are as much concerned with value added as with revenue from sales.

Although extraordinary profits and losses are usually shown separately on the income statement, the definition as to what they are varies among countries. The early definition outlined in U.S. APB Opinion #9 issued in 1966 has been adopted in a number of countries. The change in the definition specified in APB Opinion #30 in 1973 which stresses the criteria of UNUSUAL NATURE AND INFREQUENCY OF OCCURRENCE has not yet been adopted. Obviously the many variations in income statement presentation will continue to plague the investment analyst's interpretation of a company's results of operation until an internationally defined standard is established.

## THE FUNDS STATEMENT

### #5-7....Funds Statement

In the U.S. the Funds Statement, a third financial statement, has become basic to the report package required for a complete presentation of a company's financial position. This statement is referred to most frequently as the STATEMENT OF CHANGES IN FINANCIAL POSITION.

A typical Funds Statement is illustrated in the AICPA book PROFESSIONAL ACCOUNTING IN 30 COUNTRIES, p. 693, as shown in Figure 5-3. The Funds Statement became required in the U.S. with the promulgation of APB Opinion #19 in 1971. It has since

```
========================================================================
                            FIGURE 5-3
        ILLUSTRATIVE CONSOLIDATED STATEMENT OF CHANGES IN
            FINANCIAL POSITION OF A U. S. COMPANY
                FOR THE YEAR ENDED DEC. 31, 19____
```

WORKING CAPITAL WAS PROVIDED BY:
   Operations:
      Income Before Extraordinary Items
      Depreciation and Amortization of Fixed Assets
      Deferred Federal Income Taxes
      Deferred Receivables
   FUNDS PROVIDED BY OPERATIONS
   Extraordinary Items
   Increase in Long-Term Debt
   Retirement of Property, Plant, Equipment
   Decrease in Other Assets
   Proceeds from Exercise of Options & Warrants & Sale of Stock
   TOTAL FUNDS PROVIDED
WORKING CAPITAL WAS USED TO:
   Purchase Property, Plant, Equipment
   Retire Long-Term Debt
   Increase Investments
   Decrease Minority Equity in Consolidated Subsidiaries and
         Other Noncurrent Liabilities
   Increase (Decrease) in Working Capital
   TOTAL FUNDS APPLIED
COMPONENTS OF WORKING CAPITAL CHANGES AS FOLLOWS, ( ) indicates
        Decrease:
   Cash
   Marketable Securities
   Notes and Trade Accounts Receivable
   Inventories
   Other Current Assets
   Notes Payable and Long-Term Debt
   Accounts Payable and Accrued Liabilities
   Accrued Federal Income Taxes
   Other Current Liabilities
   Increase (Decrease) in Working Capital

Source: PROFESSIONAL ACCOUNTING IN 30 COUNTRIES, page 693. Copyright ©
    1975 by the American Institute of Certified Public Accountants,
    Inc. Reprinted with permission.

been adopted as required in Canada, Peru, Panama, and recommended in Australia, England, Mexico, and a number of other countries. A universal utilization should occur pursuant to the adoption of IASC #7, issued in July 1977 to become effective after Dec. 31, 1978, entitled STATEMENT OF CHANGES IN FINANCIAL POSITION.    IASC #7 requires that financial statements include one summarizing the financing and investing activities of an enterprise. Basically the Standard conforms to U.S. GAAP. However, it differs from APB #19 in that it requires the Statement of Changes to accompany EVERY income statement, whereas APB #19 requires the Statement only when BOTH an income statement and a balance sheet are presented.  Under IASC #7, unusual items and funds provided from operations should be  separately disclosed. However,  an enterprise may adopt whatever  format is most  informative for its own particular situation.

## STATEMENT OF CHANGES IN SHAREHOLDERS' EQUITY

### #5-8....Statement of Changes in Shareholders' Equity

In the NEW YORK  CERTIFIED PUBLIC  ACCOUNTANT, 41,  No.  12, Jan.  1971, pp. 887-890,  it is pointed out  that another basic statement that is emerging, particularly  in  the U.S., is the Statement of Changes in Shareholders' Equity. This is a comprehensive illustration of changes in  a number  of  shareholders' equity accounts.  Such a statement is illustrated in Figure 5-4 as  taken from the  1975 Annual Report  of the  Martin Marietta Corp., p. 27.

Figure 5-4 shows the changes in the retained earnings, paid-in capital,  preferred legal capital, common legal capital, and treasury stock accounts.  A statement presenting all changes in shareholders' equity accounts may be particularly useful to the international investor  who may not be  familiar  with  all the various  types of equity  capital  accounts. For example,  the statutory and legal reserve accounts discussed in Chapter 3 may be strange to American investors.

The  Statement of Changes  in Shareholders' Equity could replace the combined  Statement of Income  and  Retained Earnings utilized in some countries.  Such a combined statement tends to obstruct the comprehensibility of the income statement section. Furthermore, the  income statement is regarded as of sufficient importance to stand alone.  In addition, a comprehensive Statement  of  Changes in Shareholders'  Equity  would alleviate the need  to present more than one equity statement,  e.g., a separate statement  for Retained Earnings and  one for Capital Surplus. Such separate statements of retained earnings are normally presented with the annual financial statements in many countries.

There are two major advantages of  a  separate Statement  of Changes in  Shareholders' Equity:  (1)  it  presents  a simple, clearcut analysis of changes in  the  investor's own equity interest in the corporation; and  (2) it serves as an aid in synchronizing the world-wide reporting of equity changes.

FIGURE 5-4
STATEMENT OF SHAREHOLDERS' EQUITY

| | 4% CUM. PFD. STOCK | COMMON STOCK | ADDL. PAID-IN CAPITAL | RETAINED EARNINGS | TREASURY COMMON STOCK | TOTAL STKHLDRS EQUITY |
|---|---|---|---|---|---|---|
| Balance, 12/31/73 | 1,680 | 25,528 | 171,999 | 377,510 | 73,561 | 503,156 |
| Net Earnings 1974 | | | | 80,801 | | 80,801 |
| Pfd. Stock Dividends | | | | (63) | | (63) |
| Com. Stock Dividends | | | | (27,755) | | (27,755) |
| Stk. Options Exercised | | 31 | 384 | (416) | 755 | 754 |
| Pfd. Stock Retired | (1,150) | | | | | (1,150) |
| Shares Issued in Merger | 530 | 25,559 | 172,383 | 426,791 | (41,609) | 583,654 |
| Net Earnings for 1975 | | | | 55,367 | | 55,367 |
| Pfd. Stock Dividends | | | | (18) | | (18) |
| Com. Stock Dividends | | | | (30,583) | | (30,583) |
| Stk. Options Exercised | | 86 | 1,067 | (704) | 1,656 | 2,105 |
| Pfd. Stock Retired | (530) | | | | | (530) |
| Adj. Shares Issd. Merger | | | | 197 | (928) | (731) |
| BALANCE, 12/31/75 | | 25,645 | 173,450 | 451,050 | (40,881) | 609,264 |

(All of the above figures expressed in thousands of dollars)

Source: 1975 Annual Report of the Martin Marietta Corporation, page 27.

# CONSOLIDATED FINANCIAL STATEMENTS

## #5-9....Consolidated Financial Statements

Until 1976, consolidation policies were not consistent within the countries around the world. Three specific types of consolidation policies could be identified: (1) required consolidated financial statements for the parent company stockholders, as practiced in the United States; (2) consolidated statements supplementary to parent company financial statements, as practiced in the United Kingdom; and (3) the presentation of parent company statements only to the parent company stockholders. It is expected that this diversity of consolidation policy differences will be alleviated by the establishment of IASC #3, CONSOLIDATED FINANCIAL STATEMENTS, issued March 1976 to take effect after December 31, 1976.

IASC #3 requires a parent company to consolidate all subsidiaries except where (1) control is temporary, or (2) the subsidiary operates under conditions in which severe long-term restrictions on the transfer of funds impair the parent's control. Subsidiaries described in item (2) should be shown in the financial statements under the equity method at their carrying amount at the date they cease to be consolidated.

IASC #3 does not provide any guidance on accounting for subsidiaries under temporary control. A subsidiary whose activities are so dissimilar from those of other companies in the group may be excluded from consolidation on the basis that a better presentation would result from separate financial statements. Such dissimilar subsidiaries not consolidated are to be accounted for by the equity method, and separate financial statements should be presented for them.

IASC #3 further provides that companies over which an investor can exercise significant influence, known as ASSOCIATED COMPANIES, should be accounted for by the equity method. What indicates the exercise of significant influence is defined by APB #18, EQUITY METHOD OF ACCOUNTING FOR INVESTMENTS IN COMMON STOCK, which provides that ownership of less than 20% creates the presumption that the investor does not exercise such influence. However, the investor must intend to retain its interest in the investee company as a long-term investment.

IASC #3 indicates when the parent should cease to accrue its share of the investee's earnings:
(1) when an investee ceases to be a subsidiary and does not become an associated company;
(2) when an investee no longer meets the criteria for an associated company; or
(3) when a subsidiary ceases to be consolidated because it operates under severe long-term restrictions on the transfer of funds.

## COMPARATIVE FINANCIAL STATEMENTS

### #5-10....Comparative Financial Statements

International Accounting Standards may also be necessary for other presentation policies. Thus IASC #1 (1974) recommends publication of Comparative Financial Statements presenting the results of the preceding accounting period along with the current year's results. The practice of presenting comparative statements is widespread but not universal. Other presentation policy differences may require more study before transnational financial statement readability can be simplified.

## SEGMENT REPORTING

### #5-11....Segment Reporting

In Sept. 1981, IASC #14 was released (REPORTING FINANCIAL INFORMATION BY SEGMENT). In the Sept. 14, 1981, CPA LETTER, Volume 61, No. 15, page 2, it is pointed out:
The new standard is compatible with U.S. requirements except that its application is stated in terms of "publicly traded and to other economically significant entities, including subsidiaries." Other economically significant entities are those whose levels of revenue, profits, assets, or employment are significant in the countries in which their major operations are conducted. IASC #14 requires the enterprise to:
(a) Describe the activities of each reported industry segment and indicate the composition of each geographical area;
(b) Disclose for each reported industry and geographical segment the sales or other operating revenue--distinguishing between outside revenue and that derived from other segments, segment results, segment assets employed (expressed as money amounts or percentages of consolidated totals) and the basis of inter-segment pricing;
(c) Provide reconciliations between the sum of the information on individual segments and the aggregated information in the financial statements; and
(d) Disclose material changes in identification of segments and changes in accounting practices for reporting segment information, the reasons for the changes and, if determinable, the effects of the changes.
In its ACCOUNTING NEWS BRIEFS, Vol. 6, No. 3, April 1980 issue page 3, Arthur Andersen & Co. comments, with respect to Segment Reporting, as follows:
If a company whose securities are traded publicly operates in different industry segments or geographic areas, it must

provide information about both. Management could determine which segments to report separately based on profitability, risk, growth, and relative impact on the company as a whole. Disclosures would include a segment's sales or other revenues, operating results, and assets in money amounts or as a percentage of consolidated totals. Any company that now complies with FASB #14, FINANCIAL REPORTING FOR SEGMENTS OF A BUSINESS ENTERPRISE, would be in compliance with this new standard.

An example of a geographical segment report is given in the APPENDIX at the end of this chapter.

## DISCLOSURE OF ACCOUNTING POLICIES

### #5-12....Nature of the Disclosure Principle

Besides the financial statements, other disclosures may be required. For example, there may be a disclosure of the effects of post balance sheet events which substantially alter the reader's interpretation of the financial position of the enterprise. The disclosure of significant subsequent events is required in the U.S. and at least a dozen other countries. The requirements for footnote disclosures vary considerably. The underlying concept that tends to create some demand for footnote disclosures is the materiality concept with its inherent disclosure requirements.

One disclosure requirement that should be universally adopted is that of basic accounting policies. Such disclosure will aid the financial statement reader in the interpretation of operational results and financial position. A secondary effect is that it will reveal any unique accounting practices and eventually lead to a rather universal concept as to the fairness of financial statement presentation.

### #5-13....Disclosing Accounting Policies

The foregoing problem was considered in the first step taken by the IASC which was to promulgate the disclosure of accounting policies. Thus, IASC #1 (1974) states:
  (a) Financial statements should include clear and concise disclosure of significant accounting policies which have been used.
  (b) The disclosure of the significant accounting policies used should be an integral part of the financial statements. The policies should normally be disclosed in one place.
  (c) Wrong or inappropriate treatment of items in balance sheets, income statements or profit and loss accounts, or other statements is not rectified either by disclos-

ure of accounting policies used  or by notes or explanatory material.
This standard was  subsequently supplemented by  requiring also
the disclosure of changes in accounting policies.

## #5-14....Changes in Accounting Policies

Chapter 3 pointed  out  that consistency  in the utilization
of accounting  policies was  declared  a fundamental accounting
assumption.   However, a change in accounting policy may be necessary if  the adoption of a new accounting policy  is required
by statute or by an accounting standard setting body.  Alternatively,  a  change may be desired  if the newly adopted  policy
would result in a more appropriate presentation  of a financial
statement.
Changes in accounting  policy can be accomplished  basically
in one of three manners: (1) the new policy may be applied prospectively to current  and  future  financial  statements;  (2)
retroactively, as  though the policy had always been in use; or
(3) currently only, by presenting the amount of  the cumulative
effect on retained  earnings at the beginning of the  period in
which the change is made, with the total amount to be presented
as a single item on the income statement.

## #5-15....IASC Standard for Changes in Accounting Policies

When the policy change is applied currently, and/or prospectively,  pro forma supplementary information  is appropriate in
order  to show the affects on income of the prior  periods that
would have been affected.  When the change is  applied retroactively,  the  presentation dictates that  all  previous periods
affected be adjusted  to reflect the new  policy.  These situations are  provided for by IASC  #8,  UNUSUAL  AND PRIOR PERIOD
ITEMS AND  CHANGES IN ACCOUNTING POLICIES, issued Oct. 1977 effective after Dec. 31, 1978.   Because of the different methods
that are utilized around the world, IASC #8 declares:
  (a) A change in accounting policy should be made only if the
      adoption of a different accounting policy is required by
      statute or by an accounting standard setting body, or if
      it  is considered that the change would result in a more
      appropriate  presentation of  financial statements of an
      enterprise.
  (b) If there is a change in an accounting policy that has  a
      material  effect  in the current period,  or may have  a
      material effect in subsequent periods, the effect of the
      change should  be disclosed and quantified together with
      reasons for the change.
This declaration is further expanded by requiring disclosure of
changes in accounting estimates.

## #5-16....Changes in Accounting Estimates

A change in an accounting estimate is not a change in accounting policy. In the preparation of financial statements, estimates are based on circumstances existing at the time they are made. Estimates of such items as uncollectible accounts, inventories obsolescence, or the useful lives of depreciable assets may need to be revised in subsequent periods, when changes in the circumstances take place. Such changes in estimates are normally handled currently and prospectively. IASC #8 specifically indicates:

(a) A change in an accounting estimate should be accounted for as part of income from ordinary activities of the enterprise in the period of change and future periods if the change affects both. Revision of an estimate that relates to an item that is treated as an unusual item should itself be reported as unusual.

(b) If there is a change in an accounting estimate that has a material effect in the current period, or may have a material effect in subsequent periods, the effect of the change should be disclosed and quantified.

## #5-17....Effects of Policy Disclosure

Since significant variations in accounting practices exist around the world, two important points may be made. First, the harmonization work of the IASC can be expected to be persuasive in achieving a high degree of comparability in financial statements. Secondly, until the harmonization process is completed, if ever, the investor analyst does receive the benefit of full disclosure of the accounting policies in the analytic work for the investment decision.

This disclosure requirement may be particularly beneficial when new accounting practices are adopted because of new circumstances and types of transactions occurring in international commerce. For that matter, the disclosure is even important for highlighting an accounting policy that may be unique to a particular country because of special environmental conditions and for which an international standard would seem inappropriate.

## EEC FINANCIAL STATEMENT PRESENTATION REQUIREMENTS

## #5-18....EEC Financial Statement General Observations

In the book ACCOUNTING FOR THE MULTINATIONAL CORPORATION, Mr. Watt points out on page 171:

Following prevailing practice in such countries as Germany and France, the proposed Fourth Directive prescribes financial statement format in considerable detail. Companies are given a choice between two forms of balance sheet, neither of which bears any marked resemblance to U.S. format, and four forms of profit and loss presentation. Some variations in the prescribed formats are permitted, but these appear to be in the area of detail rather than overall structure. All four profit and loss formats require disclosure of sales (turnover) and cost of sales--a feature observed in varying degrees in present-day financial reporting in the areas. There is also provision for deferred (future) taxes.

Comparative financial statements are required but a Statement of Changes in Financial Position is not required to be presented as a part of the annual accounts. The concept that consolidated statements are necessary for fair presentation is recognized in the proposed 4th Directive which does not, however, make their preparation a requirement. This subject is dealt with in the proposed 7th Directive which provides that where, within the Community dependent group, companies or subgroups, independent of each other, are dominated by an undertaking outside the Community, consolidated accounts must be prepared for the dependent undertakings within the EEC. For example, if a company in France and a company in Germany, independent of each other, were both dominated by an American company, consolidated accounts would be required in respect of these two companies plus any of their own dependent undertakings.

#### #5-19...EEC General Requirements for Financial Statement Presentation

As indicated by Mr. Watt, because there are substantial differences between EEC financial statements and those in the U.S., there will be presented in the discussion of EEC requirements for financial statements the reference to and general titles respecting the statements. This should give the reader a sufficient basis for knowing the composition of the statements and how they compare with U.S. financial statements.

These requirements are set forth in the proposed 4th Directive in Sections 2 through 6. Basically these sections are set up as follows: Sec. 2--LAYOUT OF THE ANNUAL ACCOUNTS, comprises Articles 3 through 6; Sec. 3--BALANCE SHEET LAYOUT, Art. 7-11; Sec. 4--SPECIAL PROVISIONS RELATING TO CERTAIN ITEMS IN THE BALANCE SHEET, Art. 12-18; Sec. 5--LAYOUT OF THE PROFIT AND LOSS ACCOUNT, Art. 19-24; and Sec. 6--SPECIAL PROVISIONS RELATING TO CERTAIN ITEMS IN THE PROFIT AND LOSS ACCOUNT, Art. 25-27. Obviously the details of these sections and articles would not warrant the extensiveness of the discussions of these provisions. However, it is not deemed inappropriate to indicate the principal divisions of these items.

## #5-20...EEC 4th Dir.--Section 2--Layout of Annual Accounts

Article 3 forbids a change in the form of presentation of the statements from year to year, indicating the principle of consistency. Departures are permitted only in exceptional cases. Provisions 1, 2, and 3 of Article 4 relate to the showing of certain items in Arabic numerals, and Provision 4 requires the showing of figures on the balance sheet and income statement for the preceding year. Article 6 states that "any set-off between assets and liabilities, or between expenditure and income, is prohibited."

## #5-21...EEC 4th Directive--Section 3--Balance Sheet Layout

Articles 7, 8, and 9 go into a specific listing of the various asset, liability and owners' equity accounts. The headings are as follows:

ASSETS: (a) Subscribed Capital unpaid; (b) Formation Expenses; (c) Fixed Assets -- Intangible--consisting of research and development costs, concessions, patents, licenses, trademarks, goodwill; and Tangible--consisting of land and buildings, plant and machinery, fixtures, tools and equipment, and equipment in process of construction, participating interests, and other financial assets; (d) Current Assets -- consisting of inventories, debtors, securities; (e) Prepayments.

LIABILITIES: (a) Subscribed Capital; (b) Reserves, including legal, share premium, revaluation, statutory, and optional; (c) Total Subscribed Capital and Reserves; (d) Provisions for Contingencies and Reserves; (e) Creditors; (f) Accruals; (g) Profit, for the year and accumulated.

Article 10 of Sec. 3 provides for disclosure of joint assets and/or liabilities to relate the components to their proper attachment; Art. 11 stipulates that commitments by way of guarantee be set out below the balance sheet or in the notes, distinguishing between the various types of guarantee legally recognized.

## #5-22...EEC 4th Directive--Section 4--Special Provisions Relating to Certain Balance Sheet Items

Article 12 makes provision for the showing of value adjustments to be shown in the balance sheet as a deduction from the relevant item or in the notes for fixed and current asset accounts. Article 13 states: "Under the term 'land and buildings' shall be shown land not built on as well as land built on and the buildings thereon, together with fixtures and fittings." Article 14 defines the term "participating interests" as rights in the capital of other undertakings, whether or not represent-

ed by certificates which, by creating a durable link with them,
are intended to contribute to the activities of the company.  A
holding of 10% of the subscribed capital of another undertaking
shall be presumed to constitute a participating interest.

Article 15 requires that under the heading PREPAYMENTS there
"shall be shown expenditure incurred during the year but relating to a subsequent year,  together with the earnings  relating
to the year to the extent that they  will not be received until
after the close  of the year which may  be shown under debtors.
Where the amount involved is considerable, an  explanation must
be given in the notes." Article 16 defines VALUE ADJUSTMENTS as
"items relating to elements  of assets and are intended to take
account of  depreciation established at the date of the balance
sheet whether definitive or not."

Article 17  indicates that the  provisions for contingencies
and  charges are intended to cover  major maintenance  work  or
repairs to be incurred in  subsequent  years, but indeterminate
as to amount on the  date on which they will arise.  Article 18
provides  for ACCRUALS  FOR LIABILITIES  which are  received in
cash in advance but  to be performed  in the  future and  for
charges  received  in the  current  period to be paid in subsequent periods.

#5-23...EEC 4th Dir.--Section 5--Profit and Loss Account Layout

Articles 19 through 23 detail the specific listing and  layout  of the Profit  and Loss Statement accounts.  There are six
divisions that make up the Profit and Loss Statement: (I) Operating Result,  (II) Financial Result, (III) Exceptional Result,
(IV) Sub-Total, (V) Taxes, and (VI) Result for the Year.
(I).    OPERATING  RESULT -- The components of the Operating Re-
        sult  are specifically listed  as  (1) Net Turnover; (2)
        changes in stocks of finished and semifinished products;
        (3) work effected by the undertaking for its own account
        and  shown under assets;  (4) other operating  receipts;
        (5)  cost  of raw  and auxiliary  materials;  (6)  staff
        costs; (7)  value  adjustments of current  assets and of
        tangible and intangible fixed  assets; (8) other operat-
        ing expenses; and (9) Operating Result.
(II).   FINANCIAL  RESULT --  The  components  are (10) earnings
        from participating interest including those derived from
        associated undertakings; (11) earnings from other secur-
        ities;  (12) other interest and  similar  earnings; (13)
        value adjustments of other financial assets  and securi-
        ties part of the current assets; (14) interest and simi-
        lar charges; and (15) Financial Results.
(III).  EXCEPTIONAL RESULT--comprises (16) exceptional earnings;
        (17) exceptional charges; and (18) Exceptional Result.
(IV).   is the SUB-TOTAL.
(V).    TAXES -- consists of (19) taxes on the results  that are

actual and future; and (20) Other Taxes.
(VI).   RESULT FOR THE YEAR -- commonly referred to  as the Bottom Line.

## #5-24...EEC 4th Directive--Section 6--Special Provisions Relating to Certain Profit and Loss Account Items

Article  25 of Sec. 6 provides that "the net count of  turnover includes  receipts from sales of products, goods and services falling within the usual  operations of the company, after allowing for any price reduction in respect of those sales, and for value  added tax and other taxes directly tied to the turnover." Art. 26 permits earnings and charges that are attributable to another year together with any earnings and charges that do not arise out of the  usual operations of the undertaking to be shown under the items Exceptional  Earnings and  Exceptional Charges.  Art. 27 states: "Under the item 'Taxes on the Result' shall be shown the actual amount of taxes payable for the year, and separately, the amount of the future liability to tax."

## #5-25...EEC Disclosure Principles

With respect to disclosure requirements discussed in Chapter 3, relating to GAAP, it  was pointed out that the EEC  has gone into great detail with respect to the requirements of footnotes to financial statements,  when they would be  required, and the extent of their disclosures.

The 4th Directive requires sufficient  comments in footnotes to  meet the requirement of a TRUE AND FAIR VIEW.  The specific minimum requirements under the Directive are a proper  description of valuation methods; disclosure of rates used for foreign currency  translation; information  regarding  investments that are 10% or  more in other companies;  amounts of financial commitments; sales  reported by geographical markets  and  product lines;  taxes  attributable to operations,  to financial operations, and to exraordinary items.

## #5-26...EEC 4th Dir.--Sec. 8--Contents of Notes on the Accounts

Section  8 embraces Articles 40  through  42.    Article  40 states:  "The notes on the accounts shall contain commentary on the balance sheet and profit and loss in such manner as to give a TRUE AND FAIR VIEW of  the company's assets, liabilities, financial position and results."

Art. 41  provides for the information to  be  set out in the notes:    (1) The valuation methods applied to the various items in the annual accounts; for foreign currency debtors  and creditors, the  method used  for calculating the rate of  exchange must be  shown; (2) the names of companies  in which 10% of the capital  is  owned,  showing the proportion of  capital  held, amount of reserves, and results for the latest business year of the undertaking concerned; (3) the way in which the authorized capital has been employed; (4) entitlements carrying the right to a share of the profits, any convertible debentures or similar securities or rights; (5) the overall amount of the financial commitments not shown in the balance sheet for the purpose of assessing the financial position; (6) net amount of turnover broken down by categories of products and activities and by geographical markets; (7) number of persons employed broken down by categories and total personnel costs for the period; (8) taxes included in operating results, financial result or exceptional result; (9) amount of changes in the result for the year due to application of fiscal laws; (10) emoluments granted during the year to members of administrative, managerial and supervisory bodies and any commitment of retirement pensions; and (11) amount of advances and credits granted to members of administrative, managerial and supervisory bodies and guarantees to them of any kind.

Art. 42 provides for the right to omit any particulars regarding the name and head office of each company in which at least 10% of the capital is owned when the nature is such that in the view of a reasonable businessman they would be seriously prejudicial to any of the undertakings to which this provision relates. Such omission of the particulars shall be mentioned in the notes on the accounts. In conclusion, it is apparent that the EEC is quite extensive in its provisions of disclosure.

## APPENDIX TO CHAPTER 5

=====================================================================

X COMPANY -- INFORMATION ABOUT THE COMPANY'S OPERATIONS IN DIFFERENT
GEOGRAPHIC AREAS FOR THE YEAR ENDED DECEMBER 31, 1977

|  | United States | Geo-graphic Area A | Geo-graphic Area B | Adjust-ments & Elimi-nations | Consoli-dated |
|---|---|---|---|---|---|
| Sales to unaffiliated customers | $3,000 | $1,000 | $ 700 |  | $ 4,700 |
| Transfers between geographic areas | 1,000 |  |  | $(1,000) |  |
| Total Revenue | $4,000 | $1,000 | $ 700 | $(1,000) | $ 4,700 |
| Operating Profit | $ 800 | $ 400 | $ 100 | $( 200) | $ 1,100 |
| Equity in net income of Z Co. |  |  |  |  | 100 |
| General corporate expenses |  |  |  |  | ( 100) |
| Interest expense |  |  |  |  | ( 200) |
| Income from continuing operations before income taxes |  |  |  |  | $ 900 |
| Identifiable assets at 12/31/77 | $7,300 | $3,400 | $2,450 | $( 150) | $13,000 |
| Investment in net assets of Z Co. |  |  |  |  | 400 |
| Corporate assets |  |  |  |  | 1,600 |
| Total assets at 12/31/77 |  |  |  |  | $15,000 |

(See accompanying "Note" on following page.)

**"Note":**

Transfers between geographic areas are accounted for by (describe basis of accounting for such transfers). Operating profit is total revenue less operating expenses. In computing operating profit, none of the following items has been added or deducted: general corporate expenses, interest exp., income taxes, equity in income from unconsolidated investee, loss from discontinued operations of West Coast division (part of Company's U.S. operations), extraordinary gain (relates to Company's operations in Geographic Area B), and the cumulative effect of the change from straight-line to accelerated depreciation (relates entirely to Company's operations in U.S.).

Identifiable assets are those assets of the Company that are identified with the operations in each geographic area. Corporate assets are principally cash and marketable securities.

Of the $3,000 U.S. sales to unaffiliated customers, $1,200 were export sales, principally to Geographic Area C.

(SOURCE: Exhibit C, FASB #14)

====================================================================

## SUMMARY OF FOOTNOTE REFERENCES
(References are to Paragraph #'s)

#5-1 thru #5-11:  "Financial Statements, Consolidated Statements, Comparative Statements, and Segment Reporting," adapted from Norlin G. Rueschhoff, INTERNATIONAL ACCOUNTING AND FINANCIAL REPORTING, 1976, Praeger Publishers, Inc., by permission.

#5-2   AICPA, PROFESSIONAL ACCOUNTING IN 30 COUNTRIES, pp. 51, 125-126, 169, 629, 746-749. Copyright © 1975 by the American Institute of Certified Public Accountants, Inc. Reprinted with permission.

#5-4   IASC #13, CURRENT ASSETS AND CURRENT LIABILITIES, 1979

#5-6   AICPA, op.cit., pp.52, 350, 351, 630, 750-753, by permission

#5-7   Ibid., p. 693, by permission

#5-8   "Statement of Changes in Shareholders' Equity," NEW YORK CERTIFIED PUBLIC ACCOUNTANT, 41, No. 12 (Jan. 1971): 887-890

#5-8   1975 Annual Report, Martin Marietta Corp., p. 27

#5-9   IASC #3, CONSOLIDATED FINANCIAL STATEMENTS, 1976

#5-11  "IASC #14, Reporting Financial Information by Segment, 1981," CPA LETTER, Vol. 61, No. 15 (Sept. 14, 1981): 2

#5-11  Arthur Andersen & Co., ACCOUNTING NEWS BRIEFS, Vol. 6, No. 3 (April 1980): 3

#5-13  IASC #1, 1974

#5-15  IASC #8, UNUSUAL AND PRIOR PERIOD ITEMS AND CHANGES IN ACCOUNTING POLICIES, 1977

#5-16  Ibid.

#5-18  George C. Watt, ACCOUNTING FOR THE MULTINATIONAL CORPORATION, p. 171. Copyright 1977 by Financial Executives Research Foundation (FERF), Morristown, N.J. Reprinted with permission.

#5-19  George C. Watt,  EEC 4th Directive, Secs. 2 through 6, Ibid.
#5-20  EEC Fourth Directive, Sec. 2
#5-21  EEC Fourth Directive, Sec. 3
#5-22  EEC Fourth Directive, Sec. 4
#5-23  EEC Fourth Directive, Sec. 5
#5-24  EEC Fourth Directive, Sec. 6
#5-26  EEC Fourth Directive, Sec. 8

## BIBLIOGRAPHY

Cummings, Joseph. "Beware of the Pitfalls in Foreign Financial Statements," Peat, Marwick, Mitchell & Co., WORLD, 6, No. 1 (Winter 1972): 45-47

Emmanuel, C.R. and Gray, S.J. "Segmental Disclosures By Multibusiness Multinational Companies: A Proposal," ACCOUNTING AND BUSINESS RESEARCH (Summer 1978): 169-177

Fitzgerald, Richard D. "International Disclosure Standards--The United Nations Position," JOURNAL OF ACCOUNTANCY, AUDITING, AND FINANCE, 3 (Fall 1979): 5-20

Golub, S.J. "A Global Perspective to Financial Reporting," INTERNATIONAL JOURNAL OF ACCOUNTING EDUCATION & RESEARCH (Fall 1982): 37-44

Gray, S.J. "Segment Reporting and the EEC Multinationals," JOURNAL OF ACCOUNTING RESEARCH, 16 (Autumn 1978): 242-253

Riise, A. "Norwegian Standards for Annual Reporting Requirements and Chart of Accounts," INTERNATIONAL JOURNAL OF ACCOUNTING EDUCATION & RESEARCH (Spring 1982): 103-120

Sharp, I.N.S. "International Variations in Presentation and Certification of Accounts," THE ACCOUNTANT, 165, No. 5040 (July 1971): 124-126

## THEORY QUESTIONS
(Question Numbers are Keyed to Text Paragraph #'s)

#5-2   Make a critical comparative analysis of the Balance Sheet formats in Canada, England, Australia, and West Germany.

#5-4   How are Current Assets and Current Liabilities defined under IASC #13? How does this compare with U.S. practice?

#5-5   What provision is made for Occurrences After the Balance Sheet Date in IASC #10 and how does this compare with U.S. practice?

#5-6   Make a critical comparative analysis of the Income Statement forms in Japan, England, Australia, and West Germany.

#5-7   What is the status of the Funds Statement under IASC #7?

#5-8   What information is disclosed by the Statement of Changes in Shareholders' Equity? What are its two major advantages?

#5-9   What are the rules of consolidation under IASC #3?

#5-10  What provision is made for Comparative Financial Statements under IASC #1?

#5-11   What provision is made for Segment  Reporting under IASC
        #14?

#5-13   Under IASC #1,  how should the Disclosure  of Accounting
        Policies be handled?

#5-14   State the three ways  in  which  changes  in  accounting
    .   policy can be accomplished.

#5-15   How should Unusual and Prior Period Items and Changes in
        Accounting Policies be handled under IASC #8?

#5-16   Distinguish between a  change in  an  accounting  policy
        and an accounting estimate.

#5-21   Discuss the Balance Sheet layout prescribed by Section 3
        of the EEC 4th Directive.

#5-23   What provision is made for Income Statement layout under
        Section 5 of the EEC 4th Directive?

#5-26   How are Contents  of Notes on the Accounts handled under
        Section 8 of the EEC 4th Directive?

## EXERCISES

### EX-5-1

For proper disclosure international  financial statements,  the
following statement is false:

  a. Financial statements should include clear and concise dis-
     closure of all  significant accounting policies that  have
     been used.
  b. The significant  accounting  policies  should  normally be
     disclosed with  each footnote that describes each  balance
     sheet item.
  c. Financial  statements  should  have  corresponding figures
     for the preceding period.
  d. A  change  in accounting policy that has a material effect
     in  subsequent periods should  be disclosed  together with
     the reasons.

### EX-5-2

In the presentation  of inventories in  international financial
statements,

  a. The profit and loss of the  period should be charged  with
     the amount of  inventories sold  and  used  and  with  the
     amount of any  writedown  in the period  to net realizable
     value.
  b. Inventories should be grouped  into  one classification on
     the statement of financial position.
  c. The  accounting policies adopted for the purpose of valua-
     tion  of inventories, except for  the cost  formula  used,
     should be disclosed.
  d. Exceptional  amounts of wasted  material, labor, or  other
     expenses should be included as part of the inventory cost.

EX-5-3
The following inventory accounting method may be used in international financial statements in accord with International Accounting Standard No. 2 only if disclosure is given between the amount presented and the current cost or net realizable value:
  a. Specific identification      c. Standard cost
  b. Base stock                   d. FIFO retail

EX-5-4
On a financial statement prepared in accordance with international standards, the cost of manufactured goods should be reported
  a. At prime cost                c. At absorption cost
  b. At direct cost               d. At variable factory cost

EX-5-5  (CPA EXAM, 11/74, THEORY, #1-38)
Lochlann Company purchased with U.S. dollars all the outstanding common stock of Dey Company, a Canadian corporation. At the date of purchase, a portion of the investment account was appropriately allocated to goodwill. One year later, after an exchange rate decrease (U.S. dollars have become less valuable), the goodwill should be shown in the consolidated balance sheet at what amount?
  a. An increased amount, less amortization
  b. The same amount, less amortization
  c. A lesser amount, less amortization
  d. An increased or lesser amount depending on management policy, less amortization

EX-5-6  (CPA EXAM, 5/79, THEORY, #5)
PART (A). In order to properly understand current generally accepted accounting principles with respect to accounting for and reporting upon segments of a business enterprise, as stated in FASB #14, it is necessary to be familiar with certain unique terminology.
Required:
With respect to segments of a business enterprise, explain the following terms:
  1. Industry segment
  2. Revenue
  3. Operating profit and loss
  4. Identifiable assets
PART (B). A central issue in reporting on industry segments of a business enterprise is the determination of which segments are reportable.
Required:
  1. What are the tests to determine whether or not an industry segment is reportable?
  2. What is the test to determine if enough industry segments

have been separately reported upon and what is the guideline on the maximum number of industry segments to be shown?

## PROBLEMS

### P-5-1

Norbert Corporation is a U.S.-based international company with operations in Canada and Mexico. In each country it has a 100 percent-owned subsidiary that owns all the operations in that country.                                                          *22 500 COS to SUB*

Last year Norbert had sales of $120,000, of which $30,000 were to the Mexican subsidiary and $20,000 to a German import- *12 000 COS* er. Norbert's cost of sales were $90,000 with a standard 25 percent gross profit rate. Expenses were $15,000 for opera- tions, $5,000 for interest, and $1,000 general parent company overhead. Norbert's total assets were $300,000, of which $250,000 were identifiable with U.S. operations. *50 000 Investment acct*

The Canadian subsidiary had sales of $30,000 with a cost of sales of $18,000 and other operating expenses of $1,000. The identifiable Canadian assets were $100,000.

In Mexico the sales were $50,000. That subsidiary's cost of sales was $30,000, all of which were obtained from the parent company at a negotiated price of U.S. cost plus one-third. The ending inventory of the Mexican subsidiary was $6,000 which was part of its total identifiable assets of $125,000. The Mexican company's operating expenses were $8,000.

Required:

In proper format, present the information about Norbert Corpo- ration's foreign operations including appropriate footnotes.

### P-5-2

The Nilron Company is a U.S.-based international company with operations in Europe and Latin America. For each of these two areas it has a 100 percent-owned subsidiary that owns all the operations in each area. The U.S. parent company also has oper- ations in the United States.

During 1978 the U.S. company had $8,000 in sales, of which $2,000 were to Latin America affiliates, $1,000 were to the U.S. government, and $1,500 were to a Japanese importer. Its cost of sales were $6,000 with a standard 25 percent gross profit ratio. Expenses were $1,000 for operations, $400 for interest, and $200 for general corporate overhead. Its total assets were $18,000, $15,000 of which were identifiable with U.S. operations.

The European subsidiary's consolidated 1978 sales were $2,000, with cost of sales of $1,200 and other operating ex- penses of $100. The identifiable European assets were $6,000. The European subsidiary had a $200 loss on disposal of its Dan- ish operations in 1978.

In Latin America the 1978 sales were $3,500, all of which were reported by the Latin American subsidiary. That subsidiary's cost of sales were $2,100, all of which were obtained from the U.S. company at a negotiated price of U.S. cost plus one-third. Its ending inventory was $400 which was part of the total identifiable Latin American assts of $9,000. Its 1978 operating expenses were $500.

**Required**:

Present, in proper format, information about Nilron Company's operations in different geographic areas. Include appropriate accompanying footnotes.

# International Accounting Reporting Standards

#6-1....Assurance of Fairness of Financial Statement
Presentation

The mere establishment of a standard set of international
financial statement presentation principles will not in itself
lead to international harmony in transnational financial reporting to investors. Besides comparability, the international
investor may also want an assurance as to the fairness of the
presentation which may be obtained through certification by a
competent outside auditor. This assumes a high level of universally applied professional standards for auditors. In this
chapter we will review the reporting standards as applied in
transnational financial reporting which will be designed to
permit a familiarization with the present status of professional standards for public accountants.

ACCOUNTING REPORTING STANDARDS*

#6-2....The Certified Auditor's Report

A fairness in financial statement presentation depends not
only on full disclosure but also on high standards of auditing
and professional competence. Fairness and truth in public
financial reporting is possible only through respect for, and
trust in, the professional auditor and accountant. The trust is
fulfilled through the mechanism of the Certified Auditor's
Report.

------

*See Summary of Footnote References -- #6-1 thru #6-11

## #6-3....Audit Certification

In practically every developed, as well as developing, country, some type of law or regulatory provision requires regular
submission of financial statements to certain governmental
bodies, regulatory agencies, or similar institutions. Further,
for corporations with stocks listed on official securities exchanges, regulations require submission of the financial statements to the shareholders too. In most cases, such submitted
financial statements must be certified, or otherwise attested
to, by a qualified auditor.

## #6-4....Short-Form Audit Report

The form of the certification varies. The most prevalent
type of audit report is the SHORT-FORM REPORT used in the U.S.
The form was approved by members of the InterAmerican Accounting Conference held in 1965 in Argentina. Thus, the short-form
report has widespread adoption in most of the Western Hemisphere. An illustration of the Short-Form Report is given in the
AICPA book, PROFESSIONAL ACCOUNTING IN 30 COUNTRIES, pp. 653-
654, as follows:
==================================================================

### FIGURE 6-1
### UNITED STATES ILLUSTRATIVE AUDIT REPORT FORMAT

We have examined the balance sheet of X Company as of December 31, 19__, and the related statements of income and retained
earnings and changes in financial position for the year then
ended. Our examination was made in accordance with generally
accepted auditing standards, and accordingly included such
tests of the accounting records and such other auditing procedures as we considered necessary in the circumstances.

In our opinion, the aforementioned financial statements present fairly the financial position of X Company at December 31,
19__, and the results of its operations and changes in its financial position for the year then ended, in conformity with
generally accepted accounting principles applied on a basis
consistent with that of the preceding year.

------------------------------------------------------------

==================================================================

## #6-5....Fairness and Truth Report

Another prevalent type of audit report is the certification
as to FAIRNESS AND TRUTH in accordance with specified regula-

tory acts. An illustration of this kind of report is that used
in Switzerland, as given in the AICPA book PROFESSIONAL AC-
COUNTING IN 30 COUNTRIES, pp. 585-586:
=================================================================
FIGURE 6-2
SWITZERLAND ILLUSTRATIVE AUDIT REPORT FORMAT

As auditors of your company, we have examined the accounts
for the year ended 19___ in accordance with the provisions of
the law. We have come to the conclusion that:
* the balance sheet and profit and loss account are in
  agreement with the books;
* the books of account have been properly kept;
* the financial position and the results of operations
  are presented in accordance with the principles of evaluation prescribed by the law and the requirements of the
  statutes.
Based on the result of our examination, we recommend that the
accounts submitted to you be approved.
We further confirm that the proposals of the Board of Directors for the disposal of the available profits are in agreement
with the law and the statutes.
-----------------------------------------------------------
=================================================================


#6-6....True and Fair View Report

The True and Fair View Report is used in New Zealand. Typi-
cal of this type of report is illustrated on p. 426 of PROFES-
SIONAL ACCOUNTING IN 30 COUNTRIES, as follows:
=================================================================
FIGURE 6-3
NEW ZEALAND ILLUSTRATIVE AUDIT REPORT FORMAT

We have obtained all the information and explanations that
we have required. In our opinion, proper books of account have
been kept by the company so far as appears from our examination
of those books. In our opinion, according to the best of our
information and the explanations given to us and as shown by
the said books, the balance sheet and the profit and loss accounts are properly drawn up so as to give respectively a true
and fair view of the state of the company's affairs as at ____,
19__ and the results of its business for the year ended on that
date.
According to such information and explanations, the accounts, the balance sheet, and the profit and loss account give

the information required by  the Companies Act of 1955  in   the
manner so required.

---

(Copyright © 1975 by the American Institute  of Certified Public Accountants.  Reprinted with permission.)

====================================================================

Slight   variations of the New Zealand "true and fair  value"
report can  be  found  in  the U.K., South Africa,  Sweden, and
other countries that have had some British influence. It should
also be noted that the New Zealand report is similar to that of
Switzerland in  that it states  compliance  with the  Companies
Act. In this respect, whether the short-form report used in the
U.S. and many other countries is  adopted in lieu of the legalistic "true and fair" attestation is a  controversial issue  in
developed countries.

## #6-7....Simplistic Reports

The simplest type of audit report is a SIGNATURE ONLY report
used in Spain.  Next most simple is that used in Denmark, which
is also used in  a few other countries, as presented on  p. 177
of the AICPA book PROFESSIONAL ACCOUNTING IN 30 COUNTRIES:

====================================================================
FIGURE 6-4
DENMARK ILLUSTRATIVE AUDIT REPORT FORMAT

The above profit and loss  account  and balance sheet that I
have examined are in accordance with the books of the company.

---

(Copyright © 1975 by the American Institute of  Certified Public Accountants.  Reprinted with permission.)

====================================================================

## #6-8....Long-Form Report

In many countries, typically Germany, a very elaborate long-
form report is used.   In the AICPA book, PROFESSIONAL ACCOUNT-
ING IN 30  COUNTRIES, pp.  731-734, while  no standard   form is
presented, the following remarks indicate the nature and extent
of the audit report:

Standards of reporting evolved  in   response  to the requirements  of the Companies  Act.  The wording for the   accountant's report (Bestatigungsvermerk)  is laid down in the
Companies Act, and the German Institute has recommended that
it be universally  used.  It states  that  "according to the
audit, made  in conformity with the professional duties, the
accounting and  the annual financial statements  and the re-

port of the board of management comply with German law and the company's statutes."

The general outline and content of the long-form report prescribed by law for corporations and other firms whose financial statements are required to be audited contains any details that in American practice would be found only in the audit working papers. The requirements are prescribed by the Companies Act and cover the following matters:

(1) Whether accounting, annual financial statements, and the report of the board of management are in accordance with the law;

(2) Whether the management has supplied all necessary documents and other items of substantiation and has responded to all requests for information;

(3) Details of composition of, and comments on, items in annual financial statements;

(4) Remarks on facts either jeopardizing the existence of an enterprise or inhibiting its development;

(5) Major violations by the board of management of law or company statutes.

## #6-9....Professional Competence

The certification or attestation must normally be by a qualified registered accountant. Just as there are variations in the qualifications necessary for certification among the states in the U.S., so also are there variations among countries. Sanctioned requirements include some combination of practical experience, formal education, successful examination, and institute or statutory registration, as pointed out by Cesar Salas in the article, "Accounting Education and Practice in Spanish Latin America," INTERNATIONAL JOURNAL OF ACCOUNTING, 3, No. 1, Fall 1967, pp. 67-85. Needless to say, within the requirements such as experience and formal training, variations will always exist.

In most cases the financial statements of corporations with shares listed on an official securities exchange must have an attestation by a certified, chartered, or registered public accountant. Other corporation financial statements may be attested to by accountants with lower minimum qualifications, similar to the registered but not certified, public accountants in some U.S. states.

## #6-10....Auditing Standards

To attain a high level of standards in certification the auditor, in addition to professional competence, must also exert diligence and integrity in performing the audit. This means he must use substantive auditing procedures before the certifi-

cation can be given. Though auditing procedures are required in
most countries, the extent and thoroughness of the audit tests
are not always at the high level that one might expect from the
reading of the short-form audit report.

Thus the lack of inventory observation or receivables confirmation is quite common in most countries. Also in a few
countries, such as Belgium and Italy, there is not internal
control review nor direct confirmation of bank balances. Nevertheless, the auditor does testify to the accuracy of the financial statement as derived from the company's accounts. No doubt
the standardization of audit tests and procedures seems necessary for certification of reports for companies with shares
listed on international securities exchanges.

### #6-11...Importance of High Standards in the International Investment Arena

The movement of international investments among the world's
citizens is increasing, particularly in the amount of direct
investments among countries. They are more than just movements
of unilateral investments from developed countries to the developing nations, because they exist between the developed
countries too.

The movement in international direct investments has caused
a demand for exchanges of investments in a secondary market
whether through securities exchanges, in the over-the-counter
market, or in private negotiations. For the exchanges in investment to take place, there must be some understanding as to
the intrinsic values--the proper exchange prices--of the investments. This understanding can best be monitored through the
review of the financial positions and results of operations of
the enterprise involved.

Indeed, the international investor is demanding the authen-
tication of financial statements on which trust can be based
for the negotiations in the investment exchange price. High
levels of professional competence and reporting standards are
expected if these international investment exchanges are to be
handled in a mutually understanding, trustful manner. In THE
CPA LETTER, Sept. 1979, the IFAC has issued a proposed international auditing GUIDELINE describing the basic principles governing the auditor's professional responsibilities to be exercised whenever an audit is carried out. The basic principles
stated in "Basic Principles Governing an Audit" are integrity,
objectivity, independence, confidentiality, competence, documentation, planning, reviewing, and reporting. As of 1980, IFAC
membership was 73 accountancy bodies from 55 countries. As of
Aug. 1982, there were 80 bodies from 59 countries representing
750,000 qualified accountants. As of 1985, there were 91 bodies
from 66 countries representing 900,000 accountants.

## EEC COUNTRIES REPORTING STANDARDS

### #6-12....Reporting Standards Clusters

While there may be a variation of reporting standards in the nine original EEC countries, they do appear to cluster into three groups that are somewhat similar: (1) the English Group, (2) the French Group, and (3) the German Group. Included in the English Group are the United Kingdom, Ireland, the Netherlands, and Denmark. The French Group comprises France, Belgium, and Luxembourg. The German Group is virtually itself. And Italy is strictly in a developmental stage.

### #6-13....English Group: (1) The United Kingdom

It is natural to expect that the professional bodies will exert great influence on reporting standards. The five principal bodies in the U.K. are The Institute of Chartered Accountants in England and Wales; Institute of Chartered Accountants of Scotland; Institute of Cost and Management Accountants; Chartered Institute of Public Finance and Accountancy; and the Assoc. of Certified Accountants. In May 1974, the 5 bodies formed a joint Consultative Committee on Accountancy Bodies (CCAB), which was also joined by The Institute of Chartered Accountants of Ireland, with a total membership of over 80,000.

In Chapter 2 it was pointed out that much accounting in the U.K. was extracted from the Companies Acts, a series of which was enacted between 1844 and 1967. The only requirement under these Acts was that financial reporting was required to be a "true and fair" statement; no specific standards or principles were promulgated. As a result, the Chartered Accountants Institutes issued recommendations beginning with 1942, which, like the FASB's in the U.S., were not binding.

The bankruptcies of many large British firms in the 1960s precipitated the formation of the Accounting Standards Steering Committee (ASSC) in 1970, which currently, like the FASB, promulgates what are called STATEMENTS OF STANDARD ACCOUNTING PRACTICE (SSAP's), which must be conformed to by all members of the five professional bodies.

These SSAP's bear a marked resemblance to the U.S. version of FASB's and are similar in substance. They have gone even further than the U.S., as evidenced by the recommendation of the 1975 Sandilands Committee Report advocating that historical cost valuation be replaced by current cost.

### #6-14....English Group: (2) Ireland

The professional body is The Institute of Chartered Accountants in Ireland, which joined the British CCAB in 1974. The

membership comprises some 3,000 accountants and is bound by the
SSAP promulgated by the ASSC.

Like the United Kingdom, there are the Irish Companies Acts
which are aimed at a "true and fair view" of the transactions
and affairs of business entities being disclosed from the books
of account. The Companies Act states that the books of account
must record (1) all cash receipts and disbursements and their
source and application; (2) all sales and purchases; and (3)
all assets and liabilities. All books and records must be kept
at the registered office of the company and be available for
inspection where kept outside the country.

Despite the absence of an express requirement that books be
audited, in cases of those companies incorporated under the
Companies Act, independent auditors must be used. The Irish
Companies Act is thus similar to the United Kingdom's in the
express provision that: "every balance sheet of a company shall
give a true and fair view of the state of affairs of the company as at the end of the financial year, and any profit and loss
account of a company shall give a true and fair view of the
profit or loss of the company for the financial year." However,
the Companies Act does not provide any specific accounting
principles to be observed.

## #6-15....English Group:  (3) The Netherlands

In the Netherlands the professional body is the Dutch Institute of Register Accountants comprising some 3,500 members. The
Dutch has a subsidiary group of student members because admission to membership in the Dutch Institute comes through study
with the Institute of Register Accountants. University graduates require less time with the Institute than those with no
college work.

Like the United Kingdom and Ireland, the Netherlands has its
Dutch Commercial Code whose provisions are similar to the
Irish. It requires proper record keeping and issuance of fair
and true financial statements. Also since these provisions are
general in nature, like the British and Irish, the Dutch Institute has promulgated accounting and auditing standards on its
own for the purpose of supplementing the Commercial Code.

The consequence of these proposed standards by the Dutch
Institute was the passage of the ACT ON ANNUAL ACCOUNTS in 1970
effective as of May 1, 1971. The important provisions of the
ACT include: (a) financial statements must abide by "sound business practice"; (b) based on full disclosure of the principles
used in stating assets, liabilities, profit, and loss; (c) prepared on the basis of consistency with full disclosure of
changes; (d) with financial statements presenting a "fair picture" of financial condition and operating results appropriate-

ly grouped and titled; and (e) statements must be prepared on a comparative basis with the preceding period.

Like the CCAB and the ASSC in Britain and Ireland, business executives, labor officials, and government officers have joined into an official study group. Its purpose has been to make recommendations for accounting standards similar to the SSAP and the U.S. FASB.

The Dutch accounting standards appear to be on as high a level as those in the U.S. and Britain. As we do, they separate the tax accounting from the financial accounting. They also use the equity method for intercorporate investments in the presentation of consolidated financial statements.

Just as the British, who as a result of the Sandilands Committee Report recommended in 1975 that historical cost valuation be replaced by current cost, the Dutch have incorporated the current replacement value method of valuing inventories and depreciable fixed assets as GAAP. In fact one of the largest Dutch corporations, Philips Company, has been using this method in its accounting practice since 1951. As previously indicated, where replacement cost is used, the resultant reserves are carried in the owners' equity section of the balance sheet. Finally, since 1970 with the passage of the ACT ON ANNUAL ACCOUNTS, statutory audits are compulsory, requiring that all audits be made by Register Accountants or other experts expressly deemed to be qualified.

## #6-16....English Group: (4) Denmark

The final country in the English cluster is Denmark whose professional body is the Danish Foreningen, with approximately 1,000 members. Like England, Ireland and the Netherlands, Denmark enacted its COMPANIES LEGISLATION on June 4, 1973, to be effective as of Jan. 1, 1974.

The basic provisions of the Danish Companies Law include similar requirements to those stated in the Dutch ACT, such as full disclosure in all financial statements, preparation of financial statements in accordance with good accounting practices, consistency, and fair picture of condition and results of operations.

Additionally, the Danish Companies Legislation makes provision for such specific items as (a) Marketable Securities, which may be valued at current market value; (b) capitalization of research and development costs where significant in amount, subject to minimum annual amortization of 20%; (c) capitalization of goodwill subject to minimum annual amortization of 10%; (d) fixed assets valuation subject to maximum cost; (e) treasury stock to be shown, if at all, at acquisition cost, and shown as an asset; and (f) current assets to be valued at lower of cost or market with write-ups allowed only if in accordance with "good accounting practices."

Like the British, Irish, and Dutch, the Danish Foreningen
established an accounting standards committee in Dec. 1973 to
make recommendations of "good accounting practices." As a result, the Auditing Standards Committee of the Danish Foreningen
has promulgated a series of recommendations on auditing standards and procedures on a par with the British and the Dutch.
Among the important provisions are the requirement of at least
one auditor by all companies and at least two auditors by
quoted companies, one of whom must be certified.

#6-17....French Group:    (5) France

There are two groups of professional accountants in France--
Experts Comptables, and the Commissaires Aux Comptes, known as
statutory auditors. The Experts Comptables are a more qualified
group of approximately 4,000 members whose primary concern is
opinion audits for the larger French corporations concerned
about attracting capital in international capital markets.  Experts Comptables may act as Commissaires Aux Comptes who have
their own institute.    The Commissaires serve the purpose of
statutory auditors who are required by law of April 1, 1975, to
be appointed as auditors for all French corporations whose capital exceeds 300,000 Francs.

France has been a leading proponent of uniform accounting as
evidenced by its PLAN COMPTABLE, the first of which was approved in Sept. 1947 by the Ministry of National Economy.   The 1947
Plan was revised in 1957 and again in 1977 and is somewhat comparable to the British Company Laws.

The PLAN was required by the law of Dec. 1958 to be applied
to over 50 trades and industries covered.  This was further implemented by a decree of April 1962 making it mandatory for
committees in the various industries to adapt the plan to their
respective industries.  Among the more important provisions of
the PLAN are (a) terminology definitions, (b) valuation principles, (c) explanation of forms of entries, (d) National Uniform
Chart of Accounts, (e) financial statements standard forms, and
(f) cost accounting methods. The Uniform Chart has further value as a requirement for schedules used for income tax returns,
and in addition serves as the basis for French accounting education.

As is the case with the British Group, prominent members of
the French accounting profession have joined together with
prominent members of industry, commerce, labor unions, and
high public officials to form 2 bodies-the Conseil National de
la Comptabilite (National Council of Accountancy), and L'Ordre
National des Experts Comptables (French Professional Institute)
-- to promulgate recommendations and opinions on accounting
principles to effectuate the Plan Comptable.  As with the Brit-

ish and   U.S. opinions, they are not mandatory like   the Danish
Companies Legislation.  The  opinions cover such   topics, inter
alia, as:  "Research and Development costs; Income and Expenditure Allocations; profit  sharing plans;  statements of sources
and application  of  funds; investment tax credits; value added
taxes; leasing; and employees welfare benefits accounting."

The PLAN results from the French Code de Commerce  which was
revised in July 1966 to make  more stringent  requirements for
statutory  auditors and require stricter financial  disclosure.
It was revised again in  1968 in  the direction of the U.S. SEC
laws by creating the Commission des Operations de Bourse (COB).
The  purpose of the COB  is to improve French financial reporting by  requiring opinion audits of  corporations attempting to
have their securities listed on the French Stock Exchange.

#6-18....French Group:   (6) Belgium

The professional group in Belgium is   the COLLEGE NATIONAL
DES  EXPERTES COMPTABLES, which like the French favors national
uniform accounting for Belgium.  The law in Belgium is the Commercial Code, which is patterned after the  French Code de Commerce.  Up to 1975 there were  no  laws relating  to accounting
practices so   that  annual  financial  statements were prepared
under the direction of the  corporate directors.  Because  they
were held responsible for reliability, it was customary to find
an overconservative  attitude in  statement presentation.   The
standard practices  followed  the pattern  required  by the tax
laws  which have set out the accounting  practices hence became
the principles generally followed.  As a result, tax and financial accounting coincided in Belgium.  One exception to the tax
laws resulted from the reporting requirement under the Conseils
d'Enterprises (Work Councils) which were created  by the law of
September 1948.

In  November 1973 the Work  Councils were  required by Royal
Decree  to receive periodic economic  and financial information
of the reporting companies. The reports to be submitted were to
include data on such  items as  productivity, production,  cost
methods, budgeting, personnel expense, research and development
costs.

In 1964 the College National des  Experts Comptables  recommended a National Accounting Plan  patterned  after the  French
PLAN favoring national uniform accounting.  However, it was not
until April of 1973 that  the  Central  Council of the Economy
issued a proposal for  a Plan Comptable General  Belge (Belgian
National Accounting Plan),  which became  effective  in October
1976 by Royal Decree. The  July 1975 law of the Commercial Code
stipulates in detail the content and form of accounting records
and financial statements.

The French Plan  Comptable 1968 revision was directed toward

control of corporations attempting to have their securities
listed on the French Stock Exchange and pursuant thereto the
COB was created. So too those companies in Belgium whose securities are traded publicly must appoint a Reviseur d'Enterprises
(RDE) whose functions parallel those of the COB in France. The
RDE must be a member of that institute which is recognized as
qualified accountants.

#6-19....French Group:  (7) Luxembourg

The professional body in Luxembourg, which did not receive
public regulation until a decree advanced in March of 1970, is
the Expertes Comptables. It consists of about two dozen members. Obviously the scope of accounting in Luxembourg is quite
limited because the country is small both in size and in economic magnitude. In recent years, however, there has been a great
surge of banking in this country making it a prominent financial center.

In the past the law regulating accounting, known as the Code
de Commerce, was somewhat similar to that in Belgium. Thus Luxembourg accounting, like the Belgium type, had its financial
accounting follow its taxation accounting, as there was no code
or other authority to set forth accounting principles and/or
standards.

The only requirement of the Luxembourg Code de Commerce was
that each corporation was required to appoint one or more statutory auditors. As seen above, because there were no strict
requirements regarding good accounting practices, the statutory
auditor was not required to be an Expert Comptable, of which
there were none before their establishment in March of 1970.
Nor was the statutory auditor even required to be a company
employee. However, each statutory auditor was required to own
the same specified number of qualification shares as a director
of the corporation. Where statutory auditors were not qualified, they were permitted to engage qualified accountants to
carry out the audit.

#6-20....German Group:  (8) Germany

The professional certified public accountants in Germany
are referred to as WIRTSCHAFTSPRUFER. This is one of the most
difficult positions to attain because of the stringency and
rigidity of German requirements for admission. Nowhere in the
world are the educational requirements higher than in Germany,
resulting in a far more limited number of CPA equivalents than
in other similar countries. All statutory auditor appointments
are required by law in Germany to go to Wirtschaftsprufer. The
German Institute comprises over 3,000 members.

Financial accounting in Germany is covered by three components: accounting principles, German Commercial Code, and Stock Corporation Law of 1965.  Accounting principles related to the rules of accounting for books, ledgers, etc., are referred to as Ordnungsmassige Buchfuhrung and are geared to tax laws and regulations.  Thus failure to keep records in accordance with tax regulations may result in refusal to recognize the records for tax purposes and permit the tax authorities to impose their own estimate as to what the tax should be.  Under such circumstances accountants hew to the line with record keeping to see that they are kept according to what is expected of the tax authorities.

The second component governing accounting principles in Germany is covered by the German Commercial Code, which provides the rules for preparation of annual financial statements and procedures for physical verification of assets and inventories. The German financial statements are similar to those of the English Group and the U.S., with the exception that disclosure through notes is absent from the statements, but is included in a Management Report. This is required by the Corporate Publicity Law of 1969 requiring corporations to issue them where they meet two of the three following requirements: (1) balance sheet statutory total exceeding 125 million German Marks; (2) annual sales exceeding 250 million German Marks; (3) an average monthly staff of more than 5,000 employees.

The third component governing accounting principles in Germany is the 1965 Stock Corporation Law which covers basic accounting principles for corporations. The Stock Corporation Law is subject to interpretations made by the German Institute of Accountants (Wirtschaftsprufer), the more prominent of which relate to: "writing off of deferred charges against income in the year in which incurred; nonrecognition of income tax allocation; minimum amortization of 20% of goodwill per year; retained earnings to be carried in a reserve account; not all pension liabilities fully recongized; and exclusion of foreign subsidiaries from consolidations."

Some of the regulations that are mandatory in the Stock Corporation Law are (a) current assets to be valued at lowest of cost, net realizable value, or replacement cost; (b) fixed assets to be stated at cost less depreciation; (c) intangible assets are capitalizable only if purchased from third parties; (d) all liabilities must be fully provided for; and (e) no recognition of unrealized profits.

In "Public Accounting in West Germany," Arlene Wenig and Godehard Puckler, in the JOURNAL OF ACCOUNTANCY, April 1982 issue, page 83-86, inter alia, note that:

Public accounting is a highly respected profession in West Germany. At present, there are approximately 3,900 WPs, 2% of whom are women.  There are also related professional classifications, such as Steuerberater (Stb) and Steurbe-

vollmachtiger (StBev)--certified tax advisers. The Great Depression was the catalyst leading to the emergence of public
accounting.    When   a premier bank   fell into bankruptcy, in
1931, the nation was shocked. One of the bank's largest customers, Nordwolle, was extended   credit   based   on falsified
financial statements. As a result, the Stock Corporation Law
was enacted in 1931, revised   in   1965,   and further changes
are expected shortly as   the Fourth, Seventh, and Eighth Directives of European Economic Community (EEC) are implemented.
     The EEC Fourth Directive issued   in 1978, pending imple-
mentation into   West   German law,   will modify   existing accounting rules and standards.   If two of the following three
criteria are   met under the Fourth Directive, a company will
have   to be audited:   (1) Net sales greater than DM 5.6 million; (2) Total   assets   greater   than DM 2.8   million; (3)
Average   number of employees more than   50.   Under   existing
West German   law, only statements of financial position   and
profit   and   loss   are necessary in a statutory   audit.   The
wording of the accountant's report and the   format and   captions of the financial statements are specified in the Stock
Corporation Law.
     On   April   9,   1981, the results of a survey prepared by
various West   German   business   organizations   on the effect
implementation of the   4th   Directive would have   on the accounting profession was reported in a leading German newspa-
per. Based on the survey, it was estimated that an additional   30,000 limited liability companies would be required   to
be audited under the   new regulations.   Approximately 43% of
the 30,000 companies are already being audited by WPs, leaving 17,000 to be   audited for the first time. It is believed
that   the West German   Parliament will   pass   a law in which
only WPs are qualified to audit financial statements.
     Enormous change is taking   place in the West German pub-
lic accounting profession.   The   next few years will be piv-
otal in the further development of public accounting in West
Germany. International accounting firms will find themselves
in greater demand as a result of these changes.
That the prediction made in the   preceding sentence   is already
bearing fruit may be evidenced   by a note in the JOURNAL OF AC-
COUNTANCY, February 1979, pages 28-30, which indicates that:
     Several major European accounting firms are holding dis-
cussions with the goal of establishing an organization which
they believe could be one of the world's largest in the profession.   Klynveld Kraayenshof, a major firm in Holland, and
Deutsche   Treuhand, a major firm in Germany, have had a series   of   meetings with Thomson McLintock & Co., a major firm
in the United Kingdom, initially formed at forming a European group based on these three firms.

Thomson McLintock is one of the five principal firms that form the foundation of the McLintock Main LaFrentz-International (MML) organization, which comprises 36 firms in 39 countries. Pelser, Hamelbert, Van Til & Co. of Holland, also one of the five principal firms of MML, has also been involved in the discussions as have Fiduciare de France in France, Fides in Switzerland and the Jespersen firm in Denmark.

Main LaFrentz & Co. in the U.S., Thorne Riddell & Co. in Canada and Hancock & Offner in Australia complete the five principal firms of MML. Klynveld Kraayenshof and Deutsche Treuhand are presently affiliated with other firms in the U.S., Canada, and Australia.

James A. Halsey, international partner for Main La Frentz, stressed that the talks are still exploratory and he observed that Main LaFrentz is considering joining the discussions. Archibald MacKay, chairman of Main LaFrentz, said the objective of the discussions would be a FEDERATION OR GROUPING and there wouldn't be any sharing of equity or profits among members. Current members of McLintock Main LaFrentz do not split equity or total fees but share costs of administration, supervision and quality control of MML.

## #6-21....(9) Italy

There are three organizations comprising the group of Italian professional accountants: College of Accountants and Commercial Experts; Order of Graduates in Economics and Commerce; and Official Auditors of ACCOUNTS (sindaci). Requirements for the College of Accountants and Commercial Experts is merely a high school diploma, which would make this group the equivalent of bookkeepers. The Order of Graduates in Economics and Commerce are required to attain a university degree.

Requirements for Official Auditors of Accounts are (1) Italian citizenship; (2) no less than five years' experience in a recognized professional organization, serving either as an accountant, attorney, director, statutory auditor, or administrative manager for a corporation which has a legal base of not less than 50 million Lira. A member of the Order of Graduates in Economics and Commerce need only have 3, instead of the 5, year requirement of experience. None of the three groups of accountants has issued any pronouncements regarding accounting or auditing standards.

At the beginning of the discussion of the groupings of accountants in the EEC, it was pointed out that the original nine EEC countries fall within three groups--British, French, and German--making up only eight of the countries. Italy was not included because it is strictly in the developmental stage. Accounting in Italy is in a jumbled and confused state. Investigation has disclosed that in much of the Italian accounting there exist such practices as decreased reports of sales revenue, understatement of assets and overstatement of liabilities of which many are of a fictitious character. All of this is directed toward the end of reducing profits to avoid taxes. There is no requirement of consistency in an absence of comparative results. There has been talk of Italian businesses keeping two sets of books, as there has in other Mid- and Near-East countries, where this is almost common knowledge.

The reasons for this state of affairs are basically two: (1) statements are primarily prepared only for tax purposes; and (2) the lack of any substantial numbers of stockholders and investors to whom reports must be issued. Thus it was not until 1974 that somewhat of an improvement took place in Italy. Laws were enacted, in June 1974 and March 1975, under the Civil Code, to establish a committee to control corporations whose stock is quoted on Italian Stock Exchanges. This committee, somewhat similar to the French COB and the RDE in Belgium, as well as the SEC in the U.S., is the Commissione Nazionale per LeSocieta e la Borsa (CONSOB).

The principal purpose of CONSOB is to attempt to give a greater degree of credibility to Italian financial statements than has heretofore been the case. The Civil Code also requires all limited liability companies whose capital is one million Lira or greater to submit annual statutory audits. The law is implemented by giving CONSOB complete control over the eligibility and appointment of auditing firms and requiring every audit appointment to be approved by it. Further, CONSOB has complete authority over accounting principles and auditing standards to be applied. One feature of the law is unique in that there is no other country that has such a requirement, viz., a system of independent auditor rotation.

No auditor can act for a period of longer than nine years, after which time there must be an interval of five years before there can be a reappointment. Also in companies whose capital exceeds 50 billion Lira legal capital, the appointment may be for one year; where the capital is between 10 and 50 billion Lira, it may be for two years; for all other companies, the appointment may be for four years. It should be interesting to observe the progress to be made accounting-wise in Italy under the CONSOB arrangement. Certainly if Italy is to be an integral factor in the EEC Community, this plan would be the least to be expected.

Some indication as to the progress being made by Italy may be gleaned from an article entitled "Accounting Italian-Style" appearing in WORLD, published by Peat, Marwick & Mitchell, issue of Autumn 1980, pages 2-12:

Italians have been wise in the ways of accounting at least since the Renaissance days of Fra Luca Paciolo, who wrote the first treatise on double-entry bookkeeping in 1494. Until the present day, however, the Italian business and financial communities treated accounting very much as a family matter. What passed for an audit was more of a statutory compliance review than the expression of a professional opinion. Independent audits were considered meddlesome interference in company affairs. But change is imminent.

Beginning in 1983, financial statement audits that adhere to international standards will become a legal requirement for all major Italian companies. Groundwork for this seemingly revolutionary change was laid through much of the 1970s, and can be pegged to the 1973 Tax Reform Act. One year later, Parliament created a securities regulatory authority known as CONSOB. Subsequent laws make audits mandatory for holding companies that control nearly half of Italian industry, including Alitalia, Alpha Romeo, steel, energy, utility, shipyards, telephone and television companies.

But is Italy really ready for generally accepted accounting principles? Foreign readers of the business press may be excused for thinking the Italian economy inefficient and undisciplined. For a good part of 3 decades the economy has supposedly been on the brink of collapse. Italians may not be surprised that it keeps humming right along, but nearly everyone else is.

The new accounting and auditing regulations are winning general acceptance in the Italian business community, again to the surprise of many foreign observers. Accountants are enthusiastic, welcoming the opportunity to build a profession from almost the ground up and to enjoy the rewards of an enormous untapped pool of public audit. The trouble is that for the next few years the demand for audit services will be far greater than the supply of auditors. George Loli, a partner in Peat Marwick's Milan office, believes the Italian accounting profession, with indispensable help from the international firms, will reach full maturity within ten years.

## IASC PROFESSIONAL BODIES

### #6-22....IASC Country Representatives

There were nine founding member countries represented on the IASC, to which a substantial number of members were admitted to associate status. It should be observed that every country represented in the IASC has a recognized professional accounting body of reputable standing. Since these bodies have had an impact on reporting standards, a listing of them and the countries they represent should be in order.

#6-23....Founder Member Countries

   The  founder member countries  and their respective  professional accountancy bodies are listed:
(1)  Australia - Institute of Chartered Accountants in Austral-
     ia, and Australian Society of Accountants
(2)  Canada - Canadian Institute of Chartered Accountants,  the
     General  Accounts' Association, and Society of Industrial
     Accountants of Canada
(3)  France -  Ordre des Experts  Comptables et des  Comptables
     Agrees
(4)  Germany  -  Institut  der Wirtschaftsprufer in Deutschland
     E. V. Wurtschaftspruferkammer
(5)  Japan - Japanese Institute of Certified Public Accountants
(6)  Mexico - Instituto Mexicano de Contadores Publicos, A.C.
(7)  Netherlands - Nederlands Instituut van Resiter-accountants
(8)  United Kingdom and  Ireland - Institute  of Chartered  Ac-
     countants  in England  and Wales,  Institute of  Chartered
     Accountants of  Scotland,  Institute of Chartered Account-
     ants  in  Ireland, Association  of Certified  Accountants,
     Institute of Cost and Management Accountants, and Charter-
     ed Institute of Public Finance and Accountancy
(9)  U.S.A.- American Institute of Certified Public Accountants

#6-24....Additional Member Countries

   The member countries and  their respective professional  accountancy bodies admitted by 1979 were:
(10) Bangladesh - Institute of Chartered Accountants of Bangla-
     desh
(11) Belgium -  College National des Experts Comptables de Bel-
     gique, Institut des  Reviseurs d' Enterprises,  Institut
     Belge des Reviseurs de Banques
(12) Denmark - Foreningen Af Statsautoriserede Revisorer
(13) Fiji - Fiji Institute of Accountants
(14) Ghana - Ghana Institute of Chartered Accountants
(15) Greece-Institute of Certified Public Accountants of Greece
(16) Hong Kong - Hong Kong Society of Accountants
(17) India - Institute of Chartered Accountants of India
(18) Israel-Institute of Certified Public Accountants in Israel
(19) Jamaica - Institute of Chartered Accountants of Jamaica
(20) Korea - Korean Institute of Certified Public Accountants
(21) Luxembourg - Ordre des Experts Comptables Luxembourgeois
(22) Malaysia - Malaysian Association of  Certified Public Ac-
     countants
(23) Malta - Malta Institute of Accountants
(24) New Zealand - New Zealand Society of Accountants
(25) Nigeria - Institute of Chartered Accountants of Nigeria
(26) Pakistan  - Pakistan Institute  of Industrial Accountants,

Institute of Chartered Accountants of Pakistan
(27) Philippines  -  Philippine Institute of  Certified  Public
     Accountants
(28) Sierra Leone - Association of Accountants in Sierra Leone
(29) Singapore - Singapore Society of Accountants
(30) South Africa - National  Council  of Chartered Accountants
     of South Africa
(31) Sri Lanka- Institute of Chartered Accountants of Sri Lanka
(32) Trinidad and Tobago - Institute of  Chartered  Accountants
     of Trinidad and Tobago
(33) Yugoslavia - Yogoslav Association of Accountant and Finan-
     cial Experts, and Social Accounting Service of Yugoslavia
(34) Zambia - Zambia Association of Accountants
(35) Zimbabwe - Zimbabwe Society of Chartered Accounts

## #6-25...Relationship of IASC Member Countries
## to Type of Political Order

A 1978 survey made by Freedom House, a nonpartisan voluntary
organization, rated all the nations in the world by  the degree
of freedom on the basis of political and civil  rights it gives
its citizens  (Dec. 4, 1978,  U.S. NEWS &  WORLD REPORT,  pages
32-33).  All  nations  are  divided into three  groups  -- FREE,
PARTLY FREE, and NOT FREE.
There were 43 nations listed in the  FREE GROUP:  Australia,
Austria, Bahamas,  Barbados,  Belgium,  Botswana, Canada, Colom-
bia, Costa  Rica, Denmark, Fiji, Finland, France, Gambia, Great
Britain, Greece,  (Grenada), Iceland, India,  Ireland,  Israel,
Italy, Jamaica,  Japan, Luxembourg,  Malta, (Mauritius), Nauru,
Netherlands, New Zealand, Norway, Papua-New  Guinea,  Portugal,
Spain, Sri  Lanka, (Surinam), Sweden, Switzerland, Trinidad and
Tobago, (Turkey), U.S.A., Venezuela, and West Germany.
The PARTLY FREE GROUP comprises 48 nations: Bahrain, Bangla-
desh,  Bhutan, (Bolivia),  Brazil, Comoros,  Cyprus,  Djibouti,
(Dominican Republic),  (Ecuador), Egypt, El  Salvador, (Ghana),
Guatemala, Guyana, Honduras, Indonesia, Kenya, Kuwait, Lebanon,
Lesotho,  (Liberia),  (Madagascar), Malaysia, Maldives, Mexico,
Morocco, Nepal, Nicaragua, (Nigeria), (Pakistan), (Peru), Phil-
ippies, Qatar, Senegal, (Seychelles), Sierra Leone, Singapore,
South Africa,  (South Korea),  Swaziland, (Syria),  (Taiwan),
(Tonga), United Arab Emirates, Upper Volta, Western Samoa,  and
Zambia.
The NOT FREE GROUP consists of 64 nations:  Afghanistan, Al-
bania, Algeria, Angola, Argentina, Benin, Bulgaria, Burma, Bur-
undi, (Cambodia), Cameroon, Cape Verde, Central African Empire,
Chad,  (Chile), China,  Congo, Cuba, Czechoslovakia, East  Ger-
many, Equatorial -Guinea, Ethiopia, Gabon,  Guinea, Guinea-Bis-
sau, Haiti, Hungary, (Iran), Iraq, (Ivory Coast), Jordan, Laos,
Libya, Malawi, Mali,  Mauritania,  Mongolia, Mozambique, Niger,

North Korea, Oman, (Panama), (Paraguay), (Poland), Rumania, Rwanda, Sao Tome and Principe, Saudi Arabia, Somalia, (Sudan), Tanzania, (Thailand), Togo, (Transkei), (Tunisia), (Uganda), U.S.S.R., (Uruguay), Vietnam, Yemen-Aden, Yemen Sana, Yugoslavia, Zaire, and (Zimbabwe).

In concluding this chapter, it should be noted that of the member country professional bodies of IASC, eight of the nine founder member countries (all except Mexico) are listed in the FREE NATION GROUP, and Mexico, the ninth, is in the PARTLY FREE GROUP. Thirteen of the newly admitted member countries are listed in the FREE NATION GROUP, and eleven countries in the PARTLY FREE GROUP. Only two of the new member countries--Zimbabwe and Yugoslavia--are listed in the NOT FREE NATION GROUP.

Thus, of a total of 35 IASC member countries, 2 are Not Free, 12 are Partly Free, and 21 are Free Nations; or, 33 are either Free or Partly Free, and only 2 Not Free. Some of the classifications may be debatable by political scientists. But certainly there is sufficient evidence to warrant some sort of inference that there is a strong correlation between good accounting practices and the establishment of professional accounting bodies, as well as the nature of the democracy of the government involved.

In an update of the foregoing study made by Freedom House (reported July 13, 1982 in the CHICAGO TRIBUNE), some slight shiftings took place in a handful of countries, but substantially the classification remained the same. Seven new island countries that sprung into existence were added to the Free Group: Dominica, Kiribati, Solomons, St. Lucia, St. Vincent, Tuvalu, and Vanuatu. Five of the Partly Free Countries were advanced to the Free Group: Dominican Republic, Ecuador, Ghana, Nigeria, and Peru. Three countries were demoted from the Free Countries to partly Free Countries: Grenada, Mauritius, and Turkey. Thirteen countries were advanced from Not Free to Partly Free: Chile, Iran, Ivory Coast, Poland, Sudan, Thailand, Transkei, Tunisia, Uganda, Uruguay, Panama, Paraguay, and Zimbabwe. A big jump down from Free to Not Free was Surinam. And 7 countries went down from Partly Free to Not Free: Bolivia, Cambodia, Liberia, Madagascar, Pakistan, Seychelles, and Syria.

## IFAC GUIDELINES

### #6-26....IFAC Practitioner Counterpart of IASC

With the admission of two new member bodies to the IFAC in 1984--the Norges Registrerte Revisorers Forening and the Federacion de Colegios de Contadores Publicos del Peru--the IFAC totals 85 bodies from 63 countries, representing 800,000 professional accountants, with permanent offices at 540 Madison Avenue, New York.

## #6-27....IFAC Guideline Committees

In order to coordinate the activities of such a vast number of members, the IFAC has set up three committees to issue guidelines in connection with international accounting practices: Auditing Practices; Ethics; and Education. Each of the three committees is commissioned to issue GUIDELINES for their particular area.

The objective of the INTERNATIONAL AUDITING GUIDELINES is to help improve the degree of uniformity of auditing practices throughout the world. The objective of the INTERNATIONAL ETHICS GUIDELINES is to attempt to coordinate practices of accountants world-wide. And the objective of the INTERNATIONAL EDUCATION GUIDELINES is to promote uniformity of practice among accountants throughout the world.

## #6-28....International Auditing Guidelines

By the end of 1984, the International Auditing Practices Committee issued the following 18 International Auditing Guidelines:

#1 Preface and Guideline: Objective and Scope of the Audit of Financial Statements (1980)
#2 Audit Engagement Letters (1980)
#3 Basic Principles Concerning an Audit (1980)
#4 Planning (1981)
#5 Using the Work of Another Auditor (1981)
#6 Study and Evaluation of the Accounting System & Related Internal Controls in Connection with an Audit (1981)
#7 Control of the Quality of Audit Work (1981)
#8 Audit Evidence (1982)
#9 Documentation (1982)
#10 Using the Work of an Internal Auditor (1982)
#11 Fraud and Error (1982)
#12 Analytical Review (1983)
#13 The Auditor's Report on Financial Statements (1983)
#14 Other Information in Documents Containing Audited Technical Statements (1984)
#15 Auditing in an EDP Environment (1984)
#16 Computer-Assisted Audit Techniques (1984)
#17 Related Party Transactions (1984)
#18 Using the Work of an Expert (1984)

## #6-29....International Ethics Guidelines

The International Ethics Committee issued the following seven International Ethics Statements of Guidelines:

#1 Statement on Advertising, Publicity & Solicitation(1981)
#2 Statement on Professional Competence (1981)

#3  Statement on Integrity, Objectivity & Independence(1982)
#4  Statement on Confidentiality (1982)
#5  Ethics Across International Borders (1983)
#6  Statement on Conditions for Acceptance of Appointment
    When Another Accountant is Already Carrying Out Work for
    Same Client (1983)
#7  Statement on Conditions for Superseding Another Account-
    ant (1983)

## #6-30....International Education Guidelines

These education guidelines will have influence on practice
as well as in the academic sphere. The International Education
Committee has issued only four Guidelines in three years:
#1  Guideline on Prequalification Education & Training(1982)
#2  Guideline on Continuing Professional Education (1982)
#3  Guideline on Test of Professional Competence (1984)
#4  Guideline on the Core of Knowledge--Professional Sub-
    jects (1984)

### SUMMARY OF FOOTNOTE REFERENCES
(References are to Paragraph #'s)

#6-1 thru #6-11:   "Accounting Reporting Standards," adapted from
        Norlin G. Rueschhoff, INTERNATIONAL ACCOUNTING AND FINANCIAL
        REPORTING, 1976, Praeger Publishers, Inc., by permission.
#6-4    AICPA, PROFESSIONAL ACCOUNTING IN 30 COUNTRIES, pp. 653-654.
        Copyright © 1975 by the American Institute of Certified Pub-
        lic Accountants, Inc.  Reprinted with permission.
#6-5    Ibid., pp. 585-586, by permission
#6-6    Ibid., p. 426, by permission
#6-7    Ibid., p. 177, by permission
#6-8    Ibid., pp. 731-734, by permission
#6-11   AICPA, THE CPA LETTER (September 1979)
#6-20   Arlene Wenig and Godehard Puckler, "Public Accounting in
        West Germany," JOURNAL OF ACCOUNTANCY (April 1982): 83-86.
        Copyright © 1982 by the American Institute of Certified Pub-
        lic Accountants, Inc.  Opinions expressed in the JOURNAL  OF
        ACCOUNTANCY are those of editors and contributors.  Publica-
        tion in the JOURNAL OF ACCOUNTANCY does not constitute en-
        dorsement by the AICPA or its committees.
#6-20   JOURNAL OF ACCOUNTANCY (February 1979): 28-30
#6-21   "Accounting Italian-Style," Peat, Marwick, Mitchell & Co.,
        WORLD (Autumn 1980): 2-12
#6-25   U.S. NEWS & WORLD REPORT (December 4, 1978): 32-33
#6-25   "Freedom House Report," CHICAGO TRIBUNE (July 13, 1982)

### BIBLIOGRAPHY

Anderson, J.V.R.  "True and Fair in the EEC," THE ACCOUNTANT, 174
    (March 4, 1976): 284-286

Barrett, M. Edgar. "Financial Reporting Practices: Disclosure and Comprehensiveness in an International Setting," JOURNAL OF ACCOUNTING RESEARCH (Spring 1976): 10-26

Chang, L.S.; Most, K.S.; and Brain, C.W. "The Utility of Annual Reports: An International Study," JOURNAL OF INTERNATIONAL BUSINESS STUDIES (Spring-Summer 1983): 63-84

Collins, John D. "Understanding Europe's Statutory Audit Requirements," Peat, Marwick, Mitchell & Co., WORLD (Autumn 1974)

Court, Peter. "The Multinational Audit Team: Who Holds the Reins?", ACCOUNTANCY, 91 (October 1980): 85-88

Crum, William F. "The European Public Accountant," MANAGEMENT ACCOUNTING, 56 (March 1975): 41-55

Dahmash, N.H. "Public Auditing Developments in the Arab States: A Comparative Study," INTERNATIONAL JOURNAL OF ACCOUNTING EDUCATION & RESEARCH (Fall 1982): 89-114

Dev, Susan and Eno, Inanga. "Educating Accountants in Nigeria," ACCOUNTANCY, 90 (April 1979): 127-129

Fantl, Irving L. "Control and the Internal Audit in the Multinational Firm," INTERNATIONAL JOURNAL OF ACCOUNTING EDUCATION & RESEARCH, 11 (Fall 1975): 57-65

Fitzgerald, Richard D. "International Harmonization of Accounting and Reporting," INTERNATIONAL JOURNAL OF ACCOUNTING EDUCATION & RESEARCH, 17 (Fall 1981): 21-32

Flint, David. "The Audit of Local Authority in Scotland," THE ACCOUNTANTS MAGAZINE, 85 (August 1981): 257-258

Kullberg, Duane R. "Management of a Multinational Public Accounting Firm," INTERNATIONAL JOURNAL OF ACCOUNTING EDUCATION & RESEARCH, 17 (Fall 1981): 1-6

Liick, W. "The Impact of International Standards and Other Developments on the German Accounting Profession," INTERNATIONAL JOURNAL OF ACCOUNTING EDUCATION & RESEARCH (Fall 1982):45-56

Mueller, Gerhard and Walker, Lauren. "The Coming of Age of Transnational Financial Reporting," JOURNAL OF ACCOUNTANCY (July 1976): 67-74

Nobes, C.W. "A Judgmental International Classification of Financial Reporting Practices," JOURNAL OF BUSINESS FINANCE AND ACCOUNTING (Spring 1983): 1-19

Pomeranz, Felix. "International Auditing Standards," INTERNATIONAL JOURNAL OF ACCOUNTING (Fall 1975): 1-13

Salas, Cesar. "Accounting Education and Practice in Spanish Latin America," INTERNATIONAL JOURNAL OF ACCOUNTING, 3, No. 1 (Fall 1967): 67-85

Stamp, Edward and Moonitz, Maurice. INTERNATIONAL AUDIT STANDARDS. London: Prentice-Hall, Intl., 1978

## THEORY QUESTIONS
(Question Numbers are Keyed to Text Paragraph #'s)

#6-3  Discuss the rationale of Audit Certification.
#6-4  Make a comparative analysis of the following audit reports: (a) Short Form, (b) Fairness & Truth, (c) True &

Fair View, (d) Simplistic, (e) Long Form.
#6-11  Discuss the importance of high standards in the interna-
       tional investment arena.
#6-13  What    is    the Consultative Committee    on    Accountancy
       Bodies?  What is the Accounting  Standards Steering Com-
       mittee (ASSC) and to which U.S. body is it similar? What
       are  Statements of  Standard Accounting Practice  (SSAP)
       and what U.S. pronouncements are they similar to?
#6-14  What  is the  status  of professional   accountancy in the
       English Cluster of EEC countries: (a) Ireland, (b) Neth-
       erlands, (c) Denmark?
#6-17  Discuss the impact of the Plan Comptable on professional
       accounting in France.
#6-18  What  is  the status of professional  accountancy in Bel-
       gium and Luxembourg?
#6-20  Why  is the West  German accounting  profession regarded
       as superior amongst all the countries in the world? Dis-
       cuss the  three  components  of financial accounting  in
       Germany.
#6-21  Why has Italian accounting failed to measure  up to that
       of other EEC countries and  how is the Italian situation
       improving?  Discuss the  impact of CONSOB on Italian ac-
       counting.
#6-25  Discuss the relationship between professional accounting
       in the IASC member countries and the nature of the poli-
       tical order existing in them.
#6-26  Discuss the impact that the IFAC has had on Internation-
       al Accounting.

## EXERCISES

### EX-6-1  (CPA EXAM, 11/44, AUDITING, #8)

You are making  an examination  of the  accounts of an importer
as  of Dec.  31, 1943.  Draft a form of confirmation letter for
submission to the sole bank with which your  client  does business.

### EX-6-2  (CPA EXAM, 11/82, AUDITING, #23)

Morgan, CPA, is  the principal auditor for a multinational corporation.  Another CPA has examined and reported on  the financial statements of a significant subsidiary of the corporation.
Morgan is satisfied with the independence and professional rep-
utation of the other  auditor, as well  as the  quality  of the
other auditor's examination. With respect to Morgan's report on
the consolidated financial statements, taken as a whole, Morgan
   a. Must <u>not</u> refer to the examination of the other auditor.
   b. Must refer to the examination of the other auditor.

c. May refer to the examination of the other auditor.
d. May refer to the examination of the other auditor, in which case Morgan must include in the auditor's report on the consolidated financial statements a qualified opinion with respect to the examination of the other auditor.

## EX-6-3  (CPA EXAM, 11/30, AUDITING, #5)

The following certificate was appended to the consolidated balance sheet of the Blank Corporation and its subsidiaries:

"We have examined the books and accounts of the Blank Corporation and its domestic and South American subsidiaries and affiliated companies for the year ended December 31, 1929, and have had submitted to us the audited statements of the remaining foreign subsidiary companies. The assets and liabilities of subsidiary companies other than the South American companies are embodied in the above balance sheet. South American and affiliated companies are treated as investments. In accordance with the decision of the directors, no charge for depreciation of plants was made during the year. We certify that upon the foregoing basis the balance sheet is in our opinion correctly prepared so as fairly to set forth the financial position of the companies at December 31, 1929."

What qualifications are there in the above certificate?

## PROBLEMS

## P-6-1  (CPA EXAM, 11/67, AUDITING, #9)

Ivy Corporation has a subsidiary company in a foreign country. An independent auditor in that country issued an unqualified opinion on the subsidiary's financial statements. Although the CPA is unaware of the standards of the practice of public accountancy in the foreign country, he is willing to accept full responsibility for the independent auditor's opinion on the subsidiary company's financial statements because he believes Ivy Corporation's internal staff performed an adequate check on the operations of the subsidiary company during the year. The CPA would be willing to express an unqualified opinion on the financial statements of Ivy Corporation alone, but he must express an opinion on the consolidated statements of Ivy Corporation and its subsidiaries.

What type of opinion should be expressed for Ivy Corporation's consolidated statements?

**P-6-2** (CPA EXAM, 11/69, AUDITING, #6)

Pace Corporation, an audit client of yours, is a manufacturer of consumer products and has several wholly-owned subsidiaries in foreign countries which are audited by other independent auditors in those countries. The financial statements of all subsidiaries were properly consolidated in the financial statements of the parent company and the foreign auditor's reports were furnished to your CPA firm.

You are now preparing your auditor's opinion on the consolidated balance sheet and statement of income and retained earnings for the year ended June 30, 1969. These statements were prepared on a comparative basis with those of last year.

**Required**:

a. How would you evaluate and accept the independence and professional reputations of the foreign auditors?

b. Under what circumstances may a principal auditor assume responsibility for the work of another auditor to the same extent as if he had performed the work himself?

c. Assume that both last year and this year you were willing to utilize the reports of the other independent auditors in expressing your opinion on the consolidated fin. stmts. but were unwilling to take full responsibility for performance of the work underlying their opinions. Assuming your examination of the parent company's financial statements would allow you to render an unqualified opinion, prepare (1) the necessary disclosure to be contained in the scope paragraph and (2) the complete opinion paragraph of your auditor's report.

d. What modification(s), if any, would be necessary in your auditor's opinion if the financial statements for the prior year were unaudited?

# PART II


## SECTION TWO

## MICRO INTERNATIONAL FINANCIAL ACCOUNTING PRACTICE

# The Basic Ingredient in International Business Transactions — Foreign Exchange

NATURE AND CHARACTERISTICS OF FOREIGN EXCHANGE

#7-1....Need for Foreign Exchange

If all the trading in the world were conducted only on a within-the-country basis, and there was no business transacted between individuals or enterprises in one country with those in another, there would be no international transactions. In such case, all business would be transacted on the basis of the local currency of the country in which the transaction took place and there would be no need for foreign currency.

However, it is common knowledge that business is transacted not only by the nations between themselves but also by individuals and enterprises in different countries. Under such circumstances, two alternatives exist with respect to payments to be made in international transactions: (1) either the parties to the transaction may refuse to recognize the validity of the currency of each others' country; or (2) they may be willing to recognize and accept the foreign currency in the consummation of the transaction.

The former situation would result in bartering by which each party would merely transfer the commodity or service it has to offer in exchange for the commodity or service to be received. Bartering, of course, was the method used in the early stages of the development of our economic societies, and before international trade became sophisticated. The second alternative would be the recognition of the foreign currencies relating to the parties involved in the transaction and their willingness to accept them in payment.

Obviously, of the two alternatives, the recognition of foreign currency is by far the more practical, convenient, efficient and logical, especially in the light of the shrinkage of the globe due to the jet age. And, if the second alternative is to be recognized as the most effective method, then it becomes necessary to have foreign currency, or Exchange, as it is commonly known.

## #7-2...Dual Nature of International Business Transactions

Using the simplest illustration, when a tourist desires to make a purchase in a foreign country, he in essence must engage in two transactions: first he must, with the currency of his own country, buy the foreign currency of the country in which the goods he desires to buy are sold; and then he engages in the second transaction by transferring the foreign currency he has purchased as payment for the goods he buys priced in the foreign currency. Because the foreign currency is first purchased from the currency dealer and then used to pay for the merchandise or services purchased, currency assumes the nature of a commodity that is freely bought and sold.

## FOREIGN EXCHANGE MARKETS

## #7-3....Need for Foreign Exchange Markets

Since bartering would not be able to absorb the volume and extent of current international trade, thereby requiring the use of foreign exchange, and since foreign exchange is in the nature of a commodity, it therefore becomes necessary to facilitate the flow of the various foreign currencies in the world. This has been accomplished through the establishment of FOREIGN EXCHANGE MARKETS, similar to commodity and stock markets.

The DUAL NATURE of international business transactions, as illustrated above in connection with a tourist, also applies to trading transactions such as imports and exports. The importer must buy foreign currency with which payment will be made to the foreign vendor, and the exporter will convert the foreign currency he has received from the sale into his own local currency. In order to carry out these currency conversions it is necessary to deal with the foreign exchange market mechanism.

The foreign exchange markets are especially a sine qua non because of foreign exchange, which simply is the national currency of another country. Since each country has its own national currency, and each national currency has its own value which most likely will be different than that of any other country, it therefore becomes necessary to give each currency a value relative to that of other currencies, in order to reduce them to a common denominator. This relative value is known as the EXCHANGE RATE. To have any semblance of order there must be someone who can marshall together all currencies and relate their respective values to each of the other currencies in the form of an exchange rate. The mechanism for performing this function of establishing exchange rates is the FOREIGN EXCHANGE MARKET.

## #7-4....Purposes of Foreign Exchange Markets

Foreign exchange and its market come into play only where international relations are involved. If we did not have tourism, trading, capital investments, economic missions, political ties, military involvements, or diplomatic groups in foreign countries, there would be no need for foreign exchange or foreign exchange markets. It is the foreign exchange market that guarantees that foreign exchange will be able to be purchased and sold freely in recognized facilities, without which condition international trade would hardly be able to function. In order to have a proper comprehension of how the foreign exchange markets operate, how foreign exchange rates are set, and what causes foreign exchange to fluctuate, there should be an understanding of how the markets were established, their history and development, how they operate, and the effect of external forces on them.

## #7-5...History of Development of Foreign Exchange Markets

In the article "Early Accounting Problems of Foreign Exchange," in the ACCOUNTING REVIEW, Oct. 1944, pp. 381-407, Raymond de Roover points out that foreign exchange dealings had their origins with the beginning of foreign trade and of coinage. Foreign trade and exchange was carried over into the Middle Ages, and the problems encountered at that time are stated by R.G. Hawtrey, the former Asst. Sec. of the U.K. Treasury, in "Money and Money of Account," in THE ACCOUNTANT, Jan. 6, 1940, page 15:

In the Middle Ages international traders were required to determine the fineness and weight of foreign coins and they would be accepted only for their intrinsic value, viz.; metal content. Various devices therefore had to be developed to avoid having to receive and transport metal more often than was unavoidable. The way to get around this was for international traders to give one another credit for a short period and settle accounts at the great international fairs. Or a merchant would have an agent or factor in a foreign country with which he traded. The agent would receive and hold money on a merchant's account and the merchant could direct him by letter to whom to make payments.

Eventually merchants took to giving such directions not to their own agents but to the foreign purchasers of the goods, and the letters giving such directions acquired the characteristics of the modern negotiable instrument known as the Bill of Exchange.

Notwithstanding the above arrangements, there always appeared to be some balances resulting from the international transactions, and, to meet this contingency, the Bank of Amsterdam was established in the early 17th century to attempt to find a method of getting around the necessity of reassessing the value of different coins whenever they were used in the settlement of obligations.

Thus the Bank of Amsterdam was not established as a lending institution but rather to settle bills of exchange by silver deposits. By retaining the silver deposits, it was able to settle its liabilities by the silver reserve by setting the silver content as the unit of measurement for settling its accounts. In this way it created the modus operandi for establishing a money of account for international transactions, which served as a pattern for the modern foreign exchange market. Thus the net effect, as Hawtrey points out, was that "the Bank of Amsterdam was simply a debtor of its depositors, and the essence of the system was that the debt due to the depositor was an asset that could be assigned by him to someone else, and so used as a means of payment." Continuing with the history of the development of Foreign Exchange Markets, Mr. Hawtrey goes on:

Banks were established in imitation of the Bank of Amsterdam at other centres, such as Hamburg, Venice and Nuremburg. But in England the problem of providing a convenient medium for the settlement of mercantile transactions was solved on different lines.

In the absence of any officially established central agency, the function of assessing the value of consignments of coins devolved on the goldsmiths. It was part of their business not only to appraise but to buy gold and silver, and in the 17th century the London goldsmiths adopted the practice of allowing merchants and others who sold them gold and silver to leave the proceeds of sale on deposit with them. As soon as a debt due from a goldsmith became recognized as the most convenient medium of payment in trade, the goldsmiths found they could create this medium out of nothing.

If a merchant wanted to make a payment, he need not deposit gold or silver with the goldsmith, or sell something to another trader in exchange for a credit with a goldsmith. If he had good security to offer, he could BORROW from the goldsmith. That was an exchange of debts. The merchant became indebted to the goldsmith for a sum payable at an agreed future date, while the goldsmith became indebted to the merchant for a sum payable on demand, which the mercahnt could draw upon, that is to say, he could assign the goldsmith's debt to another creditor and so use it as a means of payment.

It is significant that the early goldsmiths in London did not establish their own separate unit of account but used the standard measures for pounds, shillings and pence--the English currency. In this context it should be noted that there are two

methods by which records of international accounts may be kept:
first, in relationship to some national currency generally
recognized as the base currency; or by a fictitious currency
unit agreed to by the parties, as will be seen later.

## #7-6....Constituency of Foreign Exchange Markets

To accomplish the purpose of the Foreign Exchange Market to
facilitate the flow of money credits and currency in international transactions, capitals and major cities around the world
(such as London, New York, Paris, Frankfurt, Rome, Madrid,
etc.) have established markets directly interested in foreign
exchange. These markets consist of banks dealing in foreign
currency and credits, foreign exchange traders, money changers,
and foreign exchange clubs. It is thus readily apparent that
the foreign exchange market is indeed the most basic element
involved in international business transactions.

## #7-7....Objectives of the Foreign Exchange Market

The foreign exchange market determines the rate at which one
currency is exchanged for another currency. Foreign exchange
rates as established by this market are used for the determination of exchange prices in the recording of international
transactions. Foreign exchange rates are also used to measure
the amounts of foreign currency items, such as unsettled open
account balances which are reported in financial statements.
Since exchange rates fluctuate, foreign currency may go down in
value causing risks especially with the holding of open account
balances. For such a situation, as will be seen later, a forward market has been created which, similar to the case of
grain futures, permits the hedging against such exchange rate
risks.

## FOREIGN EXCHANGE TERMINOLOGY

## #7-8....Foreign Exchange Definition

Foreign exchange has loosely been used to have a dual connotation, which is particularly the case with the term EXCHANGE.
In its ordinary signification, exchange means the trading of
property between two or more parties; in this sense foreign
exchange means engaging in a transaction whereby the party desiring the exchange is trading his home currency for the currency of another country for the purpose of using the acquired
currency to pay for merchandise bought or to be bought in the
foreign country in that country's currency.
The term foreign exchange has also been used loosely quite

universally to simply mean foreign currency, in which case the
term "exchange" is being used as synonymous with "currency."
Under this signification it is commonly understood that foreign exchange consists simply of the monies of another country
offered for sale in the money market of a given country. Thus
the net effect of the exchange is that the exchanger is merely
holding currency of a foreign country in lieu of his local
currency that he exchanges for it, i.e., foreign exchange is
tantamount to being foreign money or currency.

Thus in the U.S., the purchase or sale of British Pounds
Sterling or Mexican Pesos for U.S. Dollars constitutes foreign
exchange. In a similar way the purchase or sale of U.S. Dollars
in the London market would constitute foreign exchange to the
British businessman.

#7-9....Classification of Currency

Currency may be designated as local or foreign. As used
hereafter, Local Currency is defined as currency of a specific
domicile country. It is distinguished from Foreign Currency,
which is any currency other than the local currency. For example, the local currency of West Germany is the German Mark; for
Great Britain, the Pound Sterling. However, from the standpoint
of the U.S., both German Marks and British Pounds Sterling are
foreign currencies. Also, in West Germany the Pound Sterling is
a foreign currency.

#7-10....Foreign Currency and International Transactions

Not all international business transactions require the exchange of local currency for foreign currency. A U.S. exporter
may sell goods to a French importer and receive payment in
French Francs. If the U.S. exporter then uses the Francs to
purchase French goods which he imports, no further foreign exchange is required inasmuch as payment is made in Francs, which
of course is the local currency of France.

#7-11....Foreign Exchange Conversion

Accountants also are concerned with the recording of foreign
exchange transactions and of transactions involving foreign and
local currencies. When one currency is actually exchanged for
another, the exchange is referred to as a CONVERSION. Thus conversion is the term used to describe money-changing, and in
such case, in essence the foreign money is regarded as similar
to a commodity being purchased in the same vein as a purchase
of merchandise.

## #7-12....Foreign Exchange Translation

Accountants must also record transactions in foreign currencies where no money-changing (i.e., no conversion) takes place.
Because two or more currencies may be involved, in order to
avoid confusion the currency must be identified as to situs or
domicile. In this respect currency is designated as Local or
Foreign.

Thus in the illustration above of a U.S. exporter billing
the French importer in French Francs for his goods, the transaction is recorded in U.S. Dollars, the currency of his domicile enterprise. It therefore becomes necessary to TRANSLATE
the French Franc billing into U.S. Dollars in order to record
the billing on the exporter's records in terms of dollars. In
such case the foreign currency is said to be TRANSLATED into
the currency commonly used by the businessman. In addition,
where financial statements are expressed in terms of foreign
currency, they must be translated into the local currency to be
meaningful in the domicile country.

## #7-13....Distinction Between Conversion and Translation

It is therefore important to make a distinction between the
terms CONVERSION and TRANSLATION. In conversion, a transaction
for the purchase or sale of foreign money, with local money
being given or received, is involved. In translation, no currency transaction whatever takes place; there is merely a restatement of a foreign currency value or figure on the records
of the enterprise in terms of local currency.

## INSTRUMENTS OF FOREIGN EXCHANGE*

## #7-14....Bank Transfers

The main device for effecting foreign exchange transactions
is the BANK TRANSFER. The principal method of transferring a
deposit to or from a bank abroad is either by a CABLE TRANSFER
across the ocean or a TELEGRAPHIC TRANSFER over land. Such
transfers can also be made by mail. But, the speed of a cable
or telegraphic transfer gives them tremendous advantage over
the mail transfer.

------

*See Summary of Footnote References -- #7-14 thru #7-23

## #7-15....Cable Transfers

A cable transfer is an order transmitted by a domestic bank by cable to a foreign correspondent bank to make payment to a designated payee. It directs the foreign bank to debit the account of the seller of a particular currency and to credit the account of the payee designated by the buyer. Thus the U.S. exporter who receives a Paris bank deposit in French Francs in payment of his goods may desire to sell the Francs by means of a cable transfer to his New York bank account in Dollars. The conversion rate for the transfer is determined by the current market rate between the two currencies. If the exporter has no French Franc bank account, he may ask the payer to transfer the amount by cable directly to his New York bank, which purchases the exchange and credits the equivalent dollars to the exporter's account. The cost of sending the cable is charged by the bank to the sender.

## #7-16....Bills of Exchange

In addition to the cable, telegraphic, or mail transfers of bank balances, there are various bills of exchange used in foreign exchange instruments. Among these, checks, money orders, and sight drafts effect immediate cash payments; time drafts provide for deferred payments.

## #7-17....Personal Checks and Money Orders

Personal checks have become increasingly important as a means of international cash payment, and those of reputable international corporations are commonly accepted in all parts of the world. Dividend and bond interest payments are often sent by check to foreign stockholders and bondholders as well as to domestic holders. Travelers checks and money orders in desirable hard currencies are also widely accepted. The acceptor of the check normally sells it to his local bank for local currency. The local bank in turn sends the check to its foreign correspondent bank in the country of the check's currency. There it is presented to the drawee bank for payment and credit to the correspondent bank's account.

## #7-18....Bank Drafts

Bank drafts, similar to checks, are used when a foreigner wants to remit funds directly without going through a foreign bank. A New York bank may sell a French purchaser of U.S. goods a draft on the bank's balance abroad. Many U.S. banks have overseas branches for such purposes. The draft may then be mailed directly to the U.S. exporter, who is able to cash it like any check.

## #7-19....Sight Drafts

Other bills of exchange regularly used in international commerce are sight drafts and time drafts. A sight draft is an order drawn by a domestic bank upon a foreign correspondent bank to pay on demand a sum certain in money to the bearer or to the order of a designated payee. The use of drafts has evolved mostly in the commercially developed countries. One type of draft--the commercial bill--arises when an exporter draws a draft directly on the foreign purchaser for the amount of the export sale.

## #7-20....Letters of Credit

Through the issuances of letters of credit, a banker's bill becomes another type of draft. A Banker's Bill arises when the exporter draws a draft directly on the foreign purchaser's bank or its correspondent bank. The Letter of Credit is an assurance by the bank that the designated party's check or draft will be paid by the bank upon presentation. If a letter of credit is issued, the exporter has greater assurance of collection for the goods shipped to the foreign purchaser.

A letter of credit is an instrument issued by a bank at the request of one party authorizing that party or designated second party to draw a check or draft against the bank, or one of its correspondents, for a designated sum payable on demand, at a specified time, or upon presentation of specified documents which usually give title to the goods. These include the papers covering the shipment, such as the bill of lading, plus other documents essential to the export or import of the goods.

## #7-21....Documentary Bills

Usually a banker's bill or commercial bills are documentary bills--i.e., a bill of lading or other document of title for the goods accompanies the draft. The title document is to be surrendered only after the draft is paid if it is a sight draft, or accepted if it is a time draft.

## #7-22....Time Drafts

Time drafts are similar to sight drafts except that instead of being payable on demand, they are payable a certain number of days after presentation. Commercial letters of credit previously given to the exporter assure him that the time draft will be paid at the end of a 30, 60, 90, or 180-day period. Time drafts, like sight drafts, can be documentary bills, but they may also be CLEAN BILLS. Clean bills unaccompanied by title documents are utilized if the exporter is willing to pass title

to the goods prior to payment or acceptance by the foreign purchaser or his bank.

#### #7-23....Foreign Currency Notes and Coins

Besides the use of bank transfers and bills of exchange,
foreign transactions can also be settled by payment in the actual currency, i.e., the currency notes and coins of the foreign country. Tourists traveling abroad use this means of international cash payment as their chief foreign exchange instruments. Also U.S. merchants and others, particularly those
in the border areas, use a fairly large volume of Canadian and
Mexican currency. The use of foreign currency notes as an instrument of foreign exchange is an important one, but it is
practically limited to smaller transactions.

### FOREIGN EXCHANGE RATES

#### #7-24....Establishment of Foreign Exchange Rates

The rates of exchange for the currency of any particular
country are normally established by the National Central Banks
of the country involved. Generally the rates are established by
determining the direct and indirect precious metal content of
the currency, or by the reserves of stable currencies, other
than the local, used to support the international changeability
of the currency. It then becomes necessary for the exchange
markets in each country to set up a communications system that
will reach all the other exchanges instantaneously.

In the process of the prodigious sums of money that are in
continuous exchange, there will result very substantial profits
or losses on the differentials in the interest, premium, or
discount rates, which come to relatively insignificant frac-
tions. This may be examined further by referring to the Federal
Reserve Bank of New York Study made in 1959 by Allen R. Holmes,
entitled "The New York Foreign Exchange Market."

#### #7-25....History of Foreign Exchange Rate Determinations

In order to have a good understanding of the subject of foreign exchange rates, it is necessary to examine the history of
the metamorphoses and fluxes in bases and criteria for setting
of foreign currency market rates.

Early in this century, before World War II, the determination of the foreign exchange rate was made in terms of the gold
content of a national unit of currency. This resulted in what
was referred to as the INTERNATIONAL GOLD STANDARD, which established rules for national monetary and fiscal policies within the framework of the larger international economy. The rules
of the international economy were based on the freedom of the

flow of both goods and gold between trading countries. The rates of exchange were tied to what was called "gold-export-import points." When a given currency moved outside the points to a point below the required condition of monetary and fiscal policies neutral to the gain or loss of gold, the free flow of gold, acting as a gold regulator, would be invoked.

The invocation would guarantee deflationary action in the country where the gold-losing took place and inflationary action in the country where the gold-gaining took place. The consequence would be that the gold-gaining country would experience a weakening in terms of trade and the gold-losing country would experience a strengthening in terms of trade. This would result in either a stoppage of the gold flow or an increase in the gold flow, thereby bringing about an equilibrium in the foreign exchange market.

Only extraordinary changes, such as those involving the structural basis in national economies, would require a significant or permanent change in the foreign exchange rates. Thus under ordinary circumstances rate changes took place only when there were temporary fluctuations around an equilibrium rate. Under the international gold standard, exchange rates were found to be generally quite stable. Thus for many years it was common knowledge that a French Franc was always the equivalent of 5 to the dollar or 20 cents each, and a German Mark was always 4 to the dollar or 25 cents each.

However, during the decades of 1920 and 1930, there were some very serious international difficulties that caused the abandonment of the gold standard. The result has been that foreign exchange rates are subject to artificially managed structures because national economic policies have been removed from international adjustment mechanisms, so that we find permanent inflationary tendencies in many countries. Inflationary tendencies in turn have caused a swing away from stability in a continuous upward direction which seems to go in one way, resulting in a weakening of the gold equivalents.

Under such circumstances, foreign exchange rates are controlled by central banks which negotiate agreements with various groups, such as currency areas, international payments unions, and international monetary institutions such as the International Monetary Fund (IMF). These agreements result in the foreign exchange rates being termed AGREEMENT RATES, which specify that the relative value of a foreign currency will be restrained from fluctuating outside certain predetermined limits. In those cases where the currency does so fluctuate beyond the limits thereby making the agreement rate unrealistic, then there is an elaborate system of international borrowing that comes into play, which is augmented by the cooperation of friendly countries who may adjust their monetary policies in order to strengthen the currency that has come under pressure.

Thus foreign exchange rates had been kept on a more or less stable level (making allowances for inflation within countries), through a complex control of supply and demand factors and the cooperation of various governments to keep the variations under control. Currencies of countries which followed the IMF agreement were anchored to a common standard of value consisting of gold and those reserve currencies readily convertible into gold under the Bretton Woods System. The IMF member countries agreed to control the fluctuation of their exchange rates within certain required limits, which, when they appeared to be exceeding them, caused intervention to stabilize the exchange rates by certain methods.

However, fixed exchange rates were abandoned resulting in the termination of the Bretton Woods System in 1971. In its wake a system was created known as FLOATING EXCHANGE RATES, under which currencies are free to find their own value relative to one another, and an absence of any—or relatively little—intervention by the governments to moderate the fluctuations.

## #7-26....Effect of Floating Exchange Rates on World Trade

A Reuters Despatch in the September 29, 1980 issue of the NEW YORK TIMES indicates that:

Floating exchange rates since 1973 have had only a minor effect on world trade, and there is no evidence that a government can manipulate its currency to gain unfair advantage, the General Agreement on Tariffs and Trade (GATT) reported.

World trade continues to suffer, however, from the lack of a single currency with stable purchasing power, a role first played by the British Pound and later by the U.S. Dollar, it said.

The study by GATT, the agency which monitors world trade, said complaints by economists and businessmen that the present system of flexible exchange rates had distorted trade patterns and undermined efforts to reduce trade barriers were unfounded.

## #7-27....Flexible Exchange Rates Best

Flexible rates began in 1973. Since that time, exchange rate movements of 1% a day, 5% a week, or 25% a year have not been uncommon. This volatility was largely because of the price controls on crude oil. Despite criticisms, however, some good things did emerge from this flexibility -- for example, the oil price revolution did not drastically limit world trade; international trade of industrial countries rose by 32%; real gross national product rose by 20%; and international capital movements were not seriously hampered.

Floating rates have greatly absorbed various price changes, and overshooting exchange rates became stabilizing agents. In 1983, French President Mitterrand and Representative Jack Kemp advocated a return to the Bretton Woods fixed-rates system, a return to the gold standard of exchange. Since the economies of the world are interrelated in a complicated matrix of national and international economic policies, fixing the rates might lead to more rate adjustments. This would in turn free the underlying problem of coordinating economic policies, causing it to become a greater political problem. This is compounded by enormous gold reserves held by Russia, which would be a threat to national economic security. To correct the situation, former West German central bank president, Otmar Emminger, prescribes "better management of floating." It may thus be argued that there has not been a failure of flexible rates, but the true culprit has been government inability to design and implement acceptable internal and external stabilizing policy decisions.

## #7-28....Currency Devaluations

In tracing the history of determination of foreign exchange rates, it was pointed out that the IMF member countries committed themselves to attempt to restrain fluctuations of rates within certain agreed limits. Where the fluctuations proved beyond containment within the limits set, the country which experienced the pressure had to take action to remedy the situation. If loans and policy shifts were unable to alleviate the situation, this required an alteration in the rate of exchange. In cases where more local currency units are required to obtain a given number of units of another currency, the value of the local currency depreciates. Hence the setting of the new rate requiring more units is known as DEVALUATION, because each unit has less value and the foreign exchange rate of the currency has dropped. Notable examples in the 1970s have been Mexico and Israel, which have spilled over into the 1980s.

## #7-29....Effect of Devaluations on Currency

In the article "Devaluation and Inflation and Their Effect on Foreign Operations," in ACCOUNTANCY, Aug. 1965, Michael T. Wells states the effect of devaluation on foreign operations:

Devaluation and inflation are intimately connected. Exchange problems generally arise because devaluation takes place when the financial authorities of a country decide that its currency is OVERVALUED, and that the country's balance of payments would benefit from a lower value of the currency internationally. A currency normally becomes overvalued because the supply of money has been increased without a corresponding increase in the amount of goods and

services  available  for  consumption--in  other  words,  when
INFLATION exists.
    The timing of these steps  is not  invariable.  Normally
the inflation comes first and then devaluation is prescribed
as the remedy for  the ill, but  there  are situations where
the reverse  takes  place--devaluation comes first  and  the
inflation comes later.  We are concerned with the effects of
devaluation and inflation on business and on our operations.
For this  reason a full understanding of the exchange  problems involved is essential to the successful manager.
The causes of foreign exchange fluctuations resulting in devaluations will be treated in Chapter 8.

#### #7-30....Relative Nature of Devaluation

    It should be pointed out that devaluation is relative in the
sense that  a devaluation does  not necessarily take  effect in
relation to all currencies.   As previously indicated there appear to be clusters of countries revolving around a major country, which relate their currencies to  the major country.  As a
result, when the devaluation takes place, it is relative to the
major  country  in  the cluster.  Two  recent examples are  the
Indian Rupee  and  the Jamaican  Dollar.  In the Dec. 24,  1978
issue of the CHICAGO TRIBUNE, it is pointed out:
    The  Indian  Rupee  has  been devalued  by 2.12% against the
    British Pound,  the  Reserve Bank of India reported.  At the
    new rate, a  Pound is worth 16.5  Rupees compared with 16.15
    Rupees before  the devaluation. There was  no immediate word
    on how the  United States Dollar-Rupee  rate  would  be  af-
    fected.
And a United Press International  report dated January 15, 1979
states:
    In a  further sign of weakening in  Jamaica's economy,  the
    sagging Jamaican Dollar has been devalued a few more percen-
    tage  points.  Government spokesmen  said, however, that the
    latest was one of  the regular monthly  sliding devaluations
    of the currency against  the U.S. Dollar.  The  devaluations
    are one of the conditions of a  loan  package of hundreds of
    millions of dollars from the Washington-based  International
    Monetary Fund that  is saving the Caribbean island nation of
    2 million persons from outright bankruptcy.  Before the lat-
    est devaluation, one U.S.  Dollar bought 1.65 Jamaican  Dol-
    lars;  with this latest devaluation, one U.S. Dollar  bought
    1.71 Jamaican Dollars.

#### #7-31....Currency Revaluations

    REVALUATION  is  the  opposite  of  devaluation, causing  the
local currency to increase in value  and thereby requiring less

units to obtain a given number of units of another currency. In revaluation, the setting of the new rate requiring less units thereby increases the value of the revaluation units.

## SUMMARY OF FOOTNOTE REFERENCES
(References are to Paragraph #'s)

#7-5    Raymond de Roover, "Early Accounting Problems of Foreign Exchange," ACCOUNTING REVIEW (October 1944): 381-407

#7-5    R. G. Hawtrey, "Money and Money of Account," THE ACCOUNTANT (January 6, 1940): 15

#7-14 thru #7-23:  "Instruments of Foreign Exchange," adapted from Norlin G. Rueschhoff, INTERNATIONAL ACCOUNTING AND FINANCIAL REPORTING, 1976, Praeger Publishers, Inc., by permission.

#7-26   Reuters Despatch,  NEW YORK TIMES (September 29, 1980)

#7-29   Michael T. Wells, "Devaluation and Inflation and Their Effect on Foreign Operations," ACCOUNTANCY (August 1965)

#7-30   CHICAGO TRIBUNE (December 24, 1978)

#7-30   United Press International  (January 15, 1979)

## BIBLIOGRAPHY

Abs, Herman J. "Bretton Woods: Temporarily Suspended or Obsolete?", COLUMBIA JOURNAL OF WORLD BUSINESS, 7 (Jan-Feb 1982): 7-12

Brittain, Bruce.  "Tests of Theories of Exchange Rate Determination," JOURNAL OF FINANCE (May 1977): 519-529

Evans, Thomas G. THE CURRENCY CAROUSEL. Princeton, N.J.: Dow Jones, 1977

Giddy, Ian H.  "Research on the Foreign Exchange Markets," COLUMBIA JOURNAL OF WORLD BUSINESS, 14 (Winter 1979): 4-6

Holmes, Allen R.  "The New York Foreign Exchange Market," FEDERAL RESERVE BANK OF NEW YORK STUDY (1959)

Kohlhagen, Steven W.  "The Performance of the Foreign Exchange Markets," JOURNAL OF INTERNATIONAL BUSINESS STUDIES, 6 (Fall 1975): 33-40

Kubarych, Roger M. "Foreign Exchange Markets in the United States," FEDERAL RESERVE BANK OF NEW YORK (August 1978)

Lindsay, L.G. "A Primer on Foreign Exchange," CANADIAN BANKER (June 1983): 14

Makin, John H.  "Fixed vs. Floating: A Red Herring," COLUMBIA JOURNAL OF WORLD BUSINESS, 14 (Winter 1979): 7-14

Tygier, C.  BASIC HANDBOOK OF FOREIGN EXCHANGE. London: Euromoney Publications, 1983

Wallich, Henry C.  "What Makes Exchange Rates Move?", CHALLENGE (July-August 1977): 39-40

Weisweiller, R. INTRODUCTION TO FOREIGN EXCHANGE. Cambridge, England and Dover, N.H.: Woodhead-Faulkner, 1983

## THEORY QUESTIONS
(Question Numbers are Keyed to Text Paragraph #'s)

#7-1   Discuss why there is a need for foreign exchange.

#7-2   Why does foreign exchange give international business transactions a dual nature?

#7-3   What causes the need for foreign exchange markets in international transactions?

#7-4   What are the purposes of foreign exchange markets?

#7-8   Define the term FOREIGN EXCHANGE.

#7-9   Classify currency.

#7-11  What is meant by Foreign Exchange CONVERSION?

#7-12  What is meant by Foreign Exchange TRANSLATION?

#7-13  Distinguish between Foreign Exchange Conversion and Translation.

#7-14  Discuss the relation of each of the following types of instruments to the carrying on of foreign exchange transactions: (a) Bank Transfers, (b) Cable Transfers, (c) Bills of Exchange, (d) Personal Checks and Money Orders, (e) Bank Drafts, (f) Sight Drafts, (g) Letters of Credit, (h) Documentary Bills, (i) Time Drafts, (j) Foreign Currency.

#7-24  How are Foreign Exchange Rates established?

#7-26  What effect do floating exchange rates have on world trade?

#7-28  What are Currency Devaluations and what causes them?

#7-29  What effect do devaluations have on a currency?

#7-31  What are Currency Revaluations, their causes, and effect they have on a currency?


## EXERCISES

### EX-7-1   (CPA EXAM, 11/23, LAW, #3)
Define (a) an inland bill of exchange; (b) a foreign bill of exchange. In what circumstances does the determination as to whether a bill of exchange is inland or foreign become a vital point?

### EX-7-2   (CPA EXAM, 5/62, LAW, #3C)
The requirement of "a sum certain in money" is fulfilled even though:
   a. The instrument is payable in stated installments.
   b. Attorney's fees and other costs of collection are included in the instrument.
   c. It is payable in Mexico in Mexican Pesos.
   d. The instrument states that it will carry the maximum legal interest rate.
   e. The instrument is payable in something other than money at the option of the maker or drawer.

## PROBLEMS

### P-7-1 (CPA EXAM, 5/69, LAW, #30,D)

The following handwritten instrument was negotiated by Elmer Dodd for value to Jane Maples:

> Toronto, Canada,  May 5, 1969
> Sixty days after date pay to the order of Elmer Dodd, one hundred and fifty dollars ($150), payable at New National Bank, U.N. Plaza, New York, N.Y. Value received and charge the trade account of Olympia Sales Corporation, New York, N.Y.
>
> W. Stark

Answer which of the following is True (T) or False (F).

_____ a. The instrument is a negotiable foreign time draft.

_____ b. In the event of dishonor a formal protest is required to hold secondarily liable parties.

_____ c. A timely presentment for payment can be made at any time within a week following the expiration of 60 days from the May 5, 1969 issue date.

_____ d. Olympia Sales has primary liability on the instrument.

_____ e. In the event Olympia Sales is insolvent and cannot pay, Stark will be liable to Jane Maples if she has complied with the proper procedural steps and sues him.

### P-7-2 (CPA EXAM, 5/77, LAW, #20)

Examine the following instrument:

| Diana Davidson | |
| 21 West 21st Street | No. 111 |
| Toronto, Canada | |

April 1, 1977

Pay to the order of Stanley Stark          $1,000.00

One thousand & no/100's Canadian Dollars

Diana Davidson

FIRST NATIONAL TRUST
Buffalo, New York

For Finder's Fee

Required:

Which of the following conclusions is correct?

a. It is non-negotiable because it is payable in Canadian money.

b. It is a demand instrument but does not qualify as a negotiable instrument because it is drawn in Canada and payable by a bank in the United States.

c. The instrument is  a negotiable foreign check (draft), and
   in the event of dishonor  a formal protest must be made by
   the party seeking recovery.

d. Diana Davidson is  the maker of the instrument and as such
   is primarily liable thereon.

## P-7-3  (CPA EXAM, 11/76, THEORY, #1, II)

When preparing combined  or consolidated  financial  statements
for a domestic  and a foreign company, the account balances expressed in  the foreign  currency  must  be translated into the
domestic currency.  The objective of the translation process is
to obtain currency valuations that

a. Are conservative.

b. Reflect current monetary equivalents.

c. Are expressed in domestic units of measure and are in conformity with domestic generally  accepted accounting principles.

d. Reflect the translated account at its unexpired historical
   cost.

# The Basis for Implementation of International Business Transactions – Foreign Exchange Rates and the Foreign Exchange Market

### #8-1....Foreign Exchange Market Rates

The market rates for foreign exchange vary slightly for the different foreign exchange instruments. THE WALL STREET JOURNAL, for example, regularly quotes the selling prices for bank transfers in the U.S. for payment abroad. These are SPOT PRICES quoted for IMMEDIATE DELIVERY in the interbank market.

The rates for cable transfers are the BASIC SPOT RATES. The rates for other transactions such as mail transfers or bills of exchange are based on the cable transfer rate. Since the cable transfer rate is the main device for currency conversion, the spot rate becomes the most relevant to financial accounting measurement.

### #8-2....Classification of Rates

Because foreign currency in international transactions is regarded as a commodity, and as such is freely traded by international departments of all large banks, a market with quotations of fluctuating prices causes market rates to be quoted. These rates may be classified according to Time, Nature of Transaction, or Governmental Fiat.

## TIME RATES

### #8-3....Time Rates Classification

Time-wise market rates may be referred to as SPOT RATES or FORWARD RATES.

## #8-4....Spot Rates

As seen above, Spot Rates are the most relevant to financial accounting measurement and those which are quoted as in effect at the time the exchange transaction is to take place--on the spot, so to speak.

## #8-5....Forward Rates

Forward Rates are those resulting from a FORWARD EXCHANGE CONTRACT that is to take effect at a future date resulting from a hedging arrangement. A forward exchange contract between a bank and a customer, or between two banks, specifies delivery of a certain sum in foreign currency at a future date and at a designated rate which is stipulated at the time the contract is entered into. This rate is the FORWARD RATE. THE WALL STREET JOURNAL regularly quotes the forward rate for 30-day and 90-day futures of British Pound Sterling. Canadian Dollars and several continental European currencies are also active in the forward market.

Most forward exchange contracts are made over the telephone and later confirmed in writing. The forward rate designated in the contract may be more or less than the spot rate on the date the contract is consummated. Similarly the forward exchange rate may also be more or less than the spot rate on the date that the contract must be fulfilled. An illustration of the accounting procedures involved in forward exchange contracts will be given in connection with a discussion involving export and import transactions in the next chapter.

## #8-6....Forward Option Rates

If a buyer or seller knows only approximately when the foreign currency is needed or received, he may execute a FOREIGN OPTION CONTRACT. Such contracts may be arranged for delivery at the beginning of a month (from the 1st to the 10th), the middle (11th to the 20th), or the end (from the 21st on), or in another requested period of time. In such case, although the cost to the customer may be slightly higher, the customer is afforded more leeway in timing.

Forward Exchange and Forward Option Contracts shift the risk of future purchases or sales of foreign currencies to the banker-dealer. Because of the risk involved, the credit-worthiness of the customer is an important element in the forward exchange business. For the customer anticipating the receipt or delivery of foreign exchange, the forward exchange market serves a highly useful purpose.

## TRANSACTION RATES

### #8-7....Nature of Transaction Rates

By nature of transaction, rates are classified as BUYING and SELLING RATES. The buying rate is the price the foreign exchange dealer will pay for buying foreign currency. The selling rate is what he will charge for selling the foreign currency. When the terms "buying" and "selling" are used, the transaction must be looked at from the viewpoint of the foreign exchange dealer. Thus tourists frequently become confused by these quotations, thinking that the buying rate is what they pay for buying, which is not the case. The buying rate for the tourist is the selling rate of the foreign exchange dealer, hence the price the tourist pays is the selling rate (of the dealer), not the dealer's buying rate.

## GOVERNMENTAL FIAT RATES

### #8-8....Classification of Governmental Fiat Rates

Governmental Fiat Rates are those set by governments to obtain advantages for their countries. There are three types: Preferential, Penalty, and Differential.

### #8-9....Preferential Rates

These are established for essential or desirable imports which are differentiated from less preferred imports and dividend remittances. They are, in effect, favorable rates. They act as a form of GOVERNMENT SUBSIDY to maintain lower selling prices to the public in a foreign country. Rebates are sometimes also given to encourage imports of essential food.

An illustration of Preferential Rates is the devaluation of the Mexican Peso on August 5, 1982. The effect on the rates is described in Section 11, page 7 of the CHICAGO TRIBUNE, August 22, 1982:

> With the recent Peso devaluation, the Mexican travel industry is predicting an influx of foreign tourists looking to take advantage of an exchange rate ranging from 65 to 150 pesos to the dollar. Before the Aug. 5 devaluation, a dollar was worth only 47 pesos.
> The current devaluation has put the peso at 65-70 pesos to the dollar. The official rate is 69.5. This is a gain in strength from the initial 82-85 pesos to the dollar of Aug. 5. The country now is working under a two-tiered exchange rate. The system contains a PREFERENTIAL EXCHANGE RATE under which the government theoretically will sell dollars at 49.5 pesos to businesses that can prove they will use them to

pay off  dollar debts resulting from purchases of nationally
useful  goods and machinery abroad or to pay for foodstuffs,
raw materials and other high priority imports.
     The other half of the system will be used for non-essen-
tial purchases  and  will let the peso float  freely against
the dollar, allowing the exchange rate to be fixed by supply
and demand.
Another  illustration  is  the  Sudan, which  has  two  exchange
rates:
     The OFFICIAL  RATE, fixed at 50 pt  to  the  U.S. Dollar, is
     used  for  government transfers and  economically  strategic
     commercial transactions, while the  PARALLEL RATE,  fixed at
     80 pt  to the U.S.  Dollar, is used for other commercial and
     all private transactions.

## #8-10....Penalty Rates

     These  are  less favorable than the free market and official
exchange rates. They constitute a TAX ON IMPORTS. In some cases
the difference is  actually levied as a tax.  Also the purchase
of the proceeds from exports of designated products by the central  banks  at a specified  less  favorable rate constitutes a
type of export duty.

## #8-11....Differential Rates

     A  few currencies  are  traded in the black market,  but the
most prominent divergent exchange  rates  are  local government
sponsored.  Because they differ from the market rates, they are
referred to as DIFFERENTIAL RATES.  Actually, both preferential
and penalty rates are in effect differential rates because they
differ from the market rates.

## FOREIGN CURRENCIES AND THEIR RATES

## #8-12....Foreign Currencies

     Every country has its  own  unit of currency, usually called
by a different name.  However, in  clusters of countries having
some common bond such  as a common  language  or cultural background, the currency name  may be the  same.  Thus  in English-
speaking countries they are  called  the Dollar or Pound.  Most
Spanish-speaking  countries  use the Spanish  word  for  Dollar,
viz., Peso.  In French colonies, the Franc is commonly used for
the unit of  currency.  Most  currencies have  fractional units
such as the British Pound subdivided into Pennies,  the Spanish
Peso  into Centavos, the  German Mark  into  Pfennigs, and  the
French Franc into Centimes.
     International  accounting students are concerned with inter-

national currencies. A listing of currencies of most nations in the world, along with their values, appearing on page 214 in the 1984 Diary published by the American Express Company, is shown in Figure 8-1.

#8-13....Foreign Exchange Rate Quotations

Monthly reports of major currency rates are issued by the larger banks. The Federal Reserve Bank issues a statistical release on the last day of each month showing the average rates of 24 major currencies for the month together with comparable figures for other months. The averages are based on daily noon buying rates for cable transfers in New York City certified for customs purposes by the Federal Reserve Bank of New York. The rates are quoted in terms of U.S. cents. An illustration of the Federal Reserve Release is shown in Figure 8-2.

#8-14....Types of Currency Rate Quotations

Rates can be quoted in two ways -- DIRECTLY or INDIRECTLY.

#8-15....Direct Quotations

Direct Quotations are those which state the value of one foreign currency unit in local currency. Assuming that a British Pound is worth $2 U.S., a French Franc is worth 20 cents U.S., and a German Mark is worth 50 cents U.S., Direct Quotations for each of the countries would be as follows:

UNITED STATES

| 1 British Pound | = | $2.00 U.S. |
| 1 French Franc | = | $0.20 U.S. |
| 1 German Mark (DM) | = | $0.50 U.S. |

FRANCE

| 1 British Pound | = | 10 French Francs |
| 1 U.S. Dollar | = | 5 French Francs |
| 1 German Mark | = | 2-1/2 French Francs |

GERMANY

| 1 British Pound | = | 4 (DM) German Marks |
| 1 French Franc | = | 40 Pfennigs (.40 DM) |
| 1 U.S. Dollar | = | 2 (DM) German Marks |

GREAT BRITAIN

| 1 U.S. Dollar | = | 50 Pence (1/2 Pound) English |
| 1 French Franc | = | 10 Pence English |
| 1 German Mark | = | 25 Pence English |

The Direct Quotation method tells what one unit of a foreign currency is worth in the local or domestic currency. Therefore, when you observe a French Franc you have 20 cents; or if you

FIGURE 8-1 -- INTERNATIONAL CURRENCIES

| Country/Monetary Unit | Approximate Number Equal to One U.S. Dollar | Country/Monetary Unit | Approximate Number Equal to One U.S. Dollar | Country/Monetary Unit | Approximate Number Equal to One U.S. Dollar |
|---|---|---|---|---|---|
| Afghanistan/Afghani | 50.51 | Costa Rica/Small Colon | 40.00 | Greece/Small Drachma | 83.33 |
| Algeria/Dinar | 4.69 | Cuba/Peso | .85 | Greece/Large Drachma | 83.33 |
| Angola/Kwanza | 30.30 | Curacao/Guilder | 1.80 | Guadeloupe/Franc | 6.85 |
| Argentina/New Peso | 59880.24 | Cyprus/Pound | .50 | Guatemala/Quetzal | 1.00 |
| Australia/Dollar | 1.16 | Czechoslovakia/Kroner | 10.36 | Guiana-French/Franc | 6.85 |
| Austria/Schilling | 16.81 | Dahomey/CFA-FC-West | 340.14 | Guyana/Dollar | 2.94 |
| Bahamas/Small Dollar | 1.00 | Denmark/Krone | 8.62 | Haiti/Gourde | 5.00 |
| Bahrain/Dinar | .38 | Djibouti/Franc CFA | 340.14 | Holland/Guilder | 2.65 |
| Barbados/Small Dollar | 2.00 | Dominican Rep./Small Peso | 1.00 | Honduras Rep./Lempira | 2.00 |
| Belgium/Franc | 50.00 | Dubai/Dirham | 3.68 | Hong Kong/Dollar | 6.62 |
| Belize/Dollar | 2.00 | East Caribbean/Small Dollar | 2.70 | Hungary/Forint | 38.31 |
| Bermuda/Dollar | 1.00 | Ecuador/Small Sucre | 69.93 | Iceland/New Small Krona | 19.05 |
| Bolivia/Peso Boliviano | 44.44 | Egypt/Pound | .83 | India/Large Rupee | 9.76 |
| Brazil/New Cruzeiro | 387.60 | El Salvador/Colon | 2.50 | Indonesia/Rupiah | 689.66 |
| British West Indies/Dollar | 2.70 | England/Pound | .66 | Iran/New Rial | 83.33 |
| Bulgaria/Leva | .97 | Ethiopia/Birr | 2.00 | Iraq/Dinar | .31 |
| Burma/Kyat | 7.63 | Falkland/Pound | .66 | Ireland/Small Pound | .72 |
| Cameroun-Rep./Franc CFA | 340.14 | Fiji/Dollar | .95 | Israel/Shekel | 37.17 |
| Canada/Dollar | 1.22 | Finland/Small Markka | 5.38 | Italy/Small Lire | 1418.44 |
| Cayman Islands/Dollar | .83 | France/Franc | 6.85 | Italy/Large Lire | 1418.44 |
| Central Africa Rep./CFA-FC-EQ | 340.14 | Gabon/CFA-FC-EQ | 340.14 | Ivory Coast/CFA-FC-West | 340.14 |
| Chad/CFA-FC-EQ | 340.14 | Gambia/Dalasi | 2.60 | Jamaica/Dollar | 1.79 |
| Chile/Peso | 80.00 | Germany E./Ostmark | 2.40 | Japan/Yen | 237.53 |
| China-People's Rep./Renminbi | 1.96 | Germany W./Mark | 2.40 | Jordan/Dinar | .36 |
| Colombia/Small Peso | 71.43 | Ghana/Cedi | 2.74 | Kenya/Shilling | 12.99 |
| Congo-Brazzaville/CFA-FC-EQ | 340.14 | Gibraltar/Pound | .66 | Korea/Won | 740.74 |

**Important:** These numbers only approximate actual values, and are not to be used for foreign exchange transactions.

| Country/Monetary Unit | Approximate Number Equal to One U.S. Dollar |
|---|---|
| Kuwait/Dinar | .29 |
| Laos/Kip | 10.00 |
| Lebanon/Pound | 3.97 |
| Libya/Dinar | .30 |
| Luxembourg/Franc | 50.00 |
| Macao/Pataca | 6.90 |
| Malagasy Rep./Franc | 357.14 |
| Malawi/Kwacha | 1.11 |
| Malaysia/Small Dollar | 2.28 |
| Mali/Franc | 666.67 |
| Malta/Pound | .42 |
| Martinique/Franc | 6.85 |
| Mauritania/Ouguiya | 54.05 |
| Mauritius/Rupee | 10.00 |
| Mexico/Small Peso | 158.98 |
| Mexico/Large Peso | 158.98 |
| Morocco/Dirham | 6.45 |
| Mozambique/Metical | 30.30 |
| Nepal/Rupee | 13.16 |
| Neth. Guiana/Surinam Guilder | 1.79 |
| New Caledonia/CFP Franc | 117.65 |
| New Zealand/Small Dollar | 1.53 |
| Nicaragua/Cordoba | 10.00 |
| Niger/CFA-FC-West | 340.14 |
| Nigeria/Large Naira | .68 |
| Norway/Small Krone | 7.14 |
| Oman/Riyal Omani | .34 |
| Pakistan/Small Rupee | 12.74 |
| Papua/Kina | .78 |
| Paraguay/Guarani | 160.00 |
| Peru/Small Sol | 1117.32 |
| Philippine Islands/Piso | 9.51 |
| Poland/Zloty | 86.96 |
| Portugal/Small Escudo | 95.24 |
| Qatar/Ryal | 3.64 |
| Roumania/Leu | 12.50 |
| Rwanda/Franc | 92.59 |
| Saint Pierre/Franc | 6.85 |
| Samoa-Western/Tala | 1.25 |
| Saudi Arabia/Riyal | 3.44 |
| Scotland/Small Pound | .66 |
| Senegal/CFA-FC-West | 340.14 |
| Seychelles/Rupee | 6.62 |
| Sierra Leone/Leone | |
| Singapore/Dollar | 2.08 |
| Somalia/Somali Shilling | 6.35 |
| South Africa/Rand | 1.09 |
| South West Africa/Rand | 1.09 |
| South Yemen/Dinar | .34 |
| Spain/Small Peseta | 131.58 |
| Sri Lanka/Rupee | 22.22 |
| Sudan/Pound | 1.33 |
| Sweden/Small Krona | 7.43 |
| Sweden/Large Krona | 7.43 |
| Switzerland/Franc | 2.05 |
| Syria/Pound | 3.92 |
| Tahiti/Franc | 117.65 |
| Taiwan/Dollar | 40.00 |
| Tanzania/Shilling | 9.52 |
| Thailand/Baht | 22.99 |
| Togo/CFA-FC-West | 340.14 |
| Trinidad & Tobago/Small Dollar | 2.41 |
| Tunisia/Dinar | .64 |
| Turkey/Large Pound | 192.31 |
| Uganda/Shilling | 200.00 |
| United Arab Emirates/Dirham | 3.68 |
| Upper Volta/CFA-FC-West | 340.14 |
| Uruguay/New Peso | 25.00 |
| U.S.S.R./Rouble | .71 |
| Vanuatu/Vatu | 100.00 |
| Venezuela/Bolivar | 15.38 |
| Viet Nam/Dong | 2.17 |
| Yemen/Arab.Rep.Rial | 4.60 |
| Yugoslavia/Large Dinar | 66.67 |
| Zaire Republic/Zaire | 5.85 |
| Zambia/Kwacha | 1.17 |
| Zimbabwe/Dollar | .98 |

**Important:** These numbers only approximate actual values, and are not to be used for foreign exchange transactions.

Source: Adapted from INTERNATIONAL CURRENCIES, 1984 Diary, American Express Company, page 214.

look at a German Mark you are  looking  at 50 cents;  or if you
have a British Pound this is equivalent to $2.   This method is
used  in  Figure 8-2, indicated  by the remark "Rates  In  U.S.
Cents Per Unit of Foreign Currency."

=================================================================
FIGURE 8-2

FOREIGN EXCHANGE RATES
OCTOBER 1978

(Rates in U.S. Cents Per Unit of Foreign Currency)

| Country | Monetary Unit | 1978 October | 1978 September | 1978 August | 1977 October |
|---------|------|------|------|------|------|
| Australia | Dollar | 116.8656 | 115.2929 | 115.4108 | 111.8989 |
| Austria | Schilling | 7.45257 | 7.01020 | 6.94902 | 6.15674 |
| Belgium | Franc | 3.45032 | 3.22073 | 3.18344 | 2.82290 |
| Canada | Dollar | 84.5461 | 85.7389 | 87.6901 | 91.0096 |
| Denmark | Krone | 19.5837 | 18.4108 | 18.1712 | 16.3592 |
| Finland | Markka | 25.4538 | 24.5859 | 24.3805 | 24.1368 |
| France | Franc | 23.7665 | 22.9094 | 22.9982 | 20.5739 |
| Germany | D. Mark | 54.4297 | 50.7777 | 50.0836 | 43.9044 |
| India | Rupee | 12.6433 | 12.4450 | 12.4826 | 11.6050 |
| Ireland | Pound | 200.7541 | 195.9529 | 194.0596 | 177.1079 |
| Italy | Lira | 0.123173 | 0.120495 | 0.119521 | 0.113527 |
| Japan | Yen | 0.544776 | 0.526563 | 0.530021 | 0.392626 |
| Malaysia | Dollar | 45.6273 | 43.6025 | 43.4328 | 41.0882 |
| Mexico | Peso | 4.3904 | 4.3907 | 4.3758 | 4.4069 |
| Netherlands | Guilder | 50.0167 | 46.7331 | 46.2025 | 41.0482 |
| New Zealand | Dollar | 107.3689 | 105.5849 | 105.4182 | 98.1524 |
| Norway | Krone | 20.3254 | 19.1893 | 19.0180 | 18.2319 |
| Portugal | Escudo | 2.23421 | 2.19481 | 2.20423 | 2.46012 |
| South Africa | Rand | 115.0000 | 115.0000 | 115.0000 | 115.0359 |
| Spain | Peseta | 1.43168 | 1.36054 | 1.33441 | 1.19021 |
| Sri Lanka | Rupee | 6.3757 | 6.3855 | 6.3926 | 11.6180 |
| Sweden | Krona | 23.3489 | 22.5919 | 22.5226 | 20.8464 |
| Switzerland | Franc | 65.1172 | 63.7652 | 60.0130 | 43.9093 |
| United Kingdom | Pound | 200.7541 | 195.9529 | 194.0596 | 177.1079 |

The above table shows the average rates of exchange of 24 currencies in
October 1978 together with comparable figures for other months.   Aver-
ages are based on daily noon buying rates for  cable  transfers in  New
York City certified for customs purposes by the Federal Reserve Bank of
New York.

Source:  Federal Reserve Statistical Release,  October 31, 1978
=================================================================

## #8-16....Indirect Quotations

Indirect Quotations are stated in terms of how many foreign currency units can be purchased with one unit of the local (domicile) currency. Using the illustrations from the Direct Quotations, the Indirect Quotations would be as follows:

UNITED STATES

| 1 U.S. Dollar | = 1.00 ÷ 2.00 | = 1/2 British Pound |
| 1 U.S. Dollar | = 1.00 ÷ 20¢ | = 5 French Francs |
| 1 U.S. Dollar | = 1.00 ÷ 50¢ | = 2 German Marks |

GERMANY

| 1 German DM | = 50¢ ÷ 2.00 | = 25 British Pence |
| 1 German DM | = 50¢ ÷ 20¢ | = 2-1/2 French Francs |
| 1 German DM | = 50¢ ÷ 1.00 | = 1/2 U.S.$, or 50 U.S.¢ |

FRANCE

| 1 French Franc | = 20¢ ÷ 1.00 | = 20¢ U.S. |
| 1 French Franc | = 20¢ ÷ 2.00 | = 10 British Pence |
| 1 French Franc | = 20¢ ÷ .50 | = 40 German Pfennigs |

GREAT BRITAIN

| 1 British Pound | = 2.00 ÷ 1.00 | = 2 U.S. Dollars |
| 1 British Pound | = 2.00 ÷ 20¢ | = 10 French Francs |
| 1 British Pound | = 2.00 ÷ 50¢ | = 4 German Marks |

For 1 U.S. Dollar we can buy either 1/2 British Pound, 5 French Francs, or 2 German Marks. For 1 German Mark we can buy 25 British Pence or 2-1/2 French Francs or 50 U.S. cents. For 1 French Franc we can buy 20 U.S. cents or 10 British Pence or 40 German Pfennigs. For 1 British Pound we can buy 2 U.S. Dollars or 10 French Francs or 4 German Marks. The Indirect Method is then the opposite of the Direct Method; thus saying directly that 1 Pound is the equivalent of 2 U.S. Dollars is the same as saying indirectly that 1 U.S. Dollar is the equivalent of 1/2 Pound. And saying directly that 1 Franc is the equivalent of 20 cents U.S. is the same as saying indirectly that 1 Dollar is the equivalent of 5 Francs.

## #8-17....Summary of Quotation Methods

When we take one unit of the foreign currency to be equated in terms of the value of the domestic or local unit, the quotation is DIRECT. When we express one unit of the domestic currency in terms of the NUMBER OF UNITS of the foreign currency, the quotation is INDIRECT.

Basically then, the Direct Method expresses both currencies in terms of financial values, whereas the Indirect Method expresses the local currency financially but the foreign currency in numbers of units. The method that is used in the daily press

for foreign exchange market currency quotations is the Indirect
Method, i.e., the number of foreign units to be bought with one
domestic unit is the customary quotation.  In such case, in order to ascertain the value of one foreign unit, the number of
foreign units must be divided into the local currency unit,
viz., $1 U.S.  Thus the German Mark is listed in Figure 8-2 as
being worth 54.4297 cents; the dealer would divide the 54.4297
cents into a dollar, which would determine the number of Marks
one dollar would buy (roughly 1.84).  Hence, the dealer would
quote by the Indirect Method the rate as 1.84 Marks to the Dollar.
     Figure 8-3 shows an example of an Exchange Rate Table, which
conveniently quotes both Direct and Indirect Rates for major
world currencies.

## FOREIGN EXCHANGE MARKET RATE FLUCTUATIONS

### #8-18....Market Rate Fluctuations

     Because foreign exchange is subject to market operations,
like any market the rates will fluctuate.  In the last several

```
===========================================================
                        FIGURE 8-3
                       AN EXAMPLE OF
                 DOLLAR EXCHANGE RATES ABROAD
                        JUNE 1984
```

|                    |                |  U.S. $    |
| Country/unit       | Per 1 U.S. $   | Equivalent |
|--------------------|----------------|------------|
| Australia dollar   | 1.15           | .8696      |
| Austria schilling  | 19.00          | .0526      |
| Belgium franc      | 55.55          | .0180      |
| Brazil cruzeiro    | 1675.00        | .000597    |
| Britain pound      | .73            | 1.37       |
| Canada dollar      | 1.29           | .7752      |
| Colombia peso      | 125.00         | .008       |
| Denmark krone      | 10.00          | .1000      |
| France franc       | 8.29           | .1206      |
| Greece drachma     | 104.00         | .0096      |
| Holland guilder    | 3.07           | .3257      |
| Ireland pound      | .8900          | 1.235      |
| Israel shekel      | 235.00         | .00425     |
| Italy lira         | 1645.00        | .000608    |
| Japan yen          | 234.00         | .004275    |
| Mexico peso        | 180.00         | .00555     |
| Norway krone       | 7.80           | .1282      |
| Portugal escudo    | 133.00         | .0075      |
| Spain peseta       | 147.00         | .0068      |
| Sweden krona       | 8.09           | .1236      |
| Switzerland franc  | 2.29           | .4366      |
| West Germany mark  | 2.77           | .3610      |

```
===========================================================
```

years there have been severe fluctuations in the price of several currencies. In the early 1970s the U.S. dollar was so severely depreciated that many foreign tourists found German, French and Spanish shopkeepers, inter alia, unwilling to honor traveler's checks issued in Dollars.

After recovering, the U.S. Dollar again in 1978 took a beating against the German Mark, the Japanese Yen, and the Swiss Franc. Where there previously were 360 Yen to the Dollar, the number dropped to below 190. Similarly, where there had been 4 German Marks to the Dollar, the drop was to less than 2. Conversely, the British Pound, which was set for one equal to U.S. $2.40, dropped to a value of around U.S. $1.59. As previously pointed out, severe changes such as these may result in devaluations, such as occurred with the Mexican Peso and the Israeli Pound (known as the Shekel in the 1980s). These severe fluctuations in the past have been emphasized daily in the financial sections of the press, and an inquiry into the factors which cause them is necessary.

## #8-19....Causes of Foreign Exchange Rate Fluctuations

There are six basic rate fluctuation causes: balance-of-payments deficits or surpluses; differing global rates of inflation; money market variations from interest rates in individual countries; capital investment levels; national economic characteristics; and extrapolated expectations.

## #8-20....Balances of Payments

Perhaps the most important cause of fluctuations in currency is the country's balance-of-international-payments. This has been emphasized in an article published by the Chemical Bank of New York, entitled "Foreign Exposure Management," 1972, p. 4:

The fundamental determinant of the supply/demand relationship among currencies is, of course, long run developments in the balance of payments of individual countries, particularly the major trading nations. A basic balance of payments disequilibrium, whether it takes the form of persistent surpluses or deficits, inevitably leads to pressures resulting in parity changes in the form of revaluations or devaluations.

Such a disequilibrium can result from numerous sources. These include, to name only a few, interest rate differentials, the loss of a key export market, changes in the propensity to import, the existence of differential rates of inflation among key trading nations, a desire to invest heavily abroad, foreign military commitments and aid programs, and tariff and anti-tariff restrictions on trade. Of these causes, the most basic is the development of differential rates of inflation among a group of trading nations. If

prolonged, such a development will invariably erode the competitive position of the country with the most rapid rate of
inflation. Exchange rates are certain to flow from such a
situation.
This is precisely the situation of the U.S. entering the decade
of the 1980s; inflation is virtually coequal in importance with
balance-of-payments as the major cause of currency downward
fluctuations.

## #8-21....Global Rates of Inflation

The most important problem facing the U.S. in 1980 was inflation. Of equal rank, as well as adding to the inflation pot,
was the balance-of-payments, which over a period of many months
was greatly unfavorable and unfortunately shows no signs of
let-up in the near future.
Inflation causes the purchasing power of the local currency
to decrease at home, thereby losing the power to maintain its
value against other currencies. Since the balance-of-payments
deficits require repeated outflows of monetary reserves, this
necessitates more currency outlays than would be the case without inflation, bringing a corresponding pressure on the international value of the currency.

## #8-22....Interest Rate Money Market Variations

Interest (the cost of borrowing money) will naturally be a
determinant in the outflow of funds between countries. Where
interest rates become high, they restrict the propensity to
borrow and the unfavorable rates act as a deterrent to free
flow of the currency. The result is the same as in the case of
inflation.

## #8-23....Capital Investment Levels

The investment in foreign plants and facilities by various
countries has an effect on the economic prosperity of the nation in which the investments are made. Like inflation and interest rates, the level of capital investments will have a definite effect on the value of the currency.

## #8-24....National Economic Characteristics

Another cause of currency fluctuation is the national economic characteristics of the particular country involved. Industrial nations whose manufacturing processes suffer may have no
other source to fall back on, resulting in economic recession.
Similarly, a country totally agricultural in its economy can
suffer severely from failing harvest crops.

## #8-25....Extrapolated Expectations

In the article "Inflation--Interest Rates Seen as Part of the Answer to Currency Fluctuations," in THE WALL STREET JOURNAL, June 1976, p. 1, Richard F. Janssen declares that EXTRAPOLATED EXPECTATIONS is a major cause of exchange rate fluctuations. His definition of the term is that "whatever speculators and other traders in foreign currency think the market is most likely to do in the future is what it will do."

An excellent article summarizing the reasons why currencies come under pressure is "Foreign Currencies: Gordian Knot of World Trade," by Franz Pick and Alexander Stanley, in DUN'S REVIEW AND MODERN INDUSTRY, August 1957, page 90.

## EFFECT OF MARKET FLUCTUATIONS ON CURRENCIES

## #8-26....Classification of Currencies

An important consideration in dealing in foreign currencies is the determination of where the exchange of currencies should take place. The question is frequently asked by tourists, travelers and students when and where to convert American dollars into the foreign currencies of the countries they are going to visit. Herbert J. Teison, publisher of a travel newsletter entitled TRAVEL SMART says: "Money is a commodity and there's nothing holy about it. It simply fluctuates with supply and demand when it's left alone."

Where the exchange of currencies should take place--whether at home or in the country of the currency to be purchased--depends upon the nature of the currency. From this viewpoint countries are classified as HARD, STABLE, or STRONG, currency countries, and SOFT, UNSTABLE, or WEAK, currency countries.

## #8-27....Hard, or Strong, and Soft, or Weak, Currencies

Leonard Sloane in an article in the CHICAGO TRIBUNE, April 11, 1976, defines a Hard Currency as that:
which is freely convertible into any other currency. Among such currencies are the U.S. Dollar, the Swiss Franc, the Netherlands Guilder, and West German Mark.

Currencies are considered Soft when they are not freely convertible and restrictions on changes to hard currencies have been imposed. Hard currencies, which are usually in demand, show few differences between the official exchange rate set by the government and the free market rate. But in soft currencies, there is typically a gap between the official rate within the country and the free market elsewhere.

Thus if you are going to countries that have soft currencies, there is little doubt that the initial conversion

should be done in the U.S. before departure. The exchange
rates in the soft currency countries, such as Italy, Portugal, and most of the South American nations, is generally
lower than it is in the unofficial market in America.

Thus a vacationer in Italy would probably now receive
about 830 lira to the dollar from a bank in Italy even
though the OFFICIAL rate may be somewhat higher. Yet money
brokers and dealers in New York recently were quoting 865
lira to the dollar in the unofficial market.

Other examples are Portugal--28-1/2 Escudos to the Dollar in Portugal and 30 in the U.S.; Brazil--9.6 Cruzeiros to
the Dollar in Brazil and 12-1/2 in the U.S.
In addition, many soft currency countries have established limits on the amount of their currencies that a visitor can legally bring in. It should be remembered that some countries have
restrictions on the amount of their currencies that can be reconverted to dollars, or require exchange receipts for reconversion. In such cases it is advisable not to exchange too much
and by all means to keep the records of how much is involved.

## ACCOUNTING FOR FOREIGN EXCHANGE*

### #8-28....Nature of the Foreign Exchange Account

When a business enterprise does business overseas and re-
.ceives payment in the foreign currency of the party with whom
it has dealt, the holding of this foreign exchange or currency
must be reflected in the accounts on the balance sheet date.
Foreign exchange is regarded as a type of cash account. Thus
for external reporting, the balance sheet nomenclature CASH ON
HAND AND IN BANK includes the holdings of any foreign exchange
whether in the form of foreign exchange instruments or foreign
bank accounts. As long as there are no restrictions BLOCKING
the purchase or sale of the foreign exchange, the foreign exchange instruments are as liquid as other cash items. Blocked
currency accounts (viz., those restricted from conversion into
other currencies by the foreign central monetary authority)
must be disclosed on the balance sheet if the amounts are
material. The disclosure may be by footnote, by parenthetical
remark, or by setting forth the amount in a separate category.

### #8-29....Market Transactions

The bank's rates for customers tend to be less favorable
than the cable transfer rates. Nevertheless, competition is

------

*See Summary of Footnote References -- #8-28 thru #8-33

keen among bankers in the retail market.  The  bulk of the foreign exchange business with firms and individuals is transacted
by telephone.  Many firms shop around for the best price before
making  the actual sale or purchase.  Though the quoting of the
rate is nearly automatic, it represents a careful assessment of
the market factors as weighted  with the customer's present and
potential business.  The foreign exchange trader knows the current  state of the market, its  expected  future trend, and the
current exchange position of the bank.

### #8-30....Commissions on Foreign Exchange Transactions

    In the interbank or  wholesale market, the banks  ordinarily
do  not charge a commission  on foreign  exchange transactions.
The small spread  between the buying and selling  rates provide
the revenue for the bank.   This SPREAD, known as the AGIO, includes the  foreign  exchange broker's commission which must be
paid on transactions between the banks.

### #8-31....Recording Foreign Exchange

    Foreign exchange is a  type of  cash account and the holding
of foreign exchange on the balance sheet date must be reflected
in the accounts.  There are two  methods of keeping foreign exchange accounts:  the Cost Method and the Standard Rate Method.

### #8-32....Cost Method of Recording Foreign Exchange

    The  Cost Method records transactions in  both the  domestic
and the foreign currencies at the actual amounts.  The  foreign
currency columns constitute a perpetual inventory.  This method
requires an adjustment at the monthend to bring the  ending domestic balance in line  with  the  current value of the foreign
currency balance.  The adjustment is recorded in a Foreign  Exchange Gain and Loss Account.
    To illustrate the Cost Method, assume the U.S. Corp. engages
in the following transactions in December:

Dec.1    Purchases 3,500 Jordanian Dinars  at spot rate of  U.S.
         $5.00 per Dinar, for $17,500
Dec.10   Issues  sight draft for purchases of imported Jordanian
         merchandise payable in Jordanian  Dinars in  the sum of
         400  Jordanian  Dinars  at market  rate of 1  Jordanian
         Dinar = U.S. $4.99
Dec.23   A 30-day time draft in  the sum of 500 Jordanian Dinars
         received  from  a  Jordanian customer came due  and was
         paid for  by the customer on Dec. 23  on which date the
         market rate was 1 Jordanian Dinar = U.S. $4.95

Using the Cost Method, the journal entries would be:

Dec.1  Jordanian Dinar Frgn. Exch.
                (3,500 x $5)            17,500
            Cash                                    17,500

Dec.10 Purchases (400 x 4.99)         1,996
            Jordanian Dinar Frgn.Exch.             1,996

Dec.23 Jordanian Dinar Frgn. Exch.
                (500 x 4.95)            2,475
            Draft Receivable                        2,475

Assume that as of Dec. 31 the Market Rate of the Jordanian Dinar was $4.99. The adjustment entry to be made to bring the foreign exchange account into balance with its current value would be:

Dec.31 Foreign Exch. Gains & Losses      15
            Jordanian Dinar Frgn. Exch.              15

The basis for such adjustment entry can be observed by setting up a Jordanian Dinar Foreign Exchange Account in the ledger and recording the above journal entries in the account, which would appear as follows:

JORDANIAN DINAR FOREIGN EXCHANGE ACCOUNT (COST METHOD)

| Date | Explanation | Jordanian Dr. | Jordanian Cr. | U.S.Rate | U. S. Dr. | U.S. Cr. |
|------|-------------|---------------|---------------|----------|-----------|----------|
| Dec.1 | Cable Transfer | 3,500 | | $5.00 | $17,500 | |
| Dec.10 | Sight Draft Payable | | 400 | 4.99 | | $1,996 |
| Dec.23 | 30-Day Draft Receivable | 500 | | | 2,475 | |
| Dec.31 | Totals | 4,000 | 400 | | $19,975 | $1,996 |
| BALANCES--Dr. | | 3,600 | | | $17,979 | |
| Dec. 31 | Adjustment of Balance to Current Value | | | | | $15 |
| MARKET BALANCE | | 3,600 | | x 4.99 | $17,964 | |

#8-33...Standard Rate Method of Recording Foreign Exchange

The Standard Rate Method reduces all transactions to a standard rate. The difference between the standard rate and the actual cost or proceeds is immediately recorded in the Exchange Gain and Loss Account. An adjustment is required at the month-end  only if the standard  rate is  changed.  The standard rate usually  represents an average rate around  which most  current transaction prices are fluctuating.

To illustrate the Standard Method,  assume the same transactions as for the Cost Method  and that the  standard rate is to be 1 Dinar = $4.99 U.S.  Under the Standard Method, the journal entries would be:

```
Dec.1   Jordanian Dinar Frgn. Exch.
             (3,500 x 4.99)              17,465
          Exchange Gains & Losses Variance    35
          Cash (3,500 x 5.00)                      17,500

Dec.10  Purchases (400 x 4.99)           1,996
          Jordanian Dinar Frgn. Exch.              1,996

Dec.23  Jordanian Dinar Frgn. Exch.
             (500 x 4.99)               2,495
          Exchg. Gains & Losses Variance           20
          Draft Receivable (500x4.95)            2,475

Dec.31  Exchange Gains & Losses            15
          Jordanian Dinar Frgn.Exch.               15
        (To bring actual cost to current value)
```

The basis for the  $15 adjustment on Dec. 31 is the debit of $35 on Dec. 1 less the credit of $20 on Dec. 23.

The Jordanian Dinar Ledger  Account under  the Standard Rate Method would appear as  follows:

JORDANIAN DINAR FOREIGN EXCHANGE ACCOUNT (STANDARD METHOD)

| | | Actual Cost | | | Standard Rate (4.99) | | |
|---|---|---|---|---|---|---|---|
| | | Dinars x Rate | Jordanian | | | U. S. | |
| | | | Dr. | Cr. | Rate | Dr. | Cr. |
| Dec. 1 | Cable Trans-fer | 3,500 x 5.00 = | 17,500 | | 4.99 | 17,465 | |
| Dec.10 | Sight Draft Payable | (400) x 4.99 = | | 1,996 | 4.99 | | 1,996 |
| Dec.23 | 30-Day Draft Rcble. | 500 x 4.95 = | 2,475 | | 4.99 | 2,495 | |
| TOTALS | | 3,600 | 19,975 | 1,996 | | 19,960 | 1,996 |
| Current Value (Exchg. Loss) | | | | 15 | | | |
| TOTALS | | 3,600 | 19,975 | 2,011 | | 19,960 | 1,996 |
| BALANCES | | | 17,964 | | | 17,964 | |

It should be noted that no adjusting posting is made to the Standard Rate section of the Account, and also that when the adjusting entry is made only to the Actual Cost, the balances in the account are exactly the same for the Actual as for the Standard. The $15 adjustment to the Actual is accounted for in the journal entries showing an Exchange Loss on Dec. 1 of $35 and an Exchange Gain of $20 made on Dec. 23, leaving a net loss of $15 as evidenced by the adjustment entry.

## SUMMARY OF FOOTNOTE REFERENCES
(References are to Paragraph #'s)

#8-9    CHICAGO TRIBUNE, Section 11 (Aug. 22, 1982): 7
#8-12   AMERICAN EXPRESS COMPANY DIARY, 1984
#8-13   Federal Reserve Statistical Release, N.Y. (Oct. 31, 1978)
#8-20   Chemical Bank of N.Y., "Foreign Exposure Management," 1972,
        p. 4
#8-25   Richard F. Janssen, "Inflation--Interest Rates Seen As Part
        of the Answer to Currency Fluctuations," THE WALL STREET
        JOURNAL (June 1976): 1
#8-26   Herbert J. Teison, TRAVEL SMART, newsletter
#8-27   Leonard Sloane, CHICAGO TRIBUNE (April 11, 1976)
#8-28 thru #8-33:  "Accounting for Foreign Exchange," adapted from
        Norlin G. Rueschhoff, INTERNATIONAL ACCOUNTING AND FINANCIAL
        REPORTING, 1976, Praeger Publishers, Inc., by permission.

## BIBLIOGRAPHY

Brittain, Bruce. "Tests of Theories of Exchange Rate Determina-
        tion," JOURNAL OF FINANCE (May 1977): 519-529
Evans, Thomas G. THE CURRENCY CAROUSEL. Princeton, N.J.: Dow Jones,
        1977
Giddy, Ian H. "Research on the Foreign Exchange Markets," COLUMBIA
        JOURNAL OF WORLD BUSINESS, 14 (Winter 1979): 4-6
Kohlhagen, Steven W. "The Performance of the Foreign Exchange Mar-
        kets," JOURNAL OF INTERNATIONAL BUSINESS STUDIES, 6 (Fall
        1975): 33-40
Kubarych, Roger M. "Foreign Exchange Markets in the United States,"
        FEDERAL RESERVE BANK OF NEW YORK (August 1978)
Makin, John H. "Fixed vs. Floating: A Red Herring," COLUMBIA JOUR-
        NAL OF WORLD BUSINESS, 14 (Winter 1979): 7-14
"The New York Foreign Exchange Market," BANKERS MAGAZINE (January-
        February 1984): 67
Pick, Franz and Stanley, Alexander. "Foreign Currencies: Gordian
        Knot of World Trade," DUN'S REVIEW AND MODERN INDUSTRY (Aug-
        ust 1957): 90
Wallich, Henry C. "What Makes Exchange Rates Move?", CHALLENGE
        (July-August 1977): 39-40

## THEORY QUESTIONS
(Question Numbers are Keyed to Text Paragraph #'s)

#8-2  How are exchange rates classified according to time? Define Spot Rates and Forward Rates.

#8-7  How are exchange rates classified according to nature of transaction? Define Buying Rates and Selling Rates.

#8-8  How are exchange rates classified according to government fiat? Define Preferential Rates, Penalty Rates, and Differential Rates.

#8-14 How many types of currency rate quotations are there? Illustrate each.

#8-19 What are the six common causes of foreign exchange fluctuations? Briefly explain the nature of each.

#8-26 Into what two classes is currency classified? Define each of them.

#8-28 Where a firm holds foreign currency at statement date, how is it classified, what statement should it appear on, as what?

#8-31 How many methods are there of keeping foreign exchange accounts, what are they, and briefly discuss how they operate?


## EXERCISES

### EX-8-1  (CPA EXAM, 11/45, LAW, #12)
An accountant, in making a cash audit of the John Jones Company, finds in the cash drawer a note payable to John Jones Co. from a customer in England payable in New York in English pounds, shillings, and pence. Give your opinion as to its classification, negotiability, and valuation.

### EX-8-2  (CPA EXAM, 5/70, THEORY, #4)
Although cash generally is regarded as the simplest of all assets to account for, certain complexities can arise for both domestic and multinational companies.
**Required**:
   a. What are the normal components of cash?
   b. Under what circumstances, if any, do valuation problems arise in connection with cash?
   c. Unrealized and/or realized gains or losses can arise in connection with cash. Excluding consideration of price-level changes, indicate the nature of such gains or losses and the context in which they can arise in relation to cash.

### EX-8-3
The U. S. Import Co., a U. S. importer, purchased merchandise from the Tokyo Exporting Co. of Japan in the sum of Y 70,000

Japanese Yen payable in Japanese Yen. Payment date is Jan. 3 on
which date the spot rates were:

       Selling Rate:  1 Japanese Yen   =     $.0045
       Buying Rate:   1 Japanese Yen   =     $.0042

**Required**:
How many U.S. dollars will be required to settle the account?
(show computations)

### EX-8-4

On March 1 the U.S. Mfg. Co., a U.S. firm, purchased merchandise from the Manila Corp. on 30-days account in the sum of
90,000 Philippine Pesos. On March 1 the exchange rate for
Philippine Pesos was as follows:

       Buying Rate:   1 Philippine Peso =    $.115
       Selling Rate:  1 Philippine Peso =    $.120

**Required**:
As accountant for the U.S. Mfg. Co., what entry in terms of
U.S. dollars would you record for the purchase? (show computa-
tions)


## PROBLEMS

### P-8-1

On June 30, ABC Corp., a U.S. company, sold merchandise costing
$75,000 to the Lisbon Co. of Portugal taking a note receivable
in Escudos which at the prevailing rate of exchange on the date
of the sale had a fair market value of $100,000. On Dec. 31,
due to a change downward in the rate of exchange, the note was
worth $75,000. On March 15 of the following year the note was
paid in full, and when immediately converted to U.S. dollars,
ABC Corp. received $125,000.

**Required**:
Prepare journal entries for June 30, December 31, and March 15,
assuming ABC reports on a calendar-year basis.

### P-8-2  (CPA EXAM, 11/17, PRAC. II, #7)

The XYZ Corp., the accounts of which you are auditing, is an
American company and has as its principal asset an industrial
plant purchased many years ago located in Mexico. It also has
capital locked up in current inventories, accounts receivable,
etc., incidental to the operation of such Mexican plant. For
many years the Mexican accounts were reflected on the head office books on the basis of $2 Mex. to $1 U.S.A.

**Required**:
   Do you consider this proper at a time when Mexican exchange
stands at, say $1 Mex. equal to 18 cents U.S.A.?
   Assuming you feel that the situation requires adjustment,
how would you proceed to correct the American balance sheet?

## P-8-3 (CPA EXAM, 11/18, PRAC. I, #3)

A dealer in foreign exchange finds from his books that he has had the following transactions in London exchange during a particular month, viz:

Exchange bought in local market:
*Purchase of Foreign Currency*

Jan. 1    30-day bill, payable in *Buy currency or give note* London ₤3,000 at                2.375

Jan. 15   Bill due at sight in London ₤2,500 at                         2.38

Exchange sold in local market:
*Sale of Curr For Currency*

Jan. 5    Bill due in London at sight ₤1,000 at *Dr. Receivable Cr. Cash - FE*     2.385

Jan. 20   Cable transfer ₤2,000 at        2.39

Foreign correspondents' draft honored and paid:
*Sale of currency*

Jan. 20   Bill at 30 days after sight accepted Dec. 21 ₤500 at          2.39

At January 31 the rate for cable transfers is $2.40.

**Required**:

a. Prepare the general journal entries for the foregoing transactions.

b. Construct a ledger sheet for the foreign exchange account using the Cost Method showing the gain or loss from the foreign exchange transactions.

c. Using a standard rate of $2.05 *$2.40* = ₤1, construct a ledger sheet for this account using the Standard Rate Method.

d. Is the profit or loss so stated final?

## P-8-4 (CPA EXAM, 5/66, THEORY, #4, 25 MIN.)

The Overseas Trading Company, a U.S. corporation with several foreign subsidiaries, appended the following footnote to its December 31, 1965 financial statements:

"'Marketable securities' includes $15,100 of freely transferable import certificates issued by the government of a foreign country. The certificates entitle the bearer to import into the foreign country certain restricted luxury items (costing up to 40% of the invoice prices of the exports on which the certificates were issued) that cannot otherwise be imported. They were issued by the foreign government as an incentive to export goods from the foreign country and were valued at market on the dates received (current market, $15,250). Our foreign subsidiary does not import luxury items and expects to sell all certificates during the operating period. The foreign government's policy is expected to continue indefinitely."

**Required**:
  a. Discuss the propriety of valuing the certificates at market on the dates they are received.
  b. Discuss the propriety of treating the credit arising from the receipt of the certificates as
    1. A reduction of Cost of Goods Sold.
    2. An addition to Stockholders' Equity.
    3. An addition to Other or Special Income.
    4. An addition to Gross Sales.

P-8-5

A French Exchange Trader quotation as of March 1 is
      Buying Rate     =   $1 U.S. =         8.0 F.F.
      Selling Rate    =   $1 U.S. =         8.5 F.F.

**Required**:
  a. How much will the trader pay for $100 U.S.?
  b. What is the Agio?
  c. What would the profit be if the trader sold the U.S. $100 for French Francs?

P-8-6

The Oslo Co. deals with the Karachi Corporation. On May 11 the spot rates for the currencies of the two countries in terms of U.S. $ Dollars are:
      1 U.S. $           =    8 Norwegian Krone
      1 Norwegian Krone =    U.S. 12-1/2 cents
      1 U.S. $           =    16 Pakistan Rupees
      1 Pakistan Rupee  =    U.S. 6-1/4 cents

**Required**:
What are the Direct and Indirect quotes in terms of
  a. the Norwegian Krone?
  b. the Pakistan Rupee?

# Accounting for International Foreign Trade and Investment Business Transactions

## FOREIGN OPERATIONS*

### #9-1....Nature of Foreign Operations

Basically, foreign operations may be conducted on a LOCAL or an INTERNATIONAL level. By LOCAL OPERATIONS is meant that a local business operator may conduct transactions with a foreign business operator with each being based in his own home country, such as exporting and importing, as well as foreign investments in international ventures. By INTERNATIONAL OPERATIONS is meant that a local company opens a branch operation or subsidiary in a foreign country. In Chap. 9 we will treat the principles relative to the operation on a local basis followed by a discussion of operations on an international basis.

## FOREIGN TRADE

### #9-2....Nature of Export-Import Operations

The export and import business of the U.S. with relation to other parts of the world originated in colonial days. The procedures for handling foreign trade shipments are rooted in early commercial practices. Modern banking, transportation, and communications have facilitated the negotiation, movement and financing of foreign trade. The export-import balance of trade is a significant element in the international balance-of-payments position of any country. As seen in Chap. 8, it is one of the most weighty elements that causes currency market rate fluctuations. The importance of foreign trade cannot be overemphasized.

------

*See Summary of Footnote References -- #9-1 thru #9-21

#9-3....Export-Import Financing

Like domestic trade, overseas trade can be financed through open account, consignments of merchandise, or advance cash deposits. However, the greatest part of overseas trade transactions are handled through the use of letters of credit and bank drafts. Each of these financing methods, along with the specialized authority-to-purchase procedure, serves a purpose in foreign trade.

#9-4....Letters of Credit

Sec. 5-103(1) of the U.S. UNIFORM COMMERCIAL CODE defines a Letter of Credit as "an engagement by a bank or other person that the issuer of the letter will honor drafts or other demands for payment on him, upon compliance with the conditions specified in the credit." In international transactions, the letter of credit is an instrument issued by a bank, at the request of one party, authorizing that party or a designated second party to draw a check or draft against the bank or one of its correspondents, for a designated sum, payable on demand, at a specified time, or upon presentation of specified documents which usually give title to the goods. These include the papers covering the shipment such as the bill of lading, plus other documents essential to the export or import of goods.

#9-5....Types of Letters of Credit

Generally there are three main types of Letters of Credit: the Cash Letter, the Traveler's Letter, and the Commercial Letter. Each is issued upon the request of an individual after the bank's approval of his application.

#9-6....Cash Letter of Credit

The Cash Letter of Credit is a definite demand instrument. It expedites international cash payment.

#9-7....Traveler's Letter of Credit

*Travelers Checks*

This is a variant of the Cash Letter. It allows a traveler abroad to carry substantial amounts of funds with safety. In effect it is a world-wide bank account. The person to whom it is issued may draw demand drafts on the issuing bank at any of its foreign branches or correspondents. Both the Cash and the Traveler's Letters may be classified as Commercial Letters of Credit. However, Commercial Letters also are executed for delayed international payments, and may be used for exports and imports.

#9-8....Commercial Letter of Credit

This is issued by a bank at the request of a buyer of merchandise in favor of the seller of the merchandise. It provides for payment to the seller upon his presentation of the specified shipping documents. The usual documents are the invoice, the bill of lading, and the insurance policy or certificate. Other required documents may be certificates of origin, weight lists, various types of certificates of analysis, and packing lists. Commercial Letters of Credit may be classified as Commercial Export Letters and Commercial Import Letters of Credit.

#9-9....Commercial Export Letters of Credit

These may be either Revocable or Irrevocable. The irrevocable letter may be either confirmed or unconfirmed. The confirmed irrevocable straight credit is issued by a foreign bank and confirmed irrevocably by the exporter's domestic bank. The domestic bank is obligated to honor drafts against the irrevocable letter. No changes in terms may be made without the consent of all parties.

The unconfirmed letter of credit may be the domestic bank's own irrevocable commercial letter of credit. Such a letter is similar to the confirmed irrevocable credit except that the latter is the obligation of two banks whereas the bank's own irrevocable letter carries the obligation of only one bank.

The other type of unconfirmed irrevocable letter is the correspondent's irrevocable straight credit. This letter is issued by the foreign bank without the responsibility or engagement of the exporter's domestic bank. The domestic bank simply transmits the advice of its issuance on behalf of the foreign bank. For the exporter, this method is not as preferred as the confirmed irrevocable straight credit or the domestic bank's own irrevocable letter of credit.

The least frequently used method is the revocable letter of credit. Because no bank will guarantee a letter that may be cancelled by the issuing bank, such a letter is unconfirmed. It usually serves as a means of arranging payment. Because it may be amended or cancelled without the consent of or notice to the beneficiary, it provides no protection prior to payment.

#9-10....Commercial Import Letters of Credit

The irrevocable import letter is used to finance a large part of the imports into the U.S. The irrevocable letter's principal advantage is that it gives the foreign shipper the protection of a bank obligation. Also the domestic importer is able to use the purchased merchandise as security in obtaining credit to finance the transaction.

The import letter may be fixed, revolving, or increased. A
FIXED IMPORT LETTER OF CREDIT is for a certain amount and is
exhausted when the amount has been drawn or accepted. In a RE-
VOLVING IMPORT LETTER OF CREDIT the original amount is replen-
ished after each draft until the expiration date. For an IN-
CREASED IMPORT LETTER OF CREDIT each increase is authorized
specifically by an amendment. In most cases, the privilege is a
matter of continuous agreement between the bank and its customer. The revolving or the increased import letter enables the
use of the same letter for all transactions with a specified
shipper.

#### #9-11....Outline Classifying Letters of Credit

All of the letters of credit presented above may be classified into a convenient chart which has been produced here in
Figure 9-1.

#### #9-12....Authority to Purchase

Somewhat similar to the commercial letter of credit is the
AUTHORITY TO PURCHASE. It is used mainly by Far Eastern banks
to finance exports from the U.S. and other countries. It gives
the exporter a specific domestic bank where he may negotiate
drafts on the foreign buyer or his bank abroad. It is an authority extended by the foreign bank to a domestic bank to buy
the drafts and documents of a specified shipment. The authority
to purchase may be issued irrevocably or revocably on the part
of the foreign bank. The irrevocable authority to purchase may
be confirmed by the domestic bank.

#### #9-13....Drafts

A substantial volume of U.S. exports is financed by dollar
drafts. For imports, drafts are used only in specific appropriate circumstances. The dollar draft, a foreign exchange instrument, may be either a time draft or a sight draft. In foreign
trade transactions, such drafts are often accompanied by the
shipping documents.

#### #9-14....Advance Deposits

A very small amount of foreign trade is financed by advance
deposits. This method is used when credit risks are doubtful.
Certain conditions, such as foreign exchange restrictions or
political and economic disturbances, may force the seller into
negotiating the no-risk transaction by demanding cash in advance.

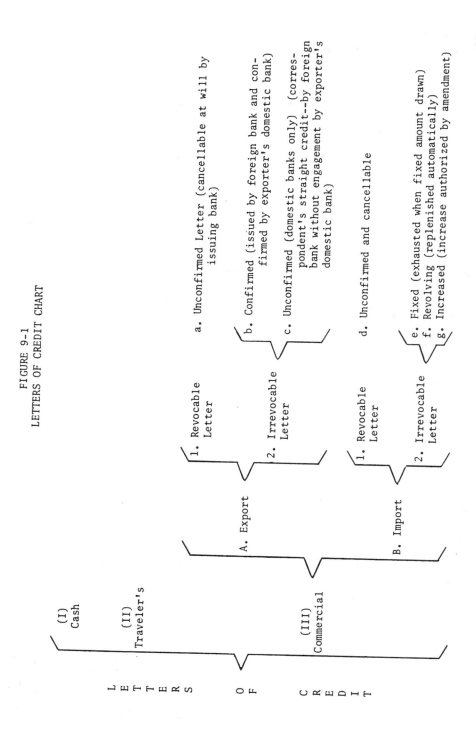

FIGURE 9-1
LETTERS OF CREDIT CHART

LETTERS OF CREDIT

(I) Cash

(II) Traveler's

(III) Commercial

A. Export
1. Revocable Letter
2. Irrevocable Letter
    a. Unconfirmed Letter (cancellable at will by issuing bank)
    b. Confirmed (issued by foreign bank and confirmed by exporter's domestic bank)
    c. Unconfirmed (domestic banks only) (correspondent's straight credit—by foreign bank without engagement by exporter's domestic bank)

B. Import
1. Revocable Letter
2. Irrevocable Letter
    d. Unconfirmed and cancellable
    e. Fixed (exhausted when fixed amount drawn)
    f. Revolving (replenished automatically)
    g. Increased (increase authorized by amendment)

## #9-15....Credit on Open Account

For a few well-known reputable international firms, foreign trade, like domestic transactions, is handled on an open-account basis. In addition to the delayed payment risk associated with domestic transactions, there is the disadvantage in foreign trade of the added time involved in the goods shipment. Without a concrete obligation upon shipment of the goods, the exporter may be hindered in using the immediate export sale as a basis for obtaining credit from a financial institution.

## #9-16....Goods on Consignment

Goods on a consignment basis are usually limited to shipments to foreign branches or subsidiaries. With the credit risks thoroughly examined and known, consignments are occasionally made to select agents, representatives, or import houses abroad. Since a consignment involves no tangible obligation upon shipment, the consignment basis has the same financing disadvantage as the open account credit transactions.

## #9-17....Foreign Shipment Terms

In the negotiating of foreign trade transactions, the quoted price specifically excludes or includes certain related shipping costs. Besides the customary domestic freight shipment terms—F.O.B. (free on board) Shipping Point and F.O.B. Destination—there are several other terms commonly used in foreign trade practice. They include FAS (free alongside), C.& F. (cost and freight), and CIF (cost, insurance and freight). The standard U.S. definitions of the main foreign trade terms used are published by the International Chamber of Commerce.

Unless otherwise specified, just as in domestic trade, the seller must bear all risks and all costs until title passes to the buyer at the stipulated point of transfer. Export costs include such items as packing, transportation to point of transfer, documentation fees, sailing registration fees, and insurance as designated by the terms. Usually the foreign duties and export taxes must be paid by the buyer.


## FOREIGN INVESTMENTS

## #9-18....Nature of Foreign Investments

Investments in international ventures may take one of several forms. In accounting, a distinction is made between two kinds of investment: temporary and permanent.

Temporary investments, which take the nature of marketable securities, are purchased with temporarily excessive cash. Such excess cash may derive from seasonal or cyclical movements of volume and working capital, or may be accumulated for a future capital investment.

Permanent, or long-term, investments may take the form of investments in branches, joint ventures, partnerships, or corporations. They are acquired with the intention of holding them for a number of years. Whereas short-term investments are classified as current assets, permanent investments are classified (in a separate category below the current asset section) as long-term investments or simply "investments."

#9-19....Foreign Marketable Securities

When a firm decides to acquire foreign marketable securities as an investment of excess cash, it has practically as many alternatives as for a domestic investment. Foreign common stock investments can be acquired through the registered stock exchanges in the U.S. There are about 25 foreign stocks listed on the New York Stock Exchange and approximately 65 on the American Stock Exchange. If the security broker is a member of a foreign stock exchange such as the Toronto Stock Exchange (the leading one in Canada), he may purchase the securities for the corporation. Needless to say, the foreign securities also can be acquired privately and in the over-the-counter market.

Over-the-counter foreign securities may be represented by AMERICAN DEPOSITARY RECEIPTS (ADRs), representing ownership of securities physically deposited abroad. The ADRs are quoted in U.S. Dollars and are valid only for securities supported by validation certificates showing proof of compliance with tax and ownership regulations.

#9-20....Foreign Direct Investment

Permanent (or long-term) foreign investments are negotiated with the intention of holding them for a period of years. A foreign direct investment may consist of capital transferred, or an advance or loan, or the direct investor's share of the reinvested earnings of an affiliated foreign entity.

A direct investor may own as much as 10 percent or more of the voting power, earnings, or capital of the foreign entity. The entity may be a corporation, partnership, or branch engaged in business in a foreign country. The amount of direct investment is dependent on both the history of direct investment policy of a firm and the economic development of the foreign country, or the fiscal relationship of that country with the home country.

## #9-21....Foreign Joint Ventures

Joint ventures may be incorporated or unincorporated. APB Opinion No. 18 describes a corporate joint venture:

CORPORATE JOINT VENTURE refers to a corporation owned and operated by a small group of businesses (the joint venturers) as a separate and specific business or project for the mutual benefit of the members of the group.

The purpose of a corporate joint venture frequently is to share risks and rewards in developing a new market, product, or technology; to combine complementary technological knowledge; or to pool resources in developing production or other facilities.

A corporate joint venture also usually provides an arrangement under which each joint venturer may participate, directly or indirectly, in the overall management of the joint venture. Joint venturers thus have an interest or relationship other than as passive investors.

An entity which is a subsidiary of one of the joint venturers is not a corporate joint venture. The ownership of a corporate joint venture seldom changes, and its stock is usually not traded publicly. A minority public ownership, however, does not preclude a corporation from being a corporation joint venture.

The Opinion further declares that the equity method should be utilized to account for investments in common stock of corporate joint ventures, whether foreign or domestic.

A joint venture may be established because a 50 percent ownership is the maximum that a particular foreign government would allow under its foreign investment laws. Also, joint ventures may be negotiated because the parent company needs a strong local partner. However, there are some drawbacks in a strict 50-50 arrangement. Who, for example, assumes final responsibility? And what happens when there is a tie vote? To bypass such barriers, special arrangements are made. Among them are the use of two kinds of stock; allowing a small percentage of ownership in the hands of a friendly mediator; establishing a special by-law which extends the management power to one of the venturers; or simply the awarding of a management contract.

## ACCOUNTING FOR FOREIGN TRADE BUSINESS TRANSACTIONS

## #9-22....Foreign Trade Transactions

Foreign trade basically consists of export and import transactions and is LOCAL in the sense that each of the parties to the export-import relationship maintains his business domicile in his home country. Although the export-import relationship is reciprocal, the entries on the books of the exporter may not necessarily be the opposite of those made by the importer due to the factor of exchange risks.

## FOREIGN EXPORT SALES

### #9-23....Export Sales

There are two possible methods of billing sales by exporters: in the local currency of the exporter, or in the foreign currency of the importer purchaser. From the viewpoint of the exporter, the more desirable method is to bill in his local currency, e.g., U.S. Dollars for a U.S. exporter. In such case, because the foreign purchaser must pay in U.S. Dollars, the exporter avoids the risk resulting from any exchange rate fluctuation occurring between the date of the invoice and the date of payment.

### #9-24....Export Sales Billed in Exporter's Currency

To illustrate, assume that on July 1 the U.S. Exporting Co. sells merchandise to the Australian Corp. in the sum of U.S. $11,150 to be paid in 30 days in U.S. Dollars. On July 31 the Australian Corp. sends remittance on its account for $11,150 U.S. Dollars. The entries on the books of the U.S. Exporting Co. would be:

| | | | |
|---|---|---|---|
| 7/1 | Accts. Rcble., Australian Corp. | 11,150 | |
| | Sales | | 11,150 |
| 7/31 | Cash | 11,150 | |
| | Accts. Rcble., Austr. Corp. | | 11,150 |

### #9-25....Export Sales Billed in Importer's Currency

However, where the export sale is billed in the foreign currency of the importer, any change in the rate of the foreign currency between the sales date and the payment date will result in an EXCHANGE GAIN OR LOSS, which is regarded as a revenue or expense to the exporter. To illustrate, assume that on July 1 the U.S. Exporting Co. sells merchandise to the Australian Corp., billing it for A$10,000 Australian Dollars to be paid for in Australian Dollars in 30 days. The spot rate for Australian Dollars on July 1 is U.S. $1.115. On July 31 when the Australian Corp. sends remittance on its account for A$10,000, the spot rate for Australian Dollars was $1.117 U.S. The entries on the books of the U.S. Exporting Co. would be:

```
7/1    Accts. Rcble., Australian Corp.   11,150
         Sales                                      11,150
       (Sale of 10,000 A$ at spot
       rate of U.S. $1.115)

7/31   Austral.Dollars Foreign Exchange  11,170
         Accts. Rcble., Austr. Corp.              11,150
         Exchange Gain or Loss                        20
       (Receipt of Payment of 7/1 invoice
       of A$10,000 at spot rate of
       A$ = U.S. $1.117)
```

The U.S. Exporting Co. now has U.S. $11,170 on hand which would appear as Cash on the balance sheet of July 31. If the Australian Foreign Exchange was converted to U.S. Dollars on July 31, the entry to be made would be:

```
7/31   Cash                              11,170
         Austr. $ Foreign Exchange              11,170
```

Any costs of conversion would be charged to exchange expense.

## #9-26....Export Sales Exchange Gains and Losses

It may be observed that since the spot rate of the Australian Dollar was $1.115 on July 1 (the date of sale) and increased to $1.117 on July 31 (the date of payment), the exporter received the equivalent of $.002 more for each dollar than what was called for on the invoice. This resulted in a gain of 10,000 x .002, or $20. The sale billed at $11,150 resulted in the receipt of $11,170. The extra $20 came from a fluctuation upward in the exchange rate, hence is regarded as an EXCHANGE GAIN. If the exchange rate at payment date had declined from July 1, an EXCHANGE LOSS would have resulted.

In comparison with the previous situation where the billing was in local U.S. currency, there was no gain or loss because the foreign importer paid in U.S. currency. At the U.S. $1.117 rate, it actually cost the foreign importer only A$9,982.10 to remit the U.S. $11,150; so that instead of having to send A$10,000, he had to remit only A$9,982.10--a gain of $17.90 for the foreign importer where remittance was made in U.S. Dollars.

## #9-27....Classification of Foreign Exchange

As indicated above, if the exporter is paid in foreign exchange and it is held on the balance sheet date, it must be reflected in the accounts. As seen, Foreign Exchange is a type of cash account, so that for external reporting it would be included as part of the balance sheet nomenclature, CASH ON

HAND AND IN BANK.  It would include the holdings of any foreign exchange, whether in the form of foreign exchange instruments or foreign bank accounts.  Any Blocked Currency amounts restricted from conversion into other currencies by the foreign central monetary authority must be disclosed on the balance sheet if the amounts are material.  The disclosure may be by footnote, by parenthetical remark, or by setting forth the amount in a separate category.

As long as there are no restrictions blocking the purchase or sale of the foreign exchange, the foreign exchange instruments are as liquid as any cash items. Any gains or losses from the foreign exchange fluctuations are realized gains or losses. They should be charged against or credited to ordinary operations and, if material, should receive financial statement disclosure.

## FOREIGN IMPORT PURCHASES

### #9-28....Foreign Import Purchases

As is the case with a foreign sale, conversely a foreign exporting firm may invoice a domestic importer in the foreigner's currency or in the importer's local currency.  If the foreign exporter desires to bear no risk, he will bill the importer in his own country's currency.  In such case, the importer must bear the gain or loss from any currency fluctuation between the invoice date and the payment date. If the foreign exporter bills in the importer's local currency, the foreign seller will bear any gain or loss between the two currencies.

### #9-29....Import Purchases Billed in Importer's Currency

Assume that on July 1 the U.S. Importing Co. buys merchandise from the Australian Corp. in the sum of $11,150 payable in 30 days in U.S. Dollars.  On July 31 the U.S. Importing Co. sends remittance to the Australian Corp. on its account for $11,150 in U.S. Dollars.  The entries on the books of the U.S. Importing Co. would be:

| | | | |
|---|---|---|---|
| 7/1 | Purchases | 11,150 | |
| | Accts. Pybl., Austr. Corp. | | 11,150 |
| 7/31 | Accts. Pybl., Austr. Corp. | 11,150 | |
| | Cash | | 11,150 |

### #9-30....Import Purchases Billed in Exporter's Currency

Assume that on July 1 the U.S. Importing Co. buys merchandise from the Australian Corp. in the sum of A$10,000 payable

in 30 days in Australian Dollars. On July 31 the U.S. Importing
Co. sends remittance to the Australian Corp. for A$10,000. The
spot rate for Australian Dollars on July 1 was U.S. $1.115 and
on July 31 was U.S. $1.117. The entries on the books of U.S.
Importing would be:

| 7/1 | Purchases (10,000 x 1.115) | 11,150 | |
|---|---|---|---|
| | Accts. Pybl., Austr.Corp. | | 11,150 |

| 7/31 | Austr.Dollars Foreign Exchange | 11,170 | |
|---|---|---|---|
| | Cash | | 11,170 |
| | (To record purchase of 10,000 | | |
| | A$ at 1.117) | | |

| 7/31 | Accts. Pybl., Austr. Corp. | 11,150 | |
|---|---|---|---|
| | Exchange Gain or Loss | 20 | |
| | Austr.Dollars Forgn.Exchg. | | 11,170 |

Thus the billing in foreign currency cost the U.S. importer an
EXCHANGE LOSS, because on July 1 the spot rate of the Australian Dollar was U.S. $1.115 and rose to U.S. $1.117 on July 31.
Therefore the importer had to pay the equivalent of $.002 more
for each unit of U.S. Dollar to satisfy the account payable,
making a total of 10,000 x .002, or $20. In other words, while
the purchase was made for $11,150 U.S., the importer had to pay
$11,170 due to the fluctuation downward in the exchange rate,
resulting in an exchange loss of $20. In this case the contrast
should be made with the previous situation involving the export
sale where the billing was made in U.S. Dollars netting the
foreign merchant only 9,982.10 in Australian Dollars, so that
the Australian exporter had to absorb the exchange loss due to
the decline in the value of the U.S. Dollar in relation to the
Australian Dollar.

### #9-31....Recording Foreign Receivables and Payables

The general rule followed in the recording of foreign sales
and purchases of goods in the foregoing transactions was that
each phase is recorded at the exchange rate prevailing on the
date of the invoice of purchase or sale or payment. The payment
on a subsequent date was recorded at the rate prevailing at
that time. Any exchange gain or loss due to changes in the rate
prevailing between the two dates is reported separately.

When the time period between the purchase or sale date spans
two periods, an allocation problem arises. There are two dimensions to the allocation problem: (1) the valuation of the foreign receivable or payable is necessary for proper balance
sheet presentation; (2) the disposition of any exchange gain or
loss must be properly reported.

## APPROACHES TO RECORDING FOREIGN PURCHASES AND SALES

### #9-32....Recording Foreign Purchases and Sales

There are two approaches to the nature of the export-import transactions that will affect both the balance sheet presentation and the question of exchange gain or loss: the one-transaction approach, or perspective; and the two-transaction approach, or perspective.

### #9-33....One-Transaction Approach

This approach dictates that the FINAL amount of the import or export transaction not be determined until the final settlement. Thus the original amount of the sale or purchase is regarded as being recorded as an ESTIMATE which is to be adjusted when the cash payment is made on the account. This will result, in effect, in a CASH BASIS of accounting. Thus, although two transactions have been involved--viz., the purchase or sale, and the payment--only one will be recognized--viz., either a sale or purchase AS OF THE DATE PAYMENT IS MADE.

Under the one-transaction, or single-transaction, approach (or perspective) the Exchange Gain or Loss is totally disregarded. If in the case of a purchase there is a GREATER payment required due to an increase in the value of the foreign exchange, such extra payment will be added to the amount of the original purchase price. Conversely, if in the case of a purchase there is a LESSER payment required due to a decrease in the value of the foreign exchange, such lesser amount will be deducted from the amount of the original purchase price by the amount of the difference.

In the case of a sale, if a GREATER payment is received from the account receivable due to an increase in the value of the foreign exchange, the extra amount in the payment received will be added to the amount of the original sale price. Conversely, in the case of a sale, if a LESSER payment is received from the account receivable due to a decrease in the value of the foreign exchange, such lesser amount will be deducted from the original sale price by the amount of the excess.

### #9-34....Accounting for the One-Transaction Approach

This approach totally disregards exchange gains or losses, which arise only where the billing is done in a foreign currency. Using the above illustration of the export sale billed in the currency of the importer, the entries on the books of the exporter under the one-transaction approach would be:

| 7/1 | Accts. Rcble., Austr. Corp. | 11,150 | |
| | Sales | | 11,150 |
| | (Sale of 10,000 A$ at spot rate of U.S. $1.115) | | |

| 7/31 | Foreign Exchange, Austr.Dollars | 11,170 | |
| | Accts.Rcble., Austr.Corp. | | 11,150 |
| | Sales | | 20 |
| | (Receipt of A$10,000 in payment of 7/1 invoice at spot rate 7/31 of A$ = U.S. $1.117) | | |

| 7/31 | Cash | 11,170 | |
| | Forgn. Exch., AustrDollars | | 11,170 |
| | (To record conversion of foreign exchange less any conversion expense) | | |

Using the same transactions illustrated above for the import purchase billed in the currency of the exporter, the entries on the books of the importer would be:

| 7/1 | Purchases | 11,150 | |
| | Accts. Pybl., Austr.Corp. | | 11,150 |

| 7/31 | Austr. Dollars, Forgn. Exch. | 11,170 | |
| | Cash | | 11,170 |
| | (To purchase 10,000 A$ to pay off account payable) | | |

| 7/31 | Accts. Pybl., Austr. Corp. | 11,150 | |
| | Purchases | 20 | |
| | Austr.Dollars Forgn. Exch. | | 11,170 |

In essence, what the one-transaction approach means as related to exchange gains or losses is that in the case of a sale, an exchange gain increases the amount of the sale and an exchange loss decreases the amount of the sale, and in the case of a purchase, an exchange gain reduces the cost of the purchase and an exchange loss increases the cost of the purchase; or expressed in terms of exchange gains or losses:

an exchange gain in the case of a sale increases the sale;
an exchange gain in the case of a purchase reduces the cost of the purchase;
an exchange loss in the case of a sale decreases the sale;
an exchange loss in the case of a purchase increases the cost of the purchase.

## #9-35....Accounting for the Two-Transaction Approach

The entries presented in #9-25 for export sales billed in the importer's currency and in #9-30 for import purchases billed in the exporter's currency followed the two-transaction approach resulting in exchange gains and losses. The two-transaction approach reflects the view that the collection of the receivable or payment of a payable is a transaction separate from the original sale or purchase, viz., the purchase or sale is one transaction and the payment is a second one. The first transaction is translated at the exchange rate in effect on the date of the sale or purchase. Any change in the exchange rate does not affect the amount recorded as export revenue or import cost at the time of the original transaction. This change results in an exchange gain or loss.

Several theoretical questions arise concerning the acceptance of the two-transaction approach, particularly the proper classification of the income and expense and their allocation where the fluctuation arises over two or more accounting periods. The problem is to ascertain whether gains or losses are realized or unrealized and when. These are financial reporting problems.

## #9-36...Theoretical Pros and Cons of One-Transaction vs. Two-Transaction Approach

As to import purchases, it would seem that the general cost definition would be applicable. Cost means the sum of the applicable expenditures and charges directly or indirectly incurred to bring the article to its existing condition and location under ARB No. 43, RESTATEMENT AND REVISION OF ACCOUNTING RESEARCH BULLETINS, 1953, page 28. Fluctuations in exchange rates occur after the article is brought to its existing location. They have no effect on the article's condition.

The exchange gain or loss is not a function of procurement but one of finance, viz., a decision to accept or avoid the risk involved in delayed payment. As will shortly be seen, this risk can be managed through hedging by means of a FORWARD EXCHANGE CONTRACT. As a financial expense or revenue, the exchange gain or loss should not be charged directly to the foreign sales or purchases account. The method of settlement of an open account balance is a decision separate from the original import or export transaction, and therefore should be recorded separately as an exchange gain or loss in the period that the exchange rate changes. This squares with the two-transaction approach and as a result is receiving world-wide support in practice. Since October 1975, under FASB #8, para. 27, it is expressly provided that "the two-transaction method is required in all situations not hedged for specific transactions," thereby barring the use of the one-transaction approach.

## BALANCE SHEET VALUATION OF RECEIVABLES AND PAYABLES*

### #9-37...Valuation Methods of Foreign Receivables and Payables

Under the two-transaction approach, foreign currency monetary balances of foreign receivables and payables are translated at the exchange rate prevailing on the balance sheet date. There are two methods of recording the change in balance sheet valuation of a foreign receivable or payable: (1) the DIRECT CHARGE METHOD, under which it may be recorded directly in the pertinent account; or (2) the ACCRUAL METHOD, under which it can be recorded in a separate accrual or contra-account.

### #9-38...Foreign Receivables Valuation:  Direct Charge Method

Assume the U.S. Exporting Co. sells the Australian Corp. merchandise on Dec. 1, billing A$10,000 payable in 60 days. On Dec. 1 the current exchange rate was Australian 1$=U.S.$1.115. At the end of the fiscal period (Dec. 31) the current rate was A$1=U.S.$1.112. On Jan. 30, the due date of the account receivable, the U.S. Exporting Co. received remittance from the Australian Corp. of 10,000 Australian Dollars. On Jan. 30 the current exchange rate was A$1=U.S.$1.113. The entries using the DIRECT CHARGE METHOD would be:

| | | | |
|---|---|---|---|
| 12/1 | Accts. Rcble., Austr. Corp. | 11,150 | |
| | Sales | | 11,150 |
| | | | |
| 12/31 | Exchange Gains or Losses | 30 | |
| | Accts.Rcble.,Austr.Corp. | | 30 |
| | (To adjust year-end balance | | |
| | to current rate value) | | |
| | | | |
| 1/30 | Forgn. Exch. Austr. Dollars | | |
| | (10,000 x 1.113) | 11,130 | |
| | Accts.Rcbl.,Austr.Corp. | | |
| | (11,150 - 30) | | 11,120 |
| | Exchange Gains or Losses | | 10 |

It should be noted that the difference between the original accounts receivable in the sum of 11,150 and the payment received of 11,130 (or $20) is the net amount of the difference

------

*See Summary of Footnote References -- #9-37 thru #9-43

between the adjustment made to show a $30 loss at the end of the year to be charged to last year's period, and the gain of $10 shown on January 30 to be credited to the current year's period.

## #9-39....Foreign Receivables Valuation: Accrual Method

Using the same data immediately above, under the ACCRUAL METHOD the journal entries would be:

```
12/1    Accts. Rcble., Austr. Corp.
                (10,000 x 1.115)        11,150
            Sales                                   11,150

12/31   Exchange Gains or Losses       30
            Allownc for Loss on Frgn.Exch           30
        (To adjust year-end acct. rcble.
        balance to current rate value)

1/30    Foreign Exchange, Australia
                (10,000A$ x 1.113)      11,130
        Allownc for Loss on Frgn Exch.     30
            Accts.Rcble.,Austr.Corp.                11,150
            Exchange Gains or Losses                    10
```

## #9-40...Foreign Payables Valuation: Direct Charge Method

Assume the U.S. Importing Co. buys merchandise from the Australian Corp. in the sum of 10,000 Australian Dollars on Dec. 1 payable in 60 days. On Dec. 1 the current exchange rate was 1 Australian $=U.S.$1.115. On Dec. 31, the end of the U.S. Importing Co. fiscal year, the current rate of exchange was A$1= U.S.$1.116. On Jan. 30, when the current exchange rate was A$1= U.S.$1.117, the U.S. Importing Co. sends remittance for Australian $10,000 in payment of its account payable to the Australian Corp. Under the DIRECT CHARGE METHOD the entries to be made would be:

```
12/1    Purchases (10,000 x 1.115)     11,150
            Accts.Pybl., Austr.Corp.                11,150

12/31   Exchange Gains or Losses       10
            Accts.Pybl., Austr. Corp.               10
        (To adjust year-end balance
        to current value)

1/30    Foreign Exchange,Austr.Dollars 11,170
            Cash                                    11,170
        (To record purchase of 10,000
        A$ at 1.117 to remit to Aus.Corp)
```

```
1/30    Accts. Pyble., Aust. Corp.
                (11,150 + 10)          11,160
        Exchange Gain or Loss             10
            Frgn.Exch., Aust.Dollars              11,170
```

#9-41....Foreign Payables Valuation:  Accrual Method

Using the same data  as that immediately above, the  journal entries would be:

```
12/1    Purchases (10,000 x 1.115)     11,150
            Accts.Pybl., Aust.Corp.               11,150


12/31   Exchange Gains or Losses           10
            Accrued Liability on
                Frgn. Exch. Loss                      10


1/30    Accts. Pybl., Austr. Corp.     11,150
        Accrued Liab. on Frgn.Exch.Loss    10
        Exchange Gains or Losses           10
            Foreign Exchange, Aus.Dollars
                (10,000 x 1.117)                  11,170


1/30    Foreign Exchange, A$           11,170
            Cash                                  11,170
        (To record purchase of 10,000A$
        at 1.117 to remit to Aust.Corp)
```

#9-42...Evaluation of Direct and Accrual Methods of Valuation

Because  the  documents  substantiating  the  balance  sheet amount are in  terms of foreign currency, the  more appropriate method is to record the  change in  domestic currency valuation directly  into the accounts.  This  method has the advantage of showing the  present translated value which  should be reported on the balance sheet.

#9-43...Reporting Exchange Gains and Losses Resulting
        From Valuation of Receivables and Payables

As stated in #9-31, the second dimension to the period allo-cation problem is the  proper disposition of the  recorded  ex-change gains and losses.  Since the actual gain or  loss is at-tributable to a financial management decision separate from the trade transaction, the gains or  losses derived from  valuation of the  receivables or payables at the time of an exchange rate change are recognized as current operating gains or losses, and as such  are separated on the income statement.  If the amounts are material, disclosure of them on the income statement may be necessary for a fair presentation.

## HEDGING AGAINST EXCHANGE FLUCTUATION LOSSES

### #9-44....Forward Exchange Contracts

As indicated in #9-36, the importer, in the illustrated transaction of purchase in #9-30, could have avoided the loss by making a loan in the foreign currency as a means of hedging against such losses, or, as is frequently done, by purchasing the foreign exchange forward. A forward exchange transaction, resulting in a FORWARD EXCHANGE CONTRACT, involves the purchase or sale of foreign exchange for delivery in the future. No cash transaction occurs at the time the contract is negotiated. Each party agrees to deliver one foreign currency in exchange for the other currency at the rate specified on the contract's designated delivery date. Each party acquires a liability in one currency and a receivable in the other currency.

A Forward Exchange Contract "involves the purchase or sale of foreign exchange for delivery in the future." In such case the future delivery is associated with an import purchase or export sale transaction because its purpose is to act as a HEDGE. Therefore, ordinarily the forward exchange contract entered into in connection with an IMPORT PURCHASE TRANSACTION would be for the PURCHASE OF FOREIGN EXCHANGE in order to hedge against the foreign exchange rising in value. In such case the importer would have a higher cost of purchasing the foreign exchange at the date of payment of the Import Purchase account payable should he not be protected by the forward exchange contract. Accordingly it is expected, though not always the case, that the forward exchange rate will be HIGHER than the spot rate for the import purchase.

Conversely a forward exchange contract entered into in connection with an EXPORT SALE TRANSACTION would be for the SALE OF FOREIGN EXCHANGE in order to hedge against the foreign exchange falling in value. In such case the exporter would have a lower price for selling the foreign exchange at the date of receipt of the export sale account receivable should he not be protected by the forward exchange contract. Therefore it is expected, though not always the case, that the forward exchange rate will be LOWER than the spot rate for the export sale.

### #9-45....Classification of Forward Exchange Contracts

In the situation above, the Forward Exchange Contract was identified as being directly associated with a purchase or sale of merchandise and their resultant account receivable and account payable. Basically the relationship involves export and import transactions. However, forward exchange contracts may also be resorted to for other transactions, which in FASB #52

(1983) entitled FOREIGN CURRENCY TRANSLATION, may be classified
into four types: (1) Contracts to hedge a net investment in a
foreign entity; (2) Contracts to hedge IDENTIFIABLE foreign
currency commitments meeting specified conditions; (3) Contracts for foreign currency SPECULATION; (4) Contracts to hedge
a foreign currency exposed net asset or net liability position.

Type 4 contracts are associated with M/N companies consolidated financial statements and therefore not related to trading
business transactions. Type 3 contracts are also not concerned
with trading transactions. Although Types 1 and 2 are both associated with trading transactions, the distinction between
them is that Type 1 is GENERAL in nature, whereas Type 2 is a
hedge of an IDENTIFIABLE commitment. Type 1 contracts apply
where an enterprise ANTICIPATES entering into merchandise sales
or purchases commitments over a designated period of time and
enters into a forward contract for a large designated sum expected to cover one or several sales or purchases transactions
between the date the forward contract is entered into and the
date of its termination. Such a situation is not a hedge of an
identifiable foreign currency commitment, because it had no
specific commitment made at the time the forward contract was
entered into. Thus the basic forward contract we are concerned
with is the IDENTIFIABLE Type 2 contract. Before illustrating
the accounting for Type 2 contracts, let us examine that for
the Type 3 SPECULATION contract and the Type 1 GENERAL commitment contract.

#9-46....Type 3 Speculation Forward Exchange Contracts

Assume that the U.S. Securities Co. purchases a 60-day Forward Exchange Contract on May 1 for 1,000,000 French Francs.
The rates for French Francs during the 60-day period the contract was in effect were: *FF 1000 000 × .223 = $223,000*

| Date | Spot Rates 1 F.F. = U.S. | | Forward Market Rates 1 F.F. = U. S. | |
|------|--------|---------|--------|--------|
|      | Buying | Selling | 30-Day | 60-Day |
| May 1   | $.184 | $.192 | $.207 | $.223 |
| May 31  | $.179 | $.188 | $.202 | $.218 |
| June 30 | $.186 | $.196 | $.217 | $.225 |

The journal entries for the Forward Exchange Speculation
Contract would be:

```
5/1    Forwd.Exch.Contract F.F. Rcble    223,000
          Forwd.Exch.Contr.U.S.$ Pybl              223,000
       (1,000,000 F.F. x .223;
       60-day forward rate on May 1)
```

5/31    Exchange Gains or Losses        21,000
            Forwd.Exch.Contr.F.F.Rcble                  21,000
        <1,000,000 F.F. x (.223 - .202)>=
        <1,000,000 x (60-day forward rate
        as of 5/1 - 30-day forward rate
        as of 5/31)>

6/30    Forwd.Exch.Cont.U.S.$ Pybl      223,000
            Cash                                        223,000
        (In payment of Forwd.Contr.Pybl)

6/30    French Franc Foreign Exchange   202,000
            Forwd.Exch.Contr.F.F.Rcble                  202,000
        (Receipt of French Francs
        223,000 - 21,000)

6/30    Cash (1,000,000 F.F. x .186
                June 30 Buying Rate)    186,000
        Exchange Gains or Losses
                <1,000,000x(.202-.186)>  16,000
            French Francs Frgn.Exch.                    202,000

The net result of the SPECULATION was that the amount of
cash paid out was $223,000 and the amount received was
$186,000, for a loss of $37,000. This equals the sum of the
loss on May 31 of 21,000 plus that on June 30 of 16,000.


## #9-47....Forward Exchange Hedge Discounts and Premiums

In hedging forward exchange contracts, normally there is a
difference between the Forward and the Spot Rates, which is
referred to as the SPREAD. A distinction should be made between
the Spread in a Forward Rate and that previously discussed in
connection with the AGIO, which is the difference between the
buying and selling rates of a foreign currency dealer, representing the gross profit in trading in foreign currency. Where
the Forward Rate is <u>less</u> than the Spot Rate, the foreign currency is said to be selling at a DISCOUNT, representing a gain.
Where the Forward Rate is <u>greater</u> than the Spot Rate, the foreign currency is said to be selling at a PREMIUM, which is regarded as an expense. Discounts and premiums are therefore applicable to Types 1 and 2 Forward Exchange Contracts. FASB #52
regards the discounts and premiums as the cost of the hedge and
therefore to be treated as an expense, which has been labeled
Interest Expense or Financial Expense, though in reality it is
a hedging or insurance expense, and is to be entered in the
books as of the date of entry of the forward exchange contract.

### #9-48...Type 2 Forward Exchange Contracts to Hedge Identifiable Foreign Currency Commitment

Assume that on Aug. 1 the U.S. Importing Co. enters into a commitment with the Paris Corp. to purchase merchandise, agreeing to pay in French Francs subsequently on Sept.30, the date on which the merchandise purchase transaction is to be consummated. Desiring to hedge against a possible loss due to currency fluctuation, the U.S. Importing Co. on Aug. 1 enters into a forward exchange contract for 1,000,000 French Francs in U.S. currency on Sept. 30. The spot rates on the respective dates were as follows:

                Aug. 1      1 F.F. = U.S. $.198
                Aug. 31     1 F.F. = U.S. $.202
                Sept. 30    1 F.F. = U.S. $.205

For 60-day contracts the forward rate on Aug. 1 was 1 F.F.=U.S. $.209; and the contract was for 1,000,000 French Francs. The journal entries for the above transactions would be:

| | | | |
|---|---|---|---|
| 8/1 | Forwd.Exch.Contr.F.F.Rcble | | |
| | (1,000,000 x .198) | 198,000 | |
| | Deferred Premium (Interest) Exp. | | |
| | (.209 - .198 = .011); | | |
| | (1,000,000 x .011) | 11,000 | |
| | Forwd.Exch.Contr.U.S.$ Pybl | | |
| | (1,000,000 x .209) | | 209,000 |
| | | | |
| 8/31 | Forwd.Exch.Contr.F.F.Rcbl. | 4,000 | |
| | Deferred Exchange Gain | | 4,000 |
| | (To record increase in F.F. | | |
| | from .198 on Aug. 1 to .202 | | |
| | on Aug. 31) (1,000,000 x .004) | | |
| | | | |
| 9/30 | Forwd.Exch.Contr.F.F.Rcbl. | 3,000 | |
| | Exchange Gain | | 3,000 |
| | (To record increase in F.F. | | |
| | from .202 on Sept. 1 to .205 | | |
| | on Sept. 30) (1,000,000 x .003) | | |
| | | | |
| 9/30 | Purchases (1,000,000 x .205) | 205,000 | |
| | Accounts Payable | | 205,000 |
| | (To record merchandise purchase) | | |
| | | | |
| 9/30 | Forwd.Exch.Contr.U.S.$ Pybl | 209,000 | |
| | Cash | | 209,000 |
| | (To record payment of U.S.$ | | |
| | liability on Forward Contract) | | |

| 9/30 | Foreign Exchange F.F. | 205,000 | |
|---|---|---|---|
| | Forwd.Exch.Contr.F.F.Rcble | | 205,000 |
| | (To record receipt of F.F. | | |
| | under Forward Contract) | | |

| 9/30 | Accounts Payable | 205,000 | |
|---|---|---|---|
| | Foreign Exchange F.F. | | 205,000 |
| | (To record payment of | | |
| | account payable with F.F.) | | |

| 9/30 | Deferred Exchange Gain (8/31) | 4,000 | |
|---|---|---|---|
| | Exchange Gain (9/30) | 3,000 | |
| | Purchases | 4,000 | |
| | Deferred Premium Expense | | 11,000 |
| | (To close premium expense and | | |
| | exchange gains to Purchases) | | |

Closing the premium and exchange gains to Purchases brings their cost to 205,000 + 4,000, or 209,000, which was the amount of the cash outlay therefor. If the U.S. Importing Co. had not entered into the Forward Exchange Contract, it would have had to pay only 205,000, which would be 4,000 less than the forward contract price of 209,000. This additional 4,000 was the cost of the hedge, which is tantamount to Insurance Expense in that the U.S. Importing Co. was assured what the maximum cost to it for the merchandise would be. This premium expense is attached to the cost of the merchandise as a product cost rather than as a period expense.

In order for a Forward Exchange Contract to be regarded as a hedge of a foreign currency commitment, two conditions must be met under FASB #52, FOREIGN CURRENCY TRANSLATION, para. 21, pages 9-10:

(1) The foreign currency transaction is designated as, and is effective as, a hedge of a foreign currency commitment.

(2) The foreign currency commitment is firm.

A gain or loss on a forward contract or other foreign currency transaction that is intended to hedge an identifiable foreign currency commitment (for example, an agreement to purchase or sell equipment) shall be deferred and included in the measurement of the related transaction (for example, the purchase or sale of the equipment).

In para. 18, FASB #52, it states that if a gain or loss on a forward contract is deferred, the forward contract's discount or premium that relates to the commitment period may be included in the measurement of the basis of the related foreign currency transaction when recorded.

#### #9-49...Type 4 Forward Exchange Contracts
####        to Hedge Net Exposed Foreign Currency
####        Positions

Forward exchange contracts to hedge a net exposed foreign currency position are the type of forward exchange contracts we are concerned with here in connection with export and import transactions. These contracts are applicable to export sales and import purchases discussed immediately below. The procedure for forward exchange contracts related to merchandise sales transactions will be the reverse of that for merchandise purchases transactions. A better grasp of the accounting illustrations for these transactions can be had by setting forth the chronological steps that take place in consummating the transactions. They are as follows:

FOR MERCHANDISE SALES TRANSACTION HEDGES
(1) Export Merchandise Sale transaction
(2) Forward Exchange Contract transaction
(3) Receipt of Foreign Exchange from Accounts Recvble
(4) Payment of Forward Contract Payable Liability with
    Foreign Exchange
(5) Receipt of Cash from Forward Exchange Dealer

FOR MERCHANDISE PURCHASES TRANSACTION HEDGES
(1) Import Merchandise Purchase transaction
(2) Forward Exchange Contract transaction
(3) Payment of Cash Local Currency on Forward Exchange
    Contract Payable
(4) Receipt of Foreign Currency from Forward Contract
    Receivable
(5) Payment of Accounts Payable with Foreign Currency

Experience has shown that there are two areas that cause difficulty in carrying out the five steps stated above. The first is a tendency to use the terms FOREIGN EXCHANGE and FORWARD EXCHANGE interchangeably, because of their similarity, which causes confusion with entries. The second is in connection with the Receivable and the Payable in the forward exchange contract. The impression is created that the Forward Receivable and Forward Payable are both in the same currency of the country of the enterprise for which the entries are made. This is not the case, as the Forward Receivable is in one currency and the Forward Payable is another reciprocal currency. Which is which depends on whether the transaction is a sale or a purchase, in which case the currency for a sale will be the opposite of that for a purchase. Therefore in order to clarify which is which, the Receivable will have the currency which is to be received identified in the following accounting

illustrations and the Payable  will have the currency which  is
to be paid identified.

### #9-50...Classification of Type 4
###         Forward Exchange Contracts

Broadly, Type 4 Forward Exchange Contracts are classified as
those associated with a MERCHANDISE SALE  transaction and those
associated with  a  MERCHANDISE PURCHASE transaction.  Both the
Sales and Purchases transactions may be subclassified as  those
in which  the  currency  fluctuations  are  treated as Exchange
Gains or Losses,  and those  in which they are treated as mixed
Financial Expenses (Interest  or Insurance) and  Exchange Gains
or  Losses.  Both the sales and  purchases transactions may  be
classified according to the  relationship of  the  Forward  Exchange Rate  to both the  merchandise Sales and Purchases  Date
Spot Rate and the  Sales Collection  and Purchases Payment Date
Rate.  Three situations exist for each.
For the merchandise <u>sales</u> hedge transaction they may be:
(1)  Forward Exchange Contract Rate is Less Than Merchan-
     dise Sales Date Spot  Rate and THE SAME AS the Sales
     Accounts Receivable Collection Date Rate
(2)  Forward Exchange Contract Rate is Less Than Merchan-
     dise Sales Date Spot Rate and GREATER THAN the Sales
     Accounts Receivable Collection Date Rate
(3)  Forward Exchange Contract Rate is Less Than Merchan-
     dise  Sales Date Spot Rate and LESS  THAN  the Sales
     Accounts Receivable Collection Date Rate
For the merchandise <u>purchases</u> hedge transaction they may be:
(1)  Forward Exchange Contract Rate  is Greater Than Mer-
     chandise Purchases  Date  Spot Rate and  THE SAME AS
     the Purchases Accounts Payable Payment Date Rate
(2)  Forward Exchange Contract Rate is  Greater Than Mer-
     chandise Purchases Date Spot Rate  and GREATER  THAN
     the Purchases Accounts Payable Payment Date Rate
(3)  Forward Exchange Contract  Rate is Greater Than Mer-
     chandise Purchases Date Spot  Rate and LESS THAN the
     Purchases Accounts Payable Payment Date Rate

## IDENTIFIABLE FORWARD EXCHANGE CONTRACTS FOR SALES TRANSACTIONS

### #9-51...Accounting For Export Sales Forward Exchange Contracts

To illustrate the accounting  entries for EXPORT SALES  Forward  Exchange Contracts, assume that  the U.S.  Exporting  Co.
engages in the following transactions:

July 1      Sale  of  exported merchandise to the Berlin  Co. of
            Germany for 20,000 German Marks  (DM)  on account,
            payable in 30 days

July 1      Enters   into   a 30-day Forward Exchange  Contract to
            sell 20,000 DM on July 31
July 31     Received payment from the Berlin Co. of 20,000 DM on
            its account
July 31     Delivers 20,000 DM to the  bank  in payment  of its
            liability under the Forward Exchange Contract
July 31     Receives from the bank U.S. Dollars  cash for the DM
            foreign  exchange sold  under  the Forward  Exchange
            Contract

The  exchange rates for DM under the  three possible situations
outlined in #9-50 are as follows:

|  | Mdse. Sales Date Spot Rates | Forward Rates | Collection Date Rates |
|---|---|---|---|
| (1) | 1 DM=U.S. $0.50 | 1 DM=U.S. $0.49 | 1.DM=U.S. $0.49 |
| (2) | 1 DM=U.S. $0.50 | 1 DM=U.S. $0.49 | 1 DM=U.S. $0.48 |
| (3) | 1 DM=U.S. $0.50 | 1 DM=U.S. $0.49 | 1 DM=U.S. $0.51 |

   The journal entries  for  each of the  two possible  forward
exchange export sales  transactions  are outlined below for (A)
Fluctuations Treated as Exchange Gains or Losses, and (B) Fluctuations Treated as Combined Financial (Interest or  Insurance)
Hedging Expenses and Exchange Gains or Losses.

************************************************************
### EXPORT SALES TRANSACTIONS
============================================================
            (A)   CURRENCY FLUCTUATIONS TREATED AS
                  EXCHANGE GAINS OR LOSSES
------------------------------------------------------------
   Rate Structure:   (1) Forward Rate Less Than Spot Rate
            and SAME AS Collection Date Rate
RATES:
Spot Rate                     1 DM = U.S. 50 cents
Forward Rate                  1 DM = U.S. 49 cents
Collection Date Rate          1 DM = U.S. 49 cents
JOURNAL ENTRIES:
7/1    Accts. Rcble. (20,000 x $.50)      10,000
          Sales                                       10,000
7/1    Forwd.Exch.Contr.U.S.$ Rcble.
              (20,000 x $.49)              9,800
          Forwd.Exch.Contr. DM Pybl               9,800
7/31   Frgn.Exch.DM (20,000 x $.49)       9,800
       Exchange Gains or Losses             200
          Accounts Receivable                     10,000
7/31   Forwd.Exch.Contr. DM Pybl.         9,800
          Foreign Exchange DM                      9,800
7/31   Cash (20,000 x $.49)               9,800
          Forwd.Exch.Contr.U.S.$ Rcble             9,800
------------------------------------------------------------

**JOURNAL ENTRIES:**

| | | | |
|---|---|---|---|
| 7/1 | Purchases (20,000 x $.50) | 10,000 | |
| | Accounts Payable | | 10,000 |
| 7/1 | Forwd.Exch.Contr.DM Rcble | 10,200 | |
| | Forwd.Exch.Contr.U.S.$Pybl | | |
| | (20,000 x $.51) | | 10,200 |
| 7/31 | Forwd.Exch.Contr.U.S.$ Pybl | 10,200 | |
| | Cash | | 10,200 |
| 7/31 | Frgn.Exch. DM (20,000 x $.49) | 9,800 | |
| | Exchange Gains or Losses | 400 | |
| | Forwd.Exch.Contr. DM Rcble | | 10,200 |
| 7/31 | Accounts Payable | 10,000 | |
| | Foreign Exchange DM | | 9,800 |
| | Exchange Gains or Losses | | 200 |

-------------------------------------------------------------

### Rate Structure: (3) **Forward Rate Greater Than Spot Rate and LESS THAN Payment Date Rate**

**RATES:**

| | |
|---|---|
| Spot Rate | 1 DM = U.S. 50 cents |
| Forward Rate | 1 DM = U.S. 51 cents |
| Payment Date Rate | 1 DM = U.S. 52 cents |

**JOURNAL ENTRIES:**

| | | | |
|---|---|---|---|
| 7/1 | Purchases (20,000 x $.50) | 10,000 | |
| | Accounts Payable | | 10,000 |
| 7/1 | Forwd.Exch.Contr. DM Rcble | 10,200 | |
| | Forwd.Exch.Contr.U.S.$ Pybl | | |
| | (20,000 x $.51) | | 10,200 |
| 7/31 | Forwd.Exch.Contr.U.S.$ Pybl | 10,200 | |
| | Cash | | 10,200 |
| 7/31 | Frgn.Exch. DM (20,000 x $.52) | 10,400 | |
| | Forwd.Exch.Contr. DM Rcbl | | 10,200 |
| | Exchange Gains or Losses | | 200 |
| 7/31 | Accounts Payable | 10,000 | |
| | Exchange Gains or Losses | 400 | |
| | Foreign Exchange DM | | 10,400 |

=============================================================

### (B) CURRENCY FLUCTUATION ENTRIES TREATED AS COMBINED FINANCIAL (INTEREST OR INSURANCE) HEDGING EXPENSES TOGETHER WITH EXCHANGE GAINS OR LOSSES

-------------------------------------------------------------

### Rate Structure: (1) **Forward Rate Greater Than Spot Rate and SAME AS Payment Date Rate**

**RATES:**

| | |
|---|---|
| Spot Rate | 1 DM = U.S. 50 cents |
| Forward Rate | 1 DM = U.S. 51 cents |
| Payment Date Rate | 1 DM = U.S. 51 cents |

**JOURNAL ENTRIES:**

| | | | |
|---|---|---|---|
| 7/1 | Purchases (20,000 x $.50) | 10,000 | |
| | Accounts Payable | | 10,000 |

| 7/1 | Forwd.Exch.Contr.DM Rcble | | |
| | (20,000 X $.50) | 10,000 | |
| | Financial Expense | 200 | |
| | Forwd.Exch.Contr.U.S.$Pybl | | |
| | (20,000 x $.51) | | 10,200 |
| 7/31 | Forwd.Exch.Contr.U.S.$ Pybl | 10,200 | |
| | Cash | | 10,200 |
| 7/31 | Frgn.Exch. DM (20,000 x $.51) | 10,200 | |
| | Forwd.Exch.Contr.DM Rcble | | 10,000 |
| | Exchange Gains or Losses | | 200 |
| 7/31 | Accounts Payable | 10,000 | |
| | Exchange Gains or Losses | 200 | |
| | Foreign Exchange DM | | 10,200 |

---

### Rate Structure: (2) Forward Rate Greater Than Spot Rate and GREATER THAN Payment Date Rate

RATES:

| | |
|---|---|
| Spot Rate | 1 DM = U.S. 50 cents |
| Forward Rate | 1 DM = U.S. 51 cents |
| Payment Date Rate | 1 DM = U.S. 49 cents |

JOURNAL ENTRIES:

| 7/1 | Purchases (20,000 x $.50) | 10,000 | |
| | Accounts Payable | | 10,000 |
| 7/1 | Forwd.Exch.Contr.DM Rcble | 10,000 | |
| | Financial Expense | 200 | |
| | Forwd.Exch.Contr.U.S.$Pybl | | 10,200 |
| 7/31 | Forwd.Exch.Contr.U.S.$ Pybl | 10,200 | |
| | Cash | | 10,200 |
| 7/31 | Frgn.Exch. DM (20,000 x $.49) | 9,800 | |
| | Exchange Gains or Losses | 200 | |
| | Forwd.Exch.Contr. DM Rcble | | 10,000 |
| 7/31 | Accounts Payable | 10,000 | |
| | Foreign Exchange DM | | 9,800 |
| | Exchange Gains or Losses | | 200 |

---

### Rate Structure: (3) Forward Rate Greater Than Spot Rate and LESS THAN Payment Date Rate

RATES:

| | |
|---|---|
| Spot Rate | 1 DM = U.S. 50 cents |
| Forward Rate | 1 DM = U.S. 51 cents |
| Payment Date Rate | 1 DM = U.S. 52 cents |

JOURNAL ENTRIES:

| 7/1 | Purchases (20,000 x $.50) | 10,000 | |
| | Accounts Payable | | 10,000 |
| 7/1 | Forwd.Exch.Contr. DM Rcble | 10,000 | |
| | Financial Expense | 200 | |
| | Forwd.Exch.Contr.U.S.$ Pybl | | 10,200 |
| 7/31 | Forwd.Exch.Contr.U.S.$ Pybl | 10,200 | |
| | Cash | | 10,200 |

```
7/31    Frgn.Exch. DM (20,000 x $.52)      10,400
          Forwd.Exch.Contr. DM Rcbl                    10,000
          Exchange Gains or Losses                        400
7/31    Accounts Payable                   10,000
          Exchange Gains or Losses            400
          Foreign Exchange DM                          10,400
```
*****************************************************

## #9-53...Nature of Forward Exchange Contract Rcvbl & Pybl Accts

The two accounts involved in the Forward Exchange Contract--
one the Receivable and the other the Payable--have received
different terminology from various authors. The Receivable account in the Forward Exchange Contract entry has been called,
inter alia, DUE FROM EXCHANGE BROKER ON FORWARD EXCHANGE CON-
TRACT, as well as INVESTMENT IN FORWARD EXCHANGE CONTRACT. The
Payable account entry has been called, inter alia, CONTRACTS
PAYABLE, as well as LIABILITY FOR EXCHANGE SOLD.

Some confusion appears to have resulted from the fact that
both the Forward Exchange Contract Receivable and the Payable
are recorded in terms of the local currency of the exporter or
importer. However, as can be observed from the export or import
transactions recorded above, the Receivable represents currency
which is the reciprocal of that for the Payable. If the Receivable pays in local currency, the reciprocal payable will be
paid in foreign currency, and vice versa. If the Payable is
paid in local currency, the reciprocal Receivable will be paid
in foreign currency, and vice versa. Notwithstanding, the foreign currency will be entered into the books at the translated
local currency value. To compound the situation, what currency
will be Receivable and Payable will be the reverse in connection with a sales transaction as it will be for a purchase
transaction. Under the foregoing circumstances it can be quite
confusing to merely label the Receivable or Payable as resulting from a Forward Exchange Contract. That is why the Forward
Receivables and Payables accounts in the export sales and import purchases transactions have been more precisely labeled to
declare the type of currency--Local or Foreign--that is Receivable or Payable, as follows:

Export Sales Transaction:
    (1) Dr. - Forward Exchange Contract Local Currency Rcvbl
    (2) Cr. - Forward Exchange Contract Frgn. Currency Pybl
Import Purchases Transaction:
    (3) Dr. - Forward Exchange Contract Frgn Currency Rcvbl
    (4) Cr. - Forward Exchange Contract Local Currency Pybl

It should also be noted that in the Forward Exchange Contract
entry, where a Finance Expense is shown, the Receivable is recorded at the Spot Rate, whereas the Payable Credit is always
recorded at the Forward Rate.

In practice, the liability for exchange sold may be offset against the amount due from the exchange broker. This makes the liability for exchange sold a contra-asset. However, where there is a revaluation due to an exchange rate change, if the liability exceeds the offsetting amount due from the broker, only the net amount is reported as liability and the amount due from the broker becomes a contra-liability account.

Whether or not the amounts should be fully disclosed would then depend on the materiality of the possible effects on the firm's financial position. Thus many industrial companies do not record the forward exchange contract at all. In such case they would accrue only the net difference between the receivable and the liability at the time of an exchange rate change. Then later only the receipt of the foreign exchange and its conversion into domestic cash would be recorded.

## ACCOUNTING FOR FOREIGN INVESTMENTS*

### #9-54....Classification of Investments

As is the case with domestic investments, foreign investments may be classified as SHORT-TERM, or TEMPORARY; and LONG-TERM, or PERMANENT.

### #9-55...Accounting for Temporary Short-Term Foreign Investments

The same accounting principles used for domestic investments are applicable to foreign investments. Generally the cost-or-market rule applies to industrial enterprises which acquire the securities as an investment of idle cash. The costs of acquisition, including any interest equalization tax, are recorded as an asset. Costs paid in foreign currency are translated at the conversion rate in effect at the time of the acquisition.

Sales proceeds from foreign investments are recorded at the realized value. If the amount received is in foreign currency, it is translated at the conversion rate in effect at the time of sale. Also, in applying the cost-or-market rule to determine market price, the foreign market price on the balance sheet date is translated at the rate of exchange prevailing on that date.

### #9-56....Accounting for Long-Term Investments

There are two principal methods of accounting for long-term investments: the Cost Method, and the Equity Method. Both

------

*See Summary of Footnote References -- #9-54 thru #9-58

methods are  presented in APB Opinion  No. 18 (1971) summarized
below.

#9-57....The Cost Method

An investor records an investment in the  stock of an investee at cost.  Dividends received that are  distributed from net
accumulated earnings of the investee after the date of acquisition by the investor are recognized as income.  The net accumulated earnings of an investee subsequent to the date of investment are recognized by the investor only to the extent distributed by the investee as dividends. Dividends received in excess
of earnings subsequent to the date of investment are considered
a return of investment and are recorded  as  reductions of cost
of the  investment.  Where a  series of operating losses  of an
investee or other factors may indicate that a decrease in value
of the investment has occurred which  is  other than temporary,
it should be recognized.

#9-58....The Equity Method

Initially  an investor in the stock  of  an investee records
the investment at cost.  The  carrying amount of the investment
should be adjustd  to  recognize the investor's  share  of  the
earnings or losses of  the investee after the  date of acquisition. The amount of the adjustment is included in the determination of net income by the investor.  Such amount   reflects adjustments  similar  to  those  made in  preparing consolidated
statements. They include: (a) elimination of intercompany gains
and losses; (b) amortization, if appropriate, of any difference
between investor cost  and  underlying  equity  in net assets of
the investee  at the date of investment;  and (c) adjustment of
investment  to reflect the  investor's share of changes  in the
investee's capital. Dividends received from the investee reduce
the carrying amount of the investment.

A series of operating losses of an investee or other factors
may indicate  that a decrease in value  of  the  investment has
occurred which is other than temporary. Such decrease should be
recognized even though the  decrease in value is  in  excess of
what would otherwise be recognized by application of the equity
method.  APB  Opinion #18 is quite specific  in extending these
accounting principles  to  investments in  common  stock of all
unconsolidated subsidiaries, foreign as well as domestic.

Neither of the two methods--Cost or  Equity--is a valid substitute for consolidation  and should  not be  used  to justify
exclusion  of a subsidiary when consolidation is  otherwise appropriate. The equity method should be followed when the investor  has the ability to exercise significant influence over operating  and  financial policies of an investee even though  he

holds 50% or less of the voting stock. In order to achieve a
reasonable degree of uniformity, a significant degree of influence is presumed to exist when an investor holds 20% or more of
the voting stock of the investee. Thus the promulgated guidelines are summarized as follows:
   If ownership is less than 20 percent, use the cost method
   for recording;
   If ownership is 20 percent to 50 percent, use the equity
   method for recording;
   If ownership is more than 50 percent, consolidate the financial statements.

## SUMMARY OF FOOTNOTE REFERENCES
(References are to Paragraph #'s)

#9-1 thru #9-21:   "Foreign Operations and Investments," adapted
      from Norlin G. Rueschhoff, INTERNATIONAL ACCOUNTING AND FI-
      NANCIAL REPORTING, 1976, Praeger Publishers, Inc., by per-
      mission.
#9-4  U.S. UNIFORM COMMERCIAL CODE, Sec. 5-103(1)
#9-21 APB Opinion No. 18
#9-36 FASB #8, para. 27, October 1975
#9-37 thru #9-43:   "Receivables and Payables Valuation," adapted
      from Norlin G. Rueschhoff, op. cit., by permission.
#9-45 FASB #8; FASB #20, ACCOUNTING FOR FORWARD EXCHANGE CON-
      TRACTS, (1978), para. 27, p. 11
#9-49 FASB #20, Ibid., para. 13, p. 5
#9-54 thru #9-58:   "Accounting for Foreign Investments," adapted
      from Norlin G. Rueschhoff, op. cit., by permission.
#9-56 APB Opinion No. 18, 1971

## BIBLIOGRAPHY

Collier, Philippe. "Speculation and the Forward Foreign Exchange
      Rate," JOURNAL OF FINANCE, 35 (March 1980): 173-176
Folks, William R., Jr. "Optimal Foreign Borrowing Strategies With
      Operations in Forward Exchange Markets," JOURNAL OF FINAN-
      CIAL AND QUANTITATIVE ANALYSIS, 13 (June 1978): 245-254
Frey, Karen. "Management of Foreign Exchange Risk With Forward Con-
      tracts," MANAGEMENT ACCOUNTING, 58 (March 1977): 45-48
Kahnamouyipour, Heydar. "Foreign Exchange: Hedge, Speculation or
      Swap?", ACCOUNTANCY, 91 (October 1980): 52-53
Polimeni, Ralph S. "Accounting for Forward Exchange Contracts,"
      INTERNATIONAL JOURNAL OF ACCOUNTING EDUCATION & RESEARCH, 13
      (Fall 1977): 159-168
Ryder, Frank R. "Challenges to the Use of the Documentary Credit in
      International Trade Transactions," COLUMBIA JOURNAL OF WORLD
      BUSINESS, 16 (Winter 1981): 36-41

## THEORY QUESTIONS
(Question Numbers are Keyed to Text Paragraph #'s)

#9-1    On how many levels may foreign operations be conducted? Explain each.

#9-2    Discuss the significance of Export-Import Operations.

#9-11    Make up an outline classifying Letters of Credit.

#9-17    Enumerate the common types of foreign shipment terms, defining each.

#9-18    Classify Foreign Investments and define each.

#9-19    How may foreign marketable securities be acquired? What are American Depositary Receipts?

#9-21    How does APB #18 define a corporate Joint Venture?

#9-23    What methods may exporters use in billing for sales made by them? Which method is the more desirable?

#9-28    What methods may importers use in recording charges for purchases made by them? Which method is the more desirable?

#9-31    What is the general rule followed in the recording of foreign sales & purchases of goods as exports & imports?

#9-32    What are the two approaches to recording foreign trade transactions? Describe how they operate and make a critical comparative analysis of the two.

#9-37    What are the two methods of recording the change in balance sheet valuation of foreign receivables or payables? Describe how each method operates in the case of receivables and in the case of payables.

#9-42    Make a critical comparative analysis of the Direct Charge and Accrual Methods of Receivable and Payable Valuation.

#9-44    What is a Forward Exchange Contract and how does it operate?

#9-45    How are Forward Exchange Contracts classified under FASB #20? Explain each type.

#9-47    What are Forward Exchange Hedge Discounts and Premiums and how are they handled?

#9-53    Discuss the nature of the Forward Exchange Contract Receivable and Payable accounts.

#9-55    Discuss how temporary foreign investments should be handled on the books of account.

#9-56    Discuss the treatment of long-term foreign investments under (1) the Cost Method and (2) the Equity Method.

## EXERCISES   ALL

### EX-9-1 (CPA EXAM, 5/20, PRAC. II, #9)
A merchant going abroad to purchase goods secures from his bank, on the strength of his general financial standing, a let-

ter of credit for use in his contemplated purchases of
$500,000. How should the issuance of this letter of credit be
shown in the accounts of the bank?

## EX-9-2 (CPA EXAM, 11/31, AUDITING, #7)

You are auditing an importer's accounts in behalf of a bank
which has established commercial letters of credit for large
amounts in favor of the importer. The latter signs "trust receipts" when he receives the goods he imports. How far would
you pay attention to the practice of the importer in paying the
bank drafts drawn under these credits, and why?

## EX-9-3 (CPA EXAM, 11/81, PRAC. I, #32)

U.S. Importers, Inc., bought 5,000 dolls from Latin American
Exporters, S.A., at 12.5 pesos each, when the rate of exchange
was $.08 per peso. How much should U.S. Importers record on
its books as the total dollar cost for the merchandise purchased?

## EX-9-4 (CPA EXAM, 5/77, PRAC. I, #4)

The Marvin Co. has a receivable from a foreign customer which
is payable in the local currency of the foreign customer. The
amount receivable for 900,000 local currency units (LCU) has
been translated into $315,000 on Marvin's Dec. 31, 1975, bal-
ance sheet. On Jan. 15, 1976, the receivable was collected in
full when the exchange rate was 3 LCU to $1. What journal entry
should Marvin make to record the collection of this receivable?

## EX-9-5 (CPA EXAM, 11/78, THEORY, #25)

A change in the foreign currency exchange rate between the date
a transaction occurred and the date of the current financial
statements would give rise to an exchange gain or loss if

   a. The asset or liability being translated is carried at a
      price in a current purchase or sale exchange.
   b. The asset or liability being translated is carried at a
      price in a past purchase or sale exchange.
   c. The revenue or expense item relates to an asset or liabil-
      ity that is translated at historical rates.
   d. The revenue or expense item relates to a deferred asset or
      liability shown on a previous statement of financial posi-
      tion.

## EX-9-6

Give the journal entry to be made by International Trade Co. to
record its $5,000 share of its income in Easy Money Joint Ven-
ture, assuming the joint venture has a separate set of accounting records and the investing company follows the principles
set forth in APB Opinion No. 18.

EX-9-7 (CPA EXAM, 5/82, PRAC. II, #7)

Dale, Inc., a U.S. corporation, bought machine parts from Kluger Co. of West Germany on March 1, 1981, for 30,000 marks when the spot rate for marks was $.4895. Dale's year-end was March 31, 1981, when the spot rate for marks was $.4845. Dale bought 30,000 marks and paid the invoice on April 20, 1981, when the spot rate was $.4945. How much should be shown in Dale's income statements as foreign exchange gain or loss for the years ended March 31, 1981 and 1982?

EX-9-8

On Nov. 1, Nexon Co. acquired 100,000 shares of Subcess Corp. common stock at a total cost of $500,000. Subcess Corp. has 1,000,000 shares of common stock outstanding. Nexon plans to hold these shares for a long time. On Dec. 31 of that same year the Subcess common stock was listed on the World-Wide Stock Exchange at $4.50 per share.

**Required:**
 a. Record the journal entry for November 1.
 b. Record the adjustment entry for December 31.
 c. How will the financial statements read after making the foregoing entries?

## PROBLEMS

P-9-1 (CPA EXAM, 5/82, PRAC. I, #2)

On Jan. 2, 1981, Portela, Inc., bought 30% of the outstanding common stock of Bracero Corp. for $258,000 cash. Portela accounts for this investment by the equity method. At the date of acquisition of the stock, Bracero's net assets had book and fair value of $620,000. The excess of Portela's cost of investment over its share of Bracero's net assets has an estimated life of 40 years. Bracero's net income for the year ended Dec. 31, 1981 was $180,000. During 1981 Bracero declared and paid cash dividends of $20,000. On Dec. 31, 1981, Portela should have carried its investment in Bracero in the amount of
 a. $234,000      c. $304,200
 b. $258,000      d. $306,000

P-9-2 (CPA EXAM, 5/82, PRAC. I, #10)

On Jan. 2, 1980, Troquel Corp. bought 15% of Zafacon Corporation's capital stock for $30,000. Troquel accounts for this investment by the cost method. Zafacon's net income for the years ended Dec. 31, 1980, and Dec. 31, 1981, were $10,000 and $50,000 respectively. During 1981 Zafacon declared a dividend of $70,000. No dividends were declared in 1980. How much should Troquel show on its 1981 income statement as income from this investment?
 a. $1,575      c. $ 9,000
 b. $7,500      d. $10,500

International Accounting 255

**P-9-3 (CPA EXAM, 11/81, PRAC., #11)**
On Jan. 1, 1980, Rey Corp. paid $150,000 for 10,000 shares of
Rio Corporation's common stock, representing a 15% investment
in Rio. Rio declared and paid a dividend of $1 a share to its
common stockholders during 1980. Rio's net income was $130,000
for the year ended Dec. 31, 1980. At what amount should Rey's
investment in Rio appear on Rey's balance sheet as of Dec. 31,
1980?
    a. $140,000               c. $159,500
    b. $150,000               d. $169,500

**P-9-4 (CPA EXAM, 5/84, PRAC. I, #4)**
On Jan. 1, 1983, Miller Co. purchased 25% of Wall Corporation's
common stock; no goodwill resulted from the purchase. Miller
appropriately carries this investment at equity, and the balance in Miller's investment account was $190,000 at Dec. 31,
1983. Wall reported net income of $120,000 for the year ended
Dec. 31, 1983, and paid common stock dividends totaling $48,000
during 1983. How much did Miller pay for its 25% interest in
Wall?
    a. $172,000               c. $208,000
    b. $202,000               d. $232,000

**P-9-5 (CPA EXAM, 5/84, PRAC. II, #31)**
On Jan. 4, 1982, Wynn, Inc., bought 15% of Parr Corporation's
common stock for $60,000. Wynn appropriately accounts for this
investment by the cost method. The following data concerning
Parr are available for the years ended Dec. 31, 1982 and 1983:

|              | 1982     | 1983     |
|--------------|----------|----------|
| Net Income   | $30,000  | $90,000  |
| Dividends Paid | None   | $80,000  |

In its income statement for the year ended Dec. 31, 1983, how
much should Wynn report as income from this investment?
    a. $4,500               c. $12,000
    b. $9,000               d. $13,500

**P-9-6**
The U.S. Trading Co., a U.S. corporation, purchased merchandise
on May 1 on 30-day open account in the sum of 60,000 Dutch
Guilders (DG) from the Holland Corp. of Amsterdam. On May 1 the
spot rates of exchange were:
    Buying Rate:     1 DG =    U.S. 30 cents
    Selling Rate:    1 DG =    U.S. 33 cents
On May 31 the U.S. Trading Co. purchased a draft in the sum of
60,000 DG for remittance to the Holland Corp. The spot exchange
rates on May 31 were:
    Buying Rate:     1 DG =    U.S. 31 cents
    Selling Rate:    1 DG =    U.S. 34 cents

**Required**:
Using the Single One Transaction Perspective Approach, what entries are to be recorded on the books of the U.S. Trading Company (show computations)
   a. as of May 1.
   b. as of May 31.


## P-9-7
Using the data in P-9-6, prepare journal entries to record the transactions on May 1 and 31 using the Two Transaction Perspective Approach. (show computations)


## P-9-8
The American Exporting Co., a U.S. corporation, sold merchandise on July 1 on 30-day open account in the sum of 125,000 Canadian Dollars to the Toronto Importers. The spot rate for Canadian Dollars on July 1 was 1 U.S. Dollar = 1.25 Canadian Dollars. On July 31 the Toronto Importers paid its account by remitting 125,000 Canadian Dollars to American Exporting Co. The spot rate on July 31 was 1 U.S. Dollar = 1.26 Canadian Dollars. The American Exporting Co. deposited the Canadian draft to its bank account.
**Required**:
Using the Single One Transaction Perspective Approach, what entries are to be recorded on the books of the American Exporting Company (show computations)
   a. as of July 1.
   b. as of July 31.


## P-9-9
Using the data in P-9-8, prepare journal entries to record the transactions on July 1 and 31 using the Two Transaction Perspective Approach. (show computations)


## P-9-10
On Aug. 1 the U.S. Importing Co., a U.S. corporation, purchased merchandise from the Belgian Supply Co. of Brussels on 30-day open account in the sum of 120,000 Belgian Francs (BF). On Aug. 1, the date of the purchase, the U.S. Importing Co. also entered into a FORWARD EXCHANGE AGREEMENT by purchasing a 30-day Forward Exchange Contract in the sum of BF = 120,000. The exchange rates on Aug. 1 were:
   Buying Rate:          1 BF  =     U.S. 2 cents
   Selling Rate:         1 BF  =     U.S. 2-1/2 cents
   30-day Forward
      Market Rate:       1 BF  =     U.S. 3-1/3 cents
On Aug. 31 the U.S. Importing Co. honored the Forward Exchange Contract with the bank and then settled its account with the

Belgian Supply Co.  On Aug. 31 the spot rate for Belgian Francs
was 1 BF = U.S. 3-1/2 cents.
**Required**:
Prepare journal entries of the U.S. Importing Co. for
    a. the purchase of the merchandise.
    b. the Forward Exchange Contract.
    c. the honoring of the Forward Exchange Contract.
    d. settlement of the account payable.

**P-9-11**
On August 1 the  U.S. Finance Corp. purchased  a 60-day forward
exchange  speculation  contract  for 500,000 Swiss Francs (SF).
The rates  for Swiss Francs during the 60-day  period  the contract was in effect were as follows:

| | | | | |
|---|---|---|---|---|
| Aug. 1 | Spot Rate Buying: | 1 SF | = | U.S. 44 cents |
| | Spot Rate Selling: | 1 SF | = | U.S. 48 cents |
| | Forward Rate--30-day: | 1 SF | = | U.S. 47 cents |
| | Forward Rate--60-day: | 1 SF | = | U.S. 50 cents |
| Aug. 31 | Spot Rate Buying: | 1 SF | = | U.S. 42 cents |
| | Spot Rate Selling: | 1 SF | = | U.S. 46 cents |
| | Forward Rate--30-day: | 1 SF | = | U.S. 49 cents |
| | Forward Rate--60-day: | 1 SF | = | U.S. 50 cents |
| Sept. 30 | Spot Rate Buying: | 1 SF | = | U.S. 46 cents |
| | Spot Rate Selling: | 1 SF | = | U.S. 48 cents |
| | Forward Rate--30-day: | 1 SF | = | U.S. 49 cents |
| | Forward Rate--60-day: | 1 SF | = | U.S. 50 cents |

**Required**:
    a. Prepare  entries in General  Journal form for the  forward
exchange speculation contract.
    b. Make up a Summary Statement showing  the net result of the
forward exchange speculation contract.

**P-9-12**
The  American Exporting Co.  engages in the following  transactions during the month of October:
    Oct. 1:  Sale  of exported merchandise to the Paris Co.
          of  France for 100,000 French  Francs  (FF) on
          account receivable in 30 days
    Oct. 1:  Enters into a 30-day forward exchange contract
          to sell 100,000 FF on October 31
    Oct. 31: Receives payment of 100,000 FF  from the Paris
          Company on its account
    Oct. 31: Delivers the 100,000 FF to the bank in payment
          of  its liability  under the  forward exchange
          contract
    Oct. 31: Receives cash from the bank for the FF foreign
          exchange delivered under the forward  exchange
          contract
The spot rate for FF on the date of the sale of the merchandise

was  1 FF = U.S.  20  cents; the forward rate for FF on the date
of  the sale  of the merchandise  was 1 FF = U.S. 19 cents; the
spot rate on Oct. 31, the date of the collection of the account
receivable, was 1 FF = U.S. 19 cents.

**Required**:

Prepare  entries  in  General  Journal form  for  the  foregoing
transactions on the basis that fluctuations are treated

    a. as Exchange Gains or Losses.

    b. as combined Financial  Hedging Expenses and Exchange Gains
       or Losses.

## P-9-13

Assume that in  P-9-12 the spot rate on Oct. 31 was 1 FF = U.S.
18 cents.  Prepare entries in General Journal form on the basis
that fluctuations are treated (a) as  Exchange Gains or Losses;
and  (b)  as  combined Financial Hedging Expenses and  Exchange
Gains or Losses.

## P-9-14

Assume that in P-9-12 the spot rate on Oct. 31 was  1 FF = U.S.
21 cents.  Prepare entries in General Journal form on the basis
that fluctuations are treated  (a) as Exchange Gains or Losses;
and  (b) as combined  Financial Hedging  Expenses and  Exchange
Gains or Losses.

## P-9-15

The  American Importing Co. engages in the  following  transactions during the month of October:

    Oct. 1:  Purchase  of  imported  merchandise  from  the
           Paris Co. of France for 100,000  French Francs
           (FF) on account payable in 30 days

    Oct. 1:  Enters into a 30-day forward exchange contract
           with the bank to buy 100,000 FF on Oct. 31

    Oct. 31: Pays cash  on  forward  exchange contract  for
           liability to  pay in 30  days  for foreign ex-
           change to be delivered

    Oct. 31: Receives  100,000  FF  under  forward exchange
           contract

    Oct. 31: Turns over 100,000 FF received  to  the  Paris
           Co. in payment of its accounts payable

The spot  rate for FF on the date of  the purchase of the  merchandise was  1 FF  = U.S. 20 cents; the forward rate for FF on
the date of the purchase  of the merchandise was 1 FF = U.S. 21
cents; the spot rate on  Oct.  31, the date of the  payament on
the account payable, was 1 FF = U.S. 21 cents.

**Required**:

Prepare  entries  in  General  Journal form  for  the foregoing
transactions on the basis that fluctuations are treated

    a. as Exchange Gains or Losses.

b. as combined Financial Hedging  Expenses and Exchange Gains or Losses.

## P-9-16

Assume that in P-9-15 the spot rate on Oct. 31  was 1 FF = U.S. 19 cents.  Prepare entries in General Journal form on the basis that fluctuations are treated (a) as Exchange Gains  or Losses; and  (b) as combined  Hedging Expenses and Exchange  Gains  and Losses.

## P-9-17

Assume that in P-9-15 the spot rate on Oct.  31 was 1 FF = U.S. 22 cents.  Prepare entries in General Journal form on the basis that  the fluctuations are  treated (a)  as  Exchange  Gains or Losses;  and (b)  as  combined  Hedging  Expenses and  Exchange Gains or Losses.

### CASES

### CASE-9-1  (CPA EXAM, 11/74, THEORY, #3)

Hawkes Systems, Inc., a  chemical processing company, has  been operating  profitably for many years.  On March 1, 1974, Hawkes purchased 50,000 shares of Diversified Insurance  Co. stock for $2,000,000.  The 50,000 shares represented 25% of Diversified's outstanding stock.  Both  Hawkes and Diversified operate on  a fiscal year ending Aug. 31.

For the fiscal year ended Aug. 31, 1974, Diversified report-ed net income of $800,000  earned ratably  throughout the year. During  November 1973, February, May, and August 1974, Diversi-fied paid its regular quarterly cash dividend of $100,000.

**Required**:

a. What criteria should Hawkes consider in determining wheth-er its investment in Diversified should be classified as  (1) a current asset (marketable security)  or (2)  a noncurrent asset (investment) in Hawkes' Aug. 31, 1974, balance sheet?   Confine your  discussion to the  decision criteria for  determining the balance sheet classification of the investment.

b. Assume the investment should be classified as a  long-term investment  in the noncurrent asset  section of Hawkes' balance sheet. The cost of Hawkes' investment equaled its equity in the recorded values  of Diversified's  net  assets; recorded values were not materially different from fair values (individually or collectively).  For  the fiscal year  ended Aug. 31,  1974, how did the  net income  reported and dividends paid by Diversified affect  the  accounts of Hawkes  (including Hawkes'  income tax accounts)? Indicate each account affected, whether it increased or decreased, and explain the reason  for the change in the account balance (such as Cash, Investment in Diversified, etc.). Organize your answer in the following format:

| Account Name | Increase or Decrease | Reason for Change in Account Balance |
| --- | --- | --- |

## CASE-9-2  (CPA EXAM, 5/32, LAW, #3)

A contract, signed by the seller and accepted in writing by the buyer, contained the following matter:

New York, Jan. 2, 1932
        To:   A. W. Jones Corp.
              2 Broadway, New York, N.Y.

Dear Sirs:

Herewith we  confirm sale to you for the account of ourselves, through C.S.  Smith & Co., 25 tons (each 2,240 lbs. net) Chinese Antimony  Regulus, 99%, @ 21-3/4 cents per lb., c.i.f. New York.

Shipment:   Promptly from Hamburg
Duty:       For account of buyers
Insurance:  For account of sellers
Payment:    Net cash against shipping documents payable upon arrival of steamer.  No arrival, no sale, but proof of shipment to be given by sellers.

At the time this contract was signed, the goods were in transit between China and Hamburg.  The shipment arrived in Hamburg and was transshipped to New  York.  The shipment reached  New  York within the contract time.  The invoice,  receipt for  freight, bills  of lading, and other documents were not forwarded by the seller to the buyer but  were tendered to  the buyer  after the goods had arrived. The insurance policies were issued to bearer "for account of whom it may concern" and were never tendered to the  buyer.  The bills of lading were  through  bills of lading and did not contain the name of the buyer as assignee.

**Required**:
  a. What does "c.i.f." mean?
  b. Is this contract a c.i.f. contract?

# International Foreign Operations – The Multinational Entity

**THE BASIC INTERNATIONAL ACCOUNTING ENTITY --**
**THE MULTINATIONAL CORPORATION**

**#10-1...International Foreign Operations**

Having treated international transactions on the local level involving basically export and import trading, we turn next to the discussion of international transactions on the international level. Foreign operations on the international level exist where a foreign branch, agency or subsidiary is set up to operate in a foreign country. In such case the domestic parent company is involved with its subsidiary operating in a foreign country.

**#10-2...Evolution of International Business Operations**

Shortly after World War II, most international operations took the form of exports and imports resulting predominantly in an exchange of goods and services on markets spread around the world. Because such operations were tantamount to mere sales and purchases transactions, they were restricted to transporting, insuring, and financing functions. In the 1960s there was a significant shift to international operations, which involved not only the service functions but also the setting up of facilities for distributing goods and installation of plants for manufacturing and assembling products. Symbolic of this situation is the following remark by the Proctor & Gamble Company in its annual report for 1965:

> Proctor & Gamble has become a truly international organization, now doing business in just about every country in the free world, with consumers asking for our products in scores of different languages and dialects, and paying for them with the currencies of more than 140 countries.

In addition to operations, international investments have expanded to a very great degree as evidenced by the greater number of securities being traded on the major stock exchanges.
The 1966 NEW YORK STOCK EXCHANGE FACT BOOK indicates that there
were 268 foreign securities worth over $11 billion listed on
its exchange. Conversely, such giant U.S. corporations as General Motors, Ford, Standard Oil, IBM and ITT were listed on
foreign stock exchanges. In fact, in an Address before the 8th
Intrntl. Congress of Accountants, N.Y., 1962, Frederick Donner,
Chairman of General Motors, advocated that corporate stock certificates be printed in several different languages for more
comprehensibility on the part of foreign investors.

A third factor causing expansion in foreign operations was
the increase in the number of international institutional investors. All of the major New York banking institutions hold
substantial interests in foreign government operations as well
as private corporations all over the world including the less
developed countries. The International Finance Corporation has
proffered many investment opportunities including international
subsidiaries of major U.S. banks, and the EEC will have an impact on international activities expansion.

#10-3...Foreign Branch Operations

The international explosion of the 1960s resulted in the
general internationalization of business through the establishment of agencies, branches and subsidiary operations in foreign
countries. The branch operation is basically an arm of the organization that created it and lacks any real separation of
existence by itself. Therefore the accounts of the branch must
be regarded as part and parcel of those of the parent home operation. This means that neither the parent nor the branch accounts can stand by themselves but are regarded as a joint integrated whole. In order to have a complete and fair presentation of the entire structure, they must be combined into one.
This close relationship between the branch and its parent indicates that foreign branches are essentially similar to the
domestic variety.

Like the domestic branch, foreign branch activities are
closely planned, controlled and administered by the parent. As
a result the subservient branch operation accounts must be
merged into those of the dominant parent. This requires the
branch accounts to be made available in the terms of the home
office currency and joined with the home office in terms of its
currency.

#10-4...Foreign Subsidiary Operations

Normally, parent organizations exercise planning, administering and operating control over subsidiaries either wholly or

majority owned.  However, because  the  subsidiaries  generally
have a separate legal existence from the  parent, they do enjoy
a degree of operational autonomy.  As a result they have  their
own sets  of books and financial statements indicating the comparative  results from period to  period, which are joined with
the results of the parent operations.

In order  for the parent to properly plan and administer the
affairs of the  subsidiary, appropriate accounting  reports are
required.  The subsidiary, like the branch,  is regarded as  an
extension of the parent.   Therefore the results of the  operations  of both must  be  translated into a  common currency  in
order to draft proper  consolidated statements to show a single
operations result. This does not mean a total disregard for the
identity  of the subsidiary.  It  will not only  have  its  own
statements for its own operations but also will be  able to observe its role as part of  the parent totality through the consolidated statements.

Furthermore, it  is  customary to find local managerial personnel having a  considerable  say in the  foreign  operations.
This requires a strong accounting orientation in the local foreign concepts, terms, and practices in order for the local managers to have a better grasp of the results of their operations
in terms they  are familiar with.  Local accounting methodology
will also enable a better comparison  to  be made  with the results of competitors of the subsidiary.

## INTERNATIONAL CORPORATIONS

### #10-5...The International Corporation

In addition to setting up subsidiaries  in foreign countries
and  the taking over,  through purchase,  of foreign operations
as subsidiaries, the large international corporations have been
able to  attract  foreign corporations in different fields  of
operation as subsidiaries, resulting in conglomerates. Thus the
process of  internationalization of  business in  general  has
evolved into the creation of the INTERNATIONAL CORPORATION.  It
combines a multifaceted arrangement  of transnational,  political,  social and  geographical factors and has resulted  in  an
economics and business global orientation. The magnitude of the
expansion by  international businesses all  over the world  has
created a condition whereby the former export and import activities  have been dwarfed  by the subsidiary  and  branch operations. The result has been a dissipation of what was traditionally known as foreign operations.

### #10-6...Business Internationalization vs. Foreign Business

International businesses are no  longer regarded as  foreign
but as  integral parts of the overall international corporation

operations. In the article "The Administrative Structure of International Business With Special Reference to Foreign Based Affiliates," in the UNIVERSITY OF WASHINGTON BUSINESS REVIEW, Feb. 1963, pp. 38-50, Endel J. Kolde points out that the former so-called foreign operations are now regarded as international in the fullest sense of the term.

#10-7...Extent of International Operations

By 1971 the growth in foreign operations by the larger corporations in the world impelled the U.N. Dept. of Economic and Social Affairs to make a study of their characteristics. The results were published in the Dec. 1973, FINANCIAL EXECUTIVE, p. 32. Figure 10-1 shows the 25 largest corporations ranked by volume of sales, number of countries operated in, foreign sales and percentage of total profits.

In 1973 the U.S. Senate Committee on Finance made a survey which indicated that the sales volume of General Motors in 1969 was greater than all of the countries in the world but the top 22. Indeed if the sales volume of the largest corporations were equated with the volume of the output of goods and services of the largest nations, a listing of the non-Communist world's 100 largest money powers would contain 53 international corporations and only 47 countries, and the multinational corporations account for approximately 1/6 of the world's gross national product. Figure 10-2 shows the 100 biggest money powers and their sales volume in billions of dollars.

The movement by U.S. corporations into foreign domains has not been unilateral as indicated by a subsequent study reported in the Nov. 1, 1975 issue of FORBES MAGAZINE, which elicits a substantial reversal of the original trend under which U.S. corporations dominated the international scene. The FORBES study indicates an invasion of the U.S. by foreign enterprises numbering some 85 large corporations from a widespread area including the following countries: United Kingdom, Netherlands, South Africa, Germany, Canada, France, Switzerland, Belgium, Japan, Sweden, Saudi Arabia, Kuwait, United Arab Emirates, and Italy. As recently as 1979 the oil rich Arab countries have been investing substantially in U.S. enterprises, notably banks, real estate, hotels, etc. Ironically, the FORBES article is entitled "The U.S.' Unnaturalized Citizens." This has resulted in a turn-around of the viewpoint from which decisions are made. The April 18, 1977 issue of U.S. NEWS & WORLD REPORT, pp. 92-93, states that more and more business decisions that affect the economy "are being made abroad, as foreigners plunge into the U.S. This trend is apt to continue. Foreign direct investment has multiplied more than 3-1/2 times since 1966. Foreign affiliated firms based in the U.S. now handle about 30%

FIGURE 10-1
25 LARGEST CORPORATIONS IN THE WORLD

| Rank/Company/Country | Sales in Billions $ | Subsidi- aries in No. Countries | Foreign Sales % | % of Total Profits |
|---|---|---|---|---|
| 1 General Motors/ U.S. | $ 28.3 | 21 | 19% | 19% |
| 2 Exxon/U.S. | 18.7 | 25 | 50% | 52% |
| 3 Ford Motor Co./ U.S. | 16.4 | 30 | 26% | 24% |
| 4 Royal Dutch Shell/ U.K. Dutch | 12.7 | 43 | 79% | -- |
| 5 General Electric/ U.S. | 9.4 | 32 | 16% | 20% |
| 6 I.B.M./U.S. | 8.3 | 80 | 39% | 50% |
| 7 Mobil Oil/U.S. | 8.2 | 62 | 45% | 51% |
| 8 Chrysler/U.S. | 8.0 | 26 | 24% | -- |
| 9 Texaco/U.S. | 7.5 | 30 | 40% | 25% |
| 10 Unilever/U.K. Dutch | 7.5 | 31 | 80% | -- |
| 11 I.T.&T./U.S. | 7.3 | 40 | 42% | 35% |
| 12 Gulf Oil/U.S. | 5.9 | 61 | 45% | 21% |
| 13 British Petroleum/ Britain | 5.2 | 52 | 88% | -- |
| 14 Philips Gloeilampen- fabrieken/Dutch | 5.2 | 29 | -- | -- |
| 15 Standard Oil Cali- fornia/U.S. | 5.1 | 26 | 45% | 43% |
| 16 Volkswagenwerk/ Germany | 5.0 | 12 | 69% | -- |
| 17 U.S. Steel/U.S. | 4.9 | -- | 54% | 52% |
| 18 Nippon Steel/Japan | 4.1 | 5 | 31% | -- |
| 19 Standard Oil Indi- ana/U.S. | 4.1 | 24 | -- | -- |
| 20 DuPont/U.S. | 3.8 | 20 | 18% | -- |
| 21 Siemens Electric/ Germany | 3.8 | 52 | 39% | -- |
| 22 Imperial Chemical/ England | 3.7 | 46 | 35% | -- |
| 23 Hitachi/Japan | 3.6 | -- | 39% | -- |
| 24 Goodyear Tire & Rubber/U.S. | 3.6 | 22 | 30% | 30% |
| 25 Nestle/Switzerland | 3.5 | 15 | 98% | -- |

Source: Study of U.N. Dept. of Economic and Social Affairs. Reprinted
   by permission from FINANCIAL EXECUTIVE, copyright December 1973
   by Financial Executives Institute.

# FIGURE 10-2
## 100 BIGGEST MONEY POWERS IN THE WORLD
## AND THEIR SALES VOLUME IN BILLIONS OF DOLLARS

| Name | Sales Bil.$ | Name | Sales Bil.$ | Name | Sales Bil.$ |
|------|------|------|------|------|------|
| United States | 961.6 | CHRYSLER | 9.8 | DU PONT | 4.4 |
| Japan | 256.4 | IBM | 9.5 | GENERAL | |
| West Germany | 235.5 | UNILEVER | 8.9 | TELEPHONE | 4.3 |
| France | 176.7 | TEXACO | 8.7 | Malaysia | 4.3 |
| United Kingdom | 146.9 | I.T.&T. | 8.6 | Bangladesh | 4.3 |
| Italy | 108.2 | South Korea | 8.5 | I.C.I. | 4.2 |
| Canada | 92.4 | Indonesia | 8.4 | TOYOTA | 4.2 |
| India | 57.8 | Philippines | 7.7 | DAIMLER-BENZ | 4.2 |
| Australia | 43.3 | GULF OIL | 7.6 | GOODYEAR | 4.1 |
| Brazil | 41.2 | Chile | 7.5 | NESTLE | 4.1 |
| Spain | 39.4 | Portugal | 7.4 | FARBWERKE- | |
| Netherlands | 39.4 | Egypt | 7.0 | HOECHST | 4.1 |
| Sweden | 38.0 | Thailand | 7.0 | Morocco | 4.0 |
| Mexico | 35.7 | Colombia | 6.8 | MITSUBISHI | 4.0 |
| Belgium | 31.7 | Nigeria | 6.7 | NISSAN | 4.0 |
| GENERAL MOTORS | 30.4 | Peru | 6.7 | Libya | 3.9 |
| Argentina | 27.2 | STANDARD (CAL.) | 6.5 | Saudi Arabia | 3.9 |
| Switzerland | 26.3 | A.&P. | 6.4 | R.C.A. | 3.8 |
| EXXON | 22.1 | PHILIPS | 6.2 | KRESGE | 3.8 |
| A.T.&T | 21.0 | Taiwan | 6.2 | ATLANTIC | |
| FORD | 20.2 | SAFEWAY STORES | 6.1 | RICHFIELD | 3.8 |
| Denmark | 18.2 | BRITISH PETR. | 5.7 | KROGER | 3.8 |
| Austria | 17.8 | Israel | 5.6 | BASF | 3.7 |
| South Africa | 17.5 | J.C. PENNEY | 5.5 | CONTINENTAL OIL | 3.6 |
| ROYAL DUTCH | | U.S. STEEL | 5.4 | FIAT | 3.6 |
| SHELL | 14.1 | STANDARD (IND.) | 5.4 | BRITISH SHEEL | 3.6 |
| Norway | 13.6 | NIPPON STEEL | 5.4 | MONTEDISON | 3.6 |
| Turkey | 13.0 | Algeria | 5.3 | PROCTOR & | |
| Iran | 12.6 | WESTINGHOUSE | 5.1 | GAMBLE | 3.5 |
| Finland | 11.5 | VOLKSWAGEN | 5.0 | I.H. | 3.5 |
| Venezuela | 11.2 | Ireland | 4.9 | EASTMAN KODAK | 3.5 |
| SEARS ROEBUCK | 11.0 | SHELL OIL | 4.8 | Kuwait | 3.5 |
| Greece | 10.8 | Pakistan | 4.7 | RENAULT | 3.5 |
| GENERAL ELECTRIC | 10.2 | SIEMENS | 4.7 | MATSUSHITA | 3.5 |
| MOBIL OIL | 10.2 | HITACHI | 4.4 | L.T.V. | 3.4 |

Source: Survey of U.S. Senate Committee on Finance, 1973.

of the country's total imports and 24% of its exports. As a
result, more and more business decisions that affect the economic health of America are being made in board rooms overseas."

#10-8...Emergence of the Multinational Corporation

The shifting of international business to operations on an
international scale together with the opening of new plants and
facilities in the functional areas of manufacturing, assembling, shipping, financing, and distributing of goods all over
the world made it inevitable that springing out of this expansion should be the international corporation. It has come to be
referred to as MULTINATIONAL or TRANSNATIONAL CORPORATION, designated as M/N/C, T/N/C, or M/E for Multinational Enterprise.

Many books and articles have been written regarding the
M/N/C. In the various countries in which they operate, almost
as much attention is given to the social, political, and cultural apsects as to their basic economic function. Many of
these books have accused U.S. M/N/Cs of exploiting labor,
usurping raw materials, and generally abusing the people and
economies of the countries in which they operate, all for their
own personal gains. The result has been to require them to regard national, geographic, social, cultural, and political aspects of their own operations with almost equal importance as
their economic aspects. This has resulted in the development of
theories about Socio-Economic, Political and Inflation Accounting, all of which have sprung out of the nature of the M/N/C
and are treated later in this book.

MULTINATIONAL CORPORATIONS

#10-9...Definition of Multinational Corporation

There appears to be some difficulty about expressing a precise definition of a multinational corporation. In the MULTINA-
TIONAL ENTERPRISE IN TRANSITION by A. Kapoor and P. Grub, Dar-
win Press, 1972, p. 18, after presenting several definitions,
it is declared that "in summary, the multinational corporation
means different things to different people, and different phenomena are called by the same name. It seems essential that
those interested in international business clarify their meaning when discussing the multinational corporation."

In the May 1970 issue of the CENTER MAGAZINE, Vol. III, No.
1, Neil Jacoby says: "A Multinational Corporation owns and manages businesses in two or more countries. It is an agency of
DIRECT, as opposed to PORTFOLIO, investment in foreign countries, holding and managing the underlying physical assets
rather than securities based upon those assets."

## #10-10...Classification of Multinational Corporations

Many narrow definitions of Multinational Corporations have sprung up based on the VIEWPOINT from which they are examined. Under such criterion, M/N/Cs may be classified as Operational, Ownership, Nationality, Behavioral, and Accounting.

## #10-11...M/N/C Operational Viewpoint

As indicated in a paper given before a "Symposium on Management and Corporations in 1985" at Carnegie Institute in April 1960, David Lilienthal looks at the operational definition as "corporations which have their home in one country but operate and live under the laws and customs of other countries as well," which in effect simply means a firm operating in more than one country.

## #10-12...M/N/C Ownership Viewpoint

Another definition has evolved from an ownership viewpoint, as presented by Olivier Giscard d'Estaing, the Director General of INSEAD of Fontainbleu, in his report of the Crotonville Conference, as follows: "A multinational firm means a firm owned by persons from many nations: "multi" meaning consisting of many, and "national" meaning consisting of many nations."

## #10-13...M/N/C Nationality Viewpoint

Still another definition from the nationality of top management viewpoint, as stated by Business International Corp. in its book ORGANIZING FOR WORLD-WIDE OPERATIONS, 1965, follows:

A multinational corporation is one whose top management is composed of nationals of various countries, on the basis that such a firm will be presumably less apt to keep the interest of one country above everything, and will have a pure world-wide outlook.

## #10-14...M/N/C Behavioral Viewpoint

In his book THE CONCEPT OF THE CORPORATION, New American Library, 1964, at p. 244, Peter Drucker defines a multinational corporation as "one with corporate headquarters in the U.S., but in their organization, their business, their scope, they are world-wide. Top management is not concerned with any one region or territory but demands that they think and act as international business in a world in which national passions are as strong as ever."

## #10-15...M/N/C Accounting Viewpoint

For accounting purposes a simple definition would be that a
M/N/C is a business entity which operates in more than one
country through branches, divisions, and/or subsidiaries. This
definition invokes the question as to why corporations should
want to operate on an international level. There are six basic
reasons:
(1) to obtain raw materials in countries where such resources
    are found in abundance;
(2) to procure equity capital in countries where such capital
    is available and not necessarily in the base domicile
    country;
(3) to obtain debt financing otherwise not available in the
    domicile or other countries;
(4) to conduct manufacturing in countries where labor costs
    are far lower than in other countries;
(5) to fabricate products in countries where operating costs
    are far lower than in the domicile country;
(6) to operate in countries where the products may be sold and
    marketed on a higher profit ratio than obtainable else-
    where.

## #10-16...Types of International Corporations

The Multinational Corporation is not necessarily the only
exclusive type of international operation. In the article
"Joint Ventures of Transnational Business," in the INTERNATION-
AL MANAGEMENT REVIEW, Vol. 1, No. 1, 1964, Richard Robinson
pointed out that the term INTERNATIONAL as used in connection
with business could be refined to include 3 different types:
(1) WORLD-WIDE CORPORATION--A corporation registered in sev-
    eral countries, doing business in these countries, re-
    taining one corporate identity--a LEGAL view;
(2) MULTINATIONAL CLUSTER--A group of corporations, each
    created in the country of operation, but all controlled
    by one headquarters;
(3) MULTINATIONAL CORPORATION--A corporation which controls
    a multinational cluster, in a minimum of countries,
    which number must be large enough to involve the multi-
    national corporation in the international field. They
    may be subclassified on the basis of
    (a) OPERATIONS--as exporters, importers, transporters,
        petroleum, manufacturers, or traders
    (b) SIZE--total assets controlled, or relative to total
        operations
    (c) AREAS OF OPERATIONS--regional or multiregional.
Prof. George Scott, in the article "Financial Control and Reporting in Multinational Enterprises," in ACCOUNTING FOR MULTI-

NATIONAL ENTERPRISES, Bobbs-Merrill, pp. 143-145, points out:
Multinational enterprises are widely viewed as the most efficient organizational vehicles that have ever existed for
mobilizing the world's scarce resources. There are significant differences between multinational enterprises (M/E) and
other international companies. The mushrooming growth of
international business is sometimes regarded as a rival of
the Industrial Revolution in importance. In 1957, 2,800 parent companies of the U.S. controlled 10,000 foreign affiliates abroad--about 3.5 affiliates per parent. In 1971, 3,500
parent companies controlled 25,000 foreign affiliates--a
growth from 3.5 to 7 foreign affiliates per U.S. parent company. Thus the total number of foreign affiliates increased
by a factor of 2-1/2 during this 14-year period and the
average number of foreign affiliates per company doubled. At
present, approximately 1/6 of the world's GNP is generated
by the foreign affiliates of international companies, so the
world is becoming multi-nationalized.

### #10-17...Distinction Between Multinational Enterprises and International Companies

Prof. Scott goes on to say that there are significant differences between multinational enterprise operations and other
international companies. He points out that "the M/E is a
unique form of entity with respect to the way it conducts its
business and the differences are subtle and difficult to pinpoint but are critical to an understanding of the M/E." These
differences follow:
The M/E--as opposed to other international companies--is
characterized by: (1) significant operations abroad and operations in several countries--arbitrarily, at least 20% of
total sales abroad and operations in six or more countries;
(2) foreign operations which encompass the full range of
domestic activities, including foreign sourcing, production,
and marketing; (3) activities which are integrated across
national borders at the operations and financial levels, as
well as in terms of managerial control;(4)coordination on a
global basis--by means of a management system which forces
the component parts of the total entity to cooperate rather
than to go their separate ways.

### #10-18...International Accounting vs. Multinational Accounting

A distinction should be made between an international corporation and a national corporation with international operations. This was done at the beginning of this chapter to differentiate between _trading_ in foreign countries and _operating_
in foreign countries. In the article "Creating a World Enter-

prise" in the HARVARD BUSINESS REVIEW, Nov.-Dec. 1959, pp. 77-
89, Gilbert Clee and Alfred DiScipio admonish that there is a
difference between an international corporation and a national
corporation with international operations.

The difference is in perspective--the international corporation is an international entity with a global perspective, with
international horizons, and an international point of view. The
national corporation doing international business, on the other
hand, has a single country perspective with a major business
orientation tied to one country. It may have an international
division or perhaps a few international branch operations but
they will be held in the same vein with domestic divisions or
branches. The multinational corporation will have different
accounting procedures than the national corporation with international transactions. The international corporation has been
defined by Prof. Mueller in "Accounting Problems of International Corporations" in the Apr.1965, CANADIAN CHARTERED AC-
COUNTANT, pp. 271-274, as "one owned and controlled in two or
more countries."

It therefore behooves us to make a distinction between the
two terms INTERNATIONAL ACCOUNTING and MULTINATIONAL ACCOUNT-
ING, which have been used interchangeably in accounting literature. INTERNATIONAL ACCOUNTING is broader in scope than Multinational Accounting and is applicable both to multinational
corporations and their branches and subsidiaries as well as to
national corporations engaging in international transactions.
MULTINATIONAL ACCOUNTING applies only to accounting for multinational corporations, hence is narrower in scope; it is embraced in, and is a significant though not total, part of international accounting.

#10-19...Multinational Corporation Future Problems

In the Spring 1974 issue of WORLD in the article "Challenges
for the Multinationals," E.C. Palmer indicates that Multinational Corporations face four challenges:
Perhaps the most significant challenge facing the MNCs
today is the prospect of increased government intervention
and control.
The second challenge facing the MNCs is the need to develop information systems which meet the requirements: of
management in order to control the organization and make
decisions; of the investors in order to make investment decisions; and of national governments in order to measure the
impact and contribution of the MNC's domestic operations.
The third challenge facing the MNCs is people. People
qualified to perform in international business are not readily available. As one executive puts it: "These people have
to be grown." During the last several months the MNCs have

found themselves faced with a brand new challenge. Recent
events have vividly illustrated what can happen to the world
economy and the economics of individual countries when they
come to rely too heavily on external sources of supply.

#10-20...International Organizations Monitoring and Regulation

An invaluable reference source of international organizations monitoring is the INTERNATIONAL ORGANIZATIONS REGULATORY
GUIDEBOOK (1981 Edition), which has been compiled to indicate
the nature and extent they are regulated and monitored. Some of
the matters presented therein will give an indication of the
importance of this subject: challenge to MNCs from regulatory
activities of international organizations; major MNC functional
issues; international organizations, e.g., OECD, U.N., UNCTAD,
ECOSOC, WIPO, EEC, UNIDO, ITU, ILO, OAS, WHO, U.S. government
policy.


ACCOUNTING PROBLEMS ARISING FROM CURRENCY DIFFERENCES*

#10-21...Added International Environmental Complexities

Foreign branch and subsidiary accounting is generally much
the same as the domestic. The added international environmental
complexities are the accounting problems arising from the differences in currency of which there are three: the Financial
Accounting Problem; the Managerial Accounting Problem; and the
presentation of the proper financial statements.

#10-22...The Financial Accounting Problem

If the accounting data of the foreign operations are to be
incorporated into combined financial statements, the foreign
currency data must be expressed in terms of homogeneous monetary units, that is, in the currency of that of the home office.

#10-23...The Managerial Accounting Problem

Management is accustomed to thinking in terms of the home
office currency. Thus the foreign investment must be expressed
in the home office currency in order to evaluate the return on
the investment.


------
*See Summary of Footnote References -- #10-21 thru #10-34

#10-24...Proper Statement Presentation

The public corporation operating in the international environment must provide meaningful financial statements for the
international investor. In doing so the financial executive is
faced with the SELECTION OF A PROPER REPORTING CURRENCY. When
there are international operations, an appropriate approach to
the translation of the foreign currency transactions and foreign currency financial statements must be considered. Consistent with this translation process, the financial executive
must decide upon a proper perspective for consolidation of foreign currency financial statements.

#10-25...Financial Accounting Relationship of Foreign
         Operations to Home Office Operations

For a U.S. firm, financial statements of foreign operations
may be translated at the company's headquarters or at the foreign operational level. At this point it should be remembered
that the term TRANSLATION is to be distinguished from CONVER-
SION, in which latter case one currency is actually exchanged
for another, i.e., money-changing. Here we are concerned with
translation, a process by which accountants must take transactions recorded in terms of foreign currencies and then merely
restate them in terms of local currency so that no conversion
takes place. In addition to translation of transactions, financial statements expressed in foreign currency terms must also
be translated to terms of home office currency. If performed in
the U.S., key figures are returned to management in the foreign
countries. Also, various regular and special reports concerning
foreign exchange are prepared in the U.S. and sent to the foreign managers.

#10-26...Managerial Accounting Relationship of Foreign
         Operations to Home Office Operations

Usually the foreign executives are rather autonomous in managing the foreign operations. Awareness of financial position
and operational results is fostered by translating the financial statements before transmission to the U.S. Even when the
treasury function of exchange risk control is centralized, the
reports in dollars are prepared locally for transmission to the
U.S. headquarters. The translation into the language and currency of the parent company aids in communication of results
and directives.

Though the foreign operations may be managed rather autono-
mously, the usual accounting assumption is that the foreign
operations are considered to be extensions of the home country
operations. The financial statement presentation is based on

the pervasive accounting principle which dictates that the initial recordings of assets and liabilities be measured at exchange prices. The exchange rate prevailing AT THE TIME EACH TRANSACTION IS ENTERED INTO must then be used to translate the transaction negotiated in a foreign currency. As will be seen in the next chapter, because THE TIMES OF THE TRANSACTION are determinant in the recording process, this method of translation for foreign currency financial statements is called the TEMPORAL APPROACH.

## THE REPORTING CURRENCY

### #10-27...Selection of the Reporting Currency

In providing meaningful financial statements, the financial executive is faced with the selection of a proper reporting currency. The enterprise operating in the international environment must have a reporting currency which most clearly reflects its transactions. It is necessary to use one currency so that the total entity provides financial information based upon a common denominator. This is required both for the management of the enterprise and for proper interpretation by the international investor.

### #10-28...Approaches to Selection of Reporting Currency

Generally there are considered to be six different approaches as to what currency should be used as the reporting currency: (1) the LEGALISTIC APPROACH--the currency of the country of incorporation; (2) the BUSINESS TRANSACTIONAL APPROACH--the currency in which the majority of the business transactions are negotiated; (3) the OWNERSHIP APPROACH--the currency of the country where the majority of the stockholders are domiciled; (4) the DIVIDEND APPROACH--the currency in which the dividends are paid; (5) the STRONG-CURRENCY APPROACH--the currency that has world-wide recognition as a strong currency; and (6) the CENTRAL-UNIT CURRENCY APPROACH--an established or imaginary currency unit which may be in terms of a monetary unit of a precious metal content or involve the mix of several strong currencies.

### #10-29...The Legalistic Approach

The most normal situation is that where a corporation uses the currency of the country in which it is incorporated. The laws of some countries such as Germany indeed require that firms incorporated there have their financial statements prepared in the currency of that country. However, the home cur-

rency is not always used. For example, there are a number of
foreign companies listed on the New York and American Stock
Exchanges which use U.S. dollars as their reporting base because the majority of their business transactions are in U.S.
dollars.

#### #10-30...The Business Transaction Approach

Basing the reporting currency selection on the majority of
the monetary transactions in which the enterprise operates has
a strong practical support. It eliminates the need to hedge a
large quantity of foreign risk exposure in a country in which
it holds its majority of assets.

#### #10-31...The Ownership Basis

The citizenship of the shareholders may be considered in the
determination of the proper recording currency. Ownership would
seem to be a popular basis for a choice of currency. After all,
the annual reports are prepared for the owner--that is, the
stockholder. But serious shortcomings beset the use of ownership as a basis for choosing a currency. For one thing, ownership interest may change; and for another, a multinational corporation may have shareholders domiciled in many countries.
Moreover, the firm may not necessarily invest and operate in
any particular country at a continuous or stable rate. Thus the
ownership basis is not a good criterion for selecting the currency of account.

#### #10-32...The Dividend Approach

The dividend approach could also be used as an alternative
for choosing the currency base. Financial statements prepared
under this concept would preferably be stated in the currency
in which the dividends are paid. As a matter of fact, there are
corporations that do issue dividends in a currency other than
the one used as the reporting currency. For example, in 1970
three Canadian corporations listed on the New York and American
Stock Exchanges paid dividends in Canadian Dollars but used the
U.S. Dollar as the reporting currency.
On the other hand, two other Canadian corporations paid U.S.
Dollar dividends but continued to express their financial
statements in Canadian currency, as indicated in the article by
Norlin Rueschhoff, "U.S. Dollar Based Financial Reporting of
Canadian Multinational Corporations," in the INTERNATIONAL
JOURNAL OF ACCOUNTING, 8, No. 2, Spring 1973, pp. 108-109. One
can thus conclude that the dividend considerations are not the
key element in the reporting currency decision.

## #10-33...The Strong-Currency Approach

As previously pointed out, the nature of currency has a considerable influence on the freedom of its transferability. Thus
it was noted that currencies are classified as HARD CURRENCIES
and SOFT CURRENCIES. The HARD CURRENCY is one that is freely
convertible into any other currency, whereas SOFT CURRENCIES
are not freely convertible and usually have restrictions imposed on them for conversion to hard currencies. Like any commodity, to which foreign currency has been likened, it fluctuates
with supply and demand on a free market when it is left alone.

Hard currencies--principal of which are the U.S. Dollar,
the Swiss Franc, the West German Mark and the Netherlands Guil-
der--are freely convertible not only between one another but
also to soft currencies. On the other hand, soft currencies--
typical of which are the Italian Lira, the Portuguese Escudo,
the Brazilian Cruzeiro, and most of the other South American
currencies--are not only difficult to convert to hard currencies but even to one another of the soft currencies. In addition, hard currencies (which are usually in demand) show few
differences between the official exchange rate set by the government and the free market rate. With soft currencies there is
typically a gap between the official rate within the country
and the free market rate elsewhere.

Another factor to be considered is that many soft currency
countries have established limits on the amount of their currencies that visitors can legally bring into the country. For
example, Italy has a limit of 35,000 Lira and Portugal's is
1,000 Escudos. In addition there is a commission or service
charge for exchanging money. In the U.S. most money dealers
charge 1% for amounts up to $1,000, 1/2% up to $10,000 and 1/4%
over $10,000. Banks overseas also charge for such an exchange,
either a fixed fee or a percentage ranging from 2 to 3%.

Finally, in some countries there are restrictions on the
amount of their currencies that can be reconverted to dollars
or the currency that was originally converted. Other countries
require exchange receipts demanding the keeping of records of
purchases in order to reconvert. From the foregoing observations it should be apparent that the Strong-Currency Approach
is an important one in the selection of a reporting currency.

## #10-34...The Central Unit Currency Approach

A currency unit such as the Special Drawing Rights (SDRs) of
the IMF, or the basket currencies used in the Euromarket or in
Central America, could be used as a generally accepted world-
wide currency. For example, the European Currency Unit (ECU),
the official European Unit of Account (EUA 17), and the unofficial European Unit of Account (EUA 9) are used in the transac-

tions of governments  in  the EEC.  In fact, on Dec. 5, 1978 in
Brussels, after  months of extensive negotiations, the European
Common Market nations formed the EUROPEAN MONETARY SYSTEM (EMS)
to take effect on Jan. 1, 1979.  All EEC country members except
Great Britain, which  temporarily  abstained  from joining  the
group, were full-fledged members. European countries other than
EEC members may join  by invitation as associate members.   The
purpose of the EMS is to help stabilize  the value of their respective currencies so  as to  assist  in  terminating the wild
fluctuations in currency values.

## THE EUROPEAN MONETARY SYSTEM

### #10-35...The European Currency Unit

The plan of the  EMS is for the members to set up a new fund
of currencies worth some 33  billion dollars permitting Central
Banks to borrow from this fund within certain limits.  The currency of each member will be set in terms of every other member
currency and a new ECU was created.  The ECU is the key unit of
value against  which  all  member  nations'  currencies  are
measured.

The ECU is  a  basket of  all  nine EEC currencies which is
weighted according to  the strength of each country's  economy.
On such basis the percentage weight that has  been attached  to
each currency in one ECU is as follows:

| | | | |
|---|---|---|---|
| German Mark | 33.0% | Belgium Franc | 9.2% |
| French Franc | 19.8% | Danish Kroner | 3.1% |
| Pound Sterling | 13.4% | Irish Pound | 1.15% |
| Dutch Guilder | 10.5% | Luxembourg | |
| Italian Lira | 9.5% | Franc | .35% |

At first  only Central Banks of  the member  nations are to  be
permitted  to use the ECU,  with the possible eventuality  that
it  may be open for use for  business purposes.  The method in
which  the system is  to  operate, involving  what is termed  a
"Parity  Grid," is described in  the U.S.  NEWS & WORLD REPORT,
issue of Dec. 25, 1978, p. 92:

Changes  in a currency's value against the ECU will tell
countries when  to begin buying and selling  currencies  in
the open market.  Transactions between the members  and with
the central fund will be accounted for in terms of ECUs. For
most countries, currencies will be allowed to fluctuate only
2.25% from an agreed rate.  In a few  cases,  the allowable
deviation may be larger.

Example:  Assume that 1 guilder  is supposed to equal 1
mark.  If the guilder's  value rises in the foreign-exchange
markets until it is worth more than 1.025 marks, or falls to
less than 0.975, steps will be taken to bring it closer into
line.

If the guilder falls too much, the Central Bank of Germany or the Netherlands will have to buy guilders with marks until the exchange rate has been bid up enough. If the guilder rises too high, then the Central Banks will buy marks with guilders to drive down the Dutch rate.

It is possible, though not probable, that the ECU will some day rival the dollar as the world's major reserve asset—but only if the Europeans are more successful than the U.S. in combating inflation.
A EUROPEAN MONETARY COOPERATION FUND (EMCF) has been established by the EMS members to aid in the stabilization of exchange rates to keep them within the upper and lower limits. This fund is to be resorted to for use in support or intervention in cases where a crisis should arise in the hope of stabilizing member nations' exchange rates.

#10-36...European Composite Unit (EURCO) System

Contrary to the EMS which is intended only for the EEC countries, the EURCO is used for private contracts. The EURCO is an established mix of currencies with specific values and proportional weightings changing on a day-to-day basis in line with fluctuations in the foreign exchange markets. In the article "A Common European Currency," in MANAGEMENT IN A WORLD PERSPECTIVE, Univ. of Southern California School of Business, 1975, pp. 30-39, Brian Williams points out that the constituency of the 1 unit of EURCO comprises the sum of:

| | |
|---|---|
| 0.90 German Marks | 4.50 Belgian Francs |
| 1.20 French Francs | 0.20 Danish Kroner |
| 0.075 Pound Sterling | 0.005 Irish Pound |
| 80.0 Italian Lira | 0.50 Luxembourg Francs |
| 0.35 Dutch Guilders | |

The percentage that each of the currencies bears to the total EURCO UNIT is:

| | | | |
|---|---|---|---|
| German Mark | 29.9% | Belgian Franc | 9.4% |
| French Franc | 22.3% | Danish Kroner | 2.7% |
| Pound Sterling | 14.6% | Irish Pound | 1.0% |
| Italian Lira | 9.9% | Luxembourg | |
| Dutch Guilder | 10.1% | Franc | 1.0% |

The advantage of the use of such a reporting currency is that the financial statements would tend to have a more stable common denominator, particularly if the majority of business is transacted in the several countries constituting the currency mix.

#10-37...The Eurodollar Market

The largest market for banking currency outside of its local country is Europe, and such currency has therefore been referred to as EUROCURRENCY. Since the largest volume in such cur-

rency is in U.S. Dollars, the market, which was established in
the latter 1950s, has been called the EURODOLLAR MARKET. The
dollars can be deposited or invested either in Europe or the
U.S. The operation of the Eurodollar Market has been successful
for four reasons: the overwhelming sums of U.S. Dollars banked
outside the U.S.; capital restrictions imposed by other countries; the free operation of the market unfettered by restrictions or any regulations; and its greater accessibility and
lower costs.

The EURODOLLAR MARKET serves three classes of financing:
Short-term, Medium-term, and Long-term. The greater source is
the short-term offerings used commonly by multinational corporations with loan maturities ranging from as little as 30 days
to as long as 3 to 5 years based on floating instead of fixed
interest rates. The medium-term loans range from 5-8 years and
are used mainly by countries experiencing difficulty with payments for oil prices. The long-term loans are evidenced by
EUROBONDS wich are sold in a currency other than that of the
issuing country but are issued in terms of dollars. An illustration would be a German subsidiary of a U.S. multinational
corporation issuing German Mark bonds in the Netherlands. Because Eurodollars are an important source of financing and an
important part of the international capital market, companies
dealing with the market must be careful to ensure accurate financial reporting.

#### #10-38...Appraisal of Currency Approaches

Perhaps some day such an accepted world-wide common currency
unit can be used for financial reporting. In the meantime, the
use of the currency in which the majority of business transactions takes place would appear to be the most theoretically
sound. For international corporations operating from a center
in one country, the transaction basis would coincide with the
legal basis representing the currency of the country of incorporation. In any case, the reader of the international financial statements should not be misled in the analysis of the
statements. The country of incorporation and the currency base
should clearly be stated on the face of the financial statements.

### SUMMARY OF FOOTNOTE REFERENCES
(References are to Paragraph #'s)

#10-2   Proctor & Gamble Company, Annual Report, 1965
#10-2   NEW YORK STOCK EXCHANGE FACT BOOK, 1966
#10-6   Endel J. Kolde, "The Administrative Structure of Interna-
        tional Business With Special Reference to Foreign Based Af-
        filiates," UNIV. OF WASH. BUSINESS REVIEW (Feb. 1963): 38-50

#10-7   U.N. Dept. of Economic  and Social  Affairs Study, FINANCIAL
        EXECUTIVE (Dec. 1973): 32.  Reprinted by permission from FI-
        NANCIAL EXECUTIVE, © 1973 by Financial Executives Institute.
#10-7   "The U.S.' Unnaturalized Citizens," FORBES MAGAZINE (Nov. 1,
        1975)
#10-7   U.S. NEWS & WORLD REPORT (April 18, 1977): 92-93
#10-9   A. Kapoor and  P. Grub,  MULTINATIONAL ENTERPRISE IN TRANSI-
        TION (Darwin Press, 1972), p. 18
#10-9   Neil Jacoby, CENTER MAGAZINE, Vol. III, No. 1 (May 1970)
#10-11  David Lilienthal,  "Symposium on Management and Corporations
        in 1985" at Carnegie Institute (April 1960)
#10-12  Report of Crotonville Conference, Olivier Giscard d'Estaing,
        INSEAD OF FONTAINBLEU
#10-13  Business International  Corporation, ORGANIZING FOR  WORLD-
        WIDE OPERATIONS (N.Y.: 1965)
#10-14  Peter Drucker, THE CONCEPT OF THE CORPORATION, (New American
        Library, 1964), p. 244
#10-16  Richard Robinson, "Joint  Ventures of  Transnational  Busi-
        ness," INTERNATIONAL MANAGEMENT REVIEW, Vol. 1, No. 1 (1964)
#10-16  George  Scott,  "Financial Control and Reporting in Multina-
        tional Enterprises," ACCOUNTING  FOR MULTINATIONAL  ENTER-
        PRISES (Indianapolis: Bobbs-Merrill, 1978), pp. 143-145
#10-17  Ibid.
#10-18  Gilbert Clee  and Alfred DiScipio,  "Creating a World Enter-
        prise," HARVARD BUSINESS REVIEW (Nov-Dec 1959): 77-89
#10-18  Gerhard Mueller, "Accounting Problems of International Corp-
        orations,"CANADIAN CHARTERED ACCOUNTANT (April 1965):271-274
#10-19  E.C.  Palmer,  "Challenges  for  the Multinationals," WORLD
        (Spring 1974)
#10-20  INTERNATIONAL ORGANIZATIONS REGULATORY BOOK, 1981 edition
#10-21  thru #10-34:  "The Reporting Currency," adapted from Norlin
        G.  Rueschhoff, INTERNATIONAL ACCOUNTING AND  FINANCIAL  RE-
        PORTING, 1976, Praeger Publishers, Inc., by permission.
#10-32  Norlin Rueschhoff, "U.S. Dollar Based Financial Reporting of
        Canadian Multinational Corporations," INTERNATIONAL  JOURNAL
        OF ACCOUNTING, 8, No. 2 (Spring 1973): 108-109
#10-35  "Parity Grid," U.S. NEWS & WORLD REPORT (Dec. 25, 1978): 92
#10-36  Brian Williams, "A Common  European Currency," MANAGEMENT IN
        A WORLD PERSPECTIVE (Univ. of So. Calif. School of Business,
        1975), pp. 30-39

## BIBLIOGRAPHY

Dawson, Steven M.  "Eurobond Currency Selection: Hindsight," FINAN-
    CIAL EXECUTIVE, 41 (November 1973): 72-73
De La Mahotiere, Stewart.  "The Multinational's Role in  a Changing
    World," ACCOUNTANCY (March 1976): 28-30
Findlay, M.C. and Kleinschmidt, Elko. "Error--Learning in the Euro-
    dollar Market," JOURNAL OF FINANCIAL AND QUANTITATIVE ANALY-
    SIS, 10 (September 1975): 429-446
Finney, M.J. "Euro--Sterling Issues," THE ACCOUNTANT, 178 (June 1,
    1978): 732-734

Goodman, Stephen H.  "No Better Than the Toss of a Coin," EUROMONEY
    (December 1978): 75-85
Greenberg,  R.D.  "The Eurodollar  Market,"  CALIFORNIA LAW  REVIEW
    (September 1983): 1492
Meadows,  Edward.  "How the Euromarket  Fends  Off Global Financial
    Disaster," FORTUNE (September 24, 1979): 122-135
Periton,  Paul.  "The European Monetary System and Its Relationship
    to the U.K.," THE ACCOUNTANT, 183 (August 28, 1980): 348-351
Pinsky, Neil and Kvasnicka, Joseph. "The European Monetary System,"
    ECONOMIC PERSPECTIVES (Nov-Dec 1979): 3-10
Scorey, Michael.  "Eurobonds: Investments You're  Not Supposed  to
    Know About," ACCOUNTANCY, 92 (January 1981): 48-50
Severn, Alan K. and Meinster, David.  "The Use of Multicurrency Fi-
    nancing By the Financial  Manager," FINANCIAL MANAGEMENT, 7
    (Winter 1978): 45-53
Turner, J. Horsfall. "The Eurocurrency Loan," ACCOUNTANCY, 85 (Aug.
    1974): 64-66
Turnovsky, Stephen J. "A Determination of the Optimal Currency Bas-
    ket," JOURNAL OF INTERNATIONAL ECONOMICS (May 1982): 333

## THEORY QUESTIONS
(Question Numbers are Keyed to Text Paragraph #'s)

#10-8  Trace the development  of international business culmin-
       ating in the Multinational Corporation.
#10-9  Why is it difficult to define a MNC? Express definitions
       of a MNC from the following viewpoints: (a) operational,
       (b)  ownership, (c) nationality, (d) behavioral, (e) ac-
       counting.
#10-16 Classify and define the different types of INTERNATIONAL
       CORPORATIONS?
#10-17 Distinguish between Multinational Enterprises and Inter-
       national Companies.
#10-18 Distinguish between International  Accounting and Multi-
       national Accounting.
#10-19 With what four challenges are MNC's faced?
#10-21 What three accounting problems arise from  currency dif-
       ferences?  Explain the nature of the problems.
#10-27 Discuss the  problem of Selection of a Reporting Curren-
       cy.
#10-28 Briefly discuss the six  different  approaches as to the
       selection of a reporting currency.
#10-34 Trace the development  of the  European  Monetary System
       and its role in the EEC.
#10-35 What is the European Currency Unit (ECU) and how does it
       function?  What is the  purpose of the European Monetary
       Cooperation Fund and how does it operate?
#10-36 Describe the operation  of  the European  Composite Unit
       System.

#10-37 Outline the function of the Eurodollar Market, its currency and reasons for its success.

#10-38 Make a critical comparative analysis of the various currency approach selections. Which do you think is the most effective?

## EXERCISES

### EX-10-1
On Sept. 30 the Silko Co. acquired a 25,000 British Pounds financial futures contract for speculative purposes. The contract stipulated the delivery of pounds by Silko on Dec. 30 at the agreed rate of $1.50 per pound. On Dec. 30 the spot rate was $1.30 per pound.

Required:
Prepare the general journal entry to record the settlement of the contract on the Silko books on Dec. 30.

### EX-10-2
The U.S.A. Company, whose fiscal year ends Dec. 31, purchased 1,000 boxes of chocolate on Dec. 1 from the Swiss Co., payable on Jan. 31. The spot rates were as follows:

| | | | |
|---|---|---|---|
| Dec. 1 | 1 Swiss Franc | = | U.S. 40 cents |
| Dec. 31 | 1 Swiss Franc | = | U.S. 41 cents |
| Jan. 31 | 1 Swiss Franc | = | U.S. 39 cents |

Required:
a. Assuming the billing is in U.S. dollars at $4.00 per box, prepare the general journal entries to record the transactions on the books of the U.S.A. Company.

b. Assuming that the billing is in Swiss Francs (SF) at 10 SF per box, prepare the general journal entries to record the transactions on the books of the U.S.A. Company.

## PROBLEMS

### P-10-1
On Dec. 15, John Johnson, who was planning a trip to Mexico City, purchased 12,500 Mexican pesos at the rate of 24.87 pesos = $1.00. On Dec. 27 he decided not to take the trip and reconverted the pesos back to dollars when the rate was 25.02 pesos = $1.00.

Required:
a. Prepare general journal entries for December 15 and December 27.

b. Assuming he postponed the trip until January instead of the reconversion on December 27, and the year-end closing rate was 24.95 pesos = $1.00, record the adjusting entry as of December 31.

## P-10-2 (CPA EXAM, 5/82, PRAC. II, #1)

On Nov. 30, 1980, Tyrola Publishing Co., located in Colorado, executed a contract with Ernest Blyton, an author from Canada, providing for payment of 10% royalties on Canadian sales of Blyton's book. Payment is to be made in Canadian dollars each January 10 for the previous year's sales. Canadian sales of the book for the year ended Dec. 31, 1981, totaled $50,000 Canadian. Tyrola paid Blyton his 1981 royalties on Jan. 10, 1982. Tyrola's 1981 financial statements were issued on Feb. 1, 1982. Spot rates for Canadian dollars were as follows:

|  |  |
|---|---|
| November 30, 1980 | $.87 |
| January 1, 1981 | $.88 |
| December 31, 1981 | $.89 |
| January 10, 1982 | $.90 |

**Required:**
How much should Tyrola accrue for royalties payable at December 31, 1981?

## P-10-3 (CPA EXAM, 11/83, PRAC. I, #11)

On July 1, 1981, Stone lent $120,000 to a foreign supplier, evidenced by an interest-bearing note due on July 1, 1982. The note is denominated in the currency of the borrower and was equivalent to 840,000 local currency units (LCU) on the loan date. The note principal was appropriately included at $140,000 in the receivables section of Stone's Dec. 31, 1981, balance sheet. The note principal was repaid to Stone on the July 1, 1982, due date when the exchange rate was 8 LCU to $1. In its income statement for the year ended Dec. 31, 1982, what amount should Stone include as a foreign currency transaction gain or loss?

a. $0
b. $15,000 loss
c. $15,000 gain
d. $35,000 loss

## P-10-4

MB Dealers, a U.S. importer, purchased Mercedes Benz cars from the Mercedes Benz Mfg. Co. of Stuttgart, Germany, on Dec. 15, 1984, to be paid for in 30 days on Jan. 15, 1985. The spot rate on Dec. 15 was 1 DM = U.S. 51 cents. On Dec. 31, 1984, the spot exchange rate was 1 DM = U.S. 50 cents, and on Jan. 15, 1985, the spot exchange rate was 1 DM = U.S. 52 cents. The purchase invoice of MB Dealers indicates that the total purchase price for the cars bought on Dec. 15 came to DM 100,000, the merchandise being billed in German currency.

**Required:**
a. Journal entry on books of MB Dealers on December 15, 1984.
b. December 31, 1984: What, if any, entry would be made? Why?
c. On January 15, 1985: Journal entry to be made for payment of purchase.

## CASES

CASE-10-1

Alcan Aluminum Ltd., a Canadian corporation with shares listed on stock exchanges in the United States, Canada, and Europe, switched from Canadian dollar reporting to U.S. dollar reporting. An excerpt from its June 1970 interim financial report is as follows:

### Results for the Six Months Ended June 30, 1970

Reporting the Company's results in U.S. dollars rather than Canadian dollars, Alcan Aluminum Ltd. had consolidated net income of U.S. $45.6 million in the first half of 1970 as compared with $37.8 million restated in U.S. dollars for the like period of 1969. The $45.6 million consolidated net income for the first half includes an exchange profit of $2.5 million. Net income per share excluding this exchange profit was U.S. $1.27 compared with U.S. $1.11 per share for the first half of last year. The decision to change the Company's reporting to a U.S. dollar basis was made by the Directors after the Company had consulted its auditors and certain regulatory bodies.

### Alcan's Adoption of U.S. Dollar Reporting

When reporting to shareholders, Alcan has in the past expressed its financial statements and earnings in terms of Canadian dollars. The Directors have now decided that to provide these statements and earnings in terms of U.S. dollars will give a fairer picture of the Company's worldwide business.

A company such as Alcan clearly needs a scale for measuring its results in the many parts of the world where it operates, which will present an accurate and consistent picture of the Company's operations to its shareholders and the investing public. The Canadian dollar constituted such a scale as long as its exchange value moved within a narrow range from an official rate of U.S. $.925. However, on June 1 the Canadian government decided to let the foreign exchange value of the Canadian dollar "float" and it is not known when a new fixed rate of exchange may be established. Even if such a rate is established, it is the U.S. dollar which is the basic international currency to which all others relate and which provides the best vehicle for international reporting.

In making the decision to give results in U.S. dollars, the Directors took into account that, although Alcan is a Canadian company, about 60 percent of the Company's assets, 55 percent of shareholders, 85 percent of sales and operating revenues, and 60 percent of net income are non-Canadian. Additionally, aluminum, like most materials sold internationally, is normally quoted at a U.S. dollar price and, since 1950, Alcan's dividends have been paid in U.S. dollars.

The consolidated statements of income for the second quarter and first half of 1970 are expressed in U.S. currency following the same accounting principles used in the past for the translation into Canadian dollars of foreign currency accounts. The comparable statements for 1969 have been restated in U.S. currency on the same basis. The indicated first half 1970 earnings of U.S. $1.35 per common share include a profit of U.S. 8 cents per share arising from translating of Alcan's Canadian working capital at the higher exchange rate for the Canadian dollar. If the June 30 value of the Canadian of U.S. $.97 were maintained until the end of 1970, a further profit of U.S. 15 cents per share would be recorded in the second half as Alcan's Canadian inventories at May 31 are sold. This exchange profit in 1970 would more than offset the adverse impact of the higher Canadian dollar on export sales margins during the second half of this year, although the latter impact will continue beyond 1970 if the Canadian dollar remains at present levels.

If Alcan had continued to report to shareholders in Canadian dollars, common share earnings would have amounted to Can. $1.28 for the first half of 1970 as compared with Can. $1.21 for the same period of 1969. These 1970 earnings would have reflected an adverse impact amounting to Can. 2 cents per share arising from the conversion of Alcan's non-Canadian working capital at the June 30 exchange rate. Assuming continuation of this exchange rate through 1970, a further loss of Can. 31 cents per share would have been recorded over the balance of the year as non-Canadian inventories existing at May 31 were sold. However, over the long-term this loss would have been more than offset by profit on the repayment of debt payable in currencies other than Canadian dollars, which profit would have amounted to Can. 71 cents per share.

**Required**:

a. List the different bases or approaches that the company could have used to select its currency reporting base. Give justifications for each.

b. What was the primary basis for the company's switching its reporting currency to the U.S. dollar? Explain.

c. What was the basis that provided the justification for the previous use of the Canadian dollar as the reporting currency? Would this basis still be valid?

**11**

# Foreign Exchange Financial Statement Translation

#11-1...Dual Nature of Translation

Once the financial executive has selected the reporting currency, he must then use the appropriate method of translating
foreign currency business transactions and/or foreign currency
account balances. Thus there is a dual aspect to the translation process: (1) as seen in the export and import transactions, sales and purchases made and billed in foreign currency
must be translated in order to be entered at the amount of the
exporter's or importer's local currency in their respective
books; (2) when foreign currency financial statements are to be
combined with the home office financial statements, the former
statements must have their amounts translated in terms of the
home office currency to create the homogeneity required to be
able to merge the two into one figure.

Thus if there are international operations managed through a
branch or subsidiary whose financial statements are accumulated
in a foreign currency, they must be translated into the reporting currency. The degree of centralization of control will play
a part in the translation process.

#11-2...Transaction Approach to Translation of
        Foreign Currency Financial Statements

When a firm expands its export and import business by setting up a branch or subsidiary, it must translate the foreign
currency financial statements in order to combine them with the
home office statements. In order to preserve the historical
cost concept in translation, a transaction approach similar to
the two-transaction perspective has developed. Through experience, the approach has been refined and has received various
names: (1) Current-Noncurrent; (2) Monetary-Nonmonetary, (3)
Temporal (previously mentioned), and (4) Current Rate.

## CURRENT-NONCURRENT TRANSLATION METHOD

### #11-3...Current-Noncurrent Method of Translation

The current-noncurrent method of translating foreign currency financial statements of  position evolved in the early   20th
century in the U.S.    Until 1956  it was  regarded   as the most
authoritative method  of translating foreign currencies in   accounts under its description in Chapter 12 of the AICPA ARB No.
43.   Up to  the early  1960s the current-noncurrent method of
translation  was regarded as   a GAAP   not only in   the U.S. but
also in many other countries where it is still advocated.

Basically, the current-noncurrent  method provides that current assets and liabilities in the  balance sheet be translated
at the current rate of exchange, i.e.,  the rate  prevailing as
of the date of the construction of the balance sheet. Long-term
assets and liabilities are to be translated at historical rates
of exchange, viz., the  rates existing at  the  date the assets
were acquired or  the liabilities incurred. An   exception  was
made  under APB Opinion No. 6 in the case  of  long-term, which
was translated at the current rate.

Income Statement operating items were to be translated at an
average exchange rate which is to be applied to each operational month, or, if for the entire reporting period, on a weighted
average basis.  Depreciation and amortization items, being tied
to their  respective  fixed assets,  would  correspondingly be
translated at the historical rate in effect when the respective
assets were acquired.   Gains or losses resulting from  foreign
exchange  fluctuations would  be  classified as Realized or Unrealized, and according  to AICPA ACCOUNTING RESEARCH AND   TER-
MINOLOGY   BULLETIN, Final   Edition,   1961, "realized  gains   or
losses are  recommended  to be  charged against  or credited to
operations, and unrealized gains or losses should preferably be
carried to a suspense  account,  except to the extent that they
offset prior provisions  for unrealized  losses, in  which  case
they may be credited to the account previously charged."

### #11-4...Current-Noncurrent Method Shortcomings

Many shortcomings sprang up in the current-noncurrent method
during the  time it became the  traditionally accepted translation method.  They were enumerated by  Prof. Samuel Hepworth of
the Univ. of Mich. in  his 1956 book,  REPORTING FOREIGN OPERA-
TIONS.  One  severe shortcoming pointed out  by  Prof.  Gerhard
Mueller in the article "Are Traditional Foreign Exchange Translation Methods Obsolete?", in the CALIFORNIA MANAGEMENT REVIEW,
Summer 1956, pp. 41-46, was that a fluctuating foreign exchange
may produce distorted operating results between accounting periods in inventory translations.  Other shortcomings pointed out

by Prof. Hepworth are that  the current-noncurrent concepts are
not indicative of the propriety of the rate used based  on such
a  classification, and the distortion caused by the lack of association  of foreign exchange gains  and  losses  with overall
operating results of international business operations.

As a consequence, Prof.  Hepworth  made the following recommendations:  (1) to replace the current-noncurrent concept with
a more accurate one based on monetary-nonmonetary concepts; (2)
to translate inventories  at historical rates rather  than current rates;  (3) to translate long-term  liabilities at current
rather than historical rates;  and (4)  to consider foreign exchange gains and  losses as part of  the  overall international
business operating results even if they are reported separately
from the daily business activity results.

In the wake  of the  conclusions reached by Prof.  Hepworth,
the NAA Research Report #36 (1960), MANAGEMENT ACCOUNTING PROB-
LEMS  IN FOREIGN OPERATIONS,  p. 17, described the current-noncurrent method as "one that seems  to reflect the use of an established balance sheet  classification for a purpose  to which
it is not relevant." The result was the launching of the monetary-nonmonetary method of translation.


## MONETARY-NONMONETARY TRANSLATION METHOD

### #11-5...Monetary-Nonmonetary Method of Translation

A summary  of the results of Prof.  Hepworth's  findings and
those of the NAA, stated above, was issued in a booklet on CUR-
RENT  FOREIGN EXCHANGE INFORMATION, published  by the  international CPA firm, Price Waterhouse & Co.  The following language
in the summary  provides the basis for the monetary-nonmonetary
terminology:

Balance Sheet  accounts  other than  stockholder equity  accounts should  normally be divided into those accounts which
are  of a FINANCIAL NATURE and those that are  PHYSICAL IN
NATURE.  For purpose of translating FINANCIAL ITEMS, a year-
end  rate will generally provide the most reasonable  dollar
equivalent of the related local currency account.  Translating long-term  receivables and payables at the current  rate
presents  the receivable  or payable in terms of the amounts
of dollars which at the present time  would  be required for
settlement.  The PHYSICAL ITEMS,  for which historical rates
should be used,  are  such that their value in terms of dollars  would generally  tend  to be  recovered over the years
through increased selling prices in local currency. Deferred
charges and prepaid expenses,  since  they represent  costs
already  incurred,  are not  susceptible to  future exchange
fluctuations; in this sense  they  are  like physical  items

such as  fixed assets, and should also be translated at historical  rates.  The capital  stock portion  of stockholders
equity  is generally translated at  the rates in effect when
the capital was invested.  This preserves the historical relationship of the invested  capital to the dollar investment
on the parent company books. The retained earnings should be
expressed in the  dollar  relationship which existed  as the
earnings accumulated.   The basic  theory behind translating
income and  expense accounts is to reflect individual transactions  at  the  rates of exchange in effect at the time of
each transaction; in  most  cases,  adequate  representative
results can  be obtained by the  use of some type of average
rates.  Depreciation would be  translated at the appropriate
historical rates, as should inventories included in cost  of
goods sold, and amounts amortized  from  deferred charges or
credits when such rates are used for balance  sheet translations, otherwise an average rate should be used.

## #11-6...Difference Between Current-Noncurrent and
## Monetary-Nonmonetary Methods

The basic difference between the current-noncurrent  and the
monetary-nonmonetary methods, then, is the substituting of  the
classification  of items as monetary and nonmonetary instead of
current and  noncurrent.  The  monetary-nonmonetary  method was
formally advocated by the issuance  of Opinion No. 6 by the APB
in 1965.    However, the  translation problem  was  subsequently
studied in  depth, culminating  in the publication by the AICPA
of ARS No. 12 in 1972. This study by Leonard Lorenson, "Reporting Foreign Operations of U.S. Companies in U.S. Dollars," con-
ceptualized  the  monetary-nonmonetary  method  in  the  theory
founded on the temporal principle.
Thus the modification of ARB No. 43 permitted the use of the
monetary-nonmonetary method of translation.  This is emphasized
by the NAA  Research Report No. 36, MANAGEMENT ACCOUNTING PROB-
LEMS  IN FOREIGN  OPERATIONS, which basically  divides  balance
sheet items into FINANCIAL  (MONETARY) ITEMS and PHYSICAL (NON-
MONETARY) ASSETS. The FINANCIAL ITEMS consist of local currency
and claims  to  receive or pay a fixed number of local currency
units, and  the PHYSICAL ASSETS constitute such physical  items
as inventories and fixed assets. The rationale is stated by the
NAA as follows:

The dollar equivalent of local currency financial assets
and  liabilities  is immediately affected by a change in the
rate of exchange because if the local currency declines relative to the U.S. dollar, financial assets in local currency
will yield fewer dollars on conversion and debts  payable in
local currency can be  satisfied  with fewer dollars.  Local

currency financial assets are always at risk from unfavorable movements in the exchange rate. Because financial items
are directly affected by exchange rate fluctuations, the
exchange rate prevailing on the balance sheet date yields
the best translation for financial items expressed in a foreign currency.

Physical items tend to be unaffected by exchange rate
fluctuations. Since a substantial decline in value of a foreign currency unit relative to the dollar is usually a consequence of inflation in the foreign country, prices in that
country may be expected to rise and physical assets will
command increased selling prices in the devalued currency.
Such assets are logically translated at the rate of exchange
current on the date the foreign subsidiary acquired the
assets.

#### #11-7...Monetary-Nonmonetary Method Shortcomings

Lorenson's study culminated in the publication of ARS No. 12
in 1972 and the establishment of the monetary-nonmonetary method. In this study, Lorenson points up the shortcomings, basic
of which (somewhat similar to the current-noncurrent) is that
it depends on an account classification scheme rather than the
substance of the matter. In essence this means that the classic
classification of accounts is not necessarily the basis for a
method of translation.

As a result, ACCOUNTING FOR THE TRANSLATION OF FOREIGN CUR-
RENCY TRANSACTIONS AND FINANCIAL STATEMENTS, in FASB #8, on
pages 58-59, points out that "no comprehensive principle of
translation can be derived solely from the monetary-nonmonetary
distinction."

In ARS No. 12, Lorenson indicates that the process of translation is merely a restatement of a given figure in terms of
another supposedly similar figure. It is thus a change in a
unit of measurement, but has no impact whatever on the nature
or character of the item, which in the final analysis should be
the true test. The net result is merely a currency restatement
but has no effect on the valuation of the item. Under GAAP in
the U.S., the showing of the assets in the balance sheet is
tied to a time concept related to the money values stated; thus
cash is the amount owned at the balance sheet date, receivables
and payables are amounts expected to be received or paid at
some future date, other assets are expressed in the amount paid
for them at a past date when they were acquired. It is simple
to see that this description fits the three aspects of time,
viz., cash representing present, fixed assets the past, and
receivables and payables the future. It is this time dimension
that is not given consideration under the monetary-nonmonetary
method.

## THE TEMPORAL TRANSLATION METHOD

### #11-8...The Temporal Method of Translation

In attempting to cure the defects pointed out above, Lorenson promulgated what he termed the TEMPORAL PRINCIPLE OF TRANSLATION. In his opinion the manner best suited for keeping the accounting bases that are used in the measurement of foreign currency items is to use the exchange rates in effect at the dates which are applicable to the foreign money measurements in translating their foreign money amounts. The objective of Lorenson is to translate assets and liabilities in a way that will retain their original measurement bases, viz., those which existed at the time the transaction took place. The translation process is thus concerned with the TIMES--the TEMPORAL EVENTS-- during which the transactions are recorded. It assumes that all transactions of subsidiaries and branches are controlled and recorded by the parent company and are thereby based on a parent company perspective. In essence, the approach is an extension of the two-transaction approach for translating international export and import transactions.

Thus the historical exchange rate which prevails at the time of each transaction is used to translate original transactions. However, monetary items and balance items representing current values are updated with each exchange rate change. Exchange gains and losses occur as exchange rate changes take place and are recorded as current income items. Lorenson states that under the temporal principle "money, receivables, and payables measured at the amounts promised should be translated at the foreign exchange rate in effect at the balance sheet date, and assets and liabilities measured at money prices should be translated at the foreign exchange rate in effect at the dates to which the money prices pertain."

As a result, the procedure recommended by Lorenson is that cash, receivables and payables are to be translated at the current rate; foreign statement assets stated at historical cost are translated at the historical rate; assets stated at current values are translated at the current rate; revenues and expenses are translated at historical rates that prevailed when the transactions took place; and voluminous revenue and expense transactions are translated at average rates. With the issuance of FASB #8 in 1975, the temporal method was formally adopted thereby eliminating the choice of method previously existing in the U.S. Under FASB #8, all U.S. companies were required to espouse the temporal principle of translation.

It should be noted that under the historical cost theory of accounting, the translation procedures under the temporal method are virtually the same as those under the monetary-non-monetary principle. This has caused many accounting writers to

indicate that the temporal method  is synonymous with the monetary-nonmonetary method,  with the  use  of  both  being interchangeable.  Under a replacement cost, discounted cash flow, or
market value arrangement, however, the two methods would differ
substantially in results.

Thus, under the temporal method, FASB #8 recommends the following division between Current Translation Rates  and Historical:

## CURRENT

Cash
Marketable Securities Carried at Market Price
Accounts & Notes Receivable and related Unearned Discount
Allowance for Doubtful Accounts and Notes Receivable
Inventories Carried  at Current Replacement  or Current Selling
    Price
Inventories Carried at Net Realizable Value
Inventories  Carried at Contract  Price (Produced  Under  Fixed
    Price Contract)
Refundable Deposits Paid Out
Advances to Subsidiaries
Life Insurance Cash Surrender Value
Accounts and Notes Payable
Accrued Expenses Payable
Accrued Losses on Firm Purchase Commitments
Refundable Deposits Received
Bonds Payable or Long-Term Debt
Unamortized Premium or Discount on Bonds or Notes Payable
Convertible Bonds Payable
Accrued Pension Liabilities
Obligations Under Warranties

## HISTORICAL

Marketable Securities Carried at Cost
Inventories Carried at Cost
Prepaid Insurance, Advertising, and Rent
Property, Plant and Equipment
Accumulated Depreciation on Property, Plant & Equipment
Patents, Trademarks, Licenses and Formulas
Goodwill
Other Intangible Fixed Assets
Deferred Income

## THE CURRENT RATE TRANSLATION METHOD

### #11-9...Current Rate Approach to Translation

Unlike the  methods discussed  to this  point, all  of which
were formulated  in the U.S., the  CURRENT RATE METHOD had  its

origin outside the U.S.  Its first support came from the Institute of Chartered Accountants in  England  and Wales in 1968 in
STATEMENT N25, in a document entitled "The Accounting Treatment
of Major Changes  In  The Sterling Parity of  Overseas  Currencies."  In its MEMBER'S HANDBOOK STATEMENT N25, para. 14, 1968,
the pronouncement was made that  "the  Current Rate, or Closing
Rate, method was acceptable as well as the Historic  Rate, Current-Noncurrent Method."

The Scottish Institute of  Chartered Accountants,  in a  research study  entitled  "The  Treatment in Company Accounts  of
Changes in the  Exchange  Rates  of International  Currencies,"
published in THE  ACCOUNTANT'S MAGAZINE, Sept. 1970,  pp.  415-
423, goes further than the British view by announcing  that the
only method  acceptable  for  translation  is the Current  Rate
method.  Although Canada has taken no definitive  action on the
subject, in a research monograph published in 1972, the Canadian Institute's Accounting and  Research Committee supports  the
Current Rate Method though not under all conditions.  There are
circumstances  indicating  that Australia may also support this
method.

Under the Current  Rate Method,  all of the foreign subsidiary's assets, liabilities,  revenues  and expenses--in essence,
ALL financial statement accounts--are translated at the current
rate of exchange prevailing on the balance sheet date. It utilizes  a  local perspective by viewing the  foreign-based operations as autonomous business enterprises.  The  unit of measure
is the currency of the foreign country of domicile.  The translation process is then reduced to a mechanism for restating the
financial statements in the common reporting currency.

The  exchange  adjustment resulting  from  the  current rate
translation process  is regarded as an adjustment to the shareholders' equity.  The adjustment is derived in  the updating of
the beginning owners' equity.  Dividends paid by the subsidiary
to the parent,  as well as other intercompany transactions, may
affect the amount of the translation adjustment. Of importance,
however, is that under this approach the subsidiary remittances
and  other  intercompany payments are viewed as  a sacrifice of
the working capital of  the subsidiary.  The dividend is viewed
as  a  payout of the local currency to  be paid to  the  parent
stockholders.

## #11-10...Hybrid Current Rate Transaction Approach

A variation of the current rate method is  to use the transaction approach for translating the income statement  accounts.
Being the equivalent of the temporal method, the exchange gains
or losses derived under the transaction approach would justifi-
ably  be  reported as  current income statement items.  In  any
case, the extent of any  utilization  of  the Current Rate  Ap-

proach may depend upon the perspective which, if local and representative of the proper multinational perspective, may develop into the most appropriate for the truly multinational enterprises.

## USAGE EXPERIENCE OF TRANSLATION METHODS

### #11-11...Translation Methods Usage Experience

Outside the U.S. a study was made in 1975 of international
practice by Price Waterhouse International entitled A SURVEY
IN 46 COUNTRIES: ACCOUNTING PRINCIPLES AND REPORTING PRACTICES,
which indicates that the methods used are quite diverse, and
may be summarized as follows:

| Method | Countries Represented by Majority of Firms |
|---|---|
| Current-<br>Noncurrent | Bermuda, Canada, Colombia, Iran, Paki-<br>stan, South Africa |
| Monetary-<br>Nonmonetary | Argentina, Australia, Brazil, Chile, Fiji,<br>Mexico, New Zealand, Uruguay, Venezuela |
| Current Rate | Denmark, France, India, Japan, Nether-<br>lands, Norway, Switzerland, United Kingdom |

These results were confirmed in the article "Foreign Currency Translation Practices Abroad" by Evans in THE CPA JOURNAL,
June 1974, pp. 47-50. A chart of graphic panorama of the comparative features of each of the translation methods is presented in Figure 11-1.

## TRANSLATION RATES UNDER FASB #8

### #11-12...Basis for FASB #8

In the article "Currency Translation: A New Blueprint," in
the JOURNAL OF ACCOUNTANCY, June 1982, p. 82, Professors Thomas
Ratcliffe and Paul Munter point out:
In the 9-year period from 1966 to 1975, U.S. exports expanded 266%, from 23 billion to 85 billion, and sales by foreign
U.S. subsidiaries rose 369% from $98 billion to $458 billion. In addition devaluations of the dollar and establishment of floating exchange rates significantly altered the
environment of U.S.-based multinational companies, causing
constant currency exchange rate fluctuations. Currency re-
alignments coupled with multinational expansion has made the
related accounting complex and important, and resulted in
the issuance of FASB #8, ACCOUNTING FOR THE TRANSLATION OF
FOREIGN CURRENCY TRANSACTIONS AND FOREIGN CURRENCY FINANCIAL
STATEMENTS in October 1975. From its inception, FASB #8 was
extremely controversial, despite the need for guidance in

FIGURE 11-1
GRAPHIC PANORAMA OF THE COMPARATIVE FEATURES
OF EACH OF THE TRANSLATION METHODS

| ACCOUNT C=Current Rate H=Historical Rate R=Residual Balance | Current- Non- Current | Monetary- Non- Monetary | Temp- oral | Current | Current Temporal Hybrid | Monetary Temporal Hybrid |
|---|---|---|---|---|---|---|
| Cash | C | C | C | C | C | C |
| Accounts Receivable | C | C | C | C | C | C |
| Inventories-Cost | C | H | H | C | C | H |
| Inventories-Market | C | H | C | C | C | H |
| Investments-Cost | H | H | H | C | H | H |
| Investments-Market | H | H | C | C | H | H |
| Fixed Assets | H | H | H | C | H | H |
| Other Assets | H | H | H | C | H | H |
| Accounts Payable | C | C | C | C | C | C |
| Long-Term Payables | H | C | C | C | C | H |
| Common Stock | H | H | H | C/H | H | H |
| Retained Earnings | R | R | R | R | R | R |

Source: Pages 47-50, Evans, "Foreign Currency Translation Practices Abroad." Reprinted with permission of THE CPA JOURNAL, copyright June 1974, New York State Society of Certified Public Accountants.

translating foreign currency statements due to the diversity
of existing standards.  Criticism of FASB #8 caused the FASB
to restudy the matter  and led to the issuance  of FASB #52,
FOREIGN CURRENCY TRANSLATION.
Thus FASB #8, sanctioning  the temporal  method of translation,
was the required  method of translation from 1975 to 1981  when
FASB #52 was issued.

#11-13...FASB #8 Translation Rates

Under the temporal  approach, balance sheet items which represent current  values are translated at current balance-sheet-
date  exchange rates, and items  representing historical values
are translated at the rate prevailing at the time of the transactions.  FASB #8 had a rather comprehensive recommended sample
list of rates used to translate various assets and liabilities,
which follows:

RATES USED TO TRANSLATE ASSETS AND LIABILITIES
FASB #8 - OCTOBER 1975, PAGE 20

| | Translation Rates | |
| Item | Current | Histor- ical |
|---|---|---|
| ASSETS: | | |
| Cash on Hand & Demand & Time Deposits | x | |
| Marketable Equity Securities: | | |
|    Carried at Cost | | x |
|    Carried at Current Market Price | x | |
| Accounts and Notes Receivable and Related | | |
|    Unearned Discount | x | |
| Allowance for Doubtful Accounts and | | |
|    Notes Receivable | x | |
| Inventories: | | |
|    Carried at Cost | | x |
|    Carried at Current Replacement Price | | |
|     or Current Selling Price | x | |
|    Carried at Net Realizable Value | x | |
|    Carried at Contract Price (produced | | |
|     under fixed price contracts) | x | |
| Prepaid Insurance, Advertising, & Rent | | x |
| Refundable Deposits | x | |
| Advances to Unconsolidated Subsidiaries | x | |
| Property, Plant and Equipment | | x |
| Accumulated Depreciation of Property, | | |
|    Plant and Equipment | | x |
| Cash Surrender Value of Life Insurance | x | |
| Patents, Trademarks, Licenses & Formulas | | x |
| Goodwill | | x |
| Other Intangible Assets | | x |

LIABILITIES:
```
Accounts & Notes Payable & Overdrafts       x
Accrued Expenses Payable                     x
Accrued Losses on Firm Purchase Commitments x
Refundable Deposits                          x
Deferred Income                                        x
Bonds Payable or Other Long-Term Debt        x
Unamortized Premium or Discount on
        Bonds or Notes Payable               x
Convertible Bonds Payable                    x
Accrued Pension Obligations                  x
Obligations Under Warranties                 x
```

## FASB #8 BALANCE SHEET ITEMS TRANSLATION*

### #11-14...Foreign Monetary Assets and Liabilities

The principles for recording the international financial items are the same as those used for the domestic. As indicated in the discussion of exports and imports, the value of foreign receivables is translated at the rate prevailing at the balance sheet date. This is consistent with the principle of valuating at net realizable value. Cash and other financial assets are also translated at the current rate, assuming that these items are readily convertible into the home office currency. In using the prevailing balance sheet rate for translating payables, liabilities are recorded at current liquidation value. The underlying going-concern concept is involved in the application of these financial accounting principles.

### #11-15...Foreign Investments

One item that was used to demonstrate the shortcomings of the monetary-nonmonetary method was a foreign investment. In FASB #8, pages 58-59, it is pointed out:

Nonmonetary assets and liabilities are measured on different bases, e.g., past prices or current prices, under different circumstances, and translation at a past rate does not always fit. Translating nonmonetary items at a past rate produces reasonable results if the items are stated at historical cost, but not if they are stated at current market price in foreign currency. For example, if a foreign operation purchases as an investment 100 shares of another company's stock--a nonmonetary item--for FC 1,000 when the rate is

------
*See Summary of Footnote References -- #11-14 thru #11-27

FCl=$1, the cost of that investment is equivalent to $1,000. If the investment is carried at cost by the foreign operation, treating the investment as a nonmonetary item and translating it at the historical rate is appropriate. However, if the investment is carried at market price, translating that basis by the historical rate usually produces questionable results. For example, if the current market value of the investment is FC 1,500 and the current rate is FCl= $1.25, translating FC 1,500 into $1,500 by using the historical rate does not result in the current market value measured in dollars (FC 1,500 x 1.25 = $1,875) or the historical cost in dollars. The monetary-nonmonetary method can produce the $1,875 current market value only if it recognized that, under the method, the current rate is the applicable historical rate for nonmonetary assets at current prices. One way to solve this issue under the monetary-nonmonetary method is to declare that nonmonetary assets, such as investments and inventories, should become monetary assets if carried at market price.

## #11-16...Foreign Inventories

The accounting principles for foreign inventories remain the same as those for domestic operations. For example, if inventories are kept on a FIFO cost basis in domestic operations, the same basis should be used for the same type of merchandise sold through the foreign entity to be consistent. With respect to foreign inventories, FASB #8 at pages 22-23 provides:

To apply the rule of cost or market, whichever is lower, translated historical cost shall be compared with translated market. Application of the rule in dollars may require write-downs to market in the translated statements even though no write-down in the foreign statements is required by the rule. It may also require a write-down in the foreign statements to be reversed before translation if the translated market amount exceeds translated historical cost; the foreign currency cost shall then be translated at the historical rate. Once inventory has been written down to market in the translated statements, that dollar amount shall continue to be the carrying amount in the dollar financial statements until the inventory is sold or a further write-down is necessary.

In the application of this principle there are two requirements: the original cost must be recorded and translated, and second, the market value must be computed and translated.

The merchandise sold through a foreign entity may be shipped to that entity from headquarters or purchased locally by the entity. Because the purchase of resale merchandise abroad requires the acquisition of foreign exchange at the free market buying rate, the transfer of merchandise from the home office also should be at the free market buying rate prevailing at the time of transfer. To illustrate, assume the U.S. Corp. has a Paris Branch and that merchandise of 1,000 French Francs is involved, with an exchange rate of 4FF=$1U.S. The Home Office and Paris Branch book entries would be:

(1) MERCHANDISE SHIPPED FROM HOME OFFICE:
    Entries on Branch Records:
    Inventory                          FF 1,000
        Home Office                              FF 1,000
    (To record receipt of merchandise
    from Home Office costing $250
    translated at current spot rate)

    Entries on Home Office Records:
    Paris Branch                       $250
        Inventory                              $250
    (To record shipment of merchandise
    to Paris Branch)

(2) MERCHANDISE PURCHASED LOCALLY:
    Entries on Branch Records:
    Foreign Exchange                   FF 1,000
        Home Office                              FF 1,000
    (To record cable transfer of funds
    from Home Office at current rate)

    Inventory                          FF 1,000
        Foreign Exchange                         FF 1,000
    (To record local purchase of merchandise)

    Entries on Home Office Records:
    Paris Branch                       $250
        Cash                                   $250
    (To record cable transfer of
    funds to Paris Branch)

#11-17...End of Period Inventory Valuation

If the inventory is still on hand at the end of the fiscal accounting period, the 4FF=$1 rate would be used to translate the foreign inventory into U.S. Dollars. The translated value of $250 (FF 1,000 divided by 4) would equal the original cost. However, the year-end rate could change upward or downward, and under either of these circumstances the question arises as to how the inventory should be valued. If the year-end rate becomes FF4.2=$1, should the translated inventory value be $238.10? Or conversely, if the rate should change to FF3.6=$1, should the translated value be increased to $277.78? A strict cost interpretation would dictate the continued use of the FF4= $1 rate. To analyze the effects of the various rate changes upward or downward, examples showing the gross profit resulting if the total inventory is sold for FF 2,000 in the following period, when the prevailing exchange rate is still at the year-end rate, are presented below.

| Income Statement | Branch Records | Translated Rate Values | | |
|---|---|---|---|---|
| | | $1 = 4 FF. | $1 = 4.2 FF. | $1 = 3.6 FF. |
| Sales | FF 2,000 | $500.00 | $476.20 | $555.56 |
| Cost of Goods Sold | 1,000 | 250.00 | 250.00 | 250.00 |
| Gross Profit | FF 1,000 | $250.00 | $226.20 | $305.56 |
| | | | | |
| Cash Foreign Exchange | FF 2,000 | $500.00 | $476.20 | $555.56 |
| Home Office | 1,000 | 250.00 | 250.00 | 250.00 |
| Gross Profit | FF 1,000 | $250.00 | $226.20 | $305.56 |

The entries to close the branch records and transfer the cash to the Home Office would be as follows:

```
Sales                                    FF 2,000
     Inventory (or Cost of Goods Sold          1,000
     Income Summary                            1,000
(To close sales and COGS to Income Summary)

Income Summary                           FF 1,000
     Home Office                                1,000
(To close Income Summary to Home Office)

Home Office                              FF 2,000
     Foreign Exchange                           2,000
(To record cable transfer of 2,000 FF to
 Home Office at prevailing rate of exchange)
```

The corresponding entries to record the above information on the records of the Home Office under the three different remittance rates would be as follows:

| | Translated Value at Remittance Rates | | |
|---|---|---|---|
| | 4 FF=$1 | 4.2FF=$1 | 3.6FF=$1 |
| Foreign Branch | Dr:$250.00 | Dr:$226.20 | Dr:$305.56 |
| Brnch Net Incme | Cr:$250.00 | Cr:$226.20 | Cr:$305.56 |

(To record Branch Net Income)

| | | | |
|---|---|---|---|
| Cash | Dr:$500.00 | Dr:$476.20 | Dr:$555.56 |
| Foreign Branch | Cr:$500.00 | Cr:$476.20 | Cr:$555.56 |

(To record receipt of cash from branch by cable transfer)

## #11-18...Gross Profit Under Cost Basis

Under the cost basis, the gross profit constitutes the difference between the sales price translated at the rate prevailing at the date of sale and the original cost translated at the rate prevailing at the time of acquisition. Thus any changes in the exchange rate are reflected directly in the gross profit. In some cases of foreign currency devaluations, this could mean a postponement of loss. For example, if the selling price is less than FF 1,050, there would be a negative gross profit. The cost-or-market rule then applies in translating foreign inventories.

## #11-19...Valuation of Inventory Under Current Replacement Cost

If market (that is, current replacement cost) remains the same in local currency, translating the acquisition cost at the balance sheet exchange rate would have the effect of reducing the inventory to the current replacement cost in dollars. For example, when the exchange rate declined from 4FF=$1 to 4.2FF=$1, the inventory would be valued at $238.10 (FF 1,000 divided by 4.2). No entry should be made in the branch records. The entry on the Home Office records at year-end would be:

| | | |
|---|---|---|
| Exchange Gains and Losses | $11.90 | |
| French Branch | | $11.90 |

(To record reduction of foreign
inventory to current replacement cost)

## #11-20...Historical Cost Valuation of Inventory

Where the exchange rate would rise to 3.6FF=$1, the historical cost would be used. Since the inventory then would be FF 1,000 divided by 3.6, or $277.78 at the current rate, the market value would be higher than the cost. Translating at the historical rate of 4FF=$1 would maintain the inventory at the lower of cost or market at $250 on the Home Office records. A comparison of the three situations under these assumptions would be:

| | | Translated Values | | |
|---|---|---|---|---|
| Item | Branch Records | $1 = 4 FF | $1 = 4.2 FF | $1 = 3.6 FF |
| Sales | FF 2,000 | $500.00 | $476.20 | $555.56 |
| Cost of Goods Sold | FF 1,000 | $250.00 | $238.10 | $250.00 |
| Gross Profit | FF 1,000 | $250.00 | $238.10 | $305.56 |

In the case of the write-down of the inventory to 4.2FF= $1 translation rate, the effect is to maintain the 50% normal gross profit rate in the year of sale. The exchange loss would be taken in the year the exchange rate dropped.

#11-21...Unrealized Exchange Gain

It may be considered desirable to continue to report the 50% normal gross profit also when the exchange rate rose. The year-end adjustment on the Home Office records would then be:

```
Foreign Branch                          $27.78
    Unrealized Exchange Gain                         $27.78
(To adjust inventory to current replace-
ment cost -- at 3.6 = 277.78 minus
at 4.0 = 250.00 = 27.78)
```

The unrealized exchange gain is a deferred credit reported in the liability section of the balance sheet. Proper parenthetical or footnote disclosure would be necessary to indicate that the inventory of the foreign branch is reported at current replacement cost, which is higher than original cost. In the year of sale the exchange gain would become realized and be reported on the income statement as Other Revenue.

#11-22...Original Cost vs. Replacement Cost

In the above illustrations the assumption was that the foreign selling price and replacement cost remained the same in the local currency. A more realistic assumption is that the market price also fluctuated in the foreign country. For example, if the replacement cost of the merchandise rose to FF 1,050 when the exchange rate dropped to 4.2FF=$1, the original cost of $250 (FF 1,000 divided by 4) is the same as the replacement of $250 (FF 1,050 divided by 4.2). Provided the selling price also rose by 5 percent to FF 2,100, the dollar profit would be the same. However, the entries in the records would differ. If original cost is used, no entry would have to be made in the records. When the inventory is translated, the historical rate of 4FF=$1 is used. But if the replacement cost is

used, the branch office would have to record the   inventory increase.   The entry is as follows:

        Inventory                          FF 50
            Home Office                            FF 50
        (To record increase in inventory
          as credit to the Home Office)

The effect would be in the income statement of the branch.   Under the two methods it would appear as follows:

|              | Original Cost | | Replacement Cost | |
|              | Branch | Translated | Branch | Translated |
|--------------|--------|------------|--------|------------|
| Sales        | FF 2,100 | $500     | FF 2,100 | $500     |
| Cost of Goods | | | | |
|    Sold      | FF 1,000 | $250     | FF 1,050 | $250     |
| Gross Profit | FF 1,100 | $250     | FF 1,050 | $250     |

The  use of  replacement cost has the advantage of  showing the
normal 50% profit margin on the branch statement.
    If  the replacement price in local currency  did not rise as
much as  the exchange rate declined, the replacement cost would
be less than the original cost. The rate of exchange prevailing
on the balance sheet date  should be used to translate  the inventory.    Similarly, if the local currency  replacement  price
increased  more than the exchange  rate declined, the  original
cost would  be  lower than the replacement  cost; the inventory
should be translated at the  historical exchange rate.   Also if
the difference  between the  selling  price percentage increase
and the replacement price percentage increase is  greater  than
the exchange rate  percentage decline,  the  replacement  price
should be reduced to net realizable value--which is the selling
price less a  reasonable percentage to cover selling and  local
expenses.

#11-23...Permanent Investments

    For permanent  investments  accounted for under  the  equity
method,  the foreign statement balances also must be translated
at the exchange rates appropriate for foreign branch or subsidiary operations.

#11-24...Fixed Assets

    The cost principle is the underlying  concept in the record-
ing of fixed  assets.  The fixed assets of a foreign entity may
be recorded  in the foreign entity ledger or  only  in the home
office ledger.    If the records are kept  in the foreign entity
ledger, the  balance  should be translated  into dollars at the

exchange rates current when the assets were acquired--the historical rate.

In order to translate the long-term asset balances at historical rates, the acquisition dates must be known. This entails additional subsidiary records. Rather than keeping records of all acquisition dates, the acquisitions are often grouped into years. A representative exchange rate is then applied to all acquisitions of each year. Another method is to maintain dual currency accounts showing the acquisition cost in both U.S. dollars and local currency.

## #11-25...Depreciation Allowances

Depreciation on foreign assets is computed on the original cost as stated in U.S. dollars. This method is designed to ensure adequate charges to cover equivalent dollar cost in cases of later devaluation or decline in the exchange rate.

## #11-26...Asset Retirements

Since the original cost and the related accumulated depreciation accounts are translated at historical rates, the elimination of retired fixed assets must be at the same rate. However, if proceeds are received in salvaging the assets, the proceeds must be translated at the rate prevailing at the time of sale. This may mean that a loss in local currency is a gain in dollars or vice versa. For example, assume a machine with a book value of FF 1,000, acquired when the exchange rate was 4FF=$1, was sold for FF 1,200 when the exchange rate was 5FF=$1 U.S. The results would be as follows:

|  | Local Currency | Rate | U.S. Currency |
|---|---|---|---|
| Proceeds on Disposal | FF 1,200 | .20 | $240 |
| Book Value of Asset | FF 1,000 | .25 | $250 |
| Gain or Loss on Sale | FF 200 | (.05) | ($ 10) |

Companies with assets invested in countries with declining exchange rates must be aware of, and budget for, the erosion of such assets.

## #11-27...Intangibles and Prepaid Expenses

Since the cost principle is generally applicable to intangible assets and to prepaid expenses, the same rules used for fixed assets apply to these assets as well. Amortization and depletion charges also are based on the original cost in dollars.

## INCOME STATEMENT ACCOUNTS*

### #11-28...Income Statement Accounts General Rules

The cost principle and the going-concern concept also apply in the translation of income statement accounts. The depreciation, depletion and amortization charges are based on the original cost in dollars. Revenues and other expenses also should be based on the rates prevailing at the time of each transaction. However, in many cases the large volume of transactions involved makes the practical application of this principle rather difficult. Short cuts through the use of average rates are devised to derive fairly accurate approximations. Specifically, the FASB position as stated in FASB #8 is as follows:

Revenue and expense transactions shall be translated in a manner that produces approximately the same dollar amounts that would have resulted had the underlying transactions been translated into dollars on the dates they occurred. Since separate translation of each transaction is usually impractical, the specified result can be achieved by using an average rate for the period. However, revenue and expenses that relate to assets and liabilities translated at historical rates shall be translated at the historical rates used to translate the related assets or liabilities.

When the exchange rate does not fluctuate during the year, translating the accumulated totals at closing rates will produce the same result as in the individual translation of each transaction. To be consistent, however, items charged to revenues or expense from previous periods must be translated at historical rates. The items translated at historical rates will depend on the time of original recording of balance sheet items. When the exchange rate fluctuates during the year, the closing rate translation may yield results which would vary from the rates prevailing during the year.

### #11-29...Types of Rates

There are several different types of rates applied in practice: Month-End Closing; Monthly Average; Standard Current; Remittance; Historical; Penalty; Preferential.

### #11-30...Month-End Closing Rates

Month-end closing rates are often used to determine the average rate. This may be accomplished in two ways. One method is to apply the year's average rate to the year's accumulations of

------

*See Summary of Footnote References -- #11-28 thru #11-36

revenue and cost.    Under the second method, a weighted average
may be necessary if the revenues and/or  costs  are seasonal or
sporadic.

#11-31...Monthly Average Rates

The month-end  closing rate is  particularly applicable when
the exchange rate is  stable or has  shown only minor  fluctuations. Under such conditions the month-end closing rate is preferred  because of its simplicity in  computation  and clerical
application. If the closing rate does not satisfactorily represent  the rates prevailing during  the  month, an average  rate
applicable to each month must be computed. This may be a simple
average of the daily  rates.    When  the volume of transactions
tends to be rather  steady throughout the  period  and  the exchange  rates tend to be  evenly dispersed around  the average,
the simple average rate is the most representative.

The simple average is  determined by adding each day's average of  the high and low rates  of  exchange for the period and
dividing this sum by the number of days making the total. As in
the  application  of  the month-end closing  rates, the monthly
average rates may be applied in two principal ways.   First, the
average of daily rates may be applied to the applicable month's
accumulated  revenues  and costs.  The resultant dollar figures
for each month  are added together to determine the  dollar totals for the period. When  exchange  rates  and volume tend to
fluctuate appreciably from month  to month, this  procedure  is
preferred.   The result is  a weighted monthly average. Second,
the unweighted monthly average is merely the sum of the monthly
average rates in the  period divided by the number of months in
the period.   This  average is then  applied to the accumulated
totals of the revenue and costs  for the period.  When the rate
movement and transaction volume tend to be steady, this average
rate would be quite representative.

#11-32...Standard Current Rates

For some stable currencies, the  market rates  merely oscil-
late around a pegged rate.  To make minor adjustments for small
fluctuations may be confusing for management and adds to compu-
tational cost. Many companies then use a standard rate throughout the year.

The rate may be the pegged rate, or, in the case of the Ber-
mudan Dollar, the par.   If necessary, the rate may  be rounded
off to the nearest  cent. Such bookkeeping rates  are reviewed
regularly, but would not be adjusted unless clearly inappropriate.  At year end, the closing rate, which may also be  rounded
off to the nearest whole unit, is computed. If applicable, this
rate becomes the standard rate for the following year.

#11-33...Remittance Rates

Dividends are translated at the rate at which the foreign
currency remittance is realized in dollars. Very occasionally
such remittance rates are used as the rate of translating current revenue and costs of foreign operations.

#11-34...Historical Rates

The historical rate is universally used to translate current
charges for depreciation, depletion and amortization. This is
necessary to cover equivalent dollar cost determined at the
date of acquisition. The historical rate is determined and applied in the same manner as the rate used to translate the related asset account. This also applies to prepaid expenses
which are translated at historical rates at the year-end.
The historical rate may be used on the balance sheet date
for inventories shown at historical cost. In such instances,
the same historical rate must be utilized in the translation of
that portion of the cost of goods sold in the subsequent
period.

#11-35...Penalty Rates

In some cases certain imports of inventories or fixed assets
are taxed by requiring that the import be paid at exchange
rates higher than the free market rate. The difference between
the higher exchange rate and the free market rate results in a
penalty. In these instances the difference between the rates is
charged to the related inventory or fixed asset item. Such penalty charges are equivalent to transportation or installation
costs.

#11-36...Preferential Rates

Some countries encourage essential or desirable dollar imports into the local economy by allowing a favorable rate of
exchange for purchase of dollars to settle the payments for the
imports. Such favorable rates on imported products act as a
form of government subsidy designed to maintain lower selling
prices to the local consumer and are reverse of the penalty
rates.
Inventories and liabilities derived from such special imports must be translated at the preferential exchange rates.
However, unless the liability and the related asset at the
preferential rates are matched in amounts, debit or credit balances may arise in the translation into dollars. Such debit or
credit balances would be erroneous exchange gains or losses.
There are two methods by which such errors are avoided, as

pointed out in the NAA Research Report #36, N.Y., 1960, MANAGE-
MENT ACCOUNTING PROBLEMS IN FOREIGN OPERATIONS, pp. 47-55.

One method (the MATCHING TECHNIQUE) is to continue to match
the assets and liabilities connected with the preferential
rate in making the translation. If the liability is paid for
before the related asset is disposed of, only that asset portion equivalent to the liability outstanding is translated at
the preferential rate.

The other procedure, referred to as the DEFERRED ACCOUNTING
TECHNIQUE, is to set up deferred charges or credits in the balance sheet. In translation, if the asset acquired at preferential rates is less than the related liability still existing, a
deferred charge would be established. If the dollar component
of the inventory exceeds the related debt, an additional deferred credit must be established.

## THE CONSOLIDATION CONCEPTS*

### #11-37...Factor Affecting Consolidation Viewpoint

The perspectives taken under the various translation methods
parallel the two most widely accepted consolidation concepts--
Parent Company Concept and the Entity Concept. The factor that
causes different views in consolidation is the handling of
minority interests, the financial statement treatment of which
in the consolidation process depends upon the view taken.

### #11-38...Parent Company Concept for Consolidation

Under the Parent Company Concept, the consolidated statements are viewed as extensions of the parent company statements, in which the investment account of the parent is replaced by the individual assets and liabilities underlying the parent's investment. The subsidiaries are viewed as equivalent to
branches. For partially-owned subsidiaries, the minority interest is viewed as an outside group, and reported as a liability
in the consolidated financial statements. Further, the minority
interest share of the subsidiary income is viewed as an expense
to the consolidated entity comprising the parent and its proportionate share of the consolidated subsidiaries.

At the date of acquisition, any difference between the cost
of the parent's investment and the parent's interest in the net
assets of the subsidiary is attributed entirely to the parent
company and does not affect the minority interest in the acquired company. Further, when intercompany transactions are

------
*See Summary of Footnote References -- #11-37 thru #11-41

eliminated in consolidation, only the parent's share of an intercompany transaction is eliminated, because the minority
share in such transaction is considered to be a transaction
with outsiders.

#11-39...Entity Concept for Consolidation

Under the Entity Concept, consolidated statements are viewed
as those of an economic entity with two classes of shareholders' equity--the majority interest and the minority interest.
These interests are treated consistently as an entity and thus
are both treated as portions of the shareholders' equity. The
earnings of the entity then are shared proportionately between
the two types of interest. The minority interest is considered
not as an outside group but as part of the total ownership
equity.

In the elimination of interecompany transactions, all intercompany profits are eliminated, because only transactions outside the consolidated entity are relevant. Also any excess of
the cost of the parent's investment over the parent's interest
in the net assets of the subsidiary is used as a basis for re-
valuing all the assets of the subsidiary, and the minority interest is also revalued accordingly. This concept views the
consolidated entity with international operations as a single
multinational enterprise with autonomous, decentralized activities in various countries, with variant classes of ownership
interests.

#11-40...Selection of the Appropriate Concept

A comparison of the 2 consolidated concepts is shown below:

PARENT COMPANY CONCEPT
(1) Minority interest treated as a liability on the balance
    sheet
(2) Minority interest share of net income treated as an ex-
    pense to the consolidated group
(3) Only the parent company proportionate share of unrealized
    intercompany profits is eliminated
(4) Any difference between the parent's investment and the
    parent's interest in the net assets of a subsidiary is
    allocated to identifiable assets with any remainder shown
    separately on the consolidated balance sheet

ENTITY CONCEPT
(1) Minority interest is treated as a class of owner's equity
(2) Minority interest income is treated as a divisional share
    of the consolidated income
(3) Total elimination of unrealized intercompany profits is

(4) achieved by prorating to minority and majority interest
The excess of the cost of the parent's investment over the parent's interest in the net assets of the subsidiary is used as a basis for determining the fair value of the entire subsidiary with a proportionate amount allocated to the minority interest

The selection of the appropriate concept will depend on the perspective. In this regard most international corporations now view their overseas operations as extensions of the parent company. Further, the parent shareholders are considered to be the primary readers of the consolidated statements. Thus it is not surprising to note that the accounting professions in the U.S., the United Kingdom, and Canada prefer the parent company concept as evidenced by the statement of the AISG, para. 73, "Consolidated Financial Statements", AICPA, N.Y., 1973.

## #11-41...The Overall Perspective

Upon contemplation of the different alternatives involved in the decisions to report consolidated international financial statements, an underlying postulate appears to surface in the various choices, viz., the perspective taken. Strangely enough there is always a choice between the two main perspectives: the parent company and the local. In order to determine what the choice should be in maintaining one perspective that is to be based on some consistency, the various components should be listd for each of the two perspectives as follows:

### FOREIGN SUBSIDIARY CONSOLIDATION CONCEPTS UNDER TWO PERSPECTIVES

#### THE PARENT COMPANY PERSPECTIVE
(1) The reporting currency is the currency of the country of incorporation.
(2) The temporal approach to translation of foreign currency financial statements is utilized for subsidiaries viewed as extensions of the parent company.
(3) The parent company consolidation concept views the foreign subsidiary operations as extensions of the parent similar to branches.
(4) The translate-restate method is utilized for price-adjusting translated foreign currency financial statements.

#### THE MULTINATIONAL PERSPECTIVE
(1) The reporting currency is the currency in which the majority of the business transactions occur.
(2) The current-rate approach to translation of foreign currency financial statements views the foreign subsidiaries

as autonomous operations.
(3) The entity concept for consolidation views the consolidated entity as one enterprise with various classes of shareholder interest.
(4) The restate-translate method is utilized for consolidating
translated foreign currency price-adjusted financial
statements.

## SUMMARY OF FOOTNOTE REFERENCES
(References are to Paragraph #'s)

#11-3  AICPA, ARB No. 43, Chapter 12; APB Opinion No. 6
#11-3  AICPA ACCOUNTING RESEARCH AND TERMINOLOGY BULLETIN, 1961
#11-4  Samuel Hepworth, REPORTING FOREIGN OPERATIONS, 1956
#11-4  Gerhard Mueller, "Are Traditional Foreign Exchange Transla-
tion Methods Obsolete?", CALIFORNIA MANAGEMENT REVIEW (Summer 1956): 41-46
#11-4  NAA Research Report #36, MANAGEMENT ACCOUNTING PROBLEMS IN
FOREIGN OPERATIONS, (N.Y.: 1960)
#11-5  Price Waterhouse & Co., CURRENT FOREIGN EXCHANGE INFORMATION
#11-6  Leonard Lorenson, "Reporting Foreign Operations of U.S. Com-
panies in U.S. Dollars"
#11-6  NAA Research Report #36, op. cit.
#11-7  Lorenson, op. cit.
#11-7  FASB #8, ACCOUNTING FOR THE TRANSLATION OF FOREIGN CURRENCY
TRANSACTIONS AND FINANCIAL STATEMENTS, 1975, pp. 58-59
#11-8  Lorenson, op. cit.
#11-9  Institute of Chartered Accountants in England and Wales,
"The Accounting Treatment of Major Changes in the Sterling
Parity of Overseas Currencies," MEMBER'S HANDBOOK STATEMENT
N25, para. 14, 1968
#11-9  Scottish Institute of Chartered Accountants, "The Treatment
in Company Accounts of Changes in the Exchange Rates of In-
ternational Currencies," THE ACCOUNTANT'S MAGAZINE (Sept.
1970): 415-423
#11-11 Price Waterhouse International, A SURVEY IN 46 COUNTRIES:
ACCOUNTING PRINCIPLES AND REPORTING PRACTICES, 1975
#11-11 Evans, "Foreign Currency Translation Practices Abroad," THE
CPA JOURNAL (June 1974): 47-50. Reprinted with permission of
THE CPA JOURNAL, copyright 1974, New York State Society of
Certified Public Accountants.
#11-12 Thomas Ratcliffe and Paul Munter, "Currency Translation: A
New Blueprint," JOURNAL OF ACCOUNTANCY (June 1982): 82. Reprinted with permission. Copyright © 1982 by the American
Institute of Certified Public Accountants, Inc. Opinions
expressed in the JOURNAL OF ACCOUNTANCY are those of editors
and contributors. Publication in the JOURNAL OF ACCOUNTANCY
does not constitute endorsement by the AICPA or its committees.
#11-14 thru #11-27: "Balance Sheet Items Translation," adapted
from Norlin G. Rueschhoff, INTERNATIONAL ACCOUNTING AND FI-

NANCIAL REPORTING, 1976, Praeger Publishers, Inc., by permission.

#11-15 FASB #8, pp. 58-59

#11-16 FASB #8, pp. 22-23

#11-28 thru #11-36: "Income Statement Items Translation," adapted from Norlin G. Rueschhoff, op. cit., by permission.

#11-28 FASB #8

#11-36 NAA Research Report #36, op. cit. pp. 47-55

#11-37 thru #11-41: "Consolidation Concepts," adapted from Norlin G. Rueschhoff, op. cit., by permission.

#11-40 AICPA, "Consolidated Financial Statements," AISG, para. 73 (1973)

## BIBLIOGRAPHY

Arnic, Joel H. "Foreign Currency Translation," CA MAGAZINE (March 1982): 30

Beaver, William and Wolfson, Mark. "Foreign Currency Translation Gains & Losses: What Effect Do They Have and What Do They Mean?", FINANCIAL ANALYSTS JOURNAL (March-April 1984): 28-36

Bindon, K.R. INVENTORY AND FOREIGN CURRENCY TRANSLATION REQUIREMENTS (Ann Arbor, Mich: UMI Research Press, 1983)

Fantl, Irving L. "The FASB Currency Translation Bungle," THE WOMAN CPA, 37 (October 1975): 5-7

Fantl, Irving L. "Problems With Currency Translation," FINANCIAL EXECUTIVE, 47 (December 1979): 33-37

Goodman, H. and Lorenson, L. ILLUSTRATIONS OF FOREIGN CURRENCY TRANSLATION. N.Y.: AICPA, 1982

Miller, Stephanie. "International Accounting--Users Beware," MANAGEMENT ACCOUNTING (August 1984): 46-56

Mueller, Gerhard. "Translating Foreign Currency Financial Statements: Accounting Points of View," PROCEEDINGS OF ANNUAL MEETING OF ACADEMY OF INTERNATIONAL BUSINESS. New York, 1976

Nobes, C.W. "A Review of the Translation Debate," ACCOUNTING AND BUSINESS RESEARCH, 10 (Autumn 1980): 421-431

Schweikart, James A. "We Must End Consolidation of Foreign Subsidiaries," MANAGEMENT ACCOUNTING, 63 (August 1981): 15-25

Walker, R.G. "International Accounting Compromises: The Case of Consolidation Accounting," ABACUS, 14 (December 1978):97-111

Wurst, Charles M. and Alleman, Raymond. "Translation Adjustments for a Strong Dollar," FINANCIAL EXECUTIVE (June 1984): 38-41

## THEORY QUESTIONS
(Question Numbers are Keyed to Text Paragraph #'s)

#11-3 Discuss the history and operation of the Current-Noncurrent Method of foreign currency translation.

#11-4 What are the shortcomings of the Current-Noncurrent

Method?

#11-5 Discuss the history and operation of the Monetary-Non-monetary Method of foreign currency translation.

#11-6 What are the differences between the Current-Noncurrent and the Monetary-Nonmonetary methods?

#11-7 Discuss the shortcomings of the Monetary-Nonmonetary Method.

#11-8 Discuss the history and operation of the Temporal Method of foreign currency translation.

#11-8 (a) Under the Temporal Method of FASB #8, what items are attributable to translation at the current rate and what under the historical rate?

#11-9 Discuss the operation of the Current Rate Method of translation.

#11-10 Describe the Hybrid/Current Rate Transaction Approach.

#11-11 What has been the actual usage experience with the various translation methods?

#11-13 At what rate are foreign assets and liabilities translated under FASB #8?

#11-14 At what rate are foreign monetary assets and liabilities translated under FASB #8?

#11-15 At what rate are foreign investments translated under FASB #8?

#11-16 At what rate are foreign inventories translated under FASB #8?

#11-23 At what rate should Permanent Investments accounted for under the Equity Method be translated?

#11-24 What rate should be used for translation of Fixed Assets?

#11-25 What rate should be used for translation of Depreciation Allowance?

#11-27 What rate should be used for Intangibles and Prepaid Expenses?

#11-28 What are the general rules applicable to translation of Income Statement accounts under FASB #8?

#11-29-36. What 7 different rates are there that have been applied in practice for translation of Income Statement accounts? Briefly discuss their nature.

#11-37 What factor causes different views of the consolidation viewpoint?

#11-38 Outline and discuss the Parent Company Concept for consolidation.

#11-39 Outline & discuss the Entity Concept for consolidation.

#11-40 Make a comparative analysis of the two consolidation concepts.

#11-41 Compare the foreign subsidiary consolidation concepts under the parent company perspective and the multinational perspective.

## EXERCISES

### EX-11-1  (CPA EXAM, 5/79, THEORY, #2)
The year-end balance of  accounts receivable on the books  of a
foreign subsidiary should be  translated by  the parent company
for consolidation purposes at the
   a. Historical rate
   b. Current rate
   c. Negotiated rate
   d. Spot rate

### EX-11-2  (CPA EXAM, 5/78, THEORY, #2)
When translating an amount for fixed assets shown on the statement of financial  position of a foreign subsidiary, the appropriate rate of translation is the
   a. Current exchange rate.
   b. Average exchange rate for the current year.
   c. Historical exchange rate.
   d. Average exchange rate over the life of each fixed asset.

### EX-11-3  (CPA EXAM, 11/65, THEORY, #1-4)
In the conversion of the trial balance of  a foreign  branch to
domestic currency, the average rate of exchange for the current
year should be applied to
   a. Home office current.
   b. Notes payable.
   c. Sales.
   d. Accumulated depreciation.

### EX-11-4  (CPA EXAM, 5/67, THEORY, #1-12)
Which of the following accounts in a foreign subsidiary's trial
balance may  not  be converted to domestic currency in terms of
the current rate of exchange?
   a. Sales.
   b. Intercompany accounts payable incurred during the year.
   c. Long-term liabilities incurred several years ago.
   d. Long-term receivables obtained several years ago.

### EX-11-5  (CPA EXAM, 5/76, THEORY, #1-20)
A company is translating account balances from another currency
into dollars for its  Dec. 31, 1975, statement of financial position and its calendar year 1975 earnings statement and statement of  changes in financial  position.   The average exchange
rate for the year 1975 should be used to translate
   a. Cash at December 31, 1975.
   b. Land purchased in 1973.
   c. Retained earnings at January 1, 1975.
   d. Sales for 1975.

### EX-11-6  (CPA EXAM, 11/71, THEORY, #1-17)
Tree Co.  acquired 80% of the outstanding stock  of Limb Co., a
foreign company. In preparing consolidated statements the paid-

in capital of Limb Co. should be translated into dollars at the
   a. Exchange rate effective when Limb Co. was organized.
   b. Current exchange rate.
   c. Average exchange rate for the period Tree Co. has held the
      Limb Co. stock.
   d. Exchange rate effective at the date Tree Co. purchased
      the Limb Co. stock.

## EX-11-7  (CPA EXAM, 11/71, THEORY, #1-16)
The account(s) in a foreign subsidiary's trial balance that
should not be translated to domestic currency in terms of the
current rate of exchange would be
   a. Sales.
   b. Intercompany accounts payable incurred during the year.
   c. Long-term liabilities incurred several years ago.
   d. Long-term receivables obtained several years ago.

## EX-11-8  (CPA EXAM, 11/81, THEORY, #27)
At what translation rates should the following balance sheet
accounts in foreign statements be translated into United States
dollars?

|     | Equipment | Accum. Deprec. of Equipment |
|-----|-----------|-----------------------------|
| a.  | Current | Current |
| b.  | Current | Average for year |
| c.  | Historical | Current |
| d.  | Historical | Historical |

## EX-11-9  (CPA EXAM, 5/22, PRAC. I, #4)
In consolidating the statements of a foreign branch with the
statements of the home office, it is necessary to make conversions from foreign to domestic currency. At what rates should
the balances of the following accounts be converted? Give your
reasons.

      Fixed Assets
      Inventories at the beginning of the period
      Current assets
      Current liabilities
      Nominal accounts

## EX-11-10  (CPA EXAM, 11/33, AUDITING, #7)
You are auditing the books of a company incorporated in the
U.S. and of its Canadian subsidiary for the year 1981. You find
that the accounts of the subsidiary have been consolidated with
those of the parent company on the basis of par of Canadian
exchange throughout the year, in spite of the fact that the
Canadian dollar has been below par most of the year, and was at
83% of the U.S. dollar on Dec. 31, 1931.
   a. Should any exchange gain or loss be recognized? If so,

should it be reflected in the consolidated accounts?
b. Upon what bases should the conversion of fixed assets (including the credits to the fixed asset accounts for property retirements and the provision for depreciation) be made?
c. Upon what basis would you convert the funded indebtedness, subject to what exception?
d. Upon what basis would you convert an inventory of goods of the Canadian company purchased during 1930?

## EX-11-11 (CPA EXAM, 11/53, THEORY, #7)
a. State the rule followed by a company in converting foreign currency into U.S. dollars on:
1. Fixed assets of branches in foreign countries.
2. Inventory of merchandise bought by the foreign branch in that country.
b. If your basis of conversion differs as to the two items listed in a., explain why there is such difference, including a discussion of the accounting principles that are involved.

## EX-11-12 (CPA EXAM, 5/78, THEORY, #3)
PART (a). The Financial Accounting Standards Board discusses certain terminology essential to both the translation of foreign currency transactions and foreign currency financial statements in its Statement No. 8. Included in the discussion is a definition of and distinction between the terms "measure" and "denominate."
**Required**:
Define the terms "measure" and "denominate" as discussed by the FASB and give a brief example that demonstrates the distinction between accounts measured in a particular currency and accounts denominated in a particular currency.
PART (b). There are several methods of translating foreign currency transactions or accounts reflected in foreign currency financial statements. Among these methods are current/non-current, monetary/nonmonetary, current rate, and temporal method (the method adopted by the FASB).
**Required**:
Define the temporal method of translating foreign currency financial statements. Specifically include in your answer the treatment of the following four accounts:
1. Long-term accounts receivable
2. Deferred income
3. Inventory valued at cost
4. Long-term debt

## EX-11-13 (CPA EXAM, 5/80, THEORY, #31)
When translating foreign currency financial statements, which of the following items would be translated using current ex-

change rates?
   a. Inventories carried at cost
   b. Prepaid insurance
   c. Goodwill
   d. Marketable equity securities carried at current market
      price

## EX-11-14 (CPA EXAM, 5/80, THEORY, #32)
When translating foreign currency financial statements, which
of the following items would be translated using historical
exchange rates?
   a. Notes payable             c. Deferred income
   b. Long-term debt            d. Accrued expenses payable

## PROBLEMS

### P-11-1 (CPA EXAM, 5/76, PRACTICE I, #17)
The Jem Co. used the monetary-nonmonetary approach when translating foreign currency amounts at Dec. 31, 1975. At that time
Jem had foreign subsidiaries with 1,500,000 local currency
units (LCU) in long-term receivables and 2,400,000 LCU in long-
term debt. The rate of exchange in effect when the specific
transactions occurred involving those foreign currency amounts
was 2 LCU to $1. The rate of exchange in effect at Dec. 31,
1975 was 1.5 LCU to $1. The translation of the above foreign
currency amounts into U.S. dollars would result in long-term
receivables and long-term debt, respectively, of
   a. $750,000 and $1,200,000
   b. $750,000 and $1,600,000
   c. $1,000,000 and $1,200,000
   d. $1,000,000 and $1,600,000

### P-11-2 (CPA EXAM, 11/76, PRAC. I, #1)
The Dease Co. owns a foreign subsidiary with 3,600,000 LCU of
property, plant, and equipment before accumulated depreciation
at Dec. 31, 1975. Of this amount, 2,400,000 LCU were acquired
in 1973 when the rate of exchange was 1.6 LCU to $1, and
1,200,000 LCU were acquired in 1974 when the rate of exchange
was 1.8 LCU to $1. The rate of exchange in effect at Dec. 31,
1975 was 2 LCU to $1. The weighted average of exchange rates
which were in effect during 1975 was 1.92 LCU to $1. Assuming
that the ppty., plant, and equip. are depreciated using the
straight-line method over a 10-year period with no salvage
value, how much depreciation expense relating to the foreign
subsidiary's property, plant, and equipment should be charged
in Dease's income statement for 1975?
   a. $180,000                  c. $200,000
   b. $187,500                  d. $216,667

**P-11-3  (CPA EXAM, 11/76, PRAC. I, #2)**
The Clark Co. owns a foreign subsidiary which had net income
for the year ended Dec. 31, 1975 of 4,800,000 LCU, which was
appropriately translated into $800,000. On Oct. 15, 1975, when
the rate of exchange was 5.7 LCU to $1, the foreign subsidiary
paid a dividend to Clark of 2,400,000 LCU. The dividend represented the net income of the foreign subsidiary for the 6
months ended June 30, 1975, during which time the weighted
average of exchange rates was 5.8 LCU to $1. The rate of ex-
change in effect at Dec. 31, 1975 was 5.9 LCU to $1. What rate
of exchange should be used to translate the dividend for the
Dec. 31, 1975 financial statements?
  a.  5.7 LCU to $1            c.  5.9 LCU to $1
  b.  5.8 LCU to $1            d.  6.0 LCU to $1

**P-11-4  (CPA EXAM, 5/81, PRAC. I, #17)**
Certain balance sheet accounts in a foreign subsidiary of Rose
Co. at Dec. 31, 1980, have been translated into U.S. dollars as
follows:

|  | Translated at | |
| --- | --- | --- |
|  | Current Rates | Historical Rates |
| Accounts receivable, current | $200,000 | $220,000 |
| Accounts receivable, long-term | 100,000 | 110,000 |
| Prepaid insurance | 50,000 | 55,000 |
| Goodwill | 80,000 | 85,000 |
|  | $430,000 | $470,000 |

What total should be included in Rose's balance sheet at December 31, 1980, for the above items?
  a.  $430,000                c.  $440,000
  b.  $435,000                d.  $450,000

**P-11-5  (CPA EXAM, 11/79, PRAC. I, #19)**
On Jan. 1, 1978, the Ben Co. formed a foreign subsidiary. On
Feb. 15, 1978, Ben's subsidiary purchased 100,000 LCU of inventory. The entire inventory on Dec. 31, 1978, was made up of the
original 25,000 LCU inventory purchased on Feb. 15, 1978. The
exchange rates were 2.2 LCU to $1 from Jan. 1, 1978, to June
30, 1978, and 2 LCU to $1 from July 1, 1978, to Dec. 31, 1978.
The Dec. 31, 1978 inventory balance for Ben's foreign subsidiary should be translated into U.S. dollars of
  a.  $10,500                 c.  $11,905
  b.  $11,364                 d.  $12,500

**P-11-6  (CPA EXAM, 5/80, PRAC. I, #9)**
A foreign subsidiary of the Satelite Corp. has certain balance
sheet accounts at Dec. 31, 1979. Information relating to these
accounts in U.S. dollars is as follows:

|                                          | Translated at |            |
|                                          | Current Rates | Historical Rates |
|------------------------------------------|---------------|------------------|
| Marketable securities carried at cost    | $ 75,000      | $ 85,000         |
| Inventories carried at average cost      | 600,000       | 700,000          |
| Refundable deposits                      | 25,000        | 30,000           |
| Patents                                  | 55,000        | 70,000           |
|                                          | $755,000      | $885,000         |

What total should be included in Satelite's balance sheet at
Dec. 31, 1979, as a result of the above information?
   a. $770,000                    c. $870,000
   b. $780,000                    d. $880,000

## P-11-7  (CPA EXAM, 5/79, PRAC. I, #10)

The France Co. owns a foreign subsidiary with 2,400,000 LCU of
property, plant, and equipment before accumulated depreciation
at Dec. 31, 1978. Of this amount, 1,500,000 LCU were acquired
in 1976 when the rate of exchange was 1.5 LCU to $1, and
900,000 LCU were acquired in 1977 when the rate of exchange was
1.6 LCU to $1. The rate of exchange in effect at Dec. 31,
1978, was 1.9 LCU to $1. The weighted average of exchange rates
which were in effect during 1978 was 1.8 LCU to $1. Assuming
that the ppty., plant, and equip. are depreciated using the
straight-line method over a 10-year period with no salvage
value, how much depreciation expense relating to the foreign
subsidiary's property, plant, and equipment should be charged
in France's income statement for 1978?
   a. $126,316                    c. $150,000
   b. $133,333                    d. $156,250

## P-11-8  (CPA EXAM, 11/80, PRAC. I, #11)

A wholly-owned foreign subsidiary of Union Corp. has certain
expense accounts for the year ended Dec. 31, 1979, stated in
local currency units (LCU) as follows:

|                                                                  | LCU     |
|------------------------------------------------------------------|---------|
| Amortization of patent (related patent was acquired January 1, 1977) | 40,000  |
| Provision for doubtful accounts                                  | 60,000  |
| Rent                                                             | 100,000 |

The exchange rates at various dates are as follows:

|                                      | Dollar equivalent of 1 LCU |
|--------------------------------------|----------------------------|
| December 31, 1979                    | $.20                       |
| Average for year ended Dec. 31, 1979 | $.22                       |
| January 1, 1977                      | $.25                       |

What total dollar amount should be included in Union's income
statement to reflect the above expenses for the year ended De-

cember 31, 1979?
  a. $40,000                          c.  $44,000
  b. $42,000                          d.  $45,200

## P-11-9  (CPA EXAM, 5/55, THEORY, #8)

a. The ABC  Mfg. Corp. during the current year opened a manufacturing and selling branch in X country.  At year-end the official  rate of currency exchange  with country  X was 12 to $1
and the unofficial free market rate was 15 to $1.  In combining
the statements of the branch with  those of the parent at year-
end, at what value would the  following branch accounts be  reflected in the combined balance sheet?
                (1).  Accounts receivable
                (2).  Fixed assets
                (3).  Inventories
                (4).  Short-term debt
                (5).  Long-term debt
b. How is the gain or loss resulting from the  translation of
the foreign currency  into U.S. currency reflected  in the balance sheet of ABC Corp. at year-end?
c. On June 30, 1954, ABC sold  merchandise costing $75,000 to
Z located in Y country, taking a note  payable in Y  currency,
which at the official rate of exchange on  the date of sale had
a fair market value of $100,000. On Dec. 31, 1954, the note was
worth $75,000 due to a change in the rate of exchange. On March
15, 1955, the note was paid  in full and, when immediately converted  to  U.S.  dollars, ABC received $125,000.  What journal
entries are required at June 30, 1954, Dec. 31, 1954, and March
15, 1955?  Explain.

## P-11-10  (CPA EXAM, 11/76, THEORY, #11)

When preparing combined  or  consolidated financial  statements
for a  domestic and a foreign company, the account balances expressed  in the  foreign currency must  be translated into  the
domestic currency.  The objective of the translation process is
to obtain currency valuations that
  a. Are conservative.
  b. Reflect current monetary equivalents.
  c. Are expressed in domestic units of measure and are in con-
     formity with domestic  generally accepted accounting prin-
     ciples.
  d. Reflect the translated account at its unexpired historical
     cost.

## P-11-11  (CPA EXAM, 5/60, THEORY, #1(B))

On Jan. 1, 1958, the Janetrude  Corp. opened a manufacturing
and  selling branch  in  country X.  All current  transfers of
funds are executed at the free market rate.
     You  are  preparing a comined balance  sheet and a  combined

earnings statement as of Dec. 31, 1959, which is the end of the corporate year. Examine each of the general ledger accounts of the foreign branch. Decide at which currency rate (listed below) each should be converted.

  E. The official rate of currency exchange at the date of payment, acquisition or entry.
  F. Official rate of currency exchange at Dec. 31, 1959.
  G. The free market rate at the date of acquisition, entry or payment.
  H. The free market rate at December 31, 1959.
  I. Average rate of official currency exchange for 1959.
  J. The average free market rate for 1959, or for each month of 1959.
  K. None of the above.

**Required**:

Print next to each branch ledger account below the single capital letter of the currency rate at which the accounts should be converted in preparing combined statements.

_____ Sales
_____ Remittances from home office
_____ Accounts receivable--trade
_____ Office equipment (purchased in the U.S. and paid for in U.S. dollars
_____ Factory building
_____ Inventory of finished goods--December 31, 1959 (use general rule)
_____ Mortgage payable on factory building (due December 31, 1983)
_____ Inventory of finished goods--Jan. 1, 1959
_____ Note payable to bank (due Jan. 31, 1960)
_____ Accumulated depreciation on factory building


**P-11-12  (CPA EXAM, 11/75, THEORY, #4)**

Dhia Products Co. was incorporated in the State of Florida in 1960 to do business as a manufacturer of medical supplies and equip. Since incorporating, Dhia has doubled in size about every 3 years and is now considered one of the leading medical supply companies in the country.

During Jan. 1971, Dhia established a subsidiary, Ban, Ltd., in the emerging nation of Shatha. Dhia owns 90% of the outstanding capital stock of Ban; the remaining 10% is held by Shatha citizens, as required by Shatha constitutional law. The investment in Ban, accounted for by Dhia by the equity method, represents about 18% of the total assets of Dhia at Dec. 31, 1974, the close of the acounting period for both companies.

**Required**:

  a. What criteria should Dhia Products use in determining whether it would be appropriate to prepare consolidated financial statements with Ban for the year ended Dec. 31, 1974? Explain.

b. Independent of your answer to **a.**, assume it has been appropriate for Dhia and Ban to prepare consolidated financial statements for each year 1971 through 1974. But before consolidated fin. stmts. can be prepared, the individual account balances in Ban's Dec. 31, 1974, adjusted trial balance must be translated into the appropriate number of U.S. dollars. For each of the 10 accounts listed below, taken from Ban's adjusted trial balance, specify what exchange rate (for example, average exchange rate for 1974, current exchange rate at Dec. 31, 1974, etc.) should be used to translate the account balances into dollars and explain why that rate is appropriate. Number your answers to correspond with each account below.

1. Cash in Shatha National Bank
2. Trade accounts receivable (all from 1974 revenues)
3. Supplies inventory (all purchased during the last quarter of 1974)
4. Land (purchased in 1971))
5. Short-term note payable to Shatha National Bank
6. Capital stock (no par or stated value and all issued in January 1971)
7. Retained earnings, January 1, 1974
8. Sales revenue
9. Depreciation expense (on buildings)
10.Salaries expense

c. Identify standards of financial statement disclosure of foreign currency translations that Dhia must consider as required by the FASB Statement No. 1.

## P-11-13

Using International Accounting Standard No. 3 as a guide for each of the following circumstances, indicate whether preparation of consolidated statement is desirable (Yes) or undesirable (No), and why.

a. General Corporation is an automobile manufacturer which owns 80% of the common stock of the Prudence Life Insurance Company
b. Jonathan Inc. owns 52% of the voting common stock of the Metwell Corp. but the Oddside Co. owns 48% of the common stock of Metwell Corp. and all of Metwell's preferred stock
c. Hettel Co., a large wholesale merchandising firm, owns 43% of the issued and outstanding stock of Hinz Corp., a small wholesaler
d. White Woodworking Co. is operated by General Contractors Inc. which owns 60% of White's voting stock
e. Clark Equipment Co., located in Michigan, owns 100% of the common stock of Scheid Machinery Co., located in West Germany

    f. Franklin Mint Corp., whose fiscal year-end is Dec. 31, owns all of the stock of the Jefferson Mint Corp., whose fiscal year-end is August 31

    g. The National Transportation Co. owns 60% of the stock of the Eastern Railroad, which is currently being operated by a receiver until a final reorganization agreement is accepted by the courts

## P-11-14

Apex Co. acquired 70% of the outstanding stock of Nadir Corp. Immediately after the acquisition the separate balance sheet of Apex and the consolidated balance sheet are as follows:

|  | Apex | Con-solidated |
|---|---|---|
| Current Assets | $106,000 | $146,000 |
| Investments in Nadir (cost) | 100,000 | 0 |
| Goodwill | 0 | 8,100 |
| Fixed Assets (net) | 270,000 | 370,000 |
|  | $476,000 | $524,000 |
|  |  |  |
| Current Liabilities | $ 15,000 | $ 28,000 |
| Capital Stock | 350,000 | 350,000 |
| Minority Interest | 0 | 35,100 |
| Retained Earnings | 111,000 | 111,000 |
|  | $476,000 | $524,000 |

Ten thousand dollars of the excess payment for the investment in Nadir was ascribed to undervaluation of its fixed assets; the balance of the excess payment was ascribed to goodwill. Current assets of Nadir included a $2,000 receivable from Apex which arose before they became related on an ownership basis.

**Required:**

    a. Compute the total of the current assets on Nadir's separate balance sheet at the time Apex acquired its 70% interest.

    b. Compute the total stockholders' equity on Nadir's separate balance sheet at the time Apex acquired its 70% interest.

## P-11-15

On Jan. 1 the U.S. Corporation opened a foreign branch which purchased and resold merchandise in a foreign country. Each month of the first year of operations the branch purchased resale merchandise costing LC 100,000. The exchange rate was stable throughout the year except for a devaluation on Dec. 1. On that date the rate changed from LC 2 = $1 to LC 2.50 = $1.

    The Dec. 31 inventory was LC 200,000. The company used the lower-of-FIFO-cost-or-market method for inventory valuation. The replacement price of the inventory was LC 220,000.

**Required:**

    a. Compute the translated dollar cost of the ending inventory.

b. Compute the dollar valuation of the ending inventory to be included on the translated dollar balance sheet.

**P-11-16  (CPA EXAM, 11/77, PRAC. I, #4c)**

On Jan. 1, 1975, the Franklin Co. formed a foreign subsidiary which issued all of its currently outstanding common stock on that date. Selected captions from the balance sheets, all of which are shown in LCU, follow:

|  | Dec. 31, 1976 | Dec. 31, 1975 |
|---|---|---|
| Accounts receivable (net of allowance for uncollectible accounts of 2,200 LCU at Dec. 31, 1976, and 2,000 LCU at Dec. 31, 1975) | 40,000 LCU | 35,000 LCU |
| Inventories, at cost | 80,000 | 75,000 |
| Property, plant and equip. (net of allowance for accumulated depreciation of 31,000 LCU at Dec. 31, 1976, and 14,000 LCU at Dec. 31, 1975) | 163,000 | 150,000 |
| Long-term debt | 100,000 | 120,000 |
| Common stock, authorized 10,000 shares par value 10 LCU per share, issued and outstanding 5,000 shares at Dec. 31, 1976, and Dec. 31, 1975 | 50,000 | 50,000 |

Additional information is as follows:

>>>Exchange rates are as follows:

| Jan. 1, 1975 - July 31, 1975 | 2.0 LCU to $1 |
|---|---|
| Aug. 1, 1975 - Oct. 31, 1975 | 1.8 LCU to $1 |
| Nov. 1, 1975 - June 30, 1976 | 1.7 LCU to $1 |
| July 1, 1976 - Dec. 31, 1976 | 1.5 LCU to $1 |
| Average monthly rate for 1975 | 1.9 LCU to $1 |
| Average monthly rate for 1976 | 1.6 LCU to $1 |

>>>An analysis of the accounts receivable balance is as follows:

| Accounts Receivable | 1976 | 1975 |
|---|---|---|
| Balance at beginning of year | 37,000 LCU | --- LCU |
| Sales (36,000 LCU per month in 1976 and 31,000 LCU per month in 1975) | 432,000 | 372,000 |
| Collections | 423,000 | 334,000 |
| Write-offs (May 1976 & Dec. 1975) | 3,200 | 1,000 |
| Balance at end of year | 42,200 LCU | 37,000 LCU |

| Allowance for Uncollectible Accounts | 1976 | 1975 |
|---|---|---|
| Balance at beginning of year | 2,000 LCU | --- LCU |
| Provision for uncoll. accts. | 3,400 | 3,000 |
| Write-offs(May 1976 & Dec.1975) | 3,200 | 1,000 |
| Balance at end of year | 2,200 LCU | 2,000 LCU |

>>>An analysis of inventories, for which the first-in, first-out (FIFO) inventory method is used, is as follows:

| | 1976 | 1975 |
|---|---|---|
| Inventory at beginning of year | 75,000LCU | --- LCU |
| Purchases(June 1976 & June 1975) | 335,000 | 375,000 |
| Goods available for sale | 410,000 | 375,000 |
| Inventory at end of year | 80,000 | 75,000 |
| Cost of goods sold | 330,000LCU | 300,000LCU |

>>>On Jan. 1, 1975, Franklin's foreign subsidiary purchased land for 24,000 LCU and plant and equipment for 140,000 LCU. On July 4, 1976, additional equipment was purchased for 30,000 LCU. Plant and equipment is being depreciated on a straight-line basis over a 10-year period with no salvage value. A full year's depreciation is taken in the year of purchase.
>>>On Jan. 15, 1975, 7% bonds with a face value of 120,000 LCU were sold. These bonds mature on Jan. 15, 1981, and interest is paid semiannually on July 15 and Jan. 15. The first payment was made on Jan. 15, 1976.
**Required:**    *Use SFAS # 8 for Translation Purposes*
Prepare a schedule translating the selected captions above into U.S. dollars at Dec. 31, 1976, & Dec.31, 1975, respectively. Show supporting computations in good form.

## CASES

### CASE-11-1
On Jan. 2 Asch Corp. paid $1,000,000 cash for all of Bacher Company's outstanding stock. The recorded amount (book value) of Bacher's net assets on Jan. 2 was $880,000. Both Asch and Bacher have operated profitably for many years, both have Dec. 31 accounting year-ends, and each has only one class of stock outstanding. This business combination should be accounted for by the purchase method in which Asch should follow certain principles in allocating its investment cost to the assets acquired and liabilities assumed.
**Required:**
  a. Describe what principles Asch should follow in allocating its investment cost to the assets purchased and liabilities assumed for a Jan. 2 consolidated balance sheet. Explain.
  b. Independent of your answer to a., assume that on Jan. 2 Asch acquired all of Bacher's outstanding stock in a stock-for-

stock exchange and that all other conditions prerequisite to a
pooling of interest were met. Describe the principles Asch
should follow in applying the pooling of interest method on
this business combination when combining the balance sheet accounts of both companies in preparing a consolidated balance
sheet on Jan. 2.

# Accounting for Multinational Branch Operations

#12-1....Multinational Branch Operations

The principles enunciated above may be demonstrated by a comprehensive illustrative problem involving branch operations. Accounting for multinational branch operations is similar to that for domestic branches. The principal distinction is that in foreign operations the books of the Home Office are kept in terms of domestic currency whereas those of the Branch are kept in foreign currency.

#12-2....Branch Transactions

Assume that on Jan. 1, 1982, the Chicago Corp. opens a branch operation in Frankfurt, Germany, and engages in the following branch transactions for the year 1982:
1.  The Chicago Corp. purchases a draft sent to the Frankfurt Branch in the sum of DM (German Marks) 10,000 which is deposited in an account opened in a Frankfurt bank at current rate of exchange of 1 DM = $.50 U.S. on Jan. 2 (date of deposit)
2.  On Jan. 20 the Chicago Home Office sends merchandise costing $51,000 to the Frankfurt Branch; current spot rate 1 DM = $.51 U.S.
3.  On Jan. 30, the Chicago Home Office sends bank draft in the sum of $10,400 U.S., which was deposited in the Frankfurt Branch bank account; current exchange rate was 1 DM = $.52 U.S.
4.  Branch local merchandise purchases during the year made on account came to DM 80,000
5.  Branch Equipment costing DM 10,000 was bought on Dec. 20; current rate of exchange 1 DM = $.50 U.S.
6.  Sales on account during the year came to DM 250,000
7.  Payments received from Accounts Receivable during the year were DM 240,000

8.  On June 1 the Branch purchased a Bank Draft in the sum of
    U.S. $20,160, which was remitted to Home Office; current
    exchange rate was 1 DM = $.48 U.S.
9.  Payments made during the year to Accounts Payable were DM
    70,000
10. Cash payments during the year for operating expenses were
    DM 30,000
11. Remittance on Oct. 1 by Branch to Home Office in sum of DM
    50,000; current rate 1 DM = $.52 U.S.
12. Branch Ending Inventory on Dec. 31 was DM 10,000; current
    rate 1 DM = $.50 U.S.

#12-3....Branch Transactions Journal Entries

The journal entries to be made on the Branch books, all in
terms of German Marks (DM), would be as follows:

(1)  Cash (DM)                              10,000
         Home Office (Remittance Recd)              10,000
(2)  Mdse. Shipment--Home Off. Recd     100,000
         Home Office Equity                        100,000
     ($51,000 divided by $.51=100,000DM)
(3)  Cash (DM)                              20,000
         Home Office (Remitnc Recd)                 20,000
     ($10,400 divided by $.52=20,000DM)
(4)  Purchases                              80,000
         Accounts Payable                           80,000
(5)  Branch Equipment                       10,000
         Cash (DM)                                  10,000
(6)  Accounts Receivable                   250,000
         Sales                                     250,000
(7)  Cash (DM)                             240,000
         Accounts Receivable                       240,000
(8)  Home Office (Remitnc Paid)             42,000
         Cash                                       42,000
     ($20,160 divided by $.48=42,000DM)
(9)  Accounts Payable                       70,000
         Cash                                       70,000
(10) Operating Expenses                     30,000
         Cash                                       30,000
(11) Home Office (Remitnc Paid)             50,000
         Cash                                       50,000
     (50,000DM x $.52U.S.=$26,000U.S.)

#12-4....Branch Ledger Accounts

After posting the foregoing entries, the ledger accounts
would appear as follows:

BRANCH LEDGER

| Dr. | | Cr. | | Dr. | | Cr. | |
|-----|-----|-----|-----|-----|-----|-----|-----|

Cash

Home Office (Remittances Received)

| (1) | 10,000 | (5) | 10,000 |
|-----|--------|-----|--------|
| (3) | 20,000 | (8) | 42,000 |
| (7) | 240,000 | (9) | 70,000 |
| | | (10) | 30,000 |
| | | (11) | 50,000 |

| | | (1) | 10,000 |
|---|---|-----|--------|
| | | (3) | 20,000 |

Home Office Shipments Received

Home Office Equity

| (2) | 100,000 |
|-----|---------|

| | | (2) | 100,000 |
|---|---|-----|---------|

Operating Expenses

Purchases

| (10) | 30,000 |
|------|--------|

| (4) | 80,000 |
|-----|--------|

Sales

Accounts Payable

| | | (6) | 250,000 |
|---|---|-----|---------|

| (9) | 70,000 | (4) | 80,000 |
|-----|--------|-----|--------|

Equipment

Accounts Receivable

| (5) | 10,000 |
|-----|--------|

| (6) | 250,000 | (7) | 240,000 |
|-----|---------|-----|---------|

Home Office (Remittances Paid)

| (8) | 42,000 |
|-----|--------|
| (11) | 50,000 |

## #12-5....Branch Trial Balance

The trial balance then taken would be:

FRANKFURT BRANCH -- CHICAGO CORPORATION
TRIAL BALANCE -- 12/31/82 (DM)

| Account | Dr. Balance | Cr. Balance |
|---------|-------------|-------------|
| Cash | 68,000 | |
| Accounts Receivable | 10,000 | |
| Equipment | 10,000 | |
| Remittances Paid to Home Office | 92,000 | |
| Shipments Recd from Home Office | 100,000 | |
| Accounts Payable | | 10,000 |
| Remittances Recd from Home Off. | | 30,000 |
| Home Office Equity | | 100,000 |
| Sales | | 250,000 |
| Purchases | 80,000 | |
| Operating Expenses | 30,000 | |
| TOTALS | 390,000 | 390,000 |

## #12-6....Branch Closing Entries

```
Home Office Equity                         92,000
    Remittances Paid to Home Office                    92,000

Remittances Rcvd From Home Office          30,000
    Home Office Equity                                 30,000

Branch Inventory                           10,000
Cost of Goods Sold                        170,000
    Shipments From Home Office                        100,000
    Purchases                                          80,000

Sales                                     250,000
    Income Summary                                    250,000

Income Summary                            170,000
    Cost of Goods Sold                                170,000

Income Summary                             30,000
    Operating Expenses                                 30,000

Income Summary                             50,000
    Home Office Equity                                 50,000
```

## #12-7....Branch Post-Closing Trial Balance

After posting the closing entries, the Post-Closing Trial Balance would be:

|                      | Dr. Balance | Cr. Balance |
|----------------------|------------:|------------:|
| Cash                 | 68,000      |             |
| Accounts Receivable  | 10,000      |             |
| Inventory            | 10,000      |             |
| Equipment            | 10,000      |             |
| Accounts Payable     |             | 10,000      |
| Home Office Equity   |             | 88,000      |
| TOTALS               | 98,000      | 98,000      |

## #12-8....Statement of Branch's Home Office Equity

```
Shipments Received From Home Office       100,000
Home Office Remittance Received            30,000
    Total Received From Home Office       130,000
Home Office Remittances Paid               92,000
    Net Home Office Equity                 38,000
    Add: Net Income                        50,000
Home Office Equity -- 12/31/82             88,000
```

## #12-9....Branch Financial Statements

The balance sheet and income statement for the Frankfurt Branch would be:

### BALANCE SHEET AS OF 12/31/82

| ASSETS | | EQUITIES | |
|---|---|---|---|
| Cash | 68,000 | Accounts Payable | 10,000 |
| Inventory | 10,000 | Home Office | |
| Equipment | 10,000 | Equity | 88,000 |
| Accounts Rcvbl | 10,000 | | |
| TOTAL ASSETS | 98,000 | | 98,000 |

### INCOME STATEMENT FOR 1982

| | | |
|---|---|---|
| Sales | | 250,000 |
| Cost of Goods Sold: | | |
| Home Office Shipment | 100,000 | |
| Purchases | 80,000 | |
| | 180,000 | |
| Ending Inventory | 10,000 | |
| Cost of Goods Sold | | 170,000 |
| Gross Profit | | 80,000 |
| Operating Expenses | | 30,000 |
| NET INCOME | | 50,000 |

## #12-10...Branch Transactions Involving Home Office Accounts

In the branch books, all transactions were recorded in DM, the currency of Germany, where the transactions took place. In those transactions in which the Frankfurt Branch was involved with local businesses, all transactions are considered local (or domestic) for the Frankfurt Branch. However, five of the 1982 transactions involved the Home Office, viz.:

(1)  1/2/82 -- the remittance of 10,000 DM to the Branch;
(2)  1/20/82 -- the merchandise shipment by the Home Office to the Branch costing U.S. $51,000;
(3)  1/30/82 -- the remittance of U.S. Cash $10,000 by the Home Office to the Branch;
(8)  6/1/82 -- the remittance of U.S. $20,160 by the Branch to the Home Office; and
(11) 10/1/82 -- the remittance by the Branch to the Home Office of DM 50,000.

Because these five transactions were entered into with the Home Office, they will have to be recorded on the books of the Home Office in terms of U.S. dollars as follows:

(1)      Remittance to Branch              5,000
              Cash                                    5,000
         (DM 10,000 at current rate of
         1 DM = $.50 U.S.;
         10,000 x $.50 = $5,000)

(2)      Branch Receivable               51,000
              Shipment to Branch                   51,000
         (Shipment in U.S. Dollars which
         was recorded in Branch books as
         51,000 divided by $.51 current
         rate or 100,000 DM)

(3)      Remittance to Branch             10,400
              Cash                                   10,400
         (Remittance in U.S. Dollars which
         was recorded in Branch books at
         10,400 divided by $.52 current
         rate or 20,000 DM)

(8)      Cash                             20,160
              Remittance From Branch               20,160
         (Remittance in U.S. Dollars which
         was recorded in Branch books at
         20,160 divided by $.48 current
         rate, or 42,000 DM)

(11)     Cash                             26,000
              Remittance From Branch               26,000
         (Remittance in DM recorded on
         Branch books as 50,000 DM;
         rate 1 DM = $.52 U.S. =
         50,000 x $.52 = $26,000 U.S.)

#12-11...Branch Trial Balance Translation Statement

     The Trial Balance, Balance Sheet, Income Statement, and
Statement of Home Office Account will all be sent to the Chicago Corp. Home Office after completion. The Home Office must
then translate from Marks to Dollars the Frankfurt Branch Trial
Balance and Inventory, which contain the data required for all
statements. This will enable the Chicago Corp. Home Office to
record the Net Income on the Home Office books, and consolidate
the Branch Financial Statements with those of the Home Office.
     The first step in the procedure of consolidation is to
translate the Branch Trial Balance as follows:
     (a) set out the branch trial balance in terms of DM;
     (b) set forth the conversion symbols in terms of the ap-
         proach to be used, which in this case will be under FASB

#8, the Temporal Method;
(c) determine translation rate from the symbols used;
(d) multiply the trial balance figure by the translation rate, which should
(e) wind up with the translated amount for each account in terms of U.S. Dollars.

Under the Temporal Method of FASB #8 the symbols for the rates on the Trial Balance will be: (C) for Current; (H) for Historical; (A) for Average; and (R) for Reciprocal. The "(R)" rate will be applicable to balances in Reciprocal Accounts on the books of the Home Office. Under the temporal method, the accounts in these four categories would be the following. The translated Trial Balance would appear as Figure 12-1.

| | |
|---|---|
| (C) CURRENT: | Cash |
| | Accounts Receivable |
| | Accounts Payable |
| (H) HISTORICAL: | Equipment |
| (A) AVERAGE: | Sales |
| | Purchases |
| | Operating Expenses |
| (R) RECIPROCAL: | Remittances to Home Office |
| | Remittances From Home Office |
| | Home Office Equity |
| | Shipments From Home Office |

It should be noted that the amounts in the Rate Column of Figure 12-1 were derived as follows:

(C) The Current Exchange Rate on 12/31/82 was quoted as 1 DM = $.50 U.S. Hence this rate is used for all current items.

(A) The Average Rate was determined by taking the total Remittances From Branch to Home Office expressed in terms of Dollars and dividing that figure by DM value of the Remittances. There were two remittances resulting from transactions (8) and (11) as follows:

| | Dollars | DM |
|---|---|---|
| Transaction (8) | $20,160 | 42,000 |
| Transaction (11) | $26,000 | 50,000 |
| TOTALS | $46,160 | $\div$ 92,000 = 50.174¢ Avg. Rate |

(H) To determine the Historical Rate, reference would have to be made to the current rate on the date the transaction giving rise to the account took place.

(R) The Reciprocal Rate is determined from the books of the Home Office as shown in the journal entries made on the books of the Home Office in the transactions with the Branch.

## FIGURE 12-1
## STATEMENT OF TRANSLATION OF FRANKFURT BRANCH
## TRIAL BALANCE -- 12/31/82

| ACCOUNT | (DM) DR. BAL | (DM) CR. BAL | SYMBOL | RATE | TRANSLATION $ DR. BAL | TRANSLATION $ CR. BAL |
|---|---|---|---|---|---|---|
| Cash | 68,000 | | C | 50¢ | 34,000 | |
| Accounts Receivable | 10,000 | | C | 50¢ | 5,000 | |
| Equipment | 10,000 | | H | 50¢ | 5,000 | |
| Remittances to Home Office (8)+(11) | 92,000 | | R | 50¢ | 46,160 | |
| Accounts Payable | | 10,000 | C | 50¢ | | 5,000 |
| Remittances From Home Office (1)+(3) | | 30,000 | R | | | 15,400 |
| Home Office Equity (2) | | 100,000 | R | | | 51,000 |
| Sales | | 250,000 | A | 50.174¢ | | 125,435 |
| Shipments From Home Office (2) | 100,000 | | R | | 51,000 | |
| Purchases | 80,000 | | A | 50.174¢ | 40,140 | |
| Operating Expenses | 30,000 | | A | 50.174¢ | 15,050 | |
| TOTALS | 390,000 | 390,000 | | | 196,350 | 196,835 |
| Exchange Adjustment | | | | | 485 | |
| TOTALS | | | | | 196,835 | 196,835 |

The Average Rate can of course be derived in a number of ways. The one used above was regarded as most appropriate for the transactions presented.

#12-12...**Exchange Adjustments**

In examining the last two columns of Figure 12-1 it may be observed that the debit total came to $196,350 and the credit total to $196,835. Although the Branch Trial Balance in terms of DM was in balance (390,000 DM), the rate variations used in translation caused the trial balance to fall out of balance. It is therefore necessary to make an adjusting entry on the side of the smaller total in an amount required to bring the smaller total up to the greater total. This amount is known as an EXCHANGE ADJUSTMENT, and in this case would amount to $196,835 (the credit total) minus $196,350 (the debit total), or $485.

#12-13...**Exchange Gains and Losses**

The Exchange Adjustment measures the gain or loss resulting from exchange rate fluctuations. If the debit total is greater than the credit total, the difference is regarded as an EXCHANGE GAIN. If the credit total is greater than the debit total (as was the case with the Frankfurt Branch), the difference is regarded as an EXCHANGE LOSS. The exchange gain or loss in this case, resulting merely from translation without any transactions having taken place, is distinguished from those illustrated in export and import sales and purchases where the gain or loss resulted from business transations.

#12-14...**Types of Exchange Adjustments**

There are 2 types of exchange adjustments: Transactional and Translational. A TRANSACTIONAL EXCHANGE ADJUSTMENT is one resulting from a conversion of currency required to conclude a transaction. A TRANSLATIONAL EXCHANGE ADJUSTMENT, on the other hand, is a theoretical computation taking place within the organization itself and not involving any dealings with outside parties; it results merely from restating one figure at another value.

#12-15...**Realized Gains and Losses**

Transactional Gains and Losses, resulting only from transactions, are concrete, definite and conclusive. Hence they have been referred to as REALIZED GAINS OR LOSSES because they have actually been realized. Consequently such realized gains or losses should definitely be shown immediately in the period of income determination, and either charged against or credited to operations as items of revenue or expense.

#12-16...Unrealized Gains and Losses

Because they do not  result from transactions, Translational
Gains and Losses have been  called UNREALIZED GAINS AND LOSSES.
While the REALIZED Gains  and Losses  have unquestionably  been
regarded  as REAL  and therefore  taken  cognizance  of on  the
books,  the  question arises  as to what should be done with the
UNREALIZED Gains and Losses.
The  disposition of the Unrealized  Gains and Losses depends
upon the  viewpoint from which they are being examined.  If regarded from the  local  foreign branch  company viewpoint, they
may be ignored for two reasons:    (1) if the foreign branch  or
subsidiary would  maintain such  Exchange Gains or  Losses,  it
would be misleading by distorting original financial  relationships; and (2) because  a more  realistic method of translation
than the Temporal Approach (which  was used to  create  the Exchange Adjustment) would be to use the Current Rate Method.  By
not treating the  exchange adjustments as gains or losses, they
would be handled  by direct  charges or  credits to the Owners'
Equity.
However, if we view the Unrealized Gains and Losses from the
viewpoint of the Parent, then they may be handled in two ways:
    (1) as  gains or  losses,  similar  to  Realized  Gains  and
        Losses; or
    (2) as Deferred Items on the balance sheet.
The  former is supported in the U.S. and Canada,  and is called
the  North American  view; the Deferred  view  is supported  in
Continental European and British Commonwealth countries.
The North American view follows the precept that any gain or
loss  resulting from  current period  transactions that  can be
measured objectively  should  be recorded as part of the income
for that period.  Thus, with respect to the timing of recording
exchange adjustments, the  STATEMENT OF  POSITION ON ACCOUNTING
FOR FOREIGN  CURRENCY  TRANSLATION,  AICPA, N.Y., 1974, page 3,
provides:  "In general, exchange adjustments should be recorded
when exchange rate changes occur in  order  to record  exchange
gains or  losses in the  period of the event--the exchange rate
change--rather than the date the account balance  is  settled."
Under this concept, unrealized gains or losses would be treated
similarly to realized gains or losses.
The British Continental Deferred view adheres to the principle that in order to  be regarded as gains or losses they  must
result strictly from business  operations.  The gains or losses
are debited or credited to Reserve  Accounts which are  part of
the Owners' Equity  section of the balance sheet.  The Exchange
Adjustment Reserve Account  would  be debited  for  losses  and
credited  for gains resulting from the end-of-the-period translation procedure.

#### #12-17...Approaches to Translated Unrealized Gains and Losses

The North American viewpoint has resulted in a variety of accounting treatments as pointed out in an FASB DISCUSSION MEMORANDUM entitled "An Analysis of Issues Related to Accounting for Foreign Currency Translation," 1974, pp. 82-100. This has resulted in difficulties encountered by accountants in disposing of translation gains and losses from the parent viewpoint. Basically there are two approaches: the TRADITIONAL APPROACH and the FULL RECOGNITION APPROACH.

#### #12-18...The Traditional Approach

This recognizes LOSSES immediately when sustained, but suspends the recognition of GAINS until they are realized. The recognition of gains under this method is virtually impossible for two reasons: (1) the difficulty, if not impossibility, of determining the date the gain is realized; and (2) how much of the gain is realized. To overcome these objections, accountants have merely offset losses against gains and deferred the difference.

#### #12-19...The Full Recognition Approach

This approach is simply that both the translated gains and losses be reflected in current income when determined. Under this method, the translation gains and losses are handled similarly to transactional (conversion) gains and losses. This is the viewpoint followed in FASB #8, which requires foreign exchange translation gains and losses to be considered as part of the overall operating results of the M/N/C whose foreign accounts are translated. This means no deferrals or realizations are recognized, because the moment they are calculated they are to receive full recognition. The only condition imposed by FASB #8 is that they are to be reported separately.

#### #12-20...Exchange Adjustment Reporting

With respect to the reporting, it is declared in the STATEMENT OF FINANCIAL ACCOUNTING STANDARDS, FASB #1, entitled "Disclosure of Foreign Currency Translation Information," 1973, p. 5, that "the effects of material exchange adjustments should be shown in an OTHER REVENUES AND EXPENSES section of the Income Statement. Such disclosure is supported by the AICPA in its STATEMENT OF POSITION ON ACCOUNTING FOR FOREIGN CURRENCY TRANSLATION, page 12."

What about extreme exchange adjustments resulting from Revaluations and Devaluations? Because such exchange adjustments

have generally resulted in substantial amounts, they had been
treated as EXTRAORDINARY GAINS OR LOSSES. However, APB Opinion
#30, "Reporting the Results of Operations," AICPA, N.Y., 1973,
p. 566, prohibits such treatment:

> Certain gains and losses should not be reported as extra-
> ordinary items because they are usual in nature or may be
> expected to recur as a consequence of customary and continu-
> ing business activities. Examples include: *** (b) gains or
> losses from exchange of translation of foreign currencies,
> including those relating to major devaluations and revalua-
> tions.

## #12-21...Results Experienced Under FASB #8
### Full Recognition Approach

The FASB #8 translation rule discussed above went into effect on Jan. 1, 1976. During 1976 the M/N/Cs that adhered to
the Standard produced a cacophony of pandemonium on the part of
their financial executives and controllers. A very graphic illustration was reported in "Learning to Live With Currency
Fluctuations" (in BUSINESS WEEK, Jan. 20, 1976, pp. 48-52),
where it was pointed out that in mid-1975, when the U.S. Dollar
was greatly strengthened, International Harvester had its third
quarter earnings of 16 cents a share totally expunged by a
translation loss of $4-1/2 million, and the figure for I.T.&T.
came to a loss of $52 million.

A lengthy article by Philip Revsin in THE WALL STREET JOUR-
NAL, Dec. 8, 1976, pp. 1 & 28, is headed "New Accounting Rule
Makes Multinationals Alter Their Strategies--Corporations Com-
plain That Profits Are Held Hostage to Revaluations Abroad." A
brief but significant portion of this article declares:

> A year old accounting rule designed to make it easier
> for everybody to understand the foreign activities of multi-
> national companies is causing a belated uproar among operat-
> ing executives and mass confusion among the investing pub-
> lic. The rule is FASB Statement No. 8 (known irreverently in
> corporate circles as "Section 8," a reference to old Army
> terminology for an insanity discharge). At first glance, the
> FASB rule reads like a typically harmless exercise in ac-
> countantese. And, after a first glance, and a few initial
> gripes, many operating executives shrugged off the new rule
> as just another headache for the crew in green eyeshades.
> But now, after nine months of living with Statement 8, a
> crescendo of yelps is coming from the highest corporate lev-
> els. For Statement 8 drastically alters the means of report-
> ing foreign business results in quarterly financial state-
> ments. As a result, widely fluctuating values of pesos,

pounds, marks, Canadian and Australian dollars, and other
foreign currencies often are having far more impact on quarterly profit and loss statements than are the sales or
profit margins of multinational manufacturers' product
lines.

Quarterly earnings reports have been bouncing about un-
predictably ever since Statement 8 took effect on Jan. 1,
1976. "It will be years before anybody can work with a comparative financial statement with any degree of certainty
again," grumbles Herbert Knortz, Executive V.P. of I.T.&T.;
and adds Charles Allen, V.P. and Chief Financial Officer of
TRW, Inc., "Our Profit and Loss Statement now depends to a
large degree on the political factors that go into the various currency revaluations in foreign countries."

The article goes on to point out wild fluctuations in profits
both upward and downward for such companies as F.W. Woolworth,
Hoover Co., Gillette, Textron, Firestone, and Sperry Rand.
These outbursts came in the immediate wake of the adoption of
FASB #8 so that perhaps when adjustments to it were made over
time, the financial executives could adjust to it. In fact,
accounting experts were of the opinion that so long as the
nature of translation gains and losses were fully disclosed,
statement readers and intelligent investors would be able to
fully comprehend the implications, and in time adjustment to
the situation would smooth matters out. Samuel Hepworth's RE-
PORTING FOREIGN OPERATIONS, p. 72, observes: "It seems appropriate to conclude that gains or losses resulting from altered
dollar value of foreign money value assets should be considered
as representing a proper component of the overall operating
results of the foreign subsidiary, and that such gains or losses should be given recognition in connection with the translation of foreign currency balances into dollars when they occur
as evidenced by exchange rate movements, with no attempt being
made to distinguish between realized and unrealized gains or
losses."

#12-22...Branch Statements Expressed in Translated Terms

Reverting to our illustrative problem, after the Branch
Trial Balance has been translated from the branch foreign cur-
rency to the U.S. dollar Home Office currency, the next step in
the procedure is to construct Branch Financial Statements in
Home Office translated figures. The inventory of DM 10,000 hav-
ing been carried at cost would be translated at the Historical
Rate under the Temporal Method and be valued at 51 cents under
LIFO, and at the current rate on 12/31 of 50 cents, or 10,000
DM x $.50 = $5,000 U.S.

FRANKFURT BRANCH TRANSLATED BALANCE SHEET ($)
DECEMBER 31, 1982

| ASSETS: | | EQUITIES: | |
|---|---|---|---|
| Cash | 34,000 | Accounts Payable | 5,000 |
| Accounts Rcble | 5,000 | Home Office | 44,000 |
| Mdse. Inventory | 5,000 | | |
| Equipment | 5,000 | | |
| TOTAL ASSETS | 49,000 | TOTAL EQUITIES | 49,000 |

The Home Office Balance of $44,000 was derived as follows:

| | |
|---|---|
| Balance Per Branch Trial Balance | 51,000 |
| Add: Remittance From Home Office to Branch | 15,400 |
| TOTAL | 66,400 |
| Less: Remittances From Branch to Home Office | 46,160 |
| Balance Before Net Income | 20,240 |
| Add: Net Income | 23,760 |
| ENDING HOME OFFICE BALANCE | 44,000 |

The Net Income figure of 23,760 was derived from the following Income Statement:

FRANKFURT BRANCH TRANSLATED INCOME STATEMENT ($)
FOR THE YEAR 1982

| | | |
|---|---|---|
| Sales | | 125,435 |
| Less: Cost of Goods Sold: | | |
| Home Office Shipments | 51,000 | |
| Purchases | 40,140 | |
| Goods Available for Sale | 91,140 | |
| Less: Ending Inventory | 5,000 | |
| COST OF GOODS SOLD | | 86,140 |
| GROSS PROFIT | | 39,295 |
| Operating Expenses | 15,050 | |
| Exchange Adjustment | 485 | |
| TOTAL EXPENSES | | 15,535 |
| NET INCOME | | 23,760 |

On Dec. 31, 1982 the Home Office will make an entry to record the Net Income (or loss where one occurs) as follows:

| | | | |
|---|---|---|---|
| 12/31/82 | Branch Equity | 23,760 | |
| | Branch Net Income | | 23,760 |
| | (To close Branch Net Income | | |
| | to Branch Equity Account) | | |

## #12-23...Home Office and Branch Consolidated Statements

To conclude the illustrative problem, the Home Office Trial Balance would be joined with the translated Frankfurt Branch Trial Balance, from which consolidated statements would be constructed.

The Home Office Trial Balance figures which were derived from the Home Office ledger are as follows:

CHICAGO CORPORATION HOME OFFICE
TRIAL BALANCE AS OF 12/31/82

| Account | Dr.Bal.($) | Cr.Bal.($) |
|---|---|---|
| Cash | 160,000 | |
| Accounts Receivable | 90,000 | |
| Beginning Inventory, 1/1/82 | 80,000 | |
| Equipment (Net) | 70,000 | |
| Remittances Recvd From Branch | | 46,160 |
| Accounts Payable | | 40,000 |
| Remittance Sent to Branch | 15,400 | |
| Branch Receivable | 51,000 | |
| Sales | | 750,000 |
| Shipments to Branch | | 51,000 |
| Purchases | 570,000 | |
| Operating Expenses | 40,760 | |
| Capital Stock | | 150,000 |
| Retained Earnings, 1/1/82 | | 40,000 |
| TOTALS | 1,077,160 | 1,077,160 |

The ending Inventory of the Home Office on Dec. 31, 1982 came to $90,000.

Joining the Home Office Trial Balance with that of the Frankfurt Branch would result in consolidated statements such as Figure 12-2.

## #12-24...Footnote Disclosure of Foreign Currency Translation

The guidelines for disclosure of foreign currency translation are presented in FASB #1 (1973), pages 5-6:

The FASB has concluded that certain disclosures shall be made in financial statements that include amounts denominated in a foreign currency which have been translated into the currency of the reporting entity. The amounts may result from transactions, the consolidated subsidiaries, and the equity method of accounting for investees. The following information shall be disclosed:

(a) A statement of translation policies including identification of (1) the balance sheet accounts that are translated at the current rate and those translated at the historical rate; (2) the rates used to translate income statement accounts (e.g., historical rates for specified accounts and a weighted average rate for all other accounts); (3) the time of recognition of gain or loss on forward exchange contracts; and (4) the method of accounting for exchange adjustments (and if any portion of the exchange adjustment is deferred, the method of disposition of the deferred amount in future years).

(b) The aggregate amount of exchange adjustments originating in the period, the amount thereof included in the determination of income and the amount thereof deferred.

(c) The aggregate amount of exchange adjustments included in the determination of income for the period, regardless of when the adjustments originated.

(d) The aggregate amount of deferred exchange adjustments, regardless of when the adjustments originated, included in the balance sheet (e.g., such as in a deferral or in a "reserve" account) and how this amount is classified.

(e) The amount by which total long-term receivables and total long-term payables translated at historical rates would each increase or decrease at the balance sheet date if translated at current rates.

(f) The amount of gain or loss which has not been recognized on unperformed forward exchange contracts at the balance sheet date.

## TRANSLATION UNDER FASB #52

### #12-25...Launching of FASB #52

Dissatisfaction with FASB #8 has resulted in a replacement standard that had been continuously worked on for over four years. The JOURNAL OF ACCOUNTANCY, July 1981, page 110, in an article entitled "Foreign Currency Translation: The Controversy Continues," indicates that:

Accountants and financial executives eagerly anticipated action by the FASB to replace Statement No. 8. A 1980 poll by Louis Harris of some 400 business leaders found that 59% deemed Statement 8 "neither wise nor sound," according to an article by John Thackray in the INSTITUTIONAL INVESTOR, Dec. 1980.

Thackray says that "from its very unveiling, Statement No. 8 generated determined opposition in the corporate community." Critics noted that the Statement had "two terrible defects." The first was the requirement that nonmonetary assets be reported at historical cost not current cost, and that monetary assets be reported at current rates of exchange--a requirement which, according to Melvin Howard,

## FIGURE 12-2
### CHICAGO CORP. AND FRANKFURT BRANCH CONSOLIDATED FINANCIAL STATEMENTS
### FOR THE YEAR ENDED DECEMBER 31, 1982

| | TRIAL BALANCES | | | | ADJUSTMENTS AND ELIMINATIONS | | CONSOLIDATED | |
| --- | --- | --- | --- | --- | --- | --- | --- | --- |
| | HOME OFFICE | | FRANKFURT BRANCH | | | | | |
| | Dr. | Cr. | Dr. | Cr. | Dr. | Cr. | Dr. | Cr. |
| **INCOME STATEMENT** | | | | | | | | |
| Sales | | 750,000 | | 125,435 | | | | 875,435 |
| Inventory 1/1 | 80,000 | | | | | | 80,000 | |
| Home Offc. Shpmt | | 51,000 | | | | (a) 51,000 | | |
| Shpmt to Branch | | | 51,000 | | (a) 51,000 | | | |
| Purchases | 570,000 | | 40,140 | | | | 610,140 | |
| Inventory 12/31 | | 90,000 | | 5,000 | | | | 95,000 |
| Expenses | 40,760 | | 15,050 | | | | 55,810 | |
| Exch. Adj. | | | 485 | | | | 485 | |
| TOTALS | 690,760 | 891,000 | 106,675 | 130,435 | | | 746,435 | 970,435 |
| Bal.-Net Income | 200,240 | | 23,760 | | | | 224,000 | |
| TOTALS | 891,000 | 891,000 | 130,435 | 130,435 | | | 970,435 | 970,435 |
| **RETAINED EARNINGS STATEMENT** | | | | | | | | |
| Ret. Earnings 1/1/82 | | 40,000 | | | | | | 40,000 |
| Net Income | | 200,240 | | 23,760 | | | | 224,000 |
| Ret. Earrngs 12/31/82 | | 240,240 | | 23,760 | | | | 264,000 |

BALANCE SHEET

| Account | | | | | | | | |
|---|---|---|---|---|---|---|---|---|
| Cash | 160,000 | | 34,000 | | | | 194,000 | |
| Account Receivable | 90,000 | | 5,000 | | | | 95,000 | |
| Inventory 12/31 | 90,000 | | 5,000 | | | | 95,000 | |
| Equipment | 70,000 | | 5,000 | | | | 75,000 | |
| Branch Receivable | 51,000 | | | | | (d) 51,000 | | |
| Remittance to Branch | 15,400 | | | | | (b) 15,400 | | |
| Remittance to Home Office | | | 46,160 | | | (c) 46,160 | | 45,000 |
| Accounts Payable | | 40,000 | | 5,000 | | | | |
| Remittance From Branch | | 46,160 | | | (c) 46,160 | | | |
| Remittance From Home Office | | | | 15,400 | (b) 15,400 | | | |
| Home Office Eq. | | | | 51,000 | (d) 51,000 | | | |
| Capital Stock | | 150,000 | | | | | | 150,000 |
| Retained Earnings | | 240,240 | | 23,760 | | | | 264,000 |
| | | | | | | | | |
| TOTALS | 476,400 | 476,400 | 95,160 | 95,160 | 163,560 | 163,560 | 459,000 | 459,000 |

chief financial officer of Xerox Corp., "doesn't describe
what goes on in the real world." The second flaw is the requirement that monetary exchange translations flow through
the parent company income statements, which means deflated
earnings during periods when the dollar is in decline.
In Aug. 1980 the FASB responded with a new exposure draft entitled FOREIGN CURRENCY TRANSLATION and invited comment thereon
to Oct. 1, 1981. The new Standard FASB #52 was issued Dec. 8,
1981 to take effect in 1983, although companies would be permitted to adopt it earlier if they so desired.

#12-26...Reaction to FASB #52

The above July 1981 article stated on page 110:
    First reaction to FASB #52 was good, according to Thack-
ray. Herbert Knortz, V.P. of I.T.&T., an opponent of Statement No. 8, says that exposure draft "goes right down the
line of what we have been recommending--a single rate of
exchange translation for both monetary and nonmonetary assets and liabilities." John Ostrem, HFC V.P., calls the new
draft a "very good one overall."
    But negative reaction to the new exposure draft has also
been expressed by many companies. The article reports that
most seem to agree with FASB task force member Gerald White:
"If adopted in its present form, the draft will create different problems which will be as hard as any have been under
Statement No. 8."
    Critics of the new draft point out that it has two large
practical problems. The first one is the use of functional
currencies necessitated by the draft's requirement that companies report net investment gain or loss on a country-by-
country, subsidiary-by-subsidiary basis. Eugene Flegm, accounting director for GMC, illustrates: "If we have $100
million in Euro-dollar debt in Brazil, and the cruzeiro
drops 20%, we have to book a $20 million loss. Where's the
realism in that?" Another corporate executive is quoted as
saying that "these new rules create a whole set of artificial gains and losses. They make no economic sense."
    The second problem noted is the balance sheet effect of
translating assets at curent exchange rates in hyperinfla-
tionary times. Critics say this will cause another "yo-yo
effect" similar to that caused by Statement No. 8. Beyond
these two problems, some executives expressed concern that
the draft represents profound changes in accounting practices. "This is the most bullish accounting standard ever
published by the FASB," says Thornton O'Glove, Chairman of
Reporting Research Corporation, who adds: "As far as accounting goes, you can hold your nose, this new draft stinks
so bad." But he also notes that "it will allow corporations

to smooth out and manage their earnings and show stability."
In a later development, as published in the Feb. 1981 edition of the JOURNAL OF ACCOUNTANCY, page 10, FASB Chairman,
Donald J. Kirk, said during hearings on the draft that "a
popular solution may well be impossible." FASB #52 was
passed by a narrow margin of a 4 to 3 vote.

#### #12-27...Keeping Retained Earnings Clean

One of the first objections raised to FASB #52 was by Frank
Murphy, V.P. Economic Development Corp., who in a letter to the
JOURNAL OF ACCOUNTANCY, May 1982 issue, page 114, contends that
FASB #52 "is a model of inconsistency. It gives a company the
election to avoid in the income statement net translation losses for a period of time, but permits translation gains to be
recognized currently. By reason of the transition period and
the net translation gain or loss, a company is permitted to
report these items either currently or as a surplus adjustment.
In my view this hurts the financial statement comparability and
consistency."
To this view, Paul Pacter, executive assistant to the FASB
chairman, responds:
Translation adjustments that are excluded from net income
are not buried in retained earnings, as Mr. Murphy suggests.
Rather, they are reported separately and accumulatively in a
separate component of consolidated shareholders' equity until the parent's net investment in the foreign entity is
sold or liquidated. In a sense they may be viewed as an unrealized component of comprehensive income--the change in
net assets of an entity during a period from all transactions other than those with owners. Retained earnings continues to be kept CLEAN under Statement 52.

#### #12-28...Early Test Case

Almost immediately in the wake of the adoption of FASB #52,
Occidental Petroleum Corporation's 1981 Annual Report, page
49, says:
Occidental has elected, as recommended by the FASB, early adoption of the method. The new statement requires that a
functional currency be determined for each entity and that
the exchange gain or loss from translating the functional
currency balance sheets to the U.S. dollar at the rates of
exchange in effect at the end of each period shall be charged or credited to a new category within the shareholders'
equity section entitled "Cumulative Foreign Currency Translation Adjustments." The cumulative effect of translating
such balance sheets at Dec. 31, 1981 was to reduce "Other
Shareholders' Equity" by $6 million.

Assets and liabilities of an entity denominated in currencies other than its functional currency are translated at
the rates of exchange in effect at the end of each period.
Revenues and expenses of an entity denominated in currencies
other than its functional currency are translated at the
average rates of exchange prevailing during the period. Foreign currency translation of such transactions resulted in a
gain of $89 million for the year ended Dec. 31, 1981. The
effect on the year ended Dec. 31, 1981 of applying FASB #52
rather than #8 was to increase net income by $79 million.

#### #12-29...Key Objective of FASB #52

The basic objective of FASB #52 is to try to cure the major
defects of FASB #8. Under the heading ACCOUNTING PROBLEMS ARIS-
ING FROM CURRENCY DIFFERENCES discussed in #10-21, it was
pointed out that there are basically three: (1) selection of a
proper reporting currency; (2) translation of currency for
proper statement presentation; and (3) transaction translation.
FASB #52 appears to address these problems.

#### #12-30...Selection of Proper Reporting Currency

Para. 4 of FASB #52 provides that the objectives of FOREIGN
CURRENCY TRANSLATION (its title) are to:
Provide information that is generally compatible with the
expected economic effects of a rate change on an enterprise's cash flows and equity; and to reflect in consolidated statements the financial results and relationships of the
individual consolidated entities as measured in their FUNC-
TIONAL CURRENCIES in conformity with U.S. generally accepted
accounting principles.
This introduces the new concept of a FUNCTIONAL CURRENCY to be
employed in carrying out the translation process. Therefore
under FASB #52 the preliminary procedure requires that the balance sheet and income statement components be first measured in
terms of the functional currency of the business entity. Para.
5 defines functional currency as "the currency of the primary
economic environment in which the entity operates and generates
net cash flows." If a subsidiary or branch operates in France,
the functional currency would be the Franc. Accordingly, if
there are several branches each operating in different countries, each branch would have its own functional currency. An
exception would be in cases where the subsidiary or branch
would be operating as an extension of the parent company's operation, in which case the currency of the parent would be the
functional currency. The ultimate decision as to what the functional currency should be rests in the judgment of management.
To aid in this determination, Appendix A of #52 presents a set

of guideline questions:
   (1) Are cash flows related to the foreign entity's assets
      and liabilities primarily in the foreign currency? Are
      these cash flows independent from parent company cash
      flows?
   (2) Are the sales prices of the foreign entity's products
      related to local market conditions rather than changes
      in exchange rates?
   (3) Is there an active local sales market for the foreign
      entity's products?
   (4) Are labor, materials and other costs for the foreign
      entity's products local rather than imported from the
      parent company?
   (5) Is the foreign entity's primary financing in terms of
      functional currency?
   (6) Is there a low volume of intercompany transactions be-
      tween the parent and the foreign subsidiary?
The functional currency would be deemed to be the foreign currency if the answers to the above questions were YES. Should
the answers be NO, the parent company's currency would be deemed to be the functional currency. Once the functional currency
has been established, it should be consistently applied; however, where there is a material change in the economic facts and
circumstances, a change may be warranted.

    Appendix B requires REMEASUREMENT OF THE BOOKS OF RECORD
INTO THE FUNCTIONAL CURRENCY in cases where the books have not
been kept in their functional currencies before being translated. The purpose is to obtain the same results as would have
occurred if the functional currency had been used in the first
place, which in essence is a reversion to the translation rules
used under FASB #8. Para. 48 of Appendix B lists the accounts
which should be remeasured using the historical rate:
   (a) Marketable securities carried at cost: (1) Equity secur-
      ities; (2) Debt securities not intended to be held until
      maturity
   (b) Inventories carried at cost
   (c) Prepaid expenses, e.g., insurance, advertising, rent
   (d) Property, Plant and Equipment
   (e) Accumulated depreciation on prop., plant, & equip.
   (f) Patents, trademarks, licenses, formulas, & goodwill
   (g) Other tangible assets
   (h) Deferred charges and credits, except deferred income
      taxes and policy acquisition costs for life insurance
      companies
   (i) Deferred Income
   (j) Common Stock, and Preferred Stock carried at issuance
      price
   (k) Revenues and expenses related to nonmonetary items: (1)
      cost of goods sold; (2) depreciation of tangibles; (3)

amortization of tangibles; (4) amortization of deferred
charges or credits except deferred income taxes and policy acquisitions costs for life insurance companies
Para. 11 of FASB #52 provides for the establishment of the
functional currency in highly inflationary economies:
The financial statements of a foreign entity in a highly
inflationary economy shall be remeasured as if the functional currency were the reporting currency. Accordingly, the
financial statements of those entities shall be remeasured
into the reporting currency according to the requirements of
Para. 10. For the purposes of this requirement, a highly
inflationary economy is one that has cumulative inflation of
approximately 100 percent or more over a 3-year period.

#### #12-31...Classification of Foreign Currency Translation

FASB #52 makes a distinction between two basic situations
involving the translation procedure: Translation of Foreign
Currency TRANSACTIONS, and Translation of Foreign Currency FI-
NANCIAL STATEMENTS. Translation of the transactions is provided
for in para. 15 and 16, and that for financial statements in
para. 12, 13, and 14. The former are related to the impact of
foreign currency fluctuations on income, and the latter to
proper financial statement presentation.

#### #12-32...Acctg. For Foreign Currency Transactions Translation

The Jan. 1, 1982 issue of THIS WEEK IN REVIEW, #82-1, pp.
1-2, published by Deloitte, Haskins & Sells, states:
Foreign currency transactions are transactions denominated
in a currency other than the enterprise's functional currency. Foreign currency transactions may produce foreign currency receivables or payables that are fixed in the amount
of foreign currency to be received or paid. A change in exchange rates between the functional currency and the currency in which a transaction is denominated will increase or
decrease the amount of the functional currency expected to
be received or paid. These increases or decreases in the
expected functional currency cash flow are considered as
foreign exchange gains and losses and are included in the
determination of income for the period in which the transaction takes place, or, if the transaction is unsettled, the
period in which the rate change takes place.

EXAMPLE: Assume Biltrite, Ltd., a British corporation, borrowed, for general purposes, 1,000,000 Swiss Francs (SF) on Sept.
30, 1980. Further, assume the exchange rates for SF are as follows:

Sept. 30, 1980          1 SF = .24 Ł
Dec. 31, 1980           1 SF = .23 Ł
July 31, 1981           1 SF = .25 Ł

The entry on Sept. 30, 1980 (the transaction date) is:
    Cash (SF 1,000,000 x Ł .24)        Ł 240,000
        Notes Payable (SF 1,000,000)                   Ł 240,000

Now assume that  SF 200,000 of notes are paid at Dec. 31, 1980.
The entry as of the transaction date would be:
    Notes Payable
        <(SF 200,000/1,000,000) =
        ((1/5) x Ł 240,000) =
        Ł 48,000>                 Ł 48,000
        Cash (SF 200,000 x Ł .23)                      Ł 46,000
        Exchange Gain                                     2,000

No part of the exchange gain  on these transactions is deferred
because the original transaction  was  not  intended  to  be  a
hedge.
    To continue the illustration:
Assume  Biltrite, Ltd.,  does  not repay any  more of the Swiss
notes.  Accordingly, on July 31, 1981  (the  fiscal year  end)
Biltrite still owes SF 800,000.  An entry would be made to recognize the amount at which those  notes could  be settled as of
that date, and a new carrying amount determined as follows:
    Balance, Swiss Franc Notes              SF 800,000
    Exchange Rate as of 7/31/81             Ł      .25
    Carrying Amount in Ł                    Ł   200,000
    Balance Per Books (Ł 240,000 - 48,000)      192,000
        EXCHANGE LOSS                        Ł     8,000

The entry to record the exchange loss and the adjusted carrying
amount would be as follows:
    Exchange Loss                       Ł 8,000
        Swiss Notes Payable                     Ł 8,000

    In  the article  "Accounting  for the Translation of Foreign
Currency Transactions  and  Financial  Statements,"  Sept.  22,
1980, published  in Arthur  Young's CLIENT MEMORANDUM, page  7,
it is observed:
        The accounting  for foreign currency transactions gener-
    ally will be the same under FASB #52 as under  FASB #8, that
    is, the translation  gains  or losses generally will  be in-
    cluded in net income  for  the period in  which the exchange
    rates change.   In two cases, however, the gains  and losses
    from foreign currency  transactions will be reported  in the
    separate component of stockholders' equity along with finan-
    cial statement translation adjustments.

The two exceptions are (a) when the foreign currency transaction (including a forward exchange contract) is intended to be, and is effective as, an economic hedge of a net investment in a foreign entity; and (b) when the foreign currency transaction is between an investor and an investee, when the latter is consolidated, combined, or accounted for by the equity method in the investor's financial statements.

#### #12-33...FASB #52 Accounting for Translation of Foreign Currency Statements

As shown above in Sec. #12-30, FASB #52 enunciates two objectives of translation in para. 4. To accomplish these objectives, two major changes from FASB #8 are made in FASB #52: (1) all of the assets and liabilities in foreign currency financial statements, in most cases, are translated at the CURRENT RATE; and (2) the EXCHANGE ADJUSTMENTS resulting from such translations, with a few exceptions, would be reported in a separate component of stockholders' equity rather than reflected in income.

With respect to TRANSLATION ADJUSTMENTS, para. 13 provides: "Translation adjustments shall not be included in determining net income but shall be reported separately and accumulated in a separate component of equity." Para. 14 goes on to declare that "upon sale or liquidation of an investment in a foreign entity, the amount attributable to that entity and accumulated in the translation adjustment component of equity shall be removed from the separate component of equity and shall be reported as part of the gain or loss on sale or liquidation of the investment for the period during which the sale or liquidation occurs."

To demonstrate the differences between translation of balance sheets under FASB #8 and #52, the following illustration is presented in Arthur Young's CLIENT MEMORANDUM, Sept. 22, 1980, page 5:

A U.S. company has a West German subsidiary that was started on Jan. 1, 1974, at which time all fixed assets were acquired. The exchange rate on Jan. 1, 1974 was DM 2.70 = U.S. $1. The current rate is DM 1.80 = U.S. $1. The average historical rate for inventory and retained earnings are DM 2.00 and DM 2.10 = U.S. $1, respectively.

|  | DM | Translation to U.S. Dollars | |
|---|---|---|---|
| Accounts | Balances | FASB#8 | FASB#52 |
| ASSETS: | | | |
| Cash and Receivables | 2,700 | $1,500 | $1,500 |
| Inventory | 3,240 | 1,620 | 1,800 |
| Net Fixed Assets | 4,050 | 1,500 | 2,250 |
| Total Assets | 9,990 | $4,620 | $5,550 |

```
LIABILITIES & STOCKHOLDERS'
EQUITY:
  Accounts Payable              1,350      $  750    $  750
  Debt                          2,700       1,500     1,500
  Capital Stock (Origi-
    nal Inv.)                   3,375       1,250     1,250
  Retained Earnings
    Statement                   2,565       1,120     1,220
  FOREIGN CURRENCY/
    TRANSLATION EQUITY
    ADJUSTMENT                                           830
  Total Liabilities & Equity    9,990      $4,620    $5,550
```

Under FASB #8 the translation loss has been reflected in income and retained earnings over the period of the decline in the exchange rate. Under FASB #52 the translation gain from the strengthening of the DM would be credited directly to a separate equity account that would not be amortized. Annually such translation gains and losses result from translating a foreign entity's financial statements using a CURRENT EXCHANGE RATE that differs from (a) the average exchange rates used in the income statement for the period, & (b) the rate at the end of the previous period.

A comprehensive illustration of foreign currency financial statement translation is presented in an Appendix to an article by Professors Thomas Ratcliffe and Paul Munter in the JOURNAL OF ACCOUNTANCY, June 1982, pp. 82-89, entitled "Currency Translation: A New Blueprint." The article points out on page 85 that TRANSLATION ADJUSTMENTS may result from either

(a) translating a foreign entity's financial statements using a current exchange rate that differs from the exchange rates used during the period, or

(b) translating a foreign entity's financial statements using a current exchange rate that differs from the exchange rate used to translate the foreign entity's financial statements at the end of the previous period.

The amount of the translation adjustment is computed as follows:

(a) Multiply the amount of net assets at the beginning of the period by the change in exchange rates during the period;

(b) Multiply the increase or decrease in net assets for the period by the difference between the average exchange rate and the end-of-period exchange rate;

(c) Where a net asset increase or decrease is attributable to a capital transaction, the translation adjustment is equal to the increase or decrease in net assets multiplied by the difference between the end-of-period exchange rate and the exchange rate at the time the capital transaction occurred.

The sum of the three results stated immediately above equals the total translation adjustment.

## APPENDIX:
## ILLUSTRATION OF FOREIGN CURRENCY STATEMENT TRANSLATION

On Jan. 1, 1981 MR Corporation created a wholly-owned foreign subsidiary. The balance sheet and income statement for the year ended Dec. 31, 1984, expressed in foreign currency units (FCU), are:

### BALANCE SHEET, 12/31/84

| | |
|---|---|
| Cash | 8,000 (FCU) |
| Accounts Receivable | 4,000 |
| Inventory | 12,000 |
| Property, Plant, & Equipment | 20,000 |
| TOTAL ASSETS | 44,000 (FCU) |
| | |
| Notes Payable | 12,000 (FCU) |
| Capital Stock | 20,000 |
| Retained Earnings | 12,000 |
| TOTAL EQUITIES | 44,000 (FCU) |

### INCOME STATEMENT, 12/31/84

| | | |
|---|---|---|
| Sales | | 40,000 (FCU) |
| Expenses: | | |
| Cost of Goods Sold | 22,000 (FCU) | |
| Depreciation | 4,000 | |
| Other Expenses | 10,000 | 36,000 |
| NET INCOME | | 4,000 (FCU) |

The capital stock was issued and the property, plant & equipment acquired when the subsidiary was created on Jan. 1, 1981.

The inventory at Jan. 1, 1984 was 14,000 FCU and was acquired during the fourth quarter of 1983. Purchases of 20,000 FCU, sales, and other expenses occurred evenly during 1984.

The Exchange Rates were as follows:

| | |
|---|---|
| January 1, 1981 | 1.3 FCU = $1 |
| 4th Quarter 1983 Average | 1.3 FCU = $1 |
| 1984 Average Rate | 1.1 FCU = $1 |
| 4th Quarter 1984 Average | .8 FCU = $1 |
| December 31, 1983 | 1.3 FCU = $1 |
| December 31, 1984 | .7 FCU = $1 |

## CASE 1:

Assuming that the enterprise reporting currency is the U.S. dollar and that the functional currency for the subsidiary is FCU, the translation of the financial statements would be shown in Figure 12-3.

```
================================================================
```

FIGURE 12-3
TRANSLATION OF FINANCIAL STATEMENT
CASE 1

| | FCU Balance | Translation Rate | Translated U.S. $ |
|---|---|---|---|
| Balance Sheet Elements: | | | |
| Cash | 8,000 FCU | .7 FCU = $1 | 11,429 |
| Accounts Receivable | 4,000 | .7 FCU = $1 | 5,714 |
| Inventory | 12,000 | .7 FCU = $1 | 17,143 |
| Property, Plant & Equipment | 20,000 | .7 FCU = $1 | 28,571 |
| Notes Payable | 12,000 | .7 FCU = $1 | 17,143 |
| Capital Stock | 20,000 | .7 FCU = $1 | 28,571 |
| Income Statement Elements: | | | |
| Sales | 40,000 FCU | 1.1 FCU = $1 | 36,364 |
| Cost of Goods Sold | (22,000) | 1.1 FCU = $1 | (20,000) |
| Depreciation | ( 4,000) | 1.1 FCU = $1 | ( 3,636) |
| Other Expenses | (10,000) | 1.1 FCU = $1 | ( 9,091) |
| Net Income | 4,000 | | 3,637 |
| Retained Earnings 1/1/84 | 8,000 | 1.3 FCU = $1 | 6,154 |
| Translated Retained Earnings 12/31/84 | | | 9,791 |
| Reported Retained Earnings | 12,000 FCU | .7 FCU = $1 | 17,143 |
| TRANSLATION ADJUSTMENT | | | 7,352 |

Source: Adapted from Case 1 of Appendix in "Currency Translation: A New
        Blueprint," by Professors Thomas Ratcliffe and Paul Munter,
        JOURNAL OF ACCOUNTANCY (June 1982), pages 82-89. Reprinted with
        permission. Copyright © 1982 by the American Institute of Cer-
        tified Public Accountants, Inc. Opinions expressed in the JOUR-
        NAL OF ACCOUNTANCY are those of editors and contributors. Pub-
        lication in the JOURNAL OF ACCOUNTANCY does not constitute en-
        dorsement by the AICPA or its committees.

```
================================================================
```

The translated balance sheet and income statement would appear
as follows:

BALANCE SHEET, 12/31/84

| | | | |
|---|---|---|---|
| Cash | $11,429 | Notes Payable | $17,143 |
| Acct. Rcvble | 5,714 | Capital Stock | 28,571 |
| Inventory | 17,143 | Retd. Earnings | 9,791 |
| P.,P. & E. | 28,571 | Transl.Adjust. | 7,352 |
| TOTAL ASSETS | $62,857 | TOTAL EQUITIES | $62,857 |

INCOME STATEMENT, 12/31/84

| Sales | | $36,364 |
|---|---|---|
| Less: Expenses: | | |
| Cost of Goods Sold | $20,000 | |
| Depreciation | 3,636 | |
| Other Expenses | 9,091 | |
| Total Expenses | | 32,727 |
| NET INCOME | | 3,637 |

CASE 2:

Assuming that the foreign country has had a cumulative inflation rate in excess of 100 percent for the past three years, under para. 11 of FASB #52, the financial statements of the entity would be remeasured as if the functional currency were the reporting currency (U.S. $) and the nonmonetary items would be remeasured using the historical rate. The remeasurement into U.S. dollars is shown in Figure 12-4.

The remeasured balance sheet and income statement would appear as follows:

BALANCE SHEET, 12/31/84

| Cash | $11,429 | Notes Payable | $17,143 |
|---|---|---|---|
| Accts. Rcble | 5,714 | Capital Stock | 15,385 |
| Inventory | 15,000 | Retained Earnings | 15,000 |
| P., P. & E. | 15,385 | | |
| TOTAL ASSETS | $47,528 | TOTAL EQUITIES | $47,528 |

INCOME STATEMENT, 12/31/84

| Sales | | $36,364 |
|---|---|---|
| Expenses: | | |
| Cost of Goods Sold | $13,951 | |
| Depreciation | 3,077 | |
| Other Expenses | 9,091 | |
| Total Expenses | $26,119 | |
| Translation Loss | 1,399 | |
| Total Expenses | | 27,518 |
| NET INCOME | | $ 8,846 |

#12-34...FASB #52 Disclosure Requirements

Para. 30, 31 and 32 require the aggregate transaction gain or loss included in determining net income for the period to be disclosed in the financial statements and notes. Included are gains or losses recognized on forward contracts, discussed below. At a minimum, the analysis shall disclose (a) beginning and ending amount of cumulative translation adjustments; (b)

FIGURE 12-4

REMEASUREMENT OF FINANCIAL STATEMENT
CASE 2

| | FCU Balance | Translation Rate | Translated U.S. $ |
|---|---|---|---|
| **Balance Sheet Elements:** | | | |
| Cash | 8,000 FCU | .7 FCU = $1 | 11,429 |
| Accounts Receivable | 4,000 | .7 FCU = $1 | 5,714 |
| Inventory (Historical Cost) | 12,000 | .8 FCU = $1 | 15,000 |
| Property, Plant, & Equipment (Histor) | 20,000 | 1.3 FCU = $1 | 15,385 |
| Notes Payable | 12,000 | .7 FCU = $1 | 17,143 |
| Capital Stock (Hist. Cost) | 20,000 | 1.3 FCU = $1 | 15,385 |
| **Income Statement Elements:** | | | |
| Sales | 40,000 FCU | 1.1 FCU = $1 | 36,364 |
| Cost of Goods Sold: | | | |
| Beginning Inventory (Histor. Cost) | (14,000) | 1.3 FCU = $1 | (10,769) |
| Purchases | (20,000) | 1.1 FCU = $1 | (18,182) |
| Ending Inventory (Histor. Cost) | 12,000 | .8 FCU = $1 | 15,000 |
| Total Cost of Goods Sold | (22,000) | | (13,951) |
| Depreciation (Histor. Cost) | ( 4,000) | 1.3 FCU = $1 | ( 3,077) |
| Other Expenses | (10,000) | 1.1 FCU = $1 | ( 9,091) |
| Income Before Translation Adjustment | 4,000 | | 10,245 |
| Retained Earnings 1/1/84 | 8,000 | 1.3 FCU = $1 | 6,154 |
| Total Retained Earnings Before Trans. Adj. | | | 16,399 |
| Retained Earnings 12/31/84 (Resid. Amt. = net assets minus Capital Stock) | 12,000 FCU | .8 FCU = $1 | 15,000 |
| TRANSLATION ADJUSTMENT LOSS | | | 1,399 |

Source: Adapted from Case 2 of Appendix in "Currency Translation: A New
Blueprint," by Professors Thomas Ratcliffe and Paul Munter,
JOURNAL OF ACCOUNTANCY (June 1982), pages 82-89. Reprinted with
permission. Copyright © 1982 by the American Institute of Certified Public Accountants, Inc. Opinions expressed in the JOUR-
NAL OF ACCOUNTANCY are those of editors and contributors. Publication in the JOURNAL OF ACCOUNTANCY does not constitute endorsement by the AICPA or its committees.

the aggregate adjustment for the period resulting from translation adjustments; (c) the amount of income taxes for the period
allocated to translation adjustments; and (d) the amounts
transferred from cumulative translation adjustments and included in determining net income for the period as a result of the
sale or liquidation of an investment in a foreign entity. A
typical illustration of such disclosure is that of Occidental
Petroleum Corp. discussed in #12-28.

## #12-35...FASB #52 Forward Exchange Contracts

Para. 17, 18 and 19 provide for Forward Exchange Contracts.
In a booklet entitled FOREIGN CURRENCY TRANSLATION, FASB #52,
Dec. 1981, p. 13, examples are presented for computation of
gains or losses on forward exchange contracts (see Chapter 9).
The booklet published by Deloitte, Haskins & Sells, indicates
on p. 12 that:

Accounting for forward exchange contracts has not been
changed from the provisions of Statement No. 8, but the
rules for consideration of such contracts as hedges have
been liberalized. A forward contract or other foreign currency transaction may be considered to hedge an identifiable
foreign currency commitment if the following conditions are
met: (a) the foreign currency transaction is designated as,
and is effective as, a hedge of a foreign currency commitment, and (b) the foreign currency commitment is firm.

Gain or loss on a forward exchange contract is to be
computed as previously required by the provisions of Statement No. 8. An illustration of the computation of the gain
or loss and discount or premium on a forward exchange contract is as follows:

HEDGES -- FORWARD EXCHANGE CONTRACT -- GAIN OR LOSS

Assume that on July 1, 1981, Biltrite, Ltd, a British
corporation, enters into a contract to purchase equipment in
the amount of $1,000,000 to be delivered and paid for on
Dec. 31, 1981. To fully hedge the foreign currency commitment, Biltrite purchases a forward exchange contract. The
relevant rates per U.S. $ are:

July 1,1981   Spot Rate                          Ł .52
Dec. 1981     Contract Forward Rate              Ł .51
July 31,1981  Spot Rate(Balnc Sheet Date)        Ł .54

The deferred gain on the forward exchange contract is
computed as follows:

Foreign Currency Amt. of Forward Contract    $1,000,000
Spot Rate July 31, 1981             Ł .54
Spot Rate July 1, 1981              Ł .52 x              .02
Deferred Gain on Forward Exch. Contract      Ł    20,000
         loss

HEDGES -- FORWARD EXCHANGE CONTRACT -- DISCOUNT OR PREMIUM
The discount on the forward exchange contract is computed as follows:

| | | |
|---|---|---|
| Foreign Currency Amt. of Forward Contract | $1,000,000 | |
| Contract Forward Rate July 1, 1981 | Ł .51 | |
| Spot Rate July 1, 1981 | Ł .52 x | .01 |
| Discount on Forward Exchange Contract | Ł | 10,000 |

NOTE: Both the gain and discount are deferred and included in the cost of the equipment; alternatively the discount could be included in income over the life of the contract.

#12-36...Flowchart Summary of Statement No. 52

A "Flowchart Summary of FASB #52" in the JOURNAL OF ACCOUNTANCY, June 1982, p. 86, is reproduced in Figure 12-5.
An excellent summary of FASB #52 by Professors Richard Veazey and Suk Kim appears in the Winter 1982 issue of the COLUMBIA JOURNAL OF WORLD BUSINESS, pp. 17-22, entitled "Translation of Foreign Currency Operations: SFAS No. 52." Figure 12-6 illustrates the changes wrought in FASB #8 to produce FASB #52.
The CONCLUSION of the article indicates that "many financial executives applaud the new rule, but they do not believe that it will resolve all the problems related to the translation of foreign currency financial statements into the reporting currency. Nevertheless SFAS No. 52 ended the Board's painstaking process of changing an accounting standard which did not reflect economic reality. Under SFAS No. 8, erratic exchange rates caused erratic earnings for two major reasons: first, the receivables, payables and monetary items were translated at current exchange rates, while inventories and fixed assets hedging these monetary items were translated at historical exchange rates; second, companies were required to reflect foreign exchange gains or losses from balance sheet translations in the income statement. Since SFAS No. 52 has corrected these two problems, it is expected to significantly reduce fluctuations in earnings that existed under SFAS No. 8."

IASC #21

#12-37..."IASC #21 -- Accounting For the Effects of
          Changes in Foreign Exchange Rates"

The latest expression of foreign translation appears in the JOURNAL OF ACCOUNTANCY, June 1983, page 24:
The International Accounting Standards Committee (IASC) has issued IASC #21, ACCOUNTING FOR THE EFFECTS OF CHANGES IN FOREIGN EXCHANGE RATES. The IASC noted that the standard isn't substantially different from its exposure draft,

# FIGURE 12-5
## A FLOWCHART SUMMARY OF STATEMENT NO. 52

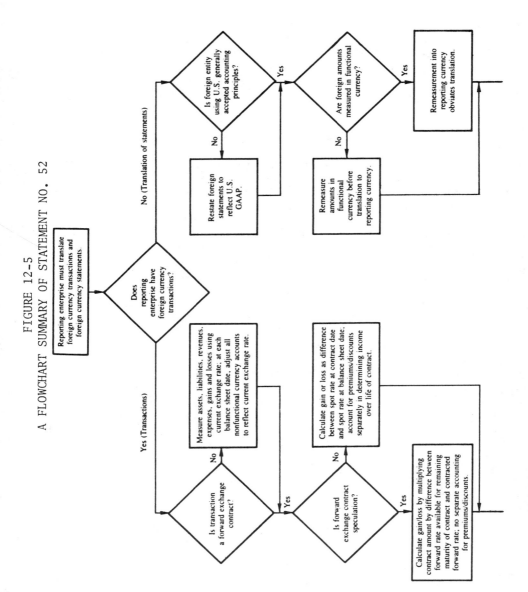

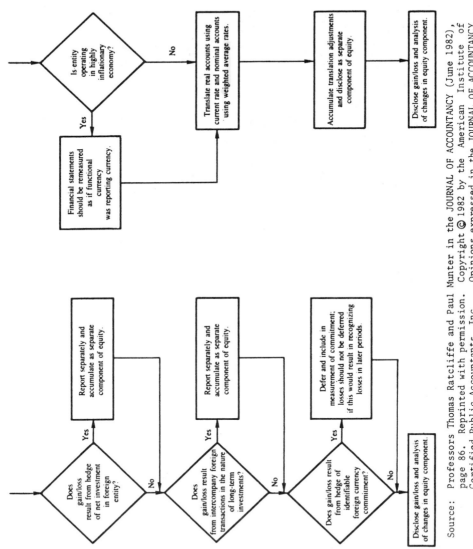

Source: Professors Thomas Ratcliffe and Paul Munter in the JOURNAL OF ACCOUNTANCY (June 1982), page 86. Reprinted with permission. Copyright © 1982 by the American Institute of Certified Public Accountants, Inc. Opinions expressed in the JOURNAL OF ACCOUNTANCY are those of editors and contributors. Publication in the JOURNAL OF ACCOUNTANCY does not constitute endorsement by the AICPA or its committees.

FIGURE 12-6
COMPARISON OF THE MAJOR PROVISIONS OF
SFAS NO. 8 AND SFAS NO. 52

| Provision | SFAS No. 8 | SFAS No. 52 |
|---|---|---|
| Translation method | Temporal method | Current exchange rate method |
| Functional currency | Not used | The currency of the primary economic environment in which an entity generates and expends cash |
| Foreign-exchange gains or losses from balance sheet translations | Included in current income | Placed directly in stockholders' equity on the balance sheet |
| Translation of operations in highly inflationary economies | Normally not serious under the temporal method | The financial statements of a foreign entity are remeasured as if the functional currency were the reporting currency |
| Gains or losses from foreign currency transactions | Included in current income | Included in current income |
| Realization of the separate component of equity | Not applicable | Upon sale or upon complete or substantial liquidation of the investment |
| Gains or losses from transactions intended to hedge a net investment | Included in current income | Placed directly in stockholders' equity on the balance sheet |
| Gains or losses from intercompany transactions | Included in current income | Accumulated as a separate component of stockholders' equity for all intercompany transactions that are of a long-term investment nature. Included in current income for other intercompany transactions |

Source: Adapted from pages 17-22, "Translation of Foreign Currency Operations: SFAS No. 52," by Professors Richard Veazey and Suk Kim in COLUMBIA JOURNAL OF WORLD BUSINESS (Winter 1982), by permission.

JOURNAL OF ACCOUNTANCY, March 1982, page 20.

IASC #21 requires that a transaction in a foreign currency be recorded by using the exchange rate applicable at the time of the transaction or a rate that approximates the actual rate. Also, monetary items resulting from such transactions are to be reported at the closing rate at each balance sheet date.

According to the IASC, the main changes in IASC #21 from Exposure Draft #23 include:
- Restriction of circumstances under which gains or losses on long-term monetary items may be deferred;
- A requirement that hedges should be designated as such and should provide effective offset;
- Permission to use a method similar to the temporal method of translation for entities affected by high rates of inflation.

The IASC says that comments on the exposure draft indicated "general support around the world for the net investment method of accounting for foreign operations whose activities aren't an integral part of those of the parent." This method requires that most foreign financial statement amounts should be translated at current exchange rates.

IASC #21 was published on July 1, 1983 and becomes effective January 1, 1985.

## SUMMARY OF FOOTNOTE REFERENCES
(References are to Paragraph #'s)

#12-11 FASB #8, 1975

#12-16 AICPA, STATEMENT OF POSITION ON ACCOUNTING FOR FOREIGN CURRENCY TRANSLATION (1974), p. 3

#12-17 "An Analysis of Issues Related to Accounting for Foreign Currency Translation," FASB DISCUSSION MEMORANDUM, 1974, pp. 82-100

#12-20 FASB #1, STATEMENT OF FINANCIAL ACCOUNTING STANDARDS, "Disclosure of Foreign Currency Translation Information," 1973, p. 5

#12-20 APB Opinion #30, "Reporting the Results of Operations," (N.Y.: AICPA, 1973), p. 566

#12-21 "Learning to Live With Currency Fluctuations," BUSINESS WEEK (Jan. 20, 1976): 48-52

#12-21 Philip Revsin, "New Accounting Rule Makes Multinationals Alter Their Strategies--Corporations Complain That Profits Are Held Hostage to Revaluations Abroad," THE WALL STREET JOURNAL (Dec. 8, 1976): 1, 28

#12-21 Samuel Hepworth, REPORTING FOREIGN OPERATIONS, p. 72

#12-24 FASB #1, 1973, pp. 5-6

#12-25 "Foreign Currency Translation: The Controversy Continues," JOURNAL OF ACCOUNTANCY (July 1981): 110. Reprinted with permission. Copyright © 1981 by the American Institute of Cer-

tified Public Accountants, Inc.   Opinions expressed in  the
JOURNAL OF ACCOUNTANCY   are   those   of editors and contributors.   Publication in the JOURNAL OF  ACCOUNTANCY does   not
constitute endorsement by the AICPA or its committees.
#12-26 Ibid., by permission.
#12-27 Frank Murphy,  JOURNAL OF ACCOUNTANCY (May 1982): 114
#12-27 Paul Pacter,  Executive Assistant to FASB Chairman
#12-28 Occidental Petroleum Corp., Annual Report, 1981, p. 49
#12-30 FASB #52, para. 4; Appendix A; Appendix B; para. 11
#12-32 Deloitte, Haskins & Sells,  THIS WEEK IN REVIEW, #82-1 (Jan.
       1, 1982): 1-2
#12-32 Arthur Young & Company,  "Accounting  For the Translation of
       Foreign  Currency Transactions  and  Financial  Statements,"
       CLIENT MEMORANDUM (September 22, 1980): 7
#12-33 FASB #52, para. 4, para. 13, para. 14
#12-33 Arthur Young & Company, op. cit., p. 5
#12-33 Thos. Ratcliffe and  Paul  Munter,  "Currency Translation: A
       New  Blueprint," JOURNAL OF  ACCOUNTANCY (June 1982): 82-89.
       Reprinted with permission.  Copyright © 1982 by the American
       Institute  of  Certified Public  Accountants, Inc.  Opinions
       expressed in the JOURNAL OF ACCOUNTANCY are those of editors
       and contributors.  Publication in the JOURNAL OF ACCOUNTANCY
       does  not constitute endorsement by the AICPA or its commit-
       tees.
#12-35 Deloitte, Haskins &  Sells,  FOREIGN CURRENCY TRANSLATION,
       FASB #52 (December 1981): 12-13.  Reprinted with permission.
#12-36 Richard Veazey and Suk Kim, "Translation of Foreign Currency
       Operations: SFAS  #52," COLUMBIA  JOURNAL OF WORLD BUSINESS
       (Winter 1982): 17-22.  Reprinted with permission.
#12-37 "IASC #21--Accounting For  the Effects of Changes in Foreign
       Exchange Rates,"  JOURNAL  OF ACCOUNTANCY (June  1983): 24.
       Copyright © 1983 by the American Institute of Certified Pub-
       lic  Accountants, Inc.  Opinions expressed in the JOURNAL OF
       ACCOUNTANCY are those of editors and contributors.  Publica-
       tion in the JOURNAL  OF ACCOUNTANCY does not  constitute en-
       dorsement by the AICPA or its committees.


## BIBLIOGRAPHY

Adkins, Lynn.  "A New Management Headache," DUN'S REVIEW (Oct.1977)
Alleman, Raymond H. "Why ITT Likes FASB #52," MANAGEMENT ACCOUNTING
       (July 1982): 23-29
Bender, Douglas E.  "Foreign  Currency  Translation--FASB #52," CPA
       JOURNAL (June, July, August 1982)
Coopers & Lybrand.  FOREIGN CURRENCY TRANSLATION: AN IMPLEMENTATION
       GUIDE,  N.Y. (January 1982)
Deloitte, Haskins & Sells. FOREIGN CURRENCY TRANSLATION, N.Y. (Dec.
       1981)
Ernst & Whinney,  "Foreign Currency Translation," FINANCIAL REPORT-
       ING DEVELOPMENTS, Cleveland (January 1982)
Jansz, Rodney.  "Foreign Currency  Translation," THE AUSTRALIAN AC-

COUNTANT, 51 (February 1981): 18-21
McCord, Sammy O.  "SFAS No. 8 vs. SFAS No. 52: An Assessment," MID-
    ATLANTIC JOURNAL OF BUSINESS (Summer 1984)
Parkinson, R. McDonald.  TRANSLATION OF FOREIGN CURRENCIES: A RE-
    SEARCH STUDY.  Toronto Canadian Institute of C.P.A.s, 1972
Rodriguez, Rita.  "FASB #8: What Has It Done For Us?", FINANCIAL
    ANALYSTS JOURNAL (March-April 1977): 40-47
Taussig, R.A.  "Impact of SFAS No. 52 on the Translation of Foreign
    Financial Statements of Companies in Highly Inflated Econo-
    mies," JOURNAL OF ACCOUNTING, AUDITING & FINANCE (Winter
    1983): 142
Walker, David.  "Currency Translation: A Pragmatic Approach," AC-
    COUNTANT, 9 (March 1978): 311-313
Wojciechowski, Stanley.  "DuPont Evaluates FASB #52," MANAGEMENT
    ACCOUNTING (July 1982): 31-35

## THEORY QUESTIONS
(Question Numbers are Keyed to Text Paragraph #'s)

#12-12 What is an Exchange Adjustment, how is it determined,
    and what are its consequences?
#12-14 How many types of Exchange Adjustments are there, what
    are they, and define each of them.
#12-15 What are Realized Gains and Losses and how should they
    be handled?
#12-16 What are Unrealized Gains and Losses, how do they differ
    from Realized Gains and Losses, and how should they be
    handled?
#12-17 Discuss the pros and cons of the North American view vs.
    the Continental Deferred view for handling unrealized
    gains and losses.
#12-18 What has been the procedure for handling gains and loss-
    es under the Traditional Approach?
#12-19 What has been the procedure for handling gains and loss-
    es under the Full Recognition Approach under FASB #8?
#12-21 What results have been experienced under the FASB #8
    Full Recognition Approach? Comment on the significance
    of these results.
#12-24 What Footnote Disclosure is required for foreign curren-
    cy translation under FASB #1?
#12-25 Discuss the launching of FASB #52.
#12-26 What were the first reactions to FASB #52?
#12-29 What are the key objectives of FASB #52?
#12-30 What provisions are made by FASB #52 for selection of
    the proper reporting currency?
#12-30 (a) Where the books of record have not been kept in
    their functional currencies before being translated,
    what provision does Appendix B of FASB #52 make for re-
    measurement of the books of record into the functional

currency?

#12-30 (b) What provision is made by FASB #52 for the establishment of the Functional Currency in highly inflationary economies?

#12-31 Between what two basic situations involving the translation procedure does FASB #52 make a distinction and what is it?

#12-33 Compare accounting under FASB #8 with FASB #52.

#12-34 What disclosure requirements are made under FASB #52?

#12-38 What provision is made in IASC #21 for Accounting for the Effects of Changes in Foreign Exchange Rates?

## EXERCISES

### EX-12-1 (CPA EXAM, 5/75, THEORY, #1-18)
A material loss arising from the devaluation of the currency of a country in which a corporation was conducting foreign operations through a branch would be reflected in the company's year-end financial statements as
a. An asset to be subsequently offset against gains from foreign currency revaluations.
b. A factor in determining earnings before extraordinary items in the year during which the loss occurred.
c. An extraordinary item on the earnings statement of the year during which the loss occurred.
d. A prior period adjustment unless the operations of the foreign branch had begun during the year in which the loss occurred.

### EX-12-2 (CPA EXAM, 5/77, THEORY, #22)
How should exchange gains and losses resulting from translating foreign currency financial statements into U.S. dollars be accounted for?
a. Included as an ordinary item in net earnings for the period in which the rate changes.
b. Included as an extraordinary item in net earnings for the period in which the rate changes.
c. Included in the statement of financial position as a deferred item.
d. Included as an ordinary item in net earnings for gains, but deferred for losses.

### EX-12-3 (CPA EXAM, 11/78, PRAC. I, #8)
Seed Co. has a receivable from a foreign customer which is payable in the local currency of the foreign customer. On Dec. 31, 1976, this receivable was appropriately included in the accounts receivable section of Seed's balance sheet at $450,000. When the receivable was collected on Jan. 4, 1977, Seed converted the local currency of the foreign customer into

$440,000. Seed also owns a foreign subsidiary in which exchange gains of $45,000 resulted as a consequence of translation in 1977. What amount, if any, should be included as an exchange gain or loss in Seed's 1977 consolidated income statement?

a. $0
c. $35,000 exchange gain
b. $10,000 exchange loss
d. $45,000 exchange gain

**EX-12-4  (CPA EXAM, 11/79, PRAC. I, #9)**
Fore Co. had a $30,000 exchange loss resulting from the tansla-tion of the accounts of its wholly-owned foreign subsidiary for the year ended Dec. 31, 1978. Fore also had a receivable from a foreign customer which was payable in the local currency of the foreign customer. On Dec. 31, 1977, this receivable for 500,000 local currency units (LCU) was appropriately included in the accounts receivable section of Fore's balance sheet at $245,000. When the receivable was collected on Feb. 5, 1978, the exchange rate was 2 LCU to $1. What amount should be in-cluded as an exchange gain or loss in the 1978 consolidated income statement of Fore Co. and its wholly-owned foreign sub-sidiary as a result of the above?

a. $ 5,000 exchange gain
c. $25,000 exchange loss
b. $20,000 exchange loss
d. $30,000 exchange loss

**EX-12-5  (CPA EXAM, 5/80, THEORY, #9)**
A foreign exchange gain that is a consequence of translation should be

a. Included in net income in the period it occurs.
b. Deferred and amortized over a period not to exceed forty years.
c. Deferred until a subsequent year when a loss occurs and offset against that loss.
d. Included as a separate item in the equity section of the balance sheet.

**EX-12-6  (CPA EXAM, 11/80, THEORY, #14)**
Exchange gains and losses resulting from translating foreign currency financial statements into U.S. dollars should be in-cluded as

a. A deferred item in the balance sheet.
b. An extraordinary item in the income statement for the per-iod in which the rate changes.
c. An ordinary item in the income statement for losses but deferred for gains.
d. An ordinary item in the income statement for the period in which the rate changes.

**EX-12-7  (CPA EXAM, 5/83, PRAC. II, #18)**
Palo Corp. incurred the following losses, net of applicable taxes, for the year ended Dec. 31, 1982:

\*Loss on disposal of a segment
   of Palo's business                          $400,000
\*Loss on translation of foreign
   currency due to major devaluation               $500,000
How much should Palo report as extraordinary losses on its 1982
income statement?
   a. $0                           c.  $500,000
   b. $400,000                      d.  $900,000

**EX-12-8  (CPA EXAM, 5/84, PRAC. I, #36)**
Blackwood Corp.  had a $200,000 translation loss adjustment re-
sulting from the translation  of the accounts  of  its  wholly-
owned  foreign  subsidiary for  the  year ended Dec.  31, 1983.
Blackwood also had a  receivable from a foreign  customer which
was payable in the local currency  of the foreign customer.  On
Dec. 31, 1982, this  receivable  for $100,000 LCU was appropri-
ately  included in Blackwood's  balance sheet at $55,000.  When
the receivable was collected  on Feb.  10, 1983,  the  exchange
rate was  2 LCU to $1.  In Blackwood's 1983 consolidated income
statement,  what amount should be included  as foreign exchange
loss?
   a. 0                            c.  $20,000
   b. $5,000                        d.  $25,000

**EX-12-9  (CPA EXAM, 5/84, THEORY, #27)**
Losses resulting from the process  of translating a foreign entity's financial statements from the functional currency, which
is experiencing a 3% inflation rate, to  U.S. dollars should be
included as
   a. A deferred charge.
   b. A separate component of income from continuing operations.
   c. A component of income from continuing operations.
   d. An extraordinary item.

**EX-12-10  (CPA EXAM, 11/83, THEORY, #25)**
A sale of goods, denominated in a currency other than the entity's functional  currency,  resulted in  a  receivable that was
fixed in terms of the amount  of foreign currency that would be
received.  Exchange rates between the  functional currency  and
the currency  in which the transaction was denominated changed.
The resulting gain should be included as
   a. A separate component of stockholder's equity.
   b. A deferred credit.
   c. A component of income from continuing operations.
   d. An extraordinary item.

**EX-12-11  (CPA EXAM, 5/66, THEORY, #12)**
In the conversion of the  trial  balance  of  a foreign branch,
increases in the translated value of foreign net current assets

resulting from an upward fluctuation in the foreign exchange
rate should be
  a. Credited to current income.
  b. Debited as a current expense of operations.
  c. Offset against prior provisions for unrealized losses,
     the excess of the increase being credited to a suspense
     account.
  d. Credited to retained earnings in order to state the income
     from operations fairly.

### EX-12-12 (CPA EXAM, 11/39, AUDITING, #5)

A large U.S. concern owns foreign companies or branches that
own and operate plants and sell their products in their respective countries. Their balance sheets include among other accounts the following:
  1. Cash in Restricted Currencies
  2. Accounts Receivable
  3. Inventories
  4. Capital Assets
  5. Current Liabilities
  6. Intercompany Accounts Payable
The accounts of the foreign companies or branches were all converted at the official rates of exchange at the close of the
fiscal year and the exchange differences in consolidation carried forward as a debit under deferred charges. In auditing the
accounts (a) what rates of exchange would you use in making
conversions of the above balances, and (b) how would you recommend handling exchange differences?

### PROBLEMS

### P-12-1 (CPA EXAM, 11/19, PRAC. II, #2)

The Pan-American Chemical Co., a New York corporation, owns a
plant in Chile where nitrate of soda is manufactured and shipped to the U.S. The accounts in Chile are kept in the local
currency (pesos) and the following is a summary of the transactions during 1918:
>>>1/1/18 New York remitted by telegraphic transfer
         $30,000, which realized 120,000 pesos.
   4/1/18 N.Y. remitted $30,000; realized 150,000 pesos.
   7/1/18 N.Y. remitted $30,000; realized 180,000 pesos.
  10/1/18 N.Y. remitted $30,000; realized 150,000 pesos.
>>>There were paid in wages for plant construction 120,000
pesos.
>>>There was paid for operating, 300,000 pesos.
>>>At Dec. 31, 1918, the unpaid payroll for operating labor
amounted to 60,000 pesos and one-sixth of the nitrate produced
during the year remained in inventory.
>>>You may assume that the production, construction and ship-

ments were spread evenly over the whole 12 months, and that the only element entering into costs of production and construction in Chile was labor.

>>>The average quoted exchange rates in Chile and New York were as follows:

| | |
|---|---|
| 1/1/18 to 6/30/18 | 3 pesos = $1 |
| 7/1/18 to 12/31/18 | 5 pesos = $1 |
| At the close of business 12/31/18 | |
| the rate suddenly dropped to | 6 pesos = $1 |

>>>You are required to show the accounts affected in both pesos and American dollars and to prepare a trial balance as at 12/31/18 for the purpose of incorporating the Chilean accounts on the New York books.

## P-12-2  (CPA EXAM, 5/68, PRAC. I, #3)

Copra Trading Co. established a foreign Branch Office on Arpoc Cay in 1960 to purchase local products for resale by the Home Office and to sell Company products.

You were engaged to examine the Company's financial statements for the year ended Dec. 31, 1967, and engaged a chartered professional accountant in Arpoc to examine the Branch Office accounts. He reported that the Branch accounts were fairly stated in pesos, the local currency, except a franchise fee and any possible adjustments required by the Home Office accounting procedures were not recorded. Trial balances for both the Branch Office and Home Office appear below.

### COPRA TRADING COMPANY AND BRANCH OFFICE
### TRIAL BALANCES
### AT DECEMBER 31, 1967

| Debits | Branch Office Trial Balance (in Pesos) | Home Office Trial Balance (in Dollars) |
|---|---|---|
| Cash | 110,000 | $   90,000 |
| Trade Accounts Receivable | 140,000 | 160,000 |
| Branch Current Account | | 10,000 |
| Inventory | 80,000++ | 510,000++ |
| Prepaid Expenses | 10,000 | 18,000 |
| Fixed Assets | 1,000,000 | 750,000 |
| Investment in Branch | | 12,000 |
| Purchases | 1,180,000 | 3,010,000 |
| Purchases from Branch | | 140,000 |
| Operating & General Expenses | 190,000 | 680,000 |
| Depreciation Expense | 100,000 | 50,000 |
| Total Debits | 2,810,000 | $5,430,000 |
| | | |
| Credits | | |
| Allowance for Depreciation | 650,000 | $  350,000 |
| Current Liabilities | 220,000 | 240,000 |
| Home Office Current Account | 30,000 | |

| Long-Term Indebtedness | 230,000 | 200,000 |
|---|---|---|
| Capital Stock | | 300,000 |
| Retained Earnings | | 145,000++ |
| Sales | 1,680,000 | 4,035,000 |
| Sales to Branch | | 160,000 |
| Total Credits | 2,810,000 | $5,430,000 |

++at January 1, 1967

Your examination disclosed the following information:

1. The peso was devalued July 1, 1967, from 4 pesos per $1 to 5 pesos per $1. The former rate of exchange had been in effect since 1959.

2. A billing of $4,000 was included in the Branch Current Account covering a shipment of merchandise made on Dec. 29, 1967, which was not received or recorded by the Branch in 1967. Sales to the Branch are marked up 33-1/3% and shipped F.O.B. Home Office. Branch sales to Home Office are made at Branch cost.

3. The Branch had a beginning and ending inventory on hand valued at 80,000 pesos of which 1/2 at each date had been purchased from the Home Office. The Home Office had an inventory at Dec. 31, 1967 valued at $520,000.

4. The Investment in Branch is the unamortized portion of a $15,000 fee paid in Jan. 1966 to a U.S. firm for marketing research for the Branch. Currency restrictions prevented the Branch from paying the fee, which was paid by the Home Office. The Home Office agreed to take merchandise in repayment over a 5-year period during which the fee is to be amortized.

5. The Branch incurred its long-term indebtedness in 1962 to finance its most recent purchase of fixed assets.

6. The government of Arpoc imposes a franchise fee of 10 pesos per 100 pesos of net income of the Branch in exchange for certain exclusive trading rights granted. The fee is payable each May 1 for the preceding calendar year's trading rights and had not been recorded by the Branch at Dec. 31.

**Required**:

Prepare a worksheet to present the combined income statement and combined balance sheet of Copra Trading Co. and its foreign Branch Office with all amounts stated in U.S. dollars. Formal statements and journal entries are not required. Supporting computations must be in good form. Number the worksheet adjusting and elimination entries.

**P-12-3    (CPA EXAM, 5/27, PRAC. I, #1)**

The Arlington Silk Mills incorporated a selling company in France, as of Jan. 1, 1926, to take over the assets and liabilities of their Paris office at that date, which were as follows:

                              Assets
Cash                                                Fcs.    134,000
Accounts Receivable                                         680,000
Merchandise at invoice price plus freight, etc.           1,050,000
Furniture and Fixtures                                       40,000
                                                    Fcs. 1,904,000

                            Liabilities
Accounts Payable                                    Fcs.     23,800
Arlington Silk Mills--Current Account                     1,780,200
Capital Stock                                               100,000
                                                    Fcs. 1,904,000


The exchange rate at Jan. 1, 1926, was 3.70 cents to the franc.
During the year, merchandise costing $160,000 was shipped by
the Arlington Silk Mills and billed at 10% above cost, and remittances amounting to 5,000,000 francs were made by the French
company, the details being as follows:

| Merchandise Invoiced | Remittances |
|---|---|
| 1/16.....$30,000 @ .0373 | 2/20.....Fcs. 500,000 @ .0356 |
| 3/27..... 20,000 @ .0342 | 6/12..... 1,000,000 @ .0287 |
| 5/6...... 50,000 @ .0324 | 7/10..... 800,000 @ .0254 |
| 8/14..... 40,000 @ .0275 | 8/28..... 1,000,000 @ .0284 |
| 10/16.... 36,000 @ .0286 | 11/27.... 700,000 @ .0360 |
|  | 12/12.... 1,000,000 @ .0379 |
| $176,000 | Fcs.5,000,000 |

The trial balance of the French company at Dec. 31, 1926, forwarded to the American company, was as follows:

| Account | Dr. | Cr. |
|---|---|---|
| Sales |  | Fcs. 7,730,000.00 |
| Merchandise Purchased | Fcs. 5,645,581.46 |  |
| Merchandise Inventory | 1,050,000.00 |  |
| Freight Charges | 580,000.00 |  |
| Warehouse Charges | 213,000.00 |  |
| Salaries | 474,000.00 |  |
| General Expenses | 306,000.00 |  |
| Selling Expenses | 117,000.00 |  |
| Accounts Receivable | 1,610,000.00 |  |
| Cash | 284,000.00 |  |
| Furniture and Fixtures | 50,000.00 |  |
| Accounts Payable |  | 73,800.00 |
| Arlington Silk Mills |  | 2,425,781.46 |
| Capital Stock |  | 100,000.00 |
|  | Fcs.10,329,581.46 | Fcs.10,329,581.46 |

The inventory at the end of the year amounted to 1,412,000
francs, which included freight charges, etc., of 140,000
francs, the exchange rate at that date being 3.90 cents to the
franc.

**Required:**
Prepare a balance sheet and profit and loss account, in dollars, for consolidation with the accounts of the American company and submit the journal entries necessary for the purpose on the books of the company.

**P-12-4   (CPA EXAM, 5/32, PRAC. I, #7)**
The Products Co., Ltd., Canada, keeps its records on a nominal dollar basis, and presents the following balance sheet as at Dec. 31, 1930:

### Assets

| | |
|---|---:|
| Cash | $ 10,000 |
| Accounts Receivable | 300,000 |
| Inventories | 250,000 |
| Fixed Assets (U.S. dollar cost at date of acquisition) | 100,000 |
| | $660,000 |

### Liabilities

| | | |
|---|---:|---:|
| Notes Payable | | $ 15,000 |
| Accounts Payable | | 150,000 |
| Due to Parent Company (U.S. dollars) | | 200,000 |
| Capital | | 150,000 |
| Surplus: | | |
| Beginning of year | $ 25,000 | |
| Profit for year | 120,000 | 145,000 |
| | | $660,000 |

You are requested to convert this statement to a U.S. currency basis for consolidation with the parent company's balance sheet. Assume that the Canadian dollar is worth $.80 in U.S. funds. Explain your treatment of each item. The following information is available:
 Accounts Receivable--all Canadian funds
 Notes Payable--all Canadian funds
 Accounts Payable--$30,000 payable in Canadian funds and
  $120,000 in United States funds
 Inventories--
  Raw material purchased in Canadian funds = $ 20,000
  Raw material purchased in U.S. funds =     $100,000
  Goods in process =                         $130,000
  This item includes material purchased both in United States and Canada, with labor performed in Canada. The total purchases for the year average approximately 85% from U.S. and 15% Canadian. The labor cost approximates 13% of the cost of materials.
Assume no intercompany profit on materials purchased from the parent company.

## P-12-5  (CPA EXAM, 5/34, PRAC. II, #2)

From the following balance sheets and income accounts of the Universal Machinery Co. and its Canadian subsidiary company, prepare a consolidated balance sheet and income account and submit the working papers relative thereto:

### UNIVERSAL MACHINERY COMPANY
### BALANCE SHEET
### DECEMBER 31, 1932

#### Assets

| | |
|---|---:|
| Land | $ 130,000 |
| Buildings and Equipment | 400,000 |
| Investments in Universal Machinery Co. of Canada, Ltd. | 200,000 |
| Advances to Universal Machinery Co. of Canada, Ltd. | 30,000 |
| Investment in stock of Universal Machinery Co.-- 500 shares at cost | 10,000 |
| Inventories | 260,000 |
| Accounts Receivable | 240,000 |
| Cash | 150,000 |
| Deferred Charges | 25,000 |
| | $1,445,000 |

#### Liabilities

| | | |
|---|---:|---:|
| Capital Stock: | | |
| Common, no par value, 10,000 shares outstanding | | $1,000,000 |
| Reserves for Depreciation | | 110,000 |
| Accounts Payable | | 185,000 |
| Surplus: | | |
| Balance January 1, 1932 | $140,000 | |
| Net Profit for Year | 70,000 | |
| | $210,000 | |
| Dividends Paid--$6 a share | 60,000 | |
| | | $ 150,000 |
| Balance December 31, 1932 | | $1,445,000 |

### UNIVERSAL MACHINERY COMPANY OF CANADA, LTD.
### BALANCE SHEET
### DECEMBER 31, 1932

(Accounts stated in Canadian currency)

#### Assets

| | |
|---|---:|
| Land | $ 55,000 |
| Buildings and Equipment | 130,000 |
| Inventories | 80,000 |
| Accounts Receivable | 60,000 |
| Cash | 50,000 |
| Deferred Charges | 5,000 |
| | $380,000 |

Liabilities

Capital Stock:
Common, $100 par value, 2,000 shares outstanding    $200,000
Reserves for Depreciation                               30,000
Accounts Payable                                        50,000
Universal Machinery Company--Advances                   30,000
                                                      $310,000

Surplus:
Balance January 1, 1932              $100,000
Net Profit for Year                    20,000
                                     $120,000
Dividend Paid                          50,000
Balance December 31, 1932                            $ 70,000
                                                     $380,000

INCOME ACCOUNT FOR THE YEAR 1932

|  | Universal Machinery Company | Universal Machinery Company of Canada, Ltd. |
|---|---|---|
| Net profit from operations | $47,000 | $25,000 |
| Depreciation @ 5% of buildings & equipment at Jan. 1, 1932 | 20,000 | 5,000 |
|  | $27,000 | $20,000 |
| Miscellaneous Income: |  |  |
| Dividend received from Universal Machinery Co. of Canada, Ltd. | $50,000 |  |
| Dividend on Universal Machinery stock held as an investment | 3,000 |  |
|  | $53,000 |  |
|  | $80,000 |  |
| Provision for federal income taxes | $10,000 |  |
| Net profit for year | $70,000 | $20,000 |

(1) The Canadian dollar was quoted at 90 cents on Dec. 31, 1932, and at par on Jan. 1, 1932. The average rate for the year was 95 cents.

(2) The investment of the Universal Machinery Co. in the real estate, plant and equipment of the Canadian company at Jan. 1, 1932, amounted to $155,000 U.S. currency.

(3) Additions to the real estate and plant of the Canadian company during 1932 amounted to $30,000 Canadian currency.

(4) The question of income taxes need not be further considered.

## P-12-6  (CPA EXAM, 11/48, THEORY, #4)
The Inter-Continental Corp., with its home office in the U.S. and branches in foreign countries, prepares consolidated financial statements which reflect the assets and liabilities and the operating results in such locations. The accounts of the foreign branches are kept in the respective currencies of the countries in which they are situated.

a. Explain the basis of converting the statements prepared in foreign currencies for purposes of consolidation with that of the Home Office,with respect to each of the following items:
        Accounts Receivable--Trade Debtors
        Sales
        Factory Building
        Accrued Payroll
        Depreciation of Building
        Home Office Account
b. Explain the nature of any difference between the two sides of a foreign branch trial balance after it has been converted to the currency of the Home Office.

## P-12-7  (CPA EXAM, 11/58, PRAC. I, #2)

Trial balances as of Dec. 31, 1957, of the Parent Company and its two subsidiaries are shown below.

| | Parent Company | | Domestic Subsidiary | | Mexican Subsidiary (Pesos) | |
|---|---|---|---|---|---|---|
| | Dr. | Cr. | Dr. | Cr. | Dr. | Cr. |
| Cash | $ 10,000 | | $ 1,500 | | P 10,000 | |
| A/R--Trade | 30,000 | | 8,000 | | 35,000 | |
| A/R--Merchandise in Transit to Domestic Subsidiary | 4,000 | | | | | |
| Inventories | 20,000 | | | | 83,000 | |
| Investments at cost: | | | | | | |
| Domestic Subsidiary, 900 shares acquired 12/31/56 | 9,000 | | | | | |
| Foreign Subsidiary, 1,000 shares acquired 12/31/56 | 12,000 | | | | | |
| Fixed Assets | 45,000 | | 3,500 | | 175,000 | |
| Goodwill | | | 2,000 | | | |
| Cost of Sales | 300,000 | | 15,000 | | 300,000 | |
| Depreciation | 3,000 | | 200 | | 7,000 | |
| Taxes | 15,000 | | 400 | | 15,000 | |
| Selling Expenses | 42,000 | | 2,400 | | 27,000 | |
| Administrative & General Exp. | 35,000 | | 2,000 | | 18,000 | |
| Dividends declared | | | 1,000 | | | |
| Sales--Trade | | 400,000 | | 21,000 | | 381,000 |
| Sales--Domestic Subsidiary | | 10,000 | | | | |
| Accounts Payable--Trade | | 25,000 | | | | 7,000 |
| Dividends Payable | | | | 1,000 | | |
| Long-Term Debt due 1/1/60 | | | | | | 100,000 |
| Reserve for Depreciation | | 15,000 | | 2,000 | | 75,000 |
| Capital Stock | | 50,000 | | ++10,000 | | ++100,000 |
| Surplus 1/1/57 | | 25,000 | | 2,000 | | 7,000 |
| | $525,000 | $525,000 | $36,000 | $36,000 | P670,000 | P670,000 |

++1,000 shares issued and outstanding

## Data:
In April 1957 the Mexican peso was devalued from U.S. $.12 (the prevailing rate of exchange on Dec. 31, 1956) to $.08 (which was also the prevailing rate of exchange on Dec. 31, 1957).

## Required:
Prepare working trial balance in U.S. dollars for the Mexican subsidiary.

## P-12-8 (CPA EXAM, 5/65, PRAC. I, #2)

The Wiend Corp. acquired the Dieck Corp. on Jan. 1, 1963, by the purchase at book value of all outstanding capital stock. The Dieck Corp. is located in a Central American country whose monetary unit is the peso. Dieck's accounting records were continued without change; a trial balance, in pesos, of the balance sheet accounts at the purchase date follows:

### THE DIECK CORPORATION
### TRIAL BALANCE (IN PESOS)
### JANUARY 1, 1963

|  | Debit | Credit |
|---|---|---|
| Cash | P 3,000 | |
| Accounts Receivable | 5,000 | |
| Inventories | 32,000 | |
| Machinery and Equipment | 204,000 | |
| Allowance for Depreciation | | P 42,000 |
| Accounts Payable | | 81,400 |
| Capital Stock | | 50,000 |
| Retained Earnings | | 70,600 |
| | P 244,000 | P 244,000 |

The Dieck Corporation's trial balance, in pesos, at December 31, 1964, follows:

### THE DIECK CORPORATION
### TRIAL BALANCE (IN PESOS)
### DECEMBER 31, 1964

|  | Debit | Credit |
|---|---|---|
| Cash | P 25,000 | |
| Accounts Receivable | 20,000 | |
| Allowance for Bad Debts | | P 500 |
| Due from Wiend Corporation | 30,000 | |
| Inventories, December 31, 1964 | 110,000 | |
| Prepaid Expenses | 3,000 | |
| Machinery and Equipment | 210,000 | |
| Allowance for Depreciation | | 79,900 |
| Accounts Payable | | 22,000 |
| Income Taxes Payable | | 40,000 |
| Notes Payable | | 60,000 |
| Capital Stock | | 50,000 |
| Retained Earnings | | 100,600 |
| Sales--Domestic | | 170,000 |
| Sales--Foreign | | 200,000 |
| Cost of Sales | 207,600 | |
| Depreciation | 22,400 | |
| Selling and Administration Expenses | 60,000 | |
| Gain on Sale of Assets | | 5,000 |
| Provision for Income Taxes | 40,000 | |
| | P 728,000 | P 728,000 |

The following additional information is available:
1. All of the Dieck Corporation's export sales are made to its parent company and are accumulated in the account, Sales-- Foreign. The balance in the account, due from the Wiend Corp., is the total of unpaid invoices. All foreign sales are billed in U.S. dollars. The reciprocal accounts on the parent company's books show total 1964 purchases as $471,000 and the total of unpaid invoices as $70,500.
2. Depreciation is computed by the straight-line method over a ten-year life for all depreciable assets. Machinery costing P20,000 was purchased on Dec. 31, 1963, and no depreciation was recorded for this machinery in 1963. There have been no other depreciable assets acquired since Jan. 1, 1963, and no assets are fully depreciated.
3. Certain assets that were in the inventory of fixed assets at Jan. 1, 1963, were sold on Dec. 31, 1964. For 1964 a full year's depreciation was recorded before the assets were removed from the books. Information regarding the sale follows:

| | |
|---|---|
| Cost of Assets | P14,000 |
| Accumulated Depreciation | 4,900 |
| Net Book Value | P 9,100 |
| Proceeds of Sale | 14,100 |
| Gain on Sales | P 5,000 |

4. Notes payable are long-term obligations that were incurred on December 31, 1963.
5. No entries have been made in the Retained Earnings account of the subsidiary since its acquisition other than the net income for 1963. The Retained Earnings account at Dec. 31 1963, was converted to $212,000.
6. The prevailing rates of exchange follow:

| | Dollars per Peso |
|---|---|
| January 1, 1963 | 2.00 |
| 1963 average | 2.10 |
| December 31, 1963 | 2.20 |
| 1964 average | 2.30 |
| December 31, 1964 | 2.40 |

**Required**:
Prepare a worksheet to convert the Dec. 31, 1964, trial balance of The Dieck Corp. from peso to dollars. The worksheet should show the unconverted trial balance, the conversion rate, and the converted trial balance. (Do not extend the trial balance to statement columns. Supporting schedules should be in good form.)

**P-12-9**
The London Co., Ltd., a British corporation, received a loan from the Barclay Bank of London on June 30, 1983, in the sum of 1,000,000 German Marks (DM). On Dec. 31, 1983, payment was made on 200,000 DM of the notes. At the end of the fiscal year, June

30, 1984, the balance due of 800,000 DM remains unpaid. The
exchange rates for DM are as follows:

|  |  |
|---|---|
| June 30, 1983: | 1 DM = .20 Ł |
| December 31, 1983 | 1 DM = .19 Ł |
| June 30, 1984 | 1 DM = .21 Ł |

**Required**:
Prepare entries in general journal form to record the transactions on June 30, 1983, and on Dec. 31, 1983. Draft a schedule
to show the carrying amount of the note as of June 30, 1984
adjusted for the exchange fluctuation, and the journal entry
for the exchange fluctuation.

## P-12-10

The U.S. Multinational Corp. created The Paris Corp. in France
as a subsidiary on Jan. 1, 1982. The Balance Sheet of the Paris
Corp. as of Dec. 31, 1982, was as follows:

| ASSETS: | FF Balances | LIABILITIES: | FF Balances |
|---|---|---|---|
| Cash & Receivables | 50,000 | Accounts Payable | 25,000 |
| Inventory | 60,000 | Long-Term Debt | 50,000 |
| Net Fixed Assets | 100,000 | Capital Stock | 70,000 |
|  |  | Retained Earnings | 65,000 |
| TOTAL ASSETS | 210,000 | TOTAL LIAB. & EQUITY | 210,000 |

The fixed assets were acquired on January 1, 1982. The exchange
rates were as follows:     *Franc is appreciating in relation to US $*

|  |  |
|---|---|
| On January 1, 1982: | $1 U.S. = 5 FF |
| On December 31, 1982: | $1 U.S. = 4.5 FF |
| Average Historical Rates for Inventory: | $1 U.S. = 4.7 FF |
| Average Historical Rates for Retained Earnings: | $1 U.S. = 4.8 FF |

**Required**:
Construct a 3-column worksheet showing the account balances,
translation to U.S. dollars under FASB #8, and the translation
to U.S. dollars under FASB #52, and the disposition of the Exchange Gain or Loss.

## P-12-11

The London Co., Ltd., a British corporation, entered into a
contract for the purchase of equipment on July 1, 1983, in the
sum of $500,000. The equipment was to be paid for on Dec. 31,
1983. On July 1, 1983, the London Co. purchased a forward exchange contract to fully hedge the foreign currency commitment.
The relevant rates of exchange were as follows:

| July 1, 1983: | Spot Rate = | $1 U.S. = Ł .52 |
|---|---|---|
|  | Forward Rate, 6 months = | $1 U.S. = Ł .51 |
| July 31, 1983 (balance sheet date): |  |  |
|  | SpotRate = | $1 U.S. = Ł .54 |

*If revalued, they have liability)*
*So they have a loss deferred.*
*Will have no impact since hedged*
*+ ups + downs will cancel out.*

*$ has gone up*
*$ is the foreign*
*currency*

**Required**:
Prepare a schedule showing
   a. the deferred gain on the forward exchange contract as of the balance sheet date; and *but a deferred gain / is a deferred loss from Br perspective*
   b. discount on the forward exchange contract as of the balance sheet date.
   c. How should the gain be handled on the books?
   d. In what alternative ways may the discount be handled?

<h2 style="text-align:center">CASES</h2>

### CASE-12-1 (CPA EXAM, 5/25, PRAC. I, #5)

In the course of an examination of the accounts of a corporation having two foreign branches operated through subsidiary companies, the accounts of which are consolidated with those of the parent company, you are given the following comparative balance sheets of the two branches -- one in Great Britain, the other in France:

**BRITISH BALANCE SHEET**

| Assets | 1923 | 1922 |
|---|---|---|
| ++Fixed Assets | £ 5,000 | £ 4,500 |
| Current Assets | 20,000 | 19,500 |
| Deferred Charges | 1,000 | 1,000 |
| | £26,000 | £25,000 |
| **Liabilities** | | |
| Current Liabilities | £ 8,000 | £ 8,000 |
| Capital Stock | 5,000 | 5,000 |
| Surplus | 13,000 | 12,000 |
| | £26,000 | £25,000 |

     ++No additions to fixed assets were made from
       the date of incorporation to Dec. 31, 1922.

The investment in the capital stock of the British company is carried on the books of the head office at $24,300 representing the value at the rate of exchange current at the date of incorporation. The rate of exchange as at the end of 1922 was 4.50 and at the end of 1923, 4.20.

**FRENCH BALANCE SHEET**

| Assets | 1923 | 1922 |
|---|---|---|
| ++Fixed Assets | Fr.500,000 | Fr.475,000 |
| Current Assets | 180,000 | 165,000 |
| | Fr.680,000 | Fr.635,000 |
| **Liabilities** | | |
| Current Liabilities | Fr. 40,000 | Fr. 30,000 |
| Capital Stock | 600,000 | 600,000 |
| Surplus | 40,000 | 5,000 |
| | Fr.680,000 | Fr.635,000 |

     ++No additions to fixed assets were made from
       the date of incorporation to Dec. 31, 1922.

The investment in the capital stock of the French company is carried on the books of the head office at $114,000, representing the value at the rate of exchange current at the date of incorporation. The rate of exchange at the end of 1923 was .04 cents and that of 1922 was .06 cents.

The current liabilities of the foreign corporations include, in the case of the British company, ⅃ 1,000 and in that of the French company 5,000 francs, due to the head office at the end of each year.

The treasurer of the company proposes to convert each item on the 1923 balance sheet at the rate of exchange current at the close of that year and to use these figures in preparing the consolidated balance sheet. The difference between the value at which the capital stock of the foreign subsidiaries is carried on the books of the head office and the net worth thus determined, he proposes to add to the consolidated fixed assets.

Criticize or justify the proposed method of handling these accounts. Explain and illustrate what method, if any, you would consider preferable.

### CASE-12-2 (CPA EXAM, 11/33, PRAC. II, #2)

You are appointed by the board of directors to examine the accounts relating to the assets and liabilities of The Goodenough Corp., New York, and its domestic subsidiaries, as at Dec. 31, 1932. Prepare a consolidated balance sheet as at Dec. 31, 1932.

The Goodenough Corp. has one foreign subsidiary (wholly owned), the accounts of which have been examined by another firm of accountants whose report, which has been submitted to you, is as follows:

### THE BRITISH GOODENOUGH COMPANY, LTD.
### BALANCE SHEET AS AT DECEMBER 31, 1932

LIABILITIES

| | | |
|---|---:|---:|
| Share Capital: | | |
| Authorized: | | |
| 600,000 shares of ⅃ 1 each | ⅃ 600,000 | |
| Issued: | | |
| 600,000 shares of ⅃ 1 each | | ⅃ 600,000 |
| Current Trade Liabilities | | 78,500 |
| Reserve for Income Tax Payable: | | |
| Due January 1, 1933 | | 90,000 |
| Due January 1, 1934 | | 74,500 |
| Indebtedness to Affiliated Company | | 2,500 |
| Profit-and-Loss Appropriation Account: | | |
| Balance January 1, 1932 | ⅃ 12,145 | |
| Net Profit for Year | 298,000 | |
| | ⅃ 310,145 | |
| Less: Dividends | 200,000 | 110,145 |
| TOTAL | | ⅃ 955,645 |

NOTE:   There is a liability  not  included in this balance sheet
        in respect to machinery which this  company has agreed to
        purchase.

### ASSETS

| | |
|---|---:|
| Property, Plant and Equipment at Cost, Less Reserve of Ŀ 250,000 for Depreciation | Ŀ 450,000 |
| Stock on Hand at Cost | 170,000 |
| Customers' Accounts Receivable, Less Reserve of Ŀ 10,000 for Bad and Doubtful Accounts | 250,383 |
| Cash at Bank and In Hand (Of this amount the sum of Ŀ 80,000 is earmarked for a guarantee given on behalf of the company) | 85,262 |
| TOTAL | Ŀ 955,645 |

### Auditor's Report

We report to the members  that  we have examined the  above
balance sheet with the books of the company and have obtained all
the information and explanation we have required.We are not satisfied  as  to the adequacy of the  reserve for bad  and doubtful
accounts.

Subject to this remark  we are of opinion that the  balance
sheet is properly drawn up so as to  exhibit  a true and correct
view of the state of the  company's affairs as at Dec. 31, 1932,
according to the best of our information  and explanations given
to us, and as shown by the books of the company.

A.B.C. and Co.

London, England,
January 31, 1933

You have communicated with the English  company  and  with  its
auditors and have ascertained the following:

a. With the  exception of machinery  costing Ŀ 100,000, which
was installed in Nov. 1932 when the  average  rate  of  exchange
was $3.50, the property, plant and equipment were acquired when
the company was  formed, when the rate  of exchange was  at par
($4.86).  The established policy  of the company is to charge a
full  year's depreciation on additions  made  in  the  first  6
months of any year and to charge depreciation commencing Jan. 1
of  the  year  following the year of addition on additions  made
in the second six months of any year.

b. Of the  stock on hand Ŀ 160,000 represents goods purchased
from The Goodenough Corp.,  the parent company, at  its cost of
$540,000 plus freight to England of $36,000 paid by  the parent
company at the time of shipment. Cost of the remaining Ŀ 10,000
of British stock approximated  market at Dec. 31, 1932.  (Note:
There had been no change in freight rates to Dec. 31, 1932, and
the rate of exchange on that date was $3.40.  You find that The
Goodenough Corp. had reduced the cost  of  its inventory by 10%

in order to reflect the lower of cost or market value as at Dec. 31, 1932. The directors have agreed that for the purpose of the consolidated balance sheet the inventory as a whole should be valued at the lower of cost or market value.)

c. The auditors of The British Goodenough Co. feel that an additional reserve of ₤ 50,000 should be provided against the accounts receivable. Neither the directors of the British company nor those of the American corporation can agree that any further reserve is necessary.

d. The note on the British balance sheet refers to machinery which it has been agreed shall be purchased from the parent company at its cost less depreciation -- net $120,000.

As a result of your examination of the accounts of The Goodenough Corp. and its domestic subsidiaries, you have prepared the following consolidated trial balance as at Dec. 31, 1932, together with your list of audit notes:

CONSOLIDATED TRIAL BALANCE
AS AT DECEMBER 31, 1932

| | DR. | CR. |
|---|---|---|
| Cash in Banks and On Hand | $ 880,000 | |
| U.S. Government Securities | 504,000 | |
| Accounts Receivable | 1,910,000 | |
| Reserve for Doubtful Accounts | | $ 210,000 |
| Inventories | 1,325,000 | |
| Property, Plant and Equipment | 6,600,000 | |
| Reserve for Depreciation | | 2,500,000 |
| Company's Own Shares | 275,000 | |
| Due from The British Goodenough Co.,Ltd. | 10,000 | |
| Accounts Payable and Accrued Liabilities | | 2,320,000 |
| Provision for Federal Income Tax | | 275,000 |
| Dividend of 50 cents a share, payable Jan. 2, 1933 | | 500,000 |
| Capital Stock--common, no par, authorized and issued | | 5,000,000 |
| Surplus | | 3,615,000 |
| Investment in Subsidiary Company at Cost | 2,916,000 | |
| | $14,420,000 | $14,420,000 |

Audit Notes

1. Cash includes a special deposit of $100,000 in the Y Bank & Trust Company. This deposit is subordinate to claims of all other depositors but not to claims of stockholders.

2. The government securities are stated at cost, although the market value at Dec. 31, 1932, was only $490,000. However, on Feb. 28, 1933, the market value had recovered to $507,000.

3. The intercompany account is debited or credited at the actual rate of exchange on the date of each transaction, but the balance at the end of each month is adjusted on the books of the parent company by a debit or credit to profit-and-loss

account, to bring the account to the basis of a fixed rate of exchange, viz., $4. The actual dollar cost of the Ł 2,500 shown on the British company's balance sheet was $9,250. There were no items in transit.

4. In addition to customers' accounts the following items are included in accounts receivable:

    (a)  Loan to officer $87,000

    (b)  Customers' accounts aggregating $370,000, on which payments are deferred by special arrangement until 1934; $50,000 of reserve is allotted to these accounts.

5. Company's own shares represent 7,000 shares carried at cost and held for resale to employees under employees' stock purchase plan. The market value on Dec. 31, 1932, was $3 per share but the directors will not agree to writing down this asset to market value.

6. The life of Mr. B., President, is insured for $1,000,000 in favor of the company and the policy at Dec. 31, 1932, had a cash-surrender value of $75,000. All premiums have been charged to expense, as the directors object to setting up cash-surrender value on the books.

7. There are claims pending against the company which are estimated not to exceed $150,000.

8. The property, plant and equipment accounts are stated at cost.

9. Accounts payable include employees' savings deposits, $392,000.

# PART II

## SECTION THREE

## MICRO INTERNATIONAL MANAGERIAL CONTROL ACCOUNTING

# International Investment Accounting

## INTERNATIONAL MANAGERIAL ACCOUNTING CONTROL*

### #13-1...Nature of International Managerial Control Accounting

Having concluded the discussion of International Financial Accounting Theory and Practice, we turn to the control aspects of international accounting through managerial accounting techniques. Managerial accounting on the international level includes all matters of managerial accounting on the domestic basis. However, because of the natural risks inherent in foreign operations, there are three additional aspects of international managerial accounting, viz., (1) foreign investment decision-making; (2) foreign working capital management; and (3) the foreign intercorporate transfer system, which involves sales and purchases between the parent company and its foreign subsidiaries, as well as between the foreign subsidiaries themselves.

Because managerial accounting on the domestic basis is treated as part of the regular accounting curriculum, it will not be repeated here. In this chapter attention will be focused on international investment accounting, followed by international working capital management accounting in Chap. 14 and international intercorporate transaction accounting in Chap.15.

## M/N/C FOREIGN INVESTMENT DECISION-MAKING

### #13-2....Foreign Investment Decision Procedure

In foreign investment decision-making, international accountants are giving more and more attention to control of foreign exchange risks, projection of exchange risks, as well as

------
*See Summary of Footnote References -- #13-1 thru #13-24

risk evaluation methods in continuing international operations.
While each of these segments of the international management
accounting process is important, of great significance is the
efficient integration of the investment decision-making into
the multinational firm's control program. This objective is
accomplished by using the established foreign exchange risk
which is designed to integrate the financial control and management accounting reporting system.

The financial statement model is used to budget the amount
at risk. This allows an analysis and evaluation of the projected risk. There are two steps involved: (1) measurement of the
amount of risk, and (2) evaluation of the risk in conjunction
with the financial control and budgeting function, referred to
as EXCHANGE EXPOSURE ANALYSIS.

#13-3....Measuring the Amount At Risk

The first management step in the information system involves
the measurement of the amount at risk--a financial reporting
and budgeting problem. Local currency budgets must be prepared,
viz., balance sheet, owners' equity, earnings, and financial
assets flow.

#13-4....Risk Measurement Procedural Steps

First the amount of capital investment in plant and equipment must be determined in the capital expenditure budget. The
capital expenditure amounts are then integrated into the pro
forma balance sheets and income statements for the life of the
investment. The income statements show not only the depreciation charges but also the funds flow from internal operations.
External equity capital sources are shown on the separate pro
forma statements of owners' equity. Then the sources and disposition of funds must be determined in budgeting the foreign
exchange exposure. Various relationships and trends must be
assumed in projecting the amount at risk. Underlying assumptions must be made in preparing the local currency pro forma
financial statements, and each assumption must be carefully
weighted in the final determination of local currency budgets.

To illustrate the procedure, assume that the U.S. Corp. is
desirous of making a foreign investment in Canada. The following data is projected:
(1) An initial investment of $6,000 U.S. ($1 U.S. = $1 Canadi-
    an) is made through equipment import and foreign exchange
    transfer
(2) Local financing is available for the initial financial
    assets
(3) The plant investment has a 5-year life with no salvage
    value and straight-line depreciation is used

(4) Dividends are paid in local currency at year-end for the amount of local currency earnings
(5) Local currency net profit margin of 20% is maintained before depreciation charges
(6) Canada has a 10% annual inflation rate; costs rise with inflation and selling prices are increased as costs rise
(7) During the 5-year span, production and inventories are stable, and output is readily sold at the established prices
(8) Repatriation of capital is available at the end of the 5th year

Figure 13-1 reveals the pro forma Balance Sheet, Owners' Equity, Income Statement, and Financial Flow Statement for the projected foreign investment. The procedure for constructing these is detailed below:

## (I) BALANCE SHEETS

It is necessary first to construct the Investment Balance Sheet in order to project the balance sheet items for the proposed 5-year length of the venture. The Investment Balance Sheet components are (1) Financial Assets; (2) Inventory; (3) Net Plant Assets; (4) Total Assets (12/31); (5) Financial Liabilities; (6) Equity Capital; and (7) Total Equities (12/31). The following figures are to be plugged for these seven items:

(6) Investment in Equity Capital = $6,000
(3) Investment in Net Plant Assets = $5,000
(1) Balance of Investment in Financial Assets = $1,000
(5) Financial Liabilities = $1,000
(7) Total Equities = $1,000 + $6,000 = $7,000
(4) Total Assets = $7,000
(2) Inventory = <Total Assets - (Financial Assets + Net Plant)> = $1,000

The resultant Investment Balance Sheet is as follows:

| | | | |
|---|---|---|---|
| Financial Assets | 1,000 | Financial Lia- | |
| Inventory | 1,000 | bilities | 1,000 |
| Net Plant Assets | 5,000 | Equity Capital | 6,000 |
| TOTAL ASSETS | 7,000 | TOTAL EQUITIES | 7,000 |

The procedure to be followed would then be:
From the Investment Balance Sheet as a springboard can be projected the 5-year period balance sheet by components: The Financial Liabilities remain constant at $1,000 as does the Equity Capital at $6,000, making Total Equities $7,000, which will make the Total Assets $7,000 also. The Net Plant Assets to be depreciated straight line at 20% over 5 years would reduce at the rate of $1,000 per year. The Inventory would increase at the rate of 10% per year. The Financial Assets figure would

then be forced by subtracting  the sum of the Inventory and Net
Plant Assets from the Total Assets.

## (II) INCOME STATEMENTS

Sales for the 1st year are projected at $10,000.  With a 10%
increase yearly, sales for the next 4  years would  be $11,000;
$12,100;  $13,310; and $14,641.

Beginning Inventory as projected  on the balance sheet for 5
years is $1,000; $1,100;  $1,210;  $1,331; $1,464.

Projected  Gross Profit or the Funds Flow From Operations is
20%  of  sales.  For the  five years  the numbers  are  $2,000;
$2,200;  $2,420;  $2,662; and $2,928.

Depreciation is at the rate of $1,000 per year.  The Net In-
come for  5 years  would be $1,000;  $1,200;  $1,420;  $1,662; and
$1,928.

Net Cost of Sales is sales minus gross profit, $10,000 minus
$2,000, or $8,000 the  first year which increases  by 10%  each
year to $8,800 the 2nd year; $9,680  the  3rd year; $10,648 the
4th year; and $11,713 the 5th year.

The Ending Inventory is the Beginning Inventory of  the next
year as above.  The numbers for the five years would be $1,100;
$1,210;  $1,331;  $1,464;  and  completely  disposed  of in the
fifth year.

The Net Cost of Sales plus Ending Inventories gives us Goods
Available for Sale for the  five  years:   $9,100;  $10,010;
$11,011;  $12,112; and $11,713.

Net Income is Projected Gross  Profit above minus  depreciation.  The numbers for the five  years would be $1,000; $1,200;
$1,420;  $1,662;  and $1,928.  All  are distributed as Dividends
for each year.

## (III) OWNERS' EQUITY STATEMENTS

Since all  earned  income is  distributed as  dividends, the
Owners' Equity balance for each year would be the Investment of
$6,000 as shown in Figure 13-1.

## (IV) STATEMENTS OF FINANCIAL ASSETS FLOW

Begins with the Funds  Flow From Operations which appears on
the  Income Statement as Projected Gross Profit which is 20% of
Sales. To the Funds Flow From Operations is added the Beginning
Inventory (on Income Statement), and from which is deducted the
Ending Inventory (on Income Statement) to derive the Operations
Financial Assets  Flow.  The Dividends representing the Net In-
come are then deducted  resulting in the Increase  in Financial
Assets which is added to the beginning Financial Assets balance
to derive the Dec. 31 Ending Net Financial Assets.

After carrying  out the above procedures, the pro forma Balance  Sheets, Income  Statements, Owners' Equity, and Financial

FIGURE 13-1
## BUDGETED LOCAL CURRENCY FINANCIAL STATEMENTS

| | | | Year | | | |
|---|---|---|---|---|---|---|
| | 0 | 1 | 2 | 3 | 4 | 5 |
| *Balance Sheets* | | | | | | |
| Financial assets | 1,000 | 1,900 | 2,790 | 3,669 | 4,536 | – |
| Inventory | 1,000 | 1,100 | 1,210 | 1,331 | 1,464 | – |
| Plant assets (net) | 5,000 | 4,000 | 3,000 | 2,000 | 1,000 | – |
| Total assets, December 31 | 7,000 | 7,000 | 7,000 | 7,000 | 7,000 | – |
| Financial liabilities | 1,000 | 1,000 | 1,000 | 1,000 | 1,000 | – |
| Equity capital | 6,000 | 6,000 | 6,000 | 6,000 | 6,000 | – |
| Retained earnings | – | – | – | – | – | – |
| Total equities, December 31 | 7,000 | 7,000 | 7,000 | 7,000 | 7,000 | – |
| *Statements of Owners' Equity* | | | | | | |
| Balance, January 1 | – | 6,000 | 6,000 | 6,000 | 6,000 | 6,000 |
| Capital contribution | 6,000 | – | – | – | – | (6,000) |
| Add earnings | – | 1,000 | 1,200 | 1,420 | 1,662 | 1,928 |
| Less dividends | – | (1,000) | (1,200) | (1,420) | (1,662) | (1,928) |
| Balance, December 31 | 6,000 | 6,000 | 6,000 | 6,000 | 6,000 | – |
| *Earnings Statements* | | | | | | |
| Sales | – | 10,000 | 11,000 | 12,100 | 13,310 | 14,641 |
| Less cost of sales | | | | | | |
| Beginning inventory | – | 1,000 | 1,100 | 1,210 | 1,331 | 1,464 |
| Costs and expenses | 1,000 | 8,100 | 8,910 | 9,801 | 10,781 | 10,249 |
| Less ending inventory | (1,000) | (1,100) | (1,210) | (1,331) | (1,464) | – |
| Net cost of sales | – | 8,000 | 8,800 | 9,680 | 10,648 | 11,713 |
| Funds flow from operations | – | 2,000 | 2,200 | 2,420 | 2,662 | 2,928 |
| Less depreciation | – | (1,000) | (1,000) | (1,000) | (1,000) | (1,000) |
| Net income | – | 1,000 | 1,200 | 1,420 | 1,662 | 1,928 |
| *Statements of Financial Assets Flow* | | | | | | |
| Funds flow from operations | – | 2,000 | 2,200 | 2,420 | 2,662 | 2,928 |
| Add beginning inventory | – | 1,000 | 1,100 | 1,210 | 1,331 | 1,464 |
| Less ending inventory | (1,000) | (1,100) | (1,210) | (1,331) | (1,464) | – |
| Financial assets flow from operations | (1,000) | 1,900 | 2,090 | 2,299 | 2,529 | 4,392 |
| Add capital investments | 6,000 | – | – | – | – | (6,000) |
| Less capital expenditures | (5,000) | – | – | – | – | – |
| Dividends | – | (1,000) | (1,200) | (1,420) | (1,662) | (1,928) |
| Increase in financial assets | – | 900 | 890 | 879 | 867 | (3,536) |
| Financial assets, January 1 | – | – | 900 | 1,790 | 2,669 | 3,536 |
| Financial assets, December 31 | – | 900 | 1,790 | 2,669 | 3,536 | – |

Flow Statements for the projected foreign investment  would result as combined in Figure 13-1.

## #13-5....Projecting the Risk Itself

After  making the financial statement projections, the  next
information system requirement is  the measurement  of the risk
itself.   The real risk has  two parameters: (1) the  estimated
size  of future devaluations or revaluations,  and (2) the projected timing of these occurrences. Economic and political considerations  are the determinants.   The key  economic factor is
the inflation rate, particularly in relation to the parent company's economy. Besides internal political factors, such external factors as  changes in the rules of the international monetary system must be  weighted.  Nevertheless the  risk  must be
projected in order to provide the exchange rates to be used for
translation of budgeted statements in the local currency.

## #13-6....Translated Statements Exposure

The next step in  the procedure is to  construct  translated
statements that will  expose  the amounts of foreign  exchange
gains and losses. Assuming an exchange rate which is constantly
decreasing  at an annual rate of 10%, the translation would result in the BUDGETED TRANSLATED DOLLAR FINANCIAL STATEMENTS  in
Figure 13-2, expressed in Canadian currency.
The procedure  for constructing the Budgeted Translated Dollar Financial Statements is detailed below:

### (I) BALANCE SHEETS
The 100%  constant  decrease in the exchange  rate is applicable only to the Financial Assets and Liabilities.
Financial Assets. Thus for the 1st year, financial assets of
$1,900 divided  by 110% equals $1,727; the 2nd  year, financial
assets  of $2,790 divided by 110%  derives  $2,536 which  would
again be divided by 110%, resulting in $2,306; the  third year,
financial assets of $3,669 divided by 110% equals  $3,335 which
in turn is divided by 110% giving $3,032, which again is divid-
ed by 110% equaling  $2,756; the  fourth year, financial assets
of $4,536 would be divided by applying the 110% to the  declin-
ing figure 4 times, to arrive at $3,098.
Financial Liabilities.  For the 1st year,  the $1,000 finan-
cial liabilities divided by 110% becomes $909; the 2nd year the
$909 balance  divided by 110% gives $827; the  $827  divided by
110%  gives $751 for the 3rd year; and the $751 balance divided
by 110% is $683 for the 4th year.
Inventory would be constant at $1,000 for all 4 years.
Plant Assets would decrease at the rate of $1,000 per year.
Equity Capital remains constant at $6,000 all 4 years.

Retained Earnings. The total assets for the 4 years are
$6,727; $6,306; $5,756; and $5,098. Deducting the sum of the
Financial Liabilities and Equity Capital from the Total Assets
results in negative Retained Earnings for each of the 4 years
of $182; $521; $995; and $1,585.

## (II) STATEMENT OF OWNERS' EQUITY

The beginning first year balance of Owners' Equity was the
$6,000 investment. Deducting the $182 negative Retained Earnings from the $6,000 gives an Ending Owners' Equity balance of
$5,818, the beginning balance for the 2nd year. Dividends paid
in the 1st year of $1,000 divided by 110% makes net dividends
of $909, which when added to the $5,818 balance is $6,727. Thus
$6,727 minus $6,000 represents earnings of $727 for the 1st
year. For the 2nd year the negative retained earnings of $521
is deducted from the $6,000 investment leaving an Owners' Equi-
ty balance of $5,479; dividends of $1,200 divided by 110% +
110% make net dividends of $992, which added to the $5,479 balance totals $6,471. Deducting the beginning balance of $5,818
from the total of $6,471 gives an earnings figure of $653 for
the 2nd year. For the 3rd year the negative retained earnings
of $995 is deducted from the $6,000 investment leaving an Owners' Equity balance of $5,005; dividends of $1,420 divided by
110% + 110% + 110% make net dividends of $1,067, which added to
the $5,005 balance totals $6,072. Deducting the beginning balance of $5,479 from the $6,072 gives an earnings figure of $593
for the 3rd year. For the 4th year the negative retained earnings of $1,585 is deducted from the $6,000 investment leaving
an Owners' Equity balance of $4,415; dividends of $1,662 divided by 110% + 110% + 110% + 110% make net dividends of $1,135
which added to the $4,415 totals $5,550. Deducting the beginning balance of $5,005 from the $5,550 gives an earnings figure
of $545 for the 4th year.

The 5th year beginning balance of Owners' Equity is $4,415
from which dividends of $1,928 are paid divided by 110% + 110%
+ 110% + 110% + 110% making net dividends of $1,197, which when
deducted from $4,415 leaves an Equity balance of $3,218. Since
the payout for the conclusion of the investment came to $3,726,
the earnings for the 5th year were $3,796 minus $3,218 or $508.

## (III) INCOME STATEMENTS

The figures for all items on the Income Statement would be
constant for all 5 years. Both the Beginning and Ending Inventories would be $1,000 and the Depreciation would also be
$1,000 per year. The Sales of $10,000 per year constant would
be divided by an average 105% to set Sales at $9,524 for the 5
years. The Cost and Expenses of Sales in the sum of $8,100
would also be divided by 105% average to derive the figure of
$7,714. The Funds Flow From Operations (Projected Gross Profit)

## FIGURE 13-2
## BUDGETED TRANSLATED DOLLAR FINANCIAL STATEMENTS

| | | | Year | | | |
|---|---|---|---|---|---|---|
| | 0 | 1 | 2 | 3 | 4 | 5 |
| ***Balance Sheets*** | | | | | | |
| Financial assets | 1,000 | 1,727 | 2,306 | 2,756 | 3,098 | — |
| Inventory | 1,000 | 1,000 | 1,000 | 1,000 | 1,000 | — |
| Plant assets (net) | 5,000 | 4,000 | 3,000 | 2,000 | 1,000 | — |
| Total assets, December 31 | 7,000 | 6,727 | 6,306 | 5,756 | 5,098 | — |
| Financial liabilities | 1,000 | 909 | 827 | 751 | 683 | — |
| Equity capital | 6,000 | 6,000 | 6,000 | 6,000 | 6,000 | — |
| Retained earnings | — | (182) | (521) | (995) | (1,585) | — |
| Total equities, December 31 | 7,000 | 6,727 | 6,306 | 5,756 | 5,098 | — |
| ***Statements of Owners' Equity*** | | | | | | |
| Balance, January 1 | — | 6,000 | 5,818 | 5,479 | 5,005 | 4,415 |
| Capital contribution | 6,000 | — | — | — | — | (3,726) |
| Add earnings | — | 727 | 653 | 593 | 545 | 508 |
| Less dividends | — | (909) | (992) | (1,067) | (1,135) | (1,197) |
| Balance, December 31 | 6,000 | 5,818 | 5,479 | 5,005 | 4,415 | — |
| ***Earnings Statements*** | | | | | | |
| Sales | — | 9,524 | 9,524 | 9,524 | 9,524 | 9,524 |
| Less cost of sales | | | | | | |
| Beginning inventory | — | 1,000 | 1,000 | 1,000 | 1,000 | 1,000 |
| Costs and expenses | 1,000 | 7,714 | 7,714 | 7,714 | 7,714 | 6,668 |
| Less ending inventory | (1,000) | (1,000) | (1,000) | (1,000) | (1,000) | — |

| | | | | | |
|---|---|---|---|---|---|
| Net cost of sales | 7,714 | 7,714 | 7,714 | 7,714 | 7,668 |
| Funds flow from operations | 1,810 | 1,810 | 1,810 | 1,810 | 1,856 |
| Less depreciation | (1,000) | (1,000) | (1,000) | (1,000) | (1,000) |
| Less exchange losses | (83) | (157) | (217) | (265) | (348) |
| Net income | 727 | 653 | 593 | 545 | 508 |

*Statement of Financial Assets Flow*

| | | | | | |
|---|---|---|---|---|---|
| Funds flow from operations | 1,810 | 1,810 | 1,810 | 1,810 | 1,856 |
| Add beginning inventory | 1,000 | 1,000 | 1,000 | 1,000 | 1,000 |
| Less ending inventory | (1,000) | (1,000) | (1,000) | (1,000) | – |
| Financial assets flow from operations | 1,810 | 1,810 | 1,810 | 1,810 | 2,856 |
| Add capital investments | 6,000 | – | – | – | – |
| Less capital expenditures | (5,000) | – | – | – | (3,726) |
| Dividends | (909) | (992) | (1,067) | (1,135) | (1,197) |
| Increase in net financial assets | 901 | 818 | 743 | 675 | (2,067) |
| Add financial assets, January 1 | – | 818 | 1,479 | 2,005 | 2,415 |
| Less exchange losses | (83) | (157) | (217) | (265) | (348) |
| Financial assets, December 1 | 818 | 1,479 | 2,005 | 2,415 | – |

would be $2,000 divided by 110%, or $1,810. The Net Cost of
Sales is $7,714 (Beginning Inventory plus Cost and Expenses,
less Ending Inventory). The Funds Flow From Operations is the
Sales of $9,524 minus the Net Cost of Sales of $7,714, or
$1,810; deducting the Depreciation of $1,000 gives Net Income
Before Exchange Fluctuation of $810. The earnings for the 5
years respectively as shown on the Owners' Equity Statement
were $727; $653; $593; $545; and $508. Deducting these 5 fig-
ures from the Net Profit of $810 gives us the Exchange Losses
as follows: $83; $157; $217; $265; and $348.

### (IV) STATEMENTS OF FINANCIAL ASSETS FLOW

The Funds Flow From Operations is constant at $1,810 for
four years, and $1,856 for the fifth year.

Beginning Inventory is constant at $1,000 for 5 years.

Ending Inventory is constant at $1,000 for four years, with
no balance for the fifth year.

Dividends as per Owners' Equity Statement are $909; $992;
$1,067; $1,135; and $1,197.

Increase in Financial Assets is Funds Flow From Operations
of $1,810 minus the dividends -- $901; $818; $743; and $675.
For the fifth year the Operation Financial Asset Flow of
$2,856 is deducted from the return of Capital Investment of
$3,726 giving $870, which when added to the dividends of $1,197
gives a total decrease in Financial Assets of $2,067.

When the Increase in Financial Assets is added to the Beginning Balance of Financial Assets, the total Financial Assets
for year one are $901 plus zero, or $901, from which is deducted the Exchange Loss of $83, leaving the Ending Financial Asset
Balance of $818 (year two beginning balance). The $818 Beginning Balance added to the increase of $818 in Financial Assets
totals $1,636 from which is deducted the $157 Exchange Loss,
leaving an Ending Balance of Financial Assets for year two of
$1,479 (year three beg. bal.). The $1,479 Beg. Bal. added to
the increase of $743 in Financial Assets equals $2,222 from
which is deducted the $217 Exchange Loss, leaving an Ending
Bal. of Financial Assets for year three of $2,005 (year four
beg. bal.). The $2,005 Beg. Bal. added to the increase of $675
in Financial Assets totals $2,680 from which is deducted the
$265 Exchange Loss, leaving an Ending Bal. of Financial Assets
for year four of $2,415 (year five beg. bal.). From the $2,415
Beg. Bal. is deducted the Decrease in Financial Assets of
$2,067 as computed above, leaving a balance of $348, which is
expunged as an Exchange Loss for year five of $348.

After carrying out the above procedure, the BUDGETED TRANS-
LATED DOLLAR FINANCIAL STATEMENTS (Balance Sheet, Owners' Equi-
ty, Income Statement, and Financial Assets Flow) are shown in
Figure 13-2.

### #13-7....Remedies for Reducing Foreign Exchange Risk Loss

With fluctuating exchange rates, exchange gains and losses will result in the course of the translation process. The amounts of these gains and losses appear as separate items on the translated dollar income statements and the statements of financial assets flow. It should be noted that the exchange losses will continually be increasing unless remedies are sought to stop their flow. Common remedies for reducing the foreign exchange risk losses are local borrowing, use of forward exchange contracts, prompt remittance of excess cash, and use of cash to purchase goods for resale or use. Also the selling price may be increased to compensate for higher costs. However, it should not normally be raised merely as an additional source of absorbing exchange losses. Such a pricing policy would be self-defeating because it would be contributing to the inflationary trend. If possible, the exchange losses should be hedged or budgeted in the normal operations management. Thus the budgeting of the future risk is the key to a successful foreign exchange risk control program.

## EXCHANGE EXPOSURE ANALYSIS

### #13-8....Evaluation of the Risk

The next step in the information system is the evaluation of the risk in conjunction with the financial control and budgeting function. The amount of the exchange gain or loss depends on the firm's definition of exchange risk exposure, of which there may be different international views.

### #13-9....Exchange Exposure Definition

The exchange exposure in a foreign currency is the amount of net financial assets. in that currency. Inventories may or may not be included with the financial assets. To differentiate between inventory exclusion and inclusion, exposure may be categorized as MINIMUM EXPOSURE (excluding inventories) or MAXIMUM EXPOSURE (including inventories) as pointed out in the NAA Research Report #36, 1960, entitled MANAGEMENT ACCOUNTING PROBLEMS IN FOREIGN OPERATIONS, page 66.

Alternatively, exchange exposure can be presented inversely. Thus maximum exposure can be defined as total net foreign assets less net foreign fixed and intangible assets; and minimum exchange exposure is the maximum exposure less the inventories. Thus minimum exchange exposure is not often defined as equal to net financial assets, and maximum exposure would include the inventories. Ideally the maximum exposure should be zero. To

avoid losses on  devaluation,  zero exposure must exist  at all
times, not only at the reporting date.  This means that any inflow must be as carefully managed as are the amounts on hand.

## ANALYSIS AND EVALUATION OF THE PROJECTED RISK

### #13-10...Accomplishment of the Control

The control is accomplished through a proper analysis of the
potential losses.  An effective  analytical means  is to  use a
funds flow approach, under which  we first translate the annual
funds  statements  at  rates expected to prevail at the time of
the transactions.  Then the statements are again translated but
at the expected year-end closing rates. The differences derived
from this dual translation show the sources  of  exchange gains
and losses.  They also  show the importance of  budgeting both
the source and use of funds.  An illustration of the  STATEMENT
OF ANALYSIS OF FOREIGN EXCHANGE LOSSES ON A BUDGETED INVESTMENT
VENTURE is presented in Figure 13-3.  The decisive elements for
the evaluation of the project are (1) the cost of placing capital, (2) the  availability  and cost of financing, and (3)  the
availability and cost of foreign currency remittances.

### #13-11...Cost of Placing Capital

Capital placement in  a foreign  country can be accomplished
through (a) foreign  exchange transfer, (b) investment in kind,
(c) reinvestment of earnings, and (d) loans or  other nonequity
financing.

### #13-12...Foreign Exchange Transfer

The cost of the  investment  is determined  by  the exchange
rate  at  which the  foreign capital  investment is transacted.
This cost  must be compared with the long-run return on investment.  The return on investment is measured by the ultimate repatriation of  that  investment plus  the dollar withdrawals of
earnings.  The investor assumes the risk of exchange rate fluctuations from the time of investment until the time of earnings
withdrawal or capital repatriation.

### #13-13...Investment in Kind

If  an investment is accomplished  by supplying equipment or
machinery, the exchange rate existing at the time of investment
is generally considered to be the determinant of the investment
cost.

#13-14...Reinvestment of Earnings

Also when earnings are reinvested, the capital cost is calculated at the exchange rate prevailing at the time of earnings
realization.   Again, this cost must be compared with the ultimate rate  of return that is  expected to  be derived  from the
added investment.

#13-15...Loans or Other Nonequity Financing

A relatively  less  costly method of investment may be local
currency borrowing, particularly if the loans are used to minimize the amount of net financial assets at risk. Sometimes such
loans may be obtained at preferential or guaranteed rates which
are registered  with the appropriate local governmental  agency
or the  Central Bank.  The exchange rate may be higher than the
free  market rate.  Also the interest rate on such loans may be
higher than interest rates available in other countries.   But,
in the  face  of possible  devaluations, the added cost  may be
offset by potential savings in foreign exchange losses.

#13-16...Sources of Financing

Loans appear to be  the most widespread source of  funds  in
the international scene and there are a large  number of potential sources, both external and internal.  A list  of financing
sources would include:

**EXTERNAL SOURCES**

Letters of Credit
Commercial Bank Loans:
     parent country  bank;  local  country  bank; third country
     bank; branch of an  international bank; international bank
     group or consortium
Credit Through Government Institutions:
     export-import bank;  agency for international development;
     overseas private investment  corp.;  foreign credit insur-
     ance association
Eurodollar or Asian-Dollar Financing:
     commercial bank  intermediary; foreign finance subsidiary;
     Eurobond and Euroequities market
Financing Through World Bank Group:
     International  Bank  for  Reconstruction and  Development;
     International  Development Corporation; International  Fi-
     nance Corporation
Credit Through Development Banks:
     regional development banks (e.g.,  Inter-American Develop-
     ment Bank);  national development banks;  private develop-

# FIGURE 13-3

## BUDGETED INVESTMENT VENTURE ANALYSIS
## OF FOREIGN EXCHANGE LOSSES

| | Per Local Currency Statement | Per Budgeted Trans. Statement | Closing Rate Transl. | Exchange Gain or Loss ($) |
|---|---|---|---|---|
| **FIRST YEAR:** | | | | |
| Funds Flow From Operations | 2,000 | 1,810 | 1,818 | 8 |
| Add: Beginning Inventory | 1,000 | 1,000 | 909 | ( 91) |
| Less: Ending Inventory | (1,100) | (1,000) | (1,000) | -- |
| Financial Assets Flow | 1,900 | 1,810 | 1,727 | ( 83) |
| Less: Dividends | (1,000) | ( 909) | ( 909) | -- |
| Exchange Loss | -- | ( 83) | -- | 83 |
| Financial Assets, Dec. 31 | 900 | 818 | 818 | -- |
| **SECOND YEAR:** | | | | |
| Funds Flow From Operations | 2,200 | 1,810 | 1,818 | 8 |
| Add: Beginning Inventory | 1,100 | 1,000 | 909 | ( 91) |
| Less: Ending Inventory | (1,210) | (1,000) | (1,000) | -- |
| Financial Assets Flow | 2,090 | 1,810 | 1,727 | ( 83) |
| Less: Dividends | (1,200) | ( 992) | ( 992) | -- |
| Exchange Loss | -- | ( 157) | -- | 157 |
| Net | 890 | 661 | 735 | 74 |
| Add: Financial Assets, Jan. 1 | 900 | 818 | 744 | ( 74) |
| Financial Assets, Dec. 31 | 1,790 | 1,479 | 1,479 | -- |

## THIRD YEAR:

| | | | | |
|---|---|---|---|---|
| Funds Flow From Operations | 2,420 | 1,810 | 1,818 | 8 |
| Add: Beginning Inventory | 1,210 | 1,000 | 909 | (91) |
| Less: Ending Inventory | (1,331) | (1,000) | (1,000) | -- |
| Financial Assets Flow | 2,299 | 1,810 | 1,727 | (83) |
| Add: Financial Assets, Jan. 1 | 1,790 | 1,479 | 1,345 | (134) |
| Total | 4,089 | 3,289 | 3,072 | (217) |
| Less: Dividends | (1,420) | (1,067) | (1,067) | -- |
| Exchange Loss | -- | ( 217) | -- | 217 |
| Financial Assets, Dec. 31 | 2,669 | 2,005 | 2,005 | -- |

## FOURTH YEAR:

| | | | | |
|---|---|---|---|---|
| Funds Flow From Operations | 2,662 | 1,810 | 1,818 | 8 |
| Add: Beginning Inventory | 1,331 | 1,000 | 909 | (91) |
| Less: Ending Inventory | (1,464) | (1,000) | (1,000) | -- |
| Financial Assets Flow | 2,529 | 1,810 | 1,727 | (83) |
| Add: Financial Assets, Jan. 1 | 2,669 | 2,005 | 1,823 | (182) |
| Total | 5,198 | 3,815 | 3,550 | (265) |
| Less: Dividends | (1,662) | (1,135) | (1,135) | -- |
| Exchange Loss | -- | ( 265) | -- | 265 |
| Financial Assets, Dec. 31 | 3,536 | 2,415 | 2,415 | -- |

## FIFTH YEAR:

| | | | | |
|---|---|---|---|---|
| Funds Flow From Operations | 2,928 | 1,856 | 1,818 | ( 38) |
| Add: Beginning Inventory | 1,464 | 1,000 | 909 | ( 91) |
| Financial Assets Flow | 4,392 | 2,856 | 2,727 | (129) |
| Add: Financial Assets, Jan. 1 | 3,536 | 2,415 | 2,196 | (219) |
| Total | 7,928 | 5,271 | 4,923 | (348) |
| Less: Dividends | (1,928) | (1,197) | (1,197) | -- |
| Exchange Losses | -- | ( 348) | -- | 348 |
| Balances | 6,000 | 3,726 | 3,726 | -- |
| Less: Capital Repatriation | (6,000) | (3,726) | (3,726) | -- |
| Financial Assets, Dec. 31 | -- | -- | -- | -- |

ment banks (e.g., Atlantic Development Group for Latin
   America)
Equity Financing:
   parent company; subsidiary; joint ventures

## INTERNAL SOURCES

Generated from operations (retained earnings before deduction
   for depreciation and depletion)
Extended from the parent, through informal cash advances, formal loans, or supplied inventory
Extended from another subsidiary or an affiliate by advancing
   cash or supplying inventory

When loans are utilized, the interest cost must be measured
against the projected savings on foreign exchange devaluations.

## #13-17...Swap Transactions

Another source of financing is known as SWAP TRANSACTIONS.
Swaps are temporary financial operations most commonly arranged
between a parent company and its foreign subsidiary. Under such
an arrangement, U.S. Dollars would be delivered to the Central
Bank or, in some cases a private bank, in a foreign country
where the subsidiary is located. Then local currency is received by the foreign subsidiary from the bank at a special rate of
exchange, with the understanding that at the end of a specified
period of time the reverse operation will take place--i.e., the
bank will return the amount of dollars it received in exchange
for the amount of local currency it had delivered.

## #13-18...Accounting For Swap Transactions

To illustrate the accounting for swap transactions, assume
that the MNC Corp. engages in the following swap arrangements
with the French Central Bank for its Paris subsidiary:

3/1/81   Delivers 10,000 U.S. Dollars to the foreign central
         bank in a Swap Agreement to receive a return of the
         dollars upon return of the 40,000 French Francs to be
         received from the bank on 3/1/81; on 3/1/81 the spot
         rate was 1 FF = U.S. 25 cents.
3/1/81   Received 40,000 FF under the Swap Agreement that the
         $10,000 U.S. will be returned upon the delivery of the
         40,000 French Francs by 3/1/83.
3/1/82   The French Franc was devalued to 20 cents U.S.
3/1/83   The MNC Corp. delivered 40,000 French Francs to the
         Central Bank in fulfillment of the Swap Agreement and
         received the $10,000 return.

The journal entries for the foregoing transactions would be as follows:

```
3/1/81   U.S. Currency Swap Rcvble     10,000
              Cash                                10,000
         (To record the delivery of
         dollars to French Central
         Bank in Swap Agreement to
         receive dollars upon return
         of FF received within 2 yrs)

3/1/81   FF Frgn. Exchg. (40,000
                     x $.25)           10,000
              FF Swap Payable                     10,000
         (To record receipt of 40,000
         FF at exchange rate of 4 FF
         = $1 under the swap agree-
         ment that U.S. $10,000 will
         be returned on delivery of
         40,000 FF within 2 yrs)

3/1/82   Frgn.Exchg.Gain & Loss(40,000
                     x $.05)            2,000
              FF Frgn. Exchg.                      2,000
         (To record loss on foreign
         exchange due to devaluation)

3/1/82   FF Swap Payable               2,000
              Frgn.Exchg.Gain & Loss               2,000
         (To record revaluation of
         Swap Pybl to current ex-
         change rate and record gain
         due to devaluation resulting
         in decrease in Swap Pybl)

3/1/83   FF Swap Pybl(40,000 x $.20)   8,000
              FF Foreign Exchange                  8,000
         (To record delivery of
         40,000 FF in fulfillment
         of Swap Agreement)

3/1/83   Cash                          10,000
              U.S.Currency Swap Rcvbl             10,000
         (To record receipt of dollars
         from delivery of FF at ex-
         change rate agreed to in
         Swap Agreement)
```

To view the effect of a devaluation, the above shows such effect one year later. This illustrates that a Swap Agreement can protect the foreign assets in the case of devaluation. Whether the foreign assets are in cash or in another financial asset form makes no difference.

### #13-19...Nature of Swap Accounts

The Swap Receivable account is a dollar receivable whereas the Swap Payable account is due in the foreign local currency. It would seem that these amounts are separate assets and liabilities on the balance sheet. However, in consolidated financial statements, corporations generally offset one against the other. In this manner the Swap Payable is a type of contingent liability, similar in nature to discounted notes receivable. If the amounts are material, full disclosure would be necessary. When swap arrangements are utilized, the interest cost must be measured against the projected savings on foreign exchange devaluations.

### #13-20...Equity Capital Sources

Finally, equity capital sources may be utilized. The availability of local equity financing will depend on the sophistication of the foreign capital market, the availability of local private capital, and the opportunities in joint ventures. The cost of equity capital must be weighted against the advantages of local participation.

### #13-21...Cost and Availability of Foreign Currency Remittances

In some countries local financing may not be obtainable. Where this is the case, the cost of the capital investment is directly related to the cost and availability of foreign currency remittances. The foremost thought before investment is the feasibility of the earnings withdrawals. Coupled with the availability of the withdrawals is the exchange rate at which the remittances can be transacted. The next consideration is the availability and cost of the eventual repatriation.

### #13-22...Blocked Earnings

The lack of availability of remittances causes blocked earnings. If such blocked amounts cannot be invested locally at favorable rates of return, currency devaluations will cause a continuing erosion of the investment. A way to avoid blocked foreign exchange is for the parent company to obtain foreign currency remittances through exports by simply having the foreign subsidiary imports billed in the parent company's currency. However, such procedures are often prohibited, or at least regulated, by a country's trade laws. Finally, availability of remittances will depend on the earnings potential and working capital position of the foreign enterprise.

## THE FINAL DECISION PROCESS

### #13-23...Additional Management Accounting Techniques

After the available resources and projected return are determined, the investment decision model can be adjusted accordingly. If more than one alternative appears feasible, additional management accounting techniques should be used. First, the
projected flows of funds initially and as repatriated could be
adjusted to present values, with discounting at a normal rate
of return. Furthermore probabilities could be established for
each of the alternatives. The final solution may be an optional
multiple approach to financing.

### #13-24...Use of Financial Statement Model for Budgeting

The use of the financial statement model for budgeting the
amount of risk allows a view of the outcome based on certain
assumptions. By formalizing this model, perhaps through a computer routine, the assumptions can be changed slightly for
testing the sensitivity of the outcomes to minor changes in the
assumed facts. Further, the model can be used to establish a
flexible budgeting system whereby changes in the environmental
factors can be analyzed. Once the final investment decision is
made with its assumed environmental criteria, the established
budget can be utilized for comparison with actual data accumulated over time. The investment decision-making model will then
serve also as a control device.

## NATIONS' CREDIT RISKS

### #13-25...Credit Ratings of World's Nations

A very important factor in foreign investment decision-making is the credit rating of the country in which operations are
projected. Regularly, the INSTITUTIONAL INVESTOR magazine com-
piles a list of how the various countries in the world rank as
credit risks. They are of the opinion that such a list of ratings is becoming crucial because of the growing world indebtedness and rising oil prices. The resulting list compiled is
called by it "the most comprehensive and representative samp-
ling of bankers' views on country credit worthiness ever compiled." The magazine indicated that "banks, no matter how big,
face a monumental task in compiling realistic assessments of
COUNTRY RISK, while more complete compilations by international
organizations like the International Monetary Fund are infrequently shared."

FIGURE 13-4
COUNTRY CREDIT RATINGS

| Rank | Country | Credit Rating | Rank | Country | Credit Rating |
|------|---------|---------------|------|---------|---------------|
| (1) | United States | 9.89 | (48) | Thailand | 5.47 |
| (2) | West Germany | 9.83 | (49) | India | 5.42 |
| (3) | Switzerland | 9.82 | (50) | Chile | 5.42 |
| (4) | Japan | 9.69 | (51) | Nigeria | 5.41 |
| (5) | Canada | 9.35 | (52) | Philippines | 5.37 |
| (6) | France | 9.11 | (53) | Israel | 5.37 |
| (7) | United Kingdom | 9.06 | (54) | Indonesia | 5.32 |
| (8) | Netherlands | 8.97 | (55) | Ecuador | 5.32 |
| (9) | Norway | 8.89 | (56) | Portugal | 5.20 |
| (10) | Australia | 8.77 | (57) | Oman | 5.20 |
| (11) | Belgium | 8.62 | (58) | Tunisia | 5.00 |
| (12) | Austria | 8.57 | (59) | Poland | 4.95 |
| (13) | Saudi Arabia | 8.54 | (60) | Ivory Coast | 4.82 |
| (14) | Sweden | 8.42 | (61) | Kenya | 4.56 |
| (15) | Kuwait | 7.93 | (62) | Panama | 4.55 |
| (16) | Singapore | 7.89 | (63) | Morocco | 4.55 |
| (17) | U. S. S. R. | 7.88 | (64) | Jordan | 4.47 |
| (18) | New Zealand | 7.82 | (65) | Costa Rica | 4.47 |
| (19) | Hong Kong | 7.73 | (66) | Paraguay | 4.34 |
| (20) | Denmark | 7.53 | (67) | Uruguay | 4.10 |
| (21) | Finland | 7.49 | (68) | Liberia | 4.07 |
| (22) | Italy | 7.38 | (69) | Cyprus | 3.94 |
| (23) | Ireland | 7.33 | (70) | Syria | 3.93 |
| (24) | Venezuela | 7.24 | (71) | Dominican Republic | 3.64 |
| (25) | Mexico | 7.18 | (72) | Iran | 3.62 |
| (26) | South Korea | 7.12 | (73) | Egypt | 3.39 |
| (27) | China | 7.11 | (74) | Gabon | 3.33 |
| (28) | Spain | 7.03 | (75) | Bolivia | 3.16 |
| (29) | Malaysia | 7.03 | (76) | Peru | 3.07 |
| (30) | United Arab Emirates | 6.62 | (77) | Senegal | 2.85 |
| (31) | Taiwan | 6.58 | (78) | Lebanon | 2.75 |
| (32) | Qatar | 6.58 | (79) | Pakistan | 2.63 |
| (33) | Brazil | 6.49 | (80) | Seychelles | 2.52 |
| (34) | Bahrain | 6.29 | (81) | Tanzania | 2.50 |
| (35) | Hungary | 6.26 | (82) | Jamaica | 2.40 |
| (36) | Czechoslovakia | 6.26 | (83) | Zimbabwe | 2.38 |
| (37) | Greece | 6.26 | (84) | Sierra Leone | 2.26 |
| (38) | Argentina | 6.24 | (85) | Angola | 2.16 |
| (39) | South Africa | 6.20 | (86) | Zambia | 2.07 |
| (40) | Colombia | 6.07 | (87) | Congo | 1.95 |
| (41) | Iraq | 6.04 | (88) | Sudan | 1.85 |
| (42) | Libya | 6.00 | (89) | Turkey | 1.48 |
| (43) | Algeria | 5.86 | (90) | Ethiopia | 1.38 |
| (44) | Iceland | 5.85 | (91) | Nicaragua | 1.04 |
| (45) | Trinidad and Tobago | 5.83 | (92) | Zaire | 0.98 |
| (46) | Yugoslavia | 5.75 | (93) | Uganda | 0.87 |
| (47) | Romania | 5.48 | | | |

Source: Adapted from a study by INSTITUTIONAL INVESTOR, 1979.

## #13-26...Compilation of Credit List

The list is updated every six months by polling 75-100 leading international banks, on  a confidential basis, asking  that
they  rate the countries by rank on a 1-to-100  scale, with one
representing the least creditworthy countries with the greatest
chance  of default,  and 100 indicating  the most  creditworthy
with least chance of default. Responses are weighted based on a
bank's degree of  world-wide exposure and sophistication of its
country analysis  system.  The magazine has indicated that with
some  countries,  resources (such as  oil and  gold  producers)
count heavily, and in some cases sentiment is a factor.
Figure 13-4 shows the top 93 countries (in 1979) in order of
rank, along with their respective credit ratings.

## #13-27...Comments on Ratings

In 1979, observations made by INSTITUTIONAL INVESTOR regarding some  of the ratings  that appear anomalous are that  Spain
and Portugal were relatively low because of political instability  and uncertainties and that Russia was 17th (below  Kuwait
and Singapore) despite its record of paying its bills on time.
A recent observation made by INSTITUTIONAL INVESTOR magazine
regarding the 1985 rating is  that the overall  rating  of 40.3
rose somewhat since  early 1984, a turnaround  that  ended four
years of steady deterioration of creditworthiness.  The driving
force  behind the current upward trend  is Eastern Europe.  In
contrast, the developed countries have recently remained totally unchanged.

### SUMMARY OF FOOTNOTE REFERENCES
(References are to Paragraph #'s)

#13-1 thru #13-24:   "International Managerial Accounting Control,"
    adapted from Norlin G.  Rueschhoff, INTERNATIONAL ACCOUNTING
    AND FINANCIAL REPORTING, 1976, Praeger  Publishers, Inc., by
    permission.
#13-9 NAA Research Report #36,   MANAGEMENT ACCOUNTING PROBLEMS IN
    FOREIGN OPERATIONS, 1960, p. 66
#13-25 INSTITUTIONAL INVESTOR, 1979

### BIBLIOGRAPHY

Antl, B.  "Swap Financing Techniques," EUROMONEY, London (1984)
Black, Fischer.  "The Ins and  Outs of Foreign Investments," FINAN-
    CIAL ANALYSTS JOURNAL, 34 (May-June 1978): 25-32
Bradford, Samuel R.  "Foreign Exchange Exposure," ACCOUNTANCY,  86

(September 1975): 74-78

"Country Risk," EUROMONEY (September 1982): 71

Fantl, Irving L. "Europe's Need: A Workable Capital Market," FINAN-
    CIAL EXECUTIVE, 44 (Sept. 1976): 22-30

Gray, S.J. "European Investment Analysis," ACCOUNTANCY, 88 (October
    1977): 92-101

Heckman, C.R. "Measuring Foreign Exchange Exposure," FINANCIAL
    ANALYSTS JOURNAL (Sept-Oct 1983): 59

Jucker, James and DeForo, Clovis. "The Selection of International
    Borrowing Sources," JOURNAL OF FINANCIAL AND QUANTITATIVE
    ANALYSIS, 10 (September 1975): 381-407

Kettell, Brian. "Foreign Exchange Exposure," ACCOUNTANCY, 89 (March
    1978): 83-89

Malkoff, Alan R. "Foreign Acquisition Analysis: A Suggested Ap-
    proach," MANAGEMENT ACCOUNTING, 60 (June 1979): 32-41

Richards, Ferry E. "The Multinational Corporation's Borrowing Deci-
    sion," MANAGEMENT ACCOUNTING, 57 (Feb. 1976): 51-52

Shapiro, Alan C. "Defining Exchange Risk," THE JOURNAL OF BUSINESS,
    50 (January 1977): 37-39

Soenen, Luc. "Foreign Exchange Exposure Management," MANAGEMENT
    INTERNATIONAL REVIEW, 19 (1979)(2): 31-38

Srinivasulu, S.L. "Classifying Foreign Exchange Exposure," FINAN-
    CIAL EXECUTIVE (February 1983): 36-44

Stockton, R.J. "Borrowing Foreign Currency," THE AUSTRALIAN AC-
    COUNTANT, 49 (December 1979): 769-773

## THEORY QUESTIONS
(Question Numbers are Keyed to Text Paragraph #'s)

#13-1  Discuss the nature of managerial control accounting on
       the international level and what additional aspects
       arise that do not exist in local managerial accounting.

#13-2  What is meant by Exchange Exposure Analysis and what two
       steps are involved in carrying it out?

#13-3  How is the first step of measuring the amount at risk
       effected?

#13-4  Outline the steps involved in the measurement of the
       risk.

#13-5  What are the two parameters involved in projecting the
       risk itself?

#13-9  Define the term EXCHANGE EXPOSURE.

#13-9  (a) Classify Exchange Exposure and define the classes.

#13-10 How is control of the risk accomplished?

#13-10 (a) What are the three decisive elements for the evalua-
       tion of a project?

#13-11 How can placement of capital in a foreign country be
       accomplished?

#13-12-15. Describe capital placement in a foreign country
       through (a) Foreign Exchange Transfer, (b) Investment in
       Kind, (c) Reinvestment of Earnings, and (d) Loans or

Other Nonequity Financing.
#13-16 Discuss the different sources of financing.
#13-17 Define Swap Transactions and explain how they serve as a source of financing.
#13-19 What are the nature of the Swap Receivable and Payable accounts?
#13-22 What are Blocked Earnings & what problems do they pose?
#13-25 What role does nations' credit risks pose in foreign investment decision making?
#13-27 Comment on the Country Credit Ratings compiled by INSTI-TUTIONAL INVESTORS magazine.

## EXERCISES

### EX-13-1 (CPA EXAM, 5/18, PRAC. I, #8)
You are called upon to advise a client who has large dealings, both buying and selling, with foreign countries, involving questions of foreign moneys and exchange. What general principles would guide you in advising him?

### EX-13-2 (CPA EXAM, 11/37, PRAC. II, #5)
John Smith borrowed 2,000,000 francs in Paris for 150 days at 3%, interest in the United States being at 5% (interest payable on due date of loan). The rate of exchange was $.06 on the date the loan was made and was $.061 on the date of repayment. Commission on purchase or sale of exchange was 1/20% for each transaction. The cable charge for each transfer of funds was $20.

How much did Mr. Smith save or lose by borrowing abroad at the lower interest rate? Submit the worksheet supporting your answer.

### EX-13-3
MULTIPLE CHOICE: Circle the answer which is least applicable.
1. The following items are quite important in the management of foreign exchange risk:
   a. The foreign inflation rate.
   b. The amount of depreciation on foreign plant.
   c. The availability of foreign currency remittances.
   d. The availability of local currency financing.
2. In the decision to borrow abroad, the following factors have direct effects in determining the cost or savings:
   a. The interest rate differential between the home country and the foreign country.
   b. The costs of currency conversions.
   c. The exchange rate fluctuations.
   d. The comparative inflation rates between the home country and the foreign country.

3. The availability of foreign equity financing in the host
country depends on:
  a. The opportunity for joint ventures.
  b. The number of credit institutions within the foreign econ-
     omy.
  c. The availability of local private capital.
  d. The sophistication of the foreign capital market.

## PROBLEMS

### P-13-1

The U.S. Co., a corporation, is contemplating making a foreign
investment in Australia, repatriation of which will be available at the end of 5 years. The current rate of exchange at the
original initial investment date was $1 U.S. = A $1. In attempting to measure the amount at risk, the following data is
projected:
  1. The initial investment through equipment import and foreign exchange transfer is U.S. $30,000;
  2. Local financing is available for initial financial assets;
  3. Plant investment has a 5-year life with no salvage value,
to be depreciated by the straight-line method;
  4. Dividends in local currency are paid at the year-end in
the amount of the local currency earnings;
  5. Profit margin of 20% in local currency is maintained before depreciation charges;
  6. The annual inflation rate in Australia is 10%, and costs
rise with the inflation rate; selling prices increase with
rise in costs;
  7. Production and inventories during the 5-year span are
stable, with output readily salable at the established prices.
  8. Additional data presented: Investment in: financial as-
sets--$5,000; net plant assets--$20,000; inventory--$10,000;
financial liabilities--$5,000; equity capital--$30,000; first-
year sales--$30,000; costs & expenses--$25,000. Sales and inventory have a 10% yearly increase.
**Required**:
From the foregoing data, draft pro forma Budgeted Local Currency Financial Statements, consisting of (a) Balance Sheets, (b)
Statements of Owners' Equity, (c) Income Statements, and (d)
Statements of Financial Assets Flow.

### P-13-2

Using the data in P-13-1 and assuming that the exchange rate is
constantly decreasing at an annual rate of 10%, construct
Translated Financial Statements consisting of (a) Balance
Sheets, (b) Statements of Owners' Equity, (c) Income Statements, (d) Statements of Financial Assets Flow, that will expose the amounts of foreign exchange gains and losses.

**P-13-3**

Using the data in the preceding two problems, draft a Statement of Analysis of Foreign Exchange Gains/Losses on Budgeted Investment Venture.

**P-13-4 (CPA EXAM, 5/33, PRAC. I, #4)**

From the following data, prepare entries for the corporation's books to record all exchange transactions, the exchange position, and profits realized. Show also what the result would have been had the exchange risk not been covered.

A United States corporation, owning the entire capital stock of a foreign company, sells its raw material to this company at cost. From this raw material the foreign company manufactures a certain product which it sells exclusively in its own country. It pays for the raw material bought, and remits the net profits as soon as they are realized in cash.

The unit of this foreign currency is the crown, worth sixty cents at par of exchange.

The rate of exchange declining, the customary measures are taken by the U.S. corporation to guard against exchange losses. These measures consist principally of selling forward the foreign currency to be collected. For this reason and purpose the company's costs and expenses, as well as the proceeds from its sales, must necessarily be determined as nearly as possible in advance.

Crowns are freely bought and sold in the U.S., there being no restriction by the foreign government on the transfer of domestic funds to other countries.

On Oct. 1, when the crown was selling at 30, the U.S. corporation shipped raw material which cost $30,000 and billed the foreign company for the equivalent of 100,000 crowns, payable Dec. 30.

It was estimated that all manufacturing, selling, administration and other expenses applicable to this venture would be 120,000 crowns and that the product would be all sold by Dec. 30 for 250,000 crowns. The estimate proved to be correct with one exception, viz.--the goods were actually sold and delivered Dec. 30 for 255,000 crowns, spot cash, f.o.b. factory.

The rate of exchange had in the meantime fallen to 20.

**P-13-5**

John Smith borrowed 1,000,000 guilders in Amsterdam for 180 days at 6%, interest in the United States being at 7% (interest payable on due date of loan). The rate of exchange was $.275 on the date the loan was made and was $.276 on the date of repayment. Commission on purchase or sale of exchange was 1/20% for each transaction. The cable charge for each transfer of funds was $30.

**Required**:
Prepare a schedule showing the amount of savings or loss derived by Mr. Smith's borrowing abroad at the lower interest rate.

**P-13-6**
On Jan. 1 the Mark Equip. Corp., a U.S. corporation, delivered $28,000 to the London bank and received Ł 10,000 under an agreement whereby the $28,000 would be returned upon the delivery of Ł 10,000 in six months. On May 1 the British pound was devalued to $2.40 = Ł 1. On June 30, Ł 10,000 was returned to the London bank by the Mark Corp.
**Required**:
Prepare journal entries to record the above transactions.

# International Working Capital Management Accounting *

#### #14-1....International Working Capital

As seen in Chap. 13, multinational enterprise control not only consists of the stewardship of global investments for an optimized return but also includes the management of the international working capital to assure its protection against exchange risk. The working capital management is further linked to international investment decision-making as previously discussed and also to multinational transfer administration to be discussed in the material following, and is integrated into the global information system of the firm.

#### #14-2....Constituency of Working Capital Management

Working capital management involves the international management of cash movements, the temporary investment of idle cash, control of inventories and trade receivables, and the direction of trade payables and other current liabilities including tax obligations. Such management is complex and must be handled in a systematic manner.

#### #14-3....Relation of Exchange Gains and Losses
####            (Exchange Risk Exposure) to Working Capital

In the international environment, the flow of working capital is affected by inflation, remittance restrictions, exchange rate fluctuations, business practices, and government regula-

------

*See Summary of Footnote References -- #14-1 thru #14-17

tions that are culturally different from those of the home
country. The criterion of the efficacy of working capital management decisions is the size of the exchange gains and losses,
the amount of which depends on the firm's definition of exchange risk exposure. Though there may be different international views as to its definition, the most common approach
presented herein coincides with the temporal approach to translation of foreign currency working capital.

## EXCHANGE EXPOSURE ANALYSIS

### #14-4....Exchange Exposure

The exchange exposure in a foreign currency is the amount of
net financial assets in that currency. Inventories may or may
not be included with the financial assets. To differentiate
between inventory exclusion and inclusion, exposure may be
classified as MINIMUM EXPOSURE (excluding inventories) and MAX-
IMUM EXPOSURE (including inventories). Alternatively, exchange
exposure can be presented inversely so that maximum exposure
can be defined as net foreign assets less net foreign fixed and
intangible assets, and minimum exposure is the maximum exposure
less the inventories.

### #14-5....Determination of Foreign Exchange Exposure

In order to determine the foreign exchange exposure in a
particular currency, it is necessary to separate the dollar
items from the other currency items on the local currency balance sheet. Two statements must be prepared: a Balance Sheet
Breakdown Statement and a Statement of Exchange Exposure. To
illustrate these, assume that the following data appears on the
records of the Canadian Corporation expressed in Canadian Dollars:

| | | | |
|---|---|---|---|
| Cash | 10,000 | Current Liabil. | 20,000 |
| Accts. Rcble | 12,000 | Long-Term Liabil. | 10,000 |
| Notes Rcble | 13,000 | U.S. $ Frgn Exchng | 2,500 |
| Inventories | 35,000 | Other Frgn Exchng | |
| Net Fixed | | (Currency U.S. $) | 300 |
| Assets | 20,000 | Due Home Office | |
| | | (U.S. $) | 1,000 |

The BALANCE SHEET BREAKDOWN STATEMENT, with the separation of
nonlocal currency items, appears as follows:

|  | Local Currency | U.S. $ | Other Currency $ |
|---|---|---|---|
| **ASSETS:** | | | |
| Cash | 10,000 | | |
| Foreign Exchange | | 2,500 | 300 |
| Accts. Rcble. | 12,000 | | |
| Notes Rcble | 13,000 | | |
| Inventories | 35,000 | | |
| Net Fixed Assets | 20,000 | | |
| TOTAL ASSETS | 90,000 | 2,500 | 300 |
| | | | |
| **LIABILITIES:** | | | |
| Current Liabil. | 20,000 | | |
| Long-Term Liabil. | 10,000 | | |
| Due Home Office | | 1,000 | |
| TOTAL LIABILITIES | 30,000 | 1,000 | |
| NET ASSETS | 60,000 | 1,500 | 300 |
| TOTAL LIABILITIES AND NET ASSETS | 90,000 | 2,500 | 300 |

The STATEMENT OF EXCHANGE EXPOSURE (two methods of calculating) resulting from the Balance Sheet Breakdown Statement would appear as follows:

### STATEMENT OF EXCHANGE EXPOSURE

|  | Local Currency | Other Foreign Currency U.S. $ |
|---|---|---|
| **FINANCIAL ASSETS:** | | |
| Cash | 10,000 | |
| Foreign Exchange | | 300 |
| Accounts Receivable | 12,000 | |
| Notes Receivable | 13,000 | |
| TOTAL FINANCIAL ASSETS | 35,000 | 300 |
| | | |
| Less: | | |
| **FINANCIAL LIABILITIES:** | | |
| Current Liabilities | 20,000 | |
| Long-Term Liabilities | 10,000 | |
| TOTAL FINANCIAL LIABILITIES | 30,000 | |
| MINIMUM EXPOSURE | 5,000 | 300 |
| Add: Inventories | 35,000 | |
| MAXIMUM EXPOSURE | 40,000 | 300 |

RECONCILIATION

| Item | Local Currency | Other Currency |
|---|---|---|
| NET ASSETS (Per Balance Sheet) | 60,000 | 300 |
| Less: Net Fixed Assets | 20,000 | |
| MAXIMUM EXPOSURE | 40,000 | 300 |
| Less: Inventories | 35,000 | |
| MINIMUM EXPOSURE | 5,000 | 300 |

Since prepaid expenses reduce the cash exposed, they are not included in the computation of exchange exposure. Besides manifesting the exposure to foreign exchange risk, further schedules showing the amounts of assets covered by forward exchange contracts may be presented. Daily records of quoted exchange rates may also be charted. Such charts help in determining the rates to be used in translating the financial statements.

#14-6....Analysis of Exchange Gains and Losses

There are two broad approaches that may be used for the analysis of foreign exchange gains or losses. They may be illustrated in connection with the Income Statement or the Funds Flow Statement. In connection with the Income Statement, there are two methods that may be used: SEPARATE ANALYSIS STATEMENT and INTEGRATED INCOME STATEMENT. Thus, if the latter two are used, there in effect are three approaches for analysis of foreign exchange gains or losses: SEPARATE ANALYSIS STATEMENT, INTEGRATED INCOME STATEMENT, and FUNDS FLOW STATEMENT.

To illustrate the three approaches, assume The Paris Corp., a subsidiary, shows Comparative Balance Sheets during the year 1984 (Figure 14-1), using the following Translation Rates: C = Closing Rate; H = Historical Rate; R = Remittance Rate. The Income Statement in Figure 14-1 uses these Exchange Rates: H = Historical; A = Average.

Figure 14-1 presents hypothetical balance sheets at the beginning and end of the year along with the accompanying income statement. It shows the foreign subsidiary amounts in local currency and translated into dollars. The translation dates are indicated. Without a breakdown of the exchange gain or loss, the balance sheet in dollars must be plugged for the amount of the net income in dollars. The beginning balance of the retained earnings in translated dollars is the balance as computed at the previous year end; the ending balance of retained earnings and the net income amounts are those derived from plugging, i.e., they are forced, in order to have the dollar balance sheet balance. On the income statement, the exchange gain or loss is derived by plugging to force the income statement to show the amount of derived net income as it appears on the balance sheet.

#14-7...Separate Statement of Analysis of Exchange Gain or Loss

The analysis of exchange gain or loss may be  presented in a separate statement.  Using the data above for The  Paris Corp., the STATEMENT OF ANALYSIS OF EXCHANGE GAIN OR LOSS would appear as Figure 14-2.

A  RECAPITULATION OF  THE STATEMENT OF  ANALYSIS OF  FOREIGN EXCHANGE GAINS AND LOSSES would appear as:

CLOSING FINANCIAL ASSETS:

|  |  |
|---|---|
| Cash | 10,000 |
| Receivables | 25,000 |
| Total Financial Assets | 35,000 |
| Current Liabilities | 25,000 |
| Long-Term Loans | 20,000 |
| Total Liabilities | 45,000 |
| Closing Balance of Net Financial Assets | (10,000) |

| Exchange | Losses and Gains |
|---|---|

EXCHANGE GAINS:

|  |  |  |
|---|---|---|
| Financial Assets |  | 750 |
| Income & Depreciation |  | 1,100 |
| Investments |  | 200 |
| Dividend Remittances |  | 100 |
| EXCHANGE LOSSES: |  |  |
| Inventory Held During Yr. | 1,500 |  |
| Cap. Stk. Issue Increase | 500 |  |
| TOTAL GAINS |  | 2,150 |
| TOTAL LOSSES | 2,000 |  |
| NET EXCHANGE GAINS |  | 150 |
| (Per Income Statement) |  |  |

#14-8...Components of Separate Statement of Analysis
        of Exchange Gains or Losses

As  demonstrated  in  the statement above, it commences with the breakdown of  financial  assets.  This includes  long-term loans  financial  debt  and  excludes physical  assets including inventories.  Where the net financial assets is a negative fig-ure, a GAIN occurs as a  result of the decline  in the exchange rate.

The  statement then proceeds  to show  the  effects of other balance sheet  items.  The  decline in the  historical exchange rate for inventories shows an exchange loss.  Since fixed assets

## FIGURE 14-1
## THE PARIS CORPORATION

### COMPARATIVE BALANCE SHEETS FOR 1984

| Item | JANUARY 1 Local Currency | Tr. Rate | U.S. $ | DECEMBER 31 Local Currency | Tr. Rate | U.S. $ |
|---|---|---|---|---|---|---|
| Cash | FF 10,000 | .25 C | $ 2,500 | 10,000 | .20 C | $ 2,000 |
| Receivables | 20,000 | .25 C | 5,000 | 25,000 | .20 C | 5,000 |
| Inventories | 30,000 | .27 H | 8,100 | 35,000 | .22 H | 7,700 |
| Fixed Assets | 50,000 | .30 H | 15,000 | 50,000 | .30 H | 15,000 |
| Additions | | | | 10,000 | .21 H | 2,100 |
| Accd. Deprec. | (15,000) | .30 H | (4,500) | (20,000) | .30 H | (6,000) |
| TOTAL ASSETS | FF 95,000 | | $26,100 | 110,000 | | $25,800 |
| Current Liabilities | FF 25,000 | .25 C | $ 6,250 | 25,000 | .20 C | $ 5,000 |
| Long-Term Loans | 20,000 | .25 C | 5,000 | 20,000 | .20 C | 4,000 |
| Capital Stock | 20,000 | .30 H | 6,000 | 20,000 | .30 H | 6,000 |
| Additions | | | | 10,000 | .25 H | 2,500 |
| Retained Earnings Jan. 1 Balance | 30,000 | | 8,850 | 30,000 | | 8,850 |
| Net Income | | | | 10,000 | | 550 |
| Dividends Paid | | | | (5,000) | .22 R | (1,100) |
| TOTAL LIABILITIES AND EQUITY | FF 95,000 | | $26,100 | 110,000 | | $25,800 |

## INCOME STATEMENT FOR 1984

| Item | Local Currency | Exchange Rate | U.S. Dollars |
|------|---------------|---------------|--------------|
| Sales | 100,000 | .23 A | $ 23,000 |
| Cost of Goods Sold: | | | |
| Inventory, Jan. 1 | 30,000 | .27 H | 8,100 |
| Purchases | 60,000 | .23 A | 13,800 |
| Inventory, Dec. 31 | (35,000) | .22 H | ( 7,700) |
| Cost of Goods Sold | 55,000 | | 14,200 |
| GROSS PROFIT | 45,000 | | 8,800 |
| Wages and Expenses | 30,000 | .23 A | 6,900 |
| Depreciation | 5,000 | .30 H | 1,500 |
| TOTAL EXPENSES | 35,000 | | 8,400 |
| Income From Operations | 10,000 | | 400 |
| Net Income From Balance Sheet | 10,000 | | 550 |
| Exchange Gains | | | 150 |

FIGURE 14-2

STATEMENT OF ANALYSIS OF FOREIGN EXCHANGE GAINS OR LOSSES

| | Local Currency (FF) | Dollar ($) Loss or Gain |
|---|---|---|
| (a) NET FINANCIAL ASSETS | | |
| Cash | 10,000 | |
| Receivables | 20,000 | |
| Total Financial Assets | 30,000 | |
| Current Liabilities | 25,000 | |
| Long-Term Loans | 20,000 | |
| Total Financial Liabilities | 45,000 | |
| NET FINANCIAL ASSETS | (15,000) | |
| x Exchange Rate Decline = | | |
| Ending Rate .20 | | |
| Beginning Rate .25 | | |
| Decline (.05) x (15,000) = | | +Gain: 750 |
| (b) NONMONETARY FINANCIAL ASSETS | | |
| Beginning Inventory | 30,000 | |
| Ending Inventory | 35,000 | |
| Inventory Held During Year | 30,000 | |
| x Exchange Rate Decline = | | |
| Ending Rate .22 | | |
| Beginning Rate .27 | | |
| Decline (.05) x 30,000 = | | -Loss: (1,500) |
| INCOME FROM OPERATIONS | | |
| (c) Net Income | 10,000 | |
| (d) Depreciation | 5,000 | |
| Total Per Income Statement | 15,000 | |
| Translated at Closing Rate: 15,000 x .20 = | | $3,000 |
| $ Net Income Per Income Statement | 400 | |
| $ Depreciation Per Income Statement | 1,500 | |
| Total Per Income Statement | | $1,900 |
| Exchange Gain (3,000 - 1,900) | | +Gain: 1,100 |

## INVESTMENTS

(e) Inventories:
Ending Inventory                35,000
Beginning Inventory             30,000
Increase in Inventory            5,000

Rate Increase =
(Hist.)    .22
(Closing)  .20
Increase   .02  x 5,000          =          +Gain: 100

(f) Fixed Assets:
Ending Fixed Assets             60,000
Beginning Fixed Assets          50,000
Increase in Fixed Assets        10,000

Rate Increase =
(Hist.)    .21
(Closing)  .20
Increase   .01  x 10,000         =          +Gain: 100

Total Exchange Gain From Investments ($200)

## EQUITY INCREASE AND DISINVESTMENTS

(g) Capital Stock Issue         10,000
Rate at Date of Issue     .25
Closing Rate              .20
Decrease in Rate        (.05)  x 10,000    =     -Loss: (500)

(h) Dividend Remittances        ( 5,000)
Rate at Remittance Date   .22
Closing Rate              .20
Decrease in Rate        (.02)  x (5,000)   =          +Gain: 100

continue to be translated at the same historical rate, there is
no exchange loss on their holding. The related depreciation is
also translated at the historical rate. The local currency and
dollar amount of depreciation must be added back to net income
to derive the cash flow. There is a gain from the cash flow
because the revenue translation rate is lower than the
translation rates for costs and expense. The gain derives from
the recovery of costs and expenses at favorable rates.

Other balance sheet changes show the investments or disin-
vestments and their effect on the exchange position. Investments in inventories and fixed assets at rates more favorable
than the closing rate shows a gain. Also the remittance of dividends to the parent company at a favorable rate shows a gain.
In contrast, the issue of capital stock adds to financial
assets. With the decline in exchange rate following the capital
stock issue, an exchange loss results.

Finally, the summation of funds inflow and outflow with the
beginning net financial assets gives the amount representing
the ending net financial assets. This is verified with the accompanying schedule of individual financial assets and liabilities. In the summation, the exchange gains and losses are netted to arrive at the amount which agrees with the figure plugged on the income statement.

## #14-9....The Integrated Income Statement

Another method of showing the exchange gain and loss analysis is to present it as part of the income statement. This
method has the advantage of showing the complete breakdown of
the exchange gain or loss in the income statement. As pointed
out by William Furlong, in "How to Eliminate the Plugging of
Net Worth for Translated Foreign Currency Financial Statements," in MANAGEMENT ACCOUNTING, 49, No.8, 1968, pp. 39-45, it
also eliminates the plugging. The final dollar net income
amount is then the figure reported on the retained earnings
statement.

The exchange gain and loss breakdown is computed on the
sources of balance sheet changes. Net income, capital stock
issues, dividend remittances, depreciation or appreciation of
the translated value of beginning net assets and changes in
the physical assets all reflect in exchange gains or losses.
The analysis is similar to that shown in the separate statement; however, no correlation with the flow of net financial
assets is presented.

Using the above data for The Paris Corp., the integrated
income statement showing the analysis of the exchange gains
and losses appears in Figure 14-3, which uses the following
Exchange Rates: A = Average; H = Historical.

## FIGURE 14-3
### INTEGRATED INCOME STATEMENT SHOWING
### ANALYSIS OF EXCHANGE GAINS AND LOSSES

| Item | Local Currency | Exchange Rate & Amount | Dollar Amount |
|------|---------------|-----------------------|---------------|
| Sales | 100,000 | .23 A | 23,000 |
| Cost of Goods Sold: | | | |
| Inventory, Jan. 1 | 30,000 | .27 H | 8,100 |
| Purchases | 60,000 | .23 A | 13,800 |
| Goods Avail. for Sale | 90,000 | | 21,900 |
| Ending Invntry, Dec.31 | 35,000 | .22 H | 7,700 |
| Cost of Goods Sold | 55,000 | | 14,200 |
| Gross Profit | 45,000 | | 8,800 |
| Wages and Expenses | 30,000 | .23 A | 6,900 |
| Depreciation | 5,000 | .30 H | 1,500 |
| Total Expenses | 35,000 | | 8,400 |
| Net Income | 10,000 | | 400 |

EXCHANGE GAIN AND LOSS ANALYSIS

| | | | Losses | Gains |
|---|---|---|---|---|
| (a) From Net Financial Assets: Beg. Rate | .25 | (3,750) | | |
| Less: Year End Rate | .20 | (3,000) | | 750 |
| (b) Beg. Inv. Held During Yr: Yr.End Rt | .22 | 6,600 | | |
| Less: Beg. Rate | .27 | 8,100 | 1,500 | |
| (c) Net Income From Oper.: Yr.End Rate | .20 | 2,000 | | |
| Less: Per Income Statement Above | | 400 | | 1,600 |
| (d) Depreciation Charges: Year End Rate | .20 | 1,000 | | |
| Less: Historical Rate | .30 | 1,500 | 500 | |
| (e) Inventory Increase: Historical Rate | .22 | 1,100 | | |
| Less: Year End Rate | .20 | 1,000 | | 100 |
| (f) Fixed Asset Incr.: Prevail. Rate | .21 | 2,100 | | |
| Less: Year End Rate | .20 | 2,000 | | 100 |
| (g) Capital Stock: Year End Rate | .20 | 2,000 | | |
| Less: Prevail. Rate | .25 | 2,500 | 500 | |
| (h) Dividend Remittance: Remittnc Rate | .22 | 1,100 | | |
| Less: Year End Rate | .20 | 1,000 | | 100 |
| TOTAL EXCHANGE GAINS | | | | 2,650 |
| TOTAL EXCHANGE LOSSES | | | 2,500 | |
| NET EXCHANGE GAINS | | | 150 | |
| TOTALS | | | 2,650 | 2,650 |

## #14-10...The Integrated Funds Statement

A simplified method of showing the breakdown of exchange gains and losses is by a columnar funds statement. In such a statement, the local currency figures are translated at the proper prevailing rate and then into dollars, but the rate that is used for all amounts is the closing rate. The resulting dollar gain and loss amounts represent the differences between the translated historical amounts and translated closing amounts.

The usual format for the funds statement is followed. It shows first the funds flow from operations, followed by additional inflow items. The total receipts are added to the beginning balances to derive the total funds available. Inventories are shown separately because they are translated at historical rates. However, this would not be necessary if the inventories were treated as a financial asset and were translated at the closing rate.

The disposition of the funds is shown in the bottom part of the statement. Because the inventories are not financial assets, they must be shown separately. The ending net financial assets is the difference between the funds available and the funds outflow. The amount of the exchange gain or loss is verified by deducting the net exchange gain or loss from the historically translated amounts.

Assuming the data for The Paris Corp., the format for the INTEGRATED FUNDS STATEMENT ANALYSIS OF EXCHANGE GAINS AND LOSSES would appear as Figure 14-4.

## #14-11...Statement of Exchange Exposure in Local Currency

The Net Financial Assets in local currency that appear in Figure 14-4 may be verified by constructing a separate STATEMENT OF EXCHANGE EXPOSURE IN LOCAL CURRENCY. Such statement is designed not only to show this verification but also to present to management a report on the exchange risk in that currency. From the data for The Paris Corp., the STATEMENT OF EXCHANGE EXPOSURE IN LOCAL CURRENCY would appear as follows:

### STATEMENT OF EXCHANGE EXPOSURE IN LOCAL CURRENCY

| Item | Jan. 1 | Dec. 31 |
|------|--------|---------|
| Cash | 10,000 | 10,000 |
| Receivables | 20,000 | 25,000 |
| TOTAL MONETARY ASSETS | 30,000 | 35,000 |
| Current Liabilities | 25,000 | 25,000 |
| Long-Term Loan | 20,000 | 20,000 |
| TOTAL MONETARY LIABILITIES | 45,000 | 45,000 |
| NET FINANCIAL ASSETS -- | | |
| MINIMUM EXPOSURE | (15,000) | (10,000) |
| Inventories | 30,000 | 35,000 |
| MAXIMUM EXPOSURE | 15,000 | 25,000 |

FIGURE 14-4

INTEGRATED FUNDS STATEMENT EXCHANGE GAINS AND LOSSES ANALYSIS

| | | FUNDS | FLOW | | |
|---|---|---|---|---|---|
| Item | In Local Currency | Translated At Closing Rate | As Shown On Statements | Exchange Losses | Gains |
| Source of Funds (Fund Inflow): | | | | | |
| Income from Operations | 10,000 | 2,000 | 400 | | 1,600 |
| Depreciation | 5,000 | 1,000 | 1,500 | 500 | |
| Funds Flow From Operations | 15,000 | 3,000 | 1,900 | | |
| Proceeds From Stock Issue | 10,000 | 2,000 | 2,500 | 500 | |
| Total Receipts | 25,000 | 5,000 | 4,400 | | |
| Add: Beg. Net Fincl.Assets | (15,000) | (3,000) | (3,750) | | 750 |
| Beg. Inv. | 30,000 | 6,000 | 8,100 | 2,100 | |
| Total Funds Available | 40,000 | 8,000 | 8,750 | | |
| Disposition of Funds (Fund Outflow): | | | | | |
| Ending Inv. | 35,000 | 7,000 | 7,700 | | 700 |
| Dividend Paid | 5,000 | 1,000 | 1,100 | | 100 |
| Fixed Asset Incr. | (10,000) | (2,000) | (2,100) | | 100 |
| Total Outflow | 30,000 | 6,000 | 6,700 | | |
| End. Bal. Net Fin. Assets 12/31 | 10,000 | 2,000 | 2,050 | | |
| Funds Outflow | 40,000 | 8,000 | 8,750 | | |
| TOTAL GAINS AND LOSSES | | | | 3,100 | 3,250 |
| NET EXCHANGE GAIN | | | | 150 | |
| TOTALS | | | | 3,250 | 3,250 |

#14-12...Exchange Exposure Report Purpose

The purpose of the EXCHANGE EXPOSURE REPORT is to serve as a
management report for working capital decisions.  The decision
process assumes the establishment of cash flow centers, the
movement through which is directed by responsible financial
counsel.  Knowing the amounts of exchange risk and exposure enables proper measures to be taken to respond to projected exchange rate fluctuations.

EXCHANGE RISK CONTROL

#14-13...Means of Offsetting Foreign Exchange Risk

The direction of the exchange risk control measures will
depend on the trend of the exchange rate movements.  A tendency
for devaluation will require a different, and opposite, reac-
tion from a measure to avoid an exchange loss on an upward revaluation.  The following measures might be used to protect
against imminent devaluation of a currency:
(1)  Minimize the foreign cash balances by:  (a) transferring
     excess cash to the parent company through payment of pro-
     visional dividends; (b) paying accounts payable due in
     other currencies as rapidly as possible; (c) purchasing
     goods for resale or use; (d) investing excess cash in hard
     currencies; (e) reducing the parent company investment.
(2)  Maximize conversion of foreign currency receivables into
     cash by:  (f) reducing credit terms; (g) offering generous
     cash discounts; (h) discounting the receivables.
(3)  Optimize the inventory risk by:  (i) accumulating invento-
     ries of types on which prices can be raised; (j) maintain-
     ing low levels of inventories with inelastic price struc-
     tures; (k) invoicing export sales in harder currencies.
(4)  Maximize use of local short-term liabilities by:  (l) ob-
     taining local borrowing to offset local monetary asset
     exposure; (m) gaining more generous terms for trade pay-
     ables; (n) delaying tax payments where possible.
(5)  use other hedging devices such as:  (o) forward exchange
     contracts, and (p) swap arrangements.
Where a currency has a tendency toward an upward revaluation,
the same measures in reverse can be used to minimize the exchange loss or maximize the exchange gain.

IMPLEMENTING THE WORKING CAPITAL CONTROL PROGRAM

#14-14...Need for Formalized Information Systems

To attain effective control of the foreign exchange risk,
formalized information systems directed to such end must be

employed. Interviews with accounting executives of several multinational industrial corporations bear out the fact that a threefold approach is essential to a successful working capital program. The three requirements for implementation are (1) a formally established policy and reporting procedure, (2) local participation, and (3) a central financial counsel.

#### #14-15...Formal Policy and Reporting Procedure

The best formal policy is one in writing. It should include delineation of administrative responsibility, methods of hedging, exposure control techniques, and instructions and formats for the reporting procedures. These should include statement formats for exchange exposure, present coverage, and the details of intercompany accounts. The reporting should be promptly at month's end.

#### #14-16...Local Participation

The reports should be translated into the parent company currency before submission by the subsidiary officials. The translation requirement is the one key to the success or failure of such a program. The most help in the administration of the program can come when the local managers see the translated reports initially. Another important local duty is the reconciliation of the intercompany accounts with other subsidiaries as discussed in Chapter 15. Copies of intercompany account recapitulations should be forwarded to affected subsidiaries and reconciled before final submission.

#### #14-17...Central Financial Counsel

The whole program must be administered by a central financial counsel, which can be an individual or a committee, and located in the headquarters or a regional office. Such counsel must also be versed in foreign exchange market trends. Although international banks may provide advisory assistance, determination and authority for actual currency conversion must emanate from the central financial counsel. Finally, the program for managing foreign exchange risk should be an open-end decision model, a skeleton, but comprehensive, one that is simple yet adaptive to many situations.

### SUMMARY OF FOOTNOTE REFERENCES
(References are to Paragraph #'s)

#14-1 thru #14-17: "International Working Capital Management Accounting," adapted from Norlin G. Rueschhoff, INTERNATIONAL ACCOUNTING AND FINANCIAL REPORTING, 1976, Praeger Publish-

ers, Inc., by permission.
#14-9  William Furlong, "How to Eliminate the Plugging of Net Worth
       for Translated Foreign Currency Financial  Statements," MAN-
       AGEMENT ACCOUNTING, 49, No. 8 (1968): 39-45

## BIBLIOGRAPHY

Bardsley, R. Geoffrey.  "Managing International Financial  Transac-
     tions,"  INTERNATIONAL JOURNAL OF ACCOUNTING EDUCATION & RE-
     SEARCH, 8 (Fall 1972): 67-76
Choi, Frederick. "Multinational Finance and Management Accounting,"
     MANAGEMENT ACCOUNTING, 58 (October 1976): 45-48
Dyment, John J.  "International Cash  Management," HARVARD BUSINESS
     REVIEW, 56 (May-June 1978): 143-150
Edmunds, J.C.   "Working Capital Management in Multinational Compa-
     nies," MANAGEMENT INTERNATIONAL REVIEW, 3 (1983): 73
Goeltz, Richard K.  "Managing Liquid Funds Internationally," COLUM-
     BIA JOURNAL OF WORLD BUSINESS, 7 (July-Aug 1972): 59-65
Obersteiner, Erich.  "The Management of Liquid Fund Flow Across Na-
     tional  Boundaries,"  INTERNATIONAL  JOURNAL  OF  ACCOUNTING
     (Spring 1976): 91-101
Rutenberg, D.  "Maneuvering Liquid Assets in a Multinational Compa-
     ny: Formulation and Deterministic Solution Procedures," MAN-
     AGEMENT SCIENCE (June 1970): 671-685
Sangster, Bruce. "International Funds Management," FINANCIAL EXECU-
     TIVE, 45 (December 1977): 46-52
Shen, Paul.  "Cash Flow Budgeting for the Importer," MANAGEMENT AC-
     COUNTING, 62 (September 1980): 33-35

## THEORY QUESTIONS
(Question Numbers are Keyed to Text Paragraph #'s)

#14-2  What elements  are involved in Working  Capital  Manage-
       ment?
#14-3  What  is  the  relationship of Exchange Risk Exposure to
       Working Capital Management?
#14-5  What  two statements must be prepared  to determine  the
       foreign exchange exposure?
#14-6  What three approaches are there  for analysis of foreign
       exchange gains and losses?
#14-8  What are the  components  of  the separate  Statement of
       Analysis of Exchange Gains or Losses?
#14-9  What  statement  may  be used for presenting an analysis
       of exchange gains or losses and how does it operate?
#14-10 Discuss the showing of  the breakdown of Exchange Gains
       or Losses by a Columnar Funds Statement.
#14-12 What  is  the  Exchange  Exposure Report and what purpose
       does it serve?
#14-13 What measures might be used to protect against  imminent

devaluation of a currency?
#14-14 What are the three requirements for implementation of a successful working capital program? Briefly explain each.

## PROBLEMS

### P-14-1  (CPA EXAM, 5/35, PRAC. I, #1)

The U.S.A. Co., a domestic corporation, purchased on Jan. 1, 1931, a 90% interest in the capital stock of X Company Ltd., an English corporation, for the sum of $550,000. The U.S.A. Co. acquired a further 5% interest in X Co. Ltd. on June 30, 1932, for $25,000. The following is a summary of the position of X Co. Ltd., as shown by the reports of the local auditors:

|  | Jan. 1, 1931 | Dec. 31, 1931 | Dec. 31, 1932 | Dec. 31, 1933 |
|---|---|---|---|---|
| Current Assets | ₤ 100,000 | ₤ 110,000 | ₤ 115,000 | ₤ 125,000 |
| Current Liabilities: |  |  |  |  |
| To U.S.A. Company | 4,000 | 6,250 | 6,000 | 4,000 |
| (due in dollars) | ($20,000) | ($25,000) | ($21,000) | ($20,000) |
| To others (due in sterling) | ₤ 36,000 | ₤ 58,750 | ₤ 69,000 | ₤ 61,000 |
|  | ₤ 60,000 | ₤ 45,000 | ₤ 40,000 | ₤ 60,000 |
| Fixed Assets, less reserves | ₤ 75,000 | ₤ 70,000 | ₤ 65,000 | ₤ 65,000 |
| Funded Debt | 20,000 | 20,000 | 20,000 | 20,000 |
| Net Fixed Positions | ₤ 55,000 | ₤ 50,000 | ₤ 45,000 | ₤ 45,000 |
| Total Equity | ₤ 115,000 | ₤ 95,000 | ₤ 85,000 | ₤ 105,000 |
| Capital Stock | ₤ 100,000 | ₤ 100,000 | ₤ 100,000 | ₤ 100,000 |
| Earned Surplus: |  |  |  |  |
| Balance, Jan. 1 | ₤ 15,000 | ₤ 15,000 | ₤ 5,000 | ₤ 15,000 |
| Profit or loss for year |  | (15,000) | (10,000) | 20,000 |
| Dividend paid June 30 |  | 5,000 |  |  |
|  | ₤ 15,000 | ₤ 5,000 | ₤ 15,000 | ₤ 5,000 |
| Total Capital and Surplus | ₤ 115,000 | ₤ 95,000 | ₤ 85,000 | ₤ 105,000 |

NOTE:

| | | | | |
|---|---|---|---|---|
| Earned Surplus, June 30, 1932 |  |  | (₤ 10,000) |  |
| Exchange rates on balance sheet dates | 5 | 4 | 3.50 | 5 |
| Do. on June 30 |  | 5 | 4 |  |

## Prepare:

1. A columnar statement whereon the U.S.A. Company's entries to its investment and surplus accounts are shown. Give full explanations on the statement.

2. A statement of revenue surplus showing the ultimate profit or loss on exchange with proper explanation of how it came about.

3. State briefly in what manner the exchange risks could have been averted.

P-14-2

The U.S. Corp. commenced foreign operations in Zalania on Jan. 1 through a newly incorporated Zalanian subsidiary. The closing trial balance of the foreign subsidiary at Dec. 31 in Zalanian local currency (ZLC) showed the following:

| | |
|---|---:|
| Cash | ZLC 2,000 |
| Accounts Receivable | 15,000 |
| Inventories | 50,000 |
| Fixed Assets (less ZLC 5,000 | |
| accumulated depreciation) | 25,000 |
| | ZLC 92,000 |
| | |
| Accounts Payable | ZLC 12,000 |
| Long-Term Debt | 20,000 |
| Capital Stock | 40,000 |
| Retained Earnings (after payment | |
| of ZLC 5,000 dividend on Aug. 31) | 20,000 |
| | ZLC 92,000 |

The Capital Stock account represents the original investment of cash in U.S. dollars. The rate throughout the year was ZLC 4 = U.S. $1, but at the market closing on Dec. 31 the currency was devalued to ZLC 5 = U.S. $1.

Required:

a. Prepare a statement of exchange exposure in local currency and translated into dollars as of Dec. 31 showing both minimum exposure and maximum exposure.

b. Present an analysis of the exchange gain or loss using the temporal approach.

c. Present an analysis of the exchange gain or loss using the current rate approach.

d. Give several techniques that the corporate financial executive could have used to result in a zero exchange gain or loss for the year in each case.

P-14-3

The following data expressed in terms of Australian dollars appears on the records of The Australian Corp.:

| | | | |
|---|---:|---|---:|
| Cash | 50,000 | Current Liabilities | 100,000 |
| Accts. Rcbl. | 60,000 | Long-Term Liab. | 50,000 |
| Notes Rcbl. | 65,000 | U.S. $ Forgn. Xchg. | 12,000 |
| Inventories | 175,000 | Other Forgn. Xchg. | |
| Net Fixed | | (U.S. $) | 1,500 |
| Assets | 100,000 | Due Home Office | |
| | | (U.S. $) | 5,000 |

Required:

From the foregoing data construct a Balance Sheet Breakdown Statement for Determination of Foreign Exchange Exposure.

**P-14-4**

From the Balance Sheet prepared in the foregoing problem, construct a Statement of Foreign Exchange Exposure.

**P-14-5**

The Berlin Corp., a subsidiary of the U.S. Co., a United States corporation, presents the following comparative balance sheets for the year 1984:

| ASSETS: | | JAN. 1 | | DEC. 31 |
|---|---|---|---|---|
| Cash | DM | 20,000 | DM | 20,000 |
| Receivables | | 40,000 | | 50,000 |
| Inventories | | 60,000 | | 70,000 |
| Fixed Assets | | 100,000 | | 100,000 |
| Additions | | | | 20,000 |
| Accd. Deprec. | | (30,000) | | (40,000) |
| TOTAL ASSETS | DM | 190,000 | DM | 220,000 |

| LIABILITIES AND EQUITY: | | | | |
|---|---|---|---|---|
| Accounts Payable | DM | 50,000 | DM | 50,000 |
| Long-Term Loans | | 40,000 | | 40,000 |
| Capital Stock | | 40,000 | | 40,000 |
| Additions | | | | 20,000 |
| Retained Earnings: | | | | |
|   Jan. 1 Balance | | 60,000 | | 60,000 |
|   Net Income | | | | 20,000 |
|   Dividends Paid | | | | (10,000) |
| TOTAL LIABILITIES AND EQUITY | DM | 190,000 | DM | 220,000 |

The Income Statement of The Berlin Corp. for 1984 was as follows:

| | |
|---|---|
| Sales | DM 200,000 |
| Cost of Goods Sold: | |
|   Inventory, Jan. 1 | 60,000 |
|   Purchases | 120,000 |
|   Inventory, Dec. 31 | (70,000) |
| Cost of Goods Sold | 110,000 |
| GROSS PROFIT | 90,000 |
| Wages and Expenses | 60,000 |
| Depreciation | 10,000 |
|   Total Expenses | 70,000 |
| NET INCOME FROM OPERATIONS | 20,000 |

The currency translation rates that existed during the year 1984 were as follows:

**As of January 1, 1984:**

Current Rate: 1 DM = U.S. 50 cents

Historical Rate for Inventory:  1 DM = U.S. 54 cents
Historical Rate for Fixed Assets: 1 DM=U.S. 60 cents
Historical Rate for Capital Stock:1 DM=U.S. 60 cents
**As of December 31, 1984:**
Current Rate:  1 DM = U.S. 40 cents
Historical Rate for Inventory:  1 DM = U.S. 44 cents
Historical Rate for Fixed Assets: 1 DM=U.S. 60 cents
Historical Rate for Fixed Assets Additions:
        1 DM = U.S. 42 cents
Historical Rate for Capital Stock:1 DM=U.S. 60 cents
Historical Rate for Dividends Pd.:1 DM=U.S. 44 cents
**For Income Statement Items:**
Historical Rate for Beg. Invty: 1 DM = U.S. 54 cents
Historical Rate for End. Invty: 1 DM = U.S. 44 cents
Historical Rate for Depreciation: 1 DM=U.S. 60 cents
Average Rate for Sales, Purchases and Wage and
        Expenses:  1 DM = U.S. 46 cents

**Required:**
Draft a columnar worksheet translating the German mark comparative balance sheets and income statement into U.S. dollars.

**P-14-6**
From the comparative balance sheets and income statement drafted in the preceding problem,
    a. construct a Statement of Analysis of Foreign Exchange Gains or Losses for the Berlin Corporation.
    b. from the Statement of Analysis of Foreign Exchange Gains or Losses draft a Recapitulation Summary of the Statement of Analysis of Foreign Exchange Gains or Losses.

**P-14-7**
Using the data for The Berlin Corp. in P-14-5, draft an Integrated Income Statement Analysis of Exchange Gains or Losses.

**P-14-8**
Using the data for The Berlin Corp. in P-14-5, draft an Integrated Funds Statement Analysis of Exchange Gains or Losses.

**P-14-9**
Using the data for The Berlin Corp. in P-14-5, draft a Statement of Exchange Exposure in Local Currency.

# 15

# International Intercorporate
# Transactions Accounting*

#15-1....Nature of the Transfer Problem

For many multinational companies, the transfer of goods and services among overseas units is an almost daily occurrence. The primary type of transfer is the movement of manufactured goods. However, there also can be transfers of raw materials acquired in a single country, as well as royalties, service fees, and home office allocations. There are two management issues in the transfer process: (1) a determination of the amount of the transfer as dictated by the transfer price or fee, and (2) the settlement of the transaction.

**TRANSFER POLICY**

#15-2....The Principle of Equity

The underlying philosophy in establishing a formal transfer policy is the principle of equity, as pointed out by James Greene and Michael Duerr in "Intercompany Transactions in the Multinational Firm," N.Y., National Industrial Conference Board, 1970, pages iv-vi. Under this principle, the multinational firm sets its tranfer policy on the basis of a reasonable and equitable allocation of the profits among the overseas units, as can be justified by a long-run host country interest in development and investment growth in the foreign country. Although the principle of equity may seem to militate against a goal of total corporate profit maximization, nevertheless short-run sacrifices may be feasible when the eventual effects of a fair, equitable, transfer policy optimize the long-run profit goal and firm survival.

------
*See Summary of Footnote References -- #15-1 thru #15-19

#15-3....Policy Considerations

Uniformity in policy administration appears to cease once the goal of equitable distribution is established. The many factors considered in an equitable allocation cause the transfer policies to remain somewhat flexible. Thus the income tax factor may cause variations in policy administration among subsidiaries. However, just as important are such factors as export subsidies and tax incentives; customs duties; exchange rate risk; expropriation risk; inflation risk; exchange controls; the level of competition; and the financial appearance of the subsidiary.

When the transfer policy conflicts with the performance evaluation system, dual records may be necessary to reflect the effects of the transfer policy as compared to the effects under an accurate profit center concept. Such concept also may be somewhat adjusted to link profit with an effort such as the maintenance of quality. Also, further record keeping may be required in some countries in order to comply with federal and local regulations.

#15-4....The Transfer Price

The use of "arm's length" prices emerges as the most prevalent practice when the policy considerations are coupled with the principle of equity. Their use allows a flexibility in favorably weighing a particular country's considerations in an equitable fashion. This may cause variations in application among countries. Nevertheless, because policies based on "arm's length" prices are the most easily justified, they are the most widely used.

Further, methods used to apply the transfer price policy are NEGOTIATED PRICES AND PRICES BASED ON COST-PLUS. Negotiated prices are arranged between the buying and selling units and may become necessary when the product is not sold to outsiders. Where the price is based on cost-plus, it includes an allocation of home office overhead to cover the marketing, distribution and promotion expenses.

BELOW-COST PRICING may be considered profitable from a firmwide profit maximization viewpoint where its use is based on relevant incremental variable costs. This is particularly the case when such pricing leads to additional sales to provide incremental profits through the use of duplicated idle facilities. However, such a pricing policy may be criticized as a low-price dumping of products in the importing country.

INFLATED PRICES on the other hand may be used to cover costs of royalties and other service fees which cannot be taken as deductible business expenses in some countries. The inflated price method may also be utilized to offset the blocking of dividend remittances.

Whether prices should be set as equitable, inflated or depressed is a policy determination.  What is important to note,
however, is that the price determines the amount of the fund
transfers among countries as well as the profit allocation. The
settlement of transfers has a direct effect on a country's balance of payments.

**TRANSFER SETTLEMENT**

**#15-5....The Settlement Policy**

The multinational's intercompany account settlement may involve payments of foreign currencies among a dozen or more
overseas units.  There may be many unnecessary currency conversions, particularly if each foreign subsidiary receives payment
for its intercompany receivables and makes payment of its intercompany payables.  The quantity and amount of such conversions should be minimized, requiring a settlement policy that
is clear and consistent.  A clear policy puts the transfer settlements on a routine basis, and consistent policy makes the
settlements less vulnerable to losses from exchange rate fluctuations. An optimal settlement policy also requires the establishment of a reporting procedure as well as a decision
process.

**#15-6....The Reporting Procedure**

Information on the intercompany account balances should be
an integral part of the subsidiary reporting system. The month-
end intercompany balances must first be reconciled by each
subsidiary.  If any intercompany accounts between subsidiaries
do not agree, the controllers of the units are responsible for
reconciling the differences and determining what the proper
amounts should be.  This will preclude the omission or double-
reporting of any in-transit items in the overall reconciliation
of the amounts.  After the relevant information has been transmitted to the appropriate subsidiary units, the adjusted reports are forwarded to headquarters.

**#15-7....The Netting Process**

In an article entitled "Payments Netting in International
Cash Management," by Alan C. Shapiro, in the JOURNAL OF INTER-
NATIONAL BUSINESS STUDIES (JIBS), Vol. 9, #2, Fall 1978, pages
51-58, it is stated:
    Multinational operations involve a highly coordinated
    international interchange of material, parts, subassemblies,
    and finished products among the various units of the MNC
    with many affiliates both buying from and selling to each
    other.  The importance of these physical flows to the inter-

FIGURE 15-1

INTERCOMPANY PAYMENTS MATRIX

(IN MILLIONS $)

| RECEIVING COMPANIES | Paying Companies | | | | | | | Row Totals |
|---|---|---|---|---|---|---|---|---|
| | United States | England | Germany | France | Switzerland | Sweden | Belgium | |
| United States | x | 21 | 18 | 0 | 7 | 10 | 17 | 73 |
| England | 25 | x | 16 | 10 | 2 | 8 | 5 | 66 |
| West Germany | 13 | 10 | x | 18 | 6 | 9 | 7 | 63 |
| France | 9 | 15 | 0 | x | 1 | 0 | 15 | 40 |
| Switzerland | 6 | 0 | 12 | 7 | x | 5 | 4 | 34 |
| Sweden | 5 | 14 | 11 | 0 | 0 | x | 0 | 30 |
| Belgium | 8 | 18 | 1 | 15 | 2 | 0 | x | 44 |
| COLUMN TOTALS | 66 | 78 | 58 | 50 | 18 | 32 | 48 | 350 |

Source: "Payments Netting in International Cash Management," Alan C. Shapiro, JOURNAL OF INTERNATIONAL BUSINESS STUDIES (JIBS), Vol. 9, #2, Fall 1978, pages 51-58. Reprinted with permission.

national financial executive is that they are accompanied by a heavy volume of intercompany fund flows. Of particular importance is the fact that there is a measurable cost associated with these cross-border fund transfers. Thus, there is a clear incentive to minimize the total volume of intercorporate fund flows. This can be achieved by PAYMENTS NETTING.

The idea behind a NETTING SYSTEM is very simple. Payments between affiliates normally would go back and forth, whereas in most cases only a netted amount need be transferred. For example, if affiliate A buys $2 million worth of parts from B, and B in turn buys $1 million worth of goods from A, the combined flows total $3 million. On a net basis, however, A would only pay B $1 million.

## #15-8....Prof. Shapiro States Benefits From Netting:

The benefits from netting can be substantial. For example, Monsanto estimates that it is saving $2.25 million annually by using a multilateral netting system which reduces interaffiliate payments from $300 million gross to $150 million net with a savings of 1.5% on the amount not transferred. Similarly Baxter Labs estimates that it is saving $200,000 per year by eliminating approximately 60% of its intercompany transactions through netting. Thus, in view of the potential cost savings, while not a widespread practice, the value of netting has apparently been recognized by a number of M/N/Cs. A 1976 survey of 194 M/N/Cs by Business International revealed that 28% of the U.S. and 33% of the European-based firms have a multilateral netting system.

## #15-9....Information Requirements

The information requirements essential to any netting process are a centralized control point to collect and record detailed information on the intercompany accounts of the participating affiliates. Prof. Shapiro declares:

The control point will use a matrix of payables and receivables to determine the net payor or creditor position of each company. Assuming a U.S. parent corporation with subsidiaries in France, England, Belgium, Switzerland, Sweden and West Germany, an example of the matrix would appear as shown in Figure 15-1. Each of the amounts due to and from sister companies are converted into a common currency, viz., the U.S. Dollar, and entered into the matrix. The next step is to calculate the net outflow from each affiliate, by totaling up the matrix rows for each subsidiary and the parent, and the matrix columns. The difference between total payments, the COLUMN TOTALS, and total receipts, the ROW TOTALS, becomes the net outflow for that unit, as follows:

NETTING SCHEDULE (IN MILLIONS $)

| Country | Pays | Receives | Net |
|---------|------|----------|-----|
| United States | 66 | 73 | - 7 |
| England | 78 | 66 | 12 |
| West Germany | 58 | 63 | - 5 |
| France | 50 | 40 | 10 |
| Switzerland | 18 | 34 | -16 |
| Sweden | 32 | 30 | 2 |
| Belgium | 48 | 44 | 4 |

The netting system should be tailored to the particular company. To do this, the following precise information is needed regarding the internal flow of funds: (a) the amounts and
currencies of flows; (b) the origins and destination of
flows; (c) the timing of these flows; (d) the average size
of payments; (e) the per unit costs involved in sending
funds between any two points.

## #15-10...Foreign Exchange Controls

Prof. Shapiro goes on to point out that "before implementing
a netting system, a company needs to know whether any restrictions on netting exist. Firms may sometimes be barred from netting, or required to obtain permission from the local monetary
authorities. Although netting will not affect a nation's balance of payments, domestic banks may exert pressure on the local government if they are heavily dependent on income from
foreign exchange transactions. For example, netting is not permitted by the Australian government if it leads to a significant decrease in foreign exchange purchases."

In the April 28, 1978 issue of BUSINESS INTERNATIONAL MONEY
REPORT, a listing is made of the various major countries and
the limits set by them on Netting:

| Country | Netting | Country | Netting |
|---------|---------|---------|---------|
| Argentina | Not Permitted | Netherlands | Permitted |
| Australia | Permission Required | New Zealand | Permission Required |
| Belgium | Permitted | Norway | Permission Required |
| Brazil | Not Permitted | | (Available) |
| Canada | Permitted | Pakistan | Not Permitted |
| Denmark | Permitted | Philippines | Permission Required |
| France | Permission Required | Singapore | Permitted |
| | (Hard to get) | Spain | Permission Required |
| Germany | Permitted | South Africa | Not Allowed (Spe- |
| Ireland | Permission Required | | cial Permission) |
| | (Available) | Sweden | Permission Required |
| Italy | Not Permitted | Switzerland | Permitted |
| Japan | Not Permitted | Taiwan | Not Possible |
| Korea | Permitted | United Kingdom | Permitted |
| Malaysia | Permitted | United States | Permitted |
| Mexico | Permitted | Venezuela | Permitted (Not Cus- |
| | | | tomary) |

#15-11...Reconciliation Recapitulation of Intercompany Account
      Net Balances of Parent and Foreign Subsidiaries

When the subsidiaries submit their Schedules of Accounts
Receivable and Payable with other subsidiaries and the Parent
Company, the inter-subsidiary-home-office accounts receivable
and payable balances are then recapitulated at headquarters to
determine net balances. The intercompany balances received from
the subsidiaries are then translated into the parent company
currency, showing each subsidiary's receivables and payables
offset by either the total receivable or payable, whichever is
lower. After deducting the offset, the net balance receivable
or payable is derived. The amounts of the offsets are communicated to each subsidiary because only the net balances need to
be transferred to accomplish complete settlement of the intercompany balances. An illustrative case as to how the netting
process is applied to intercompany settlements is presented
below.
      Assume the U.S. Multinational Corp. has three subsidiaries:
The Paris Corp. of France, the Berlin Corp. of Germany, and the
Rome Corp. of Italy. At the end of the fiscal year, each of
the subsidiaries submits in report form to the U.S. Parent
Corp. office in New York, the following data regarding its Accounts Receivable and Accounts Payable intercompany balances:

THE PARIS CORP.:
      Accounts Rcvble from Parent Corp - FF        5,120
      Accounts Rcvble from Berlin Corp - FF        10,240
      Accounts Rcvble from Rome Corp - FF          51,200
      Accounts Payable to Parent Corp - $          10,000
      Accounts Payable to Berlin Corp - DM         9,660
      Accounts Payable to Rome Corp. - IL          1,746,000
THE WEST BERLIN CORP.:
      Accounts Rcvble from Parent Corp. - DM       6,440
      Accounts Rcvble from Paris Corp. - DM        9,660
      Accounts Rcvble from Rome Corp. - DM         28,980
      Accounts Payable to Parent Corp. - $         8,000
      Accounts Payable to Paris Corp. - FF         10,240
      Accounts Payable to Rome Corp. - IL          1,164,000
THE ROME CORP.:
      Accounts Rcvble from Parent Corp. - IL       582,000
      Accounts Rcvble from Paris Corp. - IL        1,746,000
      Accounts Rcvble from Berlin Corp. - IL       1,164,000
      Accounts Payable to Parent Corp. - $         2,000
      Accounts Payable to Paris Corp. - FF         51,200
      Accounts Payable to Berlin Corp. - DM        28,980

The books of The Parent Corp. disclose the following accounts
receivable and accounts payable:

```
Accounts Rcvble from Paris Corp. - $        10,000
Accounts Rcvble from Berlin Corp. - $        8,000
Accounts Rcvble from Rome Corp. - $          2,000
Accounts Payable to Paris Corp. - FF         5,120
Accounts Payable to Berlin Corp. - DM        6,440
Accounts Payable to Rome Corp. - IL        582,000
```

**#15-12...Summary of Translated Currency Schedule
of Intercompany Receivables and Payables**

Before constructing the INTERCOMPANY RECONCILIATION RECAP-
ITULATION OF ACCOUNTS RECEIVABLE AND PAYABLE, it is necessary,
as a preliminary step, to make the required foreign currency
translations from the foregoing data to reduce all figures to
common denominator U.S. Dollars. This is done in Figure 15-2,
assuming the following currency rates:

$$\$1 \ U.S. \ = \ 5.12 \ French \ Francs$$
$$\$1 \ U.S. \ = \ 3.22 \ German \ Marks$$
$$\$1 \ U.S. \ = \ 582 \ Italian \ Lira$$

**#15-13...Reconciliation Recapitulation of Intercompany
Receivables and Payables**

The Reconciliation Recapitulation Statement resulting from
the Netting Process is shown in Figure 15-3.

**#15-14...The Netting Process and Its Advantages**

In Figure 15-3 only two subsidiaries--The Paris Corp. and
The Rome Corp.--must forward payments of $3,000 and $15,000
respectively. The Berlin subsidiary will receive $2,000 of the
$18,000 total and the $16,000 remainder will go to the Parent
Corp. Note that the net balances amount to only one-third of
the total payables.

The netting process may reduce the number of currency conversions but always reduces the amounts of the transfers. For
example, if the next month-end recapitulation is the same as
above except that the amount owed by the Berlin Corp. to the
Paris Corp. is $2,000 more, then the offset of the Paris Corp.
increases the Accounts Receivable to $15,000 and the Berlin
Corp.'s offset decreases the Accounts Receivable to $12,000.
The net result is that only the Parent Corp. is to receive its
$16,000 payment--the amount to be sent from the Paris Corp. of
$1,000 plus the Rome Corp. amount of $15,000. Thus the number
of conversions is reduced to only two, and the amount of the
transfers are reduced by more than 70 percent.

FIGURE 15-2

SUMMARY OF TRANSLATED CURRENCY REPORT OF INTERCOMPANY RECEIVABLES AND PAYABLES

| Corporation | Company | Accounts Receivable From | | | Accounts Payable To | | |
|---|---|---|---|---|---|---|---|
| | | Amount Local Currency | U.S. $ Translation Rate | Amount | Amount Local Currency | U.S. $ Translation Rate | Amount |
| PARIS CORP. | Parent | FF 5,120 | 5.12=$1 | $ 1,000 | ($) $10,000 | - | $10,000 |
| | Berlin | FF 10,240 | 5.12=$1 | 2,000 | (marks) 9,660 | 3.22=$1 | 3,000 |
| | Rome | FF 51,200 | 5.12=$1 | 10,000 | (lira) 1,746,000 | 582 =$1 | 3,000 |
| | TOTAL | FF 66,560 | | $13,000 | | | $16,000 |
| WEST BERLIN CORP. | Parent | DM 6,440 | 3.22=$1 | $ 2,000 | ($) $8,000 | - | $ 8,000 |
| | Paris | DM 9,660 | 3.22=$1 | 3,000 | (FF) 10,240 | 5.12=$1 | 2,000 |
| | Rome | DM 28,980 | 3.22=$1 | 9,000 | (lira) 1,164,000 | 582 =$1 | 2,000 |
| | TOTAL | DM 45,080 | | $14,000 | | | $12,000 |
| ROME CORP. | Parent | IL 582,000 | 582 =$1 | $ 1,000 | ($) $2,000 | - | $ 2,000 |
| | Paris | IL 1,746,000 | 582 =$1 | 3,000 | (FF) 51,200 | 5.12=$1 | 10,000 |
| | Berlin | IL 1,164,000 | 582 =$1 | 2,000 | (DM) 28,980 | 3.22=$1 | 9,000 |
| | TOTAL | IL 3,492,000 | | $ 6,000 | | | $21,000 |
| PARENT CORP. | Paris | $10,000 | - | $10,000 | (FF) 5,120 | 5.12=$1 | $ 1,000 |
| | Berlin | $ 8,000 | - | 8,000 | (DM) 6,440 | 3.22=$1 | 2,000 |
| | Rome | $ 2,000 | - | 2,000 | (IL) 582,000 | 582 =$1 | 1,000 |
| | TOTAL | $20,000 | | $20,000 | | | $ 4,000 |

FIGURE 15-3

RECONCILIATION RECAPITULATION OF INTERCOMPANY RECEIVABLES AND PAYABLES RESULTING FROM NETTING PROCESS

### ACCOUNTS RECEIVABLE

| From Corp. Account | Accounts Receivable To Parent Corporation L/C | $ | Accounts Receivable To Paris Corporation L/C | $ | Accounts Receivable To Berlin Corporation L/C | $ | Accounts Receivable To Rome Corporation L/C | $ |
|---|---|---|---|---|---|---|---|---|
| Parent | - | - | FF 5,120 | $ 1,000 | DM 6,440 | $ 2,000 | IL 582,000 | $ 1,000 |
| Paris | $10,000 | $10,000 | - | - | DM 9,660 | $ 3,000 | IL 1,746,000 | $ 3,000 |
| Berlin | $ 8,000 | $ 8,000 | FF 10,240 | $ 2,000 | - | - | IL 1,164,000 | $ 2,000 |
| Rome | $ 2,000 | $ 2,000 | FF 51,200 | $10,000 | DM 28,980 | $ 9,000 | - | - |
| TOTAL RCBLES. | $20,000 | $20,000 | FF 66,560 | $13,000 | DM 45,080 | $14,000 | IL 3,492,000 | $ 6,000 |

### ACCOUNTS PAYABLE

| To Corp. Account | Accounts Payable By Parent Corporation L/C | $ | Accounts Payable By Paris Corporation L/C | $ | Accounts Payable By Berlin Corporation L/C | $ | Accounts Payable By Rome Corporation L/C | $ |
|---|---|---|---|---|---|---|---|---|
| Parent | - | - | $10,000 | $10,000 | $ 8,000 | $ 8,000 | $ 2,000 | $ 2,000 |
| Paris | FF 5,120 | $ 1,000 | - | - | FF 10,240 | $ 2,000 | FF 51,200 | $10,000 |
| Berlin | DM 6,440 | $ 2,000 | DM 9,660 | $ 3,000 | - | - | DM 28,980 | $ 9,000 |
| Rome | IL 582,000 | $ 1,000 | IL 1,746,000 | $ 3,000 | IL 1,164,000 | $ 2,000 | - | - |
| TOTAL PYBLES. | | $ 4,000 | | $16,000 | | $12,000 | | $21,000 |

EXCESS:

| | Parent | Paris | Berlin | Rome |
|---|---|---|---|---|
| Receivables Over Payables | $16,000 | $ 3,000 | $ 2,000 | |
| Payables Over Receivables | | | | $15,000 |

## #15-15...The Cost-Benefit Decision

The netting report provides the information for the international money management decision process. The responsibility for the decision making is preferably centralized at the headquarters. The netting process may effect direct cost savings, for example, by reducing conversion costs through mere transfers in an international bank, as indicated in the article "Are Currency Exchange Costs Nibbling at Your Overseas Profits," in BUSINESS ABROAD, 95, #2, 1970, pp. 14-15. Further savings may be achieved by international hedging, i.e., by withholding intercompany transfers to increase exchange exposure positions in countries with a high probability of predicting an expected currency revaluation. However, such savings must be measured against the benefits of an efficient movement of working capital and the costs of borrowing if a subsidiary's working capital position becomes inadequate. Nevertheless, without a deliberate settlement policy and procedure, such cost-benefit factors may be neglected in the intercompany transfer settlement decisions.

## #15-16...Direction and Control

Once a decision is made, however, the central authority directs the payments to be processed. Instructions are advanced to the units as to the amounts to be transferred. The instructions may not necessarily require complete monthly settlements if internal hedging is practiced. For example, in the above illustration the German subsidiary prior to the floating of the Deutsche Mark may have been required to withhold its intercompany payables even though its receivables were settled.

Thus the conversions are directed in the light of the exchange exposure position of each country and the related currency risk predictions. Feedback on the performance of the instructions then becomes the final step in the reporting procedure. It is accomplished by merely reviewing the intercompany positions as communicated in the subsequent monthly reports.

## THE NEED FOR CENTRALIZED CONTROL

## #15-17...Rationale for an Integrated Control System

Foreign exchange is one of the greatest risk factors in multinational financial management. Product and service transfers to, from, and among foreign subsidiaries complicate the control of this risk. Intercompany transfers require a cybernetic system that not only discloses the quantity and amounts of the transfers, but also directs the movement of the settlements. Such a system is best controlled by a central financial authority.

FIGURE 15-4

## The Movement of Funds

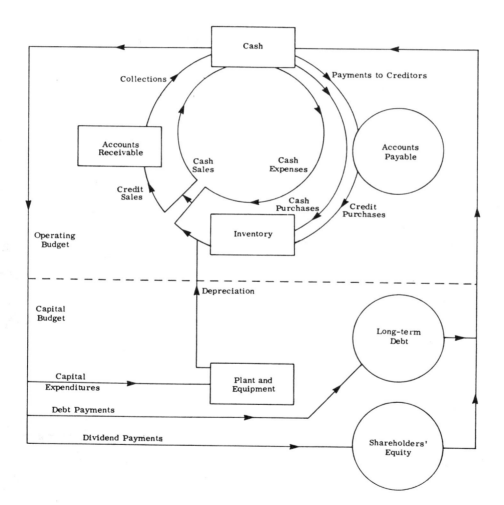

The flow of intercompany transactions has a direct contribu-
tory influence on the  short-run performance of the foreign operating unit. The performance is affected not only by the movement of  intercompany  transfers, but also by the settlement of
the transfer transactions  and by the price that determines the
amount of the fund movement. The centralized authority can best
evaluate the inflationary, exchange market, cost structure, and
fund movement factors within an integrated control system.

#### #15-18...The Control System

With a dependence on the modern instant data-moving communi-
cative methods, the budget becomes the main core in centralized
control. The budget is used in control by comparing its projections with the actual results as time passes.  The total budget
procedure includes the capital budget as well as an operational
budget as depicted in a chart constructed by Prof. Norlin Rueschhoff reproduced in Figure 15-4.  The  budget system breakdown
is necessary to  separate the  working capital  and operations
control functions from the investment decision-making and capi-
tal-control functions.  Each subsidiary may be given  autonomy
within the operational budget.
The  budget  must  be  in consonance with the  international
strategic plan that involves  investment decision-making, which
requires problem-solution techniques and should present projections for several years in the future.  In the general plan, as
well  as  in  routine  decision-making,  social  responsibility
should be included as a qualitative factor, as will be discussed in the chapter on Social Accounting.  Examples of the social
responsibility awareness include the local employment considerations  that  help  the community, as  well as the national and
international nature  of the firm's output, which benefit society in general. The determination of the social consequences of
possible alternatives may need to be accomplished intangibly.
The strategic plan  is  a general future  plan with specific
projections  for  the capital budget.  In  contrast, operations
control is quite concrete and is  centered on the financial reporting system as  a  key  to the system  of operational budget
performance.  Operational control is primarily a responsibility
of the foreign  management with the coordination integration of
the reporting system as part of the duties of the international
controller.

#### #15-19...The Control Centrum

Although operational control may be centered on the overseas
profit  center,  international  coordination  is  accomplished
through the centralized control center in the headquarters. The
centralized control is  necessary to enhance an expedient move-

FIGURE 15-5

## The Movement of Intercompany Transfers

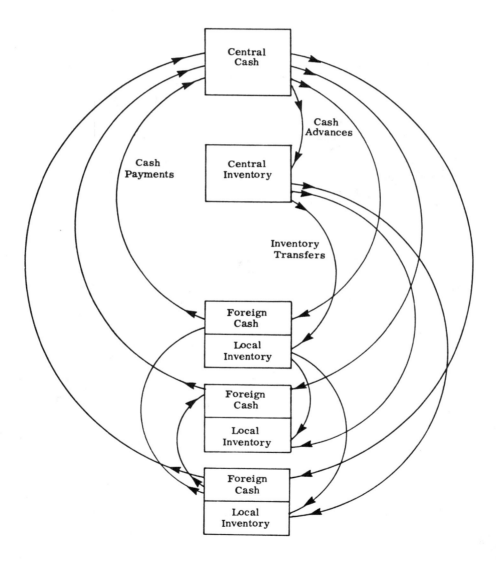

ment of goods and services among the affiliates. As illustrated in Figure 15-5, the flow of goods and services initiates the movement of funds. International reporting and instructional dissemination of the movement of funds is integrated into a centralized information system. Centralized control may not be popular for a multinational corporation, but it may be necessary to assure minimization of currecy conversion costs and foreign exchange losses. With the current flux in the international monetary scene, the centralized control of the currency conversions may indeed be an important financial management responsibility.

## SUMMARY OF FOOTNOTE REFERENCES
(References are to Paragraph #'s)

#15-1 thru #15-19:   "International Intercorporate Transactions Accounting," adapted from Norlin G. Rueschhoff, INTERNATIONAL ACCOUNTING AND FINANCIAL REPORTING, 1976, Praeger Publishers, Inc., by permission.

#15-2   James Greene and Michael Duerr, "Intercompany Transactions in the Multinational Firm," N.Y., National Industrial Conference Board, 1970, pp. iv - vi

#15-7   Alan C. Shapiro, "Payments Netting in International Cash Management," JOURNAL OF INTERNATIONAL BUSINESS STUDIES (JIBS), Vol. 9, #2 (Fall 1978): 51-58. Reprinted with permission.

#15-8   Ibid., by permission.

#15-9   Ibid., by permission.

#15-10  Ibid., by permission.

#15-10  BUSINESS INTERNATIONAL MONEY REPORT, April 28, 1978

#15-15  "Are Currency Exchange Costs Nibbling at Your Overseas Profits?", BUSINESS ABROAD, 95, #2 (1970): 14-15

## BIBLIOGRAPHY

Arpan, Jeffrey S. "International Intracorporate Pricing: Non American Systems and Views," JOURNAL OF INTERNATIONAL BUSINESS STUDIES (Spring 1972): 1-18

Benke, Ralph and Edwards, James Don. "Transfer Pricing: Techniques and Uses," MANAGEMENT ACCOUNTING (June 1980): 45-47

Burns, Jane. "Transfer Pricing Decisions in U.S. Multinational Corporations," JOURNAL OF INTERNATIONAL BUSINESS STUDIES, 11 (Fall 1980): 23-39

Coburn, David; Ellis, J. III; and Milano, Duane. "Dilemmas in MNC Transfer Pricing," MANAGEMENT ACCOUNTING, 63 (Nov.1981):53-8

Elam, Rick and Hanid, Henaidy. "Transfer Pricing for the Multinational Corporation," INTERNATIONAL JOURNAL OF ACCOUNTING EDUCATION & RESEARCH, 16 (Spring 1981): 49-65

Fantl, Irving. "Transfer Pricing--Tread Careful," THE CPA JOURNAL, 44 (December 1974): 42-46

Fowler, D.J.  "Transfer Prices and  Profit Maximization in Multina-
     tional Operations," JOURNAL OF INTERNATIONAL  BUSINESS STUD-
     IES, 9 (Winter 1978): 9-26
Kim, Seung and Miller, Stephan.  "Constituents of the International
     Transfer Pricing Decision," COLUMBIA JOURNAL OF WORLD BUSI-
     NESS (Spring 1979): 69-77
Lamp, Walter.  "The Multinational Whipping Boy,"  FINANCIAL  EXECU-
     TIVE, 44 (December 1976): 44-47
Malmston, Duane.  "Accommodating Exchange Rate Fluctuations  in In-
     tercompany Pricing and Invoicing," MANAGEMENT ACCOUNTING, 59
     (September 1977): 24-28
Merville, Larry and Petty,  William II.  "Transfer Pricing  for the
     Multinational Firm," ACCOUNTING REVIEW (Oct. 1978): 935-951
Milburn,  J.  Alex.   "International  Transfer  Transactions:  What
     Price?", CA MAGAZINE (December 1976): 22-27
Nagy, Richard J.  "Transfer Price Accounting for MNC's," MANAGEMENT
     ACCOUNTING, 59 (January 1978): 34-38
OECD.  "Transfer  Pricing  and  Multinational Enterprises,"  Paris:
     OECD, 1979
Rodney, Earl.   "Financial  Controls for Multinational Operations,"
     FINANCIAL EXECUTIVE, 44 (May 1976): 26-29
Samuelson, L.  "The  Multinational Firm With Arm's  Length Transfer
     Pricing  Limits," JOURNAL OF INTERNATIONAL ECONOMICS  (Nov.
     1982): 365
Shulman, J.S. "Transfer Pricing in the Multinational Firm," EUROPE-
     AN BUSINESS (January 1969): 46-54
Stewart, J.C. "Multinational Companies and Transfer Pricing," JOUR-
     NAL OF BUSINESS FINANCE & ACCOUNTING, 4(Autumn 1977):353-371
Tang, Roger.  "Canadian Transfer  Pricing  Practices," CA MAGAZINE,
     113 (March 1980): 32-38
Tang, Roger.  "Multinational Transfer Pricing," Scarborough, Ontar-
     io: Butterworths, 1981
Tang, Roger and Chen, K.H. "Environmental Variables of Internation-
     al  Transfer Pricing: A  Japan-U.S. Comparison," ABACUS,  15
     (June 1979): 3-12
Thomas, Arthur L.  "Transfer Prices of the Multinational Firm: When
     Will They Be Arbitrary?", ABACUS (June 1971): 40-53
Wu, Frederick and Sharp, Douglas.   "An Empirical Study of Transfer
     Pricing Practices," INTERNATIONAL JOURNAL OF ACCOUNTING EDU-
     CATION & RESEARCH, 14 (Spring 1979): 71-100

## THEORY QUESTIONS
(Question Numbers are Keyed to Text Paragraph #'s)

#15-1  What is the  nature  of the multinational Intercorporate
       Transfer System? How many management issues are there in
       the transfer process and what are they?
#15-2  Discuss the Principle of Equity in the transfer policy.
#15-4  Discuss the various methods in use for establishing  the
       Transfer Price.

#15-5  Discuss  the  problems  arising  in  connection  with  the
       Transfer Settlement Policy.
#15-6  What  reporting  procedure  should be  followed  regarding
       intercompany account balances?
#15-7  What is the Netting Process and how does it operate?
#15-8  Specify  the  benefits  that  result  from the use of  the
       Netting Process.
#15-9  Outline  the  information requirements that are essential
       to the operation of the Netting Process.
#15-10 Why is it  important  to know whether  any  restrictions
       exist before attempting to implement the Netting System?
#15-15 Discuss  the relationship of the  Netting Report to  the
       international money management decision process.
#15-17 Discuss the rationale for an integrated control system.

## EXERCISES

### EX-15-1
MULTIPLE CHOICE:  Circle the best answer.
   1. The principle under which  a multinational firm  sets  its
transfer  policy on the basis of a reasonable and equitable allocation of the profits among its overseas units is called
   a. The principle of conservatism.
   b. The goal of profit maximization.
   c. The matching principle.
   d. The principle of equity.

   2. In the netting process as applied  to intercompany account
settlements, the following statement is false:
   a. Direct cost savings may be affected by reducing the amount
      of currency conversions.
   b. Each overseas unit offsets its payable against the receiv-
      ables of each  other unit and immediately forwards payment
      to the  unit owed or forwards a statement  of balance  due
      from the unit which owes.
   c. A central  financial counsel can best give instructions as
      to the movement of funds among overseas units.
   d. Gains  in the foreign exchange  market may  be achieved by
      delaying certain intercompany account settlements.

## PROBLEMS

### P-15-1
The Pattern Co., a U.S. parent  corporation, has 3 subsidiaries
--Santo Co., Simple Co., and Sunny  Co.--in Countries A, B, and
C, respectively.  The exchange rates on Jan. 31 are:

          3  A Currency (AC)    =     U.S. $1
          4  B Currency (BC)    =     U.S. $1
          5  C Currency (CC)    =     U.S. $1

On Jan. 31 the following intercompany balances exist:
    Pattern owes Simple $1,000 and Sunny $3,000
    Santo owes Pattern $5,000; Simple BC12,000; and
        Sunny AC30,000
    Simple owes Pattern BC8,000; Santo BC24,000; and
        Sunny BC40,000
    Sunny owes Pattern $8,000; Santo CC30,000; and
        Simple CC10,000
**Required**:
  a. Prepare a report showing the amount of net receivables and payables among the parent and the subsidiaries.
  b. State the directions of the movement of funds in order to settle the Jan. 31 intercompany account balances.

## P-15-2
The Humbo Co., a U.S. parent corporation, has wholly-owned subsidiaries in Japan named Jumbo Co. and in Mexico called Mumbo Co. At month-end the spot exchange rates were 250 Japanese yen to one dollar and 50 Mexican pesos to one dollar. At that date, Humbo owed $3,000 to Jumbo and 100,000 pesos to Mumbo; Jumbo owed 250,000 yen to Humbo and 2,000,000 yen to Mumbo; and Mumbo owed $5,000 to Humbo and 50,000 pesos to Jumbo.
**Required**:
  a. Prepare a report showing the net payables and receivables among the three entities.
  b. Explain how the intercompany accounts should be settled at month-end to minimize the number of conversions.
  c. Give reasons why a total settlement may not be specified at a particular month-end.

## P-15-3 (CPA EXAM, 5/38, PRAC. II, #1)
On Jan. 3, 1936, Eastern Mfg. Corp. organized a subsidiary, Eastern Sales Co. of France, to operate at retail in Paris. Not having had any previous experience with foreign exchange, the treasurer of Eastern Mfg. Corp. consults with you in Feb. 1937, concerning the valuation to be placed on the inventory of Eastern Sales Co. of France at Dec. 31, 1936, and the handling of intercompany transactions. The following data are furnished:
>>>Sales of product by Eastern Mfg. Corp. to Eastern Sales Co. of France at $5 per unit, payable in dollars:
|            |             |
|------------|-------------|
| Feb. 15, 1936 | 200,000 units |
| Apr. 4, 1936  | 10,000 units  |
| July 20, 1936 | 20,000 units  |
| Nov. 16, 1936 | 50,000 units  |

>>>Freight and duty paid by Eastern Sales Co. of France on such purchases amounted to 10 francs per unit.
>>>The cost to Eastern Mfg. Corp. of the product manufactured by it is $4 per unit.

>>>The wholesale replacement value (f.o.b. Paris) of a more or less similar article of French manufacture was 110 francs per unit during the months of Dec. 1936 and Jan. 1937.

>>>Remittances made by Eastern Sales Co. of France to Eastern Mfg. Corp. were:

| | |
|---|---|
| Oct. 1, 1936 | 4,000,000 francs |
| Dec. 11, 1936 | 5,000,000 francs |

>>>The published exchange rates per franc were:

| | | | |
|---|---|---|---|
| Jan. 3, 1936.... | $.0660 | Oct. 1, 1936.... | $.0487 |
| Feb. 15, 1936... | .0668 | Nov. 16, 1936... | .0465 |
| Apr. 4, 1936.... | .0659 | Dec. 11, 1936... | .0466 |
| July 20, 1936... | .0662 | Dec. 31, 1936... | .0467 |

**Required**:

The following information is requested:

1. A statement showing the transactions in the intercompany dollar account with Eastern Mfg. Corp. as they should be recorded in the books of Eastern Sales Co. of France.

2. The value at which 100,000 units on hand at Dec. 31, 1936, should be carried on the balance sheet of Eastern Sales Co. of France. This balance sheet is to be made up in francs and in dollars and the inventory must therefore be valued in both currencies.

3. The amount of intercompany profit which should be eliminated from inventories at Dec. 31, 1936, upon the consolidation of the balance sheets of the two companies.

# PART III

# MACRO INTERNATIONAL ACCOUNTING

Having completed the discussion of Micro International Accounting, we turn next to the treatment of Macro International Accounting. As previously indicated, the primary distinction between Micro and Macro is that the former is basically concerned with the private enterprise profit-motive aspects of the business, whereas the latter is related to the governmental welfare-of-the-public concepts unrelated to the profit-motive interests of the enterprise.

It has been pointed out that it is difficult, if not impossible, to draw a clear line between micro and macro, indicating the sphere in which each lies. In situations where the macro aspects arise as a result of the micro operations, and thereby become inextricably attached thereto, such macro aspects must be treated as supplemental to the micro aspects. Strictly speaking, when standing alone they are not macro, but become macro only when attached to the micro which gives rise to them. These are therefore in the nature of QUASI MACRO ACCOUNTING and have arisen as ancillary to multinational operations that have accounting implications. They have resulted in the sprouting of new areas of accounting--principal of which are Socio-Economic, Political, and Inflation Accounting.

In Part III, therefore, the subject of Macro International Accounting is treated in two sections. Section One discusses the Pure or Regular Macro Accounting aspects dealing with econ-

omies in which the macro aspects are dominant in both controlled economies and free-enterprise societies (Chapter 16).  Section Two deals with the ancillary aspects resulting in QUASI
MACRO ACCOUNTING. They have arisen because many books and articles have accused multinational corporations of exploiting
labor, usurping raw materials, and in general abusing the people and economies of the countries in which they operate, all
for their own personal gains.

     This has had the tendency to make multinational corporations
treat their operations--with respect to their national, geographic, social, cultural and political aspects--with almost
equal importance as their economic aspects.  These concepts are
geared to National Public Policy and the Public Interest and
are therefore macro in character.  However, they are completely
applicable to private enterprises whose basic motive is profits.  Hence, although macro related, they are not pure macro in
character.

     Quasi Macro International Accounting has resulted in three
areas--Socio-Economic, Political and Inflation, each of which
has two aspects.  International Socio-Economic or Social Accounting may be related to Social Accounting (Chapter 17) or
Developmental and Behavioral Accounting (Chapter 18).

     International Political Accounting may be classified as
Bribery and Extortion Accounting (Chapter 19), or Political
Risk Accounting, an emerging and relatively new and very dy-
namic area, especially since the Iran issue, detailed in
Chapter 20.

     International Inflation Accounting is covered in two chap-
ters.  Chapter 21 outlines the basic principles of Inflation
Accounting tracing the historical aspects around the world,
followed by the presentation of the accounting procedures of
Inflation Accounting in Chapter 22.

# PART III

# SECTION ONE

# REGULAR MACRO
# INTERNATIONAL
# ACCOUNTING

# International Macro-Accounting Principles

MACRO-ACCOUNTING ASPECTS

### #16-1....Nature of Macro-Accounting

Macro-Accounting is an area that extends the traditional entity stewardship to total governmental reporting. In the treatment of identifying emerging trends it was pointed out that it is quite difficult to pinpoint the precise point where micro-accounting stops and macroaccounting commences. Perhaps the basic distinction is one of orientation--micro-accounting adopts a private-enterprise-free-market, profit-seeking viewpoint, whereas macro-accounting espouses a governmental, total-public, non profit-seeking, public welfare philosophy.

Typically, accounting for governmental units, such as townships, school districts, and government-owned enterprises, has been treated as an element of micro-accounting--that is, as accounting for a firm. At least the entity concept of a firm is postulated to apply to such governmental entities; other accounting concepts such as the going-concern and the accrual are not utilized in pure form in accounting for all such entities.

### #16-2....Classification of Macro-Accounting

Macro-accounting may be classified as (1) Pure, or Regular, Macro-Accounting, which may be sub-classified as (a) Free Market Enterprise Macro-Accounting, and (b) Controlled Economy Macro-Accounting; (2) Quasi Macro-Accounting; and (3) Mixed or Hybrid Micro Macro-Accounting.

### #16-3....Free Market Enterprise Macro-Accounting

This may be LOCAL or NATIONAL in character. Local macro-accounting is that applicable to governmental agencies or bodies in a free market society which are subdivisions of and within a particular government. National macro-accounting is that applicable to the national government operating in a free market society, and includes National Income Accounting and Balance-of-Trade Accounting.

#16-4....Controlled Economy Macro-Accounting

This is applicable to countries in which enterprises appear
to be operated on a private individual basis, but may be
nationalized or taken over by the government or are under
government fiat.    Pure macro-accounting exists when all
business enterprises are owned and controlled by the
government.

FREE MARKET ENTERPRISE MACRO-ACCOUNTING

#16-5....Local Free Market Enterprise Macro-Accounting

This has also been called Governmental Accounting or Fund
Accounting. It is designed to facilitate control over expenditures of a particular governmental unit. The units include
countries, townships, municipalities, school districts, and
special districts such as port authorities, libraries and public buildings, as pointed out by the AICPA in AUDITS OF STATE
AND LOCAL GOVERNMENTAL UNITS, N.Y., 1974, page 4.
Accounting for such units is segregated into the following
types of funds: General, Special Revenue, Debt Service, Capital
Project, Enterprise, Trust and Agency, Intragovernmental Service, and Special Assessment. The principles for Governmental
Accounting are quite well developed in the U.S. Many universities offer separate courses on the subject which are generally
required for the accounting major.

#16-6....National Free Market Enterprise Macro-Accounting

Absent from the groups of entities covered in typical governmental fund accounting discussions are national governments.
However, attention is being given to this matter too. A proposal for presentation of consolidated financial statements for
the U.S. government was formulated by Arthur Andersen & Co. in
1975. In a pamphlet entitled SOUND FINANCIAL REPORTING IN THE
PUBLIC SECTOR, pp. 7-21, sample consolidated financial statements are given, presented here in Figures 16-1, 16-2, and
16-3.
Governmental financial statements on the national level can
be very useful and informative not only for the very developed
countries, but to show the financial responsibility of countries in which future investment is contemplated. With additional effort and counsel from the accounting profession, governmental reporting may be expected in the future to be more
responsible and receptive to the social interests of the tax-
paying public. An example of such reporting from page 57 of
U.S. NEWS & WORLD REPORT, February 25, 1985, is reproduced in
Figure 16-4.

## #16-7....National Income Accounting

A second type of national macro-accounting is known as National Income Accounting. It is concerned with movements of
funds: (a) in the business, households, and government sectors
of the economy; (b) in domestic savings and investments; and
(c) in the rest of the world. It is also concerned with the
computation of the Gross National Product, which includes:
wages, rental income of persons, net interest paid to households, profits, indirect business taxes, business transfer payments, and capital consumption. The system determines national
income which is the GNP less capital consumption and indirect
business taxes.

National income accounting has traditionally been an endeav-
or associated with economists. Only recently has the accounting
profession taken cognizance of its importance and begun to give
it much attention. Recent accounting textbooks in the area of
Advanced Accounting have included this topic and will hopefully
reinforce the trend toward inclusion of macro-accounting concepts as part of the basic knowledge of the accountant. Further
extension of the concepts will predictably set forth a system
for preparation of balance sheets for the whole economy and
eventually for the whole world.

## #16-8....Balance-of-Payments Accounting

At the present time international accounting at the national
level is limited to Balance-of-Payments Accounting which reports the movements in trade and finance among countries. Each
nation is particularly interested in achieving a favorable balance of trade, whereby merchandise and service exports exceed
merchandise and service imports.

By nature, not all countries can have favorable trade movements at the same time. As macro-accounting concepts are extended beyond national income accounting to financial position
and funds flow reporting, the frontier will soon be opened to
simulation of national macro-accounting reports in a global
system. Perhaps the balance-of-payments analysis can then be
more receptive to the social goals of a world-wide society.

## #16-9....Definition of Balance-of-Payments Accounting

Like national income accounting, international balance-of-
payments accounting has also been associated with economists.
The U.S. State Dept. defines the U.S. international balance-of-
payments as "the record of financial transactions which take
place between the United States and the rest of the world during a particular period of time; the balance-of-payments statement covers receipts and payments for both private and govern-

FIGURE 16-1

UNITED STATES GOVERNMENT
ILLUSTRATIVE CONSOLIDATED BALANCE SHEET
JUNE 30, 1974 AND 1973

|  | Millions of Dollars | |
|---|---|---|
|  | 1974 | 1973 |

### A S S E T S

|  | 1974 | 1973 |
|---|---|---|
| CASH AND CASH EQUIVALENTS | 18,127 | 22,797 |
| GOLD, At Official Rate (Note 3) | 11,567 | 10,410 |
| RECEIVABLES (Net of Allowances): | | |
| Accounts | 5,490 | 4,859 |
| Taxes (Note 4) | 14,960 | 12,844 |
| Loans (Note 5) | 65,836 | 62,985 |
| TOTAL RECEIVABLES | 86,286 | 80,688 |
| INVENTORIES (At Cost) (Note 6): | | |
| Military & Strategic System Supplies | 28,019 | 25,173 |
| Stockpiled Materials & Commodities | 11,526 | 12,693 |
| Other Materials & Supplies | 11,026 | 12,012 |
| TOTAL INVENTORIES | 50,571 | 49,878 |
| PROPERTY & EQUIPMENT (At Cost): | | |
| Land (Note 7) | 6,686 | 6,415 |
| Buildings, Structures and Facilities (Note 8) | 88,649 | 86,129 |
| Strategic and Tactical Military Assets (Note 9) | 119,913 | 117,670 |
| Nonmilitary Equipment (Note 9) | 39,708 | 37,377 |
| Construction in Progress | 19,400 | 17,169 |
| Other Property and Equipment | 2,118 | 1,848 |
| TOTAL PROPERTY & EQUIPMENT | 276,474 | 266,608 |
| Less: ACCUMULATED DEPRECIATION (Note 10) | 129,000 | 122,000 |
| NET PROPERTY AND EQUIPMENT | 147,474 | 144,608 |
| DEFERRED CHARGES AND OTHER ASSETS | 15,297 | 15,369 |
| TOTAL ASSETS | 329,322 | 323,750 |

(continued)

FIGURE 16-1 (continued)

|  | Millions of Dollars | |
|  | 1974 | 1973 |

L I A B I L I T I E S   A N D   D E F I C I T

| | | |
|---|---|---|
| FEDERAL DEBT (Note 11): | | |
| Gross Debt Outstanding | 486,247 | 468,426 |
| Less:  Intragovernmental Holdings: | | |
| Trust Funds | (129,745) | (114,852) |
| Federal Reserve | ( 80,649) | ( 75,182) |
| Other | ( 10,449) | ( 10,529) |
| Debt Outstanding With the Public | 265,404 | 267,863 |
| Less:  Unamortized Discount | 2,506 | 2,243 |
| TOTAL FEDERAL DEBT | 262,898 | 265,620 |
| | | |
| FEDERAL RESERVE LIABILITIES: | | |
| Federal Reserve Notes Outstanding | 64,263 | 58,754 |
| Deposits of Member Banks | 26,760 | 25,506 |
| Other | 2,286 | 1,725 |
| TOTAL FEDERAL RESERVE LIABILITIES | 93,309 | 85,985 |
| | | |
| ACCOUNTS PAYABLE AND ACCRUED LIABILITIES: | | |
| Accounts Payable | 32,491 | 30,757 |
| Accrued Interest, Annual Leave and | | |
| Other | 11,187 | 11,819 |
| Deferred Revenue | 6,734 | 6,565 |
| TOTAL ACCOUNTS PAYABLE AND | | |
| ACCRUED LIABILITIES | 50,412 | 49,141 |
| | | |
| OTHER LIABILITIES | 18,991 | 19,836 |
| | | |
| RETIREMENT AND DISABILITY BENEFITS (Note 12): | | |
| Civil Service | 108,000 | 97,000 |
| Military | 80,380 | 70,950 |
| Veterans | 110,980 | 110,850 |
| TOTAL RETIREMENT & DISABILITY BENEFITS | 299,360 | 278,800 |
| | | |
| ACCRUED SOCIAL SECURITY (Note 13) | 416,020 | 340,930 |
| | | |
| CONTINGENCIES (Note 14) | | |
| | | |
| TOTAL LIABILITIES: | 1,140,990 | 1,040,312 |
| Less:  ACCUMULATED DEFICIT | 811,668 | 716,562 |
| | | |
| TOTAL LIABILITIES AND DEFICIT | 329,322 | 323,750 |

Source: Adapted from SOUND  FINANCIAL  REPORTING  IN THE  PUBLIC SECTOR,
Arthur Andersen & Co., 1975, pp. 7-21, by permission.

FIGURE 16-2

UNITED STATES GOVERNMENT
ILLUSTRATIVE CONSOLIDATED STATEMENT OF CHANGES IN
CASH AND CASH EQUIVALENTS
FOR THE YEAR ENDED JUNE 30, 1974
(IN MILLIONS OF DOLLARS)

SOURCES OF CASH:

| | | |
|---|---|---|
| Excess of Expenses Over Revenues | | (95,106) |
| Plus or Minus Items Not Affecting Cash: | | |
| Depreciation (Note 10) | | 13,200 |
| Provision for Retirement and Disability Benefit Expense (Notes 12 & 13) | | 95,650 |
| Revenue Attributable to Change in Gold Valuation (Note 3) | | ( 1,157) |
| Increase in Accrued Corporate Income Taxes Receivable | | ( 2,116) |
| Effect of Other Accrual Adjustments (Net) | | ( 151) |
| CASH PROVIDED BY OPERATIONS | | 10,320 |
| Increase in Federal Reserve Liabilities | | 7,324 |
| TOTAL SOURCES OF CASH | | 17,644 |

USES OF CASH:

| | | |
|---|---|---|
| Decrease in Net Federal Debt - Increase in Gross Debt Outstanding | 17,821 | |
| Less: Increase in Intragovernmental Holdings: | | |
| Trust Funds | 14,893 | |
| Federal Reserve | 5,467 | |
| Other | ( 80) | |
| Total Increase | 20,280 | |
| Decrease in Debt Outstanding With Public | 2,459 | |
| Increase in Unamortized Debt Discount | 263 | 2,722 |
| Additions to Property and Equipment | | 16,066 |
| Increase in Loans Receivable | | 2,851 |
| Net Change in Other Assets & Liabilities | | 675 |
| TOTAL USES OF CASH | | 22,314 |

| | |
|---|---|
| DECREASE IN CASH | ( 4,670) |
| CASH AT BEGINNING OF YEAR | 22,797 |
| CASH AT END OF YEAR | 18,127 |

Source: Adapted from SOUND FINANCIAL REPORTING IN THE PUBLIC SECTOR,
Arthur Andersen & Co., 1975, pp. 7-21, by permission.

FIGURE 16-3

UNITED STATES GOVERNMENT
ILLUSTRATIVE CONSOLIDATED STATEMENT OF REVENUES AND EXPENSES
FOR THE YEARS ENDED JUNE 30, 1974 AND 1973
(IN MILLIONS OF DOLLARS)

|  | 1974 | 1973 |
|---|---|---|
| REVENUES: | | |
| Individual Income Taxes | 118,952 | 103,246 |
| Social Security and Unemployment Taxes and Retirement Contributions | 76,780 | 64,541 |
| Corporate Income Taxes | 40,736 | 37,588 |
| Excise Taxes | 16,844 | 16,260 |
| Estate and Gift Taxes | 5,035 | 4,917 |
| Outer Continental Shelf Rents and Royalties | 6,748 | 3,956 |
| Other (Note 3) | 6,539 | 4,970 |
| TOTAL REVENUES | 271,634 | 235,478 |
| EXPENSES AND TRANSFER PAYMENTS: | | |
| National Defense: | | |
| Military Personnel | 23,728 | 23,246 |
| Operations and Maintenance | 27,698 | 24,980 |
| Research and Development | 8,582 | 8,157 |
| Depreciation (Note 10) | 11,100 | 10,800 |
| Other | 1,371 | 3,091 |
| Total National Defense | 72,479 | 70,274 |
| Other Operating Expenses (Note 10) | 41,982 | 36,328 |
| State & Local Governments Grants-in-Aid | 41,500 | 40,400 |
| Transfer Payments to Individuals: | | |
| Income Security, Retirement, Unemployment and Social Security Payments | 69,381 | 60,373 |
| Health Care | 11,300 | 9,000 |
| Veterans' Benefits & Services | 10,400 | 9,700 |
| Other | 6,900 | 4,800 |
| Total Individuals Transfer Payments | 97,981 | 83,873 |
| Noncash Provision For Retirement and Disability: | | |
| Social Security (Note 13) | 75,090 | 63,670 |
| Other (Note 12) | 20,560 | 13,360 |
| Total Noncash Provisions | 95,650 | 77,030 |
| Interest Expense (Net of Interest Income) | 17,148 | 14,146 |
| TOTAL EXPENSES | 366,740 | 322,051 |
| EXCESS OF EXPENSES OVER REVENUES (Note 15) | 95,106 | 86,573 |

Source: Adapted from SOUND  FINANCIAL  REPORTING  IN THE  PUBLIC SECTOR,
    Arthur Andersen & Co., 1975, pp. 7-21, by permission.

FIGURE 16-4

# The Government's Red-Ink Ledger

Once again, the bottom line on the federal government's balance sheet is written in red.

A financial statement released by the Treasury for the fiscal year that ended Sept. 30, 1983, the latest available, shows the government's liabilities exceeding its assets by nearly 3.5 trillion dollars—an amount almost as large as the gross national product. The figure is 395 billion dollars bigger than the imbalance on the asset-liability ledger that existed a year earlier.

The widening gulf between what the government owns and what it owes does not mean, however, that Washington is going broke. The government not only can keep borrowing from private investors but it also can raise new funds through taxes.

Moreover, all the numbers cannot be taken at face value. Many assets are understated, such as the 263 million ounces of gold listed as worth only $42.22 an ounce—a fraction of the current market price. Nearly 700 million acres of public-domain land aren't even counted in the Treasury's evaluation.

On the other hand, liabilities of 4.3 trillion dollars also are understated, since they do not include 3 trillion of potential liabilities caused by loan and credit guarantees, insurance programs and other commitments.

## The Federal Balance Sheet

### Assets

(What the government owned—resources available to pay liabilities or provide public services in the future.)

**Cash and monetary reserves**
Operating cash in the Treasury . . $ 37.1 bil.
International monetary
reserves . . . . . . . . . . . . . . . $ 26.1 bil.
Other cash . . . . . . . . . . . . . . . . . $ 16.5 bil.
$ 79.7 bil.

**Receivables** (net of allowances)
Accounts receivable . . . . . . . . . . $ 31.9 bil.
Accrued taxes receivable . . . . . . . $ 24.7 bil.
Loans receivable . . . . . . . . . . . . . $221.5 bil.
Advances and prepayments . . . . . $ 7.8 bil.
$285.9 bil.

**Inventories**
Goods for sale . . . . . . . . . . . . . . . $ 44.7 bil.
Work in progress . . . . . . . . . . . . . $ 2.3 bil.
Raw materials . . . . . . . . . . . . . . . $ 13.9 bil.
Materials, supplies for
government use . . . . . . . . . . . . . $ 67.1 bil.
Stockpiled materials,
commodities . . . . . . . . . . . . . . . $ 15.5 bil.
$143.5 bil.

**Property and Equipment** (at cost)
Land . . . . . . . . . . . . . . . . . . . . . . . $ 10.5 bil.
Buildings, structures, facilities . . . $139.6 bil.
Military hardware . . . . . . . . . . . . . $292.0 bil.
Equipment . . . . . . . . . . . . . . . . . . $ 82.0 bil.
Construction in progress . . . . . . . . $ 37.3 bil.
Leasehold improvements . . . . . . . $ 2.3 bil.
Other . . . . . . . . . . . . . . . . . . . . . . $ 4.6 bil.
Less accumulated
depreciation . . . . . . . . . . . . . . . . −$280.4 bil.
$287.9 bil.

**Deferred charges and**
other assets . . . . . . . . . . . . . . . $ 86.1 bil.
**TOTAL ASSETS** . . . . . . . . . . . . . . . $883.1 bil.

### Liabilities

(what the government owed)

Accounts payable . . . . . . . . . . . $ 143.5 bil.
Unearned revenue . . . . . . . . . . . $ 28.5 bil.
Borrowing from the public . . . . $1,130.4 bil.
**Accrued pension and disability liabilities**
Military personnel . . . . . . . . . . . $ 444.3 bil.
Civilian employes . . . . . . . . . . . $ 514.6 bil.
Social Security . . . . . . . . . . . . . $1,778.4 bil.
Veterans' compensation . . . . . . $ 223.0 bil.
Federal employes'
compensation . . . . . . . . . . . . $ 10.8 bil.
Other pension plans . . . . . . . . . $ 16.4 bil.
Contingent liabilities . . . . . . . . . $ 2.4 bil.
Other liabilities . . . . . . . . . . . . . . $ 56.7 bil.
**TOTAL LIABILITIES** . . . . . . . . . . $4,349.0 bil.

Liabilities . . . . . . . . . . . . . . . . . . $4,349.0 bil.
Assets . . . . . . . . . . . . . . . . . . . . . −$ 883.1 bil.
**LIABILITIES LESS ASSETS** . . . . $3,465.9 bil.

*USN&WR—Basic data: U.S. Dept. of the Treasury*

Government's Net Liabilities
$1,439 bil.
'77 '78 '79 '80 '81

mental transactions, whether they are settled in cash or financed by credit."

The New York Federal Reserve Bank defines balance-of-payments as "the result of countless private and public decisions
to buy or sell, lend or borrow, abroad. The total of all our
receipts from exports of goods and services, including investment income, is not sufficient to cover the amounts spent in
imports, travel, military aid, and investments. The result is
an overall deficit in our balance-of-payments."

The breadth of the activity inherent in balance-of-payments
is indicated in these definitions to embrace every transaction
engaged in by a nation, its business enterprises, its governmental and military agencies, and the activities of its private
citizens, with similar counterparts of a foreign nation.

#16-10...Source of Balance-of-Payments Accounting

The BALANCE-OF-PAYMENTS DIVISION in the Office of Business
Economics of the Department of Commerce is responsible for as-
similating the data that is required for U.S. balance-of-payments accounting. As a general proposition in other non-social-
ist countries, balance-of-payments accounting is directed by
the BALANCE-OF-PAYMENTS MANUAL of the INTERNATIONAL MONETARY
FUND. Part of the data required is substantiated by official
documents. But where these are unavailable, as is the case with
financial accounting principles, estimated techniques are employed (such as, for example, foreign military personnel expenditures, foreign travel, foreign transportation, income from
foreign investments and private remittances).

#16-11...Balance-of-Payments Accounting Basic Equation

Just as is the case with traditional micro financial accounting, balance-of-payments accounting has its basic financial equation:          **Receipts = Payments**
The Payments are the debits and the Receipts the credits. The
Payment debits result from imports or outflows and are regarded
as DECREASES. The Receipt credits result from exports or inflows and are regarded as INCREASES. If we are to follow conventional accounting procedures which place debits on the left
and credits on the right, then the basic balance-of-payments
equation would be
          **Payments (Debits) = Receipts (Credits)**
Thus balance-of-payments accounting is a bit confusing in terms
of traditional accounting because under the latter, receipts
are normally entered as debits and payments as credits; and it
is expected that the receipts of a specific item will exceed
the payments, and not be in balance.

## #16-12...Balance-of-Payments Accounting Procedures

First, the basic procedure is to record as credits the receipts resulting from exports or inflows, and as debits the
payments resulting from imports or outflows. Second, total the
receipts credits and total the payments debits, which will normally not balance. Third, the difference between the total debits and credits, or the balance, is then added to the smaller
of the debit total or credit total which constitutes the figure
required to bring the credits and debits in balance. Fourth,
this figure is the BALANCE-OF-PAYMENTS, viz., the figure needed
to bring the payments in balance with the receipts, which gives
us the name BALANCE-OF-PAYMENTS STATEMENT.

If the credit total exceeds the debit total, the difference
is a CREDIT BALANCE, which is considered favorable or desirable; and if the debit total exceeds the credit total, then
there is a DEBIT BALANCE, which is unfavorable or undesirable.
A continuous string of debit balances such as those being experienced by the U.S. over the past several years is one of the
potent causes that was previously pointed out as having an unfavorable effect on the foreign exchange rate of the U.S. dollar. Thus, in effect, under the balance-of-payments principle,
the payments balance always must balance. The excess credit
balance results in a balance-of-payments SURPLUS, and the excess debit balance results in a balance-of-payments DEFICIT. It
is these deficits that cause currency values to depreciate.

## #16-13...Balance-of-Payments Concepts

Because there has been considerable disagreement as to what
are regarded as "REGULAR ITEMS" in the reckoning of balance-of-
payments accounting, there are many different BALANCE-OF-PAY-
MENTS CONCEPTS. The three most widely used are Basic Balance
Concept, Liquidity Balance Concept, and Official Balance Concept. The structural pattern of items under each method is presented below, as reported by THE BALANCE-OF-PAYMENTS STATISTICS
OF THE U.S. by the Review Committee for Balance-of-Payments
Statistics.

## #16-14...Basic Balance Concept

Under this concept, the balance-of-payments statement would
be based on the following equation:

Goods & Services + Remittances & Pensions + U.S. Government
    Grants & Capital Movements + (Private U.S. & Foreign
    Long Term Capital - Foreign Holdings of U.S. Govt. Bonds
    & Notes) + Balance on Basic Transactions

= Private U.S. & Foreign Short Term Capital + Foreign Hold-
ings of U.S. Govt. Bonds & Notes + Foreign Official
Short Term Capital + U.S. Gold & Convertible Currency
Reserves & IMF Position + Errors & Omissions

## #16-15...Liquidity Balance Concept

Under this concept, the balance-of-payments statement would
be based on the following equation:

Goods & Services + Remittances & Pensions + U.S. Government
Grants & Capital Movements + (Private U.S. & Foreign
Long Term Capital - Foreign Holdings of U.S. Govt. Bonds
& Notes) + U.S. Private Short Term Capital + Foreign
Commercial Credits + Errors & Omissions + Balance on
Liquidity Basis
= Foreign Holdings of U.S. Govt. Bonds & Notes + Foreign
Official Short Term Capital + (Foreign Private Short
Term Capital - Commercial Credits) + U.S. Gold & Con-
vertible Currency Reserves & IMF Position

## #16-16...Official Balance Concept

Under this concept, the balance-of-payments statement would
be based on the following equation:

Goods & Services + Remittances & Pensions + U.S. Government
Grants & Capital Movements + (Private U.S. & Foreign
Long Term Capital - U.S. Govt. Bonds & Notes Held by
Foreign Official Monetary Institutions) + Private U.S.
and Foreign Short Term Capital + (Foreign Official Short
Term Capital - That of Official Monetary Institutions) +
Errors & Omissions + Balance on Official Reserve Trans-
actions
= Foreign Official Monetary Institutions' Holdings of U.S.
Govt. Bonds & Notes + Foreign Official Monetary Institu-
tions' Short Term Capital + U.S. Gold & Convertible Cur-
rency Reserves & IMF Position

## #16-17...Appraisal of Concepts

The Basic Balance Concept was in use through World War II;
but when it was found that short-term capital movements had a
greater bearing on major country financial positions than ex-
hibited by the statement, it was no longer used after 1950. The
other two concepts--Liquidity Balance and Official Balance--are
published periodically by the U.S. Dept. of Commerce as indicators of the international balance-of-payments position.

## #16-18...Connotation of "Balance" in Balance-of-Payments

If the balance-of-payments statements always balance, the question arises as to what significance there is to the term BALANCE in the statement. The "balance" basically is derived by plugging it as the difference between the greater of either of the debits or credits against each other. The emphasis is not on the figure plugged to derive the balance, but on whether it is a DEFICIT or a SURPLUS, and also on what to do about it after this is determined.

In attempting to solve this, economists classify the items into two categories, as evidenced from the formulas for the three concepts above--viz., REGULAR ITEMS or SETTLEMENT ITEMS. The REGULAR ITEMS include international payments and receipts arising from normal foreign currency deficits, or surpluses emerging from imbalances between international economic relationships. The SETTLEMENT ITEMS are those arising from international receipts or payments required to balance foreign currency surpluses or deficits arising from imbalances between the regular items of the financial transactions of a nation with other countries.

## #16-19...Balance-of-Payments Accounting Anomalies

A considerable amount of difficulty is experienced with balance-of-payments accounting because of the idiosyncracies of the arrangement. Five troublesome areas are encountered: (1) unilateral situations which do not conform to basic double-entry accounting philosophy; (2) clear-cut classification of the items involved; (3) identification of items as to long- or short-term or direct or indirect; (4) classification of the type of transaction involved; and (5) classification of transactions based on the entity of origin. Before clarifying these problems we must first examine the operation of the basic system.

## #16-20...The Basic Balance-of-Payments Accounting System

The basic items may be classified as Debits or Credits as follows:

### DEBIT ITEMS
1. Increase in U.S. investment abroad (acquisition of a claim on a foreign government, company, bank, person)
2. Service performed by foreigners for U.S. residents
3. Accounts Receivable of debts owed by foreigners to U.S. residents
4. Decrease of foreign asset holdings in U.S. (e.g., payment made out of a foreign deposit in the U.S.)
5. Foreign transactions in U.S. private assets (e.g.,

capital raised abroad for expansion overseas by a U.S.
corporation and deposited in a foreign bank)

## CREDIT ITEMS

1. Increase in a foreign investment in the U.S. (con-
   tracting of debt to a foreign government, company,
   bank, person)
2. Service performed by U.S. resident to foreigners
3. U.S. merchandise exports
4. Foreign assets in U.S.
5. Transaction in foreign assets in U.S. (e.g., capital
   raised abroad for expansion overseas by a U.S. corporation)

## #16-21...Unilateral Anomaly

Conventional double-entry accounting has its basis in the
recording of business transactions, which, as the term double-
entry implies, is a bilateral situation. There is always a debit and an equal credit, resulting in "the Balance." But there
are many international transactions that are unilateral in
character, e.g., grants, transfer payments and gifts. In many
cases where we find there is a bilateral situation, different
source documents must be referred to ascertain the basis--typi-
cal being an export, which is recorded as a receipt in the statistics of the Bureau of the Census, but at the same time is
recorded by the Federal Reserve Bank as an increase in foreign
exchange balance in the bank account of the exporter. The result is that the item may be double counted, or in reverse situations totally excluded. It is items such as these that are
recorded under the category ERRORS AND OMISSIONS in the three
formulas. This lack of balance is alien to the conventional
accounting format.

## #16-22...Lack of Clear-Cut Classification of Items

A very typical illustration is that the fare of an airline
passenger who flies overseas on an American carrier is disregarded for balance-of-payments accounting, but if the same passenger flies on a foreign carrier it is treated as a transportation payment. Another illustration is in connection with the
balance-of-payments item IMPORTS OF GOODS AND SERVICES, which
includes U.S. Embassy State Dept. employees' salaries abroad,
U.S. overseas Embassy building rental payments, wage remittances by U.S.-employed foreign migrant workers to their home
countries.
The converse is in connection with EXPORTS OF GOODS AND
SERVICES, which includes fees charged by U.S. Embassies for
issuing visas, rental receipts from U.S. films shown in foreign

countries, Panama Canal tolls income, revenues of engineering firms operating abroad, and receipts from United Nations operations.

## #16-23...Identification of Items as Long- or Short-Term, and as Direct or Indirect

A typical illustration is in connection with securities or loans which mature after a one-year period being regarded as long-term, even though they may mature in less than a year from the date of the originating transaction.

## #16-24...Classification by Type or Entity

Typical is whether or not to classify by the type of transaction, such as one arising from travel, or by the entity or origin, such as the U.S. government, in cases where travel is involved.

## #16-25...Conclusions

Edward Bernstein has said that "the balance-of-payments deficit (i.e., the balance-of-payments problem) can't be measured. It can only be analyzed, that is to say, that there will be big differences of opinion as to the size of the deficit." The reason is that no one indicator is right or wrong.

If such be the case, why have balance-of-payments statements? The answer is that they do serve a useful purpose because they do report to all segments of a nation what the nature and the size of international financial transactions are. However, it must be cautioned that their value is predicated directly upon their serving the use for which they are being employed.

## #16-26..Relationship of Balance-of-Payments to Macro-Accounting

An example of how balance-of-payments statements affect the policies of international corporations in the direction of the linkage between national economic policies and the goals of private business enterprise is the U.S. situation between 1960 and 1965. The U.S. had very substantial deficits resulting from military and international aid commitments. The resultant gold outflow seriously affected the value of the U.S. dollar causing the President to caution international corporations to refrain from further expansion and investments abroad, and repatriation of foreign dollars to the U.S.

This set the national economic policy for such period and it behooved U.S. M/N/Cs to heed the presidential admonitions. Failure to do so would militate against the best interests of

the private corporations because it would  inevitably result in
direct  presidential intervention in  foreign  operations.  It
would also precipitate  a devaluation of the dollar which would
cause  serious  losses on international current  asset  values,
and it could blunt the effectiveness of competitive operability
to the extent of lost business  opportunities and  general cur-
tailment of U.S. economic activity.

The proof of the propinquity between national economic policy  and  operational  activities  of  M/N/Cs  was  dramatically
brought home in this  illustration.  Such situations are recur-
rable, and therefore when they  do arise point up the relationship between balance-of-payments and macro-accounting.

## #16-27...Illustrative Balance-of-Payments Statement

A Balance-of-Payments Summary for 1975 expressed in terms of
billions of  dollars issued by the Dept. of Commerce,  International  Economic Report  of  The President, is shown  in Figure
16-5.

## FREE ENTERPRISE SOCIETY MACRO-ACCOUNTING

## #16-28...Accounting as a National Economic Policy Instrument

In those  free economy countries which believe that  private
business enterprises  are public in character because  they are
regarded by the governments as instruments of national economic
policy, accounting regulations are  superimposed  upon business
enterprises  on the ground that they are subordinate and ancillary to the government.

## #16-29...The Swedish Case

Prof. Dhia Al Hashim points  to Sweden as a country that illustrates this situation.  In ACCOUNTING FOR  MULTINATIONAL EN-
TERPRISES, Bobbs-Merrill, 1978, page 9, he points out:
In Sweden it is considered good accounting practice to  provide for investment fund reserves up to 40% of profit before
tax in profitable years and then to use these funds in periods when the economy is under stress.  Thus corporations can
avoid up to 40% of their  annual tax bill through the establishment of these fund reserves. To benefit from these anti-
cyclical investment funds, companies have  to deposit 46% of
the allocation to the funds in non-interest-bearing accounts
in the Sveriges Riksbank Central Bank, which  is about  what
it actually saved in tax. These funds cannot be used by corporations without  the approval  of the  Labor Market Board.
Based on the  need of the economy, this Board  then  decides
when and for what purposes these funds can be used. However,

FIGURE 16-5
U. S. BALANCE-OF-PAYMENTS SUMMARY STATEMENT
FOR THE YEAR 1975 (IN BILLIONS OF DOLLARS)

| DEBITS (PAYMENTS) | | | | CREDITS (RECEIPTS) | | | |
|---|---|---|---|---|---|---|---|
| Item | Amt. | Net | Net Bal. | Item | Amt. | Net | Net Bal. |
| I. GOODS AND SERVICES: | | | | | | | |
| TRADE:<br>Imports | 98.2 | -- | | TRADE:<br>Exports | 107.3 | 9.1 | |
| MILITARY:<br>Expenditures | 4.8 | 0.8 | | MILITARY:<br>Sales | 4.0 | -- | |
| INVESTMENTS:<br>Income Payments | 11.7 | -- | | INVESTMENTS:<br>Income Receipts | 16.9 | 5.2 | |
| TRAVEL:<br>Expenditures | 8.8 | 2.7 | | TRAVEL:<br>Income | 6.1 | -- | |
| OTHER SERVICES: | | | | OTHER SERVICES:<br>Net | 4.8 | 4.8 | |
| TOTAL AMOUNTS | 123.5 | | | TOTAL AMOUNTS | 139.1 | | |
| TOTAL NET | | 3.5 | | TOTAL NET | | | 19.1 |
| TOTAL NET BALANCE ON GOODS AND SERVICES | | | | | | | 15.6 |
| II. CURRENT ACCOUNT ITEMS: | | | | | | | |
| Non-Military<br>Remittances | 1.7 | 1.7 | | | | | |
| U.S.Govt Grants | 2.8 | 2.8 | | | | | |
| TOTAL CURRENT<br>ACCOUNT ITEMS | 4.5 | 4.5 | | | | | 4.5 |
| | | | | BALANCE ON CURRENT ACCOUNT | | | 11.1 |
| III. LONG-TERM PRIVATE CAPITAL FLOWS: | | | | | | | |
| U.S. Direct In-<br>vestment<br>Abroad | 5.9 | 4.7 | | Foreign Direct<br>Investments<br>in U.S. | 1.2 | | |
| Net Portfolio<br>Investment | 2.3 | 2.3 | | | | | |
| Other Long-<br>Term Private<br>Capital | 1.7 | 1.7 | | | | | |
| TOTALS | 9.9 | 8.7 | | TOTALS | 1.2 | -- | |
| NET LONG-TERM PRIVATE<br>CAPITAL FLOWS | | 8.7 | | | | | |
| IV. U.S. GOVERNMENT CAPITAL FLOWS: | | | | | | | |
| U.S. Govt Capi-<br>tal Flows | 2.0 | 2.0 | 2.0 | | | | |
| TOTAL U.S. GOVT<br>& PRIVATE<br>CAPITAL FLOWS | | 10.7 | 10.7 | | | | |
| BALANCE ON BASIC<br>TRANSACTIONS | | 0.4 | 0.4 | | | | |
| TOTAL | | | 11.1 | TOTAL | | | 11.1 |

Source: Adapted from Dept. of Commerce, International Economic Report
of The President, 1975.

after five years of its deposit in  the Central Bank, a company  can withdraw 30% of the  amount on deposit without the
prior approval of the Board.  Upon the release of the funds,
corporations can take additional tax deductions equal to 10%
of the funds  released.  However, a corporation cannot claim
depreciation expense  on the  asset purchased out  of  these
funds, resulting in an increase in its future taxes.

## #16-30...Swedish Investment Reserves

It  is apparent  that Swedish business operations in general
are oriented  toward governmental stability  as  a prime objective.  This  in essence is a macro-concept. Since 1945, Swedish
business  executives have been very conscious of great fluctuations resulting from business cycle movements.  This has caused
an economic philosophy oriented toward attaining  the objective
of leveling out business  activity to avoid booms and busts for
the purpose of attaining greater economic stability.
This illustration of investment fund reserves is cogent evidence of  such intent on  the part of the Swedish business community.  Thus  the investment reserve has a double-edge advantage. It provides a tax shield which reduces taxes, on the condition that such  savings  be  set aside for  potential capital
investments needed to stimulate  the national economy where  it
becomes depressed. It is consequently manifestly an income-lev-
eling device, which, as pointed out in Swedish articles, helped
Swedish businesses  to increase investments  and decrease unemployment in the global economic recession of 1957-58.

## #16-31...Swedish Inventory Reserves

In  addition to the  investment reserve, Sweden  also  makes
arrangements for inventory reserves.  Under this plan, inventories established on  the  lower of cost or market basis (or the
FIFO method) may be reduced, after a 5% allowable reduction for
unsalable or obsolete stock, by up to 60%. This may result in a
maximum inventory of 40% of its value. In addition the inventories may  arbitrarily be increased or  decreased from period to
period, the objective being to level income between periods.

## #16-32...Swedish Depreciation Allowances

Investment and inventory reserves are not  the  only devices
used to level incomes in Sweden.  Provision is also  made  for
liberal  depreciation allowances.  An example is that which was
allowed during the  period from  1938  to 1951 when the Swedish
government gave carte-blanche permission to Swedish enterprises
to use  any  known method  or rate for its determination.  With
what appears to be a manipulation of expenses and establishment

of reserves, Swedish businesses were apparently able to present
income statements in such a manner as to effectuate the macro
objective of having stable reporting patterns. This followed a
trend toward uniformity, and is regarded as in the national
economic interest.

#16-33...Attaining the Desired Income in Sweden

Interestingly enough, what the whole scheme means is the
setting of what the enterprise feels or believes to be the
desired or appropriate income figure for the period, and then
manipulating the three factors--investment reserve, inventory
reserve, and depreciation--to attain the desired figure.

An appraisal of this situation is made by Prof. Gerhard
Mueller in ACCOUNTING PRACTICES IN SWEDEN, College of Business
Administration, University of Washington, 1962, page 47, where
it is pointed out:

Use of the investment reserve provides a somewhat limited flexibility only since the reserve cannot be drawn down
at will. Also it has a cash flow consequence since it trig-
gers a deposit requirement for some cash resources. On the
other hand a 10% tax break becomes available when some or
all of these reserves are properly used.

The inventory reserve is more flexible since it allows
ready upward or downward adjustments. However, use of this
reserve also has some attendant complications in periods of
relatively low profitability when one might wish to draw
from existing inventory reserves in order to compensate for
low period profitability. In such case, tax liabilities are
created from the paper transfer that would be involved,
which is generally undesirable in periods of restricted economic activity. This resembles the LIFO situation in the
U.S.

Finally, flexible depreciation allowances have a draw-
back in that they allow primarily one-directional flexibility in that it is difficult to reverse previously allowed
depreciation. This limits the usefulness of free depreciation allowances to high-profit periods when high compensat-
ing expense amounts are desired.

#16-34...The Swedish Audit Report

Obviously the natural question arising as a consequence of
the Swedish practice would be what kind of report could be rendered by the independent auditors. The answer is that it is
vague and general, containing a statement that the officers of
the company and management have given the auditors no cause for
criticism. This is followed by a general absolving of any responsibility for derelection in duties.

As readily seen, the statements are negative in character and wind up with the conclusion that the business has been operated in conformity with the best interests of the stockholders. What it boils down to is a review of the financial transactions, events, and conclusions to be drawn therefrom. Again, this reveals that the key consideration is not the individual enterprise but rather the public interest, clearly a macro-concept.

## #16-35...Swedish Macro-Concepts

The Swedish experience can be summarized as being predicated upon the following macro-concepts: first, that all of the economic enterprises in the economic order consist of the individual economic entities that make up the order; second, that the national economic policies can best be effectuated by directing the activities of the individual entity toward the national goal; and third, by relating the conduct of business enterprises directly to the national economic policies, the public interest will best be served.

## CONTROLLED ECONOMY MACRO-ACCOUNTING

## #16-36...Types of Controlled Economy Macro-Accounting

There are two types of controlled economy macro-accounting countries: (1) those in which enterprises appear to be operated on a private individual basis, but may be totally controlled by government fiat, or be nationalized or taken over by the government; and (2) totalitarian countries in which all business enterprises are completely and totally owned and controlled by the governemnt.

An illustration of the first type would be Egypt under President Nasser. Illustrations of the second type would be Totalitarian Germany, Russia, and Peoples Republic of China.

## 16-37...Nature of Controlled Economy Governmental Accounting

Because the governmental enterprise in a controlled economy includes not only the governmental administration but also all the industrial, financial, transportation, and utility enterprises of the nation, this situation is probably the pure case of macro-accounting.

If the financial statements of these divers enterprises in the controlled economy were all consolidated, many of the accounts would be eliminated in consolidation. The intercompany accounts, including accounts with other enterprises and with the central administration, consist of distributive assets, monetary assets (except for cash on hand), receivables, cred-

FIGURE 16-6

## ALNASER COMPANY
## CURRENT OPERATIONS ACCOUNT
### (For the Year Ended June 30, 1971)

### Left side — Value of Production & Services

| 1969-70 Egyptian Pounds | Uniform Account No. | | Egyptian Pounds | Egyptian Pounds | Egyptian Pounds |
|---|---|---|---|---|---|
| | | *Value of Production & Services* | | | |
| | | Production at selling price: | | | |
| 7,021,300 | 411 | Net sales of finished goods | 8,518,483 | | |
| (197,271) | 412 | Cost of the difference between beginning and ending finished goods | | 382,506 | |
| (155,420) | 413 | Changes in value of the difference between beginning and ending finished goods | (486,329) | | 8,414,660 |
| 6,668,609 | | | | | |
| 16,711 | 414 | Cost of the difference between beginning and ending work in process | (17,386) | | |
| 230 | 416 | Revenues from others | — | | |
| 28,757 | 417 | Services sold | 26,364 | | 8,978 |
| 45,698 | | | | | |

### Right side

| 1969-70 Egyptian Pounds | Uniform Account No. | | Egyptian Pounds | Egyptian Pounds |
|---|---|---|---|---|
| | | *Wages* | | |
| 429,201 | 311 | Monetary wages | 452,158 | |
| 100,865 | 312&313 | Nonmonetary wages | 107,013 | 559,171 |
| 530,066 | | | | |
| | | *General Expenditures* | | |
| 4,568,221 | 32 | Raw materials & supplies used | 5,633,766 | |
| 174,615 | 33 | Services acquired | 178,586 | |
| 179,694 | 34 | Finished goods purchased for sale | — | 5,812,352 |
| 4,922,520 | | | | |
| | | *Current Transferred Expenditures* | | |
| 363,743 | 3511 | Custom duties | 371,939 | |
| 9,399 | 3514 | Other taxes (e.g., tax on franchises) | 4,348 | 376,287 |
| 373,142 | | | | |
| | | *Depreciation* | | |
| 60,181 | 3522 | Bldg., construction & roads | 76,421 | |
| 315,958 | 3523 | Equipment | 347,857 | |
| 25,514 | 3524 | Cars | 26,126 | |
| 3,422 | 3525 | Tools | 4,988 | |
| 3,308 | 3526 | Furniture | 2,793 | |
| — | 3528 | Deferred revenue expenditure | 32,774 | 491,959 |
| 408,383 | | | | |
| 11,639 | 353 | Rent expense | 9,991 | |
| 102,316 | 354 | Difference between assumed rents for depreciable assets and their depreciations | 100,638 | 110,629 |
| 113,955 | | | | |

## Left side

| 1969-70 Egyptian Pounds | Uniform Acount No. | | Egyptian Pounds | Egyptian Pounds |
|---|---|---|---|---|
| | | **Furnished Goods Purchased for Sale** | | |
| 240,455 | 4181 | Net sales | — | |
| (31,278) | 4182 | Cost of the difference between beginning and ending finished goods | — | |
| (6,053) | 4183 | Changes in value of goods purchased for sale on hand | — | |
| | | | — | |
| 203,124 | | | | |
| 6,917,431 | | | | 8,423,638 |
| 113,852 | | Income from normal operations | | 1,036,374 |
| | | **Transferred Revenues** | | |
| 256,121 | 441 | Interest earned | — | |
| 6,437 | 442 | Rents earned | 3,903 | |
| 23,091 | 444 | Prior years' revenues | 28,106 | |
| — | 445 | Fines earned | 66 | |
| 915 | 446 | Other revenues | 413 | |
| 102,316 | 447 | Difference between assumed rents for depreciable assets and their depreciations | 100,638 | |
| 370,609 | 448 | Difference in interest | 288,843 | 421,969 |
| 759,489 | | | | |
| 873,341 | | | | 1,458,343 |

## Right side

| 1969-70 Egyptian Pounds | Uniform Acount No. | | Egyptian Pounds | Egyptian Pounds |
|---|---|---|---|---|
| | | **Interest Expenses** | | |
| 204,277 | 355 | Local interest | 197,353 | |
| 42,360 | 356 | Foreign interest | 36,999 | |
| 370,609 | 357 | Difference in interest | 288,843 | 523,195 |
| 616,976 | 358 | Changes in value of finished goods produced on hand | | |
| (155,420) | | | | (486,329) |
| (6,053) | 359 | Changes in value of goods purchased for sale on hand | | — |
| 113,852 | | Income from normal operations | | 1,036,374 |
| 6,917,431 | | | | 8,423,638 |
| | | **Current Transfers** | | |
| 252 | 361 | Gifts | 20 | |
| 101 | 362 | Contributions to others | — | |
| — | 363 | Fines | 1,969 | |
| 99,592 | 365 | Prior years' expenses | 32,666 | |
| 454,819 | 367 | Additional allowance for depreciation | 1,342,591 | 1,377,246 |
| 554,764 | | | | |
| 318,577 | 228 | Profits for the period | | 81,097 |
| 873,341 | | | | 1,458,343 |

Source: Adapted from material by Professor Dhia Al Hashim, ACCOUNTING FOR MULTINATIONAL ENTERPRISES (Indianapolis: Bobbs-Merrill, 1978), pp. 10-11.

its, obligations and internal source accounts. The resulting
consolidated balance sheet would present a total of all the
assets in the country. The preparation of an equivalent statement of financial position for a noncontrolled economy goes
beyond national income accounting.

## #16-38...Egyptian Accounting

Egypt illustrates how practices in socialist countries differ from those in free-enterprise economies. Through the process of the nationaliation decrees of 1961 under President Nasser, the Egyptian government acquired control of about 80% of
the country's economic resources. The government took steps to
establish a uniform system of reporting financial statements
for nationalized businesses. As indicated by Prof. Al Hashim
in the book ACCOUNTING FOR MULTINATIONAL ENTERPRISES, pp. 9-13:
   because it is difficult, if not impossible, for a central
   government to find out which sector of the economy is lagging in efficiency and productivity without comparable accounting information, the tendency toward accounting uniformity is present in controlled economies. Therefore, to
   help achieve the objectives of the Egyptian National Planning Board, the Uniform Accounting Law of 1966 was written
   with unusually explicit detail. In fact, it is more in the
   nature of an accounting handbook as it traces the movement
   between accounts, sets norms for accounting classifications,
   and spells out valuation and reporting methods.
      The stated objectives of this uniform system of accounts
   in Egypt are the following: (a) to facilitate national planning and control; (b) to permit the screening of inefficient
   enterprises; and (c) to provide information to management.
      Through the first objective, financial and social ac-
   counting are coordinated in order to facilitate the preparation of the Gross National Product and other statistical
   data used to analyze the economy and to control its direction.
The application of the Uniform Accounting Law is illustrated
by the Statements of Current Operations Account presented in
Figure 16-6. It is of interest to note that this 1966 Law requires enterprises to use replacement-cost accounting in order
to maintain the integrity of the invested capital.

## #16-39...German Accounting

It was previously pointed out that Germany, from 1937 to
1945, was as clear cut an example of pure macro-accounting as
could be experienced because of the total domination of business by the government. All industrial operation was totally
geared to national policy considerations. Thus a 1937 decree

made uniform accounting mandatory as pointed out by Hans Singer
in STANDARDIZED ACCOUNTANCY IN GERMANY, Cambridge Univ. Press,
1944, p. 15.  The decree provided:

> The new aims of the German economy call for increased output
> and efficiency from business undertakings.  The fulfillment
> of this great task requires a thorough knowledge and a close
> control of all business transactions.  Thus a well-developed
> accounting system is a primary  factor in the reorganization
> of industry.  The public interest, and in particular the aim
> of the four-year plan, demand that  the accounting system of
> all firms should be arranged on uniform principles. Systema-
> tic mutual exchange of experience, especially in the form of
> comparative analysis  of companies,  will  help toward  this
> end.

## RUSSIAN ACCOUNTING*

### #16-40...Russian Accounting

The dominant feature of the totalitarian accounting approach
was the requirement that the accounting systems of all firms be
uniform.  Central Economic Planning  virtually demands a system
of uniformity of accounting for  two reasons:  (1) to be worth-
while the plan must be predicated on credible data; and (2) the
interdependence of the heterogeneous  activities, all dominated
by a master plan, with one another.

Accordingly  central  planning  decrees  complete  uniform accounting.  This  is emphasized by Robert Campbell in ACCOUNTING
IN SOVIET PLANNING AND  MANAGEMENT, Harvard Univ. Press,  1963,
in  which  he  points out that the best illustration is Russia,
where "accounting  is more important in the Soviet economy than
it is in the Western economies."

Soviet accounting has to be uniform  even  though experience
has  evidenced a decided lack of control data from its accounting practice which  plague the Russian accounting system.   For
example, in the early part  of the 1960s, when a study of  Russian  accounts  indicated that the system used was outdated and
recording  techniques resulted in an  unrepresentative carrying
value  of asset accounts, a completely new start for asset values was carried out.

### #16-41...Russian Versus U. S. Accounting

The basic difference between Russian  and U.S. accounting is
that in free  economies the whole system of costs and prices is

------

*See Summary of Footnote References -- #16-40 thru #16-44

established through the market processes whereas in the Russian central system they are set by the accounting systems and procedures. The single enterprise is not geared toward the bottom line of the income statement nor are financial resources available on such a basis.

#16-42...Deficiencies of Russian Accounting

Professor Campbell summarizes the deficiencies of Russian Accounting as follows:
(1) cost accounting results from faulty depreciation estimates;
(2) lack of proper allocation of current expenditures to various kinds of output;
(3) omission of charges to product costs;
(4) poorly traced expense flows through the manufacturing processes;
(5) inascertainability of process or product costs;
(6) inability to account for land, all of which belongs to the government.
Under these conditions there can be no such thing as the U.S. balance sheet accounting. Hence Russian accounting is really working capital accounting.

#16-43...Efficacy of Russian Accounting

The irony of Russian accounting is that its prime objective is control, and it fails by a wide margin to attain it. This may be evidenced by the statement by R.H. Mills and A. L. Brown who pointed out in the JOURNAL OF ACCOUNTANCY, June 1966, pages 40-46, that:
The purpose of such rigidly constructed accounting reports is to facilitate better centralized control and planning. The reports are used in the evaluations of the administrative organizations and resource allocation process and are an integral tool in developing regional and national economic plans.
One area of considerable interest and importance is cost accounting. The virtual absence of the influence of the market mechanism on prices necessitates the determination and fixing of prices primarily on the basis of cost accounting reports. These reports are valid only to the extent that they have been properly prepared and reflect accurate cost data.

#16-44...Russian Balance Sheet Account Classification

A sample list of balance sheet account classifications presented by Bertrand Horwitz in ACCOUNTING CONTROLS AND SOVIET

ECONOMIC REFORMS OF 1966, American Accounting Association, 1970, pp. 11 & 13, is shown in Figure 16-7. The unique items are the Distributive Assets and Special Purpose Sources. The accounts listed could be used to draw up a balance sheet that would be similar to the statement of financial position for a governmental enterprise fund.

## CHINESE ACCOUNTING

### #16-45...Chinese Accounting

In using the term "Chinese," it is intended to be that for the People's Republic of China as differentiated from that of Taiwan. It includes accounting for mainland China, which of course is a controlled economy as contrasted with Taiwan, a free-market economy.

### #16-46...Chinese Economy

Since Jan. 1975, when a new constitution was adopted, the Chinese economy has undergone alternating periods of upheaval and stagnation, but a July 1979 INFORMATION GUIDE issued by Price Waterhouse & Co. points out that:
reasonably close estimates can now be made of economic per-
formance. The economy is predominantly agricultural and is
characterized by centralized planning, administration and
control. All industrial buildings, land and equipment belong
to the State. Workers are paid wages in cash, in contrast to
the peasants whose labor is paid principally in kind. ***
Coal is the principal source of energy. In 1978, 1,600 new
oil wells commenced production. Principal industries are
iron & steel, textiles, food processing & machine products.
Foreign trade is a state monopoly conducted principally through ten foreign trade organizations. China's major trading partners in 1977 were Japan, Hong Kong, West Germany, U.S., U.K., France, Soviet Union, Italy, Australia, and Canada. Exports comprise mainly foodstuffs, textiles and clothing, crude oil, chemicals and handicrafts. Principal imports are machinery and equipment, grain, steel, textile fibers, nonferrous metals, and fertilizers.

### #16-47...Chinese Currency and Exchange Rates

The Price Waterhouse INFORMATION GUIDE, July 1979, indicates:
The currency of China is the RENMINBI (RMB) or PEOPLE'S
CURRENCY. The basic unit is the YUAN which is divided into
10 JIAO (pronounced MAO); the smallest subdivision is the
TEN, or cent. Thus, 1 YUAN = 10 JIAO; 1 YUAN (Y) = 100 TEN
(cents); and 1 JIAO = 10 TEN. The RMB is an inconvertible

FIGURE 16-7
RUSSIAN BALANCE SHEET ACCOUNT CLASSIFICATION

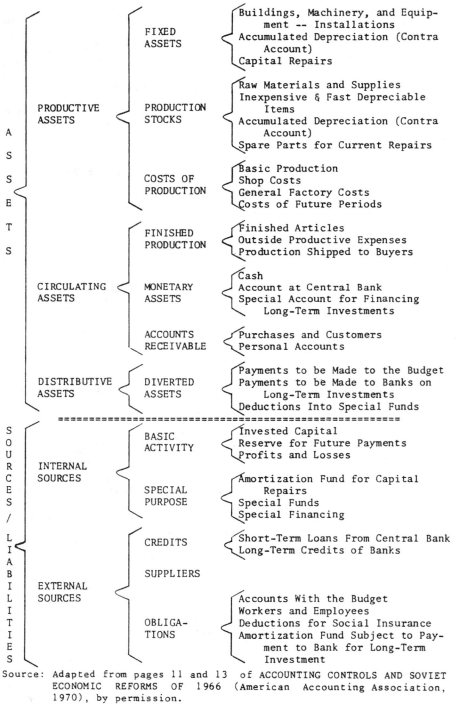

Source: Adapted from pages 11 and 13 of ACCOUNTING CONTROLS AND SOVIET
ECONOMIC REFORMS OF 1966 (American Accounting Association,
1970), by permission.

currency. Bank deposits can be maintained at the Bank of
China, but usually RMBs are bought and sold as needed for
commercial or travel purposes. The exchange value of the RMB
is determined by the Bank of China and changes periodically,
generally in response to international monetary conditions.
The Bank of China posts bid and offer rates for the RMB
against major Western currencies. The offering price of the
RMB has risen recently from 59.01 U.S. cents on Jan. 4, 1978
to 63.56 on Dec. 30, 1978. During 1978 it fluctuated between
57.6 and 63.6 U.S. cents.
     Since Aug. 1975, the Bank of China has permitted busi-
ness people with RMB denominated contracts to purchase RMBs
forward. However, the relatively high cost of forward RMBs
(30% for a 6-month contract), the availability of dollar
denominated contracts, and the stability of the RMB-U.S.
dollar exchange rates have combined to minimize forward
transactions. The RMB is NOT traded on international exchange markets and its use in foreign exchange transactions
is solely as a unit of account.
The People's Bank of China has published the following Renminbi
Exchange rates for major currencies for January in years 1977,
1978 and 1979:

| Country and Currency | | | Yuan 1977 | Yuan 1978 | Yuan 1979 |
|---|---|---|---|---|---|
| Australia | $A1 | = | 2.047 | 2.059 | 2.059 |
| Canada | Can$1 | = | 1.860 | 1.562 | 1.335 |
| France | Franc 1 | = | 0.382 | 0.360 | 0.369 |
| Germany | DM 1 | = | 0.796 | 0.836 | 0.845 |
| Japan | Y 1,000 | = | 6.422 | 7.078 | 7.871 |
| Netherlands | FL 1 | = | 0.712 | 0.748 | 0.783 |
| Switzerland | S Fr. 1 | = | 0.773 | 0.979 | 0.929 |
| United Kingdom | ₺ 1 | = | 3.198 | 3.283 | 3.161 |
| United States | $1 | = | 1.880 | 1.695 | 1.591 |

## #16-48...Chinese Foreign Trade System

     Foreign trade in China is a state monopoly controlled by the
Ministry of Foreign Trade. It is conducted exclusively through
a network of corporations organized on a commodities or services basis. It may be carried on through Joint Ventures, Barter
(or Switch Trade), or Counter-Trade or Compensation Trading.
     On July 1, 1979, a new LAW ON JOINT VENTURES USING CHINESE
AND FOREIGN INVESTMENT was adopted and became effective on July
8, 1979. The Joint Venture Law contains 15 articles, the first
three of which state purposes and objectives; Articles 4 and 5
relate to CAPITAL; Article 6 defines BOARDS OF DIRECTORS; Articles 7 and 8 provide for PROFIT; Articles 9 through 12 describe
PRODUCTION; Article 13 relates to LOSSES; Article 14, ARBITRA-
TION OF DISPUTES, and Article 15, EFFECTIVE DATE OF LAW.

Under the Barter or Switch Trade arrangement, China is interested in importing equipment or foodstuffs in exchange for a commodity in abundance in China. A notable example is the shipment of coal (which China has in abundance) for Japanese products.

Under Counter-Trade or Compensation Trading arrangements, China will provide factory premises and a stable work force to manufacture products in exchange for equipment, technical services and required raw materials of the foreign trade partner, which will receive the manufactured product as payment. In return, China is paid a discounted processing fee applied against initial cost of the equipment, subsequently taking ownership of the equipment and receiving the full processing fee.

### #16-49...The Chinese Accounting Profession

In the article "Observations of a CPA in China" in the JOURNAL OF ACCOUNTANCY, Jan. 1980, p. 80, Bernard Barnett, former president of the N.Y. State Society of CPAs and national director of tax practice of Seidman & Seidman, states that he "never met or spoke to a professional Chinese accountant (such an arrangement was not encouraged)." In response to the question asked "Is there an association of professional accountants or auditors in China?", the answer was, "What are accountants and auditors?" In reply to that question Mr. Barnett stated that they were "professionals who examine the books and records of an enterprise in order to verify the financial data," to which the following interrogatory response was, "Why should such persons be needed?" In response to the answer to this question, viz., that it was "to make certain that the financial statements accurately reflect the income and expenses--to ensure that the proper profits are turned over to the goverment," the response was, "Oh, no--that is totally unnecessary. No one in China would ever cheat his own government."

Mr. Barnett pointed out that "further questioning elicited that there was indeed some sort of audit function in the Economics Ministry or the national bank. Such an audit entity would apparently function as a super General Accounting Office."

### #16-50...Chinese Accounting Methods

The accounting methods in China are based on socialist principles. All former privately-owned businesses were nationalized in 1949 and thousands of new state-owned enterprises in the areas of merchandising, manufacturing, utilities, transportation, agriculture, housing, etc., were set up by the state, under the communist principle that the profit motive is subordinated to the "social welfare of the people" goal.

In the article "Cash Control System in Communist China," in

the Oct. 1955 ACCOUNTING REVIEW, p. 602, Stephen T. Smith notes that after the Communists assumed power in 1949, Chinese accountants who had been using Western accounting methods shifted to the Soviet accounting systems. This however was altered during the proletarian cultural revolution which took place in the late 1960s. As indicated in an article by Paul Kircher, "Accounting Revolution in Red China," in the FINANCIAL EXECUTIVE, Feb. 1967, p. 39, the Chinese accountants did not believe that the imported accounting methods were suitable for the communist economy, resulting in unfavorable effects, and they sought accounting reform.

#16-51...Chinese Accounting

It has already been pointed out on several occasions that a controlled economy must begin its accounting system with a Chart of Accounts. As no exception, China in late 1977 prescribed a uniform accounting system including a Chart of Accounts. Such charts denominate the general ledger account titles approved for business enterprises, and serve as a control device by limiting the number of control accounts, aid in uniformity in reporting and analysis, and establish uniform titles for business transactions.

#16-52...Chinese Uniform Chart of Accounts

Accounts are divided into four categories, viz., (I) Sources of Funds; (II) Applications of Funds; (III) Revenues; and (IV) Costs and Expenses. Each of the four categories is divided into general ledger accounts, which in turn are subdivided into detailed subsidiary accounts for control and managerial purposes. The Chinese, at the very root, have converted the debit-credit system we know toward its internal environment to make the basic accounting equation read
    **Total Source of Funds = Total Application of Funds**
so that the sum of the totals of categories (I) and (III) equals the sum of the totals of categories (II) and (IV).
    The Commercial Accounting Editorial Board, in the book COMMERCIAL ACCOUNTING, People's Press, Shanghai, China, 1977, p. 21, lists a chart of account such as Figure 16-8.

#16-53...Chinese Basic Accounting Equation

From Figure 16-8, it may be seen that the basic equation in Chinese accounting is

**Total Source of Funds = Total Application of Funds; or**
**Sources of Funds + Revenues = Application of Funds +**
**Expenditures**

FIGURE 16-8

CHINESE UNIFORM CHART OF ACCOUNTS

I. SOURCES OF FUNDS:

1. State Operating Fund
2. Special Reserve Fund
3. Other Operating Fund
4. Bank Loans
5. Accounts Payable
6. Revenue Clearance
7. Improvement & Construction
   Fund
8. Capital Repairs Fund
9. Workers' Welfare Fund
10. Production Assistance Fund
11. Distributive Earnings
12. Capital Fund
13. Cost-price Differentials
14. Net Earnings Summary
15. Operating Loss Subsidy
    From the Treasury
16. Earnings Remitted From
    Subunits
17. Operating Loss Subsidy
    From the Higher Unit

II. APPLICATIONS OF FUNDS:

22. Merchandise in Transit
23. Merchandise Inventory
24. Special Reserve Merchandise
25. Finished Goods
26. Goods in Process
27. Agriculture & Dairy Products
28. Raw Materials
29. Containers
30. Supplies and Small Tools
31. Furniture & Consumable Equipment
32. Allocating Expenses
33. Cash on Hand
34. Cash in Bank
35. Collection by Bank
36. Revolving Fund for Operations
37. Advanced Payments
38. Accounts Receivable
39. Unsettled Receivable
40. Loss Clearance
41. Disputable Fund
42. Construction Materials
43. Capital Fund Projects
44. Advances to Workers' Welfare Fund
45. Advances to Production Assis-
    tance Fund
46. Fixed Assets
47. Earnings Remitted to the Treasury
48. Deductions From Earnings
49. Earnings Remitted to the Higher
    Unit
50. Operating Loss Subsidy to
    Subunits

III. REVENUES:

18. Operating Revenue
19. Subcontract Operating
    Revenue
20. Assets Overage
21. Other Revenue

IV. COSTS AND EXPENSES:

51. Cost of Operations
52. Operating Expenses
53. Taxes
54. Subcontract Operating Cost
55. Assets Shortage
56. Support to Agriculture
57. Aid to Industry
58. Other Expense

Source: Adapted from material on page 21 in COMMERCIAL ACCOUNTING, Com-
        mercial Accounting Editorial Board (Shanghai, China:    People's
        Press, 1977).

This of course recognizes that the double-entry system is ac-
knowledged as being amenable to the financial accounting of a
socialist economy. The difference lies however in the fact that
Chinese accountants are of the opinion that the Western-and-
Soviet concepts of debit and credit are confusing. Therefore,
they have replaced it with a new increase-decrease system based
on the principle that all business transactions can be classified into the four basic groups of the Chart of Accounts. Thus
in order to maintain equilibrium, any transaction must fall
within one of four categories:

1. An increase in the Source of Funds and an increase in Application of Funds;
2. A decrease in Source of Funds and a decrease in Application
of Funds;
3. An increase in one Source of Funds item and a decrease in
another Source of Funds item; or
4. An increase in one Application of Funds item, and a decrease
in another Application of Funds item.

## #16-54...Recording Chinese Business Transactions

Prof. Philip C. Cheng of East Carolina Univ. made a study of
"Chinese Accounting Methods and Standards" which is reported in
the JOURNAL OF ACCOUNTANCY, Jan. 1980, pp. 76-85. In accordance
with the increase-decrease concept stated above, the entries
for four business transactions are illustrated as follows:

(1)  Working fund is appropriated from the state:
This transaction involves increase in both the Source of
Funds and the Application of Funds, expressed as:
Increase: State Operating Fund     xxx
Increase: Cash in Bank                    xxx
(2)  A piece of equipment is retired:
This transaction involves decreases in both the Source of
Funds and the Application of Funds expressed as:
Decrease: Capital Fund             xxx
Decrease: Fixed Assets                    xxx
(3)  Money is borrowed from the bank for payment of an account
payable:
This transaction involves only one side of the equation--
Source of Funds--and is expressed as:
Increase: Bank Loans               xxx
Decrease: Accounts Payable                xxx
(4)  Cash Purchases of Merchandise:
This transaction involves only one side of the equation--
Application of Funds--and is expressed as:
Increase: Merchandise Inventory    xxx
Decrease: Cash in Bank                    xxx

International Accounting

## #16-55...Recording Chinese Sales and Purchases

Prof. Cheng goes on to illustrate the entries for merchandising transactions as follows:
Assume that goods amounting to Y10,000 are shipped from Shanghai to Peking and the selling company paid freight of Y500 and all bank collection procedures have been arranged. The entry to record the transaction on the books of the selling firm would be as follows:

```
Increase: Sales Revenue          10,000
    Increase: Collection by
        Bank (Peking Supply
        (Depot)                          10,500
    Decrease: Cash in Bank                  500
```

When the selling company receives the collection memo from the bank, it would prepare an entry to record the collection as follows:

```
Increase: Cash in Bank           10,500
    Decrease: Collection by
        Bank (Peking Supply)
        Depot)                           10,500
```

After the buying company receives a copy of the collection memo from its bank and other documents related to the purchase, it must first make the necessary verifications and then prepare an entry as follows:

```
Increase: Mdse. Inventory        10,000
Increase: Operating Expenses
        (freight)                   500
    Decrease: Cash in Bank               10,500
```

Commodity markups also become part of the cost of merchandise inventory for accounting purposes at retail and are subsequently passed on to consumers. The markups are recorded in the cost-price differentials account, which is essentially an unrealized gross profits account, when the merchandise is received by the retailer. Markdowns are also entered in the cost-differentials account.

An illustrative entry to record a purchase for the retailer would be as follows:

```
Increase: Accounts Payable
        (Hangchow Supply
        Depot)                      10,000
Increase: Cost-Differentials
        (Clothing Dept.)             1,000
    Increase: Merchandise In-
        ventory (Sweaters)                  11,000
```

#16-56...Recording Chinese Fixed Assets Transactions

Because all land is owned by the Chinese government, it poses no valuation problems and does not appear on any accounting books or financial statements of a business. Fixed assets are defined as those having a cost of Y500 or more and an economic life of more than one year. Although the straight-line or composite rates of depreciation are used, they are oriented toward the communist philosophy, viz., depreciation is regarded as a transfer to the product cost. Prof. Cheng describes the entries for transactions involving fixed assets as follows:
  (1) Construction of a new warehouse at a cost of Y250,000 is approved and appropriated from the state:
      Increase: Improvement & Con-
                struction Fund      250,000
          Increase: Cash in Bank                    250,000
  (2) Construction payments are made:
      Increase: Capital Fund Pro-
                jects               250,000
          Decrease: Cash in Bank                    250,000
  (3) (a) Construction Work Completed:
      Decrease: Improvement & Con-
                struction Fund      250,000
          Decrease: Capital Fund
                    Projects                        250,000
  (3) (b) Warehouse is Recorded:
      Increase: Capital Fund        250,000
          Increase: Fixed Assets
                    (Warehouse)                     250,000
  (4) Current Depreciation is charged and funded to current operations:
      Increase: Improvement & Con-
                struction Fund        6,000
          Increase: Operating
                    Expenses (Dep.)                   6,000
  (5) Funded Depreciation is remitted to Higher Unit Per centralization of finance:
      Decrease: Improvement & Con-
                struction Fund        6,000
          Decrease: Cash in Bank                      6,000

#16-57...Recording Chinese Taxes and Earnings

In the book INDUSTRIAL SOCIETY IN COMMUNIST CHINA, N.Y., Random House, 1969, pages 503-504, Barry M. Richman indicates that about 90% of China's national revenue budget comes from transaction taxes and business earnings remitted by all types of enterprises except agriculture. The other 10% comes from house rentals and agricultural production. Because there is no corporate income tax, tax planning and managerial decisions are nonexistent.

According to Prof. Cheng:

Transactions taxes levied at 3% of sales price must be remitted by the tenth of the month following the date of sale. Since wholesalers are not regarded as transaction taxable entities, retailers are required to remit their monthly transaction taxes to the state. For accounting purposes, transaction taxes are deducted from earnings by retailers as illustrated:

(1) Assume that a retail company has sales of Y100,000 during the month and must pay transaction taxes of Y3,000. The entry would be:

Increase: Accounts (Taxes)
        Payable                3,000
Increase: Taxes Expense            3,000

(2) The transaction taxes are closed to the net earnings summary account at the end of the month:

Decrease: Net Earnings
        Summary                3,000
Decrease: Taxes Expense            3,000

(3) The transaction taxes are remitted to the state in the early days of the next month:

Decrease: Accounts (Taxes)
        Payable                3,000
Decrease: Cash in Bank              3,000

## #16-58...Chinese Financial Reporting

Unlike the U.S. and free economies, Chinese accounting serves the information users in four related ways:

(1) To reflect the information as to whether the economic activities of a business have complied with the overall objectives of the state;

(2) To use the information to develop plans and exercise controls;

(3) To furnish financial data to the central bank and commerce and finance departments to review national economic plans and monetary policies;

(4) To enable workers to have a better understanding and wider participation in implementation of national plans and policies.

To the above ends, the financial statements required are a complete report on financial position and operating results for the year. This results in four major required reports: (1) Telephone and Telegram Reporting of Primary Financial Indicators; (2) Schedule of Improvement and Construction Fund; (3) Statement of Operations; and (4) Statement of Funds Position. According to Prof. Cheng:

(1) The Telephone and Telegram Report is the effectuation of the principle that accounting is fundamentally a means of communicating financial information, and effective reporting involves, basically, getting the right information to the right persons at the right time. Therefore all businesses must report monthly the 13 financial indicators (such as bank loans, owned operating funds, sales, gross margin, distribution costs, transaction taxes and net earnings) by telephone or telegram to the higher unit.

(2) The Schedule of Improvement and Construction Fund sets forth in detail the deposits into and withdrawals from the improvement and construction fund. All changes in the fund, such as remittances to the state or a higher unit, appropriations to subunits and the acquisition or construction of fixed assets, will disclose whether the transactions are in conformity with financial rules and economic plans.

(3) The Statement of Operations summarizes the revenues and related costs and expenses of a business for a stated period of time. In addition, the statement has a group of supplementary data that is necessary to reflect some important economic events in the socialist economy, such as tax remittances to the state and wage payments to workers during the period.

(4) The Statement of Funds Position reflects the sources and applications of funds and the remittance of operating earnings to the state or appropriation from the state due to operating losses. This report can be used as a measure of success or failure in the reasonable, efficient use of resources and in fulfillment of prescribed financial rules.

Figure 16-9 is an illustration of a STATEMENT OF FUNDS POSITION based on material appearing in the book COMMERCIAL ACCOUNTING, by the Commercial Accounting Editorial Board, People's Press, 1977, Shanghai, China, page 235.

## #16-59...Future of Chinese Accounting

Prof. Cheng concludes his survey of Chinese accounting with the following observations:

It is evident that Communist China is attempting to break away from the traditional accounting concepts of the Western world. Where this path will lead is probably more dependent on political events than on whether the accounting systems are found to work or require substantial changes. As the world grows smaller, the West should be aware of these differences so that the accounting profession can better assess the impact of such changes on practices and research efforts.

The authors are of the opinion, from the great leap forward in business relations between the U.S. and China, that this is

FIGURE 16-9
STATEMENT OF FUNDS POSITION
AS OF DECEMBER 31, 1978

| SOURCES OF FUNDS: | | APPLICATIONS OF FUNDS: | |
|---|---|---|---|
| 1. OWNED OPERATING FUNDS | 378,400 | 1. MERCHANDISE & SUPPLIES | 388,756 |
| State Operating Fund | 378,400 | Merchandise in Transit | 2,500 |
| Special Reserve Fund | -- | Merchandise Inventory | 384,856 |
| Other Operating Fund | -- | Special Reserve Goods | -- |
| | | Finished Goods | -- |
| | | Goods in Process | -- |
| | | Agriculture and Dairy Products | -- |
| | | Raw Materials | 1,400 |
| 2. BANK LOANS | 2,667 | 2. NONMERCHANDISE RESOURCES | 16,658 |
| Merchandise Financing | 2,667 | Containers | 1,504 |
| Advanced Payments Loan | -- | Supplies & Small Tools | 1,935 |
| Capital Repairs Financing | -- | Furn.&Consumable Equip. | 13,189 |
| Special Loan | -- | Allocating Expense | -- |
| Sundry | -- | Cash on Hand | 30 |
| 3. NONBANK FINANCING | 13,795 | 3. EXPENDABLE RESOURCES | 4,528 |
| Accounts Payable | 13,650 | Cash in Bank | 1,582 |
| Revenue Clearance | 145 | Collection by Bank | -- |
| | | Operations Revolving Fund | 60 |
| | | Advanced Payments | -- |
| | | Accounts Receivable | 2,786 |
| | | Unsettled Receivables | -- |
| | | Loss Clearance | 100 |
| | | Disputable Fund | --- |
| 4. SPECIAL FUNDS | 5,282 | 4. USES OF SPECIAL FUNDS | 3,700 |
| Improvement & Construction Fund | 3,800 | Construction Materials | 2,000 |
| Capital Repairs Fund | -- | Capital Fund Projects | 1,200 |
| Workers' Welfare Fund | 1,482 | Advances to Workers' Welfare Fund | 500 |
| 5. CAPITAL FUND | 54,000 | 5. FIXED ASSETS | 54,000 |
| 6. EARNINGS & REMITTANCES | 165,662 | 6. DEFICITS & APPROPRIATIONS | 152,164 |
| Earnings of the Year | 165,662 | Losses of the Year | -- |
| Unremitted Last Year's Earnings | -- | Unappropriated Last Year's Losses | -- |
| Operating Loss Subsidy From the Treasury | -- | Earnings Remitted to the Treasury | 152,164 |
| | | Deductions from Earnings | -- |
| GRAND TOTAL | 619,806 | GRAND TOTAL | 619,806 |

Source: Adapted from material on page 235 in COMMERCIAL ACCOUNTING,
Commercial Accounting Editorial Board (Shanghai, China: People's Press, 1977).

necessarily going to involve  the stationing of  the Big 8 professional accounting firms on China soil. It is inevitable that
the  requirement that  the  accounting from the  U.S.  business
firms  kept  by U.S. methods will arouse  the curiosity of  the
Chinese. They will slowly but surely subscribe to and adopt our
accounting methodology.  Evidence of this is sprouting from the
report in the July  1980 JOURNAL OF ACCOUNTANCY, p.24, where it
is indicated:

> The Chinese Accounting Society, newly formed in the People's
> Republic of China, wishes to establish a  friendly relation-
> ship with the American Institute of  CPAs that would include
> "an academic  exchange  of knowledge," according to a letter
> from CAS Secretary Yeung Gee Un to LeRoy  J. Herbert, outgo-
> ing chairman of  the AICPA international  practice executive
> committee.  Herbert recently visited  China on business and,
> shortly after  returning home, received Yeung Gee  Un's let-
> ter.  As  part of the "academic exchange," the AICPA library
> now receives three Chinese-language copies of the CAS month-
> ly publication, FINANCE AND ACCOUNTING.

Hugh L. Marsh,  Jr., senior  vice-chairman of  the board of the
Institute of Internal Auditors, and general manager of internal
audit for  the Aluminum Company of America, was invited in Nov.
1983 by the Audit  Agency of the People's Republic of  China to
visit that country to discuss  the Institute of Internal Auditors' activities, training  programs, publications and research.
In  Feb.  1984 he met with officials  of  the  Foreign  Affairs
Dept., many other government officials, and academicians.  In a
report to the  JOURNAL OF ACCOUNTANCY, May 1984, pp.  24-25,  he
noted that a number of the largest U.S. international CPA firms
have already established representative  offices  in China, and
provided in the report a first-hand view of the differences  in
accounting  and auditing practices between the U.S. and  China.
Some of the highlights of Mr. Marsh's report, inter alia, indicate that:

> The CPA  in China must be  chartered by the Ministry  of
> Finance.  Applicants to the profession must pass a certified
> examination.  The estimated 8 million accountants  have been
> trained at some 30 universities or colleges  or some 250 vo-
> cational middle schools in China that  offer  courses in ac-
> countancy.  A great number of new accountants are turned out
> also by evening  classes, TV university classes, correspond-
> ence courses, seminars, and other  advanced education class-
> es.

> China's  first Auditor General  was appointed by the 6th
> National People's Congress in June 1983. Organizing and set-
> ting up the various levels of  the Audit Agency in the  pre-
> fectures,  provinces,  counties &  municipalities throughout
> China involved  some 30,000 individuals, which is planned to
> be increased to 60,000 in the next 2 years.  This number may

increase because the new Constitution requires all business entities to have internal auditors, and it is estimated that the number of entities in China exceeds 500,000.

Generally, China applies internationally accepted principles and standards of accounting to govern joint venture operations, including the standard calendar year and the double-entry system. Some of the largest U.S. international CPA firms are represented in China, five in Peking, two in Shanghai, and one in Fuzhou. The government allows only one office per firm within the country, which is usually little more than hotel rooms converted into office space. However, the independent audits normally associated with such firms can be performed only by authorized government agencies.
As indicated above, China is on the way toward an explosion in the area of accounting. Because of its vast size, the future of the accounting profession in China may change significantly.

## SUMMARY OF FOOTNOTE REFERENCES
(References are to Paragraph #'s)

#16-5 AICPA, AUDITS OF STATE AND LOCAL GOVERNMENTAL UNITS (1974), p. 4

#16-6 Arthur Andersen & Co., SOUND FINANCIAL REPORTING IN THE PUBLIC SECTOR, 1975, pp. 7-21. Reprinted with permission.

#16-6 Reprinted with permission from U.S. NEWS & WORLD REPORT (Feb. 25, 1985): 57. Copyright, 1985, U.S. News & World Report, Inc.

#16-27 Dept. of Commerce, International Economic Report of The President, 1975.

#16-29 Dhia Al Hashim, ACCOUNTING FOR MULTINATIONAL ENTERPRISES (Indianapolis: Bobbs-Merrill, 1978), p. 9

#16-33 Gerhard Mueller, ACCOUNTING PRACTICES IN SWEDEN (College of Business Administration, Univ. of Washington, 1962), p. 47

#16-38 Dhia Al Hashim, op. cit., pp. 9-13

#16-39 Hans Singer, STANDARDIZED ACCOUNTANCY IN GERMANY (Cambridge University Press, 1944), p. 15

#16-40 thru #16-44: "Russian Accounting," adapted from Norlin G. Rueschhoff, INTERNATIONAL ACCOUNTING AND FINANCIAL REPORTING, 1976, Praeger Publishers, Inc., by permission.

#16-40 Robert Campbell, ACCOUNTING IN SOVIET PLANNING AND MANAGEMENT (Harvard University Press, 1963)

#16-43 R.H. Mills and A.L. Brown, JOURNAL OF ACCOUNTANCY (June 1966): 40-46. Copyright © 1966 by the American Institute of Certified Public Accountants, Inc. Opinions expressed in the JOURNAL OF ACCOUNTANCY are those of editors and contributors. Publication in the JOURNAL OF ACCOUNTANCY does not constitute endorsement by the AICPA or its committees.

#16-44 Bertrand Horwitz, ACCOUNTING CONTROLS AND SOVIET ECONOMIC REFORMS OF 1966 (American Accounting Association, 1970), pp. 11, 13. Reprinted with permission.

#16-46 Price Waterhouse, INFORMATION GUIDE FOR CHINA (July

1979)
#16-47 Ibid.
#16-48 LAW ON JOINT VENTURES  USING  CHINESE AND FOREIGN INVESTMENT
        (July 1, 1979)
#16-49 Bernard  Barnett, "Observations of a CPA in China," JOURNAL
        OF ACCOUNTANCY (January 1980): 80.     Reprinted with permis-
        sion.  Copyright © 1980 by  the American Institute of Certi-
        fied  Public Accountants, Inc.   Opinions  expressed in the
        JOURNAL OF  ACCOUNTANCY  are those  of editors and contribu-
        tors.  Publication in  the  JOURNAL OF ACCOUNTANCY  does not
        constitute endorsement by the AICPA or its committees.
#16-50 Stephen  T. Smith, "Cash Control System in Communist China,"
        ACCOUNTING REVIEW (October 1955): 602
#16-50 Paul Kircher, "Accounting  Revolution in Red China,"  FINAN-
        CIAL EXECUTIVE (February 1967): 39
#16-52 Commercial Accounting  Editorial  Board, COMMERCIAL ACCOUNT-
        ING (Shanghai, China: People's Press, 1977), p. 21
#16-54 Philip C. Cheng, "Chinese Accounting Methods and Standards,"
        JOURNAL OF ACCOUNTANCY (January 1980): 76-85. Reprinted with
        permission.   Copyright © 1980 by  the American Institute of
        Certified Public Accountants, Inc. Opinions expressed in the
        JOURNAL  OF ACCOUNTANCY are  those of editors  and contribu-
        tors.  Publication in  the  JOURNAL OF ACCOUNTANCY  does not
        constitute endorsement by the AICPA or its committees.
#16-55 Ibid., by permission.
#16-56 Ibid., by permission.
#16-57 Barry  M.  Richman,  INDUSTRIAL  SOCIETY IN COMMUNIST  CHINA
        (N.Y.: Random House, 1969), pp. 503-504
#16-57 Cheng, op. cit., by permission.
#16-58 Ibid., by permission.
#16-58 Commercial Accounting Editorial Board, op. cit., p. 235
#16-59 Cheng, op. cit., by permission.
#16-59 JOURNAL OF ACCOUNTANCY (July 1980): 24
#16-59 Hugh L. Marsh,  Jr., Report  to JOURNAL  OF ACCOUNTANCY (May
        1984): 24-25

## BIBLIOGRAPHY

Al Hashim, Dhia.  "Social Accounting in Egypt," INTERNATIONAL JOUR-
        NAL OF ACCOUNTING EDUCATION & RESEARCH (Spring 1977):127-141
Bailey,  D.T.   "The Accounting Profession in Russia," ACCOUNTANCY,
        88 (March 1977): 70-73
Bailey,  D.T.  "Accounting in Russia: The European Connection," IN-
        TERNATIONAL JOURNAL OF ACCOUNTING EDUCATION & RESEARCH (Fall
        1982): 1-36
Berry, M.H.  "The Accounting Function in Socialist Economies,"  IN-
        TERNATIONAL JOURNAL OF ACCOUNTING EDUCATION & RESEARCH (Fall
        1982): 185-198
Chastain, C.E.  "Soviet Accounting  Lags Behind the Needs of Enter-
        prise Managers," INTERNATIONAL MANAGEMENT  REVIEW (April
        1982): 12

Conference Board. UNDERSTANDING THE BALANCE OF PAYMENTS. N.Y.: Con-
    ference Board, 1970
Gorelik, George. "Soviet Accounting, Planning, and Control," ABA-
    CUS, 10 (June 1974): 13-25
Hoyt, Ronald and Maples, Lawrence. "Accounting for Joint Ventures
    With the Soviet Bloc and China," INTERNATIONAL JOURNAL OF
    ACCOUNTING EDUCATION & RESEARCH, 16 (Fall 1980): 105-124
Lederer, Walther. "How the U.S. Balance of Payments Affects the
    Dollar," EUROMONEY (March 1978): 85-93
Motekat, Ula K. "The Accounting Cycle for a People-Owned Enter-
    prise," THE WOMAN CPA, 41 (April 1979): 16-23
National Foreign Trade Council, Inc. THE BALANCE OF PAYMENTS, Memo-
    randum 9845 (April 22, 1971)
Reichmann, Thomas and Lange, Christoph. "The Value Added Statement
    As Part of Corporate Social Reporting," MANAGEMENT INTERNA-
    TIONAL REVIEW, 21 (1981): 17-22
Yang, Chi-Liang. "Mass Line Accounting in China," MANAGEMENT AC-
    COUNTING, 62 (May 1981): 13-21

## THEORY QUESTIONS
(Question Numbers are Keyed to Text Paragraph #'s)

#16-1  Discuss the nature of Macro International Accounting.
#16-2  How may International Macro Accounting be classified?
#16-7  Discuss the nature of National Income Accounting.
#16-8  Explain Balance-of-Payments acctg. and how it operates.
#16-9  How has International Balance-of-Payments been defined?
#16-11 What is the Balance-of-Payments basic equation?
#16-18 What is the significance of the term BALANCE as used in
       connection with Balance-of-Payments?
#16-25 Make an appraisal of the efficacy of the balance-of-pay-
       ments accounting, indicating why have balance-of-pay-
       ments statements in the light of the many inconsisten-
       cies and discrepancies that exist.
#16-26 Discuss the relationship of balance-of-payments to Macro
       Accounting.
#16-28 Discuss the operation of accounting as a National Econo-
       my Policy Instrument. What country illustrates such
       usage of accounting?
#16-30-31. Discuss the macroconcept of the Swedish Inventory
       Reserves and Depreciation Allowances.
#16-38 Explain how Egypt exercises control of businesses
       through accounting.
#16-40 Explain the importance of accounting to the Soviet Rus-
       sia economy.
#16-41 Make a comparative analysis of Russian accounting with
       that in the U.S.
#16-42-43. What are the deficiencies of Russian accounting and
       how effective is it?
#16-46 Discuss the nature of the Chinese economy.

#16-47 Discuss Chinese currency and exchange rates.
#16-49 What is the  status of the Chinese accounting profession and what is its future?
#16-52-53. Explain  the Chinese Uniform Chart  of Accounts and the operation of the Chinese Basic Accounting Equation.
#16-58 In how  many ways does Chinese accounting serve informa- tion users?  What  four major  reports are required and explain the nature of each.
#16-59 Discuss the future of Chinese accounting.

## EXERCISES

### EX-16-1

With  respect to consolidated  financial  statements,  proposed for the U.S. government, the following are some of the account- ing and reporting questions that arise.

1. Are the criteria established therein for including govern- ment and quasi-government  entities in the statements appropri- ate to best reflect the overall financial position  and operat- ing results of the government?

2. Should  future retirement and Social Security  benefits be treated as liabilities?

3. Should increases in the official  rate for gold be treated as income?

4. Should individual  income  taxes receivable be recorded on an accrual basis?

5. Does the government have  adequate procedures  to properly account for inventory items on hand?

6. Have "excess materials  awaiting  disposition" been stated at net realizable values?

7. Does the  government have adequate procedures to  properly account for capital assets?

8. Is  it appropriate for the  government to  capitalize  and depreciate the cost of assets?

9. Are reserves for loan guarantee defaults and other contin- gencies required to reflect potential losses or present liabil- ities?

**Required**:
For each of the above, answer "yes" or "no", and explain.

### EX-16-2  (CPA EXAM, 5/21, AUDITING, #2)

You are called upon to audit the accounts of  Dec. 31, 1920, of a company incorporated in the state of New York, which owns all the capital stock of  two other companies, one  incorporated in Great  Britain  and the other in Russia.  No reports have  been received from the Russian company since Dec. 31, 1917.  All the intercompany  transactions have been  recorded on the  books at the pre-war rates of exchange.

Before giving an unqualified certificate to the consolidated

balance sheet of these companies at Dec. 31, 1920, on what basis would you require the accounts to be stated in regard to
fluctuations in exchange and possible loss on Russian assets,
assuming that the balance sheet of each company revealed the
following assets and liabilities?

| | |
|---|---|
| Goodwill | Capital Stock |
| Plant & Equipment | Accounts & Notes Payable |
| Inventories | Surplus |
| Accounts Receivable | Cash |

## PROBLEMS

### P-16-1

The United States Government Ledger shows the following account
balances in billions of dollars for the fiscal year ending September 30, 1985:

Accounts Receivable....35
Accrued Taxes Receivable....25
Advance Prepayments....10
Accounts Payable....150
Accrued Military Personnel Pension & Disability
      Liabilities....450
Accrued Civilian Personnel Pension & Disability
      Liabilities....500
Accrued Federal Employees Compensation....10
Accrued Social Security Pension & Disability
      Liabilities....1,800
Accrued Veterans' Compensation Pension & Disability
      Liabilities....225
Public Borrowing....1,200
Buildings, Structures and Facilities....140
Cash--Treasury Operating....40
Cash--International Monetary Reserves....25
Cash--Miscellaneous....15
Construction in Progress....40
Contingent Liabilities....5
Deferred Charges and Other Assets....85
Equipment....85
Inventories--Goods for Sale....45
Inventories--Materials and Supplies....70
Inventories--Raw Materials....15
Inventories--Stockpiled Commodities....16
Inventories--Work in Progress....4
Land....10
Leasehold Improvements....5
Loans Receivable....220
Military Hardware....300
Other Liabilities....60
Other Pension Plans....15

```
        Other Property and Equipment....4
        Accumulated Depreciation....300
        Unearned Revenue....30
```
**Required**:
Using the  above data, construct  a Federal Government  Balance
Sheet in good form.

**P-16-2**
The following items in billions of dollars appear in the International Economic Report of the U.S. Department of Commerce for
the year 1984:

(I). GOODS IN SERVICES:

| From | Item | Receipts | Item | Pay-ments |
|------|------|----------|------|-----------|
| Trade: | Exports | 130 | Imports | 100 |
| Military: | Sales | 6 | Expenditures | 8 |
| Investments: | Income Recpts | 25 | Income Pymts | 20 |
| Travel: | Income | 10 | Expenditures | 12 |
| Other Services: | Net | 5 | --- | -- |

(II).  CURRENT ACCOUNT ITEMS:

| | | | |
|---|---|---|---|
| Non-Military Remittances | -- | | 2 |
| U.S. Government Grants | -- | | 3 |

(III).  LONG-TERM PRIVATE CAPITAL FLOWS:

| | | | |
|---|---|---|---|
| Foreign Direct Invest-ments in U.S. | 2 | U.S. Investments Abroad | 6 |
| Net Portfolio Investment | -- | | 4 |
| Other Long-Term Private Capital | -- | | 2 |

(IV).  U.S. GOVERNMENT CAPITAL FLOWS:

| | | |
|---|---|---|
| U.S. Govt. Capital Flows | -- | 4 |

**Required**:
Using  the above  data, construct a Balance-of-Payments Summary
Statement for 1984.

**P-16-3**
The Vodka Co. of Moscow has the following accounts in its ledger:

```
        Account at Central Bank
        Accounts With the Budget
        Accumulated Depreciation
        Amortization Fund for Capital Repairs
        Amortization Fund to Bank for Long-Term Investment
        Basic Production
        Buildings, Machinery and Equipment
        Capital Repairs
        Costs of Future Periods
        Cash
        Deductions for Social Insurance
        Deductions into Special Funds
```

    Finished Articles
    General Factory Costs
    Inexpensive & Fast Depreciating Items
    Invested Capital
    Long-Term Bank Credits
    Outside Productive Expenses
    Payments to the Budgets
    Payments to Long-Term Banks
    Personal Accounts Receivable
    Production Shipped to Buyers
    Profits and Losses
    Purchases and Customers Accounts Receivable
    Raw Materials and Supplies
    Reserve for Future Payments
    Special Account for Long-Term Investments
    Special Financing
    Special Funds
    Short-Term Loans
    Shop Costs
    Spare Parts for Current Repairs
    Workers and Employees Accrued Wages

**Required**:
Using the above data, construct in good   form a Russian Balance
Sheet for the Vodka Co.


**P-16-4**
The Great Wall Co. of Peking engages  in the following merchandising transactions in the month of September:
  (1) Merchandise  valued  at  Y 20,000 (Yuan)  shipped to  the
      Lotus Co. of Shanghai.   The Great Wall Co. paid  freight
      charge of Y 400.
  (2) The Great Wall  Co. receives the collection memo from the
      bank.
  (3) The Lotus Co. receives a copy of the collection memo from
      its bank and makes the necessary verification.
  (4) The Lotus Co. records the purchase on its books.
**Required**:
    a. Record the journal entries for transactions (1) and (2) on
the books of the Great Wall Co., vendor.
    b. Record the journal entries for transactions (3) and (4) on
the books of the Lotus Co., vendee.


**P-16-5**
The Canton  Co. engages in the following  Fixed  Asset Transactions during October:
  (1) The State approves and appropriates for construction of a
      new plant valued at Y 500,000.
  (2) The Y 500,000 construction payments are made.

(3) The construction work is completed.
(4) Plant value is recorded on the books.
(5) Current Depreciation of Y 12,000 is charged and funded to current operations.
(6) Per Centralization of Finance, funded Depreciation is remitted to Higher Unit.

**Required:**
Prepare journal entries for the foregoing six Fixed Asset Transactions.

**P-16-6**
The balances in the accounts of the Won Ton Co. of Canton as of December 31, 1984, are as follows:

        State Operating Fund....400,000
        Merchandise Financing Bank Loan....3,000
        Accounts Payable....14,000
        Improvements and Construction Fund....5,000
        Capital Fund....50,000
        Merchandise Inventory....400,000
        Raw Materials....2,000
        Containers....2,000
        Tools and Supplies....2,000
        Furniture and Fixtures....15,000
        Cash in Bank....1,700
        Accounts Receivable....3,000
        Construction Materials....2,000
        Capital Fund Projects....1,500
        Fixed Assets....50,000
        Earnings Remitted to Treasury....192,800

Earnings of the year came to 200,000 Yuan.

**Required:**
Construct a Statement of Funds Position for the Won Ton Co. as of December 31, 1984.

# PART III


# SECTION TWO

# QUASI MACRO ANCILLARY INTERNATIONAL ACCOUNTING ASPECTS

# International Social Accounting

SOCIAL ACCOUNTING CONCEPTS

#17-1....Nature of Social Accounting

A new pattern of development concerned with expanding the accounting dimension to include SOCIAL RESPONSIBILITY (frequently referred to as S/R) stewardship has emerged since the later 1960s and early 1970s. This development has had the effect of broadening the traditional financial statements for user audience by expanding the accounting process to include new types of social reporting. A review of these emerging social accounting concepts is relevant to the study of comparative international accounting principles.

#17-2....Classification of Social Accounting Concepts

Social accounting concepts fall into three main categories: Social Responsibility (S/R) Reporting; Developmental Accounting; and Behavioral Accounting.

S/R Accounting represents an extension of the financial statement audience to those readers who have an interest in the social effects of the policies of the public-owned enterprise. Developmental Accounting is concerned with the promotion of economic development and the reporting of the effects and stages of such development. Behavioral Accounting, of very recent vintage, deals with the behavioral science relationship to accounting. Developmental and Behavioral Accounting are treated in the next chapter.

SOCIAL RESPONSIBILITY ACCOUNTING

#17-3....Socio-Economic Accounting

The expansion of social responsibility has impelled the accountant to consider reporting the effects of certain social

costs, expenditures and benefits. Welfare accountability is
coupled with environmental accountability as a new dimension
for accountants, making for the birth of Socio-economic Accounting.

## #17-4....Definition of Social Accounting

Social Accounting has received definitions by many writers.
In the article "Corporate Social Accounting in the U.S.A.:
State of the Arts and Future Prospects," in Vol. 1, No. 1, AC-
COUNTING ORGANIZATIONS AND SOCIETY, 1976, pp. 23-42, Epstein,
Flamholtz and McDonough define Social Accounting as "the iden-
tification, measurement, monitoring and reporting of the social
and economic effects of an institution on society."

At the 4th International Conference of Accounting Education
in Berlin (1977), a considerable part of the program was devoted to the matter of introducing Social Accounting into the accounting curriculum. Three groups were appointed to study the
subject and report on it--German, French, and English-speaking.
At page 47 of the published BERLIN CONFERENCE PROCEEDINGS,
Prof. Sieben summarized the results of the German-speaking
group:

> Social Accounting is in fact the comprehensive accounting
> system; the other areas, such as Financial Accounting, being
> simply sub-areas of Social Accounting in its broad interpre-
> tation. The discussion, however, was based on the tradition-
> al definition, that is, Social Accounting was seen as an
> extension of existing accountancy.

On page 48 Prof. Perridon reported on the results of the
French-speaking discussion group:

> The first issue which was considered was what is expected
> of Social Accounting. As in the German-speaking group, we
> agreed that the term ACCOUNTING is not well chosen. It does
> not take into consideration that the company influences the
> environment and the environment the company. We defined So-
> cial Accounting as a management tool with which the aims of
> a social policy can be determined and carried out and with
> which the fulfillment of these aims can be measured. ***
> Social Accounting should be included in the accounting edu-
> cation programme, both in basic and continuing education,
> and it should be offered as a specialization.

The views of the English-speaking discussion group are expressed on page 49 by Prof. Brummet as follows:

> The only concensus we could come to in our discussion was
> that we had an interesting subject to talk about. Otherwise
> everyone had a different point of view. *** The main ques-
> tions involving Social Accounting seemed to be: Why and to

what extent do we need Social Accounting? How can Social
Accounting be defined and what are its goals? *** I would
like to emphasize that Social Accounting is a field which
absolutely requires an interdisciplinary approach, for example, in the elaboration of suitable measurement techniques.
This is the only way we will be able to clearly define Social Accounting.  *** In conclusion I would like to stress
that Social Accounting is still in the experimental stages.
There is still much research to be done before we have the
answers to all our questions.
It should be observed that there was little if any agreement
between the three major-language-speaking country representatives as to what Social Accounting really is.  The only clear-
cut conclusion of all was that there is a need for Social Accounting even though no one apparently seems to know precisely
what it is.  In SUBJECT 5, p. 7, of the Conference Proceedings,
Prof. Brummet refers to a definition in the 1957 DICTIONARY FOR
ACCOUNTANTS prepared by Eric Kohler:
      Social Accounting is the application of double-entry
      bookkeeping to socio-economic analysis; it is concerned with
      the construction, estimation, and analysis of national and
      international balance sheets, and the design of a system of
      component accounts.
      The activity contemplated by this definition continues
      to be important for both public and private policy deci-
      sions, but let us note that it is purely economic in nature.
      It is appropriately labeled social accounting only to the
      extent that social well-being is economic based.  *** It is
      totally sterile with regard to human perceptions and thus
      human welfare per se.  Thus my concern is for a different
      definition of social accounting.

Prof. Brummet proceeds to point out what he believes to be the
modern concept of Social Accounting:
      K.V. Ramanathan, writing in the ACCOUNTING REVIEW, defines
      Social Accounting as "the process of selecting firm-level
      social performance variables, measures, and measurement pro-
      cedures; systematically developing information useful for
      evaluating the firm's social performance; and communicating
      such information to concerned social groups, both within and
      outside the firm." This is the modern concept of social ac-
      counting.  It focuses on the essence of human well-being
      rather than solely on the financial or economic aspects of
      that well-being.
In SUBJECT 5, p. 8, Prof. Brummet points out that the AICPA
has set up a Committee on Corporate Social Measurement,
which, in a publication issued by it, sets up an explanation
of an IDEAL system of Social Accounting:
      (1) An ideal system of social measurement would, in fact, be

a SYSTEM based on MEASUREMENT. (2) It would produce information about each and every cause/effect relationship arising out of the impact of any defined entity on the quality of life of all significant segments of society. (3) The resulting information would be expressed in quantitative terms that not only would be separately useful for the immediate purposes of the measurements, but also would be initially expressed in, or converted to, a single common measurement unit. (4) Measurements would be made for the duration of the impacts, in a manner giving appropriate recognition to timing differences, using direct methods without surrogates; they would be consistently applied across entities and constituencies, and over time, in a manner neutral toward any particular set of social objectives, and requiring only a minimal expenditure for measurement costs. (5) The information thus produced would permit both the entity's management and outsiders to engage in efficient decision-making, using sound socio-economic planning and control procedures; to evaluate an entity's past, present, and intended actions using both normative and non-normative bases of comparison; and to continue, or, if need be, to modify the entity's "contract with society."

Prof. Brummet makes the following comments on the above Report: "While totally idealistic and incapable of total solution, these statements should give us a clear focus on our subject, viz., assessing an entity's contribution to human welfare."

Prof. Brummet indicates that "some members of our profession may believe that we should not venture into this new area." He prefers to go along with the opinion expressed by the NAA, which in a recent article states:

Accountants can either choose to accept the challenge and develop concepts and tools to help business meet the challenge of dealing with the pluralistic and political realities of its environment more systematically and responsibly, or they can ignore the challenge and continue to hide behind a special-interest perspective which frustrates efforts to extend the capacity of accounting to serve multiple interest. There is little doubt in our minds that the latter alternative is irresponsible and makes little sense from a strategic point of view for the long-term viability of the accounting profession.

After discussion of all groups at the Berlin Conference, Prof. Brummet finally arrives at the following definition of Social Accounting:

There are already many definitions but I would like to suggest the following simple definition which relates to organizations both in the private and public sector: "Social Accounting should be thought of as the keeping track, or the monitoring, of efforts and results of activities of organi-

zations in the social sphere, or of the externalities, the
social externalities that relate to mainstream activities of
organizations." Thus social accounting implies interdisciplinary support.

#17-5....Relationship of Socio-Economic Accounting
        to Social Programs and Institutions

Socio-economic accounting reports on the performance of social programs and social institutions. Social institutions employ a system of fund accounting. Social programs can be integrated with the fund accounting system of a not-for-profit entity, or within a governmental unit. The types of funds are
current unrestricted, restricted, endowment, loan, annuity,
plant and agency. The stress on the fund arrangement and its
data accumulation is designed to report on the stewardship accountability for expenditures funded. Audit guides have been
published to deal with the financial reporting problems, e.g.,
AICPA'S AUDITS OF COLLEGES & UNIVERSITIES, 1973, and HOSPITAL
AUDIT GUIDE, 1972. However, socio-economic accounting should
extend beyond a mere reporting of expenditures.

#17-6...Socio-Economic Accounting Principles and Precepts

Socio-economic accounting should also be designed to measure
the social benefits, and/or costs involved in connection with
social programs. A set of socio-economic principles must be
established, which has been proposed by David Linowes in the
JOURNAL OF ACCOUNTANCY, #136, No. 1, 1973, page 34, in "The
Accounting Profession and Social Progress," as follows:
(1) Clearly set forth standards for measurement when making
fund appropriations for those objectives for which the social program or agency exists. (2) Keep changing the mix of
resource inputs--viz., the kind of things being sought with
the budgeted funds--until satisfactory results are achieved.
(3) Use the existing qualitative measurement standards in
the social, education, and welfare areas--standards which
are now being overlooked in assessing these non-business
operations. (4) Establish a marketplace mechanism, or at
least create feedback reporting procedures among the clients
of the social programs. (5) Use discretionary fund allocations as an executive incentive device. (6) Merge two or
more agencies which are too small to be effective. (7) Divest deficient units of an otherwise effective agency. (8)
Prepare social reports regularly for qualitative accomplishments, as well as the usual financial reports. (9) Fix responsibility for applying socio-economic accounting principles. (10) Establish a regular program of socio-economic
audits by independent outsiders.

FIGURE 17-1
CHRYSLER U. S. EMPLOYMENT

| Job Category | Year End | Total No. Employees | Women | | Minority Groups | | | | | |
|---|---|---|---|---|---|---|---|---|---|---|
| | | | No. | % | Black | Asian | Amer. Indian | His-panic | Total Min. Employees | % |
| Officials and Managers | 1975 | 11,116 | 156 | 1.4 | 1,058 | 21 | 5 | 37 | 1,121 | 10.1 |
| | 1976 | 11,944 | 260 | 2.2 | 1,313 | 19 | 9 | 50 | 1,391 | 11.6 |
| | 1977 | 12,529 | 312 | 2.5 | 1,388 | 23 | 10 | 68 | 1,489 | 11.9 |
| Professionals | 1975 | 7,691 | 356 | 4.6 | 214 | 91 | 5 | 24 | 334 | 4.3 |
| | 1976 | 7,680 | 468 | 6.1 | 265 | 108 | 4 | 26 | 403 | 5.2 |
| | 1977 | 8,152 | 646 | 7.9 | 366 | 144 | 3 | 37 | 550 | 6.7 |
| Technicians | 1975 | 3,735 | 113 | 3.0 | 106 | 21 | 1 | 11 | 139 | 3.7 |
| | 1976 | 4,676 | 162 | 3.5 | 141 | 28 | 2 | 14 | 185 | 4.0 |
| | 1977 | 5,737 | 245 | 4.3 | 223 | 33 | 1 | 21 | 278 | 4.8 |
| Office and Clerical | 1975 | 7,830 | 4,291 | 54.8 | 699 | 12 | 10 | 59 | 780 | 10.0 |
| | 1976 | 7,779 | 4,384 | 56.4 | 756 | 18 | 10 | 53 | 837 | 10.8 |
| | 1977 | 7,947 | 4,615 | 58.1 | 854 | 20 | 15 | 61 | 950 | 12.0 |
| TOTAL WHITE COLLAR | 1975 | 30,372 | 4,916 | 16.2 | 2,077 | 145 | 21 | 131 | 2,374 | 7.8 |
| | 1976 | 32,079 | 5,274 | 16.4 | 2,475 | 173 | 25 | 143 | 2,816 | 8.8 |
| | 1977 | 34,365 | 5,818 | 16.9 | 2,831 | 220 | 29 | 187 | 3,267 | 9.5 |

| Category | Year | | | | | | | | | |
|---|---|---|---|---|---|---|---|---|---|---|
| Craftsmen Skilled | 1975 | 13,614 | 9 | .06 | 894 | 23 | 11 | 80 | 1,008 | 7.4 |
| | 1976 | 15,569 | 14 | .09 | 1,132 | 22 | 12 | 110 | 1,276 | 8.2 |
| | 1977 | 16,044 | 15 | .09 | 1,119 | 23 | 13 | 121 | 1,276 | 8.0 |
| Operatives (Semi-Skilled) | 1975 | 82,063 | 8,595 | 10.5 | 30,942 | 170 | 52 | 921 | 32,085 | 39.1 |
| | 1976 | 88,353 | 10,963 | 12.4 | 32,560 | 171 | 65 | 1,028 | 33,824 | 38.3 |
| | 1977 | 90,318 | 12,646 | 14.0 | 32,602 | 188 | 59 | 1,089 | 33,938 | 37.6 |
| Laborers (Unskilled) | 1975 | 1,243 | 12 | 1.0 | 646 | 4 | 0 | 25 | 675 | 54.3 |
| | 1976 | 1,376 | 50 | 3.6 | 747 | 5 | 0 | 48 | 800 | 58.1 |
| | 1977 | 2,023 | 64 | 3.2 | 1,018 | 7 | 0 | 53 | 1,078 | 53.3 |
| Service Workers | 1975 | 2,985 | 171 | 5.7 | 1,130 | 3 | 1 | 14 | 1,148 | 38.5 |
| | 1976 | 3,341 | 219 | 6.6 | 1,224 | 4 | 0 | 24 | 1,252 | 37.5 |
| | 1977 | 3,203 | 268 | 8.4 | 1,129 | 3 | 1 | 25 | 1,158 | 36.2 |
| TOTAL BLUE COLLAR | 1975 | 99,905 | 8,787 | 8.8 | 33,612 | 200 | 64 | 1,040 | 34,916 | 34.9 |
| | 1976 | 108,639 | 11,246 | 10.4 | 35,663 | 202 | 77 | 1,210 | 37,152 | 34.2 |
| | 1977 | 111,588 | 12,993 | 11.6 | 35,868 | 221 | 73 | 1,288 | 37,450 | 33.6 |
| GRAND TOTALS | 1975 | 130,277 | 13,703 | 10.5 | 35,689 | 345 | 85 | 1,171 | 37,290 | 28.6 |
| | 1976 | 140,718 | 16,520 | 11.7 | 38,138 | 375 | 102 | 1,353 | 39,968 | 28.4 |
| | 1977 | 145,953 | 18,811 | 12.9 | 38,699 | 441 | 102 | 1,475 | 40,717 | 27.9 |

Source: REPORT TO SHAREHOLDERS, 1978, Chrysler Corporation.

## SOCIAL RESPONSIBILITY ILLUSTRATIVE CASES

### #17-7....Social Responsibility Cases

To illustrate the foregoing principles and their emergence on the accounting scene, three cases will be presented: Chrysler Corporation; Sears Roebuck; & Westinghouse. In all three cases the declaration of the social aspects is made in the Reports to the corporate shareholders as part of their regular reporting procedures.

### #17-8....The Chrysler Case

In its mid-year REPORT TO SHAREHOLDERS for the six months ended June 30, 1978, the Chrysler Corp. states:

#### CHRYSLER COMMITTED TO EQUAL OPPORTUNITY

Chrysler Corporation is committed to a policy of equal opportunity for all people. Chairman John Riccardo reaffirmed that commitment recently in Detroit when he said: "Chrysler will continue to support and expand its employment, training, and upgrading programs that offer the rewards, promise, and human dignity of meaningful job opportunities for all people. We made our decision to be involved long ago. Nothing will change that now."

The table <shown in Figure 17-1> provides recent employment information and reflects the results of the company's affirmative action program.

### #17-9....The Sears Roebuck Case

The statistics provided in Figure 17-1 follow the job categories as required by the EQUAL EMPLOYMENT OPPORTUNITY COMMISSION created by Congress to see that minorities are not discriminated against. All of the larger corporations are required by law to keep these statistics and report them to the EEOC. Within the past several years there have been a multiplicity of federal employment policies which like an octopus has stretched out in all directions and engulfed itself in a maze of contradictions and inconsistencies. This became so onerous and unbearable as to cause Sears Roebuck & Co., which employed over 430,000 workers as of Jan. 1978, to file a suit in the Federal Court naming 10 federal government agencies as defendants. The bill of complaint charged that "the government itself, by laws and regulations dating back over three decades has made it impossible for Sears to comply with the laws regarding employment of minorities and women."

The reason the suit was filed is that the EEOC had been giving Sears a rough time. In 1977 the Commission accused Sears of

discriminating against blacks, women  and Spanish Americans  in
some jobs, a suit that was still pending in 1979. The basis for
this suit was statistical evidence  of disparities  between minority and women representation in various parts of Sears' work
force and the work force as a whole.

Sears was of the opinion  that it was  being  scrutinized by
EEOC because of its size and national visibility and that there
was  no foundation in  fact to  support any great deficiency in
its employment practices. In  order  to avoid any controversy,
Sears instituted a strict quota system in 1974, but the Commission was not satisfied. The suit therefore requested the federal agencies to cease their harassment of Sears and to present a
coherent  and realistic policy with respect  to the proper  employment system to be used to comply with the law.  The statistics furnished to EEOC  regarding its minority hiring practices
are presented in Figure 17-2.

Commenting on  the  litigation,  the  CHICAGO  TRIBUNE,  in
an editorial presented on Jan. 26, 1979, states:

The lawsuit depicts  Sears  as a  beleaguered  Gulliver,
fettered  by scores  of  legal and bureaucratic Lilliputians
tugging at it from different directions. Veterans preference
and  education benefit laws encouraged the  company to  draw
employees  from  the  predominantly  male military services.
Equal opportunity regulations then stepped in  and told  the
firm it had too few women employees.  Then Congress  turned
around and ordered the company not to retire anyone until he
is  70 years old, thus  decreasing the number  of  positions
available for minority and female applicants.  And to top it
all,  Sears charges,  the federal government  has failed  to
take steps to create a society  in  which the work force includes sufficient numbers  of well-qualified minority applicants.

If we have any quibble  with Sears' lawsuit, it is  only
that  the suit does  not specifically attack  quota  systems
which are at odds with the American ideal of  quality of opportunity, the very ideal they are now said to advance.  The
frustration this suit  represents, the sheer outrage at government  policy  divided against itself,  and  the light  it
sheds on the  smug irresponsibility of federal bureaucracies
that  want to saddle  private business  with  the burden  of
their own  failures of  vision are worth the Sears'  effort.
When a company with as deep a concern for its social responsibility as Sears is committed to social justice, there  appears to be a wrong that needs to be exposed and corrected.

It  is apparent that  the point made by Sears is that while Social Responsibility may be a good thing when carried ·out in the
proper perspective, it may nevertheless result  in  a  possible
destruction  of a  business  enterprise  where capriciously and
injudiciously exploited.  On June 9, 1981, in a CHICAGO TRIBUNE

FIGURE 17-2

SEARS ROEBUCK AND COMPANY EMPLOYMENT

(Percentage of female and minority employees in each EEOC job category)

| Job Category | Period | Female % | Black % | Asian American % | Native American % | Hispanics % | Total Employees (thousands) |
|---|---|---|---|---|---|---|---|
| Officials & Managers | Feb. 66 | 20.0 | .4 | .2 | .1 | .7 | 33.4 |
| | Jan. 78 | 36.0 | 7.2 | .4 | .2 | 2.7 | 52.5 |
| Professionals | Feb. 66 | 19.2 | .8 | .5 | .0 | .4 | 1.3 |
| | Jan. 78 | 59.2 | 5.5 | 1.3 | .0 | 2.3 | 2.0 |
| Technicians | Feb. 66 | 48.1 | 1.1 | 1.5 | .0 | .7 | 1.5 |
| | Jan. 78 | 50.6 | 12.1 | 1.3 | .1 | 4.7 | 2.3 |
| Sales Workers | Feb. 66 | 56.9 | 3.2 | .6 | .1 | 1.5 | 98.7 |
| | Jan. 78 | 64.9 | 11.9 | .7 | .2 | 4.3 | 143.6 |
| Office & Clerical | Feb. 66 | 86.0 | 3.1 | .6 | .1 | 2.0 | 78.6 |
| | Jan. 78 | 86.6 | 13.2 | .9 | .2 | 5.2 | 115.7 |
| Craft Workers | Feb. 66 | 3.8 | 2.8 | .7 | .1 | 2.8 | 20.8 |
| | Jan. 78 | 8.1 | 8.9 | 1.0 | .4 | 5.7 | 30.2 |
| Operative | Feb. 66 | 12.0 | 13.8 | .8 | .1 | 3.5 | 23.4 |
| | Jan. 78 | 22.4 | 19.0 | .9 | .2 | 6.9 | 12.8 |
| Laborers | Feb. 66 | 34.3 | 18.4 | .3 | .1 | 6.5 | 15.2 |
| | Jan. 78 | 30.7 | 23.9 | .7 | .3 | 7.0 | 56.1 |
| Service Workers | Feb. 66 | 32.3 | 44.9 | .5 | .1 | 2.0 | 9.9 |
| | Jan. 78 | 44.4 | 32.1 | 1.0 | .3 | 6.8 | 15.1 |
| ALL CATEGORIES | Feb. 66 | 50.7 | 5.9 | .6 | .1 | 2.1 | 282.8 |
| | Jan. 78 | 56.7 | 13.9 | .8 | .2 | 5.0 | 430.3 |

Source: Adapted from statistics furnished EEOC by Sears, Roebuck & Co.

editorial it was reported that Sears and the EEOC arrived at an
agreed settlement of the four suits  filed against  Sears.  The
editorial  points out that the final settlement amounted  to  a
victory for Sears, and  that the litigation should serve to diminish future harassment of large corporations.

#17-10...The Westinghouse Electric Case

A fairly substantial portion of the Second Quarter 1978  Report to the Stockholders of the  Westinghouse Electric Corporation involves: "Social  Responsibility -  What Westinghouse is
Doing."  The report states:
   Corporations were originally formed as economic entities
whose primary responsibility was providing goods  and  services at  a profit.   In  carrying out this economic function
they provided jobs and  paid taxes which, in turn, supported
government services.   Until the 1930s these were considered
the only legitimate activities of a  corporation.  But since
then the public has begun to  expect and then press corporations to act, to give, and to do.  Westinghouse responses to
the needs of society add up to an impressive show of  corporation Social Responsibility and can be proud of its  accomplishments in contributing to  the good  of its various pub-
lics. In fact, more often than not, it is impossible to separate Westinghouse's own economic interest  from  society's.
Many areas of our concerns and expertise serve both corporation and society--energy, transportation, broadcasting,  and
education.
   A  Social Responsibility Committee at the senior management level reviews  major Westinghouse  programs and actions
and the effects on our three broad constituencies--internal,
employees and  stockholders;  customers  and suppliers;  and
society at large.
   INTERNAL SOCIAL  RESPONSIBILITY.  The interests of Westinghouse are in a very real sense identical to the interests
of the people who work here.  Now, more than ever, people at
Westinghouse come  from every part of society.  Westinghouse
had  affirmative action plans well before they were required
by law.  In  the past two years, some  32%  of the  incoming
class of college graduates consisted of  minorities  and women.  A special placement program has in two years increased
the number of minority managers by 26%, minority professionals by 34%, women managers by 28% and women professionals by
41%.  Minority  and women engineers are hard to  come by, so
Westinghouse  has often taken  the initiative  in developing
technical talent.
   Westinghouse encourages all its employees to continue
their education through a tuition-refund program.  In  some
cases it actually brings college classes to the  plant.  Al-

though not required  by any labor agreement, it has periodically increased pension benefits for its retired workers.
     CUSTOMERS AND SUPPLIERS. Westinghouse began a program of
product safety before government regulation was   introduced.
It  has an excellent record of compliance  with the Consumer
Product Safety Act   and   with   the   Occupational   Safety and
Health Act. It has also designed training courses in product
safety for the Department of Energy.  Among suppliers, Westinghouse has increased the number of minorities represented.
Since 1975, purchases from  minority  suppliers have quadru-
pled.  The corporation publishes a minority suppliers direc-
tory; every month tax payments  averaging  over $21  million
are deposited  in  20 black-owned banks,  and life insurance
coverage  with black-owned insurance  companies  amounts  to
$102 million.
     PUBLIC AT LARGE.  Westinghouse's interface with the com-
munity at large is made in hundreds of ways. In the field of
broadcasting and program production, it has had a  long tradition  of serving "in the public interest, convenience  and
necessity," as prescribed by the Federal Communications Commission. Throughout the years it has taken positions against
crime,  violence and sex in  television programming  and has
protested the ever-increasing commercial content  of television.  It has won critical acclaim for many special programs
and for public service work done.  It also contributes money
and  equipment through  its corporate contributions program,
such  as United Way.  Some  $800,000  goes to education and
$600,000  to hospital  grants. We have been  sponsoring the
Science Talent Search for 37 years, and  give  over $138,000
to  symphonies, theaters, ballets and  the allied arts. More
than $52,000 went to the  Urban League and the NAACP.  Along
with the National Endowment for the Humanities it has funded
the production  of two films, HOW CONGRESS  WORKS and AN ACT
OF CONGRESS  which will be broadcast nationally.  The SOCIAL
RESPONSIBILITY  COMMITTEE will continue  to look at Westinghouse's  responsibilities  to our various  constituencies to
determine  what the important problems are, where our mutual
interests lie, and what are the appropriate priorities.
The Westinghouse Report  is a  fairly comprehensive  picture of
what the social responsibilities of a M/N/C can be.

#17-11...Financial Format of S/R Statements

     It is interesting to note that the Westinghouse Report enum-
erates the  various S/R endeavors or activities it  engages in,
but  does  not  present, except very broadly, any  figures  or
statements involving costs and expenditures. The question that
arises is whether or not MNCs  should contrive to  issue statements  in financial terms as accounting reports specializing in

the S/R aspects of the enterprise.  In an article entitled "The Challenge for International Business," California State University at San Jose, Oct. 25, 1972, Harvey Kapnick, chairman of Arthur Andersen & Co., says:

> Information of this type (S/R) would provide a realistic basis for the public to evaluate the progress of a particular business in helping to solve the social problems in each country in which it operates, the priority it has given to those social goals, and the clear indication of the social liabilities under which it is operating in each country and the cost of those liabilities. Such information would also supply the fact to those who believe that multinational businesses are insensitive to the business practices and social needs of the countries in which they operate.

Specifically, Mr. Kapnick suggests that the following information be included in such reports:  (1) General Objectives (expected rate of growth, priorities & social problems being solved); (2) Employee Data (new jobs created, countries & costs, employees training costs, employee productivity);  (3) Product Development (planned product changes, research & development costs); (4) Taxes Paid to Foreign Governments;  (5) Investors' Returns (interest paid, dividends);  (6) Government Regulation Costs.

## #17-12...Social Responsibility Financial Statements

There are two questions associated with the matter of S/R Financial Statements:  (1) what information should be included and how should it be presented; and (2) what seems to be the experience in this area.  Both of these questions are addressed by a study made by the international accounting firm, Ernst and Ernst, of the 500 largest corporations listed in FORTUNE magazine, known as the FORTUNE 500.

## #17-13...S/R Financial Statement Categories

Deriving from the overall survey of the corporations, it appears that there are six general categories reported:  Environment, Equal Opportunity, Personnel, Community Involvement, Products, and Other S/R Disclosures.  The following enumerates the specific areas under each:
(1) Environment:  pollution control, reduction of pollutive effects arising from use through product development, environment repair, waste material recycling, other environment disclosures
(2) Equal Opportunity: minority employment, minorities advancement, women employment, women advancement, minority business, other disadvantaged groups, other equal opportunity statements

(3)  Personnel: employee health and safety, training, other
     disclosures of personnel responsibility
(4)  Community Involvement: community activities, public
     health, art and education, other disclosures of community
     activity
(5)  Products: safety, quality, other disclosures product re-
     lated
(6)  Other S/R Disclosures: corporate S/R objectives, compli-
     ance with applicable governmental regulations, business
     ethics, participation in self-regulatory trade associa-
     tions, additional S/R material offer.

It should be observed that in the presentation of the Westinghouse case, virtually all of the 6 categories were presented
in report form, whereas the Chrysler report embraced items 3
and 6 only. It should be noted further that in item 6, involving compliance with applicable governmental regulations, the
Sears case indicates the apparent overemphasis and conflict of
governmental regulations, making for a negation of compliance
with some regulations as contradictory to compliance with others.
   The Ernst and Ernst study of the FORTUNE 500 corporations
elicits the following response with respect to the making of
S/R disclosures:

| Year | S/R Company Disclosures Made | No S/R Company Disclosures Made | Not Available | Total |
|------|------------------------------|----------------------------------|---------------|-------|
| 1971 | 239 | 226 | 35 | 500 |
| 1972 | 286 | 206 | 8  | 500 |
| 1973 | 298 | 198 | 4  | 500 |
| 1974 | 346 | 151 | 3  | 500 |
| 1975 | 425 | N/A | 75 | 500 |

It appears as though there is a steady, though not sharp,
increase in the number of companies making disclosures.

#17-14...Experience of Types of S/R Financial Statement
         Presentation

   S/R DISCLOSURE STATEMENTS may be presented in report form or
in financial statement form. The Westinghouse Statement is a
very good illustration of the Report Form which verbally describes what the corporation is doing and how much in expenditures are being made. The Financial Statement Form would be one
which enumerates the various categories in columns and inserts
the money costs involved under each category, as will shortly
be illustrated by the GERMAN SHELL CASE. Of course, S/R Dis-

closure Statements may report certain activities engaged in
without the corresponding costs expended. The Ernst and Ernst
study discloses the following information with respect to the
form the S/R Disclosure Statement was presented for the year
1975:

| S/R Category Reported | S/R Report Form Statement | S/R Financial Statement Form |
|---|---|---|
| 1. Environment | 103 | 117 |
| 2. Equal Opportunity | 66 | 11 |
| 3. Personnel | 59 | 7 |
| 4. Community Involvement | 54 | 52 |
| 5. Products | 10 | 2 |
| 6. Other S/R Disclosures | 1 | 0 |

Most likely it is only a matter of time before all S/R Disclosure Financial Statements will be presented as another Exhibit, added to the long list now extant, of Statements or
Schedules drafted to support other major statements to which
they are subordinate.

#17-15...Accounting Orientation and the Public Interest

S/R Accounting brings a new dimension that has been conspic-
uously absent from the science of accounting, viz., to correct
the accounting to date that has been ignoring the public interest. Since an economic entity goes to make up the national economic order, a business enterprise should be geared to coordinating its activities with national economic policies. As Prof.
Mueller has stated:
    If we add the accounting dimension which asserts that ac-
    counting measures, directs, controls and reports the econo-
    mic activities of the firm, it would seem to follow that
    firm goals have a close relationship to the public interest
    by virtue of their correspondence with national economic
    policies. While it is generally agreed that the corporation
    must recognize its primary responsibility to its stockhold-
    ers, there are also parallel corporate obligations to socie-
    ty at large, regarding the corporation as the standard bear-
    er for maintaining satisfactory levels of economic well-be-
    ing; for the creation of more economic wealth than what is
    used up in its productive processes; and for scientific,
    technical, and social innovations which make human life in-
    creasingly more pleasurable.
In the final analysis the true value of S/R Disclosure Accounting is in its advancement of the science of accounting to true
professionalism as pointed out by Prof. Mueller:
    A very real question exists about the extent to which ac-

countants and accounting should be concerned with the public
interest. As accountants move closer and closer to professional status for their services and activities, concern
with the public interest should grow correspondingly. It
seems rather clear that a key pillar of professionalism is
recognition and defense of the public interest. The classical professions of law, medicine, and theology demonstrate
this concept amply. Writers of a later age will no doubt say
the same about accounting.
Surely, S/R Accounting falls within this caveat.

## GOVERNMENTAL INVOLVEMENT IN SOCIAL RESPONSIBILITY

### #17-16...Codes of Conduct and Social Responsibility

One device used in foreign countries to attempt to attain
social responsibility on a high level is through the employment
of CODES OF CONDUCT. The countries in which the foreign operations are conducted set up such codes expecting the MNC to adhere to their guidelines and thereby attain a degree of harmony
between the MNC and the government. Because these Codes are
established in concert with government officials, this aspect
may be more greatly geared to the political aspects than the
social, although it is definitely social in character. Further
treatment of Codes of Conduct will be made in the Political
Accounting chapter.

### #17-17...Socio-Economic Operating Statement

Social programs are administered directly by social not-for-
profit enterprises and governmental entities. They are not restricted to social institutions, but are also fulfilled through
business enterprises. They may be directly administered through
contributions to social organizations or indirectly by expenditures that benefit society. One method of socio-economic reporting is to prepare a SOCIO-ECONOMIC OPERATING STATEMENT,
tabulating separately the expenditures made voluntarily for
improving the welfare of employees, the public safety of the
company's products or services, and the conditions of the environment, pointed out by David Linowes in his book THE CORPORATE
CONSCIENCE, 1974, Hawthorn Books, pages 104-137. Such a STATE-
MENT may be particularly applicable to MNCs which participate
in the social progress of foreign countries. The Statement may
be designed to fulfill the requirements of a Code of Conduct
for M/Es. Political Contributions could also be reported in
these Statements.
Socio-Economic Financial Statements for Germany, France,
England and The Netherlands are presented below.

## #17-18...German Socio-Economic Financial Statements

It appears that Germany and France claim to have made much
more progress in this area than the U.S. or anywhere else in
the world. In an article entitled "The Corporate Social Report:
The Deutsche-Shell Experience," in ACCOUNTANCY, Dec. 1976,
Richard Van den Bergh points out:

The Consultation Document "Aims and Scope of Corporate
Reports" produced by the Department of Trade is only the
most recent of an increasing number of proposals on this
subject in the industrial world. The overall conclusion is
that corporate social responsibility is moving, slowly but
surely, from being a phrase of convenience and goodwill to
an accountable reality. Companies will, within the foreseeable future, have to account publicly for their total performance.
The strongest move in the expansion of corporate reporting has taken place in Germany. Since 1972, ten companies
have published so-called SOCIAL BALANCES OR REPORTS, and it
is known that many of the 200 largest industrial companies
are in the process of preparing reports. Employers' and Industry Associations, among others, are also undertaking research in this area. Falling short of full potential, the
German Reports are designed to show the activities and performances of the companies for and on behalf of specific
constituent groups. The corporate social report as it is
developing in Germany tries to give a more comprehensive
view of what the company is doing, without restrictions to a
narrow financial or economic analysis.
*** The report which is to serve as an example of German practice is that produced by Deutsche Shell AG (DSAG), a
wholly owned operating company within the Shell Group. It is
one of the most comprehensive reports produced to date and,
as part of the annual report, has a unique structure. In
comparison with the CORPORATE REPORT PROPOSALS and the consultation paper, it certainly is the most interesting.
Deutsche Shell's 1975 Annual Report is not a financial
report with a few sections added describing activities of a
social nature. It is a report which sets out to assess its
activities in the year measured against explicit stated corporate objectives. It differs from previous German reports
of this kind by integrating the SOCIAL ACCOUNT into the annual report and by using its corporate objectives as a basis
of accounting.

## #17-19...Deutsche Shell AG Report

After stating the objectives by putting the year into perspective, the report is divided into six parts, the first five

referring to each corporate  objective and the sixth being   the
financial statements.

The five objectives established  by DSAG in 1974,   each considered of equal value, were as follows:

(1) supplying the consumer in line with market conditions;

(2) development of new processes and products;

(3) achievement of an adequate return on capital;

(4) consideration of the interests of employees; and

(5) attention to public concerns.

A  description of each of the five objectives is  then detailed
in expository fashion in the report.  Mr. Van den Bergh goes on
to point out that:

of most  interest to  accountants,  however, is not the  descriptive report  but the financial  statements.   Three new
accounts have been added, intended to put the financial performance of  Shell  into perspective, given both its  objectives and the interests of its constituencies.

Figure 1:  The SOCIAL ACCOUNTS, or using its German mis-
nomer, the SOCIAL BALANCE, is a structured  presentation  of
the costs incurred for  the  activities relevant to  the employees.  This type of account was first adopted by the mining company STEAG in  1972 and has been used  and adapted by
almost  all the companies producing social reports to  date.
It is a cost account restructuring the expenditures in terms
of their purpose. Where applicable the postings are referred
back to the text which  serves as notes to the accounts, and
their positions in the profit and loss account.

Figure 2:  RELATIONS TO INVESTORS shows the transactions
in both the  p/l account  and balance  sheet which  directly
affect the investors.  It is the first time that such an account has been produced  in Germany  and may become the subject of much discussion in the future.

Figure 3:  PERFORMANCE ACCOUNT  serves to reconcile the
social accounts with the financial  statements,  and at  the
same  time is  a type of  value-added  statement.   It shows
clearly  in summary  form the changing  allocation of corporate resources.

Illustrations  of  the accounting statements  for each of these
are shown in Figure 17-3, consisting of 3 pages.

## #17-20...Criticisms of German Social Reports

Mr. Van den Bergh  points out three criticisms of the social
reports  produced  to date, which are  applicable to the  Shell
Report, as follows:

First, certain issues have  been omitted, in most  cases
intentionally on grounds of practicality.  The degree of objectivity of these reports will  remain questionable  until
suitable methods of assessment and presentation are developed.

```
============================================================
```

FIGURE 17-3
DEUTSCHE SHELL AG SOCIAL ACCOUNTS

F i g u r e   1 -- S o c i a l   A c c o u n t s

| Item | Report Page | P&L Position | Cost (000 DM) 1975 | Cost (000 DM) 1974 |
|---|---|---|---|---|
| **RELATIONS TO PERSONNEL:** | | | | |
| I. Wages | 24 | 16 | 60,725 | 58,894 |
| Salaries | | 16 | 133,249 | 131,341 |
| TOTAL I | | | 193,974 | 190,235 |
| II. Benefits Accruing Directly to Employees (Excluding Wages and Salaries) | | | | |
| 1. General | | | | |
| (a) Christmas Bonus (13th month) | | 16 | 16,055 | 15,764 |
| (b) Holiday Pay | | 17 | 5,750 | 4,590 |
| (c) State Sponsored Saving Scheme (employer contribution) | | 16 | 3,099 | 3,262 |
| (d) Other (Inc. rebate on Shell products) | | 1,26 | 1,821 | 1,753 |
| 2. For Special Reasons | | | | |
| (a) Suggestions Scheme | 28 | 16 | 90 | 64 |
| (b) Long Service Bonus | | 16 | 300 | 395 |
| (c) Birth Grant | | 18 | 32 | 32 |
| (d) Marriage Grant | | 18 | 173 | 131 |
| (e) Work Safety Competition | 26/28 | 16 | 646 | 712 |
| (f) Rent Subsidies | | 16 | 398 | 424 |
| TOTAL II | | | 28,364 | 27,127 |
| III. Benefits Accruing Indirectly to Employees | | | | |
| 1. Employer Contribution: | | | | |
| (a) Pension Insurance )( | | | | |
| (b) Health Insurance )( | | 14,16,17 | 20,857 | 13,852 |
| (c) Unemployment Ins. )( | | | | |
| 2. Employer's Liabil. Ins. | | 17 | 1,670 | 1,643 |
| 3. Work Undertaken for Co. Health Scheme (Salaries, Rent, etc.) | | Various | 622 | 612 |
| TOTAL III | | | 23,149 | 16,107 |
| IV. Benefits Accruing Directly To Personnel as a Group | | | | |
| 1. Miscellaneous | | | | |
| (a) Co. Medical Serv. | 28 | Various | 806 | 799 |
| (b) Accid. Prevention | 26-28 | Various | 2,000 | 2,000 |
| (c) Holiday Homes | | Various | 130 | 112 |
| (d) Sports Assn. Subsidies | 25 | Various | 514 | 493 |
| | | | 3,450 | 3,404 |

|  |  |  |  |  |  |
|---|---|---|---|---|---|
| 2. | Education & Training |  |  |  |  |
|  | (a) Training Centre | 25 | Various | 523 | 546 |
|  | (b) Language Courses | 25 | Various | 64 | 46 |
|  | (c) Other Training | 25 | Various | 1,401 | 1,372 |
|  | (d) Trainees and Apprentices | 25 | Various | 1,136 | 1,289 |
|  |  |  |  | 3,124 | 3,253 |
| 3. | Other |  |  |  |  |
|  | (a) Work Clothes |  | 26 | 624 | 538 |
|  | (b) Cost of Canteen |  | 26 | 4,023 | 4,400 |
|  |  |  |  | 4,647 | 4,938 |
|  | TOTAL IV |  |  | 11,221 | 11,595 |

| V. | Benefits to Pensioners and Dependents |  |  |  |  |
|---|---|---|---|---|---|
| 1. | Pension Payments | 24 | 18 | 27,030 | 22,772 |
| 2. | Transfer to Pension Reserves | 24 | 18 | 77,329 | 74,017 |
| 3. | Insolvency Ins. | 24 | 18 | 669 | -- |
|  | TOTAL V |  |  | 105,028 | 96,789 |

| VI. | Work Council's Relations With Personnel |  | Various | 1,579 | 1,559 |
|---|---|---|---|---|---|

| TOTALS I THROUGH VI |  |  |  | 363,315 | 343,412 |
|---|---|---|---|---|---|
| Less Double Counting (especially personnel costs) |  |  |  | ( 6,507) | ( 7,012) |
|  |  |  |  | 356,808 | 336,400 |

## ATTENTION TO PUBLIC CONCERNS:

| I. | Relations to the Consumer |  |  |  |  |
|---|---|---|---|---|---|
| 1. | Research & Develop. | 18/19 | Various | 35,717 | 32,578 |
| 2. | Cost to Secure Splies | 11 |  | NA | NA |
|  | TOTAL I |  |  | 35,717 | 32,578 |

| II. | Relations to Environment |  |  |  |  |
|---|---|---|---|---|---|
| 1. | Air Purification )( |  |  |  |  |
| 2. | Noise Control )( |  |  |  |  |
| 3. | Preservation of )( Countryside )( | 33/34 | Various | 62,000 | NA |
| 4. | Waste-Water Control)( |  |  |  |  |
|  | TOTAL II |  |  | 62,000 | NA |

| III. | Relations to the Public |  |  |  |  |
|---|---|---|---|---|---|
| 1. | Youth Work | 30/31 | Various | 722 | 590 |
| 2. | Donations & Charitable Contributions | 32 | 26 | 390 | 363 |
| 3. | Publications , etc. | 28/29 | Various | 1,791 | 2,697 |
| 4. | Taxation & Rates (including capital gains tax) | 35 | 24a,b,c | 138,870 | 209,782 |
| 5. | Subscriptions to Assns, Institutes, etc. |  | 26 | 5,225 | 4,705 |
| 6. | Other Contributions |  | 26 | 3,721 | 2,786 |
|  | TOTAL III |  |  | 150,719 | 220,923 |

| TOTALS I THROUGH III |  |  |  | 248,436 | 253,501 |
|---|---|---|---|---|---|
| Less: Double Counting |  |  |  | (10,747) | (11,109) |
|  |  |  |  | 237,689 | 242,392 |

Figure 2 -- Relations To Investors

|  | Cost (000 DM) | |
|---|---|---|
|  | 1975 | 1974 |
| **I. Results Effective** | | |
| Dividends | 100,000 | 153,000 |
| Genußscheinbedienung | -- | 136,732 |
| Interest Expense | 51,725 | 55,117 |
| Less: Interest Income | (17,770) | (22,421) |
| Net Interest Expense | 33,955 | 32,696 |
| Capital Gains Tax - Results 1973 | -- | (40,992) |
| Results 1974 | (43,460) | -- |
|  | 90,495 | 281,506 |
|  | | |
| **II. Balance Sheet Effective** | | |
| Increase in Capital | (100,000) | -- |
| Loans - Taken Up | (186,679) | (48,514) |
| Repaid | 112,500 | 12,500 |
|  | (174,179) | (36,014) |


Figure 3 -- Performance Accounts

|  | | 1975 | | 1974 | |
|---|---|---|---|---|---|
|  | Page | (000 DM) | % | (000 DM) | % |
| **DISTRIBUTIONS TO:** | | | | | |
| Employees | 23-29 | 356.8 | 4.8 | 336.4 | 3.8 |
| Community | 20-34,35 | 237.7 | 3.2 | 242.4 | 2.8 |
| Company Rein- vestment | 22 | 107.1 | 1.4 | 493.8 | 5.7 |
| Investors | 20-22 | 90.5 | 1.2 | 281.5 | 3.2 |
| Suppliers | 35 | 6,695.4 | 89.4 | 7,375.0 | 84.5 |
| TOTALS | | 7,487.5 | 100 | 8,729.1 | 100 |

|  | P&L Position | 1975 (000 DM) | 1974 (000 DM) |
|---|---|---|---|
| **SOURCES:** | | | |
| Proceeds From Turnover (Excl. duty, excise and tax) | 1 | 7,321.6 | 7,793.6 |
| Change in Levels of Inventories | 2 | ( 117.1) | 398.0 |
| Capitalised Cost of Co. Prod. Assets | 3 | 4.0 | 2.9 |
| Income From Profit Pooling Contracts | 7 | 76.8 | 282.0 |
| Income From Investments | 8 | 1.6 | 0.9 |
| Income From Other Financial Invest. | 9 | 3.5 | 3.3 |
| Other Income | 14 | 258.3 | 260.3 |
| TOTAL BEFORE LOSSES | | 7,548.7 | 8,741.0 |
| Less: Losses Assumed According to Profit & Loss Pooling Contracts | 25 | 61.2 | 11.9 |
| NET TOTAL | | 7,487.5 | 8,729.1 |

Source: Adapted from Richard Van den Bergh, "The Corporate Social Report: The Deutsche-Shell Experience, " ACCOUNTANCY (Dec. 1976)
==========================================================

Second, the virtual omission of environmental impact  by
companies in industries where  pollution control is a  major
issue reduces the social relevance of their reports.

Third, and most fundamental, this type of  report covers
the  activities of the company and a more  or  less detailed
account  of how resources and surpluses are allocated within
a societal context.  They do not show the social benefits or
costs that accrue except in general verbal terms,  i.e., the
net societal contribution or impact of  corporate operations
is not assessed.

He concludes that certainly there are a  number of improvements
that can be made on the social  reports  in their present form,
both by  modifying the accounts themselves and by supplementing
them.

## #17-21...French Socio-Economic Reporting

In  the article "Social  Accounts:  France  Sets the Pace,"
(WORLD ACCOUNTING REPORT, Feb. 1978), John Moore points out:

The decree of Dec. 8, 1977, following up the recommendations of the Sudreau Report on French Company Law Reform, at
last  codifies what  many companies in other  countries have
regarded to be a confused and confusing area--that of social
reporting.

Nevertheless, the previous absence of detailed  guidance
on  social  reporting has not prevented some  of the largest
French companies experimenting with  such  reports in  a sophisticated  and inventive manner which  leaves whatever attempts that  have  been made in this direction in many other
countries look sadly inept.

It would  be  unfair  to blame other companies elsewhere
out  of hand for not  taking more initiative, for what  most
have lacked is encouragement.  But if France is the hare in
this field, the UK is a tortoise.  ***

*** What attempts that have been made on social reporting in the UK are limited.  Most reports are designed as if
to  be  read  by children rather than fully literate adults.
These are usually printed as  pull-outs  from  the  main accounts and are primarily addressed to the employees. *** The
whole effect  is larded  with a dollop  of  paternalism--the
chairman  usually exhorts the virtues of hard work, and con-
demns the latest  iniquities of an uncaring government--in a
tone hardly credible for the late 1970s.

Three French  companies (Moet-Hennessy, Creusot-Loire and Rous-
sel Uclaf) have  done  some of the  best work to date in social
reporting.  Mr. Moore indicates that in all of the presentation
of the material of these companies, the reports serve as a
compact  management  and workers  consultative document,  as
well as a useful  reference for  shareholders, which clearly

explains not only company policy in relation to the individual, but its relationship with other industry and government policy. Roussell Uclaf since 1975 has published in addition to its annual financial report, rather than as a part of, a social policy statement to give a complete panorama of its activities, over 48 pages crowded with densely factual and statistical, but very clearly presented, information.

#17-22...French Government Decree of 1977

Before passage of the Decree of 1977, Employees Work Councils (comites d'enterprise), which were obligatory for businesses with more than 50 employees, already have a general right under the FRENCH COMPANY LAW REFORM published in 1975, to certain financial information such as the annual accounts. The new Decree, however, gives the employee representatives the right to their own annual report containing information primarily designed for employee needs. The new Decree is part of the French Industrial Code but does not form part of the Company Law. It requires all enterprises employing more than 750 employees to supply their works councils with an annual Social Report covering in great detail matters relating to employment, wages, social costs, safety conditions, training and industrial relations. A detailed list required by the Law calls for the following disclosures beginning in 1979:

I.   EMPLOYMENT:  (11) Payroll; (12) Outside Workers; (13) Hiring Policy; (14) Leavers; (15) Promotion; (16) Unemployment; (17) Disabled and Handicapped; (18) Days of Absence.
II.  WAGES AND RELATED COSTS:  (21) Wage Bill; (22) Wage Hierarchy; (23) Wage Calculation; (24) Ancillary Costs; (25) Total Wages Cost.
III. HEALTH AND SAFETY CONDITIONS:  (31) Industrial Injuries and Road Accidents; (32) Allocation of Casualties; (33) Industrial Sickness; (34) Health & Safety Committee; (35) Safety Costs.
IV.  OTHER WORKING CONDITIONS:  (41) Working Hours; (42) Work Organization; (43) Working Conditions; (44) Working Organization; (45) Costs Incurred to Improve Labor Organization; (46) Factory Physician; (47) Inept Employees.
V.   TRAINING:  (51) Training; (52) Training Leavers; (53) Apprenticeship.
VI.  INDUSTRIAL RELATIONS:  (61) Representatives of Employees; (62) Information and Communication; (63) Disputes on Industrial Law.
VII. OTHER WORKING CONDITIONS:  (71) Social Benefits; (72) Other Social Expenditures.

In concluding this discussion, the French Code merely equates Social Reporting with Employee Reporting. The authors are of the opinion that notwithstanding the continental and

European claims that their social reporting exceeds that of any countries, the reports of Westinghouse, Sears, and Chrysler certainly do as much if not more in the way of social disclosure than what is required in Europe.

#### #17-23...UK Socio-Economic Reporting

It was pointed out above that in commenting on the German Shell Statement, Mr. Van den Bergh indicated:
In contrast the UK theme seems to tend to limit the scope of corporate reports to the economic performance, orientated to the interests of each of the different constituencies. To the UK, widening the scope to include other areas of accountability is of secondary importance.
In commenting above on the French Code requiring S/R accounting, Mr. John Moore similarly attacks the UK for its lackadaisical attitude toward this type of reporting:
If France is the hare of this field, the UK is the tortoise. UK professional bodies put social reporting low on their list for accounting reform. The UK Stock Exchange regards any proposals for further disclosure, no matter how innocuous, as a nasty and brutish manifestation of state intervention.
These opinions issued respectively in 1976 and 1978 have had a reversal in the decade of the '80s, evidenced by the March 31, 1981 Quarterly Report of the British Petroleum Company, which contains a rather full and detailed report under the following headings: BP's Traditional Involvement With the Community; What is Corporate Social Responsibility?; Two Key Issues: (1) The Education System, and (2) Unemployment; Principles For Action; Implementation of BP's Community Affairs Programme; The Community & Educational Affairs Group: (a) Education, (b) Unemployment, (c) Donations & Sponsorships; and The Future.

#### #17-24...The British Petroleum Corporation Report

The BP Report headed "BP AND SOCIETY IN THE UNITED KINGDOM" is presented in Figure 17-4.

========================================================================
#### FIGURE 17-4
#### BP AND SOCIETY IN THE UNITED KINGDOM
(The following is an abridged version of a BP Briefing Paper published as of March 31, 1981, for the information of BP group staff.)

#### BP'S traditional involvement with the community
In recent years the BP group has substantially expanded its interest in the UK. More than one-fifth of total group assets

are now located there. In 1980 BP's capital expenditures in the
UK amounted to over $1,680 million, which was more than in any
other country. The company now employs almost 40,000 people in
the UK (excluding those employed in its UK-based fleet), or
about one-third of the group's total employees world-wide.

BP has a long history of helping educational and community
activities through links with schools and universities and
through sponsorships and donations. Since the early 1970s it
has also been active in educational liaison through its School
Link Scheme and BP Schoolteacher Fellowships.

Many BP centres have a tradition of involvement with their
local communities, often supporting and initiating community
projects such as work experience schemes, vacation training
and teachers-in-industry programmes.

## What is corporate social responsibility?

The debate about corporate social responsibility arises from
the premise that corporations should be seen as an integral
part of the society in which they operate. The corporation thus
has a vested interest in the prosperity of society.

When considering their attitudes to corporate social responsibility companies have been mindful that in most advanced industrial countries there already exists a substantial welfare
system and that this should not be duplicated by the private
sector. Such social spending is made possible to a significant
degree by taxes paid by companies: in the UK, not least those
paid by oil companies via royalties, petroleum revenue tax and
corporation tax. For example, BP's contribution to the UK Government in 1980 by way of taxes and royalties was $3,739 mil-
lion and the estimate for 1981 is in excess of $5,600 million.

Following a comprehensive appraisal of its approach to corporate social responsibility in the UK, BP concluded that it
should be based on enlightened self-interest. Its community
programme would therefore feature contributions to the wider
community designed to help create the environment the company
needs in order to survive and operate efficiently.

## Two key issues

BP's researches indicated that two of the most important
issues directly affecting the relationship between business and
the community were:

(1) The Educational System -- students and teachers both
have a limited knowledge and appreciation of industry and of
the importance of its function as a wealth creator. Equally,
industry should be more aware of, and responsive to, current
educational trends.

(2) Unemployment -- the concentration of unemployment among
the young, unskilled, disabled and minority groups was viewed
as a particularly worrying trend, which could lead to the re-

jection of many of the cultural and social values associated
with work and business.

**Principles for action**
   In developing its programme of corporate social responsi-
bility BP adheres to the following principles:
   -   Local management and employees should be involved as
       fully as possible.
   -   Projects should be carefully selected with attention
       being paid to the analysis of local needs and priori-
       ties.
   -   Support should be concentrated in areas where the compa-
       ny has a large or long-standing presence.
   -   Support should not be limited to cash funding; manpower
       and its skills will often represent BP's major contribu-
       tion to projects.
   -   BP should be willing to enter into joint initiatives
       with other companies and organisations to support appro-
       priate projects.

**Implementation of BP's community affairs programme**
   For BP, two important principles underlying its social responsibility policy are that the funding should be on a scale
that does not jeopardise the company's investment in its day-
to-day business and that it should be at a level which the company is prepared to sustain for a reasonable period of time.
   Moreover, a successful community affairs programme can only
develop if management, employees and the public understand the
interdependence of industry and society.
   Accordingly, in order to increase this mutual understanding,
existing contacts between the company and such groups as members of Parliament, the unions, the Civil Service, academics
and teachers, have been extended.
   One of the most significant contributions a company can make
to a local community is through the individual efforts of its
employees, and BP encourages this sort of involvement. For
example, during the International Year of Disabled People, the
company is offering to match pound for pound all the money contributed by BP employees in the UK through their involvement
with the disabled, up to a combined company and employee total
of $179,200. The company has also provided the four organising
bodies in the UK with $22,400 towards their publicity costs.
   Discussion of BP and its relationship with the community is
now a regular part of internal management courses.

**The Community and Educational Affairs Group**
   Most BP group subsidiaries have been involved with community
affairs activities, on their own behalf, for many years. In the
UK in 1980 the company spent slightly over $4.5 million on its

community affairs activities. In 1981 this total will be an estimated $5.8 million. In order to help coordinate and implement company policy towards the community in the UK, BP has established a Community and Educational Affairs Group in the Public Affairs and Information Department at head office.
The areas covered by this Group include:

## (a) Education

For many years BP has striven to improve links between the academic world and industry through its education liaison team, and now, in order to encourage a greater mutual understanding, it is:
- Increasing the number of schools in the BP School Link Scheme from 120 to 200.
- Increasing from 8 to 20 places, the opportunities for teachers to gain industrial experience by secondment to BP sites.
- Creating more places on its Schoolteacher Fellowship Scheme (an increase from 6 to 9).
- Extending the provision of work experience and courses about industry for secondary school pupils and teachers.
- Expanding the BP Educational Service, which provides educational institutions with subsidised teaching materials related to industry, energy and associated subject.

In higher education BP is:
- Increasing the number of places for company-sponsored sandwich and vacation students.
- Working with selected educational institutions and professional bodies in order to consider the mutual dependence of industry and education.
- Providing facilities for academic staff to gain industrial experience, and increasing support for joint research projects with universities.
- Encouraging employees to involve themselves with institutions of higher education.

## (b) Unemployment and support for small business

BP believes that its primary contribution to alleviating the problem of unemployment must be through the direct contribution it makes to the UK economy as an employer, purchaser of materials and services from other companies, investor, taxpayer and generator of employment throughout the nation's economy.
The company provides direct support for such bodies as the London Enterprise Agency ("LENTA") and Rainform Venture Capital in their attempts to encourage new business enterprises, and thus to increase employment prospects. BP also seconds employees to organisations concerned with unemployment where their management expertise may be beneficial in helping to alleviate

the problem. In certain circumstances the company provides direct help in the form of technical and commercial advice to small businesses.

## (c) Donations and sponsorships

Financial donations and sponsorship remain an important means by which industry can fulfil some of its social obligations. When considering appeals for donations and sponsorships, preference is given to activities in local communities where BP has a strong presence, and emphasis is placed on activities which fall into one or more of the following categories:
- Health and welfare.
- Challenging activities that encourage young people to meet the highest standards of excellence.
- Educational support.
- Environmental protection.

BP's arts sponsorships include music, drama, museums, cultural festivals and the visual arts.

In the field of science BP has recently produced the Faraday Lecture, illustrating the use of electricity and electronics in the exploration and production of oil. The company is also sponsoring an International Energy Research Prize, and a major exhibition at the Science Museum in 1982.

Examples of sponsorships by BP group UK subsidiaries include BP Oil's influential "Challenge to Youth" project, which seeks to foster technological inventiveness in schoolchildren; a coaching scheme for young people in sport; and the "BP Get-around" scheme run in association with CORAD (Committee on Restrictions Against Disablement), during the International Year of Disabled People.

## The future

BP's main contribution to society will continue to be the successful, efficient and responsible management of its business. By improving conditions in society, and by achieving a better understanding with all sections of the community, BP can help create a more favourable environment for its business operations. Therefore, the aims of BP's community and educational affairs policy are an integral part of the overall commercial objectives of the company.

---

Copies of all BP Briefing Papers can be obtained from BP North America Inc., 620 Fifth Avenue, N.Y., N.Y. 10020

---

## #17-25...Netherlands Social Reporting

In the article "Employees and the Corporate Social Report: The Dutch Case," in ACCOUNTING REVIEW, Vol. LVI, No. 2, Apr. 1981, pp. 294-308, Prof. Hein Schreuder points out:
> Corporate Social reporting is rapidly becoming normal business practice in the Netherlands. These reports are primarily addressed to the employee constituency and contain information on the personnel policy of the firm.
> In the last decade, corporate social reporting has become a widespread phenomenon in the Netherlands. Whereas before 1970 only a few companies published a social report, estimates of the number of such reports run from 100 to well above 200. In the Dutch context, "social reporting" refers to the provision of information on the relations between the organization and its employees. These reports are addressed primarily to the employee constituency.
> In these reports, the Dutch social reports resemble those published in France and West Germany. In general, European social reports are more employee-oriented than their American counterparts, which contain more items of a general societal nature.

Obviously the authors do not agree with the statement that U.S. social reports are not personnel-oriented in the light of the Chrysler, Sears and Westinghouse reports heretofore presented, which are full of personnel figures and data.

## #17-26...Corporate Social Responsibility Update

"The Current Status of Corporate Social Reporting Disclosures" is an article published in the Nov.-Dec. 1979 MASSACHUSETTS CPA REVIEW, by Susan Szepan, reprinted in the July 1980 JOURNAL OF ACCOUNTANCY, pp. 77-80, which is an update of corporate S/R reporting in the U.S. Ms. Szepan indicates that "public attitudes and expectations about corporations have changed in recent years, and this reversal to the 'dirty business' attitude is forcing corporations to account publicly for their actions." Prof. Lee Seidler's definition of Social Accounting is presented in "Dollar Values in the Social Income Statement," in WORLD, Spring 1973, p. 4: "Social Accounting measures the change in the general welfare resulting from the activity being measured."

## FUTURE OF SOCIAL ACCOUNTING

## #17-27...Social Accounting Progress

John C. Biegler, senior partner in Price Waterhouse & Co., has pointed out in the PRICE WATERHOUSE REVIEW, 1978, Vol. 23,

No. 3, pages 4-5, that "more systematic social accountability
will depend partly on the continuing development of workable
methods of measurement. The accounting profession is already at
work.  In 1977 the AICPA published a book entitled THE MEASURE-
MENT OF CORPORATE SOCIAL PERFORMANCE. I believe it is an important beginning."

Quoting from this book issued by the AICPA's Committee on
Social Measurement, the JOURNAL OF ACCOUNTANCY, Nov. 1978, says
on page 104:

There is little likelihood that a system will be devised
in the foreseeable future that can measure the social impacts of business actions with anything approaching the re-
finement of financial accounting systems. Nevertheless, substantial strides can be expected to result in more useful
social information.

Both the number of subject areas being given attention
and the specific problems receiving study are increasing.
Standards for the development and disclosure of social information will be enunciated over time.  Knowledge of the
manner in which business actions impact on society will continue to grow. Better measurement techniques will be devised
and used by accounting and other disciplines in order to
produce useful information at reasonable cost. Social information will become more important to the managerial function
not only as an ingredient of economic decision-making but
also as a means for meeting the public's social expectations
of private enterprise.

#17-28...Conference Board Study

In 1983 a study was made by E. Patrick McGuire for the Conference Board, a business research agency. In this study he
points out that after years of the U.S. as being characterized
as "ugly Americans" in many underdeveloped countries, there has
been a significant change in the "Yankee Go Home" syndrome.
Investment projects of transnational corporations have clearly
helped the local economies by building schools, hospitals,
roads, water systems, etc. This was not done as an altruism; it
was good business because it provided jobs and a healthy and
reliable work force.

The U.S. multinational corporations have learned to be more
flexible in working with the widely different political regimes
of underdeveloped countries.  In turn, the local leaderships
have also found that they must cooperate with U.S. MNCs to
avoid their own social and political instability.

As a result of the Third World debt situation, underdeveloped countries need and want Americans. And American businesses have learned to deal with whatever administration is in
power.

#17-29...**Social Responsibility as a Firm Asset**

In an article entitled "Social Responsibility Called Asset to Firms," in the NEW YORK DAILY NEWS, Peter Lowry, poet and social worker, is quoted as saying:
"A well-run company that is socially responsible to the environment, to workers and to human rights will be successful and outperform the stock market. When a company gets entangled in employee rights lawsuits, product-safety disputes, or controversies involving nuclear power, defense contracts, or pollution, their productivity and profits will fall. The basic problem has always been getting information about the social values of companies." *** Last fall Lowry founded the Center For Economic Revitalization, Inc., which researches a company's social activities. They report their findings in a bimonthly newsletter. The information is designed to supplement other research. For example, a broker familiar with Atlantic Richfield Co.'s impressive earnings record might not know that the company goes beyond federal pollution control rules by spending $8 million to prevent gas and oil leaks at offshore drilling sites.

**SUMMARY OF FOOTNOTE REFERENCES**
(References are to Paragraph #'s)

#17-4   Epstein, Flamholtz and McDonough, "Corporate Social Accounting in the USA: State of the Arts and Future Prospects," ACCOUNTING ORGANIZATIONS AND SOCIETY, Vol.1,No.1(1976):23-42

#17-4   Prof. Sieben, 4th International Conference of Accounting Education, BERLIN CONFERENCE PROCEEDINGS (Oct. 1977): 47

#17-4   Louis Perridon, BERLIN CONFERENCE PROCEEDINGS, Ibid., p. 48

#17-4   Lee Brummet, BERLIN CONFERENCE PROCEEDINGS, Ibid., p. 49

#17-4   Ibid., p. 7

#17-4   Eric Kohler, DICTIONARY FOR ACCOUNTANTS, 1957

#17-4   Brummet, op. cit., p. 8

#17-6   David Linowes, "The Accounting Profession and Social Progress," JOURNAL OF ACCOUNTANCY, #136, No. 1 (1973): 34. Copyright © 1973 by the American Institute of Certified Public Accountants, Inc. Opinions expressed in the JOURNAL OF ACCOUNTANCY are those of editors and contributors. Publication in the JOURNAL OF ACCOUNTANCY does not constitute endorsement by the AICPA or its committees.

#17-8   REPORT TO SHAREHOLDERS, 1978, Chrysler Corporation

#17-9   CHICAGO TRIBUNE (Jan. 26, 1979); CHICAGO TRIBUNE (June 9, 1981)

#17-10  Westinghouse Electric Corp., 2nd Quarter, 1978 Report to Stockholders

#17-11  Harvey Kapnick, "The Challenge for International Business," Calif. State Univ. at San Jose (Oct. 25, 1972)

#17-13  Ernst & Ernst Study of FORTUNE 500 Corporations, 1975

#17-15 Prof. Gerhard Mueller
#17-17 David Linowes, THE CORPORATE CONSCIENCE (N.Y.: Hawthorne
       Books, 1974), pp. 104-137
#17-18 Richard Van den Bergh, "The Corporate Social Report: The
       Deutsche-Shell Experience," ACCOUNTANCY (Dec. 1976)
#17-19 Ibid.
#17-20 Ibid.
#17-21 John Moore, "Social Accounts: France Sets the Pace," WORLD
       ACCOUNTING REPORT (Feb. 1978), Financial Times Business In-
       formation, Ltd., London, England
#17-22 FRENCH COMPANY LAW REFORM, 1975
#17-23 Van den Bergh, op, cit.
#17-23 John Moore, op. cit.
#17-23 British Petroleum Co., Quarterly Report, March 31, 1981
#17-24 BP AND SOCIETY IN THE UNITED KINGDOM, Ibid. Reprinted by
       permission of The British Petroleum Company p.l.c, London,
       England
#17-25 Hein Schreuder, "Employees and the Corporate Social Report:
       The Dutch Case," ACCOUNTING REVIEW, Vol. LVI, No. 2 (April
       1981): 294-308
#17-26 Susan Szepan, "The Current Status of Corporate Social Re-
       porting Disclosures," MASSACHUSETTS CPA REVIEW (Nov-Dec
       1979); also in JOURNAL OF ACCOUNTANCY (July 1980): 77-80
#17-26 Lee Seidler, "Dollar Values in the Social Income Statement,"
       WORLD (Spring 1973): 4
#17-27 John C. Biegler, PRICE WATERHOUSE REVIEW, Vol. 23, No. 3
       (1978): 4-5
#17-27 AICPA Committee on Social Measurement, THE MEASUREMENT OF
       CORPORATE SOCIAL PERFORMANCE, 1977, quoted in JOURNAL OF
       ACCOUNTANCY (Nov. 1978): 104. Copyright © 1978 by the Ameri-
       can Institute of Certified Public Accountants, Inc. Opinions
       expressed in the JOURNAL OF ACCOUNTANCY are those of editors
       and contributors. Publication in the JOURNAL OF ACCOUNTANCY
       does not constitute endorsement by the AICPA or its commit-
       tees.
#17-29 Peter Lowry, "Social Responsibility Called Asset to Firms,"
       NEW YORK DAILY NEWS.

## BIBLIOGRAPHY

AICPA. AUDITS OF COLLEGES AND UNIVERSITIES. 1973
AICPA. HOSPITAL AUDIT GUIDE. 1972
Beresford, Dennis and Feldman, Stewart. "Companies Increase Social
    Responsibility Disclosure," MANAGEMENT ACCOUNTING (March
    1976): 51-55
Brown, Andrew. "Social (R)Evolution and the EEC," THE ACCOUNTANTS
    MAGAZINE, 85 (March 1981): 83-84
Chastain, Clark F. "Environmental Accounting--U.S. & U.K.," AC-
    COUNTANCY, 84 (December 1973): 10-13
Ernst & Whinney. SOCIAL RESPONSIBILITY DISCLOSURE: 1977 SURVEY OF
    FORTUNE 500 ANNUAL REPORTS. Cleveland: 1977

Gray, Rob and Perks, Bob. "How Desirable is Social Accounting?",
    ACCOUNTANCY (April 1982): 101-102
Jaggi, Bikki. "An Analysis of Corporate Social Reporting in Ger-
    many," INTERNATIONAL JOURNAL OF ACCOUNTING EDUCATION & RE-
    SEARCH, 15 (Spring 1980): 35-45
Linowes, David F. "The Accounting Profession and Social Progress,"
    JOURNAL OF ACCOUNTANCY (July 1973): 32-40
Schoenfeld, Hanns-Martin. THE STATUS OF SOCIAL REPORTING IN SELECT-
    ED COUNTRIES. Urbana, Ill: Center for International Educa-
    tion and Research in Accounting, 1978
Seary, Bill. "EEC Finance--Is There Anything for Charities," AC-
    COUNTANCY, 92 (September 1981): 61-62
Siegal, Joel and Lehman, Martin. "Own Up to Social Responsibility,"
    FINANCIAL EXECUTIVE (March 1976)
Task Force on Corporate Social Performance. CORPORATE SOCIAL RE-
    PORTING IN THE UNITED STATES AND WESTERN EUROPE. Washington,
    D.C.: Department of Commerce, July 1979
Van den Bergh, Richard. "Time to Speed Corporate Social Account-
    ing," ACCOUNTANCY, 87 (April 1976): 50-53
Wells, Louis. "Social Cost/Benefit Analysis for MNC's," HARVARD
    BUSINESS REVIEW, 53 (March-April, 1975): 40-50

## THEORY QUESTIONS
(Question Numbers are Keyed to Text Paragraph #'s)

#17-1-2. Discuss, define, and classify Social Accounting.

#17-5 Describe the relationship of Socio-Economic Accounting
    to social problems and institutions.

#17-6 What set of principles must be established as a frame-
    work for Socio-Economic Accounting?

#17-11 What should be the format for Social Responsibility
    Statements?

#17-13 What six general categories should be included as part
    of the S/R Financial Statements?

#17-15 Discuss the relationship of Social Responsibility Ac-
    counting to the public interest.

#17-16 Discuss the relationship of Governmental Codes of Con-
    duct to Social Responsibility Accounting.

#17-17 What is the nature of the Socio-Economic Operating
    Statement?

#17-18 Discuss the treatment of S/R Accounting in Germany.

#17-19 Make a critical analysis of the Deutsche Shell AG Re-
    port.

#17-20 What criticisms have been made of the Deutsche Shell AG
    Report?

#17-21 Discuss the treatment of S/R Accounting in France.

#17-22 Discuss the effect of the French Government Decree of
    1977 on French S/R Accounting.

#17-23 Discuss the treatment of S/R Accounting in England.

#17-25 Discuss Social Reporting in the Netherlands.

#17-27 Discuss the future of Social Responsibility Accounting.

## EXERCISES

**EX-17-1**
Into what six categories does the Kapnick Report divide Social
Responsibility reporting?  Briefly describe the nature of each.

**EX-17-2**
Into what six categories does the Ernst & Ernst FORTUNE 500
Study divide Social Responsibility reporting?  Briefly describe
the nature of each category.

**EX-17-3**
What categories of SOCIAL COSTS are required under the French
Company Law Decree of 1977?Briefly describe the nature of each.

**EX-17-4**
Make a critical comparative analysis of the Kapnick, Ernst &
Ernst, and French Decree.

**EX-17-5**
Write a critique as to how you compare the Kapnick, Ernst &
Ernst, and French Decree, with the DEUTSCHE SHELL AG REPORT.

### PROBLEMS

**P-17-1**
Records of Simon Electric Corp. of Frankfurt, Germany, disclose
the following data in terms of millions of DM:

### PERSONNEL RELATIONS:

| | | | |
|---|---|---|---|
| Wages | 60 | Medical Service | 1 |
| Salaries | 140 | Accident Prevention | 2 |
| Christmas Bonuses | 20 | Sports Subsidies | 1 |
| Holiday Pay | 5 | Education and | |
| Birth Grant | 30 | Training | 3 |
| Marriage Grant | 180 | Work Clothes and | |
| Rent Subsidies | 400 | Canteen | 4 |
| Employer Contribution to | | Pension Payments | 30 |
| Health, Pension, & Un- | | Pension Reserves | 80 |
| employment Insurance | 20 | | |

### PUBLIC RELATIONS:

| | | INVESTORS RELATIONS: | |
|---|---|---|---|
| R & D | 35 | Dividends | 100 |
| Environment | 65 | Net Interest | 35 |
| Donations & Charities | 1 | Loans Repaid | 100 |
| Publications | 1 | | |
| Taxation | 150 | | |
| Subscriptions | 5 | | |

PERFORMANCE RELATIONS:

| Distributions: | | Sources: | |
|---|---|---|---|
| Employees Distributions | 3 | Proceeds From Turnover | 7 |
| Community Distribution | 2 | Income From Investments | 4 |
| Suppliers Distribution | 6 | | |

**Required:**

From the foregoing  data prepare a Corporate Social Report  for the Simon Electric Corporation.


**P-17-2**

Using the list of items related to  Social  Reporting  provided for under the French Company Law Reform  Act of 1977, construct a SOCIAL RESPONSIBILITY REPORT for a typical French corporation using whatever figures you wish to supply for each item.

**P-17-3**

Using the list of items related to the British Petroleum Briefing Paper of March 31, 1981, construct a SOCIAL  RESPONSIBILITY REPORT for the British Petroleum Company using whatever figures you wish to supply for each item.

# International Developmental and Behavioral Accounting

ACCOUNTING IN DEVELOPMENT

#18-1....Nature of Developmental Accounting

Accounting in Development has been receiving attention due to its reflection of the world-wide social responsibilities of idealistic citizens. The efforts toward a Code of Conduct for M/Es show the significance that is being placed in assistance to development. Accounting information plays an important role in determining and monitoring the financial requirements and economic effects in the various stages of development of firms and their operations within an economy.

#18-2....Stages of Development Process

Three stages may be identified in the development process of an economy: the TAKE-OFF STAGE, the DRIVE-TO-MATURITY STAGE, and the MATURE STAGE.

In the preliminary stage, prior to the first stage of development, the economy assumedly has many small firms with limited operational capacities. They probably use a type of cash-basis accounting with a major emphasis on the flow of immediate return to the owner-manager. In the first stage of development-- the TAKE-OFF STAGE--new products and/or capacity expansion are introduced. After that, in the second stage, the economy enters a DRIVE-TOMATURITY STAGE. In the third stage, the economy enters the MATURE STAGE of high mass production and consumption.

Firms may enter stages of development that parallel the development of an economy. However, they also can enter similar stages of development regardless of the stage of economic development, as pointed out by Surendra Singhvi, in an article "Corporate Financial Management in a Developing Economy," Univ. of Washington Graduate School of Business, 1972, pp. 48-49.

## #18-3....Accounting in Development-Stage Enterprises

As indicated in FASB #7, 1975, ACCOUNTING AND REPORTING BY
DEVELOPMENT STAGE ENTERPRISES, particular attention is now being given in the U.S. to accounting in development-stage enterprises. The problem involves the expending of start-up costs,
which include financial planning; raising capital; exploring
for natural resources; developing natural resources; establishing sources of supply; acquiring property, plant, and equipment; recruiting and training personnel; developing markets;
and starting up production. When these costs are immediately
charged to income in the period incurred, a retained earnings
deficit will accumulate before net profits commence. Full disclosure of the nature of such enterprises must be given in the
financial statements.

The principles for development-stage enterprises assume a
successful operational performance in due time. Hence the going-concern assumption prevails. Costs are deferred only if
they are recoverable and matchable with specific future benefits. Thus specific disclosures are required in order to identify the development-stage reasons for a temporarily reflected
poor performance.

## #18-4....Accounting During Development

As firms develop within themselves and in relation to a developing economy, the accounting requirements exert a broadening responsibility for both the management accountant and the
professional public accountant. The primary functions of accounting in developing countries should be financial reporting
to various individuals and groups external to the firm, financial reporting to management, and business advising to management, as pointed out by George Scott in his article "Accounting
and Developing Nations," Univ. of Washington, Graduate School
of Business, 1970, page 75.

As the economy grows, and firms grow in size and development, additional sources of financing usually are sought. The
main ones may be financial institutions. Another source may be
issuances of bonds or stocks to the public. In any case, external reporting becomes more and more important as a firm develops, particularly within a developing economy.

As the complexity of the firm grows, the need for extensive
internal management reporting becomes essential. Management
reporting focuses on internal control, cost control, pricing
decision-making and working capital management. Internal management reports may also provide data for investment decisions
through use of such techniques as break-even analysis, sensitivity analysis, market analysis, and personnel performance
evaluation.

Finally, business advisory services by accountants may be extended to management in developing companies. They may include tax counseling as well as management advisory services regarding management control and financial management. Such services may be performed by the firm's controller and treasurer, or by the outside professional accountant.

#18-5....Functions of Accountant During Development

During development the functions of the accountant broaden to take in the more complex responsibilities and sophisticated counsel. Education becomes essential in assuring that the practicing accountant has the professional competence to perform the developmental duties. Thus emphasis on education and training is very important in accounting in development. Another important aspect is the overall need for accounting information in administering developmental programs.

#18-6....Economic Evaluation Accounting

Economic evaluation accounting assumes an accounting structure that is designed to provide information which facilitates the economic evaluation of an enterprise's activities by management, investors, and government. It provides information for analysis of the firm's activities in relation to the economic goals of a nation. It requires that accounting for the effects of certain economic incentives be in accord with their objectives. Economic incentives for development may be in the form of subsidies, tax credits, or regulatory control.

The incentives may be rather direct and for a special purpose, such as an investment tax credit or a dividends exclusion provision. Or they may be rather general, such as subsidy for location in a certain underdeveloped area. What is important is that the reporting be so designed as to allow ready analysis of the results and effect of the incentive utilization. The implications are that the accounting for economic evaluation must enhance the control of economic incentives and the achievement of economically designed goals. As previously seen, idealistically the economic evaluation accounting objective should be linked with a macro-accounting system.

#18-7....Developmental Accounting and The Third World

In the Proceedings of the 4th International Conference on Accounting Education in 1977 at page 18 is a commentary of Prof. Adolf J. H. Enthoven which declares:

My main concern is accounting and accounting education in the Third World Nations. It is obvious that the accounting system in the Third World deviates from the systems in the industrialized countries. The major task of accounting in the developing countries is to be seen as a tool to assist social and economic plans and planning. An expedient accounting system both of a prospective and retrospective nature is needed in order to carry out adequate cost-benefit analyses and to aid decision-making regarding the future, especially relating to investments. This information is based on micro- and macro-accounting. Macro accounting deals with the national income accounts, the input and output analyses, the flow of funds accounts, the national balance sheet and the balance-of-payments accounts. The linkage between micro- and macro-accounting has been neglected in the past, in particular the measurement of value added which is in fact the proper medium to aggregate micro- and macro-accounting. The Third World needs this sort of accounting whereby decisions can be made in the total economic context.

A second consideration is that of the close linkage between the private and public sector of accounting in the developing countries. In many Third World nations, industries are either partly or fully nationalized. Public enterprise accounting differs in several aspects from private enterprise accounting: Parastatal Accounting forms the link between public accounting and micro-accounting. The multinational concerns are a further important aspect for the developing countries. Information on this topic can be found in the TRANSNATIONAL REPORT OF THE UNITED NATIONS.

Also unfortunately it is generally the case that neither the so-called "Performance Budgeting" nor the "Regular Accounting Administration" is very well developed. Social Accounting must also be discussed in this context, the same as the problem of multinational concerns. *** In the Third World nations, accounting should be more effectively geared towards the social economic growth patterns. There is a need for an Economic Development Accountancy which is both the horizontal and vertical integration of the various dimensions of accounting.

How the U.S. can participate in the development of accounting in Third World countries is described by Prof. Enthoven in the article "U.S. Accounting and the Third World" in the June issue of the JOURNAL OF ACCOUNTANCY, pp. 110-118.

In a discussion of the "Development and State of Conventional Accounting Education Systems," SUBJECT 1 of the Berlin Conference, Prof. Enthoven continues at page 41:

Previously we described the scope for ECONOMIC DEVELOPMENT ACCOUNTANCY and the close linkage of accounting with economic decision-making aspects of both a micro and macro nature. Accordingly, the educational setup in Third World countries requires a base with as pillars the accounting and economic disciplines to cope with socio-economic issues. The interaction between economics and accounting may well have to be enlarged.

### #18-8...Relationship of Developmental Acctg. to Social Acctg.

On page 37, Prof. Enthoven describes the relationship of Developmental Accounting to Social Accounting (and in the process affords another definition of Social Accounting) in the following terms:

SOCIAL ACCOUNTING, also referred to as socio-economic or societal accounting, meaning the societal evaluations of private and public activities, and the reflection of social indicators for evaluative purposes, also tends to be carried out on a haphazard basis and void of proper systematization. Measurement of externalities and social welfare measurements, either in the micro or macro accounts, to supplement the national (macro) accounts, for example, the 1968 UN system, is an area where accountants all over the world have not been actively involved. Our present national (macro) accounting systems do not portray welfare or well-being aspects between countries and over time, to indicate successful performances of an economic and social nature, and the achievement of a country's aim on a national comparative basis.

### #18-9...Recent Experiences of Third World Enhancement Programs

The Sullivan Code is in the Oct. 8, 1979 issue of U.S. NEWS & WORLD REPORT, page 80, under the title "U.S. Firms' Aim: Equality For Blacks," written from Port Elizabeth, South Africa. It points out how far U.S. MNCs have gone in attempting to carry out socio-economic equality between black and white workers:

A U.S. executive explains why many American firms here are focusing on meeting the educational and training terms of a voluntary U.S. EMPLOYERS' CODE that, among other things, requires equal treatment for blacks. The Code was drawn up by the Rev. Leon Sullivan, a black member of the General Motors board of directors. "Blacks have told me," says the executive, "they'll continue to eat in separate canteens and go to separate toilets. What they really want is upward mobility -- and that means training."

A black worker here concurs with the American assessment, stressing: "You can't get equal pay unless you have equal qualifications." U.S. companies have poured millions of dollars into facilities and programs aimed at raising the qualifications of black workers.

General Motors, Ford, Firestone, and other companies here in the automotive center of South Africa are investing

$2 million in a technical college for blacks.   Goodyear and Volkswagen are building a similar school. Goodyear also pays the   university expenses   of a dozen   children of   non-white employees and guarantees them jobs on graduation.   Firestone teaches English to  blacks on its assembly line and picks up the tab  for school fees and books for children of its black workers. It supports some black engineering students at university levels.

Concerned by  the lack  of   scientific  background among blacks, IBM is asking government approval to spend $2.7 million on  120  videotape machines for high schools in Soweto, the restive black township near Johannesburg.   Also in Soweto, the Chamber of Commerce of the U.S. is moving to build a $3.5 million commercial high school for 600 black  students. A graduate  could either go to a university or be guaranteed a job in an American company.

One growing practice  among American firms is the "adoption" of black schools. Colgate-Palmolive works with parents at one school to determine the most critical needs. The company has also replaced broken windows and installed electrical  and  heating  systems.  Corn Products Company  built  a classroom,  supplied a water  tank  and  painted a  poverty-stricken rural school near Durban.

One American auto executive and his wife adopted a rural school entirely on their own.  Harold Sims, an American  who helps  monitor compliance of  the Sullivan Code,  emphasizes this  point:  "The most  revolutionary  thing you can do in South  Africa  is to accelerate the  creation  on a  massive scale  of  opportunities  for  blacks  to  be  educated  and trained."

In the  discussion of the relationship of  CODES  OF CONDUCT to S/R in Chapter 17, it was pointed out that the codes imposed on MNCs  were those in  which the  foreign  governments had a hand either in their construction or imposition.  It was stated that discussion of  such  Codes would  be made in the Political Accounting chapter.  However, it may  be seen  that  the Sullivan Code resulted  from the  action  of a  member  of  the Board of Directors  of  General Motors, and was in no way related to any governmental action, hence the Sullivan Code is related  to S/R rather than Political Accounting.

#### #18-10...Progress Under the Sullivan Code

An updated report as  to  the progress that  has  been  made under the Sullivan Code was  presented in  the  April 28, 1980 edition of U.S. NEWS & WORLD REPORT, pages 43 and  46, entitled "Crucial Stakes For U.S. Firms in South Africa." From such report it  appears that the issue of  apartheid has had a braking effect on  the development of progress under the Sullivan Code.

The following excerpts from the report indicate there is still a long way to go to achieve any lasting success:

In New Brighton, a black community in the South African city of Port Elizabeth beside the sea, a $2 million technical school built with American money opened in Jan. for 600 black students. Not far away, a U.S. auto maker has built a golf course, a cycling stadium, and almost 100 houses for blacks. And in Soweto, the explosive black township near Johannesburg, there are plans to erect a $4 million commercial high school for blacks with funds raised by the American Chamber of Commerce in South Africa.

With moves such as these and by endorsing fair-employment rules, U.S. companies doing business here hope to counter efforts at home to compel them to sever their lucrative commercial links with South Africa because of this nation's policy of apartheid--separation of the races. The drive by religious and antiapartheid groups in the U.S. to force a withdrawal from this racially troubled nation is in high gear; dozens of firms face shareholder pleas to curtail or abandon activities in South Africa; American colleges debate the propriety of retaining stock in companies operating here; labor unions have urged members to boycott banks doing business in South Africa.

The outcome is uncertain, but the U.S. economic commitment here cannot be eliminated easily. American firms are deeply entrenched and are major employers, especially of non-whites. American direct investment in South Africa totals about $2 billion, roughly 16% of all foreign investment in the country. Some 350 U.S. firms have offices in South Africa. The number of employees of American subsidiaries last year topped 97,000, including 70,000 blacks and mixed races. U.S. shareholders own 25% of all stock in South African gold mines. About 6,000 U.S. companies do business with South Africa with two-way trade running at approximately $4 billion a year. But in the face of rising opposition at home and the danger of black-white confrontation here, few U.S. companies are moving in. Since 1976, 76 American firms have entered South Africa and 60 have left.

According to a Dept. of Commerce survey in 1979, the South African share of total U.S. investment abroad is only 1.1%. However the opponents of withdrawal stress that U.S. imports from South Africa involving 37 minerals are deemed vital to a modern society. In 1979, one-third or more of American imports of chromite ore, antimony, vanadium and platinum metals, vital in making alloy steel, came from South Africa. Adding to South Africa's importance is the fact that such critical minerals as chrome, manganese, gold flourspar, vanadium and platinum could only be obtained from the Soviet Union as an alternative source.

For three years many U.S. companies have been trying to
safeguard their investments here through the so-called Sullivan Code--6 principles written by a black director of General Motors. These are designed to ensure racial equality at
work and to help put an end to apartheid. The Code's results
have been patchy so far. Only 135 out of 350 eligible U.S.
firms have signed it. Of these, just 22--about 6%--were
deemed to be "making good progress" in implementing the Code
when it was reviewed in Nov. 1979. Still the report noted
greater effort by signatories to live up to the Code.

Living up to the Code means achieving integration of all
work and recreational facilities at U.S. factories. Also
that there be equal employment practices for all workers,
sizable training programs for blacks as well as better housing, education and transportation. Finally, it means equal
pay for equal work and promotion of increasing numbers of
blacks to supervisory-managerial jobs. Yet at Ford Motors,
one of the companies trying hardest to meet the Sullivan
goals, only 8% of the supervisory staff is black; Caltex has
no blacks in management; and Firestone has fewer than 50
salaried blacks on a staff of 2,500.

The Sullivan Code also has encouraged local and other
foreign-owned companies to match its principles, and it has
helped persuade Pretoria that some labor reforms recently
introduced by the government were unlikely to stir up much
resentment among South African whites. Ford, with 5,200
workers and annual South African sales of about $350 mil-
lion, has experienced both success and setbacks in trying to
live up to the Sullivan Code. Ford had no non-white foremen
in 1975; today they are a common sight. Six years ago there
were no black management people; now there are more than
100. Outside academic researchers called in by Ford to "audit" compliance with the Sullivan Code had warned earlier
that blacks were irked by the slow pace of advancement, real
though it was. One of the Ford auditors points up the problem that what Ford has done in the last few years was to
raise black expectations beyond its ability to fulfill them.
There also is a campaign among black intellectuals and some
black union leaders to convince U.S. firms to pull out. Pol-
aroid did pull out in 1977 and General Motors, Control Data
and Eastman Kodak indicated they would not expand, while
General Electric reduced its involvement.

Most analysts are convinced that a total American withdrawal would prompt officials in Pretoria to block repatriation of U.S. assets and order local firms to take over
existing facilities. The biggest effect would be to swell
the ranks of the jobless. To critical outsiders, the pace of
change still leaves much to be desired. But within South
Africa, American firms are widely perceived as leaders in

breaking down apartheid--at least in the workplace. To
executives of these companies, this justifies a continued
presence in this troubled land.

The foregoing appraisal indicates that the problem is not confined to being strictly developmental in character; it is also
social, economic, and political.

#18-11...Developmental Accounting and the Fourth World

In 1976 studies made by the Overseas Development Council
resulted in a new classification of underdeveloped countries
with the creation of what it has termed the "Fourth World."
This distinction between Third and Fourth World nations is
based on either a per capita national output, a physical quality of life, or an annual output per person.

Nations, territories, or colonies with either a per capita
national output of less than $2,000, or a relatively low physi-
cal quality of life as ranked by the Council are regarded as
Third World countries. These include Albania, Algeria, Angola,
Argentina, Bahamas, Bahrain, Barbados, Belize, Bolivia, Botswana, Brazil, Brunei, Chile, China, Colombia, Congo, Costa Rica,
Cuba, Cyprus, Djibouti, Dominica, Dominican Republic, Ecuador,
El Salvador, Equatorial Guinea, Fiji, French Polynesia, Gabon,
Ghana, Grenada, Guadeloupe, Guam, Guatemala, Guyana, Honduras,
Hong Kong, Iran, Iraq, Ivory Coast, Jamaica, Jordan, North Ko-
rea, South Korea, Kuwait, Lebanon, Liberia, Libya, Macao, Ma-
laysia, Malta, Martinique, Mauritania, Mauritius, Mexico, Mon-
golia, Morocco, Namibia, Netherlands Antilles, New Caledonia,
Nicaragua, Nigeria, Oman, Pacific Islands Trust Territory, Pan-
ama, Papua New Guinea, Paraguay, Peru, Philippines, Portugal,
Qatar, Reunion, Roumania, St. Lucia, Sao Tome & Principe, Saudi
Arabia, Senegal, Seychelles, Singapore, South Africa, Surinam,
Swaziland, Syria, Taiwan, Thailand, Tonga, Trinidad & Tobago,
Tunisia, Turkey, United Arab Emirates, Uruguay, Venezuela,
Western Samoa, Yugoslavia, Zambia, Zimbabwe Rhodesia.

The Overseas Development Council rates the Fourth World
countries as those which are the poorest of the poor countries,
and are so poverty-stricken--with less than a $300 annual out-
put per person--that they are placed in the special Fourth
World category. These countries with their dollar per capita
national output are as follows:

Afghanistan-160; Bangladesh-110; Benin-130; Bhutan-70; Bur-
ma-120; Burundi-120; Cambodia-70; Cameroon-290; Cape Verde-
260; Central African Empire-230; Chad-120; Comoros-180;
Egypt-280; Ethiopia-100; Gambia-180; Guinea-150; Guinea-Bis-
sau-140; Haiti-200; India-150; Indonesia-240; Kenya-240;
Laos-90; Lesotho-170; Madagascar-200; Malawi-140; Maldives-
110; Mali-100; Mozambique-170; Nepal-120; Niger-160; Paki-
stan-170; Rwanda-110; Sierra Leone-200; Solomon Islands-250;

Somalia-110; Sri-lanka-200; Sudan-290;  Tanzania-180;  Togo-260; Uganda-240; Upper Volta-110;  Vietnam-160; North Yemen-250; South Yemen-280; Zaire-140.

Because of the poverty of these nations it is not too difficult to see that MNCs attempting to operate in any of them are going to be the target for espousing such corporations to the governmental  plans,  particularly  in  the Social Sphere, which also embraces the economic aspects.  The June 25, 1979 issue of U.S. NEWS & WORLD REPORT, page 53, states:

Booming population growth and a declining  rate  of economic expansion are  putting  enormous social restraints on  Third World countries everywhere. *** Instead of the "new international economic order" that emerging nations demanded nearly a decade ago, events have shaped a kind  of global disorder, with high  oil  prices a driving force  behind  simultaneous inflation and recession.  Industrialized economies have been hurt, but developing economies have suffered even more. With Third  World  indebtedness  approaching  $300  billion, many countries are facing bankruptcy or cutbacks in growth plans. Thus, slowly  the U.S.  policy  toward  the  Third  World is shifting.

## BEHAVIORAL ACCOUNTING

## #18-12...Relationship of Behavioral Acctg. to Social Acctg.

Closely related to  the area of Social Accounting is that of Behavioral Accounting, a latter  date  development in expansion of accounting horizons. The nature of Behavioral Accounting was discussed  at  the  4th  International  Conference on Accounting Education. In the PROCEEDINGS published pursuant to the Conference at page 29, Prof.  Andre Zund offers the following suggestions:

The expansion in accounting  can  be explained primarily by the growing needs of all stakeholders of the business, as Mr. Lorton  has also pointed out.  In  general,  traditional accounting no longer meets these requirements.  The question is whether accounting  education should  even take these new trends into  account, and, if  so, which tendencies are best suited  for teaching purposes.  There are  three  such  new trends  but I would like to  concentrate  on Behavioural Accounting.

In order to fulfill the  growing information needs,  the accountants must have a better knowledge than in the past of human behaviour both inside and outside the company. This is the purpose of Behavioural Accounting.  Behavioural Accounting studies the behaviour of those who produce,  analyze and make use of accounting data. In this way, the new discipline is  to familiarize  management with  accounting theory.  In

other words, Behavioural Accounting is the SCIENCE of behavioural implications of accountancy.

Although there are no evaluations which show to what
extent an accountant's knowledge of these behavioural implications allows him to be more successful in his work, there
is no doubt that knowledge of dysfunctional reactions leads
to the development of a behaviour-oriented information system which cannot be infiltrated. The accountant familiar
with these behavioural implications knows, for example, that
the budget is not a tool of pressure but a guideline and
that demanding, but still attainable, goals have a stimulating effect. He also knows that no motivation is produced if
goals set too low are continually exceeded or goals set too
high are never reached.

Of course, one could raise the objection that Behavioural Accounting is still poorly developed and that the existing empirical studies are not sufficient to establish a system of doctrines consisting of proven findings. But if
teaching were always to wait until research has supplied
irrefutable results, it would fail to meet the current
needs. Particularly in practice-oriented disciplines like
accountancy, teaching and research go hand in hand. And furthermore, we possess specific knowledge in various disciplines, such as general psychology, social psychology, and
industrial psychology, which may be applied very well to the
accounting field. This has been neglected in the past. Various empirical studies conducted in the U.S. indicate this
quite clearly.

#### #18-13...Nature of Behavioral Accounting

The function of behavioral accounting is to establish a set
of behavioral rules or assumptions to be related to the discipline of conventional management accounting. There are two
views regarding human behavior in business organizations: (1)
the Traditional, or Classical, and (2) the Modern Organization
Theory.

The TRADITIONAL, or CLASSICAL, view is predicated on concepts of profit maximization, economic incentives,and minimization of work effort of personnel due to lack of total interest
in accomplishments of management personnel (as evidenced by the
basis of departmentalization, responsibility, authority and
control). The profit maximization concept is generally regarded
as the test of generally accepted favorable accounting systems.
The Traditional View represents the behavior found in common
practice and is embedded in, and permeates, our general accounting education and practice. It is founded on the single
view of human behavior that has existed in business organizations from the time of the industrial revolution to the present

which has  been adopted by management accounting  as an unques-
tioned tenet.

The MODERN ORGANIZATION THEORY is now  surfacing, and should
it become more realistic  with respect to business organization
behavior, the scope of management theory and practice will have
to be expanded and broadened. Under this theory the future will
require much research to set forth principles for measuring how
effectively management accounting systems perform the functions
of motivating, predicting and explaining human behavior.

#### #18-14...Relationship of Behavioral Accounting
####          to Business Organization

Chapter 1 pointed out that  there is a  close  relationship
between economics, business, and  accounting; and  that the development of accounting  has been parallel with the development
of business. Business in turn is closely related to management,
which makes accountants amenable to  the study of  organization
theory required  to comprehend  the functioning of business enterprises.   However, as pointed out by Prof. Zund, accountants
have failed almost completely  to take  cognizance of the relationship of management  behavior and accounting.   The development of management theory and practice  is predicated on an understanding  of the interrelationship  and application  of  the
behavioral aspects to actions by management.

In "Behavioral  Assumptions of Management  Accounting," published  in the ACCOUNTING  REVIEW,  July 1966, pages  496-509,
Prof. Edwin Caplan declares:

The management of a business enterprise is faced with an
environment--both internal and external to the firm--that is
in a perpetual state of  change.  These  include  physical
changes (climate,  availability of  raw  materials,  etc.);
technological  changes (new  products  and processes, etc.);
social changes (attitudes  of employees, customers, competitors,  etc.);  and  financial  changes  (asset  composition,
availability of funds, etc.). An important characteristic of
"good" management is the  ability to  evaluate past changes,
to  react to current changes, and to predict future changes.
However, it is  inconceivable that any workable  information
system  could provide data  relative to all, or even a  substantial  portion, of  the changes occurring inside and outside of the organization.

The  essential  point is  that  decisions regarding what
information is  the most critical, how it should be processed, and who  should receive  it  are almost  always made by
accountants.  In addition they  are often directly involved,
as participants, in the management  decision-making  process
itself.  Accountants exercise choice in  the design of their
systems and the  selection of data for admission into  them.

Thus the entire management accounting process can be viewed
from the standpoint of attempting to  INFLUENCE THE BEHAVIOR
of others, performing these functions with certain  expectations with respect to  the reactions of others to what  they
do, resulting in some explicit or implicit ASSUMPTIONS about
human behavior in organizations.

## #18-15...Historical Aspects of Traditional Determinants of Organizational Human Behavior

Prof. Caplan declares that having  established that the management  accounting function by  necessity  involves behavioral
assumptions, these assumptions  are  based  on the premise that
current management accounting is  the product of three  related
conceptual forces, viz., (1) individual engineering technological, (2) classical organization theory, and (3) economic  "theory of the firm." Notwithstanding,  there has only been recognized a  single view  of business  organization  human behavior
since the Industrial Revolution.

Robert  L. Heilbroner  in his book THE WORLDLY PHILOSOPHERS,
Simon & Schuster, 1961, pp. 7-8,  suggests that from the beginnings of recorded history the traditional determinants of human
behavior in organizations  have been either CUSTOM  or PHYSICAL
FORCE.  The simplistic nature of these concepts  makes it unnecessary  to  explain  any behavioral actions.  However, as  the
structure of society changed as a result of the Industrial Revolution, Prof. Caplan indicates that:

The new entrepreneurial class of the 18th century sought not
only a  social  philosophy to  rationalize  its actions, but
also practical solutions to  the problems of motivating, coordinating, and  controlling  the members  of  its organizations.  The coordinating problem resulted in the development
of  the classical organization theories which  is the second
of the three  conceptual forces  mentioned in  the preceding
paragraph.

Interjected were  the theories of the economists whose explanation of human behavior was economic motivation and profit maximization. These were  incorporated into the industrial community
thought patterns which in turn provided  the  philosophical and
psychological  foundations  of the scientific management  movement, founded at the beginning of the 1900s  by Frederick  Taylor.  Prof. Caplan points out that:

Taylor's  scientific  management  movement combined  the
basic  behavioral assumptions  of the economic theory of the
firm with the  viewpoint  of  the engineer  seeking the most
effective  utilization of the physical resources at his disposal, and became interested in maximizing the  productivity
of the  worker  through  increased  efficiency  and  reduced
costs. The scientific management movement flourished and for

many years virtually dominated the scene as most of Taylor's
views are still widely accepted today. The scientific management movement led into detailed studies of factory costs
and provided an important stimulus for the development of
modern cost-and-management accounting.

About 1920 a second major pattern of organization the-
ory--the ADMINISTRATIVE MANAGEMENT THEORY--evolved adopting
a departmentalized approach. The primary objective was the
efficient assignment of organization activities to individual jobs and the grouping of these jobs by departments. This
school was concerned with such matters as lines of authority
and responsibility, specialization, span of control, and
unity of command. It appears that with respect to philosophy
and techniques, much of contemporary management accounting
is a product of and geared to the scientific management and
administrative theories, and can be termed the traditional
management accounting model of the firm.

#### #18-16...Traditional Management Acctg. Behavioral Assumptions

Prof. Caplan goes on to conclude that:
It should now be possible to postulate some of the fundamental behavioral assumptions that appear to underlie the traditional management accounting model. These assumptions with
their major conceptual sources are as follows:
I.   ASSUMPTIONS WITH RESPECT TO ORGANIZATION GOALS:
     A.  The principal objective of business activity is
         profit maximization (economic theory).
     B.  The principal objective can be segmented into sub-
         goals to be distributed throughout the organization
         (principles of management).
     C.  Goals are additive--what is good for the parts of
         the business is also good for the whole (principles
         of management).
II.  ASSUMPTIONS WITH RESPECT TO THE BEHAVIOR OF PARTICI-
     PANTS:
     A.  Organization participants are motivated primarily
         by economic forces (economic theory).
     B.  Work is essentially an unpleasant task which people
         will avoid whenever possible (economic theory).
     C.  Human beings are ordinarily inefficient and wasteful
         (scientific management).
III. ASSUMPTIONS WITH RESPECT TO THE BEHAVIOR OF MANAGEMENT:
     A.  The role of the business manager is to maximize the
         profits of the firm (economic theory).
     B.  In order to perform this role, management must con-
         trol the tendencies of employees to be lazy, waste-
         ful, and inefficient (scientific management).
     C.  The essence of management control is authority. The

ultimate authority of management stems from its
ability to affect the economic reward structure
(scientific management).

D. There must be a balance between the authority a person has and his responsibility for performance
(principles of management).

IV. ASSUMPTIONS WITH RESPECT TO THE ROLE OF MANAGEMENT AC-
COUNTING:

A. The primary function of management accounting is to
aid management in the process of profit maximization
(scientific management).

B. The accounting system is a "goal-allocation" device
which permits management to select its operating
objectives and to divide and distribute them
throughout the firm, i.e., assign responsibilities
for performance. This is commonly referred to as
"planning" (principles of management).

C. The accounting system is a control device which permits management to identify and correct undesirable
performance (scientific management).

D. There is sufficient certainty, rationality, and
knowledge within the system to permit an accurate
comparison of responsibility for performance and
the ultimate benefits and costs of that performance
(principles of management).

E. The accounting system is "neutral" in its evalua-
tions--personal bias is eliminated by the objectivity of the system (principles of management).

## #18-17...Behavioral Accounting Experiences

At the 4th International Conf. on Acctg. Education, Prof.
Andre Zund describes experiences with behavioral accounting:
I would like to briefly discuss a few didactic experiments. Students of WIRTSCHAFTSSCHULEN (business high school
students) in Germany were not in favor of integrating Behavioural Accounting into accounting training. This was not
due, however, to a lack of interest on the part of the students but rather because its integration would have further
increased the already heavy workload. Nevertheless, it still
seems necessary that students at this early stage be made
familiar with this subject matter, although the necessary
teaching aids are still lacking today.
At the university level, a series of seminars was conducted jointly with the Psychology Dept. at the Univ. of
Saint Gallen during the winter semester of 1976/77. These
seminars dealt with accountancy and human behaviour. The
course was received very favorably, and not only by students
of accountancy. The preparation of these doctoral seminars

was facilitated by the fact that professors and practitioners have been working closely together for many years. It was interesting to note that the behavioural implications of accountancy were best understood by those persons who had already been active several years on higher hierarchical levels of a company and had been involved with accountancy on a daily basis. This is a valid possibility for further education in this field.

#### #18-18...Future of Behavioral Accounting

Prof. Zund makes the following conclusions:
(1) Considering the behavioural aspects of accountancy is of practical relevance because modern accountancy is marked more by an instrumental rather than a documentary character;
(2) Because students as well as teachers lack the necessary practical experience, Behavioural Accounting is not appropriate for commercial or business high schools;
(3) Behavioural Accounting is suitable subject matter for interdisciplinary courses at the highest university level;
(4) Seminars for the further education of practitioners are especially rewarding.

Behavioural Accounting is still in the beginning stages. Many empirical research studies and teaching experiments will be necessary before behavioural aspects are an integral part of accounting education.

### SUMMARY OF FOOTNOTE REFERENCES
(References are to Paragraph #'s)

#18-2  Surendra Singhvi, "Corporate Financial Management in a Developing Economy," Univ. of Washington Graduate School of Business Administration, 1972, pp. 48-49

#18-3  AICPA FASB #7, ACCOUNTING AND REPORTING BY DEVELOPMENT STAGE ENTERPRISES, 1975

#18-4  George Scott, "Accounting and Developing Nations," Univ. of Washington Graduate School of Business Admin., 1970, p. 75

#18-7  Adolph J.H. Enthoven, 4th International Conference on Accounting Education, Berlin, 1977, PROCEEDINGS, p. 18

#18-7  Enthoven, "Development and State of Conventional Accounting Education Systems," Subject 1, Ibid., p. 41

#18-8  Enthoven, Ibid., p. 37

#18-9  Sullivan Code, "U.S. Firms' Aim: Equality for Blacks," U.S. NEWS & WORLD REPORT (October 8, 1979): 80

#18-10 "Crucial Stakes for U.S. Firms in South Africa," reprinted with permission from U.S. NEWS & WORLD REPORT (April 28, 1980): 43,46. Copyright 1980, U.S. News & World Report, Inc.

#18-11 Overseas Development Council Study, "Fourth World," U.S.

NEWS & WORLD REPORT (June 25, 1979): 53
#18-12 Andre Zund, 4th Conference PROCEEDINGS, op. cit., p. 29
#18-14 Edwin Caplan, "Behavioral Assumptions of Management Account-
    ing," ACCOUNTING REVIEW (July 1966): 496-509. Reprinted with
    the permission of the publisher, American Accounting Assn.
#18-15 Ibid., by permission.
#18-15 Robert L. Heilbroner, THE WORLDLY PHILOSOPHERS (N.Y.: Simon
    & Schuster, 1961), pp. 7-8
#18-16 Caplan, op. cit., by permission.
#18-17 Zund, op. cit.
#18-18 Ibid.

## BIBLIOGRAPHY

Al Hashim, D.D. "International Dimensions in Accounting and Impli-
    cations for Developing Nations," MANAGEMENT INTERNATIONAL
    REVIEW (April 1982): 4
Briston, Richard J. "The Changing Role of Government Audit in De-
    veloping Countries," THE ACCOUNTANT'S MAGAZINE, 83, (August
    1979): 325-327
Enthoven, A.J.H. "U.S. Accounting and the Third World," JOURNAL OF
    ACCOUNTANCY (June 1983): 110-118
Leff, Nathaniel. "Multinational Corporate Pricing Policy in the
    Developing Countries," JOURNAL OF INTERNATIONAL BUSINESS
    STUDIES, 6 (Fall 1975): 55-64
Lelievre, Thomas and Lelievre, Clara. "Accounting in the Third
    World," THE WOMAN CPA, 39, (October 1977): 3-5
Mirghani, M.A. "A Framework for a Linkage Between Microaccounting
    and Macroaccounting for Purposes of Development Planning in
    Developing Countries," INTERNATIONAL JOURNAL OF ACCOUNTING
    EDUCATION & RESEARCH (Fall 1982): 57-68
Samuels, J.M. and Oliga, J.C. "Accounting Standards in Developing
    Countries," INTERNATIONAL JOURNAL OF ACCOUNTING EDUCATION &
    RESEARCH (Fall 1982): 69-88
Scott, William R. "The Role of Accounting in Economic Development,"
    CA MAGAZINE (July 1974)

## THEORY QUESTIONS
(Question Numbers are Keyed to Text Paragraph #'s)

#18-1-2. Describe the nature of Developmental Accounting, enum-
    erating the stages of the development process.
#18-3-4. What accounting problems exist in connection with de-
    velopment enterprises and what problems arise during
    development?
#18-5 How does the development process affect the functions
    of the accountant?
#18-6 What is Economic Evaluation Accounting?
#18-7 Discuss the relationship of Developmental Accounting to
    the Third World.

#18-8   What is the relationship of Developmental Accounting to
        Social Accounting?
#18-9   Briefly outline some significant recent experiences of
        Third World Enhancement programs.
#18-11  Discuss the relationship of Developmental Accounting to
        the Fourth World.
#18-12  What is the relationship of Social Accounting to Behav-
        ioral Accounting?
#18-13  Discuss the nature of Behavioral Accounting, explaining
        the Traditional, or Classical, and the Modern Organiza-
        tion Theory views of human behavior in business organi-
        zations.
#18-14  Explain the relationship of Behavioral Accounting to
        business organization.
#18-15  Outline the historical aspects of the traditional deter-
        minants of organizational human behavior.
#18-16  Outline the fundamental behavioral assumptions that ap-
        pear to underlie the traditional management accounting
        model.
#18-17-18. Relate some accounting experiences with behavioral
        situations and their indication of the future of behav-
        ioral accounting.


## EXERCISES

### EX-18-1
Discuss the relationship of Codes of Conduct to Developmental
Accounting.

### EX-18-2
What is the Sullivan Code and what impact has it had in its
experiences with emerging nations? How do you appraise the future of the success of the Sullivan Code?

### EX-18-3
What is your opinion of the new classification of developing
countries into what are called "Fourth World" nations? Should
the former Third World nations be subclassified to create the
Fourth Nation group and on what basis?

### EX-18-4
Make a critical analysis of the four classes of traditional
Management Accounting Behavioral Assumptions.

# International Political Bribery and Extortion Accounting

IMPACT OF GOVERNMENT POLITICS ON THE ACCOUNTING PROCESS

#19-1....Emergence of International Political Accounting

In the article "The Politicization of Accounting" published in the Nov. 1978 JOURNAL OF ACCOUNTANCY, pp. 65-72, Dr. David Solomons points out:

> There was once a time, not so many years ago, when accounting could be thought of as an essentially non-political subject. If it was not as far removed from politics as was mathematics or astronomy, it was at least no more political than psychology or surveying or computer technology or statistics. Even in areas of accounting such as taxation, which might be thought to be most relevant to questions of public policy, practitioners were generally content to confine themselves to technical issues without getting involved as accountants in the discussion of tax policy.
>
> Today, to judge from current discussions of the standard-setting process, accounting can no longer be thought of as non-political. The numbers that accountants report have, or at least are widely thought to have, a significant impact on economic behaviour. Accounting rules therefore affect human behaviour. Hence the process by which they are made is said to be political. It is then only a short step to the assertion that such rules are properly to be made in the political arena, by counting heads and deciding accounting issues by some voting mechanism.

When the Structure Committee of the Financial Accounting Foundation was confronted with the question as to the nature of the task of setting standards, its study of "The Structure of Establishing Financial Accounting Standards," April 1977, reported at page 19:

> Because the process of setting accounting standards *** re-

quires some perspective it would not be appropriate to establish a standard based solely on a canvass of the constituents. Similarly, the process can be described as legislative because it must be deliberative and because all views must be heard. But the standard setters are expected to represent the entire constituency as a whole and not of a specific constituent group. The process can be described as po-litical because there is an educational effort involved in getting a new standard accepted.

This viewpoint of the Structure Committee is reaffirmed by Robert May and Gary Sundem in the Oct. 1976 ACCOUNTING REVIEW, page 750, where, in the article "Research for Accounting Policy: An Overview," it is stated:

In practice as well as in theory the social welfare impact of accounting reports apparently is recognized. Therefore it is no surprise that the Financial Accounting Standards Board is a political body and, consequently, that the process of selecting an acceptable accounting alternative is a political process. If the social welfare impact of accounting policy decisions were ignored, the basis for the existence of a regulatory body would disappear. Therefore the FASB must consider explicitly political (i.e., social welfare) aspects as well as accounting theory and research in its decisions.

## #19-2....Nature of Political Accounting

In the July 1973 ACCOUNTING REVIEW (in "Research, Intuition and Politics in Accounting Inquiry"), Dale Gerboth states:

When a decision-making process depends for its success on public confidence, the critical issues are not technical; they are political. In the face of conflict between competing interests, rationality as well as prudence lies not in seeking final answers, but rather in compromise--essentially a political process. ***

A politicization of accounting rule-making is not only inevitable but just. In a society committed to democratic legitimization of authority, only politically responsive institutions have the right to command others to obey their rules.

## #19-3....Political Versus Social Accounting

The preceding quotations appear to indicate that because of the Social Aspects discussed in Chapters 17 and 18, the public at large is affected, with the result that the people in general, or government, is involved, which automatically makes the matter political. Under such thinking, it may be difficult, if not impossible, to draw an exact line as to where Social Accounting ends and Political Accounting begins.

#19-4....Political Versus Macro-Accounting

Another factor that enters into the picture is whether political accounting is a strict concept related to the accounting
profession alone, as represented by the FASB, or a broader concept that involves the goals of the national government. In
this regard Prof. David Hawkins, in the lecture "Financial Accounting, The Standards Board and Economic Development," published in Apr. 1975 by Baruch College of the City University of
New York, pp. 7-8, declares:

> Congress and the executive branch are becoming more and
> more aware of the behavioural aspects of corporate reporting
> and its macro economic implications. Increasingly these pol-
> icy makers will demand that the decisions of those charged
> with determining what constitutes approved corporate report-
> ing standards result in corporate reporting standards that
> will lead to individual economic behaviour that is consist-
> ent with the nation's macro economic objectives. *** This
> awareness on the part of economic planners brings accounting
> standards-setting into the realm of political economics. ***
> Corporate reporting standards should result in data that
> are useful for economic decisions provided that the standard
> is consistent with the national macro economic objectives
> and the economic programs designed to reach these goals.
> *** Because the FASB has the power to influence economic
> behaviour it has an obligation to support the government's
> economic plans.

Commenting on the last remark of Prof. Hawkins, Dr. Solomons is
of the opinion:

> In that last passage, the word BECAUSE is noteworthy,
> implying as it does that the power to influence economic
> behaviour always carries with it an obligation to support
> the government's plans. Even if the matter under discussion
> were, say, pricing policy or wage policy or some aspect of
> environmental protection, the assertion would be open to
> argument. In relation to accounting, where the end product
> is a system of measurement, the position which Hawkin urges
> on the FASB could, I believe, threaten the integrity of fi-
> nancial reporting and deprive it of whatever credibility it
> now has.
> There is no question as to the sensitivity of *** the
> issues that have been on the agenda of the FASB. The finan-
> cial community is not indifferent to the accounting rules
> imposed on it by the FASB. *** Few if any accounting stand-
> ards are without some economic impact. *** One of the most
> sensitive standards has been that dealing with foreign cur-
> rency translation #8. Under the so-called temporal method,
> mandated by the Board, monetary assets and liabilities of a

foreign subsidiary of a U.S. corporation have to be translated, for consolidation purposes, at the rate of exchange
current at the balance sheet date. Assets which, in accordance with generally accepted accounting principles, are carried at cost have to be translated at the rate current at
the time they were acquired. Exchange gains and losses, realized and unrealized, have to be brought into the income
statement. For companies that formerly used a current/non-
current classification, the important changes lie in the
treatment of inventories and of long-term debt. Inventories,
as current assets, were formerly carried at the current rate
and are now carried at the historical rate; long-term debt,
as a noncurrent liability, was formerly carried at the historical rate and now, as a monetary item, is carried at the
current rate. Moreover, unrealized translation gains, formerly kept out of the income statement, now have to be
brought in. The result has been greatly to increase the volatility of the reported earnings of companies with important
foreign operations. Criticism of Statement #8 has focused on
this increased volatility rather than on whether the new
rules result in a better or worse representation of financial performance. ***
     Numerous other politically sensitive accounting issues
could be cited, but none has received as much attention as
accounting for inflation, for none has such widespread potential repercussions throughout the business world. Each
method which has been proposed to replace or to modify traditional methods would affect different companies differently, making some look more prosperous than they are under
present methods and others less prosperous. For example,
current purchasing power adjustments to historical cost accounting (general price level accounting) tend to make utilities with heavy debt capital look better off; replacement
cost accounting tends to make companies with a large investment in depreciable assets, such as steel companies, look
relatively less profitable. A system using exit values
(e.g., continuously contemporary accounting, or COCOA) would
make firms using assets that are not readily salable look
bad. Though the protracted arguments about the relative merits of these and other rival systems have not generally
overtly recognized the vested interests that stand to gain
or lose by the way the argument goes, the political implications of inflation accounting have probably had as much responsibility for the difficulty in reaching agreement on the
direction in which to move as have the technical problems
involved. ***
     The above examples will serve to illustrate some of the
points of contrast between accounting and politics.

#### #19-5....Distinction Between Political Accounting
#### and Macro-Accounting

In the discussion above, the term POLITICAL appears to be
used in both a broad sense, associated with national policy,
and a narrower sense, as related to the formulation of accounting precepts by what is regarded as a quasi political body,
viz., the FASB. It could be said that all accounting would be
political in character under the latter interpretation. However
there should be a distinction between the narrower strict accounting aspects and the broader best-interests-of-the-na-
tional-public aspects. In the material to follow, the term PO-
LITICAL ACCOUNTING will be used to discuss the relationships
that exist where governmental groups have direct contact with
individuals and corporate operations. The term MACRO-ACCOUNTING
has been used previously to denote the situation where the private sector has no alternative but to comply with the policies
aimed at promoting the national public interest.

The national interest aspects under the heading of INTERNA-
TIONAL MACRO-ACCOUNTING have previously been discussed. There
are two aspects of International Political Accounting: (1) Political BRIBERY AND EXTORTION (in this chapter), and (2) Political RISK (in the next chapter).


**POLITICAL ASPECTS**

#### #19-6...Relationship of Political Accounting to
#### Socio-Economic Accounting

Political Accounting is concerned with accounting as related
to political situations with which both individuals and enterprises may be confronted. The political accounting aspects may
therefore be related to individuals who are attempting to seek
office, and its corollary--the contributions made for political
purposes--as well as contributions made by individuals as corporate officers; or, it may be concerned with the relations
that MNCs have with subsidiaries operating in foreign countries, and the responsibility of such corporations to the law
of such foreign countries controlling the foreign operations.
Since the political aspects are necessarily involved with the
national public welfare, it should be apparent that many of the
social accounting problems are intertwined with, and regulated
by, government fiat. Because of this propinquity to the social
aspects, which are rather inextricably interwoven with political philosophies, political accountability like social responsibility represents a further addition for the accounting profession.

## #19-7....Nature of Political Accounting

Political Accounting involves the principles of accounting
related to (1) the individual politician, (2) individual contributions for political office seekers, (3) individual political contributions by corporate officers, (4) corporate political contributions, and (5) political climate in foreign countries in which MNCs operate, which has a dual aspect (a) operation under the laws of the foreign country, and (b) liability
to seizure by nationalization and/or expropriation by the foreign countries.

## #19-8....Personal Political Accounting

Accounting for the politician is centered on the principles
for preparation of personal financial statements. In the U.S.
the accounting profession has sanctioned the use of current
values in personal financial statements. Current values tend to
provide more relevant data for the voting citizen than do historical costs, particularly when the disparity is considerable.
The promulgated report is a two-column financial statement
showing both the cost basis and the current-value basis, as
demonstrated by the AICPA article "Audits of Personal Financial
Statements," 1968, pp. 2-3. The purpose is to give the citizen
a relevant financial presentation so as to allow a judgment
about a politicians's possible conflict of interest and the
inherent personal integrity capabilities.

## #19-9....Political Contributions

The other element of political-seeking accounting is the
stewardship accounting for political contributions. More and
more attention is being given to suggesting the publication of
a financial statement of the total campaign contributions and
expenditures by each political candidate. Further, public-owned
corporations are being asked to report political contributions
and favors, if given, in financial statements to shareholders.
As a corollary there have been a rash of contributions made
in the decade of the '70s to foreign country rulers and officials, and their representatives for the purpose of consummating large purchase orders, which has resulted in the enactment
of the FOREIGN CORRUPT PRACTICES ACT.

## POLITICAL BRIBERY AND EXTORTION -- FCPA

## #19-10...The Foreign Corrupt Practices Act (FCPA)

The Act was passed in the wake of the disclosures that many
MNCs were paying what was tantamount to bribes for the purpose

of getting orders and doing business in foreign countries. While the basic reason for the law was to bar foreign payoffs, it went into great detail in prescribing a system of internal accounting controls required to be adhered to by these corporations. The record discloses that between 1975 and Dec. 1977, when the Act was passed, some 300 corporations had made some form of sensitive payments. In its May 1976 report to Congress, the SEC disclosed that there was an attempt on the part of those making the illegal payments to cover up by failing to properly record them on the records of the company. The internal accounting system was such as to prevent these payments from being brought to the attention of the board of directors.

The paradox of the Act is that although it is referred to as Foreign Corrupt Practices, corporations that do not have any foreign operations or corrupt practices notwithstanding are held to fall within its purview. The Act is not limited to foreign activities.

The Act has two sections, the first relating to the foreign corrupt practices; and the second, which has no relation to the first, strictly speaking, the accounting provisions. It is the second section that is onerous and causing much concern on the part of public accounting firms. These accounting provisions impose new responsibilities on public companies to maintain accurate books and records, and a system of internal accounting controls that conform to the rules specifically set forth in the Act. The office of the Chief Accountant of the U.S. SEC (which advises the SEC) works with its enforcement division with respect to matters involving possible violations of the Act. Paradoxically the first suit brought under the Act did not involve either a foreign operation or a corrupt practice in the customary sense of the term.

#19-11...Internal Accounting Controls System

The reason for the uproar amongst accountants is that the Act requires companies to "devise and maintain a system of internal accounting controls," but fails to define what constitutes an adequate system of control. In fact, the term "adequacy" was specifically omitted, and the SEC contends that by adequacy is meant the REASONABLE ASSURANCE TEST, which is basically a cost-benefit tradeoff that is regarded as a management determination. Under this test, the SEC contends that it is incumbent on management to determine if there is a weakness in the internal control system through which assets could be dissipated or financial statements misstated, or unauthorized transactions materialized, and, after discovery of these defects, to correct them.

The SEC contends the procedure is quite simple but admits it is very subjective which compels the decision of "adequacy" to

be made only by management. For example, SEC says, if the installation of the system of controls costs more than the savings resulting from misappropriated or lost assets, there would
be no requirement to institute the controls and the test of
reasonable assurance would then be met. In the light of the
fact that the accounting profession and auditing procedures now
go through a review of internal controls before conducting an
audit examination, they have set up a number of task forces to
determine what is an adequate system. Paradoxically it is
admitted by the SEC and the accounting profession that all publicly-held companies almost universally have some degree of
internal accounting control.

The SEC to date has issued no additional guidelines to be
followed by corporations to meet the requirements of the Act.
The only document published so far by SEC is an Accounting Series Release, which merely calls attention to the readers that
the Act has been passed and that they should review their accounting controls to make sure they comply with it. A special
advisory committee of the AICPA has published a tentative draft
which furnishes fairly substantial guidelines as to what should
be encompassed by the review with suggestions on how to conduct
it. Thus the SEC not only has not published any official advice
but also has made it clear that it has no intention to do so.
The reason for this attitude is that it is relatively new and
unusual with respect to public companies in general because it
goes beyond the objectives of the SEC to assure full and fair
disclosure. It really is directed to the responsibility of corporations and their officers and directors to maintain corporate accountability.

#### #19-12...The Aminex Resources Corporation Case

The first complaint filed under the Act was against the Aminex Resources Corp., in which it was alleged that spurious
bookkeeping was used to disguise fraud by two of its executives. Paradoxically the Aminex Case is an illustration as to
how the Act was used with a company in a nonforeign situation.
However it appears to be the opinion of the accounting profession that the motive behind the passage of the Act was for Congress to solve the foreign payments slush fund problems. Some
of the staff reports definitely indicate such intent. The wording used in the Act was taken by Congress from auditing literature, extracted and inserted, with the result that there appears to be a decided vagueness in the wording. Many professionals queried about it definitely state they do not know the
meaning of some of the language in the Act. Vague terms will
likely be clarified from future litigation.

## #19-13...Foreign Corrupt Practices Act Observations

As was the case in connection with S/R Accounting, the firm of Ernst & Ernst has also made a study of the Act and issued two reports dated Feb. 1978. One is entitled "Foreign Corrupt Practices Act of 1977" and the other, as supplementary to the Act, is "Evaluating Internal Control, A Guide for Management and Directors."

To discuss the great detail presented in these two studies would consume too much space and certainly be beyond the scope of this material. However, the high spots that involve the basic considerations are presented. In an informal presentation before the accounting faculty of Roosevelt Univ., Robert G. Streit, partner in the firm of Ernst & Ernst, presented an overview of the Act and its implications for the accounting profession.

### (1) SUMMARY

The law became effective Dec. 19, 1977. All U.S. companies and officers, directors, employees, agents, or stockholders are prohibited from bribing foreign governmental or political officials. And, all PUBLICLY-HELD companies must meet the law's internal control and recordkeeping requirements. Management's responsibility for maintaining internal control is not new. However, subjecting public companies and their officers and employees to civil liability and criminal prosecution under federal securities laws for not having a sufficient system of internal control is a significant development. Any company doing business in foreign countries, and all public companies, should consider discussing the effects of the law with legal counsel.

BACKGROUND. The law primarily stems from disclosures of questionable or illegal foreign payments by many U.S. companies. Senator Proxmire, who originally introduced the legislation, viewed these practices as adversely affecting the financial integrity of U.S. corporations and the efficient functioning of our capital markets. The law reflects information in the 1976 REPORT OF THE SECURITIES AND EXCHANGE COMMISSION on "Questionable and Illegal Corporate Payments and Practices," and testimony before Congress by a former SEC chairman, representatives of the AICPA, and others. In considering the need for legislation, Congress rejected the approach of requiring disclosure of these payments with criminal penalties for failure to do so, similar to the SEC's voluntary disclosure program. Instead, the legislators concluded that prospectively outlawing certain acts was the most effective and least burdensome deterrant.

FOREIGN BRIBERY. Foreign bribery is defined as a direct or indirect payment or offer intended to promote business interests. The law does not, however, prohibit "grease" or "facilitating" payments to relatively low-level foreign government employees. Companies making bribes can be fined up to $1 million; individuals face a maximum $10,000 fine, imprisonment of up to five years, or both.

INTERNAL CONTROL. The law requires publicly-held companies to (1) devise and maintain a system of internal control sufficient, inter alia, to provide reasonable assurance that transactions are properly authorized and recorded, and (2) keep records which "accurately and fairly" reflect financial activities in reasonable detail.

## (2) OUTLINE OF THE LAW
## (A) FOREIGN CORRUPT PRACTICES

SCOPE OF THE LAW. The foreign bribery provisions of the law apply to all U.S. companies and officers, directors, employees, agents, or stockholders acting on behalf of such companies. The law is comprised of two similar sections—one covers publicly-held companies and the other applies to all other domestic concerns.

FOREIGN SUBSIDIARIES. Although foreign subsidiaries of U.S. businesses are not specifically mentioned in the law, the conference report on the final legislation includes the following statement: "The conferees recognized the inherent jurisdictional, enforcement, and diplomatic difficulties raised by the inclusion of foreign subsidiaries of U.S. companies in the direct prohibitions of the bill. However, the conferees intend to make clear that any issuer or domestic concern which engages in bribery of foreign officials indirectly through any other person or entity would itself be liable under the bill." Thus the law appears to encompass foreign subsidiaries by prohibiting INDIRECT (as well as direct) foreign corrupt payments or offers.

The conference report also indicates that U.S. companies and their officers, directors, or employees "will be liable when they act in relation to the affairs of any foreign subsidiary." This could affect many multinational corporations that appoint their U.S. officers and employees as directors or officers of foreign subsidiaries. If a foreign subsidiary were to make a prohibited payment at the direction of, or which is known to, any such officer or employee, a question would arise as to whether the U.S. company and the officer or employee violated the law.

DEFINITION OF CORRUPT PRACTICES. Prohibited acts consist of the "corrupt" use of interstate commerce to offer, pay, promise to pay, or authorize giving ANYTHING OF VALUE to any of the following for certain prohibited purposes: (1) foreign official, including any person acting in an official capacity for a foreign government, department, agency or instrumentality; (2) foreign political party, official or candidate for foreign political office; or (3) other person, while knowing or having reason to know, the offer or payment will ultimately go to either of the above two categories.

PROHIBITED PURPOSES. The offer payment must be to influence an act or decision by a foreign government, politician, or political party to assist in obtaining, retaining, or directing business to any person. The word "corrupt" is used to clarify that the offer, payment, promise, or gift must be intended to induce the recipient to misuse his or her official position in order to wrongfully direct business. Political contributions in foreign countries apparently would not necessarily be prohibited under the terms of the law if they are not intended to assist in obtaining or retaining business.

FACILITATING PAYMENTS EXCLUDED. The law is not intended to cover "facilitating" or "grease" payments, made to relatively low-level government employees. The law specifically excludes foreign government employees whose duties are "essentially ministerial or clerical" from the definition of "foreign official." The purpose of facilitating payments is different from that of payments prohibited by the law. Facilitating payments merely move a matter toward an eventual act or decision and do not involve discretionary action. They are made to secure prompt and proper performance of duties, rather than to cause an official to exercise other than free will in a decision-making process. Examples of facilitating or grease payments consist of payments to (1) expedite shipments through customs or to speed processing of customs documents, (2) secure required permits or licenses, or (3) obtain adequate police protection. However, the foreign official's function must be essentially ministerial or clerical for the exclusion to apply.

PENALTIES. A company convicted of making an illegal foreign bribe, which does not have to be "willful," can be fined up to $1 million. Any officer or director or stockholder acting on behalf of the company, who "willfully" violates the bribery provisions may be fined up to $10,000, imprisoned for up to five years, or both, as may also any employee or agent subject to U.S. jurisdiction if the violation is "willful" and the company has violated the antibribery provisions. The law prohibits a corporation from directly or indirectly paying a fine imposed on an individual.

## (2) OUTLINE OF THE LAW
### (B) ACCOUNTING REQUIREMENTS FOR PUBLIC COMPANIES

The law amends the Securities and Exchange Act of 1934 by requiring PUBLICLY-HELD companies to meet recordkeeping and internal control standards intended to help prevent the concealment of foreign corrupt payments.

RECORDKEEPING STANDARD. The law places the responsibility on publicly-held companies to "make and keep books, records, and accounts, which, IN REASONABLE DETAIL, accurately and fairly reflect the transactions and dispositions of the assets of the issuer." Considerable disagreement on the part of the accounting profession was expressed with the term IN REASONABLE DETAIL, on the grounds of vague and indefinite connotations, but the conference committee report states that this phrase was added to clarify that the issuer's records should reflect transactions in conformity with "accepted methods of recording economic events." And the Senate committee report stated that "accurately" does not mean exact precision as measured by an abstract principle. Rather it means that transactions be reflected in conformity with generally accepted accounting principles or other applicable criteria.

INTERNAL CONTROL STANDARD. The internal control objectives set forth in Statement of Auditing Standards No. 1, Sec. 320.28 are now incorporated in Sec. 13(b) of the Exchange Act as follows: (1) Transactions are executed in accordance with management's general or specific authorization; (2) Transactions are recorded as necessary (a) to permit preparation of financial statements in conformity with generally accepted accounting principles or any other criteria applicable to such statements, and (b) to maintain accountability for assets; (3) Access to assets is permitted only in accordance with management's general or specific authorization; & (4) The recorded accountability for assets is compared with the existing assets at reasonable intervals and appropriate action is taken with respect to any differences. Management's responsibility for maintaining internal control is not new. However, subjecting registrants and their officers and employees to civil liability and criminal prosecution under federal securities laws for not having a sufficient system of internal control is a significant development. Evaluating whether an internal control system provides reasonable assurance that the objectives outlined above are met is a highly subjective process in which knowledgeable individuals can arrive at different conclusions.

DISCLOSURE REQUIREMENTS. While the law imposes new requirements on public companies with respect to maintenance of internal control and outlaws certain foreign corrupt practices, it does not alter existing obligations to disclose material questionable and illegal corporate payments and practices, as required under SEC Accounting Series Release No. 242, dated Feb. 16, 1978.

### (3) IMPLICATIONS OF THE LAW
In this third section of the study, interpretations of
the Law are discussed. These, of course, are the opinions of
the staff which composed the study, and will result in verifications from future practices. For this reason only the
headings of the topics discussed will be stated to give the
reader somewhat of an idea as to the various ramifications
that may result from the operation of the FCPA:
(A). PREVENTION OF FOREIGN BRIBES. Management Actions;
Corporate Codes of Conduct; Monitoring Compliance; Auditors'
Responsibilities for Detection
(B). SUFFICIENCY OF INTERNAL CONTROL. Management's Responsibility; AICPA Advisory Committee; Example of a Management Report; Auditors' Responsibility; Internal Control Circumvention; Management Actions; Documentation.

### (4) TEXT OF PUBLIC LAW 95-213 -- FOREIGN CORRUPT PRACTICES ACT OF 1977 -- TITLE I
This section, of course, contains the precise wording of
the Act. That part applicable to Foreign Corporations is
presented in an Appendix.

## #19-14...Implementation of Foreign Corrupt Practices Act

To accompany the foregoing study of the FCPA, Ernst & Ernst
issued a supplementary "Guide for Management and Directors to
Evaluate Internal Control" for compliance with the FCPA, which
describes in great detail a thorough system of internal control. This guide consists of the following four parts: (1) Key
Information for Management and Directors, (2) Approach to Evaluating Internal Accounting Control, (3) Guides for Evaluation,
and (4) Accounting Provisions of the FCPA. The most detailed
section is the third (pages 13-61), which categorizes all accounting details into four functional areas: (1) Sales (S); (2)
Production or Services (P); (3) Finance (F); and (4) Administration (A). A listing is then made of every item falling within each of these four functional areas with a reference number
assigned to each item. Under the Sales category there are numbers S-1 through S-7 representing 7 items; under Production are
numbers P-1 through P-15; under Finance are F-1 through F-11;
and under Administration are A-1 through A-8. Each of these
items receives a detailed description with respect to internal
auditing control. The culmination of the entire fabric is presented on pp. 58 and 59 as geared to the Balance Sheet and Income Statement, which is stated below:

RELATIONSHIP OF CONTROL OBJECTIVES TO FINANCIAL STATEMENT
CLASSIFICATIONS: Balance Sheet and Income Statement formats
in Figure 19-1 are useful to determine that all control ob-

jectives affecting important account classifications are being evaluated. For example, accounts receivable balances are affected by various control objectives in both the Sales and Finance components.

## #19-15...Provisions in the FCPA Relating Directly to Accounting

The provisions in the FCPA that relate directly to accounting are stated on page 62 of the Guide entitled "Evaluating Internal Control," as follows: "SEC 102, Section 13(b) of the Securities Exchange Act of 1934, 15 U.S.C. 78q(b) is amended by inserting "(1)" after "(b)" and by adding at the end thereof the following:"

(2) Every issuer which has a class of securities registered pursuant to Section 12 of this title and every issuer which is required to file reports pursuant to Section 15(D) of this title shall

(A) make and keep books, records and accounts, which, in reasonable detail, accurately and fairly reflect the transactions and dispositions of the assets of the issuer; and

(B) devise and maintain a system of internal accounting controls sufficient to provide reasonable assurances that

(i) transactions are executed in accordance with management's general or specific authorization;

(ii) transactions are recorded as necessary (I) to permit preparation of financial statements in conformity with generally accepted accounting principles or any other criteria applicable to such statements, and (II) to maintain accountability for assets;

(iii) access to assets is permitted only in accordance with management's general or specific authorization; and

(iv) the recorded accountability for assets is compared with the existing assets at reasonable intervals and appropriate action is taken with respect to any differences.

(3) (A) With respect to matters concerning the national security of the U.S., no duty or liability under para. (2) of this subsection shall be imposed upon any person acting in cooperation with the head of any federal department or agency responsible for such matters if such act in cooperation with such head of a department or agency was done upon the specific written directive of the head of such department or agency pursuant to Presidential authority to issue such directives. Each directive issued under this paragraph shall set forth the specific

FIGURE 19-1

RELATIONSHIP OF CONTROL OBJECTIVES TO FINANCIAL STATEMENT CLASSIFICATIONS

BALANCE SHEET - CONTROL OBJECTIVES

| ASSETS: | Debit | Credit |
|---|---|---|
| **Current Assets:** | | |
| Cash | F-1,F-2,F-5, F-6,F-7,F-9 | F-3,F-4,F-8 |
| Accounts Receivable | S-1,S-3,S-4, S-5,S-6 | S-2,S-7, |
| Allowance for Bad Debts | | F-1,F-2 |
| Inventories | S-1,P-1,P-2, P-3,P-4,P-5 P-6,P-7 | S-1,S-2 S-3,S-5,S-6, P-7,P-8,P-9, P-10 |
| Prepaid Exp & Other Assets | A-1,A-2, P-1,P-2 | A-2,P-2 |
| **OTHER ASSETS:** | | |
| Notes Receivable | F-4 | F-1,F-2 |
| Investments | F-8 | F-8,F-10, F-11 |
| Goodwill and Intangibles | | A-6 |
| Interco. Accts | F-7 | F-7 |
| Deposits & Other | A-1,A-2, | A-1,A-2 |
| Land | P-11,P-12 | P-13 |
| Buildings | P-11,P-12 | P-13,P-14 |
| Machy. Equip. | P-11,P-12 | P-13,P-14 |
| Allow. Deprec. | P-13,P-14 | P-15 |

| LIABILITIES: | Debit | Credit |
|---|---|---|
| **Current Liabilities:** | | |
| Notes Payable | F-4 | F-5 |
| Trade Accts. Paybl & Accrued Liab. | F-4 | F-5 |
| Accrued Payroll | F-4 | A-3,A-4,A-5, P-3,P-4,P-5 |
| Taxes (Excl. Inc.) | F-4 | A-1,A-2 |
| Accrued Interest | F-4 | F-5 |
| Income Taxes | A-7,F-4 | A-7 |
| Long-Term Debt | F-4 | F-5 |
| Deferred Inc. Tax | A-7 | A-7 |
| **STOCKHOLDERS EQUITY:** | | |
| Preferred Stock | | F-6 |
| Common Stock | | F-6 |
| Addl. Pd-In Cap. | | F-6 |
| Retained Earnings | F-6 | F-6 |
| Commitments and Contingencies | A-8 | A-8 |

# INCOME STATEMENT - CONTROL OBJECTIVES

| | Debit | Credit |
|---|---|---|
| Sales | S-1, S-4, S-7 | S-1, S-3, S-4, S-5, S-6, F-1 |
| Cost of Sales | A-8, S-3, S-5, S-6, S-7, P-1, P-2, P-3, P-4, P-5, P-6, P-7, P-8, P-9, P-10, P-15 | S-7 |
| Selling, General and Administrative Expenses | A-1, A-2, A-3, A-4, A-6, A-8, S-2, P-15, F-5 | |
| Provision for Income Taxes | A-7 | A-7 |
| Other | P-13, P-14, F-8, F-10, F-11 | P-8, P-13, F-8, F-1, F-9 |

Source: Adapted from Ernst & Ernst, "Guide for Management and Directors to Evaluate Internal Control", page 58-59.

facts and circumstances with respect to which the provisions of this paragraph are to be invoked. Each such
directive shall, unless removed in writing, expire one
year after the date of issuance.
**(B)** Each head of a federal department or agency of the
U.S. who issues a directive pursuant to this paragraph
shall maintain a complete file of all such directives
and shall, on Oct. 1 of each year, transmit a summary of
matters covered by such directives in force at any time
during the previous year to the Permanent Select Committee on Intelligence of the House of Representatives and
the Select Committee on Intelligence of the Senate.

#### #19-16...The Minahan Report

To examine the problem of the FCPA as related to the urgency
of the situation outlined above, the AICPA appointed a special
advisory committee on internal accounting control. This committee (MINAHAN COMMITTEE) issued its MINAHAN REPORT. The newsletter ACCOUNTING EVENTS AND TRENDS published by Price Waterhouse
& Co., Dec. 1978, Vol. 5 No. 8, page 2, points out:
    Of the audiences who will look to the Minahan Report
for guidance in real-life evaluations, none is more important than management and directors of publicly-held companies who bear ultimate responsibility for internal control
systems. As the foundation for public reporting on those
systems, the Minahan Report must provide guidance intelligi-
ble to those primarily responsible, guidance that reflects
the way businesses are organized and run. Changes are therefore needed in the tentative report in three areas.
    ADMINISTRATIVE CONTROLS. Almost as an aside, the tenta-
tive report discusses administrative controls--e.g., organization structure, delegation of authority, budgeting, and
internal auditing--relegating them to the background. In our
view, they belong in the foreground. They are fundamental to
an effective control system, and assessment of the system
should start with them--a business-oriented review of the
control environment of the entity as a whole. Fine distinctions between "accounting" and "administrative" controls
elevate control techniques over control objectives. Regardless of label, controls that help achieve objectives are
ACCOUNTING controls, and controls that do not are not.
    FUNCTIONAL APPROACH. The tentative report stresses the
"cycle approach" to evaluation, focusing on classes of
transactions--e.g., revenue cycle--rather than on people and
departments responsible for transactions. We think that focus is faulty. The cycle concept is an abstraction, more
meaningful to auditors than to management. Companies are
organized along functional lines and controlled through

functional authority. The logical approach to internal accounting control follows those functional lines with the
emphasis on WHO is responsible. Management knows what a
shipping department and billing clerk are; the head of the
revenue cycle exists only in the imagination. The tentative
report uses functional concepts implicitly but brushes off
the functional approach as "another way." We think it should
be the primary means of evaluation, because it interfaces
directly with the structure of business.

FOCUSES ON OBJECTIVES. Drawing on auditing literature,
the federal securities laws recognize four basic control
objectives which, if achieved, should satisfy public expectations. Thus it seems obvious that these objectives must be
the main focus. The tentative report properly recognizes
that the four basic objectives must be interpreted for application in practice. Nevertheless, interpretations must
not be confused with objectives, and the cycle evaluation
criteria in the tentative report are in fact interpretations
which, as presented, appear to be objectives. The Minahan
Report should stress the concept of starting with broad objectives, breaking them into manageable pieces to set detailed criteria that fit the characteristics of the entity
and its control system. To keep the focus clearly on objectives, all examples of specific criteria--for functions or
for cycles--should be associated with them. The message
should be that particular criteria are less important than
methodology, and that the particular methodology is less
important than achieving objectives. The final Minahan Report can be very valuable to management and auditors who
must meet important responsibilities, old and new.

## #19-17...Reactions to Minahan Report

In the May 1979 issue of its newsletter ACCOUNTING NEWS
BRIEFS, after the final Minahan Report was issued, Arthur Andersen & Co. comments:

The AICPA Special Advisory Committee on Internal Accounting Control--the Minahan Committee--has issued its final report on the evaluation of internal accounting controls, with special attention to the needs of management.
Although the committee's recommendations are advisory only
and lack official standing with the AICPA, they should help
management to appraise the company's internal accounting
controls and consider whether it is complying with the accounting provisions of the FCPA.

As in its tentative report, the committee suggests that
"an effective way for management to approach an evaluation
of control procedures and techniques is to (a) classify
transactions by functions, operating units, or cycles; (b)

convert the broad objectives of internal accounting control
into relevant specific objectives appropriate for those
classifications of transactions; and (c) identify and evaluate the control procedures and techniques in place to determine whether they meet specific objectives, giving appropriate consideration to the internal accounting control environment."

This is essentially the same approach we follow in our
audit practice and refer to as Transaction Flow Auditing
(TFA). The Committee's final report notes that the manner in
which a company groups its transactions will depend on its
circumstances. However, "the committee has found the cycle
approach to be a convenient way for it to develop illustrative specific objectives and examples of control procedures
and techniques." An Appendix to the report provides examples
for a hypothetical manufacturing company using five cycles--
revenue, expenditure, production or conversion, financing,
and external financial reporting.

#19-18...Relationship of FCPA to Corporate Accountability

In a speech by Harvey Kapnick, chairman of Arthur Andersen
& Co., before the NAA, AICPA, and FEI on Feb. 14, 1979 in Tam-
pa, published in the EXECUTIVE NEWS BRIEFS Vol. 7, No. 2, Arthur Andersen & Co., entitled "Improving Corporate Responsibility Through Stronger Internal Auditing," it is pointed out that
a distinction is to be made between a REFORM and a REVOLUTION,
and that there is an impact of this distinction on the accounting profession:

A 19th century British statesman once remarked: "A reform is a correction of an abuse; a revolution is a transfer
of power." As we examine dramatically changing concepts of
corporate governance, we are likely to conclude that some of
the results of current "reform" efforts actually may be revolutionary. Two recent trends have set in motion what I believe is an irreversible "transfer of power" as opposed to a
"correction of abuses" in the corporate environment.

The first trend is symbolized by Congressional enactment
of the FCPA of 1977. The Act is revolutionary because it
goes far beyond regulating public actions and consequences.
It imposes profound changes in the management relationships
WITHIN corporations themselves in an effort to improve their
accountability to the public. The disturbing aspect of this
trend is government's transfer of power and drawing of new
lines of responsibility inside companies. The new law resulted from the perceived need to correct bribery and other
abuses overseas, but the accounting provisions apply to ALL
SEC registrants and thus affect companies whether or not
they have foreign operations. The power of the SEC to moni-

tor and regulate the behaviour of the American corporate business community has been radically expanded.

The second trend is the mounting pressure to ensure a more active role and greater independence for boards of directors and audit committees. This too involves a transfer of power. *** Strong and independent boards are not a threat to responsible managements, but they can challenge managements that are unable to perform effectively in today's environment.

The FCPA requires all companies to devise and maintain a system of internal control sufficient to provide reasonable assurance that accountability over assets and operations is maintained. It is the Congressional response to government investigations, litigation, and the disclosures relating to the so-called "sensitive payments" of about 500 American corporations. While this Act includes antibribery provisions, the accounting provisions are even more far-reaching. The Act imposes two basic accounting requirements: companies must maintain accurate books and records, and a sufficient system of internal accounting controls. Despite the persuasive arguments against further government regulation and intrusion into daily business decision-making, I believe the accounting provisions of the Act, if properly applied within the corporate community, will not represent a set-back for American business but a great potential opportunity for progress. Indeed, by improving its internal controls, the business community can stage a constructive "revolution" within its own corporate operations.

These views of Mr. Kapnick are not shared by Peat, Marwick, Mitchell & Co., which, in its EXECUTIVE NEWSLETTER, Vol. V, No. 6, Aug. 7, 1979, declares:

Mandatory reporting on internal accounting controls is "unnecessary and not justified in terms of cost to registrants or usefulness to investors," PMM & Co. has told the SEC in response to its proposals for annual statements on these controls by management, attested to by independent auditors. PMM & Co. did not quarrel with the SEC's assertion that the establishment and maintenance of an effective system of internal accounting controls "have always been important responsibilities of management." It does not follow from the fact that management has these responsibilities that management and independent accountants should be required to report annually on the system of internal accounting control. *** Nothing in the legislative history of the FCPA of 1977 indicates a congressional intent to require the kind of reports proposed by the SEC.

In objecting to the proposed reporting mandate for all registrants, the SEC has presented no persuasive evidence "indicating that users of financial statements desire the

proposed reports, need them, or would benefit from them."
The cost is not justified by any incremental benefits users
might receive. Investors might be misled by the proposed
requirement for management to represent that the system provided "reasonable assurance" that certain specified objectives were met. "Reasonable assurance" would require highly
subjective cost-benefit judgments, and such a representation
might imply a higher degree of assurance than it is practical to provide.

Registrants would incur significant internal costs in
addition to their costs for the proposed examination by independent auditors. Also the additional costs would have an
unfavorable impact on the capital formation process by de-
terring companies from becoming subject to the federal securities laws. We do not consider ANY mandatory reporting
necessary or justifiable.

## #19-19...Recent FCPA Developments

In Vol. III, No. 1 of Arthur Young & Company's newsletter
VIEWS, Feb. 1979, it is pointed out that:
Interest in the FCPA is likely to continue unabated for
some time. In particular, the accounting provisions of the
Act have made it even more important than before that members of boards of directors (and especially members of audit
committees) and senior executives of companies to which the
Act applies give increased attention to their companies'
internal accounting controls. In an effort to clarify the
issues and to offer corporate management a practical course
of action on an approach to complying with the accounting
provisions of the Act, Arthur Young & Company has just issued a second booklet on the subject, which suggests that companies subject to the Act would be well advised to devise
formal programs for dealing with its accounting provisions,
but emphasizes that there is no "one right approach" to a
program for complying with these provisions. It reiterates
the Arthur Young view that, while a major undertaking over a
relatively short period of time may be appropriate for some
companies, it would be an expensive overreaction for others.
The publication recommends a reasoned approach based on a
company's own particular circumstances and a program for
compliance which may cover: how responsibilities for a program may be assigned within an organization; how a company's
system of internal controls may be reviewed and strengthened
by correction of significant weaknesses identified; and how
continuing operation and suitability of the system may be
monitored.

The Arthur Young publication states that the overall
objectives of a program for responding to the internal ac-

counting control provisions should be to develop a reasonable basis for believing that a company is complying with the provisions and to prepare a supporting record. This record should include documentation of actions taken by the board, the audit committee, and senior management. Such documentation, in the firm's view, should go a long way toward demonstrating compliance with the accounting provisions of the Act.

In the Feb. 1979 JOURNAL OF ACCOUNTANCY, p. 28, in a discussion at a New York conference, "Accounting and Legal Implications of the FCPA," Attorney Alan B. Levenson reminded the conference that the accounting standards provisions "apply to transactions of all kinds and these transactions need not be corrupt." He pointed out that although certain transactions may not be unlawful under the Act, they may still be material and thus reportable under SEC regulations.

At the 1979 June meeting of the International Institute of Internal Auditors held in New York City, Benjamin Fisburne III indicated that because the FCPA is a law, and it is going to need much interpretation, as matters now stand it is going to be difficult for auditors, management and accountants to determine a definite course to pursue. Where laws are involved, it has been customary to develop a fund of cases tried in the courts to extract interpretations of the law that will make for more positive situations. Until such a fund of cases is built up, it will be difficult to determine in advance what is the proper course to pursue with respect to questionable audit situations.

## #19-20...The Holcar Oil Corporation Case

The June 1979 JOURNAL OF ACCOUNTANCY, page 22, reports the first suit under the FCPA:

The Justice Department's first civil injunctive proceeding brought under the FCPA of 1977 was settled recently when two U.S. businessmen charged with the violation agreed to an injunction against any further actions in violation of the Act. The businessmen neither admitted nor denied the allegations in agreeing to the consent judgment.

The Justice Dept. had alleged that an illegal payment of $1.5 million had been made by Carver and Holley, owners of Holcar Oil Corp., a Cayman Island corporation, to the former director of petroleum affairs for Qatar, a Persian Gulf emirate. The payment was allegedly made to obtain an oil drilling concession in Qatar. The Justice Dept. also alleged that the businessmen were prepared to make further payments to retain the concession.

Early in 1978 Qatar told Holcar, which had run into financing and technical problems, that the concession would be

terminated. At this point, the Justice Dept. said in its
complaint, former Budget Director Bert Lance allegedly used
his White House connections to help the businessmen. Lance
was not named in the complaint.

## #19-21...The Kenny Case -- 1st Criminal Case

An editorial in the CHICAGO TRIBUNE, Aug. 9, 1979, states
that:
      The first criminal conviction under the FCPA was attain-
ed when Finbar B. Kenny of New York pleaded guilty to spending $337,000 to rig an election in the Cook Islands. The Act
makes it illegal for American businessmen to pay bribes
overseas.  Why would any New Yorker want to invest $337,000
in an election in the Cook Islands--area 93 sq. miles, population 21,317 in 1976? Because export of Cook Island postage
stamps yields $1.5 million a year, and Mr. Kenny had an ex-
clusive franchise to sell these stamps. If Sir Albert Henry,
the prime minister, lost the election, this cozy franchise
might be disturbed. So Mr. Kenny was willing to pay for fly-
ing a few hundred voters back to the Cook Islands for the
election.
      All this sounds like a comic opera. When one thinks of
Americans' bribes abroad, one is more likely to think of
munitions contracts than of franchises to sell postage
stamps, of foreigners more sinister than the Cook Islands'
Sir Albert. But the Kenny case is serious because it established that the U.S. government can successfully prosecute
for the offense of overseas bribery. Today Mr. Kenny and the
Cook Islands. Tomorrow, perhaps, bigger fish will be fried,
and honest Americans dealing in commodities more vital than
Cook Island stamps will be less likely than before to have
to compete with makers of crooked deals.

## #19-22...Legal Aspects of FCPA

Arthur Andersen & Co. on p. 2 of its Jan. 1979 newsletter,
ACCOUNTING NEWS BRIEFS, details the involvement of the American
Bar Association with the FCPA:
      A committee of the American Bar Assn. has issued a guide
to the accounting standards provisions of the FCPA as an aid
to lawyers and others who must interpret and apply the Act.
The ABA Committee on Corporate Law and Accounting said it
prepared the guide "because of the importance of the new
accounting provisions, their vagueness, the complete lack of
interpretive guidelines or experience with these provisions
at present, the technical character of the field, and the
peculiar, almost accidental, character of their legislative
origins."

The guide analyzes the standards and traces their legislative history. It concludes that the only practical way to
deal with the accounting standards of the FCPA is through a
close cooperative effort among legal counsel, internal auditors, independent auditors and management. An auditor should
not be expected to advise a company on whether it complies
with the accounting standards provisions of the FCPA; that
is a legal question says the guide. But auditors "must be
the source of professional knowledge as to what accounting
and control practices and systems are currently considered
to constitute good practice."

The guide outlines these roles that an outside auditor
can play in assisting management and legal counsel in evaluating and documenting a company's internal accounting control systems:

1. Confirm that as of a given date he knows of no "material
   weaknesses" in internal auditing controls, or that, if
   he does, they have been communicated to management. "Errors or irregularities" would be treated the same way.
2. Report any other weaknesses in internal accounting controls which, while not "material weaknesses," are sufficiently important "to cause concern about the reliability" of the control system.
3. Conduct special studies of particular accounting controls, with objectives agreed to by management.
4. Perform a comprehensive study of a company's internal
   accounting control systems "to assess whether they accord with good practice."
5. Review and comment on management's cost-benefit analysis
   or other studies of internal accounting controls, "recognizing that management must make the final decision
   whether or not to make changes in the control systems."

If a company discovers errors in its books and records or
weaknesses in its system of internal accounting controls,
the ABA guide says companies "must be encouraged to correct
them." It would be short-sighted and self-defeating, the
guide says, for companies not to correct discovered errors
out of fear that the correction itself would constitute an
admission of violation of the statute. "Issuers should be
given every incentive to correct their errors, not to per-
petuate or conceal them," the guide says. It is "absolutely
essential," it continues, that the fact that a company
adopts constructive suggestions for improving its internal
control systems "not be read by a court or other public
agency to mean that the company had theretofore failed to
satisfy the 'sufficiency' standard."

## #19-23...SEC Proposals on Internal Control Reporting

In the Vol. 59, No. 9 issue of the semi-monthly news report published by the AICPA entitled THE CPA LETTER, May 14, 1979, it was pointed out that:

At an open meeting late last month, the Securities & Exchange Commission approved in principle a proposal which would require management to include a statement on internal accounting control in certain SEC filings and in annual reports to stockholders. The rules, designed to reinforce the accounting requirements of the 1977 FCPA, provide for a two-step implementation process:

Phase 1, for fiscal years ending between Dec. 15, 1979 and Dec. 15, 1980, would require management to state whether its internal accounting control system, as of the final day of its fiscal year, was sufficient to assure compliance with the law. Also the proposal would require management to disclose any uncorrected material weaknesses brought to its attention by the outside auditors.

Phase 2, for fiscal years ending after Dec. 15, 1980, requires more stringent disclosure. Management would have to comment on the adequacy of its internal control system for the entire fiscal year rather than as of fiscal end. Auditors would also be required to issue an opinion on management's report on internal accounting controls.

## #19-24...The Arthur Andersen & Co. Response

That there would be unfavorable repercussions emanating from the various large CPA firms was inevitable, and without exception all of them strenuously objected. Comments from 2 of the Big 8 firms follow. The May 1979 letter of Arthur Andersen & Co. ACCOUNTING NEWS BRIEFS, Vol. 5, No. 5, p. 1, "SEC Does a Two-Step Toward More Disclosure of Internal Controls," states:

For companies that must file with the SEC, business life has become a bit more complicated. In a long-awaited move made in response to the accounting provisions of the FCPA, the SEC has proposed a two-step program in which public companies would have to tell more about their internal accounting controls.

## #19-25...SEC 2-Step Approach; Arthur Andersen Continues:

Step One applies to fiscal years ending between 12/15/79 and 12/15/80. In the annual report to shareholders and 10-K filing with the SEC, management would be required to: (1) state its opinion that the company's system of internal controls provides reasonable assurance that the objectives of internal accounting control outlines in the FCPA are being met, and (2) disclose any material weaknesses in internal controls that were uncorrected as of year-end. Weaknesses that had cropped up during the year but were settled by year-end would not have to be reported. And the company's outside auditor would function only as a backstop to report year-end material weaknesses that management did not disclose.

By comparison, Step Two requires more from both management and auditor. The second step would apply to fiscal years ending after 12/15/80. Management's opinion on the company's internal accounting controls would span the whole year, not just conditions at year-end. The auditor would be directly involved in Step Two. He would express two opinions—one on whether the representations of management about the system of internal control are consistent with the results of management's evaluation of the system, and the other on whether the representations of management are reasonable with respect to transactions and assets in amounts that would be material when measured in relation to the company's financial statements.

In proposing to require management's opinion on internal accounting control, the Commission did not set forth detailed, prescriptive rules for control procedures and techniques that will ensure compliance with the internal accounting control provisions of the FCPA. The Commission believes, however, that the control procedures and techniques that will provide for compliance with those provisions must be determined in the context of the circumstances of each company, and that it is management's responsibility to make those determinations.

In discussing the approach managements should use to evaluate their itemized systems of accounting control, the commission emphasizes the need for an evaluation of the overall control environment, a specific review of the systems and control procedures, an ongoing program to monitor compliance with these control procedures and, finally a determination of "reasonable assurance" by reference to cost-benefit relationships. "Appropriate documentation is important to each aspect of an evaluation of internal accounting control."

## #19-26...The Arthur Young & Company Response

Arthur Young & Company, in its newsletter VIEWS, Vol. III, No. 5, July 1979, declares:

As reported in the last issue of VIEWS, the SEC recently made a proposal that would require management of a publicly-held company to report on its internal controls and for the independent accountant, in turn, to examine and report on

management's report. We do not believe that the benefits of
the Commission's proposal would justify the costs of complying with it. We oppose the rule proposed because in our
opinion the proposed reports would not add information useful to investors but would instead be likely to lead to un-
warranted conclusions and would entail much greater cost--
both financial and social--than the release has recognized.
The proposed rule is particularly undesirable insofar as it
applies to immaterial matters.

However, if a rule is to issue, we believe it should be
changed to reduce its adverse consequences. Our two principal recommendations for such change are (1) Limit reporting
to controls over matters that are material in relation to a
registrant's financial statements; (2) Define and explain
the term "reasonable assurance" as an integral part of the
rule.

## #19-27...Clarification of FCPA Antibribery Section

In Vol. IV, No. 2 of Arthur Young and Company's VIEWS, April
1, 1980, pages 3-4, it is pointed out, under the heading "SEC
Seeking to Clarify 'Antibribery' Section of FCPA":
The SEC is seeking comments on the ANTIBRIBERY section
of the FCPA, in particular whether provisions in that section have presented ANY IMPEDIMENTS TO LEGITIMATE CORPORATE
ENTERPRISE. The Commission isn't about to reconsider the
underlying objective of the Act--to prohibit payments or
bribes to foreign officials in connection with obtaining or
retaining business. Rather it wants to better administer the
Act by resolving uncertainties.

In particular, the Commission's release notes that some
commentators have raised concerns about the meaning and
scope of certain of the operative provisions of the statute,
such as the requirement that payments not be made "corrupt-
ly;" the effect of the phrase "obtaining or retaining business;" the scope of the definition of "foreign officials;"
and the exclusion of "facilitating" or grease payments reflected in that definition. Comments should reach the Commission by June 30, 1980, and be as "specific as possible
and reflect actual experiences under the Act."

In another development, the Justice Dept. has announced
that companies can obtain a statement from the Department
indicating whether it would bring a civil or criminal action
with respect to a proposed foreign payment or favor. The
Department plans to respond to such requests within 30 days
and would be bound by any commitments given. Although both
the SEC and the Justice Dept. share responsibility for administering the FCPA, the SEC has previously indicated that
it will not be so bound by the Justice Dept.'s Statements.

As a result many companies are likely to be wary of a commitment from the Department when no similar assurances can be obtained from the SEC.

## #19-28...Justice Dept. Procedure:  The FCPA Review Letter

The April 1980 issue of Arthur Andersen & Co. ACCOUNTING NEWS BRIEFS, Vol. 6 No. 3, page 3, indicates:

The Justice Dept. has established a procedure under which any person subject to the antibribery provisions of the FCPA may request a statement of the Department's enforcement intent with respect to proposed business conduct. The request must be in writing and must contain a detailed description of all relevant information. The Justice Dept. may request additional information or documents as needed.

The FCPA REVIEW LETTER is binding on the Department to the extent the disclosures contained in the company's request were accurate and complete and continue to be so following the issuance of the review letter. The letter is not binding, however, on other governmental regulatory agencies. The review procedure does not apply to questions concerning compliance with the accounting provisions of the FCPA, nor does a Justice Dept. review letter change responsibilities for complying with those provisions.

## FCPA EXPERIENCE

## #19-29...FCPA Bribery Experience

In the March 1980 JOURNAL OF ACCOUNTANCY, pp. 50-63, Alan R. Sumutka, in the article "Questionable Payments & Practices: Why? Who? Detection? Prevention?", declares:

In the last year, hundreds of U.S. corporations voluntarily have disclosed their participation in such dubious activities as creating slush funds, accepting kickbacks, and making illegal payments to foreign or domestic officials. This information has been gleaned from such sources as annual reports, proxy statements and audit committee reports from 117 corporations, and the findings are discussed in this article.

The most common reason for questionable corporate payments was found in the FACILITATING or GREASE type of payment to low-level governmental employees whose duties are essentially ministerial or clerical. The second most common reason was to obtain or retain business. Next were questionable political contributions. Another reason was to obtain favorable tax treatment.

Questionable payments and practices were recorded in the accounting records and transacted through four general meth-

ods:  (1) payment of  cash;  (2) transfer of merchandise; (3)
granting a price reduction; and (4) use of a questionable or
illegal business practice.
The accounting treatment for  the  payments  is  illustrated in
Figure 19-2.
Mr. Sumutka concludes that outright detection and prevention
of these illegal activities  appears unlikely  unless  corporations comply with the  accurate recordkeeping provision  of the
FCPA.

## #19-30...U. S. Corporate Experience

In the  June 16,  1980 issue  of U.S. NEWS &  WORLD  REPORT,
pages  67-68,  entitled "Why U.S.  Business  Is Losing  Markets
Abroad," it states:
    Business leaders  charge that billions  of dollars worth
    of sales have  been forfeited to  their  competitors because
    of antitrust  and antibribe laws; taxes on Americans working
    abroad; trade restrictions to promote  human rights; prevent
    compliance  with  Arab boycotts; avoid the spread of nuclear
    explosives; slow  the  conventional arms  race; protect  the
    environment.  Critics  don't quarrel with the  goals of the
    restrictions but insist that little is  achieved by shunning
    sales that competitors will make anyway.
    Intense, cut-throat competition for global  markets is a
    fact of life,  says Senator  Lloyd Bentsen, chairman of  the
    Joint  Economic Committee.  "We still approach the challenge
    with the misty idealism, unilateral, self-imposed restraints
    and  lack of  commitment that have  gradually diminished our
    competitive position for most of the past decade."

After mentioning several of the causes of loss of business, the
article goes on to say:
    Hobbling businesses, too, is  the Foreign Corrupt  Prac-
    tices Act.  The law, passed in the wake of corporate bribery
    scandals in the mid-'70s, is designed to prevent U.S. compa-
    nies from making under-the-table  payments  to foreign offi-
    cials.
    Everyone agrees with the NOBLE INTENT of the  Act, Sena-
    tor Bentsen asserts,  but unless other countries observe the
    same standards, the law does little more than force American
    businessmen into "pre-emptive capitulation" to foreign  com-
    petitors.
    Sales have been  lost for Americans in  the Philippines,
    Indonesia and Thailand, in particular. One U.S. company with
    an office in Manila  no longer sells to the  Philippine gov-
    ernment because of the Act, he reports. Japanese come in and
    wine and dine Philippine  officials and get their  business,
    but officials of the American firm are afraid to do that.

FIGURE 19-2
REASON FOR QUESTIONABLE PAYMENT OR PRACTICE

| Account Charged | Facilitating payments | Obtain or retain business | Political contributions | Political fund-raising | Influence governmental decisions or payment for price increase | Obtain favorable tax treatment or settle tax disputes | Import unauthorized goods or obtain reduction in duty | Secure confidential competitor or customer information | Meet competition |
|---|---|---|---|---|---|---|---|---|---|
| Advertising exp. | | X | | | | | | | |
| Bonuses | | | | | | | | | |
| Business exp. | X | | X | | X | | | X | |
| Consulting fees | | X | | | | X | | | |
| Cost of sales | | X | | | | | | | |
| Donations of gifts | X | X | X | | | | | | |
| Freight | X | | | | | | | | |
| General expense | | | | | | X | | X | |
| Government promotional exp. | | X | X | | | | | | |
| Gratuities | X | | | | | | | | |
| Legal & administrative exp. | X | X | X | X | | | | | |
| Miscellaneous Expense | | X | X | | | | | | |
| Political contr. | | | X | | | | | | |
| Professional services | | X | | | X | | | | |
| Research & Devel | X | | | | | | | | |
| Salary exp. | | | X | | | | | | |
| Sales or export commissions, commission exp | X | X | | | | X | X | X | X |
| Sales discounts or allownc, or other contra-revenue acct | | X | | | | | | | |
| Sales promotion | | X | | | | | | | |
| Selling expense | X | X | | | | | | | X |
| Suspense | | X | | | | | | | |
| Tax expense | | | X | | | X | | | |
| Travel or trav. & entertain. | X | X | X | | | | | | |
| Technical service costs | | X | | | | | | | |
| Unsupported payments | | | | | | X | | X | |

What concerns many who have studied the law is that its
ambiguities are having a chilling effect on legitimate ventures. "It leads us to have to take incredible precautions,"
said Ford Motor Co.'s President Donald E. Peterson, who,
before his recent promotion, ran Ford's international operations. "We couldn't even hand our annual report to one official for fear it might be misunderstood."

## #19-31...Bribery Equalization Effort

In the June 1980 issue of the CHICAGO TRIBUNE, reporter Bill
Neikirk points out that:
Pres. Carter is expected to urge the leaders of 6 industrial nations to support an international agreement on corporate bribery when he attends the economic summit in Venice
June 22-23. American efforts to seek such an agreement in
the U.N. have run into solid opposition, officials said, so
Carter is being urged to attempt a political push at the
summit. One official said that we have been unsuccessful
because a lot of developed countries don't want it since
they accept payments as a business practice, and because the
developing countries want to link any agreement with a treaty on multinational corporations. The proposed treaty would
impose unacceptable limits on multinational corporations.
Carter is being urged to press for the agreement on
grounds that American companies, because of the FCPA, think
they are at a disadvantage in foreign markets, since the
illicit payments are widely used by companies in other countries as a way of obtaining business. U.S. companies must
follow a law that prohibits such payments, although the law
is vague. In fact in response to the uncertainty, the Justice Dept. has adopted a procedure enabling companies to
find out in advance whether payments would violate the law.
American companies were found to be making payments in the
Middle East, Japan, Europe, and Africa in an effort to obtain international contracts. Generally, officials said most
other countries condone the practice making it much more
difficult for Carter to achieve success with his proposal.
There can be no doubt that the FCPA has lost billions of dollars of business for U.S. MNCs. It will continue to do so,
unless other countries enact a similar law. However, they are
not disposed to do this since it has been customary procedure
in the Middle East, Africa, and the Orient to operate on the
basis of accepting bribes.

## #19-32...Bribery Practices Outside the U. S.

The big problem with the FCPA is that bribery has been a way
of life in almost all parts of the world, including the U.S.,

for many years.  How do countries other than the U.S. look upon bribery?

If all other countries  resort to it, the U.S.  MNCs will be at a decided disadvantage in getting foreign orders. Alice Siegert, West German correspondent for the CHICAGO TRIBUNE, in the column "International Bribery A  Corporate Necessity?" (Aug. 6, 1979), points out:

A German manufacturer who  sold  10,000 railroad ties to the government of Gabon paid $55,000 in cash to three visiting officials from Libreville.  Customs officials in Indonesia have devised  a special  procedure for  receiving  kickbacks.  They  open their  desk drawers and when a sufficient amount of cash is  deposited, the drawer is  closed and  the request is granted.  In Saudi Arabia a  sealed envelope containing  money or a check and discreetly placed on  an official's  desk is  an essential condition  for doing business. These examples of  bribery were disclosed recently in  a report by STERN magazine published in Germany.

A substantial number of German firms have been  involved in such  questionable payments, which are  not prohibited by law and  furthermore can  be  deducted from  the company tax bill.  According to conservative estimates, German companies last  year paid more than  $250 million in bribes  and kickbacks.  If the  figure is roughly accurate, this would be a fraction of 1% of the total export volume of $158 billion.

The usual argument businessmen use is that paying bribes is a routine method in many countries and unless German companies do it they will lose contracts abroad.  The magazine noted that several years ago a German corporation had to pay a $10  million  commission to Imelda Marcos, wife of Philippine President  Ferdinand Marcos, for the sale  of  a  plant making prefabs.

Payoffs  are particularly  popular  in  Eastern  Europe, where the granting of "baksheesh"  is  a  time-honored tradition.  However, businessmen report that trade officials there frequently  are  content with such  gifts as a fur  coat,  a Swiss watch or a sophisticated pocket calculator.

The Bonn government wants to control bribery in cooperation with other major trading  nations, but it does not want to act unilaterally and hurt export business and jobs.

## #19-33...The Chafee Bill

The  dilemma has received the attention of Sen. John H. Chafee who has proposed a  bill (S-708) intended to remedy the unfair advantage that FCPA presents to foreign MNCs. The case for American business is  well presented by Marvin Stone, editor of U.S. NEWS & WORLD REPORT, who on June  22, 1981, declares in an editorial ("Doing Business Abroad"):

Here's a thorny question: In the interest of selling
more goods overseas, is the U.S. going to have to relax its
law that forbids American companies to pay off foreign officials and influence peddlers? Three and a half years ago the
FCPA passed through Congress without a dissenting vote. That
law, strictly barring bribery, accurately expressed the
American consensus at that time--and it still does. Of
course, we still oppose bribery.

But now, after watching the effects of that 1977 law,
many Americans are having second thoughts about the way it
was written and the ways it is being applied. They see U.S.
firms losing billions of dollars worth of sales abroad because they can't make payments that foreigners demand. The
business they lose is going to foreign firms that are will-
ing--and able--to make such payments. The American share of
world markets is decreasing, and the U.S. trade balance is
suffering as a result. So it is not surprising that moves
are afoot in Congress to modify the 1977 law.

Such changes are proposed in S-708, a bill sponsored by
Sen. John Chafee and 13 other members of the Senate. At the
outset of any discussion of this bill, it should be made
clear that it would not legalize bribery or other corrupt
activities. What the bill will do is clarify the 1977 law
and make it easier for businessmen to know what they may or
may not do in making sales abroad. It would also reduce the
complexity and cost of the bookkeeping a company must do to
prove it is obeying the law. To reduce this confusion, the
bill adopts what seems to be a reasonable test: A payment is
a bribe only if it is intended to induce a person to do
something that violates the law or his legal responsibility.
One such change is this: It would not forbid Americans to
make payments that are considered legal in the country where
they are made, even though they might be illegal in the U.S.

Sponsors of the measure point out that many countries,
especially in the so-called Third World, do not have the
same code of business ethics as the U.S., and payments called criminal here are accepted in those countries as normal
business expenses. American firms, barred from making such
payments, are at a disadvantage because their foreign competitors are under no such restrictions. Several businessmen
told the subcommittee that they lost rich sales abroad because they could not match payments that foreign bidders
make as standard practice. Further, foreigners tend to resent this country's attempt to impose its own code of conduct on their traditional ways of doing business, and often
are reluctant to deal with American firms. When the FCPA was
passed, it was hoped that other countries would follow suit
in regulating business. But that hasn't happened, and until
it does, officials say, foreign companies will continue to

profit at American expense under the present law. The Chafee Bill seems a reasonable attempt to give U.S. businessmen a better chance--without giving them a license to bribe.

## #19-34...Chafee Bill Relation to Internal Control Requirements

It was pointed out that the Chafee Bill "would also reduce the complexity and cost of the bookkeeping a company must do to prove it is obeying the law." The alarm this has caused amongst businessmen in every segment of the business world is summed up by SEC Chairman Harold M. Williams in the Jan. 26, 1981 issue of THE CPA LETTER, Vol. 61, No. 2, as follows:
Speaking before some 500 attendees at the AICPA 8th national conference on current SEC developments held earlier this month, Williams noted that the concerns created by the FCPA, as expressed by lawyers, accountants and corporate executives, have been "without equal." For the most part, he added, this anxiety can be attributed to the spectre raised by some "of exposure to commission enforcement action, and perhaps criminal liability, as a result of technical and insignificant errors in corporate records or weaknesses in corporate internal controls." Such uncertainty can have a "debilitating effect" on companies trying to comply with the law.

Elaborating further on Mr. Williams' comments, Vol. VII, No. 1 of the Peat, Marwick, Mitchell & Co. EXECUTIVE NEWSLETTER, page 1, adds:
Anxieties created among businessmen by the FCPA may have led to a diverting of business resources "from more productive uses to overly-burdensome compliance systems which extend beyond the requirements of sound management or the policies embodied in the Act." Some of the commentators "claim that because of the broad strokes with which the accounting provisions are fashioned, no corporate executive can ever feel fully confident that his corporation is in compliance with the law."

## #19-35...Proposals Under the Chafee Bill

In the PMM & Co. EXECUTIVE NEWSLETTER, Vol. VII, No. 4, June 3, 1981, page 1, it is pointed out that according to U.S. Trade Representative William Brock:
"The current generally, overly-broad recordkeeping standards in the FCPA are unnecessary and executive." He further argued that the FCPA recordkeeping provisions "represented a significant extension of the jurisdiction of the SEC over business practices unrelated to the protection of investors and unnecessary for the effective operation of the prohibitions against illicit payments overseas."

Sen. Chafee's Bill (S-708) would redesignate the FCPA as
the BUSINESS PRACTICES AND RECORDS ACT, and would introduce
a standards of MATERIALITY in these provisions. The term
MATERIAL would be used in the same sense as in GAAP when
those principles are applied to the preparation and presentation of financial statements of the issuer. The meaning of
the term "reasonable" in the FCPA, as applied to records and
internal accounting controls, has been a main source of confusion, and Sen. Chafee's Bill would define "reasonable detail" and "reasonable assurances" as meaning "such level of
detail and degree of assurance as would satisfy prudent individuals in the conduct of their own affairs, having in
mind a comparison between benefits to be obtained and costs
to be incurred in obtaining such benefits." The Chafee Bill
would also pinpoint certain conduct as being outside the Act
and would permit giving "an item of value that constitutes,
or is intended as no more than, an item given as a courtesy,
a token of regard and esteem, or in return for hospitality."

## #19-36...FCPA Internal Audit Experience

In the Aug. 25, 1980 issue of THE WALL STREET JOURNAL, Professors Michael Maher and Bernard White, who were part of a
Univ. of Michigan research team that interviewed some 350 executives of 50 companies, and received questionnaire information
from executives in 673 companies, found that in 21 of the 50
companies, "a major reorganization" of the internal audit function had taken place recently. The report states that:

While the antibribery provisions of the FCPA may have received more publicity, it was the internal control requirements of the FCPA which spurred corporate officers and directors to action and resulted in changed company control
policies. In all cases, internal audit emerged as a more
powerful and influential force within the company, even
though only 10% of the companies studied had added any significant new control procedures as a result of FCPA. Of
course, not all of these changes can be attributed directly
to the FCPA, but it does seem to have played an important
part in stimulating a general trend toward greater internal
accountability and control by senior management and the
board of directors. Many financial and accounting executives
are pleased that the Act gives them the club to make operating management more responsible for internal control. However, many executives expressed concern that in the long run
the Act may spur centralization of authority and control at
senior management levels.

Commenting on the implications of the Maher and White study,
the JOURNAL OF ACCOUNTANCY, Jan. 1981, declares:

The authors note that in 80% of the companies the primary response to the FCPA has been to establish documentation which can be used if their systems and environment of internal control are ever challenged in court. A majority of the companies have also recently implemented employee codes of conduct, including conflict-of-interest statements; statements of intent to comply with laws and regulations; and bans on accepting gifts, using insider information, and misusing corporate assets.

## #19-37...Future Action on Extortion and Bribery

The foregoing discussion points to the fact that international debate has focused on extortion and bribery in international business transactions. The result of such debate has been to spur many governments, as well as the U.N., to consider ways and means of combating such practices in a more vigorous fashion than has actually taken place both nationally and internationally. Contemporaneously, the international business community has given high priority to the consideration of the issues involved as well as to the action required to solve them. The International Chamber of Commerce (ICC) has set up an ad hoc commission composed of representatives from both developed and developing countries under the chairmanship of Lord Shawcross of Great Britain. This Commission has investigated the extent to which individual countries have enacted legislation to prohibit extortion and bribery. The results of the survey have clearly shown that while such laws exist in most countries, the effectiveness of their enforcement varies considerably. The publication contains (1) a set of recommendations drawn up by the ICC on measures to be taken by governments, nationally and internationally, to foster the elimination of bribery and extortion in business transactions; and (2) rules of conduct for voluntary application by enterprises.

The activity of the ICC has resulted in the development of a Code of Conduct to combat extortion and bribery. As indicated in "Combating Extortion and Bribery in Business Transactions," in the PRICE WATERHOUSE REVIEW, Vol. 23, No. 4, 1978, pp. 40-45, Richard D. Fitzgerald, who was quite involved with the drafting of the Code, states that:

the world business community, through the ICC, has come up with a Code of Ethics that lays down specific codes of conduct for business enterprises and establishes a review panel to oversee the application of the code.

The ICC report includes both rules of conduct for business and equally important recommendations to governments, and points out that there can be no "bribe" without a "bribee" and that much bribery is in fact a response to extortion. A coordinated and mutual reinforcing program by both government and business is needed to deal effectively with the problem of corruption.

The rules of conduct are voluntary and provide for self-regulation. The ICC recognizes that the Code will not stamp out bribery and extortion throughout the world but it should offer a beginning as well as provide common standards for business to apply.

The BASIC PRINCIPLE OF THE CODE reads as follows: "All enterprises should conform to the relevant laws and regulations of the countries in which they are established and in which they operate, and should observe both the letter and spirit of these rules of conduct."

Recommendations to governments in the ICC report are (1) Affirmation by governments of their commitment against extortion and bribery; (2) National measures to be taken by governments; (3) International cooperation and judicial assistance in instances of extortion and bribery.

The BASIC RULES of the ICC'S code consist of five Articles:

**ARTICLE 1 - EXTORTION.** No one may demand or accept a bribe.

**ARTICLE 2 - BRIBERY.** No enterprise may, directly or indirectly, offer or give a bribe in order to obtain or retain business, and any demand for such a bribe must be rejected.

**ARTICLE 3 - KICKBACKS.** Enterprises should take measures reasonably within their power to ensure that no part of any payment made by them in connection with any commercial transaction is paid back to their employees or to any other person not legally entitled to the same.

**ARTICLE 4 - AGENTS.** Enterprises should take measures reasonably within their power to ensure: (a) that any payment made to any agent represents no more than an appropriate remuneration for the services rendered by him; and (b) that no part of any such payment is passed on by the agent as a bribe or otherwise in contravention of these RULES OF CONDUCT.

**ARTICLE 5 - FINANCIAL RECORDING.** (a) All financial transactions must be properly and fairly recorded in appropriate books of account available for inspection by boards and auditors; (b) there must be no "off the books" or secret accounts, nor may any documents be issued which do not properly & fairly record the transactions to which they relate.

As of 1982, Congressional efforts to amend the FCPA, although approved by S-708 in the Senate, were stalled in the House. A House bill sponsored by Representative Matthew Rinaldo similar to the Chafee Bill was effectively tabled during the 1982 ses-

sion,   thereby stalling the desired correction   proposed by the
Chafee Bill.

### #19-38...Heinz Bill No. S-414

Since   the Chafee Bill did not appear to make much progress,
Sen. John Heinz introduced a   bill   entitled THE   BUSINESS   AC-
COUNTING AND FOREIGN TRADE SIMPLIFICATION ACT, written to amend
and clarify certain sections of the FCPA.   On May 24, 1983, the
Senate Banking Committee   reported out Senate   Bill S-414.   SEC
Chairman   John Shad expressed the support by SEC of the bill in
testimony before a Senate subcommittee as follows:
> Most of the concerns   expressed   to   the SEC have arisen
> from difficulty   in interpreting the reach of the accounting
> provisions   of   the   FCPA.   Amendments to   these provisions
> should   accomplish two   goals in addition to   ensuring   that
> the   statutory objectives   of the FCPA are met.   They should
> provide greater certainty in order   that   persons subject to
> the Act know   what it permits and what it   prohibits.   And,
> amendments should reduce compliance   requirements   that   are
> not necessary to the accomplishment of its objectives.
The key features of S-414 would cure   the ostensible objections as follows:

(1) Revise   the FCPA accounting   provisions   by   merging the
    recordkeeping and internal   accounting controls require-
    ments, and   permitting a Cost-Benefit test   to apply   in
    order to attain the objectives of the FCPA.
(2) Replace the REASON TO KNOW standard in the FCPA by hold-
    ing a U.S. company liable when it DIRECTS OR AUTHORIZES,
    EXPRESSLY OR BY A COURSE   OF CONDUCT,   that   an   illegal
    payment be made.
(3) Exempt   payments to foreign officials in certain circum-
    stances that   are specified,   such as the   expediting of
    the performance of a routine governmental action.
(4) Divide the responsibility for implementation of the FCPA
    into   two areas--enforcement of   antibribery provisions,
    and accounting   compliance provisions, with jurisdiction
    over the former lodged in the Department of Justice   and
    over the latter in the SEC.

Such is the status of the FCPA as of the middle of 1984.   It is
devoutly to be hoped that Congress will follow through on S-414
in   1984 to help reduce trade deficits and promote   business of
U.S. MNCs. In the BAYLOR BUSINESS STUDIES, 134, Vol. 13, No. 4,
pp.   7-19, is a summary   entitled "What   American Business Managers Should Know and Do About International Bribery," by Hsin-
Min Tong and Priscilla Welling.

## SUMMARY OF FOOTNOTE REFERENCES
(References are to Paragraph #'s)

#19-1   David Solomons, "The Politicization of Accounting," JOURNAL
        OF ACCOUNTANCY (November 1978): 65-72. Reprinted with per-
        mission. Copyright © 1978 by the American Institute of Cer-
        tified Public Accountants, Inc. Opinions expressed in the
        JOURNAL OF ACCOUNTANCY are those of editors and contribu-
        tors. Publication in the JOURNAL OF ACCOUNTANCY does not
        constitute endorsement by the AICPA or its committees.
#19-1   Structure Committee of the Financial Accounting Foundation,
        "The Structure of Establishing Financial Accounting Stand-
        ards," April 1977, p. 19
#19-1   Robert May and Gary Sundem, "Research For Accounting Policy:
        An Overview," ACCOUNTING REVIEW (Oct. 1976): 750
#19-2   Dale Gerboth, "Research, Intuition and Politics in Account-
        ing Inquiry," ACCOUNTING REVIEW (July 1973)
#19-4   David Hawkins, "Financial Accounting, The Standards Board
        and Economic Development," Baruch College of the City Uni-
        versity of New York, April 1975, pp. 7-8
#19-4   Solomons, op. cit., by permission.
#19-8   AICPA, "Audits of Personal Financial Statements,"1968,pp.2-3
#19-13  Ernst & Ernst, "Foreign Corrupt Practices Act of 1977," pre-
        sentation at Roosevelt Univ. by Robert G. Streit, Feb. 1978
#19-14  Ernst & Ernst, "Guide for Management and Directors to Evalu-
        ate Internal Control Under FCPA"
#19-15  Ibid., p. 62
#19-16  Price Waterhouse & Co., ACCOUNTING EVENTS AND TRENDS, Vol.
        5, No. 8 (Dec. 1978): 2. Reprinted with permission.
#19-17  Arthur Andersen & Co., ACCOUNTING NEWS BRIEFS (May 1979).
        Reprinted with permission.
#19-18  Harvey Kapnick, "Improving Corporate Responsibility Through
        Stronger Internal Auditing," Arthur Andersen & Co., EXECU-
        TIVE NEWS BRIEFS, Vol. 7, No. 2 (Feb. 14, 1979). Reprinted
        with permission.
#19-18  Peat, Marwick, Mitchell & Co., EXECUTIVE NEWSLETTER, Vol. V,
        No. 6 (August 7, 1979)
#19-19  Arthur Young & Company, VIEWS, Vol. III, No. 1 (Feb. 1979).
        Reprinted with permission.
#19-19  Alan B. Levenson, "Accounting and Legal Implications of the
        FCPA," JOURNAL OF ACCOUNTANCY (Feb. 1979): 28
#19-20  "Holcar Oil Corporation Case," JOURNAL OF ACCOUNTANCY (June
        1979): 22
#19-21  "The Kenny Case," CHICAGO TRIBUNE, editorial (Aug. 9, 1979)
#19-22  Arthur Andersen & Co., ACCOUNTING NEWS BRIEFS (Jan 1979): 2.
        Reprinted with permission.
#19-23  AICPA, THE CPA LETTER, Vol. 59, No. 9 (May 14, 1979)
#19-24  Arthur Andersen & Co., "SEC Does a Two-Step Toward More Dis-
        closure of Internal Controls," ACCOUNTING NEWS BRIEFS, Vol.
        5, No. 5 (May 1979): 1. Reprinted with permission.
#19-25  Ibid., by permission.

#19-26 Arthur Young & Company, VIEWS, Vol. III, No. 5 (July 1979). Reprinted with permission.

#19-27 Arthur Young & Company, "SEC Seeking to Clarify 'Antibribery' Section of FCPA," VIEWS, Vol. IV, No. 2 (April 1, 1980): 3-4. Reprinted with permission.

#19-28 Arthur Andersen & Co., ACCOUNTING NEWS BRIEFS, Vol. 6, No. 3 (April 1980): 3. Reprinted with permission.

#19-29 Alan R. Sumutka, "Questionable Payments and Practices: Why? Who? Detection? Prevention?", JOURNAL OF ACCOUNTANCY (March 1980): 50-63. Reprinted with permission. Copyright © 1980 by the American Institute of Certified Public Accountants, Inc. Opinions expressed in the JOURNAL OF ACCOUNTANCY are those of editors and contributors. Publication in the JOURNAL OF ACCOUNTANCY does not constitute endorsement by the AICPA or its committees.

#19-30 "Why U.S. Business Is Losing Markets Abroad," U.S. NEWS & WORLD REPORT (June 16, 1980): 67-68

#19-31 Bill Neikirk, CHICAGO TRIBUNE (June 1980)

#19-32 Alice Siegert, "International Bribery A Corporate Necessity?", CHICAGO TRIBUNE (Aug. 6, 1979)

#19-33 Marvin Stone, "Doing Business Abroad." Reprinted with permission from U.S. NEWS & WORLD REPORT (June 22, 1981). Copyright 1981, U.S. News & World Report, Inc.

#19-34 Harold M. Williams, THE CPA LETTER, Vol. 61, No. 2 (Jan. 26, 1981)

#19-34 Peat, Marwick, Mitchell & Co., EXECUTIVE NEWSLETTER, Vol. VII, No. 1, p. 1

#19-35 Peat, Marwick, Mitchell & Co., EXECUTIVE NEWSLETTER, Vol. VII, No. 4 (June 3, 1981): 1

#19-36 Michael Maher and Bernard White, THE WALL STREET JOURNAL (Aug. 25, 1980); JOURNAL OF ACCOUNTANCY (Jan. 1981)

#19-37 Richard D. Fitzgerald, "Combating Extortion and Bribery in Business Transactions," PRICE WATERHOUSE REVIEW, Vol. 23, No. 4 (1978): 40-45. Reprinted with permission.

#19-38 SEC Chairman John Shad, testimony before Senate subcommittee, 1983

## BIBLIOGRAPHY

Abdel-Khalik, A. INTERNAL CONTROL AND THE IMPACT OF THE FOREIGN CORRUPT PRACTICES ACT. Gainesville: Univ. Press of Florida, 1982

Aggarwal, R. and Kim, S.H. "Should the FCPA Be Abolished?", INTERNAL AUDITOR (April 1982): 20-23

Bagby, J.W. "Enforcement of Accounting Standards in the Foreign Corrupt Practices Act," AMERICAN BUSINESS LAW JOURNAL (Summer 1983): 213

Baird, Byron N. and Michenzi, A.R. "Impact of the Foreign Corrupt Practices Act," INTERNAL AUDITOR (June 1983): 20-22

Baruch, Hurd. "The Foreign Corrupt Practices Act," HARVARD BUSINESS REVIEW, 57 (January-February 1979): 32-51

Bradt, John D. "The Foreign Corrupt Practices Act and the Internal

Auditor," INTERNAL AUDITOR, 36 (August 1979): 15-20

Carmichael, D.R. "Internal Accounting Control--It's the Law," JOUR-
     NAL OF ACCOUNTANCY, 149 (May 1980): 70-76

Chazen, Charles.    "An Accountant Looks at the FCPA," THE CPA JOUR-
     NAL, 50 (May 1980): 38-45

Ernst & Ernst. THE FOREIGN CORRUPT PRACTICES ACT: FOCUS ON INTERNAL
     CONTROL   (September 1978)

Greanias,  George C. and Windsor, Duane.   THE FOREIGN CORRUPT PRAC-
     TICES ACT.  Lexington, Mass: Lexington Books, 1982

Kim, Suk.  "On Repealing  the Foreign Corrupt Practices Act: Survey
     and  Assessment," COLUMBIA JOURNAL  OF  WORLD BUSINESS,  16
     (Fall 1981): 16-21

Marsh, Hugh L. "The Foreign Corrupt Practices Act: A Corporate Plan
     for Compliance," INTERNAL AUDITOR, 36 (April 1979): 72-76

McKee, Thomas.  "Auditing Under the Foreign Corrupt Practices Act,"
     THE CPA JOURNAL (August 1979): 31-35

Neumann, Frederick L.  "Corporate Audit Committees and the  Foreign
     Corrupt  Practices  Act," JOURNAL OF ACCOUNTANCY, 151 (March
     1981): 78-80

Reavell, Fraser M. "The U.S. Foreign Bribery Act Gives Headaches to
     Accountants," ACCOUNTANCY, 91 (Sept. 1980): 58-60

Ricchiute, David.  "Foreign Corrupt Practices: A New Responsibility
     for Internal Auditors," INTERNAL AUDITOR, 35(Dec.1978):58-64

Root,  Steven J.  "Foreign Corrupt Practices Act," INTERNAL AUDITOR
     (April 1983): 28-30

Sanderson,  Glen  and Varner, Iris.  "What's Wrong  With  Corporate
     Codes of Conduct," MANAGEMENT ACCOUNTING (July 1984): 28-35

Solomon,  Kenneth.   "Illegal Payments: Where  the Auditor Stands,"
     JOURNAL OF ACCOUNTANCY (January 1977)

Tong, Hsin-Min and Welling, Priscilla. "What American Business Man-
     agers Should Know and Do About International  Bribery," BAY-
     LOR BUSINESS STUDIES, 134, Vol. 13, No. 4, pp. 7-19


## THEORY QUESTIONS

(Question Numbers are Keyed to Text Paragraph #'s)


#19-2-5.  Explain the  nature of  Political Accounting. Compare
     Political with Social and Macro Accounting.

#19-10 Discuss the causes and reasons for enactment of the For-
     eign Corrupt Practices Act.

#19-11 What ramification  of the  FCPA was the cause  of uproar
     amongst accountants?  Explain.

#19-13 How does the FCPA define foreign bribery?  Corrupt Prac-
     tices?  Facilitating Payments?

#19-15 What are the FCPA recordkeeping standards? Internal Con-
     trol standards?

#19-16 Discuss the nature, implications and effect of the Mina-
     han Report on the FCPA.

#19-17 What has been the reaction of the accounting practition-
     ers to the Minahan Report?

#19-18 What is the relationship of the FCPA to corporate re-
        sponsibility?
#19-20 Discuss the first civil case under FCPA (Holcar Oil Cor-
        poration).
#19-21 Discuss the first criminal case under the FCPA (The Ken-
        ny Case).
#19-23 What proposals on internal control reporting have been
        made by the SEC? What responses have been offered by
        Arthur Andersen and Arthur Young?
#19-28 Discuss the nature of the FCPA Review Letter under the
        Justice Department procedure.
#19-29 What has been the experience with bribery under the
        FCPA?
#19-30 What has been the corporate experience with respect to
        business dealings under the FCPA?
#19-31 What effort has been made toward bribery equalization
        between countries?
#19-32 What have been the bribery practices outside the U.S.
        and their effect on U.S. business?
#19-37 What proposals have been made by the International Cham-
        ber of Commerce for future action on extortion and brib-
        ery? What three recommendations to governments are made
        in the ICC Code of Conduct? What five basic rules of
        conduct are proposed under the ICC Code?

## PROBLEMS

### P-19-1   (CPA EXAM, 11/80, LAW, #44)

The Foreign Corrupt Practices Act of 1977 prohibits bribery of
foreign officials. Which of the following statements correctly
describes the Act's application to corporations engaging in
such practices?
   a. It only applies to multinational corporations.
   b. It applies to all domestic corporations engaged in inter-
      state commerce.
   c. It only applies to corporations whose securities are reg-
      istered under the Securities Exchange Act of 1934.
   d. It applies only to corporations engaged in foreign com-
      merce.

### P-19-2   (CPA EXAM, 5/82, AUDITING, #11)

The Foreign Corrupt Practices Act requires that
   a. Auditors engaged to examine the financial statements of
      publicly-held companies report all illegal payments to
      the SEC.
   b. Publicly-held companies establish independent audit com-
      mittees to monitor the effectiveness of their system of
      internal control.
   c. U.S. firms doing business abroad report sizable payments

to non-U.S. citizens to the Justice Dept.
    d. Publicly-held companies devise and maintain an adequate system of internal accounting control.

## P-19-3  (CPA EXAM, 5/82, AUDITING, #3)

Jones, CPA, who has been engaged to examine the financial statements of Ajax Inc., is about to commence a study and evaluation of Ajax's system of internal control and is aware of the inherent limitations that should be considered.
**Required:**
    a. What are the objectives of a system of internal control?
    b. What are the reasonable assurances that are intended to be provided by the system of internal accounting control?
    c. When considering the potential effectiveness of any system of internal accounting control, what are the inherent limitations that should be recognized?

## P-19-4  (CPA EXAM, 11/82, AUDITING, #59)

When an auditor issues an unqualified opinion on an entity's system of internal accounting control, it is implied that the
    a. Entity has not violated provisions of the FCPA.
    b. Likelihood of management fraud is minimal.
    c. Financial records are sufficiently reliable to permit the preparation of financial statements.
    d. Entity's system of internal accounting control is in conformity with criteria established by its audit committee.

## P-19-5  (CPA EXAM, 11/82, LAW, #30)

Under the FCPA, an action may be brought which seeks
    a. Treble damages by a private party.
    b. Injunctive relief by a private party.
    c. Criminal sanctions against both a corporation and its officers by the Department of Justice.
    d. Damages and injunctive relief by the Securities and Exchange Commission.

## P-19-6  (CPA EXAM, 11/83, LAW, #45)

Which of the following corporations are subject to the accounting requirements of the FCPA?
    a. All corporations engaged in interstate commerce.
    b. All domestic corporations engaged in international trade.
    c. All corporations which have made a public offering under the Securities Act of 1933.
    d. All corporations whose securities are registered pursuant to the Securities Exchange Act of 1934.

## P-19-7  (CPA EXAM, 5/84, LAW, #32)

The FCPA provisions relating to the maintaining of a system of internal accounting controls apply to

a. All domestic corporations that do  an annual foreign trade business in excess of $1 million.
b. All corporations that are registered or reporting corporations under the Securities Exchange Act of 1934.
c. Only those corporations engaged in foreign commerce.
d. All corporations engaged in interstate or foreign commerce.

## CASES

### CASE-19-1  (CPA EXAM, 5/81, LAW, #4A)

Delwood is the Central American representative of Massive Mfg., Inc., a large diversified conglomerate listed on the New York Stock Exchange. Certain key foreign government and large foreign manufacturing company contracts were in the crucial stages of bidding and negotiation. During this crucial time, Feldspar, the CEO of Massive, summoned  Delwood to the company's home office for an urgent consultation. At the meeting, Feldspar told Delwood that corporate sales and profits were lagging and something definitely had to be done. He  told Delwood that his job was on the  line and that unless major contracts were obtained, he would have  to reluctantly accept his resignation. Feldspar indicated  he was aware of both  the competition and  the legal problems that were involved. Nevertheless, he told Delwood "to do what is necessary in order to obtain the business." Delwood flew back to Central America the  next day and began to  implement  what  he believed  to be the instructions he had received from Feldspar.  He first contacted influential  members  of the ruling parties  of the  various  countries  and  indicated  that large discretionary contributions to their re-election campaign funds  would be forthcoming  if Massive's bids for foreign government contracts  were approved. Next, he contacted the large foreign manufacturers and  indicated  that loans were available to them on  a non-repayment basis if they placed their business with Massive. These payments were to be accounted for by charging  certain  nebulous accounts  or by listing the payments  as legitimate loans to purchasers. In any event the true nature of the expenditures was not to be shown on the books. All this was accomplished, and Massive's  sales improved markedly in Central America.

Two years later the  Securities and Exchange Commission discovered the facts described above.

**Required**:

Answer the following, setting forth reasons for any conclusions stated:

What  are the legal  implications of  the  above to Delwood, Feldspar, and Massive Manufacturing?

# International Political Risk Accounting

## NATURE AND CAUSES OF POLITICAL RISK

### #20-1....Inherent Nature of International Operations

In the early years of establishing foreign operations by an MNC, foreign countries were quite receptive to them. Such countries appeared to be content with the many advantages flowing to them from the creating of products not locally developed, financial and economic flows, and social advancements. As a result the political risk involving the investment was more or less negligible.

However, with the passing of time, various agitation cropped up in the form of declarations that the developers were imperialists, colonialists, and exploiters. Aided and abetted by dictatorial military and/or communist regimes, there sprung up a rash of invasions by the local authorities into the ownership of the properties developed by the foreign companies. This was accentuated in the developing countries which did not have the technology and/or capital to exploit the products indigenous to the country where discovered--principally oil. A considerable number of countries have been involved, and in many other countries all business operations were nationalized, a euphemism for plain takeover of private business by the government.

### #20-2....Extent of Foreign Operations Takeovers

According to Jay Shapiro, managing director of the JLS Group, a New York-based insurance risk management company, contracts have been expropriated or frustrated in some way over the last 15 years in more than 20 countries. The list includes: Algeria, Angola, Argentina, Bolivia, Brazil, Chile, Colombia, Cuba, El Salvador, Egypt, India, Iran, Iraq, Libya, Maldive Islands, Mozambique, Nigeria, Pakistan, Portugal, Sri Lanka, Syria, Tanzania, Venezuela, and Zaire.

In the June 1981 NEWSLETTER  of the American  Society of International Executives, page 2, it is indicated that:
  Singapore, Japan, Netherlands, and the U.S.  are  the SAFEST
  countries for investment, says Business International Corp.,
  a consulting concern that assesses such risks annually.  The
  riskiest countries  are Iran,  Zaire, Ghana, and  Angola, it
  asserts. Risks include political instability, currency weakness,  restrictions  on repatriation  of  profits, and other
  factors.

## #20-3....Political Aspects of Economic Relationship

It has now become  common knowledge that the previous econo-
mic-climate-of-a-country factor has turned political in nature,
and  under  the rules of political  expediency,  countries  have
arbitrarily seized business operations  without  any  equitable
justification for so doing.  The takeover  complex has extended
to every continent.  Thus the political aspects  have  become a
part of the economic just  as the social aspects have been seen
to be inextricably interwoven with the political. This makes it
difficult to determine precisely where one begins and the other
ends.  For example in  Aug. 1979, Nigeria  nationalized British
Petroleum on the ground  that England was sympathetic to  South
Africa.  A London Reuters Agency Despatch  dated  Aug. 13, 1979
furnishes another example:
  Persian Gulf Arab  oil  producers are  prepared  to  discuss
  long-term  oil supplies for the  European Economic Community
  only if the EEC  nations  are willing to discuss  the Middle
  East conflict, involving possible  discussion of recognition
  of the PLO.  The Arab refusal to SEPARATE ECONOMIC AND POLI-
  TICAL issues was confirmed  by United Arab Emirates oil minister Mana  Al-Oteiba, who said there  were  no plans for an
  EEC-Arab meeting specifically to discuss oil prices and production.  The official  said "You cannot discuss oil without
  dealing with Political and Economic  Officials, even if such
  a meeting was to be held."
All  of  these seizures  that have taken place  fall under  the
heading of POLITICAL RISK, which becomes an extremely important
factor in the determination as  to  whether or not a MNC should
set up an operation in a particular foreign country.

## #20-4....Nature of Political Risk

Experience has now shown that  when a MNC foreign  operation
is created, it automatically  becomes exposed to a multiplicity
of political risks.  Unfortunately  the MNC need do nothing and
yet be subjected to the risks.  Its mere creation or existence

causes it to become a target for foreign forces—governmental, economic and/or social. In some cases there may be some justification for complaints, but they become invalid and untenable after corrective action is taken pursuant to the advice, requests or instructions of the foreign government sources.

However, based on the theory of political sovereignty, the MNC has no recourse against the takeover perpetrator, even if the justification has no validity. In effect this theory says: "If you want to operate in our country, you will have to take and like anything we dish out to you, regardless of what kind of argument we make or of its validity. The mere fact of sovereignty over the territories over which we exercise control is sufficient rationalization for us to impose any possible action, no matter how adverse, that we may take."

While there may be some cases in which takeovers are justified, they are far outweighed by the number that are not, and in most cases the bases or reasons are specious and spurious. Nevertheless they are seriously proposed as justifications, which merely enhances their untenability. Regardless of their justification, the matter of sovereignty over the land takes first priority so that once the MNC commences operations, it becomes irrevocably subordinated to the will of the government in whose territory it operates.

## #20-5....Causes of Political Risk

Ostensibly the fundamental overall cause of political risk is a conflict between the national interests of the foreign government and the corporate objectives of the MNC. In effect the foreign government says to the MNC operator: "Your modus operandi and/or your purposes or objectives appear to clash with our aspirations; therefore, either you must cease and desist from these practices, or eliminate them, or be eliminated." There are about a dozen different bases used for justification of conflicts. Many of these are impressed in the armour of justification of the complaining country after being successfully used by another country.

The more prominent and most basic causes are (1) national sovereignty; (2) control of key industries; (3) economic development; (4) conversion of business operations to the style of government, e.g., socialistic, communistic, strongly nationalist; (5) contribution to balance-of-payments; (6) control of export markets; and (7) local participation in ownership.

Most of the takeover cases result where the MNC originates in the more affluent countries, notably Britain, France, Germany and the U.S., and operates in the less developed countries. Nevertheless there have been conflicts between two developed country operations.

## #20-6....Definition of Political Risk

Political Risk may be  defined as "the risk to be assumed by a MNC in setting up a subsidiary operation in a foreign country which will  be amenable to either control, partial takeover, or full takeover, on some political pretense, generally untenable, and under which the risk of losing the foreign operation may be slight, substantial, or total." This definition indicates that there are two factors involved in political risk--one involving the degree or extent of action taken by  the foreign government in attempting  control  of the foreign operation, and the other involving the  degree or extent of the loss resulting  from action.   There have been  a multiplicity of  different forms  or types of  action  arising  out  of political risk, running  the gamut from virtually innocuous  effects  to  total takeover resulting from nationalization.

## #20-7....Classification of Political Risk

Political Risk may be  classified  from four different viewpoints:  (I) As To Source;  (II) As To  Action Taken By Foreign Government; (III) As To Degree Of Takeover; and  (IV) As To Effect On Operations.

## #20-8....(I) Political Risk As To Source

There are four different  sources from which political  risk may emanate:  (A) the foreign government as a political entity; (B)  an influential business segment of the foreign government; (C) an influential social  segment of  the foreign  government; and (D) private individuals seeking ransom through kidnapping.

## #20-9...(II) Political Risk As To Action Taken
## By Foreign Country

There  are three  types of action that may be  taken by  the foreign government  with  respect to political risk,  viz., (A) Control of  Operations of Foreign Subsidiary; (B) Partial Takeover; or (C) Full or Total Takeover.
(A) AS TO CONTROL OF OPERATIONS: The foreign government may not have an  actual  hand in  the foreign subsidiary operations but  may impose conditions that act  as restrictions and  exert some degree of control over such operations.
The following practices fall  under such restrictive category:  (1) discriminatory taxes; (2)  management  position quotas for domicile nationals; (3) restrictions on funds  transfer out of the country; (4) continuous revisions  of terms of contracts extracting greater percentages of the profits; (5) breaches  in

terms resulting in lower MNC income; (6) visa and work permit
limitations; (7) limitations of supplies and materials; (8)
negotiating transfer prices designed to favor the foreign country's tax base; (9) requiring export industries to sell in the
home market at breakeven price to subsidize local consumption;
(10) making host country currency temporarily inconvertible;
and (11) requiring the MNC to construct social and economic
facilities.

(B) AS TO PARTIAL TAKEOVER: Partial Takeover may result from
(1) ownership localization under which plan the government
forces the MNC to sell ownership interests in part or all of
the assets to local citizens; or (2) partial takeover may be
only of functional activities such as personnel, production, or
marketing.

(C) AS TO FULL OR TOTAL TAKEOVER: Full Takeover may result
from (1) Expropriation, which may be (a) by a single act by the
foreign government, or (b) by Creeping Expropriation; (2) Confiscation; (3) Nationalization; (4) Socialization; (5) Intervention and Requisition; or (6) Forced Sale.

(1) Expropriation: (a) Under Expropriation, the actual
transfer of ownership is preceded by a formal writing--eith-
er declaration, decree, or law--generally under a legal proceeding which stipulates the government's intention to expropriate the specific MNC foreign operation. The purpose of
the formal enactment of the law is supposedly to lend credibility to the action under the guise of due process of law.
Expropriation may be with or without compensation generally
set by the foreign government.

(b) Under Creeping Expropriation, nations sometimes impose a series of restrictions and edicts over an extended
period of time which result in a virtual takeover of business control by the foreign government. Illustrations of
such acts are profit repatriation constraints; pricing restrictions; local personnel requirements; R&D restrictions;
elimination of profits by levy of tax, royalty, or other
charges; claiming large compensation for past alleged in-
equities from concession agreements made by a previous government ousted from power.

(2) Confiscation: The basic characteristic of a Confiscation is the absence of compensation to the former owners
of the seized property. Thus expropriated property becomes
confiscated where there is an absence of adequate effective
prompt compensation contemporaneously with the seizure.

(3) Nationalization: While it is legally in essence the
same as other types of expropriation, Nationalization differs in scope and extent. Whereas expropriation is customarily a discriminatory action on a single enterprise basis,
nationalization is a broader measure, general in scope,
which arrogates a whole sector of the economy into public

ownership by the foreign government.

(4) Socialization: Socialization also has the same <u>scope and extent</u> concept as nationalization although basically it has the same legal connotation. Whereas nationalization embraces the transfer of a whole industry from private to public ownership, socialization is the nationalization of ALL industries in a country.

(5) Intervention and Requisition: The U.S. State Dept. has defined intervention as "an action by a government to assume managerial control, without ultimate determination of legal ownership,which may or may not lead to expropriation."

Requisition is similar to Intervention but implies <u>temporary</u> governmental control of an enterprise for a specific public purpose.

(6) Forced Sale: The U.S. State Dept. has defined a forced sale as "an action, or threat of action, by a government, to induce a firm's owners to sell all or part of their property to a governmental entity or private citizens of the country in question--sometimes at lower than market value."

## #20-10...(III) Political Risk As To Degree of Takeover

As to degree of takeover, Political Risk may be classified as (A) Micro, and (B) Macro.

(A) MICRO POLITICAL RISK occurs when only selected fields of business activity, or foreign enterprises with specific characteristics, are affected, such as the takeover of foreign banks in Mexico, an action directed only at the banking industry as a specific sector of the economy.

Micro specified enterprises may be taken over (1) <u>with due process</u>, resulting in expropriation with compensation, or (2) <u>without due process</u>, resulting in confiscation without compensation.

(B) MACRO POLITICAL RISK is general in nature. It refers to politically motivated environmental changes that affect <u>all</u> foreign enterprises. Examples are the Iranian and Cuban takeovers of all private enterprises.

Macro Political Risk, or entire sector or industry takeover, may be (1) <u>with due process</u>, resulting in (a) Nationalization with compensation, or (b) <u>with due process</u>, resulting in <u>Forced Sale</u>, or <u>Socialization with compensation</u>, or (c) Requisition or Integration; (2) <u>without due process</u>, resulting in (a) Nationalization without compensation, or (b) Socialization without compensation, or (c) Requisition or Integration.

## #20-11...(IV) Political Risk As To Effect on Operations

Political risk may be classified as (A) <u>Restrictive</u>, or <u>Functional</u>, on the basis of the business function affected by foreign government restriction; and (B) <u>Analytical</u>, on the basis of explaining changes in government behavior.

(A) RESTRICTIVE POLITICAL RISKS result from uncertainty with respect to host government actions that restrict the transfer of capital, payments, products, technology and personnel into or out of the foreign country. The most common types of transfer restrictions are exchange controls and import restrictions in the form of tariffs and non-tariff trade barriers.

Restrictive Risks are classified as (1) Transfer Risks and (2) Operational Risks, both of which can be sub-classified by the business function affected, since foreign government restrictions permeate through every functional area of business.

(1) Transfer Risks: (a) The Financial Function is confronted with the following restrictions: borrowing; local equity requirements; currency inconvertibility; discriminating tax treatment; and profit repatriation constraints.

(b) The Marketing Function is confronted with the following restrictions: pricing; exporting; advertising; product selection constraints; license cancellations; and contract repudiations.

(c) The Production Function faces the following restrictions: material procurement; technology transfer; and research and development.

(d) The Personnel Function faces the following restraints: demands to hire nationals for management and other positions; wage policy restraints.

(2) Operational Risks: (a) Functional Risks: Like transfer risks, Operational Risks permeate all the business functional areas--Finance, Marketing, Production and Personnel. The following restrictions must be faced in operational risks: monetary and fiscal policies; price controls; taxation; labor codes and regulations; local content requirements; general administrative behavior. (b) Ownership Control Risks result from uncertainty about government policies and actions regarding ownership and managerial control of the subsidiary. This type of risk includes: possible shifts in discriminatory treatment of foreign-owned enterprises; official requirements or pressures for joint ventures with nationals; and expropriation policies.

(B) ANALYTICAL POLITICAL RISKS result from uncertainty with respect to changes in government behavior. Analytical Risks are (1) Political/Economic, or (2) Political/ Social. In the book MULTINATIONAL ENTERPRISE IN TRANSITION, edited by A. Kapoor and Phillip Grubb, pp. 357-358, Prof. Franklin Root points out that (1) Political/Economic Risks are associated with the actions of a host government that are primarily a response to largely unanticipated internal and external changes in the national economy. Sooner or later any government must come to terms with economic realities, or it must give way to a new government that will have to deal with the situation.

Transfer Risks tend to be political/economic in nature excepting restrictions on foreign personnel. Operational risks also tend to be political/economic, though somewhat less so than transfer risks. For example, changes in payment restriction or fiscal policies are ordinarily a direct response to changes in the economy.

(2) <u>Political/Social Risks</u>: Ownership control risks are mainly political/social in nature since they arise from government response to non-economic changes in the national society. For example, shifts in governmental policies toward joint ventures are a response to nationalism rather than economic forces. Expropriation is always a result of nationalist or socialist ideologies, and cannot be explained in economic terms, hence is political/social in character.

#20-12...Outline of Classification of Political Risk

Figure 20-1 outlines a Summary of Classification of Political Risk.

## POLITICAL RISK EXPERIENCES

#20-13...Actual Expropriations of U.S. Foreign Affiliates

A thorough study of expropriations was made and reported by R.G. Hawkins, N. Mintz, and M. Provissiero, entitled "Government Takeovers of U.S. Foreign Affiliates," in the JOURNAL OF INTERNATIONAL BUSINESS STUDIES (JIBS), Spring 1976, pp. 3-16. The study resulted in the following conclusions: with each new year, the number of takeovers of U.S. foreign affiliates by foreign governments has been steadily increasing; the indication is that there will be an acceleration in takeovers in the future; and that MNCs must reckon with takeovers as a very important factor in establishing the risk factor for future foreign investments. These conclusions become apparent from the table presented in Figure 20-2 showing takeovers of foreign affiliates of 170 companies.

The table in Figure 20-2 indicates that while expropriations originally were centered in the extractive industries (principally oil), there has been a decline in favor of the manufacturing industries--possibly because of the limited scope of oil extractions. Also, expropriation appears to be the prevalent form either without compensation or with compensation that is substantially less in value than the property expropriated. The bulk of the expropriation, which cannot be disclosed by statistics, comes from dictatorial governments which need the resources to sustain their governments; and when, where, or how these dictators will assume leadership of their country is a totally unpredictable event.

FIGURE 20-1
SUMMARY OF CLASSIFICATION OF POLITICAL RISK

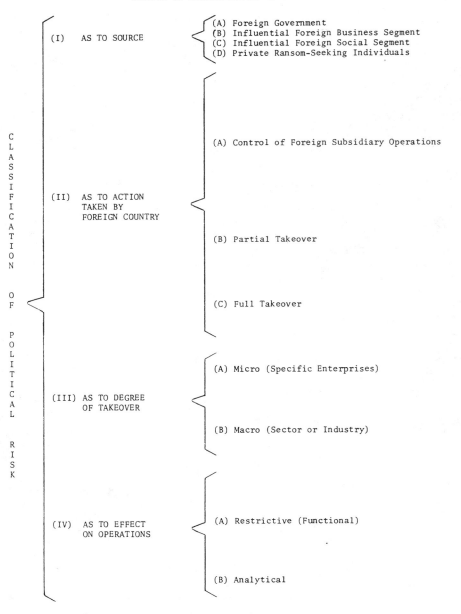

CLASSIFICATION OF POLITICAL RISK

(I)   AS TO SOURCE
    (A) Foreign Government
    (B) Influential Foreign Business Segment
    (C) Influential Foreign Social Segment
    (D) Private Ransom-Seeking Individuals

(II)  AS TO ACTION
    TAKEN BY
    FOREIGN COUNTRY
    (A) Control of Foreign Subsidiary Operations
    (B) Partial Takeover
    (C) Full Takeover

(III) AS TO DEGREE
    OF TAKEOVER
    (A) Micro (Specific Enterprises)
    (B) Macro (Sector or Industry)

(IV)  AS TO EFFECT
    ON OPERATIONS
    (A) Restrictive (Functional)
    (B) Analytical

(1) Discriminatory taxes
(2) Management position quotas for domicile nationals
(3) Restrictions on out of country funds transfers
(4) Continuous terms of contracts revisions extracting greater profits percentages
(5) Breaches in terms resulting in M/N/C lower income
(6) Visa and work permit limitations
(7) Supplies and materials limitations
(8) Transfer prices favoring foreign country tax base
(9) Export industries required to sell in home market at breakeven price to subsidize local use
(10) Making host currency temporarily inconvertible
(11) Requiring M/N/C to construct social and economic facilities

(1) M/N/C required to sell ownership interests in part or in toto to local citizens
(2) Partial takeover of functional activities

(1) Expropriation
    (a) With compensation
    (b) Without compensation
    (c) Creeping expropriation
(2) Confiscation
(3) Nationalization
(4) Socialization
(5) Intervention and requisition
(6) Forced sale

(1) With due process — (a) Expropriation with compensation
(2) Without due process — (b) Confiscation without compensation

(1) With due process
    (a) Nationalization with compensation
    (b) Forced sale - socialization with compensation
(2) Without due process
    (a) Nationalization without compensation
    (b) Socialization without compensation
    (c) Requisition (Integration)

(1) Transfer risks
    (a) Financial
    (b) Marketing
    (c) Production
    (d) Personnel
(2) Operational risks
    (a) Financial
    (b) Marketing
    (c) Production
    (d) Personnel

(1) Political/Economic
(2) Political/Social

FIGURE 20-2
FOREIGN TAKEOVERS OF U. S. FIRMS

| | No. | % | 1946-60 | 1961-66 | 1967-71 | 1972-73 |
|---|---|---|---|---|---|---|
| BY INDUSTRY: | | | | | | |
| Extractive | 69 | 41 | 50 | 50 | 39 | 37 |
| Financial | 32 | 19 | -- | 5 | 28 | 18 |
| Manufacturing | 51 | 30 | -- | 27 | 27 | 40 |
| Utilities | 18 | 10 | 50 | 18 | 6 | 5 |
| TOTALS | 170 | 100 | 100 | 100 | 100 | 100 |
| | | | | | | |
| BY REGION: | | | | | | |
| Latin America | 93 | 55 | 83 | 59 | 44 | 61 |
| Africa | 51 | 30 | 17 | -- | 51 | 16 |
| Middle East | 14 | 8 | -- | 32 | 4 | 7 |
| Asia | 12 | 7 | -- | 9 | 1 | 16 |
| TOTALS | 170 | 100 | 100 | 100 | 100 | 100 |
| | | | | | | |
| BY FORM OF TAKEOVER: | | | | | | |
| Expropriation | 103 | 60 | 67 | 95 | 63 | 42 |
| Intervention/ Requisition | 25 | 15 | -- | -- | 14 | 25 |
| Contract Re- negotiation | 20 | 12 | -- | -- | 8 | 25 |
| Forced Sale | 22 | 13 | 33 | 5 | 15 | 8 |
| | 170 | 100 | 100 | 100 | 100 | 100 |
| | | | | | | |
| BY POLITICAL/ECO- NOMIC CIRCUM- STANCES: | | | | | | |
| Leftist Change in Government | 81 | 48 | 17 | 41 | 65 | 33 |
| Right or Center Nationalist | 7 | 4 | 17 | -- | 6 | 2 |
| Natural Resource Sovereignty | 35 | 20 | 33 | 41 | 4 | 32 |
| Mature & Stand- ardized Product | 47 | 28 | 33 | 18 | 25 | 33 |
| | 170 | 100 | 100 | 100 | 100 | 100 |

Source: Adapted from a study by R.G. Hawkins, N. Mintz, and M. Provissiero, "Government Takeovers of U.S. Foreign Affiliates," JOUR-
NAL OF INTERNATIONAL BUSINESS STUDIES (JIBS), (Spring 1976) pp.
3-16. Reprinted with permission.

## AVOIDANCE OF POLITICAL RISK

### #20-14...Classification of Action Taken To Avoid Political Risk

The vast number of foreign takeovers of U.S. firms shown in Figure 20-2 indicates that political risk is a factor to be reckoned with in pursuing foreign investments. However, not much action was taken in this regard until the decade of the 1970s. The direction was more in the nature of lessening the blow of political risk rather than seeking its elimination which was regarded as unattainable.

The action taken regarding political risk is classified from the viewpoint of the timing of the taking of the action as (1) prior to making the foreign investment and (2) after the foreign investment has been made.

(1) The action taken before the investment is made may be (a) Preventive or minimization, (b) political risk insurance, or (c) analysis of the political risk. (2) The action taken after the investment has been made is in the nature of amelioration of the political risk.

### #20-15...(1)(a) Political Risk Minimization Techniques

Some management areas are of the opinion that political risks can be minimized by actions preceding the foreign investments. Among the techniques used to accomplish this purpose have been the following: (1) controlling of patents and processes strategic to the production processes; (2) controlling the key markets for the subsidiary output; (3) by entering into joint ventures with local corporations approved by the local governments; (4) rendering the local company incapable of operating successfully on its own by making the local company dependent upon the total system of the parent company's operations; (5) using an investment horizon that is quite limited in scope; (6) making the rights and duties of both the host government and foreign affiliate common in nature; and (7) international political risk insurance.

## POLITICAL RISK INSURANCE

### #20-16...(1)(b) Political Risk Insurance

That political risk is being given more and more attention is indicated by the insurance companies which are now covering political risk insurance. This is rather dramatically pointed out by Reuters News Agency in the February 19, 1979, CHICAGO TRIBUNE:

American business, anxious to protect foreign assets at a time of strife in many countries, is discovering the vir-

tues of POLITICAL RISK INSURANCE. For years, such policies
had been offered exclusively by Lloyd's of London, but last
year a member of American International Group, Inc., began
offering it to American companies, and a third private company, Insurance Co. of North America, has announced plans to
sell it.

POLITICAL RISK INSURANCE protects investors against loss
caused by political acts, such as confiscation and currency
embargo. Lloyd's of London, famous for its coverage of unusual risks, has offered political risk insurance for marine
and aviation investment for years, and certain confiscation
coverage for nearly a quarter of a century. It began promoting across-the-board political risk coverage about 1973.

## #20-17...Types of Political Risk Insurers

Political Risk Insurance may be covered by public agencies
or private insurance companies. The U.S. has three government-
related bodies covering political risk: the Overseas Private
Investment Corp. (OPIC), the ExportImport Bank (EXIM BANK), and
the Foreign Credit Insurance Association (FCIA). Although these
three agencies offer coverage for overseas investments involving some political risk, they are hampered by severe limitations, in the form of being required to evaluate such matters
as human rights, export of jobs, and/or environmental consequences in overseas projects.

Private insurers are not hampered by these political considerations as are public agencies. Although Lloyd's of London has
about 85% of the private market, as of 1980 American firms see
demand mushrooming and are emerging as competition. INA announced plans to enter this field in 1979 on the strength of
several fairly encouraging requests for coverage. INA has found
that there are tens of billions of dollars of direct investments abroad and hardly any of it is insured. In addition,
there are foreign investments by non-American firms that are
largely uninsured. Also, the American International Group, Inc.
(AIG), which began tendering the insurance in 1978, and in 1979
offers this coverage all over the world, recently announced it
would offer policies for investment in China. They have also
received feelers for this coverage from investors who are concerned in such countries as Nicaragua, Saudi Arabia, Taiwan,
Turkey and other countries located in Eastern Europe and Africa. The Frank B. Hall Co.'s Intercredit Agency, which special-
izes in export credit insurance, is of the opinion that the
growth in this business may be dramatic during 1980 and '81.

The American Society of International Executives, Winter
1982-1983 NEWSLETTER, page 1, states:

Political risk coverage--the newest and most glamourous form
of international insurance--is fast becoming a major commod-

ity. Originally designed to protect multinationals against foreign government takeovers and other kinds of expropriation, this insurance has more recently been extended to offshore trade as well as investment. Policies are now being offered to cover exportation and importation losses (including slow payments), defaults on foreign bank loans, restrictions on convertibility of earnings, and the wrongful taking of performance bonds. Private insurers offering political risk coverage include American International Political Risk, Inc. (AIGPLRK); Chubb & Son; Insurance Company of North America, based in New York; the Sivett & Crawford Group in Dallas; and Lloyd's of London.

## #20-18...Political Risk Insurance Premiums

As of 1979, premiums for political risk insurance policies written for U.S. investors by private insurers are estimated to be between 15 and 20 million dollars. However, it is extremely difficult, if not impossible, to insure multi-million-dollar investments abroad against political risk, because of the scarcity of funds and the difficulty in assessing political situations. One illustration of this pointed out by INA, where companies received coverage for more than $150 million by Lloyd's and AIG, required a great deal of scrambling and negotiation with reinsurers.

One reason corporations are reluctant to buy political risk insurance is the steep premiums charged. It is estimated that political risk premiums for $100 value could vary from a minimum of 15 to 20 cents to as high as $10, and would concentrate around 75 cents to $1.50. Fire insurance rates for similar coverage would run from a couple of cents to several dollars. A recent case, in the middle of 1979, is that of the Nello Teer Co. of Durham, N.C., which bid on a Syrian highway project with Ex-Im insurance approval; the premiums were steep coming to $1.3 million over three years for a risk exposure of $20 million. Commenting on the exorbitant premium, an executive of the company said: "Since Iran, there's apprehension the furor will spread and we're just not willing to bid a project without the security of political risk insurance." The company believed the coverage was crucial and commented "we may never need it, but it's worth the money to know the U.S. government is behind us."

## #20-19...A Typical Case Study:  Iran

R.C. Longworth in the Feb. 23, 1979, CHICAGO TRIBUNE made the following appraisal of the forecast of the political losses to be encountered in Iran:

The losses for American businesses in Iran may be just beginning. Many of these losses probably are insured. But

many others may not be, or, at best, can be recovered only
with difficulty. At this date there's been no expropriation
yet of American property in Iran but what about joint ventures where the Iranian partner has been arrested or fled
the country? Many issues regarding Iran have been raised:
(1) expropriation; (2) nonconvertibility or ban on transfer
of a firm's funds in Iran; (3) collection problems resulting
from breakdown of the Iranian banking system; (4) damage
from riots or civil war; (5) property loss of employees
forced to flee the country; (6) losses on undeliverable exports to Iran either landing in another country or returned
to the U.S.; (7) calling-in of on-demand bank guarantees
required from U.S. firms carrying out nonmilitary projects
in Iran; and (8) most important, unilateral contract cancellations by the new Iranian government, expected to run into
billions of dollars.

Most of these problems lie ahead. Nearly every contract
in Iran is under the force majeuere--political changes that
make the contract unenforceable. Julian Racliffe, British
director of Control Risks, Ltd., and an expert on negotiations with terrorists, said the political risk involved in a
fast moving situation such as that of Iran must be considered as a whole. Most U.S. firms in Iran are insured under one
of a variety of programs--private coverage through Lloyd's
or American International Group, or government coverage
through the Foreign Credit Insurance Assn. or the Export-Import Bank or Overseas Private Investment Corp. (OPIC). One
or all of these organizations will be paying out a lot of
money on Iran losses, and Ex-Im are "up to their eyeballs"
in potential losses.

Confiscation of entire businesses or of equipment and
assets left behind should be covered. Cancellation of contracts, losses in money transfers, and export losses are
covered. But much of the damage to foreign assets in Iran
was caused not by the civil war but by riots while the Shah
was still in power, and disputes regarding application of
coverage appeared inevitable.

The U.S. government itself must bear the loss of cancelled arms contracts. Cancellation of nonmilitary contracts,
especially those with work in progress, with irrevocable
subcontractor commitments, or with specialized products being made, may give rise to potentially insurable political
risk losses. Despite this, such cancellations will automatically cause a large uninsurable loss of those profits which
would have been earned if the contracts had been completed.

Corporations may feel a moral obligation, if not a legal
one, to repay employees for lost property, and most loss
potentials of this type should be insurable.

The conclusion drawn from the Iran debacle is very dramatically made by Gerald West, an official of OPIC. In his opinion "too many companies go into situations of potential political risk overseas without analyzing the risk. Companies need to talk to banks, to OPIC, to other government agencies, to anyone who can tell you which potential risks are actual risks."

## #20-20...Iranian Consequences

In the July 23, 1979 issue of the CHICAGO TRIBUNE, Janet Key points out that:

the recent collapse of the Shah's rule in Iran, the new Islamic government's subsequent repudiation of contracts made with the Shah's government, its expropriation of foreign assets, and its nationalization of all but minor industries have given many companies a painful, multi-million-dollar introduction to the term POLITICAL RISK INSURANCE, which is not exactly a common business term even among about 100 large multinational companies which account for more than half of the U.S. investments abroad.

Those companies are reluctant to release their loss figures from the revolution, but the Associated General Contractors of America, which represents some 8,000 contractors, estimates that U.S. contractors alone lost about $10 billion in cancelled or delayed projects. In light of those losses, many companies will not even bid for overseas contracts with the political risk insurance provided by the Export-Import Bank, which has received more than 500 such inquiries since it began insuring contracts last year. Other multinationals have not reached that point yet, but there is definitely an upsurge of interest in what was once considered to be a "novelty coverage."

Francis J. Corbett, manager of national sales for the international insurance services of Marsh & McLennan, Inc., the world's largest insurance brokerage firm, says that "many companies are looking for information or advice on the current costing of political risk insurance. Many are also assessing what political risk is all about, what the risks are to their investment at a given point." While companies which have foreign operations only in such "very stable" countries as Canada, Belgium, and Mexico see no reason for political risk coverage, those companies operating in volatile areas like the Middle East are beginning to line up for it.

## #20-21...Categories of Political Risk Coverage

Charles Liotta, Asst. V.P. of Marsh & McLennan, groups political risk coverage in 7 categories: Currency Inconvertibility; License Cancellation; Outright Expropriation; War, Civil Commotion, or Riot; Political Diversion;   Embargo Indemnity; & Arbitrary Letters of Credit Recall.

An example of Currency  Inconvertibility would  be  where  a company would bill a foreign country   or  company in  U.S. dollars, but could only be paid in local currency.  Some countries prohibit the export  of their currency and, in a case like Turkey, do not have  enough dollar reserves to handle the  conversion.

License  Cancellation results from an import  or  export license being cancelled by either  the  foreign government or the U.S. for political reasons.

Expropriation may be  outright or what is  termed  "creeping expropriation" through harassment.

War,  Civil Commotion, or Riot  coverage is  available  only through  the FCIA  or OPIC, not normally in the private  market except by special arrangement and for a higher premium.

Political Diversion is usually  of a  voyage particularly of seasonal goods which are rendered useless,  and is designed for ships taken  over, and has been extended  to cover airplane hijackings.

Embargo  Indemnity usually occurs  where a company falls out of favor with the government of a country such as Saudi Arabia, particularly for selling to a blacklisted country or company.

Arbitrary recall of letters of credit is becoming very popular.  The letters of credit are put up with a local  bank  by a project builder for the whole value of the project and deposited with a local bank.   A foreign government can "call  in" the letter at  any time during a project  forcing the American bank which issued  the  letter to pay it, and the company's only recourse is its insurance.  Liotta indicates:

that's where the  money comes in because London underwriters know that countries like Libya have  done this sort of thing (calling in letters of credit) before.  In the last month or so (June 1979), a lot of investors and builders  are looking for  this type of protection, particularly in  the  Middle East, in addition to insurance of license cancellation.

#### #20-22...Procurement of Political Risk Insurance

Competition in the political risk insurance field is heating up according to Janet Key.  She indicates that:

INA  is developing a risk analysis  service through  its new  subsidiary, INAMIC (INAMulti-National Investments  and Contracts);  the brokerage  firm  of Alexander & Alexander, Inc., uses its  Anistics, Inc., subsidiary; the JLS Group is expanding its  services; and a new firm, International Political Surveys, Inc.,  has  entered the growing market.  More entrants are expected as the full ramifications of Iran make their way up to corporate board rooms.

To get political risk insurance, a typical company first conducts a risk analysis of its exposure, either internally or, increasingly, by using the specialized services of an outside risk management firm, or those of an insurance company or brokerage house. Thus one petrochemical company daily monitors 400 political, social, and economic variables on its computers. Factors most commonly examined include a country's domestic instability, political climate including the number of socialists or communists active in its government, its record of foreign conflict, and its economic climate, particularly the government's attitude toward economic intervention. Methods range from the "grand tour" by company executives, to hiring an "old hand" or expert as a consultant, to so-called Delphic techniques, where aggregate variables are used to make an index of political risk.

## #20-23...Extent of Coverage

With respect to the extent of coverage, Liotta points out first that the coverage is not cheap: "The going rate for all political coverage in the U.S. and London ranges from 1 to 10% of the cost of the project. The rate depends more on the country than on the company or project involved, and also to some extent on the company's relationship with that particular country. When a company wants coverage in only one country, the cost is prohibitive--underwriters want to spread the risk by balancing a Libya with a West Germany. In addition there are certain countries that will absolutely not be covered. I don't think anyone would touch Nicaragua or El Salvador, and Iran is not being written now. Normally a regular confiscation expropriation policy's limits vary between $10 million and $20 million."

## #20-24...Extent of the Hazard

To emphasize the extent of the hazard, a Marsh & McLennan bulletin warns: "Inasmuch as the political climate in most areas of the world is subject to constant and sudden change, underwriting and rating will likewise vary continually. For this reason, quotes for premiums are given on a 'today's rate' basis and no quote is held for more than 30 days." How prophetic this statement is; and to demonstrate, the corollary action resulting from the political repercussions may be evidenced by the following article appearing in the Aug. 20, 1979, CHICAGO TRIBUNE:

KUWAIT--The chairman of Kuwait's Chamber of Commerce and Industry Sunday proposed that Persian Gulf States impose a premium on crude-oil exports to counter a recent declaration by Lloyd's of London that the area is a war zone.

Lloyd's decision to raise insurance premiums on the hulls of vessels plying the gulf, which took effect last week, has been criticized as unjustified by gulf insurance firms.

Abdel-Aziz al-Saqr, the Kuwaiti chamber's chairman, said in a statement that the proposed increase should be called a premium to cover "risks of threats, rumors, and rumor-mongers." He did not specify the size of the premium. He excluded a boycott of Lloyd's as a retaliatory measure because it was impractical, the statement said.

Representatives of Persian Gulf insurance and re-insurance companies are meeting in Baghdad to discuss the decision by the world's leading brokerage house. In a related development, the Iraq News Agency reported that that country's chamber of commerce had sent a cable to Lloyd's condemning its action as "psychological warfare against the region."

## POLITICAL RISK ANALYSIS

### #20-25...(1)(c) Nature of Political Risk Analysis

The third action that may be taken before making the foreign investment is a thorough analysis of the political risk. This is a relatively new and dynamic field of study as evidenced by its rapid development over the past 15 years. In 1984 a review of recent developments in political risk analysis shows this discipline is rapidly growing, is attaining the status of a profession, and is achieving recognition as a separate field of study in the area of international business.

The recognition of political risk analysis as a separate field of study is evidenced by the recent offering of courses in political risk at such schools as New York University and Georgetown University, and the establishment of a Ph.D. program in political risk analysis at Syracuse University.

### #20-26..Professional Status of Political Risk Analysis

That political risk analysis is attaining professional status is evidenced by the creation in 1980 of the ASSOCIATION OF POLITICAL RISK ANALYSTS (APRA). The membership of APRA consists of MNCs and their department analysts, independent political risk consultants, university professors, and other individuals involved or interested in political risk analysis. APRA serves its membership and the corporate community by sponsoring national and regional seminars, conventions, special research projects, and dissemination of valuable information via its new bimonthly publication entitled THE POLITICAL RISK REVIEW.

## #20-27...Political Risk Analysis Departments

The most significant development in political risk analysis is the proliferation of separate POLITICAL RISK ANALYSIS DE-PARTMENTS within MNCs. Such companies as General Motors, American Can Co., AT&T, and the international oil companies have their own in-house facilities to analyze political risks.

## #20-28...Sources of Political Risk Analysis

In recent years, numerous sources of political risk analysis have sprung into existence. There are subscription services that rate various countries according to their political climate's desirability. The leading subscription services are BUS-INESS INTERNATIONAL (BI); BUSINESS ENVIRONMENT RISK INFORMATION (BERI); and FROST & SULLIVAN'S, INC., WORLD POLITICAL RISK FORE-CASTS (WPRF). In addition, the following private consulting firms provide customized analyses of foreign political risks: International Business-Government Counsellors, Inc.; Intermatrix Group; International Ventures Consultants; and Bickford International Consultants, Ltd.

## #20-29...Methods of Political Risk Analysis

There are four groups of methods of political risk analysis: (1) Non-Systematic; (2) Subjective Macro; (3) Objective Macro; and (4) Company Specific Micro.

## #20-30...Non-Systematic Methods

In the article "How to Analyze Foreign Investment Climates," in the September-October 1969 HARVARD BUSINESS REVIEW, pages 100-108, R.B. Stobaugh describes the non-systematic method as a Go/No-Go Approach. Under this approach, the acceptance or re-jection of a particular country by the manager is based on an examination of one or two characteristics. Often no further study is given to the investment climate. The major shortcoming of this method is that it causes some very good investment op-portunities to be passed over because of the rejection on the initial screening.

A second non-systematic method is described by R.J. Rummel and D.A. Heenan, in the article "How Multinationals Analyze Political Risk," in the Jan.-Feb. 1978 HARVARD BUSINESS REVIEW, pp. 67-76. It is known as the Grand Tours Approach. It involves some preliminary market research followed by the dispatch of an executive or a team on an inspection tour. Local leaders are contacted and conferences held with government officials and businessmen. After surveying the political landscape for sever-al days, company representatives return home to apprise senior management of their impressions. The major shortcoming of this method is that it suffers from an overdose of selective information. In many cases company observers are briefed in form, but in fact are insulated from the political and economic realities of the country visited.

## #20-31...Subjective Macro Methods

The obvious defects of the non-systematic methods have caused many MNCs to resort to more sophisticated analysis. This has caused them to turn to the country risk ratings subscription services which base their ratings on specialists' subjective opinions of various countries. The best known subjective data based subscription services are BERI, which reviews 45 countries three times a year; BI Country Assessment Service, which surveys 71 countries twice a year; and WPRF, which summarizes 60 countries monthly.

Because BERI gathers opinions from correspondents located in the countries surveyed, or from U.S. experts who are often academics or former State Dept. officials to produce its survey, it is regarded as demonstrating the SUBJECTIVE MACRO METHOD of risk analysis. Although the three subjective risk subscription services provide some comparability between countries, their shortcoming lies in their MACRO point of view that assesses a Country as a Whole, rather than the political environment Impact Upon a Specific Industry or Company. An additional criticism of these methods is their inherent subjectivity in deriving the scores quantified for each country depending on the subjective opinions based on the expert's definition of the situation and his prior experience. Thus a pretense of objectivity is given to data derived subjectively.

## #20-32...Objective Macro Methods

Objective based systems have been contrived to avoid the problem of subjectivity inherent in the BERI, BI, and WPRF systems. There are two such methods included in this class of political risk forecasting: (1) the Political System Stability Index, and (2) the Ecological Approach.

## #20-33...The Political System Stability Index

This uses as its source data the WORLD HANDBOOK OF POLITICAL AND SOCIAL INDICATORS. This system is described by the originators, Haendel, West, and Meadow in an article entitled, "Overseas Investment and Political Risk," Philadelphia, Foreign Policy Research Institute, Monograph Series No. 21, 1975, pages 70-71.

## #20-34...The Ecological Approach

Advanced by Harald Knudsen, this is described in the article "Explaining the National Propensity to Expropriate: An Ecological Approach," in the Spring 1974 JOURNAL OF INTERNATIONAL BUSINESS STUDIES, pp. 51-71.   Knudsen utilized OBJECTIVE environmental variables of countries instead of SUBJECTIVE opinions about the investment climate.   In his study, Mr. Knudsen has gathered socio-economic information which results in ECOLOGICAL STRUCTURES in a particular foreign country.   From this information, Knudsen is of the opinion that certain political action in the form of expropriation will follow at some relatively close future time.   This is accentuated in cases of revolutionary political activity or political aggression to the point that when frustration reaches the level as to be related to prodigious foreign investments, the result is that the MNC becomes the scapegoat for all of the ills in the economy in which it operates, with the resultant takeover or expropriation.

Mr. Knudsen classified the ECOLOGICAL STRUCTURES into three groups each of which is directed to a goal which when related to one another gives a residual SCAPEGOAT FUNCTION, which finally results in the PROPENSITY TO EXPROPRIATE. This is charted in Figure 20-3.

Knudsen measures foreign investment presence by two ratios: (1) cumulative U.S. investment to gross national product; and (2) a combined measure of U.S. presence in sensitive industries derived from the ratio of exports to gross national product, the percentage of U.S. direct foreign investment in extractive and utility industries, and the concentration of U.S. direct foreign investment in any single sensitive industry.

## #20-35...Shortcomings of Objective Macro Methods

Although the objective macro methods move away from the subjective data of expert opinions to the HARD data of quantitative indicators, they do not escape the generalities of the investment climate approaches of BERI, BI, or WPRF.  Country rankings of STABILITY OR INVESTMENT CLIMATE are essentially analyses that are MACRO in character that cannot account for variations in risk exposure for different types of investments. For this reason more sophisticated techniques of forecasting political risks are needed.

## #20-36...Company Specific Micro Methods

The fourth and final approach to analysis of political risk aims at curing the fault of the macro approaches of emphasizing COUNTRY risk rather than CORPORATE SPECIFIC RISKS. Many political risk analyst experts believe that the analysis should be

FIGURE 20-3
THE ECOLOGICAL APPROACH

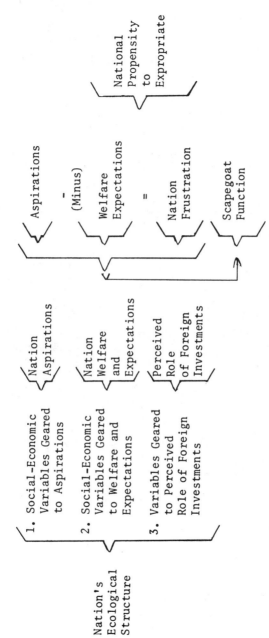

Source: Adapted from material in "Explaining the National Propensity to Expropriate: An Ecological Approach," by Harald Knudsen, JOURNAL OF INTERNATIONAL BUSINESS STUDIES (JIBS), (Spring 1974) pp. 51-71.

directed toward SPECIFIC CORPORATE RISKS.  Stephan Blank, political risk analyst for the Conference Board, says: "The idea of
rating an entire country's risk  is silly.  An extractive firm,
such as oil or mining, is almost always going to  run  a higher
risk than someone selling ice cream." Gordon Rayfield of General Motors and a founding member of the Association of Political
Risk Analysts (APRA) adds:   "I don't think there is  a lot  of
meaning in a BI or BERI kind  of study.  An analysis done for a
group of clients with different needs has to confine itself  to
such a high level of superficiality that its value is limited."
Shell Oil  Co.,  a WPRF subscriber, noted:  "Shell's experience
has been that generalized  assessments of  political risks have
very little value. The only useful analysis is tailor-made to a
specific company in a specific country."
    Numerous MNCs  are now creating in-house  political intelli-
gence  units to include  industry, corporate, product, and project factors in their analysis  of political risks.  Such firms
as  ITT, Gulf Oil,  General Motors, Shell, and  Bank of America
have such  departments set  up to forecast  political  hazards
overseas.  Although Shell's system is  similar to BERI, BI, and
WPRF in its reliance on  expert-generated data, it differs from
these surveys by focusing exclusively on the political and economic conditions that might negatively affect an OIL investment
venture.

#### #20-37...Future of Political Risk Analysts

    Obviously the  propensity  to expropriate  and macro methods
appear to be highly academic.  What they fail to take into consideration are  the unknown  factors  that spring  up magically
without any notice, all resulting purely from political considerations.  Thus in 1979 the U.S. was caught totally by surprise
when  the Islamic Revolution completely overturned the  Shah of
Iran.  Even a few weeks before it occurred,  no  one could have
foreseen such a total upheaval  as  that  which  actually  took
place.  In the Middle East and Latin America, nobody knows when
a coup will occur or where and how long it will last. The political risk factor is almost insoluble, and accountants who must
deal in concrete figures have no way whatever of knowing how to
translate political upheavals and expropriations into exact  or
even forecasted figures.  Where the  foreign country is  highly
explosive politically, the only safe way is to prepare to write
off  any  foreign investment as  a total loss, as many involved
with Iran probably will.
    If  expropriations  or nationalizations of  foreign  company
operations could be  forecast, let us ask why the Shell Oil Co.
between 1961 and 1974 had expropriations take place in the following countries:  Algeria, Ceylon, Cuba, Egypt, Guinea, Libya,
Somalia,  Syria and South Yemen.  Or why during the period from

1945 to 1973 the UniLever Co. had operations taken   over   in 17
different   countries.   So long as   the world political order is
constituted   under the U.N.   as at   present,   the insignificant
nations are naturally going to pick on the giants. This is apt-
ly stated in the Mar. 1976 JOURNAL OF ACCOUNTANCY, at page 28:
    Even the   smallest   and   most recent newcomer   to nationhood
    has   absolute, unquestioned authority over the largest   MNE.
    It can and   does monitor and control new investment.   It de-
    termines levels and distribution   and expatriation of funds.
    It imposes production quotas and controls prices at unecono-
    mic   levels   and unprofitable.   It can rule and legislate on
    every   aspect of the company's activities and in such   a way
    as to   put the   company at a trading   disadvantage vis-a-vis
    local business.

## #20-38...(2) Amelioration of Political Risks

    The discussion of political risk to this point   involved ac-
tion taken prior   to making   the   foreign investment.   Once the
investment has been made, action taken with respect   to political   risk can   no longer involve   the investment but   becomes a
question as to how   to   ameliorate, mitigate,   or minimize   the
prospective loss it is   confronted with.   From what was stated
above, the most conservative approach to the problem of POLITI-
CAL RISK is to   expect total expropriation without compensation
as occurred in Iran.
    Many MNCs   have resorted   to   practices which, while they do
not completely   eliminate   the risk, do lessen   it,   or at best
postpone it.   The following expedients have been resorted to in
this direction:   (1) Joint Venture; (2) Use of local   supply
sources; (3) Employ local citizens as the bulk of their employees   and or/managers; (4) Market   the local   production in hard
currency   countries to   improve the foreign exchange situation;
(5) Risk   diversification, vertical integration;   (6) External
financial stakeholders; (7) Technology barriers; (8) Techniques
for inevitable expropriation; and (9) Codes of Conduct.
    Joint   Ventures   improve the public image of the   subsidiary
as being a partially native firm.   The local partner could also
contribute equity capital and   access   to local borrowing, and
possibly technology and competent management.
    Concentrating foreign activity is putting one's eggs all   in
one basket. To avoid this risk, especially in third world countries,   operations   should   be spread   over several   countries,
which would result in a reduction of the percentage of loss.
    Vertical   Integration of a MNC is   among   the most   powerful
deterrents to expropriation. Under this plan the parent company
controls either the supply   channels or the   market outlets for
the   products of the subsidiary.   Foreign governments recognize
the futility of seizing a   plant that can be shut down from the

U.S. simply by halting the flow of parts or materials, or by refusing to market the finished products.

Developing external financial stakeholders in the venture is another risk minimization technique. This involves venture capital raising from the host and other governments, international financial institutions, and customers, rather than employing funds supplied by the parent company.

Advanced technology, which has proved to be an effective barrier to competition, is equally as effective as to expropriation. Although IBM stretches across 127 countries, it has not suffered a single expropriation during the past 16 years, because third world countries are not capable of duplicating IBM research and technology.

Various steps taken to minimize prospective losses of companies facing inevitable expropriation have been (a) inventories cutback; (b) complete cessation of new investment; (c) cutbacks in receivables; (d) cessation of shipments to host country; (e) payment of all commercial debt owed to U.S. suppliers; (f) reduction or elimination of guarantee by parent company on local borrowing; (g) increase in remittances to U.S.; (h) shipments to the subsidiary on letter of credit terms only; and (i) cutback in production.


## INTERNAL BUSINESS OPERATIONS CODES OF CONDUCT

### #20-39...Effect of Codes of Conduct on Political Risk

Since the basic argument used by expropriating countries has been exploitation and imperialism, one device that has been resorted to to overcome such specious arguments has been the establishment of CODES OF CONDUCT for MNCs. It is believed that if the expropriating countries set up codes of conduct for the ME operations, then they will have no cause for expropriation should the MNC enterprise live up to the codes of conduct set by such governments. This of course is tantamount to the government having a hand in the operations of foreign MEs.

This is clearly demonstrated by a survey entitled "Business & Society, 1976-2000," published by the American Management Association, which states:

There is a fundamental change coming in the relationship between business and the society it serves. The corporation will either transform itself or be transformed by the agents of the public into a unit that formally and continuously considers the desires, needs, and concerns of the individuals and forms its policies accordingly.

Thus 86% of the companies surveyed in 1976 not only adopted social responsibility programs that were mandated by the government of the country in which they operated but went even

further by instituting voluntary programs. Some even went so
far as to set up anticipatory programs.

## #20-40...Definition of Codes of Conduct

Codes of Conduct may be defined as "written documents which
prescribe the conduct, behavior, and/or actions that are either
required, or at least suggested behavior, by foreign governments to be adhered to by MNCs operating in their jurisdiction,
for the ostensible purpose of contributing to the social and
economic progress of the host country."

What they in effect do is have a foreign government say to
MNCs which operate in their jurisdictions that they are prescribing the rules of the game being played in the foreign
country to the extent that if the MNC adheres to these written
rules, the foreign government will express its satisfaction by
not punishing the MNC. Thereby at one extreme either the political risk will be eliminated, or at the least at the other
extreme it will be ameliorated by rendering it innocuous. In
effect the foreign government may say to the MNC if it adheres
strictly to the Code of Conduct "you have been a model operation and we will not attempt any serious expropriation of your
property or hamper your operations."

## #20-41...Basis of Codes of Conduct

To assure such good conduct abroad, more than 200 U.S. corporations have developed their own codes of conduct, which ex-
hort their executives to perform their management functions and
general business affairs in an ethical manner, to abide by all
laws of home and host countries, and to demonstrate exemplary
citizenship.

Addressing the International Bar Association in West Berlin
in Aug. 1980, on the subject "Codes of Conduct for Transnational Corporations--Signals of Public Expectations," page 15,
George Coombe, Jr., stated:

Voluntary codes of conduct can provide a much needed manifestation of corporate intent to engage in ethical behavior
and obey the law. *** Any such company code should include
many of the substantive matters sought to be addressed by
the several proposed multinational codes now under negotiation. In addition to disclosure and employee behavior, a
typical code might address corporate governance, functioning
of the Board, integrity of accounting and records, responsibility as an employer, description of business activities,
general rules of business behavior, responsibility to customers, and responsibility as a corporate member of the community.

## #20-42...Types of Codes of Conduct

There are three types of Codes of Conduct: Government Fiat; International Agencies; and Voluntary Individual. In addition to Codes of Conduct being established by the various governments, various international agencies and individual MNCs themselves have had a hand in developing such Codes.

The first Code was established by the Pacific Basin Economic Council in May 1972, entitled CHARTER ON INTERNATIONAL INVESTMENTS. In the same year a GROUP OF EMINENT PERSONS, numbering 20, was apppointed by the U.N. Secretary General, for the ECONOMIC AND SOCIAL COUNCIL of the U.N., for the purpose of "holding public hearings and making recommendations for some form of accountability to the international community." The purpose of such investigation was to determine the social and economic effects of the operations of multinationals on the countries in which they operate.

## #20-43...U.N. Commission on Transnational Corporations

Resulting from the public hearings conducted by the GROUP OF EMINENT PERSONS was the establishment on Dec. 4, 1974, of the U.N. COMMISSION ON TRANSNATIONAL CORPORATIONS which in turn set up a CENTER ON TRANSNATIONAL CORPORATIONS. The CENTER is an information-gathering agency whose purpose is to marshal a comprehensive system of data and information on MNCs. The classification system adopted by the U.N. T/N/C Center for Bibliography on TNCs is based on nine categories as follows:

1. Conceptual and Definitional Questions and General:
   1.0-Conceptual Questions; 1.1-Definitions; 1.2-Disclosure & Reporting Procedures & Regulations; 1.3-Reference Sources; 1.4-General Studies on TNCs; 1.5-History & Evaluation of TNCs; 1.9-Other
2. Explanations of Foreign Direct Investment, Management & Organization:
   2.0-Explanations of Foreign Direct Investments, & Management Organization; 2.1-Management & Organization; 2.10-Strategies; 2.11-Organizations & Structures; 2.12-Functions; 2.13-Teaching Case Studies; 2.14-Business in Selected Countries; 2.19-Other
3. Data and Information on Individual Enterprises:
   3.0-Individual Enterprises; 3.1-Directories; 3.9-Other
4. Aggregate TNC Activities Data & Information -- Size, Growth, Distribution, Characteristics, Trends:
   4.0-Inward Investment; 4.1-Outward Investment; 4.9-Other
5. Role of TNCs in Individual Economic Sectors:

5.0-Industrial Structure; 5.1-Agriculture, Forestry, Fishing; 5.2-Mining & Petroleum; 5.3-Manufacturing; 5.4-Construction; 5.5-Wholesale Trade, Retail Trade, Restaurants, Hotels; 5.6-Transport, Storage, Communications; 5.7-Financing, Insurance, Real Estate, Business Services including accounting, engineering, advertising; 5.8-Community, Social Personal Services; 5.9-Other

6. Role of TNCs in Individual Countries, Regions & International System:
6.0-Developing Countries; 6.1-Developed Countries; 6.2-Centrally Planned Economies; 6.3-Regional Groups; 6.4-International System

7. Impact of Transnational Corporations:
7.0-Economic Impact:
7.00-Transfer of Technology; 7.01-Industrial & Economic Development; 7.02-Employment, Training, Wages, & Working Conditions; 7.03-Finance & Balance of Payments; 7.04-Ownership & Control; 7.05-Market Structure & Restrictive Business Practices; 7.06-Transfer Pricing; 7.07-Consumption Pattern; 7.08-Environment; 7.09-Other
7.1-Political Impact:
7.10-Government-Business Relationship; 7.11-Incentives, Guarantee Programs, Investment Climate, Political Risk; 7.12-Bargaining Power; 7.13-International Relations; 7.19-Other
7.2-Socio-Cultural Impact
7.3-Legal Implications:
7.30-Regulation & Control of TNCs; 7.31-Nationalization & compensation; 7.32-Extraterritorial application of laws & regulations & antitrust; 7.33-Corrupt practices; 7.34-Contracts & agreements; 7.35-Company Laws; 7.36-Dispute Settlement; 7.39-Other

8. Transnational Corporations and Other Actors:
8.0-International & Regional Organization; 8.1-Labor Unions; 8.2-Consumers; 8.9-Other

9. Technical Assistance

It should be noted that the classification system of the U.N. Center of Transnational Corporations touches upon a variety of the international areas previously discussed such as Social Responsibility, Foreign Corrupt Practices, in addition to accounting information systems, thereby indicating a direct relationship between the Center and accounting of TNCs.

One significant early report of the U.N. Center on TNCs, titled INFORMATION ON TRANSNATIONAL CORPORATIONS, not only includes sources of information on MNCs, but also disclosure and comparability aimed at the establishment of a comprehensive world-wide information system for multinational business activities.

#### #20-44...OECD Code of Conduct

Another international public group that has delved into the area of Codes of Conduct is the 24 member Organization for Economic Cooperation and Development (OECD). In June of 1976 it established a "Code of Conduct for Multinational Enterprises." Many members of professional accounting associations in the Western governments served as advisors to the representatives of the various governments in the drafting and adoption of the OECD Code. Like the U.N. code, the OECD Code contains nine Guidelines for Multinational Enterprises:

<u>Disclosure of Information</u>: Enterprises should have due regard to their nature and relative size in the economic context of their operations and to requirements of business confidentiality and to cost, publish, in a form suited to improve public understanding, a sufficient body of factual information on the structure, activities and policies of the enterprise as a whole, as a supplement, insofar as necessary for this purpose, to information to be disclosed under the national law of the individual countries in which they operate. To this end, they should publish, within reasonable time limits, on a regular basis, but at least annually, financial statements and other pertinent information relating to the enterprise as a whole, comprising in particular:

i.      the structure of the enterprise, showing the name and location of the parent company, its main affiliates, its percentage ownership, direct and indirect, in these affiliates, including shareholdings, between them;

ii.     the geographical areas where operations are carrried out and the principal activities carried on therein by the parent company and main affiliates;

iii.    the operating results and sales by geographical area and the sales in the major lines of business for the enterprise as a whole;

iv.     significant new capital investment by geographical area and, as far as practicable, by major lines of business for the enterprise as a whole;

v.      a statement of the sources and uses of funds by the enterprise as a whole;

vi.     the average number of employees in each geographical area;

vii.    research and development expenditure for the enterprise as a whole;

viii.   the policies followed in respect of intra-group pricing;

ix.     the accounting policies, including those on consolidation, observed in compiling the published information.

Obviously the entire OECD Code is heavily accounting oriented as it is also socially, economically and politically.

While there were governmental representatives that had primary responsibility for the draft of the Code, many of the advisors to these governmental representatives were professional accountants, and the results of the Code are the first expression on the part of Western nations regarding the social aspects of corporate conduct. The question is whether there can be enforceability of the provisions of the Code on the corporations affected inasmuch as the Code is completely voluntary. However, due to the political and moral basis, it would appear that corporations failing to comply with the provisions of the Code will have considerable difficulty operating in the countries behind it.

## #20-45...Governmental Executive Agreement Codes

In addition to multigovernment codes, a more limited version is that existing between two individual countries, such as the 1976 Executive Agreement on Antitrust Cooperation between the U.S. and Germany. In the article "Antitrusters Build Bridge Between Germany and U.S." (BUSINESS EUROPE, July 16, 1976, pp. 228-229), it is pointed out that the German-U.S. Executive Agreement declares "each party will provide the other party with any significant information which comes to the attention of its antitrust authorities and which involves restrictive business practices which, regardless of origins, have a substantial effect on the domestic or international trade of other parties."

Under the executive agreement, which appears to be the first to implement the OECD Code, accomplishment of the purpose is expected through the voluntary informing of the governments to each other regarding competitive matters engaged in by corporations operating within either of the two countries. Although corporations may have the protection under national laws on confidential matters, so that a request made by one of the governments to a particular corporation cannot be enforced, leaving the corporation free to comply at its discretion--nevertheless the moral suasion factor requiring a response should certainly be quite strong.

## #20-46...Individual Multinational Operations Codes

A pioneering case of the establishment of an Individual Multinational Corporation Code is that of the Caterpillar Tractor Co., which published a comprehensive report in 1974 with respect to its world-wide activities. The general areas covered by the report were (1) ownership and investment; (2) company facilities; (3) employee relationships; (4) local law compliances; (5) public responsibility; and (6) business ethics, which is defined as follows: "the law is a floor. Ethical business conduct should normally exist at a level above the minimum required by law." It should be noted that in this Caterpillar Code are very definite correlations with Social Responsibility as well as political and legal relationships as treated in the areas of Social Accounting and Political Accounting.

In the wake of the establishment of the Caterpillar Code, the Stanford Research Institute in California published a booklet in 1975 ("International Business Principles--Codes") and another in 1976 as a follow-up booklet ("International Business Principles--Company Codes"), both of which enumerate the many companies that have emulated the Caterpillar Code.

#### #20-47...Classification of International Business Codes of Conduct

Many of the existing and proposed Codes of Conduct are presented in the Summary Classification in Figure 20-4.

### REVERSE EXPROPRIATION

#### #20-48...Privatization Around the World

A new phenomenon with respect to expropriation has sprung up in 1983 which has been termed PRIVATIZATION. The Coopers & Lybrand EXECUTIVE ALERT NEWSLETTER (Nov. 1983) contains the article "Privatization: Less Government, Better Services?". It declares that in the U.S. "the focus of the privatization has been the transfer of government-provided public services such as garbage collection, air traffic control, and fire protection. But the international perspective tends to be much broader and diverse, encompassing giant enterprises like telephone companies, mines, and steel mills."

In the June 1984 issue, pages 1-3, it appears that privatization has taken hold in a big way of many large companies spread around the world. Mexico in March 1984 reprivatized 73% of its 467 nationalized companies, including the Telephone Co. of Mexico and an affiliate of John Deere. Great Britain is preparing to offer private shares of British Telecom, and a number of developing countries are preparing companies to be put on the auction block.

#### #20-49...Causes of International Privatization

James Haybyrne, a director in Coopers & Lybrand's international management consulting group, indicates that: "the thrust of international privatization is caused by the concern about inefficiencies in state-owned enterprises and how they can be

FIGURE 20-4
SUMMARY CLASSIFICATION OF INTERNATIONAL BUSINESS
CODES OF CONDUCT

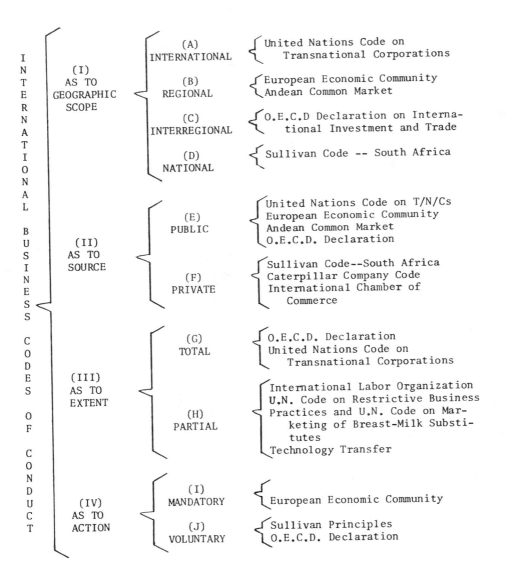

more responsive to market forces and signals.  In many developing countries,  inefficient  companies are a drain  on national
treasuries  and  contribute to  these  countries' sizeable debt
problems. *** For U.S. business, privatization offers challenges.  Foreign  investment, possible joint ventures,  and trading
opportunities are becoming more  plentiful, but risk and competition need to be weighed carefully."
     According to  Pedro-Pablo Kuczynski G., co-chairman of First
Boston  International, a  subsidiary of the investment  banking
firm:  "The burdens of state ownership have become great, sometimes overbearing.  Countries are now beginning to pursue various strategies to  improve their fiscal situation and alleviate
the burden of ownership."

#20-50...Countries Involved in Privatization

     The  June 1984 issue of the EXECUTIVE ALERT NEWSLETTER  goes
on to indicate the countries involved:
     In the People's Republic of China, liberalization of the
economy and its open-door  policy  to the world economy have
encouraged both worker incentive programs and private enterprises  such as hand-made  furniture and clothing and  other
consumer  items.  Although the self-employed make  up fewer
than  2% of China's urban  workers,  that  figure represents
about 20 million people. And private enterprises are growing
rapidly from this already substantial base of entrepreneurs.
     Great Britain is moving toward privatization in telecom-
munications, air transport, and petroleum.  In Chile 13 corporations and  18 banks valued at $940 million were sold be-
tween 1974 and late 1982.  In Peru and  Costa Rica steps are
being taken for the sale of aluminum and other manufacturing
companies.  Kenya, Liberia and  Zaire  have divested, or are
planning to divest, state-owned enterprises.

#20-51...Forms of Privatization

     Since the aim  of privatization is to alleviate the drain on
government  revenues  and  inefficiences  and other  burdens of
state ownership, countries are discovering that the divestiture
option  is not a panacea, and in  fact  isn't always practical.
With economic recession,  debt burdens, and a degree of political instability, many countries have found the timing wrong for
selling off major enterprises.  They have  therefore sought attractive alternatives that have taken the following forms:  (1)
Liquidation;  (2) Deregulation;  (3) Management Contracts  With
Performance Incentives; (4) Performance Measures Tied to Market
Signals; (5) Gradual Issuance of Public Stock; (6) Auctions, or
Major Divisions, of State-Owned Companies.

## #20-52...Future of Privatization

The EXECUTIVE ALERT NEWSLETTER is of the opinion that "the privatization movement is probably in its embryonic state and is likely to become a major influence in international business. Certainly there will be keener competition in the marketplace, with more market players and more attention to market signals. Industries and companies will become economically healthier and more efficient. And governments, especially those with existing external debt servicing requirements, will have fewer burdens."

There remains the question of the impact of privatization on the matter of political risk. Will it act as a deterrent to, or as a reduction in, expropriation? Although not all privatization is a reverse of the expropriatory process, will those countries, particularly the backward ones, recognize that expropriation isn't quite the utopia they think they are getting?

## ACCOUNTING FOR EXPROPRIATIONS AND POLITICAL RISK LOSSES

## #20-53...Political Risk Accounting Implications

Professors Arpan and Radebaugh (in their book INTERNATIONAL ACCOUNTING AND MULTINATIONAL ENTERPRISES, 1981, Warren, Gorham and Lamont) point out on pages 370-371 the central problem with respect to accounting for expropriations and political risk losses as follows:

One of the greatest risks a M/N/C faces is a government takeover of its operations and assets. While accountants can do little to prevent such takeovers, they can and do play an important role in determining the amount of compensation that should be claimed by the M/N/C. By international law, governments are supposed to pay fair compensation to companies whose assets have been taken over. In reality, however, most governments have not paid fair compensation. This then raises the question of what role can accountants play?

Thus it is up to the accountant to arrive at an estimate of the going concern value. This process takes most accountants into largely uncharted waters. It is an area where some innovative and creative accounting work can be done. With the rising nationalism and general distrust of M/N/Cs around the world, government takeovers are likely to continue, further underscoring the need for accountants to prepare for this kind of work.

To date there does not appear to be any set principles as to how expropriation losses are to be handled. Three alternatives present themselves on the books of account: (1) because it is almost an impossibility to forecast expropriation, it may be

treated as an extraordinary loss resulting from natural causes;
(2) the loss may be treated as a normal risk similar to Exchange Gains and Losses, in which case a Contingency or Other
Reserve may be set up and charged against foreign operations;
or (3) a hybrid handling of contingency and outright loss,
which many firms resort to.

There are two ramifications to the problem of accounting
for political risk:  (1) Financial Statement Disclosures, and
(2) Handling of Transactions on the Books of Account.


## FINANCIAL STATEMENT DISCLOSURES

### #20-54...Need for Financial Statement Disclosures

When expropriation of the foreign assets of a MNC becomes a
matter of concern, expression of this fact should be made as a
disclosure in the financial statements.  As a result there have
been four pronouncements issued regarding the disclosure:  ARB
#43; FASB #5; FASB #14; and SEC GUIDES #1 and #22.

### #20-55...Accounting Research Bulletin #43

Para. 6 of Chapter 12 of ARB #43 provides that "most foreign
assets stand in some degree of jeopardy, so far as ultimate
realization by United States owners are concerned. It is therefore important that full disclosure of the extent of foreign
assets be made in the financial statements.

### #20-56...FASB #5 -- Accounting For Contingencies

Para. 32 of FASB #5 declares that expropriation is a contingency.  Therefore when an expropriation appears to be PROBABLE
under para. 8a and the amount of the loss can be reasonably
estimated under para. 8b, then the amount of the loss should be
accrued.  However under para. 3 where the expropriation is only
REASONABLY POSSIBLE as opposed to PROBABLE, and where the loss
cannot be reasonably estimated, under para. 10, the circumstances should be disclosed together with an estimate of the
possible loss, or a statement to be made that an estimate cannot be made.

### #20-57...FASB #14 -- Financial Reporting for Segments
of a Business Enterprise

FASB #14 together with FASB #14 INTERPRETATION dated Sept.
1976 entitled REASONABLE ESTIMATION OF THE AMOUNT OF A LOSS
enlarges the applicable portions of FASB #5.

#### #20-58...SEC Guides #1 and #22 -- For Preparation of Financial Statements

These Guides for reporting the effects of an expropriation require that the SEC Annual Reports of Summary of Earnings and Statement of Income be followed by narrative discussions of significant changes in income and expense items and net income or loss. Such disclosure would require that the effect of an expropriation be thoroughly analyzed to determine its effect on current and future operations and net income.

## ACCOUNTING FOR POLITICAL RISK LOSS TRANSACTIONS

#### #20-59...Classification of Political Risk Losses

Political risk losses may be classified into 5 groups: expropriation; uncollectible receivables; contract repudiation and license cancellation; currency inconvertibility; and potential callings of letters of credit. Accounting rules for each of these are presented below.

#### #20-60...Accounting For Expropriation Losses

The entry recommended for expropriation losses depends upon the nature of the loss, which may fall into three categories: (a) Expropriation Loss is imminent and can be reasonably estimated; (b) Expropriation Loss is not imminent but can be reasonably estimated; (c) Expropriation Loss is imminent but cannot be reasonably estimated.

(a) Expropriation Loss Imminent and Reasonably Estimatable: A loss should be accrued in accordance with FASB #5, ACCOUNTING FOR CONTINGENCIES, as illustrated in the Sedco, Inc., case with Iran.

(b) Expropriation Loss Not Imminent But Reasonably Estimatable; or (c) Expropriation Loss is Imminent But Not Reasonably Estimatable: The political risk situation should be disclosed in the financial statements footnotes as per para. 10 of FASB #5. Where a consolidated subsidiary is involved in the expropriation, the cost method of accounting for that particular investment should be utilized in lieu of inclusion in consolidated statements per APB #18, para. 14.

Where a parent company is using the equity method of accounting for a foreign subsidiary which becomes subject to expropriatory action, the cost method should be used in lieu of the equity method, as prescribed by the footnote to para. 14 of APB #18.

Expropriation losses should be classified as extraordinary losses on the income statement, if they are material, according to APB #30, para. 23.

## #20-61...Accounting for Uncollectible Receivables

Like expropriation losses, uncollectible receivables fall within the same 3 categories so that the accounting treatment will depend upon which category is involved.

(a). If the uncollectibility of the receivable is probable but can be reasonably estimated, a loss should be accrued in accordance with FASB #5.

(b) and (c). If either the uncollectibility of the loss is not imminent and/or cannot be estimated, then under FASB #5, para. 10, the loss cannot be accrued. If the uncollectible receivable loss caused by the political risk cannot be accrued because one or both of the conditions are not met, disclosure of the political risk shall be made when there is at least a reasonable possibility that a loss may have been incurred as per para. 10 of FASB #5.

Generally, presentation of receivable write-offs in the Income Statement should not be reported as extraordinary items, because they are often usual in nature and occur frequently. However, as stated in APB #30, para. 23, write-offs or write-downs of assets can be included in extraordinary items if they are a direct result of an expropriation.

## #20-62...Accounting for Contract Repudiation and License Cancellations

The accounting for these political risks would generally follow the same principles as those stated for uncollectible receivables.

## #20-63...Accounting for Currency Inconvertibility

Deposits in foreign countries subject to immediate and unrestricted withdrawal qualify as cash. However, where the currency held in a foreign country is blocked or otherwise restricted as to use or withdrawal, together with cash in closed banks, it should be designated as claims or receivables of a current or noncurrent character. It should be reported subject to allowances for loss on their realization. Where losses of foreign currencies have occurred, they should be recorded in the books of account as losses as per ARB #43, Chapter 12, "Foreign Operations and Foreign Exchange," as was the case with the Stanwick Corp. in the Iranian inconvertibility situation.

## #20-64...Accounting for Letters of Credit

The accounting treatment for a potential calling of a letter of credit will depend upon the assessment by management of the probability and estimatability of the political risk loss occurring. If the company management thinks a loss is probable, as in the Gilbert Assoc. case with Iran, an entry should be made for a loss accrual.

Where management does not think the potential calling of a letter of credit has a determinable outcome, or is not material to the financial position, footnote disclosure of the loss contingency should be made. In such case the loss should not be accrued.

#20-65...Summary of Accounting Principles for
         Political Risk Losses

The foregoing principles recommended for the five classes of political risk losses may be summarized in Figure 20-5, as per doctoral dissertation of Dr. Mark Holtzblatt, 1984, University of Arkansas.

VALUATION OF EXPROPRIATION LOSSES

#20-66...Methods of Valuation of Expropriated Property

Four methods of valuation of expropriated property have been used in practice: Fair Market Value; Going Concern Value; Replacement Cost; and Book Value.

#20-67...Fair Market Value

In his DICTIONARY FOR ACCOUNTANTS, 5th Ed., 1975, Kohler defines fair market value as "the amount at which a seller willing to sell at a fair price and a buyer willing to buy at a fair price will trade." The difficulty with using the fair market value concept in expropriation cases is the absence of a market for the usual type of investment, in addition to being vague. Because there are seldom sales of similar enterprises to be used for comparison, market value is rarely a directly ascertainable amount.

#20-68...Going Concern Value

Because the going concern method attempts to measure earning power, it encompasses elements such as loss of future profits which may be based on projections of past earnings or estimates of future earnings. Thus in cases where an investment has a limited history of operating results, or where expropriation occurs after significant costs have been incurred but before a revenue-generating stage is reached, the going concern method is impracticable. In the article "The United States Government Perspective on Expropriation and Investment In Developing Countries," in Vol. 9, 1976, of the VANDERBILT JOURNAL OF TRANSNA-

FIGURE 20-5

SUMMARY OF ACCOUNTING PRINCIPLES FOR POLITICAL RISK LOSSES

| Type of Political Risk Loss | | Recommended Accounting Treatment | Authority | Cases |
|---|---|---|---|---|
| (I) EXPROPRIATION | A. Probable and Estimatable | Dr., Expropriation Loss Cr., Reserve for Expropriation Loss (contra-asset) Dr., Expropriation Loss Cr., Assets Involved | FASB #5, para. 8 | Iranian Cases Sedco Corp. Ensearch Reading and Bates Standard Oil (Indiana) Dow Chemical |
| | | Classify as Extraordinary Loss if Material | APB #30 para. 23 | |
| | B. Either Not Imminent or Not Estimatable | No entry, but footnote disclosure should be made | FASB #5, para. 10 | |
| (II) UNCOLLECTIBLE RECEIVABLES | | Accrue extraordinary expense if condition A. above is met | FASB #5, para. 22 | Electronic Data Systems Flexi-Van |
| | | Classify as Extraordinary if material | APB #30, para. 23 | |
| | | If condition B. exists, no entry, but footnote disclosure is needed | FASB #5, para. 10 | |
| (III) LICENSE CANCELLATION OR CONTRACT REPUDIATION | | Similar to Uncollectible Receivables treatment | Same as above | Watkins-Johnson National Homes |
| (IV) CURRENCY INCONVERTIBILITY | | Designate the blocked currency as claims or receivables of a current or non-current character or make accrual for known loss | ARB #43, Ch. 12 | Stanwick Corporation |
| (V) ARBITRARY CALLINGS OF LETTERS OF CREDIT | | Accrue a loss, or disclose Letter of Credit situation in the footnotes, depending upon whether condition A. or B. above is met. | | Gilbert Associates Rockford International |

Source: Adapted from material in doctoral dissertation of Dr. Mark Holtzblatt, 1984, University of Arkansas.

TIONAL LAW, p. 519, Richard J. Smith points out that the "going concern method of valuation is vulnerable to governmental actions which adversely affect profitability, such as increased taxes, threat of cancellation of contractual or concessionary rights, or withdrawals of privileges."

### #20-69...Replacement Cost

This method generally produces results which are at least relatively equitable from expropriation to expropriation, and is more simple to apply than the going concern method. However, because it fails to take into account the expropriated firm's earning potential, the amount of compensation will be less than that under the going concern method. The investor will therefore find it to be inadequate. Nevertheless it may yield a greater figure than the book value method, which may make it unacceptable to the expropriating state.

### #20-70...Book Value

This method values the physical assets of the enterprise at the cost of acquisition less depreciation. The book value is easily determinable and thereby enables the investor to know at all times what the extent of his investment in the foreign country is. To the investor, the obvious objection of the book value method is that as the time increases between the launching of the enterprise and the expropriation, the book value of a successful enterprise is likely to bear less relation to the value of the enterprise at the time of expropriation with its concomitant value as an income-generating force.

In the article "Book Values in Nationalization Settlements," in the UNIVERSITY OF VIRGINIA PRESS, 1973, Vol. II, page 51, Joseph McCosker states:

Generally accepted principles of accounting result in book values that normally are less than the fair values of the assets of nationalized companies. In a few instances the book value is greater than the fair value of a company's assets. *** Overall, generally accepted principles of accounting result in a book value of owners' equity that usually is less than fair value, occasionally is greater than fair value, and only by coincidence is equal to fair value. Book value is not intended to be an equitable basis for settling nationalization claims and should not be used for that purpose.

The Net Book Value is generally regarded as the best standard for the purpose of valuation by the less developed countries. Such countries claim that payment of full market value for nationalized properties would result in restraining them from exercising their sovereign and legitimate rights to reorganize their own economic system.

On the other hand, the fair market value of assets is regarded as a typical notion of laissez-faire economies. Thus it
has been a longstanding and continuing position of the U.S.
government that payment of fair market value is required by
international law, calculated on the basis that the expropriatory act neither has been threatened or occurred. Such market
value is best approximated by the going concern method. The
rationale for the U.S. position is that inadequately compensat-
ed expropriations constitute a major threat to private international investment flows. Private investors come from environ-
ments in which private property rights are recognized and assured, and will not continue to put their assets at risk in
countries in which these rights are not respected.

## POLITICAL CLASSIFICATION OF SOURCES OF INTERNATIONAL ACCOUNTING

### #20-71...World Politics Arena of Accounting

In concluding the discussion of international political accounting, in Chapters 19 and 20, it should be observed that the
sources of international accounting as discussed in Chapter 2
may be classified on a world politics basis. In the article
"Accounting in the Arena of World Politics," by Lane Daley and
Gerhard Mueller, JOURNAL OF ACCOUNTANCY, Feb. 1982, pp. 40-50,
the writers point up the "crosscurrents in the activities of
international standard-setting." The article begins:

It is no longer any secret that the affairs of accounting are inextricably intertwined with politics. Within the
profession relatively mundane items have become charged with
political emotions. Their respective resolutions will be
influenced heavily by political processes. Unparalleled in
intensity of politicization is the matter of accounting
standard-setting.

From a political perspective, national financial accounting standard-setting the world over occurs from four
different baselines: (1) The purely political approach, as
found predominantly in France and West Germany. Here national legislative action decrees accounting standards. (2) The
private professional approach, exemplified by Australia,
Canada, and the U.K. In these cases, financial accounting
standards are set and enforced by private professional actions only. (3) The public/private mixed approach, for which
the U.S. is the leading example and which countries like
Japan appear to be emulating. Here standards are basically
set by private sector bodies which behave as though they
were public agencies and whose standards are enforced
through governmental actions. (4) The broadly mixed system,
like that in the Netherlands, where not only accounting pro-

FIGURE 20-6

SELECTED REPRESENTATION ON INTERNATIONAL
STANDARD-SETTING BODIES BY INDIVIDUAL COUNTRY

| Country | AAC | AFA | CAPA | EEC | UEC | AIC | IASC | IFAC | OECD | UN** |
|---|---|---|---|---|---|---|---|---|---|---|
| **6 Group representation** | | | | | | | | | | |
| Canada | - | - | X | - | - | X | X | X | X | X |
| France | - | - | - | X | X | - | X | X | X | X |
| Germany | - | - | - | X | X | - | X | X | X | X |
| Italy | - | - | - | X | X | - | X | X | X | X |
| Netherlands | - | - | - | X | X | - | X | X | X | X |
| Great Britain | - | - | - | X | X | - | X | X | X | X |
| United States | - | - | X | - | - | X | X | X | X | X |
| **5 Group representation** | | | | | | | | | | |
| Belgium | - | - | - | X | X | - | X | X | X | - |
| Denmark | - | - | - | X | X | - | X | X | X | - |
| Ireland | - | - | - | X | X | - | X | X | X | - |
| Japan | - | - | X | - | - | - | X | X | X | X |
| Luxembourg | - | - | - | X | X | - | X | X | X | - |
| Norway | - | - | - | - | X | - | X | X | X | X |
| Philippines | - | X | X | - | - | - | X | X | - | X |
| **4 Group representation** | | | | | | | | | | |
| Australia | - | - | X | - | - | - | X | X | X | - |
| Brazil | - | - | - | - | - | X | X | X | - | X |
| Finland | - | - | - | - | X | - | X | X | X | - |
| Greece | - | - | - | - | X | - | X | X | X | - |
| India | - | X | X | - | - | - | - | X | - | X |
| Malaysia | - | X | X | - | - | X | X | X | - | - |
| Mexico | - | - | - | - | - | - | X | X | - | X |
| New Zealand | - | - | X | - | - | - | X | X | X | - |
| Nigeria | X | - | - | - | - | X | X | X | - | X |
| Panama | - | - | - | - | - | X | X | X | - | X |

3 Group
representation

| | | | | | | | | | | |
|---|---|---|---|---|---|---|---|---|---|---|
| Pakistan | - | - | x | - | - | - | x | x | - | x |
| Portugal | - | - | - | - | x | - | x | x | x | - |
| Singapore | - | x | x | - | - | - | x | x | - | - |
| Spain | - | - | - | - | x | - | x | x | x | - |
| Sweden | - | - | - | - | x | - | x | x | x | - |
| Argentina | - | - | - | - | - | x | - | x | - | x |
| Bangladesh | - | - | x | - | - | - | x | x | - | - |
| Cyprus | - | - | - | - | - | - | x | x | - | x |
| Dominican Republic | - | - | - | - | - | x | - | - | - | - |
| Fiji | - | - | x | - | - | - | x | x | - | x |
| Iceland | - | - | - | - | x | - | - | x | x | - |
| Sri Lanka | - | - | x | - | - | - | x | x | - | - |
| Thailand | - | x | x | - | - | - | - | x | - | - |
| Representatives | 1 | 5 | 14 | 9 | 16 | 7 | 32 | 37 | 21 | 19 |
| Total number of representations in body | 23 | 5 | 18 | 9 | 18 | 21 | 42 | 53 | 23 | 30 |

Adapted from United Nations Report E/C.10/AC.3/7 of September 9, 1980. Second
session of the Ad Hoc Intergovernmental Working Group on International Standards
of Accounting and Reporting-Commission on Transnational Corporations-UN Economic
and Social Council.
**Member of the UN intergovernmental working group

Source: Page 43, JOURNAL OF ACCOUNTANCY (Feb. 1982), "Accounting in the
Arena of World Politics," by Lane Daley and Gerhard Mueller.
Reprinted with permission. Copyright © 1982 by the American
Institute of Certified Public Accountants, Inc. Opinions expressed in the JOURNAL OF ACCOUNTANCY are those of editors and
contributors. Publication in the JOURNAL OF ACCOUNTANCY does
not constitute endorsement by the AICPA or its committees.

fessionals and governmental agencies, but also labor unions, industry and trade associations take an active direct hand in setting and enforcing accounting standards. No wonder, then, that the results of these various national standard-setting activities are heterogeneous and often contradictory. This is a major reason why international political attention is being visited on accounting. This is seen by many as a failure of underlying technical processes and full justification for political intervention.

Accounting standard-setting efforts are taking place in three major international arenas. The first arena is composed of international political bodies such as the U.N., OECD, EEC, and the African Accounting Council (AAC). These agencies seek to formulate requirements in a purely political manner. The selection process to choose an individual to represent a country is not based on accounting expertise but on political considerations. The second arena consists of the private standard-setting boards whose representation is from national professional accounting groups. The IASC and the Association of Southeast Asian Federation of Accountants (AFA) are in this group. The third arena consists of international professional accounting organizations that deal with various professional issues, including the IFAC, UEC, and IAA.

In all cases there is a long way to go. Formal ties between international and national governments are necessary if international standard-setters are to develop police powers to enforce their own recommendations. Greater accounting internationalization is crucial to obtaining any kind of harmonization or synchronization of reporting requirements between nations. The political representation on the various bodies attempting to set standards are presented in a chart <identified here as Figure 20-6>.

### SUMMARY OF FOOTNOTE REFERENCES
(References are to Paragraph #'s)

#20-2  American Society of International Executives, NEWSLETTER (June 1981): 2
#20-3  Reuters News Agency Despatch, London, August 13, 1979
#20-11  Franklin Root in MULTINATIONAL ENTERPRISE IN TRANSITION, ed., A. Kapoor and Phillip Grub, pp. 357-358
#20-13  R.G. Hawkins, N. Mintz, and M. Provissiero, "Government Takeovers of U.S. Foreign Affiliates," JOURNAL OF INTERNATIONAL BUSINESS STUDIES (JIBS) (Spring 1976): 3-16. Reprinted with permission.
#20-16  Reuters News Agency Despatch, CHICAGO TRIBUNE (Feb.19, 1979)
#20-17  American Society of International Executives, NEWSLETTER (Winter 1982-1983): 1

#20-19 R.C. Longworth, "Political Losses in Iran," CHICAGO TRIBUNE (February 23, 1979)
#20-19 Gerald West, OPIC
#20-20 Janet Key, "Iranian Political Loss Consequences," CHICAGO TRIBUNE (July 23, 1979)
#20-20 Francis J. Corbett, Marsh & McLennan
#20-21 Charles Liotta, Marsh & McLennan
#20-22 Janet Key, op. cit.
#20-23 Liotta, op. cit.
#20-24 "World Report on Extent of Political Hazard," CHICAGO TRIBUNE (August 20, 1979)
#20-30 R.B. Stobaugh, "How to Analyze Foreign Investment Climates," HARVARD BUSINESS REVIEW (Sept-Oct 1969): 100-108
#20-30 R.J. Rummel and D.A. Heenan, "How Multinationals Analyze Political Risk," HARVARD BUSINESS REVIEW (Jan-Feb 1978): 67-76
#20-34 Harald Knudsen, "Explaining the National Propensity to Expropriate: An Ecological Approach," JOURNAL OF INTERNATIONAL BUSINESS STUDIES (JIBS) (Spring 1974): 51-71
#20-37 JOURNAL OF ACCOUNTANCY (March 1976): 28
#20-39 American Management Assn., "Business & Society, 1976-2000"
#20-41 George Coombe, Jr., "Codes of Conduct for Transnational Corporations—-Signals of Public Expectations," p. 15, address to International Bar Assn., W. Berlin, Aug. 1980
#20-44 OECD, "Code of Conduct for Multinational Enterprises," June 1976
#20-45 "Antitrusters Build Bridge Between Germany and US," BUSINESS EUROPE (July 16, 1976): 228-229
#20-48 "Privatization: Less Government, Better Services?", Coopers & Lybrand, EXECUTIVE ALERT NEWSLETTER (Nov. 1983); EXECUTIVE ALERT NEWSLETTER (June 1984): 1-3
#20-50 Ibid. (June 1984): 1-3
#20-52 Ibid.
#20-53 Arpan and Radebaugh, INTERNATIONAL ACCOUNTING AND MULTINATIONAL ENTERPRISES (Warren, Gorham & Lamont,1981),pp.370-371
#20-55 ARB #43, Chapter 12, para. 6
#20-56 FASB #5, ACCOUNTING FOR CONTINGENCIES
#20-58 SEC GUIDES #1 and #22
#20-60 FASB #5, op. cit.; APB #18, para 14; APB #30, para. 23
#20-61 FASB #5, Ibid.; APB #30, para. 23
#20-63 ARB #43, Chapter 12, FOREIGN OPERATIONS AND FOREIGN EXCHANGE
#20-65 Dr. Mark Holtzblatt, "International Political Risk Accounting," doctoral dissertation, Univ. of Arkansas, 1984
#20-67 Eric Kohler, DICTIONARY FOR ACCOUNTANTS, 5th ed., 1975
#20-68 Richard J. Smith, "The United States Government Perspective on Expropriation and Investment in Developing Countries," VANDERBILT JOURNAL OF TRANSNATIONAL LAW, Vol. 9 (1976): 519
#20-70 Joseph McCosker, "Book Values in Nationalization Settlements, UNIVERSITY OF VIRGINIA PRESS, Vol. II (1973): 51
#20-71 Lane Daley and Gerhard Mueller, "Accounting in the Arena of World Politics," JOURNAL OF ACCOUNTANCY (Feb. 1982): 40-50. Reprinted with permission. Copyright © 1982 by the American

Institute of Certified Public Accountants, Inc. Opinions
expressed in the JOURNAL OF ACCOUNTANCY are those of editors
and contributors. Publication in the JOURNAL OF ACCOUNTANCY
does not constitute endorsement by the AICPA or its committees.


## BIBLIOGRAPHY

Bradley, David G.    "Managing Against Expropriation," HARVARD BUSI-
    NESS REVIEW, 55 (July-August 1977): 75-83
Brewer, Thomas L.    "Political Risk Assessment    for    Foreign Direct
    Investment Decisions," COLUMBIA JOURNAL  OF WORLD BUSINESS,
    16 (Spring 1981): 5-12
Choi, Frederick. "Political Risk--An Accounting Challenge," MANAGE-
    MENT ACCOUNTING, 60 (June 1979): 17-20
Haendel, West, and Meadow. OVERSEAS INVESTMENT AND POLITICAL RISK.
    Monograph Series No. 21.   Philadelphia: Foreign Policy Re-
    search Institute, 1975, pp. 70-71
Jones,  Randall J.  "A Model for Predicting Expropriation  in Latin
    America," COLUMBIA  JOURNAL OF WORLD BUSINESS, 15  (Spring
    1980): 74-80
Kline, John.  "Entrapment or Opportunity:  Structuring a Corporate
    Response to International Codes  of Conduct," COLUMBIA JOUR-
    NAL OF WORLD BUSINESS, 15 (Summer 1980): 6-13
Kobrin, Stephen J.   "When Does Political Instability Result in In-
    creased Investment Risk?", COLUMBIA JOURNAL OF  WORLD  BUSI-
    NESS, 13 (Fall 1978): 113-122
McCosker, Joseph S.  "Accounting Valuations in Nationalization Set-
    tlements," JOURNAL OF  INTERNATIONAL  BUSINESS  STUDIES,  4
    (Fall 1973): 15-29
Micallef, Joseph.  "Political Risk Assessment," COLUMBIA JOURNAL OF
    WORLD BUSINESS, 16 (Summer 1981): 47-52
Muller, Maarten. "Compensation for Nationalization," COLUMBIA JOUR-
    NAL OF TRANSNATIONAL LAW, 1 (1981): 35-78
Price Waterhouse, "Codes  of  Conduct for  Multinationals," PRICE
    WATERHOUSE--EEC BULLETIN (June 1977)
Rummel, R.J. and Heenan, David. "How Multinationals Analyze Politi-
    cal Risk," HARVARD BUSINESS REVIEW (Jan-Feb 1978):67-76
Sanderson,  Glen and Varner,  Iris.  "What's Wrong With Corporate
    Codes of Conduct," MANAGEMENT ACCOUNTING (July 1984): 28-35
Shapiro, Alan  C.   "Managing Political  Risk: A  Policy Approach,"
    COLUMBIA JOURNAL OF WORLD BUSINESS, 16 (Fall 1981): 63-70
Stanford  Research Institute, "International  Business Principles--
    Codes, 1975
Stanford Research Institute, "International  Business  Principles--
    Company Codes," 1976
Van  Agtmael, Antoine W.  "How  Business Has Dealt  With  Political
    Risk," FINANCIAL EXECUTIVE, 44 (January 1976): 26-31

## THEORY QUESTIONS
(Question Numbers are Keyed to Text Paragraph #'s)

#20-4 Discuss the nature of Political Risk as it applies to MNCs.

#20-5 Outline the causes of Political Risk.

#20-6 Define Political Risk.

#20-7 Classify Political Risk.

#20-8 Discuss political risk from the viewpoint of Source.

#20-9 Discuss political risk from the viewpoint of Action Taken by the Foreign Country.

#20-10 Discuss political risk from the viewpoint of Degree of Takeover.

#20-11 Discuss political risk from the viewpoint of Effect on Operations.

#20-13 What have been the actual experiences with government takeovers of U.S. foreign affiliates?

#20-15 What techniques have been resorted to to minimize political risk?

#20-16 Discuss the role that Political Risk Insurance plays on MNCs.

#20-17 Who are the leading types of political risk insurers?

#20-19-20. Outline the various ramifications of the Iranian Case.

#20-21 Name and describe the seven categories of political risk coverage.

#20-25-27. Discuss the nature and professional status of the discipline of political risk analysis.

#20-28 Discuss the sources of political risk analysis.

#20-29-32. Briefly explain the four methods of political risk analysis.

#20-37 Discuss the future of political risk analysis.

#20-38 Discuss the various practices that have been resorted to for amelioration of political risks.

#20-39 What is the effect of Codes of Conduct on political risk? Define Codes of Conduct.

#20-42 Classify and describe the 3 types of Codes of Conduct.

#20-43 Discuss the functions and operations of the U.N. Commission on Transnational Corporations.

#20-44 Discuss the functions and operations of the OECD Code of Conduct.

#20-45 Discuss the nature, functions, and operations of Governmental Executive Agreement Codes of Conduct.

#20-46 Discuss the nature and operations of Individual Multinational Corporations Operation Codes.

#20-48-50. What is meant by Privatization? What are the causes of Privatization and what countries have become involved with it?

#20-51-52. What forms have privatization taken and what is the future of privatization?

#20-53 What are the implications of political risk accounting
        and what are the ramifications to the problem of ac-
        counting for political risk?
#20-54-58. Discuss the need for Financial Statement Disclosures
        for political risk including ARB #43, FASB #5, FASB #14,
        and SEC Guides #1 and #22.
#20-59 Classify political risk losses.
#20-65 Summarize the accounting principles for political risk
        losses.
#20-66-70. Make a comparative analysis of the (a) Fair Market
        Value, (b) Going Concern Value, (c) Replacement Cost,
        and (d) Book Value Methods of Valuation of Expropriated
        Property.
#20-71 Make a comparative analysis and critique of the politi-
        cal classification of the sources of international ac-
        counting with the sources of international accounting
        outlined in Chapter 2.

## EXERCISES

### EX-20-1 (CPA EXAM, 11/81, THEORY, #14)
A threat of expropriation of assets which is reasonably possible, and for which the amount of loss can be reasonably estimated, is an example of
  a. A loss contingency that should be disclosed, but not ac-
     crued.
  b. A loss contingency that should be accrued and disclosed.
  c. An appropriation of retained earnings against which losses
     should be charged.
  d. A general business risk which should not be disclosed.

### EX-20-2 (CPA EXAM, 11/79, THEORY, #16)
In order to be classified as an extraordinary item in the income statement, an event or transaction should be
  a. Infrequent and material; but it need not be unusual in
     nature.
  b. Unusual in nature and material; but it need not be infre-
     quent.
  c. Unusual in nature, infrequent, and material.
  d. Unusual in nature and infrequent; but it need not be
     material.

### EX-20-3 (CPA EXAM, 5/80, THEORY, #25)
Reserves for contingencies for general or unspecified business
risks should
  a. Be accrued in the financial statements and disclosed in
     the notes thereto.
  b. Not be accrued in the financial statements but should be
     disclosed in the notes thereto.

c. <u>Not</u> be accrued in the financial statements and need <u>not</u> be disclosed in the notes thereto.

d. Be accrued in the financial statements but need <u>not</u> be disclosed in the notes thereto.

## EX-20-4 (CPA EXAM, 11/80, THEORY, #3a)

Loss contingencies may exist for companies.

**Required**:

1. What conditions should be met for an estimated loss from a loss contingency to be accrued by a charge to income?

2. When is disclosure required and what disclosure should be made for an estimated loss from a loss contingency that need not be accrued by a charge to income?

## PROBLEMS

## P-20-1 (CPA EXAM, 5/78, PRAC. II, #6)

Brower Corp. owns a manufacturing plant in the country of Oust. On Dec. 31, 1977, the plant had a book value of $5,000,000 and an estimated fair market value of $8,000,000. The government of Oust has clearly indicated that it will expropriate the plant during the coming year and will reimburse Brower for 40% of the plant's estimated fair market value. What journal entry should Brower make on Dec. 31, 1977, to record the intended expropriation?

a. Estimated loss on expropriation
    of foreign plant                        $1,800,000
  Allowance for estimated loss
    on foreign plant                                    $1,800,000

b. Estimated loss on expropriation
    of foreign plant                        $3,000,000
  Allowance for estimated loss
    on foreign plant                                    $3,000,000

c. Receivable due from foreign
    government                              $3,200,000
  Investment in foreign plant                           $3,200,000

d. Loss on expropriation of
    foreign plant                           $1,800,000
  Receivable due from foreign
    government                              $3,200,000
  Investment in foreign plant                           $5,000,000

## P-20-2

Sedco, Inc., a U.S. corporation, conducted contract drilling, pipeline construction, and ship repair operations in Iran through Iranian subsidiaries and branches. The operations were terminated due to the Iranian Revolution in Dec. 1978. Sedco described its intentions for future action and its accounting

treatment of the situation in the footnotes to its financial
statements as follows:

In the opinion of management, substantial losses will probably be involved, which is unlikely to be resolved in the
near future. Three steps of action were taken by Sedco: (1)
Sedco accounting policy was changed from one of consolidating the Iranian subsidiary and branches to one of reflecting
its investments in these entities and the results of their
operations by the equity method; (2) made a provision for
losses in Iran of $50,000,000 after income tax effects of
$9,190,000 to state investments in those entities at esti-
mated realizable value; and (3) recorded a liability for its
guarantees of the Eurocurrency loans of an Iranian associated company.

**Required**:
a. What accounting rule was Sedco following regarding consolidation of statements of foreign subsidiaries with the statements of U.S. companies?

b. What FASB rule was Sedco following in its write-down of
its investments to estimated realizable value?

c. Assuming Income Taxes Payable of $6,602,000 and Deferred
Income Taxes of $2,588,000, what journal entry did Sedco make
for the expropriation losses?

d. What journal entry was made to record payments during
1979 in the sum of $461,000 charged to the Reserve for the Loss
in Iran?

e. What rule for Reporting the Results of Operations did Sedco follow with respect to classification of the expropriation
loss?

f. Sedco's books indicated the Equity in Net Assets as
$60,729,000 as of Consolidated Balance Sheet of June 30, 1979.
How would the resultant realizable value of the Iranian assets
be presented on the balance sheet?

**P-20-3**
As a result of the turmoil in Iran, early in 1979 a shipping
line customer of Flexi-Van, serving Iran, suspended operations.
The customer owed Flexi-Van $840,000 and held approximately
2,200 units with a book value of approximately $7,000,000
slightly over one-third of which, in terms of dollars, were in
Iran. To recognize the situation, Flexi-Van recorded a provision in the 4th quarter of 1978 of $3,000,000 to reflect an
increase in its Reserve for Doubtful Accounts of $600,000 and a
write-down of Revenue Equipment of $2,400,000.
**Required**:
What entry was made by Flexi-Van to record the Uncollectible
Receivable and write-down of the Revenue Equipment?

**P-20-4**
In 1979, Granger Associates suspended work on a long-term contract for the National Iranian Radio and Television owing to the political instability in Iran. Granger Associates established a provision in the sum of $2,276,357 for estimated losses on the contract.
**Required**:
On what statement for what year should the loss appear and under what classification?

**P-20-5**
National Homes received a purchase contract in Oct. 1978 for 500 homes to be produced for ultimate delivery to the Iranian Ministry of Housing for $20,000,000. The letters of credit for which the amount was payable expired in Aug. 1979, under which National Homes had placed orders with suppliers for materials to be used prior to June 1979. In late 1978, Iranian Ministry of Housing notified National Homes that they were unable to proceed on the contract. Being unable to determine whether the contract would continue, National Homes set up a provision for a possible loss of $800,000 as a separate item in the income statement.
**Required**:
   1. What journal entry was made to reflect the loss?
   2. How would the loss be reported on the income statement under what accounting regulation, and what does it provide?

**P-20-6**
Stanwick Corp. received payments from the Iranian Navy in late 1978 and early 1979 totaling 60,950,000 Iranian Rials which were deposited in two Iranian banks. When the change in government took place in Iran, subsequent requests by Stanwick Corp. that such funds be transferred to its bank in Wash., D.C. were denied. Although Stanwick believed that such bank accounts remained intact, they decided on Jan. 31, 1980, to write-off the dollar value of such funds together with the value of cash in the Tehran office in the sum of $887,000.
**Required**:
   1. Assuming that in addition to Cash, other accounts that were affected by the currency inconvertibility were Accounts Receivable, Unbilled Receivables, and Fixed Assets, prepare the journal entry to record the loss.
   2. How would the loss be shown on the income statement?

**P-20-7**
The Gilbert Corp. sustained losses related to outstanding letters of credit. In the 4th quarter of 1979, Gilbert Corp. established a provision for loss of $2,303,000 on outstanding letters of credit which had been issued to guarantee the return

of advance payments for the projects in case performance failed
to meet contract terms. Gilbert management decided that the
company provide for anticipated losses related to the letters
of credit.
**Required**:
What journal entry did Gilbert Corporation make to record the
loss related to the letters of credit?


**P-20-8**
Like the Gilbert Corp. in P-20-7, the Rockwell Intrnl. Corp.
also sustained a loss related to outstanding letters of credit. As of Sept. 30, 1980, the company had receivables and inventories of $33 million outstanding and cash advances from
Iranian government agencies secured by letters of credit of
some $20 million. There were also outstanding performance guar-
antees secured by bank letters of credit in the sum of $23 mil-
lion. In April 1980 Iranian banks demanded payment under certain letters of credit amounting to $30 million. Rockwell filed
suit in New York to restrain the Iranian banks from presentment
of further demands and from honoring the letters of credit.
Management did not believe that an adverse resolution of the
matters related thereto would have a material effect on the
financial position of the company. Rockwell decided not to accrue a loss related to the letters of credit but to report the
loss in the footnotes to the financial statement.
**Required**:
Prepare an extensive narrative discussion of the situation outlined above to be presented in the footnotes to the financial
statements of Rockwell International.

# International Inflation Accounting Principles

## HISTORICAL ASPECTS OF INFLATION ACCOUNTING

### #21-1....Inflation Accounting Beginnings

In an article published in the ACCOUNTING HISTORIANS NOTE-
BOOK, Spring 1982, "Henry Sweeney and Stabilized Accounting,"
pages 17-20, Prof. Walker Fesmire indicates:

Since the mid-1960s, inflation has been exacting a heavy
toll from American business and the American public. During
this period the accounting profession has studied the problem of price-level changes and has issued many pronouncements upon the subject. Thus, the public assumes that the
theory of handling price-level changes is a recent development. This is an incorrect view, as accounting theorists
were concerned with and were writing about the problem as
far back as 1920. One of these early individuals, who considered price-level accounting in depth, was Henry Sweeney.

During the 1920s Sweeney reworked and consolidated the
ideas of the Europeans, who wrote during the post World War
I period, into a proposed method of inflation accounting
for America. His proposal was contained in a group of articles which later became his book, STABILIZED ACCOUNTING
(1936). Sweeney's association with the subject of stabilized
accounting extended over a period of 42 years. His involvement was intense during the early years of his career but
diminished to little involvement after 1936 because inflation was not then a problem facing American society.

It was on the basis of the experience and practice following
World War I in Germany, which experienced drastic and devastat-
ing inflation, that Sweeney's thinking was oriented to inflation accounting, which was ignored by the practitioners. His
views were published in a series of articles in the ACCOUNTING
REVIEW in the 1920s and 1930s.

## CAUSES OF INFLATION ACCOUNTING

### #21-2....Historical Cost and Inflation

Because the underlying basis for accounting reporting is historical cost, viz., that all values are entered on the books as of the date on which the transaction takes place, inflation is a factor in accounting reporting. If the dollar were like other immutable measurement units used in other areas of endeavor, such as the yard or the pound in figuring distances and weights, then the problem of inflation would not arise. However, it is common knowledge that the dollar does fluctuate in value and is not a stable unit. This has caused concern among accountants regarding the reliability of financial reporting resulting from the variances in the value of the dollar. Accounting reporting has ostensibly been predicated upon the principle that the monetary unit is stable in value and that such value must be recorded at historical rates.

### #21-3....Foreign Exchange Fluctuations and Inflation

In Chapter 5 the discussion of Foreign Exchange centered around the fact that it is in the nature of a commodity and, like all commodities, fluctuates in value. Much of such value fluctuations is tied into the inflation factor which was there discussed showing the causes of inflation and their impact on the value of foreign currency. Thus one of the most important challenges to be faced by accountants in the decade of the 1980s will be to develop new accounting techniques and principles to bring historical accounting numerical financial values into accord with their true economic values.

While there have been extreme cases of inflation in past history (most notable in the Great Depression years in Germany, when million Mark notes were disparagingly used to paper walls, and in the 1970s in Brazil), the U.S. dollar over the years has been operating on a relatively stable basis. So long as prices remain stable, or the degree of inflation is mild, the historical cost basis of recording accounting is acceptable and satisfactory. However, where inflation attains a degree of being extreme, the result of the use of historical costing may prove distorting, misrepresentative, and inaccurate.

## HISTORICAL VERSUS INFLATION REPORTING

### #21-4....Basic Objection to Historical Cost Reporting

One deleterious effect of such reporting in the face of inflation may be the representation of what are known as ILLUSORY PROFITS. Very marked illustrations of these may be (a) overinflated values of inventories resulting in profits computed as the difference between the cost of the inventory and the inflated increase in its value; which (b) as a corollary, results in what is termed income tax but actually is taxation of capital; and (c) what is tantamount to a distribution of capital which in reality is denominated as dividends, supposedly a distribution of earnings. Eventually the inflation channels in the various areas become siphoned into the overall profits report, which through higher values causes one of the most potent forces in the inflation process, viz., increases in wages for production.

## #21-5....Effects of Omission on Inflation Reporting

Because of the distortions that may result from the historical reporting in accounting currently in use, several very broad serious consequences may result. First, since accounting has been said to be the language of business and the financial statements are the language that in great measure report the results upon which managerial decision-making and action is taken, because of the resultant distortions, there could quite well be a misapplication and/or misallocation of funds toward future projections of business operations, which may produce disastrous results. Second, a misstatement of corporate liquidity might well result from a distorted statement, which could affect the ability of the corporation to pay its debts and be the cause of an economic dislocation. Thirdly, if the presumption is that the standard of living of a nation is expected to keep rising, then the overstatement of profits flowing from inflation could well produce a failure to maintain the reasonable rates required for capital formation, resulting in a decline in the standard of living of the nation. The implications are not only economic in nature but may have a serious impact on the Social Responsibility factor as well.

## #21-6....Inflation Accounting Study Recommendations

At the 4th International Conference on Accounting Education (1977), Prof. Raymond J. Chambers indicates that a failure to take the matter of inflation into consideration reveals weaknesses in the educational system in three areas. He points out:

In the first place accounting is largely based on opinion rather than proven scientific fact. *** This attitude should not be promulgated any more at universities and in textbooks because it undermines the RAISON D'ETRE of accounting itself.

The second point is that we know too little about inflation, what it is and its effects. *** The current accounting systems do not pay attention to the changes in the value of

the money  unit and of prices although we have been aware of
the fact for a long while that these changes do occur.

A  third point  is that accountants are not fully  aware
that balance sheets, assets, net worths and debt ratios represent aggregates. *** We do not pay enough attention to the
nature  of the aggregates.  There is the calculated, and the
true  replacement, and the selling prices of things.  But in
inflation accounting all of them are used side by side.  The
resulting information is  confusing and leads to false  conclusions.

These  problems  have  become more  obvious to  us  only
through the sometimes very high  and constant inflation rate
of recent years.  Accounting education will  not free itself
from its dilemma of contradictory methods and  doctrines until it  studies these fundamental  issues  more closely  and
develops a scientific accounting theory.
What Prof. Chambers is intimating  quite clearly is that inflation accounting must be  reckoned with  in any future presentation of accounting studies.

## #21-7....Early Experiences With Inflation Accounting

Price index adjusted figures have been used in  a  number of
countries in Europe,  Asia and South America for  over two decades.  There have been several causal factors that demanded the
use of  the price-index adjusted figures, among the more important of which have been (a) macro-economic considerations, such
as measurement of rates of return on invested capital in industries vital to economic development of a country; (b) relationship of  relevant price-level  changes in  industries  vital to
national  defense;  (c) evaluating the  need for export  credit
guarantees; (d) for the purposes of tax calculations; (e) proper determination of financial losses from international investments  and trade.  These various specific governmental economic
policies resulting from macroeconomic considerations have caused many of the governments to  impose upon such business enterprises various adjustments for price level in their  accounting
procedures.

## #21-8...Inflation Accounting Resulting From
## Macroeconomic Considerations

In the  late 1950s  the PLAN  COMPTABLE  GENERAL, a complete
uniform plan  of accounting, was promulgated in France and specified groups of  enterprises were required to  employ the PLAN
in their  accounting.  The macro aspect  results from the  fact
that one group  included  all enterprises which were  receiving
government subsidies exceeding the amounts  stipulated by  the
law. While the PLAN adheres to the rules of historical cost, it

allows price-level adjustments for raw materials inventories permitting the use of reserves created by asset revaluations allowing for substantial adjustments before the cutoff date of January 1, 1961.

Another macro situation existed from 1938 to 1951 in Sweden, whose national economic policies attempted to give a firm economic foundation to its enterprises by permitting capital replacement and inventory reserves, and (as pointed out in the chapter on Macro-Accounting) permitted Swedish enterprises to use any method or rate of depreciation which was completely free. Sweden has been extremely sensitive to inflationary price tendencies since the end of World War II.

When Russia found that its outdated methods of bookkeeping in the early years of the 1960 decade resulted in a complete misrepresentation of the values of assets stated in its accounts, it decided that they failed to serve important national policies effectively. This resulted in a complete revaluation of the accounts, bringing them in line with realistic current figures. Under the macro approach, any system of periodic value appraisals is acceptable, whether historical cost, price-index adjusted historical cost, or current replacement value.

## #21-9....Inflation Accounting Following World War II

In many countries the purchasing power of money deteriorated so much after World War II that the historical costs carried on the books were either misrepresentative or misleading. To make these values more realistic, it was necessary to adjust the figures by price indexes which were usually decreed to be employed by a government agency. This was particularly the case in a number of South American and Far Eastern countries. The most typical case was Brazil, where during the 1950s the unit of currency (the Cruzeiro) had sustained substantial deterioration in its purchasing power over an extended period of time. This resulted in the necessity of taking into account the very severe price-level changes of the Cruzeiro in order to have any meaning. Thus such effects of price-level changes are stated in supplementary financial statements. No single method of showing price-level changes is required in Brazil, although the basis generally used is the price coefficients allowable by the government for income tax purposes. In some cases the financial statements are adjusted directly according to price-level changes, in which case two sets of statements are prepared--the original on the historical cost basis and the supplementary containing adjustments for price-level changes.

Another severe case of hyperinflation was that which occurred in Germany resulting from the war-torn economy in the late 1940s, making historical cost financial statements practically useless. In June 1948 a major currency reform permitted all

enterprises to revalue their assets at current replacement
costs and depreciation was allowed to be taken, for financial
reporting purposes as well as tax purposes, on the revaluation
amounts. Similar statutes were enacted in France, Italy, Austria and Japan which permitted the companies to decide which
assets they wished to revalue.

The continent of South America has been afflicted with a
severe case of inflation, affecting most of the countries. In
Brazil, inflation has been so rampant that the government requires by law that companies revalue their assets each year
using a price index supplied by the government with depreciation allowed on the revaluation amounts. In addition, Brazil
regards these as authentic and primary statements and not as
supplementary statements. As is the case in Brazil, in Uruguay, where revaluation is not mandatory, it is regarded as a
generally accepted practice, although qualified opinions are
generally rendered where the revaluations and depreciation tak-
en thereon are not recorded in the financial statements. Annual
restatements of fixed assets for tax and financial reporting
became mandatory in Argentina in 1972. And in 1973 they were
required in Chile to be expanded to cover all real assets in
1975.

Outside South America, occasional revaluations occur in such
countries as Australia, Belgium, Canada, Denmark, Norway, Swed-
en and Great Britain. In a SURVEY IN 46 COUNTRIES, made by
Price Waterhouse, examples of inflation accounting are presented for such countries as Argentina, Belgium, Brazil, Chile,
Denmark, Ethiopia, Jamaica, Netherlands, Pakistan, South Africa, Switzerland, Trinidad, Uruguay and Zaire.

## INFLATION ACCOUNTING IN THE 1970s

### #21-10...Inflation Accounting in the United Kingdom

The recent history of inflation accounting originated in
England with the publication of Exposure Draft #8 (ED8) issued
by the Accounting Standards Steering Committee (ASSC). Under
ED8, listed companies were to have their annual reports include
supplementary balance sheets and income statements incorporating General Price Level Adjustments, known as CURRENT PURCHAS-
ING POWER (CPP). ED8 comments were due by July 31, 1973, but in
the last week of July the British government issued a statement
proposing to set up a committee to investigate the matter of
inflation accounting. Early in 1974 such a committee was set up
under the chairmanship of Sir Francis Sandilands, Chairman of
the Commercial Union Assurance Company. Twelve members were

selected but only three were accountants.  Before the committee
took any action, the ASC published the proposed CPP standard in
May 1974, entitled PROVISIONAL STATEMENT OF STANDARD ACCOUNTING
PRACTICE (PSSAP#7), which was similar to ED8.  Subsequently in
September 1975 the Sandilands Report was published, but it dis-
avowed the CPP Method and in its  place espoused a form of  Replacement Accounting called CURRENT COST ACCOUNTING (CCA).   CCA
in  essence provided that all company assets be  revalued regularly and that profit  determination  be  made after deductions
for inventory and depreciation adjustments.  The Sandilands Report recommended that its proposals, which were more far-reaching than those of PSSAP#7, become the standard method of inflation accounting in the United Kingdom.

The  accounting  profession  in Great  Britain supported  the
change from CPP accounting to  CCA as recommended by the Sandilands Committee, and  a Steering Committee under  the chairmanship of Douglas Morpeth, a senior partner of Touche Ross & Co.,
was set  up to establish detailed  proposals  to  carry out the
shift from CPP to CCA.  The recommendations of the Morpeth Committee  were published in December 1976 by the ASSC  taking the
form  of an  Exposure Draft--ED18, which  recommended that  the
changeover from CPP to  CCA take place in four phases beginning
July 1, 1978.  The publication of the Sandilands Report touched
off considerable debate, particularly by  several financial institutions.  They  contended that misleading implications would
result from the  deduction of adjustments for  depreciation and
inventories from  profits with no corresponding  adjustment for
the effects of inflation on monetary  assets  and  liabilities.
This would result in an overstatement  of profits for banks and
other financial  organizations but materially  understated  for
those companies whose liabilities were greater than their monetary assets.

Two  members  of the  Institute of Chartered  Accountants of
England and Wales were  of the opinion  that the switch  to CCA
was proceeding too rapidly.  They persuaded the Institute Council to poll the members for the purpose of passing a resolution
against compulsory adoption of CCA.   Such resolution was passed
in  July 1977.  To counteract the resolution, the ASC appointed
William Hyde, Chief Accountant of Oxford University,  as chairman of a subcommittee to prepare interim proposals for the partial introduction of CCA.   The Hyde subcommittee published its
recommendations  in Nov. 1977 entitled the HYDE GUIDELINES, under which listed  companies were to include  with  their annual
reports, supplementary income statements based on CCA beginning
with  1977.  The Hyde Guidelines  suggested  that  conventional
profits be  reduced by adjustments for depreciation  and inventories in line with the original recommendations of  Sandilands
and Morpeth.  It was also recommended that companies using certain methods should continue to do so, and a significant major-

ity of the large U.K. companies have followed the Hyde Guidelines although individual companies have variations in their
own detailed methods.

The most controversial item in the Hyde Guidelines involves
the recommendation by Phillips & Drew that there be a third
adjustment to take account of companies' GEARING, tantamount
to leverage. Under the preferred method the proportion of the
adjustments for depreciation and inventory financed by net liabilities and not by equity is to be added back to profits; and
where monetary assets exceed liabilities, a deduction is made
from profits based on an appropriate index.

The most recent inflation accounting development in Great
Britain is Exposure Draft 24 (ED24) issued by the ASSC which is
a watered down version of ED18, and in essence follows the Hyde
Guidelines requiring the inflation adjustments to appear in
statements supplementary to the historical statements thereby
requiring two statements. This is illustrated by the published
statement of BRITISH PETROLEUM COMPANY (see Figures 21-1 and
21-2).

The principal difference between ED24 and the Hyde Guidelines is a MONETARY WORKING CAPITAL ADJUSTMENT (MWCA). This
adjustment changes the current-cost profits and loss account by
the amount of the cost of maintaining working capital excluding
inventories in terms of current cost. The result is that the
GEARING ADJUSTMENT takes the total adjustments--the sum of the
depreciation, cost of sales, and monetary working capital--and
reduces the aggregate in the proportion that the net operating
assets are financed by net borrowings. In addition ED24, which
went into effect on Jan. 1, 1980, requires a condensed current-
cost balance sheet and statement of current-cost earnings per
share.

## #21-11...Inflation Accounting in Other Countries

Exposure Drafts and provisional accounting standards similar
to the U.K. recommendations have been provided for in 1978 in
Canada, Australia and New Zealand. The National Council of
Chartered Accountants in South Africa has issued a GUIDELINE
FOR DISCLOSURE OF EFFECTS OF CHANGING PRICES ON FINANCIAL RE-
SULTS. In Japan inflation accounting is being examined, and
Brazilian inflation accounting has been reformed in 1976 and
1978 by refining the recognition of inflation effects through
the MONETARY CORRECTION METHOD, under which price-level restatements are made of both fixed assets and permanent investments as well as deferred expenses and equity accounts. In late
1976 Australia became the first country to promulgate a professional pronouncement adopting current cost measurements.

# INFLATION ACCOUNTING IN THE U.S.

## #21-12...Inflation Accounting in the U.S.

Following in the track of the U.K. experience, and running parallel with it, has been the development of inflation accounting in the U.S. Two bodies have been responsible for setting inflation accounting rules--the SEC and the FASB. The SEC in March 1976 issued ASR 190 on DISCLOSURE OF CERTAIN REPLACEMENT COST DATA. This in effect nullified an exposure draft by the FASB in Dec. 1974 which would have required companies to supplement the historical cost information with price-level data. Under ASR 190, over 1,000 large corporations with revenues exceeding a billion dollars are required to file annual reports that provide the following information: (a) estimated inventory current replacement cost; (b) estimated productive capacity current replacement cost; (c) replacement cost basis for cost of sales; and (d) replacement cost basis of depreciation. This data is to be supplied in Form 10 K; though not required in the annual report to stockholders, about 10% of the companies voluntarily do so. These reports are a valuable source of information because the SEC has set forth a standard format as well as use of standard terminology.

In the wake of the issuance of ASR 190, two exposure drafts were issued by the FASB--one, dated Dec. 1978, entitled FINANCIAL REPORTING AND CHANGING PRICES, and the second, dated March 2, 1979, entitled CONSTANT DOLLAR ACCOUNTING. The two drafts permitted the alternatives between CURRENT VALUE ACCOUNTING and PRICE-LEVEL ACCOUNTING. Under the CURRENT VALUE draft, supplementary partial data is required limited to inventories, fixed assets, cost of sales and depreciation, but excluding marketable securities, equity investments consolidation goodwill, and intangible assets. Under the CONSTANT DOLLAR price-level draft, full prive-level techniques are required for developing disclosures on a selected basis. The matter was definitively settled with the issuance in Sept. 1979 of FASB #33 entitled FINANCIAL REPORTING AND CHANGING PRICES. Standard #33 basically (1) requires only public companies with either inventories and property, plant and equipment, before deducting accumulated depreciation of over 125 million dollars or total assets of over 1 billion dollars, after deducting accumulated depreciation, to issue the required statements; and (2) requires no changes in the basic financial statements but does require supplementary information on the effects of general inflation and on price changes of certain specific types of assets. A discussion of FASB #33 will be presented later in this chapter.

# FIGURE 21-1

## The British Petroleum Company Limited and subsidiary companies

### Group income statement on historical cost basis – Unaudited

$ million

| | July – September 1980 | July – September 1979 | January – September 1980 | January – September 1979 | Year 1979 (Audited) |
|---|---|---|---|---|---|
| **Revenues** | | | | | |
| Sales and operating revenue | 14,283 | 13,663 | 44,750 | 38,828 | 54,265 |
| Deduct: customs duties and sales taxes | 2,804 | 2,710 | 8,424 | 7,744 | 10,664 |
| Net sales and operating revenue | 11,479 | 10,953 | 36,326 | 31,084 | 43,601 |
| Other income | 220 | 232 | 841 | 576 | 784 |
| | 11,699 | 11,185 | 37,167 | 31,660 | 44,385 |
| **Operating and other costs** | | | | | |
| Cost of sales, including freight, processing and manufacturing | 7,887 | 6,197 | 23,355 | 19,130 | 26,983 |
| Distribution, selling, administrative and other expenses | 1,004 | 865 | 2,952 | 2,901 | 4,180 |
| Depreciation and amounts provided | 514 | 399 | 1,508 | 1,257 | 1,826 |
| Interest | 241 | 222 | 762 | 727 | 968 |
| | 9,646 | 7,683 | 28,577 | 24,015 | 33,957 |
| **Income before taxation** | 2,053 | 3,502 | 8,590 | 7,645 | 10,428 |
| Taxation (Note) | 1,377 | 1,800 | 5,239 | 4,077 | 5,416 |
| **Income after taxation** | 676 | 1,702 | 3,351 | 3,568 | 5,012 |
| Minority shareholders' interest | 177 | 359 | 758 | 738 | 1,138 |
| **Net income of the group** | 499 | 1,343 | 2,593 | 2,830 | 3,874 |
| Historical cost earnings per ordinary share | $0·32 | $0·87 | $1·67 | $1·83 | $2·50 |

Reprinted by permission of The British Petroleum Company, p.l.c., London, England.

**Note:**

Due to the uncertainties in computing the charge for taxation for a period of less than a year the amount shown represents the best estimate for the period January – September, and is after giving effect to the recent UK Inland Revenue proposals re stock relief.

The charge for taxation comprises:

| | | | |
|---|---|---|---|
| UK taxation | | | |
| Corporation tax | **717** | 1,106 | 1,527 |
| Overseas tax relief | **(320)** | (521) | (822) |
| Petroleum revenue tax | **397** | 585 | 705 |
| | **2,586** | 1,312 | 1,869 |
| Overseas taxation | **2,983** | 1,897 | 2,574 |
| | **2,256** | 2,180 | 2,842 |
| | **5,239** | 4,077 | 5,416 |

## Group sales figures

| | | | | | |
|---|---|---|---|---|---|
| in thousands of barrels per day* | | | | | |
| Crude oil | **620** | 930 | **666** | 1,163 | 1,071 |
| Petroleum products | **2,210** | 2,482 | **2,391** | 2,590 | 2,617 |
| | **2,830** | 3,412 | **3,057** | 3,753 | 3,688 |
| in millions of tons | | | | | |
| Chemicals | **0·9** | 1·0 | **3·4** | 3·5 | 4·9 |
| Coal | **5·6** | 4·8 | **17·3** | 14·8 | 20·7 |
| in millions of cubic feet per day | | | | | |
| Natural gas | **196** | 292 | **295** | 353 | 332 |

*Conversion of tonnes into barrels has been made at the rate of 7·5 barrels per tonne

FIGURE 21-2

## The British Petroleum Company Limited and subsidiary companies

### Group income statement
### on current cost basis – Unaudited

| $ million | July – September 1980 | 1979 | January – September 1980 | 1979 | Year 1979 |
|---|---|---|---|---|---|
| Income before taxation | **2,053** | 3,502 | **8,590** | 7,645 | 10,428 |
| Interest | **241** | 222 | **762** | 727 | 968 |
| Petroleum revenue tax and producer government taxes | **(1,104)** | (994) | **(3,422)** | (2,708) | (3,600) |
| Historical cost operating result | **1,190** | 2,730 | **5,930** | 5,664 | 7,796 |
| Current cost adjustments | | | | | |
| Cost of sales | **(203)** | 803 | **1,506** | 1,702 | 2,918 |
| Monetary working capital | **(12)** | 69 | **7** | 151 | 244 |
| Depreciation | **277** | 237 | **872** | 738 | 1,047 |
| | **62** | 1,109 | **2,385** | 2,591 | 4,209 |
| Current cost operating result | **1,128** | 1,621 | **3,545** | 3,073 | 3,587 |
| Interest | **241** | 222 | **762** | 727 | 968 |
| Income before taxation | **887** | 1,399 | **2,783** | 2,346 | 2,619 |
| Taxation | **273** | 806 | **1,817** | 1,369 | 1,816 |
| Income after taxation | **614** | 593 | **966** | 977 | 803 |
| Gearing adjustment | **7** | 375 | **686** | 882 | 1,424 |
| Minority shareholders' interest | **(155)** | (263) | **(476)** | (497) | (788) |
| Current cost income attributable to shareholders | **466** | 705 | **1,176** | 1,362 | 1,439 |
| Current cost earnings per ordinary share | **$0·30** | $0·46 | **$0·76** | $0·88 | $0·93 |

**Note:**

Figures in respect of associated companies have not been adjusted to a current cost basis as the relevant information is not available.

## Capital expenditure – including acquisitions
**$ million**

| | | | | |
|---|---:|---:|---:|---:|
| **by function:** | | | | |
| Production and exploration | **519** | 392 | **1,384** | 1,594 |
| Tankers | **–** | 2 | **24** | 17 |
| Pipelines | **76** | 10 | **108** | 60 |
| Refineries | **96** | 88 | **265** | 387 |
| Marketing | **263** | 74 | **466** | 992 |
| Total petroleum | **954** | 566 | **2,247** | 3,050 |
| Chemicals | **81** | 67 | **227** | 284 |
| Coal | **26** | 21 | **69** | 344 |
| Other | **60** | 10 | **98** | 253 |
| | **1,121** | 664 | **2,641** | 3,931 |
| **by geographical area:** | | | | |
| United Kingdom | **490** | 365 | **1,147** | 1,222 |
| Rest of Europe | **170** | 91 | **409** | 1,331 |
| Middle East and Africa | **31** | 10 | **91** | 91 |
| North and South America | **337** | 162 | **760** | 841 |
| Australasia and Far East | **93** | 36 | **234** | 446 |
| | **1,121** | 664 | **2,641** | 3,931 |
| Acquisition of Selection Trust | **973** | | **973** | |

This statement has been prepared under accounting principles generally accepted in the UK. The figures shown have been translated from the figures as reported in sterling at the September 30, 1980 exchange rate of $2·39 = £1 for convenience only and should not be construed as a representation that the amounts of the pound sterling accounts represent, or have been or could be converted into, US dollars at this or any other rate.

Registered office
Britannic House, Moor Lane, London EC2Y 9BU

Depositary for American Depositary Receipts
Morgan Guaranty Trust Company of New York, 23 Wall Street, New York, New York 10015

# INFLATION ACCOUNTING BY INTERNATIONAL GROUPS

## #21-13...Inflation Accounting and the EEC

Insofar as the EEC is concerned, the 4th Directive (1978) makes no mention of the requirement of any supplementary information with respect to inflation. However, different valuation methods in the primary financial statements are allowed to be used if clearly identified. The required disclosures elicit the historic financial position and profit and loss although valuation is allowed by the use of either the replacement-cost method or for inflation. Any provisions in the directive requiring any member country to adopt inflation accounting methods, however, has been strenuously objected to by Germany.

## #21-14...Inflation Accounting and the United Nations

There appears to be some indication that the possibility is strong in the direction of some type of rule-setting by the U.N. Group of Experts for public reports with respect to inflation accounting. This is especially so in the light of the fact that many countries are following different methods of handling accounting for changing prices or for their foreign exchange gains and losses. The first U.N. Group of Experts made hardly any effort to deal with MEASUREMENT RULES in view of the fact that in its report for 1977 all that was called for was merely the disclosure of "overall evaluation policies, such as historic cost, application of a general purchasing power index, replacement value, or any other basis." A case is being made for requiring two financial reports--one each for international and national home country standards.

## #21-15...Inflation Accounting and the IASC

In its very early discussions in 1974, the IASC placed the topic of ACCOUNTING RESPONSES TO CHANGING PRICES on its agenda. On March 1, 1977 the IASC issued a discussion paper entitled "Treatment of Changing Prices in Financial Statements: A Summary of Proposals." It was a summary of the various proposals issued by member countries as of Nov. 30, 1976. This resulted in the issuance in June 1977 of IASC #6 -- ACCOUNTING RESPONSES TO CHANGING PRICES.

IASC #6 explains the changes in relationships between specific price changes and the general level of prices, and elaborates on the number of different ways to respond to the problem of changing prices. Since there was no international consensus at that time for a single method, the committee felt that increased exposure and descriptions of accounting treatment should be made, resulting in the following declaration in

IASC #6:

> Enterprises should present in their financial statements
> information that describes the procedures adopted to reflect
> the impact on the financial statements of the specific price
> changes, changes in the general level of prices, or of both.
> If no such procedures have been adopted, that fact should be
> disclosed.

This declaration indicates that the IASC felt that further international accounting standards would be issued in the future
which would be expected to clarify how the impact of changing
prices would be reflected on financial statements. IASC #6 became effective as of Jan. 1, 1978.

## #21-16...Types of IASC Price Changes

The IASC differentiated between two different types of prices changes: (1) SPECIFIC PRICE CHANGES, similar to the CCA
method prescribed in the Sandilands Report; and (2) changes in
the GENERAL PRICE LEVEL, similar to the CPP method prescribed
in ED8, adopted in PSSAP#7. The IASC points out that financial
information could be prepared in units of money using current
values of specific prices of goods or assets, or that further
financial information could be given using historical costs
adjusted by the changes in the general level of prices, or by a
combination of the two methods.

## #21-17...Inflation Accounting and the FASB

The requirements for supplementary information are stated in
Paragraphs 29 and 30 of FASB #33:

> 29. An enterprise is required to disclose: (a) Informa-
> tion on income from continuing operations for the current
> fiscal year on a historical cost/constant dollar basis; (b)
> The purchasing power gain or loss on net monetary items for
> the current fiscal year.
> The purchasing power gain or loss on net monetary items
> shall not be included in income from continuing operations.
> 30. An enterprise is required to disclose: (a) Informa-
> tion on income from continuing operations for the current
> fiscal year on a current cost basis; (b) The current cost
> amounts of inventory, and property, plant, and equipment, at
> the end of the current fiscal year; (c) Increases or de-
> creases for the current fiscal year in the current cost
> amounts of inventory and property, plant, and equipment, net
> of inflation.
> The increases or decreases in current cost amounts shall
> not be included in income from continuing operations.

FASB #33 further requires footnote disclosure of the types of
information used to calculate current costs together with any

differences in depreciation estimates between the reported financial statements and the supplementary information. Certain
disclosures are required for each of its past five years. Of
significance to the international accountant is that whereas
FASB #33 specifies only one manner of responding to changes in
prices, under IASC #6 both methods of disclosure are required.

## #21-18...FASB #33

Arthur Young & Company in an article headed "Era of Changing
Prices About to Begin" in its monthly newsletter VIEWS, Vol.
III, No. 8, Nov. 1, 1979, declares:
    With the issuance of Statement of Financial Accounting
Standards #33, *** the long wait is over for the 1,200 -
1,500 companies that must now embark on the task of providing inflation-adjusted information in their annual reports
to shareholders. The standards Board has responded to a
sharply contentious issue that no one has ever agreed upon
and solved it in a unique way: both historical cost/constant
dollar information AND current cost information are to be
required of those public companies that meet the Statement's
size test.
    The required information will be supplementary in na-
ture; the traditional historical cost financial statements
will remain intact. While it is mandatory for companies to
provide historical cost/constant dollar information for the
first year, typically 1979, the current cost information may
be delayed until the following year's annual report. Because
of the one-year delay allowed by FASB #33, the SEC decided
in 1979 to keep its replacement cost disclosure requirements
in effect for fiscal years ending on or before Dec. 24,
1980. After Dec. 25, 1980 the current cost disclosure requirements of FASB #33 become mandatory.

## #21-19...FASB #70 Amendment to FASB #33

In the Deloitte, Haskins & Sells' THE WEEK IN REVIEW, #82-
51, Dec. 17, 1982, it is pointed out that FASB #70, entitled
FINANCIAL REPORTING AND CHANGING PRICES: FOREIGN CURRENCY
TRANSLATION, was issued to amend FASB #33. The purpose is to
implement revisions to the supplementary information about the
effects of changing prices necessitated by changes in the method of translating foreign currency financial statements set out
in FASB #52. FASB #70 has no effect on the reporting of supplementary information about changing prices by enterprises for
which the U.S. dollar is the functional currency for all significant operations, to which enterprises the provisions of
FASB #33 will continue to apply.
    Those enterprises that measure a significant part of their

operations in functional currencies  other than the U.S. dollar are exempt from the FASB #33 requirements to present historical cost information measured in units  of constant purchasing pow- er.  Those enterprises not having significant amounts of inven- tory, and property, plant and equipment,  which have used  his- torical cost information measured in units of constant purchas- ing power to satisfy  FASB #33  current cost requirements,  are permitted to continue such practice. Where an enterprise uses a functional currency other than  the U.S. dollar, it should mea- sure current cost amounts and increases or decreases therein in the functional currency.  Adjustments  to current cost informa- tion to reflect the  effects  of general inflation may be based on either the U.S. CPI(U) or functional currency general  price level  indexes.  FASB  #70 is effective for fiscal years ending after Dec. 15, 1982 for which an  enterprise has applied State- ment #52.

## #21-20...Foreign Experiences With Inflation Accounting

In contrast, the U.K. and Irish accountancy bodies published mandatory reporting standards for  large  companies as  of  the beginning  of 1980.  The new standard entitled STATEMENT OF AC- COUNTING AND AUDITING PROCEDURES #16 (SAAP #16) may be complied with by one of three ways:
(1)  Present historical cost financial  statements with supple- mentary current cost financial  statements (illustrated by British Petroleum);
(2)  Present current cost financial statements with supplement- ary historical cost financial statements; or,
(3)  Present  current cost  financial statements as  the  only statements but  accompanied  by  adequate  historical cost information to enable the user to determine the historical cost net income.
Presently  in the Netherlands both current cost and histori- cal cost statements can be obtained. For more than a decade the large  Dutch corporations have been  preparing financial state- ments using replacement costs.
An exception to the presentation of supplementary statements that is  well known is Brazil, where companies  may have to ad- just the balance sheet carrying values  by a coefficient as de- termined by a federal  authoritative body.  In  ACCOUNTING  FOR MULTINATIONAL  ENTERPRISES, pages  7-9, Prof.  Dhia Al  Hashim points out the Brazilian approach to inflation accounting:
In  Brazil,  where  a  degree  of inflation  substantial enough to  invalidate  historical  costs of assets had  been experienced, a series of governmental indexes for adjustment of assets value have been  adopted.  The  Brazilian tax law accepted the principle of accounting for inflation  in 1964. The following is an excerpt from  the Brazilian government's

policy statement  on inflation:  "The recognition of the importance of the retention and use of capital in the development  of Brazil:  This principle recognizes, in order to retain capital, its  purchasing power must remain intact  despite the fact  that the country would continue to have heavy
rates of inflation in years to come,"  as pointed out by Arthur Andersen & Co. in the BRAZILIAN METHOD OF INDEXING AND
ACCOUNTING FOR INFLATION, Chicago, Illinois, May 1975, p. 2.

The  Brazilian  government allows the  following adjustments for  inflation:  (1) Restatement of value of fixed assets, with a  credit to  a capital  account; Depreciation is
based on  the new value; (2) Recognition of loss in purchasing power on all  assets and  liabilities  other than  fixed
assets; the  loss is charged to  income; (3) Savings deposits
adjusted quarterly to  reflect the decline in the purchasing
power; for example, if one assumes a  5%  interest rate on a
saving deposit  of Cr. 1,000,  and a 35% inflation  rate for
the period, the  saving is increased from  Cr.  1,000 to Cr.
1,350 at the end of the period, and the 5%  interest is calculated  on the adjusted amount.  In order to encourage savings, special tax exemptions are granted for  the additional
interest earned due to inflationary adjustment.

The  application  of price-level accounting can  also be
seen in other countries, such as Argentina.  On July 1, 1975
the accounting profession in  Argentina  adopted price-level
adjusted financial statements.  This step was an  inevitable
response to an inflation rate in Argentina approaching 300%.

## #21-21...Banking Industry Opinion of Inflation Accounting

High officials of the  banking industry view  the  Brazilian
experience with inflation accounting with great concern. In the
ILLINOIS CPA SOCIETY NEWS JOURNAL, Vol. 29, #10, May-June 1979,
page 4, it is stated:
Roger E. Anderson, Chairman of the  Board of the Continental
Bank,  in an  address before the Illinois  Society of CPAs,
says:"Inflation itself is the all-time champion of bad bookkeeping eroding  and shifting  values in every  conceivable
way.  As accountants, you struggle to cope with  the effects
of inflation--an enormous and virtually impossible task.  As
voting  members of society at large,  you no doubt also seek
to remedy the root cause  of inflation in our national life.
The two goals are mutually reinforcing.  Certainly  we never
want to take a leaf from Brazil's experience, give up on inflation, and begin indexing it at rates of 30 or 40% a year.
Completely accounting  for  inflation is an impossible task,
and partial adjustments create distortions of their own."
And in the  Nov.  1978 issue of the JOURNAL  OF ACCOUNTANCY, at
page 16, it is declared:

"The Challenge of Accounting For Inflation by Financial Intermediaries" was the topic of A. Robert Abboud, Chairman of the First National Bank of Chicago. Abboud proposed adoption of a price index or some similar measurement by which inflation might be recognized in financial statements for tax purposes. Abboud said taxes would be paid only on the level of profits after deflation, and stockholders would receive as return of capital the amount by which profits were deflated, permitting them to exempt such amounts from taxable income. "Most bankers," Abboud said, "are skeptical of the 'myriad proposals' made for inflation-adjusted accounting." It is "far too costly, far too subjective, and probably misleading to adjust every element of the balance sheet and income statement," he asserted.

## #21-22...Inflation Accounting and the Financial Executive

"How Inflation Accounting Aids the Financial Executive" is discussed in a recent issue of FINANCIAL EXECUTIVE magazine by Allen H. Seed III, Senior Consultant at Arthur D. Little, Inc., and quoted in issue 83-19, in Deloitte, Haskins & Sells' THE WEEK IN REVIEW, May 13, 1983, pages 1-3, as follows:
Several studies have been conducted that compare the constant dollar and current cost data required by FASB #33 with comparable historical cost data. All of these studies, including my firm's studies of 29 of the 30 Dow Jones Industrial companies for the years 1979, 1980, and 1981, show similar patterns.

SUMMARY OF AGGREGATE 1981 RESULTS
REPORTED BY 29 OF 30 COMPANIES INCLUDED IN THE
DOW JONES INDUSTRIAL AVERAGE INCOME STATEMENTS
(IN BILLIONS)

| Item | Historical As Reported | Constant Dollar | Current Cost |
|---|---|---|---|
| Sales | $593.9 | $593.9 | $593.9 |
| Costs and Expenses: | | | |
| Cost of Sales | 410.6 | 413.7 | 413.0 |
| Depreciation | 27.9 | 44.1 | 42.8 |
| Other Costs & Expenses | 102.2 | 102.6 | 102.6 |
| TOTAL | $540.7 | $560.4 | $558.4 |
| Income Before Taxes | 53.2 | 33.5 | 35.5 |
| Provision For Income Taxes | 21.7 | 21.7 | 21.7 |
| NET INCOME | $ 31.5 | $ 11.8 | $ 13.8 |

Source: "How Inflation Accounting Aids the Financial Executive," by Allen H. Seed III, Senior Consultant at Arthur D. Little, Inc. Reprinted by permission from FINANCIAL EXECUTIVE, copyright 1983 by Financial Executives Institute.

What does inflation accounting tell us? As illustrated
by the data reported by the companies in the Dow Jones Industrial Average, current cost and constant dollar accounting can do the following:
- Calculate a measure of real profitability (net income)
  that is much lower than historical net income in periods
  of inflation.
- Demonstrate the extent to which capital is taxed by current income tax policies before giving effect to ITC and
  ACRS.
- Estimate a more realistic measure of net worth (net assets) than historical cost accounting, especially among
  capital-intensive companies and companies that value
  inventories using the LIFO method.
- Provide a better measure of return on investment (net
  assets) than historical net income divided by historical
  net assets.
- Indicate the funds available for dividends, growth, and
  a growth rate that can be sustained by each business.
Current cost data, when used in conjunction with historical
cost data, can provide useful information to help managers
chart the future course of a business and make better investment decisions. While current cost data may not be comprehensive or wholly accurate, it certainly can provide a
better picture of reality than historical cost information
in an inflationary environment.

## SUMMARY OF FOOTNOTE REFERENCES
(References are to Paragraph #'s)

#21-1 Walker Fesmire, "Henry Sweeney and Stabilized Accounting,"
      ACCOUNTING HISTORIANS NOTEBOOK (Spring 1982): 17-20
#21-6 Raymond J. Chambers, 4th International Conference on Ac-
      counting Education, Berlin, 1977, PROCEEDINGS, pp. 39-41
#21-10 (ASSC) Accounting Standards Steering Committee, Exposure
      Draft #8 (ED8), PROVISIONAL STATEMENT OF STANDARD ACCOUNTING
      PRACTICE (PSSAP #7)
#21-12 ASR #190, DISCLOSURE OF CERTAIN REPLACEMENT COST DATA, March
      1976; FASB #33, FINANCIAL REPORTING AND CHANGING PRICES,
      September 1979
#21-15 IASC #6, ACCOUNTING RESPONSES TO CHANGING PRICES, June 1977
#21-17 FASB #33, op. cit., Sept. 1979, para. 29, 30
#21-18 Arthur Young & Company, "Era of Changing Prices About to
      Begin," VIEWS, Vol. III, No. 8 (Nov. 1, 1979). Reprinted
      with permission.
#21-19 Deloitte, Haskins & Sells, THE WEEK IN REVIEW, #82-51 (Dec.
      17, 1982) (FASB #70 Amendment to FASB #33)
#21-20 Dhia Al Hashim, ACCOUNTING FOR MULTINATIONAL ENTERPRISES,
      pp. 7-9
#21-21 Roger E. Anderson, "Inflation Accounting," ILLINOIS CPA

SOCIETY NEWS JOURNAL, Vol. 29, #10 (May-June 1979): 4

#21-21 A. Robert Abboud, "Challenge of Accounting for Inflation by Financial Intermediaries," JOURNAL OF ACCOUNTANCY (Nov. 1978): 16. Reprinted with permission. Copyright © 1978 by the American Institute of Certified Public Accountants, Inc. Opinions expressed in the JOURNAL OF ACCOUNTANCY are those of editors and contributors. Publication in the JOURNAL OF ACCOUNTANCY does not constitute endorsement by the AICPA or its committees.

#21-22 Allen H. Seed, III, "How Inflation Accounting Aids the Financial Executive." Reprinted by permission from FINANCIAL EXECUTIVE, © 1983 by Financial Executives Institute.

## BIBLIOGRAPHY

Baden, E.J. "The Sandilands Report," THE ACCOUNTANT'S MAGAZINE, 79 (October 1975): 341-343

Baxter, W.T. "Inflation Accounting--Raising the British Standard," CA MAGAZINE, 110 (February 1977): 36-38

Baxter, W.T. "The Hyde Guide: Inflation Accounting in Britain," CA MAGAZINE, 111 (March 1978): 53-54

Beresford, Dennis and Klein, John. "Inflation Accounting in the U.S. and U.K.--A Comparison," JOURNAL OF ACCOUNTANCY, 148 (August 1979): 74-78

Brennan, W. John. "Accounting for Changing Prices," THE ACCOUNTANT, 176 (April 28, 1977): 467-469

Chambers, R.J. "Accounting for Inflation--Part or Whole?", THE ACCOUNTANT'S MAGAZINE, 80 (March 1976): 86-89

Clarke, F.L. "Australia's Current Cost Accounting: A Touch of This and Dash of That," THE ACCOUNTANT, 176,(Feb.7, 1977):190-192

Comer, Robert W. "Brazilian Price Level Accounting," MANAGEMENT ACCOUNTING, 57 (October 1975): 41-46

Drummond, C.S.R. and Stickler, A.D. CURRENT COST ACCOUNTING. Toronto: Methuen Publications, 1983

Falk, Haim, "Current Value Accounting Preferences," INTERNATIONAL JOURNAL OF ACCOUNTING EDUCATION & RESEARCH, 14 (Spring 1979): 29-46

Fleming, Robert. "New Concepts in Brazilian Accounting for Inflation," THE ACCOUNTANT'S MAGAZINE, 83 (April 1979): 162-165

Johnston, Trevor. "Current Cost Accounting in New Zealand," THE ACCOUNTANT'S MAGAZINE, 83 (Feb. 1979): 73-74

Muis, Jules W. "Current Value Accounting in the Netherlands," THE ACCOUNTANT'S MAGAZINE, 79 (Nov. 1975): 377-379

## THEORY QUESTIONS
(Question Numbers are Keyed to Text Paragraph #'s)

#21-4 Discuss the basic objection to historical cost reporting.

#21-5 What are the effects of omission of inflation reporting?

#21-10 Trace the history of inflation accounting in the U.K.
#21-12 Trace the history of inflation accounting in the U.S.
#21-13 What has been the EEC experience with inflation account-
       ing?
#21-14 What has been the U.N. experience with inflation ac-
       counting?
#21-15 What provision is made for inflation in IASC #6?
#21-18 What provision is made for inflation in FASB #33?
#21-19 What provision is made affecting inflation accounting
       in the FASB #70 Amendment to FASB #33?
#21-22 Discuss the relation between inflation accounting and
       the financial executive.


## PROBLEMS

### P-21-1  (CPA EXAM, 5/77, THEORY, #7)
Price-level adjusted financial statements (general purchasing
power) have been a controversial issue in accounting. Which of
the following arguments in favor of such financial statements
is not valid?
  a. Price-level adjusted financial stmts. use historical cost.
  b. Price-level adjusted financial statements compare uniform
     purchasing power among various periods.
  c. Price-level adjusted financial statements measure current
     value.
  d. Price-level adjusted financial statements measure earnings
     in terms of a common dollar.


### P-21-2
The Brazilian Corp. is preparing adjustments to its year-end
reports for 1985:
  1. The Fixed Assets having a book value of 5 million Cruzier-
os (CR) is revalued at 5,200,000 CR. Depreciation on the Fixed
Assets is based on the new values.
  2. All assets and liabilities other than Fixed Assets disclose a loss in purchasing power of 500,000 CR.
  3. There is a decline in Purchasing Power on Savings Deposits
which totals 5,000 CR with the inflation rate for the period
being 40% and the interest rate at 10%.
Required:
Prepare adjustment entries for the above items under Brazilian
Law permitting adjustments for inflation: (1) Revaluation of
Fixed Assets; (2) Depreciation; (3) Loss of Purchasing Power of
Non Fixed Asset items; (4) Charge for the amount of Interest
based on Adjusted Savings Deposit Increment.

**P-21-3**

The DJ Corp. presents its Historical Income Statement items for the year 1985 as follows:

Sales..........$600,000     Other Expenses....$100,000
Cost of Sales..$400,000     Provision for
Depreciation...$ 30,000        Income Taxes...$ 20,000

Under the Constant Dollar Method, the Cost of Sales is $410,000 and Depreciation is $45,000. Under the Current Cost Method, Cost of Sales is $405,000 and Depreciation is $40,000.

**Required**:

1. Prepare a Comparative Income Statement showing the Net Income under the three methods.

2. Comment on the value to management of the Statements regarding the inflationary aspects indicated.

# International Inflation Accounting

**APPROACHES TO INFLATION ACCOUNTING**

**#22-1....Approaches to Inflation Accounting**

It is evident from the preceding discussion that there are several approaches to inflation accounting. Most of them are the same under different names, but basically there are two as pointed out in IASC #6 (superseded by IASC #15), or if the two are combined, they may be regarded as a third.

The first method, as proposed under ED8 issued by the ASC was called the CURRENT PURCHASING POWER (CPP) method, which has been referred to as the HISTORICAL COST/CONSTANT DOLLAR basis in FASB #33. Because the first method was predicated on the basis of General Price Level Adjustments, it has also been referred to as the GENERAL PURCHASING POWER (GPP) approach, and along the same line has additionally been called the GENERAL PRICE LEVEL (GPL) approach.

The second method, advocated under the Sandilands Report, was the CURRENT COST ACCOUNTING (CCA) method, referred to as the CURRENT COST (CC) basis in FASB #33. Being predicated on a REPLACEMENT COST basis, the second method has also been referred to as CURRENT VALUE ACCOUNTING (CVA), or FAIR VALUE ACCOUNTING (FVA), as well as SPECIFIC PRICE ACCOUNTING (SPA) or REPLACEMENT COST ACCOUNTING (RCA). A technical distinction should, however, be made between CURRENT VALUE and REPLACEMENT VALUE, in that the latter would be applicable if a specific asset being revalued is being replaced, whereas the former would be applicable where the asset is merely being assessed a value and is not being replaced.

The basic difference between the two methods is that CONSTANT DOLLAR or CPP or GPP accounting adopts the philosophy that the value of money has gone down, whereas CCA or CVA accounting adopts the viewpoint that the value or cost of certain specific assets has gone up.

## (I)  GENERAL PRICE LEVEL (CONSTANT DOLLAR) ACCOUNTING

### #22-2....Nature of General Price Level Accounting

In 1969 the AICPA,  in its APB Statement #3 entitled  FINAN-
CIAL  STATEMENTS RESTATED FOR GENERAL  PRICE LEVEL CHANGES, set
forth the concepts  upon which  General Price Level  Accounting
were to be predicated. In Dec. 1974 the FASB issued an exposure
draft in  which a requirement was set forth of all companies to
include,  as part of their annual  reports, SUPPLEMENTAL financial statements which were to be expressed in terms of GPP.  It
should be noted that  the GPP Statements  were not intended  to
supplant  the conventional historical statements normally  presented, but  to be SUPPLEMENTAL in  character  to translate the
conventional statements in  terms  of the inflationary  results
manifested in the GPP Statements.

### #22-3....Dimensions of Historical Cost/Constant Dollar Method

This method  of responding to changes in prices restates the
historical cost measurements in  the financial statements  into
units  of  GPP.  Purchasing Power represents the quantity of  a
particular  class of goods and  services that  may be purchased
for a given sum of money at a  given time.  From the U.S. viewpoint, a unit of GPP may  be described as the power of the U.S.
Dollar to purchase  the goods and services offered for  sale in
the U.S. at a particular point in time.  The method for stating
financial statements in GPP units is referred to in FASB #33 as
the HISTORICAL COST/CONSTANT DOLLAR basis.

### #22-4....Implementation of Historical Cost/Constant $ Method

Five steps are required to implement this method:

(1)  Obtain a complete set of  financial statements prepared on
     the historical cost basis
(2)  Select  the appropriate price index to be used for the re-
     statement
(3)  Separate the monetary items from the non-monetary items
(4)  Restate  the non-monetary items in  terms of constant dol-
     lars by multiplying the items  by the conversion ratio de-
     rived by dividing the selected price index  at the time of
     restatement (the  financial statement date) as the numera-
     tor  by the value  of the index at the time of acquisition
     as the denominator
(5)  Compute  the General Purchasing Power Gain  or Loss on the
     monetary items by applying the conversion ratio,  assuming
     the acquisition  date is the beginning of the  year or the
     dates of the increases or decreases during the year

The two primary dimensions of the method are (1) the selection
of the index of GPP to be used as the constant dollar basis;
and (2) the segregation of the items to be restated.

### #22-5....Indexing Method for Price Level Measurements

The index to be used must be one that is readily available
yet representative of general price changes. Each country involved in restating financial statements for GPP must determine
which index is best suited for country-wide use.
In the U.S. the five most common GPP measurements are (1)
CONSUMERS PRICE INDEX FOR URBAN CONSUMERS (CPI-U); (2) WHOLE-
SALE PRICE INDEX; (3) GROSS NATIONAL PRODUCT IMPLICIT PRICE
DEFLATOR (GNP); (4) COMPOSITE CONSTRUCTION COST INDEX; and (5)
22 COMMODITY SPOT PRICE INDEX. All five are computed on a regular basis by U.S. government agencies and are readily available.
Of the five indices, under APB Statement #3 in 1969, the
GROSS NATIONAL PRODUCT IMPLICIT PRICE DEFLATOR (GNP) was regarded as the most comprehensive and received acceptance in
financial and economic circles as the best measure of the general price level in the U.S. economy. It was therefore designated as the only index to be used to restate historical financial statements into GPP financial statements. This however was
changed by FASB #33, under which the index required to be used
in constant dollar accounting is the CPI-U. The shift to the
CPI-U was made because it is based on a broad basket of consumers goods and services purchased for final consumption by the
consumer. For this reason, it is the most widely used index
around the world.

### #22-6....Segregation of Monetary and Non-Monetary Items

The other dimension of the indexing method is the need to
segregate the balance sheet and income statement items as either monetary or non-monetary.
Monetary items are those accounts whose values are fixed in
terms of number of dollars regardless of what change takes
place in the price level. Conversely, non-monetary items are
those accounts which will vary with changes in the price level.
Since the balance sheet fails to reflect the variance in the
price level, this can result in misrepresentations based on
the age of the items.

### #22-7...Classification of Monetary and Non-Monetary Items

Monetary items by their very nature are stated in CURRENT
dollars, while non-monetary items must be RESTATED (also referred to as TRANSLATED or CONVERTED) in terms of current dollars.

The preferable term is RESTATED to avoid confusion with Foreign Exchange transactions.

Monetary items are classified as Monetary Assets and Monetary Liabilities. Obviously Monetary Assets would include Cash, Accounts Receivable, Notes Receivable, and Investments that will be repaid at a fixed amount in the future which also pay a fixed amount of dividends and interest.

Monetary Liabilities would include Accounts Payable, Notes Payable, various Accrued Expense Items Payable, as well as Long-Term Bonds or obligations payable at a fixed amount, as well as Preferred Stockholders Equity.

Non-monetary items are all items that are not monetary for GPL accounting purposes. Like the monetary they are classified as ASSETS and LIABILITIES. Non-monetary Assets are items whose value in terms of the monetary unit may change with an elapse of time. They would include such items as Investments in Common Stocks; Inventories; Investments in Property, Plant and Equipment; and Prepaid Expense Items representing deferred charges of costs expended in the past.

Non-monetary Liabilities are items that may be paid in cash, but generally are paid in the form of services, which provide given amounts of goods and services, or an equivalent amount of Purchase Power. They would include such Deferred Credit items as Prepaid Rent Income received in advance, advances received on Subscription Contracts or Sales Agreements, or items representing reductions of prior expenses. Common Stock equity accounts and Additional Paid-In Capital are also non-monetary.

#22-8....FASB #33 Classification of Common Monetary
         and Non-Monetary Items

### MONETARY ITEMS

ASSETS:
Cash on Hand
Demand Bank Deposits
Time Bank Deposits
Accounts Receivable
   (Less Allowance for Bad Debts)
Notes Receivable
Employees' Loans
Advances to Suppliers
Nonconvertible Preferred Stock Investment
Nonparticipating Preferred Stock Investment
Nonconvertible Bonds Receivable
Deferred Income Tax Charges

LIABILITIES:
Accounts Payable
Notes Payable

Accrued Expenses Payable
Cash Dividends Payable
Customers' Advances
Refundable Deposits
Bonds Payable
Long-Term Notes Payable
Unamortized Premium or Discount on Bonds & Notes Payable
Convertible Bonds Payable
Deferred Income Tax Credits

## NON-MONETARY ITEMS

ASSETS:
Inventories
Investments in Common Stock
Property, Plant and Equipment
   (Less Accumulated Depreciation)
Patents, Trademarks, Licenses, Formulas
Goodwill
Other Intangible Assets
Deferred Charges
Deferred Property Acquisition Costs
Portion of Purchase Commitments Paid on Fixed Price Contracts

LIABILITIES:
Portion of Sales Commitments Collected on Fixed Price Contracts
Warranty Obligations
Deferred Investment Tax Credits
Common Stock
Additional Paid-In Capital

## MIXED MONETARY/NON-MONETARY ITEMS

There are certain items which are in the nature of monetary or
non-monetary which may be called Mixed Items. These items
therefore require an examination into their nature in order to
determine whether they should be assigned to the Monetary or
Non-Monetary classification.

MIXED ASSETS:
Investments in Convertible or Participating Preferred Stock
Convertible Bonds
Inventories with Stable Nonfluctuating Value
Prepaid Expenses (Ins., Rent, etc.)
Pension & Sinking Funds Enterprise Controlled

MIXED LIABILITIES:
Accrued Vacation Pay Payable
Deferred Revenue

Accrued Pension Obligations
Preferred Stock

Having segregated the monetary and non-monetary items, the monetary items on the balance sheet need not be restated. The non-monetary items will be translated or restated from historical cost to a constant dollar basis. The non-monetary items to be restated will depend upon whether PARTIAL or COMPLETE restatement is being presented.

## #22-9....Partial Restatement vs. Complete Restatement

FASB #33 permits partial restatement of the financial statements. On the balance sheet the partial items to be restated are only the inventory, plant, property & equipment accounts; on the income statement only the cost of goods sold, depreciation, and depletion and amortization expense must be restated. The index to be used under partial restatement is the average index for the year of reporting.

Comprehensive restatement may be undertaken by using a historical cost/constant dollar basis or a current cost/constant dollar basis. If an enterprise elects to use comprehensive restatement, the index to be selected may be either (a) the average-for-the-current-year constant dollar; or (b) the end-of-the-current-year constant dollar. Besides inventories and fixed assets, other non-monetary items to be considered for restatement in such case are investment in common stock, including equity investments in unconsolidated subsidiaries or other investees; certain deferred charges and credits; and long-term prepayments and deferred revenues that are not stated in fixed units of money.

## #22-10...The Restatement Formula

The general rule for restatement of non-monetary assets and liabilities may be set forth in the following formula:

$$\frac{\text{Constant Dollar Current Year Price Index}}{\text{Index at Date of Acquisition}} \quad x \quad \frac{\text{Non-Monetary Item}}{\text{Historical Cost}}$$

The application of the rule requires consideration of two elements, namely (1) the determination of the index to be used; and (2) the segregation and stratification of the items according to their acquisition dates.

The stratification is necessary for application of the proper ratio for each group of assets acquired on a specific date in order to apply the index to the amounts as of date of acquisition. This means a separate stratification for inventories, and each category of plant, property, equipment, and other non-monetary assets and liabilities.

When partial restatement is used, the constant dollar unit that must be applied is the average consumer price index for the year of reporting. For those enterprises that utilize complete restatement of financial statements, the optional year end consumer price index may be used as the constant dollar index. For amounts expressed in constant dollars of a previous period, the index of the previous period would be utilized.

## #22-11...Partial Restatement FASB #33 Requirements

As pointed out, where the historical cost/constant dollar basis is to be used, Sec. 29 of FASB #33 requires that two types of supplementary information are to be disclosed: Sec. 29(a) Information on Income from continuing operations for the current fiscal year on a historical cost/constant dollar basis; and Sec. 29(b) the PURCHASING POWER GAIN OR LOSS ON NET MONETARY ITEMS for the current fiscal year.

Sec. 29(a) is satisfied through the construction of a Supplementary Balance Sheet and Supplementary Income Statement. Sec. 29(b) is satisfied through the creation of a SCHEDULE OF COMPUTATION OF PURCHASING POWER GAIN OR LOSS ON NET MONETARY ITEMS. Illustration of the procedure for the improvisation of the Sec. 29(a) and (b) statements is presented below.

## #22-12...Procedure for Supplementary Constant Dollar Balance Sheet and Income Statement

Assume that the U.S. Foreign Auto Parts Co. desires to present its Supplemental Inflation Financial Statements as of 1982. To carry out the procedure under Sec. 29(a), it would follow the 5 steps outlined above in #22-4.

**STEP NO. 1:** Obtain a complete set of financial statements prepared on the historical cost basis. The Balance Sheet and Income Statement obtained read as follows:

### U.S. FOREIGN AUTO PARTS
### HISTORICAL COST COMPARATIVE BALANCE SHEETS

|                       |        | 12/31/81 |        | 12/31/82 |
|-----------------------|--------|----------|--------|----------|
| Cash                  |        | $ 1,000  |        | $ 2,500  |
| Receivables           |        | 3,000    |        | 3,500    |
| Inventories           |        | 10,000   |        | 12,500   |
| Office Equipment      | 5,000  |          | 5,000  |          |
| Less: Accum. Deprec.  | 2,000  |          | 2,500  |          |
|                       |        | 3,000    |        | 2,500    |
| TOTAL ASSETS          |        | $17,000  |        | $21,000  |

| | | |
|---|---|---|
| Accounts Payable | $ 3,000 | $ 4,000 |
| Capital Stock | 10,000 | 10,000 |
| Retained Earnings | 4,000 | 7,000 |
| TOTAL LIABILITIES & EQUITY | $17,000 | $21,000 |

U.S. FOREIGN AUTO PARTS INCOME STATEMENT
FOR YEAR ENDING 12/31/82

| | |
|---|---|
| Parts Sales | $40,000 |
| Less: Cost of Goods Sold | 24,000 |
| Gross Profit | $16,000 |
| Depreciation Expense | 500 |
| | $15,500 |
| Other Expenses | 12,500 |
| NET INCOME | $ 3,000 |

**STEP NO. 2:** Select the Price Index to be used. The indices for each significant measurement date follow:

| MEASUREMENT DATES | INDEX |
|---|---|
| Date of Organization | 100 |
| Date of Equipment Acquisition | 110 |
| Date of 1981 Inventory Purchase | 122 |
| Date of 1982 Inventory Purchase | 128 |
| December 31, 1981 | 125 |
| December 31, 1982 | 130 |
| Average For Year 1982 | 127 |

**STEP NO. 3:** Separate monetary from non-monetary items. The monetary items would be Cash, Receivables, and Accounts Payable. The non-monetary items would be Inventory, Office Equipment, and Capital Stock.

**STEP NO. 4:** Restate the non-monetary items in terms of constant dollars, by multiplying the amount of the items by the conversion ratio derived by dividing the selected price index at the time of restatement as the numerator by the value of the index at the time of acquisition as the denominator. The items to be restated, as indicated in Step No. 3, are Inventory (Cost of Goods Sold), Office Equipment, and Capital Stock.

(a) RESTATEMENT OF INVENTORY (COST OF GOODS SOLD): The restated amounts for the beginning and ending inventories and the cost of goods sold are as follows:

| As Stated | | Conversion Factor | As Restated |
|---|---|---|---|
| Inventory,12/31/81 | $10,000 | x  127/122 | $10,410 |
| Purchases-1982 | 26,500 | x  127/127 | 26,500 |
| Available | $36,500 | | $36,910 |
| Inventory,12/31/82 | 12,500 | x  127/130 | 12,212 |
| Cost of Goods Sold | $24,000 | | $24,698 |

(b) RESTATEMENT OF THE OFFICE EQUIPMENT AND DEPRECIATION:

| As Stated | | Conversion Factor | As Restated |
|---|---|---|---|
| Office Equip.-Cost | $5,000 | x  127/110 | $5,773 |
| Deprec. Ofc. Equip. | | 10% Annual Rate | 577 |
| Accum.Dep., 12/31/81 | 2,000 | x  127/110 | 2,309 |
| Accum.Dep., 12/31/82 | 2,500 | x  127/110 | 2,886 |

(c) RESTATEMENT OF CAPITAL STOCK:

| As Stated | | Conversion Factor | As Restated |
|---|---|---|---|
| Capital Stock | $10,000 | x  127/100 | $12,700 |

With respect to the Income Statement, insofar as such current items as Sales, Purchases, and Other Expenses are concerned, the conversion factor is 127/127, assuming a stable flow during the year. For these current income statement items, the dollar amounts actually remain unadjusted under the partial restatement procedure.

**STEP NO. 5:** Compute the GENERAL PURCHASING POWER GAIN OR LOSS on the monetary items by applying the conversion ratio, thereby fulfilling the requirement in Sec. 29(b) of FASB #33. It should be noted that in the procedure carried out in the first four steps, monetary items were not restated, but only the non-monetary items. The reason for this was that monetary items will be collected in a fixed amount of cash in the future, and therefore are reported at their dollar maturity amounts for as long as they are outstanding regardless of whether there is any inflation. Hence they are not restated in terms of GPP. Non-monetary items, on the other hand, are free to fluctuate with inflation resulting in varying amounts they will command in the marketplace. Such effects are not reflected in the balance sheet, hence serious distorions may result. Thus a realistic result is in inverse proportion to the age of the time of the

general price level.    The older the item, the more it declines
in  value.   This would also tend  to destroy the comparability
feature of financial statements covering two or more periods.

This importance  of  making  a  distinction between  monetary
and non-monetary  items is emphasized by Prof. Raymond J. Chambers in his book ACCOUNTING, EVALUATION  AND ECONOMIC BEHAVIOR,
Prentice-Hall, 1966, page 196:

> The importance of the distinction lies in the fact that mon-
> etary  assets  and  non-monetary assets are subject to quite
> different risks.  Holdings of monetary assets are subject to
> the risk of changes in the purchasing  power  of money.  If,
> for whatever reasons, the general level of prices rises, the
> purchasing power of a unit of money tends to fall; a greater
> number of units is  required to buy  a given good.  Clearly,
> then,  non-monetary assets are subject to the same influenc-
> es,  but in the  opposite direction.   If the price level is
> expected to rise, it is clearly preferable to hold goods and
> to incur fixed  obligations  than it is to hold monetary as-
> sets.

For the reason stated by Prof. Chambers, there seems to be some
opinion that constant  dollar  accounting should be equally applied  to monetary assets and liabilities as to  the  non-monetary.  As pointed out, during an inflationary period cash loses
purchasing power  because it buys less at the end of the period
than it could have bought at the beginning. Conversely, debtors
can pay their Accounts  Payable with cash that  has fallen in
value, making for less effective cash paid out.

The whole matter can be simplified as follows:   an  increase
in the monetary ASSET  position during the period  results in a
LOSS  in purchasing power, whereas an increase in the  monetary
LIABILITY position  during the period results in a GAIN in pur-
chasing power.   This  is the reason that Sec. 29(b) requires a
showing of what it refers to as the  PURCHASING POWER  GAINS OR
LOSSES ON NET MONETARY ITEMS to be computed in Step No. 5. Dif-
ferent  authorities  have designated Purchasing  Power Gains or
Losses by varied terms, most common of which are GENERAL  PRICE
LEVEL GAINS OR  LOSSES, MONETARY GAINS OR LOSSES, and INFLATION
GAINS OR LOSSES.

The  question that arises is "Where do such Gains and Losses
appear on the financial statements?"  There  are two  points of
view  expressed world-wide:   (1) as an  adjustment to invested
capital, or (2) as a holding gain or  loss on the income statement.

## #22-13...Schedule of Purchasing Power Gain or Loss
##         On Net Monetary Items

To conclude the procedure, the Purchasing Power Gain or Loss
on Net Monetary Items is computed in Figure 22-1.

FIGURE 22-1

SCHEDULE OF COMPUTATION OF PURCHASING POWER
GAIN OR LOSS ON NET MONETARY ITEMS

| Year | Monetary Item | As Stated | | Conversion Factor | As Restated | Purchasing Power Loss | Purchasing Power Gain |
|---|---|---|---|---|---|---|---|
| 12/31/82 | Cash | $2,500 | x | 127/130 | $2,442 | 58 | |
| 12/31/82 | Receivables | 3,500 | x | 127/130 | 3,419 | 81 | |
| 12/31/82 | Total Assets | $6,000 | | | $5,861 | 139 | |
| 12/31/82 | Accounts Payable | 4,000 | x | 127/130 | 3,907 | | 93 |
| 12/31/82 | Net Monetary Assets | $2,000 | x | 127/130 | $1,954 | 46 | |
| | | | | | | | |
| 12/31/81 | Cash | $1,000 | x | 127/125 | $1,016 | 16 | |
| 12/31/81 | Receivables | 3,000 | x | 127/125 | 3,048 | 48 | |
| 12/31/81 | Total Assets | $4,000 | | | $4,064 | 64 | |
| 12/31/81 | Accounts Payable | 3,000 | x | 127/125 | 3,048 | | 48 |
| 12/31/81 | Net Monetary Assets | $1,000 | x | 127/125 | $1,016 | 16 | |
| | | | | | | | |
| 12/31/82 | ANNUAL INCREASE | $1,000 | | | $ 938 | 62 | |

(1982-1981)  PURCHASING POWER GAIN OR LOSS

## #22-14...Supplementary Constant Dollar Financial Statements

All of the computations are now complete, and result in the following restated financial statements in constant dollars:

U.S. FOREIGN AUTO PARTS
SUPPLEMENTARY CONSTANT DOLLAR COMPARATIVE BALANCE SHEETS

|                          |       | 12/31/81 |       | 12/31/82 |
|--------------------------|-------|----------|-------|----------|
| Cash                     |       | $ 1,016  |       | $ 2,442  |
| Receivables              |       | 3,048    |       | 3,419    |
| Inventories              |       | 10,410   |       | 12,212   |
| Office Equipment         | 5,773 |          | 5,773 |          |
| Less: Accum. Deprec.     | 2,309 |          | 2,886 |          |
|                          |       | 3,464    |       | 2,887    |
| TOTAL ASSETS             |       | $17,938  |       | $20,960  |
|                          |       |          |       |          |
| Accounts Payable         |       | $ 3,048  |       | $ 3,907  |
| Capital Stock            |       | 12,700   |       | 12,700   |
| Retained Earnings        |       | 2,190    |       | 4,353    |
| TOTAL LIABILITIES & EQUITY |     | $17,938  |       | $20,960  |

U.S. FOREIGN AUTO PARTS
CONSTANT DOLLAR SUPPLEMENTARY INCOME STATEMENT
FOR YEAR ENDING 12/31/82

| Parts Sales            | $40,000 |
|------------------------|---------|
| Less: Cost of Goods Sold | 24,698 |
| Gross Profit           | $15,302 |
| Depreciation Expense   | 577     |
|                        | $14,725 |
| Other Expenses         | 12,500  |
| NET INCOME             | $ 2,225 |

## #22-15...Reconciliation of Constant Dollars
## Retained Earnings Statement

| Item | As Stated | As Restated |
|------|-----------|-------------|
| Retained Earnings--Per 12/31/81 Historical Balance Sheet | $4,000 | |
| Net Income--Per 12/31/82 Historical Income Statement | 3,000 | |
| Retained Earnings--Per 12/31/82 Historical Balance Sheet | $7,000 | |

| | |
|---|---:|
| Retained Earnings--Per 12/31/82 Constant Dollar Balance Sheet | $2,190 |
| Net Income--Per 12/31/82 Constant Dollar Income Statement | 2,225 |
| Total Retained Earnings--12/31/82 | $4,415 |
| Less: Purchasing Power Loss-- 12/31/82 (Per Schedule) | 62 |
| Retained Earnings--Constant Dollars As of 12/31/82 Balance Sheet | $4,353 |

The Purchasing Power Loss represents an erosion of the company's capital and may be shown as a disclosure on the supplementary income statement, but not as part of income from continuing operations. The beginning balance in retained earnings represents the accumulation of restated net income calculations and purchasing power gains and losses of past years. If dividends were paid, the index at the time of declaration would be used.

The most significant observation in the foregoing case illustration is that the net income under the priceadjusted formula is less than under the historical cost basis. As this represents an erosion of capital, a company must be careful not to declare dividends in excess of total of the restated net income and purchasing power loss.

#### #22-16...Limitations of Historical Cost/Constant Dollar Basis

The historical cost/constant dollar basis is applied to historical cost items which combine dollars spent at various times in the past with dollars spent currently. The historical cost amounts are restated into constant dollars with constant units of general purchasing power. Thus the adjustment of historical costs for price level changes by the use of price indices are still basically historical cost accounting because the accounting process has its inception in the original transaction amount.

In order for the adjustments to be made, the item must have a stipulated cost basis. It simply is a case of substituting a new adjusted value for the original cost value. The underlying principles of accounting under the historical cost assumption are left intact.

A restatement using the historical cost/constant dollar basis corrects only distortions caused by recording transactions in dollars of varying purchasing power. The restated amounts do not purport to represent appraisal values, replacement cost, or current market values. Changes in the individual prices of the assets may be more or less than, and may even be counter to, the changes in the general price level.

Indeed the changes in the individual prices of the assets

may be caused in part by changes in the general purchasing power of the dollar and in part by other supply and demand factors. If the changes in individual prices are significantly different from the change in the general price level, restatement of the non-monetary items may not be a fair presentation of the financial statement information. Other alternatives must be sought. Indeed, IASC #15 and FASB #33 both suggest the possibility of using another base--the current cost basis.

## (II) FINANCIAL REPORTING USING CURRENT COST ACCOUNTING

### #22-17...Definition of Current Cost

Under the Current Cost Method, financial statements are to be adjusted to reflect <u>current</u> rather than historical costs. What, then, are current costs? The current cost of an asset is the lowest current buying price or product cost of an asset of the same age and in the same condition as the asset owned. Current cost may not necessarily represent replacement cost which is the lowest cost of obtaining a new asset of equivalent operating or productive capability. As previously pointed out, Replacement Value would apply where a specific asset being revalued is being replaced, whereas current value applies where the asset is merely being assessed a value and not being replaced.

If the recoverable amount is lower than current cost, and if the lower value of the asset to the enterprise represents a material, permanent reduction, the recoverable amount is the amount to be reflected in current cost financial statements. The recoverable amount as used similarly in constant dollar financial statements is the estimate of the net realizable value of an asset subject to near-term sale or the net present value of future cash flows derived from an asset that is to be used in the enterprise.

The difference between GPL and CC accounting is that the former reflects historical costs restated in terms of current dollars, whereas current value accounting substitutes current value for historical amounts. Current value where related to replacement cost or purchase price has been called ENTRY VALUE, representing the current replacement cost. Where related to the selling price of the asset in the market less disposal cost, it has been termed NET REALIZABLE or EXIT VALUE. The principal basis for adopting the current value method is that it is regarded as the most appropriate measure of DISTRIBUTABLE INCOME, which is defined as the amount of dividends that can be distributed without endangering the financial stability of the business entity.

#22-18...Determination of Current Cost

Current costs may be determined by:
(1) Indexation, either by revising historical costs by using (a) externally, independently generated specific price indices for the class of assets being measured; or (b) by the use of internally generated specific price indices representing cost changes for the class of assets being measured.
(2) Direct Pricing, by using either (a) current invoice prices; or (b) vendors' firm price lists, or other quotations or estimates; or (c) standard manufacturing costs that approximate current costs.
These current costs apply not only to the asset accounts but also to the related income statement accounts, e.g., inventories and cost of goods sold, and plant, property and equipment and depreciation thereon. If recoverable amounts are used for the assets, the related income statement accounts will also be reflected in the related recoverable amounts.

#22-19...Nature of Current Value Accounting

Current Value Accounting is expected to be effectuated in a series of three transitional steps. In the first phase, it would be limited to requiring footnote disclosure of the current values of inventories, cost of goods sold, plant and equipment, and depreciation. In the second phase, supplementary financial statements would be presented stated in current value for most of the items. The third phase would be to require financial statements expressed in terms of current values which would become the PRIMARY statements of the company.

#22-20...Implementation of the Current Value Method

There are three steps required for adjusting historical cost financial statements to current costs:
(1) Determine the measurement dates of the appropriate non-monetary items
(2) Determine the current costs on the measurement dates
(3) Adjust the historical cost amounts to the lower of current costs or recovery amounts

#22-21...Illustrative Example for Supplementary
        Current Value Financial Statements

To illustrate the procedure, let us again use the U.S. Foreign Auto Parts data from above. The items to be restated are the following non-monetary accounts: Inventories, Cost of Goods

Sold, Office Equipment, Depreciation on Office Equipment, and Accumulated Depreciation on Office Equipment.

(1) <u>INVENTORIES AND COST OF GOODS SOLD</u>: The inventories and cost of goods sold would be adjusted as follows based on the assumption that the current costs were obtained from current supplier price lists:

| Item | As Stated | No. Units | Current Price Per Unit | As Restated |
|------|-----------|-----------|------------------------|-------------|
| Inventory-- 12/31/81 | $10,000 | 10,000 | 1.05 | $10,500 |
| Inventory-- 12/31/82 | 12,500 | 10,000 | 1.30 | 13,000 |
| Cost of Goods Sold | 24,000 | 22,000 | 1.12 | 24,640 |

The current price per unit is the current cost at the year-end measurement date for the inventories and the weighted-average purchase price for the cost of goods sold. If the inventories had been stated at LIFO, the cost of goods sold at LIFO may be used as a reasonable approximation of the current cost of goods sold unless previous lower cost layers were sold.

(2) <u>OFFICE EQUIPMENT</u>: For the adjustment of the Office Equipment, an indexation procedure is applied using a specific price index for office equipment as follows:

        On December 31, 1981          280
        On December 31, 1982          308
        On 1/1/78-Date of acquisition  200

Restated at Current Cost, the Office Equipment account would be as follows:

| Item | As Stated | Conversion Factor | At Current Cost |
|------|-----------|-------------------|-----------------|
| Cost as of 12/31/81 | $5,000 | 280/200 | $7,000 |
| Cost as of 12/31/82 | 5,000 | 308/200 | 7,700 |

(3) <u>DEPRECIATION ON OFFICE EQUIPMENT</u>: The related Depreciation at current cost would be as follows, assuming a straight line 10-year basis:

| Date | Equip. Restated Value | % Depreciated | Depreciated Current Cost |
|------|-----------------------|---------------|--------------------------|
| As of 12/31/81 | $7,000 | 40% | $2,800 |
| As of 12/31/82 | 7,700 | 50% | 3,850 |

(4) <u>NET OFFICE EQUIPMENT</u>: The Office Equipment net of accumulated depreciation at current cost and the 1982 depreciation is then:

| Date | Equipment Less Deprec. | Equip. Net of Accum. Deprec. |
|------|------------------------|------------------------------|
| As of 12/31/81 | $7,000 - $2,800 = | $4,200 |
| As of 12/31/82 | 7,700 - 3,850 = | 3,850 |

Average During 1982
at Current Cost --     $= \dfrac{(4,200 + 3,850)}{2} = 4,025$

Deprec. @ Current Cost --     $= 4,025 \div 5 \text{ yrs.} = 805$

Since the remaining useful life is 5 years at Dec. 31, 1982, the depreciation expense as stated at current cost is one-fifth of the average net office equipment for 1982 or $805.

## #22-22...Holding Gains and Losses

In the restatement for Item 1 above (Inventories & COGS) it should be noted that the COGS was stated as $24,000 and restated as $24,640. This means that the restated cost of goods sold was $640 more than what was actually stated. This figure may be verified as follows:

| | | |
|---|---|---|
| Ending Inventory 12/31/82, Restated | | 13,000 |
| Cost of Goods Sold, Restated | | 24,640 |
| Restated Cost of Goods Available for Sale | | 37,640 |
| Beginning Inventory 12/31/81, Restated | 10,500 | |
| Add: Purchases | 26,500 | |
| Goods Available For Sale | | 37,000 |
| Difference on Inventory Restatement | | 640 |

It should be noted that the Purchases of $26,500 was that as originally stated, so that in effect there is an increase in the amount of inventory in the purchases as follows:

| | As Stated | As Restated |
|---|---|---|
| Ending Inventory, 12/31/82 | $12,500 | $13,000 |
| Add: Cost of Goods Sold | 24,000 | 24,640 |
| Goods Available For Sale | $36,500 | $37,640 |
| Deduct: Beginning Inv., 12/31/81 | 10,000 | 10,500 |
| Purchases | $26,500 | $27,140 |

This indicates that the Inventory in the stated purchases of $26,500 was increased by $640 to $27,140.

Similarly, in the restatement for Item 4 above for Equipment Net of Accumulated Depreciation (which combines Items 2 & 3), it should be noted that the balance of the Equipment account as of 12/31/81 was $4,200 and on 12/31/82 was $3,850 after current depreciation cost of $805 was deducted. The restatement of the Equipment account less depreciation would be as follows:

| | |
|---|---:|
| Equipment Acct. Balance, 12/31/82 | $3,850 |
| Add: Depreciation Taken 1982 | 805 |
| Total | $4,655 |
| Less: Balance 12/31/81 | 4,200 |
| Increase in Value of Equipment | $ 455 |

The question that arises is what do these increased values of the Inventory and the Office Equipment in the sums of $640 and $455 respectively represent? Under the current cost basis they are recognized as income even though the inventory has not been sold and the equipment is retained. Under the historical cost basis income on inventory is not recognized until it is sold, and no income is recognized merely from holding the equipment asset. Accountants have therefore used the term HOLD-ING GAIN for the increase in current cost arising from HOLDING the inventory from one period to another. Should the value of the inventory or equipment decline in value, the result would be a HOLDING LOSS.

In the discussion of Constant Dollar Costing it was pointed out that General Purchasing Power Gains and Losses may arise from restatement of monetary items; in Current Costing the re-ciprocal is the Gains and Losses from non-monetary items, call-ed HOLDING GAINS AND LOSSES. To illustrate the comparison, where there is inflation, cash does not have the same purchas-ing power at the end of the period as it had at the beginning, and therefore losses in value. This inures to the benefit of debtors who can pay off their debts with money worth less than at the time the debt was contracted. Accordingly, if the net monetary or financial assets increase during a period, the re-sult will be a loss in purchasing power, whereas if the net monetary or financial assets decrease during a period there will be a gain in purchasing power. This means that a business entity that HOLDS monetary assets during an inflationary period will realize a loss merely from HOLDING them. So too, just as with Constant Dollar Accounting, gains and losses may result from HOLDING nonmonetary assets which are restated in value.

## #22-23...Classification of Holding Gains and Losses

Holding Gains and Losses are classified as REALIZED or UN-REALIZED. In order to be REALIZED, the asset has to be sold or consumed during the period, and the difference between the cur-rent cost of the asset at disposition and its historical cost is the realized gain or loss.

Where the asset is still in the possession of the firm at the end of the period, the loss or gain is UNREALIZED. The UN-REALIZED GAIN OR LOSS is the difference between the current cost of the asset at the end of the period and the cost at the date of acquisition of the assets. The TOTAL HOLDING GAIN OR

LOSS for a period will be the sum of the REALIZED HOLDING GAINS AND LOSSES and the UNREALIZED HOLDING GAINS AND LOSSES resulting from the end of the year current cost less the historical cost.

It may be seen then that Unrealized Holding Gains and Losses result from changes in replacement cost of the non-monetary assets. They are therefore of two types: (1) NOMINAL, or THEORETICAL; and (2) REAL. UNREALIZED Nominal Holding Gains result from changes in current costs directly attributable to changes in the GPL, whereas UNREALIZED Real Holding Gains and Losses result from changes in current costs other than the change in the GPL.


## #22-24...Statement of Unrealized Holding Gains and Losses

To illustrate the difference, assume that on Jan. 1, 1982, the X Corporation purchased a parcel of land for $100,000. The General Price Level Index was 100, and was 120 on Jan. 1, 1983, at which time the land could be sold for $150,000. A STATEMENT OF ANALYSIS OF UNREALIZED HOLDING GAINS AND LOSSES would be as follows:

| | |
|---|---|
| Current Selling Price as of Jan. 1, 1983 | $150,000 |
| Historical Cost as of Jan. 1, 1982 | 100,000 |
|    TOTAL UNREALIZED HOLDING GAIN | 50,000 |
| Less: Nominal (Theoretical) Gain = | |
|    GPL Value − Historical Value = | |
|    (120/100 x 100,000) − 100,000 = | 20,000 |
| Equals: Real Holding Gain | |
|    Current Value − GPL Value = | |
|    150,000 − 120,000 = | 30,000 |

The Statement of Unrealized Holding Gains and Losses may be expressed in terms of the following equations:

(1) Current Cost Selling Price − Historical Cost Price = Total Unrealized Holding Gain or Loss
(2) Total Unrealized Holding Gain or Loss = Unrealized Real Holding Gain or Loss + Unrealized Nominal Holding Gain or Loss
(3) Unrealized Real Holding Gain or Loss = Current Cost Selling Price − Constant Dollar Restated Cost
(4) Unrealized Nominal Holding Gain or Loss = Constant Dollar Restated Cost − Historical Cost

Applying these equations to the illustration above results as follows:

Total Unrealized Holding Gain =
  150,000 - 100,000 = 50,000
Unrealized Real Holding Gain =
  150,000 - (120/100 x 100,000) = 30,000
Unrealized Nominal Holding Gain =
  (120/100 x 100,000) - 100,000 = 20,000
Total Unrealized Holding Gain =
  30,000 + 20,000 = 50,000

It must be remembered that the Unrealized Real and Nominal Holding Gains result from NON-MONETARY ASSETS and are therefore not to be confused with the General Purchasing Power Gains and Losses which are based on MONETARY Items. Each one relates to a different class of items than the other.

## #22-25...Current Cost Financial Statements

At this point we are ready to construct the Current Cost Supplementary Financial Statements:

U.S. FOREIGN AUTO PARTS
SUPPLEMENTARY CURRENT COST INCOME STATEMENT
FOR THE YEAR ENDING DECEMBER 31, 1982

| | | |
|---|---:|---:|
| Parts Sales | | $40,000 |
| Less: Current Cost of Goods Sold | | 24,640 |
| Gross Profit | | $15,360 |
| Depreciation Expense | $ 805 | |
| Other Expenses | 12,500 | |
| | | 13,305 |
| NET INCOME | | $ 2,055 |

U.S. FOREIGN AUTO PARTS
SUPPLEMENTARY CURRENT COST COMPARATIVE BALANCE SHEETS

| | | 12/31/81 | | 12/31/82 |
|---|---:|---:|---:|---:|
| Cash | | $ 1,000 | | $ 2,500 |
| Receivables | | 3,000 | | 3,500 |
| Inventories | | 10,500 | | 13,000 |
| Office Equipment | $7,000 | | $7,700 | |
| Less: Acc. Deprec. | 2,800 | | 3,850 | |
| | | 4,200 | | 3,850 |
| TOTAL ASSETS | | $18,700 | | $22,850 |
| | | | | |
| Accounts Payable | | $ 3,000 | | $ 4,000 |
| Capital Stock | | 10,000 | | 10,000 |
| TOTAL LIABILITIES & CAPITAL | | $13,000 | | $14,000 |
| Retained Earnings | | 5,700 | | 8,850 |
| TOTAL LIABILITIES & EQUITY | | $18,700 | | $22,850 |

U.S. FOREIGN AUTO PARTS
CURRENT COST RETAINED EARNINGS RECONCILIATION STATEMENT
AS OF DECEMBER 31, 1982

| | | |
|---|---:|---:|
| Retained Earnings Balance, 12/31/81 | | $5,700 |
| Net Income Per Current Income Statement | | 2,055 |
| Total Retained Earnings & Income | | $7,755 |
| Add: Holding Gain on Inventory | $640 | |
| Holding Gain on Equipment | 455 | |
| Total Holding Gain | | 1,095 |
| Retained Earnings Balance, 12/31/82 | | $8,850 |

From the foregoing, two significant observations arise: First, the net income is less under the Current Cost method than under Historical Cost. An enterprise must be cautious about the declaration of dividends from income that exceeds the amount reported on the current cost basis, which in effect would result in the declaration of a partially liquidating dividend.

Secondly, despite the net income on a current cost basis being lower than on the historical basis, the retained earnings are higher under the current cost basis. The reason for this obviously is the effect of the Holding Gains. Again, the enterprise must be careful not to declare a dividend on the basis of these Holding Gains to avoid an erosion of operating capital which would result from the need to replace inventory and equipment at higher current future costs.

## #22-26...Limitations of the Current Cost Method

As the observations indicate, the current cost method does provide some advantages over historical cost. By showing a net income that is more realistic the tendency is created to avoid erosion of operating capital. On the other hand, the current cost method may be criticized for lacking a conservative attitude when specific prices of goods or operating assets are falling. In such case the net income will be higher than at historical cost, assuming that the historical costs are true costs.

A further disadvantage of the current cost method is its lack of objectivity for audit purposes. Historical costs are assumedly quite objectively determined. Current cost determination based on current prices or specific price indices may be more subjective. One would think, however, that as the method ferments through experience in usage, the current cost calculations may be fairly objectively attestable, particularly in consistency of determination.

## (III) CURRENT COST/CONSTANT DOLLAR ACCOUNTING

### #22-27...Refinement of Current Costs Through Constant Dollar Adjustments

Another of the weaknesses of the current cost basis is that the erosion of working capital through loss of purchasing power is not reflected. On the other hand, historical cost/constant dollar accounting is not realistic for inventories and plant, property and equipment, when specific price changes vary considerably from general price changes.

To avoid the main weaknesses of the current cost and historical cost/constant dollar methods a third method has been advocated which combines the two into a CURRENT COST/CONSTANT DOLLAR BASIS. Under this method current cost changes are considered for inventories and equipment and other non-monetary items, but changes in values of monetary items also are reflected. Then both purchasing power gains and losses and holding gains and losses are presented. Further the holding gains and losses are reflected net of the inflation effect.

### #22-28...Illustrative Case for Current Cost/Constant $ Method

Using the data of the U.S. Foreign Parts Co. as presented in the illustrations above, the following additional calculations would be necessary in order to adjust the holding gains to reflect the general price level adjustment:

| Item | | At Current Cost | Conversion Factor | | Adjusted Current Cost Restated in 1982 Dollars |
|------|---|---|---|---|---|
| Inventory, 12/31/82 | | $13,000 | 127/130 | | $12,700 |
| Cost of Goods Sold | | 24,640 | 127/127 | | 24,640 |
| Equipment, 12/31/82 | | 3,850 | 127/130 | | 3,761 |
| Depreciation | | 805 | 127/127 | | 805 |
| Totals | | $42,295 | | | $41,906 |
| Less: Inventory, 12/31/81 | 10,500 | | 127/125 | 10,668 | |
| Equipment, 12/31/81 | 4,200 | | 127/125 | 4,267 | |
| Purchases | 26,500 | 41,200 | 127/127 | 26,500 | 41,435 |
| Holding Gain at Current Cost | | $ 1,095 | | | |
| Holding Gain at Cost/Constant Dollar | | | | | $   471 |

Thus under the Current Cost/Constant Dollar Method the Holding Gain would be only $471 as against $1,095 under the Current Cost Method.

## #22-29...Nature of Holding Gains and Losses Account

Undoubtedly Holding Gains and Losses together with Purchasing Power Gains and Losses do increase or decrease the stockholders' equity. The question is whether and/or how much of these gains and losses should be reported on the income statement. This depends upon whether they are considered to be REALIZED or UNREALIZED.

As shown in discussing the Current Cost Method, Realized Gains relate to assets sold or consumed during the year. As for Inventory, the Realized portion of the Holding Gains is that which represents the adjustment to the current cost of goods sold from date of purchase to date of sale. As for Equipment, the Realized portion of the Holding Gain is that which relates to the historical cost allocation for the year.

On the other hand, the Unrealized Holding Gains relate to those held at year end. The Holding Gains for the year as shown under the current cost basis represent (1) the holding gains and losses realized during the year, and (2) the change in the Unrealized Holding Gains & Losses.

## #22-30..Calculation of Realized & Unrealized Holding Gain

To calculate the amounts of the Realized and Unrealized Holding Gains requires a breakdown of the preceding year-end unrealized amounts as well as current year-end unrealized amounts and current year realized amounts. The breakdown for the Inventory is as follows:

| Item | Historical Cost As Stated | Current Cost As Restated | Holding Difference Realized | Holding Difference Unrealized |
|---|---|---|---|---|
| Inventory, 12/31/82 | $12,500 | $13,000 | | $ 500 |
| Less: Inventory, 12/31/81 | 10,000 | 10,500 | | ( 500) |
| Unrealized Gain Increase or Decrease | | | | -0- |
| Purchases | 26,500 | 26,500 | | -0- |
| Cost of Goods Sold | 24,000 | 24,640 | $640 | |
| Realized Gain on Inventory | | | $640 | |
| TOTAL HOLDING GAIN ON INVENTORY | | | $640 | -0- |

The breakdown for the Equipment is as follows:

| Item | Historical Cost As Stated | Current Cost As Restated | Holding Difference Realized | Holding Difference Unrealized |
|---|---|---|---|---|
| Equipment Net, 12/31/82 | $ 2,500 | $ 3,850 | | $ 1,350 |
| Less: Equipment Net, 12/31/81 | 3,000 | 4,200 | | (1,200) |
| Unrealized Gain Increase or Decrease | | | | $ 150 |
| Depreciation | 500 | 805 | $305 | |
| Realized Gain on Equipment | | | $305 | |
| TOTAL HOLDING GAIN ON EQUIPMENT | | | $305 | $ 150 |

In the case of the Inventory, all of the holding gains were Realized; in the case of the Equipment, of a total of $455 of Holding Gains, $305 was Realized and $150 was Unrealized.

## #22-31...Conversion of Current Cost to Adjusted Current Cost

Having determined the Holding Gains and Losses from conversion of Historical Cost to Current Cost, the next step is to further adjust the Current Cost for general price level changes to reflect constant dollars. This is carried out in two steps: (1) Adjust Current Cost by Conversion Factor to derive the Adjusted Current Cost, and (2) Reconcile the Adjusted Historical Cost to the Adjusted Current Cost.

(1) The adjustment of Current Cost to Adjusted Current Cost is as follows:

| Item | At Current Cost | Conversion Factor | At Adjusted Current Cost |
|------|------|------|------|
| Inventory,12/31/82 | $13,000 | 127/130 | $12,700 |
| Inventory,12/31/81 | 10,500 | 127/125 | 10,688 |
| Cost of Goods Sold | 24,640 | 127/127 | 24,640 |
| Purchases | 26,500 | 127/127 | 26,500 |
| Equip,Net,12/31/82 | 3,850 | 127/130 | 3,761 |
| Equip,Net,12/31/81 | 4,200 | 127/125 | 4,267 |

(2) The Reconciliation of the Adjusted Historical Cost to Adjusted Current Cost is shown in Figure 22-2. It should be observed that the total adjusted holding gain for Inventories of $230 less $58, or $172, plus that for the Equipment of $228 plus $71, or $299, reconciles to the holding gain of $471, net of inflation, calculated at the beginning of this illustration. Also, for monetary assets and liabilities, and owners' equity capital stock, no current cost adjustments are reflected. Thus for these items the historical cost/constant dollar amounts are the same as the current cost/constant dollar amounts.

## #22-32...Reconciliation Schedule for Conversion of Current Cost to Current Cost/Constant Dollar Basis

All foregoing calculations and schedules may be integrated into a single reconciliation shown in Figure 22-3.

The Net Result of the CC/CD Schedule is:

(1)For In-
ventory: Unrealized Gain on 12/31/82
Inventory                = $ 488
Unrealized Gain on 12/31/81
Inventory                =    258

FIGURE 22-2

RECONCILIATION OF ADJUSTED HISTORICAL COST TO ADJUSTED CURRENT COST

| Item | At Historical Cost | Conversion Factor | Adjusted Historical Cost | Adjusted Current Cost | Holding Difference Realized | Holding Difference Unrealized |
|---|---|---|---|---|---|---|
| INVENTORY RECONCILIATION: | | | | | | |
| Inventory, 12/31/82 | 12,500 | x 127/130 = | 12,212 | 12,700 | | 488 |
| Less: Inventory, 12/31/81 | 10,000 | x 127/122 = | 10,410 | 10,668 | | 258 |
| Unrealized Gain Increase | | | | | | 230 |
| Cost of Goods Sold | 24,000 | x 125/122 = | 24,698 | 24,640 | (58) | |
| Purchases | 26,500 | x 127/127 = | 26,500 | 26,500 | | |
| Realized Loss on Invty | | | | | (58) | |
| TOTAL HOLDING GAIN ON INVENTORY | | | | | (58) | 230 |
| EQUIPMENT RECONCILIATION: | | | | | | |
| Equipment, Net, 12/31/82 | 2,500 | (5,773 − 2,886) = | 2,887 | 3,761 | | 874 |
| Less: Equipment, Net, 12/31/81 | 3,000 | (5,773 − 2,309) = | 3,464 | 4,267 | | 803 |
| Unrealized Gain Increase | | | | | | 71 |
| Depreciation | 500 | (5,773 x 10%) = | 577 | 805 | 228 | |
| Realized Gain on Equip. | | | | | 228 | |
| TOTAL HOLDING GAIN ON EQUIPMENT | | | | | 228 | 71 |

```
            Net Unrealized Gain on
                Inventory              =   $ 230
            Realized LOSS on Inventory =   ( 58)
            NET TOTAL INVENTORY HOLDING
                GAIN                                  $172
```

(2)For Equip-
   ment:
```
            Unrealized Gain as of
                12/31/82              =   $ 874
            Unrealized Gain as of
                12/31/81              =      803
            Net Unrealized Gain on
                Equipment             =   $  71
            Realized Gain on Equipment =     228
            NET TOTAL EQUIPMENT HOLDING
                GAIN                                  $299
            TOTAL HOLDING GAIN                        $471
```

It should be noted that under the Current Cost Method, the Retained Earnings Reconciliation Statement shows a Holding Gain
on Inventory of $640, and on Equipment of $455 for a total of
$1,095 as compared to $172 for Inventory and $299 for Equipment
for a total of only $471 under the Current Cost/Constant Dollar
Method.


#22-33...Current Cost/Constant Dollar Financial Statement


   The resulting financial statements under current cost/con-
stant dollar are as follows:


U.S. FOREIGN AUTO PARTS
CURRENT COST/CONSTANT DOLLAR COMPARATIVE BALANCE SHEETS

|                              | 12/31/81  | 12/31/82  |
|------------------------------|-----------|-----------|
| Cash                         | $ 1,016   | $ 2,442   |
| Receivables                  | 3,048     | 3,419     |
| Inventories                  | 10,668    | 12,700    |
| Equipment, Net               | 4,267     | 3,761     |
| TOTAL ASSETS                 | $18,999   | $22,322   |
|                              |           |           |
| Accounts Payable             | $ 3,048   | $ 3,907   |
| Capital Stock                | 12,700    | 12,700    |
| Retained Earnings            | 3,251     | 5,715     |
| TOTAL LIABILITIES AND EQUITY | $18,999   | $22,322   |

FIGURE 22-3

RECONCILIATION SCHEDULE FOR CONVERSION OF CURRENT COST
TO CURRENT COST/CONSTANT DOLLAR BASIS

| Item | (a) Inventory 12/31/82 | (b) Inventory 12/31/81 | (c) Cost of Goods Sold | (d) Purchases | (e) Net Equip. 12/31/82 | (f) Net Equip. 12/31/81 | (g) Deprec. |
|---|---|---|---|---|---|---|---|
| 1. Historical Cost, As Stated | 12,500 | 10,000 | 24,000 | 26,500 | 2,500 | 3,000 | 500 |
| 2. At Current Cost, As Restated | 13,000 | 10,500 | 24,640 | 26,500 | 3,850 | 4,200 | 805 |
| 3. Holding Difference (2-1) | 500 – | 500 | 640 | -- | 1,350 – | 1,200 | 305 |
| 4. Net Unrealized Gain or Loss [3(a) - 3(b) & 3(e) - e(f)] | -0- | | | | 150 | | |
| 5. Realized Gain [3(c) and 3(g)] | -- | -- | 640 | -- | -- | -- | 305 |
| 6. Total Holding Gain [5(c), 4(e) and 5(g)] | -- | -- | 640 | -- | 150 | -- | 305 |
| 7. Conversion Factor For Current Cost | 127/130 | 127/125 | 127/127 | 127/127 | 127/130 | 127/125 | 127/127 |

| | 1 | 2 | 3 | 4 | 5 | 6 | 7 |
|---|---|---|---|---|---|---|---|
| 8. Adjusted Current Cost Restated in 1982 Dollars (2 x 7) | 12,700 | 10,668 | 24,640 | 26,500 | 3,761 | 4,267 | 805 |
| 9. Adjusted Historical Cost in 1982 Dollars (Per Constant Dollar Statements) | 12,212 | 10,410 | 24,698 | 26,500 | 2,887 | 3,464 | 577 |
| 10. Unrealized Gain or Loss (8 - 9) | 488 - | 258 | -- | -- | 874 - | 803 | -- |
| 11. Realized Gain or Loss (8 - 9) | | | (Loss 58) | | | | 228 |
| 12. Increase in Unrealized Gain [10(a) - 10(b) & 10(e) - 10(f)] | 230 | | | | 71 | | |
| 13. TOTAL HOLDING GAIN (11 + 12) | (230-58) = 172 | | | | (71 + 228) = 299 | | |

TOTAL = 471

U.S. FOREIGN AUTO PARTS
CURRENT COST/CONSTANT DOLLAR 1982 INCOME STATEMENT

| | | |
|---|---|---|
| Sales | | $40,000 |
| Cost of Goods Sold | | 24,640 |
| Gross Profit | | $15,360 |
| Depreciation | $    805 | |
| Other Expenses | 12,500 | |
| Total Expenses | | 13,305 |
| NET INCOME | | $ 2,055 |

The Retained Earnings Account reconciles as follows:

| | |
|---|---|
| Balance, 12/31/81 | $3,251 |
| Add: Net Income | 2,055 |
| Net Holding Gains | 471 |
| | $5,777 |
| Less: Purchasing Power Loss | 62 |
| Balance, 12/31/82 | $5,715 |

Since retained earnings in this case include unrealized holding gains, such gain might be shown separately in a restricted or appropriated Retained Earnings account.

## #22-34...World-Wide Acceptance of Current Cost/Constant Dollar Method

This method is gaining momentum as the preferred one where historical cost data are considered inadequate. This was true in Canada several years ago, where, according to an article by John Hanna -- "Selected Alternative Accounting Models" -- published in the Fall 1972 issue of INTERNATIONAL JOURNAL OF ACCOUNTING, p. 158, a survey of sophisticated security analysts, bankers, and investment portfolio managers indicated a strong preference for current value/common dollar financial statements, as contrasted with their last preference for the historical cost/common dollar type.

## #22-35...FASB #33 Requirements

Of further note is that FASB #33 requires disclosure of results under all three methods. As previously seen, Paragraphs 29(a) and (b) require information on annual net income on a historical cost/constant dollar basis, and purchasing power gains and losses for the year. And Paragraphs 30(a) and (b) require information on annual net income as well as inventory, property, plant and equipment on a current cost basis. Finally Para. 30(c) requires disclosure of holding gains net of inflation. However, a complete set of adjusted supplementary financial statements is voluntary.

   That FASB #33 is strictly in the nebulous stage may be evidenced by a report in the Vol. 7, No. 5, July 1981 issue of ACCOUNTING NEWS BRIEFS published by Arthur Andersen & Co. page 2, as follows:

   As part of its review and monitoring of Statement #33, the board is asking for comments on the types of research it should be undertaking on the costs and benefits of disclosing the effects of inflation. The FASB will sponsor some research but also will rely heavily on outside research. It is hoped that this request for comment will encourage people to undertake projects to show, for example, whether companies are using inflation-adjusted disclosures and how, the information's effect on behavior, and estimates of how much companies spend to prepare the information.

   The Board wants to find out whether to continue to require the reporting of information about the effects of price changes, whether to continue to ask for both constant dollar and current cost information, or to pick one method, whether the information should continue to be supplementary or part of the primary financial statements, and what items companies should include in computing income adjusted for inflation's effects.

   To reduce the cost of private research, the Board will make available a data base, to include all the numerical information companies are required to publish under Statement 33. Two years of data for about 1,000 firms with fiscal years ending between Dec. 1980 and Jan. 31, 1981 should be available in Aug. 1981. Data for other firms are expected to be available next year, and the Board will update the data annually.

Arthur Young & Company has published a booklet entitled INFLATION, INSTABILITY AND ACCOUNTING from a speech by its Managing Partner, William S. Kanaga, presented at a regional conference of the Downstate New York Council, NAA, on Nov. 12, 1976 in New York. This should be a must reading for those interested in Inflation Accounting. This talk was directed primarily at the SEC requirement of the use of Replacement Cost Accounting in the form of a supplemental filing of Form 10K. Only a few brief highlights from this talk are presented to indicate the seriousness of injecting inflation accounting into the accounting framework:

   Currently we are being asked by the SEC to cope with inflation by new means of accounting--especially replacement cost accounting. The motive behind this move is to seek to make as much relevant information available to investors as possible--a laudable objective, but one that is being pursued by an incomplete, I might say dangerously incomplete, approach. According to a survey conducted by the NAA, the majority of businessmen feel not only that the new SEC rule

will be extremely expensive but also that it will not produce useful information.

Corporations are being asked to develop figures to reflect replacement costs as if everything were going to be
replaced this year. But such hypothetical figures bear no
resemblance to reality. What replaces old equipment or old
fixed assets may not be the same in productivity, in quality, nor even perhaps in function. Inflation cost information
is very different from the value-based information used in
most currentvalue financial reporting proposals. With each
company setting up its own methods for accumulating such
information, this "apples and oranges" mixture will make
financial reports even more confusing.

Over and over again, with inflation cost accounting, we
run into this problem of converting subjective, hypothetical
approximations into numbers, which become, by their very
nature, objective facts. The cynics are saying that public
accountants should love replacement cost accounting: Just
think of all that new work...think of all the increased
revenue!

## INFLATION ACCOUNTING FOR FOREIGN OPERATIONS

### #22-36...Foreign Currency Financial Statements

MNCs have a further problem, viz., how to present adjusted
financial statements on an international consolidated basis.
An enterprise may have foreign branches, subsidiaries or investees, recorded under the equity method of accounting. When
the statements of these foreign enterprises are to be restated
for price changes, the restatement process must be consistent
with the basis used in translating the foreign currency items
into the reporting currency--into U.S. dollars for U.S. firms.

Basically the method will depend on the underlying theory
involved in the price-level adjustment process. The proper SE-
QUENCE IN THE PROCESS IS DICTATED BY THE METHOD UTILIZED. There
are two different price adjustment methods: (1) the TRANSLATE-
RESTATE METHOD, for General Price-Level Accounting, and (2) the
RESTATE-TRANSLATE METHOD, for the specific price adjusted procedure.

The Institute of Chartered Accountants in England and Wales,
in the book ACCOUNTING FOR INFLATION, London, The Curwen Press,
1973, page 33, has diagrammed each of these two methods as
shown in Figure 22-4.

### #22-37...The Translate-Restate Method

When historical cost amounts are restated in general purchasing power units, as in the Historical Cost/Constant Dollar

basis, translation of the historical cost financial statements
expressed in a foreign country must first be accomplished. The
resulting translated amounts are then restated in constant purchasing dollar units. Thus FASB #33 specifically states that
"inventory, property, plant, and equipment, and related cost of
goods sold, depreciation, depletion and amortization expense
that are originally measured in units of a foreign currency
shall first be translated into U.S. Dollars in accordance with
generally accepted accounting principles and then restated in
constant dollars."

## #22-38...The Restate-Translate Method

Under the current cost basis, foreign assets and related
expense accounts should be stated at current cost before trans-

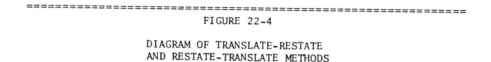

FIGURE 22-4

DIAGRAM OF TRANSLATE-RESTATE
AND RESTATE-TRANSLATE METHODS

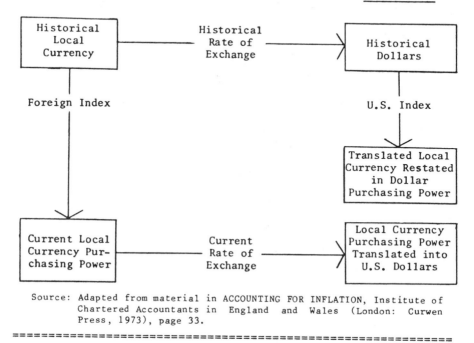

Source: Adapted from material in ACCOUNTING FOR INFLATION, Institute of
        Chartered Accountants in England and Wales (London: Curwen
        Press, 1973), page 33.

lation. Inventory, property, plant, and equipment outside the
U.S. will have to be estimated first in the foreign market and
then that current cost will be translated into U.S. dollars at
the rate in effect on the measurement date. Normally such date
will be the fiscal year end. In this connection, FASB #33 specifically provides that "if current cost is measured in a foreign currency, the amount shall be translated into dollars at
the current exchange rate, that is, the rate at the date of
use, sale, or commitment to a specific contract (in the cases
of depreciation expense and cost of goods sold) or the rate at
the balance sheet date (in the case of inventory and property,
plant & equipment)."

When currency costs of foreign assets are estimated, the
environmental factor in that foreign country must be considered. In other words, U.S. price indices would not be applicable
for restating foreign assets costs to current costs. The foreign currency amounts must be restated to current cost in terms
of foreign currency before translation into U.S. dollars at the
current rate of exchange.

### #22-39...Compatibility of Temporal Translation Method

For the historical based financial statements that are not
adjusted for price level changes, the temporal method of translation has been utilized in the U.S. Under this method, current
cost items, such as net realizable in the original unadjusted
financial statements, are translated at current exchange rates.
When foreign assets are restated to current costs under the
current cost basis for adjusting for changing prices, these
current costs are translated at current exchange rates too. In
other words, the temporal method is applicable to the current
cost basis as well as for the original historical financial
statements.

However, a different picture is presented under the historical cost/constant dollar basis for translated foreign currency
financial statements. Under the translate-restate method, restatement is actually of translated foreign currency historical
costs. Whether or not the purchasing power change for inflation rate is the same in the foreign country as it is in the
U.S. will have an effect on the restated amounts. If the inflation rates differ significantly, the restated foreign currency
translated amounts may not be very representative. Care must be
taken in properly explaining and disclosing this effect.

### #22-40...Foreign Currency Statement Translation vs.
###          Price Level Translation

The process of translation and conversion discussed above at
some length in connection with inflation accounting appears to

be similar to translation of foreign currency statements due to exchange rate variations. Although they are related, they are not interchangeable, and to avoid any confusion it is necessary to emphasize the distinctions between the two.

(1) In the first place, foreign currency statement translations are merely restatements of the value of one currency in terms of another and are totally unrelated to price-level adjustments. There is no correlation between fluctuations in the foreign currency market and the consumers price market.

(2) The translation of a cash account from one currency to another is fairly definite whereas a price-level adjustment may be subject to different interpretations. Also all cash accounts in financial statements must be in one currency only, whereas accounts could be adjusted for price-level changes on an individual basis.

(3) The orientation of price-level adjustments is in the direction of Capital Investment whereas that for foreign currency translation is Operational. This may be evidenced by the fact that some price-level adjustments go directly to retained earnings whereas Exchange Gains and Losses are regarded as current operating items. The items involved in foreign currency translations are directed at the income statement, whereas price-level translations are directed at capital items in the balance sheet.

(4) From the viewpoint of fluctuation risks, where foreign exchange currency risks are avoidable, price-level changes are clearly outside the control of the enterprise.

(5) Foreign exchange translations are TRANSACTIONS oriented due to their income statement emphasis, whereas price-level translations must be looked at from a TOTALITY of all transactions viewpoint.

## GLOBAL SURVEY OF INFLATION ACCOUNTING

### #22-41...Global Survey of Inflation Acctg. & Where It Is Going

In the Summer 1978 issue of WORLD, published by Peat, Marwick, Mitchell & Co., pages 43-51, which was reprinted in the JOURNAL OF ACCOUNTANCY, Jan. 1979, pages 70-78, is an article entitled "Inflation Accounting at the Crossroads." There is no question about this being required reading for anyone interested in the subject of inflation accounting, but to reproduce the article in its entirety would be beyond the scope of this work. Highlights are presented to indicate where inflation accounting is being practiced, the basic requirements, and what the future looks like in this area:

The subject of inflation accounting is controversial. About the only point on which there may be consensus is that inflation is here to stay. *** Some critics contend that accounting is totally inadequate to the job of reporting the impact of inflation. They say that reported earnings often are illusory because inventory profits are overstated and depreciation charges are grossly inadequate, and some assets on the balance sheet are vastly understated. Putting these charges into a global perspective, it is no wonder that inflation accounting has been called "potentially the most explosive issue facing multinational corporations and their subsidiaries."

Because of the seriousness of the inflation accounting issue, one might have expected a resolution of it by now. Clearly this is not the case. A number of difficult hurdles impede international progress in dealing with the problem. One hurdle understandably is the vested interest of managements. Then, too, there is plain old aversion to change. *** Further, there is disagreement over whether and how accounting should change to contend with inflation. Some maintain that accountants should not attempt to foster economic, social or political goals. *** Another hurdle is the great debate over theory. *** Practical considerations present another set of obstacles. *** Government influence is another hurdle because it is in part a political issue. *** Labor unions are still another hurdle.

## #22-42...Proposals Around the World

A table summarizing many of the current proposals around the world shows that current and replacement cost notions are now in vogue, contrasted to the sentiment that prevailed in the early 1970s for general purchasing power restatement. The report continues:

Also it seems that inventories and fixed assets are widely considered to be the key items affected by inflation, although there is growing sentiment for including monetary items in this group. Moreover, the focus appears more and more to be on the income statement rather than the balance sheet, and that the main objective should be to present information about how inflation or changing prices affect results of operations and long-range cash flows. Among the major industrial nations, the U.S. and the U.K. have moved relatively far, and the measures they have put into effect follow the world-wide trends. As an interim solution, however, public U.K. companies are now publishing separate profit and loss statements that reflect three adjustments to the traditional numbers: (1) A Cost of Sales Adjustment -- a charge is made for the excess of the current cost of inventories at the date of sale over the historical cost; (2) A Depreciation Adjustment -- additional depreciation based on the current replacement cost of plant and equipment is

charged; (3) A "Gearing" Adjustment -- a charge or credit is
made relating to monetary items.

The "gearing" adjustment is the most controversial of
the three. Proponents of this concept say that the cost of
sales and depreciation adjustments are overstated UNLESS
consideration is given to how a company is financed. Their
logic is that in times of inflation, if a company's monetary
liabilities exceed its monetary assets, its CREDITORS are
picking up part of the tab for inflation. In other words the
"loss" to the company's creditors must be a "gain" to its
shareholders. This follows that part of the general purchasing power concept that holds that a company gains from having debt in periods of inflation, because fewer resources in
terms of current purchasing power need be used to pay off
the debt. Conversely, under this concept, a company loses by
holding monetary assets in inflationary times. Those in the
U.K. opposing "gearing"--apparently a minority--say that
these "gains" or "losses" are merely theoretical and should
not be taken into account.

### #22-43...Table of Inflation Acctg. Proposals Around the World

This table indicates the Major Countries, the Applicability
of Inflation Accounting, the Presentation Required, Audit Implications, Tax Acceptability, and Status. The listing is as
follows:

I.   UNITED STATES: SEC ASR #190, Mar. 1976. Applicability:
     (Note--This article was written prior to issuance of FASB
     #33) Only SEC requirements stated. Presentation: Supple-
     mental statements of footnotes disclosing; replacement
     cost of inventories; replacement cost of productive capa-
     city; cost of goods sold based on replacement cost as of
     time of sale; and depreciation based on average replace-
     ment cost for the period. Audit Implications: Audit not
     required, but the auditor associated with the disclosures.
     Tax Acceptability: Not accepted. Status: FASB considering
     current values disclosures for all companies (FASB #33).

II.  UNITED KINGDOM: Interim Recommendation, THE HYDE GUIDE-
     LINES, Nov. 1977. Applicability: Voluntary for fiscal
     years ended after Dec. 1977 and directed primarily to
     listed companies. Presentation: A separate income state-
     ment showing excess of current inventories as of time of
     sale over the historical cost; additional depreciation
     based on current replacement cost; and "gearing" or lever-
     age adjustment for monetary items. Audit Implications:
     Audit recommended. Tax Acceptability: Not accepted.
     Status: English Institute of Chartered Accountants vetoed
     compulsory current cost accounting in 1977; Inflation Ac-
     counting Steering Group is drafting a long-term accounting

standard; subject to EEC requirements (below).

III.  BELGIUM: Royal Decree on Financial Statements of Enterprises, Oct. 1976. Applicability: Voluntary for all companies. Presentation: Reflect following data in the primary financial statements with footnote disclosure: replacement cost of inventories and fixed assets; cost of goods sold based on replacement cost as of time of sale; and depreciation based on current replacement cost. Audit Implications: Audit required. Tax Acceptability: Not accepted. Status: Subject to EEC requirements.

IV.   FRANCE: Finance Acts of 1977 and 1978 (application decrees to be issued April 1978). Applicability: Mandatory generally for fiscal years ended after Dec. 1977 for listed companies (optional for other companies). Presentation: Reflect in the primary financial statements the revaluation of all assets based on current replacement cost subject to a maximum limit, i.e., net book value multiplied by a given coefficient, and disclose the effect on stockholders' equity (and restrictions on distribution of earnings). Audit Implications: Audit required. Tax Acceptability: Not accepted, but a portion of the taxes relating to increases in raw materials can be deferred for 6 years. Status: Subject to EEC requirements (below).

V.    GERMANY: Pronouncement of the H.F.A. Technical Committee of the German Institute "To Maintain the Net Worth of an Enterprise at Current Value in Determining the Results of Operations" (Nov. 1975). Applicability: Voluntary for stock corporations and other companies required to publish annual reports. Presentation: Footnote disclosure of the effect on net earnings of cost of goods sold based on replacement cost as of time of sale; and depreciation based on average replacement cost. Only those inventories and fixed assets that are considered financed by equity capital are included in determining the effect on net earnings. Audit Implications: Audit required. Tax Acceptability: Not accepted. Status: Subject to EEC requirements; however implementation is likely to take a long time, since German accounting is prescribed by law which would have to be changed.

VI.   NETHERLANDS: Institute Note accompanying IASC #6, June 1977. Applicability: Voluntary for all companies. Presentation: Dutch accounting rules do not contain stringent regulations as to valuation methods other than that they must be "generally acceptable." Preference is for a current value balance sheet with historical costs in notes; and operating results on a current value basis either in the income statement or notes. Audit Implications: Audit required. Tax Acceptability: It is anticipated that at least a partial deducation will be allowed in 1978 for tax purposes. <u>Status</u>: Subject to EEC requirements; a few Dutch companies have adopted current values for accounting and reporting purposes.

VII. <u>EEC</u>: Draft 4th Directive (Revised Feb. 1974). <u>Applicability</u>: When effective, would be voluntary for all companies. <u>Presentation</u>: Reflect in the primary financial statements; replacement cost of inventories and fixed assets; cost of goods sold based on replacement cost as of time of sale; and depreciation based on current replacement cost. <u>Audit Implications</u>: Audit would be required. <u>Tax Acceptability</u>: The tax ramification would depend on the individual member states. <u>Status</u>: A final 4th Directive is expected in the near future.

VIII. <u>AUSTRALIA</u>: Provisional Accounting Standard, "Current Cost Accounting" (Oct. 1976). <u>Applicability</u>: Would be mandatory for all companies for fiscal years beginning July 1979. <u>Presentation</u>: Reflect in the primary financial statements: replacement cost of inventories and fixed assets; cost of goods sold based on replacement cost as of time of sale; and depreciation based on average replacement cost. <u>Audit Implications</u>: Audit would be required. <u>Tax Acceptability</u>: A tax deduction is allowed for one-half of the inflation amount determined by a general consumer price index included in inventories. <u>Status</u>: Current Cost Accounting Steering Group is developing working guides dealing with current cost implementation and is considering how to deal with monetary items.

IX. <u>CANADA</u>: Report of the Ontario Committee on Inflation Accounting, June 1977. <u>Applicability</u>: Would be voluntary for all companies. <u>Presentation</u>: Furnish a supplementary statement of "Funds Available for Distribution or Expansion" reflecting (a) additional funds required to replace inventory sold during the year; (b) funds required to finance the current replacement cost of plant, machinery and equipment; (c) extent to which the additional funds required to finance the increased cost of inventory and plant may be available from borrowings, assuming the maintenance of a constant ratio of equity to nonequity capital. <u>Audit Implications</u>: Audit not required. <u>Tax Acceptability</u>: Not accepted. <u>Status</u>: Proposed as an interim recommendation until a comprehensive current value accounting system is developed; The Accounting Research Committee also issued a discussion paper, "Current Value Accounting," in Aug. 1976, to encourage experimentation and debate on supplemental disclosure possibilities.

X. <u>NEW ZEALAND</u>: ED #14, "Accounting in Terms of Current Costs and Values," Aug. 1976, to be superseded by Report of the Committee of Inquiry into Inflation Accounting, "The Richardson Report," Dec. 1976. <u>Applicability</u>: When the Rich-

ardson Report would become effective, it would be mandatory for all companies; implementation would be over a
3-year period depending on whether the company is publicly
listed or, in the case of a "private company," its size.
Presentation: Reflect in the primary financial statements:
current replacement cost of all assets "essential to the
business" (broadly defined); net realizable value of other
assets; cost of goods sold generally based on replacement
cost as of time of sale; and depreciation generally based
on replacement cost of fixed assets held at the balance
sheet date. Audit Implications: Audit would be required.
Tax Acceptability: Recommends that adjustments be accepted
for tax purposes. Status: The New Zealand Society of Accountants is continuing to study the controversial issues
involved in adopting ED#14 as a standard. In preliminary
comments on the Richardson Report, the society stresses
significant implementation problems and proposed that the
earliest implementation date be April 1979.

XI.   SOUTH AFRICA: Circular to all S.A. Chartered Accountants,
      "Accounting For Inflation and Other Changes in Price Lev-
      els," Oct. 1975. Applicability: Voluntary for all compa-
      nies. Presentation: In the director's report or in a sup-
      plemental statement or footnote, present the impact of
      inflation on the enterprise. No specific guidance is pro-
      vided in the circular which permits the impact to be de-
      termined by a general purchasing power, current cost, or
      combination approach. Audit Implications: Audit not re-
      quired. Tax Acceptability: Internal Revenue Service will
      give serious consideration to using the method adopted for
      accounting purposes as the basis for tax assessments.
      Status: Circular has been ignored in practice and some
      directors' statements refer to inflation in general terms
      without any quantification. The National Council is work-
      ing on a recommendation for a supplementary current cost
      income statement.

XII.  ARGENTINA: Pronouncement of the Argentine Technical Insti-
      tute of Public Accountants (1972). Applicability: Manda-
      tory in certain provinces for all corporations with paid-
      in capital exceeding 5 million pesos ($700,000) that (a)
      have issued stock to the public; (b) are in joint ventures
      with the government; or (c) utilize public concessions or
      services. Presentation: Present complete restatement of
      all non-monetary items by means of a general price index
      as supplemental information in (a) a second column in the
      primary financial statements; (b) a footnote to the pri-
      mary financial statements; or (c) a complementary set of
      financial statements. Audit Implications: Audit required.
      Tax Acceptability: Revaluations deductible for tax purpos-
      es. Status: No changes are imminent.

XIII.BRAZIL: Brazilian Corporation Law, 1976. Applicability: Mandatory for fiscal years beginning after Jan. 1, 1978, for all companies. Under the previous law revaluations of fixed assets and working capital were required. Presentation: Reflect in the primary financial statements: revaluations of all "permanent asset accounts," including fixed assets (not inventories), investments, and deferred charges, based on an "official index," reduction of shareholder equity accounts by using the official general index; and net effect on earnings of the above revaluations and reduction. Audit Implications: Audit required. Tax Acceptability: Revaluations accepted for tax purposes. Status: No changes anticipated because of recency of enactment of the law.

## #22-44...Future of Inflation Accounting

As for the future of Inflation Accounting, the article concludes with suggestions by the authors as to how it may receive a gradual implementation:

Considering the hurdles mentioned earlier and the lessons learned from experiences in many nations, we offer the following course of action--on a global scale--for dealing with the inflation accounting issue. However, underlying the proposal is a strong belief that efforts must begin now to develop an international solution to the issue before methods adopted by individual countries become too firmly entrenched. We encourage the International Accounting Standards Committee to take the lead in this endeavor. The ultimate goal must be a reasonably uniform international standard. Our proposal includes three phases.

PHASE ONE: "Pragmatism Over Purity" may be an apt way to characterize this initial phase. By now a sufficiently common ground may exist for presenting two pieces of information on the face of the basic financial statements: (1) Cost of Sales determined on the basis of current costs of inventories at the time of their sale; and (2) Depreciation expense determined on the basis of current costs of fixed assets. *** Initially the data should be required only for enterprises whose securities are freely traded and whose inventories and fixed assts are in excess of a specified percentage, e.g., 10 to 15, of total assets. We see the end of 1979 as a realistic target date for completion of this phase.

PHASE TWO: Primarily, the second phase would involve study and experimentation, building on the initial reporting standards, and working toward the longer-term goal of a more comprehensive solution. The IASC would coordinate and monitor the implementation process. *** A number of difficult

questions would have to be considered in this phase, including these: Applicability, Gearing, Deferred Taxes, LIFO vs.
FIFO, Other Non-Monetary Assets, Forward-Looking Data. ***
Phase Two would take place over another 2-year period, so
that by the end of 1981 a sound basis would exist for formulating a comprehensive model.

PHASE THREE: The goal for this final phase would be a
comprehensive, workable, inflation-based international accounting and reporting system in the implementation stage by
the end of 1982. *** Such a system can represent a positive,
refined response to the inflation accounting issue that
would avoid the pitfalls of moving "too far too fast." ***
The quest for inflation accounting has reached a global
crossroads. It is commendable that it has reached this
point. But as it moves from the crossroads, we should resolve that it be propelled by a sound balance between theory
and practicality and that it travels forcefully in a single
direction.
Obviously the authors of this lengthy survey of inflation accounting proved to be quite a bit optimistic. As of the latter
part of 1984, Phase One, which was targeted for the end of
1979, has not been realized. Nor has Phase Two, targeted for
the end of 1981. Since inflation accounting is inevitably going
to be hitched to FASB #33, which was to be in a 3-year trial
period beginning in 1982, certainly Phase Three could never
come off by the end of 1982. Because of the highly controversial nature of inflation accounting, certainly a more cautious
timetable should have been set.

As a matter of fact, the best solution to inflation accounting is not the accounting aspects but inflation itself. One
doesn't need to be too profound to realize that if you lick
inflation, there will be no need for inflation accounting; it
would become supererogatory. And it certainly is not too recon-
dite to observe that it would be far better to lick inflation
than be forced into the inflation accounting monstrosity. The
problem basically is not an accounting one; it is a political
economic one, and will certainly require the efforts of a great
man to solve it.

As a concluding observation, there has been considerable
talk the middle of 1981 about reverting to the Gold Standard to
solve the problem. In the Aug. 17, 1981 issue of the INTERNA-
TIONAL HERALD TRIBUNE, the following remarks are interesting:

For a decade now the international financial order has
evolved a system that largely leaves the price of various
foreign currencies to the ebb and flow of supply and demand.
In many quarters this system is applauded, but increasingly
there are calls to reconsider and to return to what in any
other market would be price controls. In the market for currencies, those controls were known as fixed exchange rates,

which set and sustained the ratios at which one currency was exchanged for another.    For a  quarter century, fixed rates were the norm of the postwar world. Then ten years ago, Nixon's Administration snapped  the  link between gold  and the dollar, shattering the rock on which fixed rates rested and, in  effect, forcing a reliance on the free market to set the price of currencies. Now an increasing number of experts are calling for a re-examination of that system.  A  great  many espouse a return to some degree or another to the old system of controls.

Perhaps most  notable about the developing debate is the extreme spectrum of  proposals  on  what to do.   At one end there is the  Reagan Administration, which has  declared its belief in still greater  reliance on the free market to  set currency rates. At the other extreme are serious suggestions for an even  more rigorous gold standard than existed before Nixon ended the convertibility of dollars into gold.   In the middle, and perhaps most  numerous ,  is a cluster of experts who say they miss the greater certainty and the greater economic  discipline that fixed exchange rates purportedly provided.

The  debate seems contradictory but is hardly  academic. Fixed  exchange  rates  were  considered a  vital beacon for world trade.  Although legions  of foreign exchange  experts now help multinational business hedge against the  continual risk of untoward  currency  fluctuations,  the  uncertainty leaves an edgy discomfort.   Even from  hindsight, observers like Lord Roll, former Chancellor of  the Exchequer of Great Britain, do not disagree with President Nixon's  decision to "close the gold window," nor do they believe the world could quickly  revert to the old order.  Exchange rates, they say, can remain fixed only when  inflation rates among  countries are roughly similar and when capital flows remain even.   Arthur F. Burns, who at the  time was chairman of the Federal Reserve Board,  said "I  was  the only  one of us opposed to closing the gold window.  In retrospect, it was unavoidable. I'd  love to see a return to the gold standard, but I see no easy or quick way of attaining it."

According to Lord Roll  "the real question is  the right combination of domestic monetary policy, exchange rate policy,  and inflation  policy to get the  benefits  of flexible exchange rates without the tremendous volatility." Lord Roll favors  a fixed-rate  system with  a built-in provision for occasional change.  The search for discipline is largely behind  the current  call for a return to the  gold  standard. When  currencies can be  redeemed for gold, governments  are prevented  from printing  too  much money,  a still stricter form of discipline.  Exchange rates also become fixed;  each currency  is worth a set amount of gold.  "Paper money that

could  not be redeemed has almost always been accompanied by
unbalanced budgets, high INFLATION and high interest rates,"
said Lewis Lehrman, a businessman  economist and leading advocate of the gold standard.  As a testament to the strength
of the gold movement, the Reagan Administration has appointed  a commission  to study  restoring the  gold standard,  a
group that includes Mr. Lehrman.
On the  same subject, Mr. Lehrman is quoted in an article entitled "Time to Return to  Gold  Standard?"  in the Sept. 7, 1981
issue of U.S. NEWS & WORLD REPORT at pages 71-72:
    The  main reason for  returning to the gold standard is that
    the  present  managed  paper-dollar  standard  has  failed.
    Throughout history all paper currencies have been destroyed.
    *** A paper dollar without  any anchor  in a real article of
    wealth  is unstable. *** The gold  standard  in one  form or
    another  gave us reasonable price stability from about  1792
    to 1971--almost the entire history of the U.S. When you have
    a gold and stable dollar for approximately  170  years  with
    brief interruptions, then you  have to conclude that  it was
    more than  an accident. *** Under  the  gold standard,  the
    highest rate  of inflation between 1896 and 1913 never  ex-
    ceeded 2 to 3% per year.  It was the essence of stability.

## SUMMARY OF FOOTNOTE REFERENCES
(References are to Paragraph #'s)

#22-8   FASB #33, CLASSIFICATION OF  COMMON MONETARY AND NONMONETARY
        ITEMS
#22-12  Raymond  J. Chambers, ACCOUNTING,  EVALUATION  AND  ECONOMIC
        BEHAVIOR (Prentice-Hall, 1966), p. 196
#22-34  John Hanna, "Selected Alternative Accounting Models," INTER-
        NATIONAL JOURNAL OF ACCOUNTING (Fall 1972): 158
#22-35  Arthur Andersen & Co., ACCOUNTING NEWS BRIEFS, Vol. 7, No. 5
        (July 1981): 2
#22-35  William  S. Kanaga, "Inflation, Instability and Accounting,"
        Arthur Young & Co., Nov.12,1976, speech at N.Y. Council, NAA
#22-36  Institute of Chartered Accountants in England and Wales, AC-
        COUNTING FOR INFLATION (London: The Curwen Press, 1973),p.33
#22-37  FASB #33,  FINANCIAL  REPORTING  AND CHANGING PRICES,  Sept.
        1979
#22-38  Ibid.
#22-41  Peat,  Marwick, Mitchell & Co., "Inflation Accounting at the
        Crossroads," WORLD (Summer 1978): 43-51. Reprinted with per-
        mission.
#22-42  Ibid., by permission.
#22-43  Ibid., by permission.
#22-44  Ibid., by permission.
#22-44  "Return to the Gold Standard," INTERNATIONAL  HERALD TRIBUNE
        (Aug. 17, 1981)
#22-44  Lewis Lehrman, "Time to Return to Gold Standard?", U.S. NEWS
        & WORLD REPORT (Sept. 7, 1981): 71-72

# BIBLIOGRAPHY

Aliber, Robert Z. "Monetary Interdependence Under Floating Exchange Rates," JOURNAL OF FINANCE, 30 (May 1975): 365-376

Buckley, Adrian. "The Curate's Egg of ED 24," THE ACCOUNTANT, 181 (December 6, 1979): 810-811

Chambers, R.J. "Current Cost Accounting Does Not Add Up," THE AUS-TRALIAN ACCOUNTANT, 46 (Sept. 1976): 490-496

Choi, Frederick. "Foreign Inflation and Management Decisions," MAN-AGEMENT ACCOUNTING, 58 (June 1977): 21-27

Drury, James and Bougen, Philip. "U.K. Gearing Levels: An Investigation," ACCOUNTANCY, 91 (July 1980): 103-106

Edwards, J.R. "Inflation Accounting: The Best of Both Worlds," THE ACCOUNTANT, 174 (Jan. 15, 1976): 67-68

Fielding, John. "The Gearing Adjustment--What Is the Best Method?" ACCOUNTANCY, 90 (May 1979): 73-76

Fisher, J. "Replacement Cost Accounting--American Style," THE AC-COUNTANT, 176 (June 30, 1977): 747-751

Gibbs, Martin. "The Hyde Gearing Adjustment," ACCOUNTANCY, 89 (February 1978): 87-89

Lorenson, Leonard and Rosenfield, Paul. "Management Information and Foreign Inflation," JOURNAL OF ACCOUNTANCY, 138 (December 1974): 98-102

McCosh, Andrew M. "Implications of Sandilands For Non-U.K. Accountants," JOURNAL OF ACCOUNTANCY, 141 (March 1976): 42-50

Morpeth, D.S. "Practical Problems of Inflation Accounting," THE ACCOUNTANT, 174 (April 8, 1976): 416-418

Schmitt, G.J. "Research in Inflation Accounting," CHARTERED AC-COUNTANT IN AUSTRALIA (December 1976)

Vancil, Richard. "Inflation Accounting--The Great Controversy," HARVARD BUSINESS REVIEW (March-April 1976): 58-67

# THEORY QUESTIONS
(Question Numbers are Keyed to Text Paragraph #'s)

#22-1  Make up an outline showing the different methods or approaches to inflation accounting.

#22-2  Discuss the nature of General Price Level Accounting.

#22-3  Explain the meaning of GENERAL PURCHASING POWER.

#22-5  What are the five most common indexing methods for price level measurements and which is regarded as the most acceptable?

#22-6  Define Monetary Items and Nonmonetary Items. How are they classified?

#22-8  How does FASB #33 classify Monetary and Nonmonetary Items?

#22-10 What is the formula for restatement of Nonmonetary Assets and Liabilities?

#22-12 Explain what is meant by Purchasing Power Gains or Losses on Net Monetary Items. Where do they appear on the financial statements?

#22-16 What are the limitations of the Historical Cost/Constant Dollar basis of inflation accounting?

#22-17 Define the Current Cost Method of inflation accounting. How does it differ from General Price Level Accounting?

#22-18 How may current costs be determined?

#22-19 What three steps are required to carry out Current Value Accounting?

#22-22 What are Holding Gains and Losses? Classify them.

#22-26 What are the limitations of the Current Cost Method?

#22-27 What method has been advocated to avoid the main weaknesses of the Current Cost and Historical/Constant Dollar Methods? How does the Current Cost/Constant Dollar method operate?

#22-35 What are the requirements for inflation accounting under FASB #33?

#22-36 What further problems are multinational operations confronted with involving inflation accounting, and what two methods may be used in the price-level adjustment process?

#22-37 Explain the operation of the Translate-Restate Method.

#22-38 Explain the operation of the Restate-Translate Method.

#22-40 Outline the differences showing the distinctions between foreign currency statement translation and price level translation.

#22-41 Comment on the Peat, Marwick & Mitchell Global Survey of inflation accounting and its future.

#22-44 In your opinion what is the best solution to the problem of inflation accounting?

#22-44 (a) What do you think about the effect of returning to the Gold Standard as a solution to the inflation accounting problem?

**EXERCISES**

**EX-22-1 (CPA EXAM, 11/80, THEORY, #26)**
In accordance with FASB Statement No. 33, the Consumer Price Index for All Urban Consumers is used to compute information on
    a. an historical cost basis.
    b. a current cost basis.
    c. a nominal dollar basis.
    d. a constant dollar basis.

**EX-22-2 (CPA EXAM, 5/82, THEORY, #36)**
A method of accounting based on measures of historical prices in dollars, each of which has the same general purchasing power, is
    a. Current cost/constant dollar accounting.
    b. Current cost/nominal dollar accounting.
    c. Historical cost/constant dollar accounting.
    d. Historical cost/nominal dollar accounting.

### EX-22-3 (CPA EXAM, 5/83, THEORY, #7)
A method of accounting based on measures of current cost or lower recoverable amount, without restatement into units having the same general purchasing power, is
 a. Historical cost/constant dollar accounting.
 b. Historical cost/nominal dollar accounting.
 c. Current cost/constant dollar accounting.
 d. Current cost/nominal dollar accounting.

### EX-22-4 (CPA EXAM, 5/70, THEORY, #4)
Although cash generally is regarded as the simplest of all assets to account for, certain complexities can arise for both domestic and multinational companies.
**Required**:
 1. How might it be maintained that a gain or a loss is incurred by holding a constant balance of cash through a period of price-level change?
 2. Identify and give a justification for the typical accounting treatment accorded these gains or losses.

### EX-22-5 (CPA EXAM, 5/77, THEORY, #9)
When discussing asset valuation, the following valuation bases are sometimes mentioned: replacement cost, exit value, and discounted cash flow. Which of these bases should be considered a current-value measure?
 a. Replacement cost and exit value only.
 b. Replacement cost and discounted cash flow only.
 c. Exit value and discounted cash flow only.
 d. Replacement cost, exit value, and discounted cash flow.

### EX-22-6 (CPA EXAM, 5/77, THEORY, #6)
Asset measurement is a concept that involves the valuation or pricing of the future service of an asset. Receivables are particular assets that represent future claims to fixed amounts of monies.
**Required**:
 a. Discuss how the asset measurement concept is applied to receivables (short-term and long-term).
 b. Describe how a company that has a significant amount of receivables during an inflationary period sustains a "general price-level loss." Include in your answer an example of how such a "loss" would be computed when a $100,000 receivable exists at the beginning and end of a year that had an inflation rate of 10%.

### EX-22-7 (CPA EXAM, 11/77, THEORY, #7)
**PART (a).** Price-level adjusted financial statements are prepared in an effort to eliminate the effects of inflation or deflation. An integral part of determining restated amounts and

applicable gain or loss from restatement is the segregation of all assets and liabilities into monetary and nonmonetary classifications. One reason for this classification is that price-level gains and losses for monetary items are currently matched against earnings.
**Required**:
What are the factors that determine whether an asset or liability is classified as monetary or nonmonetary? Include in your response the justification for recognizing gains and losses from monetary items and not for nonmonetary items.
**PART (b)**. Proponents of price-level restatement of financial statements state that a basic weakness of financial statements not adjusted for price-level changes is that they are made up of "mixed dollars."
**Required**:
1. What is meant by the term "mixed dollars" and why is this a weakness of unadjusted financial statements?
2. Explain how financial statements restated for price-level changes eliminate this weakness. Use property, plant, and equipment as your example in this discussion.

## EX-22-8  (CPA EXAM, 11/79, THEORY, #24)
In current value (fair value) financial statements,
   a. General price-level gains or losses are recognized on net monetary items.
   b. Amounts are always stated in common purchasing power units of measurement.
   c. All balance sheet items are different in amount than they would be in a historical-cost balance sheet.
   d. Holding gains are recognized.

## EX-22-9  (CPA EXAM, 5/81, THEORY, #3)
Financial reporting should provide information to help investors, creditors, and other users of financial statements. Statement of Financial Accounting Standards No. 33 requires large public enterprises to disclose certain supplementary information.
**Required**:
   a. Describe the historical cost/constant dollar method of accounting. Include in your discussion how historical cost amounts are used to make historical cost/constant dollar measurements.
   b. Describe the principal advantage of the historical cost/constant dollar method of accounting over the historical cost method of accounting.
   c. Describe the current cost method of accounting.
   d. Why would depreciation expense for a given year differ using the current cost method of accounting instead of the historical cost method of accounting? Include in your discussion

whether depreciation expense is likely to be higher or lower using the current cost method of accounting instead of the historical cost method in a period of rising prices, and why.

## EX-22-10  (CPA EXAM, 11/81, THEORY, #6)
FASB Statement No. 33 requires that the current cost for inventories be measured as the
  a. Recoverable amount regardless of the current cost.
  b. Current cost regardless of the recoverable amount.
  c. Higher of current cost or recoverable amount.
  d. Lower of current cost or recoverable amount.

## EX-22-11  (CPA EXAM, 11/81, THEORY, #7)
When computing information on a historical cost/constant dollar basis, which of the following is classified as nonmonetary?
  a. Cash surrender value of life insurance.
  b. Long-term receivables.
  c. Allowance for doubtful accounts.
  d. Inventories, other than inventories used on contracts.

## EX-22-12  (CPA EXAM, 11/83, THEORY, #4)
When computing information on a historical cost/constant dollar basis, which of the following is classified as monetary?
  a. Equity investment in unconsolidated subsidiaries.
  b. Obligations under warranties.
  c. Unamortized discount on bonds payable.
  d. Deferred investment tax credits.

## EX-22-13  (CPA EXAM, 5/83, THEORY, #6)
When computing information on a historical cost/constant dollar basis, which of the following is classified as nonmonetary?
  a. Allowance for doubtful accounts.
  b. Accumulated depreciation of equipment.
  c. Unamortized premium on bonds payable.
  d. Advances to unconsolidated subsidiaries.

## EX-22-14  (CPA EXAM, 5/82, THEORY, #39)
In accordance with FASB Statement No. 33, purchasing power gain or loss results from which of the following?

|    | Monetary assets and liabilities | Nonmonetary assets and liabilities |
|----|---------------------------------|------------------------------------|
| a. | Yes | Yes |
| b. | Yes | No |
| c. | No | Yes |
| d. | No | No |

## PROBLEMS

**P-22-1  (CPA EXAM, 5/83, PRAC. II, #15)**
Loy Corp. purchased a machine in 1980 when the average Consumer
Price Index (CPI) was 180.  The average  CPI  was 190 for 1981,
and   200 for 1982.  Loy  prepares supplementary constant dollar
statements (adjusted for changing prices). Depreciation on this
machine is $200,000 a   year.   In Loy's  supplementary constant
dollar  statement for  1982 the   amount of depreciation expense
should be stated as
    a. $180,000                    c.  $210,526
    b. $190,000                    d.  $222,222

**P-22-2  (CPA EXAM, 11/83, PRAC.I #17 & 11/80, PRAC.I #17)**
On Jan. 1, 1982, Nutley Corp. had monetary assets of $2,000,000
and monetary   liabilities   of $1,000,000.   During 1982 Nutley's
monetary  inflows   and   outflows   were  relatively constant and
equal so that   it   ended the year with net   monetary assets   of
$1,000,000.  Assume   that the CPI was 200 on   Jan. 1, 1982, and
220 on Dec. 31, 1982.   In end-of-year constant dollars, what is
Nutley's purchasing   power  gain or loss on net monetary items
for 1982?
    a. $0                          c.  $100,000 gain
    b. $50,000 gain                d.  $100,000 loss

**P-22-3  (CPA EXAM, 11/80, PRAC. I, #18)**
Victor Co. purchased a machine on Dec. 31,   1977, for $100,000.
The machine   is being   depreciated on the   straight-line  basis
with   no salvage value and a five-year life.   Assume that there
was a rise   in current (replacement) cost of the machine of 10%
during  1978,   and of 10%   during   1979 (based on   the Dec. 31,
1978, current cost).   In a supplementary current cost statement
at   Dec. 31, 1979, Victor would report accumulated depreciation
for the above machine of
    a. $42,000                     c.  $46,200
    b. $44,000                     d.  $48,400

**P-22-4  (CPA EXAM, 11/78, PRAC. I, #13)**
Level, Inc., was formed on Jan. 1, 1977, when   common   stock of
$200,000  was issued for   cash   of  $50,000 and land  valued at
$150,000.  Level did   not begin operations  until   1978, and no
transactions occurred in 1977 except the recording of the issuance of common stock.   If the CPI was 100 at Dec. 31, 1976, and
averaged 110 during 1977,   what would the purchasing power gain
or loss be for Level in 1977?
    a. $0                          c.  $5,000 gain
    b. $5,000 loss                 d.  $15,000 gain

## P-22-5  (CPA EXAM, 5/79, PRAC. I, #15)

Donahue Corp. purchased a machine in 1976 when the general price-level index was 180. The price-level index was 190 in 1977 and 200 in 1978. The price-level indexes above are stated in terms of the 1958 base year. Donahue prepares supplemental general price-level financial statements (financial statements restated for changes in the general purchasing power of the dollar), as recommended by APB Statement No. 3. Depreciation is $100,000 a year. In Donahue's general price-level income statements for 1978, the amount of depreciation would be stated as

    a. $90,000               c. $105,263
    b. $95,000               d. $111,111

## P-22-6  (CPA EXAM, 5/81, PRAC. I, #1)

Details of Monmouth Corporation's fixed assets at Dec. 31, 1980, are as follows:

| Year acquired | Percent depreciated | Historical cost | Estimated current cost |
|---|---|---|---|
| 1978 | 30 | $ 50,000 | $ 70,000 |
| 1979 | 20 | $ 15,000 | $ 19,000 |
| 1980 | 10 | $ 20,000 | $ 22,000 |

Monmouth calculates depreciation at 10% per annum, using the straight-line method. A full year's depreciation is charged in the year of acquisition. There were no disposals of fixed assets. Monmouth prepares supplementary information for inclusion in its 1980 annual report as required by the FASB. In Monmouth's supplementary information restated into current cost, the net current cost (after accumulated depreciation of the fixed assets) should be stated as

    a. $58,000               c. $84,000
    b. $65,000               d. $91,000

## P-22-7  (CPA EXAM, 5/78, PRAC. I, #12)

Index Co. was formed on Jan. 1, 1977. Selected balances from the historical-dollar balance sheet at December 31, 1977, were as follows:

| | |
|---|---|
| Cash | $60,000 |
| Marketable securities, stocks (purchased Jan. 1, 1977) | 70,000 |
| Marketable securities, bonds (purchased Jan. 1, 1977 and held for price speculation) | 80,000 |
| Long-term receivables | 90,000 |

If the general price-level index was 100 at Dec. 31, 1976, and 110 at Dec. 31, 1977, these selected accounts should be shown in a general price-level balance sheet at Dec. 31, 1977, at

|    | Cash | Marketable Securities, Stocks | Marketable Securities, Bonds | Long-term Receivables |
|----|------|------|------|------|
| a. | $60,000 | $70,000 | $80,000 | $90,000 |
| b. | $60,000 | $70,000 | $80,000 | $99,000 |
| c. | $60,000 | $77,000 | $88,000 | $90,000 |
| d. | $60,000 | $77,000 | $88,000 | $99,000 |

**P-22-8 (CPA EXAM, 5/80, PRAC. I, #12)**
Dart Co. was formed on Jan. 1, 1978. Selected balances from the historical cost balance sheet at Dec. 31,1979, were as follows:

| | |
|---|---|
| Land (purchased Jan. 1, 1978) | $90,000 |
| Marketable securities, non-convertible bonds (purchased July 1, 1978, and expected to be held to maturity) | 50,000 |
| Long-term debt | 70,000 |

The average CPI was 100 for 1978, and 110 for 1979. In a supplementary constant dollar balance sheet (adjusted for changing prices) at Dec. 31, 1979, these selected account balances should be shown at

|    | Land | Marketable Securities | Long-term Debt |
|----|------|------|------|
| a. | $90,000 | $50,000 | $70,000 |
| b. | $90,000 | $55,000 | $77,000 |
| c. | $99,000 | $50,000 | $70,000 |
| d. | $99,000 | $55,000 | $77,000 |

**P-22-9 (CPA EXAM, 5/77, PRAC. I, #17 and #18)**
In 1972, Mount Hope Inc. purchased a machine for $1,000. The machine has a ten-year life and no salvage value. Mount Hope prepares supplemental general price-level financial statements (financial statements restated for changes in the general purchasing power of the dollar) as recommended by APB Statement No. 3. Indexes of the general price level appropriate for use in preparing those financial statements are as follows:

| Year | Index (1958=100) |
|------|------|
| 1972 | 148 |
| 1973 | 159 |
| 1974 | 175 |
| 1975 | 181 |
| 1976 | 185 |

a. What amount should be reflected as depreciation for this machine in Mount Hope's general price-level income statement for the year ended December 31, 1976?

b. What amount should be reflected for this machine, before accumulated depreciation in Mount Hope's general price-level balance sheet at December 31, 1976?

**P-22-10 (CPA EXAM, 5/81, PRAC. II, #1)**
The following schedule lists the average consumer price index
(all urban consumers) of the indicated year:

| | |
|---|---|
| 1978 | 100 |
| 1979 | 125 |
| 1980 | 150 |

Carl Corp.'s plant and equipment at Dec. 31, 1980, are:

| Date acquired | Percent depreciated | Historical cost |
|---|---|---|
| 1978 | 30 | $30,000 |
| 1979 | 20 | $20,000 |
| 1980 | 10 | $10,000 |
| | | $60,000 |

Depreciation is calculated at 10% per annum, straight-line. A
full year's depreciation is charged in the year of acquisition.
There were no disposals in 1980.

What amount of depreciation expense would be included in the
income statement adjusted for general inflation (historical
cost/constant dollar accounting)?

a. $6,000          c. $7,900
b. $7,200          d. $9,000

**P-22-11 (CPA EXAM, 11/81, PRAC. I, #6)**
Cartwright Corp. prepared the following data needed to compute
the purchasing power gain or loss on net monetary items for
inclusion in its supplementary information for the year ended
December 31, 1980:

| | Amount in nominal dollars | |
|---|---|---|
| | Dec. 31, 1979 | Dec. 31, 1980 |
| Monetary assets | $ 600,000 | $1,000,000 |
| Monetary liabilities | $1,566,000 | $2,449,000 |
| Net monetary liabilities | $ 966,000 | $1,449,000 |

Assumed Consumer Price Index numbers:

| | |
|---|---|
| At Dec. 31, 1979 | 210 |
| At Dec. 31, 1980 | 230 |
| Average for 1980 | 220 |

Cartwright's purchasing power gain or loss (expressed in average 1980 constant dollars) on net monetary items for the year
ended December 31, 1980, should be

a. $109,000 gain          c. $111,000 gain
b. $109,000 loss          d. $111,000 loss

**P-22-12 (CPA EXAM, 11/81, PRAC. I, #17)**
Information with respect to Roundtree Company's cost of goods
sold for 1980 is as follows:

|                          | Units  | Historical Cost |
|--------------------------|--------|-----------------|
| Inventory, Jan. 1, 1980  | 10,000 | $ 530,000       |
| Production during 1980   | 45,000 | 2,790,000       |
| Goods available for sale | 55,000 | 3,320,000       |
| Inventory, Dec. 31, 1980 | 15,000 | 945,000         |
| Cost of goods sold       | 40,000 | $2,375,000      |

Roundtree estimates that the current cost per unit of inventory was $58 at Jan. 1, 1980 and $72 at Dec. 31, 1980. In Roundtree's supplementary information restated into average current cost, the cost of goods sold for the year ended December 31, 1980, should be

a. $2,290,000

b. $2,520,000

c. $2,600,000

d. $2,880,000

## P-22-13 (CMA EXAM, 6/81, PRS 5)

In Sept. 1979, Statement of Financial Accounting Standards No. 33, "Financial Reporting and Changing Prices," (SFAS 33) was released. This statement applies to public enterprises that have either (1) inventories and property, plant, and equipment (before deducting accumulated depreciation) of more than $125 million or (2) total assets amounting to more than $1 billion (after deducting accumulated depreciation). No changes are required in the basic financial statements, but information required by SFAS No. 33 is to be presented in supplementary statements, schedules or notes in the financial reports.

**Required**:

a. A number of terms are defined and used in SFAS 33.

   1. Differentiate between the terms **constant dollar** and **current cost**.

   2. Explain what is meant by **current cost/constant dollar accounting** and how it differs from **historical cost/nominal dollar accounting**.

b. Identify the accounts for which an enterprise must measure the effects of changing prices in order to present the supplementary information required by SFAS #33.

c. SFAS No. 33 is based upon FASB Concepts Statement No. 1, "Objectives of Financial Reporting by Business Enterprises," which concludes that financial reporting should provide information to help investors, creditors, and other financial statement users assess the amounts, timing and uncertainty of prospective net cash inflows to the enterprise.

   1. Explain how SFAS No. 33 may help in attaining this objective.

   2. Identify and discuss two ways in which the information required by SFAS No. 33 may be useful for internal management decisions.

P-22-14 (CMA EXAM, 12/81, PRS)
Retail Showcase Mart was organized on Dec. 15, 1980. The company's initial Statement of Financial Position is presented below.

### Retail Showcase Mart
### Statement of Financial Position
### December 31, 1980

Assets:

| | |
|---|---:|
| Cash | $200,000 |
| Inventory (at historical cost which equals market value, FIFO, periodic) | 400,000 |
| Furniture and Fixtures | 200,000 |
| Land (held for future store site) | 100,000 |
| Total Assets | $900,000 |

Liabilities and Stockholders' Equity:

| | |
|---|---:|
| Accounts Payable | $300,000 |
| Capital Stock ($5 par; 200,000 shares authorized; 120,000 issued and outstanding) | 600,000 |
| Total Liabilities & Stockholders' Equity | $900,000 |

The Statement of Income and the Statement of Financial Position prepared at the close of business on Dec. 31, 1981, are presented below.

### Retail Showcase Mart
### Statement of Income
### For the Year Ended December 31, 1981

| | | |
|---|---:|---:|
| Sales | | $1,100,000 |
| Cost of goods sold: | | |
| Inventory 1/1/81 | $ 400,000 | |
| Purchases | 1,000,000 | |
| Goods available for sale | $1,400,000 | |
| Inventory 12/31/81 | 600,000 | $ 800,000 |
| Gross Profit | | $ 300,000 |
| Operating Expenses: | | |
| Rent | $36,000 | |
| Depreciation | 20,000 | |
| Other (all required cash expenditures) | 44,000 | $ 100,000 |
| Income before taxes | | $ 200,000 |
| Income tax expense | | 80,000 |
| Net income | | $ 120,000 |
| | | |
| Earnings per share | | $1.00 |

### Retail Showcase Mart
### Statement of Financial Position
### December 31, 1981

Assets:

| | |
|---|---:|
| Cash | $  240,000 |
| Accounts Receivable | 400,000 |
| Inventory (at historical cost, FIFO, periodic) | 600,000 |
| Furniture and fixtures (net) | 180,000 |
| Land (held for future store site) | 100,000 |
| Total Assets | $1,520,000 |

Liabilities and Stockholders' Equity:

| | |
|---|---:|
| Accounts Payable | $  800,000 |
| Capital stock ($5 par; 200,000 shares authorized; 120,000 issued and outstanding) | 600,000 |
| Retained Earnings | $   120,000 |
| Total Liabilities & Stockholders' Equity | $1,520,000 |

Retail Showcase Mart rents its showroom facilities on an operating lease basis at a cost of $3,000 per month. The rent would be $5,000 per month if it were based on the current cost of the facility. All sales and cash outlays for costs and expenses occur uniformly throughout the year.

The following information is indicative of the changing prices since Retail Showcase Mart began its operations.

* The Consumer Price Index for All Urban Consumers for the following times is:

| | |
|---|---:|
| Dec. 31, 1980 | 200 |
| Oct. 1, 1981 | 216 |
| Dec. 31, 1981 | 220 |
| Average for 1981 | 212 |

* The ending inventory was acquired on Oct. 1, 1981.
* Inventory at current costs on Dec. 31, 1981, is $700,000.
* Cost of goods sold at current cost as of date of sale is $875,000.
* Current cost of the land on Dec. 31, 1981, is $150,000.
* The sales & purchases occurred uniformly throughout 1981.
* The "net recoverable amounts" for inventories and fixed assets have been determined by management to be in excess of the net current costs.

The accounting manager of Retail Showcase Mart has decided to comply voluntarily with the reporting requirements presented in the Statement of Financial Accounting Standards No. 33, "Financial Reporting and Changing Prices."

**Required:**

a. Calculate Retail Showcase Mart's purchasing power gain or loss for 1981 in terms of Dec. 31, 1981, dollars. Round all computations to the nearest $100.

b. Prepare a constant dollar income statement for 1981 for Retail Showcase Mart in terms of Dec. 31, 1981, dollars. Round all computations to the nearest $100.

# PART IV

# MIXED MICRO-MACRO HYBRID INTERNATIONAL ACCOUNTING

The final part of this book is devoted to a discussion of
TAXATION ACCOUNTING. Taxation Accounting is a mixture of micro
and macro; obviously the macro aspects are immediately associated with the governmental function of taxation. Because such
governmental taxation has an impact on the operational results
and affects the profit-seeking objective by reducing the income, the micro aspects come into play. Hence the hybrid micro-
macro situation results.

It is inevitable that every country will seek income through
taxes. Because of the great number of countries in the world
and their diversity, the subject of International Taxation
could well result in a multiplicity of volumes if treated in
its totality. In many U.S. colleges of business, as well as
many law schools, special courses are designed for International Taxation. It would not be unreasonable to expect a tax spe-
cialist to be exposed to at least two full-credit courses in
International Taxation.

However, within the purview of the objective of this book,
the subject of International Taxation is treated in two chapters representing the two points of view from which International Taxation Accounting may be examined, viz., the Home
Country viewpoint, and from that of the Foreign Country. The
Home Country Taxation principles are treated in Chapter 23, and
those of the Foreign Country in Chapter 24.

Because of the extreme technicality of taxation principles,
to attempt to delve into the actual detailed taxation laws of
the various countries would be counterproductive. Accordingly,
only the general principles will be accentuated in the ensuing
discussion.

# International Home Country
# Taxation Accounting

NATURE OF INTERNATIONAL TAXATION ACCOUNTING

#23-1...Politico-Economic Nature of Taxation

The subject of the tax aspects of foreign operations is extremely volatile because TAXATION is Politico-Economic in character, i.e., involves political considerations as much as it
does economic. Taxation laws are so chameleonic that they are
virtually unstable insofar as presentation of international
taxation principles is concerned. For this reason the attempt
will be made to steer clear, as much as is possible, of detailed tax rates and regulations, and concentrate on the broad
politico-economic aspects of the subject of International Taxation.

#23-2..Basic Concern of International Taxation Accounting

What the basic concern will be is the tax aspects of U.S.-
based MNC foreign operations. Since such foreign operations
will be subject to the tax laws of the countries in which they
are conducted, there obviously will necessarily be two sets of
tax laws involved, viz., those of the Home Country Parent to
whom the foreign income will be attached, and those of the
country where the operations are carried on. Because of the
nature of international accounting, as pointed out in Chapter
1, the Home Country in this book is regarded as the United
States, viz., International Accounting is necessarily comparative by nature and the basis of discussion must be predicted on
the situs of the home country.
Because of the multiplicity and heterogeneity of the number
of countries in the world, the subject to international taxation could well embrace many volumes of discussion. In fact,
there are many colleges of business administration as well as

law schools which offer full term courses in International Taxation, which in the not too distant future could easily develop
into two, or even several, courses in this subject area. We
must, accordingly, confine the ensuing discussion to basic
broad principles and attempt to avoid technical detailed rules.

## #23-3...International Taxation Accounting Viewpoints

The fact that international taxation accounting may be examined from two points of view (by U.S. Tax Law, and by foreign
government operations Tax Laws) again points up the basic comparative feature of international accounting. Taxation laws of
foreign countries must necessarily involve their comparison
with U.S. tax laws which will also serve the incidental purpose
of affording some foreign tax concepts to the readers of foreign subsidiary financial statements.

## #23-4...The Basic Problem:  Double Taxation

Obviously if a corporation operates solely in the U.S., no
problem of international taxation will arise as the U.S. tax
laws will be totally applicable. It has previously been pointed
out that the foreign operations of the MNC are regarded as an
extension of the Parent Corporation operations so that the true
income is the total--both domestic and foreign. Hence it is the
foreign operation that causes international taxation to come
into play. The basic underlying reason is that the country in
which the foreign operation takes place will indubitably super-
impose a tax on such operation, inasmuch as it has always been
universally recognized that a foreign country has a prior claim
to tax income earned therein by a foreign corporation.

Thus if the U.S. Home Country also imposes a tax on the same
income, the result will be DOUBLE TAXATION. This would not only
be basically unfair but also onerous to the extent of discouraging any attempt to engage in foreign operations. If fairness
is desired, we must attain some semblance of neutrality between
domestic and foreign investment. On such basis U.S. tax laws if
they are to be equitable should be geared to in some way permit
the corporation to deduct the foreign taxes from income to
avoid double taxation. Various countries have developed different methods of avoiding double taxation, which has been done in
two ways:  (1) by TERRITORIAL LIMITATIONS, under which capital-
exporting countries exclude foreign income from its tax base
entirely, thereby having taxes on foreign income totally exempt
from the Home income; or (2) by WORLD-WIDE taxation of repatriated earnings with modifications of Home Tax rules that permit
a credit to apply against domestic income or tax. The first
method is referred to as the COMPLETE EXEMPTION TERRITORIAL
APPROACH, and the second method as the TAXATION ON REPATRIATION

INCOME FOREIGN TAX CREDIT  APPROACH, or more simply as  the DE-
FERRAL METHOD.

## THE COMPLETE EXEMPTION TERRITORIAL APPROACH

### #23-5...Nature of Complete Exemption Territorial Approach

Under this  approach  the Home Country totally  excludes the
foreign income  from  its tax  base by renouncing all claims to
tax on foreign income whether repatriated or not. The matter of
repatriation enters  into  the  picture because the income from
foreign  operations may be handled  in two ways: (1) it  may be
added to the retained  earnings of the foreign  subsidiary  and
thereby  not  be channeled to the Parent Company; or (2) it may
be  distributed  to the parent corporation in the form of dividends. In the former case the income is retained by the foreign
operation avoiding a repatriation; in the latter  case  the income is repatriated by,  or sent back  to,  the parent corporation.

### #23-6...Forms of Repatriation Operations

Whether  or not there will be a repatriation is dependent on
the form of  organization the foreign operations take.  In this
respect, it  has already been  seen that foreign operations may
be imports and/or exports, agencies, branches, or subsidiaries.

### #23-7...Agency or Branch Operation Repatriation

If the operations of the U.S. corporation in a foreign country  are carried on  by a division or branch, the U.S. corporation  will pay tax on the income earned abroad because the foreign  operation is  regarded as an extension of the  U.S.  Home
Company,  which will therefore pay  taxes  on its income world-
wide.  Conversely, losses sustained by branch operations abroad
will be deducted from the U.S.  Home Company income.  Basically
branches are utilized  by  companies engaged in  operations required  by law to use the branch form of operation  rather than
in the subsidiary form,  most  typical of which are U.S. banks.
Other  types  of operations utilizing branches are natural  resource companies, which are permitted by law to deduct incurred
drilling expenses from consolidated U.S. income; and industrial
companies permitted to deduct start-up costs.

### #23-8...Foreign Subsidiary Operation Repatriation

Where foreign  operations  are  carried on  through subsidiaries, however, the foreign subsidiary earnings per se  are not
subject to U.S. tax. It is only when the subsidiary distributes

a dividend to the U.S. Parent Company that the latter is subject to tax. This is based on the principle that the foreign
corporate subsidiary is a separate entity from the Parent Corporation and the dividend paid by the subsidiary is regarded as
income to the Parent in the same manner that an individual taxpayer is regarded as having income from dividends received as a
shareholder.

#23-9...The Deferral Privilege

There is a TIME distinction between the receipt of income
from a Branch as related to the receipt of income from a Subsidiary. This time differential is the span of the period between the income reported as of the tax due date in the case of
a Branch Operation, and the date of the payment of the dividend
by the subsidiary to the Parent, in which case the subsidiary's
income is not subject to U.S. tax until the time that the dividend is paid.
Accountants have regarded this time differential as a DEFER-
RAL and a PRIVILEGE, as such, to the parent corporation. Hence
they refer to it as the DEFERRAL PRIVILEGE, by virtue of the
fact that the parent corporation is placed in a position to
defer payment of the U.S. tax until such time as the dividend
is received. As a practical matter, however, it is common practice for the subsidiary to pay taxes to the foreign country
that are equal to or greater than what would be paid in the
U.S., hence the deferral privilege becomes academic. Should the
foreign tax rate be lower than the U.S. rate, then the foreign
subsidiary has the advantage of being able to use the earnings
in foreign expansion by not having to repatriate them in the
form of taxable dividends.

#23-10...Territorial Approach Background

The Complete Exemption Territorial Approach had its origins
in the Civil Code countries of Europe and Latin America and
over the years has been the most common in actual usage. Where
the system is one of complete or TOTAL EXEMPTION, the Home
Country Parent is permitted to exclude dividends from foreign
direct investments as well as foreign branch income from its
tax base.

THE DEFERRAL METHOD:   TAXATION ON REPATRIATION INCOME
FOREIGN TAX CREDIT APPROACH

#23-11...Nature of the Deferral Method

Under the Deferral Method any repatriated foreign income
resulting from dividends, interest and/or royalties which is

taxed in the home country is permitted to be taken  as either a
tax  credit or a  deduction from foreign income for foreign income taxes paid on such income. The deferral method is commonly
used in those countries which  do  not use the  Territorial Approach and has been referred to as a tax preference.

There are different variations of the foreign tax credit  or
deferral approach. These are illustrated by the three countries
which have used this approach extensively, viz., U.S., U.K. and
Japan.  Where the MNC has  widespread foreign  operations,  the
U.S. approach is  the  most liberal because  the tax  credit is
calculated on a world-wide basis under which all foreign income
and taxes are  combined, with carrybacks and carryforwards permitted on any excess credits (Form 1116 is reproduced as Figure
23-1).

Japan follows the U.S. pattern except  that credits are limited to first-tier  subsidiaries only, as contrasted  with  the
U.S. where restriction is to three tiers. The U.K. is even more
liberal  permitting foreign tax  credits to flow from all lower
tier companies,  but this  is offset by requiring the credit to
be computed separately for  every item of  income and disallows
carryforwards of excess credits.

Experience has  shown that relatively little revenue has resulted from the use of the tax credit system by the U.S. giving
the appearance that it could have resulted from the use  of the
Territorial Limitation Approach.  For this reason there  have
been suggestions in the U.S. advocating a modified  territorial
exemption method  in order to dispense with the complexities of
the foreign tax system.  Conversely, Canada, which had used the
territorial exemption approach, has shifted  to the foreign tax
credit system.

## OBJECTIONS TO TERRITORIAL EXEMPTION AND DEFERRAL APPROACHES

### #23-12...Criticisms of Territorial and Deferral Methods

One of the important factors entering  into the picture with
respect to tax exemptions and  credit  systems  is the taxation
philosophy underlying operations in  what are known as  low-tax
or tax-haven countries.  In such areas the  territorial and deferral  approaches have been  criticized because they encourage
accumulations of earnings in  such  tax-haven or  low-tax countries.  While taxation per se  is not the issue  in such  countries, it  is so interwoven with the political and economic aspects of such  operations as to become a central  factor to  be
considered in connection therewith.  Basically this means that
certain types of operations and/or  countries  are desirous  of
enhancing  their socio-economic  development.  Hence incentives
are offered by  both the U.S. and the foreign country to invest
and carry on business activities in such countries.  These are

FIGURE 23-1

| Form **1116**<br>Department of the Treasury<br>Internal Revenue Service | **Computation of Foreign Tax Credit**<br>Individual, Fiduciary, or Nonresident Alien Individual<br>▶ Attach to Form 1040, 1040NR, 1041, or 990-T.<br>▶ See separate instructions. | OMB No. 1545-0121<br>19**84**<br>52 |
|---|---|---|
| Name | | Identifying number as shown on page 1 of your tax return |

Use a separate Form 1116 for each type of income. Check only one box below.

| This form is being completed for credit for taxes on: | Resident of (name of country) |
|---|---|
| ☐ Nonbusiness (section 904(d)) interest income<br>☐ Dividends from a DISC or former DISC<br>☐ Distributions from a FSC<br>☐ All other income from sources outside the United States (including income from sources within U.S. possessions) | |

**Note:** If, for the box checked above, you have income from, or have paid taxes to, **more than one** foreign country or U.S. possession, you must complete and attach **Schedule A (Form 1116)**, Schedule of Foreign Taxable Income and Foreign Taxes Paid or Accrued. If you use Schedule A (Form 1116), do not complete Parts I and II below.

**Part I  Taxable Income From Sources Outside the United States**

Write the Name of the Foreign Country or U.S. Possession . . . ▶

1 Gross income from sources within country shown above (see instructions):
- a Dividends . . . . . . . . . . . . . . **1a**
- b Gross rents and royalties . . . . . . . . **1b**
- c Foreign source capital gain net income . . . **1c**
- d Wages, salaries, and other employee compensation . . . **1d**
- e Business or profession (i.e., Schedules C or F (Form 1040), K-1 (Form 1065), and K-1 (Form 1120S)) . . . **1e**
- f Gross income from trusts and estates . . . **1f**
- g Other (including interest—attach schedule) . . . **1g**
- h Add lines 1a through 1g and enter the total here . . . . ▶ **1h**

2 Applicable deductions and losses (see instructions):
- a Expenses directly allocable to the income on line 1e . . . **2a**
- b Depreciation, depletion, repairs, and other expenses directly allocable to the income on line 1b . . . **2b**
- c Other expenses directly allocable to specific income items (attach schedule) **2c**
- d Pro rata share of all other deductions not directly allocable:
  - (i) Itemized deductions (attach schedule) .
  - (ii) Other deductions (attach schedule) .
  - (iii) Add lines 2d(i) and 2d(ii) . . . .
  - (iv) Total foreign source income (see instructions)
  - (v) Gross income from all sources (see instructions) . . . . .
  - (vi) Divide line 2d(iv) by line 2d(v) . . .
  - (vii) Multiply line 2d(iii) by line 2d(vi) . . . **2d**
- e Losses from foreign sources . . . . . . . **2e**
- f Add lines 2a through 2e. Enter the total here . . . . . ▶ **2f**

3 Subtract line 2f from line 1h. Enter the result here and in Part III, line 6. (This is your taxable income or (loss) from sources outside the United States (before recapture of prior year overall foreign losses).). . . . . . . . . ▶ **3**

**Part II  Foreign Taxes Paid or Accrued (Attach receipt or copy of return)**

| | | Date Paid or Accrued | In Foreign Currency | In U.S. Dollars |
|---|---|---|---|---|
| 1 | Credit is claimed for taxes (you must check one): ☐ Paid; or ☐ Accrued | | | |
| 2 | Foreign taxes paid or accrued: | | | |
| a | Taxes withheld at source on dividends | **2a** | | |
| b | Taxes withheld at source on rents and royalties | **2b** | | |
| c | Other foreign taxes paid or accrued | **2c** | | |
| d | Add the amounts, in U.S. dollars, on lines 2a through 2c. Enter total here and in Part III, line 1 ▶ | **2d** | | |

For Paperwork Reduction Act Notice, see page 1 of separate Instructions.  Form **1116** (1984)

FIGURE 23-1 (continued)

Form 1116 (1984)

## Part III  Computation of Foreign Tax Credit

| | | | |
|---|---|---|---|
| 1 | Enter amount from Part II, line 2d, or from Schedule A (Form 1116), Part II, line 3. (This is the total amount of foreign taxes paid or accrued.) | 1 | |
| 2 | Carryback or carryover (attach detailed computation) | 2 | |
| 3 | Add lines 1 and 2. | 3 | |
| 4 | Reduction in foreign taxes (see instructions) | 4 | |
| 5 | Subtract line 4 from line 3. (This is the total amount of foreign taxes available for credit.) | | 5 |
| 6 | Enter amount from Part I, line 3, or from Schedule A (Form 1116), Part I, line 3. (This is your taxable income or (loss) from sources outside the United States.) If this is a loss, you have no foreign tax credit for the type of income you checked on page 1. Skip lines 7 through 17 | 6 | |
| 7 | Recapture of prior year overall foreign losses (attach computation) | 7 | |
| 8 | Subtract line 7 from line 6. This is your net foreign source taxable income | | 8 |
| 9 | **Individuals:** Enter amount from Form 1040, line 35, or from Form 1040NR, line 37. **Estates and trusts:** Make no entry; skip to line 11 | 9 | |
| 10 | Enter $3,400 (joint return or widow(er)), $2,300 (single or head of household), or $1,700 (married filing separate return) | 10 | |
| 11 | **Individuals:** Subtract line 10 from line 9. **Estates and trusts:** Enter on this line your taxable income without the deduction for your exemption | | 11 |
| 12 | Divide line 8 by line 11. (If line 8 is more than line 11, enter the figure "1.") | | 12 |
| 13 | **Individuals:** Enter amount from Form 1040, line 40, or Form 1040NR, line 42. **Estates and trusts:** Enter amount from Form 1041, line 26c, or Form 990-T, line 8 | 13 | |
| | **Note:** If you are liable for the alternative minimum tax, see the instructions. | | |
| 14 | Enter amount from Form 1040, line 45, or Form 1040NR, line 46 | 14 | |
| 15 | Subtract line 14 from line 13. Enter the result (but not less than zero) | | 15 |
| 16 | Multiply line 15 by line 12. (Maximum amount of credit.) | | 16 |
| 17 | Enter the amount from line 5 or line 16, whichever is smaller. (If this is the only Form 1116 you are completing, skip lines 1 through 4 in Part IV and enter this amount on line 5, Part IV. Otherwise, complete the appropriate lines in Part IV.) ▶ | | 17 |

## Part IV  Summary of Credits From Separate Parts III (See Instructions)

| | | | |
|---|---|---|---|
| 1 | Credit for taxes on nonbusiness (section 904(d)) interest income | 1 | |
| 2 | Credit for taxes on dividends from a DISC or former DISC | 2 | |
| 3 | Credit for taxes on distributions from a FSC | 3 | |
| 4 | Credit for taxes on all other income from sources outside the United States (including income from sources within U.S. possessions) | 4 | |
| 5 | Add lines 1 through 4 | | 5 |
| 6 | Reduction in credit for international boycott operations (see "Reduction of Credit for International Boycott Operations" in instructions for Part III) | | 6 |
| 7 | Subtract line 6 from line 5. This is your foreign tax credit. Enter here and on Form 1040, line 47; Form 1040NR, line 48; Form 1041, line 27a; or Form 990-T, line 9(a) ▶ | | 7 |

the low-tax or tax-haven countries.

In June 1974, the U.N. issued a report entitled THE IMPACT OF MULTINATIONAL CORPORATIONS ON THE DEVELOPMENT PROCESS AND ON INTERNATIONAL RELATIONS, in which, inter alia, tax havens and tax holidays were expressed as two matters of concern. With respect to Tax Havens, the concern expressed was that they afford the corporation the opportunity to avoid or defer the payment of taxes to the home country of the MNC. This can be done by transferring foreign company earnings to a holding company located in another country which in turn may be reinvested, thereby channeling foreign earnings away from home countries.

As previously pointed out, because foreign income is not taxed until repatriated to the Parent, the tendency is to accumulate funds in either tax havens or tax-favored holding companies. The U.S. has therefore put a stop to this possibility under Subpart F of the Revenue Act of 1962 as discussed later.

## TAX-FAVORED HOLDING COMPANIES

### #23-13...Objectives of Foreign Investment Tax Laws

In the area of foreign investment the purpose of tax laws is not only to collect revenues for the government but also to accomplish three other objectives: (1) to encourage INCOMING INVESTMENT by developing, as well as developed, countries; (2) to encourage OUTGOING INVESTMENT in general or specific areas; and (3) to encourage exports.

The most common tax incentive extant is the offering by the developing countries to attract foreign capital and exchange, expertise, economic development, industrial modernization, and employment. The incentive for such investment takes the form of TAX HOLIDAYS, which simply is a total tax exemption for a number of years.

For the developed countries, the tax incentives offered are to obtain expertise, industry modernization, capital investment, and increased employment.

With respect to INCOMING INVESTMENT, the U.S. maintains a policy of strict neutrality in not offering any specific tax incentives. With respect to OUTGOING INVESTMENT, U.S. tax laws have discouraged any U.S. investment abroad since the enactment of Subpart F in 1962.

Over the years, however, many incentives were introduced into the tax laws to meet certain emergencies that arose from time to time. Basically these incentives were confined to certain AREAS within the U.S. Western Hemisphere sphere of influence. These incentives are still in effect with respect to U.S. possessions, particularly Puerto Rico. In 1971 a tax incentive was granted for exports in the form of the DOMESTIC INTERNATIONAL SALES CORPORATION, commonly referred to as DISC.

## #23-14...Types of Foreign Operations U.S. Tax Incentives

There have been  five  types of  foreign operations  granted
U.S. tax incentives:
  (1) Operations in the Western Hemisphere--Western Hemisphere
      Trade Corporations (WHTC)--which are  concerned with in-
      come earned outside the U.S.;
  (2) POSSESSIONS  CORPORATIONS  involving  operations in U.S.
      possessions;
  (3) DOMESTIC INTERNATIONAL  SALES  CORPORATIONS, (DISC)  in-
      volving export operations;
  (4) EXPORT  TRADE  CORPORATIONS (ETC)  also involving export
      operations;
  (5) LESS  DEVELOPED COUNTRY CORPORATIONS  (LDCC) for  opera-
      tions in developing countries.
The WHTC,  Possessions Corporation,  and  DISC are all domestic
corporations of the U.S., whereas the ETC and the LDCC are foreign corporations.

## #23-15...Western Hemisphere Trade Corporation

The WHTC, a U.S. corporation trading outside the U.S. but in
the  Western Hemisphere, was taxed at a lower  rate  than other
U.S. corporations. WHTCs were permitted to reduce their taxable
income by 14/48 thereby  granting them  lower taxes.   However,
beginning with the  Tax Reform Act of 1976  the benefits of the
WHTC were phased out over a period of four years, so that as of
1980 the WHTC corporation no longer exists.

## #23-16...Possessions Corporations

A U.S. Corporation formed  as separate from its  parent  and
doing business substantially in  a U.S. possession is  not subject to U.S. tax on income earned outside the U.S. unless  such
income was  received in the U.S.  Such  a corporation is a POS-
SESSIONS CORPORATION  provided it meets  the following requirements under the  1976 law:  (1) it is  a  domestic U.S. corporation; (2) at least  80% of its  gross income  is  derived  from
within a  U.S. possession; and  (3)  at least 50%  of its gross
income is derived from the active  conduct of a trade or  business in a U.S. possession.
The following areas are deemed to be possessions to qualify:
Panama Canal Zone,  Wake  Island, Midway  Island,  and American
Samoa.  The Virgin  Islands has  its own  incentive legislation
requirements under  which a qualifying corporation receives  a
subsidy  from  the Islands' Treasury  of up to 75% of  the  tax
paid, making  the effective tax rate 25% of 48%, or 12% on Virgin Islands income.  Puerto Rico and Guam  are deemed not to be

qualified possessions. Under the 1976 Tax Reform Act, exemption
of taxation for Possessions Corporations is indirectly granted
in that the income is subject to U.S. tax which is cancelled by
the allowance of a credit for the amount of the tax. Thus
should the Possessions Corporation pay dividends to the parent
company, the latter may claim a 100% dividends-received deduction.

### #23-17...Domestic International Sales Corporation (DISC)

In order to encourage U.S. corporations to increase their
exports and to equalize business volume between exporters and
foreign subsidiaries which manufacture products abroad, the
1971 Revenue Act made provision for a new type of domestic cor-
poration--DISC. The purpose of the provision was to establish a
tax incentive for increasing exports. This was accomplished by
not taxing the DISC for its earnings and profits but reserving
the tax thereon to the stockholders when either actually distributed or deemed to have been distributed. This resulted in a
system of tax deferral under which 50% of the taxable income of
the DISC was deferred whereas the other 50% was regarded or
deemed to have been distributed resulting in a tax as a dividend to the shareholder rather than to the DISC. The shareholders in turn are entitled to claim the DEEMED foreign tax credit
for taxes paid by the DISC to foreign countries.

There are six requirements to be met to qualify as a DISC:

(1) A U.S. corporation not engaged in manufacturing;
(2) With "qualified export assets" at least 95% of total
    assets at the close of its taxable year;
(3) With at least 95% of its gross receipts for the taxable
    year being "qualified export receipts;"
(4) With only one class of stock;
(5) Having at least $2,500 of capital on each day of the
    taxable year; and,
(6) The corporation must make an election during the 90-day
    period immediately before the beginning of the taxable
    year, or 90 days after incorporation.

There are nine types of assets defined in the Code as qualified
export assets, typical of which are cash, receivables, inventory to be exported, and storage facilities; and eight types of
receipts defined as qualified export receipts, which consist of
those used to prevent the parent company from sheltering other
DISC income.
The typical DISC is customarily a subsidiary of the parent
manufacturing corporation. The DISC is permitted to lend its
deferred income to the parent which thereby may avail itself of

its use.   The   DISC may further utilize a subsidiary known as a FOREIGN INTERNATIONAL SALES SUBSIDIARY (FISS).

The   1976 Tax Reform Act has virtually eliminated the deferral   for   DISCs except for   new ones and   those   which increase their exports. A new INCREMENTAL APPROACH was instituted beginning after Dec. 31, 1975 which limits tax   deferral only to the extent to which there is an increase in the exports of the current year gross   receipts over a 4-year base period.   The first base period is   1972-1975 for the year 1979, and   after 1979 it advances one year.   Thus if   a new   DISC is   formed in 1980   or thereafter, there is   no   effective   base   period for the first four years and all export income qualifies   for   DISC benefits, and in   the fifth   year the four   preceding   years   will be the base.

The determination of   the base period years, which is important in ascertaining the deemed distribution, is illustrated by the following table:

| | | Base Period |
| --- | --- | --- |
| Year | Existing DISC | New DISC (formed in 1976 or Thereafter) |
| 1976 | 1972-1975 | 0 |
| 1977 | 1972-1975 | 0 |
| 1978 | 1972-1975 | 0 |
| 1979 | 1972-1975 | 0 |
| 1980 | 1973-1976 | 1976 |
| 1981 | 1974-1977 | 1976-1977 |
| 1982 | 1975-1978 | 1976-1978 |
| 1983 | 1976-1979 | 1976-1979 |

Under   the   1976 incremental approach, the adjusted taxable income of the   DISC   is reduced by   a   fraction, the numerator of which is 67% of average base period export gross   receipts, and the denominator   is the current   year export gross receipts; 50% of the remaining taxable   income   is eligible for deferral.   An illustrative example is   presented in ACCOUNTING FOR THE MULTINATIONAL CORPORATION by Watt, Hammer and Burge on page 424:

Assume a DISC established in 1971 has adjusted net income in 1976 of $200,000 on export gross receipts of $1,000,000:

| EXPORT GROSS RECEIPTS FOR BASE PERIOD: | |
| --- | --- |
| Year 1972 | 1,000,000 |
| Year 1973 | 1,000,000 |
| Year 1974 | 1,000,000 |
| Year 1975 | 1,000,000 |
| Base Period Total Receipts | 4,000,000 |
| Base Period Average (1/4) | 1,000,000 |
| 67% of Base Period Average | 670,000 |

```
            COMPUTATION OF DEEMED DISTRIBUTION:
Current Year Adjusted Taxable Income              200,000
Incremental Distribution
     (670,000/1,000,000 x 200,000) =              134,000
Income Qualifying for DISC benefits                66,000
Incremental Distribution                          134,000
50% Distribution                                   33,000
Total Deemed Distribution                         167,000
Tax Deferred on                                    33,000
```

Thus if export receipts have remained constant, as in the above example, the DISC deferral would be reduced to 16.5% of taxable income compared with 50% under pre-1976 law. DISCs with export profits of $100,000 or less are exempt from the incremental base period rule. Between $100,000 and $150,000 there is a reduction in the exemption.

The Tax Reform Act of 1976 provides that DISCs which make illegal payments to a foreign government official are subject to treatment as deemed distributions taxable to the DISC's U.S. shareholder. Also if a U.S. corporation or any foreign affiliate participates in an international boycott, the income eligible for tax deferral under the DISC rules is reduced by the income specifically attributable to the specific operations.

FOREIGN SALES CORPORATION AS DISC REPLACEMENT--In Oct. 1983 issue of the ILLINOIS CPA SOCIETY NEWS JOURNAL, page 24, Mr. W.R. Carnie of Staley Mfg. Co. points out:
Taxpayers who currently enjoy tax benefits as DISCs and practitioners who advise clients regarding DISCs should be aware of the proposed legislation recently introduced in Congress that would replace DISC with an entity to be known as a FOREIGN SALES CORPORATION (FSC). The legislation is to become effective January 1, 1984 and would exempt from federal income tax a portion of the foreign trading income of the FSC. Taxpayers and their advisers should analyze this proposed legislation (H.R. 3810 and S. 1804) to assess its impact on export operations.
In their THE WEEK IN REVIEW, 83-10, Mar. 11, 1983, p. 6, Deloitte, Haskins & Sells label the new corporation a FOREIGN TRADING COMPANY (FTC) instead of FSC, indicating that:
It is designed to overcome the technical objections to DISCs that have been raised. U.S. exporters could establish a subsidiary FTC in some foreign location that would serve as either a selling arm or a commission agent for export sales by the U.S. Parent.
To be eligible, the FTC must: (1) be a foreign corporation; (2) maintain a foreign office; (3) maintain books and records in that office; (4) have at least one resident di-

rector in the foreign office; (5) hold an agency agreement or distribution license; and (6) be located in either specified U.S. territories or a country that has an exchange of information agreement with the U.S.

Transfer pricing, similar to the current DISC rules, would allow for a safe-haven calculation of profit that the FTC could derive from handling its affiliates' exports. The safe-haven amount of FTC profit would be the GREATER OF 17% of combined taxable income on exports, or 1.35% of the FTC's export sales (but limited to 34% of combined taxable income.)

Exporting profits earned by the FTC would not be taxed by the U.S. and dividends paid from such profits would be tax-free to the U.S. parent. This would eliminate the cumbersome requirements on reinvestment of DISC assets, since an FTC could pay out its profits as nontaxable dividends.

In addition, some significant activities must be performed in part outside the U.S., such as soliciting orders and negotiating contracts, processing orders, or billing and collection activities, in addition to a combination of (a) disbursing export advertising expenses; (b) maintaining paid-in capital and a separate bank account; (c) holding shareholders' and directors' meetings; (d) transferring title; and (e) paying dividends, legal and accounting fees, and officers' salaries.

## #23-18...Export Trade Corporation

Prior to the enactment of the tax provisions creating the DISC, there existed tax provisions affording some tax incentives to exporting companies known as EXPORT TRADE CORPORATIONS. However, these provisions were applicable only to Export Trade Corporations that existed prior to Nov. 1, 1971, and only these can continue to operate under such provisions. Export Trade Corporations created after Nov. 1, 1971 are not eligible for treatment as such corporations for taxable years after such date.

## #23-19...Less Developed Country Corporation (LDCC)

The reasons for creation of the LDCC are that they afford tax advantages resulting from the operation in less developed countries. These advantages are
(1) Dividends, interest and certain capital gains received by the LDCC are excluded from income to the extent that they are reinvested in the less developed countries;
(2) Where a U.S. corporate shareholder receives dividends from a LDCC, they are not subject to gross-up in computing the foreign tax credit; and

(3)  Where the LDCC is a controlled foreign corporation, and if
     the stock of the company has been owned by the U.S. share-
     holders for a continuous period of ten years, and such
     stock is sold, exchanged, or liquidated by the U.S. share-
     holder, post-1962 earnings which were normally treated as
     dividends are not regarded as dividends.
The requirements for creation of an LDCC are as follows:
(1)  It must be a foreign corporation;
(2)  It must be engaged in active conduct of a trade or busi-
     ness;
(3)  Of its gross income, at least 80% must be derived from
     sources within less developed countries; and,
(4)  Of its total assets, at least 80% must consist of: (a)
     Cash and bank deposits; (b) business property located in
     less developed countries; (c) stock and certain obliga-
     tions of either another LDCC or less developed country;
     (d) assets equivalent to an insurance company's unearned
     premiums and ordinary and necessary reserves; and (e) ob-
     ligations of the U.S. and certain other U.S. property.
What constitutes a less developed country is designated by the
President. They generally comprise most of the countries in the
world except for industrialized countries of Europe, together
with Australia, New Zealand, Canada, Hong Kong, South Africa,
Japan, China & U.S.S.R.
     Under the 1976 Tax Reform Act all of the benefits of the
LDCC were eliminated, so that dividends received from a LDCC
are added to those received from a non-LDCC. Also any gains
derived from the sale, exchange or liquidation of an LDCC, and
earnings accumulated prior to Jan. 1, 1976, are taxed as capital gains.

**TAX HAVENS**

**#23-20...Tax Haven Implications**

     As previously indicated, the June 1974 report of the U.N.
expressed concern about the use of tax-haven holding companies
to avoid or defer payment of taxes to the home country of the
MNC. This is accomplished by the MNC transferring the earnings
of foreign operating companies to a holding company in another
country thereby avoiding repatriation of such earnings which
are channeled to reinvestment in countries other than the home
country. This encourages the accumulation of funds in tax-haven
and/or tax-favored holding companies.

**#23-21...Definition of Tax Haven**

     In an article by Milka Casanegra de Jantscher entitled "Tax
Havens Explained," appearing in the March 1976 issue of FINANCE

AND DEVELOPMENT, p. 31, a tax haven is defined as "a place where foreigners may receive income or own assets without paying high rates of tax upon them." Thus the prime objective of tax havens is tax reduction or elimination, which falls into four categories: (1) tax elimination, (2) low tax rates, (3) foreign source exempt income, or (4) special privileges. In an article by Jean Doucet and Kenneth J. Good entitled "What Makes a Good Tax Haven?" appearing in the May 1973 edition of the journal BANKER, p. 493, it is pointed out:

> Some countries, particularly those with few natural resources, offer permanent tax inducements. These so-called "tax havens" include: (1) the Bahamas, Bermuda, and the Cayman Islands, which have no taxes at all; (2) the British Virgin Islands and Gibraltar, which assess very low tax rates; (3) Hong Kong, Liberia, and Panama, which tax locally-generated income but exempt income from foreign sources; and (4) countries that allow special privileges that are suitable as tax havens for very limited purposes, such as Brazil which offers tax incentives for industrial development in its underdeveloped regions.

Along the same line, many countries offer a number of incentives not tax related to attract MNCs. Among them are (1) tax holidays affording relief from paying any taxes whatever for designated periods of time; (2) nontaxable cash grants which are applied to the purchase of plant and equipment for new industrial developments; (3) tax deferrals; (4) elimination or reduction of indirect taxes; (5) little or no government supervision or interference; (6) banking secrecy; (7) cost concessions in doing business; (8) no foreign exchange controls; and (9) liberal banking regulations.

#### #23-22...Tax Haven Modus Operandi

The procedure for availing the MNC of the tax-haven status is to establish a subsidiary in the tax-haven country selected in which to operate. The objective is to channel income from high-tax country operations to the tax-haven country, so that the tax-haven subsidiary becomes an intermediary. Thus a U.S. multinational manufacturing enterprise which sells its products to a dealer in France could instead sell them to its subsidiary in the tax-haven country at cost which in turn would sell to the same dealer in France; in this way the profits would arise in the tax-free tax-haven country instead of the U.S. Though it may appear that the tax-haven operation is not on the legitimate side, such is not necessarily the case, as it may very well be a perfectly legal operation.

SUBPART F INCOME

#23-23...Revenue Act of 1962 Subpart F Provision

As was pointed out above the U.S. decided to curb the possibility of avoiding taxes through accumulation of funds in non-
tax areas by enacting Subpart F of Subchapter N of the 1962
Revenue Act. Prior to 1962 the U.S. policy in the area of international taxation was one of indifference. This was ended
with the enactment of Subpart F, under which the accumulation
of foreign earnings in tax havens, which also reduced U.S. and
foreign taxes through the medium of interposed sales companies,
was stopped. Under the principle that the home country has the
right to tax any part of the income resulting from the employment of the home country's capital investment, the U.S. shareholder is taxed on earnings of a foreign subsidiary regardless
of whether or not they have been repatriated. There was some
debate at the time of the adoption of Subpart F of eliminating
deferral completely, which was not done. The result has been
that U.S. parent corporations have so restructured their operations as to circumvent it, and have used foreign tax credits to
reduce or nullify Subpart F liabilities. The consequence has
been that under Subpart F the amount of tax collection has been
negligible.
     Two disadvantages resulted from Subpart F: (1) by preventing
the sales of goods and services through tax-haven countries
between non-U.S. affiliates, the competitiveness of U.S. industry in foreign countries is severely hampered, as well as acting in the capacity of policing other countries' taxes; and (2)
the investment of surplus foreign funds in the U.S. is discouraged due to the current taxation of foreign earnings invested
in U.S. property, resulting in detriment to U.S. balance-of-
payments. Thus the TAX REDUCTION ACT OF 1975 and the TAX REFORM
ACT OF 1976 were enacted, pursuant to a "Report by the President's Task Force on Business Taxation" of Sept. 1970. They
liberalized the provisions relating to investments in U.S.
property, and extended the Subpart F rules to additional income
categories, reducing the 1962 Act relief provisions.

#23-24..Subpart F and Controlled Foreign Corporations (CFC)

The Subpart F provisions generally apply when a foreign corporation is controlled for an uninterrupted period of 30 days
or more by U.S. shareholders. A U.S. shareholder is a U.S. citizen, resident, domestic corporation/partnership/estate or
trust, who actually or constructively owns 10% or more of a
foreign corporation's voting interest. And a CFC is one in
which more than 50% of the voting interest is owned by U.S.
shareholders on any day in the corporate tax year. Thus if a

U.S. corporation owned a subsidiary more than 50% owned by U.S.
shareholders, it would be a CFC and the U.S. parent would be
amenable to be taxed on certain undistributed income of such
controlled foreign corporation. In arriving at the percentage
of control figure, a shareholder must own 10% or more of the
stock, and the aggregate of shareholders holding 10% or more
must be 51% of U.S. shareholders in order to be a CFC. Furthermore if a CFC owns more than 50% of another foreign corporation, it too would be a CFC for U.S. tax purposes.

### #23-25...Subpart F Taxable Income

Basically, then, the 1962 Revenue Act in effect classified
foreign income into two groups: (1) Non-CFC Income; and (2) CFC
Income, which in turn is classified as Active Income and Passive Income. NON-CFC INCOME is that which is automatically deferred until such income is distributed as shareholders' dividends. ACTIVE CFC INCOME is that derived from the active conduct of trade or business of a CFC and for such reason may be
elected to be deferred by the CFC. PASSIVE CFC INCOME, on the
other hand, is not deferrable and recognized by the parent when
earned regardless of when a dividend is declared. It is such
passive income that is known as SUBPART F TAXABLE INCOME.

### #23-26...Classification of Subpart F Taxable Income

There are several types of SUBPART F TAXABLE INCOME, which
may be classified as shown in Figure 23-2. The tax provisions
relating to Subpart F Taxable Income are quite intricate and
involved and beyond the scope of detailing them at this point.
A definition and description of the terms is discussed below.

### #23-27...Foreign Base Company Income

A Foreign Base Company is one which has its registration
(establishing its base) in a country not basically used for
operations. As indicated in Figure 23-2, there are four sources
of Foreign Base Company Income which is the aggregate of incomes from all four sources.
The first source--Personal Holding Company Income--generally
embraces such passive investment income as interest, dividends,
rents, royalties and gains on the sale of stock securities, or
commodities futures transactions.
The second source--Sales Income--arises from the purchase
and sale of personal property produced and sold outside the CFC
base country and is either bought from or sold to a person or
corporation to which it is related. Typical examples of such
transactions are given by Watt, Hammer and Burge in the FERF
book ACCOUNTING FOR THE MULTINATIONAL CORPORATION, page 449:

Typical examples of Foreign Base Company Sales are the sale
by a Swiss base company of goods manufactured by an affiliate in France and sold to customers in Germany; the sale by
a Panamanian company of products acquired in Brazil to an
affiliate in the U.S.; sale on a commission basis to a Canadian customer made by a Bahamian company on behalf of a U.S.
affiliate of goods it produced in the U.S. *** No foreign
base company income arises if goods produced in the U.S. are
sold by a German affiliate to customers in Germany, or if
goods manufactured in France are sold by a Belgian affiliate
to Belgian customers, or by an Italian affiliate to Italian
customers, or by the French manufacturing company to customers anywhere.

The third source--Services Income--results from performing managerial, engineering, technical or other services, except where
required in connection with the sales of goods. Thus if a U.S.
catering company with a Swiss subsidiary manages restaurants in
Dubai which pays for the services to the Swiss subsidiary, this
would be regarded as Foreign Base Company Services Income.

===================================================================

FIGURE 23-2
CLASSIFICATION OF SUBPART F TAXABLE INCOME

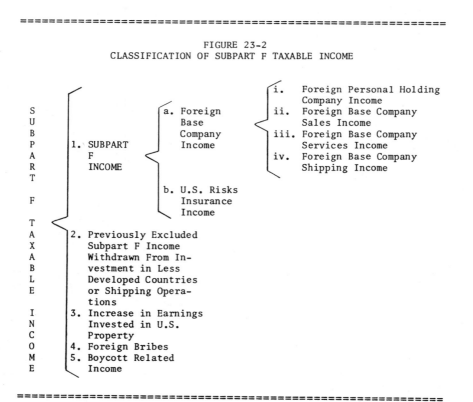

===================================================================

The fourth source--<u>Shipping Income</u>--results from income derived from the use, leasing, or hiring for use, of any vessel
or aircraft in foreign commerce, or any related services, as
well as any gains derived from the sale of such vessels or aircraft.

Taxable income in Foreign Base Company Income is subject to
what is known as the "10-70" RULE under which it is related to
the TOTAL GROSS INCOME of the CFC, and if less than 10%, then
none of the base company income is treated as income for the
period; however, if it exceeds 70%, it is then treated as foreign base company income.

## #23-28...U.S. Risks Insurance Income

Net income resulting from premiums received for insurance
on U.S. property, life insurance, or health insurance of U.S.
residents are included in a CFC Subpart F income. Such premiums
must exceed 5% of total premiums. The basis for insurance income resulted from U.S. corporations establishing foreign insurance subsidiaries in tax-haven countries to which premiums
were paid on U.S. and foreign risks. This enabled the U.S. parent to charge off the premiums as expenses whereas the income
from premiums to the subsidiary resulted in little or no tax.
Such CFC income is therefore now taxed as income to the parent.

## #23-29...Subpart F Income Previously Excluded

Income consisting of interest, dividends and capital gains,
derived from LDC corporations which were reinvested in less
developed countries and therefore had been excluded previously,
becomes taxable income under Subpart F. Such income had been
excluded because it increased the investment in a less developed country under the Tax Reduction Act of 1975 so that subsequent withdrawal of such investment income makes it amenable as
income by U.S. shareholders.

## #23-30...Increase in Earnings Invested in U.S. Property

Where earnings of a CFC are invested in stock or obligations
of a U.S. corporation, or in certain rights located in the
U.S., an amount equal to the increase over the preceding year's
earnings invested in such property must be included in the U.S.
shareholder's income under Subpart F.

## #23-31...Foreign Bribes

If a CFC makes illegal payments to foreign officials they
are regarded as Subpart F income. As previously indicated in
the discussion of International Accounting Political Bribery,

under the 1977 Foreign Corrupt Practices Act bribes paid to
foreign officials are regarded as Subpart F income notwithstanding the fact that bribes are not considered income to the
parent. The FCPA provision is purely punitive in character and
unrelated to income.

## #23-32...International Boycott Related Income

Like foreign bribes, Subpart F income resulting from corporations which cooperate in an international boycott is also
punitive in character. What constitutes participation in an
international boycott is defined by guidelines issued by the
Treasury Department. International boycott income is determined
by multiplying the earnings of the CFC by the INTERNATIONAL
BOYCOTT FACTOR, which is a fraction whose numerator is the
operations in the boycott countries and the denominator reflecting non-U.S. world-wide operations. Three elements comprise the fraction--sales, purchases and payroll.

## SUBCHAPTER C INTERNAL REVENUE CODE DEFERRAL PROVISIONS-- SECTION 367 TRANSFER OF ASSETS ABROAD

## #23-33...Section 367

Originally Sec. 367 of the Internal Revenue Code was enacted
in 1932 to cure a loophole which permitted taxpayers to avoid
capital gains taxes. An illustration of this situation is given
in the FERF book ACCOUNTING FOR THE MULTINATIONAL CORPORATION
by Watt, Hammer and Burge, page 470:

> Before 1932 it was possible to avoid the U.S. capital
> gains tax for a U.S. corporation (P) to organize a foreign
> subsidiary (S) in which it would receive 80% or more of the
> stock in exchange for the appreciated securities. This would
> be a typical tax-free transfer of property in exchange for
> stock under the provisions of Section 351. S would be in-
> corporated in a jurisdiction such as the Bahamas which does
> not tax income or capital gains. S would then sell the as-
> sets to unrelated parties free of U.S. and foreign tax. S
> would subsequently be liquidated without tax to P under the
> provisions of Sec. 332, which permits the tax-free liquida-
> tion of a subsidiary owned 80% or more into its parent com-
> pany.
> The enactment of Sec. 367 effectively closed this loop-
> hole by precluding a U.S. taxpayer from transferring certain
> appreciated assets abroad in such a manner that the gain
> when realized would escape U.S. taxation. Thus it prevents
> the tax-free transfer of certain assets, such as stocks,
> bonds, patents, and other intangibles, to a foreign subsidi-
> ary, which would subsequently generate investment income to

the foreign subsidiary. It also serves to prevent the repatriation of the earnings of a foreign subsidiary in the
form of a tax-free liquidating distribution to the U.S. parent company.

## TAXATION ON EXPATRIATE COMPENSATION OF U.S. CITIZENS WORKING ABROAD

### #23-34...Nature of Taxation on Expatriate Compensations

The development of M/N enterprises has created a personnel
problem that has been exacerbated in the U.S. by taxation of
compensation of expatriates. Many types of foreign positions
require special skills that cannot be obtained in the foreign
operations countries, and M/N enterprises are virtually required to send employees from the U.S. to the country where operations are carried on. It is a well known fact that U.S. specialists and experts are employed all over the Middle East and
in many countries in Europe. The taxation of these employees
has been handled in such a way in the U.S. as to cause much
consternation not only to the employee but to the company by
which he is employed.

The basic reason for this situation is that while every
country has the right to tax the earnings of its citizens, the
U.S. goes further than most other industrial countries by applying the individual taxes on the basis of his income world-
wide. In the Feb. 8, 1979 issue of THE WALL STREET JOURNAL, p.
2, it is pointed out that the U.S. is the only one out of eight
major Western countries that taxes expatriates on the basis of
their income world-wide. This leaves two alternatives to U.S.
companies operating abroad if they desire to equalize the tax
burden of the expatriate employee, viz., increasing the compensation to offset the increased tax, or engage local foreign
help.

This problem has been kicked around by the Congress but
reached its zenith in the late 1970s. Its nature can be determined by tracing the history of the legislation on this subject. Before 1976, the U.S. citizen working abroad was allowed
an earned income exclusion of from $20,000 to $25,000 and taxed
at the bracket reduced by the allowance; in addition the tax
credit for payment of foreign taxes was allowed. Under this
law, an expatriate earning $75,000 in a foreign country would
file Form 2555 (reproduced in Figure 23-3) with his Form 1040
personal tax return, giving him an EXEMPTION OF INCOME EARNED
ABROAD (as the November 1973 version is titled) in the sum of
$20,000. This would make his taxable income $55,000 in which
bracket he would be taxed; he would then deduct the foreign
income tax credit based on the total $75,000.

FIGURE 23-3

Form **2555**
(Rev. Nov. 1973)
Department of the Treasury
Internal Revenue Service

## Exemption of Income Earned Abroad
▶ Attach to Form 1040.

For taxable year ending ................................................

### This Form is to be Used Only by United States Citizens

| Name of taxpayer | Social security number |
|---|---|

| Foreign address (including Country) | Your occupation |
|---|---|

Name of employer ▶

| Employer's address | U.S. ▶ |
|---|---|
| | Foreign ▶ |

Give the latest year for which you filed a U.S. income tax return ▶                    Office where filed ▶

For an explanation of the provisions under which **earned income** of citizens abroad is exempt, see instructions. You may obtain Publication 54, Tax Guide for U.S. Citizens Abroad, and all forms from any Internal Revenue office, U.S. Embassy, or Consulate.

Check status under which you claim exemption of **earned income** from services abroad
☐ Bona fide residence. Complete Parts I and III.
☐ Physical presence. Complete Parts II and III.

Complete all items in the parts pertaining to your status. If an item does not apply, write "DOES NOT APPLY." Failure to submit required information may result in disallowance of the claimed exemption.

### Part I    To be Completed for Bona Fide Residence Only

1 Foreign country in which you claim bona fide residence ........................... Residence began .................., terminated ...............
      (Date)                         (Date)

2 Type of living quarters in foreign country ☐ Purchased house ☐ Rented house or apartment ☐ Rented room ☐ Quarters furnished by employer

3 Did your family live with you abroad during any part of the taxable year? . . . . . . . . . . . . . . . . ☐ Yes  ☐ No
  If "Yes," for what period? _____

4 (a) Have you made a statement to the authorities of the foreign country you claim bona fide residence in that you are not a resident of that country? . . . . . . . . . . . . . . . . . . . . . . . . . . ☐ Yes  ☐ No

  (b) Are you subject to the income tax of the country you claim bona fide residence in? . . . . . . . . . . . . . ☐ Yes  ☐ No
     If you made a statement to the authorities of the foreign country that you are not a resident, and the country holds you are not subject to its income tax, you do not qualify for this United States exemption. See Instruction 8(c).

5 Complete the following for days present in the United States or its possessions during the taxable year:

| Date arrived in U.S. | Date departed from U.S. | Number of days in U.S. on business | Amount earned in U.S. on business (Attach statement showing computation.) | Date arrived in U.S. | Date departed from U.S. | Number of days in U.S. on business | Amount earned in U.S. on business (Attach statement showing computation.) |
|---|---|---|---|---|---|---|---|
| | | | | | | | |
| | | | | | | | |
| | | | | | | | |
| | | | | | | | |

6 (a) State any contractual terms or other conditions relating to the length of your employment abroad. ..................
   ........................................................................................................

  (b) State the type of visa you entered the foreign country under. .........................................

  (c) Did your visa contain any limitations as to the length of your stay or employment in a foreign country? . . . . . . . ☐ Yes  ☐ No
     If "Yes," attach explanation.

  (d) List the places where you have resided and the dates of residence since you left the United States to establish residence abroad. ..................
   ........................................................................................................

  (e) Did you maintain a home in the United States while residing abroad? . . . . . . . . . . . . . . . ☐ Yes  ☐ No
     If "Yes," show address of your home, whether it was rented, and the names and relationships of the occupants. ..................

### Part II    To be Completed for Physical Presence Only

7 The 18-month period the exemption for physical presence in a foreign country is based on is from .............. to .............. inclusive.

8 Enter all travel abroad during the 18-month period the exemption is based on, except that you may omit travel between foreign countries that did not involve travel on or over international waters for 24 hours or more. If the last entry is an arrival in a foreign country, insert number of full days to end of 18-month period. If there was no travel to report during the period, write in schedule that you were physically present in a foreign country or countries during the entire 18-month period.

| Name of country (Including U.S.) | Date and time departed | Date and time arrived | Full days present in country | Number of days in U.S. on business | Amount earned in U.S. on business (Attach statement showing computation.) |
|---|---|---|---|---|---|
| | | | | | |
| | | | | | |
| | | | | | |
| | | | | | |
| | | | | | |

9 Enter prior years you claimed exemption for income earned abroad under section 911 ▶

# FIGURE 23-3 (continued)

Form 2555 (Rev. 11–73)

Page **2**

**Part III** To be Completed for Both Bona Fide Residence and Physical Presence

10 Enter below your total earned income, including noncash remuneration. (See instructions 7 and 8(d).)

Is part of the income (such as bonuses) attributable to services performed in past years or to be performed for years other than this year? . . . . . . . . . . . . . . . . . . . . . . . . . . . . . . . . . . . . . . . . ☐ Yes ☐ No

If "Yes," see Instructions 10(a) and 11.

Do not report exempt income on your Form 1040, but enter all taxable income in the appropriate sections of the form. For those who receive all or part of their income in foreign currency, the value of foreign currency received should be translated into terms of United States dollars on the basis of the rates of exchange prevailing at the time the income is actually or constructively received.

| Earned income (for personal services rendered in foreign countries) | Exchange rates used | Amount (In U.S. dollars) |
|---|---|---|
| 11 (a) Total wages, salaries, bonuses, commissions, etc. received during this year . . . . . . . | | |
| (b) Amount attributable to prior years or future years (See Instructions 10(a) and 11.) . . . . | | |
| (c) Balance attributable to this year. (Subtract line 11(b) from line 11(a).) . . . . . . . | | |
| 12 Pensions and annuities (See Instruction 10(d).) . . . . . . . . . . . . . . . . | | |
| 13 Allowable share of income for personal services rendered. (See Instruction 7.) | | |
| (a) In a business (including farming) or profession. Attach Schedule C or F . . . . . . . . | | |
| (b) In a partnership (State name, address, and nature of income.) | | |
| 14 Noncash remuneration (Market value of property or facilities furnished by employer. Attach statement showing how determined.) | | |
| (a) Home . . . . . . . . . | | |
| (b) Car . . . . . . . . . | | |
| (c) Other property facilities (Specify.) | | |
| 15 Other income (Specify.) | | |
| 16 Allowances or reimbursements | | |
| (a) Cost of living . . . . . | | |
| (b) Overseas differential . . . | | |
| (c) Family . . . . . . . | | |
| (d) Education . . . . . . . | | |
| (e) Home leave . . . . . . | | |
| (f) Quarters . . . . . . . | | |
| (g) For any other purpose (Specify.) | | |
| 17 Total earned income from sources outside the United States . . . . . . . . . . | | |
| 18 Amount exempt (if exempt status changed during the taxable year, complete schedule below.) . . | | |
| 19 Taxable income (Line 17 less line 18. If less than zero, enter zero.) Enter here and report on Form 1040 | | |

### Schedule for Computation of Exemption Claimed in Part III, line 18, above.

(The $20,000 and $25,000 exemptions are for full taxable years. The exemptions must be pro-rated when exempt status changes during the taxable year. See Instructions 8(a)(ii) and 10(c).)

| | A | B |
|---|---|---|
| 20 Applicable exemption . . . . . . . . . . . . . . . . . . . . . . . . | $20,000 | $25,000 |
| 21 Number of exemption qualifying days in taxable year . . . . . . . . . . . . . . | | |
| 22 Total number of days in taxable year . . . . . . . . . . . . . . . . . . | | |
| 23 Percentage applicable (Divide the number of days on line 21 by the number of days on line 22.) . . | % | % |
| 24 Allowable exemption (Multiply the amount on line 20 by the percent on line 23.) . . . . . . | $ | $ |
| 25 Total allowable exemption (Add amounts on line 24, columns A and B.) Enter here and on line 18 . . . . . . . . | | $ |

(If more space is needed for any schedule, etc., attach statement.)

The Code was changed under the Tax Reform Act of 1976 making the tax more onerous not only by reducing the EXEMPTION from $20,000 to $15,000 but also by levying the tax at a rate determined before the exemption was allowed. So that as in the case mentioned above prior to 1976, the taxable income instead of being $55,000 would be increased to $60,000, in which bracket he would be taxed, and the tax credit allowed would be based not on the $75,000 total earnings but the reduced amount of $60,000. This result made it infeasible and impracticable for many prospective employees to want to seek employment abroad, which also resulted in a great disaffection on the part of employers desirous of having U.S. employees fill such vacant foreign jobs.

Because of the hue and cry raised over the undesirable situation created by the Tax Reform Act of 1976, the FOREIGN EARNED INCOME ACT of 1978 was enacted, which eliminated the exemption completely, and substituted therefor, as a deduction from income, specific allowances for excess living costs, consisting of the following items: cost of living, housing, home leave travel, schooling, and hardship.

#### #23-35...The Expatriate Compensation Dilemma

The nature of the by-products resulting from what was stated above is well summarized by Mr. Hammer in the FERF book ACCOUNTING FOR THE MULTINATIONAL CORPORATION, page 492, as follows:

> Compensation plans for U.S. employees assigned abroad consume considerable administrative time for U.S. corporations operating internationally and the direct costs of sending employees overseas have in many cases become significant. *** The tax aspects of employee taxation have become an important element of the total compensation package because employers are adopting various policies of reimbursing their employees for excess taxes paid on foreign assignments.
>
> Local taxation levels also affect the attractiveness of various locations abroad and thus influence personal decisions of employees, particularly of senior executives, as to where to locate. *** The location of a headquarters office in a certain country quite often leads to the location of a physical plant in the same country probably because management becomes familiar with conditions there. Thus, quite important decisions from a corporate standpoint can be influenced by employees' decisions which, in turn, are based in part on personal taxation.

Thus present tax provisions relating to Americans working overseas have been subjected to very heavy criticism for both their

FIGURE 23-4

| Form **2555** | **Foreign Earned Income** | OMB No. 1545-0067 |
|---|---|---|
| Department of the Treasury<br>Internal Revenue Service | ▶ **See separate instructions.** ▶ **Attach to Form 1040.** | 19**84**<br>33 |

**For Use by United States Citizens and Resident Aliens Only**

| Name of taxpayer | Social security number |
|---|---|

| Foreign address (including country) | Your occupation |
|---|---|

Name of employer ▶

| Employer's<br>address | U.S. ▶ |
|---|---|
| | Foreign ▶ |

Employer is (check ▶ ☐ A foreign entity       ☐ A U.S. company
any that apply)    ☐ A foreign affiliate of a U.S. company   ☐ Self    ☐ Other (specify) ▶

Enter earlier years (after 1981) that you filed Form 2555 to claim either of the exclusions ▶

If you chose to claim an exclusion in 1982 or 1983, have you revoked your choice? . . . . . . . . . . . ☐ Yes ☐ No
If "Yes," give the type of exclusion and the tax year for which the revocation was effective ▶

Test under which you qualify to claim the ▶ ☐ Bona fide residence test. (Part I)     | Are you a
exclusion(s) and/or deduction         ☐ Physical presence test. (Part II)     | U.S. citizen? . . . . . ☐ Yes ☐ No

Did you maintain a separate foreign residence for your family because of adverse living conditions at
your tax home? . . . . . . . . . . . . . . . . . . . . . . . . . . . . . . . . . . . . . . ☐ Yes ☐ No
If "Yes," give city and country of the separate foreign residence. Also show the number of days during your tax year that you maintained a
second household at that address

List your tax home(s) during your tax year and date(s) established

**Complete either Part I or Part II. If an item does not apply, write "NA." If you do not provide
the information asked for, any exclusion or deduction you claim may be disallowed.**

**Part I** Taxpayers Qualifying Under Bona Fide Residence Test. (See instructions.)

1   Date bona fide residence began _____ , ended _____

2   Kind of living quarters in foreign country ▶ ☐ Purchased house     ☐ Rented house or apartment     ☐ Rented room
                                ☐ Quarters furnished by employer

3   Did any of your family live with you abroad during any part of the tax year? . . . . . . . . . . . ☐ Yes ☐ No
    If "Yes," who and for what period? ▶

4a Have you submitted a statement to the authorities of the foreign country where you claim bona fide residence that
    you are not a resident of that country? (See instructions.) . . . . . . . . . . . . . . . . . . ☐ Yes ☐ No
  b Are you required to pay income tax to the country where you claim bona fide residence? (See instructions.) . . . ☐ Yes ☐ No
    **If "Yes" to 4a and "No" to 4b, you do not qualify as a bona fide resident. Do not complete the rest of Part I.**

5   Complete the following for days present in the United States or its possessions during the tax year. (Do not include this income in Part
    III, but report it on Form 1040.)

| Date arrived<br>in U.S. | Date left<br>U.S. | Number of<br>days in U.S.<br>on business | Income earned in U.S.<br>on business (attach<br>computation) | Date arrived<br>in U.S. | Date left<br>U.S. | Number of<br>days in U.S.<br>on business | Income earned in U.S.<br>on business (attach<br>computation) |
|---|---|---|---|---|---|---|---|
| | | | | | | | |
| | | | | | | | |
| | | | | | | | |
| | | | | | | | |

6a State any contractual terms or other conditions relating to the length of your employment abroad

  b State the type of visa under which you entered the foreign country

  c Did your visa limit the length of your stay or employment in a foreign country? . . . . . . . . . . ☐ Yes ☐ No
    If "Yes," attach explanation.

  d Did you maintain a home in the U.S. while living abroad? . . . . . . . . . . . . . . . . ☐ Yes ☐ No
    If "Yes," show address of your home, whether it was rented, and the names and relationships of the occupants

**For Paperwork Reduction Act Notice, see page 1 of separate instructions.**                                  Form **2555** (1984)

FIGURE 23-4 (continued)

**Part II**  Taxpayers Qualifying Under Physical Presence Test. (See instructions.)

7  The physical presence test is based on the 12-month period from _____through_____
8  Enter your principal country of employment during your tax year ▶ _____
9  Enter all travel abroad during the 12-month period shown on line 7, except travel between foreign countries that did not involve travel
on, or over, international waters, or in, or over, the United States, for 24 hours or more. If the last entry is an arrival in a foreign country,
enter the number of full days to the end of the 12-month period. If you have no travel to report during the period, write in the schedule
that you were physically present in a foreign country or countries during the entire 12-month period. (Do not include in Part III the
income that you list here, but report it on Form 1040.)

| Name of country (including U.S.) | Date arrived | Date left | Full days present in country | Number of days in U.S. on business | Income earned in U.S. on business (attach computation) |
|---|---|---|---|---|---|
|  |  |  |  |  |  |
|  |  |  |  |  |  |
|  |  |  |  |  |  |

**Part III**  All Taxpayers

Note:  On lines 10 through 14 enter all income, including noncash income, that you earned and actually or constructively received during
your 1984 tax year for services you performed in a foreign country. If any of the foreign earned income received this tax year was
earned in a prior tax year, or will be earned in a later tax year (such as a bonus), see the instructions. Do not include income from
Part I, line 5, or Part II, line 9. Report amounts in U.S. dollars, using the exchange rates in effect when you actually or constructively
received the income.
If you are a cash basis taxpayer, report on Form 1040 all income you received during 1984 no matter when you performed
the service.

| 1984 Foreign Earned Income | | Amount (in U.S. dollars) | |
|---|---|---|---|
| 10  Total wages, salaries, bonuses, commissions, etc. . . . . . . . . . . . . . . . . . | 10 | | |
| 11  Allowable share of income for personal services performed (see instructions for Part III, line 11): | | | |
| a  In a business (including farming) or profession . . . . . . . . . . . . . . . | 11a | | |
| b  In a partnership (give name, address, and nature of income) _____ | 11b | | |
| 12  Noncash income (market value of property or facilities furnished by employer—attach statement showing how determined): | | | |
| a  Home (lodging) . . . . . . . . . . . . . . . . . . . . . . . . . | 12a | | |
| b  Meals . . . . . . . . . . . . . . . . . . . . . . . . . . . . | 12b | | |
| c  Car . . . . . . . . . . . . . . . . . . . . . . . . . . . . . | 12c | | |
| d  Other property or facilities (specify) _____ | 12d | | |
| 13  Allowances, reimbursements, or expenses paid on your behalf for services you performed: | | | |
| a  Cost of living and overseas differential . . . . . . . . . . . . . 13a | | | |
| b  Family . . . . . . . . . . . . . . . . . . . . . . . . 13b | | | |
| c  Education . . . . . . . . . . . . . . . . . . . . . . . 13c | | | |
| d  Home leave . . . . . . . . . . . . . . . . . . . . . . 13d | | | |
| e  Quarters . . . . . . . . . . . . . . . . . . . . . . . 13e | | | |
| f  For any other purpose (specify) _____ 13f | | | |
| g  Add the amounts on lines 13a through 13f . . . . . . . . . . . . . . . . . | 13g | | |
| 14  Other foreign earned income (specify) _____ | | | |
| _____ | 14 | | |
| 15  Add the amounts on lines 10 through 12d, line 13g, and line 14 . . . . . . . . . . . | 15 | | |
| 16  Value of meals and lodging included on line 12a or 12b that is excludable. (See instructions.) . . . . | 16 | | |
| 17  Subtract line 16 from line 15. This is your foreign earned income . . . . . . . . . . . ▶ | 17 | | |

Complete Part IV next if you choose to claim the housing exclusion or are claiming the housing deduction. Otherwise, skip to Part V.

# FIGURE 23-4 (continued)

Form 2555 (1984)            Page **3**

## Part IV   For Taxpayers Claiming Housing Exclusion AND/OR Deduction

| | | |
|---|---|---|
| 18 Qualified housing expenses for the tax year. (See instructions.) . . . . . . . . . . . . . . | **18** | |
| 19 Number of days in your qualifying period that fall within your 1984 tax year. (See instructions.) . . . . . . . . . . . . . . . . . . . . . . . . . . .   **19** | | |
| 20 Multiply $18.77 by the number of days on line 19, but do not enter more than $6,868.00. . . . . . . | **20** | |
| 21 Subtract the amount on line 20 from the amount on line 18. (If zero or less, do not complete the rest of Part IV or any of Part VII.). . . . . . . . . . . . . . . . . . . . . . . . . . . . . | **21** | |
| 22 Enter employer-provided amounts. (See instructions.) . . . . . . . . . .   **22** | | |
| 23 Enter the amount from line 17 . . . . . . . . . . . . . . . . . . . .   **23** | | |
| 24 Divide the amount on line 22 by the amount on line 23 and enter the percentage here. (Limited to 100%.). . | **24** | |
| 25 Housing exclusion. Multiply the amount on line 21 by the percentage on line 24, but do not enter more than the amount on line 22. Also enter this amount on line 35, Part VI . . . . . . . . . . . . . | **25** | |

**Note:** *If the amount on line 21 is **more than** the amount on line 25, complete line 26. Otherwise, skip to Part V if you choose to claim the foreign earned income exclusion.*

| | | |
|---|---|---|
| 26 Subtract the amount on line 25 from the amount on line 21 and enter here and on line 40, Part VII. (Complete Part V before Part VII, if you choose to claim the foreign earned income exclusion.) . . . . . . . . . . ▶ | **26** | |

## Part V   For Taxpayers Claiming Foreign Earned Income Exclusion

| | | |
|---|---|---|
| 27 Maximum foreign earned income exclusion . . . . . . . . . . . . . . . . . . . . . | **27** | $80,000 00 |
| 28 Number of days in your qualifying period that fall within your 1984 tax year. (See instructions for line 19.) . . . . . . . . . . . . . . . . . . . . . . .   **28** | | |
| 29 Divide the number of days on line 28 by the number of days in your tax year (usually 366) and enter the percentage here . . . . . . . . . . . . . . . . . . . . . . . . . . . | **29** | |
| 30 Multiply the amount on line 27 by the percentage on line 29 . . . . . . . . . . . . . . | **30** | |
| 31 Enter the amount from line 17 . . . . . . . . . . .   **31** | | |
| 32 Enter the amount from line 25 . . . . . . . . . . .   **32** | | |
| 33 Subtract the amount on line 32 from the amount on line 31 . . . . . . . . . . . . . . | **33** | |
| 34 Foreign earned income exclusion. Enter here and on line 36, Part VI, the amount from line 30 or line 33, whichever is less . . . . . . . . . . . . . . . . . . . . . . . . . . . . ▶ | **34** | |

## Part VI   For Taxpayers Claiming Housing Exclusion, Foreign Earned Income Exclusion, or Both

| | | |
|---|---|---|
| 35 Housing exclusion from line 25 . . . . . . . . . . .   **35** | | |
| 36 Foreign earned income exclusion from line 34 . . . . . . . .   **36** | | |
| 37 Add the amounts on lines 35 and 36 . . . . . . . . . . . . . . . . . . . . . . | **37** | |
| 38 Deductions allocable to excluded income. (See instructions and attach computation.) . . . . . . . . | **38** | |
| 39 Subtract line 38 from line 37. Enter the result here and in parenthesis on Form 1040, line 22. Next to the amount write "Exclusion(s) from Form 2555." On Form 1040 subtract the amount from your income to arrive at total income on Form 1040, line 23 . . . . . . . . . . . . . . . . . . ▶ | **39** | |

## Part VII   For Taxpayers Claiming Housing Deduction

**Note:** *Complete this part only if: (1) you entered an amount on line 26, and (2) the amount on line 17 is more than the amount on line 37.*

| | | |
|---|---|---|
| 40 Enter the amount from line 26 . . . . . . . . . . . . . . . . . . . . . . . . | **40** | |
| 41 Enter the amount from line 17 . . . . . . . . . . . .   **41** | | |
| 42 Enter the amount from line 37 . . . . . . . . . . . .   **42** | | |
| 43 Subtract the amount on line 42 from the amount on line 41 . . . . . . . . . . . . . . | **43** | |
| 44 Enter the amount from line 40 or line 43, whichever is less . . . . . . . . . . . . . . | **44** | |

**Note:** *If the amount on line 43 is **more than** the amount on line 44 and you could not deduct all of your 1983 housing deduction because of the 1983 limitation, complete the worksheet on page 4 of the instructions to figure how much of your 1983 housing deduction may be carried over to 1984. Otherwise, enter a zero (–0–) on line 45.*

| | | |
|---|---|---|
| 45 Housing deduction carryover from 1983 (from worksheet on page 4 of the instructions) . . . . . . . | **45** | |
| 46 Add the amounts on lines 44 and 45. Enter here and on Form 1040 to the left of line 31. Next to the amount on Form 1040 write "Deduction from Form 2555." Add it to the total adjustments reported on that line . ▶ | **46** | |

complexity and their adverse impact on employment of Americans abroad as well as the promotion of U.S. exports. The result has been the enactment by Congress of THE ECONOMIC RECOVERY TAX ACT OF 1981 which basically repeals the multitude of special deductions available to expatriates since 1978 such as cost of living, schooling, home leave travel and hardship area employment.

(The 1984 revision of Form 2555, entitled FOREIGN EARNED INCOME, is reproduced in Figure 23-4.)

#23-36...ERTA 1981 Provisions Relating to Expatriates

The significant provisions relating to expatriate taxation beginning with Jan. 1, 1982 are related in a pamphlet issued by Peat, Marwick, Mitchell & Co. entitled "The Economic Recovery Tax Act of 1981," issued Aug. 5, 1981, page 15, as follows:

Individuals whose tax home is in a foreign country and who are either (1) U.S. citizens establishing bona fide residence in a foreign country, or (2) U.S. citizens or residents presently outside the United States for a period of 330 days in a consecutive 12-month period, may elect to exclude earned income attributable to services performed overseas from their gross income. The maximum annual exclusion for 1982 is set at $75,000, prorated daily and increasing $5,000 per year until 1986, when the maximum exclusion will be $95,000.

Non-excluded income is to be taxed as if it were the first income earned, that is, at the lower marginal rate brackets. The exclusion of earned income can thus serve to reduce the rate of tax on non-excludable investment income.

Qualifying expatriates may also separately elect an exclusion for reasonable housing costs (excluding otherwise deductible interest and taxes) attributable to employer-provided amounts in excess of 16% of the salary paid to a U.S. government employee at the GS-14, Step 1 level. This exclusion is in addition to the maximum foreign earned income exclusion. Special rules apply where adverse conditions prevent an individual's family from residing with the individual and where excess housing costs are not attributable to employer-provided amounts.

Credits for foreign taxes and deductions allocable to excluded income, including those for moving expenses, are not allowed.

Both the exclusion of foreign earned income and the exclusion based on excess housing costs are elective. These elections apply until revoked, although a revocation precludes a new election for five years after the year of revocation, except with the consent of the Secretary of the Treasury.

## #23-37...By-Product Advantages of ERTA 1981

Three incidental advantages flow from the reduction of taxes of expatriates: (1) An increase in volume of American businesses by being more competitive in personnel recruitment; (2) Increase in Americans employed overseas; and (3) Increase in Americans employed by foreign country operators.

(1) <u>American Business Increase in Volume</u>. The ERTA 1981 will not only reduce taxes of expatriates, but will have the side effects of reducing costs of employers sending Americans overseas. This will result in an increase in the number of Americans in foreign jobs, reversing the trend of a reduction in American forces. Increasing Americans in foreign jobs will boost U.S. exports because American professionals and managers will be more apt to buy U.S.-made goods, and design projects requiring use of American equipment, than would foreign nationals. This fact is substantiated by a business research firm, Chase Econometrics, which has reported that because of the number of reduced expatriates due to the onerous tax laws, exports have been reduced by 5% of what they would have been with American expatriates. The net result is a loss in income, jobs, and taxes.

A case in point is the Idaho-based construction company, Morrison-Knudsen International, whose annual tax allowance outlay has been over $4 million. The new law will enable Morrison-Knudsen to reduce its costs and offer more competitive prices, enabling it to attract more business.

(2) <u>Increase in Americans Employed Overseas</u>. Because American firms sending employees overseas had to pay them not only their regular pay, but also additional expenses involving living costs, education, etc., the amount of the extras came to as much as the actual salary, making the excess an unnecessary cost. This forced many American firms to refrain from sending their executives and employees overseas. With the reduction in taxes, American firms will now be in a competitive position to use American personnel.

(3) <u>Increase in Hiring by Foreign Companies</u>. A third advantage of reduced expatriate taxation, according to Ward Howell International, a New York recruiting firm, is requests by four Middle East clients to recruit Americans for positions. Gilbert Dwyer, a partner in Ward Howell, says that in such countries as Belgium, Brazil, Canada, Japan, and Germany, where the tax rates are higher than those in the U.S., Americans will continue to pay the higher tax to the foreign country. This will enable them to use the foreign tax paid as a tax credit against the U.S. tax, thereby reducing it to a negligible amount or no U.S. tax at all.

On the other hand, in such countries as Saudi Arabia, Hong Kong, Great Britain, Venezuela, and developing areas of Africa

and the Middle East, where there is no tax structure or one
that is relatively minor, the savings will be dramatic. An example of such a case is given by Arthur Hayes, partner in Ernst
& Whinney:

| Item | Tax Act Prior to 1981 | Tax Act of 1981 |
|---|---|---|
| Base Salary | $ 40,000 | $ 40,000 |
| Additional Compensation | 73,110 | 73,110 |
| Total Foreign Earned Income | $113,110 | $113,110 |
| Earned Foreign Exclusion | -0- | 75,000 |
| Housing Exclusion | -0- | 38,110 |
| Excess Foreign Living Costs Deduction | 70,292 | -0- |
| Total Deductions & Exclusions | $ 70,292 | $113,110 |
| U.S. TAX | $ 6,552 | $ -0- |

#23-38...Effects on Taxes (Under ERTA 1981) of the Tax Credits
        and Exclusion

There are three situations that may exist with respect to
the effect of Foreign Tax Credits and Exclusions on taxes: (I)
No Credit for Foreign Taxes Paid and No Exclusion; (II) Low
Tax Countries; and (III) High Tax Countries. Illustrations of
the three situations are presented below, as furnished by Jack
Staley and Robert Adam, tax experts of Arthur Young & Company.

#23-39...(I) No Foreign Tax Credit and No Exclusions

Assume a family total income of $100,000, consisting of
earned income plus allowances for housing, education, etc. With
no credit for foreign taxes paid and no exclusion, the U.S.
taxes thereon comes to $35,450. However, under the 1981 Act
there would be an exclusion of $75,000, reducing the income on
which tax would be based to $25,000, on which the U.S. tax
would be $3,150.

#23-40...(II) Low Tax Countries

There are two possibilities under this situation: (a) With
No Exclusion, and (b) With the Exclusion.
        (a). With No Exclusion. Assume total income of $100,000 in a
foreign country whose income taxes are only $5,000 which can be
used as a tax credit. As seen in the preceding case, U.S. taxes
on $100,000 were $35,450. Deducting the $5,000 foreign tax
credit from the U.S. tax of $35,450 leaves the U.S. tax at
$30,450. The total tax then would be the U.S. tax of $30,450
plus the foreign tax of $5,000, or $35,450.
        (b). With the Exclusion. The income of $100,000 would be
reduced to $25,000 when the $75,000 exclusion is deducted, and

as seen in the preceding case the tax on $25,000 would be $3,150. The foreign tax credit would be 25,000/100,000 x 5,000 = $1,250. The total tax would be the sum of the U.S. tax of $3,150 plus the foreign tax of $5,000, or $8,150, less the tax credit of $1,250, or a total of $6,900. Thus under the exclusion in the new tax law, the taxpayer saves $35,450 minus $6,900, or $28,550.

#23-41...(III) High Tax Countries

As is the case with the Low Tax Countries, there are two possibilities under the High Tax Countries: (a) With No Exclusion and (b) With the Exclusion.

(a) With No Exclusion. Assume total income of $100,000 in a foreign country whose income taxes are 50%, or $50,000, which can be used as a tax credit. As previously seen, the tax on $100,000 would be $35,450. Deducting the $50,000 foreign tax credit from the U.S. tax of $35,450 would wash out the U.S. tax, making the total taxes the amount of the foreign tax, viz., $50,000. However the difference resulting in a tax overage of $50,000 minus $35,450, or $14,550, could be applied as an unused credit carryover to other years.

(b) With the Exclusion. As seen above, on income of $100,000 with an exclusion of $75,000, or net income of $25,000, the U.S. tax would be $3,150. The foreign tax credit would be 25,000/100,000 x 50,000 = $12,500. Since the foreign tax credit of $12,500 is greater than the U.S. tax of $3,150, there would be no U.S. tax. However the difference resulting in a tax overage of $12,500 minus $3,150, or $9,350, could be applied as an unused credit carryover to other years. The total tax would then be only the foreign tax of $50,000 as there would be no U.S. tax. Thus the taxpayer's current tax situation is not affected by the new exclusion, but gives him a bigger foreign tax credit carryover by not taking the exclusion.

The foregoing illustrations may be summarized as follows:

ILLUSTRATIVE CASES OF TAX SAVINGS UNDER THE
ECONOMIC RECOVERY ACT OF 1981 FOR EXPATRIATES

|  | Situation | Taxes Under Act Prior to 1981 | Taxes Under 1981 Tax Act |
|---|---|---|---|
| I. | NO CREDIT FOR FOREIGN TAXES PAID AND NO EXCLUSIONS: | | |
|  | 1. Total Income | $100,000 | $100,000 |
|  | 2. Exclusion | -0- | 75,000 |
|  | 3. Taxable Income | $100,000 | $ 25,000 |
|  | 4. U.S. Tax | $ 35,450 | $  3,150 |
|  | 5. Tax Saving | | $ 32,300 |

II.    (A). LOW TAX COUNTRIES --
       WITH NO EXCLUSION:

| | | | |
|---|---|---|---|
| 1. | Total Income | $100,000 | $100,000 |
| 2. | Exclusion | -0- | -0- |
| 3. | Taxable Income | $100,000 | $100,000 |
| 4. | U.S. Tax | $ 35,450 | $ 35,450 |
| 5. | Foreign Tax | 5,000 | 5,000 |
| 6. | Total U.S. and Foreign Taxes | $ 40,450 | $ 40,450 |
| 7. | Less: Foreign Tax Credit | 5,000 | 5,000 |
| 8. | Net Total Taxes | $ 35,450 | $ 35,450 |

       (B). LOW TAX COUNTRIES --
       WITH THE EXCLUSION:

| | | | |
|---|---|---|---|
| 1. | Total Income | $100,000 | $100,000 |
| 2. | Exclusion | -0- | 75,000 |
| 3. | Taxable Income | $100,000 | $ 25,000 |
| 4. | U.S. Tax | $ 35,450 | $ 3,150 |
| 5. | Foreign Tax | 5,000 | 5,000 |
| 6. | Total U.S. and Foreign Tax (4+5) | $ 40,450 | $ 8,150 |
| 7. | Foreign Tax Credit (Line 5) | 5,000 | 1,250 |
| 8. | Net Total Taxes | $ 35,450 | $ 6,900 |
| 9. | Tax Saving | | $ 28,550 |

III.   (A). HIGH TAX COUNTRIES --
       WITH NO EXCLUSION:

| | | | |
|---|---|---|---|
| 1. | Total Income | $100,000 | $100,000 |
| 2. | Exclusion | -0- | -0- |
| 3. | Taxable Income | $100,000 | $100,000 |
| 4. | U.S. Tax on $100,000 | $ 35,450 | $ 35,450 |
| 5. | Foreign Tax (50%) | 50,000 | 50,000 |
| 6. | Total U.S. and Foreign Tax (4+5) | $ 85,450 | $ 85,450 |
| 7. | Less: Foreign Tax Credit (U.S. Tax) | 35,450 | 35,450 |
| 8. | Net Total Taxes (Foreign Tax) | $ 50,000 | $ 50,000 |
| 9. | Less: Foreign Tax Credit (Line 7) | 35,450 | 35,450 |
| 10. | Unused Credit Carryover to Other Years (8-9) | $ 14,550 | $ 14,550 |

(B). HIGH TAX COUNTRIES--
WITH THE EXCLUSION:

| | | | |
|---|---|---|---|
| 1. | Total Income | $100,000 | $100,000 |
| 2. | Exclusion | -0- | 75,000 |
| 3. | Taxable Income | $100,000 | $ 25,000 |
| 4. | U.S. Tax | $ 35,450 | $ 3,150 |
| 5. | Foreign Tax | 50,000 | 50,000 |
| 6. | Foreign Tax Credit | 35,450 | 12,500 |
| 7. | Net U.S. Tax (4-6) | -0- | -0- |
| 8. | Total Net Taxes (U.S. + Foreign)(5+7) | $ 50,000 | $ 50,000 |
| 9. | Unused Credit Carryover to other Years (6-4) | | $ 9,350 |

#23-42...Benefits of ERTA 1981

In conclusion, it is hoped that the ERTA of 1981, effective Jan. 1, 1982, will have the following salutary effects: (1) make U.S. firms more competitive on many foreign construction and other business projects; (2) afford more and greater employment opportunities to Americans in foreign jobs and companies; and (3) reduce the costs of U.S. MNCs of sending Americans to work in their foreign operations.

## UNITARY TAXATION SYSTEM

### #23-43...Purpose of Unitary Tax

Up to this point we have been discussing taxes on a U.S. national or federal level. MNCs are now concerned with taxes on a STATE level because of a recent court decision in the State of California. This tax is known as the UNITARY TAX. The unitary tax method was first initiated in Calif. in the 1930s to prevent Hollywood movie studios from transferring assets abroad to avoid paying state taxes. The tax spread into Alaska, Colorado, Florida, Idaho, Massachusetts, Montana, New Hampshire, North Dakota, Oregon and Utah.

In order to fall within the purview of the unitary method of taxation, a company must operate as a single economic unit so that the operations in states other than the base location must be of the same type as those in the home state, such as an integrated international petroleum company.

### #23-44...Nature of Unitary Tax

In its EXECUTIVE NEWSLETTER of July 25, 1983, page 4, Peat, Marwick, Mitchell & Co. points out that:

Under the unitary system, the percentage of income subject
to tax in a particular state is based on the ratio of world-
wide payroll, sales, and property in the state. Critics
contend that such factors as lower labor costs in foreign
countries may cause a disproportionate amount of income to
be taxable in a state, resulting in taxation of income that
may have already been taxed abroad.

In 1982 the amount of unitary tax came to $600 million dollars
in state revenues. Of this amount, $500 million was collected
in Calif. alone, which prompted the Container Corporation of
America to file suit contesting its Calif. tax on the company's
world-wide earnings in 1965.

## #23-45...The Container Corporation Case

In 1965 the Container Corp. of America's earnings in Calif.
came to $32 million. The company owed the State of Calif. taxes
of 9.8%, or $174,000, under a formula taxing the in-state
sales, property and payroll. If Container Corp. figured its
obligation on a world-wide basis, it would pay at a lower rate
of 7.6% on the larger amount of its world-wide earnings which
were $47 million. Under such a formula the company would owe
$197,000 in taxes, or $23,000 more than under the traditional
method. Container Corp. filed suit against the State of Calif.,
which was decided in favor of the State, and in an appeal to
the U.S. Supreme Court, in Container Corp. of America v. Franchise Tax Board, the ruling was affirmed in favor of the State.
The decision in effect requires a Delaware Corporation, headquartered in Chicago, to report its income, for Calif. franchise tax purposes, on a unitary basis. That is, the income of
Container Corp., of Delaware, and 20 foreign subsidiaries must
be consolidated and apportioned in part to Calif., which is to
be computed by multiplying the consolidated income by a three-
factor formula designed to determine that part of the world-
wide payroll, property and sales allocable to Calif.
A distinction was made in the court ruling between the unitary system and the traditional method known as the GEOGRAPHI-
CAL or TRANSACTIONAL ACCOUNTING system. Under the latter, taxable income is determined only from the books of each corporate
entity, and income from related corporations not having business within, or income from, the taxing jurisdiction are not
included. The court stated the reason for the distinction was
that "formal accounting is subject to manipulation and impreci-
sion, and often ignores or captures inadequately the many subtle and largely unquantifiable transfers of value that take
place among the components of a single enterprise."
Three of the eight justices dissented on the ground that the
tax clearly violates the Foreign Commerce Clause, and that a

state tax should be considered  unconstitutional  if it creates
a substantial risk of international multiple taxation.

### #23-46...Unitary Tax Pros and Cons

The states having the world-wide unitary  system  argue that
it is  needed  to prevent MNCs from using bookkeeping devices to
shift their profits to other  states or  countries  to minimize
their tax burden.  Opponents  of the unitary system claim it is
a form of  double  taxation because it is imposed on income already taxed by other states or countries.

### #23-47...Political Implications of Unitary System

One  of the  principles  enunciated  by the majority opinion
was  that "the California  tax  is not preempted by federal law
or fatally inconsistent with federal policy." Under this ruling
the door is  open to present legislation in the Congress to bar
the  use of the unitary system by states.  Congressional action
has  indeed been  taken  in the form of a  Senate  Bill (S 1225)
introduced  by Sen. Charles Mathias  and in the House (HR 2918)
by Rep. Barber Conable. Both Sen. Mathias and Rep. Conable have
respectively  requested the Senate  Finance  Committee  and the
House Judiciary Committee to hold hearings on their bills. They
would  explore  the question  of  what effect the  Supreme Court
decision would have on congressional legislative action.

### #23-48...International Aspects of Unitary Taxation

In  its EXECUTIVE NEWSLETTER of Oct. 14, 1983, Vol.  IX, No.
10, page 1, Peat, Marwick, Mitchell & Co. indicates:
    A  number of  foreign nations  have been vigorously pro-
testing the unitary taxation system for some time.  Protests
have  picked up in recent months as several nations, including  Japan,  the Netherlands, and  the United Kingdom,  have
sent letters to the  U.S. government warning of possible repercussions if the system is not abandoned.
    In  a  letter to Treasury  Secretary  Donald  Regan, the
Netherlands Minister of  Finance cited Shell Petroleum  N.V.
as an example of how  unitary taxation can result in unrealistic taxation of multinational corporations.  In this case,
he  said, "a profit of about $40 million is apportioned to a
U.S. subsidiary engaged in non-oil-related business, whereas
that subsidiary has accumulated a loss of about $390 million
over the taxable years concerned."
    U.S. trading partners had begun to take a "wait-and-see"
approach while the Administration was examining initiatives.
Last month, for example, foreign ministers from the European
Economic Community had discussed unitary taxation at a meet-

ing in Brussels to determine if a protest should be sent to Pres. Reagan. They decided to postpone such action until they saw what steps the Administration would take on its own.

The decision to form the special task force to be composed of representatives from states, the federal government, and multinational corporations may be viewed by some abroad as a delaying tactic, since the Administration dropped more concrete legislative and legal initiatives in favor of letting the new group examine the issue. The day before the group was announced, a top-level British business delegation warned of retaliatory actions by the U.K. government if unitary taxation is not dropped.

## SUMMARY OF FOOTNOTE REFERENCES
(References are to Paragraph #'s)

#23-17 George C. Watt, Richard M. Hammer, and Marianne Burge, AC-COUNTING FOR THE MULTINATIONAL CORPORATION, p.424. Copyright 1977 by Financial Executives Research Foundation (FERF), Morristown, N.J. Reprinted with permission.

#23-17 W.R. Carnie, ILLINOIS CPA SOCIETY NEWS JOURNAL (Oct.1983):24

#23-17 Deloitte, Haskins & Sells, THE WEEK IN REVIEW, 83-10 (March 11, 1983): 6

#23-21 Milka Casanegra de Jantscher, "Tax Havens Explained," FINANCE AND DEVELOPMENT (March 1976): 31

#23-21 Jean Doucet and Kenneth J. Good, "What Makes a Good Tax Haven?" BANKER (May 1973): 493

#23-23 Subpart F, Subchapter N, 1962 Revenue Act

#23-23 "Report by the President's Task Force on Business Taxation," Sept. 1970, TAX REDUCTION ACT OF 1975, TAX REFORM ACT OF 1976

#23-27 Watt, Hammer and Burge, op. cit., p. 449. Reprinted by permission from FERF.

#23-33 Ibid., p. 470. Reprinted by permission from FERF.

#23-34 THE WALL STREET JOURNAL (Feb. 8, 1979): 2

#23-35 Watt, Hammer and Burge, op. cit., p. 492, by permission.

#23-36 Peat, Marwick, Mitchell & Co., "The Economic Recovery Tax Act of 1981" (August 5, 1981): 15

#23-44 Peat, Marwick, Mitchell & Co., EXECUTIVE NEWSLETTER (July 25, 1983): 4

#23-48 Peat, Marwick, Mitchell & Co., EXECUTIVE NEWSLETTER, Vol. IX, No. 10 (Oct. 14, 1983): 1

## BIBLIOGRAPHY

Arnold, B.J. "The Taxation of Controlled Foreign Corporations," CANADIAN TAXATION (Oct.-Nov. 1983): 942

Bruce, Charles M. "New Rules Taxing Americans Working Abroad," TAXES (February 1979): 79-84

Burns, Jane O.  "DISC  Accounting: An Empirical Investigation," THE
     INTERNATIONAL TAX JOURNAL, 4 (April 1978): 882-891
Casanegra de Jantscher, Milka.  "Tax Havens Explained," FINANCE AND
     DEVELOPMENT (March 1976): 31-34
Cliff, Walter C.  "Pairing: A Technique for Avoiding CFC Status and
     Other Burdens of U.S. Taxation," TAXES (Aug. 1979): 530-537
Coopers & Lybrand.  INTERNATIONAL TAX SUMMARIES. N.Y.: John Wiley,
     1983
Davis, Michael.  "The Tax Haven Company--Dispelling the Myths," AC-
     COUNTANCY, 87 (February 1976): 46-48
Delap, Richard L.  "Apportionment of Expenses to DISC Income," THE
     INTERNATIONAL TAX JOURNAL, 5 (Feb. 1979): 214-226
Deloitte, Haskins & Sells.  TAXATION OF  FOREIGN NATIONALS  BY THE
     UNITED STATES. N.Y.: Deloitte, Haskins & Sells, 1982
Deloitte, Haskins & Sells.  TAXATION OF U.S. CITIZENS ABROAD. N.Y.:
     Deloitte, Haskins & Sells, 1983
Feinschreiber, Robert.  "New Deductions  for Overseas  Americans,"
     INTERNATIONAL TAX JOURNAL, 5 (December 1978): 93-108
Gaskins, J.  Peter.  "Taxation of Foreign Source Income," FINANCIAL
     ANALYSTS JOURNAL, 29 (Sept.-Oct. 1973): 55-64
Green, Willam H.  "Planning DISC Operations in the '80s," INTERNA-
     TIONAL TAX JOURNAL, 6 (June 1980): 373-389
Howard, Frederic K.  "Overview of International Taxation," COLUMBIA
     JOURNAL OF WORLD BUSINESS, 10 (Summer 1975): 5-11
Larkins, E.P.  THE IMPACT OF TAXES ON U.S. CITIZENS WORKING ABROAD.
     Ann Arbor, Mich: UMI Research Press, 1983
Lillie, Jane.  "A New  Strategy  for Recognizing Exchange Gains  &
     Losses," INTERNATIONAL TAX JOURNAL, 4 (Aug. 1978): 1071-1080
Mihaly, Z.M. "United States Taxation of U.S. Corporations Operating
     Overseas," HASTINGS INTERNATIONAL AND COMPARATIVE LAW REVIEW
     (Spring 1982): 619
Rashkin, Michael D.  "The Branch Rule and the Subpart F Exclusion,"
     INTERNATIONAL TAX JOURNAL, 4 (June 1978): 980-994
Romito,  Edwin L.  "Amending the DISC  Return," INTERNATIONAL  TAX
     JOURNAL, 7 (April 1981): 300-308
Sale, J.  Timothy and  Carrol, Karen.  "Tax Planning Tools  for the
     Multinational  Corporation," MANAGEMENT  ACCOUNTING  (June
     1979): 37-41
Shagam, Jerome and Kolmin, Kenneth.  "Temporary Regulations Resolve
     Some Problems for U.S. Persons Working Abroad," INTERNATION-
     AL TAX JOURNAL, 5 (June 1979): 363-393
"Taxation of Americans Abroad Under  ERTA," NORTHWESTERN JOURNAL OF
     INTERNATIONAL LAW AND BUSINESS (Autumn 1982): 586

## THEORY QUESTIONS
(Question Numbers are Keyed to Text Paragraph #'s)

#23-2  Discuss the basic  concern of International Taxation Ac-
       counting.
#23-4  Discuss the nature of the basic  problem of double taxa-
       tion.

#23-5  Discuss the nature of the Complete Exemption Territorial Approach to taxation accounting.

#23-11 Discuss the nature and operation of the Deferral Method of taxation accounting.

#23-12 What criticisms have been levelled at the Territorial and Deferral Methods? What concerns were elicited by the U.N. Report on the impact of MNCs on the development process and on international relations relating to taxation?

#23-13 What is the basic objective of foreign investment tax laws? What three other objectives do the foreign investment tax laws have?

#23-14 Name five types of foreign operations that have been granted U.S. tax incentives. Briefly define and explain the nature of (a) Western Hemisphere Trade Corporations, (b) Possessions Corporations (c) DISCs, (d) Export Trade Corporations, & (e) Less Developed Country Corporations.

#23-21 Define tax havens and explain their implications and prime objectives.

#23-23 What is the nature and purpose of the Subpart F Provision of the Revenue Act of 1962? What two disadvantages have resulted from the creation of Subpart F income?

#23-26 Make up an outline classifying Subpart F taxable income. Define and explain each of the following classes of Subpart F income: (a) Personal Holding Company, (b) Sales, (c) Services, (d) Shipping.

#23-31 Discuss the treatment of foreign bribes as a Taxation Item.

#23-32 Discuss Subpart F income resulting from international boycotts.

#23-33 Discuss the relation of Section 367 of the Internal Revenue Code to the loophole permitting taxpayers to avoid capital gains taxes.

#23-34 Discuss the nature of taxation on Expatriate Compensation. What is the basic reason for the U.S. problem with Expatriate Compensation?

#23-35 What is the expatriate compensation dilemma?

#23-36 What provisions relating to expatriates have been made under the Economic Recovery Tax Act of 1981?

#23-37 What are the by-product advantages of ERTA 1981?

#23-42 What benefits have resulted from ERTA 1981?

#23-43-44. What is the nature and purpose of the Unitary Tax?

#23-45 Discuss the Container Corporation case and its impact on the Unitary Tax.

#23-46 Outline the pros and cons of the Unitary Tax.

## PROBLEMS

### P-23-1 (CPA EXAM, 5/74, THEORY, #32)

American Commercial Ventures, Inc., owns 25% of the common stock of an overseas corporation which has consistently operated profitably since the investment was made. Because the foreign corporation needs capital for growth, the foreign interests who own a majority of its stock have declared no dividends and evidently have no intent of changing this policy in the forseeable future. In light of these facts, American Commercial, which uses the equity method to account for its investment,

   a. Need not now make any provision for taxes on the foreign profits.

   b. Must accrue a provision for taxes on the foreign profits.

   c. Can, on a discretionary basis, provide for taxes on the foreign profits.

   d. Should recognize taxes only when and as foreign profits are remitted as dividends (with a resultant prior-period adjustment).

### P-23-2

When undistributed earnings of a subsidiary company have increased the pretax accounting income of a parent company because the latter consolidated the subsidiary or used the equity method to account for its investment,

   a. Income tax allocation is necessary because there is an invariable presumption that undistributed earnings will ultimately be transferred to the parent.

   b. Maximum tax rates should be applied as a matter of conservation if income tax allocation is applied.

   c. Income taxes need not be accrued where evidence shows the subsidiary will not remit undistributed earnings to the parent for an indefinite period.

   d. GAAP have been violated.

### P-23-3

The New York Corp., a U.S. multinational manufacturer, has a subsidiary operation in Bermuda. It is contemplating a transaction for sale of merchandise in the sum of $500,000 with a dealer in London. You are called in to brief management on tax implications of the transaction.

**Required:**

What would your advice be and what would be the basis for it?

### P-23-4

John Jones employed by the Zero Corp. is sent to the Euston Road branch in London in a managerial capacity in 1982 under the Tax Act of 1981. His total family income of $100,000 consists of earned income plus allowances for housing, education, etc. With no credit for foreign taxes and no exclusion, the U.S. taxes amount to $35,450. Under the 1981 ERTA Act, Jones would be allowed an exclusion of $75,000 of income which would reduce his income on which the tax is to be based to $25,000, on which the tax would be $3,150.

**Required**:
Draft a Statement showing what the U.S. tax would be for Jones under the Tax Act existing before 1981 and under the 1981 ERTA, showing the tax saving under the latter.

## P-23-5
Assume in P-23-4 that Jones is sent to a Low Tax Country and no exclusion is allowed. Jones' total income is $100,000 and his foreign income tax is $5,000 which can be used as a tax credit. U.S. taxes on $100,000 are $35,450.

**Required**:
Draft a Statement showing what the U.S. tax would be for Jones under the Tax Act existing before 1981 and that under the 1981 ERTA, showing the tax saving if any.

## P-23-6
Assume in P-23-4 that Jones is sent to a Low Tax Country which allows the exclusion. Jones' total income is $100,000, and the exclusion allowed is $75,000. The tax on $25,000 is $3,150. The foreign tax is $5,000.

**Required**:
Draft a statement showing what the U.S. tax would be for Jones under the Tax Act existing before 1981 and that under the 1981 ERTA, showing the tax saving if any.

## P-23-7
Assume in P-23-4 that Jones is sent to a High Tax Country which does not allow the exclusion. Jones' total income is $100,000. The foreign country tax is 50%, or $50,000, which can be used as a tax credit. The tax on $100,000 is $35,540.

**Required**:
Draft a Statement showing what the U.S. tax would be for Jones under the Tax Act existing before 1981 and that under the 1981 ERTA, showing the tax saving if any.

## P-23-8
Assume in P-23-4 that Jones is sent to a High Tax Country which allows the exclusion. Jones' total income is $100,000. His exclusion is $75,000, making Net Income of $25,000. U.S. tax on $25,000 is $3,150.

**Required**:
Draft a Statement showing what the U.S. tax would be for Jones under the pre-1981 Tax Act and that under the 1981 ERTA, showing the tax saving if any.

# International Foreign Country Taxation Accounting

NATURE OF FOREIGN COUNTRY TAXATION

#24-1....Complexity of International Tax Planning

Basically the material presented in the preceding chapter was predicated on U.S. tax laws. A critique of these laws is presented in a newsletter by Laventhol and Horwath called the L&H PERSPECTIVE in Vol. 6, #1, Spring-Summer 1980, page 18, where it is said:

One of the Supreme Court's least favorite activities is re-viewing complex tax cases. Although highly respected Judge Learned Hand was not a member of that Court, he probably summarized its attitude very well when he said: "The words of such an act as the Income Tax *** merely dance before my eyes in a meaningless procession; cross-referenced to cross-reference, exception upon exception--couched in abstract terms that offer no handle to seize hold of--leave in my mind only a confused sense of some vitally important, but successfully concealed, purport, which it is my duty to ex-tract, but which is within my power, if at all, only after the most inordinate expenditure of time."

This view is reiterated by James Eustice, a distinguished pro-fessor of corporate tax law, who described U.S. tax laws as a "congressional viper's tangle of words, a fourstar example of Byzantine architecure in a statue not noted for its economy of line."

When one considers the extension of the foregoing appraisals of tax laws to foreign countries, the implications to the in-ternational business executive become a horrible nightmare. In the article "The Dilemma of the International Tax Executive," Richard H. Kalish and John P. Casey (in the COLUMBIA JOURNAL OF WORLD BUSINESS, Summer 1975, p. 62) state that the problems the international business executive is confronted with

stem from  the fact that the international executive must be
a  combination of an  administrator, tax  attorney, tax  accountant, computer  expert, and a human being.  \*\*\* The complications and intricacies of the U.S. tax laws are monumental.   In addition, he is faced with sophisticated tax treaties superimposed over  U.S. law which frequently negate  its
clear implication.  The pyramid of levels of tax law priorities is further compounded by the  invariable differences in
local tax laws which  continually exert  their  influence in
eroding the "bottom  line"  of  international business.  The
dilemma is further enlarged by  the fact that  internal U.S.
law and foreign tax laws are in a continual flux of change.
In this  chapter  the tax laws of countries with which the bulk
of U.S. business is transacted will be considered.   Because of
the  great number of countries and contrariety of tax  laws, it
will be  feasible only to present the highlights framed  around
general tax principles. Russel  Moore and George Scott,  in "An
Introduction to Financial Control and Reporting In Multinational Enterprises," published by The Univ. of Texas Bureau of Business Research, 1973, p. 56, indicate  that there must be a tax
planning system that incorporates the following procedures:
  (1) Explicit statement of the objectives  of tax planning in
      international operations.
  (2) Assignment  of definite responsibilities,  at both head-
      quarters and the subsidiaries,  for  various  aspects of
      the planning.
  (3) Determination of what decisions and operating procedures
      are affected  by tax considerations,  and  how  they are
      affected, and dissemination of  this information to  the
      decision-makers.
  (4) Definition of the procedures that will ensure the inter-
      action of the tax planners with the decision-makers.
  (5) Education about the impact of  tax considerations on in-
      ternational operating  and investment  decisions and  on
      operating procedures.

## TYPES OF TAXES

### #24-2....Classification of Taxes

    Taxes  on the  operations  of  companies abroad consist of a
multiplicity  of varieties, which broadly  can be classified as
DIRECT TAXES or INDIRECT TAXES.  DIRECT TAXES are based  on IN-
COME or on CAPITAL GAINS. INCOME TAXES may be from two sources:
(a) Corporate Income Taxes or  (b)  interest  and dividend pay-
ments to foreign investors.
    INDIRECT  TAXES  are classified as:  (a) Border  Taxes,  (b)
Turnover  Taxes,  (c) Excise  Taxes, (d)  Net Worth Taxes,  (e)
Withholding Taxes, and (f) Value-Added Taxes.

## DIRECT TAXES

### #24-3....Corporate Income Taxes

Next to duties imposed on customs, corporate income taxes is the most commonly used form of taxes as may be evidenced by the fact that in the U.S. this is a major source of government revenue. Also it should be evident that in the less developed countries where personal incomes are at low levels, taxes from such source would be negligible throwing the burden of taxation on corporate businesses. Where corporate income taxes are not very lucrative, resort is had to the various indirect taxes as a source of revenue.

### #24-4....Capital Gains Taxes

Taxes on Capital Gains would be analogous to those on corporate income taxes which would be negligible in less developed countries.

## INDIRECT TAXES

### #24-5....Border Taxes

The purpose of Border Taxes is to tax imports to the extent that they make the prices of imports competitive with those of domestic prices. As a result such taxes on imports generally are found to be roughly the equivalent of indirect taxes paid by domestic producers of goods similar to the imports.

### #24-6....Turnover Taxes

Turnover Taxes are those based on total sales at some given point in the manufacturing processes. Accordingly such taxes may be assessed at different stages of production resulting in different taxes where the laws differ in different countries. The Turnover Tax is assessed in Canada at the conclusion of the manufacturing process whereas in England when the manufacturer sells the product to the wholesaler. In the U.S. it is manifested through the Sales Tax when sold to the consumer. Germany uses a multiple system under which the taxes are assessed at all stages of the production and sales cycle. Where credit is not received for the payment of any previous turnover taxes paid, all prior taxes are included in the final selling price.

### #24-7...Net Worth Taxes

Net Worth Taxes are those based on the undistributed earnings of a corporation. Obviously the purpose of such taxes is

to employ such funds in external investment  projects resulting
in the development of domestic capital markets. This results in
Net Worth Taxes being quite substantial in  amount as evidenced
by the report  in the Haskins & Sells  publication THE WEEK IN
REVIEW, July 9, 1976, page 10, indicating that "until recently,
undistributed earnings of German Companies were taxed at a rate
of 51%, and has now been increased to 56%."

#24-8....Withholding Taxes

Where investors in foreign corporations receive interest  or
dividend payments, the country where the foreign corporation is
located  will not only impose a tax  on such income but require
the issuing  corporation to  withhold  such taxes which in turn
remits the  tax  withheld to the government.  Because such tax
effectively is paid by  the investor to the foreign government,
he will be entitled to use it as a tax credit in his home country. For this reason withholding taxes have been treated in Tax
Treaties between countries (discussed later).

Withholding tax rates vary with different classes of income,
of  which there  are three:  Dividends, Interest and Royalties.
They also vary for the three types of income in different countries.  For example, for  the year 1979, Ernst  & Whinney, in a
table entitled  FOREIGN AND U.S. CORPORATE INCOME AND WITHHOLD-
ING TAX RATES, presents the following rates:

| Country | Foreign Investors Withholding Tax Rates Applicable to: | | |
|---|---|---|---|
| | Dividends | Interest | Royalties |
| Australia | 30% | 10% | 40% |
| Brazil | 25% | 25% | 25% |
| Canada | 25% | 25% | 25% |
| France | 25% | 33-1/3% | 33-1/3% |
| West Germany | 25% | -- | 25% |
| Japan | 20% | 20% | 20% |
| Mexico | 21% | 42% | -- |
| Netherlands | 24% | -- | -- |
| Switzerland | 35% | -- | -- |
| United Kingdom | -- | 33% | 33% |
| United States | 30% | 30% | 30% |

## THE VALUE-ADDED TAX

#24-9...Value-Added Taxes

Although the direct income tax is by far the greatest source
of  tax revenue in the U.S., in many European countries the indirect Value-Added  Tax, commonly referred to as VAT,  has  the
role of a very great source of revenue.

A comparison of the income derived from taxes in the U.S. with other major countries in the world elicits the differences in the types of sources and amounts derived from each. A table from the U.S. FEDERAL RESERVE BULLETIN for 1979 is presented in Figure 24-1.

By comparison the OECD has released a table of Revenue Statistics of OECD MEMBER COUNTRIES showing the PERCENTAGE OF TOTAL REVENUE COLLECTED FROM EACH TYPE OF TAX based on national, state, and local tax revenues collected in 1976.

REVENUE STATISTICS OF OECD MEMBER COUNTRIES:
PERCENTAGE OF TOTAL REVENUE
COLLECTED FROM TAXES

| Country | Taxes on Income | | | Consumption Taxes | Net Wealth and Property Taxes | Social Security Contributions |
|---------|-----------------|--|--|--------------------|-------------------------------|--------------------------------|
|         | Individual | Corporation | Total | | | |
| Austria | 21.5 | 3.3 | 24.8 | 34.8 | 2.9 | 28.9 |
| Belgium | 31.4 | 6.8 | 38.2 | 27.5 | 2.7 | 31.6 |
| Canada | 34.2 | 11.7 | 45.9 | 31.9 | 9.4 | 10.5 |
| Denmark | 54.0 | 3.5 | 57.5 | 35.7 | 5.5 | 1.1 |
| France | 12.5 | 5.8 | 18.3 | 32.4 | 3.8 | 40.2 |
| Italy | 16.5 | 6.2 | 22.7 | 28.1 | 3.3 | 45.8 |
| Japan | 24.5 | 16.6 | 41.1 | 19.0 | 9.2 | 25.5 |
| Netherlands | 27.0 | 7.0 | 34.0 | 24.5 | 3.2 | 37.8 |
| Norway | 36.6 | 4.2 | 40.8 | 37.8 | 2.0 | 18.0 |
| Sweden | 43.0 | 3.6 | 46.6 | 24.3 | 1.0 | 23.2 |
| Switzerland | 36.8 | 7.8 | 44.6 | 19.2 | 7.0 | 29.2 |
| United Kingdom | 38.0 | 4.7 | 42.7 | 23.7 | 12.1 | 19.4 |
| United States | 33.0 | 10.3 | 43.3 | 16.0 | 14.0 | 24.6 |
| West Germany | 30.2 | 4.6 | 34.8 | 25.7 | 3.3 | 34.7 |

The OECD table includes virtually all of the EEC countries. As a matter of fact they are required to use the VAT format, although different countries may use different rates. Even within EEC countries, goods are classified into different categories each of which is taxed at a different rate, which generally fall within three categories--Standard, Reduced and Higher.

The Standard Rate is that generally applicable to the rank and file of goods and services. The Reduced Rate applies to basic necessities. The Higher Rate is applicable principally to luxury items. In 1979 in the U.K. the Standard VAT Rate was 8%, but the Higher Rate on luxury goods was 12-1/2%. The Standard Rate in France was 17.6%, the Reduced Rate 7%, and the Higher Rate 33-1/3%. The Standard Rate in Germany was 12%, the Reduced Rate 6%, and there was no Higher Rate. In Belgium the Standard Rate was 16%, the Reduced Rate 6%, and the Higher Rate 25%. In Argentina the Standard Rate was 16%, and there was neither a Reduced nor Higher Rate.

FIGURE 24-1

FEDERAL FISCAL OPERATIONS:
RECEIPTS (In millions of dollars):

| Fiscal Year | Total | Individual Income Taxes | Corporation Income Taxes | Soc. Sec. Taxes | Excise Taxes | Customs | Estate and Gift | Miscellaneous Receipts |
|---|---|---|---|---|---|---|---|---|
| 1971 | 188,391 | 86,230 | 26,785 | 48,578 | 16,614 | 2,591 | 3,735 | 3,858 |
| 1972 | 208,650 | 94,737 | 32,166 | 53,914 | 15,477 | 3,287 | 5,436 | 3,633 |
| 1973 | 232,226 | 103,246 | 36,152 | 64,542 | 16,260 | 3,188 | 4,917 | 3,921 |
| 1974 | 264,932 | 118,952 | 38,619 | 76,780 | 16,844 | 3,334 | 5,035 | 5,368 |
| 1975 | 280,997 | 122,386 | 40,622 | 86,441 | 16,551 | 3,676 | 4,611 | 6,711 |
| 1976 | 300,005 | 131,603 | 41,409 | 92,714 | 16,963 | 4,074 | 5,216 | 8,026 |
| 1977 | 357,762 | 157,626 | 54,893 | 108,683 | 17,548 | 5,150 | 7,327 | 6,536 |
| 1978 | 401,997 | 180,988 | 59,952 | 123,410 | 18,376 | 6,573 | 5,285 | 7,413 |

Source: Adapted from U.S. FEDERAL RESERVE BULLETIN for 1979.

Comparatively, the Standard Rate in percentages in the major
European countries is as follows:

| | | | |
|---|---|---|---|
| Austria | 18 | Luxembourg | 10 |
| Belgium | 16 | Netherlands | 18 |
| Denmark | 20.2 | Norway | 20 |
| France | 17.6 | Sweden | 17.1 |
| Ireland | 20 | United Kingdom | 8 |
| Italy | 14 | West Germany | 12 |

Because VAT is used in the EEC countries, it should receive
more than passing attention in the discussion to follow.

## #24-10...History of VAT

The VAT was first proposed in the U.S. by T.S. Adams in 1921
but it was not until 1940 that a bill for a Value-Added Tax was
proposed in Congress. In 1970 a Presidential Task Force on Business Taxation was appointed to examine the feasability of a
VAT as part of an overall study of major tax policy issues, but
the finding was that the existing federal tax scheme be retained and the VAT was rejected. However, the Task Force did recommend that "should the need ever arise for substantial additional federal revenue, the government should turn to the value-
added tax or some other form of indirect taxation rather than
to an increase in rates of the corporate or personal income
tax." The Task Force, in giving consideration to the regres-
siveness of the Social Security Tax, which was $750 in 1970,
and the proposal to substitute the VAT in its place, came to
the conclusion that the principle of social security contributions was too important to be abandoned.

In 1979 there was considerable activity with respect to VAT
but nothing came of it. In the House, Representative Ullman,
Chairman of the House Ways and Means Committee, held many hearings on the proposal of VAT basically as an alternative to the
Social Security tax. In the Senate, Senator Long, Chairman of
the Senate Finance Committee, proposed that the VAT linked to
substantial reductions in both the income and social security
taxes, which had become increasingly more onerous, be adopted,
but did not advocate the sole use of VAT. The apparent reason
given for rejecting VAT was that it would place an inordinate
burden on those who could least stand it--the lower income
workers and those on fixed incomes--and such additional taxes
might militate against placing greater controls on government
spending. The only usage of VAT in the U.S. was in a single
state--Michigan--where a variant was employed between 1953 and
1967 and later adopted in 1975 as a Single Business Tax.

In the European theatre, France adopted VAT in 1954, but, as
stated above, it was approved by the EEC in 1967 for all member
states. As of Jan. 1, 1968, France and Germany adopted VAT; and
over a period of several years following, it was adopted by the

other member countries. Other European, South American, and
African countries--Argentina, Austria, Brazil, Chile, Egypt,
Mexico, Norway, and Sweden--have also adopted VAT.

### #24-11...Definition of VAT

VAT is a tax levied as a percentage of value that is added
to goods and/or services by each business entity in the chain
of the levels required to bring a product during the production
and distribution processes to its final disposition to the consumer. Because it is levied on consumption and therefore is
borne by the final consumer as part of the price ultimately
paid, it is an indirect tax differing from an income or inheri-
tance tax, which are direct taxes.

### #24-12...Nature of VAT

The VAT is similar to a Retail Sales Tax in that the tax
rate is a fixed rate and certain products or users are exempt.
It differs from the retail sales tax which applies only to the
final sale to the consumer whereas the VAT is applicable to
every sale made in the commercial cycle. Thus there are VATs
from the raw materials supplier to the manufacturer, from the
manufacturer to the wholesaler, and to the retailer, and to the
consumer. Theoretically the tax base applies to the increase in
value added to the product at each level of the cycle. However,
as a practical proposition it is the increase in sales price at
each level that is the determinant, with the totality of all
added taxes being included in the final sale to the consumer
who bears the full burden of the tax.

### #24-13...Modus Operandi of VAT

The procedure followed normally is for each business in the
process to collect the VAT on its sales and take credit for any
VAT it paid on its purchases, making remittance of the net
amount to the government. Any excess VAT paid over what the
business collects during the period is either credited or re-
funded for every entity in the cycle except the retail consumer
who is not entitled to any credit or refund for VAT paid. A
chart showing how the system works (presented here in Figure
24-2) is from a 1979 brochure entitled PERSPECTIVES ON THE
VALUE-ADDED TAX published by Arthur Andersen & Co.
The Miner, in selling the ore to the Converter for $10,
would charge an additional 10% or $1 VAT, thereby collecting
$11. The $1 VAT would then be remitted by the Miner to the government. The Converter, in selling the processed ore to the
Fabricator for $20, would charge an additional 10% or $2 VAT,
thereby collecting $22. Of the $2 VAT collected by the Con-

verter, he would be reimbursed for the $1 VAT paid to the Miner, thereby requiring him to remit the $2 collected less the $1 reimbursement, or $1, to the government. This procedure would be followed for the entities in the cycle, except for the Consumer who would bear the entire cumulated $14 VAT.

=================================================================

FIGURE 24-2
MECHANICS OF VAT SYSTEM
(ASSUMING A VAT RATE OF 10%)

| Cycle | Value-Added | Selling Price | VAT Collected | VAT Paid | VAT Due Government |
|---|---|---|---|---|---|
| Miner (Ore) | $10 | $ 10 | $ 1 | $ 0 | $1 |
| Converter (Steel) | 10 | 20 | 2 | 1 | 1 |
| Fabricator (file drawers) | 20 | 40 | 4 | 2 | 2 |
| Assembler (desk) | 60 | 100 | 10 | 4 | 6 |
| Wholesaler (distributor) | 20 | 120 | 12 | 10 | 2 |
| Dealer (Retailer) | 20 | 140 | 14 | 12 | 2 |
| Consumer | 0 | --- | 0 | 14 | 0 |

Source: Adapted from PERSPECTIVES ON THE VALUE-ADDED TAX, 1979, Arthur Andersen & Co., by permission.

=================================================================

## #24-14...Value-Added Financial Statements

Although VAT predominates in the EEC countries, it has been found to be an invaluable tool in controlled economies for serving as a source of controlled information. In such economies VALUE-ADDED FINANCIAL STATEMENTS are required by government fiat. Prof. Al Hashim indicates in ACCOUNTING FOR MULTINATIONAL ENTERPRISES, Bobbs-Merrill, 1978, pp. 9-12, that:

Accounting practices in socialist countries differ from those in free-enterprise countries due primarily to the difference in the political, social, cultural, legal and economic factors. The Egyptian government, for example, acquired control of approximately 80% of the country's economic resources through the nationalization decrees of 1961. *** To help achieve the objectives of the Egyptian Planning Board, the Uniform Accounting Law of 1966 has been written with unusually explicit detail, more in the nature of an accounting handbook, and spells out valuation and reporting methods.

One of the statements required under the 1966 Uniform Accounting Law was a VALUE-ADDED STATEMENT such as Figure 24-3.

FIGURE 24-3
AL NASER COMPANY
VALUE-ADDED STATEMENT FOR THE YEAR ENDED
JUNE 30, 1971 (IN 000 LBS.)

| 1969-70 Egptn. Pounds | Uniform Account No. | Value of Production and Services at Selling Price | Budgeted Egyptian Pounds | Actual Egyptian Pounds |
|---|---|---|---|---|
| | | Production at Selling Price: | | |
| 7,021 | 411 | Net Sales of Finished Goods | 7,308 | 8,518 |
| (197) | 412 | Cost of Difference Between Beginning and Ending Finished Goods | 28 | 383 |
| (155) | 413 | Changes in Value of Finished Goods Produced on Hand | 2 | (486) |
| 17 | 414 | Cost of Difference Between Beginning and Ending Work in Process | 12 | ( 17) |
| 29 | 417 | Services Sold | 19 | 26 |
| | | Finished Goods Purchased For Sale: | | |
| 240 | 4181 | Net Sales | -- | -- |
| ( 31) | 4182 | Cost of Difference Between Beginning and Ending Finished Goods | -- | -- |
| ( 6) | 4183 | Changes in Value of Goods Purchased for Sale on Hand | -- | -- |
| 6,918 | | TOTAL | 7,369 | 8,424 |
| (180) | 34 | Less: Finished Goods Purchased For Sale | -- | -- |
| 6,738 | | Value of Production & Services at Selling Price | 7,369 | 8,424 |
| | | Less: | | |
| (364) | 3511 | Custom Duties | (402) | (372) |
| ( 9) | 3514 | Other Taxes | ( 5) | ( 4) |
| 6,365 | | Value of Production & Services at Factors of Production Costs | 6,962 | 8,048 |
| | | Less: | | |
| (4,568) | 32 | Raw Materials & Supplies Used | (6,535) | (5,634) |
| (175) | 33 | Services Acquired | (240) | (178) |
| (408) | 3522-8 | Depreciation | (575) | (492) |
| 1,214 | | NET VALUE-ADDED AT FACTORS OF PRODUCTION COSTS | (388) | 1,744 |
| | | DISTRIBUTION OF VALUE-ADDED: | | |
| 530 | 311-13 | Wages | 601 | 559 |
| 114 | 353-54 | Rents | 114 | 111 |
| 617 | 355-57 | Interest | 916 | 523 |
| (155) | 358 | Changes in Value of Finished Goods Produced on Hand | 2 | (486) |
| ( 6) | 4183 | Changes in Value of Goods Purchased for Sale on Hand | -- | -- |
| 144 | | Income From Normal Operations | (2,021) | 1,037 |
| 1,214 | | | (388) | 1,744 |

Source: Adapted from material by Professor Dhia Al Hashim, ACCOUNTING
FOR MULTINATIONAL ENTERPRISES (Indianapolis: Bobbs-Merrill,
1978), pp. 9-12.

## #24-15...VAT Development in the EEC

Since the Value-Added Tax has had its greatest growth in the EEC countries, whose economic propinquity most nearly matches that in the U.S., an examination of the development of VAT in the EEC should be made. Arthur Andersen & Company, in its brochure PERSPECTIVES ON THE VALUE-ADDED TAX, page 5, indicates:

The Council of the EEC issued two directives on April 1, 1967 requiring member countries to implement the VAT system by January 1, 1970, later extended to January 1, 1971. The purpose was to harmonize the various turnover tax systems then being employed by the members to permit a better flow of imports and exports among the members with essentially equal taxation. The VAT was to replace existing taxes imposed by the various EEC members.

A certain amount of latitude was granted to the member countries in establishing the rates, items to be exempted, businesses that would be exempt, etc. However, all EEC members have hewed to the basic concept that exceptions and reduced rates should be limited. The main variations in the several VAT systems relate to the manner in which businesses are allowed to recover VAT paid on capital items, the method used in determining the tax base, and the method of allowing exemptions.

## #24-16...Methods of Recovery of VAT

There are three methods for the procedure of recovering VAT paid on capital items: (1) Consumption Method, (2) Income Method, and (3) Gross Product Method.

Under the Consumption Method, any enterprise in the chain of production is required to pay a Value-Added Tax on the purchase of capital assets, but can recover the VAT paid currently against the VAT collected on sales. This is the most widely accepted method in the EEC and the one preferred in VAT proposals in the U.S., because it avoids any tax deterrent to capital purchases.

Under the Income Method, the purchaser of capital items recovers the VAT paid over the life of the asset instead of being permitted to offset currently against the VAT collected on sales. Thus the straight line method is used to recover the VAT beginning with the year of purchase.

Under the Gross Product Method, no recovery of the VAT paid is permitted to the purchaser, who must resort to the increase in the sales price of the product by the amount of the VAT to recover it.

#### #24-17...Methods of Determination of VAT Tax Base

Before the VAT can be recovered, it becomes necessary to
determine the base to which the VAT percentage is to be applied
in order to establish the amount of the VAT. Since the Consumption Method is the most widely accepted in the EEC, there are
three methods for determination of the tax base on which the
tax is to be levied under this method: (1) INVOICE METHOD, (2)
SUBTRACTION METHOD, and (3) ADDITION METHOD.

#### #24-18...Invoice Method of VAT Tax Base Determination

The first step is determination of total taxable sales; second, this is multiplied by the applicable VAT rate; third, determination of total VAT paid on purchases of goods and services during the period; fourth, total VAT paid on purchases is
deducted from step two, which is the amount to be remitted to
the government. This is the most commonly used method in the
EEC countries.

#### #24-19...Subtraction Method

The first step is determination of total taxable sales; second, determine total purchases of goods and services on which
VAT was paid; third, subtract step two from step one; fourth,
multiply the result in step three by the applicable VAT rate.
This method has been used as a form of VAT in Michigan's old
business activities tax.

#### #24-20...Addition Method

Although the results of this method are the same as the other two, it involves the greatest amount of computations. The
first step is to accumulate the total of all items on which VAT
has NOT been paid, e.g., salaries, wages, profits, taxes, etc.;
second step is to accumulate the nontaxable receipts, capital
purchases, and changes in inventory; third, subtract step two
from step one; fourth, multiply step three by the VAT rate. It
can be seen that this is similar to the VALUE-ADDED STATEMENT
described in Figure 24-3.

#### #24-21...VAT on EEC Country Exports

The Arthur Andersen & Co. report indicates that "all members
of the EEC permit the export of goods and services free of VAT.
In effect, the last product in the chain, viz., the exporter,
is entitled to recover all VAT paid by him on items shipped out
of the country. In certain instances, the exporter does not pay
VAT on the goods he purchases."

## #24-22...VAT on EEC Country Imports

For imports the report goes on to say that "When goods and services are imported into an EEC country, the importer must pay the proper rate of local country VAT. Under the General Agreement on Tariffs and Trade (GATT), a country may adjust so-called border taxes only in the case of indirect taxes such as VAT. This rule clearly puts at a disadvantage exporters from countries, such as the U.S., that depend more heavily on direct taxation for revenue, since their products must be sold at a price that includes all the costs of the direct taxes."

## #24-23...Advantages and Disadvantages of VAT

The Arthur Andersen & Co. report sums up the advantages and disadvantages of VAT as follows:

Claimed Advantages of VAT: (1) Since the tax is based on consumption, it provides a stable revenue base. (2) It is a "neutral" tax since it falls on all types of business. (3) It provides an incentive to business to control costs. (4) A VAT encourages, or at least does not discourage, savings and investments. (5) It has the potential to raise large amounts of revenue at a low rate of tax. (6) VAT is simple to administer. (7) VAT can create incentives for exports under certain conditions. (8) Inclusion of a VAT helps create a better balanced tax system.

Claimed Disadvantages of VAT: (1) The tax is regressive. (2) It would lead to excessive spending. (3) VAT lacks a counter-cyclical balance. (4) It could be harmful to new and marginal businesses. (5) It creates administrative burdens. (6) VAT is inflationary. (7) It would be a hidden tax. (8) It conflicts with present state and municipal sales taxes. (9) In many cases it will not create meaningful incentives for exports (as pointed out above).

## #24-24...Impact of VAT on American Tax System

In concluding remarks the Andersen report projects the impact that the addition would have on the U.S. tax system:

In the last several years, the government has taken steps to better balance the total tax burden. These steps have produced a minimum income tax, a maximum tax rate on earned income, and most recently a reduction in capital gains taxes. Yet more needs to be accomplished. The tax load of the U.S. is too heavily weighted towards direct taxes. For example, in 1976 more than 88% of U.S. federal revenues came from income and payroll taxes, while only 7% came from taxes on consumption of goods and services. This compares to 1976

percentages of 54%-71% for income taxes and 19%-38% for consumption taxes for European countries.

In 1979, Senator Long predicted that should he introduce a bill
for a VAT, it could be considered by the 1981 Congress and
passed in 1982. Since Congress had agreed to ease the tax burden, one proposal was to impose a new and less visible tax in
the form of a "value-added tax" to make up for revenues that
would be sacrificed by a cut in taxes. The Value Added Tax,
which would function like a national sales tax, has the defect
of providing the government with a new reservoir of money. This
would be contrary to the Reagan policy of cutting government
spending, as a VAT would allow spending to increase. This obviously is very attractive to politicians for political reasons.
Unlike the income tax that it would partly replace, it would
hardly be noticed by buyers because the amount would not be
specified in the purchase price. Once established, it would be
very simple to increase. This invisibility is an advantage to
the politicians who levy the tax, but a disadvantage to the
taxpayers who pay it.

Because VAT places a greater proportional burden on the poor
and middle-class taxpayers than on the rich, it is regressive.
Under it, the poorer the taxpayer, the greater the share of his
income must be spent on necessities. As income tax is progres-
sive, it tends to discourage work and investment. This problem
is not solved by imposing the new regressive VAT. VAT is supposed to encourage savings, but that could more easily be done
by exempting interest income from the personal income tax. VAT
would raise the cost of investing unless all capital equipment
were exempt from VAT, thereby discouraging saving. Such exemptions would then rob the VAT of its virtue of simplicity.

VAT supporters feel that without it, Congress and the President will have to reduce spending by cutting the costs of defense and Social Security. With it, however, the government
could continue to grow without constraint. This is the source
of VAT's appeal, but the best argument against it.


## FOREIGN COUNTRY APPROACHES TO TAXATION

### #24-25...Methods of Taxation:  Classification

In Chapter 23 it was pointed out that the principal aim of
most countries is to attempt to avoid double taxation in order
to achieve some semblance of neutrality between foreign and
domestic investment. There are two methods by which this is
accomplished: the Territorial (complete exemption) Approach,
and the Deferral (taxation on Repatriation with Foreign Tax
Credit) Approach.

## #24-26...Foreign Countries Territorial Approach

The basic principles underlying the Territorial Approach and its applicability to the U.S. were discussed in Chapter 23. Comparative with other major countries, the territorial approach is in order for presentation at this point. In the FERF book ACCOUNTING FOR THE MULTINATIONAL CORPORATION, by Watt, Hammer and Burge, pp. 362-364, it is pointed out that this approach has been used in the following major areas: (a) South America, (b) France, (c) Netherlands, (d) Australia; and (e) Canada. Briefly the nature and extent for these areas is described below:

(a) <u>South American Countries</u>. Of the South American countries that still use the territorial method, Venezuela is the most extreme example. It limits its tax base to income from activities and property located in Venezuela, allows no deduction against Venezuelan taxable income for expenses incurred outside Venezuela, and allows no foreign tax credit.

Argentina and Brazil also exclude income from foreign activities and investments from the tax base of their domestic corporations, with limitations on the deductibility of expenses incurred in earning such income. Colombia, on the other hand, requires the inclusion of foreign source income and allows a deduction for foreign taxes, but no credit.

(b) <u>France</u>. France basically still uses the territorial approach with certain modifications. Foreign branch income of a French company is not subject to French tax. In 1972 France adopted a method favored by EEC countries, viz., the provisional deduction from domestic income for foreign startup expenses or losses during the first five years of operation. These losses are added back to company's income or recaptured after five years.

Under its "parent-subsidiary" rules, dividends received from subsidiaries, whether French or foreign, are virtually free of French tax. A 95% exclusion is allowed on a foreign dividend. The French system seems to favor investment abroad.

(c) <u>Netherlands</u>. A Dutch company is effectively exempt from Dutch tax on the income of a foreign branch or permanent establishment, provided the foreign branch is subject to tax in the foreign jurisdiction. Dividends and interest from foreign corporations are subject to Dutch tax, but there is an exemption for dividends received from so-called "substantial participations" under which the Dutch company owns at least 5% of the shares of the foreign company.

(d) <u>Australia</u>. The foreign branch income of an Australian corporation is exempt from Australian tax, provided that the income is subject to tax in the source country. Divi-

dends from a foreign subsidiary are virtually free of Australian tax even when repatriated. *** Interest and royalties are exempt under the same concept as branch profits if
they are subject to tax in the source country, which is
somewhat similar to the Dutch approach.

  (e) <u>Canada</u>. The territorial approach applies only to
dividends from substantial holdings. It does not apply to
foreign branches, which are subject to tax with a credit for
foreign income taxes.

## #24-27...Foreign Countries World-Wide Deferral Approach

  As was pointed out in Chapter 23, the U.S. together with the
U.K. and Japan are the three countries that have used the DE-
FERRAL and tax credit approach extensively, although each has a
different foreign tax credit system. Since the U.S. approach
has previously been discussed, only the U.K. and Japan will be
presented here:

  (a) <u>Japan</u>. The Japanese system permits a global basis of
credit calculation, with carrybacks, carryforwards, and a liberal treatment of losses, but limits credits to first-tier subsidiaries only.

  (b) <u>United Kingdom</u>. The U.K. system permits foreign tax
credits to flow up from all lower-tier companies where the requisite holding exists whereas the U.S. is restricted to three
tiers. However, the U.K. does not permit the use of the global
or overall limitation method, and requires the credit to be
computed separately for each item of income. Nor does the U.K.
permit carryforwards of excess credits.

## TAX ADMINISTRATION SYSTEMS

## #24-28...The Tax Administration Problem

  Not only does the matter of the approach used affect the
sources and amounts of taxes that are a very important consideration in tax administration, but the situation is compounded
by the imposition of different tax systems in different countries. The following features result in adjustments that have a
strong impact on the amount of income to be reported for tax
purposes: varying rates of income tax; defining explicitly what
income is; how should taxes be allocated amongst different
countries; credits and allowances for investments; special reserves to stabilize employment, as discussed in connection with
some European countries, particularly Sweden; and adjusting
assets for price level changes such as Brazil, discussed in the
chapter on Inflation Accounting. All of this results in different tax systems in different countries.

## #24-29...Classification of Tax Systems

There are two basic tax systems used globally: (1) Classical, and (2) Integrated -- which has three Variation Methods: (a) Imputation, or Tax Credit; (b) Split-Rate; and (c) Dividend Deduction.

## #24-30...Classical System

Under the Classical System income is taxed when it is received by any entity. Corporate earnings would be taxed when earned by the corporation and taxed again when distributed as dividends to the shareholder. Obviously this is the system used in the U.S., and is also in effect in British Commonwealth countries as well as in Sweden, Netherlands, Luxembourg, Italy and Spain.

## #24-31...Integrated System: (a) Imputation, Tax Credit

The basic purpose of the Integrated System is to attempt to eliminate double taxation. As indicated above, this is done through the three variation methods mentioned, first of which is the Imputation System. Under it, after the tax is levied on the corporation for its earnings, part of such tax can be used as a credit against personal income tax on the dividends. This system has been used by the U.K., France, and Belgium. In 1975 the EEC, in an attempt to harmonize taxes among the member countries, offered a proposal for the uniform adoption of the Imputation Method. Since six of the EEC countries use some form of the imputation system there would be no difficulty adjusting to it in them; the remaining three countries (Germany, Netherlands, and Luxembourg) would require a drastic change, particularly the Netherlands and Luxembourg which use the Classical System.

Historically the U.K. used the Classical System from 1965 to 1973 when it adopted the Imputation System. France adopted it in 1965, Canada in 1972, and Germany in 1977. It should be observed that even though many imputation system countries use the system and are broadly similar for domestic income, they may have great divergences both in the treatment of foreign income as well as for foreign shareholders.

## #24-32...Integrated System: (b) Split-Rate System

Under the Split-Rate System, as the name indicates, two different rates are used predicated upon the criterion as to whether the profits are retained by the corporation or distributed. Most of the major countries set rates for the two classes as STATUTORY PROFITS TAX RATES and DIVIDEND WITHHOLDING RATES.

In Japan profits distributed are taxed at a rate of 30%, whereas undistributed earnings are taxed at 40% (as of Jan. 1977).
The Split-Rate System is used by Germany and Japan. It was mentioned above that Germany used the Imputation System. However, in 1977 Germany completely restructured its corporate taxation system resulting in a hybrid system combining the imputation system with a Split-Rate differential between distributed and undistributed earnings. Such system is geared to the disadvantage of foreign shareholders because they do not receive the imputation credit which is allowed to the resident German shareholder. In the June 7, 1976, BUSINESS WEEK, (in the article "U.S. Subsidiaries Get Caught By Tax Reform", pp. 42-43), it is pointed out that corporate income tax on earnings in Germany is at 36% which German shareholders are permitted to deduct from their personal income tax, so they in effect pay no tax on dividends; however, U.S.-owned companies are not permitted to make a similar deduction and would be required to pay on earnings that would not be subject to the dividend exclusion resulting in a 10% increase in income taxes on U.S. and other foreign-owned subsidiaries in Germany.

#### #24-33...Integrated System: (c) Dividend Deduction System

The Dividend Deduction System is another method that combines corporate and personal income taxes and is greatly similar to the split-rate system whose rate of tax is predicated on distributed income. Under this method, part or all of the dividend is deductible to determine the taxable corporate income. The only difference from the split-rate system is one in the sense of degree rather than in substance, in that the amount of differential in the Dividend Deduction System is far greater in amount. This method is used in a few major countries notably Norway, Finland and Greece, and it was proposed by the Secretary of the Treasury in 1975 for the purpose of eliminating the double tax on U.S. corporate income. Norway with a 27% national corporate tax rate permits a deduction of all dividends paid and only undistributed earnings are subject to tax. Greece has a tax of over 38% on undistributed earnings, and distributed earnings are subject to a withholding tax of 30% on companies listed and 38% on those not.

#### THE FOREIGN TAX CREDIT

#### #24-34...Rationale of Foreign Tax Credit

It has been pointed out that under the political philosophy of national sovereignty, on the international level, every nation has the right to tax any income earned within its country. This basic philosophy has been exercised under two principles, the territorial and the world-wide. Under the territorial, a country will tax only earnings accruing from operations within the country and will exempt any earnings resulting from operations outside the territorial limits of the country. Under the world-wide philosophy, a country will tax all earnings of any company which is incorporated, domiciled, or headquartered in that country whether such earnings result from operations within or without the country.

The world-wide philosophy results in double taxation because such income is also taxed by the country in which it is earned. It was stated, at the beginning of the subject of International Taxation, that the primary objective is to minimize or avoid double taxation. This may be accomplished in two ways: (1) Tax Credits, and (2) Tax Treaties. Under the tax credit system, the enterprise is permitted to take a direct credit against tax it owes to its domicile country for tax paid to a foreign government, thereby avoiding double taxation. The foreign tax credit is discussed below, after which will be treated the aspects of avoidance of double taxation through tax treaties.

#24-35...Purpose of Foreign Tax Credit

The Commerce Clearing House, FEDERAL TAX COURSE, 1982 Edition, page 2403, states:

In order to avoid imposing the burden of double taxation upon a taxpayer, Code Sec. 91, adopted in 1918, allows the taxpayer a credit for the amount of income taxes imposed upon him by a foreign country or a possession of the United States where the income so taxed is also subject to taxation by the United States. *** The purpose of the credit is, in effect, to place foreign and domestic source income on an equal footing insofar as the U.S. income tax is concerned.

In the FERF book ACCOUNTING FOR THE MULTINATIONAL CORPORATION by Watt, Hammer and Burge, page 384, the effect of the credit is expressed to be that:

Under the foreign tax credit system, the U.S. relinquishes tax on income earned abroad up to the amount of the foreign tax. The result is that if the foreign tax on a dollar earned abroad and remitted to the U.S. is less than or equal to the U.S. rate of 48%, that dollar will be subject to a total tax of 48 cents. If the foreign tax rate is higher than the U.S. rate, the U.S. will get no tax on that income. This "excess" of foreign tax rate of one foreign country over the U.S. rate may be used to offset U.S. tax due on foreign source income from other countries under the "overall" limitation which requires the aggregation of foreign taxes and foreign income for this computation.

## #24-36...Foreign Tax Credit Alternatives

Continuing from the preceding quotation:
As an alternative to a credit against tax, U.S. taxpayers can treat any foreign tax paid directly as a deductible expense. For any year the taxpayer must decide whether to claim a credit or deduction for foreign income taxes, since both cannot be claimed in the same year. It will normally be more advantageous to claim a dollar-for-dollar credit against federal tax rather than a deduction. This can be illustrated as follows, assuming a U.S. corporation with $100 of foreign income, subject to a 50% foreign tax rate and a U.S. corporate tax rate of 50%:

|  | Foreign Tax Credit ($) | Foreign Tax Deduction ($) |
|---|---|---|
| Foreign Income | 100 | 100 |
| Foreign Tax (50%) | 50 | 50 |
| Net Income After Tax | 50 | 50 |
| U.S. Taxable Income | 100 | 100 |
| U.S. Tax (50%) | 50 | 25 |
| Foreign Tax Credit | 50 | -0- |
| U.S. Tax Payable | -0- | 25 |
| Total Foreign & U.S. Taxes | 50 | 75 |
| Effective Tax Rate | 50% | 75% |

## #24-37...Requirements For Foreign Tax Credit

In order to be regarded as a Foreign Tax Credit, the foreign tax cannot be one which is not based on net income. Thus a foreign Sales, Gross Receipts, or Value-Added tax cannot serve as a foreign tax credit because they are not income taxes. Moreover taxes that can be credits must be foreign INCOME taxes which the U.S. taxpayer has paid to a foreign government. Included in the term "income" are foreign branch earnings, royalties, dividends, foreign subsidiary interest income, foreign subsidiary rental income, foreign investment dividend and interest, insurance of foreign risk underwriting income, gains on sales of foreign sales of stock and personal property.

## #24-38...Classification of Foreign Tax Credits

Foreign Tax Credits may be classified as (1) Direct, and (2) Indirect or Deemed. The DIRECT FOREIGN TAX is one which is imposed directly on the U.S. taxpayer. The Indirect, more commonly referred to as the DEEMED PAID FOREIGN TAX CREDIT, a tax on foreign operations, is one which the U.S. corporation has not itself directly paid to the foreign government, but such foreign tax was paid by a foreign corporation which has paid a dividend to a qualifying U.S. corporation, discussed below.

## #24-39...Direct Foreign Tax Credit

The direct foreign tax may be paid by the foreign branch of a U.S. corporation directly to the foreign government on the earnings resulting from foreign operations or it may be imposed on the U.S. corporation through withholding on dividends remitted to the U.S. shareholders. Illustrations of each of the two situations are given in Watt, Hammer and Burge, ACCOUNTING FOR THE MULTINATIONAL CORPORATON, page 386:

### DIRECT TAX ON FOREIGN EARNINGS ($)

| | |
|---|---:|
| Income of Foreign Branch | 100 |
| Foreign Income Tax (40%) | 40 |
| Net After-Tax Income | 60 |
| Included in U.S. Income | 100 |
| U.S. Tax Thereon (48%) | 48 |
| Less: Foreign Tax Credit | 40 |
| Net U.S. Tax Payable | 8 |

### WITHHOLDING ON FOREIGN DIVIDENDS ($)

| | |
|---|---:|
| Dividend From Foreign Corporation | 100 |
| Foreign Withholding Tax (15%) | 15 |
| Net Amount Received | 85 |
| Included in U.S. Income | 100 |
| U.S. Tax Thereon (48%) | 48 |
| Less: Foreign Tax Credit | 15 |
| Net U.S. Tax Payable | 33 |

## #24-40...Deemed-Paid Credit

The Commerce Clearing House, FEDERAL TAX COURSE, 1982 Edition, page 2404, points out:

In addition to the credit for its own foreign taxes paid, a domestic corporation that receives dividends from a foreign corporation in which it owns 10% or more of the voting stock, (first-tier corporation) is entitled to a foreign tax credit for the foreign taxes DEEMED paid by that foreign corporation with respect to such dividends. ***

Similarly, if the first-tier corporation owns 10% or more of the voting stock of a second foreign corporation (second-tier corporation), and the second-tier corporation owns 10% or more of a third foreign corporation (third-tier corporation), the domestic parent may also claim a credit for taxes DEEMED paid by these foreign corporations with respect to dividends distributed through the first-tier corporation to the domestic corporation. In each instance, the indirect credit is allowed only if the domestic corporation has an indirect ownership of at least 5% in both the second- and third-tier corporations. ***

A corporation claiming the deemed-paid credit is required to "gross-up" these dividends. Thus it must increase its gross income by including in it not only the dividends but also the taxes paid by the foreign corporation.

Normally the deemed-paid credit can only be claimed by a U.S. corporation which has received a dividend. The amount that may be claimed as foreign tax that is creditable is determined by the proportion that the dividends paid to the U.S. corporation bear to the foreign corporation's earnings for the year out of which they are paid.

### #24-41...Computation of Deemed-Paid Foreign Tax Credit

An illustration of how the deemed-paid foreign tax credit is computed is presented in ACCOUNTING FOR THE MULTINATIONAL COR-PORATION, by Watt, Hammer and Burge on pages 387-388, assuming a 100 percent payout of after-tax income:

| | |
|---|---:|
| Earnings Before Tax of Foreign Corp. for 1976 | $1,000 |
| Foreign Income Tax at 30% | 300 |
| Earnings and Profits for 1976 | $ 700 |
| Dividend Paid to U.S. Parent Company in 1976 | $ 700 |
| Less: Foreign Withholding Tax of 15% | 105 |
| Net Dividend Received in U.S. | $ 595 |

FOREIGN CREDITABLE TAXES:
a. Direct Credit for Withholding Tax                    $  105
b. Deemed-Paid Credit for Subsidiary's Tax:

$$\frac{(Dividend)}{(Earnings\ \&\ Profits)} \times (Foreign\ Tax) =$$

$$\frac{700}{700} \times 300 = \qquad\qquad\qquad\qquad 300$$

Total Creditable Taxes                                  $  405

INCLUDED IN U.S. INCOME:

| | |
|---|---:|
| Gross Dividend (595 + 105) | $ 700 |
| Plus: Foreign Deemed-Paid Tax | 300 |
| U.S. Gross Dividend Included | $1,000 |
| U.S. Tax at 48% | $ 480 |
| Less: Foreign Tax Credit | 405 |
| U.S. TAX PAYABLE | $ 75 |

The rules for determining the computation of the deemed-paid foreign tax credit resulting from the above illustration are stated as follows:

This example illustrates the following rules:
(1) The formula for determining the amount of the creditable deemed-paid tax is:

Dividend (including withholding tax) divided by Net
Earnings & Profits of Foreign Corporations times Foreign
Tax;
(2) Earnings and profits are net of foreign income taxes;
(3) The foreign dividend to be included in U.S. income is
the dividend received PLUS withholding tax, PLUS deemed-
paid tax. The inclusion of the foreign deemed-paid tax
in income is known as the "gross-up."
Where the subsidiary is less than wholly owned, the investor's proportionate share of the foreign earnings and profits and foreign taxes are used in the formula.

## #24-42...Limitation on Use of Credit

Where a foreign country imposes a higher tax rate than that
of the U.S., the total creditable taxes on income received from
such foreign country may be greater than the U.S. tax on such
income. Under such circumstances the taxpayer is limited in the
amount of credit he can use to the amount of the U.S. tax on
the foreign income. The Commerce Clearing House, FEDERAL TAX
COURSE, 1983 Edition, pp. 2405-2406, states:
In computing the amount of the "credit against tax" on account of foreign taxes, taxpayers are prevented from using
foreign tax credits to reduce U.S. tax liability on income
from sources within the U.S. The method by which this limitation is computed is called the OVERALL METHOD.

## #24-43...Overall Limitation Method

The Commerce Clearing House reference continues:

Under the overall method, a taxpayer totals the taxes he
has paid to all foreign countries and possessions. *** This
total is then subjected to a limitation computed by multiplying his U.S. tax liability by a fraction which consists
of taxable income from foreign sources (after taking all
relevant deductions) over the world-wide taxable income.
Thus assume A has world-wide taxable income of $800,000
and a tentative U.S. tax liability of $370,500. From its
operations in Country M, A had $300,000 of taxable income on
which M imposed a 30% tax, and from its operations in Country T, A had taxable income of $200,000 on which a 20% tax
was imposed. To compute its foreign tax credit limitation, A
must multiply its U.S. tax by its taxable income from foreign sources ($300,000 + $200,000 = $500,000) divided by its
world-wide taxable income. Thus A's foreign tax credit is
limited to 500,000/800,000 x 370,500 = $231,562.50.
If the computed credit is less than the total credit allowed,
the domestic corporation may claim the entire amount, but if

there   is  an  excess   credit,   it   can  be  carried  back  two  years
and forward five years.

## #24-44...Determination of Income Resulting From
##           Foreign Currency Translation

Where the tax is to be based on income to be determined from
financial statements of a foreign branch or subsidiary expressed in terms of foreign currency Internal Revenue Rulings 75-107
under  the  Internal  Revenue  Code permit  two methods for determining net income:  (1) the NET WORTH, or BALANCE SHEET, METHOD,
and (2) the PROFIT AND LOSS METHOD.

## #24-45...Net Worth Method for Income Determination

This method is described in ACCOUNTING FOR THE MULTINATIONAL
CORPORATION, by Watt, Hammer and Burge, page 396, as follows:
The net worth  or balance sheet method requires assets other
than capital assets and liabilities recorded on the books in
foreign  currency to be translated into dollars at the   rate
prevailing at the   close of each taxable year.   Fixed assets
and other non-monetary assets  and long-term liabilities are
translated at historical rates.   Any increase or decrease in
opening  and closing net worth is the U.S. dollar measure of
net profit or   loss, when   added   to remittances   during the
year translated at the rate at  the time of remittance (usually the dollars received are used).   This is similar to the
Current-Noncurrent method used by some companies relative to
translating  financial  statements  of  foreign subsidiaries
before the issuance  of FASB #8.   This   method reflects so-
called unrealized gains and losses in income (no deferrals).
The translation of long-term liabilities at historical rates
tend to   offset   fixed   assets also translated at historical
rates, and the unrealized gains and losses are thereby minimized.

## #24-46...Profit and Loss Method for Income Determination

This   method applies "to a foreign branch which keeps a separate set of books and renders a financial  report to  the home
office at the end of each year.   In this situation, the profits
of the  branch are first computed  in the foreign currency  and
any remittances, expressed in local currency, made to the  head
office are deducted therefrom. To determine the dollar value of
net profit, the remittances are translated at the exchange rate
prevailing at the time of remittance (the dollars received) and
the   remaining profit is translated at the year-end   rate.   The
profit and loss method  of computing net   income is less common
than the net worth method.   Obviously this method does not pick

up unrealized gains and losses on balance sheet items and depreciation is not translated at historical exchange rates."

## #24-47...Comparative Foreign Country Allowable Foreign Tax Credits

In April 1976, Arthur Andersen & Co. presented expert testimony before the U.S. Senate Committee on Finance manifesting how the major countries in Europe handle foreign tax credits, inter alia. It was found that the U.K., Germany, France, Belgium and Italy all differed as to the limits to which foreign tax credits were allowed. Although the U.K. has a restrictive limitation, English companies are able to minimize the problem by having dividends paid to foreign holding companies. Then the foreign tax credits are averaged to derive an overall effective limitation. Japan has an overall limitation which is somewhat like that in the U.S., but losses from overseas branches are exempt in the determination of the overall limitation, thereby affording Japanese investors a comparatively higher limitation on foreign tax credits than U.S. investors. The Netherlands, like Japan, also has an overall limitation comparable to that in the U.S.

Because Germany, France and Belgium do not tax foreign branch income, no foreign tax credit is allowed for taxes paid by their branches. The Netherlands does not tax branch income. Since France, Belgium and the Netherlands do not tax dividends of foreign subsidiaries, no deemed foreign tax credit is allowed. However, the U.K., Germany and Japan do tax foreign dividends, hence allow a foreign tax credit equivalent to that of the U.S. Italy, on the other hand, taxes dividends partially and permits a credit for withholding taxes subject to limitations.

## #24-48...Internal Revenue Reduction of Tax Credits Through Allocation of Expenses--Sec. 861

The IRS, being concerned about the proper allocation of corporate expenses to foreign source income, in 1977 had incorporated in the Code Regulation 1.861.8, commonly referred to as Sec. 861. This has had the effect of reducing tax credits, because the taxable income in the U.S. becomes higher, and lower in foreign income. What Sec. 861 does is allocates the total of the expenses, losses and other deductions of a company to specific sources of income, such as Sales, Royalties and Dividends, and then apportions the expenses amongst the domestic and the foreign source income. Under Sec. 861, expenses are broken down into three major groups: interest, research and development, and general and administrative. Specific guidelines are contained in the regulation as to how each group is

to be allocated. Of course, where expenses are such as to be
identified with specific foreign income, they are charged completely to such foreign income. Otherwise the expenses must be
allocated between domestic and foreign source according to the
rules specified by the regulations.

#24-49...Illustrative Example of Operation of Sec. 861

In an article entitled "A Tool For Maximizing Foreign Tax
Credits," by James W. Schenold, appearing in the PRICE WATER-
HOUSE REVIEW 2, 1978, pages 38-51, the following illustration
is presented to demonstrate the impact Sec. 861 may have on the
tax credit.

Assume the U.S. M/N Corporation has total global income of
$3,000 from earnings and royalties, of which $1,000 is foreign
earned royalties; total expenses come to $1,500. The U.S. tax
rate is 48%, the foreign rate is 30%. Of the total expenses,
when allocated $1,000 would be charged to U.S. operations and
$500 to foreign. The comparative results under no allocation
and allocation of expenses are shown in Figure 24-4.

TAX TREATIES AS MEDIUM OF DOUBLE TAX ALLEVIATION

#24-50...Purposes of Tax Treaties

The Commerce Clearing House, FEDERAL TAX COURSE for 1982 declares:
    An alien or foreign corporation is taxed under special
Code provisions. These provisions, however, must be considered in the light of tax treaties. *** In many cases the tax
treaty will modify or even supersede the Code provisions for
taxing an alien or foreign corporation.
    Therefore, in determining the extent to which an alien
or a foreign corporation is taxable, it should first be ascertained whether a treaty is in effect and, if so, the nature of the treaty provisions. Tax treaties provide generally for a reciprocal exemption of citizens of, and corporations chartered in, the U.S. and the particular foreign
country, to avoid double taxation.

#24-51...Nature of Tax Treaties

Tax Treaties are bilateral agreements entered into between
two nations. As a result, each agreement for different nations
may contain differing provisions to meet the needs of the respective countries in their dealings. Thus in most of the hundreds of treaties now in existence which have been entered into
between developed countries, the terms are geared to capital
exporting and importing, resulting in withholding deductions of

FIGURE 24-4

COMPARISON UNDER NO ALLOCATION OR ALLOCATION OF EXPENSES

| | Before Expense Allocation | | | After Expense Allocation | | |
|---|---|---|---|---|---|---|
| | Total | U.S. | Foreign | Total | U.S. | Foreign |
| Earnings & Royalties | 3,000 | 2,000 | 1,000 | 3,000 | 2,000 | 1,000 |
| Expenses | 1,500 | 1,500 | -- | 1,500 | 1,000 | 500 |
| Taxable Income | 1,500 | 500 | 1,000 | 1,500 | 1,000 | 500 |
| Global Income | 1,500 | | | 1,500 | | |
| Tax Liabilities: | | | | | | |
| U.S. (@ 48% x 1,500) | 720 | | | 720 | | |
| Foreign (@ 30% x 1,000) | | | 300 | | | 300 |
| Tax Credit Limitation: | | | | | | |
| $\frac{1,000}{1,500} \times 720 =$ | | | 480 | $\frac{500}{1,500} \times 720 =$ | | 240 |
| Less: | | | | | | |
| Tax Credit Allowable | | | | | | |
| (Lesser of Foreign Tax or Tax Limitation) | 300 | | | 240 | | |
| U.S. Tax Liability | 420 | | | 480 | | |
| Foreign Tax Liability | 300 | | | 300 | | |
| TOTAL TAX LIABILITY | 720 | | | 780 | | |

Source: Adapted from pages 38-51, "A Tool for Maximizing Foreign Tax Credit," by James W. Schenold, in PRICE WATERHOUSE REVIEW, 2, 1978, by permission.

foreign investments income and royalties.

On the other hand, there are many less treaties entered into between developed and developing countries which are largely capital importing. To overcome this imbalance, the U.N. in 1967 established a "Group of Tax Experts on Tax Treaties Between Developed and Developing Countries." This Group issued a report in 1974 entitled "Guidelines for Tax Treaties Between Developed and Developing Countries" to assist in the development of treaties between the two classes. The Group has gone further in developing treaties for international income allocation, co-operative efforts between governments, and international business in general. Finally, the increase in trade between the U.S. and Russia, especially in the area of grain, has given rise to the need of establishing tax standards between the countries, resulting in tax treaties.

**#24-52...Model Tax Treaties**

Because all tax treaties ostensibly serve the same purposes, there has been over the past half century a concerted effort on the part of the international community to standardize treaties by creating Treaty Models. The first such model was drafted in 1928 under the auspices of the League of Nations. In 1943 Mexico issued its Model Convention followed by the London Convention in 1946. In 1963 the OECD established a Draft Double Taxation Convention on Income and Capital, which was revised in 1974, and has become a fundamental document used as guidelines for negotiators and tax advisers who seek to counsel in avoidance of double taxation.

**#24-53...The Model Income Tax Treaty Contents**

Patterned after the OECD basic tax treaty, the U.S. Treasury Department issued its own MODEL INCOME TAX TREATY in May 1976. The provisions are as follows:

ARTICLES 1 & 2:  Define the taxes, and the persons covered by the treaty.

ARTICLE 3:  Defines the terms used in the treaty, and interpretation of any terms not defined.

ADDITIONAL ARTICLES:  Cover the following topics: Industrial and Commercial Profits; Taxable Income of a Permanent Establishment; Shipping and Air Transport; Affiliated Enterprises; Investment Income; Capital Gains; Exemptions for such individuals as traveling salesmen, visiting directors, self-employed persons, students, trainees, teachers and government employees; Avoidance of Double Taxation; and finally, Exchange of Information.

The Title of a Treaty is worded as follows:

CONVENTION BETWEEN COUNTRY X AND COUNTRY Y FOR THE AVOIDANCE OF DOUBLE TAXATION AND THE PREVENTION OF FISCAL EVASION WITH RESPECT TO TAXES ON INCOME AND CAPITAL.

## #24-54...Non-Treaty Tax Cooperation Agreements

Cooperation on tax matters that are covered by agreements which do not constitute treaties exist between various countries. In 1979 the U.S., U.K., Germany, France and Canada consummated an agreement under which tax returns of MNCs would be jointly examined for the purpose of coordinating tax procedures. The agreement expressly provided for the following objectives: (1) Avoidance of double taxation where costs are shared or profits are allocated between taxpayers; (2) Determination of correct tax liabilities; (3) Transfer Pricing Practices Examination; (4) Means of improving exchange of information; (5) Intelligence sharing with respect to tax avoidance techniques; and (6) Efficient utilization of government and company personnel.

## #24-55...U.S. Income Tax Treaties

A listing of the countries with whom treaties have been signed and are being negotiated is presented on page 412 of the FERF book ACCOUNTING FOR THE MULTINATIONAL CORPORATION, by Richard Hammer, as follows:

I. Income Tax Treaties were in effect on December 31, 1976 between the U.S. and the following countries:

| | | |
|---|---|---|
| Australia | Ireland | Poland |
| Austria | Italy | Romania |
| Belgium | Japan | South Africa |
| Canada | Luxembourg | Sweden |
| Denmark | Netherlands | Switzerland |
| Finland | Netherlands | Trinidad and |
| France | Antilles | Tobago |
| Germany | New Zealand | United Kingdom |
| Greece | Norway | Barbados |
| Iceland | Pakistan | Jamaica |
| | | U.S.S.R. |

II. Income Tax Treaties have been signed between the U.S. and the following countries, but had not been ratified by December 31, 1976:

| | | |
|---|---|---|
| Egypt | Philippines | United Kingdom |
| Israel | South Korea | (revision) |

III. Negotiations are completed or are approaching completion with the following countries:

| | |
|---|---|
| Hungary | Republic of China (Taiwan) |
| Morocco | Spain |

IV. Negotiations for new treaties or revisions of existing treaties are currently in process with the following countries:

| | | |
|---|---|---|
| Bangladesh | Germany | Kenya |
| Brazil | India | Netherlands |
| Canada | Indonesia | Singapore |
| Denmark | Iran | Yugoslavia |
| France | Italy | |

By 1980 the U.S. had 26 tax treaties with some 38 countries, which is a relatively small number in comparison with the 72 countries with which the U.K. has signed treaties. Since tax treaties do cut down on taxes, it should be observed that the more treaties signed, the greater the advantage to U.S. M/Es.

A case in point is China. On March 21, 1984, representatives of the U.S. and China following two years of work by the Treasury Dept. initiated a tax treaty in Beijing. The treaty was scheduled to be signed by President Reagan during his April visit to China and to be ratified by the Congress. Because the tax treaty with China is considered one of the most liberal the U.S. has signed with a developing country, Sec. of Treasury Donald Regan expects it to lead to greater U.S. investments in China.

In an interview with the JOURNAL OF ACCOUNTANCY, appearing in the May 1984 issue, pages 24-25, a Treasury Department spokesman said:

We approached negotiations with a firm resolution of fostering stronger economic relations between the two countries. It will cover the full range of personal and corporate income tax issues and is designed to address the issue of double taxation.

Reportedly the treaty includes the customary 10% withholding tax that U.S. and Chinese companies must pay each other's country. U.S. companies currently pay a 20% withholding tax in China, while Chinese companies pay 30% in the U.S.

In recent years tax treaties signed with developing countries, such as Egypt, Morocco and Israel, have allowed a positive tax rate favoring the U.S. partner nation. Under the accord, China will probably be allowed a positive tax rate by permitting it to levy higher taxes than customary on royalties, dividends and other passive income of U.S. companies.

## MULTINATIONAL INTERCOMPANY TRANSFER PRICING

### #24-56...M/N Intercompany Transfer Pricing Dilemma

In situations where a M/E has one or more foreign subsidiaries, and sales and/or purchases are made between the M/N and its subsidiaries or between the subsidiaries themselves, it becomes necessary to set the values at which such transactions should be recorded--referred to as the TRANSFER PRICE. Where the subsidiaries are located in countries which may have low taxes and in some which have high taxes, there would appear to be a natural tendency to want to manipulate the TRANSFER PRICE by setting higher prices for the lower tax countries and lower prices for the higher tax countries. This would result in the shifting of profits, through the medium of transfer prices, from the high tax countries to the low tax countries. This has been one of the most consistent and loudest complaints voiced against M/Es. The U.S. IRS has taken cognizance of this possibility and, in order to attempt to ensure against its taking place on a large scale basis, the Congress, in the Revenue Act of 1962, issued Regulations under Sec. 482 of the Code, which was to establish guidelines for the allocation of income and expenses between related taxpayers in foreign transactions.

#### #24-57...Section 482

Section 482, which has been part of tax law for over 40 years, provides:

In any case of two or more organizations, trades, or businesses (whether or not incorporated, whether or not organized in the United States, and whether or not affiliated) owned or controlled directly or indirectly by the same interests, the Secretary or his delegate may distribute, apportion, or allocate gross income, deductions, credits, or allowances between or among such organizations, trades or businesses, if he determines that such distribution, apportionment or allocation is necessary in order to prevent evasion of taxes or clearly to reflect the income of any such organizations, trades or businesses.

Sec. 482 has been a very helpful medium through which to monitor transfer prices over the years, by compelling enterprises to demonstrate arm's-length and/or independent pricing, in the absence of which a showing must be made on the basis of cost plus a reasonable profit.

#### #24-58...Purpose of Section 482

The keystone on which the Sec. 482 enforcement program is predicated is the concept that U.S. taxpayers are to deal with affiliates on an arm's-length basis. It is to this end that the regulations are geared. This objective under Sec. 482 is somewhat akin to that discussed in the material involving reduction of tax credits through allocation of expenses as provided in Sec. 861 of the Internal Revenue Code. The distinction between the increase in taxes imposed on the M/E is that Sec. 861 deals

with the  allocation of home office expenses for foreign source
gross income, whereas Sec. 482 is concerned with the allocation
of income and expenses between more  than one separately incorporated inter-related entities. Sec. 861 and Sec. 482 appear to
be similar in that both  relate to allocations, but  where Sec.
861 relates to  allocating corporate expenses to foreign source
income, Sec. 482  is related to the  allocation  of the proper
taxable income  to the parent, based on  an arm's-length  relationship.

#24-59...Methods of Allocation

Where an allocation under  Sec. 482 is called  for, it  may
result in an  adjustment to gross income,  deductions, credits,
tax  base of assets for depreciation, or for gain or loss  purposes.  However,  deductions or credits taken may not be disallowed; it is strictly a matter of reallocating adjustments that
have already been made.
Sec. 482 classifies the guidelines for intercompany transactions  into five groups:  (1)  Intercompany loans and advances;
(2) Intercompany  performance of services; (3) Intercompany use
of tangible property; (4) Intercompany use  of intangible property; and (5) Intercompany sales of property.
Of these five types of transactions,  the fifth is very  important.  Where goods are sold to an affiliate at  a lower than
arm's-length price an allocation is called for.  The definition
of an "arm's-length  price" is that which  an unrelated  party
would have paid  if  the sale were made under the same  circumstances. Sec. 482 permits three  different methods that are regarded  as acceptable  for  determination  of  an  arm's-length
price:  (1) the comparable uncontrolled price  method;  (2) the
resale price method; and (3) the cost-plus method.

#24-60...The Comparable Uncontrolled Price Method

Under  this method the price is regarded as that charged not
only  by a U.S.  corporation to its outside customers  but also
where an unrelated  supplier charges a U.S. corporation or  any
member of the group. Included would be sales between other parties of goods  of the same type, which are comparable. What is
regarded as comparable varies depending  on  the facts and circumstances surrounding each particular case, which must be used
to make a determination.

#24-61...The Resale Price Method

This  method applies to the sale by a  manufacturer to a related sales  company that sells to an outside customer.  In determining the proper price  for the sale from the  manufacturer

to the selling company, the procedure begins with the sale
price made by the related sales company to the customer and
reduces such sales price by the amount of the appropriate markup by the selling company. This method may be used only if
there are no uncontrolled sales that may be compared with the
sales price of the manufacturing affiliate.

#24-62...The Cost-Plus Method

Like the resale price method, the cost-plus method involves
comparability with uncontrolled situations. The price under the
cost-plus method is to begin with the establishment of the
costs to the manufacturer to which is added the appropriate
markup thereby establishing the price to be charged to the
selling company by the manufacturer.

FOREIGN INVESTMENT TAX INCENTIVES

#24-63...The Impact of Taxes on Foreign Investment

The matter of decison making with respect to whether or not
a M/E should undertake the establishment of foreign operations
was previously discussed under the Managerial Control aspects.
However, many foreign governments are very interested in having
such enterprise make investments in their country, and offer
various inducements, principal of which are tax incentives.
The tax aspects are an integral part of formulating the decision as to whether or not to undertake foreign operations. This
chapter will conclude with a discussion of two aspects of tax
incentives: those in developed countries and those in developing countries.

#24-64...Tax Incentives in Developed Countries

Many highly industrialized countries in Europe such as Belgium, Italy and England have areas which are underdeveloped
resulting in inordinately high unemployment. To induce investments in such areas, they offer tax incentives for foreign investment and technical expertise.
It is pointed out in the FERF book ACCOUNTING FOR THE MULTI-
NATIONAL CORPORATION, by Watt, Hammer and Burge, p. 429, that:
    The U.K. offers cash grants toward the cost of capital
    expenditure in large areas of Northern and Western England,
    Scotland, and Wales. These grants, which are 22% of the cost
    of the capital items, do not reduce the depreciation basis
    for U.K. tax purposes, thus providing in effect a tax incen-
    tive over and above the cash grant. As a general incentive
    to capital expenditure for the modernization of its indus-
    try, the U.K. permits the expensing or 100% first-year

write-off of machinery and equipment and a 50% first-year write-off of industrial buildings. Canada permits a two-year write-off for machinery used in the manufacturing process. These incentives apply to domestic as well as incoming capital.

Brazil offers tax exemptions in certain of its vast underdeveloped regions. It permits Brazilian enterprises to invest part of their corporate tax liabilities in tax incentive programs in these regions instead of paying the taxes into the Treasury.

Some countries permit their possessions as between the Netherlands and the Netherlands Antilles to make tax-free payments of dividends. Under special provisions, French companies are permitted certain deductions with respect to operations in the overseas territories of Reunion, Martinique, Guadeloupe and Guyana.

Another way in which to encourage investment is through the allowance of the TAX-SPARING credit under the Tax Treaties, discussed above. Thus, the U.K., France, Germany, Sweden, Norway, the Netherlands and Japan each have several treaties which provide for a foreign tax credit for withholding taxes waived by developing countries.

## #24-65...Tax Incentives in Developing Countries

The most typical case is Ireland whose EXPORT SALES RELIEF ACT exempts an enterprise from all Irish corporate income taxes on profits from exported goods produced in Ireland. The exemption in the form of an abatement of taxes is granted for a period of 15 years and terminates in 1990. Ireland also does not tax repatriation of dividends.

Like Ireland, Puerto Rico has been extremely tax-incentive conscious in the area of attracting foreign investment capital. Originating in the Industrial Incentives Act of 1948, the Governor of Puerto Rico established a plan known as OPERATION BOOTSTRAP, which was carried through in the Acts of 1954 and 1963, under which foreign investors engaged in manufacturing, hotel operation, and scientific research receive total tax exemption for a period of from 10 to 25 years. However, under the Tax Reform Act of 1976, a 10% withholding tax was imposed on dividends paid to U.S parent companies of possessions corporations.

Puerto Rico appears to have set the example in the way of tax incentives for foreign investment for most of the Caribbean Islands such as Jamaica, Barbados, Haiti, and Trinidad & Tobago. All of them offer income tax exemptions to investors setting up manufacturing facilities for production of export goods. In the Bahamas and Cayman Islands income taxes are conspicuous by their absence.

In many Asian countries, such as Korea, Taiwan, Singapore and Malaysia--a good part of the ASEAN nations--tax holidays are offered as an incentive, and together with the normally much lower cost of labor which matches the tax savings, act as a double incentive for investment.

## SUMMARY OF FOOTNOTE REFERENCES
(References are to Paragraph #'s)

#24-1  "Critique of Tax Laws," Laventhol & Horwath Newsletter, L&H PERSPECTIVE, Vol. 6, #1 (Spring-Summer 1980): 18

#24-1  Richard H. Kalish and John P. Casey, "The Dilemma of the International Tax Executive," COLUMBIA JOURNAL OF WORLD BUSINESS (Summer 1975): 62

#24-1  Russel Moore and George Scott, "An Introduction to Financial Control and Reporting in Multinational Enterprises," The University of Texas Bureau of Business Research, 1973, p. 56

#24-7  Deloitte,Haskins & Sells, THE WEEK IN REVIEW(July 9,1976):10

#24-8  Ernst & Whinney, FOREIGN AND U.S. CORPORATE INCOME AND WITH-HOLDING TAX RATES, 1979

#24-9  U.S. FEDERAL RESERVE BULLETIN, 1979

#24-10 Presidential Task Force on Business Taxation, 1970

#24-13 Arthur Andersen & Co., PERSPECTIVES ON THE VALUE-ADDED TAX, 1979. Reprinted with permission.

#24-14 Dhia Al Hashim, ACCOUNTING FOR MULTINATIONAL ENTERPRISES (Indianapolis: Bobbs-Merrill, 1978), pp. 9-12

#24-15 Arthur Andersen & Co., op. cit., p. 5, by permission.

#24-21 Ibid., by permission.

#24-22 Ibid., by permission.

#24-23 Ibid., by permission.

#24-24 Ibid., by permission.

#24-26 George C. Watt, Richard M. Hammer, and Marianne Burge, ACCOUNTING FOR THE MULTINATIONAL CORPORATION, pp. 362-364. Copyright 1977 by Financial Executives Research Foundation (FERF), Morristown, N.J. Reprinted with permission.

#24-32 "U.S. Subsidiaries Get Caught By Tax Reform," BUSINESS WEEK (June 7, 1976): 42-43

#24-35 Commerce Clearing House, FEDERAL TAX COURSE, 1982, p. 2403

#24-35 Watt, Hammer and Burge, op. cit., p. 384. Reprinted by permission from FERF.

#24-36 Ibid. Reprinted by permission from FERF.

#24-39 Ibid., p. 386. Reprinted by permission from FERF.

#24-40 Commerce Clearing House, op. cit., p. 2404

#24-41 Watt, Hammer and Burge, op.cit., pp. 387-388, by permission.

#24-42 Commerce Clearing House, FEDERAL TAX COURSE, 1983, pp.2405-6

#24-43 Ibid.

#24-45 Watt, Hammer and Burge, op. cit., p. 396, by permission.

#24-46 Ibid. Reprinted by permission from FERF.

#24-47 Arthur Andersen & Co., Expert Testimony Before U.S. Senate Committee on Finance, April 1976

#24-48 Internal Revenue Code, 1977, Regulation 1.861-8, Sec. 861

#24-49 James W. Schenold, "A Tool for Maximizing Foreign Tax Cred-
       its," PRICE WATERHOUSE REVIEW,  2 (1978): 38-51.    Reprinted
       with permission.
#24-50 Commerce Clearing House, FEDERAL TAX COURSE, 1982
#24-51 Report  of U.N. Group of Tax Experts on Tax Treaties Between
       Developed  and  Developing  Countries, "Guidelines  for  Tax
       Treaties Between Developed and Developing Countries," 1974
#24-53 U.S. Treasury Dept., MODEL INCOME TAX TREATY, May 1976
#24-55 Watt, Hammer and Burge, op. cit., p. 412, by permission.
#24-55 "Treasury Department Interview With Peoples Republic of Chi-
       na," JOURNAL OF ACCOUNTANCY (May 1984): 24-25.   Copyright ©
       1984 by the American Institute of Certified  Public Account-
       ants, Inc.  Opinions expressed in the JOURNAL OF ACCOUNTANCY
       are  those of  editors and contributors.  Publication in the
       JOURNAL  OF ACCOUNTANCY does  not  constitute endorsement by
       the AICPA or its committees.
#24-56 Section 482, Internal Revenue Code, Revenue Act of 1962
#24-57 Ibid.
#24-58 Ibid.
#24-59 Ibid.
#24-64 Watt, Hammer and Burge, op. cit., p. 429, by permission.


## BIBLIOGRAPHY

American Law Institute, American Bar Association. INCOME TAX TREAT-
     IES.  Philadelphia: American Law Institute, American Bar As-
     sociation, 1982
Berg, Robert.  "Effect of the New U.K./U.S. Double Tax Treaty," AC-
     COUNTANCY, 88 (November 1977): 70-71
Binkowski,  Edward.  "Tax Consequences  of Creeping Expropriation,"
     INTERNATIONAL TAX JOURNAL, 7 (Dec. 1980): 117-126
Breecher, S.M.; Moore, D.W.; and Trasker, P.G.B.  THE ECONOMIC IM-
     PACT OF THE INTRODUCTION OF VAT. Morristown, N.J.: Research
     Foundation of the Financial Executives Institute, 1982
Burns, Jane O.   "How IRS Applies the Intercompany Pricing Rules of
     Section 482:  A Corporate Survey," JOURNAL  OF TAXATION, 52
     (May 1980): 308-314
Burns, Jane O. and Ross, Ronald. "Establishing International Trans-
     fer Pricing Standards for Tax  Audits  of Multinational En-
     terprises," INTERNATIONAL JOURNAL OF ACCOUNTING  EDUCATION &
     RESEARCH, 17 (Fall 1981): 161-180
Calhoun, Donald A. "The Foreign Tax Credit," MANAGEMENT ACCOUNTING,
     57 (Sept. 1975): 41-53
Choate, Alan G. and Moore, Michael.  "Bribes and Boycotts Under the
     Tax Reform  Act of 1976," INTERNATIONAL TAX JOURNAL, 4 (Dec.
     1977): 736-744
Christie, Andrew J.  "The  U.K./Norway Double Tax Treaty," THE AC-
     COUNTANT'S MAGAZINE, 83 (Dec. 1979): 514-515
Cinnamon, Allan. "Why Foreign Investment in the U.K. Can Be  Worth-
     while," ACCOUNTANCY, 89 (Jan. 1978): 82-85

Cowen, Scott S. "Multinational Transfer Pricing," MANAGEMENT AC-
    COUNTING, 60 (Jan. 1979): 17-22
Deloitte, Haskins & Sells. TAXATION IN JAPAN. N.Y.: Deloitte, Has-
    kins & Sells, 1982
Dilley, Steven. "Allocation and Apportionment Under Sec. 861," THE
    CPA JOURNAL, 50 (December 1980): 33-38
Dreier, Ronald. "U.S. Income Tax Treaties," COLUMBIA JOURNAL OF
    WORLD BUSINESS, 10 (Summer 1975): 21-28
FEI. PROPOSALS FOR A BETTER TAX STRUCTURE. Financial Executives
    Institute Committee on Taxation, Proposals, 1977
Feinschreiber, Robert. "Earnings & Profits Translation of Specific
    Items," INTERNATIONAL TAX JOURNAL, 5 (April 1979): 334-346
Fuller, J.P.; Chilton, F.R.; and Schrotenboer, R.B. "Foreign Tax
    Credit," HASTINGS INTERNATIONAL AND COMPARATIVE LAW REVIEW
    (Spring 1982): 633
Goldberg, H.L. "Conventions for the Elimination of International
    Double Taxation," LAW AND POLICY IN INTERNATIONAL BUSINESS,
    No. 3 (1983): 833
Gray, S.J. and Maunders, K.T. VALUE ADDED REPORTING: USES AND MEA-
    SUREMENT. London: Association of Certified Accountants, 1980
Hafele, H. "Tax Policy in the Federal Republic of Germany," EUROPE-
    AN TAXATION, No. 11 (1983): 347
Holdstock, Peter. "Some Thoughts on International Tax Planning,"
    PRICE WATERHOUSE INTERNATIONAL TAX NEWS (Dec. 1975)
Kaye, Rodney. "Transfer Pricing," THE ACCOUNTANT, 182 (April 10,
    1980): 536-538
McLeay, S. "Value Added," ACCOUNTING, ORGANIZATION AND SOCIETY, 1
    (1983): 31
Morley, Michael F. "Value Added: The Fashionable Choice for Annual
    Reports and Incentive Schemes," ACCOUNTANT'S MAGAZINE (June
    1979): 234-236
Muis, Jules W. "Inflation Accounting for Tax Purposes," ACCOUNT-
    ANT'S MAGAZINE, 82 (May 1978): 207-208
New York Institute of Federal Taxation. INTERNATIONAL TAX ISSUES
    AND CONTROVERSIES. New York Institute of Federal Taxation,
    1982
Nobes, C.W. "Imputation System of Corporation Tax Within the EEC,"
    ACCOUNTING AND BUSINESS RESEARCH, 10 (Spring 1980): 221-231
Platt, C.J. TAX SYSTEMS OF AFRICA, ASIA, AND THE MIDDLE EAST. Al-
    dershot, England & Brookfield, VT: Gower Publishing Co.,1982
"Report on Proposed United States Model Income Tax Treaty," HARVARD
    INTERNATIONAL LAW JOURNAL (Winter 1983): 219
Rosenbloom, H.D. "Tax Treaty Abuse," LAW AND POLICY IN INTERNATION-
    AL BUSINESS, No. 3 (1983): 763
Sanden, B. Kenneth. "VAT: What, How, Where?", TAX ADVISER (March
    1973): 150-157
Schartz, B.N. "Partial Income Tax Allocation and Deferred Taxation:
    An International Accounting Issue," MANAGEMENT INTERNATIONAL
    REVIEW, 20 (1980): 74-82
Seghers, Paul D. "Intercompany Pricing--Tax Audits," THE INTERNA-
    TIONAL TAX JOURNAL, 5 (August 1979): 437-441
Tomsett, Eric. "Double Taxation: The New Treaty Between U.K. and

the Netherlands," ACCOUNTANCY, 92 (July 1981): 88-90

Welch, William H. "Planning Techniques for Maximizing Foreign Cred-
    it Benefits," TAXES (Aug. 1978): 462-469

Whittaker, D.R. "An Examination of the O.E.C.D. and U.N. Model Tax
    Treaties," NORTH CAROLINA JOURNAL OF INTERNATIONAL LAW AND
    COMMERCIAL REGULATION (Winter 1982): 39

Williams, Thomas J. "The Creditability of Foreign Income Taxes: An
    Overview," TAXES (October 1980): 699-709

Wilson, L.G. "The United States and Australia Double Tax Treaty,"
    TAXES (October 1983): 679


# THEORY QUESTIONS
(Question Numbers are Keyed to Text Paragraph #'s)

#24-1   What procedures must be incorporated into a Tax Planning
        System for it to be effective?

#24-2   Make an outline classifying taxes.

#24-3   What two classes of Direct Taxes are there? Discuss the
        nature and impact of corporate income taxes. What are
        capital gains taxes?

#24-4   What are Indirect Taxes and how many kinds are there?
        Briefly describe the following indirect taxes: (a) What
        purpose does Border Taxes serve? (b) What is the nature
        and operation of Turnover Taxes? (c) What purpose does
        Net Worth Taxes serve? (d) Describe the operation of
        withholding taxes.

#24-11-12.  Define and explain the nature of VAT.

#24-13  What is the procedure that is followed for implementing
        VAT?

#24-14  What are Value Added Financial Statements and what pur-
        pose do they serve?

#24-15  Discuss the development of VAT in the EEC.

#24-16  Briefly discuss the three methods for the procedure of
        recovering VAT paid on capital items: (a) Consumption,
        (b) Income, (c) Gross Product.

#24-17-20.  Name the three methods of determination of the VAT
        tax base and define and describe each of them: (a) In-
        voice, (b) Subtraction, (c) Addition.

#24-23  Make a critical comparative analysis of the advantages
        and disadvantages of VAT.

#24-24  In 1985, pursuant to the re-election of President Rea-
        gan, the matter of raising funds to meet the prospective
        huge budget deficit arose, one source of which was VAT.
        Discuss the pros and cons of using VAT.

#24-29-33.  Make a classification of Tax Systems. Define and
        discuss (a) Classical, (b) Integrated Imputation (Tax
        Credit), (c) Integrated Split-Rate, (d) Integrated Divi-
        dend Deduction Systems.

#24-34-35. Explain the rationale and purpose of the foreign tax credit.

#24-38 Make an outline classifying foreign tax credits.

#24-40 Discuss the nature and operation of the Deemed Paid Credit.

#24-44 What are the two methods that may be used for determination of income resulting from foreign currency translation? (a) Describe the Net Worth Method; (b) the Profit and Loss Method.

#24-48 What provision is made in Section 861 of the Internal Revenue Code for reduction of tax credits through allocation of expenses?

#24-50-51. Discuss the nature of tax treaties and the purposes they serve as a medium of double taxation alleviation.

#24-52-53. What are Model Tax Treaties and how do they operate? Discuss the provisions of the U.S. Treasury Department Model Treaty.

#24-56 Explain the nature of the multinational intercompany transfer pricing dilemma.

#24-57 What provision does Section 482 make for allocation of income and expenses between related taxpayers in foreign transactions?

#24-58 Outline the purposes of Section 482 and compare it with Section 861.

#24-59 Discuss the five guidelines for intercompany transactions under Section 482.

#24-60-62. Discuss the three methods acceptable for arm's length price under Section 482.

#24-63 Discuss the impact that taxes have on foreign investment.

#24-64 Discuss tax incentives that have been offered in developed countries.

#24-65 Discuss tax incentives that have been offered in developing countries.

## PROBLEMS

**P-24-1  (CPA EXAM, 5/76, PRAC. I, #11)**
In 1975 the Chrol Co. formed a foreign subsidiary. Income before U.S. and foreign income taxes for this wholly-owned subsidiary was $500,000 in 1975. The income tax rate in the country of the foreign subsidiary was 40%. None of the earnings of the foreign subsidiary have been remitted to Chrol; however, there is nothing to indicate that these earnings will <u>not</u> be remitted in the future.

The country of the foreign subsidiary does <u>not</u> impose a tax on remittances to the U.S. A tax credit is allowed in the U.S. for taxes payable in the country of the foreign subsidiary.

Assuming the income tax rate in the U.S. is 48%, what is the total amount of income taxes relating to the foreign subsidiary that should be shown in the income statement of Chrol in 1975?

a.  $0                          c.  $200,000
b.  $40,000                     d.  $240,000

## P-24-2  (CPA EXAM, 11/81, PRAC. I, #55)
During 1980, Bell Corp. had world-wide taxable income of $675,000 and a tentative U.S. income tax of $270,000. Bell's taxable income from business operations in Country A was $300,000, and foreign income taxes imposed were $135,000 stated in U.S. dollars.

How much should Bell claim as a credit for foreign income taxes on its U.S. income tax return for 1980?

a.  $0                          c.  $120,000
b.  $75,000                     d.  $135,000

## P-24-3
The Norlin Corp. purchased 40% of the 10,000 outstanding shares of the Corb Co., a foreign corporation. The following information is relevant:

Jan. 1:   3,000 shares of Corb Co. were acquired for $60,000 cash when the carrying value of Corb's net assets were $200,000.

July 1:   1,000 shares of Corb Co. were acquired for $23,000 cash when the carrying value of Corb's net assets were $230,000.

Dec. 15:  Corb Co. paid a cash dividend equivalent of $2 per share, but Norlin Corp. received only $1.70 per share because of a dividend withholding tax of 15% held by the foreign government. Corb plans to reinvest all retained earnings for an indefinite period of time.

Dec. 31:  The carrying value of Corb's net assets were $260,000. Corb Co. had no capital transactions during the year.

Required:
Record the above transactions in journal entry form for Norlin Corp., including the accrual of the investee income at year-end under the equity method of accounting and with proper recognition of income tax considerations. Assume the ordinary income tax rate is 45% and the capital gains rate is 20%.

## P-24-4
The Worldwide Corp., a U.S. corporation, does business in the United States, has a branch in Chile, and owns 20,000 of 100,000 voting shares of Safari, Ltd., a corporation organized

in Mali. For 19X9, Worldwide has domestic taxable income of $160,000. It also earned $220,000 from its operations in Chile and paid Chilean taxes of $105,000 on this income in Chile. Worldwide keeps its books on the cash basis. The Safari invest-ment was acquired on Jan. 2, 19X8. Safari's books showed a profit of $125,000 in 19X8 and again in 19X9. On Feb. 1, 19X9, Safari declared a dividend and Worldwide received $12,000 for its share of 19X8 profits on March 1. On March 15, Safari paid its 19X8 income tax, amounting to $65,000 in U.S. currency, to the Mali government.

The 19X9 corporation tax rates are:
    On all taxable income (normal tax)     22%
    On all taxable income over $25,000 (surtax)     26%

**Required**:
Prepare the journal entry to record Worldwide Corporation's 19X9 U.S. income tax liability and expense. Assume use of Cost Method in recording the Safari investment.

## P-24-5
The Royal Chemical Co. of London involves the following stages with respect to the cycle in the disposal of its products: (1) Extractor, (2) Processor, (3) Wholesaler, and (4) Retailer. The Value Added by each of the 4 sellers in the cycle is: Extrac-tor..$500; Processor..$1,000; Wholesaler..$100; & Retailer.. $100. The VAT rate is 10%.

**Required**:
Construct a chart showing the Cycle Stage, Value Added, Selling Price, VAT Collected, VAT Paid, and VAT Due the Government.

## P-24-6
The Royal Chemical Co. of London, a British M/N/C, presents the following data in millions of pounds for preparation of its Value-Added Statement for the year 1982:

PART I--SOURCES OF INCOME: Sales..7,358; Royalties & Other In-
    come..99; Less: Materials & Services Used..5,272, to derive
    Value Added by Operations of 2,185; Net Income from Profits
    & Trade Investments..39.

PART II--DISPOSITION OF TOTAL VALUE ADDED: Employees Pay &
    Profit Sharing..1,444; Governments Disbursal..67; Capital
    Providers (for Interest & Dividends)..283; Reinvestment in
    Business (Depreciation & Retained Earnings)..430.

**Required**:
Draft a Value-Added Statement for the Royal Chemical Company for 1982.

## P-24-7
The U.S. Corp. has a branch operation in Germany. The German income for the period comes to $100,000, which is subject to a 50% foreign tax rate and a U.S. corporate tax rate of 50%.

**Required:**
   a. In what two ways can the U.S. Corporation treat the foreign tax paid directly?
   b. Draft a comparative statement for the 2 methods that can
be used showing the effective tax rate under each.

## P-24-8
The U.S. Corp. has a German branch whose earnings for the year
1985 are $100,000 on which the foreign branch pays the foreign
tax of 40% directly to the German government. The U.S. tax on
the income is 48%.
**Required:**
Draft a Statement showing the Net U.S. Tax Payable on the foreign earnings.

## P-24-9
The U.S. Corp. has a German branch whose earnings for the year
1985 are $100,000. The U.S. Corp. has the German branch dis-
tribute the earnings through dividends remitted to the U.S.
shareholders, which are subject to a Foreign Withholding Tax of
15%. The U.S. tax on the foreign income is 48%.
**Required:**
Draft a Statement showing the Net U.S. Tax Payable on the foreign earnings.

## P-24-10
The earnings before tax of the Paris Corp., a subsidiary of the
U.S. Corp., for 1985 were $10,000, on which the foreign income
tax is 30%, making earnings and profits of $7,000, which was
paid as a dividend to the U.S. parent company in 1985, less
foreign withholding tax of 15%. The U.S. tax rate is 48%.
**Required:**
Draft a Statement of Deemed-Paid Foreign Tax Credit showing
the amount of U.S. Tax Payable.

## P-24-11
The tax laws provide that where a foreign country imposes a
higher tax rate than that of the U.S., where the total creditable taxes on income received from the foreign country is
greater than the U.S. tax on such income, the taxpayer is limited in the amount of credit he can use to the amount of the
U.S. tax on the foreign income, known as the OVERALL METHOD.
The U.S. Multinational Corp. has operations in France and Belgium. The French operation had $200,000 of taxable income which
was taxed by France at 30%; the Belgian operation had taxable
income of $100,000 which was taxed by Belgium at 20%. The U.S.
corporation had world-wide taxable income of $600,000 with a
tentative U.S. tax liability of $270,000.

**Required**:
Under the Overall Limitation Method, compute the amount to which the foreign tax credit is limited.


## P-24-12
The U.S. Multinational Corp. has total global income of $6,000 from earnings and royalties of which $2,000 is foreign earned royalties. The total expenses come to $3,000. The U.S. tax rate is 48% and the foreign rate is 30%. When allocated, $2,000 of the expenses would be charged to U.S. operations and $1,000 to foreign operations.

**Required**:
Under Sec. 861 of the Internal Revenue Code requiring proper allocation of corporate expenses to foreign source income, draft a Comparative Statement showing the total tax liability before and after expense allocation.

## P-24-13
Using the format of the U.S. Treasury Department Model Income Tax Treaty, draft a treaty to be entered into between the United States and the country of Singapore.

# Glossary

## A

AAA — American Accounting Assn.
AAC — African Accounting Council
AARF — Australian Accounting Research Foundation
AAS — ASEAN Accounting Standards
AASC — Australian Accounting Standards Committee
AB — Aktiebolag (Sweden)
ABWA — Association of Accountancy Bodies of West Africa
ACA — Association of Certified Accountants U.K.
ACRS — Accelerated Cost Recovery System
AFA — ASEAN Federation of Accountants
AG — Aktien Gesellschaft (Germany)
AIB — Academy of Intnl. Business
AIC — Associasion Interamericana de Contabilidad
AICPA — American Institute CPAs
AIG — American International Group (Ins.)
AISG — Accountants International Study Group
AktG — AktienGesetz (Germany)
ANZAUAI — Australian New Zealand Association University Accounting Instructors
AO — AbgabenOrdnung (Germany)
APB — Acctg. Principles Board
APC — Auditing Practices Committee (UK)
ARB — Acctg. Research Bulletin
AS — AktienSelskab (Denmark)
ASA — Australian Society of Accountants
ASC — Accounting Standards Committee (UK)
ASEAN — Association of S.E. Asian Nations
ASSC — Acctg. Standards Steering Committee

## B

BERI — Business Environment Risk Index
BFH — BundesFinanzHof (Germany)
BGH — BundesGerichtsHof (Germany)
BGHZ — BundesGerichtsHof Entscheidingen Zivilsachen (Germany)

BI — Business International Country Assessment Service
BIAC — Business & Industry Advisory Committee (OECD)
BV — Besloten Vennootschap (Netherlands)

## C

CAAA — Canadian Association Academic Accountants
C&F — Cost and Freight
CAPA — Confederation of Asian and Pacific Accountants
CC — Current Cost Basis
CCA — Current Cost Accounting
CCAB — Consultative Committee of Accountancy Bodies
CC/CD — Current Cost / Constant Dollar
CCH — Commerce Clearing House
CFC — Controlled Foreign Corp.
CIAD — Center for International Accounting Development
CIB — Center For Intnl. Business
CIBS — Center for International Business Studies
CICA — Canadian Institute Chartered Accountants
CIERA — Center for Intnl. Education & Research in Acctg.
CIF — Cost, Insurance & Freight
CIIME — Committee on International Investment & Multinational Enterprises
CNCC — Compagnie Nationale des Commissaires Aux Comptes (France)
COB — Commission des Operations de Bourse
CoCoA — Continuously Contemporaneous Accounting
CONSOB — Commissione Nationale Per Le Societa e la Borsa (Italy)
CPI-U — Consumer Price Index-Urban
CPP — Current Purchasing Power
CSRIA — Canadian Society Registered Industrial Accountants
CVA — Current Value Accounting

## D

DD — Draft Directive
DISC — Domestic Intnl. Sales Corp
DM — Discussion Memorandum

## E

| | |
|---|---|
| EAA | European Accounting Assn. |
| ECA | European Congress of Accountants |
| ECOSOC | U.N. Economic and Social Council |
| ECU | European Currency Unit |
| ED | Exposure Drafts |
| EEC | European Economic Community |
| EFMD | European Foundation for Management Development |
| EG | Europaishe Gemeinschaften (Germany) |
| EIASM | European Institute For Advanced Studies in Management |
| EMCF | European Monetary Cooperation Fund |
| EMS | European Monetary System |
| ERTA | Economic Recovery Tax Act 1981 |
| EStG | Einkommen Steuer Gesetz (Germany) |
| EStR | Einkommen Steuer Richtlinien |
| ETC | Export Trade Corporation |
| EUA | European Unit of Account |
| EUC | Euro Currency |
| EUDM | Euro Dollar Market |
| EURCO | European Composite Unit |
| EXIM | Export-Import Bank |

## F

| | |
|---|---|
| FAF | Financial Accounting Foundation |
| FAS | Free Along Side |
| FASB | Financial Acctg. Standards Board |
| FCIA | Foreign Credit Insurance Association |
| FCPA | Foreign Corrupt Practices Act |
| FEI | Financial Executives Institute |
| FERF | Financial Executives Research Foundation |
| FIFO | First In First Out |
| FISS | Foreign International Sales Subsidiary |
| FOB | Free On Board |
| FSC | Foreign Sales Corporation |
| FTC | Foreign Trading Corp. |
| FVA | Fair Value Accounting |

## G

| | |
|---|---|
| GAAP | Generally Accepted Accounting Principles |
| GAO | General Accounting Office |
| GATT | General Agreement on Tariffs and Trade |
| GNP | Gross National Product Implicit Price Deflator |
| GoB | Grundsutze Ordnungsmassiger Buchfuhrang (Germany) |
| GPP | General Purchasing Power |
| GPLA | General Price Level Acctg. |

## H

| | |
|---|---|
| HC/CD | Historical Cost / Constant Dollar |
| HGB | Handels Gesetz Buch (Germany) |
| HFA | Haupt Fasch Ausschuss (Germany) |

## I

| | |
|---|---|
| IAA | Interamerican Acctg. Assn. |
| IAFEI | Intnl. Assn. of Financial Executives Institutes |
| IASC | International Accounting Standards Committee |
| ICAA | Institute of Chartered Accountants of Australia |
| ICAC | International Committee for Accounting Cooperation |
| ICAE | International Conferences on Accounting Education |
| ICAEW | Institute of Chartered Accountants of England and Wales |
| ICAI | Institute of Chartered Accountants of Ireland |
| ICAS | Institute of Chartered Accountants of Scotland |
| ICC | Intnl. Chamber of Commerce |
| ICCAP | International Coordination Committee for the Accountancy Profession |
| ICMA | Institute of Cost and Management Accountants |
| ICRA | International Center for Research in Accounting |
| IdW | Institut der Wirtschaftsprufer |
| IFAC | International Federation of Accountants |

| | | | | |
|---|---|---|---|---|
| IGWG | Intergovernmental Working Group | | OECD | Organization For Economic Cooperation & Development |
| IIA | Institute of Internal Auditors | | OPEC | Organization of Petroleum Exporting Countries |
| ILU | International Labor Unions | | OPIC | Overseas Private Investment Corporation |
| IMF | Intnl. Monetary Fund | | | |
| INA | Insurance Co. of North America | | | **R** |
| INSEE | Institut National Statistique et Etudes Economique | | R&D | Research & Development Costs |
| INTASI | International Accounting Studies Institute | | RCA | Replacement Cost Acctg. |
| IOE | International Organization Employees | | RDE | Reviseur d'Enterprises (Belgium) |
| ITC | Investment Tax Credit | | ROI | Return on Investment |

**J**

JAA Japan Accounting Assn.

JIBS Journal of International Business Studies

**K**

KK Kabushiki-Kaisha (Japan)

**L**

LDCC Less Developed Country Corporation

LIFO Last In First Out

LTD Limited (U.K.)

**M**

ME Multinational Enterprise

MML McLintock, Main, Lafrentz

MNC Multinational Corporation

MWCA Monetary Working Capital Adjustment

**N**

NAA National Association of Accountants

NFA Nordic Federation of Accountants

NIFO Next In First Out

NIVRA Nederlands Institut Van Register Accountants

NV Naamloze Vennootschap (Dutch)

**O**

OAS Organization of American States

OEC Ordre des Experts Comptables

**S**

SA Societe Anonyme (France)

SARL Societe A Responsibilite Limitee

SDR Special Drawing Rights

SE Societa Europa (Societe Europeene)

SEA Socio-Economic Accounting

SEC Securities and Exchange Commission

SID Society for International Development

SPA Societa Per Azioni (Italy)

SPLA Specific Price Level Acctg

S/R Social Responsibility Accounting

SSPA Statement of Standard Accounting Practice

**T**

TEFRA Tax Equity and Fiscal Responsibility Act 1982

TNA Trans National Corporation

TRA Tax Reform Act of 1984

TUAC Trade Union Advisory Committee (OECD)

**U**

UEC Union Europeenne des Expertes Comptables, Economiques et Financiers

U.K. United Kingdom

UKAUAI United Kingdom Association University Accounting Instructors

U.N. United Nations

UNCTAD United Nations Conference on Trade and Development

UNCTC  United Nations Center on
       Transnational Corporations
UNIDO  United Nations Industrial
       Development Organization
U.S.   United States

### V
VAT    Value Added Tax

### W
WHO    World Health Organization
WHTC   Western Hemisphere Trade
       Corporations
WIPO   World Intellectual Proper-
       ty Organization
WP     Wirtschaftsprufer(Germany)
WPRF   World Political Risk Fore-
       casts

# Index